GREAT LEGAL TRADITIONS

GREAT LEGAL TRADITIONS

Civil Law, Common Law, and Chinese Law in Historical and Operational Perspective

John W. Head

ROBERT W. WAGSTAFF DISTINGUISHED PROFESSOR OF LAW
UNIVERSITY OF KANSAS

CAROLINA ACADEMIC PRESS
Durham, North Carolina

Library of Congress Cataloging-in-Publication Data

Head, John W. (John Warren), 1953-
  Great legal traditions : civil law, common law, and Chinese law in historical and operational perspective / John W. Head.
       p. cm.
  Includes bibliographical references and index.
  ISBN 978-1-59460-957-2 (alk. paper)
  1. Comparative law. 2. Civil law. 3. Common law. 4. Law--China I. Title.
  K583.H43 2011
  340'.2--dc22
                          2010053972

Front Cover—The three images on the left represent the rich historical background of the three great legal traditions discussed in this book: Confucius contributed to the founding of the Chinese legal tradition with his use of the *Zhou lǐ* to prescribe a form of social governance that would contribute to cosmic harmony; Constantine, in addition to facilitating the Christianization of the Roman Empire, also founded the eastern capital of the Empire—Constantinople—from which Justinian would issue his great *Corpus Juris Civilis* in the sixth century; Blackstone, with his *Commentaries on the Laws of England*, helped preserve the vitality of the common law by making it accessible to practitioners both in England and the United States. The large image on the right shows judges on the German Federal Constitutional Court in Karlsruhe announcing a decision in 2009—thus reflecting the book's emphasis not only on the historical development but also on the contemporary operation of the legal traditions being examined here.

Carolina Academic Press
700 Kent Street
Durham, North Carolina 27701
Telephone (919) 489-7486
Fax (919) 493-5668
www.cap-press.com

Printed in the United States of America

Summary of Contents

Contents

List of Boxes and Figures

Boxes

Figures

Preface and Acknowledgments

Why This Book?

When I was a university student in the 1970s, I was fortunate enough to study law in England. Having been raised on a farm in an isolated and provincial corner of Missouri, in the heartland of the USA, I had not traveled outside North America before that. My two years in England were exhilarating for several reasons, but largely because they exposed me to a culture, including a legal culture, different from the one to which I had grown accustomed. I was permitted—indeed, obligated—to see my own culture from a different perspective, and to force my own cultural square pegs into round holes. In moving across the Atlantic, I moved across cultural "space."

I made a similar cultural move in the 1980s, working in Asia for five years as a lawyer for an international organization. Then, in the 1990s, I moved into academics, where I was able to revive my interest in history, especially legal history. This represented another type of cultural move—into the dimension of time. I have studied the legal heritage of my home country as well as that of other countries where I have lived or worked.

Why do I tell this personal story? Because it explains why I wrote this book. I believe strongly that we all have much to learn from moving across cultures. Lawyers in particular have much to learn from moving across *legal* cultures. As my own experience illustrates, such a movement across legal cultures can take two forms: (i) it can be "spatial", by which I mean a comparison of contemporary legal cultures in two or more geographical areas; and (ii) it can be temporal, by which I mean a study of earlier legal cultures. Put more simply, I believe both comparative law[1] and legal history are highly worthwhile subjects of study.[2]

This book represents my attempt to move in both directions—both "spatially" and temporally. I am writing both about comparative law and about legal history. This is my own comparison of the three greatest legal traditions in the world today—civil law, common law, and Chinese law—drawn from a historical perspective. It is a big task. How can any useful comparison be drawn between three rich and complex legal traditions that

---

1. As discussed in Chapter One, I find the term "comparative law" slightly disturbing. There is no type of law called "comparative law", in the same way as there is a type of law called "criminal law" or "water law". The more accurate term for what this book is about (in part) would be "comparison of laws" or "comparison of legal traditions". For the sake of convenience, however, I shall often refer to "comparative law".

2. Ken Pennington makes a compelling case for studying legal history and comparative law. Kenneth Pennington, *The Spirit of Legal History*, 64 University of Chicago Law Review 1097, 1112–15 (1997) (reviewing the first two volumes in a new series regarding Roman Law and Canon Law). For example, he points out that "[m]ost often law evolves under the sway of a myriad of influences" and that "[t]his truth is the best argument for studying legal history". *Id.* at 1112. For a summary of reasons why comparative law is worth studying, see section II of Chapter One, below.

represent a combined total of over six thousand years of law? It would seem to be an almost impossible undertaking, even in a treatise of many volumes—not to mention within the covers of a relatively modest book of this size.

Yet I see value in making the effort, especially for those readers seeking a general survey that is both comparative in character and "digestible" in a single effort. Who are those readers? I have designed this book primarily for law students, for upper-level and graduate students focusing on history and politics (perhaps with special concentration in European or Asian studies) or on sociology or other disciplines within the humanities. However, I expect the book also to be useful for legal practitioners wanting to gain a general understanding of the major themes and influences at work in various national legal systems that might be of special interest to them, and for a wide range of other readers curious about the world's rich diversity of views about law, rights, justice, government, and culture.

Structure and Approach of This Book

As should be clear from a brief survey of the table of contents, this book follows a two-step process of examining each of the three great legal traditions: in each case, one chapter is devoted to studying the legal tradition from a historical perspective and another chapter is devoted to studying that tradition from an operational perspective. This symmetry—in which Chapters Two, Four, and Six highlight history and Chapters Three, Five, and Seven offer an operational perspective—allows for multiple sorts of comparisons to emerge. One such comparison is between (i) the contemporary operation of a legal system in which a particular legal tradition prevails and (ii) the historical narrative that leads up to and informs the "law in action" in a country. A second comparison is across legal traditions—what I referred to above as a "spatial" comparison.

In the process of presenting these various perspectives and comparisons, I also try to create some forward motion, in the sense of identifying for the civil law and common law traditions certain features—for instance, the role of religion in law—that will prove especially useful in our survey of Chinese law. My goal has been to arrive at the end of the book not only with a general understanding of these three great legal traditions from a historical and operational perspective but also an appreciation for certain important deeper questions. What factors bear on the different roles that law plays in different societies? What will be the legal effects (or causes, for that matter) of a continuing globalization of the world? How will changing balances of power—and particularly the shifts in influence among Europe, the USA, and the People's Republic of China—affect the future development of the civil, common, and Chinese legal traditions? While this book offers few specific answers for such questions, it aims to provide the reader with some of the background needed to contemplate them intelligently.

A couple of other comments are in order regarding the "approach" of this book. As will be evident, I have tried to balance professional objectivity with personal observation. By "*professional objectivity*", I mean a careful and neutral presentation of material without personal bias. One reason I provide more footnote citations than might be expected in a text of this sort is to demonstrate my commitment to ensuring that the accounts offered here—despite their brevity because of the "survey" character of this book—are nevertheless firmly supported by credible authority. Facts matter.

On the other hand, facts can be dry without analysis and reflection. By incorporating into the book some degree of *"personal observation"*, I try to bring the facts to life by offering my own evaluation of important legal, political, and policy issues that a comparative study invites us to address. For example, in Chapter Three I make some evaluative comments about certain peculiarities of the civil law tradition; in Chapter Five I assert some of my views regarding the American myth that the US criminal justice system provides the best protections for persons accused of criminal behavior; and in Chapter Seven I provide my own speculations about the "rule of law" in China and about what lies at the center of contemporary China's legal soul. In all such cases, I identify them as my own views; and frankly I am less interested in whether readers agree with *my* views than I am in encouraging readers to formulate *their own* views on important issues that are at play here.

Lastly, I have tried to be lively. I believe the subjects this book addresses—encompassing time and space, extraordinary persons and exploding populations, the rise and fall of empires, the control that governments have over life and death, and the perspectives that different societies have on the nature of law, fairness, progress, and culture—are unparalleled in their ability to arouse our curiosity. I have tried to reflect in my accounts of these subjects the fascination that they have held for me for many years.

Acknowledgments

In writing this book I have benefitted greatly from the guidance, inspiration, and patience shown me by many people. This work, like most, is derivative in character, drawing liberally on the efforts of many others—including especially those whose books and articles are specifically cited in footnotes and in the Selected Bibliography near the end of this book. I thank them all collectively, along with my colleagues at the University of Kansas from whom I constantly draw great support, cheerfully given. As always, my wife Lucia Orth remains my most trusted and stalwart critic and conscience. In addition, I wish to add a note of gratitude to several research assistants who have provided such valuable help to me in the work that has culminated in this book. They include those who helped me compile several "generations" of teaching materials used in my Comparative Law course as well as the more recent contributors to my efforts: Marco Antonio Caporale, Enrico Greghi, Katie Lula, Maria Neal, Stefano Penasa, Jomana Qaddour, Aleks Schaefer, Erin Slinker Tomasic, Justin Waggoner, Wang Yanping, Dana Watts, and Xing Lijuan. In addition, I appreciate the generous guidance given to me by several colleagues at the University of Trento; these include in particular Roberto Toniatti, Jens Woelk, Rafaella Dimatteo, Luisa Antonielli, Carlo Casonato, Gabriella di Paolo, Sylvia Pelizzari, Elena Ioratti, Laura Baccaglini, and Cinzia Piciocchi. Support from the University of Kansas General Research Fund is also gratefully acknowledged.

Notes on Spellings, Usages, Citations, and Other Conventions

In this book I have followed certain conventions on spelling, punctuation, and usage that might be unfamiliar to some readers. These conventions include the following:

- Citations to books, articles, and other legal materials appear in a less abbreviated style than that used by many US law journals and books. I believe the heavily abbreviated style used in US legal texts can be so unfamiliar to a general audience as to create confusion or uncertainty. In addition, in the case of books, I have departed from the practice of putting the authors' names in all capital letters. Instead, authors' names for all works — books and articles and other items — appear in regular upper case and lower case letters; then titles of books appear in large and small capitals and titles of other works appear in italics or, in a few cases depending on the nature of the work, in regular font with quotation marks.

- In the case of citations to sources found on the internet, I have not included details of "last updated" and "last visited", on grounds that such information is likely to be of little use. Most of the citations to such sources were operational as of August 2010. However, it is not uncommon for a document on a website to change from one location to another within the website, so a reader wishing to retrieve such a document might wish to use the "search" function within that website in order to find the new location — bearing in mind that sometimes documents are in fact removed from the internet entirely.

- Many of the passages that I have quoted from other authors included, in their original publication, citations to authority in the form of footnotes or endnotes. Throughout this book, unless noted otherwise, I have omitted these citations without expressly indicating "(citations omitted)" or "(footnote omitted)".

- I also have omitted (in nearly all cases) citation to the authorities that support the factual accounts and explanations that I have occasionally drawn from Wikipedia. Although I am fully aware of the shortcomings of relying on Wikipedia for many types of research and analysis, I have felt comfortable drawing on such accounts and explanations if (i) they cite sources that, in my judgment, warrant confidence and (ii) they relate to general information that I am confident can easily be substantiated elsewhere if curiosity prompts someone to pursue the issue further.

- Throughout this book, the term "state" typically carries the meaning it has in international law — that is, as a nation-state and not as a subsidiary political unit such as the individual domestic states that make up federal nation-states such as India or the USA or Mexico.

- In most references to the People's Republic of China, I have used the abbreviation "PRC", rather than using the name "China". This facilitates separate reference, when necessary, to (i) the Republic of China ("ROC") on Taiwan or to (ii) China as a single social and political entity, especially in the years before 1949.

- The acronym noun "USA" is often used in this book in preference to the commonly-used noun "United States", inasmuch as there are other countries (such as Mexico) with the title "United States" in their official names. However, the term "US" has been retained for use as an adjective referring to something of or from the USA, such as "US legislation" or "US states".

- I have opted for the use of "US" and "USA" without periods, as this seems to be the more modern trend and also follows the usage found in acronyms for other political entities such as the United Nations (UN) and the People's Republic of China (PRC). Naturally, I have not changed "U.S." to "US" in any quoted material or official citations.

- The possessive form of words that end in the letter "s" have not had another letter "s" added to them—hence I have cited Thomas Hobbes' writings, not Thomas Hobbes's writings.

- I have used the abbreviation "CE", for Common Era (or Current Era), to carry the same meaning as the more outdated abbreviation "AD", for *Anno Domini*; and I have used the corresponding abbreviation "BCE", for "before Current Era", instead of "BC", for Before Christ.

- I have followed the less-used but more logical convention of placing quotation marks inside all punctuation (unless of course the punctuation itself is included in the original material being quoted). Doing so allows the text to reflect more faithfully how the original material reads.[3]

- I have used italicization in four circumstances: (i) where I wish to add emphasis (or where emphasis was already inserted in material being quoted from other authors); (ii) in textual references to titles of books (this explains italicization in the case of Justinian's *Institutes* and Justinian's *Digest*); (iii) to signify words or terms from languages other than English (mainly Latin, French, Italian, German, and Chinese); (iv) in certain "levels" of subsection headings, as a navigational aid to the reader. I assume the context will allow easy distinction between (i), (ii), and (iii).

---

3. In defense of my decision to use this approach, I would refer readers to H. W. Fowler, A DICTIONARY OF MODERN ENGLISH USAGE 591–92 (2d ed., 1965):

> Questions of order between inverted commas [quotation marks] and stops [periods] are much debated.... There are two schools of thought, which might be called the conventional and the logical. The conventional prefers to put stops within the inverted commas, if it can be done without ambiguity, on the ground that this has a more pleasing appearance. The logical punctuates according to sense, and puts them outside except when they actually form part of the quotation.... The conventional system is more favored by editors' and publishers' rules. But there are important exceptions, and it is to be hoped that these will make their influence felt. The conventional system flouts common sense, and it is not easy for the plain man to see what merit it is supposed to have to outweigh that defect; even the more pleasing appearance claimed for it is not likely to go unquestioned.

GREAT LEGAL TRADITIONS

Chapter One

Introduction to Legal Traditions and Comparative Law

Outline

Appendices to Chapter One

Study Questions

SQ #1.1   What is a legal tradition?

SQ #1.2   What is the relationship between a legal tradition, legal rationality, and legal change?

SQ #1.3   What is a legal family?

SQ #1.4   What is a legal system?

SQ #1.5   How many legal systems are there in the world today?

SQ #1.6   What are the main legal families in the world today?

SQ #1.7   Is there a "Western" legal tradition?

SQ #1.8   Are the legal traditions all converging?

SQ #1.9   For purposes of a comparative study of law, how should we define "law" and "legal system"?

SQ #1.10   In what sense is it inappropriate to use the term "comparative law" to describe the subject matter of this book?

SQ #1.11   In a "comparative law" exercise, what are we comparing?

SQ #1.12   What is the relationship between comparative law, private international law, and public international law?

SQ #1.13   What are the main purposes that a comparative study of law might fulfill?

SQ #1.14   Is "harmonization" or "unification" of law a good thing?

SQ #1.15   What is the history of comparative law as a discipline?

SQ #1.16   How many legal systems in the world today are homogenous in terms of their legal traditions — that is, how many legal systems reflect only one legal tradition?

SQ #1.17   About how old are the civil law tradition, the common law tradition, and the Chinese legal tradition?

Introductory Comment

We begin our study of comparative law by considering two fundamental issues: (1) what sort of a study it is and (2) why it is worth undertaking. As should be clear from even a quick perusal of the foregoing Study Questions — which are designed to highlight key points to be drawn from the chapter—our consideration of those two fundamental issues involves defining terms and concepts that are not as straightforward as they might at first appear. However, wrestling with these preliminary matters and emerging with some observations on these two overriding issues (observations that will naturally differ from one person's perspective to another's) will enable us to launch into the detailed historical and operational assessments beginning in Chapter Two.

I. The Concept of a Legal Tradition

As we embark on our study of three great legal traditions—civil law, common law, and Chinese law—we should first consider the meaning of the term "legal tradition". It might seem obvious what a "tradition" is, and in fact in the opening paragraphs below we shall see the relatively straightforward approach that some writers in the area of comparative law have settled on in using the term "legal tradition". As will become clear, however, there are in fact uncertainties associated with that term, and in particular there are uncertainties and differences of opinion regarding how that term—"legal traditions"—actually applies in today's world. That is, there is a wide divergence of views as to just which of several approaches should be used in dividing the world up into various traditions, and families, and systems of law. (These terms—"tradition", "family", and "system"—in fact all carry specific meanings in the context of comparative law.) We shall examine some of those different approaches to applying the term "legal tradition" to today's world, and then touch briefly on some questions of jurisprudence or legal philosophy that underlie any careful study of legal approaches in different cultures around the world. Finally, we shall identify what are the three "great legal traditions" for purposes of this book, and why they should be so regarded.

A. Defining "Legal Tradition"

1. A Straightforward Approach

Perhaps the best definition of "legal tradition"—a definition that is widely used in the literature of recent years regarding comparative law—was offered by John Henry Merryman a few decades ago. Merryman, a professor at Stanford University, posited this definition:

> A legal tradition, as the term implies, is not a set of rules of law about contracts, corporations, and crimes, although such rules will almost always be in some sense a reflection of that tradition. Rather it is a set of deeply rooted, historically conditioned attitudes about the nature of law, about the role of law in the society and the polity, about the proper organization and operation of a legal system, and about the way law is or should be made, applied, studied, perfected, and taught. The legal tradition relates the legal system to the culture of which it is a partial expression. It puts the legal system into cultural perspective.[1]

---

1. John Henry Merryman, THE CIVIL LAW TRADITION ii (2nd ed. 1985) [hereinafter Merryman-1985]. Merryman's first edition of this book appeared in 1969, and in 2007 Merryman was joined by a co-author in publishing a third edition of it. See John Henry Merryman and Rogelio Pérez-Perdomo, THE CIVIL LAW TRADITION (3rd ed. 2007) [hereinafter Merryman-2007]. In that third edition, the passage quoted above appears at *id.* at 2.

The central elements in Merryman's definition appear in the second sentence quoted above, and within that sentence the crucial noun—the direct object near the beginning—is the word "attitudes". Merryman is asserting that a legal tradition is a set of *attitudes* about law. As we shall see throughout this book, Merryman's emphasis on attitudes is in fact very well placed, for despite surface similarities between the treatment of key legal questions from one legal system to another, it remains true and important that *beneath* the surface there are often fundamental differences in attitude "about the nature of law, about the role of law in the society", and so forth.[2]

Merryman's definition of a legal tradition does not take us very far, of course, unless we also know what a legal system is. After all, his closing observation in the passage quoted above is that a legal tradition "puts the legal system into cultural perspective". So what is a legal system? The common understanding, at least in Western society, is that a legal system comprises a relatively effective mixture of rules and institutions that govern relations among individuals and groups in a society—typically the population of a nation-state or some other substantially autonomous political entity—and that also regulate the role and powers of the government of that entity. (I include the qualifying phrase "at least in Western society" in this definition because some cultures would give less prominence to rules and to effectiveness than this definition suggestions; I shall introduce some further definitions and uncertainties regarding the concept of a "legal system" later, under section IC of this chapter.)

Based on that definition, how many "legal systems" exist in today's world? Perhaps we could say on the order of 350: there are nearly 200 independent nation-states in the world, each with its own legal system; of those nation-states, there are several with federal systems (such as that in the USA) that are composed of federal "states" or "provinces" having sufficient legal autonomy to regard them as possessing their own "legal systems"; there is the international legal system (denigrated by many Americans who are ignorant of the fact that the international legal system is far more effective in practice than the legal systems of many independent nation-states); and perhaps a few other political entities also may be regarded as having their own "legal systems". All together, these might add up to about 350, or perhaps as many as 400.

---

2. Another comparative law scholar makes a similar point, but instead of using the term "attitudes" he refers to "cognitive structure" or "legal *mentalité*". See Pierre Legrand, *European Legal Systems Are Not Converging*, 45 INTERNATIONAL AND COMPARATIVE LAW QUARTERLY 52, 55–56, 60–62, 81 (1996), as reprinted in John Henry Merryman, David S. Clark, and John Owen Haley, COMPARATIVE LAW: HISTORICAL DEVELOPMENT OF THE CIVIL LAW TRADITION IN EUROPE, LATIN AMERICA, AND EAST ASIA 45–46 (2010) [hereinafter Merryman-2010]:

> In my view, neither rules nor concepts reveal as much about a legal system as appears to be assumed. Rules, for example, are largely ephemeral and inevitably contingent. They are brittle.... Likewise, concepts are deficient ... [in part because they] must of necessity be relative and, therefore, subjective.... Accordingly, rules and concepts alone actually tell one very little about a given legal system.... [Instead, the] essential key for an appreciation of a legal culture lies in an unravelling of the cognitive structure that characterises that culture. The aim must be to try to define the frame of perception and understanding of a legal community so as to explicate how a community thinks about the law and why it thinks about the law in the way it does.... It is this epistemological substratum which best epitomises what I wish to refer to as the legal *mentalité* (the collective mental programme), or the interiorised legal culture [that a community has].... Indeed, Montesquieu had already formulated the defining mission of the comparatist: "it is not the body of laws that I am looking for, but their soul".

Id. as appearing in Merryman-2010, *supra*, at 46. The point mentioned at the end of this quoted passage—that a mission for the comparativist is to search for the "soul" of a legal system—is one that will emerge later in this book, especially when we turn our attention to contemporary Chinese law in Chapter Seven.

With such a large number of legal systems in today's world, it can seem intimidating, or perhaps even impossible, to embark on any comparative study of law. Surely (one might think) there are too many details, too many differences, to bring any order out of such chaos. It is here that the concept of a "legal tradition", as well as the concept of a "legal family", can come to our rescue. As used in the literature relating to comparative law, the term "legal family" typically refers to a grouping of legal systems into classes or categories on the basis of some shared characteristics that are regarded as especially important.[3] Although the literature of comparative law is chock-a-block[4] with differences of opinion as to the method of classification and as to just which legal systems fit into what "legal families"—a matter that we shall examine in section IB of this chapter—the concept of a "legal family", as well as its usefulness in studying various legal systems, is widely accepted.

Let us bring some closure to our "straightforward approach" to defining the term "legal tradition" and the associated terms of "legal system" and "legal family". There are many, many legal systems in the world, some of them closely resembling each other and some appearing to be widely divergent in content and character. Those legal systems that share certain important features may be classified into a relatively small number of legal families—that is, groupings of legal systems *in today's world* (that is, currently in existence) that bear a certain resemblance or have a certain affinity to each other. The concept of a "legal tradition" supplies the elements of culture and history that explain such resemblance and affinity. That is, the legal systems within any particular legal family share at least to some significant degree a common "set of deeply rooted, historically conditioned attitudes" about law (to use Merryman's definition again). Hence, for reasons that we shall explore later in this section, the legal systems in today's world may be classified into a small number of legal families; and within each of those legal families, all of the member countries share one of the main legal traditions that have developed over many centuries in various parts of the world. This book focuses on the three most important ones— civil law, common law, and Chinese law.

2. A More Nuanced Approach

Let us now take a closer look at the concept of a "legal tradition". In a wide-ranging study of legal traditions, H. Patrick Glenn gives considerable attention to the notion of "tradition" in general and especially in terms of its relation to rationality. Glenn explains that although some of the great thinkers coming from the Enlightenment in 17th-century Europe regarded tradition as the opposite—perhaps even the enemy—of rationality, those thinkers were probably themselves bound up (perhaps unknowingly) in a tradition of their own:

---

3. One of the leading treatises on comparative law offers this explanation of the concept of "legal families": "The theory of 'legal families' seeks to ... [allow us to] divide the vast number of legal systems into just a few large groups ... so as to arrange the mass of legal systems into a comprehensible order". Konrad Zweigert and Hein Kötz, AN INTRODUCTION TO COMPARATIVE LAW—THE FRAMEWORK 57 (1977) [hereinafter Zweigert and Kötz].

4. The phrase "chock-a-block" means "crammed so tightly together as to prevent movement", and it is thought to derive from two terms. The first term is "chock", which is a block of wood (or some other material) used to keep a movable object from moving. The second term is "block and tackle", the system of pulleys that can be used for many purposes but particularly in sailing ships to hoist the rigging using pulleys and rope. In such a system of pulleys, the "block" is the structure that houses a pulley. The phrase "chock-a-block" describes what occurs when such a system of pulleys is raised to its fullest extent—that is, when there is no more rope free and the blocks jam tightly together. For further elaboration, see http://www.phrases.org.uk/meanings/chock-a-block.html.

Those who have studied the history of attitudes towards tradition locate the origins of a sharp dichotomy between tradition and rationality in the enlightenment of the seventeenth century. As a means of overcoming the inequalities of existing European societies, rooted in tradition, [it was thought that] tradition itself had to be overcome, or destroyed, as an operative social concept. Contemporary rationality would then prevail—forever young, as long as one accepted, albeit uncritically, the primacy of the present.

History, with its relativizing effect, tells us, however, that we are all part of a tradition, or traditions. One can perhaps distinguish between individualist or rationalist traditions—there must really be more than one of them—and communal or contextualist traditions—and there are surely more than one of them. They are all, however, traditions, and all allow our predecessors to speak to us, with more—or less—insistence. Western societies, in spite of what is often said, are thus traditional societies, and western law is traditional law, as western lawyers often explicitly acknowledge.[5]

Glenn goes on to insist that just as the perceived dichotomy between tradition and rationality is in fact a false dichotomy, likewise the perceived dichotomy between tradition and *change* is also a false dichotomy. Indeed, Glenn asserts, tradition is more accurately regarded as "a resource from which reasons for change may be derived, [and] a legitimating agency for ideas which, by themselves, would have no social resonance".[6] Ideas for change, according to Glenn, do have a claim to legitimacy if they fit within the tradition: "The past is mobilized to invent a future".[7]

This idea—that tradition serves as a powerful agent for (legitimate) change in a society—strikes me as extremely important in the context of a comparative study of law. It suggests that a legal tradition, of the sort that we shall be examining throughout this entire book, has two crucial components or functions: it both (i) provides cohesion and (ii) facilitates change. Glenn expresses it in this manner:

> Tradition is thus both disruptive *and* cohesive and rarely exclusively one or the other. Parts of society may therefore change, while others are preserved. Identity may be preserved, in an ongoing way, while reforms are effected. In this more nuanced and diversified concept of tradition, recent thinking appears to reflect still older thought, in which innovation and continuity were "inextricably fused" and which maintained that both "permanent and transitory elements" were necessary for social coherence.[8]

These views about the relationship between tradition and change—and the insistence that the former is not an impediment to the later—has also appeared in other writings on comparative law. Here is how one source expresses these ideas:

> In the minds of many people, the word "tradition" evokes the image of a frozen and static past. As we use it here, however, it denotes a vital, dynamic, ongoing

---

5. H. Patrick Glenn, Legal Traditions of the World 2–3 (2007). Glenn also explains that "in Western thought, tradition has been associated with static forms of social order. A traditional society was [thought to be] one which did not change and which was largely impervious to valid reasons for change.... [T]his manner of thought paralleled [one] which drew a sharp distinction between tradition and rationality.... Rationality and change were thus linked on one side of the dichotomy; on the other side stood tradition and stability ...". *Id.* at 22–23.

6. *Id.* at 23.

7. *Id.*

8. *Id.* at 24.

system. [We endorse] philosopher, Alastair MacIntyre's concept of a living tradition: "an historically extended, socially embodied argument, and an argument precisely about the [attitudes] that constitute that tradition. Within a tradition the pursuit of [attitudes] extends through generations, sometimes through many generations".[9]

Before moving from these definitional and theoretical issues to the more practical questions of what legal traditions exist in today's world, let us consider one last detail regarding the notion of a "legal tradition". That point is this: because some legal traditions have extremely long histories and extend over an exceptionally large geographical area — the civil law tradition in particular has these features — it is necessary sometimes to think not just in terms of a legal tradition but also in terms of several "sub-traditions" within a legal tradition. For instance, the civil law tradition is commonly regarded as encompassing five sub-traditions (or by some accounts two sub-traditions). This division of certain legal traditions into sub-traditions can be both a tool and a torment. It can be a tool in the sense that it allows for more exacting consideration of the various components of a legal tradition. It can, however, be a torment in that the introduction of the notion of sub-traditions tends to complicate the picture and to introduce some uncertainty as to which legal systems do belong to a particular legal family and which do not, based on whether such a legal system shares the requisite number of legal sub-traditions to "qualify" as a member of that legal family.

I am emphasizing these points not only to add color and nuance to the fairly straightforward definition of "legal tradition" offered above, but also to draw attention to two points that we should bear in mind as we study the three great legal traditions. First, it is not accurate — indeed, it is not very intelligent — to regard the world as a whole or any particular legal system within it as moving away from tradition and toward rationality. In other words, it is not as if our examination of (for example) the foundations of the civil law tradition in the 5th century BCE or of the Chinese legal tradition in the 11th century BCE represents some intellectual archeological dig into irrational or pre-rational times. Second, it is imperative that we recognize the importance of history as providing not only the cohesive force that tradition offers but also the basis for change that a legal tradition facilitates. After all, if a legal tradition comprises "attitudes" (as Merryman's definition posits), and if — as is surely true — no individual or society can undertake a conscious change in its attitudes without some memory of those attitudes and the identity[10] which they comprise, then surely a study and understanding of the *historical* foundations and development of a legal tradition must be undertaken by anyone who is serious about bringing change to a legal system. As we shall see later in this chapter, that ambition — to bring change to one's own (or another) legal system — is one of the foremost reasons for engaging in a comparative study of law.

Let us turn now from these definitional and theoretical issues to a discussion of what legal traditions and what legal families exist in our time.

---

9. Mary Ann Glendon, Michael W. Gordon, Paolo G. Carozza, Comparative Legal Traditions 13–14 (2nd ed. 1999) [hereinafter Nutshell-1999].

10. Glenn draws on Locke and other theorists for the proposition that "it is memory which is constitutive of identity" and that just as persons "who have lost their memory no longer know who they are", likewise the tradition of a society is itself constitutive of that society. Glenn, *supra* note 5, at 33–34. He thus equates (as I read him) a society's tradition with that society's identity, suggesting that such an identity (or tradition) cannot even exist without memory — that is, a study and understanding of its own history.

B. Legal Traditions in Today's World

1. Different Methods of Classifying Legal Traditions and Families

Different authorities offer a fairly wide variety of views as to (i) how particular legal systems — maybe as many as 350 or 400 of them that exist in today's world — can be classified logically into a manageable number of legal families, and a correspondingly wide variety of views as to (ii) what legal traditions the legal systems within those various families share. Indeed, this lack of agreement on these issues is only one of many factors that make it difficult to undertake a comparative study of law. (A number of other challenges are identified in subsection IIC of this chapter.)

Several criteria have been proposed by various authorities for classifying legal traditions and legal families. Those criteria include the following:[11]

- Substance (that is, the substantive content of the legal rules within a legal system)
- Ideology reflected in the legal system
- Conceptions of justice
- Legal technique
- Historical origins
- Juristic style
- Race and language
- Culture
- Characteristic mode of thought
- Certain distinctive institutions of the legal system
- The types of legal sources that the legal system acknowledges

It is worth recognizing that the very process of using particular criteria for classifying legal systems into separate legal families, or for identifying legal traditions more generally, necessarily introduces bias into our comparative study of law. One of the enduring masterpieces of comparative law scholarship, first written several decades ago by René David and later updated and translated into English with the assistance of J.E.C. Brierley, reflects what I regard as an undue emphasis on Western conceptions of law in its classification of legal traditions — and particularly in its treatment of legal systems of East Asia. Written at a time when the legal system in China was still largely unknown in the West — both in its traditional form and as it had changed dramatically following the collapse of the Qing Dynasty in 1911 — that book by David and Brierley[12] offers simplistic

---

11. These various criteria are drawn from several sources, most prominently from these three: Peter de Cruz, A MODERN APPROACH TO COMPARATIVE LAW 29–30 (1993) [hereinafter de Cruz 1993]; Peter de Cruz, COMPARATIVE LAW IN A CHANGING WORLD 69 (1999) [hereinafter de Cruz 1999]; Zweigert and Kötz, *supra* note 3, at 58–67. After surveying a variety of criteria, these sources settle on the following five: historical development, distinctive mode of legal thinking, certain distinctive legal institutions, sources of law (and methods of handling them), and ideology in the sense of political or economic doctrines or religious belief.

12. See René David and John E. C. Brierley, MAJOR LEGAL SYSTEMS IN THE WORLD TODAY: AN INTRODUCTION TO THE COMPARATIVE STUDY OF LAW (3d ed. 1985). The first edition by David and Brierly was published in 1968, and that edition was based on David's 1966 book GRANDS SYSTÈMES DE DROIT CONTEMPORAINS.

generalizations that in China, "law is an instrument of arbitrary action rather than a symbol of justice" and that "it is a factor contributing to social disorder rather than to social order" and that "law is not made with a view to being really applied". As we shall see later in this book, those assertions about Chinese law have some germ of truth in them, at least for purposes of distinguishing Chinese law from Western law in certain respects, but in fact they disguise more than they disclose; they overlook the fact that Chinese society was governed (and still is governed today) by a comprehensive and sophisticated system of social norms that most modern observers would consider "legal" in nature if viewed through the eyes of one who is appreciative of and respectful of the diversity of approaches toward law and society in diverse cultures. In my view, then, David and Brierley are fettered by the vocabulary and the conceptual framework they use in defining law and therefore in offering a system of classification of legal families. Indeed, their treatment of Chinese law suggests that it would most appropriately be regarded as a "non-legal" system, not truly falling within any of the families of *legitimate* "law".

My purpose in drawing attention to the approach taken by David and Brierley is not to level criticism at those two experts, whose accomplishments and reputations in the area of comparative law are far greater than mine, but instead to underscore the intrinsic limitations that we all face in classifying legal traditions and legal families in the world today. Even if we are careful not to pass judgment on the content or character of a particular legal system, the mere act of classifying them for purposes of study will itself reflect our own preconceptions—biased, culturally based—of what is important in law or a legal system. In this and other aspects of our comparative study of law, we should watch carefully and tread lightly.

2. Competing Lists of Legal Traditions and Families

With that cautionary note, let us now consider how various authorities have decided to classify legal traditions and legal families. (We should remind ourselves that a legal family is a grouping of present-day legal systems that share a legal tradition, and that a legal tradition is a set of "deeply rooted, historically conditioned attitudes" about law.) Here, in abbreviated form, are some of the competing lists of legal families:[13]

- The Romanistic, Germanic, Anglo-Saxon, Slav, and Islamic legal families;

- The continental family, the family of English-speaking countries, and the Islamic family of laws;

- The Indo-European, Semitic, and Mongolian legal families of law as well as a family of laws of "uncivilized nations", with a subdivision of the Indo-European family into Hindu, Iranian, Celtic, Greco-Roman, Germanic, Anglo-Saxon, and Lithuanian-Slav sub-groups;

- The French, German, Scandinavian, English, Russian, Islamic, and Hindu legal families;

- The families of Western legal systems, socialist legal systems, Islamic law, Hindu law, and Chinese law;

---

13. These various listings of legal families that different experts have proposed are drawn largely from Zweigert and Kötz, *supra* note 3, at 57–59. The list shown in the final bullet point is the one that Zweigert and Kötz themselves adopt.

- The Romanistic-German family, the common law family, and a family of "religious and traditional systems" that includes Islamic law, Hindu law, the law of the Far East, and African and Malagasy law;
- A family of Western legal systems, including the Romanistic and Germanic systems, the Latin American systems, the Nordic systems, and the common law systems, plus another family that would encompass socialist systems, the non-communist Asian systems, and the African systems;
- The Romanistic legal family, the Germanic legal family, the Anglo-American legal family, the Nordic legal family, the socialist legal family, the Far Eastern legal family, and Islamic law and Hindu law.

As will be evident from the discussion in subsection ID below, none of the classifications shown in the foregoing bullet points is precisely the same as the one I have used in this book. This is partly because of the emphasis I have placed on *historic continuity* as a key criterion for classifying legal traditions and legal families, a point that also will be explored below.

3. Purported Convergences in Legal Traditions

Is there a Western legal tradition? More generally, have all the different legal traditions tended in recent years to converge with one another as a consequence of the all-encompassing process of globalization that affects so many aspects of human life today? This is a useful question, or pair of questions, to address now at the very outset of our study of the world's great legal traditions. After all, if the world is experiencing a unification, or even a harmonization, of law—a sort of confluence of disparate legal traditions into one single, mighty river of "world law"—there would seem to be little point to concerning ourselves with which legal family this or that legal system happens to fit into and which legal tradition the members of that legal family share.

In my view, it would be plausible to answer the two questions posed at the beginning of the preceding paragraph with the answers "yes" and "no". It *is* reasonable, as I see things, to consider the civil law and common law traditions—to be explored in Chapters Two through Five of this book—as *moving toward* a convergence into what could be called a "Western legal tradition", at least in some areas of law. There are numerous reasons that have been adduced for such a convergence,[14] and considerable evidence of it. This is especially the case if, as I do in this book, one casts a wide net in one's definition of "law". (This point will be discussed below in subsection IC.) Expressed differently, it could be said that the differences between legal systems in the civil law family (particularly in Europe) and legal systems in the common law family (particularly those of the UK, the USA, Canada, Australia, and New Zealand) are so much less significant than the differences between any of those systems and the Chinese or Islamic or Hindu legal traditions that we might find it sensible to lump all of the common law and civil law systems into a "Western legal family".[15]

---

14. For a discussion of several "philosophies of convergence" and "strategies of convergence" that could bear particularly on a convergence of civil law and common law, see John Henry Merryman, *On the Convergence (and Divergence) of the Civil Law and the Common Law*, 17 STANFORD JOURNAL OF INTERNATIONAL LAW 357, 359–73 (1981), as excerpted in Merryman-2010, *supra* note 2, at 30–39.

15. In this regard, see David S. Clark, *The Idea of the Civil Law Tradition*, in COMPARATIVE AND PRIVATE INTERNATIONAL LAW: ESSAYS IN HONOR OF JOHN HENRY MERRYMAN ON HIS SEVENTIETH BIRTHDAY 11, 21–22 (David S. Clark ed., 1990), as excerpted in Merryman-2010, *supra* note 2, at 39–40 (noting that "our view of a legal system will largely depend on our perspective" and that therefore a person standing in China or Botswana and looking at the law of France and England would find

The main difficulty in doing so is that it would require us to smudge over the profound differences that exist between the development of English common law and European civil law. These differences will emerge from the discussions in Chapters Two and Four of this book, focusing on the historical development of each of the two traditions, even though Chapters Three and Five will illustrate many of the surface similarities between civil law and common law. A secondary difficulty with conflating common law and civil law traditions into a "Western legal tradition" is that the surface similarities just referred to are in fact uneven from one area of law to another: while business and economic laws (antitrust, intellectual property protection, commercial transactions, securities, etc.) have been subjects of very extensive harmonization and even unification—partly because of successful efforts to establish treaty regimes in these areas—much less similarity appears in areas of family law, criminal procedure, court structures, and the roles of various members of the legal profession(s) in civil law and common law countries.

On balance, then, it is plausible to refer to a "Western legal tradition" that is shared by those countries whose legal systems fall within either the common law family or the civil law family, but the disadvantages of such a classification would outweigh the advantages—except perhaps in the most general of contexts. The second question posed above—whether there is a globalization-induced convergence of legal traditions generally in the world—is easier to answer. True, there is some substantial degree of convergence in particular *rules* of law in many legal systems in the areas of business and economic regulation and transactions. As noted above, many of these similarities result from treaty regimes that have emerged in the last fifty or sixty years. Pertinent treaties in this regard would include the United Nations Convention on Contracts for the International Sale of Goods (coming into force in 1988 and now adopted by most major trading nations), the WTO-GATT treaties emerging from the Uruguay round of trade negotiations concluded in the early 1990s (encompassing now over 150 countries), and a variety of lesser-known treaties and standards on bank regulation, letters of credit, commercial trade terms, and corruption in business. In other areas of law, however, a great many differences exist among legal systems, and many of those differences are attributable to the fact that those legal systems do not share the same legal tradition.

There is another reason—a more fundamental reason—for dismissing the notion that increasing similarities between various legal systems in the world in terms of their rules and institutions would tend to make any comparative study of law unnecessary today or in the near future. Not only is there not enough similarity *on the surface* of today's legal systems to support such a notion; I venture to say that there will *never* be adequate similarity *below the surface*. And that is where legal tradition lies: below the surface. Let us bring to mind again Merryman's definition of a legal tradition. It concentrates on *attitudes*.

---

that "his looking glass likely reveals more important similarities than differences"). See also Harold Berman, Law and Revolution: The Formation of the Western Legal Tradition (1983). It is worth pointing out that some observers have asserted that there is a "Western legal tradition" and have identified its main characteristics as including such things as these: (1) a distinction between legal and other instituions, with law having an independent existence and identity from the other institutions; (2) a theoretical separation of politics and morals from law; (3) administration of the law by trained specialists—lawyers and judges; (4) legitimate contributions of legal scholarship to the development of law; (5) growth and change of law as part of a pattern of development; (6) supremacy of law over political authorities; (7) a view of the competing legal systems and jurisdictions as independently legitimate; and (8) endurance of the legal tradition even when legal systems are overthrown. *Id.* at 7–10, drawing from the writings of Alan Watson, as summarized in Colin B. Picker, *International Law's Mixed Heritage: A Common/Civil Law Jurisdiction*, 41 Vanderbilt Journal of Transnational Law 1083, 1095–1096 (2008).

C. Deeper Questions on Legal Systems

1. What Is Law?

In subsection IA1 of this chapter, I offered, in my "straightforward approach", a definition of a "legal system". I suggested there that a "legal system" could be regarded as comprising "a relatively effective mixture of rules and institutions that govern relations among individuals and groups in a society—typically the population of a nation-state or some other substantially autonomous political entity—and that also regulates the role and powers of the government of that entity". That rather straightforward definition is almost surely adequate for purposes of our investigation of how various legal systems around the world reflect the key legal traditions—especially the civil law tradition and the common law tradition (which are shared by a great many nation-states). Still, it is important to recognize that defining the term and concept of "legal system" is not as simple as might at first glance appear to be the case. This is especially true when we consider the cultural differences—sometimes quite dramatic differences—in views about what law is and what role law plays in society.

Indeed, uncertainties regarding what does or does not constitute "law", and therefore uncertainties about how to define "legal system", can come not only from cultural differences between societies but also from purely linguistic differences as well. Consider, for example, the fact that the term "law" (as we use it in English) can take on different shadings and nuances of meaning in other languages. Here is how one author has explained that fact, using French as an example:

> There are ... different words that are used for different senses of 'law': 'a law' (or statute) is *une loi*; 'the law' is *la loi* or '*la justice*' as 'to fall foul of the law'; but the law as an academic discipline is *le droit* as it is for legal systems of different countries (*le droit anglais*) and for different branches of the law (*le droit penal*, etc.)....[16]

Even more fundamental challenges and uncertainties arise in discussing the concept of "law", and therefore "legal system", where language differences are greater than that between English and French. As we shall see in Chapter Six, traditional China gives us a variety of different terms that might in some sense be translated plausibly into the English word "law", and yet several of those terms—*lǐ*, for example—were regarded for centuries both by Chinese and by non-Chinese observers to be *opposed* to law.[17]

In short, we live in a world of amazing diversity in terms of how people define "law", how they see its role in society, and even whether it should be regarded favorably or unfavorably as a social institution. This diversity of views on "law" makes it difficult to identify with any real confidence what is encompassed in the concept of a "legal system", and it ultimately throws into some question the assumptions and conceptualizations we entertain in our discussion of, and comparison of, legal traditions.

---

16. de Cruz 1999, *supra* note 11, at 64. The same passage appears also in de Cruz 1993, *supra* note 11, at 64.

17. As we shall also see in Chapter Six, even where a Chinese term is (in translation) regarded as equivalent to an English term as a *formal* matter—for example, the term "rule of law" or even the word "court"—it might still be the case that the apparent equivalence is in fact absent as an *operational* matter. One author, in addressing this interplay of law and language, issues a stern warning against being "a chronic, unthinking 'word substitutionalist,' who must obtain the assistance of the comparativist lawyer to avoid making irreparable errors". Dan Fenno Henderson, *The Japanese Law in English: Some Thoughts on Scope and Method*, 16 VANDERBILT JOURNAL OF TRANSNATIONAL LAW 601, 611 (1983), as excerpted in Merryman-2010, *supra* note 2, at 58–60.

2. Hart's Concept of Law

While we are highlighting uncertainties of this sort, we might benefit by considering briefly what many modern legal theorists would regard as the most insightful and most influential construct that has been offered in modern times for the concept of a "legal system". It is found in the writings of the great legal philosopher H.L.A. Hart, and particularly in his book *The Concept of Law*,[18] written in the late 1950s and posthumously reissued in the early 1990s with slight updating revisions. H.L.A. Hart, who held the Oxford chair in Jurisprudence for many years,[19] criticized and departed from the strict positivist approach taken by John Austin, a legal philosopher who preceded Hart by about a century and a half.[20] In Austin's view, "law" consisted of orders issued by a sovereign and backed by force or the threat of force. That positivist view—with the notion of "positivism" deriving from the view that the law had to be "posited" or promulgated by a sovereign rather than deriving from religious dogma, moral imperatives, or some supernatural source—was very widely accepted in the Western world for many decades. Hart challenged Austin's view in several respects. Perhaps the most important criticism Hart made of Austin's theory was that in reality the use or threat of force is sometimes neither a sufficient condition nor a necessary condition to the existence of what normal people would regard as "law". Instead of focusing on the element of force (or "enforcement") as an element in "law", Hart focused on *rules*.

Specifically, Hart identified two distinct types of rules that most societies (although not all societies) have: primary rules and secondary rules. Hart's concept of law asserts that law exists (or, according to many others who have commented on Hart's work, a "legal system" exists) where there is a "union of primary and secondary rules".

Such a formula as this makes no sense, of course, unless we know what Hart means by "primary rules" and "secondary rules". For Hart, primary rules offer specific direction to the persons who are subject to a legal system as to how those persons should behave. An example of a primary rule would be "stop at a red light", and another would be "pay taxes", and another would be "a will is not valid unless countersigned by two witnesses". Secondary rules, by contrast, inform the persons within the legal system as to how the primary rules are to be used and manipulated. In fact, Hart identifies three distinct sorts of secondary rules: rules of change, rules of adjudication, and rules of recognition. The first two types of rules are those that would be used to make revisions or amendments to the primary rules and those that would be used in determining whether or not a particular primary rule has in fact been adhered to or violated. A "rule of recognition" would be one that provides guidance in determining whether a particular primary rule is or is not legitimate and binding within the system.

Our interest here, of course, lies not in a close analysis of Hart's concept of law but in the fact that this formulation—or others close to it—can be found throughout Western legal thought of the last half-century. Hart's views would have us regard law as a social

---

18. H.L.A. Hart, THE CONCEPT OF LAW (1961).

19. For an elegant biography of H.L.A. Hart, written by Tony Honoré (himself also a famous legal theorist), see http://www2.law.ox.ac.uk/jurisprudence/hart.htm (referring to Hart as "the most widely read British legal philosopher of the twentieth century").

20. For a brief biography of John Austin (1790–1859), see *John Austin*, appearing in STANFORD ENCYCLOPEDIA OF PHILOSOPHY, http://plato.stanford.edu/entries/austin-john/. Among Austin's most famous books is THE PROVINCE OF JURISPRUDENCE DETERMINED (1832).

institution that is intimately bound up with the notion of rules, and also with the notion of consensus. Indeed, some minimal degree of consensus within the society about the secondary rules—especially the rule(s) of recognition—is what, for Hart, stands in the place of the use or threat of force that was central to Austin's view of "law".

3. Fuller's Morality of Law

What if there is no such consensus in the society? That is, what if the shared view within society that Hart relies on as a sort of "glue" to create the "union of primary and secondary rules" in a society—and therefore to give it "law" or a "legal system"—is in fact absent from a particular society or population that comes under a shared political control? Can there be law, and a legal system, even if the members of the society or the polity do *not* exhibit any sort of consensus as to the rules and their legitimacy?

In my view, Lon Fuller, a contemporary of H.L.A. Hart, has offered helpful answers to those questions, and the answers illustrate further the different views that can be taken as to the meaning of "law" and "legal system". In his book, THE MORALITY OF LAW,[21] Fuller offers a definition of law that does not depend either on the use or threat of force (as was essential in Austin's view) or on a consensus within society about the legitimacy and binding nature of the rules (essential to Hart's view). For Fuller, whose views are elaborated on in Box #1.1, law is present and legitimate—and constitutes a "legal system"—where rules are general, public, prospective, clear, consistent, capable of being followed, stable (over time), and administered as written. If one or more of these elements are not present, the result is, according to Fuller, something that cannot properly be called a "legal system".

Box #1.1 Lon Fuller and the "Morality" of Law[22]

In his great work, THE MORALITY OF LAW (1964), Lon Fuller argues that law is subject to an internal morality consisting of eight principles relating to the rules that purportedly comprise the legal system. These principles may be summarized in this way:

- (P1) the rules must be expressed in general terms;

- (P2) the rules must be publicly promulgated;

- (P3) the rules must be (for the most part) prospective in effect;

- (P4) the rules must be expressed in understandable terms;

- (P5) the rules must be consistent with one another;

- (P6) the rules must not require conduct beyond the powers of the affected parties;

- (P7) the rules must not be changed so frequently that the subject cannot rely on them; and

- (P8) the rules must be administered in a manner consistent with their wording.

---

21. Lon Fuller, THE MORALITY OF LAW (1964). For a brief biography of Lon Fuller (1902–1978), see *Lon L. Fuller*, appearing in WIKIPEDIA, http://en.wikipedia.org/wiki/Lon_Fuller. Fuller was a professor of law at Harvard University for many years.

22. I have drawn this description in part from an account offered at *Fuller's Morality of Law*, appearing at INTERNET ENCYCLOPEDIA OF PHILOSOPHY: A PEER-REVIEWED ACADEMIC RESOURCE, http://www.iep.utm.edu/l/legalpos/.

In Fuller's view, no system of rules that fails minimally to satisfy these principles of legality can fulfil law's essential purpose of achieving social order through the use of rules that guide behavior. A system of rules that fails to satisfy (P2) or (P4), for example, cannot guide behavior because people will not be able to determine what the rules require. Accordingly, Fuller concludes that his eight principles are "internal" to law in the sense that they are built into the existence conditions for law: "A total failure in any one of these eight directions does not simply result in a bad system of law; it results in something that is not properly called a legal system at all".

These internal principles constitute a morality, according to Fuller, because law necessarily has positive moral value in two respects: (1) law conduces to a state of social order and (2) it does so by respecting human autonomy because rules *guide* behavior. Since no system of rules can achieve these morally valuable objectives without minimally complying with the principles of legality, it follows, on Fuller's view, that they constitute a morality.

Fuller's views have attracted some criticism. For example, H.L.A. Hart has challenged Fuller's claim that the principles of legality constitute an internal morality. In Hart's view, Fuller confuses the notions of morality and efficacy. Hart expresses that criticism as follows:

> [Fuller's] insistence on classifying these principles of legality as a "morality" is a source of confusion both for him and his readers.... [T]he crucial objection to the designation of these principles of good legal craftsmanship as morality, in spite of the qualification "inner", is that it perpetrates a confusion between two notions that it is vital to hold apart: the notions of purposive activity and morality. Poisoning is no doubt a purposive activity, and reflections on its purpose may show that it has its internal principles. ("Avoid poisons however lethal if they cause the victim to vomit"....) But to call these principles of the poisoner's art "the morality of poisoning" would simply blur the distinction between the notion of efficiency for a purpose and those final judgments about activities and purposes with which morality in its various forms is concerned.

In response to Hart's criticism, it may be pointed out that while Fuller's eight principles could be regarded as being predominantly oriented toward efficiency, they do in fact double as moral ideals of fairness. For example, public promulgation in understandable terms (P2 and P4) may be a necessary condition for efficacy, but it is also a moral ideal; it is morally objectionable for a state to enforce rules that have not been publicly promulgated in terms reasonably calculated to give notice of what is required. Similarly, we take it for granted that it is wrong for a state to enact retroactive rules, inconsistent rules, and rules that require what is impossible (disallowed by P3, P5, and P6, respectively). Poisoning may have its internal standards of efficacy, but such standards are distinguishable from the principles of legality in that they conflict with moral ideals.

Nevertheless, Fuller's principles operate internally not as moral ideals, but merely as principles of efficacy. As Fuller would likely acknowledge, the existence of a legal system is consistent with considerable divergence from the principles of legality. Legal standards, for example, are necessarily promulgated in general terms that inevitably give rise to problems of vagueness. And officials all too often fail to administer the laws in a fair and even-handed manner—even in the best of legal systems. These divergences may always be *prima facie* objectionable, but they are inconsistent with a legal system only when they render a legal system incapable of performing its essential function of guiding behavior. Insofar as these principles are built into the existence conditions for law, it is because they operate as efficacy conditions—and not because they function as moral ideals.

Let us now conclude this brief glance at "deeper questions on legal systems". As noted above, the purpose of this excursion was not to study in any detail the views of particular legal theorists—Austin, Hart, or Fuller—but instead to acknowledge and understand that the most fundamental concepts and assumptions that underlie any comparative study of law or of legal traditions are themselves subject to uncertainty based on a whole range of linguistic and cultural differences. Any observer is inevitably biased in his or her observations by the culture and experience that he or she brings to such a comparative study. We cannot discard or overcome those biases completely, but recognizing them may encourage us to approach our studies with greater humility and self-awareness.

D. *"Legal Traditions" for Purposes of This Book*

1. Importance of Historic Conditioning

In the preceding paragraphs, we have seen in general terms what is meant by several complementary concepts that are all bound up in our comparative study of legal traditions. Specifically, we looked at the concepts of "legal tradition", "legal family", and "legal system". We also saw that comparative law literature is replete with disagreements over the methods by which legal systems in the world today should or could be classified into various legal families, as well as some observations as to the possible convergence reportedly taking place among certain legal traditions. In addition, we took a brief excursion into certain deeper questions on legal systems — questions that help explain such disagreements on methods of classifying legal systems into legal families.

With all that as background, we must now settle on what is meant by the term "legal traditions" for purposes of this book, which celebrates that notion in its title. I suggest that we use Merryman's definition of "legal tradition", and place special emphasis on one element of that definition.

Recall that for Merryman, a legal tradition is "a set of deeply rooted, historically conditioned attitudes about the nature of law" and its role in society. Of the various criteria that have been noted above in subsection IB1 of this chapter for identifying and classifying legal traditions and families, the criterion I find most crucial is that of the "historical conditioning" that lies at the center of Merryman's definition.

In other words, the division of the world's countries and legal systems into legal families that share certain legal traditions can most appropriately be carried out, in my view, by finding those historical trends and similarities through which the "attitudes about the nature of law" and its role in society have been *conditioned* over time. In my view, the shared history of a population — even if it includes (as is common) disharmony and violence between different segments of the population — serves as the great flowing river on the surface of which individual events and interactions occur. Great rivers, whether actual or metaphorical, differ greatly from each other. The only proof one needs of this in the case of actual rivers is found in watching the confluence of the Missouri River and the Mississippi River near St. Louis, where waters of different speeds and shades compete and then converge. Likewise, the metaphorical "river" of the civil law tradition has characteristics that distinguish it from other legal traditions, and those distinctive characteristics derive from the particular circumstances of its development over time.

2. Three Great Legal Traditions — Plus Others

With that emphasis on historic conditioning as a crucial criterion in distinguishing among legal traditions that are important in today's world, I have identified for our study in this book "three great legal traditions". They are the civil law tradition, the common law tradition, and the Chinese legal tradition. In order to ensure that we have a basic understanding of the identity of those three legal traditions, I shall devote one paragraph to each here, in anticipation of devoting two chapters to each one later in this book.

The civil law tradition, in brief, is what has developed over the course of about 2,450 years in Western Europe, originating with the famous Twelve Tables issued in 450 BCE. Indeed, for reasons that will become clear in Chapter Two, the civil law tradition could also be referred to as "the Romanist" or the "Romano-Germanic" legal tradition. These names draw attention to the fact that this legal tradition originated with Roman law and later interacted with Germanic laws and influences. I use the simpler term "civil law" in part because its characteristics are actually drawn from a great many other influences beyond the Romanist and Germanic influences—such as canon law and commercial law, for example—and therefore a label that does not try to reflect any specific individual influences seems more appropriate. In fact, as noted above, the civil law tradition has been described as comprising five sub-traditions, all of which relate to crucial historical developments and trends. They are: (1) Roman law, which matured over about a thousand years; (2) canon law, which arose in secret with Christianity but flowered when that religion gained official endorsement by the Roman authorities in the 4th century CE; (3) commercial law, which in a sense dates back into the infinite past but coalesced normatively and institutionally with the Crusades starting in the 11th century; (4) the great intellectual revolution that exploded in Western Europe around the 17th century but had its early stirrings half a millennium earlier; and (5) the "legal science" movement that gained momentum (especially in Germany) in the 19th century. Those historical developments and trends affected the law not only in Europe but, because of the campaigns of conquest and colonization undertaken by European states starting in about the 16th century, have shaped the legal systems of many countries around the world.

The common law tradition is much younger than the civil law tradition and finds its origin in 11th century England. English common law—that is, the law that was gradually seen to be (or made to be) "common" to all of England—displaced the local customary rules of behavior because of the unprecedented strength of William the Conqueror and others who followed him as monarch in England. Partly because of the much smaller geographical scope of its coverage, English common law experienced fewer external influences and therefore has fewer "sub-traditions" than does the civil law tradition, enumerated above. English common law did, however, develop in a peculiar way because of internal political developments and conflicts between the centralized monarchy and provincial political leaders as well as between the monarchy and the parliamentary (legislative) authorities. None of those peculiar and internal developments would be of lasting significance, of course, if England had not extended its political, economic, and cultural influence around the world. But it did exactly that, quickly challenging (and often out-maneuvering) those states of continental Europe in the great frenzy of conquest and colonization that occurred in the 1600s through the 1800s. Hence the common law, with its peculiar preference for judge-made rules, its penchant for "equity" (as made manifest by an entirely separate set of courts arising in about the 16th century), and its high degree of comfort with legal disorganization, clearly qualifies as one of the "great legal traditions".

Chinese law, unlike the civil law and common law traditions, did not leave its birthplace and spread widely around the world. Instead, reflecting the inward-looking nature of Chinese culture, Chinese law extended in application only over the central portion of what is today the People's Republic of China, only gradually moving northward and westward to encompass the Mongolian highlands, western deserts, and Tibetan plateau. Nevertheless, Chinese law qualifies as a "great legal tradition" for at least two reasons: (i) the size of the population subject to Chinese law has been huge for many centuries and now constitutes about one-fifth of the world's population; (ii) the level of continuity in its development, and especially in its characteristic legal codes, is unmatched by any other legal tradition. As we shall see in Chapter Six below, Chinese law is remarkable also for its highly sophisticated but (from a Western viewpoint) highly unusual internal conflict between two seemingly incompatible concepts of law and governance.

In addition to these three "great legal traditions" that this book highlights, there are several other legal traditions of greater or lesser importance in today's world. One is socialist law, which as a historical matter emerged from the civil law tradition but adopted Marxist-Leninist views of law, government, and economics that for about seventy years created such a radical departure from the rest of the civil law tradition as to warrant regarding socialist law as its own legal tradition. Indeed, most comparative law courses in the USA up until the mid 1990s—and many books on comparative law until that time— treated socialist law with the same respect as civil law and common law. That ended with the collapse of the Soviet Union and with the recognition that China's legal system embraces "socialism" in name only. (We shall examine this matter in Chapters Six and Seven, below.)

Islamic law, Hindu law, and Jewish law also may be regarded as legal traditions that have the same degree of significance in most respects as common law, civil law, and Chinese law. Islamic law and Hindu law, however, do not predominate in the legal system of any country in the world (with the arguable exception of Islamic law in Iran and perhaps one or two other states), and Jewish law has a scope of application (as a geographic and demographic matter) that is insignificant compared with that of civil law, common law, and Chinese law.

In a somewhat different category from the legal traditions listed above (and a few others, such as Scandinavian law, could also have been mentioned) might be indigenous law, in a specific meaning of that term. In one sense, of course, every legal system in the world has elements of "indigenous" law. Those are the elements that create differences between the various legal systems that are members of a particular "legal family" as defined above. What makes Belgian law different, for example, from French law, or the law of Brazil different from the law of Venezuela, is that the indigenous elements differ from one country to another even though the countries may share a legal tradition and therefore be members in the same legal family (the civil law family, in the case of the countries mentioned immediately above). In a different sense, however, we might regard certain societies on the planet that have for any number of reasons *not* come significantly under the influence of a foreign legal tradition as having their own indigenous legal traditions—unadulterated, as it were, by any other. This would apply, for example, to certain relatively small indigenous tribes and peoples who have either (i) escaped invasion by or significant interaction with other cultures, or (ii) successfully resisted absorption into a dominant culture. An example of the former would be certain aboriginal tribes that have remained hidden from view to the rest of the world in tropical rainforests. An example of the latter would be certain Native American tribes and nations that despite the brutal inhumanity by which they have been treated by European invaders have nonetheless retained their legal systems to a greater or lesser degree. To the extent that such indigenous legal systems share certain characteristics, perhaps it would be appropriate to regard those indigenous systems as sharing an indigenous "legal tradition". This is, however, a matter of speculation, both factual and theoretical.

II. The Value and Challenge of a Comparative Study of Law

This is a book on what is commonly called "comparative law". We already know from section I of this chapter that legal traditions as defined there—as well as legal systems and legal families—lie at the heart of this book. In what sense, though, will our study of such legal traditions constitute an exercise in "comparative law"? And what are we trying to accomplish by engaging in such a "comparative law" study? This second section of Chapter One opens with a consideration of those questions and then identifies some of the challenges that a comparative study of law presents and how I intend to address those challenges in this book—by integrating two perspectives: the history of each of the great legal traditions and the contemporary operation of each, all from a comparative point of view.

A. "Comparative Law" as a Term and a Discipline

1. What Comparative Law Is

It is important to note at the outset that the term "comparative law" is somewhat of a misnomer. Here is how one authority discusses the term "comparative law":

> The first question that arises is: what is the nature of comparative law? Is it a branch of law, like family law or property law? Further, since law is sometimes defined as a "body of rules", is there any identifiable body of rules known as "comparative law"? The answer to both these questions is in the negative.[23]

Hence, comparative law—or, expressed precisely, the comparative study of law—is in fact more a method than a subject. Indeed, another authority, in addressing what "comparative law" means, has explained that those "words suggest an intellectual activity with law as its object and comparison as its process".[24] The same authority elaborates on this definition of "comparative law" as follows:

> Now comparisons can be made between different rules in a single legal system, as, for example, between different paragraphs of the German civil code. If this were all that was meant by comparative law, it would be hard to see how it differed from what lawyers normally do: lawyers constantly have to juxtapose and harmonize the rules of their own system, that is, compare them, before they can reach any practical decision or theoretical conclusion. Since this is characteristic of every national system of law, "comparative law" must mean more than appears on the surface. The extra dimension is that of internationalism. Thus "comparative law" is the comparison of the different legal systems of the world.[25]

---

23. de Cruz 1993, *supra* note 11, at 2. The same author goes on to suggest that comparative law is "therefore a *method of study* rather than a legal body of rules" and that for this reason it might be preferable to describe comparative law by its French equivalent, "*droit comparé*". *Id.* at 3 (emphasis in original).

24. Zweigert and Kötz, *supra* note 3, at 2.

25. *Id.* Using the terminology that is explained in section I of this chapter, we might wish to replace the term "legal systems of the world" with "legal traditions of the world".

2. What Comparative Law Is Not

The commonly-used term "comparative law" might also be explained by identifying what it does *not* involve. For one thing, a mere study of *foreign law* is insufficient:

> One can speak of comparative law only if there are specific comparative reflections on the problem to which the work is devoted. Experience shows that this is best done if the author first lays out the essentials of the relevant foreign law ... and then uses this material as a basis for critical comparison....[26]

Likewise, comparative law is completely separate from both private international law and public international law. Private international law "is a discrete *body of law* which is also known as the *Conflict of Laws*, or the Laws of Conflicts because it is a form of *private law* which deals with situations involving private individuals in which there is a possible conflict of applicable laws".[27] Public international law, by contrast, refers to the body of law that governs relationships between nation-states and international organizations. Whereas comparative law deals almost exclusively with legal rules and institutions that exist at the national (or occasionally sub-national) level, the rules of public international law typically exist beyond the realm of the individual nation-state and indeed are often created through collective action by nation-states—most notably, of course, in the case of treaty rules.

In short, the term "comparative law" is rather odd. The term disguises the reality (i) that it refers to a *method* more than to a *subject* and (ii) that the overall aim of "comparative law" is to offer critical comparisons between corresponding elements of different legal traditions and the national legal systems that those legal traditions have influenced.

B. *Possible Aims of a Comparative Study of Law*

I have just suggested that the overall aim of comparative law—or more precisely of a comparative study of law—is to arrive at cross-tradition or cross-system comparisons. But to what end? That is, what might be the more *specific* aims of a comparative study of law? I would identify six such specific aims.[28]

1. Legal Self-Awareness and Self-Identity

Paradoxically, one of the most important reasons for embarking on a comparative study of law—at least if the comparison involves one's own legal system—is to bring a clearer understanding of that very legal system. In this respect, comparative law might be regarded as a reflective exercise. One authority explains this in the context of legal education in the USA: "[A] comparative law course often provides an American law student's first opportunity to reflect on the US legal system as a functioning whole".[29] That same authority elaborates on this point as follows:

---

26. *Id.*

27. de Cruz 1993, *supra* note 11, at 6 (emphasis in original). The same author goes on to explain that "[t]he function of private international law is to provide a solution as to which of several possible legal systems should be applied to a given case which has a foreign element". *Id.*

28. For a similar listing of such aims, see Nutshell-1999, *supra* note 9, at 7–10. For a different listing—encompassing "(1) practical or professional; (2) scientific or sociological; and (3) cultural or humanistic"—see Merryman-2010, *supra* note 2, at 52.

29. Nutshell-1999, *supra* note 9, at 10.

When we say that comparative law enables students to understand their own legal system better, we do not just mean that it will move them away from assuming their own ways are the best or the only ways of doing things. We also hope that they will acquire a better sense of what is valuable and capable of development in their own system. Above all, we are confident that those of you who are embarking for the first time on a comparative venture will have new insights that would not have occurred to you if your imagination had remained exclusively within the confines of the law of the United States.[30]

2. Law Reform

Related to the aim of gaining further awareness and understanding of one's own legal system is the aim of actually bringing improvements to that legal system by studying how various other ("foreign") legal systems offer differing solutions to similar problems. One way of characterizing this process is by likening it to a scientific experiment:

> [O]ne may say that comparative law gives us as much access to a "laboratory" as lawyers can ever have. Since controlled experimentation in law is hardly ever possible, legal scholars often use comparative law to expand their theater of observation, to see how other legal systems have dealt with problems similar to ours. The hope is that the experiences of countries at comparable stages of social and economic development will give us insight into our own situation and that they may help us to find our own paths through the maze.[31]

This "law reform" aim of comparative legal studies has a long history. According to one authority, "[p]erhaps the earliest example of the use of the comparative method for legislative purposes is when Greeks and Romans visited cities which they felt could provide them with models of laws that were worth enacting in their own country".[32] And another authority has asserted that "[l]egislators all over the world have found that on many matters good laws cannot be produced without the assistance of comparative law".[33]

3. Sociological Understanding

In some cases, of course, the specific aim of a comparative study of law has nothing to do with one's own legal system — either in the way of self-awareness or in terms of introducing improvements — but is instead undertaken for the purpose of enhancing one's

---

30. *Id.* at 6. Another source expresses the point quite bluntly: "Comparative law offers the law student [the opportunity to] understand his own law better". Zweigert and Kötz, *supra* note 3, at 15.

31. Nutshell-1999, *supra* note 9, at 7–8. Yet another authority offers a formulation that carries a closely similar meaning, asserting that one reason to study foreign and comparative law "is to deprovincialize students, broaden their perspectives, and show them that other people can do things differently and yet survive and prosper". Merryman-2010, *supra* note 2, at 1–2.

32. de Cruz 1993, *supra* note 11, at 16. Another source explains that "Classical Greeks made the earliest recorded efforts explicitly to classify legal systems.... For instance, Plato ... in his *Laws* discussed the rules of several Greek and other *poleis* (city-states) in formulating his ideal code and legal institutions for Magnesia". David S. Clark, *Comparative Legal Systems*, in I Encyclopedia of Law and Society: American and Global Perspectives 224, 225 (David S. Clark ed., 2007).

33. Zweigert and Kötz, *supra* note 3, at 12. Zweigert and Kötz refer to this process as "happy plagiarism". *Id.* at 13. They also credit Rudolph Jhering for this proposition: "No one bothers to fetch a thing from afar when he has one good or better at home, but only a fool would refuse quinine just because it didn't grow in his back garden". *Id.*

understanding of society, either of a "foreign" legal culture or of humanity at large. Here is how one authority describes that aim:

> Comparative law is also an indispensable heuristic method for legal and social theory. Montesquieu, Tocqueville, Durkheim, and Max Weber all used comparative study to illuminate the history and growth of the law, its role in society, its relation to behavior and ideas. Comparative law helps us to understand the dynamics of social, as well as legal, change.[34]

This "sociological understanding" aim of comparative law need not be so sweeping as that quoted passage suggests. It could instead focus on rather narrowly-confined topics or rules of law in different systems with an eye to understanding certain cultural values that differ from one nation to another. An example would be a comparative study of inter-country adoptions in two different countries in order to identify various social values relating to the definition of the family and the acceptance of mixed-race households. Another example would be a comparative study of the criminal treatment of juvenile offenders.[35]

4. A Tool of Construction

Whereas the first and second specific aims of a comparative study of law described above — legal self-awareness and law reform — would typically apply mainly to law students and to legislators, respectively, another possible specific aim of comparative law applies to judges. The following explanation of this point has been offered:

> The comparative method has frequently been of practical significance through courts and the judicial process, in filling gaps in legislation or in case law, in providing the background and origin to legal rules and concepts which have been inherited or transplanted from other jurisdictions, in matters which are not covered by a code provision or statute or caselaw authority.[36]

The same benefit would apply not just to judges operating at the national (or sub-national) level but also to judges and others responsible for "interpreting treaties, and in helping to understand some of the concepts and institutions of customary international law".[37]

5. Cross-Border Legal Practice

Perhaps the most obvious specific aim of a comparative study of law to most lawyers would be one that applies not to students or to legislators or to judges but instead to practitioners. As international business transactions become more and more common, most practitioners will find themselves required to deal with, and therefore to understand, at least certain principal elements of numerous legal systems and how those elements compare to corresponding elements of the practitioner's own system.

One authority has offered this explanation:

---

34. Nutshell-1999, *supra* note 9, at 8.

35. See, e.g., Jelani Jefferson and John Head, *In Whose "Best Interests"? — An International and Comparative Assessment of US Rules on Sentencing of Juveniles*, 1 HUMAN RIGHTS AND GLOBALIZATION LAW REVIEW 89 (2008).

36. de Cruz 1993, *supra* note 11, at 17.

37. Zweigert and Kötz, *supra* note 3, at 7. Those authors go on to identify certain international legal principles, such as *pacta sunt servanda* (*i.e.*, treaty and contract commitments are to be observed) and assert that "it is only through comparative law that [such principles] can be made to yield their full potential". *Id.*

The comparative law method will increasingly be useful in a practical way for the modern and up-to-date practitioner.... [W]hen you consider that so many systems have transplanted and borrowed so many concepts from the major legal [traditions] and adapted them, it is becoming increasingly necessary to be [generally familiar] with a range of traditions and doctrines, not just because of closer inter-regional cooperation and trade but also because of the setting up of transnational law firms, transnational litigation, the ever-growing influence of American corporations in foreign countries, drafting of trasnational [*sic*] contracts, and international credit arrangements.[38]

6. Contributing to a Harmonization of Law

A final specific aim of comparative legal studies refers to an urge that grows and diminishes from time to time at the international level — the harmonization or unification of law from one system to another. Let us look briefly at these two phenomena — harmonization and unification — separately, because they have attracted very different levels of interest and support over the years.

Although some efforts at wide-spread unification of laws may be seen far back in ancient history, one authority finds that unification "on a world-wide scale" dates back only about a century and a half:

> The first organised measures taken toward unification occurred simultaneously with the revival of interest in comparative law studies but were at first limited to the field of maritime and commercial law. All this was greatly assisted by the great expansion of international trade in the nineteenth century which produced various unificatory international conventions dealing with private law, commercial law, trade and labour law, copyright and industrial property law, the law of transport by rail, sea and air, [and] parts of procedural law.... It is also worth noting the work of the Hague Conference in private international law and the Rome Institute for the Unification of Law [as well as] ... the ongoing work of UNCITRAL which shows the continuing interest in some measure of unification in [the twentieth] century.
>
> ... Unlike unification which contemplates the substitution of two or more legal systems with one single system, *harmonisation of law* arises exclusively in comparative law literature and especially in conjunction with interjurisdictional, private transactions. Harmonisation seeks to "effect an approximation or co-ordination of different legal provisions or systems by eliminating major differences and creating minimum requirements or standards".[39]

Another form of harmonization involves not the creation of new (similar) laws but instead in the finding of pre-existing commonalities and harmonies in national and international legal settings. As one authority has pointed out, "comparative law is essential to the understanding of 'the general principles of law recognised by civilised nations'

---

38. de Cruz 1993, *supra* note 11, at 18. The same author goes on to emphasize the benefits that understanding a foreign legal system can yield in terms of setting up companies and dealing with dispute resolution issues. *Id.*

39. de Cruz 1993, *supra* note 11, at 19–20 (emphasis in original). By most definitions, "harmonization" would also encompass the work of the EU system of issuing "directives" for the purpose of bringing laws of member states into "approximation", even though not amounting to a full "unification" of those laws.

which are laid down as being one of the sources of public international law by art. 38(1)(c) of the statute of the international court of justice".[40]

C. Waxing and Waning Influence of Comparative Legal Studies

1. History of Comparative Law Studies

Having just identified six specific possible aims of a comparative study of law, we might assume that comparative legal studies are vigorously undertaken and enthusiastically embraced today and over recent decades. This is not the case. For a number of years, academics involved in comparative legal studies have bemoaned the perceived disinterest that the world at large has shown in their work. One author has claimed that comparative law "is experiencing something of an identity crises",[41] another has noted that comparative law "lacks form and direction" and that "confusion ... prevails",[42] and yet another says that despite the seeming significance of comparative law, it "still occupies a rather modest position in academic curricula".[43] Perhaps this tepid reception that comparative law has received reflects the legal provincialism that is referred to below as one of the principal challenges to comparative law (see subsection IIC2 of this chapter).

Whatever the reason, the discipline of comparative law may be seen as having a rather odd history, waxing and waning in interest over time. Box #1.2 offers a synopsis of the history of comparative law. As noted there, it may be seen as starting in some form in ancient times. In more modern times, it did not start building much momentum until about the year 1900.

Box #1.2 History of Comparative Law[44]

Although comparative law—the comparative study of law—had its great awakening around 1900, some early exercises in comparative law may be found in ancient Greece and Rome. For example, in his Laws, Plato compares the laws of the Greek city states. It is reported that Aristotle also examined the constitutions of over 150 city-states before writing his Politics. In Roman times, legal scholars "turned their attention to other systems of the ancient world" and examined "the different laws of Greece as well as the sense of justice common to them"; in addition, they took into account "the near Eastern [legal] systems in cuneiform ... and the recently discovered laws of ancient societies in the Mediterranean basin". [Zweigert and Kötz, *supra* note 3, at 7, quoting in part from a 1953 text by Wenger] For example, in the 3rd or 4th century CE (one source dates it as late as 400 CE), the *Collatio legum Mosaicarum et Romanarum* (also known as the *Lex Dei*) set excerpts of classical Roman legal writing next

---

40. Zweigert and Kötz, *supra* note 3, at 6. This assertion that the principal method for determining what is or what is not a "general principle of law" by conducting a comparative survey of national laws is well-accepted in the pertinent academic literature.

41. Nutshell-1999, *supra* note 9, at 3.

42. John Henry Merryman, *Comparative Law Scholarship*, 21 Hastings International and Comparative Law Review 771, 771–772 (1998).

43. Zweigert and Kötz, *supra* note 3, at 3.

44. I have drawn this summary mainly from Zweigert and Kötz, *supra* note 3, at 2–3 and 42–43 and from de Cruz 1993, *supra* note 11, at 8–15. Pinpoint citations for quoted passages appear in brackets.

to the laws of Moses, "presumably with the aim of furthering Christian belief by showing that Roman and biblical law were similar". [*Id.* at 42–43] There was insularity in Rome as well, however: Cicero is reported to have described all non-Roman law as "confused and quite absurd". [*Id.* at 42]

Some legal inquiry that may be regarded as comparative law appeared in the 17th and 18th centuries. The French social commentator and political theorist Montesquieu (1689–1755), for example, has been regarded by some as being a founder of comparative law in placing his teachings of natural law on an empirical footing. [de Cruz 1993, *supra* note 11, at 10]

The interest in comparative law quickened in the early 19th century, when German jurists founded a journal for the study of comparative law and a Chair of Comparative Law was founded at the College of France. Moreover, Sir Henry Maine may be credited with some of the earliest comparative law work in more modern times. In the preface to his *Ancient Law* (1861), Maine (who was the first occupant of the Corpus Chair of Historical and Comparative Jurisprudence at Oxford) explained that "[t]he chief object of the following pages is to indicate some of the earliest ideas of mankind, as they are reflected in Ancient Law, and to point out the relation of those ideas to modern thought". In another work, Maine declared that "[t]he chief function of comparative jurisprudence is to facilitate legislation and the practical improvement of the law". [de Cruz 1993, *supra* note 11, at 11, citing Maine's *Village Communities*] And according to some sources, the emphasis being given at about the same time (the latter half of the 19th century) to evolution and Darwinism gave further "impetus for the modern methods of comparative law"; indeed one author writing at the time hailed "the comparative method" as "the greatest intellectual achievement of our time". [de Cruz 1993, *supra* note 11, at 11, citing an 1873 work on comparative politics by Freeman]

The first scholarly organization of comparative lawyers, the French *Societé de Législation Comparée*, was established in Paris in 1869 and began publishing a journal in the next year. A German journal of comparative law began publication in 1878, and the English Society of Comparative Legislation was established in 1895. [Merryman-2010, *supra* note 2, at 3] Modern comparative law, however, is generally said to have started in Paris in 1900. In that year the International Congress for Comparative Law was founded by French scholars. "The temper of the Congress was in tune with the times, whose increasing wealth and splendour had given everyone, scholars included, an imperturbable faith in progress. Sure of his existence, certain of its point and convinced of its success, man was trying to break out of his local confines and peaceably to master the world and all that was in it. [According to this view, as expressed by legal scholars, a] world law must be created—not today, perhaps not even tomorrow—but created it must be, and comparative law must create it". [Zweigert and Kötz, *supra* note 3, at 2] In particular, "comparative law must resolve the accidental and divisive differences in the laws of peoples at similar stages of cultural and economic development, and reduce the number of divergences in law, attributable ... to historical accident or to temporary or contingent circumstances". [*Id.*]

Although the belief in progress that gripped the early part of the 20th century soon dissipated (in part because of the horrors that World War I had brought by the second decade of that century), comparative law has continued to grow over the intervening period. What has not emerged, however, is a consensus as to the most appropriate aims and methods of the discipline.

2. Challenges to a Comparative Study of Law

One of the reasons comparative law is "experiencing something of an identity crisis", as noted above, is that it is an extraordinarily challenging discipline—not simply because it is intellectually demanding (many disciplines share that feature) but because of the intrinsic difficulties in making comparisons between laws and the societies they serve. One authority has offered this enumeration of "potential pitfalls that must be borne in mind by any comparative lawyer":[45]

- linguistic and terminological perspectives [recall the earlier reference to the variety of terms used in French for "law" or "the laws"];
- cultural differences between legal systems;
- the potentiality of arbitrariness in selection of objects of study;
- difficulties in achieving "comparability" in comparison;
- the desire to see a common legal pattern in legal systems—that is, overemphasizing the validity of the theory of a general pattern of development [of the sort that Maine propounded];
- the tendency to impose one's own (native) legal conceptions and expectations on the systems being compared; and
- dangers of exclusion/ignorance of extra-legal rules [that is, the dangers of not taking into account certain types of rules that one might not easily recognize as being part of the legal system—as noted below in Chapters Six and Seven, this is a danger at work in Western studies of Chinese law until very recently].

To this list might be added two rather more obvious challenges that a comparative study of law presents. These have been touched on briefly near the beginning of this chapter.

- the sheer bulk of the material available for study, given the large number of legal systems in the world; and
- the highly personal approach that the comparativist inevitably takes in undertaking his or her study—reflecting a range of influences such as culture, general mode of education, and experience in practicing or studying law.

No wonder, with all these rather intimidating challenges, that the discipline of comparative law is, according to some observers, less robustly and less effectively embraced both in legal education and in practice than some would wish. In my view, however, those challenges can be met by combining two related methods. It is to those that I now turn.

D. Integrating Two Perspectives: History and Contemporary Operation

I propose using a two-perspective approach to undertaking a comparative study of law. This approach integrates the history and the contemporary operation of legal traditions—and in particular, the three great legal traditions of civil law, common law, and Chinese law. In the closing paragraphs of this chapter I shall elaborate slightly on these two perspectives, before embarking on an examination of those three great legal traditions, starting with the civil law tradition.

---

45. This list, as reformatted, is drawn from de Cruz 1993, *supra* note 11, at 35.

1. Comparative Legal History

Like the term "comparative law", the term "comparative legal history" is somewhat of a misnomer. The more precise term to convey the meaning of "comparative legal history" would be "comparative study of legal history". That is the exercise—the adventure—with which I believe any intelligent comparative study of law must begin.

In taking that view, I keep good company. Two eminent experts on comparative law, Zweigert and Kötz, offer these rather emphatic observations about the importance of legal history and its relationship to comparative law:

> The relationship between comparative law and legal history is surprisingly complex. At first sight one is tempted to say that while comparative law studies legal systems co-existent in space [and is in that sense "horizontal" in character], legal history studies systems consecutive in time [and is in that sense "vertical" in character]. But there is more to it than that. For one thing, all legal history uses the comparative method: the legal historian cannot help bringing to the study of his chosen system, say Roman Law, the various preconceptions of his own modern system; he is bound to make comparisons, consciously if he is alert, unconsciously if he is not. Secondly, an expanded notion of comparative law would *include* comparative legal history.... If one bears in mind that the founders of modern comparative law were nearly all great legal historians, that without a sense of history even modern comparatists cannot understand foreign solutions, that "legal history actualises the past by spanning time" ... and that we have a more "relative" sense of time and space than our predecessors, then the differences between legal history and comparative law nearly disappear.... The distinction between comparative law and legal history is therefore considerably reduced and it is only with such a qualification that one can accept the opposition between comparative legal history as "vertical comparative law" and the comparison of modern systems as "horizontal comparative law".[46]

In undertaking a comparative study of legal history in this book—particularly in Chapters Two (for civil law), Four (for common law), and Six (for Chinese law)—what specific features shall we look for most closely? For reasons that will be come clear as we proceed, I would mention these six features:

- Codes and other forms of written law. As we shall see, civil law and Chinese law are noteworthy for, and may in some respects be defined by, the rich tradition of reducing legal rules to written form and then organizing them into sophisticated codes. Such codes represent not only intellectual sophistication but also various viewpoints on the importance of written rules as opposed to oral tradition and leadership by the example of a powerful elite.

- The development of courts. We shall also see that a hallmark of the common law tradition—more so than in the civil law tradition and much more so than in Chinese law—is the development of courts in which specific disputes between private parties can be settled by a combination of prior-announced rules (either by legislation or more often by judicial pronouncements in earlier disputes) and (ii)

---

46. Zweigert and Kötz, *supra* note 3, at 7–8.

a sense of equity or fairness as determined and administered by a highly-respected officer of the law: the judge.

• The "packaging" of historical developments into eras or periods. Without some form of "shorthand" or abbreviated generalization, the sheer enormity of detail in, say, European law makes it impossible to see major trends. Hence we shall watch for, and wish to highlight, major eras, such as the "classical period" of Roman law, when (in the 2nd and 3rd centuries CE) the *jurisconsults* were most active, or the period of the "rise of Equity" in England (especially in the 16th century CE), or the Qin-Han period in China, when a grand compromise or "alloy" between two competing legal philosophies set dynastic Chinese law on a long course of stability.

• Contemporaneousness of developments in the three great legal traditions. First for curiosity and then to understand the interaction of civil, common, and Chinese law, we shall want to pay special attention to what different events and trends appear in those traditions at the same time. To assist in that effort, Appendix 1.1 (at the end of this chapter) presents a comparative time line.

• The geographical settings and coverage of the traditions. As noted above in passing, civil law and common law influences have spread throughout the world, largely through conquest and colonization, so that a great many countries on Earth share one or the other (occasionally both) of those legal traditions — and hence are members of either the civil law "legal family" or the common law "legal family" (or occasionally both). In all such countries there is a tug-of-war between these traditions and the indigenous law that predates their introduction. We shall see that in many cases the greater the geographical distance (or cultural distance) from the heartland of a legal tradition, the less influence that legal tradition has on a country's legal system.

• The significance of individuals and coincidences. Legal history is replete with instances in which the emergence of an especially influential individual human being in a particular place at a particular time facilitates an enormous shift in a legal system. Constantine, Justinian, Irnerius, Napoleon, William of Normandy, King John, Edward Coke, Blackstone, Confucius, Qin Shi Huangdi, Dong Zhongshu, Mao Zedong — these individuals unquestionably blazed the trails (sometimes knowingly, sometimes not) of the civil law, the common law, and Chinese law, respectively. In addition, the occurrence of events that at the time might have been seen as random or of only temporary importance — the rediscovery of a large old book (the *Digest*) in the late 11th century, the losing of a single battle (at Hastings, also in the latter part of the 11th century), the terms of a peace treaty (at Versailles following World War I, triggering China's May Fourth Movement) — can be seen in retrospect as having set and changed the course of legal history in these great legal traditions. We shall watch for individuals and events such as these because of the role they play as building blocks of the narrative or "folklore" that surrounds those legal traditions.

2. Contemporary Operation of Legal Systems

The other perspective that I believe makes for an intelligent and fruitful comparative study of law — working in a way that is complementary to the emphasis on *legal history* mentioned above — concentrates on the actual *operation* of legal systems that are representative of or heavily influenced by each of the three great legal traditions. If we were to view this in mathematical terms, it could be expressed in this formula: legal history + contemporary operation of representative legal systems = comparative understanding of legal traditions.

Note that the second element in the formula proposed above refers to "legal systems". In a sense, no "legal tradition" has any operations. Instead, the only one of the three related concepts introduced in subsection IA of this chapter—"legal tradition", "legal family", and "legal system"—that actually *operates* is the last of these. A legal system has actual rules and institutions and legal personnel that facilitate their use. Hence it is necessary to look at the nuts and bolts of specific legal systems, operating at the level of the nation-state, to see how each of the great legal traditions actually plays out in practice. If a legal system is likened to a large truck lumbering down the highway, the legal tradition may be regarded as the source of the truck's fuel and direction, but it is at the level of specific rules and institutions that "the rubber hits the road".

Naturally, it will be necessary to pick and choose what seem to be useful and informative illustrations, drawn from several legal systems, in order to arrive at some understanding of the contemporary manifestation of the three great legal traditions. For the most part, the legal systems to be used for this purpose in Chapters Three (civil law), Five (common law), and Seven (Chinese law) will be several European countries, the UK and the USA, and China—in today's People's Republic of China ("PRC").

What specific aspects of "contemporary operation" will our studies highlight? The following attributes:

- The sources and categories of law—to address the questions: (i) where are the legal rules of the society seen as coming from, either literally (as in the case of a legislature or a constitution) or figuratively (as in the case of custom); and (ii) into what categories or classifications are the legal rules and institutions divided for purposes of legal practice, court jurisdiction, and so forth?

- Criminal procedure—to examine the methods the society uses (through its legal system) to deal with persons who are charged with violating the rules, and in particular what comparisons exist on such issues as evidence, the role and powers of the state, the structure of the proceedings, the rights of the accused, the interests of victims, and the main purposes of prosecution.

- The legal profession(s)—to see how the legal system organizes the education, licensing, and operations of the "personnel" of the law, such as legislators, judges, government attorneys, defense attorneys, other advocates, notaries, juries, and legal scholars.

- Court structures—to compare the organization of jurisdiction, as into a single pyramidal structure or a series of largely separate systems of courts, including entities that are specifically devoted to reviewing legislative action and administrative action.

- The role of codified law—to assess how the use of legislation generally, and carefully-constructed codes in particular, reflects such values as legal certainty and case-by-case fairness.

As a final element of the "operational" aspect of legal systems, we shall also try to take account of the role of religion and ideology—that is, to dig beneath the surface of the legal rules and institutions into the non-legal foundations and beliefs that lie at the heart of the legal tradition(s) that most strongly influence the legal system.

Appendix 1.1
Comparative Time Lines for the Three Great Legal Traditions

Detailed Comparative Timeline of the Three Great Legal Traditions
Selected Relevant Legal and Political Developments

Dates (BCE = BC CE = AD)	Chinese Legal Tradition (focusing on mainland China)	Civil Law Tradition (focusing on Europe)	Common Law Tradition (focusing on England and USA)
before about 1200 BCE	earliest dynasties: Xia Dynasty (22nd century to 18th century) and Shang Dynasty (18th century to 12th century)		
1122 ? / 1027 ?	beginning of the Chou [Zhou] Dynasty; originally it is Xi Chou [Western Chou] Dynasty, with 15 emperors, until the capital moves to Laoyi in 771		
—1000 BCE—			
771	the Chou Dynasty becomes the Dong Chou [Eastern Chou] Dynasty, with 25 emperors; also the beginning of the "Spring & Autumn" period (771–481)		
551	Confucius is born (died 479 BCE)		
536	*Xíng shū* [books of punishment] are inscribed on bronze tripod vessels in state of Zheng [Cheng], followed by similar *xíng shū* in state of Chin in 513		
501	*Chu hsing* [bamboo punishments] are used in state of Zheng [Cheng]		
—500 BCE—			
450		Twelve Tables are issued	
400	Li K'uei's Canon of Laws [*Fa Jing*] are (supposedly) promulgated by prime minister of the state of Wei		

Year	China	Mediterranean / Europe	Britain
410		Sack of Rome	(Roman legions leave Britain)
420	beginning of the Nan-Bei [South-North] Dynasties, during which several states were established and then destroyed		(Jutes & Anglo-Saxons arrive in Britain)
438		Theodosian Code	
476		Fall of Rome	
—500 CE—			
506		*Lex Romana Visigothorum* is compiled	
533		Justinian's *Digest* is issued	
565		Lombards invade Italy	
581	end of the Nan-Bei Dynasties and beginning of the Sui Dynasty; but Sui Dynasty did not fully displace the preceding dynasty in the South until 589		
581	Sui Code (*Kaihuang Lü*) is issued (then revised in 583)		
596			England converted to Christianity
600			Laws of King Æthelbert (Kent)
618	beginning of the Tang Dynasty, with 24 emperors		
653	Tang Code is issued		
711		Arabs invade Spanish peninsula	
800		Charlemagne crowned	
907	end of the Tang Dynasty, and beginning of the "Five Dynasty Period", with 13 emperors		
960	beginning of the Song [Sung] Dynasty		
963	Song Code is issued (largely a copy of the Tang Code)		

—1000 CE—			
1066			Battle of Hastings (Norman "conquest")
1070–1080 (about)		Rediscovery of *Digest*	
1080s onward (about)		Irnerius lectures in Bologna	
1086			Domesday Book
1096		First Crusade is launched	
1140		Gratian writes *Decretum*	
1158		Emperor Frederick Barbarossa issues *Authentica Habita*	
1206	end of the (Northern) Song Dynasty and beginning of the Yüan Dynasty (but the Nan Song [Southern Song] Dynasty is not displaced until 1279)		
1215		4th Lateran Council prohibits clerics from participating in "ordeals"	Magna Carta signed
1240 (about)		Accursius writes *Glossa Ordinaria*	
1285			Statute of Westminster II
1290			Statute *Quia Emptores*
1291	a principal Yüan Code [*Chih-yüan hsin-ko*] is issued, followed by others in the 1320s and 1330s		
1350		Bartolus is oustanding Commentator	
1368	end of the Yüan Dynasty and beginning of the Ming Dynasty, with 17 emperors		
1374	the first Ming Code is issued		
1453		Charles VII orders French compilation of French *coutumes*	War of the Roses (1453–1485) (Chancellor gains autonomy)

403	beginning of "Period of the Warring States"	
376		*praetor* position is established
242		*praetor peregrinus* position is established
221	end of the "Period of the Warring States"; the State of Qin swallows its rivals to create the Qin Dynasty, which is the first fully centralized empire in Chinese history	
206	end of the Qin Dynasty and beginning of the Han Dynasty; originally it is the Xi Han [Western Han] Dynasty, with 14 emperors	
128	Han Code (*Chiu-chang lü* [Code in Nine Sections]) is issued	
—0 BCE / CE—		
161		*Institutes* of Gaius issued
220	end of the Han Dynasty, and beginning of the "Period of Three States" (a total of 11 emperors)	
235		end of the "Classical" period of Roman law
265	end of the "Period of Three States", and beginning of the Jin Dynasty; originally it is the Xi Jin [Western Jin] Dynasty, with 4 emperors	
285		Diocletian divides empire into east and west for administrative purposes
313		Edict of Milan
317	The Jin Dynasty becomes the Dong Jin [Eastern Jin] Dynasty, with 11 emperors	
330		Constantinople dedicated

1495	Roman law (modernized) is made applicable in German courts
—1500 CE—	
1602	*Slade's Case* starts contract law
1616	Compromise of 1616, limiting further expansion of Equity
1616	beginning of the Qing Dynasty, with 12 emperors; it is established in 1616 in northeast (Manchuria) and displaces the Ming in 1644
1641	Star Chamber abolished
1646	the first Qing Code [*Ta Qing lü*] is issued
1648	Peace of Westphalia ends Thirty Years War
1667	French *ordonnance* unifies civil procedure law
1740	the definitive version of the Qing Code [*Ta Qing lü-li*] is issued
1765	Blackstone's *Commentaries* published
1776	American Revolution
1789	French Revolution
1794	Prussian Code [*Preussisches allgemeines Landrecht*] is issued
1794	(absorption of commercial law into common law—late 1700s)
1804	French *Code Civil* adopted
1807–1811	other French codes adopted
1811	Austrian Code is issued
1815 (about)	beginning of "codification debate" in the United States
1832	procedural reforms in England
1848	The Field Code of civil procedure is adopted in New York state

1871	Germany is united
1873–1875	Judicature Acts approved (England)
1896	German *BGB* is approved
1900	German *BGB* is effective
1911	end of the Qing Dynasty
1919	May Fourth Movement
1923	beginning of the Restatement movement in the United States
1949	founding of the People's Republic of China, under Communist control
1966	Cultural Revolution begins
1972	UK enters EEC
1976	end of the Cultural Revolution, and death of Mao Zedong
1979	new Criminal Code is issued; massive legal reform effort begins
1992	Maastricht Treaty spurs further unification of EU
1997	revised Criminal Code is issued
—2000 CE—	
2001	PRC enters the World Trade Organization

Appendix 1.2
Key Dates and Epochs in the Three Great Legal Traditions

Civil Law Tradition

450 BCE	Twelve Tables issued
376 BCE	*praetor* position established
100s–200s CE	classical jurists (e.g., Ulpian)
200s	beginning of intense buildup of barbarian pressures on frontiers
313	Edict of Milan (Emperor Constantine allows Christianity)
410	sack of Rome
476	Fall of Rome (western part of empire)
533	Justinian's compilation (*Corpus Juris Civilis*)
"Dark Ages"	decentralization, feudalism, prevalence of customary "law"
800	Charlemagne tries to reclaim Holy Roman Empire
late 11th century	rediscovery of the *Digest*
1100s–1300s	Italian universities; Glossators; commercial law solidified; canon law codified
1140	Gratian's *Decretum*
1240	Accursius' *Glossa Ordinaria*
1400s–1700s	northern universities & Post-Glossators; rise of nation-states
1648	Peace of Westphalia, ending Thirty Years War
1500–1800	colonization; exporting nation-state and civil law tradition
1700–1900	national codifications
1804	French Civil Code
1896	German Civil Code

Common Law Tradition

before 1066 CE	"Anglo-Saxon" law (and the now-invisible Romans)
410	Roman legions leave Britain
420	Jutes & Anglo-Saxons arrive in Britain
600	Laws of King Æthelbert
1066	Battle of Hastings; William establishes strong central control
thru 1215	expanding royal power; "common law" courts
1215	Magna Carta signed
1285	Statute of Westminster II issued
1215–1500s	continued expansion despite Magna Carta; rise of Chancery and "equity" jurisdiction
1500s–1600s	limits on equity; two-track court system gets frozen

1616	"Compromise of 1616"
1700–1900	development of common law; "merger" of law & equity; exportation; statutes
1873–1875	Judicature Acts

Chinese Legal Tradition

1100–500 BCE	Zhou dynasty—golden age, development of *li* (rules of propriety)
500s	Confucius
536	*xíng shū* (books of punishment, on bronze tripod vessels)
400s–300s	rise of Legalism & Confucianism; Warring States
221–206	Qin Dynasty—(re)unification of China as empire
206 BCE–220 CE	Han Dynasty—another golden age
653 CE	Tang Code
1291	Yüan "code" (Mongol domination)
1368/1388	Ming Code (back to the "Han Chinese")
1646/1740	Qing Code (Manchurian control)
1911	dynastic periods ends with the fall of the Qing dynasty
1949	PRC is established
1979	Deng starts China on new course economically (and legally)

Appendix 1.3
Map of Eurasia in Outline

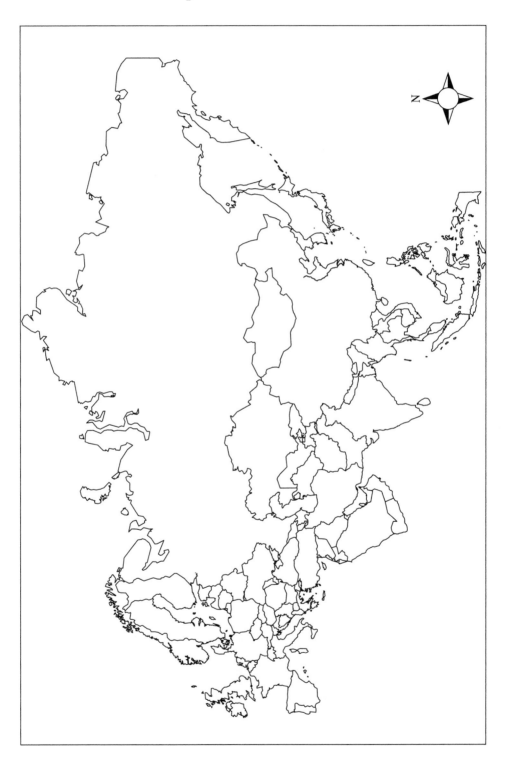

Chapter Two

The Civil Law Tradition in Historical Perspective

Outline

Study Questions

SQ #2.1   In what sense have there been "two lives" of Roman law, and when did each of those "lives" begin?

SQ #2.2   When and why were the *Lex Duodecim Tabularum* (Twelve Tables) enacted, and what is their significance?

SQ #2.3   In early Roman times, what was the main function of:

(a)   the praetor?

(b)   the jurists (*jurisconsults*)?

(c)   the *judex*?

(d)   the edict?

(e)   the formula?

SQ #2.4   How was the peregrine praetor different from the regular ("urban") praetor?

SQ #2.5   What was the *jus gentium* and what was it used for?

SQ #2.6   What was the "classical period" of Roman law, and how do we know about the writings of the classical jurists?

SQ #2.7   Why were the contributions by Gaius and Ulpian especially important?

SQ #2.8   What were some characteristics of Roman law in the century or two before the fall of Rome?

SQ #2.9   When, why, and by whom was the *Corpus Juris Civilis* prepared?

SQ #2.10   What were the four parts of the *Corpus Juris Civilis*, and how did they differ from each other?

SQ #2.11   What does Merryman mean when he says that Justinian was "a reactionary" and "a codifier"?

SQ #2.12   In what sense was the *Digest* (i) authoritative, (ii) disorganized, (iii) binding, and (iv) Christian in its outlook?

SQ #2.13   What, and when, were the "Dark Ages" (and was there light anywhere)?

SQ #2.14   How did the Roman law become "barbarized" or "vulgarized" following the fall of the Roman Empire?

SQ #2.15   What role did the Church play in law during the "Dark Ages"?

SQ #2.16   When, where, and by whom was the *Digest* rediscovered (in the West)?

SQ #2.17   How might the development of the civil law tradition have been different had the *Digest* not been rediscovered when it was?

SQ #2.18   Why was the *Corpus Juris Civilis*, and particularly the *Digest*, an attractive source to use in studying and teaching law in Bologna and other universities beginning in the 12th century?

SQ #2.19   Who were the Glossators, and what was their role — and their significance to the development of the civil law?

SQ #2.20   What was the aim of Gratian's *Decretum*, and how did that work relate to the work of the Glossators?

SQ #2.21   Who were the Post-Glossators (Commentators), and what was their role — and their significance to the development of the civil law?

SQ #2.22   What was the *usus modernus Pandectarum*?

SQ #2.23   When and why did commercial law start becoming more sophisticated in western Europe, and in what sense did it interact with Roman civil law and canon law?

SQ #2.24   What was the *jus commune*, and what were its main components?

SQ #2.25   What is the meaning (in this context) and the significance of the terms "reception" and "pluralism"?

SQ #2.26   What sort of "revolution"(s) occurred in western Europe around the 16th, 17th, and 18th centuries that dramatically changed attitudes not only toward political matters but also toward law?

SQ #2.27   How did the rise of the nation-state in Europe assure that Roman law would generally prevail over canon law?

SQ #2.28   In what ways does the French codification experience illustrate the following:

            (a)   the shift toward centralization of political and law-giving authority?

    (b)   the interaction between customary law, the law of the *jus commune*, and national law?

    (c)   the desire to bring rationality to law?

    (d)   the significance of a single powerful individual in triggering legal change?

SQ #2.29   What was the intended "audience" of the French Civil Code?

SQ #2.30   What are some important ways in which the German codification experience differs from the French codification experience?

SQ #2.31   Which of the two civil codes—German or French—was more "effective"?

SQ #2.32   What evidence is there that the process of "territorial compartmentalization" of the *jus commune* in Europe, which occurred with the rise of the nation-state, might reverse itself?

SQ #2.33   In what year did each of the following events occur?

    (a)   the issuance of the Twelve Tables?

    (b)   the division of the Roman Empire by Diocletian

    (c)   the issuance of the Edict of Milan

    (d)   the fall of Rome to the Ostragoths

    (e)   the issuance of the *Digest*

    (f)   the crowning of Charlemagne as Emperor of the Romans

    (g)   the publication of Accursius' *Glossa Ordinaria*

    (h)   the publication of Gratian's *Decretum*

    (i)   the publication of Hobbes' *Leviathan*

    (j)   the conclusion of the Peace of Westphalia

    (k)   the outbreak of the French Revolution with the storming of the Bastille

    (l)   the issuance of the French Civil Code

    (m)   the political unification of Germany

    (n)   the completion of the German *BGB*

    (o)   the reaching of the 3 billion mark for the Earth's population

    (p)   the reaching of the 6 billion mark for the Earth's population

---

Introductory Comment

Having addressed in Chapter One a range of definitional issues—concerning just what we are focusing on, and why, in undertaking a comparative study of law—we now launch on a journey of exploration in time and space. In this chapter our travels in time will span roughly two and a half millennia, and our travels in space will start near the center of the Italian peninsula and extend from the British Isles to the Bosporus. As should be evident from the foregoing Study Questions, the point of this journey is to gain an appreciation of the remarkable durability and flexibility of the civil law tradition, especially in the light of several fundamental shifts in the political and economic landscape of continental Europe. We should be especially alert to the role played by coincidence, by religion, and by the efforts (and egos) of a relatively few especially influential persons.

I. The "First Life" of Roman Law: Foundation, Maturation, Compilation

The initial phase in the great story of the civil law tradition—a story that this chapter attempts to summarize—lasted about a thousand years, from 450 BCE to the mid-500s CE. At the outset of our study of this phase, we should understand why it is regarded as the "first life" of Roman law. Here is how one authority has explained it:

> Roman law appears to have undergone two distinct periods of development, the *first period* dating from the period of the Roman Empire, and ending with the compilation by the Emperor Justinian (A.D. 527–565).... The *second period* (sometimes referred to as the *revival* or *Renaissance of Roman law* or the *Second Life of Roman law*) began with the scholarly study of Justinian's works in the Italian universities in the late eleventh century A.D. The popularity of this intellectual pursuit spread to the rest of Europe ... leaving a lasting impression on juristic terminology and legal thought as well as on the structure of European legal systems, which continued until the period of the 'great codifications' in the nineteenth century.[1]

This notion of Roman law having had two "lives" is crucial to our understanding of the civil law tradition and warrants another explanation, this one from the great Roman law scholar J.A.C. Thomas:

> [As] has so often been observed, Roman Law had two lives. First, [from its very modest beginnings] as the legal system [that regulated] the relations of a small, essentially agricultural central Italian community, [Roman law ultimately] became the law of the largest commercially-based, multiracial empire known before the peak of that of Britain.... [Then Rome and its law] declined; ... [but it] had the quintessence of its achievement summarized and condensed by a Byzantine Emperor of the sixth century A.D. who sought, successfully but ephemerally, to restore the glories of [Roman law and power as they had existed] a half-millenium or so earlier. And then, from the twelfth century A.D., through the intensive study and utilisation of the compilation of that Byzantine Emperor in the universities of continental Europe, [Roman law enjoyed its second life as] the guiding spirit and inspiration of the law and legal systems of the countries of nascent and renascent Europe so as to become a virtual *ius commune*, common law, of ... occidental Europe. Religion aside, such a resurrection is without parallel.[2]

The following subsections highlight important aspects of the first of the two "lives" of Roman law identified above. That first "life" started with a political power struggle early in the development of the Roman culture and state, and it ended with Justinian's dramatic burst of legislative effort from his base of power in Constantinople in the century following the fall of Rome in 476 CE. Let us begin with an overview of various political and related aspects of Roman times.

---

1. Peter de Cruz, A Modern Approach to Comparative Law 45 (1993) (emphasis in original).
2. J.A.C. Thomas, Textbook of Roman Law 3 (1976).

A. *Overview of Roman Times*

1. Geographic and Chronological Coverage

The maps shown in Figure #2.1 give a general view of the geographic coverage of the Roman Republic and Empire at various points.[3] The first several maps reflect developments up through the fall of Rome in 476; the other maps then continue the story with the Eastern Roman Empire—eventually called the Byzantine Empire because of its headquarters in the city of Constantinople, earlier called Byzantium. (The last two maps extend beyond the time of Justinian and therefore beyond the time of the "first life" of Roman law but have been included to show that Justinian's reclamation of the Italian peninsula was only temporary.) All dates and details on the maps are, of course, approximate.

Although the details of Roman expansion, decline, and fall will not be essential to our survey of Roman law, the seventh and eighth maps in the series shown in Figure #2.1 warrant explanation. First, the very large shaded area on the map for 450 CE represents Attila the Hun's massive empire extending into the Russian plains and pushing further to the south and west on Germanic tribes that had been pressing in on the Roman Empire in the preceding centuries—the Ostragoths, the Visigoths, the Vandals, and others. It was that pressure from Germanic tribes that resulted in the sack of Rome in 410 CE and then the fall of Rome in 476 CE. The map for 476 CE suggests that the Italian peninsula was, following the fall of Rome to the Ostragoths, still part of the Empire; but that was not exactly true. Here is an explanation of the situation:

> The fall of the western empire, reduced to little more than Italy itself by now, came about as in AD 476 a senior military officer called Odoacer led the largely German troops of the western Roman army in a revolt against the emperor. However, Odoacer chose to formally rule in the name of the eastern emperor Zeno [that is, the emperor based in Constantinople at the time. Because of this], Italy therefore formally remain[ed] part of the eastern Roman empire (even though it was in practice an independent kingdom). However, of the western empire, the area of Dalmatia still remained in independent hands, and even contained an emperor, the deposed emperor Julius Nepos. This area ... [also] was eventually absorbed into the Ostrogothic kingdom.[4]

As a political matter, the year 476 CE obviously holds a central place in the history of Rome. Let us put that date in a larger context that begins with a synopsis of that history. Some key dates and developments—with special attention to those having specific legal significance—appear in Box #2.1.

---

3. Innumerable maps of the Mediterranean and European areas during Roman times can be found on the internet—for example, by conducting a Google search for "roman empire maps". The maps shown in Figure #2.1 have been prepared by John Tomasic and Erin Slinker Tomasic, drawing general inspiration from http://www.roman-empire.net/maps/map-empire and from http://historyme-dren.about.com/gi/dynamic/offsite.htm?site=http://www.thoughtline.com/byznet/maps.htm, as prepared by Peter Dykhuis.

4. This explanation appears with a corresponding map in the website cited above in note 3, and specifically at http://www.roman-empire.net/maps/empire/extent/ad476.html.

Figure #2.1 Maps Tracing the Expansion and Contraction of Rome

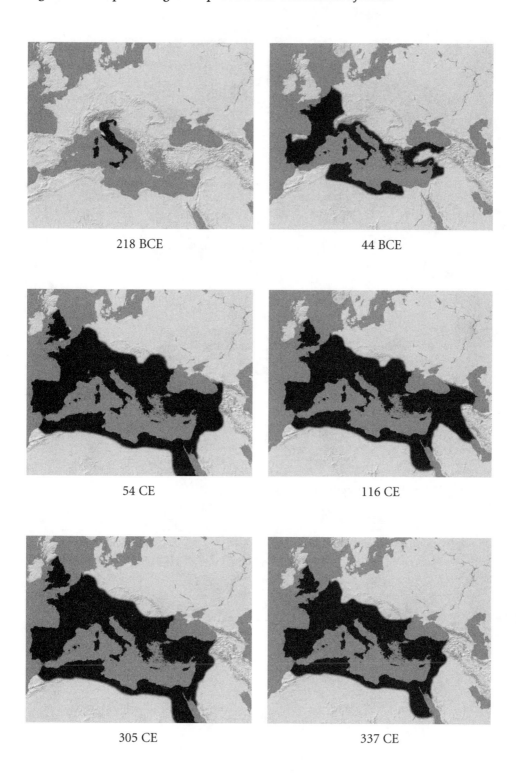

218 BCE

44 BCE

54 CE

116 CE

305 CE

337 CE

Figure #2.1 Maps Tracing the Expansion and Contraction of Rome continued

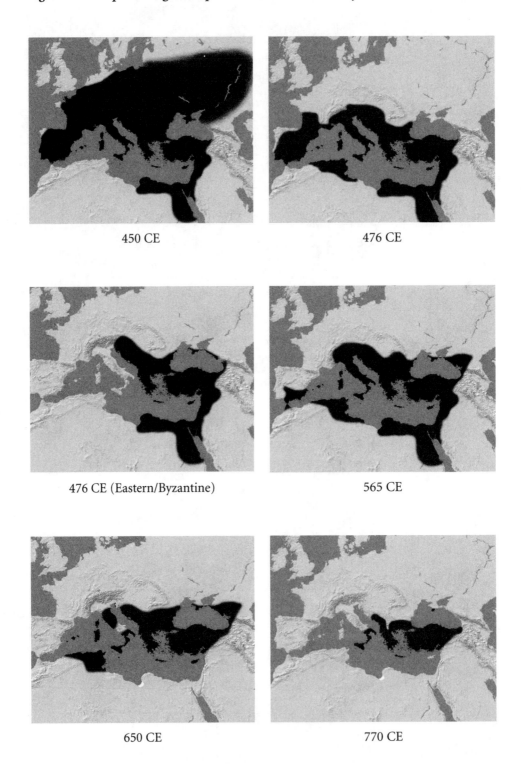

450 CE

476 CE

476 CE (Eastern/Byzantine)

565 CE

650 CE

770 CE

Box #2.1 *Key Developments in the History of Ancient Rome*

753 BCE	Legendary date for the founding of the city of Rome
509 BCE	Date assigned as the beginning of the Roman Republic, following the overthrow of the Monarchy in 510
450 BCE	Issuance of the Twelve Tables
376 BCE	The office of *praetor* is established
242 BCE	The office of *peregrine praetor* is established (some sources say 246 BCE)
27 BCE	Date assigned as the beginning of the Roman Empire (dated from the Roman Senate's granting to Octavian the honorific "Augustus"; Julius Caesar had gained appointment as permanent dictator in 44 BCE)

(all dates below are CE)

ca 117–235 CE	The "classical period" of Roman law scholarship (by *jurisconsults*)
ca 200	Barbarian pressures from the frontiers start becoming especially intense
212	Extension of Roman citizenship to virtually all free inhabitants of the empire
249	First general persecution of Christians begins
285	The emperor Diocletian divides the empire into eastern and western regions (along an axis lying just east of the Italian peninsula) for administrative purposes (in 293 CE a further division was made to create the Tetrarchy, or "rule of four")
303	The same emperor Diocletian, who was a fervent pagan and concerned over the ever-increasing numbers of Christians in the Empire, presides over the Great Persecution, which reaches a high point in this year
313	Constantine legalizes Christianity, as evidenced in the so-called Edict of Milan
330	Constantinople is dedicated as capital of the empire in the East
376	The Goths cross the Danube
395	The division of the empire into Eastern (with capital at Constantinople) and Western (with capital at Rome) is made permanent
410	Sack of Rome by the Visigoths (and the Roman legions withdraw from Britain)
402	The Western capital is moved from Rome to Ravenna
455	Sack of Rome by the Vandals
476	Fall of Rome; then, under the leadership of the Germanic (Ostragoth) chieftain Odoacer, the Western capital at Ravenna is captured, the emperor Romulus Augustus is deposed, and the remaining provinces of Italy are quickly conquered
527	Justinian's rule begins as emperor in the East (Constantinople)
530–533	Preparation of Justinian's legal compilation (later known as *Corpus Juris Civilis*)
540	Belisarius (505?–565 CE), one of the most acclaimed generals in history, carries out Justinian's ambitious project of re-conquering much of the Italian peninsula by taking control of the Ostrogoth capital of Ravenna (having conquered Naples and Rome in 536 CE)
544	Justinian's laws take effect in Italy, following his reclaiming of control over the Italian peninsula

2. Republic and Empire, East and West, Polytheism and Christianity

From the details shown in Box #2.1, it is important to identify three sets of transitions. These are (1) from Republic to Empire, (2) from unified empire to divided empire, and (3) from a secular or polytheistic state to one adopting Christianity as the state religion. The first of these, while deeply important from a political perspective, holds little interest for us from a legal perspective. Therefore we need not dwell on the transition from Republic to Empire in the 1st century BCE.

The second transition—from unified empire to divided empire—is significant because it established a political capital in Constantinople.[5] Upon the collapse of Roman power in the Italian peninsula (culminating in 476 CE), the fact that Constantinople still remained intact provided the possibility that imperial Rome might in fact survive—a possibility that Justinian pursued when he came to power as emperor in Constantinople about a half-century after the fall of Rome. And it was Justinian's great *Corpus Juris Civilis*—the legal manifestation of his efforts to reclaim the glory of Rome's past—that plays such a crucial role in the civil law tradition. (We shall examine that role later in this chapter.)

The third transition reflected in the "nutshell" account in Box #2.1 is Rome's change to a Christian state. Here is an account of the introduction, rise, repression, and ultimate acceptance of Christianity in ancient Rome:

> St. Peter and St. Paul introduced Christianity to the Romans, after Jesus was believed to have died sometime between *c.* 30–33 AD. Christian missionaries traveled across the empire, steadily winning converts and establishing Christian communities. After the Great Fire of Rome in July 64, Emperor Nero (56–68) accused the Christians as convenient scapegoats who were later persecuted and martyred. From that point on, Roman official policy towards Christianity tended towards persecution. The Roman authorities suspected Christians of disloyalty to the Emperor and of committing various crimes against humanity and nature. Persecution recurred especially at times of civic tensions and reached their worst under Diocletian (284 to 305). Constantine … ended the persecutions by establishing religious freedom through the Edict of Milan in 313. He later convened the historic First Council of Nicaea in 325, a year after ending the civil war of 324 and emerging as the victor in the war of succession. This First Council of Nicaea was formed to oppose Arius who had challenged the deity of Jesus Christ. The result was the branding of Arianism as a heresy. Christianity, as opposed to other religious groups, became the official state religion of the Roman empire on February 27, 380 through an edict issued by Emperor Theodosius I in Thessalonica and published in Constantinople. All cults, save Christianity, were prohibited in 391 by another edict of Theodosius I. Destruction of temples began immediately. When the Western Roman Empire ended with the abdication of Emperor Romulus Augustus in 476, Christianity survived it, with the Bishop of Rome as the dominant religious figure….[6]

---

5. Constantinople was founded by Constantine on the site of an already existing city, Byzantium, whose predecessor Byzantion had been settled in the early days of Greek colonial expansion, probably around 671–662 BCE. The new city of Constantinople was built over the course of six years and consecrated in May 330 CE.

6. This account is drawn from an article on Religion in Ancient Rome, available at http://en.wikipedia.org/wiki/Religion_in_ancient_Rome. Please see the Notes on Spellings, Usages, Citations, and Other Conventions, appearing at the beginning of this book, for my policies on citing Wikipedia for certain purposes.

With that exercise in historic and geographic "orienteering" completed, let us now turn in earnest to the development of the "first life" of Roman law.

B. The Twelve Tables

Our examination of Roman law in its earliest days need not be overly detailed. That is just as well, given the difficulty involved in learning about it:

> Roman law remains a challenge to modern scholarship and modern-day historians, not least because weaving a tapestry from fragments of evidence and inconclusive evidence has proved an exceedingly speculative enterprise. Buckland pinpoints the problems one encounters when trying to discover what happened in the history of Roman law when he declares that: 'Most ancient monuments and records ... perished when Rome was burnt by the Gauls, c. B.C. 390 and what passes for the history of this time is largely a fabrication of later ages, or at best a vague tradition adorned with stories of gods and heroes ... [so] we cannot have any exact knowledge of the course of events.'[7]

This paucity of resources and information also applies in part, unfortunately, to the Twelve Tables, the legal code that sits at the very foundation—chronologically and conceptually—of Roman law and therefore of the civil law tradition.

1. Political Setting

What we do know is that the Twelve Tables emerged out of a political confrontation between the plebeians and the patricians in Rome, which at the time was a small community on the left bank of the river Tiber. At the insistence of the plebeians (common people), a commission of ten citizens was appointed in 451 BCE to prepare a written text of the customary law.[8] Here is one authority's description of the political setting and what emerged from the friction of that setting:

> For the Romans the publication of these laws signalized a stage in the class conflict between the patricians and the plebeians, for the latter compelled the codification and the promulgation of what had been largely customary law interpreted and administered by the former primarily in their own interests.

> Tradition tells us that the code was composed by a commission, first of ten and then of twelve men, in 451–450 B.C., was ratified by the Centuriate Assembly in 449 B.C., was engraved on twelve tablets (whence the title), which were attached to the Rostra before the Curia in the Forum of Rome. Though this weighty witness of the national progress in jurisprudence seems to have been destroyed during the Gallic occupation of Rome in 387 B.C., yet copies must have survived, since Cicero says that in his boyhood schoolboys memorized these laws "as a required formula." However, no part of the Twelve Tables either in its original form or in an ancient copy is extant.[9]

---

7. de Cruz, *supra* note 1, at 45.
8. See Peter Stein, ROMAN LAW IN EUROPEAN HISTORY 3–4 (1999). See also de Cruz, *supra* note 1, at 48.
9. Allan Chester Johnson et al., ANCIENT ROMAN STATUTES 9 (1961).

Hence the Twelve Tables may be seen as a means of protecting the middle class from the arbitrary rule of the patrician class. That protection came in the form of a set of legal provisions regarding the legal rights and duties of the people of Rome, as well as the procedures to be followed in asserting one's rights in the course of civil disputes.

2. Content

Box #2.2 presents some excerpts from a reconstruction of the Twelve Tables that itself is drawn from fragments that have been collected and organized in a manner thought to be logical.

Box #2.2 Excerpts from the Twelve Tables[10]

Table I. Proceedings Preliminary To Trial

1. If the plaintiff summons the defendant to court the defendant shall go. If the defendant does not go the plaintiff shall call a witness thereto. Only then the plaintiff shall seize the defendant.

2. If the defendant attempts evasion or takes flight the plaintiff shall lay hand on him.

3. If sickness or age is an impediment he who summons the defendant to court shall grant him a vehicle. If [the plaintiff] does not wish he shall not spread a carriage with cushions.

4. For a freeholder [*i.e.*, a taxpayer whose fortune is valued at not less than 1,500 asses] a freeholder shall be surety [for his appearance at trial]; for a proletary [*i.e.*, a nontaxpayer whose fortune is rated at less than a freeholder's] anyone who wishes shall be surety.

5. There shall be the same right of bond and of conveyance with the Roman people for a steadfast person and for a person restored to allegiance.

   ...

8. If one of the parties does not appear the magistrate shall adjudge the case, after noon, in favor of the one present.

9. If both parties are present sunset shall be the time limit of the proceedings.

Table III. Execution of Judgment

1. Thirty days shall be allowed by law for payment of confessed debt and for settlement of matters adjudged in court.

2. After this time the creditor shall have the right of laying hand on the debtor. The creditor shall hale the debtor into court.

3. Unless the debtor discharges the debt adjudged or unless someone offers surety for him in court the creditor shall take the debtor with him. He shall bind him either with a thong or with fetters of not less than fifteen pounds in weight, or if he wishes he shall bind him with fetters of more than this weight.

Table V. Inheritance and Guardianship

1. ... Women, even though they are of full age [25 years] because of their levity of mind shall be under guardianship ... except vestal virgins, who ... shall be free from guardianship ...

2. The conveyable possessions of a woman who is under guardianship of male [family members] shall not be acquired by prescriptive right unless they are transferred by the woman herself with the authorization of her guardian ...

---

10. These excerpts are drawn from Johnson et al., *supra* note 9. For another version of the rules in the Twelve Tables, along with annotations, see http://en.wikipedia.org/wiki/Twelve_Tables.

3. According as a person has made bequest regarding his personal property or the guardianship of his estate so shall be the law.

4. If anyone who has no direct heir dies intestate the nearest male [family member] shall have the estate.

Table VII. Real Property

...

9b. If a tree from a neighbor's farm has been felled by the wind over one's farm, ... one rightfully can take legal action for that tree to be removed.

10. ... It shall be lawful to gather fruit falling upon another's farm.

11. Articles sold ... and delivered shall not be acquired by the purchaser, unless he pays the price to the seller or in some other way satisfies the seller, as, for example, by giving a surety or a pledge ...

3. Significance

The Twelve Tables may be considered profoundly important to the civil law tradition for two main reasons. The first relates to form, the second to substance.

First, the document and the political controversy that it emerged from established definitively that law should be written and promulgated, not oral and secret. For most Westerners, of course, these seem rather elementary propositions, and yet as we shall see in Chapter Six of this book, a major school of legal philosophy in China insisted just the opposite—that is, that the laws governing society should not be reduced to writing but should instead be kept under the control of a governing elite to whose highly cultivated and inspired discretion the best interests of society could be entrusted. Roman law rejected that view very early.

The fact that the Romans opted early on for written, promulgated law ensured also that there would be a need for interpretation, and therefore for experts devoting their talents to studying and advising on the laws. As we shall see, the civil law tradition places great emphasis on legal scholarship.

The second main reason to regard the Twelve Tables as so profoundly important to the development of the civil law tradition is substantive: the legal rules set forth in the Twelve Tables, and in the civil law tradition more generally, revolve primarily around private relations, not around government control or structure. In this sense Roman law may be seen as "horizontal" rather than "vertical" in character. As we shall see later, Chinese dynastic law (and still to a large degree contemporary Chinese law) is "vertical" in character, reflecting a view that law is primarily a tool to be used by the government for control of the society and its people and economy. Because of the curious course of development of English law, the common law tradition is different still, presenting a blend of public and private. But in the civil law tradition, private law prevails.

For these and other reasons, the Twelve Tables have elicited glowing accolades. Here is one:

> [T]he Twelve Tables—called *Lex Duodecim Tabulae* (Law of the Twelve Tables) ...— really forms the foundation of the whole fabric of Roman law. The importance of this code of primitive laws, whether for the Romans or for us, cannot be overestimated. For us the code is valuable for the fact that this great charter is the substructure of what Roman law is still regnant in almost half of the civilized world.[11]

---

11. Johnson, *supra* note 9, at 9.

C. Legal Practice in Early Rome

The following summary of the operation of the law in early Rome revolves around the functions of several "players"—the public government official responsible for administering the legal rules, the private elite involved in studying and advising on those rules (especially as emerging from litigation), and others.

1. The *Praetor*

The administration of the law came under the auspices of a government official, the *praetor*.[12] As noted above in Box #2.1, the office of *praetor* was established in the 4th century BCE, and then another type of *praetor*—the *praetor peregrinus*—was established in the 3rd century BCE. At that point the title of the earlier *praetor* was changed to *praetor urbanus* to distinguish the two. The term *peregrinus* means "foreigner", and this explains the difference between the two officials: the *praetor urbanus* handled (during his one-year term) the administration of legal cases arising between two Roman citizens, whereas the *praetor peregrinus* handled the administration of legal cases arising between a Roman citizen and a non-citizen of Rome or between two non-citizens of Rome.

The difference between the work of these two officials related not only to the parties appearing before them but also to the set of rules that were applied. In the case of the *praetor urbanus*, the *jus civilis* [13]—the law of the citizen (of Rome)—was applicable. In the case of the *praetor perigrinus*, the *jus gentium* was applicable. The *jus gentium* constituted those rules that were general in character, drawn from the laws of various nations under Roman control. Such rules of *jus gentium* would be used for various purposes much later in Europe, especially as the basis for formulating rules of international law (the "law of nations") by Hugo Grotius, the Dutch theorist and scholar often called the "father" of international law.

The *praetors* did not function as judges in the manner of today's judges. A separate official, the *judex* (described below in subsection IC2 of this chapter), performed that function during much of the Roman period. Nor did the *praetor* formulate and promulgate the law in the way of a legislator. In an important sense, however, the *praetors* did contribute to the development of the rules in the legal system, particularly through something called the *edict*. One authority has offered this explanation of the role of the edict:

> During the time of the Roman Republic the Urban Praetor issued an annual edict, usually on the advice of jurists [*jurisconsults*, described in subsection IC3 below] (since the Praetor himself was not necessarily educated in the law), setting out the circumstances under which he [the Praetor] would grant remedies.

---

12. For general information on the *praetor*, and on the different types of members of the *praetura*, see http://en.wikipedia.org/wiki/Praetor. The following is an introductory excerpt from that source.
   Praetor was a title granted by the government of Ancient Rome to men acting in one of two official capacities: the commander of an army, either before it was mustered or more typically in the field, or an elected magistrate assigned duties that varied depending on the historical period. The magistracy was called the *praetura* (praetorship). Its functions were described by the adjective: the *praetoria potestas* and *praetorium imperium* (praetorian power and authority) and the *praetorium ius* (praetorian law), a body of legal precedents set down by the praetors. *Praetorium* as a substantive [term] meant the location from which the praetor exercised his authority, either the headquarters of his castra, the courthouse (tribunal) of his judiciary, or the city hall of his provincial governorship.
13. This is also spelled *ius civilis*, since in Latin there is only one letter for "j" and "i"; they can be used interchangeably.

The legal provisions arising from the Praetor's Edict were known as *ius hono-rarium*; in theory the Praetor did not have power to alter the law, but in prac-tice the Edict altered the rights and duties of individuals and was effectively a legislative document. In the reign of Hadrian [emperor from 117 to 138 CE], however, the terms of the Edict were made permanent and the Praetor's *de facto* legislative role was abolished.[14]

Two examples of excerpts from edict appear below as illustration.

Whence anything is thrown out or is poured out onto that place where commonly is made a road or where persons assemble I shall grant an action, for twice as much damage as thereby is caused or done against the person who dwells there.[15]

Whoever hides for the purpose of defrauding his creditors, if he is not defended ac-cording to the judgment of an honorable man, I shall order his property pursuant to the edict to be possessed, to be advertised for sale, and to be sold.[16]

2. The *Judex*

During much of the Roman period, the person serving in the capacity of what a mod-ern Westerner would call a judge was the *judex*. The *judex* was a layperson (that is, one not trained in the law), but also typically a patrician—that is, a person with sufficient wealth and public stature as to make it possible for him to be available for service in this capac-ity on an *ad hoc* basis. The role of the *judex* was to hear the facts and arguments of the dispute and to render a judgment based on a *formulum* (formula) constructed by the par-ties and/or the *praetor*. A simplistic example of a *formulum* in a case between Mr. Hecker as a plaintiff and Mr. McAllister as a defendant, in a breach-of-sale-contract dispute, might read as follows:

If you find that Mr. McAllister failed to pay Mr. Hecker the agreed price for the horse, and that the horse was delivered by Mr. Hecker to Mr. McAllister in good condition, then you should determine that Mr. McAllister should pay Mr. Hecker the agreed price plus a fine of 50% of the agreed price.

According to the synopsis offered in the preceding paragraphs, the main persons in-volved in civil litigation in ancient Rome were the *praetor* (either *urbanus* or *peregrinus*), the *judex*, and the disputing parties themselves; and other elements in the process in-cluded the edict and the formula. The interactions of these several persons and elements, along with some further details as to how their roles changed over time, are explained more fully in the following excerpt:

In private law disputes, a State official usually officiated or ... arranged for a trial to be held after a preliminary hearing. In the conventional civil action, court proceedings commenced with a hearing before a *praetor*, a functionary who was one of a group of magistrates who were elected annually. This hear-ing identified the *issues* in dispute. The next stage consisted of a separate hear-

---

14. Barry Nicholas, An INTRODUCTION TO ROMAN LAW 22–26 (1975), cited in http://en.wikipedia.org/wiki/Praetor#Praetors_as_judges.

15. See Johnson, *supra* note 9, at 186 (showing this as a fragment of an edict, identified as being "[f]rom paragraph 61, in the second part, from title XV 'Those Goods That Are in Anyone's Prop-erty'").

16. *Id.* at 191 (showing this as a fragment of an edict, identified as being from "Paragraph 205, in the fourth part, from title XXXVIII 'Those Causes for Which a Person Enters into Possession').

ing, in the manner of a *trial* before a *iudex*, an *ad hoc* judge, a private citizen, who was selected by consent of the parties and given authority by the praetor to try the dispute, and to render a binding judgment; no appeal was available. In the majority of cases, neither praetor nor *iudex* had undergone any sort of legal training.

… A system of case-law and precedent developed in ancient Rome under the *praetor-iudex* system. Although praetors had complete freedom to decide each case on an individual basis, and could simply disregard previous rulings on similar cases, a *practice of continuity* began to develop so that new terms which were coined by the Urban Praetor were soon copied for future reference and used in subsequent cases. Clerks attached to the praetor's office kept records of the formulas used and these became available to the public.

From about the middle of the second century B.C., the litigant began to ask the praetor for a *written summary of the claim*, as well as any available defence, addressed to the judge, containing instructions on how to proceed with the case and to dispose of the issue accordingly. The plaintiff would then attempt to persuade the praetor to grant him a 'formula'. The praetor began to give advice to litigants on the conditions under which he would grant the action or allow the defence and the judge would then resolve the case on the basis of this formula.

A *consistent usage* of certain terms and synopses eventually converted them into established formulas (the *formulary system*) and they assumed an air of certainty and predictability which began to serve as guidelines to litigants and legal advisers [*jurisconsults*, discussed below] for future cases.[17]

3. The *Jurisconsults*

For several reasons—including the fact that the officials holding the office of *praetor* typically would not have had much or any legal training—there arose in ancient Rome a class of scholar-advisors known as *jurisconsults*. It was that class of scholar-advisors that would provide guidance on legal matters. Here is an account of their character and role (this account uses the term "jurists", although the more technical term would be *jurisconsults*):

In the absence of legal advisers, the *iudex* eventually turned to a select group of aristocrats, secular *jurists* who came to specialise in giving advice on legal matters. They were, in fact, self-appointed by their interest in the study and interpretation of the law and in *discussing legal problems, both actual and hypothetical, and writing about them,* they established an enduring tradition which, through their writings, was then passed from generation to generation. These jurists advised a number of different persons, ranging from parties to litigation, and lay judges to the *Urban Praetor, who was the most senior magistrate whose primary responsibility was litigation in the city of Rome.* He was therefore chief administrative officer of the judicial system that regulated litigation between Roman citizens, and in the course of his duties, [the urban praetor] began to *formulate the legal 'issues'* (or matters to be decided/resolved) which were then presented to the trial judges.

During this period, the source of private law was very seldom to be found in legislation, although the Roman assemblies could usually 'amend' private law if they

---

17. de Cruz, *supra* note 1, at 46 (emphasis in original).

wished to do so. However, the *cardinal source of law proved to be the formal edicts issued by the Urban Praetor*, which also listed the *legal remedies* available, which accorded with the legal opinions of the jurists. The remarkable fact appears to be the manner in which, for many years, these jurists simply assumed the authority to interpret the law without any official authorisation. Throughout the republic, it was the aristocratic upper class of society which controlled and ran the city....

During the course of the first phase of the classical Roman Empire (the Principate), the authority of the jurists was further strengthened. The first emperor, Augustus decided ... [to] institute a system ('patenting') which authorised a select group of jurists to give their opinions under his seal so they could 'speak' with the leader's authority or imprimatur (*ex auctoritate principis*). This merely validated a system of Roman private law which had already taken root, and the jurists simply continued to give advice as they had done in the past, modifying their advice occasionally to take account of social or economic changes.

... Juristic writings included general commentaries, analyses of specific topics, elementary treatises, collections of opinions or problems in which the jurist submitted arguments which eventually led to his particular solution. Their work ranged from the drafting of wills and contracts, advising litigants on forms of action and possible defences, to revising praetorian formulas.[18]

The contribution made by the *jurisconsults* was even greater than is described in the long preceding excerpt, for their writings served as the basis for the great compilation known as the *Corpus Juris Civilis*, commissioned by Justinian in the 6th century CE. Most of the *jurisconsults* whose work was used for this purpose were those who were active during the so-called "classical period" of Roman law—that is, the period from roughly 117 to 235 CE.

The central place that the *jurisconsults* occupy in the history of the civil law tradition is reflected in the fact that the time line diagram shown in Appendix 2.20, at the end of this chapter, begins around 100 CE, just at the dawn of the "classical period" when the *jurisconsults* were laying the substantive foundations of the civil law. As described in the explanatory notes following that time line diagram, the rather scattered work of the *jurisconsults* during that period was selectively "packaged" in Justinian's compilation.

Several of those *jurisconsults* are worthy of special mention. They include Gaius (his last name is not known, and even the name "Gaius" is surely a *nom de plume*). Another is Ulpian—it was his work on which the compilers of the *Corpus Juris Civilis* relied most heavily. A short biographical sketch of Gaius appears in Appendix 2.1, at the end of this chapter. A short biographical sketch of Ulpian appears in Appendix 2.2. Other prominent *jurisconsults* include Julius Paulus, Papinian, Marcian, Modestinus, Arcadius, and Hermogianus.

---

18. *Id.* (emphasis in original). Another type of person involved in legal practice in ancient Rome was the *advocatus*—a person who provided legal advice to a client before and during a trial, in both civil and criminal matters, and pleaded for the client in court. The latter activity (pleading) was originally reserved to persons specially trained in rhetoric. In the period of the Republic, the *advocatus* was not paid for his services, although in later periods compensation was gradually permitted. See Adolf Berger, ENCYCLOPEDIC DICTIONARY OF ROMAN LAW, available through a Google search for "advocatus Roman law".

D. Other Aspects of (Western) Roman Law

While ignoring enough details to fill many books about Roman law, let us consider three general trends that have implications for the later development of the civil law tradition. Those trends are (i) the tendency toward chaos, both in politics and in law, in the later periods of the Roman Empire, (ii) the efforts at codification during those periods, and (iii) the overlay of Christianity on Roman law starting in the 4th century CE.

1. The Tendency Toward Chaos

According to the so-called Second Law of Thermodynamics, nature tends toward "entropy"—that is, the gradual decay and dissipation of energy in a way that breaks large organized structures into small, unstructured units,[19] a condition we might consider one of "chaos".[20] (Ample evidence of the Second Law of Thermodynamics can be found in the office of any typical university professor.) Perhaps some similar tendency toward entropy, or chaos, can be observed in human structures of government and society. In any event, the highly organized and powerful imperial power of Rome—and the sophistication of Roman law—gradually suffered from decay and dissipation.

Two aspects of that decay and dissipation are important to our story. First, conflicts arose between the provinces and the central authorities. As the empire expanded (see maps in Figure #2.1, above), its control over some parts of the frontiers naturally weakened, and the legal influence of Roman law was diluted. Second, the sources of law became more complex and unmanageable. If we bear in mind the practical difficulties involved in promulgating and communicating laws in a society that was lit only by fire and that could move goods and information over land only as fast as a horse could run, we can appreciate some of the difficulties of maintaining and applying the decrees, statutes, and other forms of law—which were themselves gradually "bulking up" with the passage of time. Indeed, it would have been extremely challenging even to know what legal rules had been enacted and remained valid—in short, to answer the question, "what is the law?"

One authority offers this summary of the growing chaos and gradual degradation of Roman law:

> There were highs and lows in roman legal history; the period of the classical jurists, those whose opinions have lasted longest, ran from the first century BC to the middle of the third century AD. [Note that this is a longer period of "classical period" than was indicated earlier.] Gaius wrote his famous Institutes, or hornbook, near the end of this time. From then on things ran down; by the middle of the fifth century AD there was such a mass of opinion that a law of citations was passed (to *create* order): Papinian, Paul, Gaius, Ulpian and Modestinus

---

19. There appear to be several subsequent applications of the Second Law of Thermodynamics, but the original creator is thought to be Sadi Carnot, a French physicist who introduced the concept in an 1824 paper entitled "Reflections on the Motive Power of Fire". A later formulation of the Second Law of Thermodynamics was introduced by Rudolf Clausius. For a discussion of the Second Law of Thermodynamics, see http://en.wikipedia.org/wiki/Second_law_of_thermodynamics.

20. The word "chaos" in English derives from the Greek term *khaos*, which means "abyss, that which gapes wide open, is vast and empty". ONLINE ETYMOLOGY DICTIONARY (2010), http://dictionary.com (search "chaos").

were to be treated as authoritative; in case of conflict the majority would prevail; Papinian would prevail in the event of a tie.[21]

This chaos was further exacerbated by an ever-changing array of political and law-giving powers. One example of this mentioned earlier is the division of the Empire into East and West. Another is the rapid turnover in emperors. As one authority explains, "[t]here were something like twenty-five emperors in the first two hundred and sixty-two years of the Roman Empire and a further twenty-one emperors in the next fifty years."[22]

2. The Efforts at Codification

One approach to bringing some order out of the chaos referred to above was the preparation of legal codes—compilations designed to identify those laws that were still in force and to organize them in some logical order. These included the *Codex Gregorianus* and the *Codex Hermogenianus* issued in the late 3rd and 4th centuries CE, the *Codex Theodosianus* issued in 438 CE, and the *Lex Visigothorum* ("barbarian" code) issued in 506 CE. These might be summarized as follows:

- *Codex Gregorianus* and *Codex Hermogenianus*. It does not appear quite certain that these denote one collection or two collections. The general opinion, however, according to an entry in an 1875 encyclopedia of Greek and Roman antiquities,[23] is that there were two codices compiled respectively by Gregorianus and Hermogenianus, who are sometimes, though incorrectly, called Gregorius and Hermogenes. The codex of Gregorianus seems to begin with constitutions of Septimius Severus (196 CE) and end with those of Diocletian and Maximian (285–305 CE). The codex of Hermogenianus is apparently only quoted by titles, and it only contains constitutions of Diocletian and Maximian, with the exception of one by Antoninus Caracalla; it may perhaps have consisted of one book only, and it may have been a kind of supplement to the other. These codices were not made by imperial authority; they were the work of private individuals, but apparently soon came to be considered as being authoritative enough to be relied on in courts of justice.

- *Codex Theodosianus*. This was a compilation of the laws of the Roman Empire under the Christian emperors—that is, those since 312 CE. A commission was established by Theodosius II in 429 CE, and the compilation was published in the eastern half of the Empire in 438 CE. One year later, it was also introduced in the West by the emperor Valentinian III. It is regarded to have been rather ineffectual.[24]

- *Lex Visigothorum*. It appears that the Breviary of Alaric (*Breviarium Alaricianum* or *Lex Romana Visigothorum*) is a collection of Roman law that was compiled by order of Alaric II, King of the Visigoths, in 506 CE with the advice of his bishops and nobles, and made applicable not to the Visigothic nobles under their own law, which had been formulated by Euric, but to the Hispano-Roman and Gallo-Roman population that was living under Visigoth rule south of the Loire River. It

---

21. H. Patrick Glenn, Legal Traditions of the World 130 (2007).

22. de Cruz, *supra* note 1, at 49.

23. See http://penelope.uchicago.edu/Thayer/E/Roman/Texts/secondary/SMIGRA*/Codex_G_et_H.html.

24. This description is drawn from Wikipedia, citing works by several experts, including Boudewijn Sirks, the Regius Professor of Civil Law at Oxford and a former visiting professor at the University of Kansas.

consists of a patchwork of various previous laws and codes, including parts of the *Codex Theodosianus*, various edicts from Roman emperors, the *Institutes* of Gaius, and some elements of the Gregorian code and the Hermogenian code (also referred to in this chapter). This code appears to have been known amongst the Visigoths by the title of "Lex Romana", or "Lex Theodosii", and it was not until the 16th century that the title of "Breviarium" was introduced to distinguish it from a recast of the code that was introduced into northern Italy in the 9th century for the use of the Romans in Lombardy.

3. The Overlay of Christianity

A third development—in addition to the tendency toward chaos and the efforts at codification, discussed immediately above—also deserves our attention because of the permanent mark it has left on the civil law tradition: the Christianization of the Roman Empire. Some information about the early rejection and persecution of Christians, followed by the acceptance of the religion, was provided above in subsection IA2 of this chapter. As noted there, Christianity and its adherents suffered harsh persecution in the 3rd and early 4th centuries CE, culminating in the so-called Great Persecution in the first decade of the 4th century. The tide turned under Constantine, however, with the issuance of the Edict of Milan officially ending the persecution. Although some backsliding occurred,[25] the way was thus cleared for Christianity to become the state religion.

That step was taken near the close of the 4th century. As noted above, "Christianity ... became the official state religion of the Roman empire on February 27, 380 through an edict issued by Emperor Theodosius I in Thessalonica and published in Constantinople. All cults, save Christianity, were prohibited in 391."[26] These official acts of the acceptance and endorsement of Christianity gave a higher significance to documents of Christian doctrine that had been produced earlier, in the 3rd century CE. Two of those documents were the *Traditio Apostolica* and the *Didascalia Apostolorum*. These are summarized in Box #2.3.

Box #2.3 Early Documents of Christian Doctrine[27]

The *Traditio Apostolica*, which translates to the "Apostolic Tradition," is 3rd century writing describing Christian church life and discipline. It is believed the *Traditio Apostolica* was authored by the Roman theologian Hippolytus. Its text is the earliest description of Christianity's early forms of worship, baptism, and several other aspects of clerical action. Historians are not certain where the *Traditio Apostolica* originated (it is written in Greek), but its content was considered as authoritative in Turkey, Syria, Egypt, and Ethiopia. In fact, a modified and updated version of the *Traditio Apostolica* is presently in use in Ethiopia.

The *Didascalia Apostolorum* is a text written in Roman Syria in the 3rd century CE, although its text purports to have been written by the Apostles. The *Didascalia* was probably authored

---

25. As noted in the biographical sketch of Constantine, appearing as Appendix 2.3 at the end of this chapter, the "backslider" was another leader of the empire, Licinius, who briefly shared power with Constantine: In 320, Licinius stopped honoring the Edict of Milan and began persecuting Christians again. This led to a war. Constantine won and Licinius was executed, making Constantine the sole emperor of the Roman Empire.

26. See *supra* note 6.

27. The details in this box are drawn from Wikipedia and the following other websites: http://www.bombaxo.com/hippolytus.html (which includes a translation of the text of the *Traditio Apostolica*) and http://www.britannica.com (search "Traditio Apostolica").

by a Catholic bishop. It is significant because it was the earliest attempt to compile a code of canon law. The *Didascalia* is particularly noteworthy because of the absolute requirement of providing forgiveness to penitents, no matter what sins they had committed. The *Didascalia Apostolorum* was one of the primary sources of canon law in eastern and western Europe. Its text also dealt largely with Christian ethics.

With the adoption of Christianity as the state religion, further development of Christian dogma could occur under official auspices. Consistent with this, important councils were convened in 325 and 381 CE. The first of these, the (First) Council of Nicea (325 CE), was referred to above; it resulted in the branding of Arianism as a heresy. The second especially important council was the (First) Council of Constantinople. It was convened in 381 CE in part to complete the job of stamping out Arianism and in part to address other matters of Christian dogma. The council issued seven canons, four of which were doctrinal canons and the other three of which were disciplinary canons. The Roman Catholic Church only accepts the first four canons. The third canon asserted Constantinople's standing in the Catholic Church by declaring it to be "New Rome" and that it surpassed the patriarchs of Antioch and Alexandria. This began a chain of events that ultimately led to the "Great Schism" in 1054 between the Western Roman Catholic and Eastern Orthodox Christianity.

In sum, by the end of the 4th century CE, "Christian notions [were] interacting reciprocally with Roman law"[28] in a way that permitted the governmental authorities to exert more and more control over the ecclesiastical (Church) authorities. This created both an augmentation of imperial (governmental) power and a source of friction that would disappear with the collapse of the imperial authorities in the West (in 476 CE) but would reappear five hundred years later. A sense of that friction, as it arose beginning late in the 4th century, is conveyed by one authority as follows:

[Ecclesiastical officers (especially bishops ...) were appointed [to serve as] public functionaries by the emperor and therefore subjected to the code for the imperial civil service. The greater the public role of the ecclesiastical officers became, the greater was the scope for imperial intervention [in Church affairs] ... and the more insistently the question was asked: by what right, by what title ... did the imperial government proceed in controlling the Church? How was the appointment, dismissal and transfer of ecclesiastical officers by the emperor justified? Was he entitled to convoke councils and issue proclamations which were to all intents and purposes [Christian] dogmatic pronouncements? How could all this be squared with the basic assumption that the emperor did not only *not* stand *above* the Church, but was very much *within* the Church ...?

[From the perspective of the Church authorities (which by the fifth century had become known collectively as the papacy)] the Church universal was a new society altogether, composed as it was of beings who through baptism had shed their 'naturalness' and had become 'new creatures', 'new men' altogether [citing letters of Paul to the Corintheans, the Galatians, and the Colossians]. By losing their naturalness, they had entered a divinely created society—the Church—which ... [was subject] to the laws as given by divinity and made known through the qualified officers [of the Church, and *not* primarily through civil authorities].

---

28. Nutshell-1999, *infra* note 45, at 22.

[Hence] the emperor's role as monopolistic governor of the Church was denied [by the papacy] on grounds of insufficient qualification: it was the *pope* [and not the emperor who] alone was entitled to issue laws and to govern the Christian body public at least as far as its basic concerns demanded. It was on the question of governing the Church universal that the imperial government at Constantinople and the papal government in Rome parted ways in the fifth century. The split was to reverberate through the centuries, and was to determine the path of Europe for the subsequent millennium, if not beyond.[29]

E. Justinian and the Corpus Juris Civilis

As noted in the time line provided in Box #2.1, near the beginning of this chapter, Rome came under increasing external political and military pressure in the 4th and 5th centuries. This pressure was most manifest in the sack of Rome in 410 CE (also the year, not surprisingly, in which the Roman legions left Britain) and then in the actual fall of Rome at the hands of the Ostrogoths in the year 476. Thus the Western side of the Empire crumbled.

The Eastern part of the Roman Empire, headquartered in Constantinople, stayed in place. It is to that city that our story now shifts—and to the great codification effort undertaken by Justinian.

1. Justinian and the Eastern Roman Empire

The life story of Justinian—which is the subject of a brief biographical sketch appearing in Appendix 2.4 at the end of this chapter—involves luck, low-brow social status, a supportive but scheming spouse, and an odd combination of timidity and burning commitment.[30] It is the last of these, his burning commitment, that shows through in two specific accomplishments of Justinian.

The first of those accomplishments was the reassertion of Roman political control over the Italian peninsula. As noted in Box #2.1, this occurred around 540 CE, due to the military genius of Justinian's main general, Belisarius. That accomplishment was short-lived, as reflected in the maps appearing in Figure #2.1 above.

The second of Justinian's accomplishments also seemed short-lived. It was the legal compilation he ordered to be prepared. Within a century (probably less) of its issuance, that compilation of laws had been lost to the West, and was not to be found again for about five hundred years. And yet coincidentally—one might say miraculously—it *was* rediscovered, and it became a centerpiece for further development of the civil law tradition founded in Roman law. Hence, this second of Justinian's accomplishments, in the area of law, had a permanent influence. Indeed, the issuance of the Justinian legal compilation has been called the "most important single event for the subsequent history of Roman law in western Europe".[31]

---

29. Ullman, *infra* note 51, at 38–40 (emphasis added).

30. One authority reports that "Justinian was a thoroughly unpleasant man: deceptive, ungrateful, suspicious, and mean. But he was also ambitious, enterprising and brave." J.M. Roberts, A CONCISE HISTORY OF THE WORLD 170 (1993).

31. Arthur Taylor von Mehren and James Russell Gordley, THE CIVIL LAW SYSTEM 6 (1977).

2. The Great Compilation

Box #2.4 offers a summary of the compilation of laws that Justinian ordered, with special emphasis on the work of the commission that prepared it.

Box #2.4 *Preparation of the Corpus Juris Civilis*[32]

Less than a year into his reign as emperor, Justinian established his first law commission under John of Cappadocia, a tax expert. This commission condensed the three then-existing codes of Gegorianus, Hermogenianus, and Theodosianus [referred to above] into a single volume. A major reason for this new code, released in 529, was the hope that it could make litigation more expedient. After all, a major difficulty of operating within the Empire's legal system for many years had been the enormous body of authorities of law, many of which conflicted.

In 530, Justinian established a second, more ambitious law commission in order to clarify the law further and to restore some of the glory of Rome, by drawing heavily from the writings of the Empire's classical period.

A major barrier to accomplishing this ambitious task was the prospect that it would take at least a decade to complete. This was a substantial consideration because the work would take some of the Empire's greatest legal minds away from their other duties. Justinian put faith in Tribonian, who had demonstrated diligent efforts and impressive organizational skills while a member in the first commission, to serve as the head of the new commission. Justinian also provided Tribonian with the power to select the members of his commission.

The commission consisted of six senior commissioners and eleven junior commissioners. Two of the senior commissioner slots were filled by Tribonian and Constantinus, a law minister in Justinian's court who had also served on the first commission. Four law professors filled the other senior positions, two from Constantinople and two from Beirut, which at the time was the premier city for legal scholarship. The eleven junior commissioners were barristers from in and around Constantinople.

Tribonian divided his work into three teams, each of which was responsible for distinct sets of the Roman Empire's historic legal writings. A paced schedule was implemented for each team so they would finish at approximately the same time. Many felt the completion of the *Digest* was impracticable because of how time-consuming it would be to resolve the disputes that existed between the classical jurists. Tribonian solved this problem before the commission even began its work. He prepared a list of the 50 leading disputes and proposed that the legislature issue 50 decisions as to what the code's position would be. This was done, reducing the number of legal issues to be considered by the commission.

The work was completed entirely in Constantinople, where the Beirut guests continued to work part-time as visiting professors. The work of the commission would result in the *Digest*, a condensed collection of the best Roman jurists of the classical age. At its publication, the *Digest* consisted of five percent of the total volume of materials that it drew from, yet it was still by far the most time-consuming of the components within the *Corpus Juris Civilis*. The *Digest* was published and enacted on December 16, 533, but its draft had been completed in the middle of that year. The commission began work on the *Institutes* shortly after completing draft of the *Digest*. The *Institutes*, which was essentially an explanatory textbook of the law, was actu-

---

32. The information in Box #2.4, prepared largely by Justin Waggoner, draws mainly from the following sources: A.M. Honoré, *The Background of Justinian's Codification*, 48 Tulane Law Review 859 (1974); A.M. [Tony] Honoré, *Justinian's Digest: The Distribution of Authors and Works to the Three Committees*, 3 Roman Legal Tradition 1 (2006), *available at* http://users.ox.ac.uk/~alls0079/distribution_2007.pdf.

ally enacted approximately a month before the *Digest*. The work on the *Codex*, a compilation of prior Roman legislation declared to still be in force, was built largely upon the efforts of Justinian's first commission, with several amendments included. The *Novellae*, the final component of the *Corpus Juris Civilis*, was completed after the commission had accomplished its work. The *Novellae* included subsequent new enactments from Justinian's time (between approximately 535 and 565) used to fill the gaps in the old legislation.

All four parts of the *Corpus Juris Civilis* were made effective in the Eastern Roman (or Byzantine) Empire. Aside from the *Institutes*, which essentially gained status as a state-sponsored piece of legal education, the components of the *Corpus Juris Civilis* were given the force of law. The law contained within the *Corpus Juris Civilis* was meant to be valid forever. Thus, other than straightforward translations and cross-references, no commentary was to be made upon it. Any discrepancies or conflicts could be referred to the emperor, who could subsequently amend the law if appropriate. Within the Byzantine Empire, the *Corpus Juris Civilis* was translated to Greek and served as the basis of the law until it was superseded approximately three centuries after its issuance.

A flaw in the drafting of the *Corpus Juris Civilis* was that it was published only in Latin and not in Greek. While Latin remained the official language of the government in Constantinople, the majority of the population spoke only Greek. It is thought that Tribonian, who was likely a native Greek speaker equally fluent in Latin, overestimated the capacity of law students and barristers of his time to comprehend the Latin texts. This mistake likely contributed to the cessation of university legal education approximately twenty years after the issuance of the *Corpus Juris Civilis*; university legal education was replaced by professional legal training given by barristers. Consequently, the *Institutes* did not enjoy the decades of use within law schools that its drafters had no doubt intended, although it was still used as a means of understanding the *Digest*.

From the details included in Box #2.4, let us distill the following key points regarding the four parts of Justinian's compilation. As that compilation later acquired the "shorthand" label of the *Corpus Juris Civilis*,[33] I shall henceforth use that term—or sometimes simply *CJC*.

- The *Institutiones* (*Institutes*), which forms about one-thirtieth or one-fortieth of the entire set of books comprising the *CJC*, provided a systematic synopsis of the law designed primarily for use as an elementary textbook for first-year law students. It was based on Gaius' earlier *Institutes*. The opening page of the *Institutes* appears (in English translation) in Appendix 2.6 at the end of this chapter.

- The *Digest*—also called the *Pandectae* (meaning the complete body of law)—is by far the most significant portion of the *CJC* and represents the distillation of what, in the judgment of Justinian's jurists, was most valuable from the best Roman legal writings from all previous periods, but especially from the "classical period" during which the most outstanding *jurisconsults* were most prolific. The *Digest* is on the same order of size as the Bible, and has been called "almost as inexhaustible". (Some further comments about the *Digest* appear below.)

- The *Codex* is a collection of imperial enactments (including edicts and judicial decisions) dating from deep into Rome's past (according to some sources, they

---

33. The compilation was not known as the *Corpus Juris Civilis* until roughly a thousand years after it was created. According to one account, the appellation *Corpus Juris Civilis* occurs for the first time in 1583 as the title of a complete edition of the Justinianic compilation by Dionysius Godofredus. See Wolfgang Kunkel, An Introduction to Roman Legal and Constitutional History 157 n.2 (translated into English by J.M. Kelly, 1966).

date from about 120 CE forward but belong mainly to the 4th, 5th, and 6th centuries CE), and they are arranged chronologically within each title. The *Codex* thus represents an identification and reauthorization of still-applicable legislation.

- The *Novellae* is a collection of new imperial legislation—that is, enacted by Justinian himself—issued after the compilation of the other parts of the *CJC*.

Some further comments are in order about the content and structure of the *Digest*, which constitutes a veritable treasure chest of Roman law. First, the *Digest* reflected the law applicable to Roman citizens—the *jus civile*—as opposed to the *jus gentium* applied by the *praetor peregrinus* in cases involving non-citizens of Rome. Second, the classical law was altered substantially by Justinian's team of compilers, so that it could be seen as stating current (that is, 6th century) law. It "does not contain pure, classical Roman law."[34]

Third, whereas the *Institutes* sets out the elementary legal principles in what has been called "remarkably perspicuous order,"[35] the *Digest* is chaotic in its presentation.[36] One authority describes the *Digest* in this way:

> It is, in fact, unbelievably confusing. The precise rationale behind the structure of the *Digest* as it has come down to us remains a subject of debate and controversy. What is clear is that it was not arranged for ease of use. It is arranged neither chronologically, which would be of maximum use to a lawyer. If one turns to the *Digest* to discover the Roman legal rule on a particular topic—validity of wills, for example—one cannot find the answer easily. In fact, without help, the only way to find the answer—if one wants to be thorough—is to read the whole thing. I would suggest to you that this unwieldy, difficult, and terribly long manuscript ... [was, in modern terms,] ... simply not accessible.[37]

This account of the *Digest*—the "core of the *Corpus Juris*"[38]—as being chaotic and inaccessible seems at first blush to be inconsistent with what John Henry Merryman calls the "ideology of codification," which seems to revolve around a desire for clarity and certainty. According to Merryman, Justinian "had two principal motivations" in ordering the preparation of his Code:

> First, he was a reactionary: he considered the contemporary Roman law decadent; he sought to rescue the Roman legal system from several centuries of deterioration and restore it to its former purity and grandeur. Second, he was a codifier: the mass

---

34. von Mehren et al, *supra* note 31, at 6. It has, however, been possible to reconstruct the classical Roman law by determining, through grammatical and stylistic analysis, what changes the sixth century compilers made. *Id.*

35. F. H. Lawson, A COMMON LAWYER LOOKS AT THE CIVIL LAW 10 (1953).

36. *Id.* at 11 (describing the *Digest* as "extraordinarily ill-arranged") and 13 (referring to "the mess Justinian's servants made of [Roman juristic literature] in compiling the Digest"); René David and John E.C. Brierley, MAJOR LEGAL SYSTEMS IN THE WORLD TODAY: AN INTRODUCTION TO THE COMPARATIVE STUDY OF LAW 44 (3d ed., 1985) (referring to "the chaos of the *Digest*") and 64 (contrasting the codifications starting in the eighteenth century to "the chaotic compilations of Justinian").

37. Michael H. Hoeflich, *Legal History and the History of the Book: Variations on a Theme*, 46 UNIVERSITY OF KANSAS LAW REVIEW 415, 418–419 (1997). Hoeflich goes on then to emphasize the importance of the scholarly work in the twelfth century to develop techniques, including "glosses" and indexes, to make the *Digest* accessible. *Id.* at 419–420. The work of the twelfth century scholars is described below in section II of this chapter.

38. Lawson, *supra* note 35, at 12.

of authoritative and quasi-authoritative material had become so great, and included so many refinements and different points of view, that it seemed desirable to Justinian to eliminate that which was wrong, obscure, or repetitive, to resolve conflicts and doubts, and to organize what was worth retaining into some systematic form.[39]

How could Justinian have gotten it so wrong? That is, if he was so eager for clarity and order, how could he possibly have approved the *Digest* for promulgation given its opaqueness and disorder?

Everything is relative. We must bear in mind the enormity of the undertaking that yielded the *Digest*. Justinian's team of scholars faced several centuries of laws, commentaries, and practice[40] on a wide range of topics. Three or four years might not have given the scholars adequate time to review all the available material well enough to create the kind of code — "complete, coherent, and clear"[41] — that Merryman says is the goal of the "ideology of codification at work in the civil law world".[42] Viewed in that light — that is, relative to the enormity of the task — Justinian's *Digest* might be considered to have met the goals of clarity and order that Merryman emphasizes, in that it constituted such a vast improvement on the completely disordered state of the law that existed before the *Digest* was prepared. Thus the *Digest* may be viewed as a step along the road toward the more refined codes produced in France and Germany at the beginning and end (respectively) of the 19th century — which we shall examine later in this chapter.

A final note about the *CJC* as a whole is also in order: Justinian's legal compilation reflected the Christian ideology that had infused Roman thought since it had become the state religion in the 4th century CE. An obvious manifestation of this religious element appears in the first line of the introductory page of the *Institutes*, as appearing in Appendix 2.6 at the end of this chapter: *In Nomine Domini Nostri Jesu Christi* ("in the Name of Our Lord Jesus Christ").

F. The "Law" of the "Dark Ages"

Justinian's compilation of law disappeared from view in the western Empire only a few years after its completion. This subsection summarizes how and why that happened, and what transpired in Europe during the five centuries that elapsed before the *Digest* was rediscovered.

---

39. John Henry Merryman and Rogelio Pérez-Perdomo, THE CIVIL LAW TRADITION 7 (3rd ed. 2007).

40. As noted above, the classical period alone produced works by numerous jurists. Moreover, Justinian's jurists also reached back much further in Roman history than the classical period, as indicated by their inclusion in the *Digest* of some legislative provisions dating from the third century BCE. See Kenneth Pennington, *The Spirit of Legal History*, 64 UNIVERSITY OF CHICAGO LAW REVIEW 1105, 1101–1102 (1997). According to one source, "[t]he fifty books of the *Digest* contain material from the writings of thirty-nine jurists, the earliest of whom was Quintus Mucius Scaevola, who died in 82 B.C." Justinian, DIGEST OF ROMAN LAW: THEFT, RAPINE, DAMAGE AND INSULT 39 (Colin F. Kolbert trans., 1979).

41. Merryman, *supra* note 39, at 30 (discussing the aims of codification in post-Revolution France) and 33 (discussing the aims of codification in 19th-century Germany).

42. *Id.* at 28. We shall give closer attention to this notion of an "ideology of codification" later, in subsection IB2 of Chapter Three.

1. Partial Eclipse of Law

In the years immediately following its promulgation, of course, Justinian's codification had the force of law in the eastern Empire.[43] Indeed, as the following account indicates, Justinian's *CJC* survived in some form for nearly fourteen centuries in the area around Constantinople:

> During subsequent centuries, Greek translations and adaptations of the (originally Latin) Corpus Juris, together with commentaries and summaries based upon it, remained the basis of the Byzantine legal system. Even after the Byzantine Empire had been overrun by the Turks in the 15th century, somewhat atrophied versions of the Corpus Juris survived as the law governing the affairs of the non-Islamic subjects of the Turkish Empire; and when Greece and other Eastern European countries regained their independence from the Turks in the 19th century, the Corpus Juris naturally formed the basis of the legal systems of the reborn nations. In Greece, as in some other countries of the area, Justinian's legislation thus remained in force until it was replaced by modern codes during the [20th] century.[44]

In the West, however, the *CJC* soon fell into disuse.[45] Although it was introduced briefly into Western Europe just a decade after its promulgation,[46] when Justinian was able to expand his power temporarily into Italy, the *CJC* soon fell victim to the general breakdown of civilization commonly referred to as the Dark Ages. For definitional matters — relating especially to the "Dark Ages" and the "Middle Ages", see Box #2.5.

Box #2.5 *Defining the "Dark Ages" and the "Middle Ages"*

The terms "Dark Ages" and "Middle Ages" and the "medieval" period are often used without definitions, presumably on the assumption that the reader knows what period is being referred to with each. Here are some definitions, drawn from various online dictionaries and other authorities, intended to clarify the terms as used in this book.

Dark Ages —

- A typical definition is "the period in Europe from the fall of Rome in the fifth century AD to the restoration of relative political stability around the year 1000"; another would be "the early part of the Middle Ages".

---

43. Helmut Coing, *The Roman Law as Ius Commune on the Continent*, 89 Law Quarterly Review 505, 506–507 (1973).

44. Rudolf B. Schlesinger, Hans W. Baade, Mirjan R. Damaska, and Peter E. Herzog, eds., Comparative Law: Cases, Text, Materials 255 n.b. (5th ed. 1988) (reprinting excerpts from Coing, *supra* note 43, but adding some commentary, including note b quoted here). *See also* Merryman, *supra* note 39, at 8–9 (referring to the publication in Greek of the *Basilica*, a compilation prepared in the ninth century in the eastern Roman Empire as a result of revived interest there in Justinian's compilation).

45. John Henry Merryman, The Civil Law Tradition 8 (2nd ed. 1985). This 1985 Merryman text is the predecessor edition of Merryman, *supra* note 39 (in which a slightly different wording appears). See also Mary Ann Glendon, Michael W. Gordon, and Paolo G. Carozza, Comparative Legal Traditions in a Nutshell 20 (2nd ed. 1999) [hereinafter Nutshell-1999]. The first edition of this work was Mary Ann Glendon, Michael W. Gordon, and Christopher Osakwe, Comparative Legal Traditions in a Nutshell (1982) [hereinafter Nutshell-1982]; some citations below are to that earlier edition. The most recent edition of this work is Mary Ann Glendon, Paolo G. Carozza, and Colin B. Picker, Comparative Legal Traditions in a Nutshell (2008) [hereinafter Nutshell-2008]; some citations below are to that later edition. After the sixth century, "[t]he learning of the *Digest* was hardly known at all from the British Channel to the Danube River." Hoeflich, *supra* note 37, at 417.

46. von Mehren et al, *supra* note 31, at 7.

- One of the more comprehensive explanations (appearing in an intensely religious website but apparently avoiding any infection from that fact—see http://www.allabouthistory.org/the-dark-ages.htm), describes what was considered "dark" about the Dark Ages and why the term "Dark Ages" is less widely used now.

  The Dark Ages as a term has undergone many evolutions; its definition depends on who is defining it. Indeed, modern historians no longer use the term because of its negative connotation. Generally, the Dark Ages referred to the period of time ushered in by the fall of the Western Roman Empire. This took place when the last Western emperor, Romulus Augustulus, was deposed by Odoacer, a barbarian. AD 476 was the time of this event.

  Initially, this era took on the term "dark" by later onlookers; this was due to the backward ways and practices that seemed to prevail during this time. [Other, still later,] historians used the term "dark" simply to denote the fact that little was known about this period; there was a paucity of written history. Recent discoveries have apparently altered this perception as many new facts about this time have been uncovered.

  The Italian Scholar, Francesco Petrarca [Petrarch], was the first to coin the phrase. He used it to denounce Latin literature of that time; others expanded on this idea to express frustration with the lack of Latin literature during this time or other cultural achievements. While the term dark ages is no longer widely used, it may best be described as Early Middle Ages—the period following the decline of Rome in the Western World. The Middle Ages is loosely considered to extend from 400 to 1000 AD.

Early Middle Ages—the more modern term for "Dark Ages"

Middle Ages—

- Competing definitions (drawn from various on-line sources) include:
  - "European historical period between roughly AD 500 and 1450"
  - "from the fifth century to the sixteenth century"
  - "the period of Western history from the fall of the Roman empire (476 AD) until the fall of Constantinople to the Turks (1453 AD)"
  - "the time between the ancient and the modern times"
  - "the period in western European history from the decline and fall of the Roman Empire until the 15th century"
  - "period in European history traditionally dated from the fall of the Roman Empire to the dawn of the Renaissance"
- "The Middle Ages are sometimes divided into Early (up to the 10th century), High (10th–14th centuries) and Late Middle Ages."

High Middle Ages—

- A typical definition is "the middle part of the Middle Ages, when medieval culture may be said to have been at its height; roughly the twelfth and thirteenth centuries."
- Another definition (as suggested above) would extend the High Middle Ages to a longer period—from the 10th to the 14th centuries.

Medieval Period—

- Typically this is used synonymously with "Middle Ages."
- Some definitions assign the "medieval period" to a narrower timeframe, such as about 1000 to 1450 (that is, more in line with the "High Middle Ages", as broadly defined).

From a legal perspective, the so-called Dark Ages represented a fundamental shift in thinking. Following about a thousand years in which law—particularly written law—was regarded as a central feature of society, Europe entered a period during which just the opposite view apparently prevailed. Consider the following account of the role that law played during that time:

> ... In the West, during the Dark Ages, there was no teaching of law; and, even for practical purposes, the knowledge of law was of little use. What we might call the law of the time was made up of rules which individuals of different regions observed, more or less spontaneously, in their personal relationships, but it is doubtful that these "rules of behavior" could even be characterised as rules of law. No social authority was desirous — or even capable — of enforcing respect for them ... ; proceedings were dominated by appeals to the supernatural and by a system of non-rational proof....
>
> In the shadows of the Dark Ages, society had returned to a more primitive state. Some law might still exist ... but the reign of law had ceased. Between individuals and between social groups, disputes were resolved by the law of physical force or by the discretionary authority of the leader.
>
> Doubtlessly more important than law at this time was some form or technique of arbitration, which sought not so much to give to each his due according to fixed and pre-established rules, but rather to maintain the solidarity of the group, assure peaceful coexistence between rival groups and restore peace in the community or society.[47]

In short, the breakup of the Roman Empire in the West ushered in a time in which "[l]arge areas of human activity were no longer under law."[48] The legal and political unity provided by the Empire had disappeared, and soon the rise of Islam brought a halt to commercial activity and to urban life as it had existed up to then.[49]

Around 800 CE, some strong attempts at political re-unification — with an eye to reclaiming (or creating) a "Holy Roman Empire" — were undertaken by Charlemagne. A short biographical sketch of Charlemagne appears as Appendix 2.7 to this chapter, and the notion of a "Holy Roman Empire" is explored briefly in Box #2.6. An indication of what sort of long-term effect resulted from Charlemagne's efforts to bring about a unification of Europe as a Holy Roman Empire appears from comparing the two maps in Figure #2.2. The first map shows, in approximate fashion, the broad stretch of territory encompassed by Charlemagne's empire at the time of his death in 815 CE. The second map shows how that empire had been broken up by 843 CE.

Box #2.6 *"Holy Roman Empire"*

The Holy Roman Empire — which Voltaire is often credited as having described as "neither Holy, nor Roman, nor an Empire" — was a complicated, mainly German political quasi-institution that waxed and waned in significance over the course of about a thousand years. One source, drawing from the Britannia Concise Encyclopedia (see http://www.answers.com/topic/holy-roman-empire), offers this account:

[The Holy Roman Empire constituted a] [r]ealm of varying extent in medieval and modern western and central Europe. Traditionally believed to have been established by Charlemagne, who

---

47. David and Brierly, *supra* note 36, at 37–38.
48. von Mehren et al, *supra* note 31, at 4.
49. *Id.* at 4–5. After the Moslems took control of Africa, Spain, and some of the key islands of the Mediterranean, "Western Europe was cut off from the Byzantine Empire and lost its great avenue of communication." *Id.* at 4–5. This brought an end to commercial activity and the disappearance of the merchant class. *Id.* at 5. "The Roman cities survived only as centers of diocesan administration, losing both their economic significance and their municipal administration." *Id.*

was crowned emperor by Pope Leo III in 800, the empire lasted until the renunciation of the imperial title by Francis II in 1806. The reign of the German Otto I (the Great; r. 962–973), who revived the imperial title after Carolingian decline, is also sometimes regarded as the beginning of the empire. The name Holy Roman Empire (not adopted until the reign of Frederick I Barbarossa [in the mid-12th century]) reflected Charlemagne's claim that his empire was the successor to the Roman Empire and that this temporal power was augmented by his status as God's principal vicar in the temporal realm (parallel to the pope's in the spiritual realm). The empire's core consisted of Germany, Austria, Bohemia, and Moravia. Switzerland, the Netherlands, and northern Italy sometimes formed part of it; France, Poland, Hungary, and Denmark were initially included, and Britain and Spain were nominal components. From the mid-11th century the emperors engaged in a great struggle with the papacy for dominance, and, particularly under the powerful Hohenstaufen dynasty (1138–1208, 1212–54), they fought with the popes over control of Italy. Rudolf I became the first Habsburg emperor in 1273, and from 1438 the Habsburg dynasty held the throne for centuries. Until 1356 the emperor was chosen by the German princes; thereafter he was formally elected by the electors. Outside their personal hereditary domains, emperors shared power with the imperial diet. During the Reformation the German princes largely defected to the Protestant camp, opposing the Catholic emperor. At the end of the Thirty Years' War, the Peace of Westphalia (1648) recognized the individual sovereignty of the empire's states; the empire thereafter became a loose federation of states and the title of emperor principally honorific. In the 18th century, issues of imperial succession resulted in the War of the Austrian Succession and the Seven Years' War. The greatly weakened empire was brought to an end by the victories of Napoleon.

Figure #2.2 Charlemagne's Empire and Its Later Division[50]

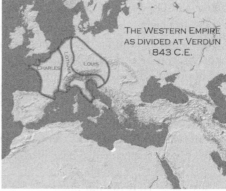

Europe in 814 CE   Europe in 843 CE

As the maps in Figure #2.2 show, Charlemagne's successes proved only temporary. Several more centuries would have to pass before a clear notion of "Europe" would emerge and prevail.[51]

---

50. These maps have been prepared by John Tomasic and Erin Slinker Tomasic. The first of the maps is based loosely on a map from The Public Schools Historical Atlas (C. Colbeck ed., 1905) as reproduced at http://historymedren.about.com/library/atlas/blatmapeur814.htm. The second map is based loosely on a map from Freeman's Atlas of the Historical Geography of Europe (3rd ed. 1903) as reproduced at http://en.wikipedia.org/wiki/File:Western_Empire_as_divided_at_Verdun_843.jpg.

51. For a different view, asserting that the idea of a European identity emerged in the ninth century—largely through the unifying influence of the Bible (and the Latin language in which it was expressed)—see Walter Ullman, Law and Politics in the Middle Ages 42–46 (1975).

Given this environment, in which the political and legal moorings had been cut away and Western Europe "became essentially a rural civilization",[52] it is hardly surprising that Justinian's *CJC* would be disregarded or even discarded:

> For five centuries after the fall of Rome a series of raiders and settlers overran the areas that had once been Roman. There were no strong, centralized states. Kingdoms rose and fell. The condition of the people sank into local self-sufficiency. It would be centuries before scholars again would be capable of picking up and putting to use the technical instruments left behind by the Classical Roman and Byzantine jurists.[53]

2. Survival and Partial Influence of Roman Law

It is important to note that although Justinian's codification of Roman law fell into disuse, some substantive elements of Roman law did continue to exercise some influence in Europe. Such elements may be seen as surviving in several forms, including two that are of special interest: in the law and culture of the Church,[54] and as an ingredient of local "vulgarized" law.[55]

The second of these, vulgarized law, warrants special attention, and this requires a slight backtracking to the 5th century, before Justinian's Code was compiled. When German tribes invaded the Italian peninsula in the 5th century, they brought with them the concept of "personal law," under which "the law of a person's nationality followed him wherever he went."[56] Therefore, the "Germanic rulers used Roman law to govern their Roman subjects, while applying their own law to their own peoples."[57] The "Roman law" used for these purposes, however, was not Justinian's great compilation; that compilation was not created until the middle of the 6th century. Instead, other sources were used. As noted above, one was the *Lex Romana Visigothorum* (also called the *Brevaiarium Alaricianum*), compiled around 506 for the Roman subjects of Alaric the Second.[58] Although it set out only a rude and fragmentary law, the *Lex Romana Visigothorum* became the standard source of Roman law for several centuries.[59] It was not the only such source: "[t]wo other statements of barbarized Roman law date from the same period: the Edicts of the Ostrogothic kings and the *Lex Romana Burgundionum*."[60]

Not surprisingly, applying the rule of "personal law" became difficult, and a fusion of Germanic tribal laws with some of the Roman legal rules gradually occurred:

> Over time it gradually became impossible to tell which group a particular person was in and the distinctions between groups disappeared. By the end of the tenth century, the rules were the same for all persons within a given territory. Crude versions of Roman legal rules had become intermingled in varying degrees with the customary rules of the Germanic invaders to the point where one can speak of the laws during this period as either "Romanized customary laws"

---

52. *Id.* at 5.
53. Nutshell-1982, *supra* note 45, at 17.
54. von Mehren et al, *supra* note 31, at 5.
55. Lawson, *supra* note 35, at 13.
56. Merryman, *supra* note 39, at 8.
57. Nutshell-1999, *supra* note 45, at 21. See also Coing, *supra* note 43, at 506, and Schlesinger et al, *supra* note 44, at 255 n.c.
58. von Mehren et al, *supra* note 31, at 6. See also subsection ID2 of this chapter.
59. *Id.*
60. *Id.*

or "barbarized Roman laws". Thus, though Roman legal science and Classical Roman law disappeared in the welter, diversity and localism of [what one authority has called a] "customary thicket", a Romanist element survived and served both as a strand of continuity and a latent, potential universalizing factor in what we now think of as the civil law tradition.[61]

As noted above, another form in which Roman law may be seen as surviving through the Dark Ages is in the law of the Church, or canon law. We shall see in section II of this chapter that canon law played an important role in the life of the universities in which the *CJC* (particularly the *Digest*) was studied beginning in the 11th century, and in the development of a *jus commune* that preceded the great European national codifications. Therefore, canon law deserves at least a brief mention at this stage. Here is an account offered by one authority:

> With the break-up of the far-flung system of Roman administration, the Church took over some of the functions of government. Indeed, after the fall of the Roman Empire, and until the revival of Roman law in the 11th century, the single most important universalizing factor in the diverse and localized legal systems of the civil law tradition was canon law. But canon law itself was a hybrid of sorts. It had been produced by Christian notions interacting reciprocally with Roman law after the Christianization of the Empire, a process during which the reign of Constantine (d. 337 A.D.) was an important marker. The Justinian Corpus, in particular, was profoundly affected by Christian ideas, but the Church, for its part, had borrowed freely from the structure, principles and detailed rules of ancient Roman law. Furthermore, just as there was some degree of amalgamation everywhere of Germanic customs, indigenous customs and debased Roman law, there was a certain penetration by canon law into the codes promulgated by German rulers....[62]

In these and other ways, some vestiges of Roman law survived the dramatic changes that swept across Europe during the Dark Ages—the fall of an empire, the retreat to a rural subsistence with a local frame of reference, and the withering of law as a feature of society. The *Corpus Juris Civilis*, however, had no role in any of that. By the forces of history, or an accident of history, it lay out of sight, beneath the surface. (It is for this reason that the diagram in Appendix 2.20, at the end of this chapter, uses a dashed line to signify the fate of Roman civil law during the period of the Dark Ages.)

II. The "Second Life" of Roman Law: Rediscovery and Change

Justinian's *Digest* was likened above to a "treasure chest" filled with the rules and reasoning of Roman law as compiled and recorded (and Christianized) under Justinian's direction but then buried (at least in the West) during the Dark Ages. Pursuing this

---

61. Nutshell-1982, *supra* note 45, at 21.
62. *Id.* at 19–20.

metaphor, we could consider the end of the Dark Ages to be the point at which that buried treasure was rediscovered and dug up. This development served as the beginning of the "second life" of Roman law, to use the other metaphor introduced above. In the paragraphs that follow we shall see how that rediscovery occurred and how the "second life" unfolded in the succeeding centuries. Those centuries saw (i) the gradual emergence of a modern Europe governed for many years by a common law that drew not just from Roman law but also from canon law (the law of the Church) and commercial law, then (ii) a series of revolutionary changes from which emerged a divided Europe in which each nation-state had its own law—several of which were reduced to a carefully codified form that reflected their debt to Roman jurists from many centuries earlier.

A. Rediscovering the Digest and Creating the Jus Commune

1. The Rediscovery of the *Digest*

The end of the 11th century "was a crucial point in the development of the civil law."[63] There occurred then in northern Italy a discovery of the *Corpus Juris Civilis*—both a literal discovery and a figurative one. The *literal* discovery occurred when an ancient manuscript containing the text of the *Digest* was found. Box #2.7 presents two accounts (mainly but not entirely consistent) about that rediscovery.[64]

Box #2.7 Rediscovery of Justinian's Digest — Two Accounts

The only surviving manuscript of the Digest was written most likely about 600, in the Byzantine part of Italy. It was carefully collated with, and corrected on the basis of, an original text of the Digest, since lost. This extant manuscript was in the possession of Pisa (hence the manuscript is called the *Pisana*) until the fifteenth century, when the Florentines captured Pisa and also took possession of this priceless jewel (hence also called the *Florentina*). There is very little evidence that the *Pisana* itself played a great role in the transmission of the Roman law before the end of the medieval period. What did play a role—and perhaps the most crucial role in the transmission of any legal work—was a copy of the *Pisana* which was made in the late eleventh century and found its home in Bologna. It was this copy of the *Pisana*, and not the *Pisana* itself, which formed the basis of teaching and of the influence of Roman law in the Middle Ages. This so-called Vulgate text of the Digest (or *Littera Bononiensis*) was copied over and over again and disseminated throughout medieval Europe. Only very rarely did the *Pisana* come to be consulted, and this not before the fourteenth century. [Ullman, *supra* note 51, at 68]

The *Pisana* (also known as the *Littera Florentina*) is a manuscript of Justinian's *Digest* rediscovered in Italy around 1070 AD. Its rediscovery is a hotly debated topic among legal historians. The *Pisana* may have been rediscovered in a monastery around the Italian coast of Amalfi, an area which had been momentarily regained by Justinian and the Byzantine/Eastern Roman Empire. The *Pisana*, which is believed to be an official copy of the *Digest*, was likely is-

---

63. Schlesinger et al, *supra* note 44, at 270.

64. See also H. J. Berman, *The Religious Foundations of Western Law*, 24 CATHOLIC LAW REVIEW 490, 492 (1975); Thomas, *supra* note 2, at 7 (asserting that the Digest was "[t]aken by the Pisans from Amalfi where it was found").

sued between 533 and 557 AD. The document itself has long been treasured by its possessors in Pisa (12th through the 15th centuries) and Florence (15th century to the present). Despite (and largely because) of its immense value to scholars, the *Pisana* was available to only the most important individuals, making it rare for scholars to gain access to the document. [http://en.wikipedia.org/wiki/Littera_Florentina]

The *figurative* discovery of the *Digest* occurred at the University of Bologna, where, beginning with lectures by a teacher there named Irnerius, the *Digest* was made the subject of study by scholars and students of law.[65] A biographical sketch of Irnerius appears as Appendix 2.8, at the end of this chapter.

This figurative rediscovery of the *Digest*, and of Roman law more generally, occurred at a time of renewal and emergence from the Dark Ages. Here is one portrayal:

> Irnerius's lecures came at a time when profound political and economic changes were already under way in western Europe. As early as the 10th century, Venice had begun to develop an important Mediterranean trade. The launching of the first Crusade in 1096 marked the beginning of the definite reopening of the Mediterranean as a western European trade route. The 12th century saw a large-scale expansion of commerce along both the Mediterranean and the northern coasts of western Europe. "The revival of maritime commerce was accompanied by its rapid penetration inland. Not only was agriculture stimulated by the demand for its produce and transformed by the exchange economy of which it now became a part, but a new export industry was born."[66]

In short, "light returned to Europe."[67] The re-emergence of political order and the economic expansion that began in the 11th century led to a renewed interest in law. "Like scholars in other fields, jurists began to turn, with the excitement of discovery, to the accomplishments of antiquity. The revival of Roman law that took place in northern Italy towards the end of the 11th century was a rediscovery, through the Justinian legacy, of Roman legal science."[68]

What did these developments—the discovery of the *Digest* and the economic and political environment in which that discovery occurred—then lead to? In a sense, they led to the modern civil law tradition. That is, the intense study of the *Digest* that began with its discovery (both literal and figurative) in the late 11th century laid the groundwork on which virtually all modern European legal systems rest, as well as (to only a slightly lesser degree) the legal systems of scores of other countries around the world. The remainder of this subsection will explain how that groundwork was laid, by summarizing these interconnected developments:

- The work of the *Glossators*, those law teachers of the 11th through 13th centuries who prepared detailed annotations on the *Corpus Juris Civilis*;

- The development of *commercial law*, prompted by greatly expanded trade within Europe;

---

65. See Schlesinger et al, *supra* note 44, at 270; Merryman, *supra* note 39, at 9; Nutshell-1999, *supra* note 45, at 20–21.

66. von Mehren et al, *supra* note 31, at 7, quoting from a 1937 treatise on the economic and social history of medieval Europe.

67. This phrase appears in the 1985 edition of the Merryman text, referred to *supra* note 45. See John Henry Merryman, THE CIVIL LAW TRADITION 8 (2nd ed. 1985).

68. Nutshell-1982, *supra* note 45, at 20.

- The work of the *Commentators*, later scholars who went beyond an explanation and systematization of the *Corpus Juris Civilis* to a practical application and modernization of it; and

- The nearly simultaneous development of *canon law* with the publication of Gratian's *Decretum*—which, together with the Roman law of the *Corpus Juris Civilis*, was fashioned into *jus commune* or common law applicable in varying degrees throughout Europe.

2. The Glossators

The term "Glossators" has been applied to the first few generations of legal scholars at the European universities, beginning at Bologna. In order to understand what they did, and why, it is necessary first to examine the nature of the universities themselves. The following excerpt highlights two aspects of the medieval universities: (i) their focus on the ancient civilization of Rome; and (ii) the significance of the University of Bologna for purposes of legal studies.

... There is quite a difference between the character of a modern university and a university of the thirteenth or fourteenth century. The modern university unites research with teaching. The main task of the medieval university was to introduce the student to traditional knowledge as laid down in a certain number of books of authority. It is characteristic of the medieval university that the knowledge it had to impart to its students[,] and the books of authority it used for this purpose, were taken from a civilisation which had long since passed away and which, nevertheless, was considered as the origin and model of all spiritual culture: Greco-Roman antiquity.

... [Accordingly,] legal education, which began in the twelfth century, was based on the greatest collection of legal materials Antiquity had left to posterity, the *Corpus Iuris* of Justinian. Modern research has shown that there may also have been political considerations which led the legists of Bologna to turn to the *Corpus Iuris Civilis*, since the medieval emperors considered themselves the successors of the Roman *imperatores*, and their partisans welcomed arguments drawn from the *Corpus Iuris* in the great struggle against the Papacy. But it is the great authority of ancient civilisation in general that is the most convincing explanation for the attitude the medieval law schools took.

The first medieval universities were not founded by act of State or church but slowly grew out of groups of students gathering around and entering into contact with individual professors. These first universities were generally restricted to one or two main subjects. They did not aim at comprehensive scientific education as most modern universities do. Theology and philosophy were taught at Paris, medicine at Salerno and Montpellier. For law, it was an Italian university which took the lead: Bologna....

Already in the twelfth century Bologna had developed into an international centre of legal studies. This can be seen in the fact that the emperor Frederick Barbarossa in 1158 gave by the so-called Authentica "Habita" very important privileges to the students of Bologna. The Emperor promises the students protection during their journey from their home country to Bologna. He grants them exemption from the city jurisdiction of Bologna, giving them a choice between the jurisdiction of the Bishop and of their own professors.... Now, if the emperor found it necessary to provide for the students of Bologna by such specific legislation, there must have been at the time a consdierable number of foreign students in Bologna. [See Box #2.8 for further details on the *Habita*.]

In fact, modern research ... [has] shown that in 1269 more than a thousand foreign students were present at Bologna.[69]

Box #2.8 The Authentica Habita[70]

The University of Bologna had been established in the late 11th century — its own website notes a founding date of (probably) 1088 — and was initially a private enterprise between teachers and their pupils. However, it soon became evident that the University needed protection from local government authorities within the city of Bologna. The *Authentica Habita* was authorized in 1155 (some sources say 1158) by Frederick I (Barbarossa), the powerful Emperor of the Holy Roman Empire. The *Habita* provided special privileges to students — in particular, law students — at the University of Bologna, allowing them to research independent from any other power. Thus, the *Habita* was instrumental in the development of Europe's preeminent law schools located within Bologna. Frederick I astutely identified the potential of utilizing jurists as advisors, enabling him to produce legal justification for acquiring greater legislative power. He became one of the first Medieval rulers to use jurists and the Roman civil law to his advantage.

An account by Merryman also tells why the *Corpus Juris Civilis* — instead of either (i) the barbarized Roman law that had been in force under the German tribes that had invaded the Italian peninsula or (ii) the body of rules followed by local towns, merchants' guilds, or petty sovereigns — was selected as the centerpiece of the law curriculum at Bologna:

> There were several reasons for this attention to the *Corpus Juris Civilis* and neglect of other available bodies of law. First, the conception of a Holy Roman Empire was very strong and real in twelfth-century Italy. Justinian was thought of as a Holy Roman Emperor, and his *Corpus Juris Civilis* was treated as imperial legislation. As such it had the authority of both the pope and the temporal emperor behind it. This made it far superior in force and range of applicability to the legislation of a local prince, the regulations of a guild, or local custom. Second, the jurists recognized the high intellectual quality of the *Corpus Juris Civilis*. They saw that this work, which they called "written reason," was superior to the barbarized compilations that had come into use under the Germanic invader. The *Corpus Juris Civilis* carried not only the authority of the pope and the emperor, but also the authority of an obviously superior civilization and intelligence.[71]

---

69. Coing, *supra* note 43, at 507–509. Although the majority of the law students at Bologna came from the continent of Europe, some of them were English clerics and laymen. Schlesinger et al, *supra* note 44, at 270 n.3, citing Theodore F.T. Plucknett, A CONCISE HISTORY OF THE COMMON LAW 296 (1956). According to one scholar, the growth of special law schools actually began "at Ravenna and shortly afterwards at Bologna". Ullman, *supra* note 51, at 78.

70. This account is drawn from principally from http://en.wikipedia.org/wiki/Medieval_university and http://faculty.cua.edu/Pennington/PoliticsWesternLaw.htm.

71. Merryman, *supra* note 39, at 9. See also Ullman, *supra* note 51, at 84–85 (emphasizing the close association of the University of Bologna with the emperors). Another reason the law curriculum looked to the *Corpus Juris Civilis*, rather than to contemporary law, reflects the state of that contemporary law in the twelfth century: "[W]hat we, today, call positive law..., in most countries, was in a chaotic, uncertain, fragmented and sometimes primitive condition. Italy and France, where the model of the new study originated, had no national law; in these countries, where feudalism prevailed, no general sovereign exercised a controlling influence. The same was true of Spain and Portugal.... Unless they were to remain schools of local procedure, without prestige, influence or power,

As noted above, however, the *Digest* (the most important part of the *Corpus Juris Civilis*) is not an easy text to understand; it is confusing and disorderly. Its titles are arranged "in an order appropriate to a system of remedies existing in the classical period but hardly intelligible to the lawyers of Justinian's day, and not at all to those of the Middle Ages."[72] Moreover, within each title, the order of the extracts from the classical jurists or other sources "gives little or no help to the student in search of his law."[73] A central task of the law teachers at Bologna, therefore, was to bring some order out of the chaos of the *Digest*. It was to this task that the Glossators applied themselves in the 12th and 13th centuries.

The term Glossator comes from the *glossae*—glosses, or annotations—that the Italian law teachers created to reveal the treasures of the *Digest*.[74] These *glossae* were systematic notations written in the margins of the text of the *Digest* in order to explain its provisions and to reconcile apparent inconsistencies between them.[75] The Glossators' "literary output thus consisted largely of short notes or glosses to particular passages in which they compared one text with another, raised a difficulty, or suggested a solution."[76]

An image of one page of such a gloss appears in Figure #2.3. The text of the *Digest* is in the center of the page, surrounded by notes and annotations.

Irnerius might be regarded as the first Glossator, and he was followed by the so-called "Four Doctors": Bulgarus, Martinus Gosia, Jacobus de Boragine, and Hugo de Porta Ravennate.[77] "The heyday of their influence was in the middle years of the twelfth century when they acted as counsellors to the imperial government as well as to other public functionaries."[78]

One of the Glossators, Accursius (1182–1259), "combined several previous glossae into the famous *Glossa Ordinaria*. It was in this annotated form that the Corpus Juris was used in practice for several centuries thereafter."[79] The date usually assigned to the *Glossa Ordinaria* (from which Figure #2.3 is drawn) is 1240 CE. A biographical sketch of Accursius appears as Appendix 2.10 at the end of this chapter.

3. Gratian's *Decretum* and the Codification of Canon Law

As the Glossators were first creating their glosses—and in fact nearly a century before the appearance of the *Glossa Ordinaria* of Accursius—another great written work ap-

---

the universities had to teach something other than the local law." David and Brierly, *supra* note 36, at 41.

72. Lawson, *supra* note 35, at 11.

73. *Id.*

74. Schlesinger et al, *supra* note 44, at 270.

75. For further discussion of the meaning of this term, see subsection ID3b of Chapter Three, *infra*.

76. von Mehren et al, *supra* note 31, at 9.

77. The works of these and other Glossators are discussed extensively in Hermann Kantorosicz, STUDIES I N THE GLOSSATORS OF THE ROMAN LAW: NEWLY DISCOVERED WRITINGS OF THE TWELFTH CENTURY (1938).

78. Ullman, *supra* note 51, at 98–99.

79. Schlesinger et al, *supra* note 44, at 270. Another source (who, incidentally, puts Accursius' death three years later, at 1263), refers to "the enormously influential *Glossa ordinaria* of Accursius…, in which he combined and synthesized the glosses of the previous century and a half" as "the greatest achievement of the Glossators." von Mehren et al, *supra* note 31, at 9. In his *Glossa Ordinaria*, Accursius "recast the efforts of his predecessors into a treatise comprising approximately 96,000 explanatory glosses." David and Brierly, *supra* note 36, at 43. A text of the *Glossa Ordinaria* is available online from the University of Heidelberg, at http://diglit.ub.uni-heidelberg.de/diglit/justinian1627bd1/. The front page of it appears as Figure #2.3.

Figure #2.3 A Gloss on the Digest*

Digeſtorum proœmium.

Digeſtorum,
SEV
PANDECTARVM
D. IVSTINIANI
SACRATISS. PRINCIPIS,
PROOEMIVM.
IN NOMINE DOMINI IESV CHRISTI.

* This image is drawn from the collection of the library of the University of Heidelberg (http://diglit.ub.uni-heidelberg.de/diglit/justinian1627bd1/0064?sid=2ba2384bdbf8ef43e48262b5295451f1). It shows the front page of Accursius' *Glossa Ordinaria*.

peared: Gratian's *Decretum*. It is here that we pick up the other main current in what became the *jus commune* of Europe: canon law.

A description of the early documents and development of the law of the Church — that is, canon law, or ecclesiastical law — appeared above in subsection IB3 of this chapter. That description highlighted how the adoption of Christianity as Rome's state religion created both (i) a strong hybrid of secular and religious law and administration and (ii) the seeds of friction between the papacy and the imperial government that would play out over many later centuries. We also saw how early councils (such as those at Nicea and Constantinople) established certain central features of Christian dogma. The most important actual *law* of the Church, however, developed not so much from such councils — that is, not so much from "conciliar decrees" — as it did from "decretals" or "decretal letters". One authority offers this comparison:

> [A] conciliar decree [that] emanated from a properly convened synod or council [such as those at Nicea in 325] ... constituted canon law in every sense of the term. [However, the importance of such conciliar decrees] lies in the field of doctrine and organization and in the formulation of basic articles of the faith.... [The councils] were convoked by imperial edict and were therefore essentially imperial assemblies in which [the papacy] played no leading part. [By contrast, the] emergence in the fifth century of the papacy as a monarchic institution acting through the instrumentality of the decretal, was of crucial significance for [the creation of canon law]....[80]

> The monarchic function of the papacy found expression in the vehicle which it borrowed from the imperial administration: the rescript or the decretal letter. The decretal letter had authoritative and binding force.... [It was] addressed either to individuals or to certain groups, [or] to bishops or princes, [and it] was the authoritative papal statement concerning a controversial point in doctrine, liturgy or discipline — in short any matter which the papacy considered relevant for the well-being of the whole Christian body public. The decretal created law both in its formal and material respects. The decretals pouring forth from the papal chancery in ever increasing quantities formulated the canon law, and the term 'canon' signified the norm of right living (*norma recta vivend*).[81]

The gradual accumulation of decretals through the centuries (beginning in the 5th century) resulted in a very complex and unwieldy body of law. After all, "[t]he decretals dealt with virtually every issue which the papacy considered vital and relevant" to Christians, and these included "royal elections, ... depositions of bishops, kings and other Rulers, sanctions against individuals and corporations..., counterfeiting of money, privileges of classes and groups, interpretation of statutes and municipal laws, fixation of crime as a public offence," and much more.[82] Several attempts were made over the centuries — especially in the 9th, 10th, and 11th centuries — to create useful compilations or codifications of the decretals (and hence of canon law).[83] But it was to be Gratian, a Camaldunensian monk, whose work proved most successful and significant in this regard.

---

80. Ullman, *supra* note 51, at 151.

81. *Id.* at 120–121. Ullman goes on to explain that "[t]he oldest extant decretal, issued during the pontificate of Siricius (in 385), was addressed to the Spanish bishops and was a formidable juristic document settling a number of disputed points authoritatively. From then onwards the output of papal decretals steadily increased". *Id.* at 122.

82. *Id.* at 140–141.

83. For descriptions of these, see *id.* at 130–133.

A biographical sketch of Gratian appears as Appendix 2.9, at the end of this chapter. Gratian, also working in Bologna, "established canonlaw as a coherent field of study"[84] by composing "an introduction to the systematic study of canon law" around 1140.[85] The second recension of this work "was immediately adopted by the teachers of all the law schools of Europe as the standard introductory text for the study of canon law."[86] From that point on — that is, beginning in the latter part of the 12th century — Roman law and canon law "comprised the curriculum of the medieval law schools,"[87] and the *Digest* and the *Decretum* served as the principal objects of study in that curriculum. One authority summarizes these developments in this way:

> Law courses began [at Bologna] at the end of the eleventh century.... The subject taught was at first only the *Corpus Iuris* of Justinian.... Canon Law, that is the law of the medieval Roman Catholic Church, was added in the twelfth century; about 1140 the Bolognese monk Gratianus completed the great collection of Canon Law materials called the *Decretum*.... Thus Bologna had two law faculties, one devoted to Roman Law (the Legists), the other to Canon Law (the Canonists). The totality of the legal material taught at Bologna was described by the term *ius utrumque*, i.e. both laws, Roman Law and Canon Law.[88]

By late in the 12th century, therefore, the curriculum of law studies had been established, centered on "the two fundamental texts needed to foster the rebirth of a legal profession in Western Europe ... and the growth of medieval legal systems throughout Europe."[89] In undertaking the task of deciphering and explaining these two great texts — especially the "unbelievably confusing" *Digest*[90] — the law teachers of the day made an enormous contribution. According to one authority, "the development of university legal education during the twelfth and thirteenth centuries was, to a large extent, the development of techniques and devices designed to make these two texts accessible, and therefore useable. The whole format of early university education was, in essence, designed to pro-

---

84. Pennington, *supra* note 40, at 1105.

85. *Id.* Gratian "called his work a *Concordia discordantium canonum*, a *Concord of Discordant Canons*," but the title was later shortened to *Decretum*. *Id.* See also von Mehren et al, *supra* note 31, at 9 (describing the *Decretum* and setting the date of its publication at 1140). See also Ullman, *supra* note 51, at 139 (stating that Gratian "composed his book in 1139–40"). Ullman says that "the effect of this book of Gratian's was the establishment of a fully-fledged canon law school at Bologna". *Id.*

86. Pennington, *supra* note 40, at 1105. See also Ullman, *supra* note 51, at 166: "The work appeared at the right time and in the right place — Bologna — and became at once recognized as a new kind of scholarship that utilized the collected law in the service of scholarly analysis and synthesis. Its 4,000 chapters relate to virtually every problem in public life that could be encountered in a Christian society." For Gratian's debt to earlier scholarship, especially that of Abelard and various Roman law authorities, see *id.* at 165. For a summary of later collections of canon law (following Gratian), see *id.* at 168–169.

87. Pennington, *supra* note 40, at at 1106. "Every student of law [in Europe] between 1200 and 1525 studied both Roman and canon law." *Id.* See also von Mehren et al, *supra* note 31, at 9 (noting that after the publication of Gratian's work, "Canon law soon took its place as a university subject at Bologna alongside the Civil Law of the Glossators"). See also Nutshell-2008, *supra* note 45, at 27 (noting that after Gratian's work, canon law "began to be taught alongside Roman civil law in universities all over Europe").

88. Coing, *supra* note 43, at 508. "The degree conferred on a student who had completed the full course of study was Juris Utriusque Doctor, or Doctor of Both Laws, referring to the civil law and the canon law. (The J.U.D. degree is still granted in some universities in the civil law world.)" Merryman, *supra* note 39, at 11–12.

89. Hoeflich, *supra* note 37, at 418.

90. *Id.*

vide tools for accessibility."[91] Specifically, the work product of the Glossators, including the famous *Glossa Ordinaria*, provided two things for the law student:

> They provide definitional help in that they explain the technical terms, and they provide cross-references to other passages in the text that permit the reader to find all of the necessary learning on a particular topic. Thus, if a lawyer can find one relevant passage in the text that is glossed, then he will, by using the gloss, be able to find other relevant passages. The gloss is, in effect, a dictionary and a finding aid. University law lectures, in which masters glossed particular sections of the fundamental texts, were, in the earliest period, specifically designed to provide these ancillary, but absolutely necessary, tools to their auditors. One needed to attend university lectures in order to acquire these tools necessary to practice law. Without the text and the finding aids, one simply could not look up the answers to questions as they arose.[92]

I have dwelt at some length in the preceding paragraphs on the rise of law studies in medieval universities, the use of the *Digest* and the *Decretum* in those studies, and the work of the Glossators in bringing order out of the chaos of the *Digest*. These are important points because they combine to form an essential link between past and present in the civil law tradition. The events occurring in northern Italy from the end of the 11th century to the middle of the 13th century brought Roman law, in the form of Justinian's great compilation, from being an object of mere "antiquarian curiosity"[93] to a position of prominence in the civil law tradition, a position it retains to this day.

4. The Commentators (Post-Glossators)

Following in the footsteps of the Glossators were the Commentators (also sometimes referred to as the Post-Glossators). These scholars, centered largely in Italy at first and then spreading north throughout Western Europe, studied the (annotated) *Corpus Juris Civilis* in the 14th and 15th centuries.[94] Their work, however, had a different objective:

> While the glossators had not ventured beyond mere exegesis and systematization of the Roman texts, the commentators' approach was primarily a practical one. They sought to adjust the law to the needs of their own time, often by taking great liberties in interpreting the Corpus Juris and in reconciling conflicting (or seemingly conflicting) passages of the original Justinian compilation as well as the glossa. In their effort to modernize the law, the commentators also took note of legal materials outside the Corpus Juris, such as statutes and local and commercial customs.[95]

Hence, through the efforts of the Commentators, "Roman law was expurgated and adapted and used for entirely new developments ... [and its] presentation was ... system-

---

91. *Id.*

92. *Id.* at 420. Sometime around 1290, "somebody had invented the best finding aid of all: the alphabetical index. While the evidence suggests that the first indices were made for biblical texts, there is also strong evidence that very soon after indices began to be made for the Bible, they began to be made for the *Digest* and the *Decretum*." *Id.*

93. *Id.* (describing what the *Digest* would have remained without the efforts of the early university scholars).

94. Schlesinger et al, *supra* note 44, at 270.

95. *Id.* Another account says that the Commentators "go beyond glosses on individual legal texts and prepare systematic comments upon legal problems. They do not ignore the existing law but achieve a synthesis with it, thereby contributing to the introduction into practice of the law contained in the Corpus juris civilis." von Mehren et al, *supra* note 31, at 9.

atised in a way which contrasts vividly with the chaos of the *Digest....*"[96] The greatest representative of the Commentators was Bartolus de Sassoferrato (1314–1357).[97] A biographical sketch of Bartolus appears as Appendix 2.11 at the end of this chapter. Other Commentators—who collectively "set the tone down to the sixteenth century" by becoming an "intellectual force on a global scale" due in part "to the proliferation of universities in the thirteenth and fourteenth centuries", giving the Commentators plenty of fora in which to create throughout Europe "a cohesive intellectual élite"—were Odofredus (a pupil of Accursius), Jacobus de Arena (d. 1298), Dynus de Mugellano, and Cynus de Pistoia (teacher of Bartolus).[98]

The work of the Commentators, building on that of the Glossators, culminated in what has been called (typically in a narrower context) the *usus modernus Pandectarum*— "a modernized Roman law, adapted to new circumstances."[99] According to Merryman, this modernized Roman law is one of the "three subtraditions within the civil law tradition."[100] A second one is canon law, which matured as an object of study with Roman law in the 12th century, as described above in subsection IIA3. These two subtraditions together are often referred to as the *jus commune*, which I discuss below in subsection IIA6. Before turning to the *jus commune*, however, I shall mention what Merryman refers to as the third subtradition of the civil law tradition—commercial law.

5. Commercial Law

At the same time that the Commentators were "adapting the law of Roman society to the problems of their own day,"[101] the "law merchant" or commercial law was entering a new phase.

> With the rise of towns, the birth of markets, fairs and banks, the rapid expansion of maritime and overland trade, and the eventual development of large flourishing commercial centers, there appeared [in the 14th and 15th centuries] the need for a body of law to govern business transactions. Since several features of Roman law proved unsuitable for this purpose, guilds and merchants' associations established their own rules and their own tribunals. The merchants' courts worked out informal rules and expeditious procedures that were practical, fair, and grounded in the usages of businessmen. These rules in time came to be recognized and applied as customary law by secular and ecclesiastical authorities.[102]

The specific method by which the merchants' rules gained the force of law is explained by another authority in this way:

---

96. David and Brierly, *supra* note 36, at 43–44.

97. Schlesinger et al, *supra* note 44, at 270; Nutshell-1999, *supra* note 45, at 24; von Mehren et al, *supra* note 31, at 9 (showing Bartolus as born in 1313).

98. For fascinating and humorous—one might even say enchanting—biographical sketches of these Commentators, see Ullman, *supra* note 51, at 105–108.

99. David and Brierly, *supra* note 36, at 44. As noted above, the Latin term for the *Digest* is *Pandectae*. The term *usus modernus Pandectarum* is typically used to refer to German scholars applying Romanist law to suit local circumstances, especially in the century or two before Germany's reunification in the late 19th century. Indeed, the term "Pandectists" was used in Germany to refer to legal scholars who concentrated their study on the *Digest*. I am using the term *usus modernus Pandectarum* in a broader sense here.

100. Merryman, *supra* note 39, at 13.

101. Nutshell-1982, *supra* note 45, at 21.

102. *Id.* at 23.

According to medieval views, the guild or corporation had the power to codify its corporate customs, and these codifications became known as *statuta mercatorum*. Confirmation of the *statuta* by the sovereign was frequently sought and granted; but it was the prevailing view that the *statuta* had the force of law even in the absence of such confirmation.[103]

The most influential of these *statuta mercatorum* were the ones adopted by the merchants' guilds in Italian commercial cities during the 14th and 15th centuries.[104]

Why would special commercial rules develop outside the Roman law or the canon law? Partly because those two systems were inhospitable to the easy transfer of property through contract.

Under the Roman system of contract law, ... only certain categories of contracts were enforceable. An executory contract which did not fit into any of these categories, was called nudum pactum and was not actionable.... Under the influence of canon law, the glossators and commentators attempted to liberalize this somewhat rigid Roman system, and to bring it closer to the expansive canon law interpretation of "pacta sunt servanda" [contracts must be observed]. As one might expect, however, these attempts to reconcile two irreconcilable approaches led to much refinement, controversy and confusion, with the result that concerning this particular subject the jus civile was, and for several centuries remained, in a very unsatisfactory state.[105]

By contrast, the separate body of commercial law placed emphasis "on freedom of contract and on freedom of alienability of movable property, both tangible and intangible; abrogation of legal technicalities; and, most importantly, a tendency to decide cases *ex aequo et bono* [according to the equities of the case] rather than by abstract scholastic deductions from Roman texts."[106]

All three of these subtraditions — Roman law (as moderized), canon law, and commercial law — thus became subjects of intense study and rapid development in the 12th through 15th centuries. It is worth reflecting on how the view of law had changed from the period of the Dark Ages. As noted above in subsection IF of this chapter, the Dark Ages were a time in which law, particularly written law, was no longer regarded as a central feature of society. Put differently, "the reign of law had ceased."[107] By the 12th century, however, the tide had turned: there was a "return to the idea of law"[108] — that is, a revival of the view "that society must be ruled by law."[109] That view had been re-established by the 13th century,[110] as illustrated by a decision within the church in 1215 to prohibit clerics from participating in procedures involving "ordeals"[111] (that is, trials by such non-rational means as "judgment of the hot iron" and "test of the cold water", the character of

---

103. Schlesinger et al, *supra* note 44, at 302.
104. *Id.* at 302 n.26.
105. *Id.* at 272.
106. *Id.* at 303.
107. David and Brierly, *supra* note 36, at 38.
108. *Id.* at 49.
109. *Id.* at 39.
110. *Id.* at 49.
111. *Id.* (referring to the Fourth Lateran Council). "Civil society could not be ruled by law so long as trials were resolved by appeals to the supernatural.... The decision of the Lateran Council to reject this vestige of the past resulted in the adoption in continental Europe of a new, rational procedure for which the Canon law served as model; its decision thus paved the way for ushering in the reign of law." *Id.*

which is probably obvious enough from their labels). In this new climate, the study, development, and application of law could flourish.

6. The *Jus Commune*

The *jus commune* was applicable in much of continental Europe for about five hundred years — although at different times in different places, and to different degrees. Between about 1200 and 1700, a common law of Europe (*jus commune, droit commune, Gemeines recht*), based on the Roman law and canon law as developed in the universities, gradually overcame many elements and rules of local law and became binding or influential in courts. The following paragraphs summarize how that process occurred by focusing on three phenomena: (i) the spread of influence from the universities to the courts; (ii) the "reception" of the *jus commune* in local legal systems, and how that "reception" differed in terms of time, place, and extent, and (iii) the notion of pluralism that facilitated such a "reception" and that eventually died with the rise of the nation-state.

The scholars who had studied law in Bologna came from all over Europe. When they returned to their home countries, some of them "established universities where they also taught and studied the *Corpus Juris Civilis* according to the style of the Glossators and Commentators."[112] Others took positions in new judicial and administrative entities that were gradually replacing medieval feudal institutions.[113] Some of these the entities were in the Church, where the number of lawyers grew steadily in the 14th and 15th centuries, and others were in the states and cities. Indeed, by as early as 1180 "some Italian city-states had university-trained lawyers as judges in their courts."[114] The following account summarizes these developments:

> [T]he continental rulers had to turn to the law faculties to supply them with men trained to become judges, lawyers and administrators. The Universities, in exchange for generous charters and privileges, willingly complied, and turned out large numbers of *doctores* well versed in Latin and in Roman law. Thus it came about … that a Roman-influenced, university-taught and university-developed *jus commune* became dominant (although perhaps in varying degrees) in almost every part of the continent. This domination (the exact period of which, again, varies from country to country) lasted for several centuries, from the middle ages to the late 18th and early 19th century.[115]

One form that the *jus commune*'s domination of Europe took was that of "reception." Merryman defines "reception" as "the process by which the nation-states of the civil law world came to include the *jus commune* in their national legal systems."[116] Reception took place through a large part of Western Europe, but it took place differently in different places. In some parts of Europe, "the Roman civil law and the writings of the Bolognese scholars were formally 'received' as binding law."[117] In other places the reception was less formal — sometimes only taking the form of customary law.[118] Special circumstances ex-

---

112. Merryman, *supra* note 39, at 9–10.
113. Coing, *supra* note 43, at 510–512.
114. *Id.* at 512.
115. Schlesinger et al, *supra* note 44, at 297.
116. Merryman, *supra* note 39, at 10.
117. *Id.*
118. *Id.*

isted in some places. For example, in certain parts of Italy, Roman law (as modernized in the universities) had actually been made the enforceable law by 1200, "at least in the sense of residual law applicable when local custom or statute did not provide the contrary,"[119] and therefore "it is perhaps not quite accurate to speak of a 'reception' there."[120] For various reasons, reception was more extensive in southern France than in northern France. In Germany, Roman law was received in 1495 *in complexu* (in its totality)[121] in a form that gave it the rank of statutory law applicable in all courts, subject to certain exceptions.[122] In short, "[t]he formality and the extent of reception in a given country and the type of interaction that occurred between the *jus commune* and [the local laws] varied considerably."[123]

In nearly all parts of Europe, however, the *jus commune* was strongly influential because of another phenomenon that is now less familiar to us, in an age of nation-states. That phenomenon is pluralism. One authority has defined "pluralism" by contrasting it with the ideas of law usually referred to as positivism—especially as developed by John Austin, whose theories on the concept of law were summarized above in subsection IC2 of Chapter One—to reflect the fact that the laws binding within a nation-state are only those that are promulgated or specifically adopted by the holders of political power in the state:

> The theories developed by Austinians are of no assistance in understanding the attitude of the lawyer of the fourteenth or fifteenth century towards the sources of law. According to those [Austinian] theories[,] legal rules are norms laid down by the sovereign for the subjects, for the citizens of the state. There is according to this view no law except what is contained in the orders of the sovereign. Consequently, no judge and no administrator is entitled to apply a rule which is not recognised by the sovereign, and the legal system is strictly territorial, strictly tied to the boundaries of the individual state. Although Austin and his school have presented this theory as a general theory of law, the historian must admit that it expresses only the attitude lawyers adopted in the nineteenth century ... when the idea of national sovereignty began to gain strength. The ideas of the Middle Ages ... were quite different. Views prevailing then can be described by the term "Pluralism" as applied to legal sources. Pluralism means first that unity of law in the modern sense is absent. There are different rules for different cities and territories and different rules for the individual professional groups like merchants, nobility, peasants, etc. But Pluralism of legal sources also means that a judge who has to decide a specific case, has to look for rules not only in the orders of the sovereign, but can

---

119. von Mehren et al, *supra* note 31, at 10.

120. Nutshell-1999, *supra* note 45, at 28.

121. von Mehren et al, *supra* note 31, at 10. "The reasons for the German reception ... still remain a mystery." *Id.*

122. *Id.* at 11. However, the degree of reception varied in the several parts of Germany. *Id.* For other observations about reception in Germany, see David and Brierly, *supra* note 36, at 55 (concluding that "[i]n Germany, a deeply divided country, Roman law was applied in order to supply a common basis to judicial decisions").

123. Nutshell-1982, *supra* note 45 at 24. One factor bearing on the likelihood of reception was whether the local customary law had been reduced to writing. David and Brierly, *supra* note 36, at 53 (explaining that "[t]he progress of Roman law was ... only contained when confronted by major statements of customary law such as those which appeared in the thirteenth century, in France with the work of Beaumanoir (1250–1296), or in Germany with the *Mirror of Saxons (Sachsenspiegel)*"). Some of the statements of customary law from France are referred to below in subsection IIB2 of this chapter.

apply rules which he finds in any book of authority, whether this has been expressly recognised by the sovereign or not. It is more important for him to find an appropriate rule than to be sure to confine himself to following the orders the sovereign has given.

It was this basic attitude of the medieval period which made it possible for the *juristae* to apply the law they had learned at the university, the Roman Canon Law [that is, the Roman law as modernized plus canon law—in short, the *jus commune*], in daily practice. The Italian law professors elaborated a convenient theory of sources of law. Broadly speaking, this theory was that a judge must first apply local customs and statutes, but whenever he could not find an appropriate rule to decide the case before him in this legal material, he could turn to [the rules of the *jus commune*] and fill the gaps found in territorial or local law by [those] rules....[124]

This, then, was the legal landscape that existed in much of Europe before the rise of the nation-state: despite a wide range of local variations, the *jus commune*—a melding of (rediscovered) Roman civil law and (codified) canon law, with an incorporation also of commercial law—was the generally applicable law of Europe. Distributed throughout the continent by university-trained lawyers, the *jus commune* enjoyed "reception" in many countries and was strongly influential nearly everywhere because of a general acceptance of the notion of "pluralism" of legal sources. In the diagram appearing in Appendix 2.20, at the end of this chapter, the emergence of the *jus commune*—or what is also referred to there as a "pan-European law"—dominates the time line of developments from the 13th century to the 18th century.

B. Replacing the Jus Commune with National Legal Systems

1. The Rise of the Nation-State and the Intellectual "Revolution"

The following paragraphs tell how the legal landscape of Europe, imprinted with the *jus commune*, changed dramatically beginning in the 17th and 18th centuries, and how those changes set the stage for the appearance of modern national codifications. I begin with a sweeping account by Merryman of how the rise of the nation-state, and the consolidation of royal power, fractured the *jus commune*. Then I turn to some specific details.

The emergence of the modern nation-state destroyed the legal unity provided by common acceptance of the Roman-canonic *jus commune* in feudal and early modern Europe. The *jus commune*, associated in many minds with the concept of the Holy Roman Empire, was a law that transcended the diversities of local tribes, communities, and nations. With the decay of feudalism, the advent of the Reformation, and the consequent weakening of the authority of the Holy Roman Empire, the centralized monarchy began to emerge as the principal claimant to citizens' loyalty. The centralized state ... tended to become the unique source of law, claiming sovereignty for itself both internally and internationally. Thus national legal systems began

---

124. Coing, *supra* note 43, at 512–513.

to replace the *jus commune*.... The content of national law might continue to be drawn largely from the *jus commune*, but its authority came from the state.[125]

Expressed differently, the rise of the nation-state brought "pluralism", as described above, to an end. There is a curious irony in the story of how this happened. The story begins with the appearance of a new breed of legal scholars, following the Commentators. These were the Humanists.[126] Unlike their predecessors in Italy (the Glossators and the Commentators), the Humanists had their principal seat of learning at the French University of Bourges.[127] In the 16th and 17th centuries they "sought to cleanse the Roman texts of the glossators' and commentators' incrustations, and by going back to the sources of the classical period of Roman law ... even to uncover the interpolations of Tribonias"[128] (that is, Tribonian, the leading codifier engaged by Justinian). This Humanist emphasis on a detailed re-scrutinizing of Roman law gradually contributed to the rise of the Natural Law school,[129] whose members took a new step: they challenged the authority of the *Corpus Juris Civilis*.[130] Instead of seeing Roman law as governing because of its pedigree as the product of a superior culture of the past, the Natural Law scholars found Roman law persuasive if, and only to the extent that, it was rational and consistent with their view of a universal law of nature. The following account summarizes the contributions of both the Humanist and the Natural Law schools:

> In the 16th and 17th centuries, as the center of legal scholarship shifted to France and Holland, the methods of the Bolognese Commentators were replaced by those of the French Legal Humanists and the Dutch Natural Law School. The Humanists used the techniques of history and philology to study Roman law. Their view of Roman law as a historical phenomenon and of the Corpus Juris Civilis as merely an ancient text (rather than as "living law" or "written reason") marked a step toward eventual displacement of the *jus commune*. This indirect challenge to the authority of Roman law was continued by the 17th century Dutch Natural Law School, whose members developed a systematic theory of law grounded in what they conceived to be the universal law of nature. The comprehensive legal system-building of these Dutch jurists was the prelude to modern codification.[131]

It is here that the irony emerges. "[O]ne product of these natural law influences is at first sight startling: this universalizing tendency helped to divide the law into national systems."[132] The Natural Law scholars, traveling widely in Europe, had urged for a rationalization of law. By this time, however, in the 17th and 18th centuries, the political de-

---

125. Merryman, *supra* note 39, at 21.

126. According to the Compact Oxford English Dictionary, "humanism" refers to "(1) a rationalistic system of thought attaching prime importance to human rather than divine or supernatural matters and (2) a Renaissance cultural movement which turned away from medieval scholasticism and revived interest in ancient Greek and Roman thought."

127. Schlesinger et al, *supra* note 44, at 271.

128. *Id.*

129. *Id.* at 271–272.

130. *Id.* at 273.

131. Nutshell-1982, *supra* note 45, at 27. The "system-building" aspect of the work by Natural Law scholars is regarded by one authority as an especially important ingredient to the rise of national codification efforts in Europe. See Schlesinger et al, *supra* note 44, at 274 (stating that the deductive method of system-building used in the Natural Law period had a profound influence on the "structure and spirit of some of the modern codes").

132. Lawson, *supra* note 35, at 33.

velopments in Europe dictated that the rationalization would be conducted through national legislation.

Those political developments, gradually leading to the emergence of the modern nation-state, had origins in earlier centuries. At the risk of over-simplification, I offer the following (non-chronological) list of several events and trends in that respect—items that might be considered mileposts in the rise of the nation-state as the dominant political unit in Europe. (Several of them revolve around the publication of books that reflect the growing independence of each nation-state in pursuing its own interests and "following its own lights" more generally.)

- The publication of Dante's *Divine Comedy*, in Italian (not Latin) in the early 1300s. For a biographical sketch of Dante, see Appendix 2.12 at the end of this chapter.[133]

- A growing use more generally of vernacular languages in universities,[134] and the corresponding decline in Latin as a universal language of scholarship.[135]

- The publication of Machiavelli's *The Prince* (written in 1513 but not published until 1532, after his death), which was written to serve as a handbook for a political leader. For a biographical sketch of Machiavelli, see Appendix 2.13 at the end of this chapter.

- The publication of Jean Bodin's *Les Six Livres de la République* (1576), setting forth an early theory of sovereignty.

- The publication of Hobbes' *Leviathan* (published in 1651), applauding the emergence of strong nation-states as the most logical and effective repositories of sovereignty. A sketch of Hobbes (with a reference to his *Leviathan*) appears as Appendix 2.14 at the end of this chapter.

- The publication of Hugo Grotius' *Laws of War and Peace* (1625) acknowledging the primacy of the nation-state as the sources of rules (*jus gentium voluntarium*) but arguing that such rules are always subordinate to rules of natural law.

- The Peace of Westphalia (1648), ending the Thirty Years War—called a "Peace" rather than a "Treaty" because in fact two (main) treaties were signed, one at Osnabrück and the other at Münster (both in Westphalia, part of modern Germany). In general terms, the end of the Thirty Years War marked a victory for secular national authorities over the Church and is seen as a watershed event after which the nation-state was recognized as the fundamental political unit of Europe.

- The American Revolution in 1776 and the French Revolution in 1789, which "were themselves the products of a more fundamental intellectual revolution."[136] One of the driving forces of that intellectual revolution was a new belief in natural law and the rights of all men to property, liberty, and life.[137] These beliefs represented a

---

133. Another of Dante's works—*Monarchia*—urged a reunification of Europe. That is, the book "took its stand against the fragmentation and atomization of what was once a consistent and united whole." Ullman, *supra* note 51, at 278. Dante's efforts in this direction obviously were of little avail.

134. Nutshell-1999, *supra* note 45, at 31; Lawson, *supra* note 35, at 43 (noting that by about the end of the eighteenth century, the "new habit of writing in various vernaculars" had contributed greatly to the "breach in the unity of the civil law").

135. Lawson, *supra* note 35, at 43.

136. Merryman, *supra* note 39, at 15.

137. *Id.* at 16.

rejection of feudalism, "which conferred social status and public office on the basis of land ownership."[138] In addition, the intellectual (and political) revolution constituted "a great step along the path toward glorification of the secular state."[139]

As is probably true of all major, long-term political changes, the rise of the nation-state cannot be pinpointed to a particular year or even century; and it is impossible to identify any discrete event or set of events that caused it or that was caused by it. However, the accumulation of many events, including those highlighted above, serves as evidence of the radical change that, certainly by the 19th century, had occurred across the political and social face of Europe. The nation-state was by then generally regarded as the fundamental political unit in Europe, the proper and sole repository of sovereignty, and hence the single source of binding law.[140] It is this change—which we might regard as the "territorial compartmentalization" of law in Europe—that is reflected in Appendix 2.20, at the end of this chapter, at around the 1800s on the time line of developments shown there.

This political change, and the "territorial compartmentalization" of law that accompanied it, set the stage for the great legal codification process that occurred in Europe in the 18th and 19th centuries. That process started with some Scandinavian legal codes, accelerated with codes enacted in Prussia and Austria, and then reached its zenith in France and Germany. Let us glance at the Prussian and Austrian codification exercises and then give special attention, in subsection IIB2 below, to the French codification experience.

Preparation of the *General Land Law for the Prussian States* was undertaken beginning early in the 18th century, but work on the project was reinvigorated and then completed in 1794 under Frederick the Great. The Prussian Code is a reflection of the Age of Enlightenment; see Box #2.9 for a summary of what and when the Age of Enlightenment was. Merryman asserts that the Prussian Code, which was extremely long, reflects a "spirit of

---

138. *Id.* One authority summarizes feudalism, as practiced in Europe, as follows:
    Feudalism was the medieval model of government predating the birth of the modern nation-state. Feudal society is a military hierarchy in which a ruler or lord offers mounted fighters a fief (medieval *beneficium*), a unit of land to control in exchange for a military service. The individual who accepted this land became a vassal, and the man who granted the land become known as his liege or his lord.... In the late medieval period, the fiefdom often became hereditary, and the son of a knight or lesser nobleman would inherit the land and the military duties from his father upon the father's death. Feudalism had two enormous effects on medieval society. (1) First, feudalism discouraged unified government. Individual lords would divide their lands into smaller and smaller sections to give to lesser rulers and knights. These lesser noblemen in turn would subdivide their own lands into even smaller fiefs to give to even less important nobles and knights. Each knight would swear his oath of fealty (loyalty) to the one who have him the land, which was not necessarily the king or higher noblemen. Feudal government was always an arrangement between individuals, not between nation-states and citizens. There was no sense of loyalty to a geographic area or a particular race, only a loyalty to a person, which would terminate upon that person's death. (2) Second, feudalism discouraged trade and economic growth. The land was worked by peasant farmers called serfs, who were tied to individual plots of land and forbidden to move or change occupations without the permission of their lord....
    Kip Wheeler, *Feudalism*, appearing at http://web.cn.edu/kwheeler/feudalism.html.
    139. Merryman, *supra* note 39, at 18.
    140. *Id.* at 20. Merryman refers to the "two faces" of sovereignty: "an outer face that excluded any law of external origin" as having any binding force within the state, unless actually imported at the order of the sovereign, and "an inner face that excluded any law of local or customary origin" such as those created by guilds or otherwise arising without the action or approval of the sovereign. *Id.* at 21–22.

optimistic rationalism" under which it was thought possible to draft systematic legislation that would be complete, coherent, and clear, so that "the function of the judge would be limited to selecting the applicable provision of the code and giving it its obvious significance in the context of the case."[141]

Box #2.9 The Age of Enlightenment[142]

A decisive change occurred in the intellectual climate of Europe in the seventeenth century: That powerful march of mind called "*The Enlightenment*" sought to free the individual from his medieval shackles by subjecting the traditional authorities in religion, politics, law and culture to rational criticism, and to make it possible for him to create a new view of the world on the basis of reason. The effects of this intellectual movement on the law were immense. It gave the lawyer a standpoint from which he could see his way through the usus modernus pandectarum [referred to above] with its variety of historically conditioned detail, purge it of obsolete legal institutions and put it in a new systematic order. One particular product of the Enlightenment is the idea of *codification*, the idea that the diverse and unmanageable traditional law could be replaced by comprehensive legislation, consciously planned in a rational and transparent order. [Zweigert and Kötz, *infra* note 148, at 136]

The Age of Enlightenment is a term used to describe a phase in Western philosophy and cultural life centered upon the eighteenth century. The term came into use in English during the mid-nineteenth century, with particular reference to French philosophy, as the equivalent of a term then in use by German writers, *Zeitalter der Aufklärung*, signifying generally the philosophical outlook of the eighteenth century. It does not represent a single movement or school of thought, for these philosophies were often mutually contradictory or divergent.

"Age of Enlightenment" and "The Enlightenment" refer particularly to the intellectual and philosophical developments of that age (and their impact in moral and social reform), in which Reason was advocated as the primary source and basis of authority.... The signatories of the American Declaration of Independence ... and the French Declaration of the Rights of Man and of the Citizen were motivated by "Enlightenment" principles.... The era is marked by political aspiration towards governmental consolidation, nation-creation and greater rights for common people, attempting to supplant the arbitrary authority of aristocracy and established churches.... The Enlightenment was less a set of ideas than it was a set of attitudes.... There is no consensus on when to date the start of the age of Enlightenment, and some scholars simply use the beginning of the eighteenth century or the middle of the seventeenth century as a default date. Other scholars ... describe the Enlightenment beginning in Britain's Glorious Revolution of 1688 and ending in the French Revolution of 1789. However[,] others also claim the Enlightenment ended with the death of Voltaire in 1778. [Wikipedia]

The Austrian civil code, which is also "founded on the idea of codification characteristic of the Age of Enlightenment",[143] was begun in the middle of the 18th century under the direction of the Empress Maria Theresia, who was embarking on fundamental administrative reforms. After several drafts, part of the code was brought into force in 1787; this then was

---

141. *Id.* at 30. For a detailed account of the Prussian code, see Ullman, *supra* note 51, at 138–139. See also Nutshell-2008, *supra* note 45, at 33.

142. This synopsis is drawn largely from two sources, as cited in the box. The first paragraph explains the relevance of the Enlightenment for law; the second and third paragraphs offer a broader explanation.

143. Ullman, *supra* note 51, at 157.

superseded by further drafts, the last of which was finalized in 1808. The final legislation was adopted in 1811. One authority has observed that the provisions of the Austrian code seem to "strike[] a happy balance between the critical rationality demanded by the times and a sound sense of the value of tradition".[144] As a *practical* matter, however, those provisions made "no attempt to curtail the numerous rights and privileges of feudal classes", and in fact even though the code asserted that "every human being is entitled to be treated as a person by reason of his intrinsic rights, made manifest by reason", the peasantry in large parts of Austria was actually "in a state of feudal dependence barely distinguishable from serfdom".[145] In short, the Austrian code did little to bring effective immediate legal change.

The French codification exercise, however, did bring about such change. Let us turn our attention now to it.

2. The French *Code Civil*

The French Civil Code of 1804 has been referred to as a model of a "modern" code,[146] inspired by revolutionary passion for enlightened legal reform.[147] Even as a literary work it has drawn great praise,[148] and it is widely regarded as the premier example of legal codification — perhaps along with the German Civil Code issued in 1896 and effective in 1900.

What were the circumstances out of which the *Code Civil* emerged? Answering this question requires us to go back about three centuries before the French Revolution of 1789. Despite France's development as a singular state in those centuries, the law of France was remarkably fragmented. As one source has put it, although "[t]he consolidation of French royal power from the end of the 15th century to the Revolution of 1789 made France the first modern [continental] nation, a *politically* unified society under strong central rule,"[149] France was far from a *legally* unified society in the period before the Revolution — known as the period of the *ancien régime*.[150] Instead, it was "a kaleidoscope of various legal systems existing contemporaneously, yet independently, in the various

---

144. *Id.* at 159.

145. *Id.* Ullman goes on to explain that the code left the rights and obligations running between landowners and peasants to the rules found at the local level, which of course tended to perpetuate the pre-existing social and economic relationships.

146. George Lee Haskins, *Codification of Law in Colonial Massachusetts: A Study in Comparative Law*, 30 INDIANA LAW JOURNAL 1, 2 (1954).

147. Merryman, *supra* note 39, at 31 (referring to the *Code Civil* as having an "essentially revolutionary" character).

148. As one authority has observed, "the Code civil is a masterpiece from the point of view of style and language.... Stendhal is said to have read part of the Code every day in order to refine his feeling for the language, and Paul Valéry described the Code civil as 'the greatest book of French literature'". Konrad Zweigert and Hein Kötz, AN INTRODUCTION TO COMPARATIVE LAW — THE FRAMEWORK 83 (1977) (citing a 1947 book by Theime on natural law and European private law).

149. Nutshell-1982, *supra* note 45, at 29 (emphasis in original). See also Francis Deák and Max Rheinstein, *The Development of French and German Law*, 24 GEORGETOWN LAW JOURNAL 551, 553 (1936), as appearing in Schlesinger et al, *supra* note 44, at 278 et seq. (noting that "mediaeval France ... [was] a 'nation,' in the modern sense of the word, for several centuries before codification").

150. Nutshell-1982, *supra* note 45, at 29. See also Deák and Rheinstein, *supra* note 149, at 553 (noting that in France "uniformity of law was not accomplished until the beginning of the nineteenth century").

provinces and districts."[151] Voltaire is often quoted as having said that a traveler in France changed laws as often as he changed horses.[152]

Within this pre-Revolutionary "kaleidoscope of various legal systems", a general distinction can be made between the north of France and the south of France.

> In the south (the *Midi*), Roman law was paramount and that section is therefore designated by French legal historians as the country of written law (*pays de droit écrit*). In the various provinces of the north, local customs were in force and this area has been termed the country of customary law (*pays de coutume*).[153]

Although the customs in the north of France were numerous and varied, they may be classified into two categories. First, there were about sixty *coutumes générales*, each of which was in force for a whole province or large district. These included the *Coutume de Paris*, the *Coutume de Normandie*, and the *Coutume d'Orléans*.[154] Second, there were perhaps about 300 *coutumes locales*, in force only within a particular city or village.[155] The various *coutumes*, both the general ones and the local ones, differed largely in matters of detail, especially regarding matrimonial property.[156]

This patchwork of local customary laws might not have had much long-term influence on French law if they had remained uncodified, but in 1453 Charles VII directed, in his ordinance of Montils-les-Tours, that an official compilation be prepared of all customs.[157] It took more than a century to accomplish this task, but "by the end of the sixteenth century the bulk of French 'customary' law was, in fact, reduced to written law"[158] — albeit rather fragmentary in character.[159]

---

151. Deák and Rheinstein, *supra* note 149, at 553. The reason for the "kaleidoscop[ic]" nature of French law, according to one source, is "fundamentally institutional": France had no "centralized administration of justice" at the time, in part because of a history of struggles (i) between feudalism and centralized power and (ii) between the Church and the State. See von Mehren, *supra* note 31, at 13–14. See also Schlesinger, *supra* note 44, at 268–269 (asserting that, in contrast to England, the reasons why no court on the European continent was able to attain the stature necessary to create a nationally unified law "can be found in the divisive struggles between ecclesiastic and secular power, and between overlord sovereignty and local or regional independence which characterize the medieval period in continental history").

152. Nutshell-2008, *supra* note 45, at 34; von Mehren et al, *supra* note 31, at 48.

153. Deák and Rheinstein, *supra* note 149, at 553. *See also* von Mehren et al, *supra* note 31, at 10 (explaining that the receptiveness of southern France to the revived Roman law beginning in the thirteenth century stemmed from the fact that "the customary law [applicable in the south at that time] was itself a vulgarized Roman law"); David and Brierly, *supra* note 36, at 54 (also distinguishing between the *pays de droit écrit* and the *pays de coutumes*).

154. Deák and Rheinstein, *supra* note 149, at 554. The *coutume de Paris* had influence "beyond the geographical limits of its actual authority." *Id.*

155. *Id.*

156. Schlesinger et al, *supra* note 44, at 265–266 note b.

157. Deák and Rheinstein, *supra* note 149, at 554. *See also* David and Brierly, *supra* note 36, at 53, 56 (referring to the order as the *Ordonnance de Montil-lez-Tours* and giving the date as 1454).

158. Deák and Rheinstein, *supra* note 149, at 554. For an extensive study of this process, see generally John P. Dawson, *The Codification of the French Customs*, 38 MICHIGAN LAW REVIEW 765 (1940).

159. David and Brierly, *supra* note 36, at 53 (noting that these compilations of customs had a "fragmentary character" in that they dealt "only with those social relationships already in existence before the thirteenth century: family relations, land law and inheritance"), 56 (observing that these compilations merely set forth "the content of the custom," thus making "evident all its gaps, archaisms and insufficiencies" and that they therefore "had the appearance of a 'special law,' that of a corrective to a system whose main principles were to be found elsewhere"). See also Lawson, *supra* note 35, at 37 (noting that the customs, even after the compilations, "were often very fragmentary" and "often

The written compilation of customs in the 16th century naturally contributed to the "kaleidoscope" character of French law. This character was only partially eroded by the creation of uniform national laws on some topics by way of several royal *ordonnances* issued in the 16th, 17th, and 18th centuries. These included the *ordonnances* of Villers-Cotterets (1539) and Moulins (1566), dealing with procedure and evidence,[160] the *ordonnance* of 1667, "which gave France for the first time a truly uniform civil procedure,"[161] the *ordonnance* of 1673 on commerce,[162] and the *ordonnances* of Chancellor D'Aguesseau governing gifts (1731), wills (1735), and family settlements (1747).[163] While these developments illustrated the increasing domination of the royal, central power from the end of the 15th century onward,[164] they did not bring unification to French law,[165] in part because such centralized legislation was often resisted by the provincial judges and *parlements*[166] — that is, governmental bodies combining some aspects of both judicial and legislative functions.[167] According to Merryman, "efforts by the crown to unify the kingdom and to enforce relatively enlightened and progressive legislative reforms ... [were often] frustrated. The courts refused to apply the new laws, interpreted them contrary to their intent, or hindered the attempts of officials to administer them."[168]

The French Revolution "shattered the old institutional structures" and centralized the machinery of government "to a degree never before known in France."[169] It marked the end of the *ancien régime* and the beginning of a short transition period called the time of the *droit intermédiaire*.[170] Legislation enacted during this time — that is, just following the outbreak of the Revolution — aimed at reform in various areas of public and private law[171] but did not immediately provide a new national private law to replace the "kaleidoscope" the had lasted for several hundred years. That was the task of codification.

---

had to be supplemented in order to make them work"). Lawson does point out, however, that the customs in the north of France gradually converged in some respects and that by 1720 they were "taking the shape of a common customary law," albeit with regional and local variants. *Id.*

160. David and Brierly, *supra* note 36, at 62.

161. von Mehren et al, *supra* note 31, at 14.

162. *Id.* at 51–52. *See also* David and Brierly, *supra* note 36, at 62 (referring to the *ordonnance sur le commerce*). The civil procedure law and the commercial law were enacted by Louis XIV "under the impulse of his enlightened minister Colbert." Lawson-1953, *supra* note 35, at 36.

163. Lawson-1953, *supra* note 35, at 36; David and Brierly, *supra* note 36, at 62.

164. von Mehren et al, *supra* note 31, at 14.

165. *Id.* at 14 (noting that "[u]nification was ... not achieved during the *Ancien régime*"), 48 (observing that except for the three eighteenth-century ordinances referred to above, "the private law of France remained as essentially diverse at the end of the 18th century as it had been at the beginning of the 15th").

166. *Id.* at 48 (stating that "the tradition of local independence remained strong in the provinces and ... increasingly found expression ... through provincial institutions, especially the Parliaments"); Deák and Rheinstein, *supra* note 149, at 555 (noting that the unifying effect of the royal ordinances "was somewhat impaired by the occasional refusal of some of the provincial *Parlements* to execute them").

167. David and Brierly, *supra* note 36, at 57–58. For a description of *parlements*, see Deák and Rheinstein, *supra* note 149, at 554 n.5 (explaining that the *Parlement* of Paris and various provincial *parlements* created between 1443 and 1775 "were chiefly courts of justice" but also "exercised legislative as well as administrative powers".).

168. Merryman, *supra* note 39, at 17.

169. von Mehren et al, *supra* note 31, at 48.

170. Deák and Rheinstein, *supra* note 149, at 555.

171. *Id.* See also de Cruz, *supra* note 1, at 59 (pointing out that under the *droit intermédiaire* "old institutional structures were destroyed and political power and the machinery of government were now centralised as never before in France. Feudal laws were abolished, ... Frenchmen were declared to have equal rights under the law, 21 was made the age of majority, marriage was secularised, divorce

It was a huge task. The fragmentary character of law in France that had, for reasons described above, persisted for centuries prompted the famous French lawyer Portalis to give this description of the scene of French law that faced the codifiers:

> What a spectacle opened before our eyes! Facing us was only a confused and shapeless mass of foreign and French laws, of general and particular customs, of abrogated and nonabrogated ordinances, of contradictory regulations and conflicting decisions; one encountered nothing but a mysterious labyrinth, and, at every moment, the guiding thread escaped us. We were always on the point of getting lost in an immense chaos.[172]

The process by which the *Code Civil* was prepared seems just as chaotic as the legal landscape it was destined to replace—at least until Napoleon took charge. In July 1790, the Constituent Assembly voted "that the civil laws would be reviewed and reformed by the legislators and that there would be made a general code of laws simple, clear and appropriate".[173] By August 1793 Jean-Jacques Cambacérès presented an incomplete draft of 715 articles, which was rejected by legislative officials as being too complicated. He presented two more drafts in 1794 and 1796, but neither of these was successful. Likewise, a draft presented in December 1799 by Jacqueminot was also unsuccessful.

Things changed in 1800. Napoleon, having concentrated great power in his hands and "harbor[ing] the ambition to be known by history as a great lawgiver,"[174] appointed a commission of four men to prepare a draft. Within four months the commission prepared a draft code, but it met strong resistance in the Tribunate, a 100-member body that included many opponents of Napoleon and that was responsible for giving recommendations to the 300-member Legislative Body (responsible for actually enacting legislation). In December, the Tribunate gave negative recommendations on two portions of the draft code; consequently, the Legislative Body voted to reject one and the other "was in jeopardy" by late December.[175] In January 1802 Napoleon withdrew the draft code to avoid its full rejection and set about securing his power more completely. The Tribunate was reduced in size to fifty members and was divided into three sections, which restricted its capacity to frustrate the government's purpose.[176]

This worked. The draft code was voted on, approved, and promulgated in 36 separate laws between March 1803 and March 1804. Then a law enacted on 21 March 1804 consolidated those separate laws into a single *Code Civil*.[177] The enacting legislation stated that upon its effectiveness, "the Roman laws, the ordinances, the general and local cus-

---

introduced, individual liberty was guaranteed and the protection of private property was reinforced"). As another authority explains, "the hectic legislation of the early years of the Revolution was sometimes too radically individualistic in the area of private law, and many of the extreme positions it adopted had to be abandoned by the more composed draftsmen of the *Code civil*" as described below. Zweigert and Kötz, *supra* note 148, at 74.

172. von Mehren et al, *supra* note 31, at 14 (quoting Portalis as reported in 1 P. Fenet, *Recueil complet des travaux préperatoires du Code Civil* xciii (1836)).

173. *Id.* at 48 (quoting from materials in the same collection of preparatory works relating to the *Code Civil* as those referred to in note 172, *supra*).

174. *Id.* at 49. See also Nutshell-2008, *supra* note 45, at 37, and Merryman, *supra* note 39, at 59 (also noting that Napoleon wanted to be remembered as a great lawgiver whose code provided the basis for a completely new legal order).

175. von Mehren et al, *supra* note 31, at 50.

176. *Id.* at 51.

177. *Id.* at 51. The *Code Civil* is also known as the *Code Napoléon*. On its enactment, its name was the *Code civil des Français* (the civil code of the French people). "Its title changed to the *Code Napoléon* in 1807, back to the *Code Civil* in 1816 following an ordinance of Louis XVIII, reverted to

toms, the charters and the regulations all cease to have the force either of general or of special law concerning the subjects covered by the present code."[178]

Two aspects of the preparation of the *Code Civil* warrant special attention. Both involve the persons most responsible for its creation: (i) the four members of the drafting commission appointed by Napoleon, and (ii) Napoleon himself.

First, as for the members of the drafting commission, it appears that various authorities on the French *Code Civil* have viewed these men differently. The four members were: Jean-Etienne-Marie Portalis, an administrative official, writer, and public orator, who is said to have represented the interests of the *droit écrit*; Tronchet, president of the *Tribunal de cassation* and said to have represented the interests of the *droit coutumier*; Bigot de Préameneu, a *Commissaire du gouvernement* in a Prize Court and a member of the *Parlement de Paris*; and Malleville, a judge of the Tribunal de cassation who served as *secrétaire rédacteur*.[179] A biographical sketch of the first of these—Portalis—appears as Appendix 2.16 at the end of this chapter.

Some authorities emphasize the fact that these men were "practitioners" instead of professors,[180] that "academic lawyers were not even asked to participate in the drafting" process,[181] and that, as a consequence, the drafting of the *Code Civil* was mainly a practical undertaking and not a scholarly one.[182] As one source puts it, "there was nothing philosophical" in the approach of the French compilers, and they "were much more concerned to sum up the teaching of the past in compendious and accessible form" than to create a complete statement of the law based on intense juristic study.[183] In contrast, Merryman says that the drafting commission, though consisting of practicing lawyers and judges, was "dominated by the work of scholars (particularly that of Robert Pothier)," and that the commission members had a "grand scholarly design."[184] My own assessment is that Merryman exaggerates in referring to a "grand scholarly design" on the part of the commission members themselves in their preparation of the *Code Civil*, but that other scholars (and their ideas) did have an important underlying influence on the commission members, in two respects: (i) the commission members did refer to earlier works by scholars (especially Pothier);[185] and (ii) the commission members relied on the structure

---

the *Code Napoléon* in 1852 under Napoleon III, and then finally renamed the *Code Civil* in 1870". Christian Dadomo and Susan Farran, THE FRENCH LEGAL SYSTEM 9 n.31 (1993).

178. Law of March 21, 1804, quoted in Schlesinger et al, *supra* note 44, at 275–276.

179. See von Mehren et al, *supra* note 31, at 49; Dadomo, *supra* note 177, at 9 n.29; Schlesinger et al, *supra* note 44, at 277 n.1.

180. Lawson, *supra* note 35, at 53, 54 (contrasting the French *Code Civil* with the German civil code, which "was drafted mainly by professors after a century of the most intense juristic study of both Roman and native German law"). Lawson notes that where the draftsmen of the *Code Civil* did consult with the writings of scholars, "they went mainly to the eighteenth century jurist Pothier, an unoriginal compiler who tried from time to time to introduce the sort of order and principle into the law which is necessary for exposition to students"). See also Zweigert and Kötz, *supra* note 148, at 76 (observing that the four draftsmen "were no revolutionary hotspurs, but experienced practitioners").

181. Schlesinger, *supra* note 44, at 305 (contrasting the French experience with that in Germany and Switzerland, where "law professors did help to prepare the codes").

182. Lawson, *supra* note 35, at 54.

183. *Id.*

184. Merryman, *supra* note 39, at 58.

185. Lawson, *supra* note 35, at 35 (stating that Pothier, who lived from 1699 to 1772, "exerted an overwhelming influence on the compilers" of the *Code Civil*). Also influential, apparently, was Domat (1625–1695). *Id.* at 36. See also Stein, *supra* note 8, at 114–115 (noting that Pothier, a magistrate and later a professor law at the University of Orleans, had done much of the detailed preliminary work necessary for the preparation of a civil code" by "reducing both the Roman and the customary laws

of Justinian's *Institutes* in organizing the French code,[186] and of course the *Institutes* reflected the work of scholars, including not only the ones employed by Justinian but also Gaius, on whose *Institutes* those Byzantine scholars had relied.

More influential than the four members of the drafting commission, at least in terms of whether the *Code Civil* would in fact be enacted, was Napoleon himself. A biographical sketch of Napoleon appears as Appendix 2.15 at the end of this chapter. Napoleon had two important attributes that I consider essential to the establishment of a new code: political power and a desire for codification. These two attributes had converged by around 1800. Napoleon had by then gained appointment as First Consul and thereby had assumed broad control over the forces of radical change that were still in the air so soon after the Revolution. When the Tribunate blocked legislative approval of the draft code in 1801, Napoleon had sufficient power to slash the Tribunate's influence. Moreover, he had a strong desire to see the *Code Civil* put in place, as indicated in a comment he is said to have made afterwards: "One Waterloo wipes out their memory, but my civil code will live forever."[187]

The codification efforts in France did not end with the *Code Civil*. By 1811, four additional codes had come into force: the code of civil procedure (1807), the commercial code (1808), the criminal procedure code (1811), and the penal code (1811).[188] The following account traces their preparation:

> The Code of Civil Procedure drew heavily on the Ordonnance of April 1667 which had, for the first time, unified the procedure of the various Parlements and other courts of justice. The draft was prepared by a committee of five, ... all of whom were either judges or practicing lawyers. The procedures followed in drafting and enacting the Code of Civil Procedure, as well as the other three codes from this period, were generally similar to those ... for the Code Civil.
>
> The committee of seven members ... [appointed] to draft a commercial code drew heavily on the Ordonnance of 1673 on commerce....
>
> A decree of ... [March 1801] charged a committee of five with drafting a single code covering both substantive and procedural criminal law. Codes had already been enacted for both aspects during the Revolutionary period.... Accordingly, the task of the drafters was essentially to adapt these codes to "a new political and social state." ... Inability to reach agreement on ... [whether to merge criminal courts with civil courts and whether to continue the institution of the jury, adopted by the Revolution], and Napoleon's preoccupation with other matters, caused consideration of the draft to be suspended until January 1808. When discussion began again, the draft was split into two parts, one dealing with substance, the other with procedure. The Code d'Instruction Criminelle was enacted late in 1808; the Code Penal in early 1810. Both Codes went into effect on January 1, 1811.[189]

---

to a rational and usable order", and stating that "[t]he compilers of the Code civil relied heavily on Pothier ... and to a lesser extent on Domat"). See also Thomas Glyn Watkin, An Historical Introduction to Modern Civil Law 134–135 (1999).

186. Nutshell-2008, *supra* note 45, at 36–37 (noting that "the formal tripartite structure of [the *Code Civil*] ... (Persons, Property and the Different Modes of Acquiring Property) remained virtually identical to that of the first three books of Justinian's Institutes," and that in formulating substantive rules "the draftsmen drew primarily ... on both customary law and the jus commune").

187. Nutshell-2008, *supra* note 45, at 37.

188. von Mehren et al, *supra* note 31, at 51.

189. *Id.* at 51–52.

Having examined the circumstances of the *Code Civil*'s enactment, let us turn to its substantive aspects. To begin with, three aspects of the structure and style of the *Code Civil* are noteworthy: (i) its organizational similarity to the *Institutes* of Justinian, (ii) its intended audience, and (iii) the character of its rules. I shall discuss those points briefly in the following paragraphs and then offer some observations about the content of the *Code Civil*.

First, the tripartite structure of the *Code Civil*—focusing on persons, things, and different modes of acquiring property—is virtually identical to the first three books of the *Institutes*.[190] Moreover, like the *Institutes*, the *Code Civil* was not written for scholars. In the case of the *Institutes*, the intended audience, as we saw above, was law students. In the case of the *Code Civil*, the intended audience was citizens of the new France. It was "written in elegant and simple language, which was expected to be fully understood by the citizens,"[191] so that the law could be "simple, nontechnical, and straightforward."[192] Merryman describes the intent in this way:

> Thus the French Civil Code of 1804 was envisioned as a kind of popular book that could be put on the shelf next to the family Bible.... It would be a handbook for the citizen, clearly organized and stated in straightforward language that would allow citizens to determine their legal rights and obligations by themselves.[193]

Consistent with this aim, the draftsmen of the *Code Civil* opted for general rules and principles rather than focusing on details and exceptions. As one authority has put it, the rules and principles of the *Code Civil* "were to serve as signposts to be followed with discretion. They were enough to give a general direction to future development, but no more."[194] Because of this general character that many of the provisions of the *Code Civil* display, it has been likened to the United States Constitution,[195] which reflects a recognition that a legislator, in promulgating a rule or principle of law, cannot foresee all possible applications of the basic principles it sets forth. Indeed, the draftsmen of the *Code Civil* were quite clear on this point: they explained that to foresee everything "is a goal impossible of attainment" and that the function of the law "is to fix, in broad outline, the general maxims of justice (*droit*), to establish principles rich in suggestiveness (*conséquences*), and not to descend into the details of the questions that can arise in each subject."[196]

Turning from the structure and style of the *Code Civil* and looking to its content, we also can see a likeness between it and a constitution. The *Code Civil* performs a constitutional function by establishing three ideological pillars: private property, freedom of contract, and the patriarchal family.[197] In doing so, the *Code Civil* carried out some of

---

190. See Zweigert and Kötz, *supra* note 148, at 84 (explaining that the *Code Civil* has in its First Book, entitled "*Des personnes*", provisions on civil rights, nationality, domicile, marriage, divorce, legitimacy, adoption, paternal power, and guardianship; in its Second Book, entitled "*Des biens et des différentes modifications de la propriété*", provisions distinguishing movables and immovables, ownership, habitation, and servitudes; and in its Third Book, entitled "*Des différentes maniéres don on acquiert la propriété*", provisions on succession, contract, evidence, unjust enrichment, delict, matrimonial property, partnership, loan, agency, suretyship, and security rights).

191. Deák and Rheinstein, *supra* note 149, at 278 n.b.

192. Merryman, *supra* note 39, at 29.

193. *Id.*

194. Lawson, *supra* note 35, at 55.

195. Nutshell-2008, *supra* note 45, at 37; Lawson, *supra* note 35, at 55.

196. Portalis, Tronchet, Bigot-Préameneu, and Maleville, "*Discours préliminaire*", in 1 J. Locré, *La Législation Civile, Commerciale et Criminelle de la France* 251, at 255 (1827), as reprinted in von Mehren et al, *supra* note 31, at 54. The statement reprinted there was prepared by the drafters of the *Code Civil* to explain the manner in which they approached their task. *Id.* at 54 n.183.

197. Nutshell-2008, *supra* note 45, at 33.

the agenda of the Revolution. For example, by guaranteeing the first of these three pillars—private property—"the Code made an abrupt break with the feudal past" and revealed the intent of the draftsmen "to break up the estates of the powerful landed aristocracy."[198]

This is one respect, then, in which the *Code Civil* was intended to make a break with the past. A broader respect in which the past was rejected appears in the wording of the final act putting the *Code Civil* in place. As noted above, it said unequivocally that all Roman laws, *ordonnances*, customs, and so forth would "cease to have the force either of general or special law." As Merryman comments, "[a]ny principles of prior law that were incorporated in the codes received their validity not from their previous existence, but from their incorporation and reenactment in codified form."[199] Another authority makes the following observation about the break with the past that the *Code Civil* was supposed to represent:

> So strong was this feeling that the Code must be treated as *res nova* that one of the early commentators, Bugnet, said, "I know nothing of civil law; I only teach the Code Napoleon." This fear lest the past should slink back again by a side-door explains Napoleon's remark *mon code est perdu* (my code is lost) when he heard of the publication of the first commentary.[200]

The fact that Roman law, customary law, and the law put in place by the *ordonnances* no longer had any direct force or effect does not mean that they were totally rejected by the draftsmen of the *Code Civil*. Indeed, just the contrary is true. As the following paragraphs indicate, all of those three sources found their way into the *Code Civil*.

First, Roman law, as modified and taking the form of the *jus commune*, had provided some uniformity to the law in France, in part because it had been summed up by a few authors (including Pothier, whose writings influenced the drafters of the *Code Civil*), and in part because large portions of it—governing ownership and possession, the transfer of movables, and the law of obligations (contract, delict, and unjust enrichment)—had been received in the north of France, thus erasing any clear line of division between the *pays de droit coutumier* and the *pays de droit écrit*.[201] Second, the law set forth in the *ordonnances* of the 17th and 18th centuries—governing commercial law, civil procedure, gifts, wills, and family settlements—was also fairly uniform (although not completely so) for the whole of France.[202] Taken together, the *jus commune* and the *ordonnances* presented the draftsmen of the *Code Civil* with a rather broad array of laws that were already more or less uniform for France. The draftsmen could draw from these two sources fairly easily, choosing between conflicting interpretation on points of detail and of course rejecting that which was considered inconsistent with the new conditions brought on by the Revolution.[203]

The customary law, of course, was far from uniform, as explained above. However, because many of the customs, as compiled in the 16th and 17th centuries, "were often very fragmentary, they often had to be supplemented in order to make them work." Guidance

---

198. *Id.*

199. Merryman, *supra* note 39, at 27. Merryman says that "the French codifiers sought to destroy prior law ... to establish an entirely new legal order." *Id.*

200. Sir Maurice Amos, *The Code Napoleon and the Modern World*, 10 JOURNAL OF COMPARATIVE LEGISLATION AND INTERNATIONAL LAW (3rd ser.) 222, 224 (1928); also quoted in Schlesinger et al, *supra* note 44, at 276, and in Merryman, *supra* note 39, at 29, 59.

201. Lawson, *supra* note 35, at 35–36.

202. *Id.* at 36.

203. *Id.*

in this regard was drawn from the *Coutume de Paris*, which "held, on the whole, a middle position among the customs." This "exerted a powerful unifying influence," so that by the middle of the 18th century, the law of northern France (where the customs were more important) "was taking the shape of a common customary law, with regional and local variants."[204]

The draftsmen of the *Code Civil* drew from all these sources, as well as from certain legislation enacted during the period of the *droit intermediare*—that is, just following the outbreak of the Revolution. The *Code Civil* reflects the influence of all these sources, so that "Frenchmen do not consider themselves to live under Roman law, but under a mixed system in which the old customs still play a very large part, and in which the Roman law has been profoundly transformed by the French mind and spirit."[205]

Several authors have drawn attention to the multiplicity of sources drawn from by the draftsmen of the *Code Civil*, as well as by those responsible for drafting other 19th century national codes, to emphasize that these national codifications created a break with the past and put an end to the *jus commune*. Here are two accounts of this:

> On one point … there can be no reasonable difference of opinion: The old adage, all-too-frequently repeated, that the civilian codes presently in force are merely a modernized version of Roman law, is simply nonsense. In many respects, the solutions adopted by the codifiers were not traditional; and of the traditional ones, many were not Roman.[206]

> An inevitable consequence of the unification of national law in these early codes was that the *jus commune* was displaced as the basic source of law. To be sure, the draftsmen of the national codes drew heavily upon the *jus commune* as well as on national law, but the authority of the law from then on was derived from the state and not from any idea of the inherent reasonableness or suitability of the legal norms themselves.[207]

Before turning from the French codification experience to the German codification experience, it is useful to reflect on the durability of the French Civil Code as a central rampart of the French legal system. Merryman explains how its special character has tended to make the *Code Civil* immune to efforts at wholesale revision, at least as an explicit matter:

> [T]he French are proud of and sentimentally attached to the Code Napoléon. It is a cultural monument. There is bound to be some resistance to proposals to replace it. Even so, there were two attempts at wholesale revision in the twentieth century. The first almost literally came to nothing. The second began bravely, in 1945, with a distinguished commission headed by a respected scholar, and with lots of fanfare, confident speeches, periodic published reports, and partial drafts. Gradually, however, the commission subsided and dropped from public view. Eventually it stopped work entirely and was quietly abolished. Since then the effort has been to amend the code piecemeal, and by now more than a third of the original provisions have been revised, replaced, or simply repealed. The process is done in such a way as to preserve, rather than replace, the monument. The original numbering of articles in the code has been retained, so that the new matter follows the old organization.[208]

---

204. *Id.* at 37 (all three quoted passages in this paragraph).
205. *Id.* at 40.
206. Schlesinger et al, *supra* note 44, at 286.
207. Nutshell-1982, *supra* note 45, at 28.
208. Merryman, *supra* note 39, at 155.

Merryman's reference to the "Code Napoléon" reflects the curious back-and-forth designation that the *Code Civil* has been given, especially in the decades following its enactment. Through various laws and decrees, the French have changed the code's title from *Code Civil* to *Code Napoléon* (in 1807), back to *Code Civil* (in 1814, with the Bourbon restoration), again to *Code Napoléon* (in 1852), and back to *Code Civil* (around 1870).[209] Throughout that period, of course—and even until the present day, as Merryman's account reveals—the basic outlines of the *Code Civil*, and still a large number of its specific provisions, have remained unchanged. Moreover, as we shall see in subsection IIIA of Chapter Three, the *Code Civil* has had a deep and lasting influence all over the world, particularly (but not solely) the civil law world.

3. The German Civil Code

Having examined the great early-19th-century masterpiece of European codification, let us now turn briefly to its late-19th-century counterpart: the German Civil Code, or *Bürgerliches Gesetzbuch*—commonly abbreviated as the *BGB*. The *BGB* may be regarded as all of the following: as a legal counterpart to the political unification of Germany, as a monument to legal science, as the crowning achievement of the legal scholar Savigny, as a counterpart to the French Civil Code, and as a competing model for civil codes in several civil law countries outside Europe.

The first of these ways of looking at the *BGB*—that is, as a legal counterpart to the political unification of Germany, reflects a historical and political peculiarity of Germany. Unlike several other countries in continental Europe (particularly France), the territory of modern-day Germany coalesced into a single nation-state only very late in the centuries-long process by which the concept of the territorial nation-state displaced the concept of cross-cutting and conflicting loyalties and power that characterized Europe during the time of feudalism and control by the Church. Only in the late 1800s did that unification occur in Germany.

German unification resulted from a process led mainly by Otto von Bismarck. Bismarck, born in April 1815, won appointments to several political and diplomatic posts until 1862, when he was named Minister-President of Prussia. This position provided the leverage he needed to press for consolidation of Prussian power through a series of agreements and military confrontations. These concluded with the unification of several independent German states into one nation in 1871. Bismarck gained further political authority and became known in his time as the "Iron Chancellor". He has also been credited with the founding of "realpolitick", a political and diplomatic strategy based primarily on practical considerations rather than on ideological or moral notions. In short, Bismarck was successful in establishing Germany as one of the most powerful countries in Europe and in building a strong sense of nationalism in a country that previously had been a weak collection of principalities.

Shortly after that political unification, the long road toward codification of "German" law arrived at its destination in the form of the *BGB*. That is, whereas political unification came in 1871, the completion of the *BGB* occurred just a quarter-century later, in 1896. The foundations of the *BGB* date back, however, much earlier in two important respects: (1) the long and intense "reception" of Roman law in the German territories a full four hundred years before the *BGB* was completed; and (2) a famous intellectual de-

---

209. *See supra* note 177.

bate that raged throughout most of the 19th century among German legal academicians as to the proper character of German law and of its codification.

We have already touched briefly on the German "reception" of Roman law,[210] but it warrants some further attention. One authority offers this assessment:

> When Germany came in contact with Roman law it was relatively late — not before the middle of the fifteenth century to any great extent, but its effect, which we call the "reception of Roman law", were much greater in Germany than in France and enormously greater than in England. This contact meant not only a widespread acceptance of legal institutions and concepts of Roman law but also a much more extensive scientific systematisation of legal thought than occurred elsewhere.
>
> The reasons which gave the reception in Germany this particular character are to be found in the political situation in Germany [in the Middle Ages]. Central imperial power was [weak, and] the power of the territorial rulers [was strong, making the conditions] very conducive to the reception of Roman law, since because of it there was no common German private law, no common German courts system and no common German fraternity of lawyers which could, as the examples of France and England show, have opposed and delayed the introduction of Roman law.[211]

Another explanation for the early and strong "reception" of Roman law into German territories — beginning officially, as noted earlier, in 1495 — lies in the fact that the so-called Holy Roman Empire resonated much more in those territories than anywhere else in Europe (a matter explored in Box #2.6, above).[212] This combination of factors may be seen as creating a shared conception of law, and a highly developed scientific understanding of Roman law in particular, that Germans would draw from in the nineteenth century to produce what became the *BGB*.

This is not to say, however, that there was a consensus among German intellectuals over the creation of a codified German law. Instead, a debate raged between two camps, which we might for simplicity's sake regard as the proponents of the Enlightenment and the proponents of "legal science". The view that prevailed in that great debate was that of "legal science", a principal champion of which was Friedrich Carl von Savigny. (A biographical sketch of Savigny appears in Appendix 2.17.) And hence the *BGB* can be regarded as a monument to legal science. What this means is worth close examination, beginning with an assessment of how the *BGB* represents a different approach from the one taken by the French Civil Code.

Recall that although the French Civil Code was drafted by experienced men who were familiar with the futility of attempting to create a legal code that actually met the ideal of being complete, coherent, and clear, and who themselves rejected the emotional extremes of the French Revolution, those men found their own realism, as Merryman explains,

---

210. See *supra* notes 121–122 and accompanying text.

211. Zweigert and Kötz, *supra* note 148, at 134. Recall from the discussion in subsection IIB2, above, that political unification (though not legal unification) came very early to France. See *supra* note 149 and accompanying text. Political unification in England came even earlier, with the Norman invasion of 1066, as discussed below in Chapter Four.

212. See Zweigert and Kötz, *supra* note 148, at 135 (noting that "Roman law was not just another foreign law, but was the law of the imperium romanum, which could claim authority on the ground that the Holy Roman Empire of the Germans, as its name suggests, was the successor of the Roman Empire, and that the German Kaiser saw himself as the heir of the Roman Caesar").

overwhelmed by the rhetoric of the Revolution and by the excesses of the "rationalism" it encouraged:

> The [French civil code thus] became a victim of the revolutionary ideology and was treated uniformly treated as though it were a conscious expression of that ideology, both in France and in the many nations in other parts of the world that were heavily influenced by the French Revolution.... In contrast to the essentially revolutionary, rationalistic, and non-technical character of the Code Napoléon, the German Civil Code of 1896 ... was historically oriented, scientific, and professional.[213]

Merryman goes on to explain that much of the credit (or blame) for the differences between the German and the French civil codes rests with Savigny, who led a group of scholars known as the Historical School. Arguing that it would be inappropriate to create a civil code along French lines—that is, by reasoning from principles of secular natural law—these scholars regarded the law of a people as being a historically determined product of that people's development, an expression of the Volksgeist or "spirit of the people". Consequently, as Merryman explains, "a thorough study of the existing German law and of its historical development was a necessary prelude to proper codification";[214] and this in turn required a thorough study of the *Roman* law (since Roman civil law as interpreted by the medieval Italian scholars had been formally received in Germany some centuries before), as well as both old and newer Germanic and German laws. Under the influence of Savigny, then, many German scholars undertook an intensive study of legal history—and they did it with a scientific mindset:

> Savigny's idea was that by thoroughly studying the German legal system in its historical context legal scholars would be able to draw from it a set of historically verified and essential principles. [Indeed, for some of his followers, the] ... components of the German legal system, in their historical context, [constituted] something like natural data. Just as natural data in biology, chemistry, or physics could be studied in order to determine the more general principles of which they were specific manifestations, so the data of German law could be studied in order to identify and extract from them those inherent principles of the German legal order of which they were specific expressions. Hence the proposed reconstruction of the German legal system was to be a *scientific* reconstruction.[215]

Another element also distinguished the German codification project from the French one: the intended "audience" of the code itself. Instead of trying to draft the law to be understood and used by the common person, as the French codifiers had done, the German codifiers wrote for the lawyers.

> [T]he Germans were convinced that it was neither desirable nor possible to rid the world of lawyers. The German view was that lawyers would be needed, that they would engage in interpreting and applying the law, and that the code they prepared should be responsive to the needs of those trained in the law.[216]

In sum, the *BGB* that emerged in 1896 was not revolutionary in the French sense. Instead of purporting to abolish the old laws and legal structures, the *BGB* was intent on codifying German law as it had matured over several centuries, in a form that the legal professionals of the new unified nation-state could understand and apply.

---

213. Merryman, *supra* note 39, at 30.
214. *Id.* at 31.
215. *Id.* at 32.
216. *Id.*

It is because of these remarkable differences between the French and the German codification experiences that we can view the German *BGB* as both (i) a counterpart to the French Civil Code and (ii) as a competing model for civil codes in several civil law countries outside Europe. These two great codes—the *Code Civil* and the *BGB*—are not entirely different, of course; for example, they both place prevailing law-making authority with legislators, not judges; they both occupy a place in the legal system that resembles the role of a constitution in some common law countries; they both share fundamental substantive rules and principles drawn from Roman law. In sum, the two codes do have both historical and operational similarities. We shall explore some of the operational aspects that show up in both of them when we turn in Chapter Three to the civil law tradition from an operational perspective. Still, the differences between the two codes are significant enough that when a country finds itself in a position to adopt a legal system, it typically will view the German and French models as competing alternatives—a matter we shall also touch on at the end of Chapter Three in surveying the distribution of the civil law tradition around the world.[217]

C. Modern Civil Law in Mass Society

Today's societies—especially in Europe but elsewhere as well—are radically different in many ways from those out of which the civil law grew over the centuries of developments surveyed earlier in this chapter. The title of this subsection—modern law in mass society—suggests two specific aspects of these differences. First, the political circumstances and the ideology in which law operates today is (or pretends to be) "modern" in certain ways that distinguish it from earlier eras. Second, as a demographic matter, societies today are "mass societies", with heretofore unimaginable populations and with unprecedented interactions—both physical and virtual—among people (including especially "ordinary" people) of all nationalities and beliefs.

Because of these two related factors, the civil law tradition finds itself today in an environment of fluidity at various levels. I wish to highlight some aspects of that "environment of fluidity" in these closing pages of this chapter. It can be an abbreviated discussion for several reasons. First, if one concludes (as I do) that the historical foundations of the civil law tradition still have a deep influence over the operation of many of the world's legal systems, then the recent changes, even dramatic changes, seen in modern society do not undercut the

---

217. As a preview of that discussion, note this observation made by one authority:
   [Although the *BGB*,] when [it] came into force in 1900 ... was much admired on all sides, more perhaps abroad than in Germany at the time, ... it really only influenced legal *theory* and legal *doctrine*; there was very little *practical* reception of the BGB, at any rate very much less than the [French] Code civil [of] a century earlier. One reason for this was that its sophisticated structure and abstract conceptualist language was seen abroad as a typical product of German scholarship which, despite its technical merits, was not likely to take root very easily in alien legal soil, but the critical fact was that the more developed states of the world outside the Common Law family had already equipped themselves with civil codes during the nineteenth century and there was therefore no widespread need to import [new] foreign models.

Zweigert and Kötz, *supra* note 148, at 153. As for the impression the *BGB* made abroad on its enactment, the same authority quotes the English jurist Maitland as declaring that it was "the best code that the world has yet seen"; "never, I should think, has so much first-rate brain power been put into an act of legislation". *Id.* at 148.

significance of those historical foundations, and therefore the usefulness of studying them. Second, we shall turn to the actual *manifestation* of this "environment of fluidity" in Chapter Three, where the civil law tradition will be examined from an operational perspective, as it appears today in civil law countries all around the world. Third, and perhaps most important as a practical matter, it is extremely difficult to gain a clear view of the present age. We can look back in time with some clarity, and that is what we have done up to now in this chapter. The process of looking backward carries the inevitable risk of bias or misperception, of course, but at least it is possible to construct a retrospective view that classifies trends and attributes causation. This is almost never possible when looking at the present; it is too close.

Therefore, in the following paragraphs I shall offer short observations, largely in a bullet-point form, about modern civil law in mass society—examining in particular the notion of modernity, the novelties that a mass society presents to the civil law today, and particularly the implications that these novelties have for the emergence of a new *jus commune*.

1. "Modern" in What Sense?

There is a new fluidity in the political and social circumstances in which the civil law operates. Consider the following points:

- In the world generally, the nation-state—that unit of political organization and legal sovereignty that has prevailed since the mid-17th century—now faces many challenges and seems to be fading in importance in the face of other forms of international organization.[218]

- This is especially true in Europe, the birthplace of the civil law tradition, as the great experiment in economic unification gradually leads toward political and legal harmonization and perhaps unification under the auspices of the EU. To a lesser extent, however, the challenges to the nation-state as the predominant unit of political organization exist also outside Europe.

- There are two main *directions* from which these challenges to the nation-state are coming—from above in the form of supranational organizations, and from below in the form of sub-national groups—tribes, sects, ethnicities, minorities, regional units, etc. As a consequence, we are witnessing a reemergence of the sorts of pluralist loyalties and ideologies that characterized society in Europe before the 17th century. That pluralism, discussed above,[219] featured an absence of a single source of law-making authority, so that rules applicable to a person could come from many sources.

- The *content and diversity* of these competing sources and rules is much greater today, however, than was true in pre-17th-century Europe. That is, the scale and variety of the differences and contradictions among the interests of different groups

---

218. For a discussion of this point, see generally John W. Head, *Supranational Law: How the Move Toward Multilateral Solutions Is Changing the Character of "International" Law*, 42 University of Kansas Law Review 605 (1994). The literature is replete with other books and articles also discussing the role of, and alleged eclipsing of, the nation-state, especially in view of the rise of so-called "non-state actors" such as public international organizations (such as the UN, the World Bank, the IMF, and the WTO), private non-governmental organizations ("NGOs"), and sub-national groups of various types.

219. See the discussion of pluralism near the end of subsection IIA6 of this chapter.

vying for person's ears and loyalties are much greater than before, because the whole world—not just Europe—contributes to the tapestry of diversity. It is, for instance, almost surely more difficult to find common ground among today's Brazilian street-cleaner, Chinese factory-worker, Indian farm peasant, Canadian government official, French banker, Nigerian oil executive, Yemeni imam, indigenous Peruvian shepherd, and Turkish lawyer than it was to find common ground among a German merchant, an Italian scientist, a Portuguese sailor, and a member of the Spanish court in 1600.

- The nation-state is a product of Europe, not naturally replicated elsewhere. That is, the world as a whole, as distinct from Europe as a tiny region of the world, has never experienced a home-grown political unification of the sort that the nation-state brought to Europe. True, the nation-state as a form of political organization was forced upon the rest of the world through colonization and conquest (followed by decolonization), but the nation-state was, and remains in some parts of the world, a foreign concept only tentatively and grudgingly accepted. In particular, those aspects of the nation-state that reflected ideas of the Enlightenment—aimed at creating a new world based on reason[220]—have grown only shallow roots in much of the rest of the world.

- Hence the ideological foundations of the civil law—born out of European experience, Christian dogma, a focus on individualism, an embrace of capitalism, and a conceptualization of law as a rational force serving the members of society in their efforts toward fulfilment—are increasingly brought under scrutiny and into question. To express this point differently: one key sense in which the social and political environment of today is "modern" is that it is increasingly non-European, non-Christian, non-individualistic, non-capitalistic, non-rational, and indeed non-legal—by which term I mean regarding law not as a manifestation of shared experience and prospects but rather as an instrument of external control and arbitrary repression.

2. The Novelties of "Mass Society"

In addition to the points made above about today's "modern" political and ideological circumstances, consider also the following points. They aim to highlight the significance of the enormous increase in sheer numbers of people, and diversities among them, to which any legal system (including those of the civil law family, of interest to us in this chapter) must accommodate itself.

- The population of the world has increased at a dizzying pace just in the last one hundred years—that is, just in the past four percent of the total time since the birth of the civil law tradition.[221] By some accounts, the world's population rose from about 1.75 billion in 1910, when my father was born, to roughly 6.90 billion today. More than four-fifths of that increase came within the last half-century, and over half of it came within the last thirty years alone. See Box #2.10 for an overview of increases in world population.

---

220. See *supra* Box #2.9.

221. If we consider the civil law tradition to be roughly 2,500 years old (beginning with the issuance of the Twelve Tables in 450 BCE), then one hundred years would be 100 ÷ 2,500 = 0.04.

Box #2.10 Increases in World Population[222]

The following figures for the historical growth in world population are excerpted from several sources. Although sources differ in some details (especially for years before about 1800), the overall trend is unmistakable: recent population increases are dramatic.

Year (CE/AD)	Population	Year (CE/AD)	Population
1	200 million	1940	2,300 million
1000	250 million	1950	2,550 million
1100	300 million	1955	2,800 million
1200	360 million	1960	3,000 million
1250	400 million	1965	3,300 million
1300	360 million	1970	3,700 million
1350	440 million	1975	4,000 million
1400	350 million	1980	4,000 million
1500	430 million	1985	4,850 million
1600	550 million	1990	5,300 million
1650	470 million	1995	5,700 million
1700	600 million	2000	6,100 million
1750	630 million	2005	6,450 million
1800	820 million	2010 (est.)	6,908 million
1850	1,130 million	2020 (proj.)	7,600 million
1900	1,550 million	2030 (proj.)	8,200 million
1910	1,750 million	2040 (proj.)	8,800 million
1920	1,860 million	2050 (proj.)	9,200 million
1930	2,070 million		

Another way of looking at these figures is by "billion-person milestones":

Year	Population
1802	1 billion
1928	2 billion
1961	3 billion
1974	4 billion
1987	5 billion
1999	6 billion

- Virtually none of the world's population growth in recent years has occurred in the areas of Europe where the civil law tradition was born. One authority, writing from an economic development perspective, made these observations in 2006:

> Today, 95 percent of population growth occurs in developing countries. The populations of the world's 50 least developed countries are expected to more than double by the middle of this century, with several poor countries tripling their populations over the period. By contrast, the population of the developed world is expected to remain steady at about 1.2 billion, with declines in some wealthy countries.[223]

222. These figures are drawn from a variety of sources. See, for example, data appearing in a US Census Bureau table at http://www.census.gov/ipc/www/worldhis.html. For a "slide show" detailing the geographical distribution of the world's population at each of the "billion-person milestones", see http://www.globalchange.umich.edu/globalchange2/index.html (follow "Lectures" hyperlink; then follow "Population Growth over Human History" hyperlink). For an overview of world and regional population figures for 2010 and for 2050 (projected), see the excerpt from *Scientific American* "*Pathways*", appearing in THE ECONOMIST, Oct. 9, 2010 (following p. 16) [hereinafter *Pathways*].

223. David E. Bloom and David Canning, *Booms, Busts, and Echoes*, 43 FINANCE & DEVELOPMENT, Sep. 2006, at 8, 9.

More recent figures show the same trend, with these details regarding percentage increases in population for various regions and countries:[224]

Region or Country	Projected % Increase from 2010 to 2050
USA	+ 27.2
Central America	+ 28.6
South America	+ 22.8
Russian Federation	− 17.3
Eastern Eruope	− 17.7
Northern Europe	+ 13.8
Southern Europe	− 0.1
Western Europe	− 2.0
Eastern Africa	+ 117.4
Middle Africa	+ 111.8
Northern Africa	+ 50.8
Southern Africa	+ 16.3
Western Africa	+ 104.4
Eastern Asia (excluding China)	+ 2.3
South-central Asia	+ 40.1
South-eastern Asia	+ 29.9
Western Asia	+ 59.8
China	+ 4.6
Japan	− 20.0

• Consider these data about the breathtaking growth in world population from another perspective: How much different is the social reality today from that in which the civil law tradition slowly developed for century upon century? The answer would be "dramatically different": today's society is a mass society in a way that simply was not true when the civil law's foundations were laid. Even the great European cities of earlier centuries were modest in size—some even quaint—compared to today's huge metropolises. For instance,

  – The largest city in all of Europe in 1500 was Constantinople, with a population of around 200,000, less than the current population of Durham, North Carolina.

  – In the 17th century, when the French Humanists and the Dutch Natural Lawyers were taking a lead in legal learning,[225] some estimates put the population of Paris at under half a million and the population of Amsterdam at about 620,000. And roughly a century later, at the time of the French Revolution (1789), the population of Paris is thought to have been about 630,000. All these populations roughly match today's population of Memphis, Tennessee—just the city alone, that is; the larger Memphis metropolitan area has a population of twice that amount, 1.2 million. Paris did not achieve population of 1.2 million until about the 1850s.

  – Even Rome, which became the world's largest city around the time of Julius Caesar and Jesus of Nazareth, had a population of only about half a million (some estimates say as much as two-thirds of a million) in the year 100 CE,

---

224. See *Pathways*, *supra* note 222.
225. See *supra* note 131 and accompanying text.

and it peaked around 800,000 in the following century before dropping in population—indeed, plummeting to well under 100,000 after the fall of Rome in the 5th century.

In short, the European urban populations during the entire formative stages of the civil law tradition were simply tiny—almost trivial—compared to today's reality. In today's Europe, the population of the metropolitan area of Amsterdam is around 2.2 million, of Berlin about 4.2 million, of Istanbul about 12.5 million, of Madrid about 6.1 million, of Milan about 3.1 million, of Paris about 10 million, and of Rome about 3.5 million.[226]

- Ours is an age that gives great weight to the values of "self-determination", both in the formal legal sense applicable in international relations,[227] and (in some regions of the world) also in the general sense of individual autonomy. Given this fact, the massive population increases of recent years tend to create a cacophony of legal views and claims—producing a sort of "leveraging" effect, so that not only does the world now hold more people, but it also purports to give a higher proportion of them a voice in how they are to be governed in their behavior.

- The ability of such voices to be heard has been increased enormously by the electronic-telecommunications revolution of the last decade or two. Take, for instance, the surge in use of Facebook and Twitter. Emerging in only the last seven years, both of these social networking services have staggering numbers of users today.[228]

3. Prospects for a New *Jus Commune*

Against the backdrop of developments described above—amounting to a dramatic transformation into a modern age of mass society—what evidence can we see of the presence, or the absence, of a new *jus commune*? Recall that we gave some initial attention to this issue earlier, in subsection IB3 of Chapter One, in considering the question of whether it makes much sense to embark on a comparative study of law if the world's legal traditions are all converging. (My own view, expressed there, is that it does make sense because they are not all converging, by the very definition of "legal tradition".) We shall also examine some related issues at the end of Chapter Three, in considering whether

---

226. The foregoing population figures appear in a variety of sources (reliable enough for illustrative purposes), including http://geography.about.com/library/weekly/aa011201a.htm. http://en.wikipedia.org/wiki/Demographics_of_Paris, http://en.wikipedia.org/wiki/List_of_largest_cities_throughout_history, and http://en.wikipedia.org/wiki/Rome#Demographics.

227. For a summary of the doctrine of self-determination in international law, see generally John W. Head, *Selling Hong Kong to China: What Happened to the Right of Self-Determination?*, 46 UNIVERSITY OF KANSAS LAW REVIEW 283 (1998).

228. Reports of the origin and expanding use of Twitter and Facebook abound on the internet. See, for example, http://www.theoriginof.com/twitter.html (noting that Twitter, "a free social networking and micro blogging service which enables its users to share and read other user's updates known as tweets, was founded in March 2006 by Obvious Group, with its [head office] in California"), http://mashable.com/2009/03/16/twitter-growth-rate-versus-facebook/ (Twitter's growth); http://thenextweb.com/socialmedia/2010/02/22/twitter-statistics-full-picture/ (asserting that as of January 2010 Twitter had 75 million users); http://www.businessinsider.com/twitter-stats-2010-4 (reporting over 100 million users as of April 2010); http://www.facebook.com/press/info.php?statistics (asserting that Facebook now has 500 million users); http://www.digitalbuzzblog.com/facebook-statistics-facts-figures-for-2010/ (noting that average users spend 55 minutes each day on Facebook, posting about 60 billion status updates every day).

from an *operational* perspective we should expect the distribution and influence of the civil law tradition around the world to diminish. There, our attention will focus on "mixed legal systems", the relationship between law and religion, and some specific operational deficiencies perceived in the civil law tradition.

For our current purposes, however, let us take a more straightforward *historical* perspective, as we have throughout this chatper. Recall that the *jus commune* of Europe drew from shared experience with Roman-canon law and from the absence of effective centralized political power to create a many-centuries-long episode of general legal harmonization. Is such a harmonization trend occurring again, either on a world-wide basis or in the European context? Can we expect to see a new *jus commune*? Consider the following points:

- In some areas of law, an impressive amount of global codification and harmonization has already occurred, especially in the past fifty years. International commercial law, for example, has matured in the form of the United Nations Convention on Contracts for the International Sale of Goods ("CISG", or "Vienna Sales Convention"), which was completed in 1980 and entered into force in 1988. The GATT/WTO system of treaties, assuming its current form at the conclusion of the Uruguay Round of trade negotiations in December 1993, stands as a monument to international rules governing international trade relations.[229] Some harmonization has also occurred in other areas beyond economic law. For instance, numerous human rights treaties, including the International Covenant on Civil and Political Rights, have been endorsed by nearly all countries of the world, thereby creating a network of mutual pledges regarding how governments will treat persons within their own borders. A casual observer might assume from this evidence that some form of a global *jus commune* is under construction.

- Despite such signs as these of harmonization of views and values, some commentators assert that modern society in the world at large is increasingly less amenable to regulation through law, or at least the kind of law that emerged in the *jus commune* of Europe several hundred years ago. There is, in the eyes of some observers, an "evolution from a monocentric to a polycentric legal system ... [which results from] the movement toward a more complex, pluralistic, and polycentric society"—indeed, a "consumer-oriented, 'disposable' society, [in which] individual laws ... also become disposable".[230] In such a setting, perhaps no global *jus commune* could possibly emerge.

- This view (discounting the possibility of any global *jus commune* developing) would seem to find support in the fact that many of the norms set forth in the treaties mentioned above date from a time in which the world's economic affairs, and even approaches toward human rights and the role of governments, reflected predominantly the views of a small cluster of countries—nearly all of them Western powers—that were then still exercising influence in a colonial or neo-colonial fashion. With the erosion of such influence, the norms themselves, as well as the institutions responsible for putting them in operation, have lost widespread support. As evidence of this erosion, witness the critical attacks of

---

229. Some of these developments in international economic law were noted also in Chapter One, near the end of subsection IB3, in examining the possible "convergence" of legal traditions.

230. Merryman, *supra* note 39, at 156–157.

231. See, e.g., John W. Head, LOSING THE GLOBAL DEVELOPMENT WAR: A CONTEMPORARY CRITIQUE OF THE IMF, THE WORLD BANK, AND THE WTO (2008).

recent years on international organizations, particularly those dealing with global economic matters.[231]

- Perhaps curiously, a perceived *decline* in the likelihood of a *jus commune* at the *global* level might be contributing to an *increase* in the likelihood of a new *jus commune* at the *European* level. That is, in reaction to developments of the sort noted above, some persons who trace their ancestry and heritage primarily to Europe (the birthplace of the civil law tradition) increasingly see themselves as more homogenous in their interests and aspirations and world-view than they ever have before. Their "intramural" differences now seem relatively slight compared to the interests, aspirations, and world-views of others in the world—the new "them". Given that fact, perhaps a new *jus commune* is in store for Europe. For some views on that subject, see Appendix #2.19, which examines the contemporary importance of the European *jus commune*.

Many of the observations made in the preceding bullet points are conditional and speculative. They must remain that way, until the passage of time allows the proper "distance" to assess more objectively what is happening in the current age. I hope these observations will, however, provide some rounding-out to this chapter's discussion of the civil law tradition in historical perspective. The long trajectory of the civil law's growth—from the Twelve Tables of Rome, through the Justinian compilation, to the rediscovery and "second life" of Roman law with the Glossators and the *jus commune* they helped create, through the territorial compartmentalization of law with the rise of the nation-state, and with the crowning achievement of legal codification in France and Germany—surely cannot be regarded as having ended with the dawn of the modern age of mass society. Evidence that it has not ended, and that in fact the historical foundations of the civil law tradition manifest themselves in the operation today of legal systems in contemporary civil law countries, will be a focus of our attention in Chapter Three.

Appendix 2.1
Biographical Sketch of the Roman *Jurisconsult* Gaius*

Gaius was a Roman jurist who lived from approximately 110 to 179 CE. Little is known of Gaius and his life. It is believed that Gaius was a foreigner (non-Roman) by birth — possibly a Greek or a Hellenized Asiatic. However, it is thought he was a citizen of Rome and may have even taught in Rome, although some historians believe part of the reason so little is known of his life (including his surname) is that he lived most of his life in a provincial town. Regardless of the reason, Gaius was not a famous jurist during his lifetime. Nevertheless, he had a lasting impact on the development of law as his writings gained wide appreciation and because he "produced a system that has come to dominate modern codified law".

That system is most evident in Gaius' most influential work, the *Institutes*. Purporting to offer a full description of the elements of Roman law, the *Institutes* is divided into four separate books, which describe the law of: (i) persons, (ii) things, (iii) obligations, and (iv) actions. A similar structure has been repeated in several codes issued later in the civil law world, most notably in Justinian's great 6th-century compilation of law and in the French Civil Code of 1804. Gaius had a very strong scholarly interest in the history and tradition of Roman law, evidence of which appears in his *Commentaries on the Twelve Tables*.

With the passage of time Gaius became a significant figure in the development of Roman law. In A.D. 426, in the *Law of Citations*, the Roman Emperor Theodosius II named Gaius as one of the five jurists (the other four were Ulpian, Papinian, Paulus, and Modestinus) whose opinions were to be followed by judicial officers when deciding cases. Consequently, the writings of Gaius became a key source of Roman law. Moreover, many quotations from Gaius' work are included in Justinian's *Corpus Juris Civilis*.

Indeed, it was only through secondary sources — for example, Justinian's compilation — that information about Gaius' *Institutes* was available for many hundreds of years. The work was lost to modern scholars until 1816, when a manuscript was discovered by B.G. Niebuhr in the chapter library of Verona, in which some of the works of St. Jerome were written over some earlier writings that then proved to be the lost work of Gaius. (Even more recently, two sets of papyrus fragments of Gaius' work have been found.) The discovery of Gaius' writings has illuminated portions of the history of Roman law which had previously been most obscure.

---

* This synopsis, prepared largely by Justin Waggoner, is drawn from several print and online sources, including especially (1) Alan Watson & Khaled Abou El Fadl, *Fox Hunting, Pheasant Shooting, and Comparative Law*, 48 AMERICAN JOURNAL OF COMPARATIVE LAW 1 (2000); W.M. Gordon and O.F. Robinson, THE INSTITUTES OF GAIUS (1988); and http://oll.libertyfund.org/?option=com_staticxt &staticfile=show.php%3Ftitle=1154&chapter=88526&layout=html&Itemid=27 (Section 21). The quoted passage in the first paragraph is drawn from the first of these sources, at page 18. The image comes from a marble bas-relief sculpted by Brenda Putnam in 1950 — one of 23 reliefs of great historical lawgivers found in the chamber of the US House of Representatives in the US Capitol building in Washington, DC.

Appendix 2.2
Biographical Sketch of the Roman *Jurisconsult* Ulpian*

Ulpian was a Roman jurist most active between 211 and 222 CE. It is thought that Ulpian was born sometime before 172 CE into a family of scholars from Tyre, in present-day Lebanon. About two-fifths of Justinian's *Digest* is attributed to Ulpian's writings.

Ulpian had a distinguished public career that spanned the reigns of five emperors. Ulpian's first known position was as an assessor in the auditorium of Papinian, another celebrated Roman jurist. Ulpian then served as a member of the council of Emperor Septimius Severus from 202 to 211. He also served as the master of the requests under the Emperor Caracalla from 211 to 217. During Egalabalus' reign, which began in 218, Ulpian was banished from Rome. However, with the accession of Alexander in 222, Ulpian was reinstated and rapidly rose to become the emperor's chief adviser and praetorian prefect. Ulpian was ultimately murdered inside the palace during an uprising. Some doubt remains as to whether his death was in 223 or 228.

Ulpian authored an impressive collection of literature, including *Ad Sabinium*, a commentary on the *jus civile*, and the *De oficio proconsulis libri*, a comprehensive exposition of the criminal law. These works and several others were drawn on extensively in Justinian's *Digest*. Even before that, Ulpian's writings had been included in the *Law of Citations* by Emperor Theodosius II in 426. The *Law of Citations* referenced the works of five Roman jurists that were to be followed by judicial officers in the decision of cases. Papinian, one of Ulpian's early mentors, also had his writings included in the *Law of Citations*, as did Gaius (as noted above in Appendix 2.1).

---

* This synopsis, prepared largely by Justin Waggoner, is drawn from several sources, including especially Bruce W. Frier, *Legal History: Law on the Installment Plan*, 82 MICHIGAN LAW REVIEW 856 (1984), along with some other online sources. For an image of a bust of Ulpian, see http://users.ox.ac.uk/~alls0079/ulpian.htm, or http://www.personenencyclopedie.info/U/ul/ulpianus-domitius/view.

Appendix 2.3
Biographical Sketch of the Roman Emperor Constantine*

Constantine, one of the most famous Roman emperors, ruled between 306 and 337 CE and was chiefly responsible for making Rome Christian. Constantine was born in 272 CE in modern-day Serbia. At his birth, Constantine's father, Constantius, was an officer in the Roman army with strong political skills. Constantine's mother was a Christian who came from a humble background and may not have been married to his father (who later married another woman). Constantius was later promoted to the position of Caesar (a junior emperor to an Augustus, under the Tetrarchy—a "rule of four" in which there were two co-junior emperors called Caesars and two co-senior emperors called Augusti on each side of the empire). Constantine, as the heir presumptive of his father's position, left the Balkans for the court of Diocletian, an Augustus who was located in Nicomedia, or modern-day Izmit, Turkey.

While in Nicomedia, Constantine received an excellent education and mingled with a diverse mixture of individuals. During his twenties, Constantine served in a variety of campaigns for Diocletian's army. In 303, Constantine was in Nicomedia for Diocletian's "Great Persecution", the most severe persecution of Christians in Roman history. Two years later Diocletian resigned due to failing health. It is believed that he intended to name Constantine as one of his successors, but was pressured into naming other individuals to these positions. Constantine, realizing his dangerous position of being a perceived threat to the current leaders in Nicomedia, sought to leave. Constantius acted promptly by requesting that Constantine join him in his campaign in Britain, which was granted. Constantine fought alongside his father for about one year, prior to his father's death in 306. Constantine was later recognized as emperor and took over his father's territory of Gaul, Iberia, and Britain.

---

* This synopsis, prepared largely by Justin Waggoner, is drawn from online sources, especially entries in Wikipedia and http://www.roman-emperors.org/conniei.htm. I took the photo of the massive bust of Constantine at the Capitoline Museum in Rome.

Although not yet a Christian, Constantine (like his father) followed a tolerant policy toward Christians. Constantine declared a formal end to the persecution of Christians and returned to Christians what they had lost during the persecutions. He was also able to increase his popularity and the prosperity of his region by refusing to participate in a civil war in Italy. Instead, he fought the Germanic tribes and Franks. In 308, a general council was called to resolve the instability in the western part of the Empire. The result was that Constantine was demoted to Caesar, which he refused to accept. This dispute was resolved in 312 when Constantine defeated Maxentius' opposing forces and entered the city of Rome. Constantine was now the leader of the western region of the Roman Empire.

In 313, Constantine met with Licinius, the emperor of the eastern region of Rome, and agreed to the Edict of Milan, which granted full tolerance to all religions in the Empire and had provisions especially beneficial to Christians. In 320, Licinius ceased to abide by the Edict of Milan and began persecuting Christians. This ultimately led to a war which Constantine won; Licinius was executed. Constantine became the sole emperor of the Roman Empire. Just before his death in 337, Constantine was baptized as a Christian.

In addition to being the first Christian emperor of Rome, Constantine is also known largely for establishing the Eastern Roman Empire as a center of learning and prosperity. Instrumental in this was Constantine's decision to rebuild the city of Byzantium, which was then named *Nova Roma* ("New Rome") and placed on equal footing with the city of Rome. While the western part of the empire would crumble in 476, the Eastern Roman Empire would thrive until the fall of Constantinople to the Ottoman Turks in 1453. *Nova Roma* was renamed Constantinople in his honor after Constantine's death in 337 and is the modern-day city of Istanbul.

Appendix 2.4
Biographical Sketch of the Roman Emperor Justinian*

Justinian, who served as emperor of the Eastern Roman Empire from 527 until his death in 565, was born a peasant in a small village in present-day Central Serbia. His uncle, Justin, who at the time was in the imperial guard, adopted Justinian, and made certain that he obtained an excellent education in Constantinople. In 518, Justin became the emperor. During Justin's five-year reign, Justinian excelled as his uncle's close confidant. He was named associate emperor shortly before Justin's death and would serve as the next emperor.

Justinian was a diligent ruler but by many accounts a most unpleasant person. Fortunately for himself and his court, he surrounded himself with individuals of extraordinary talent who were selected not on the basis of aristocratic origin, but on the basis of their skills. Like Justinian, his wife Theodora also did not come from the aristocratic class. Her father was a bear trainer for the circus and, prior to her marriage to Justinian, she was a dancer —a word that at the time was often synonymous with prostitute. Theodora was a strong and intelligent woman. Five years into Justinian's reign, a revolt formed against Justinian known as the Nika riots. While the crowd was rioting in the streets, Justinian considered fleeing the capital, but (at least according to legend) the stirring words of Theodora convinced him to order what turned out to be a brutal and successful suppression of the riot.

During his reign, Justinian sought to restore the glory of Rome. He manifested this intention in two key ways: (1) venturing west to reclaim the Roman Empire's former lands; and (2) reinstituting the law from Rome's golden age. Early on, Justinian was able to regain large stretches of land along the western Mediterranean basin, including the Italian Peninsula. However, he then found progress slow and his reclamation project would prove to be short-lived, as the Empire would eventually lose control of these lands.

---

* This synopsis, prepared largely by Justin Waggoner, is drawn from Stephanie Lysyk, *Purple Prose: Writing, Rhetoric and Property in the Justinian Corpus*, 10 CARDOZO STUDIES IN LAW & LITERATURE 33 (1998), and from online sources. The photograph of Justinian's image in mosaic, drawn from online sources, is found in the Hagia Sophia (Aya Sofia) in Istanbul. I took the photograph of the Aya Sofia.

Justinian's attempt to reestablish Roman law would prove to have more staying power. Tribonian, a member of Justinian's court, was placed in charge of an effort to codify the best of the legal works of classical Rome. (See Appendix 2.5.) This effort resulted in what is now known as the *Corpus Juris Civilis*, intended to bring order out of the chaos into which Roman law had fallen by Justinian's time.

Justinian's reign was also characterized by the construction of several great buildings, including the Hagia Sophia (Aya Sofia) pictured above. However, the Byzantine Empire also suffered from being spread too thin during Justinian's various campaigns. Moreover, the Byzantine Empire endured the bubonic plague (known as the Plague of Justinian), which greatly weakened the Empire and would had a lasting devastating effect.

Appendix 2.5
Biographical Sketch of Tribonian, Jurist for Justinian*

Tribonian was a jurist during the reign of Justinian in the Eastern Roman Empire. He is known primarily for preparing the *Corpus Juris Civilis*, which drew heavily upon the writings of classical period Roman jurists and would later serve as the principal teaching tool during the rebirth of Roman civil law after the *Digest* was discovered in the late 11th century. (Further details on the *Corpus Juris Civilis* may be found in the biographical sketch of Justinian, in Appendix 2.4.)

Tribonian was born in approximately A.D. 500 in present-day Turkey. He rapidly became a successful lawyer in Constantinople. Justinian appointed him in 528 to serve on the commission preparing the new imperial legal code. Tribonian was later appointed to head this commission and was responsible for assembling a variety of lawyers and scholars to assist in his efforts.

In addition to his role in preparing the *Corpus Juris Civilis*, Tribonian began serving as Justinian's chief legal adviser in 528; and in 529 he was appointed as quaestor, a key government official having legal and fiscal responsibilities. (The quaestor position could also be described as the chief law master, responsible for drafting legislation.) During the Nika riots in 532, Justinian was pressured into removing Tribonian from his position as quaestor due to allegations of corruption (Tribonian had earned a reputation as a briber). However, after the riots were suppressed, Tribonian was restored to his quaestor position in Justinian's administration and would complete his work on the *Corpus Juris Civilis*. Tribonian would serve under Justinian as quaestor and legal adviser until his death in 542.

---

* This synopsis, prepared largely by Justin Waggoner, is drawn mainly from David Pugsley, *On Compiling Justinian's Digest*, 20 Syracuse J. Int'l L. & Com. 161, 169 (1994), from A.M. Honore, *The Background of Justinian's Codification*, 48 Tulane Law Review 859 (1974), and from online sources. The image comes from a marble bas-relief sculpted by Brenda Putnam in 1950—one of 23 reliefs of great historical lawgivers found in the chamber of the US House of Representatives in the US Capitol building in Washington, DC.

Appendix 2.6

Opening Page of the *Institutes* (Justinian, 6th century CE) (in English translation)*

In the Name of Our Lord Jesus Christ.

THE EMPEROR CAESAR FLAVIUS JUSTINIANUS, VANQUISHER OF THE ALAMANI, GOTHS, FRANKS, GERMANS, ANTES, ALANI, VANDALS, AFRICANS, PIOUS, HAPPY, GLORIOUS, TRIUMPHANT CONQUEROR, EVER AUGUST, TO THE YOUTH DESIROUS OF STUDYING THE LAW, GREETINGS.

The imperial majesty should be not only made glorious by arms, but also strengthened by laws, that, alike in time of peace and in time of war, the state may be well governed, and that the emperor may not only be victorious in the field of battle, but also may be every legal means repel the iniquities of men who abuse the laws, and may at once religiously uphold justice and triumph over his conquered enemies.

1.   By our incessant labours and great care, with the blessing of God, we have attained this double end. The barbarian nations reduced under our yoke know our efforts in war; to which also Africa and very many other provinces bear witness, which, after so long an interval, have been restored to the dominion of Rome and our empire, by our victories gained through the favour of heaven. All nations moreover are governed by laws which we have already either promulgated or compiled.

2.   When we had arranged and brought into perfect harmony the hitherto confused mass of imperial constitutions, we then extended our care to the vast volumes of ancient law; and, sailing as it were across the mid ocean, have now completed, through the favour of heaven, a work that once seemed beyond hope.

3.   When by the blessing of God this task was accomplished, we summoned the most eminent Tribonian, master and ex-quaestor of our palace, together with the illustrious Theophilus and Dorotheus, professors of law, all of whom have on many occasions proved to us their ability, legal knowledge, and obedience to our orders; and we have specially charged them to compose, under our authority and advice, Institutes, so that you may no more learn the first elements of law from old and erroneous sources, but apprehend them by the clear light of imperial wisdom; and that your minds and ears may receive nothing that is useless or misplaced, but only what obtains in actual practice. So that, whereas, formerly, the junior students could scarcely, after three years' study, read the imperial constitutions, you may now commence your studies by reading them, you who have been thought worthy of an honour and a happiness so great as that the first and last lessons in the knowledge of the law should issue for you from the mouth of the emperor.

4.   When therefore, by the assistance of the same eminent person Tribonian and that of other illustrious and learned men, we had compiled the fifty books, called Digests or Pandects, in which is collected the whole ancient law, we directed that these Institutes should be divided into four books, which might serve as the first elements of the whole science of law.

5.   In these books a brief exposition is given of the ancient laws, and of those also, which, overshadowed by disuse, have been again brought to light by our imperial authority.

---

* This English translation is drawn from Thomas Collett Sandars, THE INSTITUTES OF JUSTINIAN (1878).

6.   These four books of Institutes thus compiled, from all the Institutes left us by the ancients, and chiefly from the commentaries of our Gaius, both in his Institutes, and in his work on daily affairs, and also from many other commentaries, were presented to us by the three learned men we have above named. We have read and examined them and have accorded to them all the force of our constitutions.

7.   Receive, therefore, with eagerness, and study with cheerful diligence, these our laws, and show yourselves persons of such learning that you may conceive the flattering hope of yourselves being able, when your course of legal study is completed, to govern our empire in the different portions that may be entrusted to your care.

Given at Constantinople on the eleventh day of the calends of December, in the third consulate of the Emperor Justinian, ever August.

Appendix 2.7
Biographical Sketch of Charlemagne*

Charlemagne, born in modern day Belgium in 747, was a King of the Franks who would ultimately conquer a large portion of western and central Europe on his way to building a Frankish Empire. Not much is known of Charlemagne's early life, aside from the fact that his father became King of the Franks in 751. Following his father's death, the Frankish kingdom was divided between Charlemagne and his younger brother Carloman, who died just three years later, leaving Charlemagne with the full kingdom.

Charlemagne's reign was characterized by almost constant battling with many foes. Early in his reign, Charlemagne captured most of Italy and also ventured into present-day Germany and defeated the Saxon forces. After winning, he was successful in converting the longstanding Germanic polytheists to Christianity—his success turned, it seems, on his issuance of rules requiring strict compliance with Christianity and the threat of beheadings for those who failed to abide. Charlemagne also succeeded in capturing a small portion of Spain from the Moors, including the city of Barcelona.

In 800, Pope Leo III crowned Charlemagne as Emperor of the Romans. Charlemagne reportedly was not completely comfortable with being proclaimed Roman Emperor, as the Byzantine Emperor in Constantinople still held a claim to that title. The Pope was willing to crown Charlemagne because the Byzantine authorities had fallen out of favor with the Pope due to religious differences. Consequently, Charlemagne would cautiously refer to himself not as "Emperor of the Romans", but as "Emperor ruling the Roman Empire."

Given the degree of division and regionalization that had characterized western Europe following the fall of Rome in 476, Charlemagne's achievements were quite significant.

---

* This synopsis, prepared largely by Justin Waggoner, is drawn from Genc Trnavci, *The Meaning and Scope of the Law of Nations in the Context of the Alien Tort Claims Act and International Law*, 26 UNIVERSITY OF PENNSYLVANIA JOURNAL OF INTERNATIONAL ECONOMIC LAW 193, 203 (2005) (especially for information about the use of the *jus gentium*), from Charles J. Reid, Jr., *Review Essay: A Brief Account of Western Constitutional History: Raoul Van Caenegem's An Historical Introduction to Western Constitutional Law* 46 EMORY LAW JOURNAL 791, 795 (1997), and from various online sources, including http://www.chronique.com/Library/MedHistory/charlemagne.htm. The image—an equestrian statue of Charlemagne by Agostino Cornacchini (1725) appearing in St. Peter's Basilica, Vatican—is attributed to Myrabella/Wikimedia Commons (CC-BY-SA-3.0 & GFDL) and is used here under a "share alike" license, the terms of which appear at http://creativecommons.org/licenses/by-sa/3.0/deed.en.

Moreover, they accorded well with the romantic views held by many Franks at the time regarding the restoration of the Roman Empire headed by their king.

A key legal feature of Charlemagne's reign was the reintroduction of the *jus gentium* as a tool for international law. The *jus gentium* was the set of legal rules the Roman Empire used for adjudicating disputes arising between Roman citizens and non-citizens. Since Charlemagne's empire comprised several tribes with varying laws, the *jus gentium* proved especially useful for handling disputes involving parties from different tribes. To this end, and in the absence of Roman law texts, Charlemagne issued a disorganized body of legislation based largely upon previous barbarian codes and also influenced by canon law.

Charlemagne's rule brought about a brief resurgence of culture and education known as the Carolingian Renaissance. He insisted on bringing knowledge into his empire, largely through travel and conquests under his leadership, in an effort to overcome the acknowledged intellectual inferiority of his empire to several of its neighbors. Although Charlemagne himself was not proficient in writing and was likely a poor reader (maybe even illiterate), he remained actively involved in learning pursuits up until his death.

Charlemagne died in 814. His empire would not last very long after his death, in part because in the pre-nation-state thinking of the time, monarchies were viewed largely as personal possessions. Charlemagne's son Louis would inherit the empire and in turn split it into what are roughly modern day France and Germany for his sons. Thus, the foundation for the modern nation-state and also the royal lines of both France and Germany trace back to Charlemagne.

Appendix 2.8
Biographical Sketch of Irnerius*

Irnerius, born in Bologna in approximately 1050, was one of the first and most celebrated professors to teach Justinian's *Corpus Juris Civilis*, after its rediscovery. After a short stint of teaching jurisprudence in Rome, he returned to Bologna, where he founded a school of jurisprudence revolving around a mastery of the *Corpus Juris Civilis*. Irnerius was reportedly a very popular teacher and, in time, students from all over Europe would come to Bologna to learn Roman civil law.

What most set Irnerius apart from his contemporaries was his teaching of Roman law through the utilization of glosses. Glosses were originally brief clarifying statements — at first between the lines of text and later in the margins of the pages — explaining the law. The use of glosses proved to be especially helpful in the challenging process of understanding Roman law, as it needed significant elucidation.

Irnerius' chief literary work was the *Summa Codicis*, which was the first systematic publication on Roman law completed in the medieval period. In the *Summa Codicis*, Irnerius sought to update Roman law by making it applicable to Europe in the 11th and 12th centuries.

Irnerius, who was also an effective litigator, would eventually cease teaching and work for the Emperor of the Holy Roman Empire. It is estimated that Irnerius died sometime between 1125 and 1140. Interestingly, he was largely forgotten by history until German legal scholars in the latter 19th century unearthed details on his importance to the development of modern civil law.

---

* This synopsis, prepared largely by Justin Waggoner, is drawn from several print and online sources, including Henry Mather, *The Medieval Revival of Roman Law: Implications for Contemporary Legal Education*, 41 CATHOLIC LAWYER 323, 330 (2002), and Duhaime's Legal Dictionary at http://www.duhaime.org/LawMuseum/LawArticle-302/Irnerius-1050-1128.aspx.

Appendix 2.9
Biographical Sketch of Gratian (author of *Decretum*)*

Gratian was a 12th century canon lawyer based in Bologna. He is best known as the author of the *Decretum*, an important textbook on, and codification of, canon law. For his work in that area, Gratian has been called the "father of the science of canon law".

Very little is known of Gratian's personal life and most of what is assumed is to at least a degree unsubstantiated. It is thought that Gratian was born in a Tuscan village near the end of the 11th century and that after reaching adulthood he became a monk and taught at a monastery in Bologna, where he devoted his life to studying canon law. In the 12th century, Bologna was not only the preeminent place in Europe to learn Roman civil law; it was also the center for canon law scholarship.

Gratian completed his *Decretum* in approximately 1140. Its official and lengthier title, "A Concord of Discordant Canons," is an apt name since it is an attempt to solve the many seemingly contradictory canons from the previous centuries of the Church. In preparing the *Decretum*, Gratian quoted a vast range of authorities, including the Bible, papal letters, church-affiliated authors, and secular law. The materials he relied on spanned an impressive breadth of more than 1,000 years. The *Decretum* would ultimately become the leading textbook for students of canon law throughout Europe. Although the *Decretum* never received any formal recognition by the papacy, it would remain the cornerstone of canon law until it was replaced by another codification published in 1917.

---

* This synopsis, prepared largely by Justin Waggoner, is drawn mainly from Charles J. Reid, Jr., *The Augustinian Goods of Marriage: The Disappearing Cornerstone of the American Law of Marriage*, 18 Brigham Young University Journal of Public Law 449, 454 (2004), from Charles Donahue, Jr., *Book Review: The Making of Gratian's Decretum*, 25 Law & History Review 401 (2007), and from various online sources. The image is of a page in what is thought to be a 13th-century version of the *Decretum* and is drawn from http://en.wikipedia.org/wiki/File:Treegratian.jpg.

Appendix 2.10
Biographical Sketch of Accursius (Glossator)*

MAGNVS ACCVRSIVS FLORENTINVS·
Ann M · CC · XXXVI ·

Born near Florence in 1182, Accursius was an Italian jurist. He was regarded by his peers as the greatest of the many acclaimed glossators. Accursius initially worked as a lawyer in his home town of Impruneta, and then he became a successful professor in Bologna, where he died in 1263.

Accursius is known largely for his authorship of the *Glossa Ordinaria* or the "Great Gloss", which was published in approximately 1235 or 1240. The *Glossa Ordinaria* was a compilation of nearly 100,000 comments and remarks upon the *Corpus Juris Civilis*. It was unparalleled in terms of its broad, thorough, and coherent discussion of the Roman civil law as it had been rediscovered in the late 11th century. While Accursius was working on the *Glossa Ordinaria*, a rival scholar had begun composing a similar book. Legend has it that, upon hearing of his rival's work, Accursius feigned sickness, ceased his lectures, and kept to himself while he fervently completed his famous work.

The *Glossa Ordinaria* was actually given the force of law in some places. As one legal historian noted, "[f]or centuries, the Accursian Gloss was the basis of any doctrine which claimed to be derived from Roman law. The maxim came to be accepted that 'What the Gloss does not recognise, the Court does not recognise.'" Unlike his predecessors and contemporaries, Accursius not only pointed out problems with the civil law, he also provided solutions. Thus did Accursius' work accelerate the development of Roman civil law in Europe.

---

* This synopsis, prepared largely by Justin Waggoner, is drawn from several print and online sources, including especially Peter Stein, ROMAN LAW IN EUROPEAN HISTORY 43 (1999) and Andrea B. Carroll, *Examining a Comparative Law Myth: Two Hundred Years of Riparian Misconception*, 80 TULANE LAW REVIEW 901, 914 (2006). The quoted passage in the last paragraph is drawn from Stein, *supra*, at 49. The first image—a statue located in the Uffizi Gallery in Florence—is drawn from http://commons.wikimedia.org/wiki/File:Accorso.jpg and attributed to Riccardo Speziari. It is used here under a GNU Free Documentation license, the terms of which appear at http://commons.wikimedia.org/wiki/Commons:GNU_Free_Documentation_License. The second image—a drawing—is attributed to the Yale Law Library, New Haven, Connecticut and is used here under a "Creative Commons Attribute 2.0 General license", the terms of which appear at http://commons.wiki media.org/wiki/ File:Flickr_-_Yale_Law_Library_-_Accursius,_glossator_(ca._1182-ca._1260).jpg and at http://creative commons.org/licenses/by/2.0/deed.en and http://creativecommons.org/licenses/by-sa/3.0/.

Appendix 2.11
Biographical Sketch of Bartolus (Post-Glossator)*

Bartolus de Sassoferrato was an Italian law professor considered to be the greatest of the "Commentators" or "Postglossators" of the civil law tradition. Born in 1313 in a central Italian village, Bartolus studied law at Perugia and Bologna, graduating as a doctor of law in 1334.

Bartolus began teaching in Pisa in 1339. After a few years there, he accepted a position at Perugia. In addition, beginning in 1355 he held an appointment from the Holy Roman Emperor Charles IV as *consiliarius* (legal accessor).

Although Bartolus died at the relatively young age of 44, he achieved extraordinary success as a jurist. The so-called "Commentators" proceeded beyond the work of their predecessors, the "Glossators", by focusing on the potential for the practical application of the law to contemporary circumstances. Bartolus' reputation as a great Commentator, and the fervor with which his views were followed, are reflected in the saying that "no one is a good jurist unless he is a Bartolist". Indeed, Bartolus was so influential that more than 80 years after his death, the civil law codes in Spain and Portugal provided that his opinions should be followed where the Roman texts and Accursius' *Glossa Ordinaria* (described above in Appendix 2.10) were silent.

One substantive area in which Bartolus' contributions were especially important involved conflicts of law issues. This work was particularly pertinent in 14th century Italy, where each city-state had its own statutes and customs. The Glossators had stated that when local customs and Roman law clashed, the Roman law would prevail. Bartolus approached this issue in a manner that was more sophisticated and also more acceptable to the city-states. First, he would extract the general principles from Roman law's very specific rules on a particular topic, as found in Justinian's *Corpus Juris Civilis*. Next, Bartolus asserted that a local custom was not automatically void if it contradicted those specific rules of Roman law; instead, it would be void only if it contradicted the underlying principles. If it did not, the local custom would be valid and operative. Under this approach, the Roman law acted as an umbrella under which the local legal systems would operate; but since the local and modern city-states best understood the appropriate specific measures for their people, local custom could produce a result dif-

---

* This synopsis, prepared largely by Justin Waggoner, is drawn from Peter G. Stein, *Judge and Jurist in the Civil Law: A Historical Interpretation*, 46 LOUISIANA LAW REVIEW 241, 246 (1985) and from various online sources. The image of Bartolus, believed to have come from an old manuscript of his work, appears at http://commons.wikimedia.org/wiki/File:Bartolo_da_sassoferrato.jpg.

fering from the particulars of Roman law that would still be considered valid. Consequently, Bartolus was one of the jurists instrumental in the further development of the *jus commune*, the law that was common to continental Europe from approximately 1200 to 1700.

In addition to his work as a commentator and his writings on conflicts of law, Bartolus was an accomplished scholar in other subjects. For example, Bartolus authored leading texts on the law relating to rivers, arms, and trademarks. Moreover, he also wrote on numerous political issues.

Appendix 2.12
Biographical Sketch of Dante*

Dante Alighieri was a Florentine poet and writer born in 1265. His works were popular enough to earn him the title of "the Supreme Poet". Dante was born into a prominent family in Florence. It is believed that Dante gained his early education at home and he was especially passionate about Latin poetry, including works by Virgil. At the age of 12, Dante was betrothed to a young girl, although he had already fallen in love with another girl named Beatrice Portinari. While it does not appear that Dante ever had any significant relationship with Beatrice and she died while both were in their twenties, his writings would continue to show his love for her. An important trend in both poetry and writing was thus born into Italy in which love was the reason for poetry and even for living.

Dante continued his own education up until his early twenties, when he fought as a soldier for the Florentine Guelph family in its victorious effort to gain power in the city. Dante then studied to become a pharmacist, although his likely true aim was to become a politician since Florence had recently set a requirement that any persons wishing to attain public office had to be enrolled in one of the "arts." Dante then served in some minor political positions.

After gaining control of the city, the Guelphs divided into two factions: the White Guelphs, of which Dante was a member, and the Black Guelphs, who were generally more closely aligned with the Pope. Tensions mounted between the Guelph factions and the Black Guelphs ultimately seized power within Florence and killed many of the White Guelphs. Dante had been sent to Rome to act as a delegate toward the Pope prior to the

---

* This synopsis, prepared largely by Justin Waggoner, is drawn from several print and online sources, including especially Matthew Pearl, *Dante and the Death Penalty* (2003), in LEGAL AFFAIRS (Jan.–Feb. 2003), at http://www.legalaffairs.org (search "Archives). The first image—an illustration (copper engraving) from a 1727 edition of *The Divine Comedy*—is drawn from http://commons.wikimedia.org/wiki/File:Dante_Alighieri_(copper_engraving).jpg, where it is attributed to the Library of Congress. The second image is a 19th-century portrait of Dante by Gustave Doré, drawn from http://commons.wikimedia.org/wiki/File:Dante_Dor%C3%A9.jpg and from http://www.stelle.com.br/pt/dore1.html. The third image is a photograph I took of a statue of Dante on the plaza at the Santa Croce basilica in Florence.

takeover by the Black Guelphs. The new Black Guelph government condemned Dante to exile for two years, imposed hefty fines, and also confiscated his property in Florence. Dante refused to pay his fine and was subsequently sentenced to perpetual exile, for which he would be killed for violating.

Dante hated his exile and in many ways considered it a death sentence. He helped the White Guelphs with several unsuccessful attempts to regain power in Florence. Over time, he grew increasingly frustrated with the ineffectiveness of the White Guelphs, leading to his dissociation with them. It was at this time that Dante began working on *The Divine Comedy*, his chief work.

The *Divine Comedy* documents Dante's journey through hell, purgatory, and paradise under the guidance of Virgil and of Damte's beloved Beatrice. Particularly vivid in *The Divine Comedy* are the excruciating punishments doled out to those in hell. Symbolism within the book is provided by displaying that no matter how creative or harsh the punishments are, they may be unable to compel penance or remorse in the mind of the recipient of such punishments. In regard to criminal law in general, and perhaps his own exile sentence in particular, Dante seems to be alluding to the fallacy underlying harsh penalties and punishments.

Dante wrote *The Divine Comedy* in Italian, thus becoming one of a handful of famous artists to break from the tradition of publishing only in Latin. As a result, a wider audience could read publications, which would help lead to higher literacy rates in future generations.

Dante died in 1321, having never been able to return to his beloved native Florence. However, the city of Florence rescinded Dante's exile sentence in 2008.

Appendix 2.13
Biographical Sketch of Machiavelli*

NICCOLÒ MACCHIAVELLI

Niccolo Machiavelli was an Italian political philosopher in the 15th and 16th centuries. He is referred to by some as the founder of political science in Europe due in large part to his book *The Prince*. The innovative strategies and beliefs included in *The Prince* have been followed by aspiring and successful government leaders since its publication.

Machiavelli was born in Florence in 1469. His education focused largely on the Latin and Italian classics, and in 1494 Machiavelli began his work as a clerk and ambassador for the Florentine government. Later that year, Florence was restored to a republican form of government as the powerful Medici family, which had ruled the city for 60 years, was driven out. In 1498 he was elected as Second Chancellor of the Republic of Florence. Then, for most of the time between 1499 and 1512, Machiavelli served as a diplomat to the courts of Louis XII in France and Ferdinand II of Aragon. Moreover, Machiavelli also was a diplomat in the court of Cesare Borgia, who used cruel methods to gain power.

---

* This synopsis, prepared largely by Justin Waggoner, is drawn from several print and online sources, including especially Lars Johansson, *Raison d'Etat: The State as a Vehicle for Self-Determination*, 2 UNIVERSITY OF CALIFORNIA AT DAVIS JOURNAL OF INTERNATIONAL LAW & POLICY 295, 303 (1996), and the Stanford Encyclopedia of Philosophy, at http://plato.stanford.edu/entries/machiavelli/. The first image — of a statue by Lorenzo Bartolini located in the Uffizi Gallery in Florence — is drawn from http://commons.wikimedia.org/wiki/File:Niccolo_Machiavelli_uffizi.jpg and is used here under a GNU Free Documentation license, the terms of which appear at http://commons.wikimedia.org/wiki/Commons:GNU_Free_Documentation_License. The second image — the famous painting of Machiavelli by Santi di Tito, now located in the Palazzo Vecchio in Florence — is drawn from http://commons.wikimedia.org/wiki/File:Santi_di_Tito_-_Niccolo_Machiavelli%27s_portrait.jpg.

Machiavelli was successful in leading the Florentine militia in the defense of the city between 1503 and 1506. However, in 1512, the Medici family, with assistance from the Pope and Spanish troops, were able to displace the republic. Due to his role in the republican government, Machiavelli was removed from office, accused of conspiracy, and arrested in 1513. He was subjected to torture, but ultimately released. Nevertheless, he was made to live outside Florence. Consequently, he spent the rest of his life in rural villages near the city, a fate that his writings indicate he detested. Machiavelli died in 1527. In addition to being a political philosopher, Machiavelli was a musician, poet, and a playwright.

The Prince focused on how an aspiring ruler could gain and retain power. Machiavelli elicits examples, based upon his experience as an ambassador and readings of rulers of ancient history, of those leaders who were the most successful in gaining and holding onto power. Machiavelli authorizes the situational use of cruel actions by a leader. He states that such actions must be swift, effective, and short-lived. An especially controversial assertion in *The Prince* is that good can result from well-coordinated evil actions. In other words, the end may justify the means. However, Machiavelli does not condone excessive evil actions and recognizes that once the ruler has sufficient control, he should seek inspiration from wise and moderate statesmen of earlier ages.

Machiavelli did not write with the intention of creating or operating within an ideal society. Rather, *The Prince* operates within a realistic society and remains grounded in the assumption that man is generally bad by nature. That assumption (which we shall see at work also in the views of the Legalist school of thought in China, described below in Chapter Six) also informs Machiavelli's views on the relationship between law and force. He acknowledges that good laws and good arms create the foundation of an effective political system. Machiavelli then notes that since coercion by the ruler creates legality, it is more important for the ruler to focus his attention on force. Consequently, in *The Prince*, Machiavelli rests the legitimacy of the law entirely upon the threat of coercive force and posits that a ruler who is merely feared by his people will be more successful than a ruler that is merely loved by them.

Appendix 2.14
Biographical Sketch of Thomas Hobbes*

Thomas Hobbes was an English philosopher and author active in the 17th century. He is famous for his book *Leviathan*, one of the great contributions to Western political philosophy. Hobbes was born in southwestern England in 1588. Hobbes' father, a vicar, abandoned his family after being involved in a fight with a clergyman; but despite this, Hobbes received an excellent education as a youth and proceeded to Oxford University, where he graduated in 1608. Following that, he traveled throughout continental Europe and extensively studied classic Greek and Latin authors.

It was this rich academic and cultural background that led Hobbes to complete an impressive translation of Thucydides' *History of the Peloponnesian War*, the first time it had been translated into English (from Greek). From about 1629, however, his interests turned more toward philosophical research, which he conducted while continuing to serve in various positions as a tutor. He participated in philosophical debates in Paris and Florence, identifying himself as a philosopher beginning in 1637.

With the combination of the early stirrings of the English Civil War in 1640 and a controversial treatise he had recently written, Hobbes became concerned for his safety in England. Consequently, he moved to Paris and would not return to his native country for eleven years. Upon moving to Paris, Hobbes fervently began writing. His various philosophical publications were well received. Some of these works included stirring critiques of Descartes, a great philosophical contemporary of Hobbes.

In 1647 and 1648, while still in Paris, Hobbes would serve as a math instructor for Charles, Prince of Wales (ultimately King Charles II). During this time, Hobbes formed a close relationship with the exiled royal family, which led him to write *Leviathan*, a book

---

* This synopsis, prepared largely by Justin Waggoner, is drawn from several print and online sources, including especially April R. Cherry, *Social Contract Theory, Welfare Reform, Race, and Male Sex-Right*, 75 OREGON LAW REVIEW 1037, 1046 (1996), and David Dyzenhaus, *Holmes and Carl Schmitt: an Unlikely Pair?*, 63 BROOKLYN LAW REVIEW 165, 171 (1997). The image—from the fronticepiece of the book *Leviathon*—is drawn from http://commons.wikimedia.org/wiki/File:Leviathan.jpg.

in which Hobbes provided his theory of civil government in relation to the political crisis resulting from war. The central theme of his book was that a strong central authority is necessary to avoid the societal ills of civil discord and civil war. Hobbes starts off his book by hypothesizing what society would be like in an anarchic state without government, known as the state of nature. This would lead to what Hobbes terms a "war of all against all."

Hobbes then claims that in order to escape from the brutality of the state of nature, people will agree to a social contract under the auspices of a sovereign authority. In turn, the people of the society will sacrifice a measure of their own rights for the protection provided by the sovereign. Thus, any abuse of power by the sovereign is the price of peace. In severe instances of abuse of power, the people can be expected to rebel against the sovereign. In *Leviathan*, Hobbes explicitly rejected the doctrine of the separation of powers, stating that an effective sovereign must control the civil, military, judicial, and ecclesiastical realms.

It is these views, in part, that associate Hobbes more with the civil law tradition than the common law tradition. Indeed, his views can be regarded as contradicting the English common law tradition for two reasons. First, Hobbes was opposed to the common law tradition because it places in judges a broad scope of authority that he believed should be reserved to the sovereign. Second, the alleged lack of predictability within the common law, and its perceived lack of order, could be likened to the chaos Hobbes saw existing in the state of nature. Therefore, from a comparative law standpoint, Hobbes' views tended to fall more in line with a civil law code being issued directly from the king, emperor, or another sovereign leader with centralized powers.

Leviathan was published in 1651, whereupon it became an extremely popular book—attracting much praise and much disparagement. In fact, its publication brought so much criticism from some quarters that Hobbes asked the government of England for protection, as he feared for his life. The secularist spirit of *Leviathan* drew the scorn of both French Catholics and Anglicans. After returning to London at the end of 1651, Hobbes continued to write on philosophical matters, as well as some highly criticized mathematics and physics publications. In 1666, the English House of Commons introduced a bill naming Hobbes as a possible heretic. The result of this action was that Hobbes could never again publish (in England) any materials on human behavior. Hobbes would continue working on various literary pursuits until his death in 1679.

Appendix 2.15
Biographical Sketch of Napoleon Bonaparte*

Napoleon Bonaparte was a French military and political leader during the very end of the 18th century and the beginning of the 19th century. Although a diminutive man, he is considered as one of the great war generals of all time. His forces conquered a large portion of continental Europe (especially western Europe) and even some of North Africa. His reign played a significant role in the development of modern Europe.

Napoleon was born on August 15, 1769 in Ajaccio on the Mediterranean island of Corsica.

He lived there until, at the age of nine, he left to attend a French military school. Prior to attending the school, he had to learn French, as Italian was his native language. Despite constantly being teased about his Italian accent, Napoleon excelled in school and graduated after five years. Subsequently, he was admitted to the elite military college in Paris, where he completed a two-year course in just one year and graduated at the age of sixteen. Napoleon joined the French army for the next four years, during which he saw the beginning of the French Revolution. Napoleon then returned to Corsica, which was experiencing political turmoil. He and his family then fled to France.

Upon returning to France, Napoleon reentered the French army and led a successful battle effort, which earned him a promotion. In October of 1795 Bonaparte repelled a violent, protesting mob in Paris, which further boosted his popularity. During the next two years, he conquered much of Northern Italy. Napoleon's military success allowed him to become influential in French politics, as did his efforts in publishing three differ-

---

* This synopsis, prepared largely by Justin Waggoner, is drawn from several print and online sources, including especially *Napoleon Bonaparte — Emperor of the French*, at http://www.lucid-cafe.com/library/95aug/napoleon.html. The first image — a lithograph by Zephyrin Billiard — is drawn from http://commons.wikimedia.org/wiki/File:Bonabarte_Premier_consul.jpg, where it is attributed to the New York Public Library. The second image — a painting by Paul Delaroche — is drawn from http://commons.wikimedia.org/wiki/File:Napol%C3%A9on_Bonaparte_par_Paul_Delaroche.jpg, where it is attributed to the Library of Congress.

ent newspapers that were circulated in France. He returned to Paris at the end of 1797 as a conquering hero, more powerful and popular than the leaders of the French government.

In the early part of 1798 Napoleon proposed a military venture to seize Egypt, which was then a part of the Ottoman Empire. Although the leaders of the French government had reservations about the cost of the venture, they wanted the popular military general out of Paris, so they acquiesced. Napoleon was able to capture Egypt, Syria, and northern Israel. However, his army was not able to maintain control in much of the area as they suffered from the bubonic plague. He returned to France in August of 1799.

When Napoleon returned to Paris, he found a public that had grown deeply dissatisfied with the French government. Bonaparte then led a *coup d'etat* that seized control of the French government and drafted a constitution in which he was First Consul, or the most powerful person in the French government. After taking power, Napoleon instituted numerous integral and lasting reforms within France. In addition to the issuance of the civil code discussed below, those actions included a centralization of governmental power, the creation of a central bank, and an increased focus on higher education. However, Napoleon recognized that France would be unable to defend its lands in North America. Consequently, in 1803 he sold approximately a quarter of the present day land mass of the United States to the Americans in the Louisiana Purchase.

Napoleon crowned himself Emperor of France in 1804 and King of Italy the following year. He was able to expand his influence throughout even more of Europe by military might and the acquisition of allies. In 1807 Napoleon signed a treaty with Czar Alexander I of Russia to divide most of continental Europe between France and Russia. Meanwhile, the United Kingdom and other European countries continued to form coalitions to attempt to loosen Napoleon's grasp on Europe. Although initially unsuccessful, these coalitions gradually gained more participants as the years wore on. However, France still remained firmly in control of much of western Europe.

In 1812, amid mounting pressures between France and Russia, Napoleon launched an invasion of Russia. Napoleon ignored advice he received not to invade the vast Russian heartland. The Russians did not meet Napoleon's advancing army and instead retreated deep into their country. The Russian army burned its fields, which caused the French to run short on food during its advance. Moreover, the long and harsh Russian winter began to set in. Both sides suffered enormous numbers of casualties in a battle outside of Moscow, which the French won. The Russians then burned much of Moscow and retreated further. The weary French army then returned to Paris because they feared losing control of France. After beginning the invasion of Russia with 450,000 troops, only 40,000 made the return journey home.

After the battle with the Russians, even more countries—including the United Kingdom, Russia, Prussia, Spain, Portugal, Sweden, and Austria—joined in the coalition against Napoleon. The coalition occupied Paris in March of 1814, and Napoleon abdicated. He was then exiled to Elba, a small island in the Mediterranean. However, Napoleon escaped Elba in February of 1815 and was able to win back the support of his army in dramatic fashion. He then arrived in Paris and ruled for what is known as "the Hundred Days." His rule ended following his defeat in the Battle of Waterloo on June 18, 1815, at the hands of the Duke of Wellington and the coalition forces. Napoleon was once again exiled, this time on the island of St. Helena in the Atlantic Ocean. While there, he lived an isolated life until his death in 1821.

During his exile, Napoleon is reported to have said, "[m]y true glory is not to have won forty battles.... Waterloo will erase the memory of so many victories.... But ... what will live forever, is my Civil Code." While his code has been altered numerous times in its more than 200 years of existence, his statement does in fact ring true. The Napoleonic Code or *Code Civil* entered into force on March 21, 1804 and has had enormous influence around the world—as described in the main text of Chapter Two.

Napoleon's life supports two competing visions of the man and his goals. He has been portrayed as a great conqueror hungry for power. Napoleon denied those accusations. He argued that he was building a federation of free peoples in a Europe united under a liberal government. Indeed, he is reported to have offered this summation of his career:

> I closed the gulf of anarchy and brought order out of chaos. I rewarded merit regardless of birth or wealth, wherever I found it. I abolished feudalism and restored equality to all regardless of religion and before the law. I fought the decrepit monarchies of the Old Regime because the alternative was the destruction of all this. I purified the Revolution.

But if Napoleon's goal was to bring improvements to the lives of ordinary people, his method of doing so was to take power into his own hands. (His view of government, in other words, was "for the people" but certainly not "by the people", to use the famous words of Lincoln's Gettysburg Address.) Napoleon's France was a police state, with spies, censorship, and repression. However, in the states he created, Napoleon granted constitutions, introduced law codes, abolished feudalism, created efficient bureaucracies for government administration, and fostered education, science, literature, and the arts.

Appendix 2.16
Biographical Sketch of Portalis*

Jean-étienne-Marie Portalis was born in April 1746 in Provence to a bourgeois family and gained his university education at Aix. By 1765 he had become a lawyer at the *parlement* of Aix-en-Provence and gained great notoriety there.

In 1793, after the First French Republic had been proclaimed, Portalis moved to Paris, where he was thrown in jail for being the brother-in-law of a political leader in Provence regarded unfavorably by the Paris authorities. He was released, however, and by 1795 was practicing law in Paris — as well taking a leadership role in the activities of a moderate party. Those activities made him a target again, forcing him to flee to Switzerland; he stayed there until after Napoleon Bonaparte consolidated his power as the established leader of France.

What happened after his return to Paris resulted in Portalis becoming known as the founding father of the French Civil Code. Napoleon named Portalis a *conseiller d'état* — a member of the Council of State, that body of government that provides the executive branch with legal advice. Portalis, along with François Denis Tronchet, Félix-Julien-Jean Bigot de Preameneu, and Jacques de Maleville, were charged with crafting the Code Civil.

Portalis recognized the shortcomings of recent civil codes from other continental states. He sought to create a code that was flexible. Portalis explained: "We have avoided the dangerous ambition to regulate and foresee everything.... The function of law is to fix in broad outline the general maxims of justice, to establish principles rich in implications, and not to descend into the details of the questions that can arise in each subject."

Portalis died in August 1807. His importance in French legal history was captured in a 1971 French postage stamp commemorating the Code Civil. The stamp depicted images Portalis and Bonaparte in the foreground, and the *Conseil d' État* in the background.

---

* This synopsis, prepared largely by Justin Waggoner, is drawn from various online sources and from these print sources: Peter Arend Jan van den Berg, THE POLITICS OF EUROPEAN CODIFICATION: A HISTORY OF THE UNIFICATION OF LAW 207 (2007); Nutshell-1999, *supra* note 45, at 37; Jean Carbonnier, *The French Civil Code, in* RETHINKING FRANCE: THE STATE 335, 336 (Pierre Nora, ed., 2001). The image — an engraving by Ambroise Tardieu (credit, H. Roger-Viollet) — is drawn from http://www.wikiberal.org/wiki/Jean_%C3%89tienne_Marie_Portalis.

Appendix 2.17
Biographical Sketch of Savigny*

Friedrich Carl von Savigny was a highly influential 19th century German jurist who was deeply involved in researching the history of law. Born in Frankfurt in 1779, Savigny was left an orphan at the age of thirteen and was thereafter raised by a guardian. He then entered the University of Marburg to study law. Savigny obtained his doctor's degree from the University of Marburg in 1800.

Following the completion of his education, Savigny lectured at Marburg on the Pandects (Justinian's *Digest*) and on criminal law. In 1803 his treatise on the law of property was published, to favorable reviews, and in the following year he began what would ultimately become a lifelong process of researching and writing about the history of law, particularly Roman civil law. Savigny was appointed by the Bavarian government to serve as the professor of Roman law at Landshut in 1808. Less than two years later, he filled the chair of Roman law at the new University of Berlin. In addition to his responsibilities as a professor, Savigny was given the task of assembling (and serving on) a *"Spruch-Collegium"* — a tribunal authorized to deliver opinions on cases remitted to it by the ordinary courts.

In 1814 Savigny published a pamphlet which spoke out against the demand for codification. It was a response to another pamphlet that urged the necessity of forming a code for Germany which should be independent of the influence of foreign legal systems. Savigny's pamphlet argued that there needed to be a comprehensive evaluation of the works completed by former generations of jurists (largely the Romans) and that there was great risk in allowing the proponents of the natural law, with their "infinite arrogance", to ruin such an evaluation.

---

* This synopsis, prepared largely by Justin Waggoner, is drawn in part from Eric H. Reiter, *Imported Books, Imported Ideas: Reading European Jurisprudence in Mid-Nineteenth Century Quebec*, 22 LAW & HISTORY REVIEW 445, 462 (2004), and from various online sources. The image—of a stamp issued by the German government in 1957—is drawn from http://commons.wikimedia.org/wiki/File:DBPB_1957_170_Savigny.jpg.

In 1815 Savigny and a cluster of other German jurists formed the German Historical School of Law, an intellectual movement standing in contrast to proponents of natural law. In a publication sponsored by that movement, Savigny identified an important text from Verona as that of Gaius, rather than, as had previously been believed, Ulpian's. Between 1817 and 1820, in addition to his position as a professor, Savigny was appointed to several positions and tasks within the Prussian government.

In 1835 Savigny begin his extensive work on a book covering contemporary Roman law, which would later have eight volumes published between 1840 and 1849. He ceased teaching in 1842 when he was appointed High Commissioner, which was the head of the judicial system in Prussia. He then resigned from that position in 1848. Savigny would continue to be a celebrated jurist throughout Germany up until and after his death in 1861, and his lasting influence provided inspiration for the exercise that culminated at the end of the century in the German Civil Code.

Appendix 2.18
Observations by J.A.C. Thomas on
"Second Life" of Roman Law*

In his *Textbook of Roman Law*, J.A.C. Thomas discusses both the "first life" and the "second life" of Roman law, as they are described earlier in this chapter. He finishes his discussion of the "first life" in this way:

> ... [O]ur principal, almost exclusive knowledge of the first life of Roman law is derived from the compilation of Justinian, more especially from the Digest. It ... was a flawed work, rapidly compiled. And, because it was intended to be not only a thesaurus of the best of the past but also a law book for contemporary use, the extracts from the juristic writings were often altered to accord with current practice, [and] indeed, Justinian directed that this should be so. After all, the last of the accepted great jurists, Modestinus, had been dead nearly three hundred years when the Digest was commissioned and life, political, social and economic, had not stood still in the interval.
>
> However successful Justinian was in imposing his nonetheless essentially Roman Law upon his Byzantine subjects,[a] later Eastern Emperors found it necessary to produce Greek versions and commentaries,[b] generally attenuating and simplifying Justinian's work. But, even thus in decline, it can be said that Roman Law lived on in the Byzantine Empire until the sack of Constantinople by the Turks in [under the leadership of Mehmet the Conqueror] A.D. 1453.
>
> [However,] in the West, soon wholly again under non-Roman domination after the death of Justinian in A.D. 565, knowledge of Roman Law [faded, and although] ... some knowledge of the Institutes and the Code and Novels remained [there, Justinian's] greatest achievement, the Digest, disappeared. In northern Europe, all trace of Roman Law virtually vanished. The dominance of Christianity, through which some knowledge of Roman Law was necessary as a preparation for study of the Canon Law, meant that the Church kept alive a frail learning. But for five centuries it seemed that Roman Law was effectively dead.

Thomas then turns his attention to the "second life" of Roman law, explaining the rediscovery of the *Digest* and its use in university legal education.

> ... And then, just as Justinian had sought, seemingly unsuccessfully, to restore the glories of bygone centuries, so the universities of Europe revived the study of Roman Law. A complete manuscript of the Digest was discovered to-

---

* This synopsis draws from J.A.C. Thomas, TEXTBOOK OF ROMAN LAW 6–12 (1976).

a. [*footnote in original*] Though published in A.D. 533, the Digest, with the rest of Justinian's compilation, was promulgated in the Italian provinces only in A.D. 544.

b. [*footnote in original*] Already in Justinian's own time, there appeared a Greek paraphrase of his elementary work, the Institutes, which is ascribed to one of his commissioners, Theophilus. The principal Greek literature is the *Basilica*, a work in sixty books, condensing and commenting upon Justinian's whole legislation, which was published by the Emperor Leo the Wise (A.D. 886–911). About A.D. 1345, Constantine Harmenopoulos, a judge at Salonica, produced a work in six books, the *Hexabiblos*, which became the basis of Greek Law, under the Turkish domination and thereafter, until the introduction of the Civil Code in A.D. 1946.

ward the end of the eleventh century[c] and its study was taken up with great enthusiasm [at] the university [of] Bologna, already a prestigious centre of learning. Over the next century and a half, its contents were mastered as they have probably never been since; scholars cited passages not by book, title and *lex* as today, but simply by the opening word or words of the passage in question; thus, for instance, *D.12.6.38* was '*frater a fratre*'; everyone knew what was meant.

The first and most illustrious of these students of the newly-discovered treasure was Irnerius…, a teacher of grammar and dialectic (*magister artium*) at Bologna who, with his disciples—notably the 'four doctors', Jacobus, Martinus, Bulgarus and Hugo—established that method of study of the sources, especially of the Digest, which was to culminate in the *Glossa ordinaria* or *Glossa magna* of Accursius who died in A.D. 1260 and which has earned its practitioners the name of Glossators.

… For all its serious achievement and its inestimable value for the future, the work of the Glossators may not unfairly be described as a colossal academic game, perhaps to be likened to the solving of a particularly difficult crossword puzzle: what had been born of the daily experience of living people became the object of intellectual satisfaction.…

… The new learning aroused enormous enthusiasm. By the middle of the twelfth century, the number of students from all over Europe who had flocked to Bologna exceeded ten thousand; and, while Bologna always remained at the forefront, the study of Roman Law spread to the other emerging universities of Italy and of Western Europe generally; even in England, the Italian Vacarius was teaching at Oxford in the mid-twelfth century. But, though necessary to familiarise scholars with the source material and thus to equip them to utilise it, the work of the Glossators was inherently sterile.…

The sterility of the work of the Glossators—and, more importantly, its lack of direct applicability to the needs of governing the emerging nation-states—led to a new development: the emergence of a new set of scholar-jurists who took a more practice-oriented interest in the *Digest*. Thomas describes this development as follows:

… The successors of the Glossators were the Post-Glossators or Commentators. The revival of Roman Law learning coincided broadly with the emergence of the nation states, such as France and England, and of the city states of Italy and the principalities of Germany. It was inevitable that the living law of these communities should be affected by what was happening in the universities and that the communities themselves should look to the results achieved in the universities to assist in the solution of the problems posed to them, especially with the rise of commerce.…

But, for the practical utilisation of the ancient law, the glossatorial method was unsuitable. Hence the emergence of more systematic commentaries and treatises in which the authors, by skilful interpretation and subtle distinctions and utilising the glosses as often as the texts on which they were a commentary, adapted the Roman material to practical modern needs and incorporated its results into

---

c. [*footnote in original*] Taken by the Pisans from Amalfi where it was found; since 1406 it has been in the Laurentian Library at Florence, hence its description as the Florentine. It is the prototype from which all other manuscripts were derived.

current law.[d] For these scholars, Justinian's compilation was not an end in itself but rather a quarry from which to extract what appeared pertinent to the problem or topic in issue; their work was facilitated by the variety of distinctions and reconciliations bequeathed by their predecessors which enabled them in fact to select what they thought the best among competing solutions while in form they appeared simply to be invoking and interpreting the definitive text. The leading figures of this form of scholarship were Bartolus of Sassoferrato (A.D. 1314–57) who, despite his brief life, was a prolific author and his pupil, Baldus degli Ubaldi (A.D. 1327–1400); and their work and that of others — not only in Italy but in other parts of continental Europe … — made for the so-called Reception of Roman Law, whereby Roman Law, as understood, expounded and adapted by its academic devotees, gradually became the virtual common law of most of Europe.…

Thomas then expands on the process of "reception" of Roman law and how that process occurred in various parts of Europe:

… Though 'Reception' is virtually a term of art, it would be more accurate in general to speak of a greater or lesser degree of infiltration of national legal systems by Roman Law.… [That is, reception was uneven, with deeper effects in different places according to the greater brought Romanist influence. The result was that, until the Code Napoleon of A.D. 1804, France had a vigorous blend of Romanist doctrine and national institutions. In the Netherlands, on the other hand, and in Germany with its mass of individual states, the new mass and consequent disunity of local customs, practices, etc.] While southern France (le pays du droit écrit) had always retained Roman institutions, northern France had well-knit bodies of customs (it was le pays des coutumes) which were codified in the sixteenth century: but the spirit of the legal profession and its university education inevitably, if gradually, law so firmly established itself that local institutions became virtually peripheral to what was now the national law; and the common, i.e. Roman, law, the gemeines Recht, was the law of Germany until the coming into force of the civil code, the B.G.B., in A.D. 1900.

… The great exception to this susceptibility to the Roman infiltration was England. Roman Law was known and taught quite early in England and … was utilised in the first comprehensive treatise of English Law [written by Bracton]: but it never came to mould the institutions, terminology and methodology of English Law as it did those of the rest of western Europe. A variety of factors account[s] for the jurisprudential isolation of England.

Thomas then explains how the intellectual history of European civil law unfolded in the 17th and 18th centuries, featuring the Humanist and Natural Law schools; and then he concludes with a description of German legal science.

… [T]he Renaissance revival of classical learning brought another approach to [Justinian's] compilation.… [Humanists focused their attention on] the law as it had existed at the various stages of Rome's history. [As part of their work,] the range of source materials studied was broadened; not only Justinian's compilation but also pre-Justinianic juristic works which had survived, notably the

---

d. To take but one example, the whole branch of law known as Private International Law or Conflict of Laws, derives from the Gloss on *C.I.1.1* and the subsequent theory of statutes which emerged with the Commentators.

Codex Theodosianus promulgated by Theodosius II in A.D. 438, and also non-juristic material like the works of Cicero....

... The eighteenth century saw the rise of what is called the School of Natural Law, [which] ... considered law to be a product of human reason which could be valid for all peoples and all times. While thus rejecting the innate authority of Roman Law as such, they nonetheless found in that law, especially its concepts of *ius gentium* and *ius naturale*, much that could be utilised; and, of course, the history of preceding centuries had produced much that was common to the states of Europe. While eschewing Roman Law in itself, they were yet the products of their education, states and general *mores*; and thus of the Europe of received Roman Law....

... The beginning of the nineteenth century was the rise of the essential German Historical School of Law, the unquestioned protagonist of which was Savigny (A.D. 1779–1861).... [T]he Historical School argued that law was not a product of reason but a manifestation of the spirit of the people who lived under it, the *Volksgeist*, and of its historical development. [Hence German legal scholarship involved both (i) an] intensive historical and philogical investigation of the *gemeines Recht* currently in force in Germany [and (ii)] ... the final elaboration of ... the law of the Pandects [*i.e.*, the *Digest*]....

Appendix 2.19

Observations by van den Bergh on the *Jus Commune**

The following observations by Govaert C.J.J. van den Bergh focus on two points: (1) the historical background to the creation of a *jus commune* in medieval Europe and (2) its relevance to modern Europe.

A body of law applied everywhere in Europe? A law curriculum that is essentially the same, whether you study in Bologna, Salamanca, Paris, Louvain, Leiden, Cologne, Leipzig, Prague or Cracow? And, as a result, broad opportunities for jurists to find jobs anywhere in Europe if they want to? Is this what we anticipate for the future of a united Europe? If so, it might be worth remembering that this has been a reality for the greater part of Europe, roughly between the twelfth and the eighteenth century....

The body of law I am referring to is called by various names. It is named *ius commune*, because it is the common law of continental Europe. It is [also] called *learned law*, because it is a body of law that had its basis in a tradition of learning. The only way you could learn to handle it was by attending a university, or by studying it on your own.... It is, finally, called *Roman law*, but that name can really be misleading [because] ... ancient Roman law, that is, in the collection of texts promulgated by the emperor Justinian in the sixth century which we are used to call the *Corpus juris civilis*[a] ... is something totally different from medieval Roman law, just as a modern motorcar is different from a coach, even though the earliest motorcars still did their best to look like coaches without a horse.

1. *Jus commune, its origin, growth and decline.*

The intellectual culture of Europe, its fundamental political ideas as well as its literary ideals, were modelled by a series of encounters with the legacy of Antiquity, which in ever[y] new generation sparked off a fervour to rediscover the lost riches of Greece and Rome, a series of renaissances, of which *the* Renaissance of the fifteenth century is only the last and best known.

The first of these renaissances took place in the Carolingian epoch in the ninth century, and to the copying activities of that period we still owe a great number of texts from classical authors. To the second, the renaissance of the twelfth century, we owe the rediscovery and intellectual capture of one of the major remains from Antiquity, the *corpus juris*, that is, a selection from the literary remains from classical Roman law promulgated in authoritative form by Justinian in the sixth century....

Mastering the *corpus juris* demanded the application of generations of students and therefore some kind of formal organisation for education and research. This organisation was provided for by the newly arising institution of the university, an institution characteristically European, if anything is. The peak of the system

---

* This synopsis is drawn from Govaert C.J.J. van den Bergh, *Ius Commune, a history with a future?*, appearing in B. de Witte and C. de Forder, eds., THE COMMON LAW OF EUROPE AND THE FUTURE OF LEGAL EDUCATION (1992), at 192 et seq.

a. [*footnote in original*] Naturally, learned law did not only consist in the study of Roman law (*ius civile*) but also in that of canon law (*Corpus juris canonici*) and feudal law (*libri feudorum*). For convenience these are not discussed here.

of education ... was formed by the higher studies which were at home in the universities.

These higher studies were threefold: theology, law and medicine. Each of them concentrated on the study of a voluminous corpus of books handed down from Antiquity. For theology this comprised the Bible and the fathers of the church, for law Justinian's *corpus juris*, for medicine the *corpus hippocraticum* and Galenus. The three studies were essentially literary studies and in a way theology and law still are today. Only medicine has changed its methodology fundamentally.... The three higher studies together covered fairly well the basic needs of medieval man: theology for the soul, medicine for the body, and law for all the rest: government, law, administration, criminal justice, international relations, etc.

... The study of the *corpus juris* along the lines just sketched, which began in Bologna towards the end of the eleventh century, had a tremendous success.... The main reason for this success was, of course, that in medieval society there was real and growing demand for the new science of learned law. Learned jurists with their expertise supported the emperor in his battles with the pope, acted as administrators and judges in Italian cities ridden with political feuds, found their way in the budding bureaucracies [and] in city governments all over Europe....

2. What of it now?

Even after this only too sketchy outline of its history, it will be evident that *jus commune* is not just a thing of the past. A system of law which has had such an impact over such a long period must have left its traces everywhere, in our codification, in our language, in our legal practice and procedure, in our ideas about what law is and what could be a proper methodology for legal reasoning, in the structure of our legal monographs as well as in our law schools. Roman law may have been abolished ... but in the background of our legal minds it is still is alive and kicking....

3. Conclusions.

Let me be frank in summing up my argument. I do not believe that *ius commune* can be revived in the united Europe of the future.... [However, I do believe] that the heritage of *ius commune* is a valuable asset for a Europe making its way toward unification. How can we best make use of it? ... I firmly believe that a European orientation in the study of law demands stimulating historical consciousness in the first place. How can Europe become a reality unless we take pride in it, our common European heritage, in stead of blindly imitating the Americans? This means that in a European legal curriculum we need more, not less, history of law....

Appendix 2.20
Diagrammatic Chronology of European Civil Law

—see explanation following diagram—

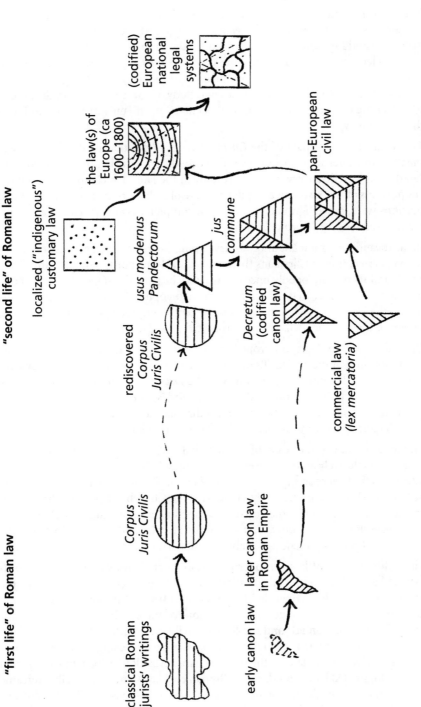

The diagram appearing on the preceding page aims to illustrate key developments in both the "first life" and the "second life" of Roman (or civil) law, as they have unfolded in Europe—culminating in today's regime of a number of codified national legal systems. The timeline at the bottom of the diagram runs from 100 CE through the present. The reasons I have drawn the diagram in this fashion are as follows:

- The classical Roman jurists' writings, appearing especially in the 2nd and 3rd centuries CE, served as the voluminous but disorganized "raw material" from which Tribonian and his commission compiled for the Emperor Justinian the most important elements of what later became known as the *Corpus Juris Civilis*—and in particular the *Digest*. That great compilation of the 6th century organized those classical Roman jurists' writings into a single body of law, changing it in the process to reflect the Christianization that had occurred in the meantime (beginning in the 4th century).

- The most important part of the *Corpus Juris Civilis*—that is, the *Digest*—was then lost in western Europe for several hundred years (during the so-called Dark Ages) until its rediscovery in northern Italy in the late 11th century. The public-law portions of the Justinian compilation were of so little relevance then that those portions were largely ignored (hence the incompleteness of the circle representing the "rediscovered *Corpus Juris Civilis*").

- In the meantime, canon law also was developing—first in secret because of official Roman persecution of Christians (hence the dashed-line borders of the "early canon law"), and then more openly once Christianity became the state religion. Following the fall of Rome, that canon law remained applicable, and developed some, during the Dark Ages, when the collapse of central imperial power into a political system of fractured feudalism gave substantial power to the Church by default.

- Upon the return of light to Europe—and spurred on by the rediscovery and rising importance of the ancient Roman law—canon law then was codified (by Gratian, in the 12th century) in the form of the *Decretum*. The simultaneous surge of economic activity (encouraged by the Crusades) brought into greater prominence the commercial law (*lex mercatoria*) that had slowly developed over the centuries largely apart from Roman civil law and canon law.

- Momentum built in the study of Roman civil law, and it was transformed from an almost exclusively academic exercise—manifest in the work of the Glossators— into a practical exercise supported (and relied on) by the secular political leaders of Europe who were increasingly vying with the Church for power. That practical exercise, carried out by the Post-Glossators (or Commentators), took the form of the *usus modernus Pandectorum*—that is, the rules and concepts found in the Pandects (*Digest*) but made applicable for modern use.

- These three bodies of law—modernized Roman civil law, canon law, and commercial law—then combined. By some accounts (reflected in this diagram), the *jus commune* that had congealed by about the 14th century and lasted through the 18th century (even longer in some regions of the continent) consists technically of just the canon law and the Roman civil law. A different characterization of the process would include in the *jus commune* the increasingly important commercial law as well. Whatever the precise characterization, a "pan-European civil law"—dominated by the modernized Roman civil law (which gradually overcame the canon law as secular nation-states gained power vis-a-vis the Church) but also including commercial law—had unmistakably emerged by the 16th century.

- That "pan-European civil law" was only part of the story, however, regarding the applicable law across the face of Europe. Localized customary law, drawing from centuries-old Germanic laws and traditions, amounted to an "indigenous" and territorially-specific (and, in some regions, codified) counterpart to the more general rules emerging from Roman, canon, and commercial law influences. Through the process of "reception", those latter influences became incorporated into the more territorially-specific customary laws, yielding by the 1600s (and extending into the 1800s in the case of still-unified Germany) a system of more or less harmonized laws in Europe—more harmonized in those regions with greater "reception", less harmonized in other regions.

- Most of that harmony was shattered with the national codification movements and the more fundamental revolutionary political changes that fueled those movements. By the beginning of the 19th century, the earliest national codification movements had insisted that the only legitimate source of law was the state—thus marking the end of "pluralism" and the victory of national sovereignty over pan-European legal and political unity. Thus did the "territorial compartmentalization" of law in Europe become the norm, resulting in a number of codified national legal systems that both (i) *share* many attributes with one another because of their common heritage of Roman law, canon law, and commercial law and yet also (ii) *differ* from one another in important ways that reflect the ideology of state sovereignty.

Appendix 2.21
History of the Civil Law Tradition in Song

Don't Know Much About History[a]
(But I want to avoid a "D")

Don't know much about history,
But I want to avoid a "D",
So I'll learn all the important dates
And the event to which each one relates.

All I have to do is learn this song.
Then I'll get those dates all right, not wrong,
And what a wonderful world this will be.

Those Roman Tables back in 450[b]
Wrote down the laws so all the folks would know[c]
The second century brought classic scholars;
Gaius and Ulpian earned fame, not dollars.[d]

Rome turned Christian when old Constantine
Said "Praise the Lord" about year 313,
And what a wonderful empire they had then.

But in 476, the Western side crumbled;
Those Ostrogoths were there to stay.[e]
In 533, though, Justinian's scholars
Gave the world the *Pandektae*![f]

It got lost until the Middle Ages,
When a monk in Pisa turned the pages.
Then with joy our friend Irnerius thundered.
(He was teaching in 1100.)[g]

---

a. I wrote these lyrics to be sung to the tune of the song "Don't Know Much About History", or "Wonderful World". The original lyrics for that song were written by songwriter and performer Sam Cooke, one of the most popular and influential African-American singers to emerge in the late '50s. (Collaborators on the music were Herb Alpert and Lou Adler.) The song has been recorded many times, with one especially popular recording by Herman's Hermits, whose other hits included "I'm Henry the Eighth, I Am" and "Mrs. Brown You've Got a Lovely Daughter"—the latter of which was a #1 hit in 1965. Cooke was inducted into the Rock and Roll Hall of Fame in 1986. To date, Herman's Hermits have not been.

b. To rhyme, this needs to be pronounced "Four Five Oh."

c. This refers to the fact that the Twelve Tables represented a victory of the plebeians over the patricians, who had theretofore exercised broad discretion in their governance rather than relying on written rules made publicly available.

d. The *jurisconsults*, including Gaius, Ulpian, Papinian, and others, reportedly did their work for the reputation, not the remuneration, that it would bring them.

e. Germanic tribes had sacked Rome before 476, most notably in 410, which had prompted the Roman military to leave Britain and return to the Italian peninsula.

f. The *Digest* is also known by the title Pandects, or *Pandektae*. It was the most important part of the great legal compilation issued by Justinian, the emperor in Constantinople devoted to winning back the glory of Rome.

g. Irnerius was the founder of the school of Glossators studying the *Digest* in great detail following its rediscovery in northern Italy in the late 11th century.

Then came Glossators and Commentators.
They set the stage for all the nation-staters,
Who won out in 1648.[h]

Then Merryman says there came a big revolution
The French took back the old Bastille,[i]
And shortly thereafter, in 1804
Napolean announced the *Code Civil!*[j]

Then the Germans had to have their fix
They wrote their Code in 1896
and what a wonderful world it revealed.

Don't know much about history,
But I want to avoid a "D",
So I'll learn all the important dates
And the event to which each one relates.

All I have to do is learn this song.
Then I'll get those dates all right, not wrong,
And what a wonderful world this will be.

---

h. The Peace of Westphalia (1648), ending the Thirty Years War, is regarded as the definitive acknowledgment of the nation-state as the fundamental political unit in Europe.

i. The Bastille was a prison in Paris, stormed on July 14, 1789. The French Revolution was only the most dramatic manifestation of a more fundamental and long-term intellectual revolution that changed Europe in the 17th and 18th centuries.

j. The French Civil Code (alternatively called the *Code Civil* or the *Code Napoleon*) was finally adopted on March 21, 1804.

Chapter Three

The Civil Law Tradition in Operational Perspective

Outline

Study Questions

SQ #3.1   What are the sources of law in the orthodox civil law tradition?

SQ #3.2   In what ways do these sources reflect the significance of (1) nationalism, (2) sovereignty, and (3) secularism?

SQ #3.3   Which of the "orthodox" sources is most important?

SQ #3.4   In what ways have recent developments changed the orthodox view on the sources and authorities of law?

SQ #3.5   In what way might caselaw and legal scholarship be regarded as "indirect" sources of law in a civil law country?

SQ #3.6   In the orthodox civil law tradition, what is the attitude toward the notion of *stare decisis*? Is the actual practice different from that orthodox attitude?

SQ #3.7   Why is the distinction between private law and public law so fundamental in the civil law tradition?

SQ #3.8   What areas of law fall within the category of "public" law? ... within the category of "private" law?

SQ #3.9   Is there a special "ideology of codification" at work in the civil law tradition?

SQ #3.10   What alternative views might be taken regarding the reason for the development of some of the great codes of the civil law?

SQ #3.11   Why might we say that the protagonist or "hero" in the civil law tradition is the scholar, and not the legislator?

SQ #3.12   In what sense might we say that various legislators in the civil law tradition, including Justinian and Napoleon, have tried to construct dams across what has been called "the great river of legal scholarship"—and why have they failed?

SQ #3.13   To what extent does the typical European civil law lawyer really view codified law as being clear, consistent, and comprehensive?

SQ #3.14   How (if at all) does the common law tradition view "certainty" differently from the view taken of "certainty" in the civil law tradition?

SQ #3.15   Why would judicial service in the civil law tradition be, as John Henry Merryman puts it, "a bureaucratic career [in which] the judge is a functionary, a civil servant [and] the judicial function is narrow, mechanical, and uncreative"?

SQ #3.16   What are some differences between (a) the legal training and career of a judge in a civil law country and (b) the legal training and career of a judge in a common law country?

SQ #3.17   What are some differences in legal training for advocates—lawyers who wish to become members of the practicing bar—in Germany, the USA, England, Italy, and China?

SQ #3.18   Why is it appropriate, in the context of a typical civil law country, to refer to the legal *professions* (plural), instead of the legal *profession* (singular)?

SQ #3.19   What are the principal functions of the public prosecutor in a typical civil law system?

SQ #3.20   What are the principal functions of the notary in a typical civil law system?

SQ #3.21   What are some ways in which legal education in Italy differs from legal education in the USA?

SQ #3.22   What is the layout of the courtroom in the "*O.J. Sampson* case" depicted in the law journal article in Appendix 3.2, and how does it differ from the layout of a courtroom in a US court for a criminal case?

SQ #3.23   Where in the courtroom do the "lay triers of fact" sit in the *O.J. Sampson* case? What does this suggest about how their role in the proceedings differs from that of a jury in a common law criminal case?

SQ #3.24   How does the role of the presiding judge in the *O.J. Sampson* case differ from the role of a judge in a criminal case in the United States?

SQ #3.25   How does the selection of judges in most civil law countries help justify giving them much greater authority than judges are given in the United States?

SQ #3.26   In the *O.J. Sampson* case, what consequences—in terms of the flow of the trial and the tone of the proof-taking—result from the fact that the presiding judge, not the adversaries, determines the order of witnesses and does most of the questioning?

SQ #3.27   Do you agree with Merryman's suggestion that the inquisitorial system typical of the civil law tradition "represents an additional step along the path of social evolution"?

SQ #3.28   Merryman has also suggested that "the evolution of criminal procedure in the last two centuries in the civil law world has been away from the extremes and abuses of the inquisitorial system". What evidence supports that proposition?

SQ #3.29   What are some *procedural* consequences of the fact that the court in the *O.J. Sampson* case will consider simultaneously both (a) the issue of culpability (guilt or innocence, and how much of each) and (b) the issue of sanction (punishment in the case of some guilt)?

SQ #3.30   What are some advantages and disadvantages of the simultaneous consideration of both culpability and sanction?

SQ #3.31   What might a lawyer trained in the common law tradition find objectionable about the criminal procedure exemplified in the *O.J. Sampson* case?

SQ #3.32   In what sense do prosecutors in a civil law system "never lose" in criminal cases?

SQ #3.33   According to the account given in the *O.J. Sampson* article, how does a typical civil law system regard:

    (a)   an accused's right not to answer questions, in order to avoid self-incrimination?

    (b)   the "exclusionary rule"—that is, the exclusion of evidence that was obtained illegally?

    (c)   the admissibility of "hearsay" evidence?

    (d)   the admissibility of the accused's prior convictions or bad acts?

    (e)   plea bargaining?

    (f)   double jeopardy and the right of a prosecutor to appeal an acquittal?

SQ #3.34   In what ways might we regard American rules of criminal procedure—especially those that divide authority among various participants in a criminal trial—as reflecting typical American attitudes toward government and authority?

SQ #3.35   Which system of criminal procedure is better—that of a typical civil law jurisdiction as exemplified in the *O.J. Sampson* article, or that of a typical state in the United States? Which system is more likely to reveal the truth in a criminal case?

SQ #3.36   What values other than the value of finding the truth are reflected in American rules of criminal procedure?

SQ #3.37   For an American lawyer involved in a criminal trial, is the quest for justice a game? Is it just a game?

SQ #3.38   What reforms to criminal procedure were attempted beginning in the 1980s in Italy, and what difficulties have those reforms faced?

SQ #3.39   What are the differences between an "inquisitorial", an "accusatorial", and an "adversarial" system of criminal procedure?

SQ #3.40   Why does a civil law system handle civil litigation in such a substantially different way from how it handles criminal cases?

SQ #3.41   Why might we say that in civil (i.e., noncriminal) procedure in a typical civil law country, there is no such thing as a "trial"?

SQ #3.42   What is meant by the observation that civil procedure in a common law country (unlike that in a civil law country) is characterized by (a) concentration, (b) immediacy, and (c) orality?

SQ #3.43   What is the historical background to the "ordinary courts" that exist in a typical civil law system? What is their role and jurisdiction?

SQ #3.44   What was the purpose in the French legal system of the former Tribunal of Cassation, and how does it represent a slight departure from the approach that a "civil law fundamentalist" would prefer in respect of legislative interpretation?

SQ #3.45   How is the Court of Cassation in today's French legal system different from the former Tribunal of Cassation?

SQ #3.46   How is the German procedure of "revision" different from the French system's use of the Court of Cassation?

SQ #3.47   In the orthodox civil law tradition, would it be common to have dissenting opinions issued by judges hearing a case *en banc*?

SQ #3.48   What is the history of the administrative courts found in a typical civil law system, and what is their main purpose?

SQ #3.49   In the French legal system, what is the difference in function between the Council of State and the Court of Cassation?

SQ #3.50   What might be done to deal with a case of apparent overlapping jurisdiction between the administrative courts and the ordinary courts in a civil law system?

SQ #3.51   Why was it considered necessary in such civil law countries as France and Germany to establish separate constitutional courts (or councils) to deal with questions of the constitutionality of legislative action, instead of simply authorizing ordinary courts to deal with such questions?

SQ #3.52   What response has the French legal system given to the need to authorize some entity to review the constitutionality of legislation?

SQ #3.53   What is the composition of the Constitutional Council established in France's 1958 Constitution? Is it primarily a legal entity or primarily a political entity?

SQ #3.54   What is the difference between "incidental" attack and "direct" attack on the constitutionality of legislation?

SQ #3.55   What would be some advantages to having the constitutionality of a law considered before it comes into effect? Why is this form of constitutional review of legislation not permitted in the US legal system?

SQ #3.56   If the Italian constitutional court declares a statutory provision unconstitutional, is that provision struck from (*i.e.*, deleted from) the statute?

SQ #3.57   What role do religion and ideology play in the actual operation of the legal system in civil law countries, and how would you assume that this differs in common law countries and in China? What about Iran?

SQ #3.58   Why is it that so many countries all over the world belong to the civil law family?

SQ #3.59   What are some key criticisms of the civil law tradition?

SQ #3.60   What are some important tendencies you see that could bear on the future of the civil law tradition? What points raised in subsection IIC of Chapter Two are most pertinent in this respect?

Introductory Comments

From the historical account of the civil law tradition offered above in Chapter Two, we turn now to an operational account—highlighting certain aspects of how civil law systems in many nations around the world actually operate. In this chapter, we need to be quite selective, identifying just some of the aspects of civil law systems that seem especially fundamental in character. Consistent with John Henry Merryman's definition of a "legal tradition" (examined above in subsection IA1 of Chapter One), the operational aspects discussed in this chapter reflect deeply rooted, historically conditioned *attitudes* taken in most civil law countries toward the concepts and sources of law—and those attitudes in turn bear directly on the content and operation of the law in those countries.

Among the most prominent themes emphasized in the pages that follow are these three:

- A *primary focus on private law*. We shall see that civil law systems, in general, are "horizontal", not "vertical", in their essential character, in the sense that the rules, both substantive and procedural, place primary importance on the relations between individuals in society. This is especially evident in what we shall come to see as the "orthodox" view (what might sometimes be disparagingly called the "folklore") of the civil law tradition. But in fact even with the growing importance of public law—revolving especially around constitutional law and administrative law, which add a more "vertical" element to a legal system by dealing with relations between the state and the individual—the civil law tradition's primary focus still remains on private law. This feature, which gets reflected in various ways, is a distinguishing mark of the civil law, especially in contrast to the Chinese legal tradition.

- An *incorporation of values emerging from the intellectual and political revolution of roughly three centuries ago* as described briefly in subsection IIB of Chapter Two. Many operational aspects of civil law systems—including even so basic a matter as what the sources of law are in such a system—reflect new ideas coming out of the great intellectual rebirth that found its most radical political manifestation in the French Revolution. The notion of participatory governance—or at least of reasonably competent rationality in governance—comes from that great intellectual rebirth, as do notions of the need for legality in the imposition of punishment, the sanctity of private property, and other aspects of classical liberalism. Several such values find their way into the content and operation of the law in modern civil law countries. Changes in social and intellectual viewpoints did not stop, however, with that revolution, and so the intensity of some such values has been blunted over time. An example is the increasingly strong urge toward social protection, with law being regarded not solely as a safeguard for private interests but also as a means of balancing those private interests with the needs of an increasingly interdependent society whose stability is essential if private interests are in fact to have any practical significance.

- More generally, *a recent urge for reform through cross-fertilization and harmonization*, yielding within the civil law world a very diverse set of experimental efforts to make law more suitable to modern circumstances. The reform efforts are visible in many aspects of how the legal systems actually operate: legal education, structure of the legal profession(s), civil and criminal procedure, and more. In this respect, we shall wish to consider—especially in anticipation of the survey of the common law tradition in Chapters Four and Five—what benefits have come thus far from the apparent willingness to seek legal improvement through borrowing and compromise.

In addition to gaining an appreciation for those three major themes, of course, our work in this chapter will not be done unless we emerge with a general understanding of a great many details as well—details of the sort reflected in the foregoing Study Questions, which are designed to identify some key points to be found in the pages that follow. Some of these details will be actual rules that operate within various civil law systems—on the admissibility of "hearsay" evidence in criminal prosecutions, for example. More of them, however, will be about institutional structures in which those rules operate. As one authority emphasizes, it is those structures, and the overall legal culture from which they have emerged, that are most important:

> [In] our view, ... it is seldom the rules of law that are truly significant or interesting about a foreign legal system; it is the social and intellectual climate, the institutional structures, the roles played by legal professionals, and the procedures characteristic of the legal system that are instructive. Often the rules of law look very much like our own—indeed, this is more and more true among the Western, capitalist nations, whether common law or civil law, that dominate the legal landscape of Europe [and elsewhere]. As with United States law, finding the rule is often less of a problem than knowing what to do with it; it is the difficult business of understanding the legal system, within which the rules exist and operate, that [warrants our greatest attention].[1]

I. Sources of Law and the Role(s) of Lawyers

A. *Sources of Law*

It is a generalization, but a useful generalization, to say that there have long been three primary sources of law in civil law countries—statutes (legislation), regulations, and (awkwardly) custom—and that in more recent decades they have been joined by such other sources as constitutions and international treaties; and that in addition to these there are also certain secondary, or indirect, sources of law, including legal scholarship and caselaw. The following paragraphs describe each of these sources of law and explain why some should be regarded as "primary" and others as "secondary", based partly on historical factors.

1. The Orthodox View

Recall from the historical account in Chapter Two that over the course of two or three hundred years, culminating most formally in 1648 with the Peace of Westphalia, Europe

---

1. John Henry Merryman, David S. Clark, and John Owen Haley, COMPARATIVE LAW: HISTORICAL DEVELOPMENT OF THE CIVIL LAW TRADITION IN EUROPE, LATIN AMERICA, AND EAST ASIA vii (2010) [hereinafter Merryman-2010].

was transformed politically. By the 17th century, the nation-state was the fundamental po-litical unit in Europe. As noted above in subsection IIB1 of Chapter Two, a key legal re-sult emerging from this transformation was that, in Professor John Henry Merryman's words, "[t]he centralized state ... tended to become the unique source of law"[2] This fact—that law-making power was concentrated in the state—is central to an understanding of the sources of law in civil law countries.

Before considering specifically what those sources are, let us explore just what it means to assert that the centralized state tended to become "the unique source" of law. As Mer-ryman explains, this assertion involves several key notions, most notably (1) national-ism, (2) sovereignty, and (3) secularism:

> The polycentric, highly decentralized, inefficient structure of the medieval po-litical world fell before the need for a more efficient, centralized governmental system—the modern nation-state. Both to bring about this kind of transfor-mation and to consolidate the accomplishments of the [intellectual and politi-cal] revolution [that flourished in the seventeenth and eighteenth centuries], an ideology was needed....[3]

The ideology that met this need was nationalism—that is, the ideology that empha-sized the power and status of the nation-state as a corporate entity (a "legal person") that was vested with a range of legal capacities; and these capacities were packaged in the concept of sovereignty.[4] As Merryman explains, the concept of sovereignty, which had existed for several centuries, was developed through the work of various legal schol-ars, including in particular Jean Bodin, Hugo Grotius, and Thomas Hobbes.[5] Their writ-ings emphasized the supremacy of the state as an entity largely free from external restraint. As a legal matter, a key notion emerging from their work (and the work of others) was that of "state positivism", under which only the state—as opposed to any other internal or external entities—has authority to posit the legal rules that are binding within the state.[6]

In addition to the concepts of nationalism and sovereignty, another concept—secu-larism—also figures into the picture of the political transformation that gripped Euro-pean by around the 17th century.

> [T]he idea that law was of divine origin—whether expressed directly, as in di-vine (i.e., scriptural) law, or expressed indirectly through the nature of human beings as created by God, as in Roman Catholic natural law—now lost most of its remaining vitality. Formal respect might still be paid to the deity in the law-making process..., but power lay in the state.... The perennial controversy be-tween natural lawyers and legal positivists ... thus was decisively resolved, for operational purposes at least, in favor of the positivists.[7]

---

2. John Henry Merryman and Rogelio Pérez-Perdomo, THE CIVIL LAW TRADITION 20 (3rd ed. 2007).

3. *Id.* at 20.

4. *Id.* As Merryman expresses it, "nationalism [became] the prevailing ideology, [and] sovereignty was the basic premise of its legal expression". *Id.*

5. *Id.* For a brief survey of the concept of sovereignty, emphasizing important alterations it un-derwent through the writings of those three theorists in particular, see John W. Head, *Supranational Law: How the Move Toward Multilateral Solutions Is Changing the Character of "International" Law,* 16 KANSAS LAW REVIEW 605, 612–614 (1993).

6. Merryman, *supra* note 2, at 20–23.

7. *Id.* at 20–21.

The result of this process is that all Western states became positivisitic and secular — in terms, that is, of the sources of their laws. What counted as law turned entirely on the will of the sovereign, whether that sovereign took the form of a prince or king or instead took the form of a legislative body chosen by some or all of the state's people. That will of the sovereign was expressed mainly through legislation, which was regarded as being subject to no external or internal authority — that is, no source that had any authority to "trump" or override the laws issued by the sovereign. If the sovereign willed it, of course, law could come from other sources, such as the *jus commune* or established custom; but those sources had no authority on their own. In short, lawmaking was concentrated in the nation-state. As Merryman summarizes it, "state positivism, as expressed in the dogma of the absolute external and internal sovereignty of the state, led to a state monopoly on lawmaking".[8]

This notion that there is a "state monopoly on lawmaking" was accompanied by another doctrine that bears on the sources of law, which is the direct object of our attention here. That doctrine relates to the separation of powers. As it developed in Europe, the separation of powers doctrine drew a bright distinction between the legislative powers of the government and the judicial powers of the government — and insisted that these two types of powers must be sharply separated from each other in order to prevent abuse. Hence, according to this view, only certain specifically designated organs of the state are entitled to make law. Merryman explains the point in this way:

> The legislative power is by definition the lawmaking power, and hence only the legislature could make law. As the only representative, directly elected branch of the government, the legislature alone could respond to the popular will.... [One clear implication of this view is that judicial decisions are *not* law, because] the familiar common law doctrine of *stare decisis* — i.e., the power and obligation of courts to base decisions on prior decisions — is obviously inconsistent with the separation of power as formulated in civil law countries and is therefore rejected by the civil law tradition.

> What, then, was law? The basic answer, which is the essence of legislative positivism, is that only statutes enacted by the legislative power could be law.... [Indeed,] in the nineteenth century law became synonymous with legislation.[9] The legislature could delegate some of that power to the executive, and it could give administrative agencies the power to issue regulations having the force of law, but such "delegated legislation" was in theory effective only within the limits provided in the delegating legislation. The legislative power was supreme.[10]

In addition to these two sources — legislation and regulations — there is a third primary source of law in the civil law world: custom. However, it is the subject of a sort of love-hate relationship:

---

8. *Id.* at 23.

9. Indeed, the term "law" is still synonymous with the term "legislation" in some civil law countries, as I discovered while working with a lawyer in the Ministry of Justice of Namibia shortly after that country gained independence from the Republic of South Africa around 1990. In drafting a new central banking statute, he and I had several confused discussions until we both realized that my use of the term "law" encompassed legislation (enacted by the parliament), regulations promulgated by agencies subsidiary to either legislative or executive authorities, and to some extent the body of caselaw built up through consistent judicial decisions — whereas his use of the term "law" was confined to only the first of these — legislation enacted by the parliament — because he was a lawyer trained and operating in the Dutch-Roman civil law tradition of South Africa.

10. Merryman, *supra* note 2, at 23–24.

Where a person acts in accordance with custom under the assumption that it represents the law, that action will be accepted as legal in many civil law jurisdictions, so long as there is no applicable statute or regulation to the contrary. The amount of writing on custom as law in civil law jurisdictions is immense, far out of proportion to its actual importance as law. The main reason for so much writing ... is the need to justify treating as law something that is not created by the legislative power of the state. To give custom the force of law would appear to violate the dogma of state positivism (only the state can make law) and the dogma of sharp separation of powers (within the state only the legislature can make law)....[11]

This sense of unease regarding the binding character of custom, and therefore regarding its inclusion in the list of sources of law, appears also in this account:

In the civil law theory of sources of law, custom is regularly listed as a primary source, but routinely dismissed as of slight practical importance, except in Spain and some of the other Spanish-speaking countries. In certain provinces of Spain, notably Catalonia, the national Civil Code does not apply to matters covered by local customary law (*fueros*). In other civil law countries, where custom is less important but still considered to have binding force, there is an apparent difference between [i] [some] systems, such as the German, which permit custom in certain cases to prevail over written law, and [ii] those [other] systems which, like the French, permit custom to supplement, but not to abrogate, the written law.... As might be expected, custom (in the form of trade usage) plays a greater role in commercial and labor law than it does in civil law generally.[12]

Stripped to its essentials, the foregoing account can be summarized as follows: civil law countries typically recognize only statutes, regulations, and custom as sources of law, and this list is arranged in descending order of importance: a statute will "trump" (that is, prevail over) a regulation that is inconsistent with it, and a custom will be "trumped" by either a statute or a regulation.[13] Box #3.1 aims to reflect this list.

Box #3.1 *Orthodox View of the Sources of Law in the Civil Law Tradition*

statutes	– rules enacted by the single legislative authority in the legal system, or
	– rules promulgated by an executive deriving authority from the legislature
regulations	– rules issued by an administrative agency deriving authority from the legislature
custom	– norms that, if relied on by persons thinking they are legally binding, are accepted as such so long as there is no applicable statute or regulation to the contrary

---

11. *Id.* at 24.

12. Mary Ann Glendon, Paolo G. Carozza, and Colin B. Picker, COMPARATIVE LEGAL TRADITIONS IN A NUTSHELL 131 (2008) [hereinafter Nutshell-2008]. This authority's use of the term "primary source" is explained below.

13. See Merryman, *supra* note 2, at 24. Another source explains that the hierarchy of "enacted law" (encompassing both statutes and regulations) calls for legislation to prevail over executive decrees pursuant to delegated legislative power, which will prevail over administrative regulations, which will prevail over local ordinances. Nutshell-2008, *supra* note 12, at 128. The same source suggests (but then throws question on the proposition) that some civil law scholars assert that "general principles" also constitute a primary source of law. *Id.* at 132.

2. The Modern View

Why have I used the term "orthodox view" in the heading to Box #3.1? Because over time, all civil law countries have in fact departed from this rather narrow view of the sources of law in a national legal system. The dogmatic conceptions of state positivism and separation of powers that gave rise to this three-item list of sources — statutes, regulations, custom — have softened and eroded over time, especially in the more highly developed civil law countries (including all those of Western Europe, where the dogmatic conceptions first emerged with such intensity). As a result, teachers and students and practitioners all over the civil law world, while recognizing the "orthodox view" as having enormous importance from a historical perspective — and while still regarding legislation as the principal and paradigm form of law — would in fact include several other items if asked to compile a list of the sources of law in their national legal systems.

Specifically, most such lawyers would regard Box #3.2 as a more accurate list of the sources of law in civil law countries.

Box #3.2 Modern View of the Sources and Authorities of Law in the Civil Law Tradition

constitution	–	fundamental substantive and structural rules which cannot be changed or overridden by regular legislative action, and with which all other rules in the legal system must be consistent
statutes	–	rules enacted by the single legislative authority in the legal system, or
	–	rules promulgated by an executive deriving authority from the legislature
regulations	–	rules issued by an administrative agency deriving authority from the legislature
custom	–	norms that, if relied on by persons thinking they are legally binding, are accepted as such so long as there is no applicable statute or regulation to the contrary
initiative & referendum	–	rules that emerge from direct lawmaking action by the people
international law	–	rules that originate outside the nation-state, as those adopted by inter-governmental organizations to which the state has transferred some degree of sovereignty, and to which nationally-promulgated rules must comply
caselaw	–	the interpretations of the rules listed above, as provided by courts in applying and sometimes expanding on those rules in the context of specific legal disputes
legal scholarship	–	the corpus of principles and doctrines underlying and explaining the rules listed above; and the process by which such principles and doctrines are developed and incorporated into the legal system

---

Two points about the list in Box #3.2 warrant close attention. First, this second list of sources of law — reflecting the "modern view" — is much longer than the first list reflecting the "orthodox" view. Second, the list includes "authorities" as well as "sources", as the title to Box #3.2 indicates.

As for the first of these points: the "modern" list is much longer because, as Merryman expresses it, "[the] dogmatic conception of what law is, like many other implications of the dogmas of the revolutionary period, has been eroded by time and events."[14] Here is what Merryman says about two specific items that have been added to the list of sources of law: constitutions and initiative and referendum:

> Perhaps the most spectacular innovation has been the strong movement toward constitutionalism, with its emphasis on the functional rigidity, and hence the superiority as a source of law, of written constitutions. Such constitutions, by eliminating the power of the legislature to amend by ordinary legislative action, impair the legislature's monopoly on lawmaking. They insert a new element into the hierarchy of sources of law, which now must read "constitution, legislation, regulations, and custom." In addition, if a court can decide that a statute is void because it is in conflict with the constitution, the dogma of sharp separation of legislative power from judicial power is impaired. The power of judicial review of the constitutionality of legislative action [therefore provides a second reason for placing "constitution" at the top of the list of sources of law in civil law countries.] ...
>
> Another complicating factor is the inclusion of the initiative and the referendum in the constitutions of some civil law countries; this necessarily involves the transfer of some lawmaking power from the legislature to the people, and further weakens the position of the legislature as the sole source of law.[15]

The inclusion of "international law" in the list of sources reflects the modern approach in many legal systems whose constitutions prescribe that (i) treaties to which the country is a party and (ii) customary international law and sometimes (iii) acts of supranational organizations (such as the European Union) to which the country belongs shall have binding effect within the national legal system.

As for the second point: Some accounts of this subject distinguish between "primary sources" and "secondary sources"—often using the term "authorities" for the latter of these. Here is one such account:

> Civil law theorists [often] make a fundamental distinction between primary sources of law, which can give rise directly to binding legal norms, and secondary sources, sometimes called *authorities*. The primary sources in all civil law systems are enacted law and custom, with the former overwhelmingly more important.... Authorities may have weight when primary sources are absent, unclear or incomplete, but they are never binding, and they are neither necessary nor sufficient as the basis for a judicial decision. Case law and the writings of legal scholars are such secondary sources....[16]

This distinction between "direct sources" and "authorities" can also be expressed in other ways, such as by using the distinction "direct/indirect" or the distinction "formal/informal". The list of sources shown in Box #3.2 reflects this distinction (however it is expressed) by including a line below "international law" and above "caselaw". Whereas the first six items on that list—that is, constitution, statutes, regulations, custom, initiative and referendum, and international law—would commonly be regarded as "direct" sources of law, the last two items on the list would be regarded as "authorities" or "indirect" sources of law. Let us consider them in turn, beginning with "caselaw".

---

14. Merryman, *supra* note 2, at 25.
15. *Id.*
16. Nutshell-2008, *supra* note 12, at 127.

3. The Significance of Caselaw

Even the term "caselaw" would be offensive to the orthodox view. As noted above, the strict separation of powers between legislative authorities and judicial authorities—a separation inspired most dramatically in the French context because of the perceived illegitimate concentration of power in the hands of the judges in pre-Revolutionary France (discussed above in subsection IIB2 of Chapter Two[17])—led to the "orthodox view" that judicial decisions simply could not constitute rules of law. As one source has expressed it, "[t]he notion goes back to Justinian that only the sovereign can make a generally applicable rule. In modern nation states, that notion developed into the idea that only a representative legislature should be able to 'make' law."[18]

Times have changed. Today in most civil law countries, judicial decisions are in fact relied on widely by lawyers and courts (and publically reported in a manner that facilitates such reliance), so that "caselaw" (in French *jurisprudence*, in German *Rechtsprechung*) plays a functional role similar to the role it plays in common law countries such as England or the USA—where, as we shall see, judicial decisions have always been regarded as a primary source of law. Hence we can draw a distinction between the civil law from an *operational* perspective and from a *theoretical* perspective. Although the orthodox view is that no court is actually bound by the decision of any other court—and hence judicial decisions cannot be regarded as a "direct" source of law—"caselaw" surely constitutes an indirect, or subsidiary source. Merryman expresses the point in this manner:

> ... Although there is no formal rule of *stare decisis*, the practice is for judges to be influenced by prior decisions. Judicial decisions are regularly published in most civil law jurisdictions. A lawyer preparing a case searches for cases in point and uses them in argument; and the judge deciding a case often refers to prior cases. Whatever the ideology of the revolution may say about the value of precedent, the fact is that courts do not act very differently toward reported decisions in civil law jurisdictions than do courts in the United States.... [Therefore,] [t]hose who contrast the civil law and the common law traditions by a supposed nonuse of judicial authority in the former and a binding doctrine of precedent in the latter exaggerate on both sides. Everybody knows that civil law courts do use precedents. Everybody knows that common law courts distinguish cases they do not want to follow, and sometimes overrule their own decisions.... [Hence the] important distinction between the civil law and the common law judicial processes does not lie in what courts in fact do, but in what the dominant folklore tells them they do. In the orthodox civil law tradition, the judge is assigned a comparatively minor, inglorious role as a mere operator of a machine designed and built by scholars and legislators.[19]

The closing comment in the passage quoted above—on the "minor, inglorious role" assigned to judges in civil law countries—is a matter we shall explore below, especially in subsection IC of this chapter. For our present purposes, the comment is important because it explains in part why "caselaw" appears below the line in Box #3.2—that is, as an indirect rather than a direct source of law in the civil law tradition.

---

17. See in particular the text accompanying notes 166–168 in Chapter Two.

18. Nutshell-2008, *supra* note 12, at 132.

19. Merryman, *supra* note 2, at 47. For further elaboration of the role that caselaw plays in civil law countries, see Nutshell-2008, *supra* note 12, at 132–136.

4. The Significance of Legal Scholarship (Doctrine)

Also appearing below the line, and therefore as an "indirect" source of law, is "legal scholarship", defined in Box #3.2 as "the corpus of principles and doctrines underlying and explaining the rules listed above; and the process by which such principles and doctrines are developed and incorporated into the legal system". Let us close our survey of sources and authorities of law in the civil law world by considering the significance given there to "legal scholarship"—also called "doctrine" (in French *la doctrine*, in German *die Rechtslehre*).

Again, Merryman offers a lively explanation. He begins by referring to "the great river of legal scholarship in the civil law tradition..., [which provides] the ideology and the basic content of legislation."[20] He then elaborates by describing a typical book on legal history in a continental European system. Such a book, he says, focuses not on changes in legislation or court structures over time but instead on schools of legal thought and disputes between legal scholars—for example, the roles of the Glossators and Commentators, or of the debates underlying German codification. In sum, he says, it amounts to intellectual history in which the protagonist is the legal scholar.

> This is what we mean when we say that legal scholars are the dominant actors of the civil law. Legislators, executives, administrators, judges, and lawyers all come under the scholars' influence. Scholars mold the civil law tradition and the formal materials of the law into a model of the legal system. They teach this model to law students and write about it in books and articles. Legislators and judges accept their ideas of what law is, and, when legislators and judges make or apply law, they use concepts the scholars have developed. Thus, although legal scholarship is not a formal source of law, the doctrine carries immense authority.
>
> In the United States, where the legislature is also theoretically supreme, there is a well-known saying (originated by a judge) that the law is what the judges say it is. This is, properly understood, a realistic statement of fact.... In a similar sense it is reasonably accurate to say that the law in a civil law jurisdiction is what the scholars say it is.[21]

In sum, legal scholarship serves as an indirect source of law in civil law countries. It has its greatest influence "when the law is unsettled or when there is no established law on a point".[22] Moreover, the "weight attached by judges to doctrinal writing varies according to a number of circumstances, including [especially] the reputation of the author".[23]

B. Classifications, Codification, and Certainty

From the subject of sources of law, we move now to three other fundamental aspects of the civil law tradition viewed from an operational perspective. The first is the classification of law into specific categories (most prominently private law and public law). The second is the civil law's remarkable record of codification and what significance that holds

---

20. Merryman, *supra note 2, at 59*.
21. Merryman, *supra* note 2, at 59–60. We shall examine below in Chapters Four and Five what it means to say that the law in a common law system is "what the judges say it is".
22. Nutshell-2008, *supra* note 12, at 137.
23. *Id.*

in practical terms. The third, closely related to the first two, is the concept of certainty, which can be seen in several practical ways to have higher value placed on it in the civil law tradition than in the common law tradition.

1. Private Law and Public Law

One way of viewing several of the developments highlighted in the historical survey offered above in Chapter Two is that they represented an effort to gain *control* over the law. Recall, for example, the various codification efforts in Roman law, culminating most gloriously under Justinian but actually beginning a couple of centuries earlier. Those efforts might, I believe, be regarded as efforts to gain control over a chaotic corpus of rules—of various origins, some effective, some superseded, many inconsistent. Likewise, the work of the Glossators and Commentators, struggling to find (or perhaps impose) internal consistency over the *Digest* and then to apply it in contemporary circumstances, may be seen as efforts at control over law in times of political uncertainty that ultimately resulted in the nation-state prevailing over the Church. Later, the enthusiasm of the Humanists and the Naturalists in the 16th to 18th centuries to find the pre-Justinian, pre-Christian essence of Roman law and use it to build a secular, rational, natural-law based law[24] also can be seen as a form of exercising control of law. And similarly, the revolutionary fervor of the French in the late 18th century fueled a radical reformulation of the law of that country—again in part to gain control over a scattered assemblage of rules and procedures rooted in medieval customs and manipulated by powerful local elites.

We turn now to a matter—the classification of law into major categories—that I believe also reflects a fundamental urge at work in the civil law world to exercise *control* over the law. Perhaps it is this urge that Merryman is describing when he explains that the division of the law into categories in the civil law tradition goes beyond mere convenience or descriptiveness and assumes a sort of dogmatic and prescriptive nature.

> One of the most characteristic aspects of the traditional civil law way of dividing law is the measurably greater degree of emphasis on, and confidence in, the validity and utility of formal definitions and distinctions. While common lawyers tend to think of the division of the law as ... the product of some mixture of history, convenience, and habit, the influence of scholars [in civil law countries] ... has led civil [law] lawyers to treat the matter of division of the law in more normative terms. [As various legal scholars have developed highly refined] definitions and categories [they] are incorporated into the systematic reconstruction of the law ... [and] become part of the systemic legal structure that is employed by legal scholars, is taught to law students, and is thereby built into the law.[25]

The reason for dwelling on this matter, which can seem overly theoretical, is precisely because it is *not* merely theoretical. Because of the enormous influence that legal scholars exert over the legal system in civil law countries—much more influence, as we shall see below in subsection IC of this chapter, than legal scholars exert in common law sys-

---

24. As described above in subsection IIB1 of Chapter Two, the Humanists of the 16th and 17th centuries sought to cleanse the Roman law of the influence of Tribonian, the Glossators, and the Commentators; and then the Natural Law scholars proceeded to challenge the very authority of Roman law, finding it acceptable only if and to the extent that it was rational and consistent with their view of a universal law of nature.

25. Merryman, *supra* note 2, at 91.

tems—the way those scholars classify the law into various legal categories has left a permanent mark on the civil law.

Specifically, that permanent mark is a fundamental distinction between private law and public law. To most lawyers and law students in common law countries, this private/public distinction is entirely foreign, not fundamental—opaque, not obvious—and yet it is probably safe to say that every lawyer and every law student in every civil law country conceives of the law in terms of that private/public distinction; and many of them would defend the validity and importance of the distinction against all critics.

Hence, it is not just the distinction itself, which we shall explore just below, but also the *stature* of the distinction in the civil law world that lawyers coming from outside that world should understand. As one authority says, the "fundamental distinction … made in all civil law systems between public and private law…, which is only latent or implicit in the common law, is basic to an understanding of the civil law."[26] Moreover, the seemingly fundamental character of the private/public distinction is central to legal education in the civil law world. "Treatises, monographs, and student manuals all contain discussions of the dichotomy…. European or Latin American law students, who encounter this sweeping division at the outset of their careers, tend uncritically to absorb it".[27]

The private/public distinction classifies civil law and commercial law as private law and classifies constitutional, administrative, and criminal law as public law. The classification can be expressed simply as in Box #3.3.

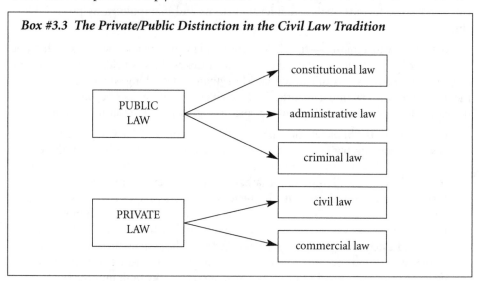

Box #3.3 The Private/Public Distinction in the Civil Law Tradition

The terms appearing on the right-hand side of Box #3.3 are familiar ones, and most of them carry no special meaning needing explanation. However, it might be useful to link each term to its historical roots, which have for the most part been noted at least briefly above in Chapter Two.

---

26. Nutshell-2008, *supra* note 12, at 108. See also Merryman, *supra* note 2, at 92 (noting that the private/public distinction strikes the typical civil law lawyer as "fundamental, necessary, and, on the whole, evident").

27. Merryman, *supra* note 2, at 92.

- *Constitutional law.* Rules, principles, and procedures found in, and applicable to, the country's constitution (usually written, although sometimes in more than one instrument) and prescribing (often among other things) how the government's structure is constituted. As explained above in subsection IA of this chapter, the introduction of such constitutions has been relatively recent in many civil law countries, and their precise status as sources of law can vary from one country to another.[28] (For a reference to constitutional courts, see subsection IIC, below.)

- *Administrative law.* Rules, principles, and procedures governing the authority and conduct of the public administration (coincident in many systems with the executive branch of government) and its relations with private individuals. With the rise of what has been called the "administrative state" in many advanced countries in recent decades, this category of law has substantially expanded in reach and volume. (For a reference to administrative courts, see subsection IIC2, below.)

- *Criminal law.* Rules, principles, and procedures relating to behavior (of persons or entities) that has been identified as so socially unacceptable or dangerous to as warrant collective response through public investigation and sanction, including restrictions on liberty and even corporal punishment. (As noted below in subsection IIC, criminal law is a subject falling within public law but falling within the jurisdiction of the ordinary courts.)

- *Civil law.* Rules, principles, and procedures relating primarily to the "horizontal" relations between members of the society and therefore including such matters as property rights, succession (disposition of property upon death), domestic relations (family law and marital property law), contracts, claims for injury outside the context of contractual relations, and the like. This category of law lies at the heart of the civil law tradition, going back to the Twelve Tables; and it was this category of law that occupied most of the attention of the Glossators following the rediscovery of Justinian's *Digest* in the late 11th century.

- *Commercial law.* Rules, principles, and procedures regarding the conduct of merchants and the settlement of disputes between them (and with their customers). Having developed for centuries separate and apart from Roman civil law, and gaining sophistication following the reawakening of commercial activity in Europe with the Crusades, commercial law eventually was merged into national legal systems in civil law countries, although some of those countries retained separate commercial courts. "Commercial law generally includes [rules governing] corporations and other business associations, securities, banking, and negotiable instruments."[29]

2. The Role of Codes and Codification

There is an obvious link between the topic discussed immediately above — classification of law (and particularly the private/public distinction) — and the topic of codes and codification: codes in most civil law countries reflect quite directly the system of classi-

---

28. One authority points out that in some civil law countries and scholarship, "[c]onstitutional law, as it pertains to the form and structure of the state and its organs, is still thought of as being akin to political science" and that therefore the category of public law is occupied mostly by administrative law. Nutshell-2008, *supra* note 12, at 112.

29. *Id.* at 122. That same authority notes that the inclusion of, and expansion of, some of these topics tends to place commercial law, by some accounts, on the border between public law and private law. *Id.*

fication described above. Specifically, a great majority of civil law countries have five codes—one each for civil law, civil procedure, criminal law, criminal procedure, and commercial law[30]—and many civil law countries also now have an administrative code[31] and a singular written constitution. Not surprisingly, this congruence between the subject-matter of the codes and the general classification of law and tends to reinforce the importance of the latter.

But there is more. That is, codification plays an especially—we might say peculiarly—large role in civil law countries, just as the private/public distinction does; and it is a role that extends beyond mere convenience, perhaps even to become a matter of ideology. Legal codification in the civil law world reflects such factors as (i) the historical importance placed on the Twelve Tables and Justinian's compilation, (ii) the role of scholars laboriously classifying and systematizing the law, (iii) the desire for rationality, coming out of the "revolution", (iv) the desire for certainty (see subsection IB3 of this chapter, below), and (v) the primacy of the legislature. Perhaps these various ingredients reflect (or maybe they have created) an "ideology" of codification that rests on the assumption (one might say "myth") that a code can in fact be clear, comprehensive, and consistent. Again, we might perceive in such an ideology, which I wish to explain further below, a desire or need or even fetish for *control* over the law.

What, specifically, are we talking about in using the terms "code" and "codification"? There can be no doubt that those terms carry different significance in the civil law than they do in the common law. Moreover, we shall see below in Chapters Six and Seven that the terms "code" and "codification" carry yet a different significance in the Chinese context. A starting-point in our consideration of what role "codes" and "codification" play in the civil law world would be to dispel the impression that civil law systems are codified and common law systems are uncodified. As Merryman points out, there "is probably at least as much legislation in force in a typical American state as there is in a typical European or Latin American nation"; and indeed, much of the American legislation takes the form of something commonly called a code, so that "California has more codes than many civil law nations, [even though] California is not a civil law jurisdiction".[32] Conversely, some civil law countries, such as South Africa, have legal systems that are predominantly uncodified[33]—so the *absence* of a codified system does not somehow bar a country from being part of the civil law family.

Taking these facts into account, Merryman asserts that what is of key importance about codes and codification in the civil law world is a matter of ideology.

> [One needs to think] of codification not as a form but as the expression of an ideology.... [If we do this, we can see that] although [codes in common law countries might] look like the codes in civil law countries, the underlying ideology—the conception of what a code is and of the functions it should perform

---

30. Some civil law systems do not have separate commercial codes but instead include commercial law matters within the civil code. As explained below, Italy provides an illustration of this approach.

31. For two illustrations of sophisticated administrative codes, see the *Code Administratif* of Luxembourg, at http://www.legilux.public.lu/leg/textescoordonnes/compilation/index.html, and the *Codice Ammistrativo* of Italy. Explanatory annotations of the latter include Francesco Bartolini, IL CODICE AMMINISTRATIVO (16th ed. 2010); Francesco Caringella & Roberto Garofoli, CODICE AMMINISTRATIVO: ANNOTATO CON LA GIURISPRUDENZA (4th ed. 2008).

32. Merryman, *supra* note 2, at 27.

33. *Id.*

in the legal process—is not the same. *There is an entirely different ideology of codification at work in the civil law world.*[34]

As we saw above in Chapter Two, two of the most ambitious and most influential codification exercises in the history of the civil law were those carried out at the direction of Justinian and Napoleon. Supporting Merryman's thesis that there is "an entirely different ideology of codification at work in the civil law world" is the fact that both of those lawgivers conceived of their codification efforts as a means of abolishing all prior law. Justinian went so far as to order a burning of some of the old texts on which Tribonian and his commission had relied in compiling the *Digest,* and to prohibit any citations to the old laws.[35] In the case of the Napoleonic Code, all previous law was formally rescinded in the legislative enactment adopting the new code,[36] and Napoleon himself (like Justinian) viewed his Civil Code as obviating any reference to prior law, or indeed any further elaboration or commentary.[37]

Why would Justinian and Napoleon view their codes in this way—that is, not needing any commentary and being in a sense "beyond history"? We can speculate (as Merryman does) that those two lawgivers saw their work as having achieved *perfection,* or at least as close an approximation to perfection as was humanly possible, so that no improvement was possible. And this (perceived) perfection, we can further speculate, had three ingredients: clarity, and comprehensiveness, and consistency. That is, both Justinian's compilation (especially the *Digest*) and Napoleon's civil code were perhaps viewed by their creators as (1) perfectly clear, in the sense of avoiding any and all obscurity or vagueness in the terms used or the rules presented, (2) perfectly comprehensive, in the sense of completely covering all topics and issues within their intentionally broad scope of coverage, and (3) perfectly consistent internally, so that no conflicts could arise in applying more than one provision to a single factual situation.

This sense of "3-C perfection" (clarity, comprehensiveness, consistency) might be viewed as the core of an "ideology of codification" at work in the civil law world. Reality, of course, is different: all thoughtful people (especially writers, teachers, students, and lawyers) know that perfection in written expression is impossible to achieve, and perhaps even to conceive. Yet reality often does not (and need not) interfere with an ideology—or, as we may wish instead to characterize it, with a myth—that provides strong bonds of cohesion within a group.

In presenting this view of an "ideology of codification", I have reflected Merryman's views. An alternative way of looking at codes and codification in the civil law tradition is sum-

---

34. *Id.* at 28 (emphasis added).

35. Merryman explains that upon the publication of Justinian's great compilation, he forbade any further reference to the works of jurisconsults relied on in the work, he also forbade the preparation of any commentaries on it, and he ordered some of the old manuscripts (from classical Roman times) to be burned. An illustration of how effective Justinian's efforts were in this regard can be seen in the fact that the deeply influential *Institutes* of Gaius was lost for many centuries; only in the early 1800s was a copy of it found in Verona. See the biographical sketch of Gaius appearing in Appendix 2.1, at the end of Chapter Two.

36. As noted above in Chapter Two, the enacting legislation of 21 March 1804 stated that upon its effectiveness, "the Roman laws, the ordinances, the general and local customs, the charters and the regulations all cease to have the force either of general or of special law concerning the subjects covered by the present code." See *supra* Chapter Two, text accompanying note 178.

37. Merryman explains that Napoleon hoped (in vain, as it happened) that no commentaries on his civil code would be published. In fact, he was so intent on this point that, according to one account, "his reaction when he was informed that the first commentary had been published was to exclaim: 'My code is lost.'" Merryman, *supra* note 2, at 59.

marized in Box #3.4. That alternative view suggests that the incidence and significance of codification in the civil law world results not from an ideology or myth but from a particular confluence of more down-to-earth historical and political conditions and factors. The thoughts expressed in Box #3.4 apply not just to the civil law tradition but to any legal tradition; and we shall consider these points further when we focus our attention later on the common law and Chinese law.[38]

Box #3.4 Conditions and Factors for Codification

In all three of the great legal traditions — civil law, common law, and Chinese law — codification has played a role. In the first and third, the issuance of codes has been a central feature. In the common law tradition, codification has played a much smaller role. Why? Merryman refers (in speaking of the civil law tradition) about an "ideology of codification". An alternative explanation or characterization would come from regarding the promulgation of codes in a legal system as resulting from a convergence of certain conditions and factors of a political, legal, and cultural nature. These conditions and factors are listed below.

Definition of Codification

simple: the enactment of a new legal code

detailed: the process by which the top authority in a political unit puts into effect for the legal system of that political unit a single, newly-conceived code of rules intended to cover all or most aspects of a major area of law within that legal system, such as civil law, commercial law, or procedural law. "Codification" *excludes* a revision of an existing code of laws currently in force, unless the revision radically changes either the structure or content of that code.

Necessary Conditions for Codification

For codification to occur, the following three conditions must exist in the legal system.

(1) *Written law is generally regarded favorably as a means of ordering society* — that is, most persons having power and influence within the political unit find it appealing, or at least acceptable, that rules of behavior take the form of official law and that they be written. [We might call this the "regard-for-written-law" condition]

(2) *The top political authority is strong enough to impose a code* — that is, the lawmaking power within the political unit is not so divided among competing players as to make it impossible to promulgate laws applicable to the entire political unit. [We might call this the "power concentration" condition]

(3) *The top political authority wants to impose a code* — that is, there is a person or a set of persons at the top of the political unit's power structure who wants to promulgate a code, or who wants to lead a movement to do so. [We might call this the "champion-of-codification" condition]

Factors Favoring Codification

Assuming the three necessary conditions for codification (as described above) are present, the following factors augur in favor of codification. Not all factors need to be present, but as more of them become present, codification becomes more likely — subject to the factors disfavoring codification as described further below.

(1) The existing law is *chaotic* or difficult to ascertain — for example, located in multiple sources, partially or largely unwritten, internally inconsistent, or tangled in its structure. [We might call this the "legal chaos" factor]

---

38. See, for example, Appendix 4.18, showing excerpts of a law journal article applying these "conditions and factors for codification" to three specific codification efforts in American legal history.

(2) The existing law is **behind the times** generally—for example, substantially out of step with the social status of one or more segments of the population, or silent on matters now important because of technological or economic advances. [We might call this the "behind-the-times" factor]

(3) The existing law is inconsistent with **radical political changes** that have just occurred—for example, change in the form of government, overthrow of a monarchy, dissolution or merger of political units, or independence of a former colony. [We might call this the "radical political change" factor]

(4) a **"model" code** from an earlier time is available and culturally relevant—either directly (for example, the country is located in a part of Europe heavily influenced by Roman law before its fall) or indirectly (for example, the country was colonized by such a European country). [We might call this the "model code" factor]

(5) **Scholars** have a dominant role in the legal system—more than practicing attorneys, judges, or perhaps even legislators; for example, scholars are usually called on to design and draft laws. [We might call this the "scholar/jurist influence" factor]

Factors Disfavoring Codification

Even if the two necessary conditions for codification are present, together with several of the five factors favoring codification (as described above), the legal environment might be too hostile for codification to occur, because one or both of the following two factors are especially strong in the legal system. One factor can be considered in spatial terms and the other in temporal terms.

(1) **Inertia.** In the physical world, a body at rest tends to remain at rest. Likewise in the world of law, an uncodified legal system (or area of law within it) tends to remain uncodified. Codification uses up many resources, and it causes disruption and short-term uncertainty. Moreover, the greater the change represented by a proposed codification, the greater the cost, disruption, and uncertainty—just as in the physical world it takes more effort to move a boulder a long distance than to move it a short distance. Hence codification will usually be resisted by many segments in the political unit unless it is considered absolutely necessary to replace the "devil we know" with a new code. [We might refer to this as the "inertia" factor]

(2) **Rootedness.** A legal system, like a tree, becomes more rooted over time, and its replacement becomes more drastic and difficult as those roots grow. This fact augurs against codification. Hence, even if the "radical political change" factor favoring codification is present, (as, for example, in the case of decolonization or political revolution), the passage of time will reduce the likelihood that codification will occur in order to replace an "inherited" legal system. [We might refer to this as the "rootedness" factor]

To summarize thus far about codes and codification: For several reasons, civil law countries generally share a deep-seated view that the law can and should find its highest expression in codified legislation. Lawyers in those countries find compelling precedent in the civil law codifications of the past (not only those of Justinian and Napoleon mentioned above but also those of the Germans and others), and they are accustomed to working with codes in all or most of the areas of private law—civil law, civil procedure, criminal law, criminal procedure, and commercial law.

Before completing this sketch of codes and codification in the civil law tradition, let us consider briefly how the picture is changing. We saw in the closing pages of Chapter Two, under the heading of "Modern Civil Law in Mass Society" that major developments of a political, demographic social, and ideological character have recently altered the trajectory of the civil law tradition—perhaps moving it toward some form of "new *jus commune*", perhaps not. At a lower plane, some of those developments are also bringing changes to codes and codification in many civil law countries, including those of Europe where the civil law tradition was born.

Merryman discusses several of these changes under the label of "decodification". He identifies four key elements of this decodification: (a) the rise of special legislation, including "micro-systems" of legislation, (b) the growing importance of judge-made law, (c) the increasing use of executive decrees, as a manifestation of the decline in legislative supremacy, and (d) the expansion of public administrations. Merryman's views may be summarized as follows:[39]

- *Special legislation* has grown up around the main codes (especially the civil code) to regulate topics not covered in those codes. Much of this legislation takes the form of "microsystems of law" that differ ideologically from the relevant code(s) and are thus incompatible with them. An example appears in the area of labor law, which a typical civil code would treat as merely one variety of contract between individuals; large systems of labor law (sometimes themselves codified into a labor law code) give labor law an entirely different treatment, so much so that in some countries the traditional civil code provision that "the contract is law for the parties" has been effectively reversed so that "the law is the contract of the parties".[40] Where conflicts arise, cases are often decided according to the provisions of the special legislation, not the civil code provisions. Obviously, this runs counter to the notion of certainty, and to the values placed on clarity and consistency referred to above.

- *Judge-made law*, offensive as that term itself might be to the orthodox civil law view of legislative supremacy, is growing steadily in importance. A prime example here is in the area of tort law, which at least the French-style codes give only rudimentary and simplistic attention. The pertinent provision in the French Civil Code, for example, states merely that "*[t]out fait quelconque de l'homme, qui cause à autrui un dommage, oblige celui par la faute duquel il est arrivé à le réparer*" — or as translated rather literally into English, that "[a]ny act whatever by a man, which causes damage to another, obliges the one by whose fault it occurred to compensate for it."[41] Judges have had to create from this broad norm a body of tort law that can be used in actual practice; and they have done so through widely published, consulted, and cited decisions. This development, like "special legislation" described above, runs counter to important values of the civil law tradition.

- *Executive decrees*, although accepted as a legitimate source of law in civil law countries — as reflected above both in Box #3.1 ("orthodox" sources) and Box #3.2 ("modern" sources) — have become so widely used in recent years as to make many contemporary legal systems the product largely of a non-parliamentary, non-public process. France leads the way in this respect, since its 1958 constitution expressly transfers a substantial portion of legislative power from the parliament to the executive branch.[42]

---

39. See Merryman, *supra* note 2, at 152–157, on which the following synopsis draws liberally.

40. *Id.* at 153, quoting from an Italian scholar.

41. *Code Civil*, article 1382. Another translation — less literal but perhaps better in reflecting the provision's meaning — would read as follows: "any loss caused to a person through the behavior of another must be repaired by the person whose fault it was that the loss occurred".

42. One authority offers this account of the French experience:

[Although] a cardinal tenet of the French Revolution was that all law-making power was to be vested in a representative assembly[,] ... it soon became apparent in France, as elsewhere, that the complexity of modern government requires the legislature to delegate substantial power to the executive to implement legislation and to issue administrative regulations.... But the 1958 Constitution ... went a step further, by putting the law-mak-

- *Expanding public administrations* constitute another manifestation of the same trend away from legislative supremacy. Even though administrative officials—which in most countries now number far more than legislative and judicial officials combined—are technically subject to the law, the opportunities for excess and misuse of administrative power are so great as to be beyond the control of those other branches. Indeed, the development in most sophisticated civil law countries of an entire body of administrative law and procedure is a testament to the power of administrative bodies, whose operations "often affect[] the lives of citizens more directly and profoundly than legislation or litigation in ordinary courts".[43]

3. Certainty and Equity

The importance of codes and codification in the civil law tradition—and the anxiety that some observers express over the sort of "decodification" referred to immediately above—reflects another value that represents a distinctive mark of the civil law tradition: the value of certainty. I have referred in earlier pages of this chapter to the value of certainty. Now let us give it somewhat closer attention, and see how it provides another point of comparison between the civil law and the other great legal traditions.

Here, reduced to its essentials, is the central proposition that I wish to explain and evaluate: The civil law tradition attaches very high value on certainty in the law—that is, clear expression, *in advance*, of what the rules are so that members of the society can be guided by them. This can be contrasted with the emphasis that common law systems are said to place on flexibility and equity—focusing on the particular fairness of the outcome (and the procedures) in settling a specific dispute between two parties.

Is that proposition convincing and true? Merryman argues that it is, asserting that while certainty is an objective in all legal systems, the civil law tradition has elevated it to "a kind of supreme value, an unquestioned dogma, a fundamental goal"; in the civil law world, he claims, "it is always a good argument against a proposed change in the legal process that it will impair the certainty of the law.... Like a queen in chess, it can move in any direction."[44]

Of course, the common law tradition also places some value on certainty. According to Merryman, however, there are three major differences between the civil law tradition and the common law tradition when it comes to the value of certainty in the law.

> First, certainty is usually discussed in more functional terms [in the common law tradition] and is not elevated to the level of dogma ... [and] it is also widely recognized that there are limits on the extent to which certainty is possible. Second, certainty is achieved in the common law by giving the force of law to judicial decisions, something theoretically forbidden in civil law. The accumulation of judicial decisions in the course of time in a jurisdiction provides a variety of concrete, detailed examples of legal rules in operation. These, together with the

---

ing power of the executive on an autonomous non-delegated basis ... [so that all] matters other than those reserved for the legislative domain ... are of an executive character. Thus, the legislative law making power, though it covers the most important matters, has become the exception and the executive-administrative jurisdiction the rule—a direct repudiation of the traditional French doctrine of legislative supremacy.
Nutshell-2008, *supra* note 12, at 129–130.

43. Merryman, *supra* note 2, at 156.

44. *Id.* at 48.

statements of the rules themselves, are likely to provide more certainty about the law than are bare legislative statements of the rules. Thus, the desire for certainty is an argument in favor of *stare decisis* in the common law tradition, whereas it is an argument against *stare decisis* in the civil law tradition. Finally, in the common law world (particularly in the United States) it is more generally recognized that certainty is only one of a number of legal values, which sometimes conflict with each other. [For example, value is placed on flexibility, which allows the law to change] in response to changed circumstances or to bend to the requirements of a particular case. In the common law, certainty and flexibility are seen as competing values, each tending to limit the other.[45]

Perhaps the most striking manifestation of the civil law's penchant for certainty is found in the role assigned to judges. As we shall explore below, judges in civil law countries are typically regarded as relatively low-level bureaucrats with the intentionally limited, rather mechanical function of applying laws that the legislature has promulgated in a manner that is (presumably) clear, comprehensive, and consistent. They (the civil law judges) are definitely not to be the repositories of substantial discretion. Therefore, the kind of discretion that common law judges routinely exercise—including the *in personam* power to compel individuals in civil actions to do or to refrain from doing certain acts under penalty of punishment (see subsection IIB, below)—would be repugnant to most civil law systems. Even more unacceptable would be judicial exercise of equitable powers of the sort that developed in the Courts of Chancery (Courts of Equity) in England, as discussed below in Chapter Four, to serve the interests of substantive justice in those circumstances where the strict application of the law seemed to cause an unduly harsh or unfair result.

In sum, the civil law tradition seems to place a distinctively high value on legal certainty, and this has several consequences and manifestations. These include the civil law tendencies to circumscribe the powers of judges, to create codified law that aims for clarity, comprehensiveness, and consistency, and to classify the law into categories that follow from the private/public distinction.

C. The Legal Profession(s)

Having surveyed some basic matters relating to the civil law tradition from an operational perspective—sources, classification, codification, and certainty—let us turn our attention to the people who do the work of the legal process in civil law countries. We shall look at the legal profession(s) first from a general standpoint; then, in subsection ID of this chapter we shall see if and how these generalizations play out in the Italian legal system.

1. Introduction

Two general observations—somewhat inconsistent with each other—can be made about the legal professionals in civil law countries. The first emphasizes unification, the second emphasizes fragmentation.

Let us begin with the "unification" observation, which is this: In the civil law world, the pathway to becoming a lawyer has traditionally been exclusively through universities,

---

45. *Id.* at 48–49.

in a way that distinguishes it from the common law world. A major textbook on comparative law, originally authored mainly by Professor R. B. Schlesinger before his death in 1996,[46] offers this explanation:

> There is one feature of legal education that is common to all civil-law systems: the monopoly position which the University occupies (at least with respect to the first part of a future lawyer's training), such that a University legal education has come to be regarded as a hallmark of the civil law.... [This distinguishes continental systems with the English system.] Beyond the Channel in England, Courts themselves educated legal professionals who would eventually practice and become the future generations of lawyers and judges.... [But in the continental systems, especially with the solidification of power of the nation-state, and particularly in Germany,] [c]entralization of power produced the notion that law students are "seedlings of the State": as judges, prosecutors, higher civil servants, and (last and least by design) as practicing lawyers. The prototype was the career judge. His training (and consequently, that of other candidates for entry into the legal professions) started with study at an approved law faculty for a minimum period of three years, followed by the "first" State law examination. If successful, the candidate then entered State service as a provisional civil servant, receiving practical training and instruction in the judiciary, the prosecutor's office, and in governmental departments. This four-year training was concluded with the "second" (or "great") state examination. Successful candidates could then apply for entry into judicial, prosecutorial, or civil service careers, or the private practice of law.[47]

This centralization of the system of legal training into the universities, although it did not always exist in Europe, "is now a standard feature of qualification for all branches of the legal profession in virtually every civil-law country."[48] In this sense, then, there is a *unification* of the process by which persons gain entry into the legal profession, thus bringing a unity to the profession itself.

On the other hand, there is also a *fragmentation* of the legal profession, and even of some aspects of legal training, in a way that is foreign to the common law, or at any rate modern American law. Lawyers in the USA are typically regarded as belonging to a single profession — *the* legal profession — in which movement from one specific type of work (that of a private practitioner, for example) to another (that of a judge, for example) is not at all unusual and requires no new or special training. By contrast, civil law countries typically have a rather high degree of separation among the legal professions, with little real opportunity to move from one career path to another. The key types of legal professionals are judges (often viewed as occupying a rather low-level bureaucratic position), prosecutors (often part of the "magistrature", along with judges), government lawyers (of various sorts), notaries (which perform much broader functions than common-law notaries), advocates, and scholars. Of these, judges are typically seen to operate at the bottom of the hierarchy, for historical and cultural reasons; and scholars are seen at the top.

---

46. Rudolf Berthold Schlesinger left Germany in 1933 to escape Nazi brutality and became a leading authority in comparative law. The most recent edition of the text, which the current authors call "the first and leading casebook on the subject in the United States for the past sixty years", is Ugo A. Mattei, Teemu Ruskola, and Antonio Gidi, SCHLESINGER'S COMPARATIVE LAW: CASES, TEXT, MATERIALS (7th ed. 2009) [hereinafter cited as Schlesinger-2009]. An earlier edition of this work has also been relied on elsewhere in this book, especially in Chapter Two.

47. *Id.* at 629, 635, citing a 1986 law journal article by Gerhard Dilcher.

48. *Id.* at 636.

Moreover, choosing which of these career paths to follow typically takes place during a person's legal training:

> [I]n civil law jurisdictions…, a choice among a variety of distinct professional careers faces young law graduates. They can embark on a career as a judge, a public prosecutor, a government lawyer, an advocate, or a notary. They must make this decision early and then live with it. Although it is theoretically possible to move from one of these professions to another, such moves are comparatively rare. The initial choice, once made, tends to be final.…[49]

Perhaps as a consequence of this fairly sharp demarcation of the career paths of various sorts of lawyers, it is relatively easy to distinguish between their various functions, and to make some observations about their relative prestige in the legal system. These observations appear below,[50] in the following order: judges, public prosecutors, government lawyers, advocates, notaries, and academic lawyers (legal scholars).

2. Judges

The functions of a judge in a civil law country are broadly similar to those of a judge in a common law country, with some important exceptions. One of the most significant of these is highlighted below in subsection IIA of this chapter, where the role of presiding judges in criminal trials is given special attention. In addition, in most civil law countries a clear distinction will exist between those judges who serve in the system of administrative courts and those who serve in the ordinary courts (a matter illuminated in subsection IIC of this chapter). Still, the judicial functions generally will include the impartial application of the law (drawing on the sources discussed above in subsection IA of this chapter), with very substantial independence from the political organs of government, to cases brought before the courts. (The degree of independence from the political organs of government will be a ground for comparing Chinese judges to those in Western countries, as will be discussed in Chapter Seven.)

How does a person become a judge in a typical civil law country? On graduation from law school (or following a period of practical training, where that is required, as suggested in the passage quoted above from the Schlesinger text), a law student who wishes to become a judge will immediately apply for admission to the judiciary; and if selected, he or she will enter that profession. In some countries, special training institutes for judges are operated to provide additional instruction pertinent to a judge's work. With years of service and seniority, a judge typically will advance within the court system (ordinary or administrative).

---

49. Merryman, *supra* note 2, at 102. He goes on to observe that it some civil law countries, the obvious disadvantages of such a system—for example, the need for young lawyers to make career decisions without an adequate basis for choice—is now being offset somewhat by requiring law graduates to spend a period of time in practical training, often including affiliations with the judiciary, with government lawyers, and in private practice before they can be licensed to practice. *Id.* at 103. An example can be seen in Germany, where all law graduates, after passing an examination, will "enter a required practical training period (*Referendarzeit*) … [which] is a two-year internship spent in different 'stations' each corresponding to a different branch of the profession", thus giving the young lawyer some experience before taking a second examination—upon successful completion of which he or she will settle upon a career path. Nutshell-2008, *supra* note 12, at 81.

50. The summary appearing in the following paragraphs draws primarily on Nutshell-2008, *supra* note 12, at 79–96, and on Merryman, *supra* note 2, at 102–111. See also Richard L. Abel, *Lawyers in the Civil Law World*, in LAWYERS IN SOCIETY: THE CIVIL LAW WORLD 1, 1–8 (Richard L. Abel & Phillip S.C. Lewis eds., 1988); Konrad Zweigert, 16 INTERNATIONAL ENCYCLOPEDIA OF COMPARATIVE LAW 40 (1982).

However, the judge will probably not be viewed as occupying a position of much prestige even after numerous years of service on the bench, for reasons that warrant separate discussion. See Box #3.5 for observations in this regard.

Box #3.5 History and Prestige of Judges and Scholars — Common Law and Civil Law

It is possible to draw some general contrasts between the relative roles and prestige accorded to two key types of legal professionals — judges and legal scholars — in civil law and common law countries, beginning with judges. One authority notes the "relatively low profile" that judges have in most civil law systems and points out that "[w]hile the common law tradition reveres the names of the great judges who created the system and accords prestige and power to their modern successors, the names of civil law judges of the past are hardly remembered and their present-day successors work largely in obscurity." [Nutshell, *supra* note 12, at 88].

Merryman offers a more expansive view. He begins with observations about judges in common law countries, with special attention on the USA:

> We in the common law world know what judges are. They are culture heroes, even parental figures. Many of the great names of the common law are those of judges.... We know that our legal tradition was originally created and has grown and developed in the hands of judges, ... building a body of law ... through the doctrine of *stare decisis*....
>
> We also know where our judges come from. We know that they attend law school and then have successful careers either in private practice or in government, frequently as district attorneys. They are appointed or elected to judicial positions ... as a kind of crowning achievement relatively late in life.... Judges are well paid ... Their opinions will be discussed in the newspapers and dissected and criticized in the legal periodicals. They are very important people. [Merryman, *supra* note 2, at 34–35.]

Contrasting with this picture of the role and prestige of judges in common law countries is a much less flattering view of the role and prestige of judges in the civil law world. There, the judge is, as Merryman explains, often seen as a civil servant and a functionary who will be treated with respect but no more than would be accorded to other civil servants. Merryman explains why this is the case by reminding us of several key historical factors:

> One of the principal reasons for the quite different status of civil law judges is the existence of a different judicial tradition in the civil law, beginning in Roman times. [In the early formative days, the judges of Rome were not] prominent people of the law [but instead] were, in effect, laypeople discharging an arbitral function by presiding over the settlement of disputes according to formulae supplied by another official, the *praetor*. [Thus, the judge] was not expert in the law and had very limited power. For legal advice the judge turned to the jurisconsult.
>
> [The power and prestige of judges did rise during] medieval and pre-revolutionary times, when it was not unusual for Continental judges to act much like their English counterparts.... [But that was seen to be a problem, especially in revolutionary France. So with that] revolution, and its consecration of the dogma of strict separation of powers, the judicial function was emphatically restricted.
>
> The picture of the judicial process that emerges [from this history] is one of fairly routine activity; the judge becomes a kind of expert clerk. Presented with fact situations to which a ready legislative response will be readily found in all except the extraordinary case, the judge's function is merely to find the right legislative provision, couple it with the fact situation, and bless the solution ... produced from the union....

> The net image is of judges as operators of a machine [that is designed by schol-ars] and built by legislators. The judicial function is a mechanical one.... [Mer-ryman, *supra* note 2, at 35–36.]

That image of the judge in the civil law world, deriving so importantly from some of the his-torical circumstances and themes that we explored above in Chapter Two, portrays the civil law judge as vastly inferior in importance to the typical common law judge. Moreover, as hinted at in the next-to-last sentence from the Merryman excerpt above, the civil law judge is like-wise vastly inferior in importance to the typical civil law scholar. Here is what one authority has to say about this contrast:

> It is the names of scholars, not judges, that have come down to us over the centuries of the civil law tradition, as the centers of high legal learning shifted from ancient Rome, to sixth century A.D. Byzantium, to thirteenth century Bologna, to sixteenth century France and Germany, to seventeenth century Holland and back to Germany in the nineteenth century. [Nutshell-2008, *supra* note 12, at 91.]

It is important to remind ourselves of each of the historical eras identified in that passage, in terms of the role played by legal scholars:

- Ancient Rome ... *Jurisconsults*, advising the persons involved in litigation before the *praetor*, wrote down their opinions, which were collected and treated as au-thoritative — and which ultimately served as the substance relied on by the com-mission responsible for compiling Justinian's *Digest*.

- 6th century Byzantium (Constantinople) ... Tribonian and others in Justinian's commission comprised mainly scholars associated with universities, and in com-piling the *Digest* they drew on the work of those classical Roman *jurisconsults*.

- 13th century Bologna ... Those responsible for reviving the *Digest* and develop-ing the *jus commune* — particularly Irnerius, the Glossators, and the Commen-tators (Post-Glossators) — were also scholars, involved at first in an almost purely academic exercise and then giving it practical application in the 14th and 15th centuries.

- 16th century France and Germany ... The Humanist School consisted of scholars applying a different system of inquiry and ideology to the study and use of law.

- 17th century Holland ... The Natural Law School likewise consisted of scholars taking yet a different approach to law.

- 19th century Germany ... German legal science, and the Historical School led by Savigny, undertook a thorough scholarly review of both Roman law and Ger-manic customs, yielding ultimately the German *BGB*.

Merryman offers a summary: "This is what we mean when we say that legal scholars are the dominant actors of the civil law. Legislators, executives, administrators, judges, and lawyers all come under the scholars' influence. Thus, although legal scholarship is not a formal source of law, the doctrine [as developed by the legal scholars] carries immense authority. [Merry-man, *supra* note MERRYNOTE1, at 56–60.]

As we shall see in Chapters Four and Five, the role of legal scholars in the common law tra-dition — whether observed in the earliest stage of English law development or in more mod-ern times — is dramatically different from the role described above. Instead, the common law legal scholar occupies, in general, a position much subsidiary to that of the common law judge.

3. Public Prosecutors (State's Attorneys)

In most civil law countries, a public prosecutor has two principal functions: (1) to serve as the prosecuting attorney in criminal cases, and (2) to represent the public interest in judicial proceedings brought to the courts by private parties. (This latter function is not typically found in common law countries.) In some civil law countries, the public prosecutors and the judges are part of a single administrative structure, sometimes called the magistrature, and a lawyer can sometimes move from serving as a judges to serving as a prosecutor (and vice versa). To become a public prosecutor, a university law graduate would ordinarily take a state-administered examination, in manner similar to (and sometimes merged with) the procedure for becoming a judge, as summarized above.

4. Government Lawyers

Practice varies among civil law countries for the appointment of lawyers to provide legal services for government agencies: in some, a central office of government attorneys provides such services; in others, agencies engage their own legal advisors. To become a government lawyer (under either approach), a university law graduate typically would — as in the case of judges and prosecutors described above — take a state-administered examination (after a period of practical training, if required) and, if successful, enter into government service, probably with the prospect of staying in that service for many years or life.

5. Advocates

Advocates may be placed in two categories — those practicing in private law firms and those serving in the legal departments of companies. Let us focus on private advocates. Two main models can be found in the civil law world, one of which is "divided" and the other of which is "unitary".

The "divided" model, traditionally associated with France, separates private practitioners of law into two kinds of advocates, similar to those kinds found in the English distinction between barristers and solicitors (as discussed in Appendix 3.1 to this chapter). The Schlesinger treatise offers this account:

> [Before 1971, the French legal profession] was characterized by a sharp distinction between two kinds of advocates. The *Avoué* was responsible of [*sic*] written pleadings and the *Avocat* was to orally address the Court.... A number of other practitioners could be seen in action, ... [including] a profession of *Agréé*, practicing in front of commercial courts. A large monopoly of Notaries on a variety of fields mainly within the law of property and successions completes the picture.[51]

> In 1971 and in 1990, two statutes attempted to simplify the system.... The 1971 reform combined several of the professions formerly involved in litigation into one, that of *Avocat*. While the *Agréés* disappeared, the *Avoués* have been able to survive this reform (as well as the 1990 one) as far as the Court of Appeals is concerned. In that intermediate jurisdiction, the *Avoué* still enjoys a lucrative monopoly. The same 1971 reform for the first time regulated the giving of legal advice in France. The new profession of *Conseil Juridique* was born. During their twenty years of existence, *Conseil[s] Juridique[s]* became quite important as legal advisers for business firms and were often organized in rather large firms.

> ... [As a result of the 1990 legislation,] the situation in France changed radically. There is no longer a separate profession, the *conseils juridiques*, authorized only to give legal advice, because they were merged with the *avocats*.

---

51. Schlesinger-2009, *supra* note 46, at 650.

... [These developments show a] trend toward a unitary profession ... in France. Not only has the *Avocat* merged with the *Conseil Juridique* ..., but the associate practice [that is, the ability to create law firms] is also developing quickly in France, ... A number of French law firms today contain more than 100 lawyers, and the largest one (Fidal) has over one thousand attorneys.[52]

Germany offers a very different picture of the legal profession, particularly in terms of the organization and practice of private attorneys. It exemplifies a "unitary" model. The following description in the Schlesinger text explains this, along with the German rules on the size of law firms:

> [T]raditionally, the entire process of legal education in Germany functions to educate a unitary jurist. The focus is still mostly to educate judges and prosecutors rather than adversary attorneys. The legal profession is as a consequence highly unitary in Germany, [especially] in the sense that there are no significant private practitioners beyond attorneys.
>
> ... There are almost 70 thousands practicing attorneys in today's Germany, and the attorney's role is highly regulated. Traditionally he was strictly forbidden from advertising. [However, today] some "decent informative advertising is now generally considered as permitted." The attorney is very restricted in his organizational form: [even with some changes in the 1990s,] the average German legal practice is still tiny. Less than 10% of the law firms contain more than five lawyers. The largest law firm today (Oppenhof and Radler) has about 200 lawyers, but any firm of 50 lawyers is still considered among the largest.[53]

Just as certain restrictions on the abilities of private practitioners (adversarial attorneys) to associate in law firms have eased (overcoming a traditional concern regarding the perceived risk of diluting the personal lawyer-client relationship), likewise certain other restrictions and regulations have fallen away now in most civil law countries. Still, specific rules on the practice of law remain within the jurisdiction of national (and subnational) government and judicial officials in most countries, so it is difficult to generalize about steps to be taken to become a member of a bar association and to practice before the courts. Moreover, these matters are the subject of substantial change in some civil law countries, especially outside Europe — including in particular Japan and Korea.[54]

For a brief comparative survey of how advocates (and certain other types of legal professionals) are trained and qualified in four countries — Germany, the USA, the UK, and

---

52. *Id.* at 650–651. The discussion in the Schlesinger text regarding the ability of foreign (non-French) lawyers to practice in France, though interesting, has been omitted here.

53. *Id.* at 648–649 (citing a 1993 publication for the quoted passage and current data).

54. For a synopsis of the recent changes undertaken in the system of legal education and the licensing of lawyers in Japan, see *id.* at 664–669. See also James R. Maxeiner, *American Law Schools as a Model for Japanese Legal Education? A Preliminary Question from a Comparative Perspective*, 24 KANSAI UNIVERSITY REVIEW OF LAW AND POLITICS 37 (2003) and several excerpts included in Chapter 2 ("The Legal Profession") in Curtis J. Milhaupt, J. Mark Ramseyer, and Mark D. West, THE JAPANESE LEGAL SYSTEM (2006). For a dated analysis of some peculiarities of the role of Japanese lawyers — some of which bear on the peculiarities of legal education in that country — see K. Hagiwara, *The Role of Lawyers in Japanese Society Against the Background of Japanese Cultural Traditions*, 29 KANAGAWA HOGAKU (REVIEW OF LAW AND POLITICS) 1 (1994). The serious challenges encountered in Japan in recent years concerning legal education have been watched closely in Korea, which is also currently in the process of reforming its system of legal training and licensing. Schlesinger-2009, *supra* note 46, at 669–670. In both countries, the overall aim is to shift toward what is perceived as an American-style system of legal education and bar examination. The Schlesinger text refers to this as an "Americanization" of the legal profession. *Id.* at 679.

China—see Appendix 3.1, which provides the text (without footnotes) of a recent law journal article on that subject. Details in this regard are offered also for Italy, in subsection ID3, below.

6. Notaries

Notaries are the lawyers that many people in civil law countries go to in order to get most routine legal work done. Unlike the position of "notary public" in the USA, a notary in the civil law world must have legal training and qualifications and in most countries must pass a national examination and serve as an apprentice in a practicing notary's office.

The reason for this level of training and qualification becomes obvious when one considers the functions of a notary. There are typically three main functions, only the first of which (as listed here) bears a resemblance to the main function of a notary in the US system: (1) to authenticate instruments, giving them thereby special legal effect, in that an instrument authenticated by a notary conclusively establishes that the instrument is genuine and accurate in recording a certain fact (so that contradictory evidence is typically inadmissible in court); (2) to draft such important legal documents as wills, contracts, deeds, and company constitutive instruments; and (3) to serve as a repository for legal instruments prepared or authenticated by them.[55]

7. Academic Lawyers (Legal Scholars)

The status and history of legal scholars has already been summarized, and placed in a comparative context, in Box #3.5 above. As noted there, the scholar is widely regarded as the protagonist, even the hero, of the civil law tradition. Naturally, such prestige would typically attach only to those relatively few academic lawyers who achieve the upper reaches of university faculty appointments, and this can prove to be a long road with many potential pitfalls. In some universities, senior law professors preside over what could, with little exaggeration, be called fiefdoms, served by a stable of graduate law students and aspirants to faculty chairs of their own. A US law professor might well be surprised by the extent and form of fealty and deference shown to senior law faculty members in a prominent university.

D. Illustrations from Italian Law

So far, this chapter has focused on certain generalizations about the sources and categories of law and lawyers in civil law countries, with only a few references to particular countries. Now let us turn our attention to one particular legal system in the civil law world and see how some of those generalizations manifest themselves in that system. Italy

---

55. For a summary of the history of the notarial profession in European civil law countries, see Schlesinger-2009, *supra* note 46, at 631–632. That account explains how certain types of notaries "became, in effect, quasi-public officials in private practice when the 'public instruments' passed by notaries became entitled to '*fides publica*' in the same manner as judicial documents, and when territorial sovereigns entrusted them with the task of serving as repositories of the public instruments recorded in their protocols." *Id.* at 633. The Schlesinger text also describes "the position of notary as a trustworthy recorder of judicial proceedings, and as a skilled and reliable draftsman and keeper of other public instruments." *Id.*

will serve our purposes well, partly because the Italian peninsula is the geographic birthplace of the civil law tradition and partly because modern Italy's legal system offers clear illustrations of many points made above. Hence, the following paragraphs (in this subsection ID) provide some details about Italy's legal system in terms of (i) the sources of law, (ii) the classifications of law (with special attention to codification), and (iii) the legal professions and the system of legal education that produces those legal professionals.[56]

1. Sources of Law in Italy

Having identified and explained the sources of law in civil law countries in very general terms—and distinguished between the "orthodox" and the "modern" views in this regard—I now offer a summary of how the Italian legal system reflects, departs from, or is silent on many of those sources. This summary takes the form of a question-and-answer "interview" with an Italian law student.[57] Naturally, more could be said about each of the following points, and not all points can be covered in this small section. However, the aim here is not to be comprehensive but instead to be illustrative, in hopes of bringing to life the generalities offered above about the sources of law.

Q: *Is it appropriate to regard statutory law as having a special status—that is, occupying a place of primary importance, among the sources of law in the Italian legal system?*

A: Yes. The Italian legal system may be regarded as having its foundation in written law ("*legge scritta*"). This means that courts always need to base their judgements on the provisions of codes and statutes from which solutions to particular cases are to be derived. In the same way, those provisions should always be respected by citizens who enter into contracts or undertake any other legal obligation. Since in the Italian legal system legislation (including the Constitution, codes, and statutes) is seen as the primary source (if not the only source) of law, it is really rare for magistrates to base their verdicts on custom; this happens only when there are *lacunae* in the system and it is impossible to fill them drawing analogies from statutory provisions. The Italian legal system is ultimately constructed for the purpose of reaching the so called "*certezza del diritto*", which means that any situation that might occur should always have a written provision to regulate it and solve it. This purpose is clearly utopian, since the possible situations are endless, but this is the aim that the Italian legislator has been trying to reach in the past centuries. This attitude often leads to the opposite problem of "overlegisla-

---

56. For more complete treatments of these and other aspects of the Italian legal system, see, e.g., Thomas Glyn Watkin, THE ITALIAN LEGAL TRADITION (1997); Mauro Cappelletti, John Henry Merryman, and Joseph M. Perillo, THE ITALIAN LEGAL SYSTEM (1967); INTRODUCTION TO ITALIAN LAW (Jeffrey S. Lena & Ugo Mattei, eds., 2002); and Guido Alpa and Vincenzo Zeno-Zencovich, ITALIAN PRIVATE LAW (2007). There are many others besides these in English, and of course countless works in Italian.

57. Most of this subsection has been prepared in collaboration with two of my Italian research assistants—Marco Antonio Caporale and Enrico Greghi. Both were students of mine in 2009 at the *Facultà di Giurisprudenza* of the University of Trento, and Mr. Greghi was also a student of mine at the University of Kansas in 2008. I have engaged in relatively little stylistic editing, in order to be as true as possible to their expressions and explanations. Some of the contents of this subsection and others appearing below also draw from an introductory course on Italian law that I attended at the University of Trento, with the kind permission of my faculty colleagues there. In that respect, I wish to give a special thanks and acknowledgment to Roberto Toniatti, Jens Woelk, Rafaella Dimatteo, Luisa Antonielli, Carlo Casonato, Sylvia Pelizzari, Elena Ioratti, Laura Baccaglini, and Cinzia Piciocchi.

tion"—that is, when a single case is regulated by more than one provision, therefore creating confusion over which one should be applied.

Q: *Your answer to my first question covered two other points that interest me about the Italian legal system: (i) the role of "custom" and (ii) the importance placed on "certainty in the law". My impression from your answer is that at least as a doctrinal matter, custom plays an extremely small role, and certainty in the law—which I assume would be the closest translation into English of "certezza del diritto"—has very great value. Is this correct?*

A: Yes, absolutely. And to expand slightly on the role of custom, let me add that in the Italian legal system, custom fills the spaces that are left out by written law; this means that custom doesn't have any authority unless the legislator omitted to regulate a particular situation (thereby leaving a *lacuna*). Custom can be defined as an unwritten law introduced by the continuous acts of the community, accompanied by a sense of obligation to behave in a certain way when a particular situation presents itself. It's important to underline that custom can be legally binding *only* if there is no applicable statute or regulation.

Q: *And I assume that "the Italian legislator" that you referred to is, at least in the context of contemporary Italian law, the parliament. What about the chief executive—does the president or the prime minister have a broad authority to enact legislation, as seems to be the case in France?*

A: In the Italian legal system the chief executive does not have the authority to issue laws but merely to propose bills that must then be approved by the Parliament. However, when a particular situation requires urgent measures to be taken, the government [*i.e.*, the executive branch] can issue a so-called "*decreto legge*" which has the same authority of a law—at least as a temporary matter—but needs to be ratified by the parliament within 60 days if it is to remain effective; otherwise it will lose its legal effectiveness *ex tunc*. This system has been created in order to respect the legislative authority of the parliament, according to the principle of separation of powers, while still permitting some matters to be handled urgently. Actually the practice of issuing *decreti legge* has become quite ordinary, and this creates problems of overregulation; and it doesn't help the speed of trials, since judges usually wait for the *decreto* to be ratified by parliament to apply that provision. The Italian Constitutional Assembly—that is, the first "parliament" who created the constitution right after the World War II—decided not to give the chief executive the power of issuing laws, keeping in mind what happened under the iron rule of Mussolini in the preceding years. Thus, only the parliament, with its democratic representation, has the ultimate power of enacting new laws and statutes.

Q: *What about regulations? In many civil law countries, regulations that are issued by administrative agencies (acting under authority delegated by the legislative authorities) are regarded as "sources" of law and in fact carry much of the real content of the law. Is this true in Italy?*

A: In the Italian legal system, regulations are rules issued by the executive power and they stand below statutes in the hierarchy of norms. Their validity and effectiveness is always subject to (that is, subsidiary to) a law issued by the parliament; therefore a regulation cannot contain provisions in conflict with a rule enacted by the legislative authority. Usually, regulations are issued after a so-called "*legge delega*" [delegating law] and they contain detailed provisions in order to give effect to the policy established in the statute. In other words, this means that each regulatory provision should fit within or match a provision of the enabling statute.

Q: *What about constitutional provisions? How do they figure among the "sources" of law in Italy?*

A: Constitutional provisions are supreme. Article 117 of the *Constituzione della Repubblica italiana* (Constitution of the Italian Republic) provides as follows:

> *La potestà legislativa è esercitata dallo Stato e dalle Regioni nei rispetto della Constituzione, nonché dei vincoli derivanti dall'ordinamento comunitario e dagli obblighi internazionali.*

Translated into English, this article provides:

> Legislative powers shall be vested in the State and the Regions in compliance with the Constitution and with the constraints deriving from European Union law and international obligations.

Hence, the laws enacted by the State through its legislative and executive powers must comply with the constitution; or, expressed differently, the constitution is at the "top of the list" of sources of law.

In fact, this topic is important enough to give it some more attention. In Italy, the constitution is seen as especially important because a special process is required to amend it. The pertinent Italian term is *rocca dura aggravare (procedimento aggravato di revisione costituzionale)*—indicating that more than the usual amount of approval is required. The details appear in Article 138 of the constitution, which calls for both a super-majority and special procedure to amend the constitution. It provides that two readings must be held, at least three months apart, in each of the two houses of the parliament. If on the second reading there is an absolute majority (50% + 1) in favor of the proposed amendment, then a referendum (country-wide) can be called by one-fifth of the members of either house or by a certain number of regional authorities. If the referendum results in a majority of voters (in Italy) in favor of the amendment, then the amendment will be promulgated. But if there is a 2/3 majority in both houses of parliament, then the referendum is not required; the amendment takes effect without the referendum.

There is another important point to make about the status of the constitution as a source of law in the Italian legal system. In addition to the special amending process just described, there is another limit on the power of the legislature—and that is the overarching power of a Constitutional Court to declare legislation unconstitutional. See Articles 134 through 136 of the constitution. Article 134 is straightforward: its opening provision (as translated into English) asserts that the Constitutional Court shall decide "[c]ontroversies on the constitutional validity of laws and enactments having the force of law adopted by the State and the Regions". Article 135 provides details about the composition and procedures of the Constitutional Court, and Article 136 underscores the power of the Constitutional Court to declare a law or other enactment unconstitutional by stating that upon such a declaration of unconstitutionality, the law "ceases to have effect".

Then, another important matter also warrants attention: the *principi supremi*— that is, the supreme principles—of the constitution. Usually considered as the first 12 articles, these fundamental principles cannot be modified, as the Constitutional Court stated more than once (see sentences n. 18/1982, 70/1984, and 1146/1988). In addition, the constitution itself states at art. 139 that the republican form of government cannot be modified; this serves to prevent the return of the monarchy or the departure from other provisions that characterize the Italian system.

In Italy, as in numerous other countries, the experience with the review of the constitutionality of legislation has been mixed. Only in 1956, after eight years of "boycotting" and uncertainty, did the Constitutional Court start exercising its right of judicial review of legislation. Two cases are usually remembered in this respect in Italy — one permitting women to enter into the judiciary and the other eliminating the crime of adultery, which had been applicable only to women. In both cases, the Constitutional Court found legislative provisions running the other direction to be unconstitutional.[58]

Q: *What about initiative and referendum? Do they figure among the "sources" of law in Italy?*

A: Article 71 of the constitution provides (as translated into English) that "[t]he people may initiate legislation through a proposal, made by at least fifty-thousand electors, of a bill drafted in Articles." So yes, this can be a source of law.

Q: *What about international law? Is it regarded as a "source" of law in the Italian system?*

A: Yes, as indicated above, Article 117 of the constitution gives specific reference to international legal obligations (without distinguishing between those created through treaty and those emerging from customary international law). Laws enacted by the State through its legislative and executive powers must comply with those obligations. Two other articles are also extremely important, though: Article 10, which provides for the recognition of international customs into the Italian system — referred to as "general recognized obligations" — and Article 11, which allows the constitution and other sources of law to be limited in sovereignty by international treaties, thus enabling the European laws and ruling to be directly binding in the Italian system.

Q: *What about "caselaw" — that is, the judgments of courts issued in the context of specific legal disputes coming before them? How, if at all, do they figure among the "sources" of law in Italy?*

A: "Caselaw" is of growing importance in Italy. In particular, court decisions play a fundamental role in completing the picture of private law. Court decisions are not formally binding in Italy — there is not a *stare decisis* rule in Italy. So judicial decisions are not considered "formally" to be sources of the law. But they are nevertheless very important, as reflected by the fact that many decisions are published in legal periodicals and reporters. Significantly, these decisions are often published together with comments written by scholars. Hence, judges will read the commentaries, learn the views of scholars, and therefore learn what the *dottrina* (doctrine) is regarding a particular area of law. As a technical matter, the *giurisprudenza* — the rules "enacted" by the courts — and the *dottrina* cannot be

---

58. Further details regarding Italy's Constitutional Court appear below in subsection IID2 of this chapter.

considered as sources of the law in and of themselves—and indeed at least until recently there was a rule in force that disallowed the citation of the *dottrina* in court decisions. Nevertheless, the *giurisprudenza* and the *dottrina* certainly *are* considered *formanti* (formants) of the law. The *formanti* can contribute to the development of law in private law (as well as in public law).

Q: *What about legal scholarship? In many civil law systems, legal scholarship—that is, the doctrine as developed by professors of law—is of fundamental importance, so that it has been said that the law is in fact "designed" by the legal scholars. Does this hold true in Italy?*

A: Yes, of course. In fact, the most famous professors of law, and their writings, are held in the very highest esteem. I already explained above the importance of *dottrina* (doctrine)—and it is the scholars in whose hands the responsibility rests for creating and developing and explaining the *dottrina*.

2. Classifications and Codification of Law in Italy

As explained earlier, the typical civil law system will draw a bright-line distinction between public law and private law. It will then further classify public law into constitutional, administrative, and criminal law (despite the fact that the last of these has such a direct effect on individuals) and will divide private law into civil law and commercial law. Complementing these legal distinctions and categories are various codes—typically a civil code, a civil procedure code, a penal code, a criminal procedure code, and a commercial code (in addition to various other more modern types of codes such as those covering administrative law or labor law). Underlying all of the classifications and codification efforts there is said to exist an "ideology of codification" that seeks great clarity, completeness, and consistency in the law—values that ultimately contribute to the fundamental aim of "certainty in the law".

How, if at all, do these various generalities offered earlier in this chapter—deriving, in turn, from a fabric of specific historical developments described in Chapter Two—manifest themselves in the contemporary Italian legal system? To address this question, I have again opted to undertake a question-and-answer "interview" with an Italian law student.[59]

Q: *How fundamental or important to Italian law is the distinction between public law and private law, and what specific types of law fit within each of these two categories?*

A: This is not an easy question to answer. As a very general matter, and certainly as a historical matter, the public-law/private-law distinction is still fundamental. In the Italian lawyer's mind, private law is the part of the law that regulates the relationship between private parties, or between private parties and public entities; the other side of the distinction is public law, which consists of rules regulating the relationships between public entities.

However, this definition is no longer very well accepted, or very useful, as a matter of reality in civil law countries. Commercial relationships in particular are very dynamic and difficult to classify into this distinction. For example, what if

---

59. Like the preceding one, this subsection has been prepared in collaboration with two of my Italian research assistants. In this case, those research assistants were Enrico Greghi, referred to *supra* note 57, and Stefano Penasa. Mr. Pesano was also a student of mine in 2009 at the *Facultà di Giurisprudenza* of the University of Trento. In addition, some aspects of this "interview" reflect discussions with numerous faculty colleagues at the University of Trento.

the regional governmental authorities need to obtain land in order to build a school? The right of expropriation is a power of the government (the state), and this would typically fall into the "public law" realm. However, the government might decide to obtain the land not through expropriation but rather through a purchase, as if it were a private entity; and this would constitute a "private law" matter.

Moreover, in different legal systems, there is generally an increase in the involvement of the state in the relationships between private individuals and entities. This is especially true in the area of employment protection. Up to about forty years ago, it was clear that a contract of employment was a matter of private law. But today it is not so clear. The same reality exists in family law, where there is a strong intervention of the state.

And so there is great debate both (1) as to whether a certain matter belongs to private law or public law and (2) over the usefulness of the distinction more generally. The distinction is seen as much less concrete and much more artificial in today's Italian law than ever before.

To the extent that it does exist, the public/private distinction is fairly clear as to its purported contents. In the Civil Code, for example, we find the main parts of private law: property, contract, tort, family law, succession, and the regulation of *società*—societies, foundations, etc. There is no Commercial Code in Italy, so all the commercial law is found in the civil code.

Q: *If there is no Commercial Code in Italy, then would I be correct to assume that the main codes are civil, civil procedure, penal, and criminal procedure?*

A: Yes. And of course there are many other laws that lie outside the codes as well. Some of these would be regarded as *leggi speciali*, special (or specialized) laws. In the area of commercial law, for example, these would include the Bank Law, the Insurance Law, the Securities Law, the Insolvency Law, and the Antitrust Law, along with two intellectual property laws (one on industrial property and one on copyright). These *leggi speciali*, although in a sense less "basic" than the civil code, in fact will prevail over the common rules found in the civil code. So, for example, the general rules in the Civil Code about the responsibilities of a member of a company's board of directors would be trumped by any specific provisions in one of the *leggi speciali*.

3. The Legal Professions and Legal Education in Italy

Having examined sources of law and classification of law in Italy, let us now turn to the subject of the "personnel" by which the legal system of that country operates. Once again, I have opted to undertake a question-and-answer "interview" with an Italian law student[60] in order to explore how the picture of legal professionals in Italy matches (or differs from) the general picture I offered earlier in this chapter. In the following "interview", because it reflects the perspective of a student, special emphasis is placed on the system of legal education, training, and qualification necessary for a person to become a

---

60. Like the preceding ones, this subsection has been prepared in collaboration with my Italian research assistants. In this case, principal input came from Enrico Greghi, referred to *supra* note 57. Mr. Greghi has, for some topics covered here, provided citations to particular statutory and regulatory provisions.

legal professional—that is, a judge, a public prosecutor, a government lawyer, an advocate, a notary, or an academic (legal scholar).

a. The Italian law student

Q: *Let's start near the beginning, after high school: what kind of education will a student have completed before going to university?*

A: In order to attend university the Italian system prescribes the successful fulfillment of a five years long high school course, thus excluding the 3-years certificate given by some schools that usually leads to the subsequent job placement.

Q: *When does the student choose law as a course of study—after two years?*

A: Immediately. In fact, in Italy law is not a graduate course and students are allowed to enter law schools *(Facoltá di Giurisprudenza)* right after the final high school exam, whose written parts are nationally decided by the Ministry of Education and given to all high school depending on their field of specialization.

Q: *So are entrance exams required to get into university, and/or into law studies?*

A: There is a high degree of autonomy of each university (see D.M. 270/04). Traditionally, some closed-number courses have been Medicine, Architecture, and some others; but after the reform of 2004 local autonomy exists for the university to decide, depending on its own resources, whether or not any courses (and if so, which ones) need an entry exam for admission and how many students may be admitted.

b. The Italian law schools

Q: *What is the difference, if any, between law "faculties" and "departments" and "law schools"?*

A: *Dipartimento* is defined by the DPR 382/1980 as "the organization of one or more sectors of research characterized by uniformity of either goals or methods and the relative disciplines of teaching." By contrast, faculties can be compared to the various schools (Law, Economics, etc.) of which the university is composed.

Q: *What role do the universities play, as a historical matter, in the study of law in Italy? Is Bologna especially important?*

A: The universities have played a fundamental role in the spread of culture in Italy and Europe, especially regarding the study and re-discovery of the *Corpus Iuris Civilis*. Recognized as founded in the 1088 by a commission of experts, Bologna is deemed probably the first university in the world and had a key role in the development of the secular university as we know it: the *Studium* was born as a free and "lay" organization of students who chose and funded their professors. They organized themselves in colleges for the mutual assistance among comrades of the same nationality *(nationes)*, split between *intra-* and *ultra-montani*. This model contrasted with the Parisian one, which featured universities of masters tied to the Church and the Monarchy. The *Studium* saw its birth thanks to the emergence of great law scholars, the Glossators, who were called to explain the ancient codes of Roman law, especially the CIC. In the Greek language, "γλῶσσα" (glossa) means "tongue" or "language." Originally, the word was used to denote an explanation of an unfamiliar word, but its scope gradually expanded to the more general sense of "commentary". The glossators used to write in the margins of the old texts (*glossa marginalis*) or between the lines (*glossa interlinearis*—interlinear glosses). Later these were gathered into large collections, first copied as separate books but then also quickly written in the margins of the legal texts. The medieval copyists at Bologna developed a typical script to enhance the legibility of both the main text and the glosses. The typically Bolognese script is called the *Littera Bononsiensis*. From the *Studium* of Bologna were, among others, Pepo, Irnerius, and Gratian, who also wrote the fist manual of Canon Law, the *Concordantia discordantum Canonum*. Subsequently in 1158 Frederic I enacted the *Constitutio Habita* with which the University became protected as place of research and study thus independent from any other power.

Q: *What distinctions are there among Italian law schools in terms of their "ranking" and attractiveness—or in terms of regional versus national reputations?*

A: A list of reputable universities is maintained by the pertinent ministry within the Italian government. The criteria it uses include international standards such as level of learning by students, their job placement, structures, research entities, quantity of external (that is, non-public) funding, and other factors. Currently, the University of Trento is at the head of this list, beating out the Polytechnics of Turin and Milan). In addition, each year there is a "Repubblica-CENSIS list": annually the CENSIS institute and *La Repubblica* newspaper release a combined list where the quality of each university and department within it is judged upon specified criteria.

Q: *What statutory or regulatory control or supervision exists—within the government, that is—over law faculties in Italy?*

A: Some provisions appear in the Constitution (Article 33) and in statutes (see L168/1989, art. 6). Under these provisions, universities have the status of being a legal person (juridical entity, *personalitá giuridica*) and have scientific, educational, organizational, financial, and accounting autonomy; and they provide for themselves their own subsidiary statutes and regulations. They also have certain degrees of statutory autonomy (power of issuing binding regulations), financial autonomy (power to manage their financial resources, mainly those coming from national funding and students' taxes), educational autonomy (capacity to determine and regulate the *corsi di laurea*—degree programs), and so forth.

c. Courses of study and degree programs

Q: *Is it usually a five-year course of study that is required to get a law degree in Italy; or has this changed recently?*

A: This is somewhat confusing because of changes that have occurred. Specifically, the law course structure has been recently renewed.[61] Before the Decree of the Minister issued in November 2005 there were two distinct law courses, one subsequent

---

61. For further details on some of the changes referred to here, see Luisa Antoniolli, *Legal Education in Italy and the Bologna Process*, 3 EUROPEAN JOURNAL OF LEGAL EDUCATION 163 (2006).

to the other. The first one—*Laurea Breve* (Low degree)—was accessible by all students who successfully finished their high school, and it provided a generic preparation about law subjects. It usually lasted three years—or, more precisely, 180 credits were needed to complete it before the discussion of a dissertation on a chosen topic of law.

This was not enough to be eligible to take the public exams required in Italy to receive the license to practice one of the legal professions such as attorney, judge, prosecutor, and so forth. Another course of study roughly comparable to the American J.D.—*Laurea Specialistica* (High, Specific Degree)—was also available; it required 120 credits and a thesis, and it provided the necessary preparation (and eligibility) to become a legal professional.

This structure, with some small changes that stress the distinction between the practical and methodological approach of the two courses (see D.M. 270/2004), still operates for the majority of the Italian university courses.

However, since 2005, the reform initiatives have condensed the two courses into one of five total years—*Laurea Magistrale*. In this course of study, students are given in their first year of studies a generic preparation—the first-year classes include philosophy of law, institutions of Roman law, private law (contracts, property, family law), public law (sources of law, constitutional settings), and history of law —and in the four following years the classes become more specific and the students must decide their own characterizing field among eight possible tracks: Constitutional, Private, Public, Historical, Commercial-Entrepreneurial, Cooperative, Communitarian (EC-EU), and Transnational. Their choice of one of these tracks entails choosing a different array of classes. In fact, in the Italian system only eight exams (courses) are non-compulsory: that is, in each year (not only the first one, as is the case in the USA), students are required to take the exams prescribed by the schedule. In order to get a *Laurea Magistrale in Giurisprudenza*—law degree —students must complete 300 "credits"; the number of credits received for each class completed varies from a minimum of six to a maximum of fifteen credits.

In addition, a doctorate program is available following a *Laurea Magistrale in Giurisprudenza*—but the admittance ratio is very low. That is, only a few law graduate students will be enrolled in a doctorate program, since the admittance ratio of the entry test is very strict. The length of this course is usually 3–4 years; during this time the future doctorates focus their study on specific topics of the chosen field of law, carry out research, and can help professors in carrying out the examinations of students seeking the *Laurea* degree.

Last but not least, law schools can set up and organize a *Scuola di specializzazione per Professioni Legali*—a School of Specialization for Legal Professions—where a two-year-long program trains the admitted students (who must already be graduates holding the *Laurea Magistrale*) in the areas of drawing legal statements, making decisions, and providing counseling. This course exists in part because the university education described above (for example, the *Laurea*) adopts a more theoretical approach to law than in is the case in the USA. The successful completion of this school will allow lawyers to skip one of the two years of *praticantato* (unpaid training in a law firm) that must be completed in order to become an effective attorney at law.

Q: *How many law students are there in Italy, and how many actually finish their law degrees?*

A: Regarding this point, here are some statistics that might interest you. All of them refer to academic year 2007–2008.

- Of the 310,000 people who enrolled for a first year at university, students who chose law were 32,360, precisely 10.5% of total, and this made law rank 3rd in percentage following economics disciplines (14.7%) and social-political disciplines (11.2%). As a related point, note that Italy is one of the most highly lawyer-populated countries at least in Europe: 210,000 lawyers, or 1 for every 283 persons—compared to Great Britain with 117,000 lawyers (1 for every 342 inhabitants) and France with 44,000 lawyers (1 for every 1,465 inhabitants).

- The total number of students enrolled in law disciplines (not just in their first year) was 103,568. This represents 5.7% of all students. Apparently some students who started their studies in law then switched to other disciplines. Indeed, in some recent years, the percentage of law students who abandon their law studies during or after their first year has ranged from about 21% to about 34% (depending on the year).

- 82.5% of law students are enrolled in a university that is located in the same region of their residence. This is similar to the percentage of all students (in all disciplines) enrolled in their nearby universities; that figure is 80%.

- The percentage of law students who had not yet passed even one exam in 2007–2008 was 21%: no other discipline showed worse figures than this.

- In 2007–2008 8.6% of total graduates were law students. Slightly more were women than were men.

- Some figures for the SJD (doctorate in law):

Admitted to start studies	1,131	8% of total doctorate-seeking students
Enrolled (all years)	3,263	8.1% of total doctorate-seeking students
Completed (with SJD degree)	797	7.8% of total doctorate-seeking students

- Foreigners (not Italian citizens) studying in Italy:

  1.6% of total law students

  2.9% of all university students

Q: *What kind of international exposure, training, and viewpoint do most Italian law students have?*

A: Typically, a student will have chances to spend a substantial period of time— usually from 3 months up to one year—studying at another European university (outside Italy) that has an agreement with the student's own home institution. This is encouraged and fostered by the European strategy and co-operation in education and training, in which politicians at the European level have recognized that education and training are essential to the development and success of today's knowledge society and economy. The EU's strategy emphasizes countries working together and learning from each other.

EU education and training policy has been given added impetus since the adoption of the Lisbon Strategy in 2000. This is the EU's overarching program focusing on growth and jobs. Knowledge, and the innovation that it sparks, are the EU's most valuable assets, particularly as global competition becomes more intense in all sectors.

While national governments are responsible for education and training, some challenges are common to all Member States. Ageing societies, skills deficits of the workforce, and the reality of global competition — all these need joint responses, with countries learning from each other. High quality pre-primary, primary, secondary, higher and vocational education and training are the fundament for Europe's success. Lifelong learning must become a reality across Europe. It is the key to growth and jobs, as well as to allow everyone the chance to participate fully in society.

EU member states and the European Commission have therefore strengthened their political cooperation. This has been done through the Education and Training 2010 work program launched in 2001 and its follow-up, the strategic framework for European cooperation in education and training ("ET 2020") adopted by the Council in May 2009.

As a practical matter, the EU fosters this mobility program by funding each student who meets the requirements (which are not onerous) with an amount of money disbursed monthly. In 2009 this sum of money was about 200 Euros.

In addition, international studies and perspectives have been encouraged by the LLP (Life-long Learning Program), which has its roots in the Maastricht Treaty establishing the EU in 1992. That agreement formally recognized education as an area of European Union competency and asserts that "[t]he Community shall contribute to the development of quality education by encouraging cooperation between member states and, if necessary, by supporting and supplementing their action, while fully respecting the responsibility of the member states for the content of teaching and the organization of education systems and their cultural and linguistic diversity."

In addition, of course, universities have freedom to negotiate bilateral agreements with other foreign universities in order to facilitate an exchange of students, scholars, and professors. Here, usually, students who meet the requirements are selected for participation in such an exchange on the basis of average grade levels, language skills, and a final test. A scholarship may be given to alleviate expenses related to mobility and life abroad costs.

So, as you can see, there is a very, very strong value placed on giving Italian law students opportunities to get international training, exposure, and viewpoint.

d. Curricular details

Q: *What courses will a law student typically take at an Italian university?*

A: As noted above, a total of 300 credits is required to get the *Laurea* degree. Usually, it is scheduled as a 5-year-long course of study for a full time student, plus the time required for the thesis that must be submitted. Each university and professor can vary the program of the courses, provided they stay within the framework of compulsory teachings given by the Ministry (see D.M. 25-11-2005 as revised from time to time). Box #3.6 shows that framework:

Box #3.6 Compulsory Law Courses at Italian Universities

	Disciplinary Sphere	Scientific Sector	Credits	
Basic	Historic-legal	Roman law and ancient law History of medieval and modern law	28	86
	Philosophical-legal	Philosophy of law	15	
	Private	Private law	25	
	Constitutional	Constitutional law Institutions of Public law Ecclesial law and Canon law	18	
Characterizing	Criminal	Criminal law	15	130
	Commercial (Business)	Commercial law	15	
	Economical and public	Science of Finance Tax law Political Economics Micro and Macro Economics Business economy Statistics	15	
	Compared law	Private Comparative law Public Comparative law	9	
	Communitarian law (EU)	EU law	9	
	Administrative	Administrative law	18	
	International	International law	9	
	Civil Trial	Civil Procedure	14	
	Criminal Trial	Criminal Procedure	14	
	Labor-Employment	Employment and Labor law	12	
Minimum bound credits				216
Credits available, decided autonomously by the universities				84
Credits required to obtain the degree				300

Box #3.7, in turn, shows a typical course of study at the University of Trento. As shown near the bottom of this table, each student is required to choose at least another 8 non-compulsory exams that determine the specialization among the 8 possible ones noted earlier: Constitutional, Private, Public, Historical, Commercial-Entrepreneurial, Cooperative, Communitarian (EC-EU), and Transnational. Students must achieve a fixed number of credits per year, regardless of the exams they take: failing to pass the scheduled year exams brings no academic sanction but the student will be forced to pay more taxes if he or she is not able to reach the minimum amount of credits per year. It is not possible to take an exam before the scheduled year.

Box #3.7 Sample Course of Study (in Law) at University of Trento

1st year (BASICS YEAR)	2nd year	3rd year	4th year	5th year
Private law I (9)	Institutions of EU law (9)	Criminal law II (6)	Civil Procedure (14)	Tax law (6)
Private Roman law (9)	Private law II (9)	Civil law (7)	Administrative law (12)	Philosophy of law II (6)
History of medieval and modern law (9)	Compared legal systems (9)	Employment-Labor law (15)	History of medieval and modern law (6)	Administrative Procedure (6)
Philosophy of law I (9)	Constitutional law (9)	Commercial law (15)	Roman law (6)	
Microeconomics (9)	International law (9)		Criminal Procedure (14)	
Public law (9)	Criminal law (9)			

Choice of 8 non-compulsory exams depending on the specialization* (6 credits each)	48
Foreign Language	5
Other skills (Advanced Languages skills, other exams, informatics, internships, …)	9
Thesis	20

Legend: (x) number of credits weighted
        "Private law" includes contract, tort, property, etc.
        "Public law" includes sources of law, constitutional institutions, local administration, etc.
        * Eight possible specialization fields: Constitutional, Private, Public, Historical, Commercial-Entrepreneurial, Cooperative, Communitarian (EC-EU), Transnational.

Q: *Do Italian law students typically attend their classes?*

A: In the Italian system of law school, attendance in each class is usually not necessary in order to take the exam; the rationale for this is to be found in the government policy that not only full-time students but also part-time students or working people should be allowed to successfully advance; hence it is regarded as best not to have them bound by compulsory attendance. Nevertheless, for some classes, the professor may require mandatory attendance or schedule written tests for attending students.

e. Career selection and preparation

Q: *Now we come to the principal underlying reason for legal education—getting qualified to become a legal professional. How is it that a law student could become prepared to become*

- *a judge?*
- *a "lawyer" (practicing attorney)*
- *a notary?*
- *a legal scholar?*

- *a government agency lawyer?*

- *a prosecutor?*

A: The answer is different, of course, for each category of legal professional. Here is a summary for each:

- a judge

  * The judge holds the public functions concerning administration of justice, interpretation of the laws and their application in the resolution of disputes. To become judge it is necessary to succeed in one of the public competitive examinations held annually and open to all law-graduated Italian citizens under the age of 40. The Constitution itself clearly states that this is the only possible way to become judge in the Italian system (Constitution art. 106).

  * It is allowed to take this public exam (and try to pass it) as many as three times. The exam is divided basically in two main steps: first three written tests on criminal, civil and administrative law; then, an oral test concerning the following subjects:

    – Private law and foundations of Roman law;

    – Civil procedure;

    – Criminal law;

    – Criminal procedure;

    – Administrative, Constitutional and Tax law;

    – Employment, Labor and Welfare law;

    – EU law;

    – International law and elements of legal informatics;

    – Foreign language, chosen by the candidate among the EU's official ones.

  * Once the competition is successfully passed, it is required that the person serve in a 2-year long paid apprenticeship (internship) as judicial auditor (*auditore giudiziario*) in an office of one Appellate Court (*Corte d'Appello*). Afterwards that person will become either judge or a prosecutor (*Pubblico Ministero*, or *PM*).

  * There have been some variations from this system. For example, a 1997 law (see D.Lgs. 398/1997) introduced the possibility that a person possessing (from after 2004) the *Diploma di Specializzazione per Professioni legali* could be admitted at the open competition in certain circumstances.

  * In general, though, the judicial-auditor-enabling open competition is a very difficult exam which requires a deep knowledge of the subjects being tested that only law school training can give. The graduate who wants to undertake this path should be ready to face an intense period of study, perhaps while attending one of the courses preparing for the exam. Since the results are unpredictable it is advisable not to close off other professional career possibilities.

- a "lawyer" (practicing attorney)
  * The practicing attorney is a self-employed person who carries out judicial services—these include defense and trial representation—as well as extra-judicial services, such as providing ongoing counseling, preparing legal opinions, assisting with arbitration, and drafting particularly complex contracts.
  * In order to enter this profession four preconditions must be met:
    1. Hold a law degree (now the *Laurea Magistrale* or previously the *Laurea Specialistica*);
    2. Complete a continuous two-year-long legal apprenticeship in a lawyer's office that shortens to just one year subsequent the successful achievement of the *Diploma di Scuola di Specializzazione per Professioni legali* (2 years long). This apprenticeship requires presence at a minimum of 20 trials per semester and the handling of at least four essays every six months concerning issues managed during the apprenticeship.
    3. Earn a Certificate of Accomplished Apprenticeship awarded by the Council of the Forensic Order;
    4. Pass the practice-enabling exam.
  * The simplest way to find a legal office in which to practice the required period of unpaid apprenticeship, in the absence of personally knowing somebody in the sector, is to ask the local Council of the Forensic Order—*Consiglio dell'Ordine forense*. As I already noted, the apprenticeship gives no right of wage or salary: only a reimbursement of expenses may be paid discretionarily by the law firm.
  * Afterwards, it is required to pass the national exam enabling the registration at the bar—*Albo degli Avvocati*—which must be taken at the Court of Appeal of the district where the apprenticeship has been performed. This exam has both theoretical and practical aspects to it, and it is both oral and written. The written tests are usually administered each December, and they focus on themes given by the Ministry of Justice. They include compilation of legal opinions on various issues (relating to both the civil code and the criminal code) and completion of other legal tasks. The oral tests, usually administered in January and February, consist of a discussion of certain issues on each of five legal subjects, at least one of which must be civil procedure or criminal procedure.
  * An individual who succeeds in this process is then eligible to practice law before all jurisdictions of the country except the so-called Superior Courts—that is, the Constitutional Court, the Supreme Court of Cassation, the Council of State, and the Superior Tribunal of Public Waters—all of which require a special license that can be obtained either after 12 years of continuous and virtuous practice or by passing another special exam.
- a notary
  * The *notaio* embodies both the figure of the public official and the self-employed person. The function of the office is above all to receive *inter vivos* and last will acts, ascribing public faith to them. To become a notary, a law graduate must have carried out an internship for a period of 18 months at a notary office or must have attended a notary course. Then he or she must pass

a national open competition conducted by the Ministry of Justice. This exam usually takes place every two years (instead of the yearly rate prescribed by the law), since a long time is needed for the grading of the written test. The first part of the exam involves a 35-question multiple choice test, and the second part involves both (i) three written tests and (ii) an oral exam about civil and commercial law, the legal aspects of the notary system, and other matters.

- a legal scholar

  * The legal scholar in the Italian system does not stand differently from the scholar of any other field. Thus, after graduation the candidate usually works toward the SJD—Doctorate of Juridical Science—which focuses the attention of the student on one subject of study. During this period, the student attends highly specialized courses and conducts research leading to the publication of writings.

  * The career of a legal scholar, which may be seen as having three levels or positions, is essentially pyramidal in shape: at the base is the Researcher status, above that is the position of Professor of Range II, and at the top of the pyramid is the position of Professor of Range I.

  * In order to become a Researcher—*Ricercatore*—the candidate must apply for that position at the university that has publicly advertised an open competition for the available place. A commission of three members of the university at issue (an ordinary professor, an associate one and a confirmed researcher) is called to judge and make a comparative decision among candidates through oral and written tests and the close examination of his/her hypothetical publications. Three years after having been hired, the researcher may obtain a confirmation of his or her status by a national commission of three members. At some point, following further evaluations and reviews before national commissions, a candidate might be advanced to a Professor II range and ultimately a Professor I range. Moreover, in some circumstances, following yet further evaluations and reviews by national commission, a professor may achieve the title of *Professore straordinario* and ultimately the title of *Professore ordinario*. See Box #3.8 for the pyramidal diagram described in the applicable law (L. 219/1998).

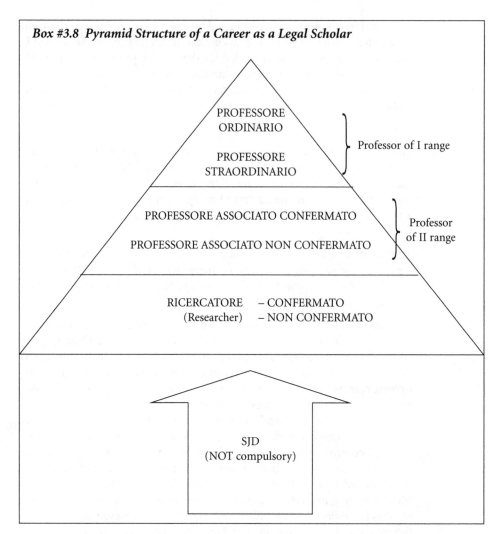

Box #3.8 Pyramid Structure of a Career as a Legal Scholar

PROFESSORE ORDINARIO

PROFESSORE STRAORDINARIO

} Professor of I range

PROFESSORE ASSOCIATO CONFERMATO

PROFESSORE ASSOCIATO NON CONFERMATO

} Professor of II range

RICERCATORE   – CONFERMATO
(Researcher)   – NON CONFERMATO

SJD
(NOT compulsory)

* Another brushstroke may be added to this picture. Professors in office may work either under a "fixed time-part time" arrangement or under or "full time" arrangement. The first of these implies 250 yearly working hours—instead of the 350 requested for a full time professor. The compensation for the former of these is lower than for the latter, but the part time professor is allowed to carry out professional activity in other contexts besides those relating to the university. Thus, a double goal may be achieved thanks to this provision: meeting the needs of professors and making sure that universities might employ people who deal with the law in action—thereby decreasing the level of academic abstraction that deeply penetrates the university system in Italy. The part time professor may not serve in certain administrative positions such as Dean and department director; these are for full time professors of Range I only.

• a government agency lawyer

* In Italy, a principal type of "government agency lawyer" is the "advocate of the State". The *Avvocatura dello Stato* is composed of a pool of specialized lawyers who represent and defend in trial the public administra-

tion and, in general, all the powers of the State when they are carrying out activities substantially administrative in nature. The *Avvocatura dello Stato* also has a consultancy function. The appointment of a person to the *Avvocatura dello Stato* occurs after an open competition published in the *Gazzetta Ufficiale*, the major source of recognition in the Italian system, where all laws and statutes are published for public knowledge. However, some preconditions must be met in order for a person to take the national exam:

– Italian citizenship;

– Membership in one of these categories:

~ Prosecutor for the State with at least two years of service,

~ Judge (in the ordinary courts),

~ Administrative judge,

~ Lawyer registered for at least six years,

~ Law professor or assistant who passed the lawyer-enabling exam,

~ Employee of local or national government agencies for at least five years, along with certain other qualifications.

* The exam itself consists of both a written portion (four tests of eight hours each, involving drafting certain documents) and an oral portion (two oral exams on a range of topics, plus an oral defense concerning a legal dispute given to the candidate 24 hours in advance).

* Only a few candidates meet these very demanding criteria to become a lawyer of the state.

• a prosecutor

* The explanation offered earlier as to how to become a judge would also apply here. Indeed, the choice confronts a successful candidate in the open competition as to whether to become a judge or to become a prosecutor.

This ends our set of "interviews" with an Italian law student. As should be clear, the Italian legal system reflects in many respects the more general observations offered earlier — particularly in the areas of sources of law, legal professions, and legal education.

II. Content and Operation

A. Criminal Procedure

A criminal trial in a civil law country typically looks very different from one in the USA. The layout of the courtroom, the roles of the participants (especially the presiding judge), the rules of evidence, the consideration of mitigating circumstances, and even the overriding aims of the exercise are different in important ways. Some of the differences might strike an American lawyer as odd, ill-advised, or even fundamentally unfair. Closer inspection might yield a different assessment. History and culture have much to do with explaining the differences

1. History, Reform, and Compromise

Criminal procedure in civil law countries reflects a fascinating interplay of key historical and conceptual developments summarized above in Chapter Two. Among the most prominent of these are (i) the rise of the nation-state as the fundamental political unit of Europe, creating a concept of legislative positivism in which the state was the sole lawgiver, (ii) the long-term influence of Christianity and of canon law procedures for handling misbehavior (particularly heresy), (iii) the legacy of a logical and comprehensive codification of laws, and the urge for certainty to which such codification responded, and (iv) the dramatic reforms of the intellectual revolution that swept across Europe in the 17th and 18th centuries. Let us begin with the last of these developments—the intellectual revolution.

Again, Merryman offers an illuminating historical review, explaining how the intellectual revolution crystallized modern principles of criminal procedure in civil law countries, especially as public criticism mounted regarding the *ancien regime*:

> Although the [intellectual revolution in Europe] profoundly affected every part of the civil law tradition, its effects are most clearly observable in public law [and especially] ... in the field of criminal procedure. Among the writers and philosophers of the eighteenth century who contributed to the ideology of revolution, most had something to say about the sorry state of criminal law and criminal procedure. The most important reformer in this field was Cesare Beccaria, whose book *Of Crimes and Punishments* exploded on the European scene in 1764 and became the most influential work on criminal law and criminal procedure in Western history.
>
> ... [Beccaria's book] begins by establishing the principle of *nullum crimen sine lege* and *nulla poena sine lege*.[62] As Beccaria states it: "Only the laws can determine the punishment of crimes; and the authority of making penal laws can reside only with the legislator, who represents the whole society united by the social compact." Thus, according to Beccaria, crimes and punishments can be established only by law, and by "law" he means "statute." Beccaria [also condemns vagueness in criminal laws, and he] goes on to establish two basic principles. The first is that there should be a proportion between crimes and punishments, so that the more serious crimes are more severely punished. The second is that punishments should apply impartially to criminals, regardless of their social station, position, or wealth.[63]

The historical survey of the civil law tradition offered above in Chapter Two featured numerous biographical sketches of persons who had broad influence over its development. So far, this chapter has not included any, given our focus here on the operational aspects of the civil law tradition. However, Cesare Beccaria has left such an indelible mark on this one particular area of the civil law tradition—criminal procedure—that we should look briefly at his life and career. See Box #3.9 for a biographical sketch.

---

62. These would translate roughly as "no crime without law (identifying the behavior as a crime)" and "no punishment without law (specifying such punishment)".

63. Merryman, *supra* note 2, at 125–126.

Box #3.9 Cesare Beccaria[64]

Cesare Beccaria was born into an aristocratic family in Milan. As a boy, he was sent to a Jesuit school at Parma, "where his 'sentiments of humanity' were 'stifled by eight years of fanatical and servile education.'" [Thomas, *supra* note 64, at xvii.] Beccaria ultimately received a degree in law from the University of Pavia in 1758. After returning to Milan, Beccaria joined an intellectual social club called the Academy of the Reformed, "one of the many academies, reading societies, salons, and lodges that flourished in the 1700s." [*Id.* at xvii.] Beccaria eventually joined the Academy of Fists, an unconventional-thinking intellectual group formed by Pietro Verri, Beccaria's friend and mentor. "To the extent that the coterie had any organizing principle, it was a commitment to free debate and a common desire to contribute to the public good." [*Id.* at xviii.] Beccaria became well-read in popular social theory of the time, including the works of Rousseau.

With the support of his friends in the Academy of Fists, Beccaria wrote his short treatise — *Dei delitti e delle pene* (*On Crime and Punishment*) — condemning torture of prisoners and the death penalty. Beccaria initially published the treatise anonymously to avoid "running into trouble with state or ecclesiastical censors." [*Id.* at xxiii.] Eventually, though, Beccaria permitted publishers to assign his name to the work. After his authorship became public, Beccaria briefly joined intellectual circles in France, but then he returned home to Milan, first accepting a position as a professor of political economy and then taking a government position in the Habsburg administration. [*Id.* at xxviii.] Beccaria never again published a significant work; he spent the remainder of his life in Milan.

On Crime and Punishment is recognized as the first published argument against the death penalty — and indeed it is also considered the first full work of penology, advocating reform of the criminal law system. *Id. On Crime and Punishment* influenced many great legal scholars. For example, Jeremy Bentham dubbed Beccaria "the first evangelist of reason." [*Id.* at xv.] Blackstone also admired Beccaria's work and drew from it when drafting his famous treatise *Commentaries on the Laws of England*, which was published only shortly later. Today Beccaria's name has come to be equated "with opposition to the death penalty and with efforts to create a more reasoned, effective, and humane approach to punishment." [*Id.* at xv.]

What were the reforms that Beccaria urged *departing* from? That is, what was the nature of the system that needed reform? At the risk of distortion through oversimplification, we might label it "absolutist inquisitorialism". The first word in that label ("absolutist") reflects the absolutism of the state, following the victory of the nation-state over the Church as the fundamental political (and hence law-making) unit in Europe. (As noted above, that victory was formally confirmed in the Peace of Westphalia of 1648.) The second word in that label ("inquisitorialism") reflects a secretive system of proof taking and judgment — inspired by canon law and leading easily to abuse of power — that the political absolutism made possible.

In order to explore the "absolutist inquisitorialism" that the criminal procedure reforms of 18th- and 19th-century Europe were meant to overcome, we must distinguish the inquisitorial system from the so-called "accusatorial" system. In an intriguing discussion of these different systems, Merryman suggests that they lie at two different places

---

64. The content of Box #3.9 is drawn principally from Aaron Thomas, *Preface* to Cesare Beccaria, On Crimes and Punishments and Other Writings (Aaron Thomas ed., Aaron Thomas & Jeremy Parzen trans., 2008) (1764). Specific references to quoted passages from Thomas are cited in square brackets. Further information is available at http://en.wikipedia.org/wiki/Cesare_Beccaria, and at *Cesare Beccaria*, on the website of the Florida State University College of Criminology and Criminal Justice, at http://www.criminology.fsu.edu/crimtheory/beccaria.htm.

along an evolutionary line. He begins by noting that although it can be inaccurate and misleading to distinguish between *contemporary* systems of criminal procedure within the civil law and common law worlds by proclaiming that the former is "inquisitorial" and the latter is "accusatorial", such a distinction does in fact have "some validity when put into *historical* context".[65] He offers this explanation:

> [T]he accusatorial system ... is generally thought by anthropologists to be the first substitute an evolving society develops for private vengeance. In such a system the power to institute the action resides in the wronged person, who is the accuser. This same right of accusation is soon extended to the accuser's relatives, and ... [ultimately to] all members of the group. A presiding officer is selected to hear the evidence, decide, and sentence; this person does not, however, have the power to institute the action or to determine the questions to be raised or the evidence to be introduced, and has no inherent investigative powers. These matters are in the hands of the accuser and the accused. The criminal trial is a contest between the accuser and the accused, with the judge as a referee. Typically the proceeding takes place publicly and orally and is not preceded by any official (i.e., judicial or police) investigation or preparation of evidence.
>
> Criminal procedure in medieval civil law also was accusatorial.... [However, the] inquisitorial procedure developed later in Church courts in cases charging the crime of heresy.[66] Under the influence of this canonical procedure and the rise of statism in the sixteenth century, all Continental criminal procedure became inquisitorial.
>
> *The inquisitorial system typically represents an additional step along the path of social evolution from the system of private vengeance.* Its principal features in-

---

65. Merryman, *supra* note 2, at 127 (emphasis added).

66. For a fascinating account of how and why "the Church was the first authority which changed from the accusatory to the inquisitorial procedure," see A. Esmein, A HISTORY OF CONTINENTAL CRIMINAL PROCEDURE: WITH SPECIAL REFERENCE TO FRANCE 78 (John Simpson trans., 2007). The author of that book provides this summary:

> The Canon law had originally recognized only the accusatory system in criminal matters, influenced in this respect both by the Roman law and by Germanic custom. In the 800s, however, it made a step forward. When, by reason of a crime committed, any one had been pointed out as suspected by public opinion, and this "mala fama" or "infamia" was established by the judge, the Canon law had admitted that this gave a certain right of action against the "infamatus." This did not allow the judge to bring witnesses against him and condemn him if he should be convicted, but the accused was obliged to exculpate himself from the crime imputed to him. This exculpation was effected, according to the circumstances of the case, by the oath of the "infamatus" supported by compugators, "co-swearers" ("purgatio canonica"), or by ordeals ("pugatio vulgaris"). If he refused, or failed, he could be condemned as convicted of the offense charged against him. These methods of proof the Canon law had borrowed from the Germanic customs, although it may at first have spontaneously adopted a similar method, allowing, in certain cases, a suspected person to exculpate himself by his own oath, but without "co-swearers." In the procedure introduced in the 800s, if the "infamatus" refused to exculpate himself, or failed in the "purgatio," he was considered convicted of the crime and could be condemned accordingly. Out of this procedure grew, by evolution, the inquisitorial procedure.

Id. at 79. Another source notes that in both the Holy Roman Empire and the German territories, "church courts were applying inquisitorial procedure from the twelfth century on, and ... these German church courts were staffed by German canon lawyers. The inquisitorial procedure which they applied was gradually adopted, with modifications, in the various German territorial courts from at least the thirteenth century." Harold J. Berman, LAW AND REVOLUTION II: THE IMPACT OF THE PROTESTANT REFORMATIONS ON THE WESTERN LEGAL TRADITION 432 (2003). See also Erwin J. Urch, THE EVOLUTION OF THE INQUISITORIAL PROCEDURE IN ROMAN LAW (1980).

clude first, attenuation or elimination of the figure of the private accuser and appropriation of that role by public officials; and second, the conversion of the judge from an impartial referee into an active inquisitor who is free to seek evidence and to control the nature and objectives of the inquiry. In addition, the relative equality of the parties that is an attribute of the accusatorial system, in which two individuals contest before an impartial arbiter, has been drastically altered. Now the contest is between an individual (the accused) and the state. Historically, inquisitorial proceedings have tended to be secret and written rather than public and oral. The resulting imbalance of power, combined with the secrecy of the written procedure, creates the danger of an oppressive system, in which the rights of the accused can easily be abused....[67]

Indeed, Merryman explains, this danger of an oppressive system did in fact materialize, and harsh abuses did occur, in the "absolutist inquisitorialist" system of pre-revolution Europe. Because the criminal action was an action by the state with proceedings that were written and secret, giving an accused person no right to counsel and often forcing testimony from the accused by the use of torture, we would regard the proceedings conducted then as being completely devoid of ordinary humanity and justice.[68]

This, then, was the nature of the system of 18th-century criminal procedure in Europe that Beccaria and others saw in serious need of reform. In the feverish social and political upheaval of the European revolutions (in France and elsewhere) of the late 1700s and early 1800s, fundamental changes were called for—and many were made—involving these elements:

- institution of the jury for criminal trials
- substitution of the oral public procedure in place of secret written procedure
- establishment of the accused's right to legal counsel
- restriction of the judge's inquisitorial powers
- abolition of the requirement that the accused testify under oath
- abolition of torture
- abolition of arbitrary intervention by the sovereign in the criminal process[69]

We shall see shortly how these reforms are reflected in the criminal procedure in modern civil law countries. First, however, we have one last preliminary point to consider.

So far, we have examined three of the four historical and conceptual developments that lie at the foundations of criminal procedure in modern civil law countries: (i) the rise of the nation-state as the fundamental political unit of Europe, creating a concept of legislative positivism in which the state was the sole law-giver, (ii) the long-term influence of Christianity and of canon law procedures for handling misbehavior (particularly heresy), and (as numbered above in the introductory paragraph of this subsection) (iv) the dramatic reforms of the intellectual revolution that swept across Europe in the 17th and 18th centuries. Let us look briefly at (iii) the legacy of a logical and comprehensive codification of laws, and the urge for certainty to which such codification responded.

---

67. Merryman, *supra* note 2, at 127–128 (emphasis added).
68. *Id.* at 127.
69. For enumerations of these reforms, and further explanation of some of them, see *id.* at 129–130.

I have already offered my views on the significance of codes and codification in the civil law tradition. See, for example, subsection IB2 above.[70] Given the central importance of codification, it should come as no surprise that reform efforts undertaken in 18th- and 19th-century Europe included codification of criminal law and procedure. As we saw above in Chapter Two, two of the five codes emerging from the great Napoleonic codification effort following the French Revolution were the criminal code and the criminal procedure code. It should be obvious that such codifications would be important ingredients to fighting some of the evils identified by Cesare Beccaria—including, for example, vagueness in the rules, which made citizens uncertain as to whether they had violated criminal laws (and, if charged with crimes, how to defend against those charges).

2. Criminal Procedure in Action in the Modern Civil Law World

Having now laid the historical and conceptual framework into which modern criminal procedure fits in the civil law world, let us look at how it operates in actual cases in a typical civil law country. Several sources will help us in that regard. Some of them appear in the following paragraphs, and another appears in Appendix 3.2, at the end of this chapter. Beyond these discussions of "typical" civil law countries' systems of criminal procedure, we shall look specifically (in subsection IID1, below) at Italy's system of criminal procedure.[71] (Much more emphasis will be laid on criminal procedure than on any of the other operational topics covered in this chapter.)

First, let us consider the very beginning of criminal proceedings—at the point just following the apparent commission of a crime. The Schlesinger text offers the following observations regarding arrest and detention. In doing so, that text starts to explode the myth that the American system of criminal procedure offers more respect of and safeguards for individual rights than is true in European civil law countries.

> In the civilian systems, as in our own, the policeman normally is the first public official to arrive at the scene of an alleged crime, or to receive a report concerning it. He may conduct an informal investigation; but his power to arrest the suspect without judicial warrant, or to proceed to warrantless searches and seizures, is seriously limited. Thus, whenever measures are contemplated by the police that affect the freedom of the suspect, it becomes necessary at a very early stage of the investigation to involve the prosecutor and the court.
>
> ... [Note the contrast with the US approach to arrest and detention:] In this country, [*i.e.*, the USA] it is still the general rule that criminal proceedings routinely "start with the harsh, and in itself degrading, measure of physical arrest." ...

---

70. For further observations along these lines, see John W. Head, *Code, Cultures, Chaos, and Champions: Common Features of Legal Codification Experiences in China, Europe, and North America*, 13 DUKE JOURNAL OF COMPARATIVE AND INTERNATIONAL LAW 1 (2003).

71. Simplified generalizations seldom match particular realities, so it should come as no surprise that the generalizations offered in the following paragraphs about criminal procedure in a "typical" civil law country will not exactly match the actual details of any particular country. That is why we shall be examining in subsection IID1 some details of criminal procedure in Italy—to counterbalance the shortcomings of these generalizations about a "typical" civil law country. For details on criminal procedure in France, see, e.g., Gerald L. Kock and Richard S. Frase, THE FRENCH CODE OF CRIMINAL PROCEDURE 1–40 (revised ed. 1988). For details on criminal procedure in Mexico, see Stephen Zamora, José Ramón Cossío, Leonel Pereznieto, José Roldán-Xopa, and David Lopez, MEXICAN LAW 345–376 (2005). Countless books and other resources are available in various languages about the criminal procedure rules in many other countries as well.

[Although there have been some modifications to this approach,] these modifications are halfhearted....

The civil-law countries, on the other hand, unanimously recognize that the initiation of a judicial proceeding, whether civil or criminal, never requires the defendant's physical arrest.... [Instead, notification of the defendant can] be effected by a summons, ... and ... it is unthinkable to use physical arrest as a routine measure against a suspect who has not yet been tried and who, consequently, must be presumed innocent.

The question whether a suspect should be detained pending trial is, in the civilians' view, completely separate and distinct from the routine of initiating the proceeding. Except in carefully defined emergency situations, a judicial order is required to detain the suspect before trial ... [and the] requirements for the issuance of such an order are strict.[72]

What do a typical civil law country's criminal procedure rules prescribe for the commencement of an investigation and trial? Traditionally, the process would comprise three stages: the investigative stage, the examining stage (sometimes called the instruction stage), and the trial.[73] The first of those stages falls within the jurisdiction of the public prosecutor. The second of those stages, which is primarily written and not public, falls under the jurisdiction of the "examining judge" but also features active participation by the public prosecutor as well. The function of the examining judge is to investigate the incident and to prepare a written account of it. If, in carrying out that function, the examining judge determines that a crime was committed and that the accused person is in fact the perpetrator, then the case would proceed to the third stage, which is the trial. If, on the other hand, the judge decides either (i) that no crime was committed or (ii) that the crime was not committed by the accused, then the matter would not proceed to the trial stage.[74]

In recent years some countries have modified or departed from this three-stage model. Germany abolished the examining stage in 1975, so that "[t]he entire pre-trial process is now in the hands of prosecutors and the police, as it is in the United States"; and more recently several other European countries and Latin American countries have adopted that German model.[75]

What is the general character and rationale of these recent departures (in some countries) from the three-stage model of criminal investigation and prosecution?

> In a very general way it can be said that the principal progress toward a more just and humane criminal proceeding in Europe in the last century and a half has come through reforms in the investigative and examining phases of the criminal proceeding. These reforms have been of two principal kinds. First, every effort has been made to develop a core of prosecuting attorneys who act impartially and objectively ... [by giving them] a security of tenure and consequent freedom from influence similar to that enjoyed by judges. Second, a number of procedural safeguards have been developed to help protect the accused's interests during the examining phase [where it still exists]. Principal among these is the right of the accused to representation by counsel throughout this phase of the proceeding.[76]

---

72. Schlesinger-2009, *supra* note 46, at 830–836 (quoting from a 1974 work by S. A. Cohn).
73. See Merryman, *supra* note 2, at 130.
74. *Id.*
75. *Id.*
76. *Id.* at 130–131.

The recent reforms referred to above have not, in most civil law countries, changed some of the core features of the criminal trial itself, which remains different in some important respects from the common law criminal trial. In a criminal trial in a civil law country, "[t]he evidence has already been taken and the record made, and this record is available to the accused and to counsel, as well as to the prosecution. The function of the trial is to present the case to the trial judge and jury [or lay triers of fact, as described below] and to allow the prosecutor and the defendant's counsel to argue their cases."[77]

Having addressed these general introductory points, let us turn to a sea of details. Appendix 3.2 draws from a law journal article written by Professor Myron Moskovitz (of Golden Gate University) in the form of a play involving four main characters: an American prosecuting attorney, an American defense lawyer, and two European law professors who advise those two American lawyers. The action in the play takes place in an unnamed European country, where a criminal trial is being conducted. The criminal trial is a special one: it is (fictionally) what the famous O.J. Simpson trial of the mid-1990s (actually conducted in California with Judge Lance Ito presiding) *would* have looked like *if* it would have been conducted in a European courtroom under the rules of criminal procedure applicable in the European country to which it has been (fictionally) transferred.

In reading the law journal article excerpted in Appendix 3.2, we should pay particular attention to these points, many of which are also reflected in specific Study Questions posed at the beginning of this chapter:

- the layout of the courtroom
- the role of the judge
- the role of the prosecuting attorney
- the role of the defense attorney
- the involvement of the victim's representative
- the selection, order, and posing of the questions and presentation of evidence
- testimony by the accused
- admissibility of evidence that was obtained illegally
- admissibility of "hearsay" evidence
- admissibility of evidence of the accused's prior convictions or other bad acts
- the simultaneous consideration of culpability and sanction
- plea bargaining
- the grounds for an appeal, including an appeal by the prosecuting attorney
- the underlying values to be served by the system of criminal justice

Some aspects of the issues listed above are summarized in Box 3.10. The synopsis offered there touches only briefly on most of the issues and will not prove especially enlightening on its own; still, it might serve as an aid in identifying some of the key points to be drawn from a close reading of the article reprinted in Appendix 3.2.

---

77. *Id.* at 131.

Box #3.10 *Criminal Trial Procedure in Civil Law Countries: Selected Operational Points*

Central to an understanding of criminal trial procedure in many civil law countries—and therefore to an appreciation of how it differs from criminal trial procedure in most common law countries—is a recognition of the particular functions performed by several key participants in a criminal trial.

First, the presiding judge plays a preeminent role, carrying most of the responsibility (and authority) for asking questions, calling witnesses, and presentation of the case more generally. In most important criminal trials, the presiding judge will be one of a panel of three professional judges.

In some countries, this three-judge panel will be accompanied, at least for some types of serious criminal trials, by several (often six) lay triers of fact. These non-professional persons serve some of the functions of a lay jury in common law criminal trials, by permitting a means by which public opinion is reflected and accountability of the professional judges to the community is safeguarded.

Closely associated with the judges and the lay triers of fact (which carry different labels in different systems) is the prosecuting attorney, a position which in some civil law countries has a very close professional and vocational affiliation with the professional judges themselves. So close is this affiliation in some systems that the prosecuting attorney will sit at a desk or table close to the raised bench where the judges (and the lay triers of fact, if any) sit. In other systems, the prosecuting attorney will sit at a desk or table on the floor of the courtroom, in a position corresponding to where the defense attorney will sit.

The role of both the prosecuting attorney and the defense attorney will vary from country to country, but in most cases will be markedly less active than in a common law criminal trial proceeding—again, because of the preeminent role occupied by the presiding judge. In many cases a representative of the victim to the alleged crime will also sit on the floor of the courtroom.

Testimony by the accused in a criminal trial in a civil law country is typically not required, but the overall structure of the proceeding often leads the accused to testify anyway. Such testimony usually is not given under oath.

One reason for testimony by the accused is related to the fact that criminal trials ordinarily combine two elements—culpability and sanction—into a seamless procedure, so that cooperation by an accused (as by offering testimony) can be seen as a ground for mitigation of punishment if the accused is found guilty. (There is nearly always, by the way, a presumption of innocence as a formal legal matter, although its precise nature and its protection of an accused will vary from one country to another.)

Questions posed to the accused can explore prior convictions and other bad acts of the accused, again because of the opportunity such questions would offer for determining what sort of sanction is to be imposed on the accused if there is in fact culpability on his or her part. An obvious objection that would be raised to the taking of evidence on prior convictions and bad acts—that such information could unduly influence the fact-finder to find culpability in current circumstances merely because the accused has behaved badly in past circumstances—is offset, at least in theory, by the fact that the professional judges are trained and experienced enough to avoid such undue implications, and the lay triers of fact (if any) can be instructed and influenced by the professional judges to do the same.

Likewise, all manner of other evidence that could be (and usually is) found objectionable on various grounds in common law criminal trials can and does get admitted into evidence in a typical civil law country. This would include (i) "hearsay" evidence (statements by one person about what s/he heard another person, not subject to cross-examination, say about some matter pertinent to the case) and (ii) evidence obtained through procedures (by the police investigators, for example) that are illegal or even unconstitutional.

> Admission of such evidence—and indeed all relevant factual evidence—is generally favored because of the overriding two-part goal that criminal trials in civil law countries are supposedly aimed to achieve. This goal is an accurate and humane determination of (1) whether the accused committed an illegal act and, if so, (2) what response society should have to that fact (through the criminal justice system) in order to mend the tear in the social fabric that such illegal behavior represents.
>
> While acknowledging that this two-part goal is partly rhetorical, difficult to achieve, and subject to competing values and pressures, civil law lawyers (including legislators and judges) commonly use this goal as a rationale for (i) resisting (and in some countries legally prohibiting) plea-bargaining procedures, at least in formal ways, and (ii) permitting an acquittal (or, for that matter, a conviction) emerging from a criminal trial to be appealed by a prosecutor is s/he believes a proper determination has not been made on the issue of either culpability or sanction.

With the summary offered in Box #3.10—and assuming the content of Appendix 3.2 has now been studied—we come to the end of our thumbnail survey of criminal procedure in "typical" European civil law countries. Let us turn to two other matters of content and operation—civil procedure and court structures—before examining the Italian legal system for some illustrations, elaborations, and exceptions.

B. Civil Procedure

Civil litigation in civil law countries is handled (i) very *differently* from criminal cases in civil law countries and (ii) very *similarly* to civil litigation in common law countries—except for a big difference: there is, in a sense, no such thing as a trial in civil proceedings in civil law countries. This stems partly from the absence of the expectation of a jury in *any* civil case. This fact has important implications for presentation of evidence and for the taking of appeals. The following paragraphs will briefly explore all these topics.

1. Where Is the Trial?

Although we have begun our survey of the content and operation of the civil law tradition by examining *criminal* procedure (see subsection IIA, above), in many respects *civil* procedure is more fundamental to the nature of the civil law tradition. This reflects in part the fact that civil procedure emerges directly from private law (recall that criminal law is typically regarded as part of public law), and in part the fact that civil procedure was not substantially affected by the intellectual revolution that brought the sweeping reforms to criminal procedure that we have seen above in subsection IIA of this chapter. In that sense, civil procedure is older than criminal procedure, more closely reflecting its origins in Roman and canon law.[78]

From this fact we could assume that civil procedure in civil law countries would retain more of the vestiges of the written, non-public features that criminal procedure in those countries has shaken off in recent centuries. And we would be correct in that assumption. Merryman offers these brief observations about civil procedure in civil law countries:

---

78. See Merryman, *supra* note 2, at 112.

A typical civil proceeding in a civil law jurisdiction is divided into three separate stages. There is a brief preliminary stage, in which the pleadings are submitted and a hearing judge (usually called the instructing judge) is appointed; an evidence-taking stage, in which the hearing judge takes the evidence and prepares a summary written record; and a decision-making stage, in which the judges who will decide the case consider the record transmitted to them by the hearing judge, receive counsel's briefs, hear their arguments, and render decision. The reader will observe that the word "trial" is missing from this description. In a very general way it can be said that what common lawyers think of as a trial in civil proceedings does not exist in the civil law world.[79]

Another authority offers this longer explanation, highlighting how the absence of a single event called a trial makes sense in the larger context of civil procedure in civil law countries:

> In a typical civil action, after the pleadings are filed, a period of evidence taking begins. From the outset, several differences from common law civil procedure appear. These differences can be summed up by noting that on the one hand, there is no real counterpart to our [US] pre-trial discovery and motion practice, while on the other hand there is no genuine "trial" in our [US] sense of a single culminating event. Rather, a civil law action is a continuous process of meetings, hearings, and written communications during which evidence is introduced, testimony is taken, and motions are made and decided....
>
> During this process, the judge plays an active role in questioning witnesses, and in framing or reformulating the issues. Although the questioning is typically done by the judge, the questions are often submitted by the parties' counsel[,] who sometimes are permitted to question a witness directly. As the action proceeds, the judge may inject new theories, and new legal and factual issues, thus reducing the disadvantage of the party with the less competent lawyer. In addition, the court may obtain certain types of evidence, such as expert opinions, on its own motion. There are no requirements that documents be formally admitted into evidence, nor are there any rules against hearsay and opinion evidence. Rather, the parties informally introduce documents after providing the other side with notice and an opportunity to inspect. The weight to be accorded the evidence is for the free evaluation of the court.
>
> ... [T]he bench is usually collegial [that is, composed of more than one judge], but as a rule only one judge will preside over the evidence-taking stage of the proceedings. In some countries, it may happen that the case is decided by an entirely different judge or panel from the one or ones who heard the parties and took the evidence. The better practice, as exemplified by Germany, requires the judge who conducted the proceedings to render the decision in the case. A money judgment on the merits is generally executed out of the defeated party's property. Costs of litigation are taxed in such a way as to discourage hopeless or frivolous causes: as a rule, the defeated party bears the cost of litigation, including attorney's fees. If each party wins and loses in part, costs are allocated proportionately.[80]

---

79. *Id.* at 112–113.
80. Nutshell-2008, *supra* note 121, at 97–99.

One important point emerging from both of the foregoing passages is that in most civil law jurisdictions, civil litigation does not include the sort of public event for the presentation of evidence and theatrical flourishes that is commonplace in common law countries (including of course the USA). That is, there is no such thing as a "trial". One way of further emphasizing this point is by visualizing civil litigation as in the diagram in Box #3.11. I find it useful to liken civil litigation in civil law countries to a string of sausages, whereas civil litigation in common law countries has as its central feature a trial, like a foot-long hot dog.

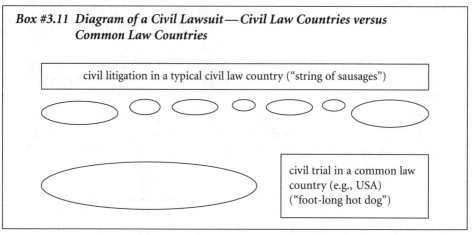

Box #3.11 Diagram of a Civil Lawsuit—Civil Law Countries versus Common Law Countries

civil litigation in a typical civil law country ("string of sausages")

civil trial in a common law country (e.g., USA) ("foot-long hot dog")

Naturally, this analogy-by-visualization suffers from oversimplification. For example, it ignores the fact that in many instances, civil disputes in common law countries often never actually go to trial because they are settled during the pre-trial stage; and indeed that pre-trial stage, which is sometimes dominated by mini-disputes over "discovery" (preparation and release of documents that one party seeks and the other wishes not to provide), can resemble the "string of sausages" described above. Still, the assumed (or threatened) destination of civil litigation in common law countries is the trial; and such a civil trial, largely identical in outward appearance to a criminal trial, is a big, singular, public event.

Another text offers this simplified view of the distinction between civil litigation in a traditional, or "orthodox", civil law system and civil litigation in a common law country, with special emphasis on the USA.

> In the legal systems in the common law tradition, procedure was historically based around a jury trial before a single judge and jury, with matters of law being reserved for the decision of the judge and matters of fact for the jury. Although the jury trial is in practice of greatly reduced significance in modern common law systems, except in the United States, the procedural system is still largely premised upon the assumption that the main purpose of the procedural rules is to prepare the parties for a trial in which all issues of law and fact arising in the litigation will be decided at a climactic hearing. In systems of this kind the dominant principles are *party control* and *party presentation*. Party control expresses the notion that it is for the parties to the litigation and not the court to determine what issues are in dispute and require resolution by the court and to decide, within a framework set by the rules of court, the pace at which the litigation proceeds to trial. The court is conceived as holding itself aloof from

these matters unless the parties choose to refer a question concerning them to the court for decision during the *pre-trail* (or *interlocutory*) procedure. Party presentation is the notion that it is for the parties to decide what evidence is to be presented to the court in order to decide the issues of fact that arise in the case and to present that evidence to the court in whatever manner they see fit, within the limits set by the rules of the law of evidence and the professional practices of the bar. Systems of this kind are sometimes said to adopt an *adversarial* procedure.

The procedural tradition in the civil law countries is quite different from that of the common law. Trial by jury is unknown in civil cases and the litigation is usually conducted before a multijudge court acting in a collegial manner to arrive at a decision that is, on the surface, unanimous. [In the purest form of this model, which many civil law countries have now departed from now, the] principle of party control is not recognized. It is for the court to decide, having received written pleadings from the parties and heard their submissions, what issues arise in the case, and for it to indicate what evidence it will require in relation to them.... The court actively manages the case throughout the procedure, indicating what steps are to be taken and when. The procedure is sometimes said to be *inquisitorial*, but this should not be misunderstood. In practice, the court's ability to conduct independent fact-finding operations is very limited and is not much greater than that of common law courts. However, it is often the case that the court will appoint its own expert witnesses in cases where expert evidence is called for.... There is no process directly equating to discovery.

There is often no trial in the sense in which that word is used in the common law, but issues of law and fact are resolved in a series of hearings. Systems of this kind often result in frequent short hearings. The emphasis is more on written evidence than oral presentation.[81]

As the foregoing excerpt makes clear, the explanation for this difference between civil litigation in civil law countries and civil litigation in common law countries can be boiled down — again, at the risk of oversimplification — to one word: juries. Whereas a defendant's right to a jury trial in civil actions is traditional in many parts of the common law world, it is largely foreign to the civil law world.[82] Recall from our discussion above that even in *criminal* cases in most civil law countries the proceedings do not involve a jury of the sort that is routine in the USA — that is, a free-standing, separately-seated group of lay people gathered to provide an accused with a right to have his case heard by "a jury of his peers". Instead, it is more usual to have community involvement reflected, if at all, by "lay triers of fact" that sit with the professional judges and are influenced by them.

In the common law tradition, however, jury trials have a long history not only in criminal cases but also in civil cases.[83] As noted above, in the modern common law world, the

---

81. Keith Uff, *Civil Procedure*, in I LEGAL SYSTEMS OF THE WORLD: A POLITICAL AND SOCIAL ENCYCLOPEDIA 308–309 (2008).

82. See Merryman, *supra* note 2, at 113.

83. For additional information on the history of jury trial in *criminal* cases in England, see TWELVE GOOD MEN AND TRUE: THE CRIMINAL TRIAL JURY IN ENGLAND, 1200–1800 (J.S. Cockburn & Thomas A. Green eds., 1988); Thomas A. Green, VERDICT ACCORDING TO CONSCIENCE: PERSPECTIVES ON THE ENGLISH CRIMINAL TRIAL JURY, 1200–1800 (1985). For a summary of the history of jury trials in *civil* litigation in common law countries, see James Oldham, TRIAL BY JURY: THE SEVENTH AMENDMENT AND ANGLO-AMERICAN SPECIAL JURIES (2006); Ellen E. Sward, THE DECLINE OF THE CIVIL JURY 67–100 (2001).

USA is a "lone ranger", or nearly so, in this regard: in most jurisdictions of the USA there is a constitutional right to a jury in civil trials,[84] even though elsewhere in the common law world the civil jury has now been abolished.[85] Moreover, even in the USA, the availability of juries in civil cases carries little *practical* significance: only a tiny proportion of civil disputes in the USA actually go through a complete trial.[86]

Still, the *traditional* significance in common law countries of having juries in (some) civil trials remains very great—great enough to exercise a continuing influence over civil litigation in those countries. What is important to us here is that it is the *absence* of this influence in civil law countries that explains much about why civil procedure in civil law countries differs so markedly from civil procedure in common law countries.

Let us now examine more closely three main features of that difference: (i) concentration versus a lack of concentration, (ii) immediacy versus mediacy, and (iii) orality versus non-orality. All three features are explained by Merryman, beginning with concentration—what I referred to earlier as the "foot-long hot dog" character of civil litigation in common law countries.

> The existence of a jury has profoundly affected the form of civil proceedings in the common law tradition. The necessity to bring together a number of ordinary citizens to hear the testimony of witnesses and observe the evidence, to find the facts, and to apply the facts to the law under instructions from a judge, has pushed the trial into the shape of an event [given the fact that the] lay jury cannot easily be convened, adjourned, and reconvened several times.... Such an event is a trial as we know it.

> In the civil law nations, where there is no tradition of civil trial by jury, an entirely different approach has developed. There is no such thing as a trial in our sense; there is no single, concentrated event. The typical civil proceeding in a civil law country is actually a series of isolated meetings of and written communications between counsel and the judge, in which evidence is introduced, testimony is given, procedural motions and rulings are made, and so on.... Comparative lawyers, in remarking on this phenomenon, speak of the "concentration" of the

---

84. See Merryman, *supra* note 2, at 113. For other discussions of the rights to civil juries in the USA, see the entry for "civil juries" in Wikipedia—an adequate source for our general purposes in this circumstance. As noted there, the initial draft of the US Constitution did not require a jury for civil cases, but the uproar that followed prompted the inclusion of the Seventh Amendment, which requires a civil jury in cases where the value in dispute is greater than twenty dollars. Although this Seventh Amendment right to a civil jury trial does not apply in state courts, all states but Louisiana do in fact preserve the right to a jury trial in almost all civil cases where the sole remedy sought is money damages to the same extent as jury trials are permitted by the Seventh Amendment (although sometimes jury trials are not allowed in small claims cases). For another discussion of the rights to *civil juries* in the USA, see Stephen N. Subrin & Margaret Y.K. Woo, Litigating in America: Civil Procedure in Context 250–252 (2006).

85. For information about the absence or abandonment of rights to civil juries in other common law jurisdictions, see International Encyclopedia of Comparative Law, Vol. 7: 54 (Gareth H. Jones, René David & Arthur Taylor Von Mehren eds., 1999) (noting that "in ENGLAND, where trial by jury in its modern form originated and to whose eighteenth century law the AMERICAN constitutions in effect refer, no such entrenched right to jury trial exists" in civil cases). See also Andrew T. Kenyon & Megan Richardson, New Dimensions in Privacy Law: International and Comparative Perspectives 5 n.22 (2006) (noting that in the U.S. both defamation and privacy litigation may be tried by a jury, whereas in England, only defamation cases may be tried by a jury).

86. My KU colleague Professor Ellen Sward has written about this. See, for example, Sward, *supra* note 83, at 338 (describing the "growing pressure within the [American] civil justice system to get parties to settle" and how too many settlements undermine the role for juries).

trial in common law countries and the lack of such concentration in civil law countries.[87]

The Schlesinger text expresses it more briefly: "the civilians do not have to divide a civil lawsuit into (a) the pretrial phase and (b) the 'trial.' A 'trial,' in the sense of single, dramatic, concentrated and uninterrupted presentation of everything that bears on the dispute, is unknown to them."[88]

The image emerging from these remarks about "concentration"—or, more precisely, the *lack* of concentration in civil law countries—coincides with the image offered in the upper portion of the diagram in Box #3.11. In other words, of the three features indicated above (immediacy and orality are still to be discussed), this feature of "concentration" is the one that has the most visible manifestation. It also has profound implications on the behavior of the lawyers for the parties to a civil action.

Assume, for example, that you are the attorney representing Dean DeRosa, the defendant in a complicated contract dispute brought before the courts in a civil law country by a plaintiff named Bruce Purdue. Despite the complication of the factual and legal issues, Purdue's complaint, and the answer that you prepare on behalf of your client in response to that complaint, can be quite general in character, since the specific issues can be further defined as the proceeding goes forward. In other words, neither you nor Purdue's attorney will need to formulate the issues and your legal positions precisely in anticipation of a concentrated event—the trial—because there will be no trial. Here are some other likely implications of that fact:

- You can spend less time preparing for a single appearance before the court, because the appearance will probably cover only one issue;

- You need not be so concerned about Purdue's counsel springing a surprise in terms of a piece of evidence or a witness' testimony, since there will be time to prepare a response before the next appearance.

- Discovery efforts (gaining information from Purdue or resisting requests for information sought by Purdue) will be less important because neither party is likely to gain an advantage by surprise.

- "Unless the court suspects you of dilatory tactics, you may always offer new evidence after some evidence has been taken."[89]

Let us turn to a second feature distinguishing civil litigation in the civil law world from civil litigation in common law countries: mediacy. Typically, civil litigation in a civil law country will involve the presentation of evidence to, and the preparation of a record by, an intermediary—that is, a person other than the judge who will ultimately decide the case. This form of "mediacy" shows how civil procedure in civil law countries still carries the mark of the medieval canon law procedures that developed in earlier centuries. Merryman offers this explanation:

> In the canon law proceeding, evidence was taken by a clerk, and it was the clerk's written record that the judge used in deciding the case. This procedure eventually was modified to place the evidence-taking part of the proceeding under the guidance of a judge, but quite often the case would still be decided by other judges, or by a panel of judges that included the judge who took the evidence.

---

87. Merryman, *supra* note 2, at 113.
88. Schlesinger-2009, *supra* note 46, at 761.
89. *Id.* at 786.

Comparative lawyers customarily contrast this form of proceeding with the custom in the common law system by which the evidence is heard and seen directly and immediately by the judge and jury who are to decide the case. Accordingly, it has become common to speak of the "immediacy" of the common law trial, as distinguished from the "mediacy" of the civil law proceeding.[90]

A third feature distinguishing civil litigation in the civil law world from civil litigation in common law countries is closely related to that of mediacy. It is non-orality. In a system (traditionally used in civil law countries) in which the person compiling the evidence was not the person deciding the case, it was obviously essential (or nearly so) to have a written record, to convey the information from the first person to the second. This tendency toward writing permeated civil litigation more generally, so that even the questions asked of a witness during the proceedings would often result from a written exercise; that is, although the judge would be asking the questions, the content of the questions themselves typically would have been written out in advance by the attorneys for the parties.[91] In short, the same historical influences that led to non-concentration and to mediacy in civil procedure in civil law countries also led to non-orality.

The Schlesinger text reminds us about what one of those historical influences was; and then it emphasizes how civil law systems have undertaken reforms in modern times.

> The Romano-Canonistic system, which dominated procedural thinking on the continent from the 13th to the 18th century, had two outstanding characteristics: First, the proceedings, including the examination of witnesses, were largely conducted *in secret*. Second, the task of hearing the parties, the witnesses, and even the lawyers was often left to subordinate officials who had to reduce everything to *writing*; the judges then based their decisions exclusively on the written record. The modern procedural codes of the civilians reflect a violent reaction, and indeed a revolt, against this medieval system. They stress that all proceedings shall be *oral* and *public* throughout.[92]

Indeed, it is not just the tradition of non-orality but all *three* of these three features—non-concentration, mediacy, and non-orality—that have been the subject of reform in many civil law countries. This reform has not emerged from any widespread enthusiasm to introduce civil juries[93] but instead from a view shared by many civil law lawyers that the concentration, immediacy, and orality present in the civil procedure used in most common law countries are superior in many ways. Hence, although the traditional system is strong in the civil law world and still widely persists, some countries—Austria and Germany are examples—are moving toward greater concentration in civil lit-

---

90. Merryman, *supra* note 2, at 130–132.

91. Merryman points out that "[f]oreign observers are sometimes confused by the fact that, in most civil law nations, questions are [often] put to witnesses by the judge rather than by counsel for the parties. This leads some to the conclusion that the civil law judge determines what questions to ask and, unlike the common law judge, in effect determines the scope and extent of the inquiry"— much like the situation in criminal trials (in civil law countries), in which the presiding judge typically takes control of the proceeding. In fact, however, "in both the civil law and the common law world ... the determination of what issues to raise, what evidence to introduce, and what arguments to make [in civil proceedings] is left almost entirely to the parties." This point is mentioned below in a slightly different context; see *infra* text accompanying note 106.

92. Schlesinger-2009, *supra* note 46, at 747.

93. See, e.g., 7 INTERNATIONAL ENCYCLOPEDIA OF COMPARATIVE LAW 54 (Gareth H. Jones, René David, & Arthur Taylor von Mehren eds., 1999).

94. See Merryman, *supra* note 2, at 113–114. See also Kuo-Chang Huang, INTRODUCING DISCOVERY INTO CIVIL LAW 74–80 (2003) (describing "a clear trend within the continental system to

igation;[94] and others are taking action to remove what Merryman calls the "documentary curtain" that separated the judges from the parties during the medieval period in hopes of reducing undue influence on the judges by interested persons. That documentary curtain, he says, "no longer seems necessary", and retaining it is seen as carrying a high cost in efficiency and accuracy, since "preparation of the record by someone other than the judge who is to decide the case ... deprives the judge of the opportunity to see and hear the parties, to observe their demeanor, and to evaluate their statements directly."[95]

This subsection opened with a question: where is the trial in civil cases in civil law countries? As the foregoing discussion explains, it is nowhere—at least in the form that is routine in common law jurisdictions—under the traditional model influenced by medieval and canon law procedures. More recently, however, some civil law countries have moved toward "blended" systems incorporating more of the concentration, immediacy, and orality that has long been typical of civil litigation as conducted in common law countries.

2. Evidence and Proof

Some of the preceding paragraphs have touched already on matters of evidence and proof. Some further points are noteworthy in this respect. They can summarized thus:

- *Hearsay.* The general rule in common law countries (subject to many exceptions) is to disallow the admission into evidence of testimony by person A that person B said "X". The prohibition on such testimony rests at least in part on the concern that a jury of lay persons might too easily accept the truthfulness of "X", without person B ever having been brought before the court to testify and therefore to subjected there to cross-examination. As noted above in subsection IIA2, civil law countries typically do not impose the same prohibition on hearsay evidence in criminal proceedings, because the professional judges are expected to discount its probity appropriately and tell the lay jurors (if any) serving on the bench with them to do the same; after all, hearsay evidence might well have at least *some* probative value in the search for truth, which is the central aim of criminal proceedings. In *civil* proceedings, where civil law countries typically have *no* lay jurors of any sort involved, even less reason exists for barring the admission of hearsay evidence. As Merryman asserts, hearsay rules "do not exist in civil law jurisdictions because of the absence of a jury in civil actions".[96]

- *Legal proof, irrebuttable presumptions, and exclusion of party testimony.* On the other hand, certain other rules of evidence are found in civil law countries—and are absent from common law countries—that do place limits on the admission of certain types of evidence, despite their potential probity. Deriving from the late medieval period, when judges in Europe were typically even less powerful people (and therefore even more susceptible to pressure through bribery or threats), certain formal and mechanical rules of "legal proof" were introduced to prescribe how specific types of testimony was to be "weighted", and certain other rules were applied to determine what types of testimony would be excluded altogether. Under the "legal proof" rules, the court "was required to give predetermined weight to

---

move toward a concentrated proceeding"). Huang also describes at length Germany's experimentation with concentration of civil litigation.

95. Merryman, *supra* note 2, at 115.

96. *Id.* at 118.

testimony based on the number, status, age, and sex of the witnesses."[97] Under the exclusionary rules, certain kinds of people were disqualified from testifying at all. These included the parties themselves, their relatives, and their friends — on grounds that testimony from such persons was intrinsically untrustworthy.[98] Such rules, in aggregate, may be seen as devices needed to protect the judge because of the absence of the involvement of civil juries, which would likely be less easily threatened and corrupted than a single judge would be. In civil law countries today, some traces of these medieval devices still exist, so that the mechanical rules of "legal proof" have evolved into rules of "irrebuttable presumptions".[99] In general, however, the principle of "free evaluation of proof" prevails, under which "the judge is free to evaluate the evidence and to reach the most appropriate conclusion."[100] Similarly, in some civil law countries the parties to a dispute — and often those closely related to them — are still disqualified from testifying.[101]

- *Decisory oaths.* The absence of a tradition of civil juries in civil law countries also led to another rule of evidence intended to provide some protection of the judge against undue pressure. The "decisory oath" rules permitted one party to put the other party on his oath to assert the truthfulness of a particular fact at issue. For example,[102] in your status as the legal counsel for Dean DeRosa (defendant in the illustration offered earlier in this chapter), you might put Bruce Purdue (plaintiff in that illustration) on his oath (that is, make him swear) as to whether the goods sold by DeRosa to Purdue had in fact been received by Purdue in a damaged condition on a specific date. If Purdue swore to this fact, it would be taken as conclusively proved in Purdue's favor. (Of course, if Purdue lied, he might be subject not only to whatever religious consequences he might fear but also criminal prosecution for perjury and civil liability for damages.) Rules of this sort,

---

97. *Id.* at 119. As Merryman explains, the testimony given by certain classes of people — nobles and property owners, for example — prevailed over that of commoners and people without property. The testimony of an older man prevailed over that of a younger man; and testimony by women was either barred or given only a fraction of the weight of a man's testimony. *Id.* For other accounts of such weightings, and of "legal proof" rules more generally, see Schlesinger-2009, *supra* note 46, at 760; J. A. Jolowicz, *Civil Procedure and the Common and Civil Law*, in Law and Legal Culture in Comparative Perspective 26, 34 (Franz Steiner Verlag ed., 2004) (explaining the "history in the civil law of 'legal proof', according to which different forms of proof have their own value fixed by law"); and Jeffrey A. Bowman, *Infamy and Proof in Medieval Spain*, in FAMA: The Politics of Talk and Reputation in Medieval Europe 95, 102 (Thelma S. Fenster & Daniel Lord Smail eds., 2003).

98. Merryman, *supra* note 2, at 119. For a more detailed treatment of this issue, see Schlesinger-2009, *supra* note 46, at 773 (noting that although "civilians hold to the idea that a party cannot be a 'witness' in the traditional sense", many civil law systems do permit party statements in open court — although the detailed rules vary dramatically from one country to another, from allowing only adverse statements to have any evidentiary effect, to permitting the court to order the parties to make an oral statement to clarify the facts of the case, to permitting the court to draw adverse inferences from the party's refusal to participate).

99. See Peter Herzog & Martha Weser, Civil Procedure in France 313–316 (1967) (describing how Article 1349 of the French Civil Code "defines *présomptions* as conclusions about unknown facts that the law or the court draws from known facts", and identifying four categories of *présomptions*: presumptions that may be rebutted freely; presumptions rebuttable only by specified persons or by proof of specified facts; presumptions that may be rebutted only by specified means of proof; and irrebuttable presumptions). See also Merryman, *supra* note 2, at 120.

100. Schlesinger-2009, *supra* note 46, at 760. See also Merryman, *supra* note 2, at 120.

101. See Merryman, *supra* note 2, at 120, 116. See also Schlesinger-2009, *supra* note 46, at 760.

102. An illustration of this sort (but not the names of my friends DeRosa and Purdue) appears in Merryman, *supra* note 2, at 119. For another description of "decisory oaths", see Schlesinger-2009, *supra* note 46, at 760.

whatever defects they might have, had the benefit of effectively shielding a judge from certain types of pressure from one party or the other, by removing a category of fact-finding responsibilities from the judge. This same system of "decisory oath" rules still exists in many civil law countries today; these include France, Belgium, Italy, and Luxembourg.[103]

- *Cross examination.* Again, the fact that the civil jury (that is, the use of a lay jury in civil litigation) did not develop as a feature of the civil law tradition also has implications for the method of examining witnesses. In particular, the spectacle of fierce, withering cross-examination so common in US courtrooms (not only in civil cases, of course, but also in criminal cases), "seems foreign to the civil law proceeding" because "[t]here has never been a jury to influence."[104] In addition, there is generally less occasion to discredit witnesses in any way (through cross-examination or otherwise) because of the disqualification of parties from testifying (mentioned above) and the filtering of questions through the judge (mentioned below).

- *Questioning by the judge.* In some civil law countries, the practice persists of having the questions in civil proceedings presented in writing (in advance) by the parties (through their legal counsel) to the judge, who will then pose the questions to the witnesses. This practice, referred to briefly above,[105] has been modified in some civil law countries; but in virtually all cases the fact that the questions are posed by the judge does not alter the reality that in civil litigation "the determination of what issues to raise, what evidence to introduce, and what arguments to make is left almost entirely to the parties".[106] This principle was referred to in an earlier passage as taking the form of both "party control" and "party presentation".[107]

- *"Management" of hearings by the judge.* On the other hand, there are some countervailing developments. "The worldwide trend in civil-law countries favors giving more power to the judge" in civil proceedings, particularly in the context of the hearing itself—leading to the model of a "managerial judge".[108] Consistent with this, but emerging for somewhat different reasons, is the "Stuttgart Model" developed in the 1970s and then finding its way into the German Code of Civil Procedure, which provides that "[a]s a rule, the case should be disposed of in a single, comprehensively prepared oral hearing (main hearing)"—a proposition that obviously places increased power into the hands of the judge presiding over a civil lawsuit.[109]

---

103. Schlesinger-2009, *supra* note 46, at 774.

104. Merryman, *supra* note 2, at 116.

105. See *supra* note 91.

106. Merryman, *supra* note 91, at 116. For another discussion of this point, giving special attention to Section 139 of the German Code of Civil Procedure, see Schlesinger-2009, *supra* note 46, at 748. "Section 139 of the German Code has been called the Magna Carta of fair procedure [because] it effectively reduces (although it cannot eliminate) the impact of the relative ability of counsel upon the outcome of litigation" since it authorizes the court "to inject new legal and factual issues into the case, and thus, in effect, to help an unprepared or incompetent attorney who did not think of those issues". *Id.* at 749.

107. See *supra* text accompanying note 81. The term "party autonomy" is also used to designate roughly the same principle, especially where it applies to setting the limits of the dispute brought before the court. Schlesinger-2009, *supra* note 46, at 762.

108. Schlesinger-2009, *supra* note 46, at 790.

109. *Id.* at 788–789.

• *Discovery (required presentation of documents)*. For various reasons, the rules of discovery have been much less broadly developed in civil law countries (in the context of civil litigation) than in the USA. In recent years, however, there has emerged "a clear trend in allowing a very limited form of discovery of documents."[110] What we might call "civil-law discovery" features these main contours:

> If a party needs a relevant document that is in the possession of the opposing party or a third person, he or she must make a request to the court, identifying the document and its contents with reasonable specificity; upon that, the document holder must either produce the document or give a legitimate reason for refusal, such as irrelevance, privilege, self-incrimination, personal embarrassment, trade or state secret, etc.[111]

• *Depositions*. The use of depositions also sets the USA apart from most other countries, including common law countries. And in civil law countries, depositions do not "fit" with the system. The Schlesinger text offers this explanation:

> The mere idea of "deposing" a witness is problematic in civil-law procedure. Since the proceeding is not structurally divided into pretrail and trial and since the gathering of evidence and its production into the official record are done simultaneously by the court (not by the parties), "pretrial" deposition as a preparatory investigation for the "trial" is of limited usefulness.... [However,] when a witness may not be available in the future, due to travel or impending death, a party may request the court to take his or her interrogation in advance. This practice is called deposition *de bene esse* in the U.S. and *ad perpetuam rei memorium* in civil-law countries. It is not a deposition in the American sense because it is not taken by the attorneys but by the court itself.[112]

3. Judgments, Enforcement, and Appeals

We may conclude our brief general survey of civil procedure in civil law countries by looking at some aspects of judgments, enforcement, and appeals. I would emphasize one point about each.

First, regarding judgments: the general tendency is to avoid separate concurring or dissenting opinions as part of a judgment. Bear in mind that judgments emerging from civil proceedings would be accompanied by written reasons, as prepared by one of the judges hearing the case. (This is often not true in US civil cases—especially, of course, if a jury is involved.) However, reflecting in part the great value placed on certainty in the civil law world—a topic discussed earlier in this chapter—that judgment is almost always singular in nature, purporting to reflect the view of the court as a whole. Although, as Merryman notes, the practice of constitutional courts in some civil law countries reveals "[a] tendency toward noting dissents and separate concurrences, and even toward the publication of separate opinions, ... the standard attitude is that the law is certain, and should appear so, and that this certainty would be impaired by noting dissents and by publishing separate opinions."[113]

---

110. *Id.* at 764.

111. *Id.*

112. *Id.* at 766.

113. Merryman, *supra* note 2, at 122. Merryman goes on to note that in some countries a judge disagreeing with a judgment might write an article for publication in a legal journal. "Even though the article is put in a scholarly or 'scientific' form, everyone—lawyers and fellow judges—knows that

Second, as for enforcement of judgments: In civil law countries, courts typically have a much narrower range of powers in ordering the satisfaction of a judgment than courts in common law countries have. The civil law courts can typically act only *in rem*—that is, they do not have the power to hold a person in "contempt of court" (and thereby compel such a person to take an action, or refrain from taking an action, on threat of a fine or imprisonment). Hence, civil remedies in civil law countries consist mainly of money-damages awards. A consequence of this limitation on the court's power relates to "discovery" in civil litigation. As noted in the preceding subsection, rules of discovery are much less developed in the civil law world than they are in the common law world—the USA in particular.[114]

Why would the enforcement powers of judges be so much weaker in the civil law world than in the common law world? By now some of the answer(s) should be rather obvious. As we have seen, the civil law tradition places judges in a much less prestigious position in general, for numerous historical reasons, than is the case in the common law tradition. Placing greater emphasis on certainty in the law and on the concentration of law-making power in the legislature have led naturally to the view that judges should be denied any more authority than is absolutely necessary to allow them to apply the law.

Recall, however, that in criminal proceedings, judges in civil law countries do in fact typically have broad authority: they control the conduct of criminal trials, for example, to a much greater degree than judges in common law countries. Why this contrast? One view is that civil law countries draw a much sharper, cleaner distinction between civil litigation and criminal proceedings.[115] Whatever the reason, the fact remains that the enforcement powers of civil law judges in civil litigation are relatively weak.

Third, as for appeals: In civil law countries, appeals from judgments emerging from civil litigation typically amount to a new trial. One authority has expressed it in this manner:

> Decisions of the ordinary civil and criminal courts of first instance may as a rule be appealed to an intermediate appellate court.... Unlike a common law appeal of a trial court's decision, the proceedings in this intermediate court may involve a full review de novo of the facts as well as the law of the case. The panel of appellate judges initially will make its independent determination of the facts on the basis of the original record. In addition, however, the appellate court may question the witnesses again, or even take new evidence or send out for expert opinions.[116]

Once again, the reason for this different concept of an "appeal" is to be found in part in the absence of the tradition of a jury in civil litigation in civil law countries. Where there *is* a civil jury, naturally, it would typically be impossible for an appellate court to re-

the article is a way of informing the legal community of the author's [that is, the judge's] dissenting views." *Id*. at 122–123.

114. See generally *id*. at 123.

115. *Id*. at 124 (asserting that in the civil law world, "[t]he line between the civil and the criminal is more sharply drawn, and morally reprehensible ... actions are matters for the criminal law rather than for the civil law").

116. Nutshell-2008, *supra* note 121, at 104. This authority goes on to point out (i) that the distinction between factual and legal issues is often difficult to draw and (ii) some civil law high courts follow the French system of "cassation" described below in subsection IIC1 of this chapter, while some follow the German system of "revision". *Id*. See also Merryman, *supra* note 2, at 123 (observing that "the appellate bench is expected to ... prepare its own fully reasoned opinion, in which it discusses both factual and legal issues").

view the factual findings made at the trial court level, since the jury does not make specific findings of fact or offer an explanation of its judgment; hence "[a]s long as there is *some* factual basis in the record to support the jury's (or the trial judge's) verdict, the appellate court in a common law jurisdiction will honor it".[117]

There is another noteworthy point regarding "appeals" in civil litigation in civil law countries. In addition to having a right to the type of appellate proceeding described above—in essence, a reconsideration of the case (both facts and law) by an intermediate appellate court—a still-dissatisfied party to a civil litigation typically also has the right to another type of hearing before an even higher court. As will be explained below in subsection IIC1 of this chapter, the highest court in the system of "ordinary" courts in most civil law countries is called the Court of Cassation (or Supreme Court of Cassation). The precise powers and functions of that court will vary from country to country, but in general the role of that court is to provide an authoritative determination of questions of law that arise in lower courts. The process by which the (Supreme) Court of Cassation plays that role is sometimes referred to as a "recourse in cassation" (by which the determination of a lower court on a question of law is "quashed") and sometimes referred to as a "revision" (which includes the additional step of revising the judgment of the lower court that relied on an incorrect determination of the question of law)[118]—but the overall effect from a litigant's perspective is about the same in either case: the right to take a civil judgment to the (Supreme) Court of Cassation amounts in essence to a separate avenue of appeal, and therefore another opportunity to prevail ultimately in the case.

C. Division of Court Structures and Jurisdiction

Instead of having a single, unified, pyramid-shaped court structure (as is largely true in the USA), most civil law countries have two main sets of courts—"ordinary" and "administrative"—and another court (or occasionally more than one) to deal with constitutional issues.[119] In general, "ordinary" courts deal with private law and criminal law matters, and administrative courts handle questions of administrative law. Constitutional courts, more recent in their development, typically have less authority than US courts have to engage in "judicial review". A general schematic representation of the typical structure of courts appears below in Box #3.12. (It can be instructive to compare the diagram in Box #3.12 with the diagram in Box #3.3, above; in each case the categories of law shown on the right-hand side are identical.)

---

117. Merryman, *supra* note 2, at 121.

118. *Id.* The conceptual and historical foundations of the process of "cassation" and of (Supreme) Courts of Cassation, are discussed more fully below. See *infra* subsection IIC1 of this chapter.

119. It is worth acknowledging at the outset of this discussion that significant exceptions exist. In some countries of Latin America, for example, the influence of the US legal system (including its constitutional structure) has led to the establishment of unified court systems. See Merryman, *supra* note 2, at 90. On the other hand, this discussion does reflect fairly closely the structure of courts in France. See generally Nicolas Marie Kublicki, *An Overview of the French Legal System from an American Perspective*, 12 BOSTON UNIVERSITY INTERNATIONAL LAW JOURNAL 57, 59–81 (1994) (summarizing the structure of the French court system).

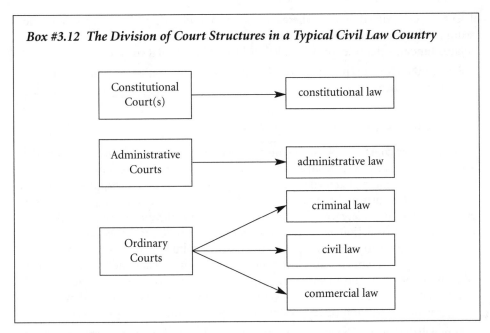

Box #3.12 The Division of Court Structures in a Typical Civil Law Country

All these differences in court structure and jurisdiction are related in large part to two points we have already examined above: (i) the fundamental division in civil law countries between private law and public law; and (ii) uneasiness about giving ordinary judges too much power. The fact that both of these two distinguishing marks of the civil law tradition are absent from the common law tradition has yielded a very different structure of courts in common law countries. Merryman offers these observations:

> The typical common law country has a unified court system that might be represented as a pyramid with a single supreme court at the apex.... It seems entirely natural to [common law lawyers] that the ultimate power to review the legality of administrative action and the constitutionality of legislative action, as well as to hear and finally decide the great range of appeals in civil and criminal disputes, should be lodged in [such a single] supreme court. [By contrast,] in the civil law world ... it is usual to find two or more separate sets of courts, each with its own jurisdiction, its own hierarchy of tribunals, its own judiciary, and its own procedure, all existing within the same nation....[120]

The division of judicial jurisdiction in civil law countries has its origin, not surprisingly, in history. In general, it can be said that the so-called "ordinary courts" in civil law countries "are the modern-day successors to the various civil and criminal courts that existed in Europe during the long period of the *jus commune*, before the modern state with its panoply of public and administrative law came into being."[121] The administrative courts have a separate genealogy: they derive from the revolutionary-era objection to permitting ordinary judges to interfere with the administrative work of the government, and from the resulting creation of an internal system (internal, that is, to the executive branch of government) by which the legality of administrative action could be tested. The constitutional courts have a yet more recent origin—as recent as sixty years ago in the case

---

120. *Id.* at 86.
121. Nutshell-2008, *supra* note 12, at 72.

of several European countries, where a need was felt following World War II to create a forum in which laws adopted by the legislature could be challenged on grounds that they violated fundamental rules or principles enshrined in national constitutions.

Each of these three types of courts—ordinary, administrative, and constitutional— is discussed in turn below.

1. Ordinary Courts

The ordinary courts are by far the most numerous in a civil law country, because their jurisdiction is the broadest. From a historical viewpoint, these are the courts that for hundreds of years in Europe handled (i) the ordinary run of secular civil disputes between individuals (that is, private law matters) and (ii) the criminal cases brought by the state against members of society whose actions were regarded as threatening to the public safety and order. The jurisdiction of these courts gradually expanded as the secular nation-state predominated over the church, whose ecclesiastical tribunals finally surrendered their control over certain types of cases involving domestic (family) law and the like. Likewise, the jurisdiction of the ordinary courts expanded also into commercial matters, as the commercial courts that had developed very early in Europe were nationalized by the ever-stronger nation-states and (in many states) merged into the ordinary court system.

Although the details of how the ordinary courts gradually inherited various aspects of their jurisdiction are bound up with the specific historical circumstances of Europe, the general theme—increasing centralization of court structures with an increasing centralization of state power—is not particularly distinctive. As we shall see in Chapter Four and Chapter Six, similar trends appear in the history of English common law and Chinese law. However, there is indeed a peculiar aspect of the ordinary courts in civil law countries that warrants our attention. It relates to the highest court in the structure, typically called the Court of Cassation or the Supreme Court of Cassation. As noted above in subsection IIB3, the role of the Court of Cassation in most civil law countries is to provide an authoritative determination of questions of law that arise in lower courts. That determination comes in some countries by way of a process referred to as a "recourse in cassation" (by which the determination of a lower court on a question of law is "quashed") and in other countries by way of a process referred to as a "revision" (which includes the additional step of revising the judgment of the lower court that relied on an incorrect determination of the question of law).

The historical foundations of both of these processes, and of the court that employs them, are the same, and they relate to the strong urge in the civil law world to prevent judges from "making law" in any way. The desire to concentrate absolutely all law-making power in the legislature led logically to a prohibition on judges engaging even in the interpretation of statutes. According to this logic, if a judge were permitted to interpret a statute, that interpretation might be inconsistent with the legislative intent, in which case the judge would in effect have exercised law-making power—particularly if an interpretation by a judge in one case were to be regarded as influential or binding on another judge in another case. In the mind of an orthodox civil law lawyer, any questions of interpretation (if a statute were vague or silent about a legal matter pertinent to a case) should be referred to the legislature for clarification, instead of being left for a judge to decide. As Merryman expresses it, "[t]he legislature would then provide an authoritative interpretation to guide the judge ... [and] in this way defects in the law would be cured, courts would be prevented from making law, and the state would be safe from the threat of judicial tyranny".[122]

---

122. Merryman, *supra* note 2, at 39.

In fact, this impulse was so strong in some systems that a special organ of the legislature was established to address questions of interpretation sent to it by the courts. This was done in Prussia, where a special "Statutes Commission" was created to address such questions.[123] The approach in France was similar but more practical: the legislature established a special organ of government—not actually part of the legislature but also not part of the court system—with authority to quash erroneous statutory interpretations made by courts, in order to protect the legislature's position supremacy against any threat of judicial usurpation.[124] The legislature called this body the Tribunal (not the Court) of Cassation ("cassation" comes from the same root word as "quash"), and describing it as "*auprès du corps legislatif*"[125] (*i.e.*, adjacent to the legislative body).

The most noteworthy element in this development in French law is what happened in terms of the relationship between the Tribunal of Cassation and the ordinary courts. Even though the Tribunal of Cassation was created by the legislature as a non-judicial body to stand apart from the courts, over time this special character was lost and the Tribunal "migrated" to take a position at the very top of the system of ordinary courts. As Merryman explains, "the highest civil and criminal court in the jurisdiction —one that is staffed by judges ...—is [thus] the direct descendant of a legislative tribunal originally created to keep the power of interpretation out of the hands of judges".[126]

Despite these historical details and oddities, the system of ordinary courts in most civil law countries today looks fairly straightforward. A great many courts of first instance, exercising jurisdiction over all types of private disputes as well as criminal cases, are scattered throughout the typical civil law country; a much smaller number of appellate courts —hearing appeals from the judgments of those courts of first instance—are located in major population centers; and a (supreme) court of cassation sits at the top of the system to review claims that the lower courts have misinterpreted or misapplied a statute or regulation.[127]

We have seen earlier that the five main codes in the orthodox civil law tradition are the civil code, the code of civil procedure, the penal code, the code of criminal procedure, and the commercial code. It should come as no surprise that these are the codes on which the ordinary courts depend in handling cases brought before those courts. As noted earlier in this chapter, many civil law countries have now seen vast bodies of law grow up outside these five traditional codes. While many of those other sources of law also find their application in the ordinary courts, others relate to administrative matters and lie entirely outside the jurisdiction of the ordinary courts. Instead, they belong to the jurisdiction of the administrative courts, to which we now turn.

---

123. *Id.*

124. *Id.* at 40.

125. *Id.*

126. *Id.* at 41.

127. For reasons explained above in subsection IIB, (i) it typically would not be appropriate to refer to the courts of first instance as "trial" courts because civil disputes often do not involve a "trial" as such; (ii) the "appeal" at the appellate-court level would in some countries amount to a new trial to review both findings of law and findings of fact that were made by the court of first instance; and (iii) because of the limited jurisdiction of the (supreme) court of cassation, a litigant would usually have difficulty getting a hearing before that court unless he or she could persuasively assert that a lower court had actually engaged in a misinterpretation of a statute—and not merely that it had misconstrued or misapplied a private legal document such as a contract. On this last point, see also Merryman, *supra* note 2, at 87.

2. Administrative Courts

Most civil law countries have a separate set of administrative courts. Their characteristics have been described as follows:

> Because modern administrative law largely took shape in the nineteenth century, the French experience was the principal model available to other countries as they searched for mechanisms to control their rapidly growing public administrations.... [T]he French revolution doctrine of separation of powers seemed to require that the actions of administrative bodies and disputes among or involving them should not be subject to control by the judiciary. Thus the administrative dispute-settling mechanism had to be located elsewhere. In Napoleonic times this authority was vested in the Council of State (*Conseil d'Etat*) which began as a body of advisors to the king under the old regime and later developed into the central organ of governmental administration.[128]

Thus was the pattern set for the Council of State to assume the role of determining the legality of administrative action — that is, of making sure that the executive organs of government were acting within authority delegated to them by the legislature. Over time, the section of the *Conseil d'Etat* that regularly exercised this power developed judicial characteristics, and the substantive and procedural rules that it applies have grown into a large and sophisticated body of administrative law.[129]

The same or similar processes occurred also in many other civil law countries, so that today most civil law countries have a separate set of laws and courts to handle governmental administrative matters. Naturally, these administrative court systems are typically much smaller than the ordinary court systems in terms of the numbers of courts, judges, cases, and judgments; but they are still quite significant, and this fact provides an important distinction between a typical civil law country and a typical common law country. In the former (a typical civil law country), ordinary courts will not exercise jurisdiction over a case in which an individual complains that a government agency has acted improperly in some respect (for example, taking private land for the purpose of building a public facility, or issuing an environmental protection rule prohibiting the dumping of hazardous waste). In the latter (a typical common law country), there is a single court structure, and the same court that handles a contract dispute between two private parties in the morning will handle an administrative law complaint in the afternoon.

What happens in the case of uncertainty as to whether a case should be brought in the ordinary courts or in the administrative courts? The answer differs from one civil law country to another. In some countries, the court in which the case is first brought determines (definitively, without review) whether or not it has jurisdiction; in some coun-

---

128. Nutshell-2008, *supra* note 12, at 69–70.

129. See *id.* at 70; Merryman, *supra* note 2, at 88. For an account of the development of the *Conseil d'Etat* in France, including its role in testing the legality of administrative action, see Charles Szladits, *The Civil Law System*, 2.2 INTERNATIONAL ENCYCLOPEDIA OF COMPARATIVE LAW 15, 28–29 (n.d.). It is worth noting that even though both the (supreme) court of cassation and the council of state in a civil law country have non-judicial origins — and indeed were expressly established (or given powers) outside the province of the ordinary courts in order to keep certain types of questions (interpretation of statutes and legality of administrative action) *out* of the hands of judges — now most civil law systems treat the officials in the (supreme) court of cassation and in the administrative courts as *judges* in largely the same way as they treat the judges in the ordinary courts. France, birthplace of the strongest separation-of-powers doctrine, is an exception in some respects.

tries, the (supreme) court of cassation is the ultimate authority on such conflicts of jurisdiction; and in some countries, a special tribunal—sometimes called a "conflicts tribunal"—has been established to address such questions.[130]

3. Constitutional Councils and Courts

In addition to ordinary courts and administrative courts, most civil law countries also have at least one constitutional court. Does the emergence of such constitutional courts parallel the emergence of administrative courts? In one sense, yes, it does: the same separation-of-powers emphasis that led to the development of a separate set of administrative courts—so that the (ordinary) judiciary would not be passing judgment over the actions of the executive branch—has led to the development of separate constitutional courts.

However, it is important to see a fundamental difference between constitutional courts and administrative courts: whereas *administrative* courts are designed, in a sense, to *protect* the legislature against both the executive branch of government (by providing a method of testing whether administrative action is in fact consistent with statutes enacted by the legislature) and the judicial branch of government (by preventing judges from assuming "law-making" powers in interpreting such statutes), *constitutional* courts are designed not to protect the legislature but to *attack* it when necessary. Constitutional courts provide (among other things) a forum and procedure for testing whether legislative action is in fact consistent with constitutional rules. These constitutional rules, as defined above in Box #3.2, are "fundamental substantive and structural rules which cannot be changed or overridden by regular legislative action". We saw above, in examining the status of such constitutional rules, that they undermine the orthodox civil law view that the legislature is the supreme, all-powerful source for the promulgation of law. Just as constitutional law stands above statutory law, likewise constitutional courts stand above the legislature—at least in those civil law countries with effective systems of judicial review of legislation.

Before turning our attention to that topic—judicial review of the constitutionality of legislation—let us look quickly at the other functions that constitutional courts typically are given in civil law countries. France offers an illustration. The pertinent provisions of the October 1958 constitution of France prescribe these most important other functions for the *Conseil Constitutionnel*[131]:

- *Elections.* The *Conseil Constitutionnel* "shall ensure the regularity of the election of the President of the Republic".[132]

- *Referenda.* The *Conseil Constitutionnel* "shall ensure the regularity of referendum procedures and shall announce the results thereof."[133]

---

130. For details on questions of jurisdictional conflicts between ordinary courts and administrative courts, see Nutshell-2008, *supra* note 12, at 69; Merryman, *supra* note 2, at 89.

131. Note that the title of this entity does not include the word "court" but instead uses the word "council" (*conseil*). This reflects the strong reluctance in the French system to use the word "court" for an entity that in fact has important political functions (and, similarly, to use the word "judge" for the persons holding positions in such an entity). In most countries, the term "constitutional court" is used. As Merryman explains, some "civil law fundamentalists have occasionally argued that these tribunals cannot really be courts or the officials who lead them judges…, [but] this view has yielded to the kind of relaxation of principle that led people to regard the Council of State as a court and the officials who run it as judges." Merryman, *supra* note 2, at 90.

132. Constitution of France, art. 58.

133. *Id.* art. 60.

The members of the *Conseil Constitutionnel*, again as prescribed in the French constitution, include the following:[134]

- three persons (who need not be lawyers, and each of which shall have terms of office of nine years, non-renewable) to be selected by the President of the Republic;

- three persons (with the same characteristics and terms noted above) to be selected by the President of the National Assembly;

- three persons (with the same characteristics and terms noted above) to be selected by the President of the Senate;

- all former Presidents of the Republic (as members ex officio for life).

While the French *Conseil Constitutionnel* offers a less "judicialized" example of a constitutional court than exists in many civil law countries,[135] it is not unusual in terms of the array of powers it is authorized to exercise. (For a summary of the powers and composition of the Constitutional Court of Italy, see below in subsection IID2.) Let us now turn to the most interesting of those powers—the power to declare legislation void for being inconsistent with the constitution.

The key pertinent provision in the French constitution makes the *Conseil Constitutionnel* responsible for ruling on the constitutionality of "organic laws" before they are promulgated, as well as on "regulations of the parliamentary assemblies" before they come into force.[136] In addition, the *Conseil Constitutionnel* is responsible for ruling on the constitutionality of any other law (that is, other than an organic law) at the initiative of (i) the President of the Republic, (ii) the chief officer of one of the parliamentary bodies, or (iii) "any sixty members of the National Assembly or the Senate".[137]

The French constitution represents one of a wide array of approaches to constitutional courts and judicial review. In particular, the French approach is rather tentative and reserved—in other words, exceptionally deferential to the majority rule as reflected in legislative action.[138] Other civil law countries have taken very different, sometimes more aggressive approaches to the issue of judicial review of legislation. One authority offers this description of the various approaches that can be taken:

> Broadly speaking judicial review conforms to one of two models, the "Austrian" and the "American". Under the former, questions of the constitutionality of legislation can be decided only by a special constitutional court on reference from an authorised person who may or may not be a judge before whom such a question is raised in the course of ordinary litigation, and the review may be *a priori* or *a posteriori*. Under the latter, it is the duty of any judge before whom such a question is raised in the course of litigation to deal with it there and then, although, no doubt, in important cases the question will finally be decided by the

---

134. These details are drawn from Constitution of France, art. 56.

135. See *supra* note 131.

136. Constitution of France, art. 61.

137. These details are drawn from Constitution of France, art. 61.

138. A frequently-cited illustration of this point is the decision by the *Conseil Constitutionnel* in the mid-1970s *not* to declare unconstitutional a law permitting abortion in France. In that decision, the *Conseil Constitutionnel* emphasized its own limited role, and the great deference it must give to the parliamentary authorities. See [1975] D.S. Jur. 529, J.O of January 16, 1975, 671, as cited and excerpted in Mary Ann Glendon, Michael W. Gordon, and Christopher Osakwe, COMPARATIVE LEGAL TRADITIONS 75–77 (1985). See also Richard E. Levy and Alexander Somek, *Paradoxical Parallels in the American and German Abortion Decisions*, 9 TULANE JOURNAL OF INTERNATIONAL & COMPARATIVE LAW 109 (2001).

Supreme Court; review of this kind is necessarily *a posteriori*. The French system can, perhaps, be regarded as a particular version of the Austrian model, for the *Conseil Constitutionnel* alone has power to pronounce a parliamentary law unconstitutional and then only on the reference of specified persons; the challenged law is referred to the *Conseil* before promulgation, and no law or part of a law declared to be unconstitutional may be promulgated. Obviously the decisions of the *Conseil Constitutionnel* have effect *erga omnes*, for a law which is not promulgated is no law, but, generally speaking, it is typical of the Austrian model that the decisions of the constitutional court have effect *erga omnes*. Under the American model, by contrast, the decision, even if of the Supreme Court, is binding as *res judicata* only between the parties. In countries of the common law tradition this is not a serious disadvantage because the doctrine *stare decisis* has the result that the decision that a law is unconstitutional will almost invariably be applied thereafter, but elsewhere as, for example, in some countries of Latin American where the American model has been followed, such a decision will be disregarded by other courts and the administration alike. On the whole, therefore, the American model is seen as unsuitable for countries of the civil law tradition.[139]

In covering some of the same topics, Merryman offers a somewhat different perspective on the different types of judicial review of the constitutionality of legislation, and distinguishes the French experience from that of three other European civil law countries:

The German, Italian, and Spanish constitutional courts were established after World War II and represent the modern trend toward constitutional review in the civil law world.... All are separate courts, distinct from all others in their respective jurisdictions. All have the exclusive power to decide on the constitutionality of legislation. In Germany, Italy, and Spain a decision by the constitutional court that a statute is unconstitutional is binding not only on the parties to the case but on all participants in the legal process. In all three instances the character of the proceedings and the rules governing the selection of judges give the constitutional court a definitely judicial character, in contrast to the political nature of the French Constitutional Council.

Generally, the procedure is this: in an action before a civil, criminal, administrative, or other court, a party can raise a constitutional objection to a statute affecting the case. At this point the action is suspended, and the constitutional question is referred to the constitutional court for decision. When that decision is published, the original proceeding is resumed and conducted in accordance with it. If the constitutional court finds the statute constitutional, it can be applied in the proceeding; if the court rules it unconstitutional, the statute becomes invalid and cannot be applied in that specific proceeding or in any other. This procedure exemplifies the so-called incidental attack on constitutionality.

The incidental procedure, which permits a constitutional attack only within the context of a specific case or controversy, is the only one available in the system of constitutional review in the United States. In Germany, Italy, and Spain (as well as other civil law countries, ...) however, a "direct" attack is also possible. Designated official agencies of government and even individuals can bring an ac-

---

139. J.A. Jolowicz, *Summary of the 1984 Scientific Colloquium of the International Association of Legal Science on "Judicial Review and its Legitimacy"*, excerpted in Glendon, Gordon, and Osakwe, *supra* note 138, at 71.

tion before the constitutional court to test the validity of a statute, even though there is no concrete dispute involving its application. In this way, the limitations inherent in the restriction to incidental review in the United States are transcended, and a hearing can be had on the abstract question of constitutionality. Even though limited by statute and decision, the direct review procedure significantly expands the availability of constitutional review beyond that available in the United States.[140]

D. *Illustrations from Italian Law*

Earlier in this chapter we examined briefly how the general observations about civil law systems *in general* regarding the sources of law, the classifications of law, and the training and practice of law manifested themselves in a *specific* legal system — that of Italy. (See subsection ID, above). Now let us examine even more briefly some of the operational topics that we have explored in the foregoing paragraphs regarding the content and operation of civil law systems. In the interest of time, we shall confine ourselves here to just two key topics: criminal procedure and constitutional review of legislation. Our aim will be to see whether, and how, today's Italian legal system illustrates the generic observations made above on those two topics.

1. Criminal Courts and Actions in Italy

The account offered above in subsection IIA2 — describing certain features of the laws governing criminal procedure in a typical modern civil law country — would perhaps trigger three reactions in an Italian lawyer with several decades of experience in that country's criminal justice system. First, she would surely find much of it familiar, even to the point of being obvious. In particular, the account of the "O.J. Sampson inquisition" appearing in Appendix 3.2 (offered as an illustration of many points made in subsection IIA2) would correspond very closely to her experience in criminal trials in Italy — at least *before* the late 1980s, when Italy's system of criminal procedure underwent a dramatic change (resisted strongly by many lawyers and others in the country) in an attempt to "import" an adversarial system and thereby displace certain aspects of the inquisitorial system.

Hence, a second reaction that an experienced Italian lawyer might have to the "generic" account offered above in subsection IIA2 is that Italy is now different in terms of the role of the judge, the role of the prosecuting attorney, the role of the defense counsel, and the selection, order, and presentation of evidence in criminal trials. (These are four of the key elements identified near the beginning of subsection IIA2.) An explanation of the changes made to Italy's criminal procedure beginning in the late 1980s, including a description of the strong resistance to those changes (featuring supreme court cases, constitutional amendments, and deep consternation) appears in Appendix 3.3.

Appendix 3.3 offers much more, however, than just a description of those late-1980s changes in Italy's criminal procedure. The main "story" in Appendix 3.3, as told by Christopher Griffith, revolves around the murder trial of Amanda Knox that concluded in Italy in late 2009. The account gives special attention to comparative aspects of the criminal

---

140. Merryman, *supra* note 2, at 140–141.

procedure rules and principles at issue in that case. Appendix 3.3 should be studied before proceeding to the next subsection in this chapter.

In particular, the account in Appendix 3.3 should be examined with an eye to identifying and understanding the following points: (i) contrasts between traditional "inquisitorial" and "adversarial" models of criminal procedure, (ii) recent moves in Italy to shift emphasis from the former to the latter, (iii) specific manifestations of the two models in the Amanda Knox trial, and (iv) criticisms—some valid and many not—leveled at the conduct of that trial, mainly by observers speaking out of ignorance of the Italian system of criminal justice.

A third reaction that an experienced Italian lawyer might have to the account offered above regarding criminal procedure in a typical civil law country is that it hardly scratches the surface in explaining the complexity of the system as it exists in Italy. For a brief description of some aspects of the law of criminal procedure in contemporary Italy, see Appendix 3.4. That description, which draws from a lecture by Professor Gabriella Di Paolo of the University of Trento, should be studied before proceeding to the next subsection in this chapter. Appendix 3.4 gives special attention to the issues of judicial organization, the relationship between judicial and other state powers, and the specific relations between judges and prosecutors. All of these organizational details have a significant impact on how the rules of criminal procedure are actually applied in practice. The account in Appendix 3.4 also examines the structure and fundamental principles of an ordinary criminal proceeding, as well as certain special procedures that have been introduced to increase the efficiency of the system (for example, by combating its perennial backlog of cases).

Taken together, the accounts offered in Appendix 3.3 and Appendix 3.4 highlight two competing themes. First, the general description of criminal procedure provided above in subsection IIA2 is borne out in practice in the context of Italian criminal procedure— up to a point. Second, because of some Italy-specific reforms made in that country over recent decades, some aspects of the general description offered above do *not* apply to Italy today. Surely the same can be said in respect of most civil law countries. As Merryman expresses it, "[c]ivil law nations share the civil law tradition, but they share it in different degrees."[141]

2. Constitutional Courts and Actions in Italy

Some basic information regarding the Constitutional Court in Italy has already appeared in the discussion of "sources" of law in Italy; see the "interview" with an Italian law student, set forth in subsection ID1, above. Box #3.13 offers further information in a bullet-point format.

Box #3.13 Italy's Constitutional Court—Powers, Structures, Operation

- Constitutional provisions: Articles 134–136
- Main task: to undertake judicial review of the constitutionality of legislation
- Membership: 15 members, appointed by
    - Parliament—in plenary session, by secret ballot, requiring a special majority;
    - President of the Republic—must have the countersignature of a minister, but as a practical matter the main authority rests with the President in this case;

---

141. *Id.* at 145.

- other Judges—of the high courts (acting via the *Consiglio Superiore Magistratura,* the entity heading the judiciary, as created in the constitution).

- Status: The Constitutional Court is an *ad hoc* court—centralizing judicial review in a single judicial body (unlike the US system).

- Jurisdiction: There must be a case or controversy in front of a judge, in which the constitutionality of a statute is challenged. The party attacking the statute's constitutionality will request the judge to send a constitutional question to the Constitutional Court. The judge can refuse that request if the judge finds the claim to be irrelevant to the case before the judge, or if the judge finds the claim to be groundless.

- Other tasks of the Constitutional Court:

  - to provide permission for the process of referendum (in the case of regular laws)—because some proposed referenda would be unconstitutional.

  - to handle matters of impeachment—for example, on grounds that the President of the Republic takes some act that is considered treasonous.

  - to serve as a referee in case of conflict ...

    - between the state and a region as to which authority has the power of legislating in a particular subject area. (For example, some regions tried to outlaw electroshock treatment.)

    - between two regions.

    - between state powers. (For example, who can grant a pardon—the President or the Minister of Justice?)

Some further points about the Italian Constitutional Court are noteworthy. Most of them relate to the effects of the rulings issued by the Court.[142]

First, in the Italian experience, if the Constitutional Court declares that a law contradicts the constitution, it puts aside the law, but it does not exactly delete the law. For instance, in 1979 the Constitutional Court declared unconstitutional Article 251 of the criminal procedure code, which requires that an oath taken before a court must refer to God. However, that provision still appears in the criminal procedure code; yet it is accompanied by a notation about the 1979 Constitutional Court's decision that the provision is unconstitutional.

Second, in some cases the Constitutional Court may be seen not only as a "negative" lawmaker—simply declaring whether a law is or is not unconstiitutional—but also as an "interpretative" lawmaker. Specifically, an "interpretative decision" is one in which the Constitutional Court construes a statute in a certain way and then states that that particular construction is the *only* construction that is constitutional (or unconstitutional). An example arose in 1965, when the Constitutional Court declared that a particular possible interpretation of a statute was constitutional, but noted that any other meaning would be unconstitutional. The law, dating from the Fascist era, provided that any activity comprising propaganda against procreation (e.g., speaking about contraception) is illegal. The Constitutional Court did not rule that this provision was unconstitutional; instead, the Court ruled that the provision has to be interpreted in the light of the constitutionally protected right of free speech—so that the statute could be constitutionally applied if the criminal punishment were to be imposed only on persons whose speech constituted indecency. Hence, in that case, the Constitutional Court was able to find an

---

142. For most of the observations made in the following few paragraphs, I have drawn from lectures and materials on Italian constitutional law provided by my colleague at the University of Trento, Professor Carlo Casonato.

interpretation of the law at issue that could "save" the constitutionality of the law, in narrowly confined circumstances.[143]

Third, in some cases, the Constitutional Court might actually go so far as to add something to the law under consideration. In other words, although the Constitutional Court might agree with a lower court judge's ruling that a statute is unconstitutional "as is", the Constitutional Court might identify further provisions that could be appended to the law to make it constitutional. A law enacted in the 1970s made abortion a crime both for the woman involved and for the doctor (or other person performing the abortion) unless a "state of necessity" existed so that the life of the woman faced a *present* danger. In the facts of a case coming before the courts under that law, a woman had faced a choice—to have an abortion or to become blind (since it was probable or certain that the process of giving birth would cause her to go blind). The Constitutional Court in a sense added a "*future* danger" provision to the law, ruling that the law could be constitutional only if the exception for "present danger" were expanded to include "future danger" as in the case of blindness that would occur upon or immediately after giving birth.

III. Closing Observations

I have already acknowledged the brevity and incompleteness of this survey of some operational aspects of the civil law tradition. Only a handful of topics—sources of law, the variety of legal professionals, criminal and civil procedure, the structure of courts, and a few others—could be covered in the few pages of this chapter. The aim of the exercise, however, is not to provide a full picture but instead to sketch out a cluster of noteworthy points that will permit us to build some comparative understanding when we turn our attention in later chapters to the common law tradition and the Chinese legal tradition.

Before doing that, let us touch on a few final topics that will underscore (i) why the operational aspects that we have addressed in this chapter are so significant globally (that is, beyond continental Europe) and (ii) what direction(s) the civil law tradition (particularly its operational dimensions) might be headed in as the environment in which it has developed continues to change. The first of these subjects (why the civil law tradition is so significant) requires a survey of one of the most momentous political and legal developments of the 20th century—decolonization. The second of the subjects (the future direction of the civil law tradition) invites us to consider the phenomenon of "mixed" legal systems and to ruminate on some of the perceived shortcomings of the civil law.

---

143. Another case provides a further illustration of this "repairing" function that the Constitutional Court has sometimes assumed: When in the 1980s a girl was refused entry into a high school at the age of 18 in hopes of repeating the first year of high school for the fifth time, her parents sued. The judge in the court of first instance sent the case to the Constitutional Court for a ruling on the constitutionality of the applicable statute, which provided that an accommodation had to be made for disabled students. The Constitutional Court, relying on certain other constitutional provisions relating to the right to education, ruled that the statute was unconstitutional because it uses the term "accommodated" and it *should* use the term "guaranteed". As a result, the law has remained unchanged, but a comment has been added to the law explaining that the Constitutional Court has ruled that the law is to be read as if it uses the term "guaranteed".

A. *Distribution of the Civil Law*

The civil law tradition was concentrated for four-fifths of its lifespan in a tiny corner of the Earth. From its beginnings around 450 BCE (when the Twelve Tables were issued) until around 1500 CE, the mixture of Roman law, canon law, and commercial law that comprise the main elements of the civil law tradition applied only slightly beyond the limits of present-day of Europe. In Roman times, Britain was a northern frontier only slightly affected by Roman law; and Roman law's influence extended only barely south of the coastal areas of northern Africa and only a short distance east of Constantinople. The European *jus commune* emerging from the universities beginning in the 11th century (in the "second life" of Roman law) had no application in the lands of India or China or South America or central Africa — until something happened that is so fundamental as to be nearly invisible today.

1. Colonization

The "something" that happened was a two-phase process of colonization and decolonization. Like a tsunami — a single, unprecedented, and unimaginably large wave — a surge of European people and ideas and control flooded the rest of the world in a frenzy of colonization and conquest that lasted roughly two or three centuries wherever it reached. The surge began around 1500, when European monarchs saw the potential for wealth and influence that the great maritime navigators brought to their attention by "discovering" new lands and trade routes. Box #3.14 offers a synopsis of how that surge developed, ultimately reaching North America, Central and South America, South Asia, Southeast Asia, East Asia, and Africa.

Box #3.14 *The Surge of European Colonization and Conquest —*
The 1500s through the 1800s[144]

North America (beginning late 1400s). In August 1492, Cristoforo Colombo, an Italian financed by the Spanish crown, sailed west from Palos de la Frontera, a Spanish port, in hopes of reaching the lands producing spices and other goods that had long teased the desires and imaginations of Europeans. Land was first spotted in October 1492. There is still debate concerning the location where Colombo first landed. Colombo called the island *San Salvador* (in what is now the Bahamas). The inhabitants called it Guanahani. Many today believe the island is either Samana Cay, Plana Cays, or San Salvador Island (named in 1925 under the belief that the location was Colombo's San Salvador).

That "discovery" served as the opening for exploration and settlement of North America by the Spanish beginning in the 1500s and then by other European powers (mainly the English and the French) through the 1600s and part of the 1700s. Ultimately, all of the continent came under the control of those foreign powers.

South America (beginning early 1500s). The surge of European conquest and colonization in the southern part of the Western Hemisphere was carried out principally by the Spanish — also beginning in the early 1500s — together with some involvement of the Portuguese and other powers. By the 1700s most of the continent was under the domination of those powers.

South Asia (late 1400s). Five years after Colombo's famous voyage, Vasco de Gama, a Portuguese explorer, was the first to successfully lead a fleet of ships with a crew of 170 men from Lisbon to India. The expedition set sail in July 1497 and arrived in Kappad (near Calicut) in

---

144. The content of Box #3.14 is drawn from a variety of sources, including various online websites accessed by Google searches for Colombo, de Gama, Magellan, history of India, imperialism in Asia, Dutch East Indies, and the Scramble for Africa.

May 1498. De Gama returned to Portugal in September 1499, where he was richly rewarded for opening a key trading route. The so-called spice trading route proved key to the growth of the Portuguese economy.

Around the world (early 1500s). Ferdinand Magellan (in Portuguese *Fernão de Magalhães*; in Spanish *Fernando de Magallanes*) was a Portuguese-born explorer who later obtained Spanish nationality to serve King Charles I of Spain. Departing in 1519, Magellan set out to discover a westward route to the Spice Islands. Traveling west toward Brazil and then rounding the southern tip of South America (passing through what is still known as the "Strait of Magellan"), the fleet reached the Spice Islands (East Indies) and eventually completed the first successful global circumvention. Magellan himself was killed along the way (in the Philippines) and his body was never recovered. His voyage, however, proved that such navigation was possible and contributed to the interest in further exploration and in the conquest it offered.

India. The sea route first discovered by Vasco de Gama led to direct and widespread Indo-European trade. The Portuguese, and then the Dutch and British, set up trading posts in India. European traders played off internal conflicts among Indian kingdoms to gain control and appropriate lands. After ongoing battles, the British East India Company moved inland, gaining control of Bengal. The British introduced a land taxation system, based on a feudal-like structure. By exploiting the existing social, political, and religious divisions, the East India Company took control of most of the Indian sub-continent (including present-day India, Pakistan, Sri Lanka, and Bangladesh) by the 1850s.

The East Indies. In 1603 the first permant Dutch trading post was established in West Java. From 1611 to 1617, the Dutch and English battled for control of the region. Each colonizing country established various trading posts. In 1620, the two countries reached a diplomatic agreement, and England, for the most part, withdrew from the region. The Dutch East India Company, the most active trading company during this period, controlled the East Indies until 1800 when the trading company went bankrupt and was dissolved. The Dutch government took control of the East Indies and expanded the territory of control over the 19th century to include the whole Indonesian archipelago.

China. During the early 1800s, China was increasingly troubled by internal weaknesses within the Qing dynasty—part of a much wider story to be told in Chapter Six of this book. Following Britain's defeat of China during the First Opium War (1839–1842), China lost control of Hong Kong and several Chinese ports were opened to British traders. China was again defeated by Britain in the Second Opium War (1856–1860), and according to the terms of the treaties the Chinese were forced to allow the British increased access to Chinese ports and Europeans were allowed to travel throughout the country's interior. Later treaties signed by China granted similar rights to foreigners from other countries, including the United States and Russia, resulting in the "extraterritorial" rights of those countries in many important parts of China.

Africa. In the 1800s, the "Scramble for Africa", also known as the "Race for Africa", brought waves of invasion, attack, occupation, and annexation of African territories by European powers. The main reason was economic: as Europe became heavily industrialized during the 19th century, Africa was increasingly seen by Europeans as a potential source for raw materials and a potential market for finished European goods. Supplementing those economic reasons, though, was a cultural and racial one: colonial expansion by Europeans into Africa was regarded (by many Europeans themselves, that is) as justified on the basis of notions of racial superiority; and it was seen by Europeans as the "White Man's Burden" to help African peoples progress out of a state of savagery. The result was a period of "New Imperialism" between the 1880s and World War I: much of Africa was colonized in just 25 years. Indeed, this most recent continent-wide surge of European conquest and colonization is reflected in the map of Africa appearing in Appendix 3.6 at the end of this chapter.

The individual details of this surge of European influence are less significant than the general trend: through a combination of effort and luck (combined, one might say, with

greed and high risk tolerance), a group of persons coming from an extremely small portion of the world's territory—Europe constitutes less than 3% of the Earth's land-mass[145]
—achieved an almost smothering domination over most of the rest of the world. The
extent of that domination is illustrated in the map[s] shown in Appendix 3.5, Appendix
3.6, and Appendix 3.7 at the end of this chapter. The first two maps show the extent of
colonial holdings as of 1800 and 1910, respectively. The third map shows European claims
and holdings in Africa as of 1914.

2. Decolonization and Nationalization of Law

That domination did not last. Whatever claims might be made that neo-colonialism
still exists—that is, that less economically developed countries are still oppressed by the
countries of the industrialized world—the legal claims and colonial holdings that the
rich "First World" countries enjoyed for a span of several centuries came to a definite end
as a legal matter over the course of just a few decades in the middle of the 20th century.
Independent countries emerged in South Asia (India, Pakistan, Bangladesh, Sri Lanka),
Southeast Asia (Indonesia, the Philippines, and others), and most of Africa, suddenly
tripling the number of countries in the world.[146]

Many of those new countries—formerly colonies, now independent states—had been
subject to the control of countries in western Europe. They shared that European connection,
of course, with the countries of Latin America, which had gained their independence
from European colonizing powers in the early 1800s. Indeed, the countries in today's
world that have a legacy of European influence—political, cultural, and legal—are spread
all around the globe.

It is the *legal* influence, of course, that should interest us most here, in two respects.
First, the concept of the nation-state—a concept forged in Europe and coming to full
maturity around the 17th century—was imposed on those territories elsewhere in the
world that had come under European domination. Second, the civil law tradition, introduced by those European powers in their far-flung territories, took root in cultural
soil very different from its original home. Like an invasive species (such as East Red Cedar
trees in the former tallgrass prairies of Kansas), the complex and sophisticated species of
law and legal thought that emerged from centuries of evolution in Europe was transplanted all around the world—and upon decolonization, the newly independent states
largely retained that new species of law and legal thought.

At a more detailed and practical level, the two great civil law codes of the 19th century—
the French Civil Code of 1804 and the German *BGB* of 1896 discussed above in Chapter
Two—have had enormous influence around the world. For reasons referred to earlier, the
French Civil Code has enjoyed more widespread adoption outside Europe than has the

---

145. See *Europe's Nature—a Rich Natural Heritage*, at http://ec.europa.eu/environment/na-
ture/info/pubs/docs/posters/enfy_overview_en.pdf.

146. The tripling of the number of countries in the world over the past several decades, largely as
a result of decolonization, is illustrated dramatically in a world map appearing recently in an AARP
magazine, drawing information from the National Geographic Society, the US Department of State,
and other sources. The map shows countries gaining independence in the 1960s (42 countries), 1970s
(another 23 countries), 1980s (a further eight countries), and the 1990s (15 more countries). See
AARP BULLETIN (November 2010), at 43 (available also at aarp.org/bulletin).

BGB[147]; but both of those codes (and other French and German codes relating to other topics) have appealed to newly-independent states that have emerged from their colonial pasts. Indeed, as will be explored further below in subsection VA of Chapter Four, the codified character of the civil law tradition helps explain why so many "new" states — even those never coming under the political control of foreign powers — are now members of the civil law family.

The overall consequence of this series of developments over several centuries is that the points we have explored in this chapter, relating to the civil law tradition from an operational perspective, apply now not just in European countries but in the majority of the nation-states of our modern world. Therefore, the observations made above regarding the role of judges, the systems of divided court jurisdiction, the distinction between private law and public law, the importance of codes, the training of lawyers, the functions of notaries, the values underlying criminal and civil procedure, and indeed a great many specific legal rules — all of these apply to a large extent in scores of legal systems and on nearly every continent. They are familiar to legal professionals in the entire civil law world.

B. The Future of the Civil Law

What implications might flow from the fact I have just emphasized — that there is a shared legal "past and present" among civil law countries? Divining the future is probably as fruitless as it is fascinating, so we need not give much attention to this topic. However, three specific points are worth considering in this regard. The first focuses on the notion of "mixed legal systems". The second focuses on the relationship between law and religion. The third focuses on certain deficiencies that have been identified in the civil law tradition.

1. "Mixed" Legal Systems

As has already been noted, most countries in the world are civil law countries — or, expressed differently, the civil law tradition is more widely distributed throughout the world than any other legal tradition. However, it is also true to say that many countries in the world are "mixed" legal systems, in which two or more legal traditions — one of them often an "indigenous" tradition — combine and compete within a single state. A straightforward example (in my view) would be Indonesia, which has a legal system today that combines (i) a heavy influence of Roman law (often referred to in that context as Dutch-Roman law) because of the colonization by the Dutch of what is now the Republic of Indonesia and (ii) indigenous law, called *adat* law. In like fashion, most African countries, particularly in West Africa, also exemplify mixed legal systems — as for example with the imprint of French law (via French and Belgian political and economic domination) combining with local indigenous laws.

We could also identify other types of mixed systems — some involving a combination of common law with indigenous law (for example, India) and some involving a combi-

---

147. See the text accompanying note 217 in Chapter Two. For an interesting account of the influence that the French Civil Code had on Latin American countries, see M. C. Mirow, *The Code Napoléon: Buried but Ruling in Latin America*, 33 DENVER JOURNAL OF INTERNATIONAL LAW & POLICY 179 (2005).

nation of both common law and civil law with indigenous law (the Philippines might well match this description, because of three centuries of Spanish domination followed by a half century of American domination, all laid atop a southeast Asian culture). Indeed, few if any legal systems could be said to be "homogoneous"; practically all are mixed.[148]

One of the possible implications of this fact relates to the future of the civil law world. We might anticipate that the integrity of the civil law world in the coming decades may well turn on how strong or weak the continuing relationship is between the former European colonial powers and their former colonies. To the extent that those relationships weaken, perhaps by the displacement of European cultural influence with other influences—such as American influence, "global" influence, or the influence of the indigenous legal culture of that country or others in its region—then the relative intensity of the civil law tradition is likely to weaken.

2. The Role of Religion and Ideology

There is another factor that is consistent with, and probably contributing to, this increasing realization that nearly all legal systems outside Europe are "mixed" legal systems. That other factor is the shift away from Christianity. Historically, Christianity permeated the civil law, for reasons we explored in Chapter Two—and indeed extending all the way back to Constantine's Edict of Milan in 313 CE. However, that religious foundation has relatively little current impact on the operation of the law in civil law countries, particularly in Europe.

That is, recent decades have brought an increasing "secularization" of many civil law systems. Even though Christianity once had a very strong *influence* on the law in European civil law countries, Christianity (and religion in general) has for many centuries been regarded as conceptually *separate* from the law in those countries. Expressed differently, religion in civil law countries has nearly always been seen as merely *related to*, not *identical with*, the law. Indeed, this distinguishes civil law from Islamic law. Were this book more comprehensive, it would offer comparisons with Islamic law in numerous respects. In lieu of that, I shall offer the simple diagram in Box #3.15, intended to reflect this fundamental difference between Islamic law and civil law (as well as common law, for that matter). The diagram in Box #3.15 depicts law in Western systems as being "influenced by religious norms but separate from them"; by contrast, Islamic teaching rests on the proposition that "law is surrounded by, part of, and subsumed by religious norms", so that there is no "distance" between theology and law—instead, law is "inside" theology.

---

148. In recent years, mixed legal systems have attracted much attention among comparative law scholars. See, e.g., Merryman-2010, *supra* note 1, at 41; Kenneth G.C. Reid, *The Idea of Mixed Legal Systems*, 78 TULANE LAW REVIEW 5 (2003); William Tetley, *Mixed Jurisdictions: Common Law v. Civil Law (Codified and Uncodified)*, 60 LOUISIANA LAW REVIEW 677 (2000). At least one observer posits that mixed legal system are similar enough to each other in certain ways as to warrant regarding them as part of their own distinct legal family. *Id.* (citing MIXED JURISDICTIONS WORLDWIDE: THE THIRD LEGAL FAMILY (Vernon V. Palmer ed., 2001)). See also Colin B. Picker, *International Law's Mixed Heritage: A Common/Civil Law Jurisdiction*, 41 VANDERBILT JOURNAL OF TRANSNATIONAL LAW 1083, 1102–1104 (2008) (citing numerous works on mixed legal systems and explaining that some authorities, including several participants at the June 2007 Second Worldwide Congress of Mixed Jurisdiction Jurists, argue that all legal systems are mixed).

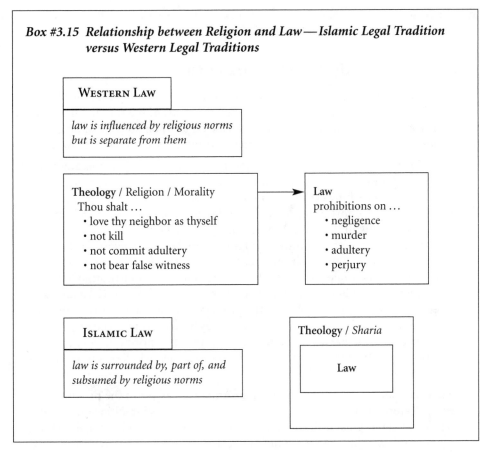

Box #3.15 Relationship between Religion and Law—Islamic Legal Tradition versus Western Legal Traditions

I would suggest that the "distance" between civil law and Christianity (or any other religion, for that matter) is constantly increasing—both (i) in Europe and, for different reasons, (ii) elsewhere, as the civil law has spread into a broad range of diverse cultures around the world. If this is true, then that increasing "distance" from Christianity would seem to make the civil law correspondingly more welcoming to other religions and ideologies. In this respect, the civil law tradition presents an ever more attractive system to many countries.

However, the opposite might also be true. Despite the increasing appeal that the civil law might have in non-Christian cultures because of the growing "distance" and disassociation between civil law and Christianity, what I regard as an expanding diversity of religious beliefs and other matters of ideology around the world might tend to have a disintegrating effect on the civil law tradition. As a principal historically shared set of values—those of Christianity—seems ever less important as an element of contemporary legal systems (certainly in Europe, the birthplace of the civil law), we can surely expect that some of the "deeply rooted, historically conditioned attitudes" of the civil law tradition will tend to fade away. Stated more simply, this would mean that as Christianity fades from the picture of the civil law tradition, so the "glue" that Christianity provided in holding that tradition together also loses its adhesive power.

In sum, there are both cohesive forces and repelling forces at work as the temporal and ideological "distance" grows ever greater between contemporary society and the European society from which the civil law tradition emerged over the course of many centuries. If the repelling forces are more powerful than the cohesive forces—and this strikes me as a reasonable possibility—then we can expect to see a growing divergence in legal systems, at least within the civil law "family".

3. Criticisms of the Civil Law Tradition

A last point that warrants some attention focuses on the content of the civil law tradition itself. Is it a good system? Does it serve well the needs of the societies that share it? Merryman, exploring the civil law tradition from the vantage point of a common law lawyer, has identified a cluster of specific criticisms that have been leveled at the civil law tradition:

> ... [C]ertain aspects of the civil law tradition have [attracted increasing criticism, either] expressly or by implication. In particular, it has been suggested that there is something excessive about the emphasis on a sharp separation of powers; that the effort to make the law judge-proof is both futile and, in the long run, socially undesirable; that the quest for certainty has become both a romantic form of snark-hunting and a meaningless, catchword argument, available to support any position; that the role of the legislature has become bloated out of all proportion, far beyond the ability of that institution to meet the demands placed upon it; that the premises and methods of German legal science have isolated the law from the problems of the society it is supposed to serve ...; that the civil law is dominated by a misdirected scholarly tradition, diverting the great potential influence and the enormous energy, creativity, and cultivated intelligence of civil law teacher-scholars into essential arid pursuits.
>
> These are not merely the reactions of an American lawyer to the prominently exotic features of an inadequately understood foreign legal tradition. Such criticisms are not original with common lawyers. They are all made by civil lawyers themselves, critically examining their own law and calling for its reform.[149]

Having surveyed the civil law tradition from a historical perspective in Chapter Two and from an operational perspective in this chapter, each of the points that Merryman enumerates in that passage should now be recognizable to us. Indeed, even our very brief survey might have unearthed additional features of the civil law (not mentioned by Merryman in the passage quoted above) that appear to today's society as somehow culturally inappropriate, impracticably anachronistic, or ideologically obnoxious. Taken together, are such criticisms and perceived shortcomings serious enough to cause a gradual abandonment of the system, or at least to reduce the appeal and erode the significance of the civil law tradition? It is a question worth ruminating on, given the fact that there are at least two other great legal traditions in the world that may be regarded—for better or for worse—to be competing with the civil law tradition. In Chapter Four we turn to one of those: the common law tradition.

---

149. Merryman, *supra* note 2, at 146.

Appendix 3.1
Training of Lawyers in Four Legal Systems
(excerpts from journal article by Szto)

This article by Professor Mary Szto provides an excellent succinct overview (as of 2004) of the training and licensing process for lawyers in four important legal systems —all of them members of "legal families" under examination in this book. The article is reprinted here with permission, in excerpted form (footnotes have been omitted, and ellipses indicate where text has, in a few segments, been omitted in the interest of space.)

Toward a Global Bar: A Look at
China, Germany, England, and the United States
14 INDIANA INTERNATIONAL & COMPARATIVE LAW REVIEW 585 (2004)
Mary C. Szto*

I. INTRODUCTION

The legal profession is globalizing rapidly. This is evidenced by the ease of world communications, burgeoning international issues, and mergers among firms of different countries. Bar admission requirements qualify attorneys to practice law. Around the world, law schools are sometimes under pressure to conform their curricula to state bar examinations. In the United States, often, applicants measure schools by their "bar passage rates."

How well do bar requirements prepare candidates for the practice of law, locally and globally? Also, do they accurately measure the knowledge, skills, and qualities an international attorney should possess?

A global look at bar requirements seeks to broaden the discussion of how best to train attorneys. By examining different country standards, any particular country can begin to "think outside the box." It also allows attorneys from different countries, who more and more are working side-by-side, to understand how they can practice law together. A third outcome might be to contribute to a dialogue for a global bar.

This article explores the requirements necessary to practice law in four countries: China, England, Germany, and the United States. These include education, practice, exam, and moral requirements. The requirements for foreign attorneys are also considered. The article concludes with observations and suggestions for future practice.

---

* B.A., Wellesley College, 1981; M.A.R., Westminster Theological Seminary, 1983; J.D., Columbia University, 1986. At the time this article was prepared, Professor Szto was serving as Visiting Associate Professor, Touro Law Center. Prof. Szto now teaches at Hamline University. Because this article was published a few years ago, it does not reflect some recent developments, such as the strategic framework for European cooperation in education and training ("ET 2020") adopted by the Council of Europe in May 2009, as referred to in the "interview" with an Italian law student appearing in subsectioin ID3b of the main text of this chapter. For a late-2008 description of such efforts, see Julian Lonbay, *The Education, Licensing, and Training of Lawyers in the European Union, Part I: Cross-Border Practice in the Member States*, THE BAR EXAMINER, Nov 2008, at 6.

In recent years, China has responded to rapid economic change and the need to produce hundreds of thousands of practitioners. England and Germany have responded to changes brought about by membership in the European Union. The United States has experienced less dramatic developments. However, foreign attorneys have long been welcome in the United States. Interestingly, the United States stands alone in not requiring supervised practice training of law candidates. This is perhaps because law training is a post-college degree in the United States.

II. The Countries

A. The People's Republic of China

Overview

China is a country with an ancient history; however, its current legal system is very young. China began developing its present legal system in the late 1970s in its efforts to achieve economic modernization. Legal education has become more widely available since 1980, which has also led to increased legal education exchanges between China and other countries with an "ever-increasing" number of law students, teachers, and scholars flowing between Chinese and foreign institutions.

China's system is a blend of civil, socialist, and increasingly American legal influences. Since the late 1970s, the legal service profession in China has also been "ever-expanding" and has become more lucrative, which continues to attract many people to the field. Whereas in 1979 there were 212 lawyers in seventy-nine firms in china, in 1999, there were 110,000 lawyers in nearly 9,000 law firms. However, there are still some aspects of the legal profession in China that need desperate help.

As China advances rapidly in the development of its legal system, we can expect additional provisions and regulations to shape the process. Most recently, in 2002, in accordance with the amended Judges Law, Prosecutors Law, and Lawyers Law, over 360,000 people took the newly instituted two-day State Judicial Exam in order to qualify for jobs as judges, prosecutors and practicing attorneys.

One of China's major concerns is that many of its judges and prosecutors have little or no university or college-level legal training. Many judges actually attended law school after they became judges.

History

In traditional China, government, law, and courts existed without the existence of lawyers as an officially recognized occupational group. Scholars of the Confucian classics dominated the ruling elite. Civil disputes were usually resolved informally through mediation, conducted by respected leaders or elders of clans, villages, and guilds in accordance with customary rules and prevailing notions of morality, which stressed harmony and the giving of concessions and discouraged litigation and the pursuit of self-interest.

Interestingly, "*songshi*, meaning experts in litigation, began to practice as early as the Tang dynasty.... They learn[ed] their knowledge of the law and of judicial proceedings through apprenticeship or self-study, and offered the services of advising on litigious matters and drafting petitions and pleadings." However, their status was not officially recognized and they had no right to represent their clients in courts or in any other capacity. "The business which these *songshi* engaged in was not considered respectable." They were sometimes labeled *daobi xieshen*, or "evil gods of the knife-pen." This is understandable in a society where the concept of legal rights was not known, where social harmony was a paramount virtue, and where litigation and conflicts involving the pursuit of self-interest were discouraged and held in contempt.

As China entered the twentieth century, it pursued attempts at Westernization of its political and legal system, including legislation for the legal profession.

Once established in 1949, the People's Republic of China (PRC) abolished the collection of laws established under the previous National Government. The first mentioning of lawyers in formal PRC legislation appeared in 1954. There was no broad statute regulating qualifications, organization, and lawyer conduct during the 1950s; however, the Ministry of Justice did establish a series of "legal advisory offices." By 1957, there were around 800 legal advisory offices throughout China and a total of about 3000 lawyers.

The anti-rightist movement brought the beginning legal movement to a halt in 1957. Many of China's legal experts were transferred to the countryside to be "reeducated" through hard labor. The Ministry of Justice was abolished and the advisory offices were closed in 1959. China had to emerge from a national nightmare during the late 1970s, the Cultural Revolution, before continuing work on the establishment of a modern Chinese legal system.

Governing Law

The governing law in China for attorneys is the Law of the People's Republic of China on Lawyers, promulgated May 15, 1996. The first of its kind, the law took effect in 1997 and clearly defines the rights and obligations of lawyers and law firms. In 2001, China amended its Judges Law, Prosecutors Law, and Lawyers Law to increase the qualifications required for these posts. In general, a lawyer must uphold the Constitution of the People's Republic of China, meet educational requirements, pass the national exam, have practice training in a law firm for one year, and be a person of good character and conduct.

Education

Legal education in China usually requires four to five years of education after the high school level. Attorneys in China are qualified by law faculties of universities and colleges or must have qualifications from other faculties of universities or colleges to show that they possess the "professional knowledge of law." They must also pass the uniform national judicial exam. A look at the curriculum and subject areas of study from China's Peking University can give us a picture of the typical law candidate's studies. Peking University runs a four-year LL.B. program. Categories of courses include Theoretical Legal Science and Applied Legal Science. The first category, Theoretical Legal Science, includes Theories of Jurisprudence, Sociology of Law, Contemporary Western Jurisprudence, and the First Amendment to the U.S. Constitution. The second category, Applied Legal Science, includes Internet Law, Technology/Economy and Law, Labor Law and Social Protection Law, General Part of Civil Law, International Financial Law, and Environmental Law. In addition, LL.B. students usually must write a thesis. [Note: Peking University and a few other universities in China have recently begun offering a J.D. degree modeled on the US J.D. degree.]

Practical Training

There is a required traineeship with a law firm for a full year. After completing the training period at a Chinese law firm a training appraisal report is issued.

Examination

From 1986 to 2001, China administered a uniform national examination formulated by the Judicial Administrative Department of the State Council for lawyers. In 2002 the State Judicial Exam was instituted. It is required for judges, prosecutors, and lawyers. The examination is administered by the Ministry of Justice, held once a year, and is a closed-book exam. Its contents include "theoretical jurisprudence, applied jurisprudence, existing legal provisions, legal practice and legal profession moralities."

Theoretical jurisprudence includes the concept of the "rule of law, basic rights and freedoms, and the relationship between the state and the individuals." Applied jurisprudence includes criminal law, civil law, family law, procedural laws, labor law, environmental law, "laws on women and children, and laws on association, trade unions, press and religions." Eligibility to take the exam requires being a PRC national, "abiding by the Constitution of the People's Republic of China, having the right to vote and stand for election, having full capacity for civil conduct," and meeting the educational requirements for either the Judges Law, the Prosecutors Law, or the Lawyers Law and being of "good character and conduct."

The profession is attracting hundreds of thousands of applicants. In 1999, 180,000 candidates registered to take the lawyers' examination. In 2000, 220,000 candidates took the last lawyers' examination. In 2002, over 360,000 took the first State Judicial Exam. This was a world history record. Of these 360,000, "about one-third were staff members of the courts, procuratorates, police departments and other workers in the field of law." Only 7% passed the examination.

Moral Character

China requires that the applicant be of good character in order to practice law. The following persons may not take the State Judicial Examination: persons who have been "subject to criminal punishment due to an intentional crime," those who have been discharged "from employment by a State organ" or whose license to practice law has been revoked, and those who cheated on the exam and have been disallowed from taking the exam for a period of time. In addition, a person will not be issued a lawyer's practice certificate if he or she has no capacity or limited capacity for civil acts.

Foreign Attorneys

Foreign attorneys are not allowed to take part in the litigation process in China. They can neither interpret Chinese laws nor provide advisory papers concerning Chinese law. Foreign attorneys can, and do, consult in China. The main work of foreign lawyers is in introducing foreign investment, representing Chinese clients in lawsuits in foreign countries, and providing advice in matters of trade, technology transfer, real estate, intellectual property rights, bonds, and securities. Even lawyers from Hong Kong are not eligible to take the State Judicial Examination.

Summary

As China continues to develop its legal system, its requirements to practice law will also develop and change. The legal profession is growing in acceptance from what was once an unpopular profession. China's desire to achieve greater economic development has led to an explosion in the number of legal personnel being trained. There is also a very critical need to provide more training for China's current judges.

B. England

Overview

England uses a common law system. There are two main types of law practitioners: barristers and solicitors. In 2000, there were around 90,000 solicitors in England and Wales and 10,000 barristers. The Law Society regulates solicitors; the General Council of the Bar (the Bar Council) regulates barristers. Traditionally, only solicitors dealt directly with clients as general agents, and only barristers could appear in the higher courts (Crown courts, High Court, Court of Appeal and House of Lords.) Barristers belong to one of the four Inns of Court described further below. Over the years, the distinction between solicitors and barristers has begun to blur.

The following deals mainly with the requirements for solicitors, with a brief summary of barrister requirements. For both solicitors and barristers there are three training paths: the law graduate path, the non-law degree path, and the non-graduate path. All three paths include a training period and a practice course.

History

... The history of the barrister dates back to the serjeant-at-law. The Crown appointed these advocates and, in the thirteenth century, only they could appear in the Court of Common Pleas. They held this privilege until 1846. Eventually these serjeants became common law judges and had their own Inns. Originally, barristers were apprentices of serjeants and they formed the four Inns still in existence today. The Inns were at first educational institutions. Barristers also received the unique privilege of appearing before the King's or Queen's Bench.

The origins of the solicitor date to the *attornatus*, who was an officer of the court in the Middle Ages. Interestingly, solicitors were expelled from the Inns in the 1500s. The Law Society was formed in 1845. Beginning in the 1800s, solicitors had to complete a formal education and apprentice for several years. An examination in law was required for solicitors in 1836.

Governing Law

The Law Society prescribes the legal education and training required to qualify as a solicitor in England and Wales in accordance with the Solicitors Act of 1974. The Training Regulations of 1990 apply the Solicitors Act.

Education

Two of the three paths to becoming a solicitor require a degree, either in law or another subject. Around 25% of solicitors do not have a law degree. After receiving a degree, students take a Legal Practice Course, before working for a solicitor's firm for two years. The Training Regulations state that a person satisfies the academic state of training by:

  (i)   graduating with a qualifying law degree incorporating a legal practice course; or

  (ii) graduating with a qualifying law degree; or

  (iii) passing a common professional examination course; or

  (iv) gaining a post-graduate diploma in law; or

  (v)   satisfactorily completing a course of study which incorporates the foundations of legal knowledge and a legal practice course.

Options (i) and (ii) are commonly known as the Law Degree Route. Options (iii) and (iv) are commonly known as the Non-Law Degree Route. There is also a Non-Graduate Route, which allows non-degreed candidates who are working in legal employment to qualify as a solicitor. They fulfill their academic stage by options (iii) or (v). Key to fulfilling the academic state is study of the Seven Foundations of Legal Knowledge. They are Obligations I (Contracts), Obligations II (Torts), Criminal Law, Equity and the Law of Trusts, the Law of the European Union, Property Law, and Public Law.

The Law Degree Route is the quickest and most common route to qualify as a solicitor. However, this route is very competitive. Applicants need high grades in any academic subject to be considered. The Non-Law Graduate can have a degree in any subject but must go through the Common Professional Examination or Post-Graduate Diploma in Law. The preparation required for the Common Profession Examination amounts to one academic year (two years for the part-time program). During this time the applicant studies the Seven Foundations of Legal Knowledge. The Common Professional Examination is given in early summer. A three-hour paper is due in each of the seven courses and an additional area of law. A candidate will normally pass the examination if all of the papers are successfully completed on the same occasion. Barring the most exceptional circumstances, a candidate may not attempt any paper on the Common Professional Exam on more than three occasions.

All candidates who are eligible for the Common Professional Examination may apply for a Diploma in Law Course. The course is approximately thirty-six weeks long and varies from institution to institution. The Non-Graduate route is open to persons who do not wish to take a degree and are working in legal employment. The process is lengthy, demanding, and academically challenging. This process requires one to qualify as a member of the Institute of Legal Executives. Study is done usually part time at local colleges or home study courses. There are several paper examinations.

Practical Training/Examination

Commonly, the academic stage of training must precede the vocational stage of training. The vocational stage of training requirement is fulfilled by:

(1) completing a legal practice course, or an integrated course, or an exempting law degree; and

(2) serving a training contract (equal to two years full-time); during which

(3) a professional skills course, and such other courses as the Law Society may prescribe, are completed.

The purpose of the Legal Practice Course is to ensure that trainee solicitors entering training contracts have the necessary knowledge and skills to undertake appropriate tasks under proper supervision during the contract. A full-time Legal Practice Course runs for one academic year; a part-time course runs for two years. The Legal Practice Course includes core courses in Ethics, Skills (advocacy, interviewing, writing and drafting, and practical research), Taxation, European Union Law, and Probate and Administration of Estates. There are also compulsory areas, which include Business Law and Practice, Conveyancing, and Litigation and Advocacy. Other areas of law fall into elective areas like Private Client and Corporate Client work and pervasive areas such as Accounts, Revenue Law, and Professional Conduct and Client Care.

Candidates are responsible for finding their own employment that will fulfill the training contract. A firm or organization carries out the Training Contract as authorized by the Law Society. Larger firms offer the majority of training places and usually recruit two years in advance. The Training Contract usually lasts for two years. Sometimes, the training contract must provide for a salary no less than that prescribed by the Society. A training establishment may have up to two trainee solicitors for each solicitor/partner or solicitor/director in private practice of each solicitor in any organization who is not forbidden to take on a trainee solicitor.

During the Training Contract it is expected that the applicant practice and learn communication skills, practice support skills, legal research, drafting, interviewing and advising and gain experience in negotiations, advocacy and oral presentation skills. Additionally the applicant must gain experience in three other areas from a list of twenty-three areas such as Banking, Employment, Family, Immigration, Personal Injury, Intellectual Property, Welfare, etc. There are checklists for each subject showing the tasks the trainee should be able to perform by the end of his or her training.

The training establishment must provide a desk available for the trainee solicitor's own work, appropriate secretarial support, and convenient access to a library or suitable material for research. A training principal ensures that each trainee solicitor maintains a training record for inspection at review of progress meetings. In addition to regular meetings with each trainee solicitor, there are adequate arrangements for daily guidance.

On a day-to-day basis, a supervisor should:

1. give the trainee tasks and work;
2. give clear instructions and check that the trainee understands them;
3. provide the trainee with sufficient factual background;
4. suggest available office or library reference materials;
5. provide the trainee with a realistic framework for the trainee to complete the task and work;
6. answer the trainee's questions;
7. assign the trainee tasks with an increasing degree of difficulty;
8. ensure that the trainee has enough but not too much work;
9. provide a balance of work across substantive and procedural areas;
10. provide work which will enable the trainee to use different skills;
11. create an environment where the trainee is not afraid to ask questions;
12. encourage the trainee to propose solutions even though they may not be correct;
13. provide regular feedback and guidance on the trainee's performance;
14. ensure that the trainee's achievements and improvements are recognized and praised;
15. ensure that aspects of the trainee's performance that need to be improved are discussed thoroughly with the trainee;
16. encourage the trainee to develop him or herself; and
17. ensure that the trainee keep any training record required by the firm of the Law Society.

In addition, the trainee has the responsibility to:

1. inform the firm if it is not fulfilling its obligations particularly with regard to basic skills and legal topics;
2. manage his/her time, effort and resources to develop good working practices;
3. seek clarification when tasks and work are ill-defined or too open-ended or the trainee is given insufficient facts;
4. inform the firm when the trainee has too much or too little work; the tasks are too challenging or not challenging enough, or there is no variety in the type of work and tasks that have been allocated to the trainee;
5. be open and honest when the trainee is given feedback or appraised on his or her performance;
6. take responsibility for his or her own self-development; and
7. inform his or her supervisor when a mistake is made.

During the Training Contract, one must also complete the Professional Skills Course. This is comprised of three compulsory courses: Advocacy and Oral Communication, Financial Awareness and Business Accounts, and Ethics and Client Responsibilities. The Law Society states, "These topics are ones which the Society believes are best studied once you have some experience of work in a solicitor's office. The Training Contract is normally waived for those pursuing the Non-Graduate Route. After the Training Contract is completed, the applicant can be added to the Roll of Solicitors.

Moral Character

The candidate applies for the Roll of Solicitors approximately eight weeks before the expected completion of the Training Contract. The application must include successful completion of all training, and the candidate and their principal supervisor must certify that there are no circumstances that may affect the character and suitability of the applicant, including criminal convictions. If the Society at any time is not satisfied as to the character and suitability of an unadmitted person to become a solicitor, it may cancel enrollment, prohibit entry into a training contract, or discharge a training contract.

Foreign Attorneys

Sections 20 and 21 of the Solicitors Act 1974 prohibit anyone other than a certified English solicitor from acting as an English solicitor. Foreign lawyers have two choices. They may practice in England under their own home title, e.g., *abogado*, *Rechtsanwalt* or attorney-at-law. Alternatively, they may re-qualify as an English solicitor. Foreign lawyers do not have a right of audience in any of the English courts except such rights as derive from European Union law. They may not employ a person to act as a solicitor for the public. However, if a foreign lawyer registers with the Law Society, they may enter into a partnership with a solicitor. The partnership of which the solicitor(s) and the foreign lawyers are members is known as a multinational partnership.

The Law Society of England and Wales maintains a list of foreign lawyers in the country who report their presence in accordance with section 89 of the Courts and Legal Services Act 1990. The Foreign Lawyers Registration Regulations 1995 set out what must be on the register, what must be done to register, renew registration, change a name on the register, and remove a name fro the register. The formalities of re-qualification depend on the jurisdiction of original qualification. It is not necessary to have British nationality in order to qualify as a solicitor. Lawyers from the European Union and European Economic Area member states, as well as from certain Commonwealth and Common Law jurisdictions, are entitled to re-qualification as solicitors by way of a special Qualified Lawyers Transfer Test. The test covers the following subjects: Property, Litigation, Professional Conduct and Accounts, and Principles of Common Law. Separate procedures exist for other lawyers.

Barristers

There are three routes to becoming a barrister: law degree, non-law degree, and non-graduate mature student. Those who do not have a law degree must take the Common Professional Examination Course. All three routes include membership in one of the four Inns of Court: the Inner Temple, Middle Temple, Gray's Inn, and Lincoln's Inn. Each student must satisfy the requirement of "term keeping" by attending twelve qualifying sessions at his or her Inn of Court. A qualifying session is an educational and collegial event. Before 1997, candidates had to dine a certain number of times at their Inn of Court in order to keep terms.

A student must complete an Academic Stage and a Vocational Stage before being "called to the bar." The Academic Stage may be fulfilled by either obtaining a law degree, or by completing the Common Professional Examination Course. Both the law degree and the Common Professional Examination Course must include a "study of the 'foundations of legal knowledge' and one other area of legal study, and assessments and examinations in those subjects." The Foundations of Legal Knowledge are:

(i)   Obligations I (Contract)

(ii)   Obligations II (Tort)

(iii)   Criminal Law

(iv)   Public Law

(v)   Property Law

(vi)   Equity and The Law of Trusts

(vii)   Foundations of EU Law.

Finishing a Vocational Course completes the Vocational Stage.

A student is then "called to the bar" after completing the Bar Vocational Course. The Vocational Course teaches "skills, knowledge and attitudes" required of barristers. The student must be at least twenty-one years of age to be called to the bar. Then the student must complete a pupilage before practicing as a barrister. The pupilage consists of a "non-practicing six months" and a "practicing six months." The practicing six months may be spent with a barrister, solicitor, or lawyer in a Member State of the European Union. A Pupil Master usually may not supervise more than one pupil at a time.

Previously, barristers took a Bar Examination. The first law examination for barristers began in 1872. In 1980, the pass rate was 87%. The Bar Examination is being faded out in favor of the Vocational Course. Solicitors may apply to become barristers. A European attorney may register with one of the Inns under his home professional title. He or she may also apply to become a barrister. This usually entails passing an Aptitude Test and attending six qualifying sessions. Applicants are ineligible for the Bar if they are engaged in an "incompatible" occupation, have been convicted of a "relevant criminal offence," have had a bankruptcy order against him, or have been prohibited from practicing any profession.

Summary

The two branches of the legal profession in England have two separate training regiments. The Law Society has prescribed detailed requirements for academic and vocational training for solicitors. There are three routes to becoming a solicitor. The most common route is to graduate with a law degree, then take a legal practice course (one year), and then enter into a two-year training contract. The two-year training contract also includes the Professional Skills Course that must be completed prior to applying for the Roll of Solicitors. The academic stage includes learning the Seven Foundations of Law and many practical courses in the skills of advocacy, drafting, and negotiations.

There are also three routes to becoming a barrister: law degree, non-law degree and non-graduate experienced student. Students must belong to and keep terms at one of the Inns of Court. Their pupilage is only one year long. They also are required to take a Vocational Course. The differences in training solicitors and barristers are blurring. In either case, the mentoring and careful supervision of trainees in England is to be particularly commended. Also, the eligibility of European Union lawyers to practice in England and the broadening of trainee options to article elsewhere will no doubt lead to further changes.

C. Germany

Overview

Germany's law is based on a civil law system. Today's requirements for attorneys (*Rechtsanwält*) trace their beginnings to eighteenth century Prussia. Federal and state law governs the requirements for attorneys. Attorneys have a long and arduous path to admission to practice including university training, state-supervised professional training, and two state examinations. Since the reunification of Germany, requirements for the legal profession have also become fairly uniform throughout Germany.

History

... The initial requirement for five years of legal education in Germany developed in 1455. In 1713, Prussia required all judges to show adequate theoretical knowledge and practical experience by observing the courts at work, leading to the preparatory service requirement as a part of the legal education requirements in Germany.

In 1749, Prussia's Codex Fridericiani Marchici established a detailed set of state exams and preparatory services for judges. In 1877, the Judiciary Constitutional Act established the legal education framework for the entire German Reich with a two-phase legal education system. The original need of eighteenth century Prussia to train a uniform, loyal, and well-qualified cadre of judges to govern a diverse and spread out geography has left its imprint on German legal training today.

Governing Law

Government control of the German legal education process exists through detailed federal and state legislation. The governing law in Germany for judges is the *Deutsches Richtergesetz*. The governing law for attorneys is the *Bundesrechtsanwaltsordnung* (BRAO), which contains the rights and obligations of attorneys.

Every major change of legal education must gain federal and state approval, making change more difficult to introduce. There are sixteen *Länder*, or states. While this system makes it more difficult to change, the quality of legal education is basically uniform throughout the country. Therefore, the reputation of the university plays a lesser role as compared to some western countries, such as the United States.

Education/Practical Training

Students usually enter a university between the ages of nineteen and twenty-two. Although university education is free, students must pass two state examinations and complete university and state-supervised practical training. Before the first state examination (*Erste Staatsexamen*), students usually take three and a half years of study. However, many students take six years to complete this first phase; the absolute minimum is two years. Most applicants are usually admitted to law school with classes of four to five hundred students.

The German Law on the Judiciary (*Deutsches Richtergesetz*; DRiG) requires certain core subjects during this first phase: Civil Law, Criminal Law, Public Law and Procedural Law, including that of the European Community, Legal History, Legal Philosophy, and Jurisprudence. Although elective courses are available, these core subjects take up most of a student's semesters. Electives may cover administrative law, labor law, company law, commercial law, or other subjects. In addition to taking required courses before the first state examination, students must also spend three periods of one month in practical training. They also usually complete written assignments (*Hausarbeiten*) and tests in the three core areas of civil law, criminal law and public law before qualifying to take the first state examination. Requirements vary among the *Länder*.

Requirements also vary among the *Länder* for the first state examination. The Court of Appeals (*Oberlandesgericht*) of each region administers the exam. Usually, the exam consists of several five-hour written tests (*Klauser*), and a one-hour oral exam. In Bavaria, students write eight five-hour papers: four in private law, one in criminal law, two in public law, and one of their choice. One practitioner and one professor grade papers. For each paper, a student must write a legal opinion for a hypothetical situation. This opinion must include all relevant legal issues and arguments.

If the student achieves a certain grade, he may take the oral exam. The oral exam is administered to between four and five students at once and takes several hours, allowing each candidate about an hour. Each panel of graders for the oral exam includes two practitioners and two professors. The oral exam covers private law, criminal law, public law, and a subject of the student's choice. Private law includes obligations, property, family law and succession, commercial law, company law, and labor law. Electives range from legal history to antitrust law.

The exams may only be retaken once, unless a *Land* allows for a "free shot," or *Freischuss*, after two and a half years of university study. Of some 15,000 law students, only approximately 7,000 complete their first phase. Of these, 25% fail the first state examination. In 1992, 33.8% had only a passing score, and only 3.2% received a "good" or "very good" score.

If students pass the first state examination, they enter a two-year training period before qualifying to take the second state examination. This professional training period is known as *Referendarzeit*. During this period, students are known as *Referendar* and are temporary civil servants. The state organizes and pays for their professional training. In 1995, they were paid around 1,800 DM a month. They must serve in four mandatory positions (*Stationen*) for a minimum of three months each and in one position of their choice for four to six months. The mandatory positions are with a civil court, a criminal court or prosecutor's office, an administrative body, and an attorneys' office. The optional placement may be with a court or public body, a notary, a trade union, a business, or in another legal jurisdiction. During the *Referendarzeit*, the students learn how to draw pleadings, draft acts, and write judgments. Trainees also attend courses run by judges or other civil servants. These sessions focus on court procedures and case analysis.

After the *Referendarzeit*, the students may return to school for additional preparation for the second state examination. The second state examination (*Zweites Staatsexamen or Grosse Staatspüfung*) is grueling and may include up to twelve written or oral exams between three and eight hours in length. This is sometimes done over a period of three weeks. Once a person has passed the second state examination, he or she is called an *Assessor* or *Volljurist*. Most *Assessoren* are close to thirty years of age. Around 20–25% will eventually become judges. They may also become notaries, prosecutors, private practitioners, and legal advisors.

Interestingly, many students (sometimes 90% in some universities) take private cram courses (*Repetitorium*) for up to eighteen months to prepare for the state examinations. Usually, students will attend weekly classes of about three to four hours. Before reunification, lawyers in East Germany were required to have four years of university study, with one year spent in practice before passing one exam. Since 1991, the new *Länder* have the same requirements as the rest of Germany.

Moral Character

Candidates applying for admission to the court can be refused admission for certain conduct and disqualifying behavior. The following offenses, if found guilty, will disqualify a candidate: unworthy conduct, which makes him appear unfit to exercise the profession; a clear breach of they duty of candor when applying for admission; use of a "doctoral" qualification which has not been earned; dishonest concealment of income from the revenue authorities; and alcoholism. Additionally, a candidate who is found to oppose the democratic order, leaving him open to criminal sanctions, or conducting activity "incompatible" with the profession can be refused admission.

Foreign Attorneys

Lawyers within the European Union may practice in other member states, including Germany. They must use the professional title of their home State but may qualify as *Rechtsanwält* after a period of three years of practicing German law or after passing an aptitude test. The examination consists of a written and oral test and is conducted in German. The written part consists of two papers on one compulsory subject and one elective subject. The oral part consists of a presentation and interview.

Summary

Lawyers in Germany undergo rigorous academic and training requirements within a framework established in eighteenth century Prussia. Of particular note are two arduous state examinations and a two-year training period where the state pays candidates to train in mandatory public and private legal offices. The use of "cram courses" is popular in Germany. Recently lawyers from member states of the European Union have been allowed to qualify as *Rechtsanwälte*.

As the European Union continues to develop and solidify, more changes will come. The EU has extensive rulemaking powers and has used them to revolutionize competition law throughout Western Europe, establish a monetary union, transform national labor workers into continent-wide labor markets, and begin the process of harmonizing private and criminal law throughout western Europe. The EU model may be a predecessor to a much larger unified global law community in the future.

D. United States

Overview

... The American Bar Association has been given the authority to oversee acceptance to the bar in the United States. Each state, however, has bar examiners who are given authority by the judiciary to administer the bar exam and regulate the requirements for admission to the bar. Two states, New York and California, will demonstrate the requirements needed for admission to the bar in the United States.

History

Compared to other countries, the United States is a new country. However, Boston and New York are over three hundred years old, and the U.S. Constitution is one of the world's oldest "living" organic laws. Today, American legal education generally takes three years for most full time students. In 1850, however, the standard course in many law schools ran for one year. The coursework later developed into two-year programs. The three-year program, an L.L.B., was a late innovation started at Harvard University. Prominent judges and lawyers constituted the faculty at the majority of the schools. In 1908, the American Bar Association adopted a canon of professional ethics.

Governing Law

The requirements for admission to practice in California are set forth in the State Bar of California Rules Regulating Admission to Practice Law in California. In New York State, the requirements are listed in the Rules of the Court of Appeals for the Admission of Attorneys and Counselors of Law Part 520.

Education

In California, every applicant has the burden of establishing that he or she has met the following legal education requirement:

(a) Graduated from a law school approved by the American Bar Association or accredited by the Committee Bar Examiners; or

(b) Studied law diligently and in good faith for at least three years in any of the following manners:

    (1) In a law school that is authorized by the State of California to confer professional degrees; is registered with the committee; and which requires classroom attendance of its students for a minimum of 270 hours a year; or

    (2) In a law office in California and under the personal supervision of a member of the State Bar of California who is, and who has been continuously, an active member of the State Bar of California for at least the last five years; or

    (3) In the chambers and under the personal supervision of a judge of a court of record of this State; or

    (4) By instruction in law from a correspondence law school requiring 864 hours of preparation and study per year and which is registered with the committee; or

    (5) By any combination of the methods referred to in this subsection.

New York has similar requirements, however, the applicant without a degree must successfully complete at least one academic year as a matriculated student in a full-time program or the equivalent in a part-time program at an approved law school and at the conclusion be eligible to continue in that school's degree program.

Practical Training

There is no additional training required in California or New York other than that listed above for those substituting supervised legal training directly for education at a law school. While many newly admitted attorneys may undergo some tutoring on the job, most, especially in larger law firms, are expected to "hit the ground running." This is in contrast to the carefully supervised English training contract and the two-year German state-supervised trainee rotations.

Examination

The bar examination is the major hurdle for most attorney candidates. New York and California are generally known to have the most difficult bar exams in the United States because of the amount of legal material that is tested and lower bar passage rates. The bar passage rate in California was 49.4% in July 2003, in New York it was 69.4%.

The New York examination is given over two days and is divided into two sections. The first day tests primarily New York state law and is prepared by the New York Board of Bar Examiners with one portion, the Multistate Performance Test (MPT), developed by the National Conference of Bar Examiners. The New York section is divided into two sessions. The morning session is three hours and fifteen minutes and includes three essay questions and fifty multiple-choice questions. The afternoon session is three hours and includes two essay questions and the MPT. The exam tests numerous areas of law that includes Contracts, Constitutional Law, Criminal Law, Evidence, Real Property, and Torts (including statutory no-fault insurance provisions). In addition, the questions may deal with Business Relationships, Conflict of Laws, New York constitutional Law, Criminal Procedure, Family Law, Remedies, New York and Federal Civil Jurisdiction and Procedure, Professional Responsibility, Trusts, Wills and Estates including Estate Taxation, and Uniform Commercial Code Article 2, 3, and 9.

The MPT is a ninety-minute essay, which requires applicants to write an answer to a problem posed by a "supervising attorney." The applicant is provided with a "file" and a "library" which contains relevant cases, statutes, and regulations. The applicant may be asked to write a memorandum, a brief, a complaint, or other legal document. The second day of testing is dedicated to the Multistate Bar Examination (MBE). The MBE portion consists of 200 multiple-choice questions prepared by the National Conference of Bar Examiners. Of the 200 questions, there are thirty-four in Contracts and thirty-four in Torts. There are thirty-three in each of the following areas including Constitutional Law, Criminal Law, Evidence and Real Property. Each question consists of a statement of facts followed by four stated alternative answers, and the applicant is required to choose the best of the stated alternatives. Almost all states require the MBE.

The California Bar Exam is a three-day exam. On days one and three, the exam's morning session consists of essay exams (three essay questions in each session) and an afternoon session testing performance skills (one performance test problem in each session). On the second day, applicants take the MBE. The subjects tested in California include MBE subjects and Civil Procedure, Corporations, Community Property, Professional Responsibility, Remedies, Trusts, and Wills and Succession.

California uses its own performance test, not the MPT. The performance section consists of "closed universe" practical problems using instructions, factual data, cases, statutes, and other reference material supplied by examiners. This examination is intended to test analysis and drafting skills of attorneys.

In the United States, many states allow for reciprocity, allowing attorneys who have passed the bar exam in another state to "waive in." New York State permits admission on motion, without examination, for applicants who have practiced for five of the preceding seven years, are admitted to practice in at least one reciprocal jurisdiction, and have graduated from an American Bar Association approved law school.

Finally, the last exam usually taken while candidates are in law school is the Multistate Professional Responsibility Exam (MPRE), which is required in most jurisdictions. The MPRE is assembled and administered by ACT, Inc., on behalf of the National Conference of Bar Examiners. The examination is administered three times per year at established test centers across the country. This exam consists of fifty multiple-choice questions and is two hours and five minutes in length.

The MPRE looks at the conduct of lawyers in certain roles that are applied in disciplinary and bar admission procedures; by courts in dealing with issues of appearance, representation, privilege, disqualification, contempt or other censure; in lawsuits seeking to establish liability for malpractice; and other civil or criminal wrongs committed by a lawyer while acting in a professional capacity. It does not attempt to test the personal ethics of the candidate.

Moral Character

California and New York both require that every applicant be of good moral character. The term "good moral character" includes qualities of honesty, fairness, candor, trustworthiness, observance of fiduciary responsibility, respect for and obedience to the laws of the state and the nation, and respect for the rights of others and for the judicial process. The applicant has the burden of establishing that they are of good moral character. New York's standards are outlined in the Rules of the Court of Appeals for the Admission of Attorneys and Counselors at Law, Section 520.12, Proof of Moral Character.

As a practical matter, candidates for both California and New York must fill in detailed forms outlining their employment history, residences, and criminal records (if any). Former employers and other references are required to fill out recommendation forms for candidates.

Foreign Attorney

Foreigners are allowed to take the New York State bar exam; however, the Board must evaluate his or her legal education according to the New York State Board of Law Examiners. In order to consider a foreign educated applicant eligible to take the bar examination under section 520.6, the Board must determine that the applicant's first degree in law was based on a period of study which is (1) the duration equivalent and (2) the substantial equivalent of the legal education obtained at an approved law school in the United States. The California rules governing foreign attorneys are similar to New York and fall under Rule 988 of the California Rules of Court.

In addition to the requirements discussed, many law schools in the United States offer graduate law degrees known as the Master of Laws or LL.M. This additional training is not required but may often increase the worth of an attorney. Depending on the state, obtaining the LL.M. may also qualify foreign attorneys to sit for the bar exam.

Summary

Usually U.S. bar candidates are required to obtain a degree from a law school accredited by the American Bar Association. This legal education requirement does not mandate a practical training component. Once bar candidates have also passed a state bar examination, they are licensed to practice law in that state. The bar examination usually consists of a multiple-choice exam given throughout the United States along with an essay portion given by the relevant state. A professional responsibility exam is also required. Some states also require a simulated practice exam, and this number is likely to increase. There are various avenues for foreign attorneys to qualify to practice in the United States.

What is curiously lacking in the bar admission process in the United States is a practical training requirement in either law school or afterwards. The careful supervision, for example, required in England and Germany is not present in the United States. A law graduate who has passed a state bar examination may "hang up their shingle" with no prior experience working for another attorney. This causes this author to surmise that there are not "too many" lawyers in America, but that there may be too many *inexperienced* attorneys, who practice without adequate supervision.

Conclusion

This article has surveyed admissions requirements in four countries. All four countries have rich historical traditions. China has had the most sweeping changes in recent years. All of the countries require some state or national standards to practice law. Germany and China have more extensive state control over the lawyer admission process. Combined education and training requirements range from five to seven years after the secondary school level.

All four countries allow for law candidates to receive either formal legal education or its practical equivalent. Curiously, only the United States seems not to require jurisprudence and legal history in its mandatory curriculum. Also, only the United States offers legal education as a post-baccalaureate program.

Three of the four countries require at a minimum one-year training or internship period. Germany and England (for solicitors) require two years. The United States does not mandate a training period either during or after law school, or after passage of the state bar exam. Law students in the United States generally try to gain some legal experience over their summer breaks; however, this is not mandatory and is not regulated by the states or the local bar associations. All four countries require that applicants be of good moral character. The definition of this varies; however, all of the countries can refuse a candidate the ability to practice law for moral reasons or defects in character such as criminal convictions.

All four countries have rigorous entrance examinations, although in England this can be avoided by obtaining a law degree. China's new State Judicial Exam had a pass rate of only 7% in 2002. In three of the countries, England, the United States, and Germany, students often use commercial "cram courses" to bridge the gap between their university training and the examination process. It will be interesting to see if China develops this industry.

Germany has no oral exam in addition to its written exams. In England, it is expected that the applicant practice and learn communication skills. In the United States, students can sharpen their oral skills during law school; however, that is somewhat dependent on the student and his or her choice of classes. Germany, England, and the United States are requiring more testing in practical skills. In the United States, the use of the Multistate Performance Test is increasing. Only the United States requires a separate exam for professional ethics.

Foreign attorneys are eligible to practice in the United States, but not in China. Germany and England allow lawyers from the European Union to practice. China may want to consider more how it may preserve its traditional preference for alternative dispute resolution. England and Germany have unique opportunities as the influence of the European Union grows. The United States may want to consider requiring jurisprudence and legal history in its curriculum and how more attorneys can be supervised and trained before they are "unleashed" on the public.

Finally, while all four countries are responding to globalization, relatively few steps have been taken to require training for international or foreign law. The time is ripe for a global dialogue on licensing requirements. There is much to be gained from learning from other countries' experiences.

Appendix 3.2
The *O.J. Sampson* Inquisition
(law journal article by Moscovitz
on comparative criminal procedure)

The following law journal article—written in the mid-1990s by Professor Myron Moskovitz of Golden Gate University and reprinted here with permission—presents a fascinating and colorful comparative survey of criminal procedure. It does so in the form of a play involving four main characters—an American prosecuting attorney, an American defense lawyer, and two European law professors who advise those two American lawyers. The action in the play takes place in an unnamed European country, where a criminal trial is being conducted. The criminal trial is a special one: it is (fictionally) what the famous O.J. Simpson trial of the mid-1990s (actually conducted in California with Judge Lance Ito presiding) *would* have looked like *if* it had been conducted in a European courtroom under the rules of criminal procedure applicable in the European country to which it has been (fictionally) transferred

---

The O.J. Inquisition: A United States Encounter with Continental Criminal Justice
Myron Moskovitz*

*Editor's Note***

October 3, 1995, marked the end of the O.J. Simpson double murder trial, which lasted 474 days and was billed "the trial of the century." After less than four hours of deliberation, the jury acquitted Mr. Simpson of all charges. The following article is a dramatization of how a case similar to the Simpson trial might be handled by a civil-law European criminal justice system.

Utilizing an unusual format, Professor Myron Moskovitz examines and illustrates the differences between the United States and civil-law European criminal justice systems. The author uses a play script inspired by the events in the trial of O.J. Simpson, set before a European Court. The script consists of fictitious conversations among a fictitious prosecutor, defense attorney, officers of a mock European Court, and two professors. The dialogue illustrates the differences between the two legal systems and the historical and sociological premises that inform them.

News Item:[1] Due to pervasive public criticism of the United States "adversarial" criminal justice system, all parties have agreed to try the double murder trial in a neutral European nation, where the case will be handled under the "inquisitorial" legal system. When

---

* Professor of Law, Golden Gate University. The author would like to thank Professors Rudolph B. Schlesinger, Mirjan Damaska, Abraham S. Godstein, Richard S. Frase, Craig M. Bradley, Lloyd L. Weinreb, Bernard Segal, Robert C. Calhoun and Joseph J. Darby for their helpful comments on an earlier draft of this article.

** Due to the unusual format of Professor Moskovitz's academic commentary, the *Journal* has chosen not to apply its standard conventions in order to preserve the dramatic nature of the dialogue.

1. To the author's knowledge, no person living or dead has engaged in any of the conversations that make up the dialogue of this perspective.

asked if it would be difficult to adjust to a new system in the short time remaining before trial, one of the attorneys replied, "No problem. There's probably a few minor differences between our systems, but we should be able to pick them up as we go along."

Scene I: A courtroom in Europe. Ms. Clare and Professor Schmrz sit at the prosecution table. Mr. Crane and Professor Grbzyk sit at the defense table. At another table sit the victims' families and their attorney, Ms. Smith. Behind the tables, guarded by bailiffs, stands the Accused, and behind him is a gallery packed with spectators. All face a long raised bench.

Crane:	I must be nuts, letting you talk me into this. What now? They put my client on the rack and turn the screw 'til he talks?
Grbzyk:	(laughing) That went out in the 18th century. You Americans have the wrong impression of the inquisitorial system. It's probably the most widely used legal system in the world today. It was started by the Catholic Church, and after the French Revolution, it was further developed by the French and the Germans. It then spread to the rest of Europe, except for the British Isles. Many African, South American, and Asian countries have also adopted it. It's used much more today than your Anglo-American "adversarial" system. It's—
Crane:	Can the lecture, Professor. Here they come.
Grbzyk:	(whispering) Straighten your robe.

Everyone stands. Nine people enter the courtroom from a side door. Three of them, wearing black robes, take the three center seats behind the bench. The other six wear red-and-white sashes, and they take the other seats. The man in the middle dons a red beret, then places a large book in front of him and opens it.

Presiding Judge:	The People of the State of California versus Mr. Sampson. Are counsel ready?
Clare:	Yes, your honor.
Crane:	(bowing) Ready, your majesty.
Smith:	Ready, your honor.
Clare:	Excuse me, your honor. I don't know who this person is.
Smith:	I'm Sally Smith, attorney for the families of the victims.
Clare:	What are you doing here? This is my case, a criminal case, not a civil case. You don't belong here.
Presiding Judge:	Ms. Clare, we allow the alleged victim to intervene and appear by counsel in our criminal trials. Who has a greater interest in seeing that justice is done than the victim?
Clare:	The State does, your honor. I represent the State, she doesn't. That's how it's done in the United States.
Presiding Judge:	But you haven't always done it that way. As I recall, in the early days of England and the United States, a criminal prosecution was usually brought by the victim, who also paid for it. Only recently, with the development of public prosecutors like yourself, has the status and the involvement of the victim withered away.
Clare:	Maybe it's coming back. Some states now allow victims to take part in sentencing hearings.

Presiding Judge: In any event, we go further here, at least in trials of serious crimes. If the defendant is convicted, he might even be ordered to pay damages to the victim. You, of course, do represent the State, but the victim may also appear by counsel. Now let's get to work. I will call as the first witness—

Crane: Uh, excuse me, my lord.

Presiding Judge: Yes, Mr. Crane?

Crane: We seem to be forgetting something.

Presiding Judge: Forgetting?

Crane: Aren't we going to *voir dire* the jurors? You know, ask them a few questions to see if they're biased? Bounce a few out on peremptory challenges? That sort of thing. That comes first, doesn't it?

The Presiding Judge stares at Crane, then cracks up laughing. The whole courtroom joins in—except for Crane and Clare.

Presiding Judge: Very good joke, Mr. Crane. We will now call the first witness. Bailiffs, please bring the Accused forward.

Crane: *(sputtering)* The Accused? That—this man is my client! The defendant! You can't make him testify—

Presiding Judge: *(annoyed)* Sit down, Mr. Crane. If you don't understand our procedure, perhaps Professor Grbzyk can enlighten you during a recess. Now, Mr. Sampson, let me ask you—

Clare: Excuse me, judge.

Presiding Judge: Now what? Yes, Ms. Clare?

Clare: I believe it's the prosecution's duty to present the state's case. So if you don't mind, I'll question the witness.

Presiding Judge: *(frowning, slamming down his gavel)* We'll take a recess, so our U.S. friends may better acquaint themselves with continental procedure.

    Scene II: A small café next to the courthouse. Crane and Grbzyk sit at one table drinking coffee. Clare and Schmrz sit at another table.

Crane: What are these people, animals? They've never heard of due process? No wonder they're always going to war. (Sipping some espresso and making a face.) Bitter, bitter, bitter.

Grbzyk: Sugar? Relax, Mr. Crane. You Americans didn't invent civilization, you know. There's more than one way to run a justice system.

Crane: You call this justice? I can't even *voir dire* my jurors.

Grbzyk: They're not jurors, at least not in the U.S. sense.

Crane: Those six people without the robes. Judges or jurors?

Grbzyk: Jurors, sort of. They're called lay assessors. They're ordinary people, like your jurors, selected at random from the population. The parties have no right to question them or to remove any of them, so long as they meet our minimal qualifications of age, citizenship, and the like. You don't need to, really, because they can't decide the case by themselves anyway.

Crane: What do you mean?

Grbzyk:	The tribunal is a "mixed panel" of professional judges—the three people in the robes—and the lay assessors. The panel decides the case by a two-thirds majority.
Crane:	Now just a minute. You're not telling me that the judges go into a room with these lay assessors and deliberate with them?
Grbzyk:	I'm afraid I am. You seem shocked.
Crane:	Of course I'm shocked. What kind of a jury do you have when judges vote with the jurors?
Grbzyk:	Well, the jurors—as you insist on calling them—can outvote the judges. There are six jurors and only three judges.
Crane:	Look, Professor, I wasn't born yesterday. Jurors think judges walk on water. When a judge—when *three* judges—tell the jurors what they think, what juror is going to disagree?
Grbzyk:	I concede that it does not occur very often.
Crane:	Why not get rid of the jurors and be done with it? Be up front and let the judges decide the case.
Grbzyk:	This does happen in minor cases. But in major cases, we want some lay involvement. Also, we have the lay people vote before the judges vote, so the lay people will not be influenced by the judges' votes.
Crane:	But they know what the judges think anyway because they heard the judges during the pre-vote discussion.
Grbzyk:	I suppose this is so.
Crane:	Where does the judge instruct these lay assessors on the law? In open court or behind closed doors, in the deliberation room?
Grbzyk:	We have no formal jury instructions, as you do. During deliberations, the judge will explain the law to the assessors. I've seen your U.S. jury instructions. They are usually in the language of statutes or appellate court opinions. They may be legally correct, but they're very difficult for lay people to understand. Your judges are reluctant to depart from them by even a single word, for fear of reversal on appeal. In our system, the judge explains the law to the assessors in simple language. If they have trouble getting it, the judge may discuss it with them informally until they understand. This all happens in the deliberation room.
Crane:	Makes sense, I guess. I've often wondered how much U.S. jurors really understand when the judge reads them those long, legalistic instructions. But in your system, the lawyers have no idea what the judge is telling the jurors. Suppose he makes a mistake? How would I ever know about it?
Grbzyk:	After the tribunal decides the case, one of the judges will write the judgment. It is not a simple "guilty" or "not guilty" verdict, as you have. It will spell out what law the tribunal applied, in detail.
Crane:	But that's written after the tribunal already voted. Maybe the judge told the jurors something different from what he wrote in the judgment.
Grbzyk:	No European judge would do a thing like that, Mr. Crane.
Crane:	You sure seem to trust these guys.

Grbzyk: I suppose we do. It's good to get an outsider's perspective on one's legal system, Mr. Crane. Perhaps we can learn a lot from each other.

                                    * * *

Clare: I can't believe this. I schlepped all the way to Europe, and I can't even question a witness?

Schmrz: Madame must have patience. Your turn will come.

Clare: Oh yeah? When? After the verdict? It's my case to try, isn't it?

Schmrz: Not exactly. Do you understand why our system is called "inquisitorial?"

Clare: After the Spanish Inquisition?

Schmrz: No, Madame. We have become a bit more civilized since then. It is inquisitorial because it is based on the tribunal's duty to inquire, to find the truth. In your adversarial system, the parties are responsible for presenting the evidence, pretty much in any way they see fit. The judge merely makes sure that everyone behaves, and the jury sits passively and listens. When the lawyers are done, the jury decides. Neither the jury nor the judge takes any active part in investigating the case, seeking out evidence, or otherwise finding out what happened. This is not so in the inquisitorial system. Here, our judges are responsible for finding the truth themselves.

Clare: Do they do that in civil cases too?

Schmrz: No. Our method of litigating civil disputes is different from yours, but it is built on the same basic premise: the state has very little stake in the outcome of civil litigation. In both Europe and the United States, the state provides a proper forum for the resolution of private disputes, but it cares little about who wins a particular case. True, the state establishes substantive rules of law, in order to cause certain results in society, and these rules are enforced partly through private litigation. But in a particular case, the state provides the playing field and the umpire, that's all. For example, if the parties choose to settle in the middle of a case—even on that which might seem unjust to an outsider—the judge will seldom hesitate to terminate the litigation. If the parties are satisfied, the state has no further interest in the matter. This is so in both of our systems. What seems odd to use, however, is that in the United States you treat *criminal* cases pretty much the same way, even though the state clearly has an interest in seeing that the guilty are convicted and the innocent are freed. In Europe, we operate openly on this principle. This is why the state inquires: the state itself cares about the outcome.

Clare: So that's why the presiding judge does the questioning?

Schmrz: Yes. When he is done, you and Mr. Crane will have a chance to ask additional questions.

Clare: If there's anything left to ask about.

Schmrz: I grant that this is unlikely, if the presiding judge is thorough.

Clare: This is ridiculous. Why am I even in the courtroom? I might as well read a book or take a nap.

Schmrz: Our prosecutors have been known to do both, on occasion.

Clare: Look, Professor, you don't seem to realize what's at stake for me here. This is *my case*. If I lose, I'm back in Compton Muni Court prosecuting parking tickets.

Schmrz: Lose? I don't understand.

Clare: What's to understand? Lose. You know, like the Super Bowl or the World Series. If you win, I lose.

Schmrz: Ah, I see. The adversarial system is speaking. But in our system, prosecutors never lose.

Clare: Never lose? So the game is fixed?

Schmrz: No. There is no "game." Prosecutors never lose, but they never win, either. They simply don't think in terms of winning or losing. If the tribunal acquits the defendant, the prosecutor feels no sense of having lost the case. He has done his job, and the tribunal has done its job. His responsibility is to assist the tribunal in finding a just result, not to "win."

Clare: How "un-American."

Schmrz: Quite so, I'm afraid.

Clare: But what about the prosecutor's career? Doesn't he move up the ladder by winning his cases?

Schmrz: Our prosecutor is a civil servant, not a political figure. He advances by faithfully performing his duties. Whether the tribunal convicts or acquits the defendant is of no consequence.

Clare: It's certainly of consequence where I come from. My community fears crime, and they want convictions. If I don't get 'em, I'm out.

Schmrz: You are employed by your community, is that correct?

Clare: Sure. The county board of supervisors pays my salary.

Schmrz: So naturally you must please them. But our prosecutors do not work for local governments. All are employed by our central government in the capital. They are not unduly concerned with the ephemeral reactions of the communities in which they happen to be based. When a prosecutor is promoted, she will probably be transferred to another city anyway.

Clare: That certainly would affect how they see their cases.

Schmrz: Madame, you should stop thinking of "my case" and "their cases." The case belongs to the tribunal, not to the lawyers.

Clare: Very lofty, Professor, but let's get down to practicalities. I question witnesses because I *know* the case, backwards and forwards. I investigated the case and I prepared for trial, so I know what to ask and how to follow up answers with more questions. The judge can't do that because he comes into court cold. He doesn't know the case.

Schmrz: This judge does.

Clare: How?

Schmrz: Did you notice the large book the presiding judge has been looking at?

Clare: Yes. I thought it was a law book.

Schmrz:	Not quite. It is called a dossier. It contains the report of the examining magistrate.
Clare:	Who's she?
Schmrz:	The examining magistrate is another judge who investigates the case before trial after the police have completed their investigation. She interviews all witnesses and writes reports on what they said. She also sees that physical evidence is gathered and any needed scientific tests are performed. She then compiles all of these documents into the dossier, which she gives to the judge who will preside at the trial. This is the French system. Some countries, like Germany, have eliminated the examining magistrate and the prosecutor prepares the dossier.
Clare:	Hold on. You mean to tell me that before the trial even begins, the judges and jurors have read a whole report on the case?
Schmrz:	Not all of them. Just the presiding judge and perhaps one other judge, who might be responsible for writing the judgment. The presiding judge needs the dossier in order to perform his job of questioning witnesses.
Clare:	But he votes, and he can influence the others during deliberations. In the U.S. of A. we would never tolerate a judge or juror who had read a whole detailed report on the case before the trial even began. I'm no bleeding heart liberal, mind you, but even a slimeball criminal defendant is entitled to a fact-finder who hasn't already made up his mind.
Schmrz:	Perhaps we trust our judges more than you trust yours.
Clare:	It's not just a matter of trust. It's a matter of the limits of the human mind. While your presiding judge is questioning the witnesses, he is also supposed to be making up his mind on how to vote. How can anyone do both at the same time? Sure, he can throw out easy, softball questions to witnesses. But sometimes the best way to get to the truth is through tough, hardball cross-examination. That's often the best way to deal with a liar. How can a judge do that and still be a neutral fact-finder? I couldn't do it, and I don't think you could either. That's why it's better to have people like me and Crane cross-examine. We can be as tough or tricky as we want, and it doesn't matter, because we don't decide the case.
Schmrz:	I see your point. Of course, keep in mind that we do allow the attorneys to question a witness when the presiding judge is done.
Clare:	So they do the cross-examining?
Schmrz:	Not in the way you describe. The presiding judge usually does such a complete job that there is little left to ask, and the attorneys don't want to offend the judge by implying that he was less than thorough. So at most, they might ask a question or two, usually very politely. Most of them have had little or no experience with U.S.-style cross-examination.
Clare:	That must make it pretty easy for someone to lie in your courts—and get away with it.
Schmrz:	The presiding judge is a very stern and prestigious figure. One would not lightly lie to him. And if the tribunal believes that the defendant has lied, that might well affect the sentence it imposes on the defendant.

Clare: In the United States, it's probably a little easier for a defendant to concoct a lie that sounds plausible, because he doesn't testify until after he's heard the prosecution case. Here, he can't do that, because he goes first.

Schmrz: He does go first, but he is nevertheless familiar with the prosecution case before he testifies. Before trial, we allow the defendant to see the complete dossier, which contains summaries of the testimony of each witness. However, those summaries might not be as detailed as the in-court testimony of witnesses, still yet to come. So our defendants might be taking a chance by inventing or embellishing stories.

Clare: You let him see the whole dossier?

Schmrz: We do. Both the prosecutor and the defense counsel may examine the dossier before trial. We believe in complete pre-trial discovery. There are no secrets.

Clare: Discovery is much more limited in the United States. We don't want to give the defendant a chance to adapt his story to what the prosecution witnesses are going to say, and we don't want him to intimidate or bribe prosecution witnesses.

Schmrz: But here the defendant has probably already told his story to the examining magistrate, as have the prosecution witnesses. They are not likely to change their stories much at trial, and if they do not appear, their written statements may be considered anyway.

Clare: Even though they're hearsay?

Schmrz: Hearsay? What is that?

Clare: Oh, boy. Toto, we're not in Kansas anymore.

* * *

Crane: OK, Professor, I'm beginning to get a glimmer of how your system works, though I can't say I like it—yet. But how can they call the Accused as the first witness? Don't you have any privilege against self-incrimination here?

Grbzyk: In a way. After your client answers some general questions about his background, the presiding judge will advise him that he has the right not to answer questions about the crime itself. But defendants rarely assert that right.

Crane: Why not? I've had a lot of clients I'd never put on the stand. Why open them up to cross-examination and have their stories ripped apart?

Grbzyk: Remember, the presiding judge has read the dossier. He knows there is evidence that the defendant committed the crime, and he wants the defendant's response.

Crane: So he's presumed guilty, before the trial even starts?

Grbzyk: No. In former times, a conviction could be based on the dossier alone. Today, however, the tribunal may not convict the defendant unless the evidence produced at the trial firmly convinces the tribunal that the defendant is guilty. But let's be practical. The person who prepared the dossier—the examining magistrate or the prosecutor—is an experienced, unbiased government official. If she has determined that there

	is sufficient evidence to go forward with the trial, everyone knows there is a good chance the defendant is guilty. In the United States, you like to pretend otherwise, but that's just pretense, isn't it?
Crane:	Well, maybe it is. I've always wondered if jurors really follow the judge's instruction to give no weight to the fact that the police have arrested the defendant and the prosecutor has brought the case to trial. I guess it's what you might call a "useful fiction."
Grbzyk:	We believe in honesty.
Crane:	Hmm. Before you get too cocky, Professor, answer this, if you will. Suppose I tell my client just to clam up when the judge questions him about the crime?
Grbzyk:	If the defendant fails to respond, the judge will assume the worst. And the defendant knows it.
Crane:	But that's using the defendant's silence against him. We don't allow that, at least not openly.
Grbzyk:	We do. Who knows more about the crime than the defendant, and what good is served by his silence? In any event, there's another reason for him to talk.
Crane:	Which is?
Grbzyk:	In your system, the trial is about guilt, and only about guilt. Sentencing comes later. We don't do it that way. Our trials are about *both* guilt and sentencing. If the tribunal finds the defendant guilty, the judgment will also contain the sentence. So the presiding judge must develop evidence not only about whether the defendant committed the crime, but also about what sentence he deserves if he did it.
Crane:	You're kidding! You mean that evidence about his prior record, his whole life—everything *we* consider in *sentencing*—comes in at his *trial*?
Grbzyk:	Quite correct. Does that bother you?
Crane:	Bother me? No, it *kills* me. How can you give a guy a fair trial on whether he committed *this* crime when you know that he has four priors, went AWOL from the Army, and stole two bits from the church collection box when he was a kid? In the United States, we call this stuff irrelevant and prejudicial and keep it out of the trial.
Grbzyk:	I suppose we trust our tribunal more than you trust yours. With our judges deliberating along with the lay assessors, the judges will make sure that the assessors do not draw any improper inferences.
Crane:	Yeah, I bet. Anyway, I see your point. At a U.S. sentencing hearing, it is better for the defendant to talk. He's already been found guilty, and if he won't cooperate now, the judge is likely to throw the book at him. If you guys *combine* guilt and sentencing into one trial, I have only one shot at showing the tribunal that the defendant isn't such a bad guy, so I'd better tell him to answer the judge's questions.
Grbzyk:	You're learning fast, Mr. Crane.
Crane:	I guess there's another reason to have him testify, or maybe a reason not to have him not testify. In the United States, if I allow my client to

testify, the D.A. can then introduce his prior felony convictions to show that he's not a very credible witness. The judge will tell the jury not to think he's committed this crime just because he committed the priors, but I don't think most jurors can draw such fine lines. So lots of times I don't put him on the stand just because I don't want the jury to hear about the priors. Over here, the tribunal will hear about the priors anyway, whether he testifies or not. So I might as well put him on.

Grbzyk: Very astute. I hadn't thought of that.

Crane: Still, it doesn't seem fair to put a defendant in a position where he has to hang himself by talking. And if they think he's lying, they can try to nail him for perjury.

Grbzyk: That cannot happen.

Crane: You don't prosecute people for lying under oath?

Grbzyk: We do. But the accused is never put under oath. We want his testimony, but we feel that the threat of perjury would unfairly put too much pressure on him.

Crane: *(shaking his head)* Weird. You people are really weird.

Grbzyk: Perhaps when you see how all the pieces fit together, we will seem less weird.

Crane: What about *before* the trial? Can the police or the examining magistrate question the defendant, get a confession out of him, and then use it at the trial?

Grbzyk: Generally, yes. But whenever a suspect is to be questioned, he must first be advised of his right to silence and his right to counsel.

Crane: Sounds familiar.

Grbzyk: It should. Some countries have explicitly based these requirements on your *Miranda*[2] decision.

Crane: Interesting. I've seen a few U.S. decisions cite European practices as authority for some new idea, but it's pretty rare.

Grbzyk: It should be rare. It's a dangerous thing to do. One shouldn't graft a feature from a different system until one fully comprehends how the entire system supports that feature.

Crane: I'm not sure I get what you're saying.

Grbzyk: You will, as you learn more about our system.

Crane: So, do your defendants exercise their *Miranda* rights, or do they waive them?

Grbzyk: Before the police, they often waive them, as do your defendants. But when the examining magistrate questions a defendant, usually she will not allow a waiver of the right to counsel.

Crane: So once the guy gets a lawyer, the lawyer tells him not to answer the examining magistrate's questions, right?

Grbzyk: Quite the contrary. The lawyer almost always advises him to answer.

---

2. *Miranda v. Arizona*, 384 U.S. 436, 86 S. Ct. 1602, 15 L. Ed. 2d 694 (1966).

Crane:	Even though his answers might be used against him in the dossier?
Grbzyk:	Yes. Don't forget, if he refuses to answer, he will be faced with the same questions at trial, and—as we discussed earlier—he will pretty much have to answer them then.
Crane:	So he might as well look cooperative from the get-go, to minimize his sentence.
Grbzyk:	Correct. And if he confesses before trial, there is not much point in refusing to confess again at the trial.
Crane:	Each aspect of this thing seems to support the other.
Grbzyk:	Quite so. And there is another reason for him to answer the examining magistrate's questions. The magistrate also has the power to decide whether the defendant is detained or released pending trial.
Crane:	So if he wants to stay out of the pokey, he'd better be nice.
Grbzyk:	You Americans are very practical, Mr. Crane.
Crane:	So are you Europeans. Your whole system seems designed to get a confession as soon as possible, even though you go through the motions of telling the guy he doesn't have to answer.
Grbzyk:	He does have the right not to answer. But we see no point in encouraging him to exercise that right, the way you Americans do. Our goal is to find the truth, and the defendant is in a very good position to help us accomplish that task. What is wrong with asking him to tell us what he knows?
Crane:	We've had some bad experiences with that, going back to the Star Chamber in England and "third degree" interrogations in the United States, with the police beating and threatening people if they won't talk.
Grbzyk:	So have we. Don't forget the Spanish Inquisition, and we did allow torture until the 19th century. But that is all behind us now, and torture and threats are illegal. So long as they are, why shouldn't we simply ask the defendant to tell what happened?
Crane:	It's just not right for the government to intrude into someone's mind, into his private thoughts.
Grbzyk:	But you intrude into private thoughts quite frequently, don't you? Any non-defendant witness may be compelled to testify about his thoughts, so long as they are relevant and no recognized privilege applies. In this very case, police officers were compelled to testify about what they thought about many things, including probable cause to search and their beliefs about race and interracial marriage.
Crane:	True, but a defendant in a criminal case is different. The government has many more resources than the defendant. They should have to prove the case without using him to help them.
Grbzyk:	So in the adversary system, you handicap the prosecution in order to make the game fair, even if this detracts from finding the truth?
Crane:	Look, the prosecution has plenty of ways to prove the truth. They have investigators, crime labs, the FBI, and the whole government apparatus when they need it. In the usual case, the defense has just one lawyer and, if you're lucky, maybe an investigator or two.

Grbzyk:	Yes, but in a given case, all the government's resources might be insufficient. In this case, for example, the prosecution must prove its case by inference, with blood samples, DNA tests, and evidence of motivation and opportunity. But only one person who is still alive saw exactly what happened and knows exactly what his mental state was when (and if) he did it. That's the defendant himself. Why not allow the court to ask him?
Crane:	Maybe it comes down to this. We don't think it's right to make people incriminate themselves with their own words.
Grbzyk:	Strange. When European parents find cookies missing from the cookie jar and ask their child what happened, they do not expect the child to answer, "It's not right to ask me to incriminate myself." Are U.S. parents different?
Crane:	Of course not, but criminal defendants aren't kids. A kid who steals cookies might be sent to his room for an hour, but a criminal defendant will be sent to a very small cell for a very long time, and maybe the gas chamber. The parents are trying to help the kid learn how to behave. The government is *not* trying to help the defendant in any way, shape, or form. It's not the same.
Grbzyk:	You seem to dislike our reliance on confessions, Mr. Crane. But U.S. attorneys advise most of their clients to confess, don't they?
Crane:	We do?
Grbzyk:	Yes. Isn't that what you do during your plea bargaining? You advise your client to plead guilty, in order to obtain the benefits of the bargain. Isn't that pretty much a confessions?
Crane:	I hadn't thought of it like that.
Grbzyk:	So perhaps your system relies on confessions just as much as ours does.
Crane:	Interesting. Even though our systems look really different on the surface, maybe there are similarities, once you look a little deeper.
Grbzyk:	Possibly. But it is risky to assume that "we are all the same, at bottom." There might in fact be some real differences. And now we must return to court.

They rise and begin walking, as do Clare and Schmrz.

Clare:	Is the inquisitorial system the same throughout Europe, Professor?
Schmrz:	Yes and no. There are fundamental features that do not vary much. Judges, not the parties are responsible for developing the evidence. The judge receives a dossier before the trial begins. There are other common features I will explain when we have more time. There are variations, however. In smaller cases, what you call misdemeanors, the tribunal might consist of only one judge and two lay assessors. Some countries use tribunals where judges outnumber lay assessors. Germany, for example, uses three judges and two lay assessors in cases of serious crime. And some countries use no lay assessors at all except in major cases. The procedure you will see in this case is somewhat typical, but other countries might differ a bit. Italy has a sort of hybrid system.
Clare:	Our adversary system also varies somewhat from state to state. I guess it's the same here.

Schmrz:	Exactly. A very good analogy.
	Scene III: The Courtroom
Presiding Judge:	Thank you for your testimony, Mr. Sampson. We appreciate your candor. A truly amazing story. Oh, excuse me. Does counsel have any further questions for the accused?
Clare:	I guess not, your honor. You seem to have asked everything I was going to ask.
Crane:	Your astute questioning would put most U.S. lawyers to shame. No questions, your grace.
Presiding Judge:	Why thank you, Mr. Crane. How very kind.

* * *

Presiding Judge:	Detective Farmer, please tell us what happened when you went to the home of the accused.
Farmer:	I went there to tell him his ex-wife had been killed. But his gate was closed, and no one answered the intercom. So I climbed over the gate. I found this glove on the driveway. (He displays a glove.) It matches a glove we found at the murder scene.
Crane:	Objection, your honor. That glove was obtained in violation of the Fourth Amendment.
Presiding Judge:	The what, Mr. Crane?
Crane:	Sorry, Judge. Wrong country. We contend that Detective Farmer conducted an illegal search by hopping the gate without a warrant.
Presiding Judge:	So?
Crane:	So? So the glove can't be used in evidence.
Presiding Judge:	Why not? It is relevant evidence, is it not?
Crane:	That doesn't matter. If it was obtained by an illegal search, it goes out. Everyone knows that.
Presiding Judge:	Not everyone in Europe knows that, Mr. Crane. We assume that the tribunal should consider all relevant evidence. We do not employ the exclusionary rule, as you call it in the United States, except in extreme cases.
Crane:	Then how do you make your police behave?
Presiding Judge:	All of our police work for the Ministry of Justice, which is part of our central government. When the Minister issues an order, every policeman in the country must obey it, or suffer demotion or termination of employment. In the United States, this cannot happen. You have many hundreds of independent cities, countries, and states, each running its own police department. The only institution you have for setting minimum standards of behavior for all policemen is your Supreme Court. And the only tool your Supreme Court has for enforcing those standards is to order that illegally-obtained evidence be excluded.
Crane:	True, your honor, but even here in Europe, with a more transient population and an increase in crime, your cops will tend to feel the pressure to harass certain people. And the cops' bosses will tend to look the other way. That's why courts need to keep out illegally-seized evidence in order to deter the police from doing that kind of stuff.

Presiding Judge: The circumstances you describe have not afflicted Europe as much as the United States.

Crane: Times change, Judge.

Presiding Judge: You're quite right, Mr. Crane. Times do change. Some European countries have begun to experience more police abuses, and some have begun to apply an exclusionary rule to evidence obtained by certain acts, such as illegal wiretapping. As yet, none has gone so far as the United States. In our tradition, the goal of a criminal trial is to find the truth, not to serve other ends. But who knows what the future will hold?

* * *

Presiding Judge: Detective Farmer, what did Mr. Crawford tell you about the activities of the accused that night?

Crane: Objection, your honor. That calls for hearsay.

Presiding Judge: Hearsay, counsel? We do not recognize such an objection.

Crane: What? I thought the point of an inquisitorial trial is to find the truth. In the United States, the key to making sure that witnesses tell the truth is cross-examination. Detective Farmer is here in court, so I can cross-examine him as to what he says he heard from Mr. Crawford. But Crawford isn't here, so if he was mistaken or lying about what he told the detective, I can't bring that out by cross-examining him. That's why we exclude hearsay, your honor, and you should too.

Presiding Judge: You give good reasons for according less weight to hearsay, Mr. Crane, but why exclude it entirely? Isn't it worth something? It might help us to see the entire picture, and what's the harm in letting Mr. Farmer tell us what he heard?

Crane: Jurors aren't well-trained and experienced enough to make the fine distinctions that you are making. They might not see the difference between hearsay and what the detective saw himself. They might give too much weight to the hearsay.

Presiding Judge: But I will be there to help them make these distinctions. Don't forget: in our system, the judges and the lay assessors deliberate together.

Crane: So you have no rules of evidence? Everything comes in?

Presiding Judge: Not everything. Evidence must still be relevant to the case, and we do recognize certain privileges, as you do. A doctor may not testify as to what his patient told him, nor may a lawyer tell what his client told him. We want to encourage patients and clients to speak freely to professionals. But your stricter rules of evidence are built on the premise that untrained lay people, your jurors, might easily become confused or distracted if you did not limit what they could hear. We have no such problem, for we do not treat our lay assessors as a separate body.

Crane: I think I'm starting to catch on to something. I can't just compare a feature of our system with a similar feature of your system. Each part is affected by other parts. I really have to consider the system as a whole.

Presiding Judge: Quite so, Mr. Crane. People often look at an isolated aspect of the system, find it attractive, and assume that it may be transferred intact to another system. This is a mistake. Both the adversarial and the inquisitorial systems are integrated systems. Each piece is affected and supported by every other piece. Transfer a piece without its support system, and it will probably fail or distort some other features that you didn't intend to affect.

* * *

Presiding Judge: Ms. Bruin, did you ever see the Accused strike his ex-wife?

Crane: Objection, your honor. Evidence of prior crimes or bad acts should be inadmissible to show that the defendant has a bad character.

Clare: But it is admissible to show that he had a motive to kill, or a pattern of behavior that is consistent with the method of killing. That's what this evidence shows, your honor.

Presiding Judge: An interesting dispute. I would expect you to make these arguments at the end of the trial, when you try to persuade the tribunal how much weight we should give to any evidence that he struck her. But why are you arguing this now?

Crane: If I'm right, then the evidence is inadmissible. You and your fellow judges and jurors shouldn't even be hearing it. It's too prejudicial. Once you hear it, you might not be able to put it out of your minds.

Presiding Judge: Mr. Crane, in U.S. bench trials, your judges often hear evidence, rule it inadmissible, and then go on to decide the case. You trust *them* to disregard such evidence. Why don't you trust *me*?

Crane: Of course I trust *you*, your honor, but I'm not so sure about these lay jurors. They don't have your training and experience. They might convict just because this evidence shows that the defendant is a bad guy, not because he committed the killings.

Presiding Judge: Recall the response I made to your hearsay objection. I will be in the deliberation room to advise the lay assessors how to perform their jobs, and to prevent them from acting improperly. Your U.S. jurors are not so well monitored as ours. Objection overruled.

* * *

Presiding Judge: Doctor, please tell us the results of your DNA testing on the hair samples.

Crane: Objection, your honor. We haven't heard any convincing evidence that DNA testing is scientifically valid.

Presiding Judge: Such evidence would be helpful, to be sure, but I am not aware of any statute that prevents us from hearing the doctor's testimony.

Crane: There's no statute, your honor, but I've got a case. In *People v. Glump*, the court held that a defendant was denied a fair trial when a technician testified about a breathalyzer test without evidence that the device they used was scientifically valid.

Presiding Judge: So?

Crane: So that case is precedent for my position, your honor. *Glump* seems to stand for the larger principle that—

Presiding Judge:	Counsel, I do not care about *Glump*. We do not treat precedent as you do in the United States. In your common-law system, the law evolves through the application of the law to specific facts, so your published decisions are very important in determining what the law is. But in our system, the law is fixed by the Legislature, and it is changed by the Legislature, not by the courts. Evolution depends on changing values, and we leave the examination of values to our legislative bodies. So we have little need for case precedent.
Crane:	All right, judge, here's my trump card. *Glump* was decided by the U.S. Supreme Court. Now will you pay a little more attention to it?
Presiding Judge:	Not much, at least in the way you want me to use it. If I am unsure as to the meaning of certain terms used in a statute, I might find guidance in a reported decision, especially from such a prestigious body as the Supreme Court. But the facts of the case—breathalyzers, DNA, whatever—mean little or nothing to me. If you can show me something in this *Glump* decision that explains the meaning of a statute that applies to our case, I'll be happy to look at it, Mr. Crane.
Crane:	Sorry, your honor, *Glump* doesn't do that.

Scene IV: On the Courthouse steps

Clare:	I needed this break. My head is still spinning.
Schmrz:	The adjustment must be difficult for you.
Clare:	I guess I can handle it. If I can handle Crane, I can do any … Speak of the devil.

Crane and Grbzyk approach.

Crane:	How you doin', Ms. D.A.?
Clare:	Not bad, Counselor. Just ruminating over the peculiarities of this inquisitorial system. Do you understand it?
Crane:	Perfectly. No problem at all. I'm a quick study.
Clare:	Yeah, sure.
Crane:	Now that you mention it, I might be a little shaky on a couple of nuances. I have to admit I'm having trouble predicting how this case is going to come out. It's hard enough to make predictions in our own courts. here, with all these foreigners—well, it worries me.
Clare:	I was thinking the same thing.
Crane:	I don't want my client convicted of two first degree murders.
Clare:	And I don't want to go back to Los Angeles with nothing but an acquittal to show for it.

They eye each other.

Crane and Clare: (together) Let's deal!

They huddle.

Clare:	Plead him guilty to just one first degree charge, and I'll drop the second charge.
Crane:	Are you kidding? He'd still get life. One charge of involuntary manslaughter. That's my absolute top offer.

Clare:	Very funny. How about—
Schmrz:	Excuse me. What are you two doing?
Crane:	We're plea bargaining.
Schmrz:	Plea bargaining?
Clare:	Yes. We do a little horse-trading, and maybe we can come to an agreement. I drop or reduce some charges, and perhaps agree to recommend a certain sentence. In return, he agrees to plead guilty.
Crane:	If, of course, my client agrees.
Schmrz:	In the United States, you bargain over justice like farmers bargain over horses? You consider this dignified?
Crane:	Is it less dignified than pushing a guy to confess, Professor?
Grbzyk:	At least our practice leads to the truth and a just result. Plea bargaining does just the opposite. According to the evidence we heard, your client is either guilty of two murders or guilty of no crime at all. How can you even consider a single manslaughter charge?
Clare:	But that's what bargaining is all about. Each side gives up something. I want two murders, and he wants no crime at all. So we cut a deal.
Crane:	And there's something you're overlooking. As I understand it, your sentences are pretty reasonable compared to ours. You mostly use fines, and when you do incarcerate people, it's usually for short terms. In the United States, our potential sentences are extremely high, and sometimes the legislature fixes the punishment and gives the judge no discretion to lower it for a particular defendant who doesn't deserve that much. So plea bargaining is our way of reaching a just result.
Clare:	Why are your sentences so low? Don't you want to stop crime?
Schmrz:	Of course we do. But we do it by curing the offender of his deviant ways and reintegrating him into society as soon as possible. The state assumes a parental role with the offender. By contrast, your system seems to be adversarial in more ways than one. Not only is the prosecutor the adversary of the defendant, so is the state itself. We prefer to see offenders as potentially decent citizens who have temporarily gone astray.
Clare:	We used to see them that way, but at some point we gave up. These days, heavy criminals are treated as permanent outcasts. We don't see "reintegration" as a realistic possibility, so we pretty much lock 'em up and throw away the key.
Grbzyk:	Do you think this is an effective way to reduce crime?
Clare:	Sure. If they're in jail, they can't commit crimes—at least not on the law-abiding community.
Grbzyk:	But they will eventually get out. When they are released, do their punishments make them less likely to commit more crimes?
Crane:	No way. They'll be *more* likely to commit new crimes. We don't spend much effort trying to teach prisoners to adjust to society and earn their way honestly, so they just learn more about being criminals. And sen-

tences being as long as they are, often these guys are pretty angry when they get out. We treat them as outcasts, so that's what they become.

Grbzyk: It seems odd. You punish your defendants more severely than we do, in order to reduce crime, and yet your crime rates are much higher than ours. What conclusions may we draw from this?

Crane: It's pretty obvious, isn't it? Harsh punishments don't work.

Clare: That's ridiculous. You could just as logically conclude that because of our high crime rates, we *need* harsher punishments to prevent them from going even higher.

Schmrz: One cannot infer causation just from correlation. High crime rates and high punishments often go together, but we cannot be sure whether either one has any causal impact on the other.

Grbzyk: Mr. Crane, earlier you seemed troubled by our quest for confessions. But a confession is an important step on the road to rehabilitation. Until the offender admits he did wrong, how can he change his ways? A good confession cleanses the soul.

Crane: So because we don't plan to do much to rehabilitate him, it doesn't matter much whether he confesses?

Clare: That's a bit of an overstatement. When a judge has discretion in sentencing, he will tend to go easier on a defendant who admits his crime. And the same is true of parole boards. So we do get a lot of confessions, at least after trial.

Grbzyk: Here in Europe, of course, the trial is about both guilt and sentencing, so he can't very well hold off confessing 'til after the trial. So it is important that he confess at trial.

Schmrz: I'd like to return to this plea bargaining for a moment. Once the lawyers arrive at a bargain, is that final? Does the judge have no say in whether the bargain does justice to the state and to the victim?

Clare: Well, the judge can reject the deal. But he's usually happy to accept it. It saves the court the expense and trouble of a trial.

Schmrz: But by reducing the charges you, the prosecutor, have effectively reduced the sentence. Is this proper? Are you trained in the sociological and psychological aspects of sentencing?

Clare: Not really, but neither are our judges. My guess is probably as good as theirs. And if they think I'm really off the mark, they can reject the deal.

Schmrz: In Europe, the prosecutor may recommend a certain sentence, but she does not make the final determination, even partially. That is for the court, not the prosecutor.

Grbzyk: This plea bargaining is legal in your country?

Clare: Legal? It's essential! In most places, less than twenty percent of our cases go to trial. The rest are plea bargained. If they weren't, we'd be up to our eyeballs in trials. We'd probably need five times more prosecutors, judges, jurors, courtrooms, bailiffs, and all the rest. Since every defendant has the right to a speedy trial, I'd have to dismiss a lot of cases if I couldn't plea bargain.

Grbzyk:	I don't understand. If people in the United States really believe that the adversary trial is the best way to achieve justice, shouldn't they be more than willing to pay whatever it takes to try *every* case?
Clare:	Tough question. I guess they're not *that* committed to the adversary trial. They may like the general idea of it, but when it comes to paying for it, they'd rather pay for more cops or more prisons, where they can *see* some effects on crime.
Schmrz:	U.S. citizens are such a peculiar lot. Because they like the general idea of the adversary trial, they have made it so elaborate that they can afford to give it to only one out of every five defendants! Strange, very strange. Wouldn't it be better to make the trial less complex, so that more defendants could have a trial? That might make plea bargaining unnecessary.
Clare:	I never quite looked at it that way. In any event, the way things are right now, we can't live without plea bargaining.
Schmrz:	And we can't live with it. Here it is illegal.
Crane:	Illegal? Why? If the parties agree to settle their case, why should that bother the court?
Schmrz:	Because the case belongs to the court, not to the parties. The tribunal may not convict or sentence the defendant unless it first hears the evidence, and if the evidence shows that the defendant committed a certain crime, the tribunal may not reduce the crime just because the prosecutor agrees to it.
Clare:	So every case goes to trial?
Schmrz:	Every case, Madame. At least every major case.
Clare:	But not if the defendant pleads guilty.
Schmrz:	There is no such thing as a guilty plea in our system. That would be permitting the parties rather than the court to determine the truth, which is not permissible. Every case goes to trial. At the trial, the defendant might well admit that the charges are true, and many do so. But the tribunal must nevertheless hear evidence, in order to determine the sentence.
Clare:	That must put a terrible burden on your courts. Trials can take weeks, even months in a murder case. It can take weeks just to pick a jury.
Grbzyk:	You forget. Our "jurors" are picked without the lengthy *voir dire* and peremptory challenges that take so much time in your courts. Most of our trials do not take very long. Because the presiding judge questions the witnesses, we do not take up much time with lawyers' cross-examination and the like. We do not allow many objections to evidence, which may save us more time. We have no need for the lengthy pre-trial hearings on the admissibility of evidence that you have. And the defendant often confesses at trial, because he confessed earlier. Even if he didn't, the dossier usually contains rather strong evidence against him, and his denials, if seen as false, would affect his sentence, so often he confesses for that reason alone. Because he confesses, very little additional testimony is needed. Most of our trials are really about the sentence, not about guilt.

Crane: So it ends up looking somewhat like one of our sentencing hearings, which we must have whether or not there is a plea bargain.

Grbzyk: Yes, I suppose it does. However, I admit that we have been seeking ways to ease the burden on our system. As our crime rates rise, the volume of cases also rises, and some European countries have adopted devices that resemble your plea bargaining. But in most countries, such things are allowed only for misdemeanors, never for major felonies, such as the present case.

Clare: If your crime rates are rising, you might have to start dealing with organized crime, like we do. Plea bargaining really helps us with that. We bust the little guys, and give them plea bargains to get them to "cooperate" and help us get the big guys. Without plea bargains, we'd have nothing to offer them.

Grbzyk: I see. So U.S. prosecutors work closely with the police?

Clare: Absolutely. Our job is to help the cops fight crime. That's what the public expects of us.

Grbzyk: This is much less so in Europe. Our prosecutors see themselves as more closely allied with the judiciary than with the police. Some countries even allow prosecutors to become judges.

Crane: That must make your judges pro-prosecution.

Grbzyk: The reverse would be more accurate: our prosecutors tend to be "pro-judge," in the sense that they are out to secure justice, not to get convictions. For example, every prosecutor has a duty to present to the court all evidence that *favors* the defendant, and they readily do so.

Clare: Shocking.

Grbzyk: I'm speaking generally, of course. Individual prosecutors vary, and so do circumstances. Italy has had a serious problem with organized crime, and prosecutors there do work closely with the police and aggressively seek to convict Mafia leaders.

Crane: If your prosecutors tend to think like judges, why not give them the power to plea bargain? You said you trust your judges.

Schmrz: We trust our officials, so long as they do not have much discretion. We fear that discretion may be abused, as has occurred during periods of dictatorship. Perhaps a prosecutor would plea bargain because of political pressure from friends of the accused. We must protect ourselves from such a possibility, so the prosecutor is obliged to bring to trial every charge supported by the evidence and the law, at least in major cases. She has no discretion.

Crane: But you give your *judges* a lot of discretion.

Schmrz: No, we really don't. Under your common-law system, the law is always changing or "evolving," as you might put it. So your judges must have discretion to change the law slightly to adapt it to new situations, as society changes. This is not so in our "civil-law" system. Here, the law is fixed by the legislature, and the judge has no discretion to change it.

Clare:	Look, we have a lot of statutes too, and our judges aren't supposed to change them. But they can *interpret* them, and when they do, they have plenty of discretion to plug in whatever policies they happen to like.
Schmrz:	I suppose our judges do the same on occasion.
Grbzyk:	But we pretend they don't! We prefer to imagine our judges as educated clerks, simply looking up the rules in the codes and telling us what they are. In truth, however, many of our statutes are quite vague, and the judge has some discretion in deciding what they mean. It is somewhat of a paradox.
Crane:	Or maybe a "useful fiction," Professor?
Grbzyk:	Quite useful, Mr. crane.
Clare:	Anyway, we can't plea bargain, so it's back to the salt mines.

Scene V: At the café

The two lawyers and their consultants sit at one table, drinking cognac.

Clare:	Usually when I finish a trial, I'm exhausted. This time, I didn't even work up a sweat.
Crane:	That's because you didn't do anything. Neither did I. Just about every time we stood up, Judge Big Shot told us to sit down and watch *him* do everything. Who needs lawyers in this crazy system? What's there for us to *do*?
Clare:	We help decorate the courtroom. That's why they give us these snazzy black robes. We're not lawyers, we're fashion statements.
Grbzyk:	Ah, you feel that you are not as important as you are in the United States. I'm sorry. But you still have significant roles here. Defense counsel may summon witnesses not called by the tribunal, though this rarely occurs. And both counsel are expected to present final arguments to the tribunal, reviewing the evidence and the law, and arguing for a certain verdict and sentence. Both of you did a fine job, by the way, as did the victim's attorney.
Clare:	And now we wait for the verdict. I *hate* this part. It drives me batty.
Crane:	What will the verdict look like? Will it be short, like "not guilty" or "guilty, life imprisonment"?
Schmrz:	No, the tribunal's judgment will be quite long. It will set out the facts of the case, in detail, and the law that applies to the case, and explain why the tribunal came to its conclusion, both about guilt and about the sentence. It will discuss the testimony of each witness.
Clare:	Who writes it?
Schmrz:	Usually the presiding judge will assign this task to one of the other judges. It is never written by a lay assessor.
Clare:	Most U.S. courts require that the verdict be unanimous. Is that so here?
Schmrz:	No. A majority vote is sufficient in some countries. We require a two-thirds vote.
Crane:	Suppose one of the judges disagrees with the judge who writes the decision. Will he write a dissenting opinion?

Schmrz: No. That would be unthinkable. It would tend to undermine the court's authority. The public must believe that every court decision is unanimous.

Crane: Even if it wasn't?

Schmrz: Even if it wasn't.

Crane: So much for honesty, Professor. What are you afraid of? Do you think people won't obey the decision or respect your courts if they know someone disagreed with it? Are your institutions so fragile that they can't stand a little dissent?

Schmrz: I admit, it is troubling.

Clare: It should be. In the United States, some states allow less-than-unanimous votes by juries in some cases, and such votes must be announced in open court. In our appellate courts, judges often write dissents. We've had some very important Supreme Court cases decided on five to four votes, and people obey them. Dissent doesn't necessarily lead to anarchy.

Schmrz: At the present time, even our highest courts never reveal that a judge dissented. I suppose a dissent implies either that the majority was incompetent, or that reasonable judges have the discretion to interpret the law in different ways. We do not want either message sent to the public.

Crane: Look, this is all very interesting, but I'm having trouble concentrating, waiting for the verdict. I hate this part too. If I lose, it's all over.

Grbzyk: Not quite, Mr. Crane. You still have your right of appeal.

Crane: What's to appeal? The presiding judge seemed to know what he was doing. I don't think he made any mistakes. With virtually no rules of evidence, what mistakes are there to make, anyway? An appellate court would throw me out: no mistakes, no reversal.

Grbzyk: You might argue that the judgment is not supported by the law or the evidence.

Crane: But then I run up against presumptions, don't I? In the United States, the appellate court looks at the reporter's transcript of the trial and presumes that the jury resolved every credibility battle in favor of the judgment, so if the cop said one thing and my client said another, I'm out of luck. And the appellate court also presumes that the jury drew any reasonable inferences that support their verdict.

Grbzyk: So even if the jury in fact did not do these things, the appellate court nevertheless presumes that they did?

Crane: Exactly. I guess that's all our appellate courts can do, because the jury never explains their verdict, they just say "guilty." So the appellate court never knows how the jury really reasoned their way to the verdict.

Grbzyk: But this is not so in our system. The judgment must fully explain the tribunal's reasoning, including why it believed one witness rather than another. So the appellate court sees what the tribunal actually thought, not what it might have thought. And if the appellate court is not persuaded by such reasoning, it might well reverse the judgment.

Crane: You talk about the tribunal's reasoning. There are nine people on this tribunal, but the judgment is written by just one of them. Is it likely that nine people would have exactly the same reasoning, especially when three of them are professional judges and the others aren't?

Grbzyk: Probably not. Another "useful fiction," perhaps.

Crane: Do the appellate judges read the transcripts of the trial to see if they support the judgment?

Grbzyk: I'm afraid there are no transcripts, Mr. Crane. We have no court reporters at our trials.

Crane: But how do the appellate judges know if the judgment correctly summarizes the testimony? If I'm arguing a case on appeal, how can I shoe that the facts stated in the judgment are inaccurate?

Grbzky: Our trial judges receive many hours of training in writing judgments, and I suppose we trust them to summarize the testimony honestly.

Crane: Amazing. Well, I hope this tribunal acquits my client, so I don't have to deal with one of your appeals.

Schmrz: Sorry, Mr. Crane, but an acquittal is no guarantee that you won't face an appeal. In our system, the prosecutor may appeal too. This is important to us, as it helps to ensure that the trial court follows the law. We strive for consistency in all of out courts. And if the appellate court reverses, your client may be tried again.

Clare: Really? In the United States, I think one or two state allow prosecutors to appeal, but only to get an advisory opinion on some important issue. And if the prosecutor wins, it doesn't affect the defendant. He can't be retired. That would violate his right against double jeopardy.

Schmrz: Here he may be retried. We do have concepts similar to your double jeopardy, but they have no application to an ongoing case. So the prosecution may appeal, and if the appellate court reverses, the defendant may be retried.

Crane: The way we see it, once a jury acquits him, that's it. A jury's verdict is sacred.

Schmrz: Sacred when it acquits, but not when it convicts? Why should you allow the defendant to appeal, but not the prosecution? How does that make sense.

Crane: We don't allow a conviction to stand if it doesn't square with the law. But if the jury acquits because the jury doesn't agree with the law, the verdict stands. The jury "nullifies" the law, just for that case. It doesn't happen often, but we view it as an outlet for public disagreement with a law that's not too popular, like laws against smoking a small amount of marijuana, for example.

Schmrz: For us, the very notion of allowing a tribunal to nullify a law is inconceivable. We would never allow it, not even in a single case. As I said earlier, we do not tolerate discretion lightly, and this seems to be discretion run wild. It could never happen here, because judges sit with out lay assessors. Even it if did happen, the tribunals written decision would reveal what they had done, and it would never stand up on appeal.

Crane: There's another reason why we allow a retrial after a conviction, but not after an acquittal. The prosecution can afford another trial, but the defendant can't. Even if he has the money for another trial, or the state is paying his lawyer, it is just too difficult emotionally. And if the prosecutor could retry him once, why would wear him down to the point that he would prpbably rater take a plea bargain. So once there is an acquittal, that has to be the end of it.

Grbzyk: Let's not forget the sentence. I believe your double jeopardy doctrine does not prevent prosecutors from appealing improper sentences. The same is true here. And the defense attorney, of course, may also appeal an improper sentence.

Crane: Thanks a lot.

Grbzyk: And even if you don't appeal, the prosecutor may appeal on the defendant's behalf.

Clare: Why would I do a thing like that?

Schmrz: Because it is your duty to do justice, Madame.

Crane: Justice? She's never heard of it.

Clare: This place is really weird.

Crane: That's what I said.

Clare: Do prosecutors really do that?

Schmrz: Not often. If the trial court might have erred against the defendant, usually the defendant will appeal.

Grbzyk: Of course, the defendant who appeals risks the imposition of further costs if he loses.

Crane: You mean his attorney's fees?

Grbzyk: Yes, of course, but not only that. Every losing defendant is assessed certain courts costs, not including the prosecutor's costs. And if the victim intervened, the losing defendant must also pay the victim's attorneys fees.

Clare: That's a lot more than most of out states require. I guess your system can discourage a defendant from dragging out the trial, or from appealing.

Grbzyk: I suppose so, but that is not its purpose, We simply feel that it is just to compel a guilty person to make the state and the victims whole.

Clare: Does it work the other way? If he is acquitted, does the state make him whole by paying his attorney fees?

Grbzyk: Yes, as a matter of fact it does.

Clare: We don't do that in the United States.

Grbzyk: Perhaps that is because you sometimes acquit people not because they are innocent, but for extraneous reasons. You release the guilty where illegally seized evidence is excluded, and without such evidence you cannot obtain a conviction. This is not likely to happen in our system. If we acquit a man, he is probably truly innocent, so he should suffer no loss at all.

Crane: In the United States, none of this stuff would matter much, as the overwhelming majority of criminal defendants are indigent. They couldn't

	even pay for my lunch. In those cases, the state has to pay for their lawyers, usually public defenders.
Grbzyk:	We do the same, at least in cases of serious crime. And indigent defendants cannot be required to pay any costs. In such cases, the issue of making the state and the intervenor whole is really moot.
Schmrz:	Your client, of course, in not indigent, Mr. Crane. In fact, some have accused him of spending so much money on his defense that he is trying to "buy an acquittal."
Crane:	Look, in the usual case the prosecution uses or has access to many more resources than the defense. They have several lawyers available in the D.A.'s office, and they have their own investigators, plus the whole police department, a crime lab, and other agencies like the F.B.I. to turn to for help. And all this against a single defense lawyer with little investigative help. Do people accuse the prosecutors of trying to "buy convictions?" Of course not. In Mr. Sampson's case the resources are almost equal for a change, so we have about as good a chance as the prosecutors to show the jury the whole story. That not unfair. What's unfair is what happens in the other ninety-nine percent of the cases.
Schmrz:	I hadn't thought of it that way.
Crane:	In some cases, a U.S. defendant doesn't even have a lawyer. Our Supreme Court has held that a defendant has a constitutional right to represent himself, without a lawyer, if he's stupid enough to go that route. It's his case, so he can handle it as he likes. Do you allow this?
Schmrz:	No. Every defendant must have counsel.
Clare:	Why? It's the defendant' neck, isn't it?
Schmrz:	Madame forgets. In our countries the proceedings are held not for the benefit of the parties, but for the state. It is the duty of the tribunal to find the truth, and defense counsel is better qualified than the defendant to aid this effort.
Clare:	Remarkable. Everything we talk about seems to keep coming back to the same fundamental concepts. Where do they come from? Why does the United States start with the notion that the parties run the trial, and Europeans start with the notion that the state runs it?
Grbzyk:	An excellent question. Perhaps the United States has a very different attitude towards government and authority than we do.
Schmrz:	I agree. To put it bluntly, Europeans trust authority, and Americans don't. Speaking generally, of course.
Crane:	That's true about us. The easiest way to get elected to government office in the United States is to attack government, especially the central governments in Washington and the state capitals.
Grbzyk:	But it goes well beyond campaign slogans. In the United States, you display your mistrust of authority by dividing it up. Europeans are not so afraid of concentrating it. Our judges have a great deal of power. They investigate the case before trial, examine all the witnesses during trial, and then deliberate right along with the lay assessors. Everyone else, the lawyers,

the lay assessors, takes a back seat to the judges. This concentrates most of the power in one institution: the judges.

Crane: I don't think U.S. citizens would tolerate that.

Grbzyk: Quite so. Your judges may be respected, but in a trial of a major crime, they have very little power compared to European judges. But your fear of the concentration of power goes even further. In your system, no one individual has much power because you divide it into so many pieces. The prosecutor, not a judge, investigates the case. The lawyers, not the judge, present the evidence at trail. The judge sits primarily as an umpire, making sure that the lawyers obey the rules. And your jury, not the judge decides who wins. But then the judge may set aside a verdict of conviction if he feels it is not supported by the evidence, and the judge, not the jury, sentences the defendant. But often your legislature has severely limited the judges discretion in sentencing, so he has little to do except apply the legislatures predetermined formula. Then an appellate court decides if the whole thing was done properly. And your press keeps watch to tell the world if any of these actors has behaved improperly. Everyone—lawyers, juror's, judges, the legislature, reporters—has a little piece of the power. No one has it all, or eve a major part of it.

Clare: You make us sound like a bunch of paranoids.

Schmrz: That's for you to decide. I'm merely stating the facts.

Crane: Perhaps this is why the U.S. system seems so complicated. Because we don't trust judges, we use a bunch of untrained amateurs: the jurors. But because we don't totally trust a bunch of amateurs we've never seen before, we have to take a lot of time questioning them and selected them. Then we need complex rules of evidence to keep them from hearing stuff we don't think they can evaluate properly. Because we don't want too much power in judges, we have the lawyers investigate the case and examine and cross-examine the witnesses, which takes more time. And because our jurors don't know the law, the judge must spend time instructing the jury on the law. You don't have any of these things under your inquisitorial system.

Clare: Our adversarial system doesn't seem very efficient.

Grbzyk: No it doesn't. Our trials usually take a fraction of the time yours take. One study showed that the average European trial for a serious crime takes about one day.

Crane: Maybe so, Professor, but a monarchy is more efficient than a democracy. Kings can make decisions a lot quicker and cheaper than a bunch of quarrelsome legislators.

Grbzyk: Touché, Mr. Crane. I catch your drift. Maybe our authoritarian mentality is showing. A vestige of the past, perhaps.

Clare: And maybe ours is a case of democracy run amok.

Crane: Wait a minute. Don't forget plea bargaining. Your trials might take less time than ours, but in your system every case goes to trial. Our trials are no longer, but over 80% of our cases don't even go to trail. Plea bargained cases are handled at least as efficiently as your trials, maybe more so.

Grbzyk:	It seems ironic. You have this elaborate structure for your trials, no doubt for good reasons, but then you totally dispense with this structure in the great majority of your cases. Apparently, whatever reasons you have for your complex trial system are not good enough to persuade you to keep it for most of your cases. Is this not weird?
Clare:	Our "elaborate structure," as you call it, is mainly for the benefit of the defendant. If he's willing to waive it, that's his right. Nothing ironic about that. We respect the right of the individual to decide what's best for him.
Grbzyk:	And we view the features of our system as being there for the state, not the parties.
Schmrz:	I suspect that the jury is the fulcrum of your system. Suppose you eliminated the jury, and all of your criminal cases were to be decided by judges. How would your citizens react?
Crane:	I'm not sure. The jury might be on the way out. In civil cases, especially business disputes, more and more cases are being handled by arbitrators. Most criminal cases are still tried by juries, but there have been changes that tend to make the jury somewhat less attractive, at least to defense attorneys. Traditionally, juries have been made up of twelve people, and their verdicts have had to be unanimous. But now some states allow juries of as few as six people, and some allow less than unanimous verdicts, like ten to two.
Clare:	Sure its cheaper with fewer people. And nonunamious verdicts make a hung jury less likely, so we have to re-try cases less often. That saves money, as well as the burden on citizens called for jury duty.
Crane:	It also means you get more convictions, and that makes me a bit less eager to have a jury trial. What kind of a jury do I get? I used to be able to *vior dire* juroros pretty extensively, to find out what these strangers were really like. Now, in a lot of jurisdictions, the judge does most or all of the *vior dire*.
Clare:	That saves a lot of time.
Crane:	It sure does. The judge asks them "Can you be fair?" Then he gets the expected answer, and swears 'em in! When I did *voir dire*, I would try to draw out a juror's true feelings about weather they would automatically believe a cop's testimony, how they feel about the crime charged, and whether they could put aside their personal feelings and follow the judges instruction on reasonable doubt.
Schmrz:	But you still have your peremptory challenges.
Crane:	Yes, but how can I exercise them intelligently if I don't know how the juror feels about these things? Sometimes I just have to go by what the juror looks like.
Clare:	Watch out with that one. Your treading on dangerous ground.
Crane:	Right. The courts have held that an attorney, criminal or civil, prosecution or defense, may not exercise a peremptory because of a juror's race or sex. So I can't go by what they look like, and I can't get into their heads. I'm flying blind.

Clare:	Come on. Don't you hire high-priced jury consultants?
Crane:	I have to, because I can't do much else, consultants give me ideas about body language, jurors occupations, and other things that indicate what these people are like. That's about all that's left for me to go on. But it's a rare case where I have a client that can afford a jury consultant. In most criminal cases, particularly where the defendant is indigent, the defense attorney has to pick jurors by the seat of his pants.
Clare:	It's no better for prosecutors. I live by the same rules you do. I need my *vior dire* and peremptories to get rid of flakes who might cause a hung jury. It's very expensive to re-try cases. It's well worth spending a little extra time and money up front to get a jury of sensible people, so we can try the case just once and get it over with.
Crane:	It's sad to see this weakening of the American jury. People used to view the jury as fundamental to our notion of individualism. A jury protects the accused from the government, and the judge is seen as part of the government.
Clare:	The prosecution needs protection too. In a lot of cases, I'd rather make my pitch to twelve ordinary citizens than to one judge, who might be some liberal appointed by a liberal governor.
Crane:	Come on. You know very well that most of them are ex-D.A.'s appointed by a conservative governor.
Clare:	Are you kidding? Let me tell you about a case I had in front of Judge....
Schmrz:	An interesting dispute. It would not arise here.
Clare:	Why not?
Schmrz:	As you indicate, your judges are usually appointed by elected official, and elected officials often have definite philosophies about crime, punishment, and the like. They will tend to select people with a similar philosophy. And those people will have displayed their outlooks by their prior work. Most of them were former prosecutors, defense attorneys, personal injury lawyers, corporate lawyers. Whatever. Your governor has a pretty good idea how each of these specialists views the world, and he appoints accordingly.
Crane:	And some of our judges are elected, usually after campaign battles over law and order.
Schmrz:	Yes. These matters are relevant to the tasks your judges perform, which often involve much discretion in fact-finding, sentencing, and establishing the law. In our system, we try to minimize the judges discretion, so her values are not important.
Clare:	How do you pick your judges?
Grbzyk:	In a way, we don't. They pick themselves. Let me explain. We do not have law schools as such, the separate post-graduate institutions that you have. Our law students are undergraduate university students, who study with the law faculty. At the end of their studies, they make a choice: to become lawyers or to become judges. If they wish to become lawyers they must apprentice with a law office for a year or tow and then take a state examination. If they choose the judiciary path, they must pass

a special state examination upon graduation, it is quite competitive, and very few are accepted. The candidate's political beliefs are wholly irrelevant to whether he or she is accepted.

Clare: Aren't they kind of young to be judges?

Grbzyk: Of course. But before they are allowed to handle cases, they must serve apprenticeships with experienced judges. Then they are assigned small civil and criminal cases. As they gain more experienced and demonstrate their competence, they may be promoted to higher courts and be assigned more significant cases. Note that all three of the judges in our case are quite mature.

Clare: So politics has nothing to do with it?

Grbzyk: Nothing at all—we hope. Our judges are civil servants, not politicians. Each has political beliefs, of course, like any citizen does, and different judges might have different attitudes towards crime, sentencing and the like. But a judge's political beliefs should have as little to do with her job as the court clerk's political beliefs affect his job.

Clare: Politics isn't necessarily a bad thing, you know. If a governor is elected on a tough-on-crime platform, he appoints tough-on-crime judges because that's what the people want.

Grbzyk: If our people choose to get tough on crime, they may elect legislators to enact statutes that do this. It is not the judges place to make such choices.

Crane: So let's get to the bottom line, Professor. Which system is better?

Grbzyk: Better? Your question is very revealing, Mr. Crane. It displays a common assumption that a legal system may be appraised apart from the society it serves. But it can't. It cannot be constructed by experts and imposed from above. A nations legal system emerges from the attitudes of its people. Asking which country's legal system is better is like asking which country's people are better.

Crane: So our system is complex and messy because we are complex and messy?

Clare: No. Our system breaks up power because Americans don't want power concentrated.

Schmrz: And our system concentrates power because this is more efficient, and because it does not particularly bother our people. We have had kings, queens, and other strong leaders for centuries, so perhaps our people have gotten used to it, even though they now claim to favor democracy. Also, as discussed earlier, we operate under the principle, or perhaps the illusion, that our judges have little discretion, that they merely apply the law mechanically.

Crane: Times change, Professor.

Schmrz: Indeed they do, Mr. Crane. Italy has recently changed its legal system. It is moving away from the inquisitorial system and toward your adversarial system. The Italians have retained their mixed panel, but they have taken away the power of judges to present the evidence, giving it to the lawyers.

Clare: Really? That's great! Why did they do it?

Schmrz:	They say that they now realize that the adversarial system gives greater respect to the rights of the individual.
Crane:	That's true. The parties have the most at stake, so their lawyers should control the presentation of the case.
Grbzyk:	Of all Europeans, I think the Italians are most similar to the United States in your dislike of concentrations of power. They would rather spread it out.
Schmrz:	These are the justifications given by the Italians, officially. But others suspect that something else is at work. For years, one of the most popular television programs in Italy has been your "Perry Mason," where a handsome trial lawyer always manages to win at the last moment. You know how Italians love a dramatic spectacle, like opera.
Clare:	So we put on a better show than you do?
Grbzyk:	That we must concede. U.S. trials have much better Nielsen ratings then European trials.
Crane:	The adversarial system demands a lot more from lawyers than the inquisitorial system does. Are Italian lawyers up to it?
Schmrz:	That remains to be seen. It will be difficult. Many Italian lawyers prepare for a trial simply reviewing their code books. They have no training in cross examination, preparation of experts, and the like.
Crane:	Those are the bread and butter tasks of U.S. lawyers. We take courses in those skills, read books on them, and practice them every day in court for years. You can't learn them in a day.
Schmrz:	The transition will not be easy.
Clare:	I've never heard of a country grafting an important feature of one system onto another type of system, like the Italians are doing. Is it really possible?
Schmrz:	A good question. I'm not sure that the Italians have thought that question through carefully enough. If and when their lawyers learn the U.S. style of trial advocacy, perhaps other aspects of their system will also have to change, or else they might have to give up the notion of letting lawyers control the evidence. I'm not sure that one can just plonk a major foreign feature into an existing system without radically altering the entire system.
Crane:	Professor, you didn't like my question about which system is better. So let me rephrase it. Which system does a better job of finding the truth?
Grbzyk:	You insist on pinning me down, eh? Well, Let me begin by passing a little saying I once heard: "An innocent defendant should prefer to be tried in Europe, while a guilty defendant should prefer to be tried in the United States.
Crane:	Wonderful! A supreme compliment to the skills of U.S. defense lawyers- like me, naturally.
Clare:	(shaking her head) Look at him. He's proud of it!
Crane:	Just kidding, Counsel. Prosecutors have no sense of humor.
Grbzyk:	The saying implies, of course, that the inquisitorial system a better job of finding the truth.

Crane:	Who said the saying, a European?
Grbzyk:	This I must admit.
Schmrz:	Let's examine the issue a little more closely. I suppose the key difference we should focus on is who decides what is the truth. You use lay jurors and we use professional judges, sometimes along with lay people. But as you pointed out, Mr. Crane, lay people tend to go along with judges. Isn't it rather obvious that professionals are better at their jobs than amateurs? Professionals have been selected for their aptitude, then they are trained, and then they spend much more time at their jobs than amateurs ever could. A research biologist stands a much better chance of finding the true cause of cancer than does some barber or baseball player. By the same token, judges are bound to be better at finding the truth at trial than jurors could ever hope to be.
Crane:	Wait a minute. Judges are trained to know and apply the law. They don't take courses in law school on how to figure out who's telling the truth. And another thing: criminal trials aren't about finding the cure for cancer.
Schmrz:	Sometimes they seem like it. In the trial we just observed, several scientists testified about the accuracy of DNA evidence. It was very technical, and I must admit that I had some difficulty following it at times. Was better able to understand it? Judges, all of whom have had university training and several years of listening to expert witnesses, or jurors, who might not have graduated from high school, and who might be seeing the inside of a courtroom for the first time?
Crane:	But this case isn't typical. Most criminal trials don't involve heavy scientific disputes. Most turn on a rather simple question: who's telling the truth and who's lying? A robbery victim points to the defendant and says, "That's the guy who robbed me," and the defendant testifies "I was home watching TV when the robbery occurred." A diploma in biology isn't going to help you figure out which one is right. And there's no reason a judge should be any better at it than a barber or a ballplayer.
Clare:	I'm not so sure about that. Judges hear defendants make up stories day in and day out. After a while, they get a pretty good ear for it. But some jurors are so naive they'll buy any cock-and-bull story.
Crane:	And some judges always believe the cops—or say they do, anyway. They have to work with the police everyday, and they want to stay on good terms with them, especially if the judge is looking for an appointment to the next court up. Judges get more points for being pro-cop then being pro-defendant. And as for defendants making up stories, sure, some do. The judge hears a few of these and then decides that all defendants are probably lying. They get jaded. That's why we need jurors. They're not prejudiced, and they bring a fresh look to things.
Clare:	You mean they're more likely to fall for your tricks. A lot of defense lawyers make a career out of confusing jurors.
Crane:	Be nice to me, Ms. D.A. Without me, there's no you. An adversarial system with only one adversary is like the Dodgers showing up for the World Series with no opponent. There's not much point to it. Under this inquisitorial system, we're both out of work.

Schmrz: Not quite, but your roles would be substantially diminished.

Clare: That's true. I'd probably get more convictions here, not having to deal with juries and exclusionary rules and the like. But 1 wouldn't have much to do with getting them. It wouldn't feel like winning. Not as much fun.

Crane: Ha! The truth comes out. You like battling me. See, we're both products of the adversarial system. Maybe U.S. prosecutors have more in common with U.S. defense lawyers than they do with European prosecutors.

Clare: Perish the though. Anyway, Professor, I see another problem with your view. Lots of times the "truth" we are looking for isn't just a "whodunit." It involves values. The law says that murder should be reduced down to voluntary manslaughter if the defendant killed because of some "reasonable provocation." So if the defendant kills because the victim recently molested the defendant's kid, we don't punish him as much as we would a Mafia hit man. But what a "reasonable" provocation is can be a tough question. It is reasonable when someone says something racist to you? It is reasonable if someone raped you last week? This isn't a question of "truth," it's a question of values. Twelve jurors might bring the values of the community into the decision better than one or even three judges could.

Schmrz: But such "values" are never considered by our tribunals. These questions are decided by our legislatures, not our courts. We expect courts to apply the law, not to make it.

Clare: Our judges make law all the time. And I guess our jurors also do it occasionally.

Crane: Jurors' experience can be important even in a whodunit case. I once had a Latino client who wouldn't look the judge in the eye when testifying because he came from a country where that was seen as a threat or an assertion of dominance. And you just don't do that with someone like a judge. The judge thought he was lying. But some of the jurors were Latino and knew about that, so they believed him, and they acquitted him.

Clare: I've had cases like that. Often twelve jurors have had experience with life that no one judge could have.

Crane: You know, some judges never get out of the courtroom, And when they do, they just hang out in country clubs with their buddies, other judges, a few doctors, and lawyers. They don't know much about real life on the streets, where most criminals defendants come from.

Schmrz: I suppose the same might be said of some of our judges.

Clare: It's more of a problem in the Untied States than here in Europe. We have a very diverse population, with racial and ethnic groups from all parts of the world. In Los Angeles, we probably have over fifty different language groups, just in one city. And these people have different cultures and customs. No single judge, no matter how much he gets out in the world, can possible know as much about these cultures as twelve jurors.

Grbzyk: Perhaps our mixed tribunal obviates some of these difficulties. Our lay assessors may bring some real life into the tribunal's deliberations.

Clare:	Sort of a compromise, isn't it? You have the benefit of professional judges running things, but you also get input from the public through the lay assessors. Sounds like a good idea.
Grbzyk:	Quite so. It satisfies both needs, Wouldn't such a compromise be an improvement over your jury system?
Crane:	Maybe, but as we saw in court today, it would probably bring a lot of other changes along with it. No more hearsay rules, no jury instruction, no *voir dire*, and no peremptory challenges. And judges telling jurors how to vote. That's a lot of baggage to bring in just to get a mixed tribunal.
Grbzyk:	Baggage, or benefits? Many people see those things you mentioned as technicalities, well worth getting rid of.
Crane:	Let's not overstate the amount of power our jurors have. Granted, they deliberate alone, without a judge with them, unlike they way you do it. But we limit them in a way you don't. Take that evidence of prior crimes which I tried to keep out. You lay assessors would hear this evidence, and then in the deliberation room the judge might try to talk them out of misusing it. In our system, the judge would screen this evidence, and keep the jury from even hearing it at all if he felt it was only marginally relevant and too prejudicial.
Schmrz:	Yes. I am quite struck by the amount of time you spend in the United States on objections and pre-trial motions involving whether jurors will be allowed to hear certain evidence. It seems to reflect a certain lack of confidence in their ability to find the truth.
Grbzyk:	You know, this problem of finding the truth is not confined to criminal cases. We deal with it all the time in everyday life. An employer discovers money missing from the petty cash box. Does she just listen to the employee's explanations, or does she try to find out the truth herself?
Clare:	Obviously the latter. Are you suggesting that the inquisitorial system is more "natural" than the adversarial system?
Grbzyk:	Perhaps.
Crane:	It's more "natural" only if you see the state in a paternalistic role. Maybe you Europeans see the state as Big Daddy, but most in the United States don't.
Schmrz:	Consider an institution may regard as quite paternalistic the Catholic Church. The Church has had experience with both models when judging whether certain people were worthy of sainthood. The Church initially used the inquisitorial model, but this became too loose, sanctifying many candidates whose qualifications were questionable. So they changed to an adversarial system, establishing the office of Promoter of the Faith to argue against any proponents of a particular candidate.
Grbzyk:	The proponents called the Promoter the "devil's advocate," didn't they?
Schmrz:	Yes. Each side had its lawyers, and the case was tried before the Pope's representatives. It worked quite well for several centuries. But the whole process became so lengthy and cumbersome that it was recently abandoned. The process is now more inquisitorial.

Grbzyk: What about scientists? Do they seek the truth through an adversarial model, an inquisitorial mode, or neither?

Schmrz: Probably through a blend of each. An individual scientist may act as an unbiased inquisitor initially, but once he publicly proposes a new thesis, the process might well become somewhat adversarial, where he defends his thesis, other scientists attack it, and the remaining scientific community sits as the tribunal. It is a tribunal of professionals, of course, not lay people.

Crane: I think we're overlooking something here. Finding the truth, whatever that is, is important. But it's not the only thing. We have juries for other reasons as well.

Grbzyk: Such as?

Crane: Well, we talked earlier about how Americans don't really trust government that much. Criminal cases are about basic moral decisions, what the morals of a community are all about. Our communities want to be involved in making those decisions. They don't want to leave it all to the judges.

Grbzyk: Don't they elect the legislators who enact the criminal laws?

Crane: Yes, but that not enough. The laws are abstract. A real case is concrete. It hits home.

Clare: I'm just trying to imagine what it would be like with no juries. People would probably think that all these judgments, both convictions and acquittals, were coming down from on high, from the top. I can just see the accusations of racism, sexism, classism, elitism, and other "isms" flooding the newspapers. When people see a case decided by fellow citizens, they are more likely to accept it.

Crane: Not always. Look at the riots resulting from the Rodney King case, when a California jury acquitted the white cops who beat up a black man.

Clare: True, but that was an aberration, an all-white suburban jury trying a case that should have been tried by a racially-mixed jury in Los Angeles. That proves my point. If a mixed Los Angeles jury had acquitted those cops, I don't think the riots would have happened.

Schmrz: Are you saying that even if your jury is more likely to be mistaken than our judges, the jury is still better because it makes the judicial system and its rulings more acceptable to your people?

Clare: Yes. Some things are more important than being right all the time.

Crane: And maybe we are saying only that it works better for us, In Europe, your local populations are not as diverse as ours. Perhaps it is less important to have a cross-section of the people deciding criminal cases. Maybe your judges are not all that different from the rest of the community, just a little better educated. So your people are more willing to accept judgments from judges.

Schmrz: Europe is changing. We now have more mobile populations, with more intermixing. So perhaps our needs will become similar to yours. Our crime rates are rising, and illegal drugs are becoming more of a problem as they have been in your country for some time. Italy is changing, and it is also changing its legal system. Maybe other countries will follow suit.

Crane:	I'm beginning to see why my question about which system is better didn't make a lot of sense. Maybe there is no "better." It all depends on what a particular society wants and thinks it needs.
Schmrz:	We see another problem with juries. It is very important to us that the law be certain, consistent, and predictable, and that our officials be seen as having very little discretion. As an institution, the jury runs counter to these objectives. Because they are untrained novices, jurors are quite unpredictable and they appear to have wide discretion, allowing them to return general verdicts, without explaining their reason, tends to confirm this.
Clare:	I'm not sure that using judges is much better. True, an individual judge might be pretty predictable. An experienced local lawyer can usually tell you how Judge X will rule, if she's been on the bench for a while. But the lawyer will also predict that Judge Y will rule just the opposite. This seems to make "the law" not very predictable. It all depends on which judge the case is assigned to.
Schmrz:	That is not so much of a problem for us. As I explained earlier, our judges are not selected for their political philosophies. In addition, they are all trained in the same way, they are required to explain their decisions, and allowing both sides to appeal tends to ensure that they will follow the law. These features make judges consistent with each other and with their own prior rulings.
Clare:	The role of juries in U.S. law is important, but let's not overstate it. Except in death penalty cases, the jury usually has no say about what sentence the defendant receives, That's for the judge, and most of our jurisdictions do allow both the prosecution and the defense to appeal sentencing decisions. This helps to make the sentencing more consistent and predictable.
Crane:	I'm trying to imagine what it would be like if our juries did the sentencing. It could get pretty wild. Each jury is made up of twelve different people, most of whom have never decided a case before. If the law gave them a lot of leeway in sentencing, say one to ten years for armed robbery, some juries would give one and some would give ten.
Clare:	The same thing can happen with judges, as a group. One judge might give one year, and another ten. But at least a given judge will tend to be pretty consistent.
Crane:	Right. If the case has been assigned to a particular judge, the sentence becomes somewhat predictable. That's very important for plea bargaining. When I try to convince a client to accept a deal, he wants to know what will happen if he rejects the bargain and goes to trial. If I can't give him a pretty good idea of this, he's likely to take his chances and go to trial.
Clare:	So if sentencing were left to the jury, we'd probably have fewer plea bargains and more trials, which would require more resources.
Crane:	This all assumes, of course, that the legislature allows leeway in sentencing. These days, a lot of them don't.
Schmrz:	Does it also assume that you will continue to bifurcate your trials, trying guilt and sentencing separately?

Crane: Yes. Even if we gave sentencing to the jury, we couldn't give it to them at the same time as the guilt issue. First, it would mean that evidence relating to sentencing would come in, maybe evidence of defendant's prior criminal lifestyle, and you just can't trust a jury to decide guilt fairly when they've heard that stuff. Second, it's just too confusing for a bunch of lay people to decide more than one issue at a time. It would take them forever to come back with a verdict. And if we required a unanimous verdict, they'd probably never come back.

Clare: Your system of combining the two issues in one trial is probably more efficient than ours.

Schmrz: Yes, but it works only because we have professional judges deliberating with the lay assessors. I agree with Mr. Crane. It would never work if we used only the lay assessors.

Clare: So maybe our jury system is really a compromise. We use juries, for all the reasons we discussed, but we limit their input to only half the case; the question of guilt. They play no part in the sentencing half, which is just as important.

Crane: With one exception.

Clare: Yes, capital cases. There the penalty is so extraordinary that we don't want the state to impose it without the consent of the community at least twelve of its members.

Grbzyk: Your comments on the truth intrigue me. Under your adversarial system, do lawyers want the tribunal to learn the truth?

Clare: I do. The truth is the defendant is guilty.

Crane: There's an unbiased opinion for you.

Clare: Actually, it is. I spend a lot of time before trial talking to witnesses and examining the physical evidence. And I get to see a lot of evidence the jury probably won't see, such as illegally seized evidence and his prior record. These things might persuade me that he's guilty even if the jury later acquits him. But if what I see convinces me that he's innocent, I don't take the case to trial. I dismiss it. I don't want to convict an innocent man. So when I take a case to trial, I know he's guilty. For me, that is the truth.

Crane: Very noble, Counsel. But you don't always know someone is innocent or guilty. Suppose you aren't sure. Suppose some guy is accused of rape, he claims the woman consented, she denies it, and you aren't sure who's telling the truth. Do you take it to trial?

Clare: That's a tough one. A lot depends on whether I think I can get a conviction. I don't like to lose. It makes it harder for me to drive a tough plea bargain if people aren't afraid that I'll win if the case goes to trial. And losing isn't much of a career booster, quite frankly. So if I think he's guilty, but I'm not sure the evidence shows it beyond a reasonable doubt. I might dismiss or plea bargain instead of trying it. I have enough trouble finding time to prosecute the guys I know I can nail. I don't need to waste time with weak cases.

Crane:	Don't dodge the issue. Suppose you have your doubts, but you're getting political pressure to prosecute—maybe from some women's group. Do you go to trial?
Clare:	My inclination is to leave it to the jury. That's their job, not mine.
Crane:	A clever way of covering your read end. If you dismiss or plea bargain, the women's group will say you sold them out. But if you go to trial and lose, maybe they'll blame the jury and not you.
Grbzyk:	Let me make sure I understand you, Ms. Clare. Even if you're not convinced he's guilty, in your role as an advocate you argue that he is? You try to persuade the jury that she's telling the truth and he isn't?
Clare:	I guess I do. Once I get into trial, I want to win.
Grbzyk:	In our system, no prosecutor would argue that the accused is lying if she did not in fact believe that he was.
Clare:	When I get to trial, defense attorneys seem to bring out the worst in me.
Schmrz:	What do you mean?
Clare:	When I first look at a case, I'm very objective, seeing all sides of it pretty fairly. At that point, I might be willing to dismiss or settle. But as I get closer to trial, I become more of an advocate, and I hone down my arguments and my rebuttles to my opponents arguments. But the odd thing is I usually convince myself with my arguments. Sometimes I look back on how I felt when I first saw the case, when I was very dubious about it and I can't figure out how I became so sure that the case should come out only one way. It's a strange transformation.
Crane:	It's not peculiar to prosecutors. It happens to me too. It happens to all U.S. litigators, even in civil cases. There's nothing wrong with it. It's inherent in the adversary system. How can you persuade a jury if they don't feel that you believe what your saying?
Schmrz:	So U.S. lawyers are all actors, pretending to believe something they don't? But you can't pretend. The jury will see through it. That's why you have to convince yourself first.
Grbzyk:	A peculiar psychological task, isn't it?
Crane:	It is, and a lot of people don't understand it. They just think lawyers are liars, saying things they don't believe just to win. It's not that simple.
Clare:	Anyway, I don't feel so bad about it. Defense counsel will urge the jury to acquit the defendant, even when he knows the defendant is guilty. He's certainly not out for the truth.
Schmrz:	I'm not convinced that either of you are out for the truth. I happened to read some newspaper reports which discussed some evidence that the accused may have become agitated by something the victims did soon before the killings. This would tend to show that he did not premeditate the killing, which would have reduced the crime to second degree murder. If it showed a reasonable provocation, it might even have reduced it to voluntary manslaughter. And yet neither of you introduced this evidence. Why?

Crane: I took the position that the prosecution couldn't prove that he even committed the killings. I didn't want to confuse the jury with any arguments that assumed that he did commit them.

Clare: I charged him with first degree murder. So naturally I wouldn't want to put in any evidence that detracted from that.

Schmrz: So each of you, for different reasons, deceived the tribunal, correct?

Clare: That's putting it pretty strong, I think he premeditated, so why should I help him by putting on evidence that tends to show that he didn't?

Schmrz: You think he premeditated, but isn't it the tribunal's task to determine whether he did or not? And you deprived it of the opportunity to do so. This would never happen in our system. The prosecutor has a duty to present all evidence which is relevant to the case, no matter which side it seems to help. The task of the tribunal is to find the truth, not to decide which side has presented the better case.

Crane: I don't think I deceive the court when I don't put on evidence I know about. Its not the job of a defense attorney to help the court find the truth. My duty is to my client. I can't tell him to lie, an I can't put on false evidence. That would be deceiving the court.

Schmrz: A fine line, to be sure.

Crane: Is it? Is it much different from refusing to plead guilty when I know he's guilty? I do that when the prosecution has a weak case. I just try to poke holes in the prosecutor's case and hold her to her burden of proving the case beyond a reasonable doubt. If I succeed and get my client off, I've done my job well, even if he is actually guilty.

Schmrz: So his guilt has no effect on you?

Crane: I wouldn't say that. Like the prosecutor, I don't like to lose. And if l lost at trial, my client's sentence will be greater than it would be if l had gotten him a decent plea bargain. So if the prosecutor has a strong case, I'll probably advise my client to bargain.

Clare: Now who's dodging the issue? Suppose I have a weak case, but you know your client is guilty. You'll still urge the jury to acquit him. You know it and I know it.

Crane: Correct.

Schmrz: Morally, you have no problem with that, Mr. Crane?

Crane: Of course not. Look, I'm no different from any other decent citizen. I don't want a rapist running loose to threaten my wife or daughter. As a citizen, I want this guy put away for a long time if he did it. But as his lawyer, I want him to walk.

Schmrz: How can you want two inconsistent results? And why put yourself in such a difficult position?

Crane: That's the same as asking me why I became a lawyer. I did it because I believe in our system, the adversary system. I think it works. Without me, or someone like me, doing what I do, the adversary system just couldn't work properly.

Schmrz:	Many people feel that U.S. criminal defense lawyers are ... how should I say it?
Crane:	I'll say it for you. We're greedy shysters, manipulators, liars, out to get mass murderers off on technicalities, et cetera, et cetera. I've heard them all.
Schmrz:	Do those accusations bother you?
Crane:	I don't mind heat. I get plenty of it from prosecutors and judges, in court. That comes with the territory. But it does other me when people don't understand how defense attorneys contribute to the rendering of justice. Basically, they just don't understand the adversary system.
Schmrz:	Justice? Are you seeking justice when you urge a jury to free a guilty man?
Crane:	See, that's the problem. You think my job is to find a just result and urge the jury to come back with that verdict. It isn't. Under the adversary system, it's the system's job to come up with a just result. That's not the job of each player in the system. Let's look at another player, the bailiff. His job is to take care of the jury. But he hears the evidence and arguments, and he might come to his own conclusions. When he escorts the jury into the deliberation room, is he supposed to tell them what he thinks is the just result? No way. That's not his role. Same with me.
Schmrz:	So justice emerges from each player carrying out his or her limited role?
Crane:	Yes, but only if every actor plays his role properly. Clare's role is to prosecute, my role is to defend, and the jury's rule is to decide who's right. If I play her role, or she plays mine, or either is us plays the jury's role, it doesn't work. We're sort of like an automobile engine. The pistons go up and down, the gears go from side to side, and some of the rods even go backwards. Everything seems to be going in a different direction, but when all of them work together properly, the whole car goes forward, just where you want it to go.
Schmrz:	An attractive analogy, Mr. Crane. But the bailiff is not actively trying to free a man who might be guilty. You are. How can you expect the U.S. public to look kindly on you?
Crane:	It's not easy. And we haven't done a very good job of explaining to the public how we help them. Look at it this way. There are two possibilities, my client will either be convicted or he'll be acquitted. Either way I help society. If he's convinced, the fact that I tried hard to get him acquitted lets us all sleep better, knowing that it's very unlikely we are punishing an innocent man, because I made sure the jury knew every weakness in the prosecution's case. And if my efforts help get him acquitted, we can be sure we're not punishing an innocent man.
Grbzyk:	But sometimes your efforts have nothing to do with guilt or innocence. When you urge the court to exclude relevant evidence because the police forgot to obtain a search warrant, or to exclude a confession because the police forgot to read the defendant his Miranda rights, you seek to prevent the jury from finding the truth about guilt or innocence. Aren't these the sorts of technicalities the public complains about?
Crane:	Look, my job is to make the arguments for my client, and that's all. I can't decide anything, and I can't make the rules. That's the court's job.

If the public doesn't like the rules, they should blame the courts and the legislatures, not me. I'm just the messenger: I tell the court when the rules have been broken.

Grbzyk: That seems reasonable. But if people don't like the rules, I suppose they'll blame the first person that mentions them. You.

Crane: Right. The basic problem is that people don't appreciate whey we have these rules. The exclusionary rule protects all of us from unreasonable searches and arrests, and the Miranda warnings make sure that the police don't coerce defendants into confessing. You can agree or disagree with these policies, but you can't fairly call them "technicalities." They're not like rules about what size paper your briefs have to be written on; they deal with fundamental rights. If they make it a little harder to find the truth in some cases, it's well worth the price. I just wish the public understood that.

Grbzyk: The U.S. public sometimes sees the arguments that lawyers present as rather fanciful. Shouldn't you take responsibility for the arguments you make?

Crane: I should, and I do. All good lawyers make creative arguments. The public doesn't realize that lawyers in an adversarial system have to push the envelope, to test the outer edges of the rules. That's part of our job. If we didn't the law would never change, and we wouldn't be representing our clients to the fullest. And don't worry, if we cross the line between creative and fanciful, the judge won't hesitate to shoot us down.

Schmrz: Intellectually, you present a persuasive case, Mr. Crane, as one might expect from an intelligent lawyer. But let's talk about your feelings for a moment. I believe that's fashionable in California these days. How do you feel when a jury acquits a man you know to be guilty?

Crane: That doesn't happen often. But when it doesn't I don't lose any sleep. I just make doubly sure my doors are locked.

Schmrz: So you feel content?

Crane: Content? When I win, I feel terrific.

Schmrz: The verdict reinforces your belief in the system, I suppose.

Crane: The system? When the jury walks through that door with a verdict, who's thinking about the system? Half the time, I'm not even thinking about my client! I'm thinking about one thing: victory. A lawyer in the adversarial system is like an athlete or a soldier, at least when we're caught up in the emotions of a trial. Who would think of asking a pro football player why he wants to win the game? We're the same way. I'm not sure whether we're born that way or the adversarial system makes us that way, but that's what happens.

Clare: During trial, I feel the same thing. I might think about the rights and wrongs of it all before the trial begins, but once the judge bangs that gavel, I just to win. Period.

Schmrz: Of course, winning is profitable for both of you is it not? Doesn't a good record enhance your careers?

Crane:	Sure it does. That's how I get clients and she gets promotions. But that's not what keeps us going during a trial. Then we're warriors, not career climbers. I'll balance my checkbook later.
Grbzyk:	Remarkable. I suppose this competitive drive is what creates the drama we spoke of earlier.
Clare:	Yes. We are very competitive, and most of out trial lawyers want to be Perry Mason, each in their own way.
Grbzyk:	I don't think our lawyers have these feelings, at least not to the degree you exhibit them.
Clare:	They don't know what they're missing. Say what you will about the adversarial system, but it sure is fun at least for the lawyers.
Grbzyk:	Even when you lose?
Clare:	Of course not. But the thrill of winning makes you forget your losses, till the next one, anyway. It is pretty much like competitive sports, I suppose.
Grbzyk:	We Europeans think competition is more suited to the soccer field than our law courts. In the United States, you seem to treat the quest for justice as just a game.
Crane:	It's a game, all right, but its not just a game. The competitive spirit is the gas that makes the car go. It's the energy that drives the adversarial system—a very good system, I might add. It gets to the truth, most of the time, while still serving other values we think are important.
Schmrz:	Does it? How can you have such faith in a system that might result in an acquittal of a client you know to be guilty? Doesn't that show that your adversarial system is faulty?
Crane:	Not necessarily. Maybe it just shows that humans aren't perfect. Until we develop an infallible lie detector machine, we'll have to rely on fallible people to decide whether other people are telling the truth. And they won't always get it right. Do your judges always get it right?
Schmrz:	Probably not, but when the defendant confesses, our judges are less likely to get it wrong. And we do get more confessions that you do.
Crane:	But look at how you get them. As I said before ...
Clare:	Please, Crane. Once is enough.
Crane:	Now wait a minute, Clare, I ...
Schmrz:	Pardon me for raising this, but I can't help noticing a certain tension between you two. Do you dislike each other?
Clare:	Not at all. Crane and I get along pretty well, considering.
Schmrz:	Considering?
Clare:	Considering we're on opposite side, of course.
Schmrz:	Opposite side? If Mr. Crane's analogy is correct, you are both parts of the same automobile engine, each working to move the car forward towards the same destination; a just result. Your goals are the same, aren't they? Why should there be any animosity at all between you?
Clare:	Good question. I guess when you represent the same side over and over, you develop certain attitudes about crimes and cops. I have mine, he has his. And the two usually conflict.

Crane: And don't forget the emotions we talked about. When you get all worked up at the trial a few times, always on the same side, it tends to worm its way inside, and it stays there.

Clare: True. Also, different personality types are attracted to one side or the other. Prosecutors' offices tend to draw in people who are straight orderly types.

Crane: So I'm crooked and disorderly?

Clare: Not necessarily. But you and your like do tend to be more like rebels. You're not too likely to pick prosecutors as your drinking buddies and vice-versa.

Crane: Conceded. We tend to distrust big government, cops and the establishment generally. You don't. You wear pin stripes and wing-tips, and we wear flashy ties and pony tails.

Grbzyk: Could either of you switch sides?

Clare: Me? Defend criminals? Never in a million years.

Crane: Actually, I used to work as a prosecutor. But I couldn't do it now. I can't work for a bureaucracy. I'm just not the organization-man type. But I'm glad I did it. It taught me a lot about how the opposition operates.

Schmrz: The "opposition" again. Is this healthy, this loyalty to one side only? And is it necessary to the adversarial system?

Clare: I never really thought about it, how could it be any different? You can't represent both sides.

Schmrz: British barristers do. A barrister might be retained by the prosecutors office in one case, and then by the accused in the next case. Some tend to specialize in representing one side or the other, but many take each case as it come. They are vigorous advocates in the particular case, put it behind them when it is over, and then become just as vigorous in the next case. It works, and no one has suggested that it diminishes the adversarial nature of British practice.

Grbzyk: Maybe the United State should try this.

Crane: Professor, didn't you warn me earlier against comparing one feature of another system with your own without looking at the whole system? I know a bit about the Brits. They separate their lawyers into solicitors and barristers. Solicitors tend to work on side of the street: either the prosecution or the defense, not both. They prepare the case for trial, just like our prosecutors and defense attorneys do. But then the solicitor brings in a barrister as a trial specialist to try it. So the lawyer with the most contact with the client, the solicitor, sticks to one side, just like our lawyers.

Grbzyk: I stand corrected, Mr. Crane.

Clare: Still, it's an intriguing idea, the more I think about it. Maybe each of us would have a little more respect for the other side if we took one of their cases occasionally. We could try it out, in some sort of test program.

Schmrz: There is something else you might try: the inquisitorial system. Some American critics of your system have proposed this, believing that it would be much more efficient. Some have even pointed to the present case as an example of how expensive and inefficient the adversarial system can be.

Crane: That might have had a chance a while ago, but not now.

Schmrz: Why is that?

Crane: Sentencing. In recent years, our sentences have gone through the roof. Mandatory minimums, consecutives, three-strikes-and-you're-out, truth-in-sentencing laws. It's getting worse all the time.

Schmrz: I don't understand. I grant that your sentences are much higher than ours, but why would this preclude your adoption of the inquisitorial system? What is the connection?

Crane: Let's forget about the lawyers for a moment and just think about the defendant. If you are charged with a crime in the United States, the prosecution is out to clobber you. They want to put you in a miserable place for a very long time, and sometimes they want to kill you. They might have good reasons for this. I appreciate people's frustrations about crime. But reasonable or not, it's clear that the prosecutors are not looking after *your* interests, so you have to do it yourself. It doesn't matter whether you're guilty or innocent. You're going to resist; it's human nature. And when you do, the government is going to fight even harder. So the system is inherently adversarial from the start — *with or without* lawyers and judges. All the lawyers and judges do is insist on some procedures that make the fight a little more civilized.

Clare: Makes sense, I guess. But I don't see how this explains the differences in systems. Doesn't the prosecution *always* want the defendant punished, even in the inquisitorial system?

Schmrz: It depends on how you are using the word "punish." When my child misbehaves, I punish him in order to reform his behavior and make him a better person, not to hurt him. I punish him because I love him.

Clare: Come on, Professor, tell the truth. When your kid wrecks the furniture, you punish him because you're angry at him, and also to cut down the expense of buying new chairs, don't you? It's not all just for him.

Schmrz: I confess, those motives are also present, along with the ones I mentioned. I want to help him, and I am also annoyed and want to protect my household. Is your decision to prosecute based on the same mixture of motives?

Clare: I guess not, at least for most major crimes. If I'm going after an adult armed robber, I try to satisfy my community's anger at people like him, and I want him off the streets for as long as possible. Usually, I'm not trying to help him at all.

Schmrz: Will he receive any help in prison?

Crane: Are you kidding? Years ago, we tried to rehabilitate prisoners: teach them to read and learn a trade, so they might get a job when they get out. In fact, rehabilitation was seen as one of the main purposes of punishment. But today people just want the two things Ms. Clare just mentioned: to hurt the guy and to get him out of the way. Any help he might get in prison is incidental, and most of them get very little.

Clare: I suppose it's true. Today, for most defendants, the sentence he receives has little to do with any notion of how long it might take to rehabilitate him.

Schmrz: You say "most." Are there exceptions?

Clare: Sure. If I have a young defendant without much of a record, I might give him a break, maybe get him into a diversion program to help him break a drug habit, or recommend a suspended sentence on condition he behaves himself and gets a job. If I don't have an angry victim pushing me, I might try to help him.

Grbzyk: This is the approach the inquisitorial system takes with almost all defendants. Perhaps I would not go so far as to say that we hurt them because we love them, as Professor Schmrz does his child. But we start with the assumption that they are redeemable.

Schmrz: Not all of them, of course. Terrorists who kill innocent people probably evoke the same response in our community that the average burglar does in yours.

Clare: Are you telling me that your defendants think the state is trying to help them by prosecuting them, so they don't have much incentive to fight?

Schmrz: I wouldn't go quite that far, but I would say this. The average robber would not feel that a state that fines him or sentences him to four or six months in prison hates him, even if it does not love him. On some level, he might believe that he did wrong and deserves some loss of freedom for a while. But if the state were to imprison him for ten years for the same crime, he might think that depriving him of a substantial part of his life was much more than just desserts.

Crane: It's worse than that. A ten-year sentence is society's declaration that he is worthless, that he has no chance for redemption, that his community *does* hate him. While a six-month sentence might conceivably reform him, there is little chance that a ten-year sentence will do so. He has effectively been declared an outcast for the rest of his life. He'll never see this as for his own benefit, and he won't take it without a fight. Any system that threatens him with this will necessarily be an adversarial system.

Grbzyk: Ms. Clare, you mentioned your occasional sympathy for young offenders. Wasn't your juvenile court system built on similar premises?

Clare: Yes. It was intended to punish juveniles like you punish your child: to protect society *and* to help the kids grow up to be good citizens. There was supposed to be an element of love in it, sort of.

Grbzyk: Did this approach affect the way juvenile court trials were handled?

Clare: Yes. They were set up to be pretty nonadversarial. No juries, no defense lawyers, and relaxed rules of evidence. The kid didn't need those things to protect him, because the court was out to help him, not to hurt him.

Crane: That was the idea, but it didn't work out that way. Kids were thrown into miserable detention homes, which were like jails, and often their "sentences" were set according to what they had done, not what they needed. It began to look so much like adult court that our Supreme Court required states to give them some of the same rights that adult defendants get, like defense lawyers. It became an adversarial proceeding because the state was trying to punish them, not help them. If the proceeding is based on hostility rather than concerns, it will always be adversarial.

Schmrz: So, I see why you said that the nature of the sentence may affect the nature of the adjudicatory system.

Crane: Yes. Earlier, I compared a U.S. adversarial trial to a baseball game. Maybe for the lawyers it is. To us, it's mainly a game—a big game, but still a game. But the defendant has much more at stake. For him, it's more like a bullfight. The matador is trying to kill the bull, and the bull is fighting for his life. That's the essence of it. You can change the weapons, the costumes, or the players. You could even give the bull a lawyer. But if they're still trying to kill the bull, the adversarial nature of the contest won't change. The bull will never quietly accept an "inquisitorial" decision that he should die. He'll always fight back.

Schmrz: The bull is innocent, of course.

Crane: True, but that doesn't matter much. Even a guilty bull, or a guilty defendant, will resist when his enemy is trying to take his life or a substantial part of it. And he should. Even if you're guilty, that doesn't mean you deserve the penalty they're trying to inflict on you.

Schmrz: How would your bull-defendant react to an inquisitorial system, if the United States were to adopt it?

Crane: I can just imagine me telling him, "Joe, I won't bother cross-examining the key witnesses against you, because we can depend on the judge to try to get to the truth. You should just get up there and confess. Don't worry, you can trust the prosecutor and the court to look out for your interests." He'd say, "Counselor, are you nuts? Those guys are trying to put me away for twenty years. That is *not* in my interests, no matter what I did. If you won't fight back for me, I'll get a lawyer who will." See, the inquisitorial system just doesn't mesh with the high sentences.

Grbzyk: Are these harsh sentences wise? I understand that your communities are concerned about crime, but they might do more to stop crime if they directed their efforts more toward rehabilitation?

Clare: Rehabilitation is pretty tough to do. When you punish your child, you can do a lot to see that the punishment helps him, or at least doesn't hurt him, because you control most of his life. You make sure that he is well-fed and housed, that he does his homework, and develops a good character and work habits. You have some say over the company he keeps. The punishment might help him, because the rest of his life is in good shape. That's just not true of most criminal defendants in the United States. They live in rough neighborhoods where they hang out with criminals, they go to lousy schools, and they often have bad home situations. A prosecutor can't do anything about this. Neither can the judge, and neither can the prison warden. We can't take "the whole person" and help him the way you help your kid. So we punish to help us, not to help the defendant. That's all we can do.

Schmrz: In our villages, or in neighborhoods of our cities, there are often support systems that enable us to help wayward offenders, even adults. Couldn't your society do something to change the conditions you describe?

Clare: Maybe we could, but we don't. Those are political questions that are much larger than the question of whether we should have an adversarial or inquisitorial legal system. Some voters think we should do more for the poor, and others think it's hopeless or too expensive to try, and they're too angry with criminals to care about helping them. Right now, the second group seems to be having its way. But whatever the people decide, we in the legal profession are stuck with their decisions. We're just the tail, not the dog. Our criminal legal system is a symptom of how those larger political questions are handled. At the moment, U.S. prosecutors can't help the defendant much. So we try to hurt him. And when we do, he fights back.

Schmrz: Does it follow that you must give him the tools to fight with, like defense lawyers and juries?

Crane: It does follow. When you have a lot of cops and prosecutors trying to hurt people rather than help them, some are bound to make mistakes and commit abuses. So the defendant needs protections. You can't allow an aggressive prosecution without giving the defendant the power to defend himself.

Schmrz: Is there a consensus on that point among your citizens?

Crane: In the abstract, I'm not sure. But when just one case of serious injustice hits the newspapers, like an innocent guy getting railroaded, most people do insist that protections be built into the system.

Clare: Same thing happens on the other side. If just one man gets off or gets out and commits another serious crime, the public demands that we change the whole way we deal with criminal cases.

Crane: Yes. We've been talking as if our system is based on a careful weighing of all the things we've been talking about. But often we set policy by sound bites. Maybe that's why we sometimes seem so erratic. Somebody commits a crime the public sees as particularly heinous, and some politician gets a lot of mileage by pushing an increase in the penalty for that crime. Over time, this happens with *several* crimes, and gradually that changes the standard. So the sentences for *all* crimes get ratcheted up, even tough we never sat down and decided that this would be a good idea for a coherent system.

Grbzyk: In Europe, where prosecutors are not so aggressively seeking long sentences, there is not as much need for protection for the defendant, which make up the heart of your adversarial system.

Crane: Right. Until we change to a sentencing approach that shows more concern for the defendant, I don't think we can change to an inquisitorial-type system.

Clare: Like what?

Clare: Well, for example, we might …

A young man comes up to Grbzyk and whispers in his ear.

Grbzyk: A fascinating question, but we must defer it to another day. Now, we should return to court. The tribunal is ready to announce its judgment.

They all rise and begin walking.

Schmrz: So, my friends, you have learned much about our inquisitorial system?

Clare: Yeah. Thanks for the tips. But the funny thing is, something else happened, something I never expected. By looking at your system and comparing it with ours, I picked up some insights into *our* system. I've been an American lawyer for quite a while, and I thought I knew our system inside out. I do, in a way, but I've been so busy climbing the trees that I never had a good look at the forest. I just took juries, hearsay rules, and opponents like Crane for granted, without seeing how it all fit together. I guess a goldfish doesn't know what her bowl really looks like until she gets out and sees another bowl.

Crane: It's been an eye-opener, all right. I thought things like the jury trial, the exclusionary rule, and the privilege against self-incrimination were engraved in stone, like the Ten Commandments. They're not. You can have a just and civilized legal system without them. You do, and you don't seem to be savages, except for your coffee. Americans view those things as fundamental rights because …

Clare: Just because they're American.

Grbzyk: And we do the same. We accept and expect certain features just because of who we are.

Schmrz: But people change. And when they do, maybe they can learn from other cultures.

All exit, into the courthouse.

—CURTAIN—

Appendix 3.3
The Foxy Knoxy Trial
(excerpts from article by Griffith on
comparative criminal law)

Note: The following article was prepared by Christopher A. Griffith, J.D. and is used here with slight editing and his permission. It offers observations regarding the Amanda Knox trial that concluded in Italy in late 2009, giving special attention to comparative aspects of the criminal procedure rules and principles at issue in the case. The article is included here for the particularly lucid account it offers of (i) contrasts between traditional "inquisitorial" and "adversarial" models of criminal procedure, (ii) recent moves in Italy to shift emphasis from the former to the latter, (iii) specific manifestations of the two models in the Amanda Knox trial, and (iv) criticisms—some valid and many not—leveled at the conduct of that trial, mainly by observers speaking out of ignorance of the Italian system of criminal justice.

The Italian criminal justice system recently attracted extensive media coverage and criticism following the trial in Perugia of American Amanda Knox and her Italian boyfriend Raffaele Sollecito over the murder of a British foreign exchange student named Meredith Kercher. The two defendants, along with a third suspect Rudy Guede, were tried and found guilty of murder, sexual violence, and other charges. The conviction of Knox, whose case received the most attention, led to outrage in some quarters.[1]

Was the outrage justified? Or was the outrage misplaced, reflecting cultural misunderstandings and sloppy legal thinking? This article addresses these questions by exploring the cultural and historical foundations of the Italian criminal justice system and by analyzing its attributes and the particular operations of most controversy in the Amanda Knox trial. The aim is to lessen the confusion over the Italian system and thereby to alleviate any anxiety that an American citizen was denied due process.

Firstly, a brief background of the case will be provided describing the relationships between the parties involved, the murder, and the outcome for the three suspects. Then, some attention will be paid to the overwhelming media response to the murder and trial, an unavoidable consequence in such a high-profile case. Then the article will penetrate this superficial layer of opinion and examine the realities of the process in the courtroom. However, one significant issue is whether negative publicity may have tainted the opinions of the "jurors" in this case, so a quick description of the feverish media coverage will also be necessary.

Essential to understanding the subtleties of the Italian criminal justice system is a foundation in civil law principles. A brief recourse of the values particular to criminal procedure in the civil law tradition will be provided. At the heart of this will be an analysis of the differences between the inquisitorial system of civil law and the adversarial system of common law. Although its foundation is built on the civil law tradition, Italy, through the 1988 version of its criminal procedure code, executed a remarkable shift from its prior inquisitorial system to a more American, adversarial system. The reasons for this departure, and for the consequent struggles at adhering to its ideologies and operations, go a long way to explaining the attitudes in Italian criminal law and its uneasy balance as a 'mixed' system.

---

1. This outrage is evident in numerous online newspaper opinion pieces. *See, e.g.,* Tim Edwards, *OJ Simpson Lawyer Slams 'Public Lynching' of Amanda Knox,* THE FIRST POST, Oct. 19, 2009, http://www.thefirstpost.co.uk/54907; Timothy Egan, *An Innocent Abroad,* NYTimes.com, June 19, 2009, http://opinionator.blogs.nytimes.com/2009/06/10/an-innocent-abroad/.

* * *

I. THE AMANDA KNOX TRIAL

A. Background of the Case

1. The murder of Meredith Kercher

Police discovered the body of a murdered 21-year-old British university exchange student, Meredith Kercher, on 2 November 2007 in the apartment she had shared with three other young women, one of whom was Knox. She lay partially clothed under a duvet in her locked bedroom, with blood on the floor, bed, and walls. Forensic investigators concluded that Kercher had been strangled, stabbed in the neck and then bled to death. Her body suffered bruises, scratches, and knife wounds on her neck and hands.

2. The three suspects, trial, and verdict

Police arrested suspects Amanda Knox and Raffaele Sollecito, Knox's Italian boyfriend of two weeks. Later, based on DNA and fingerprint evidence found near the victim's body, Rudy Guede, an Ivorian resident of Perugia, was arrested in Germany and extradited to Italy. While Sollecito and Knox faced a lengthy and enduring trial, characteristic of the Italian criminal justice system, Guede elected for what is known as a *guidizio abbreviato* or fast-track trial. He was convicted of the sexual assault and murder of Meredith Kercher and sentenced to 30 years in prison. On appeal, his sentence was reduced to 16 years. The trial of Knox and Sollecito lasted about a year in the *Corte d'Assise* in Perugia, a court, which has jurisdiction to judge the most serious crimes. Accordingly, as is traditional, the judicial panel was composed of two professional judges, *Giudici Togati*, and six lay judges, *Giudici Popolcari*, selected from the people.

On 4 December 2009, both Knox and Sollecito were found guilty of murder, sexual violence and other charges. Knox was sentenced to 26 years in prison, while Sollecito received 25 years. As of this writing, both parties are currently in process to appeal their convictions. Knox is appealing on the grounds that the forensic evidence against her was flawed.

On 4 March 2010, the *Corte d'Assise* of Perugia published the reasons for their conviction in a 427-page opinion document. The judges said there was no inconsistency in the evidence and suggested there was a sexual motive in the case. Under the influence of drugs, Knox and Sollecito "actively participated" in helping Guede subdue Kercher. However, this was a murder "without planning, without any animosity or grudge against the victim." The motive, judges said, was "erotic sexual violence." Importantly, for reasons this essay shall discuss in time, judges said that all evidence was based on forensic evidence presented.[2]

B. Italy's Trial of the Century: The Media Impact

1. The increasing role of media in high profile cases generally

Although not essential to our ultimate analysis, the media impact is nonetheless of incredible interest and a valid point of concern in such high profile cases. That the victim and suspects were all from different countries increased international attention. One BBC News opinion piece explained, "the case was media gold from the start: a pretty young victim, brutally murdered in mysterious circumstances, whose murderers were both

---

2. BBC News, *Amanda Knox murder case 'has no holes'*, March 4th, 2010, http://news.bbc.co.uk/2/hi/europe/8549724.stm.

wealthy and attractive."[3] Of Knox in particular, opinion was bitterly polarized and divided largely along national lines. Her unusual behavior following the trial led the Italian media to dub her "the angel-faced killer with ice cold eyes."[4] The Knox family, who were in the public eye throughout the trial, believed that Knox was being convicted because of a wider culture clash and even engaged the services of a public relations firm to counteract the alleged media bias against her.[5] Aggravating the situation is the fact, as part of the "Facebook generation", Knox and Sollecito exposed themselves entirely to character assassination in the media having posted photographs of themselves in situations inviting negative connotation.[6] Social networking sites have redrawn the lines of private information, and the increasingly global, persistent, and powerful media may have a profound influence on legal proceedings in the future.

> The national and international media are testing the boundaries of legality in the reporting of criminal cases and ... have set a dangerous precedent. An increasingly adversarial mainstream media seems to be emerging in [this] and other cases as the primary players in an ideological carnival where online justice and trial by media rule, the legal requirements of due process and presumed innocence cease to be a concern and the right to privacy evaporates into the 24/7 news-media ether.[7]

2. Specific Concerns in the US Media

The increasingly powerful role of media in criminal justice — not just in Italy but around the world — offers a fascinating topic. However, it is one better suited for exploration on another day. What is specifically relevant to an analysis of the "Foxy Knoxy" case is this: did the Italian media, by attacking Knox's character, impair her chance of obtaining a fair trial because the jury had not been sequestered and was exposed to such sensationalized reporting of the case? This non-sequestration approach, which is different from the approach taken in US high-profile cases,[8] fueled one of the main controversies of the trial for those unfamiliar with the Italian criminal justice system. For example, US Senator Maria Cantwell of Washington state, in a statement released after the verdict, reflected the general misunderstanding:

> I am saddened by the verdict and I have serious questions about the Italian justice system and whether anti-Americanism tainted this trial. The prosecution did not present enough evidence for an impartial jury to conclude beyond a reasonable doubt that Ms. Knox was guilty. Italian jurors were not sequestered and were allowed to view highly negative news coverage about Ms. Knox. Other flaws in the Italian justice system on display in this case included the harsh treatment

---

3. Dan Bell, *Who was the real 'Foxy Knoxy'*, BBC News, Dec. 4, 2009, http://news.bbc.co.uk/2/hi/8391199.stm. He further describes Knox as "that most-loved of villains the middle-class monster whose appearance hides a diabolical soul."

4. Richard Owen, Amanda Knox: "angel-faced killer with ice cold eyes', Times Online, Oct 28, 2008, http://www.timesonline.co.uk/tol/news/world/europe/article5034256.ece.

5. Phillip Sherwell and David Harrison, *Amanda Knox: 'Foxy Knoxy' was an innocent abroad,* say US supporters, Telegraph.co.uk, 5, December, 2009, http://www.telegraph.co.uk/news/6736512/Amanda-Knox-Foxy-Knoxy-was-an-innocent-abroad-say-US-supporters.html.

6. The Independent, *Murder in Perugia: Dangerous Games of the Facebook generation*, Nov. 11th, 2007, http://www.independent.co.uk/news/world/europe/murder-in-perugia-dangerous-games-of-the-facebook-generation-399849.html. The reference is to a photograph taken of Knox kneeling and roaring with laughter at the controls of a machine gun during a visit to a museum.

7. Chris Greer, Jeff Ferrell, and Yvonne Jewkes, *Investigating the crisis of the present*, Crime, Media, Culture, Vol. 4, No. 1, 5–8 (2008).

8. *See, e.g., Judge in Simpson Murder Trial Orders Jury to be Sequestered*, The Washington Post, Jan. 10, 1995, *available at* http://www.highbeam.com/doc/1P2-815669.html.

of Ms. Knox following her arrest; negligent handling of evidence by investigators; and pending charges of misconduct against one of the prosecutors stemming from another murder trial.[9]

These are the general concerns this essay shall address, taking the path of comparative analysis rather than a muddied walk through the cloud of misinformation presented in the media. Those covering the story in Perugia for the last two years surely recognize that stereotypes of Knox as both sinner and saint are not accurate, and that the case is so much more complex, with the truth buried beneath.[10] With this reasonable approach in hand, we begin our grand analysis of Italian criminal procedure beginning with the very fundamental philosophies that set apart the common law tradition from the civil law tradition.

II. Criminal Procedure in the Civil Law Tradition

A. Different Legal Traditions

1. The Common Law v. the Civil Law

The most important distinction between the legal system of Italy and the legal system of the United States is in their origin. The two countries are of a different 'legal tradition'.

* * * * [The article explains the concept of "legal tradition", some key distinctions between common law and civil law traditions, and specific ideologies at work in the USA.] * * * *

... Arguably at the heart of the common law tradition and especially apparent in the United States are the characteristic aspects of individualism and liberty.[11] Alternatively, the civil law is on the side of authority and order.[12] An example is the Roman maxim in Justinian's Institutes attributed to Roman Jurist Ulpian, "*quod principi placuit, legis habet vigorum*" (what please the princeps has the force of law).[13] Through its ideology of codification and structure, the civil law tradition emphasizes control. For this reason, it may be seen as characteristically paternalistic in nature as opposed to the common law tradition. The justification for this is that without order and discipline as essential elements, liberty is to give rise to anarchy.[14]

These are perhaps oversimplified explanations of the two systems' respective philosophies. [However, they do seem applicable to the "Foxy Knoxy" case and the criticisms raised against it.] ... Before he announced the life sentence he was seeking for Amanda Knox, Giuliano Mignini, the controversial and much-maligned prosecutor in the case, read the following phrase about justice from the classical Roman jurist Ulpian, "*Iustitia est constans et perpetua voluntas ius suum cuique tribuendi. Luris praecepta sunt haec: honeste vivere alterum non laedere, suum cuique tribuere.*" (Justice is the constant and perpetual will to render to every man his due. Live honestly, don't hurt others and to each his own.)[15] The civil

---

9. *Cantwell Statement on Amanda Knox Guilty Verdict*, Dec. 4, 2009, http://cantwell.senate.gov/news/record.cfm?id=320475.

10. *See* Phillip Sherwell and David Harrison, *Amanda Knox: 'Foxy Knoxy' Was an Innocent Abroad, Say US Supporters*, Telegraph.co.uk, 5, December, 2009, http://www.telegraph.co.uk/news/6736512/Amanda-Knox-Foxy-Knoxy-was-an-innocent-abroad-say-US-supporters.html. The article quotes Andrea Vogt of the Seattle Post-Intelligencer, one of the more balanced reporters who covered the trial.

11. A.G. Chloros, *Common Law, Civil Law and Socialist Law: Three Leading Systems of the World, Three Kinds of Legal Thought*, The Cambrian Law Review, pp. 11–26, 15 (1978).

12. *Id.* at 17.

13. Inst. I, II, 6.

14. Chloros, *supra* note 11, at 17.

15. Andrea Vogt, *Prosecutor Asks for Life Sentence for Knox*, SeattlePI.com, Nov. 21, 2009, http://www.seattlepi.com/local/412538_knox21.html.

law tradition has a rich heritage that is still firmly embedded in the ideologies of the modern civil law countries. This becomes more apparent as we explore the unique approaches to criminal justice taken in the orthodox civil law tradition through its inquisitorial system.

B. Inquisitorial, Accusatorial, and Adversarial

There are two main approaches to criminal procedure in most of the world, the Anglo-American accusatorial system emerging from common law, and the European inquisitorial system emerging from civil law.[16] In an accusatorial system the judge makes decisions based only on evidence collected in oral form, in his presence, and in a public trial containing adversarial dynamics.[17] In a traditional inquisitorial system, magistrates investigate, report, and make decisions over a series of phases in which the inclusion of any evidence collected is permitted, even if obtained in violation of defendant's rights and regardless of whether it was collected in oral form.[18]

1. The difference in procedure

The model of the typical criminal proceeding in the civil law world is divided into three parts: the investigative phase, the examining phase (the instruction), and the trial. Merryman best explains the pre-trial procedure in this short excerpt:

> The investigative phase comes under the direction of the public prosecutor, who also participates actively in the examining phases, which is supervised by the examining judge. The examining phase is primarily written and is not public. The examining judge controls the nature and scope of this phase of the proceeding. The examining judge is expected to investigate the matter thoroughly and to prepare a complete written record, so that by the time the examining stage is complete, all the relevant evidence is in the record. If the examining judge concludes that a crime was committed and that the accused is the perpetrator, the case then goes to trial.[19]

Most of the investigative work and fact-finding has been done behind closed doors before the trial. In terms of the evidence presented, there is no clear demarcation between the investigation and trial stages. An impartial judicial officer conducts the criminal investigation and a single judge or panel will have full access to the investigation file, the dossier, determine guilt or innocence.[20] Contrast that with the accusatorial system, in which the trial is a single concentrated event in which all evidence will be heard and ruled upon at that moment.

An accusatorial system has an inherently adversarial procedure in which two sides zealously argue opposing viewpoints. The adversarial trial is held before a neutral judge or jury, with no prior knowledge of the case and no dossier.[21] Often, the terms adversarial and accusatorial are used interchangeably. However, while accusatorial implies adversarial, the opposite is not always true. A trial could theoretically be fully adversarial, but still allow the introduction of out of court evidence such as hearsay.[22] This would breach the barrier between the investigative and trial stages, a fundamental and necessary element in a fully accusatorial system.

---

16. Craig M. Bradley ed., *Criminal Procedure: A Worldwide Study* xvii (2nd ed. 1985).

17. Michele Panzavolta, *Reforms and Counter-Reforms in the Italian Struggle for an Accusatorial Criminal Law System*, 30 N.C. J. INT'L. L. & COM. REG. 577, 582 (2005).

18. *Id.* at 583.

19. John Henry Merryman, THE CIVIL LAW TRADITION 2 (2d ed. 1985).

20. Bradley, *supra* note 16, at xvii.

21. *Id.*

22. Panzavolta, *supra* note 17, at 583.

2. The goals and philosophies

The key to these stark differences lies in the overriding goals of the criminal legal process. In the inquisitorial system, the fundamental policy is to find the truth. All evidence should be made available to the judge because no limit should be placed on this most imperative of quests.[23] Since the truth is the primary objective and such overwhelming control is placed in the judiciary, it makes sense that the inquisitorial system inexorably requires that magistrates be entirely neutral. Accordingly, there is an absence of concern for the prejudicial impact of 'out of court statements' such as hearsay on the fact-finder. The goal of the accusatorial system, on the other hand, is the resolution of conflict between parties through the principles of orality, immediacy, and concentration.[24]

3. The strengths and weaknesses

Each system has its strengths and weaknesses. To those raised in the adversarial tradition, that an examining magistrate passes along a dossier, which sets forth a detailed case for the defendant's guilt, to his judicial colleague at the trial court appears unethically close.[25] Coupled with the ideologies of efficiency, secrecy, and truth by all possible means, it is little wonder that "Americans tend to equate inquisitorial systems with coercive interrogation, unbridled search, and unduly efficient crime-control."[26] For in the accusatorial system, the adversarial approach in court preserves due process for the individual, where the final decision is not rendered by "faceless bureaucrats," but by a common sense consensus of the defendant's peers.[27] This is not to say that the accusatorial system is without its faults. It arms the defendant with rights that he may assert against the government at various stages of the proceeding, including rights against unreasonable searches, to silence, to counsel, and to confront witnesses against him.[28] However, it is cumbersome and inefficient compared to the inquisitorial system.[29] Furthermore, advocates, in their efforts to present a view of the case most favorable to their side, risk skewing the truth-finding process.[30]

4. Attitudes toward the State

Heavily influential in the two systems are fundamental assumptions and attitudes towards the state. In the inquisitorial system, "the state is the benevolent and most powerful protector and guarantor of public interest and can, moreover, be trusted to 'police' itself as long as its authority is organized in a way that will allow it to do so." In the accusatorial system, there is a "negative image of the state and a minimalist view of its functions."[31] ...

5. The due process revolution in Europe

The two approaches of criminal procedure that are the inquisitorial tradition and the accusatorial tradition are models or archetypes that are not entirely indicative of any specific country's system. This is becoming increasingly even more evident as the

---

23. *Id.*

24. *See,* Merryman, *supra* note 19, at 114.

25. Bradley, *supra* note 16, at xviii.

26. Abraham Goldstein, *Reflections on Two Models: Inquisitorial Themes in American Criminal Procedure,* 26 STANFORD LAW REVIEW 1009, 1018 (1974).

27. Bradley, *supra* note 16, at xviii.

28. *Id.*

29. *Id.* at xix.

30. *Id.*

31. Nico Jorg et al., *Are Inquisitorial and Adversarial Systems Converging?*, in CRIMINAL JUSTICE IN EUROPE: A COMPARATIVE STUDY (Phil Fennel et al, eds., 1995), at x.

two approaches are converging from different directions towards roughly equivalent mixed systems of criminal procedure.[32] Examples in the English and United States systems of movement toward the continental model are more in the form of proposal than fact.[33] However, throughout Europe, for differing reasons, civil law countries have made the transition to a more accusatorial and/or adversarial system. One such example is Italy, which through its Code of 1988, made drastic changes to part ways with its prior inquisitorial tradition. Having surveyed the differences between the model criminal justice systems of the common law tradition and the civil law tradition and extracted the underlying ideologies, it is important now to focus specifically on Italy's criminal procedure: namely its landmark 1988 code. The reasons for the code's implementation, and for the consequent struggles at adhering to its ideologies and operations, go a long way to explaining the attitudes in Italian criminal law and its uneasy balance as a 'mixed' system.

III. THE ITALIAN CRIMINAL JUSTICE SYSTEM

The modern Italian legal system has a procedural system that represents an intermediate solution between the inquisitorial style of proceeding and adversarial practices. The 1988 Italian Code burst onto the scene and quite dramatically altered the legal landscape, leading Italy tumbling down the adversarial path. In order to appreciate the importance of the change, a brief explanation of the historical background prior to the 1988 code is necessary.

A. History

Italy has in essence an inquisitorial system derived from Napoleon's Criminal Code of 1808, much like numerous civil law countries throughout the world.[34] Throughout Europe, the earlier more Draconian characteristics of the inquisitorial system had diminished by this time. Enlightenment movements had weakened the previous absolutist-inquisition process and its state abuse of power to the extent that some limited adversarial features had become necessary.[35] What emerged were modern principles of criminal procedure "permeated with state positivism, rationalism, and a concern for the rights of man as enunciated by the school of secular natural law."[36]

However, the inquisition system saw something of a revival in the 20th century. The Enlightenment movements did not cement the accusatorial system's position as the predominant model. On the contrary, the end of the 19th century saw an intellectual revolt or backlash against the supposed arbitrary nature of the adversarial due process that was beginning to creep in to civil law tradition.[37]

> Enrico Ferri, in his 1884 *Sociologia Criminale*, launched an uncompromised attack on adversarial methods, which he described as 'grotesque and often insincere contests between the prosecution and the defense to prevent or secure an acquittal.' Instead of these 'combats of craft, manipulations, declamations and

---

32. For a more detailed theory on this, *see* Merryman, *supra* note 19, 126 (suggesting the two systems lie at different places on an evolutionary line.)

33. Bradley, *supra* note 16, at xxi. In England, examples of such proposals are calls for the introduction of a pretrial truth-finder over worries about the partisan nature of policing and other proposals to include greater judicial involvement in indicating sentences and regulating deals. Jorg, *supra* note 31, at xxi. Such proposals might face more stubborn resistance in the United States.

34. Richard Vogler, A WORLD VIEW OF CRIMINAL JUSTICE 157 (2005).

35. *Id.* at 61.

36. Merryman, *supra* note 19, at 125.

37. Vogler, *supra* note 34, at 61.

legal devices, which make every criminal trial a game of chance ... a sort of spi-
der's web which catches flies and lets the wasps escape,' criminal procedure should
be a 'scientific enquiry' conducted by a judge familiar with biology, psychology
and psycho-pathology to determine which 'anthropological class' the defendant
belongs.[38]

This perspective on the criminal process proved highly seductive to the totalitarian
regimes that emerged in Europe in the early 20th century. Adversarial due process was seen
to present a direct threat. Thus, the level of control and paternalism of the traditional
inquisitorial system was implemented completely in the Italian fascist code of 1930.[39]

The Code of 1930 was a very traditional civil law inquisitorial system almost identical
to the archetypical inquisitorial model described previously in this essay. The investigating judge dominated the first phase and compiled the dossier while defense attorneys
played only a minor role in the investigation.[40] The second phase of the criminal process
under the 1930 Code was a public trial. Counsel was not allowed to cross-examine witnesses.[41] Instead, the parties could pose questions only through the judge who would formally conduct the direct and cross-examination.[42] The trial was merely a formal reception
of the evidence that had already been collected and deliberated upon in the instruction
phase.[43] Whereas investigations were conducted soon after the commission of a crime,
the trial took place considerably later. This led to the findings of the investigation naturally being given more weight than the facts presented at trial, thereby making the investigative dossier "the crucial factor in determining guilt."[44]

Even in the post-fascist republic, Italy maintained the 1930 Code of Criminal Procedure for many years. However, dissatisfaction with what was seen as a system of criminal justice that favored the State at the expense of its subjects led to calls for reform.[45]
This marked "a loss of confidence in the State as the protector of its subjects' rights, and
an acceptance that the subject sometimes needs protection against the State."[46] Finally,
after years of delay, in 1988, a new Code was born.

B. Reform: Code of 1988

Italy implemented a drastic new code of criminal procedure based largely on the Anglo-
American accusatorial system. The existing configuration of courts was almost untouched
by reforms, the purpose of the new code being to break the continuity of process in the
1930 Code.[47] The two main goals of the new code were to ensure that the prosecution
and defense were the main players in the criminal process and that the only evidence on
which a decision could be based was the evidence collected orally at trial.[48] The instruction was abolished entirely and replaced by a 'preliminary investigation.'[49] No longer was
there an examining magistrate; the pre-trial would be conducted under the surveillance
of a 'pre-trial judge' (*giudize per le indagini preliminari — 'gip'*) with almost no investiga-

---

38. *Id.*
39. *Id.* at 64.
40. Panzavolta, *supra* note 17, at 579.
41. C.P.P. art. 448 (1930).
42. *Id.* at 467.
43. Thomas Glyn Watkin 135 THE ITALIAN LEGAL TRADITION (1997).
44. Panzavolta, *supra* note 17, at 580.
45. Watkin, *supra* note 43, at 137.
46. *Id.*
47. Vogler, *supra* note 34, at 168.
48. Panzavolta, *supra* note 17, at 586.
49. Vogler, *supra* note 34, at 168.

tory role.[50] The objectives of the pre-trial were changed from 'obtaining the truth' to determining whether or not there is sufficient evidence for trial.[51] The essential accusatorial element of the demarcation between the investigation and trial phases was ensured by a 'double dossier' system (*doppio fascicolo*) in which the trial judge was never presented with the investigative dossier, but instead with a trial-dossier, to be filled only with evidence collected during trial.[52]

The reasons cited for the change to the accusatorial system vary. Some attribute it to political and ideological post-war American influence that sparked interest in the adversarial trial mode.[53] Others determine the general trend towards an adversarial process on the continent to the European Convention on Human Rights and its guarantee of certain trial rights typical of the common law style.[54] Whatever the case may be, advocates of the Code saw it as a revolutionary new system, accommodating "the competing tensions of the criminal process more consistently and more rationally than the American system upon which it was otherwise modeled."[55] This was clearly not the case as major problems undermined the procedures following their enactment.

C. Counter-Reform and Compromise

What ensued was an ideological tug-of-war, in which the very principles of the new accusatorial system were weakened one by one by Italy's Constitutional Court. Among the principles attacked were those that excluded hearsay and judge-introduced evidence.[56] The system was in very real danger of reverting back to a fully inquisitorial system. However, in efforts to curb the constitutional attacks on accusatorial process, the legislature amended the Constitution in 1999 (*Reforma de Giusto Processo*). In 2001, these reform provisions, emphasizing the equal rights of the parties to offer evidence before an impartial judge and other due process protections, were also imported directly into the Code of Criminal Procedure.[57] This proved successful in re-establishing the accusatorial system, but only to a certain degree. For the sake of pragmatism and efficiency, the inquisitorial process filtered through the system once more in areas such as petty crimes and the *guidizio abbreviato* or fast-track trial.[58] However, the most serious crimes, heard in the *Corte d'Assise*, still maintained an especially accusatorial disposition and do so to this day.

---

50. C.P.P. arts. 392–404.

51. Vogler, *supra* note 34, at 169.

52. Panzavolta *supra* note 17, at 587. There were some features of its traditional model that the 1988 Code did retain. No attempts to create a jury system were made. The sole exception is the "Corte d'Assise," a discussion of which will be very important once we look more closely at the Amanda Knox trial.

53. *See* Vogler, *supra* note 34, at 168.

54. Criminal Procedure: Comparative Aspects—Adjudication, http://law.jrank.org/pages/901/Criminal-Procedure-Comparative-Aspects-Adjudication.html. The most important of these was the defendant's right to present evidence in his defense and to confront witnesses against him (European Convention on the Protection of Human Rights and Basic Freedoms of Nov. 4, 1950, art. 6 sec. 3 lit. d).

55. L.J. Fassler, *The Italian Penal Procedure Code: An Adversarial System of Criminal Prosecution in Continental Europe*, 29(1) COLUMBIA JOURNAL OF TRANSNATIONAL LAW, pp. 244–78, 275 (1991).

56. Vogler, *supra* note 34, at 171.

57. *Id.*

58. The fast-track trial has been much criticized since a defendant who chooses this inquisitorial form of procedure, such as Rudy Guede did, will be guaranteed a one-third reduction in sentence. *See* Panzavolta, *supra* note 17, at 620.

D. Where the System Stands Today

What has resulted following the two or so decades of internal struggle within the Italian criminal justice system is a truly mixed system. This is where the system stands today, a hybrid system infused with both accusatorial and inquisitorial traits. The so-called 'shift to adversariality' in Italy was only half accomplished, leaving a criminal justice system compromised by competing ideologies and structures.[59] The relative breakdown of the purely accusatorial system in Italy has been attributed principally to cultural factors: "The magistrates not only kept thinking in terms of the old inquisitorial ideology, but they also strongly believed that such ideology was far better than the new one."[60] Such drastic change does not come easily, and the values of the inquisitorial tradition remain embedded in the Italian psyche.

Inquisitorial operations remain strong in many levels of Italian Criminal Procedure. But the remaining bastion of the adversarial and accusatorial system is still the *Corte d'Assise* in which Amanda Knox was tried. It is perhaps the most blatant example of the adversarial system in Italy. This article's trek through the history, foundation, struggles, and principles of Italian criminal procedure has led to this point, where armed with a comprehensive knowledge of what make the Italian criminal justice system tick, we may now examine the controversies raised in the American media of the Amanda Knox Trial. In some areas some myths will be dispelled, while in others American fears confirmed. While analyzing the controversies, this article shall make note to analyze whether underlying principles of inquisitorial thought might be behind some of the more peculiar actions and operations evident in the trial.

IV. CONTROVERSIES OF THE TRIAL AND CONCERNS OVER THE SYSTEM

There are two classes of criticisms or concerns to discuss in this section. First of all are some of the more lurid criticisms played out in the American media. I will address some of the concerns of Senator Cantwell and explain why these observations may be misguided. This will involve a quick look at the protections afforded by the Italian Constitution and the method of court proceedings.

Secondly, I will address some more fundamental concerns that, while not immediately observable, may exist under the surface and threaten to imbalance the Italian criminal legal system—namely, (i) whether inquisitorial operations have infiltrated the *Corte d'Assise* and threatened to tear down what remains of the accusatorial system and (ii) whether the inquisitorial psyche of Italians has lingered and proven disruptive to the adversarial style.

A. Addressing the Controversies in the Amanda Knox Trial

Quite frankly, many of the criticisms aired in the American media and echoed by Senator Cantwell are at best uninformed and at times ludicrous. But are there also some valid criticisms? There have been allegations, which might be creditable, of negligent handling of evidence by investigators. Furthermore, there were pending charges of misconduct in an unrelated case against Prosecutor Mignini, for which he was later found guilty. These are important issues, but it is beyond the scope of this article—and not central to its inquiry—to embark on an analysis of forensic evidence; and as peculiar and corrupt as it sounds having a prosecutor on indictment charges pursuing a high profile murder case, his offence had no relation to the Amanda Knox case. Accordingly, the main concerns I will address are related to the standards of the system (with special focus on the conviction), the protections for the accused, and the substantiation of due process through the trial stages.

---

59. Vogler, *supra* note 34, at 171–172.
60. Panzavolta, *supra* note 17, at 609.

1. The conviction

One of the principal accusations of injustice in the Amanda Knox trial was that the jury's verdict was not supported. To reiterate Senator Cantwell's words, "The prosecution did not present enough evidence for an impartial jury to conclude beyond a reasonable doubt that Ms. Knox was guilty."[61] This statement could be read many ways. It could either be questioning the impartiality of the jury or questioning the existence of the concept of reasonable doubt in the Italian criminal justice system or both.

(a) Reasonable doubt

At a recent forum in Rome, held by attorneys and professors and sponsored by The Italy-USA foundation in efforts to smooth over the friction created by the "Foxy Knoxy" case and to address misunderstandings, panelist Catherine Arcabascio, dean of the Nova Southeastern University Law Center, spoke of the unpredictability of trial outcomes; she went on to say, "[b]ut reasonable doubt is a standard of proof we use in both countries."[62] The standard of "proof beyond a reasonable doubt" (prova "al di là di ogni ragionevole dubbio") was introduced into the Italian Criminal Procedure Code in 2006, although prior to this, the Corte de Cassazione had used it in important decisions.[63] It is relatively recent as a formal addition, which could reinforce concerns that it is not applied correctly. It is an interesting issue, one that I shall simply raise rather than attempt to answer. To what degree the standard is a self-evident concept is a matter of debate. Perhaps there is some validity to this particular concern in regards to the Italian criminal legal system.

(b) Impartiality of the jury

To suggest that the members of the 'jury' (that is, the lay triers of fact) were not impartial is to say that they were biased or prejudiced in some regard. I will analyze two possible ways in which this could have arisen.

(i) The influence of the judges on the lay triers of fact

As noted earlier, the 'judicial panel' in the Corte d'Assise is composed of two professional judges, Giudici Togati, and six lay judges, Giudici Popolcari, selected from the people. This can be quite confusing to the Anglo-American lawyer, as it is a hybrid system — neither jury nor judge-only bench. In their deliberations, no distinction is drawn between the lay and professional judges as far as deciding issues of law and fact are concerned.[64] This uniquely 'civil law' body does not negate the adversarial process. It may, however, lead to concerns that the professional judges unduly influence the lay judges. It is important to remember, though, that the use of such lay triers of fact is a "well established institution in the criminal proceedings of civil law jurisdictions."[65] It is not a hurried implant from the common law system. Instead, it has inherent stability as a rooted entity with benefits such as permitting professional judges to assist lay judges in making informed decisions and analyzing evidence. Furthermore, this method is more compatible with the civil law philosophy of truth-finding as opposed to the common law jury instruction method.

---

61. *Cantwell Statement on Amanda Knox Guilty Verdict*, Dec. 4, 2009, http://cantwell.senate.gov/news/record.cfm?id=320475.

62. Andrea Vogt, *In Rome, a Discussion of Amanda Knox Tries to Improve U.S.-Italian Relations*, SeattlePI.com, March 18, 2010, http://www.seattlepi.com/local/416999_knox18.html.

63. Federico Picinali, *"Is "Proof Beyond a Reasonable Doubt" a Self-Evident Concept? Considering the US and the Italian Legal Cultures towards the Understanding of the Standard of Persuasion in Criminal Cases,"* Global Jurist: Vol. 9 : Iss. 4 (Topics), Article 5. (2009).

64. Watkin, *supra* note 43, at 129.

65. Merryman, *supra* note 19, at 131.

(ii) The influence of the media on the non-sequestered 'jurors'

This is perhaps the most frequent criticism played out in the American media. As noted earlier, the heavy media attention devoted to this trial, including the character assassination of Amanda Knox, make the influence of the media in the courtroom a very real concern. However, the fact is that sequestering jurors is highly impractical and costly.[66] It is also becoming less and less common in the United States.[67] Moreover, we can discern two possible safeguards against media influence in the Italian criminal legal system. The first is the aforementioned guidance from the professional judges to make informed decisions. The second is the required motivation report that must be published by the court following the conviction and that presents the exact finding on which the case was decided; this creates a further layer against partiality.

2. Protections for the accused

Controversy swirled around whether Amanda Knox had adequate protection during the police interrogation phase. During initial questioning, Knox was without an attorney. She claimed that she was coerced into implicating her boss, for whom she worked as a waitress at his nightclub, as the murderer.[68]

However, her interrogation falls into a gray area of the law because Knox had in fact voluntarily come to the police station and was being interviewed as a witness. Police have authority to obtain information relating to a crime from any individual who may have information useful to the investigation.[69] If during the course of this exchange the persons reveal incriminating evidence, the police are required to interrupt the individual and warn her that investigations may begin against her, and that she has the right to a defense attorney.[70] Amanda Knox was apparently afforded these safeguards as guaranteed by the Italian criminal justice system. Italy's Supreme Court ruled that some of her early statements were not to be used against her because they were made without an attorney.[71] Of course, we know not exactly what went on in the interrogation room. However, there is no doubt that she had individual rights that protected her from grossly unjust interrogation of a coercive nature, and all evidence points out that these were reasonably respected.

3. Due process and the trial stages

During the two years of the case, there were multiple stages of procedure. This would seem to reflect adequate fair process at least procedurally (as opposed to a precipitous rush to judgment). Amid accusations of corruption, prosecutor Mignini said: "At the various levels in this case, from the preliminary investigating judge to the trial itself, the evidence was scrutinized by no less than 19 judges."[72] This disclosure ought to at least dampen allegations that Knox was found guilt on little or no forensic evidence. However, it does go to show how incredibly complicated and laborious the trial stages have become in Italy's mixed system.

---

66. *See* Brendan I. Koerner, *When do Judges Sequester Juries*, SLATE, Nov 14, 2003, *available at http://perugiamurderfile.org/viewtopic.php?f=10&t=194&start=0.*

67. *Id.*

68. He was released because of his airtight alibi: that many had seen him at work all night.

69. C.C.P. art 351.

70. C.C.P. art 62.

71. Andrea Vogt, *Computer and crucifix: Amanda Knox's guilt will be judged in a system that is a mix of old and new*, SeattlePI.com, Dec. 3rd, 2009, http://www.seattlepi.com/local/412696_knox30.html.

72. Nick Squires, *Amanda Knox conviction: Italy strikes back at US complaints*, CSMonitor.com, Dec. 7th, 2009, http://www.csmonitor.com/World/Europe/2009/1207/p06s22-woeu.html.

There is an aspect to Italian Criminal Procedure that in fact affords more protection to the individual accused of crime than would seem available in the US system. This is the appeals process. The appeals court will review the case de novo in questions of both law and fact.[73] Furthermore, an individual may follow with one more opportunity of appeal. Article 111 of the Constitution states "recourse shall always be allowed to the Court of Cassation on the ground of any violation of any law, against judgments as well as sentences affecting personal liberty, whether pronounced by courts of ordinary or special jurisdiction." Hence the appeals process in Italy presents an extraordinary chance for an innocent Amanda Knox to reverse her conviction. An alternative view might be that it affords too much protection, thereby creating a great deal of inefficiency.

Regardless of what side of the fence one sits on, there is little to conclude that Amanda Knox did not receive due process. Her individual rights were adequately protected by the rules secured in the Italian Constitution and Code of 1988. In particular, the pre-trial stages seemed to be conducted fairly and with great scrutiny of the evidence. On the surface and in practice, all seems to have been conducted fairly.

Still, might a "subterranean analysis", looking at the underpinnings of the Italian criminal procedure, reveal ideological conflicts that undercut due process? Let us turn to that now.

B. Are Tensions of the Mixed System Evident in the Knox Trial?

1. Does the inquisitorial process infiltrate and jeopardize accusatorial principles?

The answer to this question is unclear. Although the double dossier system is very much in place, a remnant of the inquisitorial tradition still holds firm, and it threatens the very principles of the accusatorial system. While presentation of evidence is mostly in the hands of the parties, the presiding judge may intervene, even *sua sponte*, to ensure that questions are relevant, that the responses are genuine, and that the examination is conducted in a manner that is respectful of the individual.[74] As explained earlier, this is perhaps more indicative of threatening the principle of adversariality, but it is not a far cry from the judge introducing his or her own evidence, a belief still revered in an traditional inquisitorial sense.

Yet the conduct of the Amanda Knox trial does not seem to suggest a blatant disregard for the accusatorial principle of excluding 'hearsay'. This is certainly not raised as a point of controversy in the media, so the presumption is that the double-dossier system is very much intact. The real threat to the accusatorial system seems to be the efficiency and pragmatism of the inquisitorial system, which might be threatening to swallow up its ill-favored and cumbersome cohabiting judicial scheme.

2. Does the inquisitorial mindset conflict with the adversarial style?

(a) Deference by the professional judges to the prosecutor

One large point played out in the media was how relentless, vindictive, and powerful the prosecutor came across in his pursuit of the case. The prosecutor was traditionally, and still may consider himself, a magistrate or member of the judiciary.[75] Formerly, the prosecutor was an auxiliary to the judge, but since the Code of 1988, he has been relegated to the position as an advocate on one side of a conflict between parties. Whether

---

73. [See the discussion of this point in subsection IIA2 of Chapter Three, as well as in Appendix 3.2.]

74. Bradley, *supra* note 16, at 344. C.P.P. art 499 (secs. 4, 6).

75. C.P.P. art 107, Bradley, *supra* note 16, at 305.

deference is given by the professional judge to the prosecutor, as a member of the judiciary, may be a possibility, but hardly an idea we can confirm; it would most certainly not be published in the motivation report.

Before the reforms, the prosecutor was heavily involved in the truth-finding exercise. In an adversarial process, by contrast, he is to be seen as devoting his energies to only one side of the story. Perhaps we should question whether, in a culture such as Italy—steeped as it is in the inquisitorial system—today's prosecutors could have in fact made that shift in role. We can only speculate. On the other hand, it would seem more likely that the overriding aim of obtaining the truth—as embedded as it is in the Italian legal psyche—would compel the judges to undertake a a focused and careful examination of evidence, rather than deferring to the prosecution in presenting his side of the story. This view is indeed supported by the Motivation report dismissing some of the more lurid claims made by Prosecutor Mignini. Additionally, since 2006, the prosecutor is no longer a traditional magistrate and is under the supervision of the *Procura della Repubblica*.[76] Whether this makes an impact is not clear, but it does highlight that in Italy there is a recognition that the close relationship between prosecutor and judge may create a potential conflict of interest.

(b) *Deference by the lay judges to the prosecutor*

Perhaps more worrying is that lay judges (as opposed to the professional judges) might show undue deference to the prosecutor. Although the public prosecutor has primary control over the investigations, and the Code has made the public prosecutor a "party" at trial, the Italian public prosecutor has a duty to investigate facts and circumstances that exculpate or otherwise favor the defendant.[77] Again, there may be an issue where the prosecutor is supposed to be both zealous advocate and truth finder. In the Amanda Knox trial, Prosecutor Mignini does not appear to manifest this noble, truth-finding role, and most certainly does not seem to have pursued various exculpatory circumstances nearly as vigorously as he did the more incriminating ones.

V. CONCLUSION

It is simply unfair to criticize the conduct of the Amanda Knox trial from an uninformed perspective—that is, without understanding the larger setting into which the trial fits. Furthermore, although there are tensions within the Italian criminal process system following its partial adoption of an adversarial regime, they are not so evident in the Amanda Knox trial as to warrant the conclusion that she was denied her right to a fair process. Many of the American criticisms, such as the alleged media influence, underhandedness, and impartiality of the 'jurors,' are the indirect result of a democratic, open, oral and adversarial system.

Other criticisms, however, revolve around whether Italy remains unduly faithful to the underlying values of the inquisitorial system despite its recent adoption of a more adversarial system. The difficulty of making a dramatic transition of this sort is bound to create gaps and inconsistencies in practice, even though they might remain largely invisible.

Hence, although some inconsistencies do remain, and Italy may so far have only half-accomplished its structural and ideological alteration, it seems beyond reasonable question that the Italian criminal justice system—on display so publicly in the "Foxy Knoxy" trial—does in fact (i) provide not only adequate due process, but in some regards also (ii) affords more protection to the individual than would be true in the courts of the coun-

---

76. Bradley, *supra* note 16, at 346. There is no equivalent judicial authority in the United States.
77. Bradley, *supra* note 16, at 305.

try where some of the trial's principal critics come from. Some of those critics will no doubt continue to assert that the convicted Amanda Knox is innocent. If that is true, it would seem that she fell victim not to a foreign and corrupt legal system, but rather to a purely unfortunate set of circumstances that could also have easily arisen in the United States.

Appendix 3.4
Criminal Procedure in Italian Law
(by Gabriella Di Paolo, University of Trento)

[*Note: This summary is drawn from an April 2009 lecture presented by Gabriella Di Paolo at the University of Trento, as reformatted by me and with suggestions from Mr. Enrico Greghi. All errors are of course attributable to me.*]

1.   The following account offers a very brief description of the Italian criminal justice system, focusing especially on the procedural law (as opposed to substantive penal law, which is based in the Italian Penal Code).

2.   The account gives special attention to the issues of judicial organization, the relationship between judicial and other state powers, and the specific relations between judges and prosecutors—on grounds that these organizational details have a significant impact on how the rules of criminal procedure are actually applied in practice. The account also examines the structure and fundamental principles of an ordinary criminal proceeding, as well as certain special procedures that have been introduced to increase the efficiency of the system (for example, by combating its perennial backlog of cases). In concentrating on the criminal procedures, the account also highlights a matter of special interest in a comparative study, inasmuch as Italy reshaped its criminal procedure starting in 1988 by importing and transplanting some features of the Anglo-American "adversarial" system

Organization of the Judiciary System

3.   The principal legal "personnel" involved in the operation of the criminal justice system in Italy are (i) police, (ii) prosecutors (that is, *magistrati* having investigative powers and responsible for criminal prosecution), and (iii) judges (that is, *magistrati* having adjudicating powers). Let us examine each of these in terms of their structure and functions, including their independence.

Judicial Police

4.   The key functions of the police are:

- to prevent the commission of criminal offenses (the crime prevention function);
- to help ensure public order and safety (the peace keeping function); and
- to conduct investigations after the commission of a criminal offense (the criminal justice function)

5.   Structurally, the police may be regarded as operating under a "double head". On the one hand, the police corps is part of the executive department of government, subject to supervision from the Ministry of Interior and the Ministry of Defense. On the other hand, the police corps is dependent on the judiciary branch—the *Magistratura*—in carrying out its criminal justice functions.[1]

The Magistratura and Its Independence

6.   As set forth in articles 101–103 of the Constitution of the Republic of Italy (hereinafter the Constitution), the *Magistratura* comprises both judges (*giudici*) and prosecu-

---

1. See Constitution of the Republic of Italy (hereinafter Constitution), art. 109: "*L'autorità giudiziaria dispone direttamente della polizia giudiziaria*" (translated as "[t]he judiciary directly commands the judicial police", or "[t]he judiciary may use the police").

tors (*pubblici ministeri*). Expressed differently, both judges and prosecutors are *magistrati*.[2] In practice, what this means is as follows:

- Judges and prosecutors belong to the same professional group;

- Within this group, there is no career separation between judges and prosecutors (that is, they are differentiated only in terms of their functions);

- Within this group, individuals may move from one position to another (e.g., judge to prosecutor) without substantial limitations;

- Both judges and prosecutors are appointed to the *Magistratura* after a national competition;

- Both have a bureaucratic career, in the sense that promotions are based predominantly on seniority;

- Both receive the same treatment in terms of salary and other economic aspects of their appointments; and

- Both are subject to the authority and supervision of the *Consiglio superiore della magistratura* ("CSM"), the self-governing body of the judiciary.

7.   Members of the *Magistratura* (that is, judges and prosecutors) are subject to specific types of independence. The first is "external independence"; the second is "internal independence". These types of independence, which apply somewhat more fully to judges than to prosecutors, may be described as follows—as drawn from specific provisions in the Constitution.

- External independence (freedom from undue external influence, especially from the executive branch of government):

  - Article 104 (excerpt): *La magistratura costituisce un ordine autonomo e indipendente da ogni altro potere.* ("The judiciary is an order that is autonomous and independent of all other powers….")

  - Article 105: *Spettano al Consiglio superiore della magistratura, secondo le norme dell'ordinamento giudiziario, le assunzioni, le assegnazioni ed i trasferimenti, le promozioni e i provvedimenti disciplinari nei riguardi dei magistrati.* ("The High Council of the Judiciary, in accordance with the regulations of the judiciary, has jurisdiction for employment, assignments and transfers, promotions, and disciplinary measures of judges".

  - Article 112: *Il pubblico ministero ha l'obbligo di esercitare l'azione penale.* ("The prosecutor has the duty to initiate criminal proceedings"). Hence, criminal prosecution is compulsory, which would tend to insulate the prosecutor from external pressure as to whether to prosecute or withhold prosecution.

- Internal independence (to avoid a hierarchical structure that would impinge on the decisional integrity of the members of the *magistratura*):

  - Article 101: *La giustizia è amministrata in nome del popolo.* ("Justice is administered in the name of the people"); and

---

2. There is some debate under way now in Italy as to whether this structure should be retained or changed to be more in line with the moves (described below) toward an Anglo-American adversarial system.

I giudici sono soggetti soltanto alla legge. ("Judges are subject only to the law")

– Article 107: *I magistrati sono inamovibili. Non possono essere dispensati o sospesi dal servizio né destinati ad altre sedi o funzioni se non in seguito a decisione del Consiglio superiore della magistratura, adottata o per i motivi e con le garanzie di difesa stabilite dall'ordinamento giudiziario o con il loro consenso.* ("Judges may not be removed from office. Neither may they be dismissed or removed from office nor assigned to other courts or functions unless following a decision of the High Council of the Judiciary taken either for the motives and with the guarantees of defense established by the rules of the judiciary or with their consent"); and

Il Ministro della giustizia ha facoltà di promuovere l'azione disciplinare. ("The Minister of Justice has power to originate disciplinary action"); and

I magistrati si distinguono fra loro soltanto per diversità di funzioni. ("Judges are distinguished only by their different functions"); and

Il pubblico ministero gode delle garanzie stabilite nei suoi riguardi dalle norme sull'ordinamento giudiziario. ("The state prosecutor enjoys the guarantees established in his favor by the rules of the judiciary").

The Organization of Courts and Prosecutorial Offices

8.   The court system applicable to criminal justice in Italy consists of three levels: courts of first instance, courts of the second instance, and the Supreme Court of Cassazione. For each of these levels, there is a corresponding office of prosecutors (procurators). (The *Procuratore della Repubblica* is the prosecutor (*Publico Ministero*) who is in charge of the Procura—that is, the offices responsible for attending to the interests of the state and the collectivity; then there are the prosecutors (PM) who are the *magistrati* in charge of the criminal action.) The following chart details the three levels.

Courts	Prosecutorial Offices
first instance	
• Tribunal (single judge or a 3-judge panel) • Corte d'Assise (2 judges + 6 lay jurors)* • *Giudice di Pace* (justice of the peace— honorary magistrate)**	• *Procura della Repubblica*, attached to the Tribunal
second instance	
• Court of Appeal • *Corte di Assise* of Appeal***	• *Procura Generale*, attached to the Court of Appeal
review of legality (*giudizio di legittimità*)	
• Supreme Court of Cassazione	• *Procura Generale* attached to the Supreme Court of Cassazione

   * This is for crimes punishable for life imprisonment or imprisonment for more than 24 years.

   ** This is for non-serious crimes. The *giudice di pace* (justice of the peace) position was introduced only in 2001. A *giudice di pace* must have a law degree but, unlike a professional magistrate, need not have gone through the examination and training of a magistrate.

   *** This is for more serious crimes, and it includes lay triers of fact.

9.   It is worth understanding the lines of authority within the prosecutorial offices. Within a particular office of the *Procura della Repubblica*, the chief of the office gives the orders. The Ministry of Justice does not have control over the individual prosecutorial

officers. Recall that Article 112 of the Constitution (cited and quoted above) establishes that in any case of criminal activity, prosecution is compulsory. As a practical matter, however, this creates a problem of resources: some discretion needs to be exercised in order to determine which crimes need to prosecuted most urgently and most aggressively. Hence, there is often at least "technical" discretion, even if not "political" discretion at work.[3]

Private Subjects of the Criminal Proceeding

10. Although our attention has focused so far on the officials of the state who are responsible for the conducting of criminal investigations, prosecutions, and adjudications, it is important to bear in mind the other persons related in some way to criminal proceedings. They are listed below, but without further elaboration:

  * the defendant or accused party—as well as *indagato* (person under investigation);

  * the injured party (*persona offesa*)—the civil party;[4]

  * the party who has civil responsibility for the accused's action (for example, if the accused is a minor or a person who has been deemed unable to take care of its rights, as in the case of mental impairment);

  * the party who is obligated to pay any fine imposed upon the defendant's conviction of the crime (as in the circumstances covered by Articles 196 and 197 of the Criminal Procedure Code, where a fine relating to a crime is imposed on the accused but he or she is incapable of paying for it and instead the fine is paid by the natural person or legal person who was in charge of the accused's actions); and

  * for each party, legal counsel (advocate)—the assistance of counsel is mandatory, so that the defendant cannot waive the right to counsel. (Indeed, the assistance of counsel is compulsory for any party who seeks legal remedy.)

The 1988 Changes in Criminal Procedure

[**Note:** *This topic is addressed in more detail in Appendix 3.3; only an overview is provided here.*]

11. Beginning in 1988, Italy embarked on an exercise of legal "transplantation" by adopting a new set of rules for criminal proceedings, shifting from an inquisitorial system to a more "adversarial" system modeled in part on Anglo-American practice. The inquisitorial system, based originally on the French-inspired *Code d'Instruction Criminelle de 1808*, had been carried forward in laws of 1860 and 1913, and had more recently been set forth in the Italian Code of Criminal Procedure of 1930. It featured the use of a *giudice istruttore*—an "investigating judge"—whose role was to investigate the circumstances of the alleged crime and present the findings in the form of a dossier (record) that was introduced into evidence at trial. This amounted to an aggregation of prosecutorial functions and adjudicating functions, and it resulted in a system that did not allow much real input (or opportunity for defense) by the accused.

12. In order to overcome the perceived defects of that system, the sweeping changes of 1988 were introduced. The main pillars of that new system were as follows:

  * a separation of functions between prosecutors and courts;

---

3. It is noteworthy that the content of Article 112, designed to prevent political discretion, appears in statutory law that even predates the 1948 Constitution.

4. The victim can decide whether or not to bring a civil action against the defendant into the criminal proceeding, depending on whether it seems advantageous to the victim in terms of getting his or her civil claim handled quickly. (Sometimes it might not be, since in criminal proceedings more rights are given to the defendant.)

- a separation between pre-trial and trial phases, and hence the use of a "double file" system (in which the results of the investigation were not automatically entered into evidence at trial);

- other innovations in the law and procedure relating to evidence, including:

  - partisan presentation of evidence

  - certain exclusionary rules

  - cross examination conducted by the parties;[5]

- special proceedings, including plea bargaining and summary trial.

13. The reforms of 1988 faced strong resistance and opposition, including especially from some members of the judiciary. Indeed, the Constitutional Court issued rulings interfering with the implementation of those reforms. Ultimately, however, steps were taken to restore the content of those reforms. The steps included amending the Constitution. This step, taken in 1999, gave constitutional status to the following rights and guarantees (among others):

- right to an impartial and independent judge;

- right to defense (including right to self-defense, right to counsel, right to remain silent, right to have adequate time to prepare defense, etc.);

- right to the presumption of innocence;

- right to have a written opinion and to a review of the judge's decision;

- guarantee that guilt shall not be established on the basis of statements made by anyone who has freely chosen not to submit to questioning by the defendant or the defendant's counsel (subject to certain exceptions); and

- guarantee that all parties may speak in their own defense in the presence of the other parties during the taking of evidence (also subject to certain exceptions).

The Structure of an Ordinary Criminal Proceeding

Overview

14. In its simplest form, the ordinary criminal proceeding can be seen as having five possible elements (depending on whether it is appealed and whether it is sent to the Supreme Court of Cassazione for review). Those elements are:

- preliminary investigations—conducted or directed by the prosecutor, with help of the police, under control of the judge of preliminary investigations (*giudice d'indagine preliminare*) or "GIP";

- preliminary hearing—to ensure that the judge (*giudice d'udienza preliminare*), or "GUP", can prevent the prosecutor from bringing any rash charges against the accused;

- trial (first instance)—the collection of evidence, discussion of the case, and decision by the judge;

- appeal (second instance)—a full review of the case in fact and in law; and

---

5. Specifically, as explained below, this right of cross-examination by the parties (or counsel) replaces a system in which the judge simply asked for confirmation from the witness of the information included in the dossier prepared by the investigating judge.

- judgment of the Supreme Court of Cassazione — not a full review but only a review of alleged errors of law (in applying either substantive or procedural rules).

Pretrial Phase

15. The first two elements listed above — preliminary investigations and preliminary hearing — can be regarded as constituting the pre-trial phase. The preliminary investigations typically will have these features:

- the notice of a criminal offense;

- the recording of that notice in the crime register;

- duration of investigation not to exceed six months (with extensions possible);

- separation of functions between —

  - the public prosecutor, who fulfills investigative functions, and

  - the judge of preliminary investigations, whose main role is to guarantee the fundamental rights of the suspect;[6] and

- prosecutor's determination at the end of the investigations — either for:

  - request (to the GIP) for dismissal of the case (*archiviazione*), usually because of a lack of evidence; or

  - formal charge — by sending the case to a preliminary hearing (see below) in order to request the GUP that the case be referred to trial (*richiesta rinvio a giudizio*).

16. The preliminary hearing, in turn, typically has the following functions and possible outcomes:

- selects the cases to be sent to trial;

- allows the defendant to adduce exculpatory evidence in order to avoid the trial;

- allows for one of the possible alternative procedures to occur — that is, either a summary trial or a "sentencing by parties' request"); and

- can result in one of these:

  - sending the case to trial (by decree of the GUP), thus granting the request of the prosecutor;

  - dismissal of the case for lack of evidence; or

  - gathering of additional evidence.

17. As a result of the changes initiated in 1988 (see above), the acts performed during the preliminary investigations will, if the case is sent to trial, be recorded in two separate files: one file, a very thin one with only the bare facts (mainly the charges and any specially-se-

---

6. These would include the rights against improper wire-tapping, for example, or improper pre-trial detention. Rules regarding the latter (pre-trial detention) are meant to reflect the standards set forth in the European Convention on Human Rights and Fundamental Freedoms and the International Covenant on Civil and Political Rights. Among other safeguards, the rules require that pre-trial detention (and some other forms of pre-trial coercive measures) be authorized by a judge, be based on reasonable cause, and be applied only in the case of serious crimes.

cured evidence, if any), is forwarded to the trial judge; the other file (with comprehensive records) remains available only to the parties. This is the so-called "double file" system.

The Trial

18. The key features of the trial, under the system that was introduced beginning in 1988, are as follows:

- It involves extensive discovery by the parties in order to avoid the possibility of surprise evidence;
- In opening statements, the parties make their requests to the judge for the admission of evidence; and the judge decides on those requests;
- Presentation of evidence is handled primarily by the parties, and includes opportunities for cross-examination;
- Closing arguments are offered by the counsel for the parties;
- The court reaches a decision on both culpability (guilt) and punishment (sentence)—and a written opinion is mandatory.

Special Procedures

To Expedite the Case

19. In some circumstances, in order to expedite the handling of cases, it is possible for the preliminary hearing to be omitted from the process described above. In particular, the following special procedures can be used if circumstances warrant them:

- *giudizio direttissimo* (directed judgment)—in the case of a confession or an arrest;[7] and
- *giudizio immediato* (immediate judgment)—in the case of especially strong evidence. (Such an immediate judgment can be requested within 90 days from the notification of the crime to the GIP by either the prosecutor or the accused person; the main goal is to avoid the preliminary hearing, as clarified in Article 453 of the Criminal Procedure Code.)

To Avoid the Trial

20. In another set of circumstances, special procedures can be used in order to avoid the trial altogether. If one of these special procedures is used, the case is closed in the pretrial phase:

- *giudizio abbreviato* (abbreviated judgment)—in this procedure, which is available for all crimes, the decision of the case is made at the stage of the preliminary hearing—with the incentive that the penalty is reduced in amount by one-third.
- *patteggiamento* (sentencing by parties' request)—in this procedure, an agreement is reached between the prosecutor and the defendant regarding the sentence to be imposed, again with the incentive that the standard penalty for the crime is reduced in amount by one-third. Although this might seem to resemble the "plea bargaining" process in US practice, there is in fact no bargaining occurring: the *patteggiamento* is a request made by the accused to the prosecutor, allowed by the judge, and can be subordinated to the request of

---

7. Technically, an "arrest" is a measure adopted by police if a person is caught while in the process of committing a crime.

conditional suspension of the penalty (*sospensione condizionale della pena*). There are some limits to the application of the *patteggiamento*, though. Its main goal is to speed up the resolution of the case, giving the accused a penalty upon confession. It has been said that the *patteggiamento* does not have the formal value of a sentence, while still having the same effect regarding the imposition of the penalty.

- *Procedimento per decreto penale* (proceeding by penal decree) — in the case of minor offence, with only a fine punishment, this procedure is followed at the pre-trial stage, under the auspices of the GIP. This preceeding is governed by Articles 459–460 of the Criminal Procedure Code.

21. For a schematic representation of the flow of a criminal proceeding, beginning with the notice of the crime and proceeding through the trial (first instance), see the following diagram.

Flow of a Criminal Proceeding (from notice through trial) in Italy

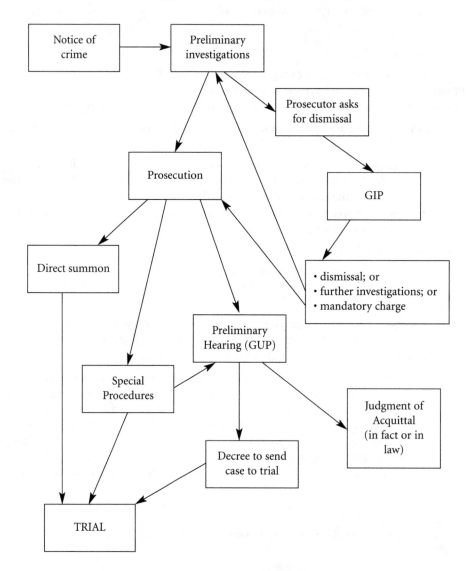

Appendix 3.5
Map of the World in 1800 (showing colonial claims)*

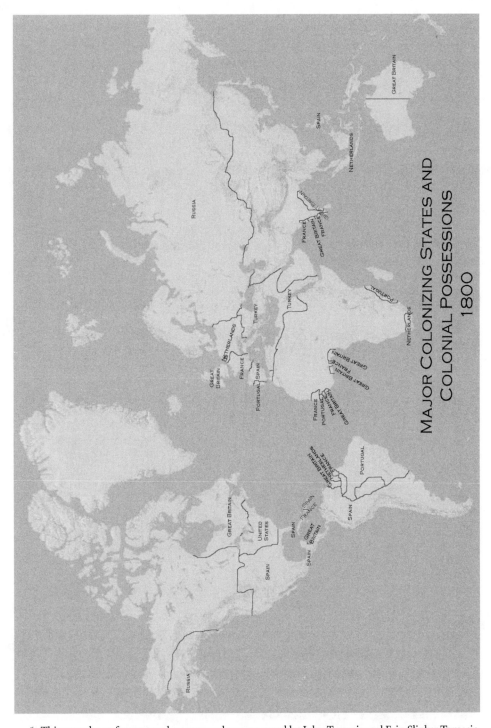

* This map draws from several sources and was prepared by John Tomasic and Erin Slinker Tomasic.

Appendix 3.6
Map of the World in 1910 (showing colonial claims)*

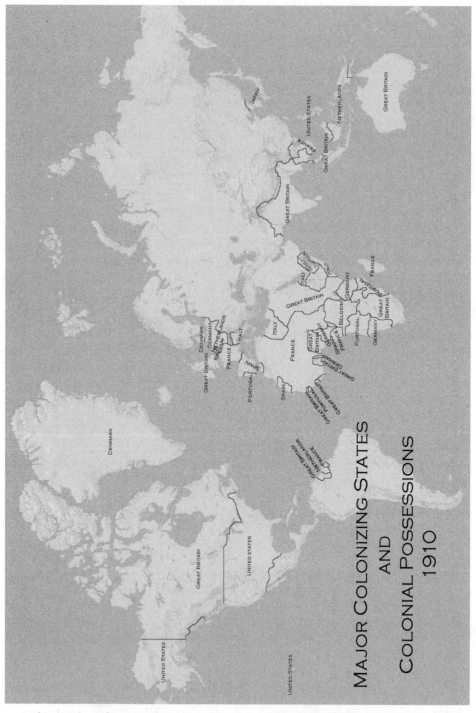

* This map draws from several sources and was prepared by John Tomasic and Erin Slinker Tomasic.

Appendix 3.7

Map of Africa in 1914 (showing European claims)*

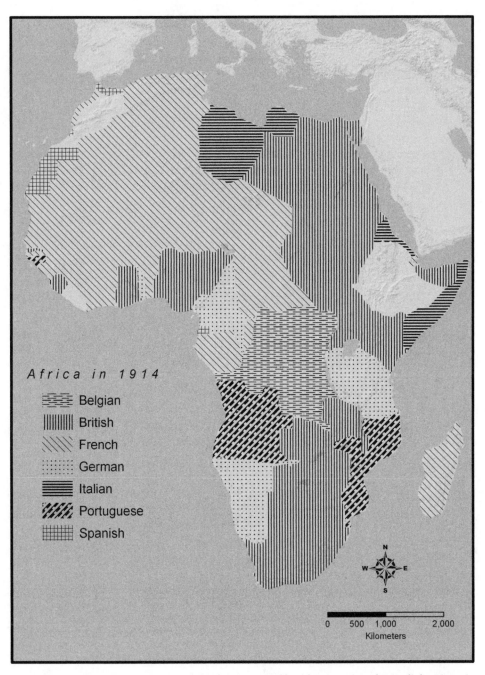

* This map draws from several sources and was prepared by John Tomasic and Erin Slinker Tomasic.

Chapter Four

The Common Law Tradition in Historical Perspective

Outline

Study Questions

SQ #4.1   When did the Roman occupation of Britain take place, and what lasting legal influence did the Roman occupation leave on the country?

SQ #4.2   When did the Anglo-Saxons come to Britain?

SQ #4.3   What law was there in England in the Anglo-Saxon period? ... what courts?

SQ #4.4   How might the history of English law been different if the Anglo-Saxon period had lasted another two hundred years?

SQ #4.5   Why did William of Normandy attack Harold at the Battle of Hastings, and why did William win?

SQ #4.6   What immediate difference did the Battle of Hastings make in the law applied in England?

SQ #4.7   Why does it makes sense to say that after the Norman "invasion", "[i]t was rather as though an army were encamped in England"?

SQ #4.8   What were the aims and significance of the Domesday Book?

SQ #4.9   Did the term "common law" mean the law of the common people within the various feudal domains that lords and barons controlled in England following the Norman "invasion"?

SQ #4.10 How did the royal courts develop?

SQ #4.11 What were the views of the barons and other local authorities regarding the general expansion in jurisdiction of the royal courts, and what action did they take in response?

SQ #4.12 What was the significance of "writs" to the development of the common law?

SQ #4.13   Why is any of this (historical background) to the growth of the common law interesting?

SQ #4.14   As a historical matter, why is the public/private distinction, which is so important in the civil law tradition, largely absent from the common law tradition?

SQ #4.15   Why did courts of equity arise in England?

SQ #4.16   What kind of law did the Chancellor apply in the early days of the rise of equity in England?

SQ #4.17   What does it mean to say that "English law ... narrowly escaped joining the European continental legal family in the sixteenth century"?

SQ #4.18   What was the compromise reached in 1616 involving Chancery and the Common Law courts?

SQ #4.19   What was the relationship between courts of equity and courts of law in the 18th century?

SQ #4.20   What role did jurists play in the development of English law, and in what sense might it be that they also helped English law "escape" joining the European continental legal family?

SQ #4.21   How does the term "jurist" in this context—that is, in the development of English common law—carry a different shade of meaning from the term "jurist" in the classical period of Roman law? ... or from the term "legal scholar" in later periods of the development of the civil law tradition?

SQ #4.22   What two main rounds of legal reforms were undertaken in 19th-century England?

SQ #4.23   What did René David point to as a "serious crisis" facing the common law?

SQ #4.24   What did René David mean in referring to a possible "*rapprochement ...* between English and continental laws"?

SQ #4.25   According to the Lord Chancellor (introducing the *Migration of the Common Law* radio series discussed in subsection VA, below), why did the common law survive after being transplanted to various other places outside England?

SQ #4.26   What other reasons might there be for the fact that the common law has survived migration (transplantation)?

SQ #4.27   Why, according to Goodhart (also in discussing the migration of the common law, in subsection VA, below), has the civil law, not the common law, been chosen whenever there has really been a choice?

SQ #4.28   Was it a foregone conclusion that the law of North America, including what became the USA, would be based on the common law?

SQ #4.29   What means were used, in the course of the reception of the common law into North America, to overcome

    (a)   the inconvenience of not having a code, as could be provided by the civil law?

    (b)   the "England-specificity" of the common law—that is, the historical idiosyncrasies appearing in the common law?

SQ #4.30   Of what significance to the development of the American legal system was Kent's *Commentaries on American Law*?

SQ #4.31   What efforts at legal codification or compilation were made in the American
colonies and just after American independence?

SQ #4.32   Did those efforts succeed or fail?

Introductory Comments

The history of English law can be divided conveniently into these four phases—the second and third of which bear directly on the common law tradition that England shares with numerous other countries around the world:

before 1066	–	Roman and Anglo-Saxon periods
1066–1400s	–	Growth & Stabilization of the Common Law
1400s–1800s	–	Growth & Stabilization of Equity
1800s to present	–	Modern Period

Here is how one authority briefly summarizes those four periods in the development of English law:

> There are four principal periods in the history of English law. The first is that before the Norman Conquest in 1066; the second, stretching from 1066 to the accession of the Tudors (1485), is that of the formation of the Common law, the period during which this new legal system was developed at the expense of local custom. The third period, running from 1485 to 1832, is that during which a complementary, and occasionally rival, system in the form of "rules of equity" developed alongside the Common law. The fourth period, beginning in 1832 and continuing up to the present time, is the modern period in which the Common law faces an unprecedented development in legislation and has to adapt itself to a society directed more and more by the intervention of governmental and administrative authorities.[1]

Box #4.1 provides a more detailed list of key dates and developments in English legal history. Several of the developments enumerated there will appear in the account that follows. (Key dates and developments in the growth of American law out of English common law will be identified in subsection VB, below).

Box #4.1 Key Dates and Developments in English Legal History

about 50 BCE	Romans arrive in Britain
43 CE	Romans establish full control over the southern part of Britain
410	Roman legions leave Britain
420	Anglo-Saxons arrive in Britain
600 (approx.)	laws of King Æthelbert of Kent
890 (approx.)	laws of King Alfred the Great

---

1. René David & John E.C. Brierly, Major Legal Systems in the World Today 309–310 (3d ed. 1985). As explained above in note 12 of Chapter One, the first edition of David's text (in collaboration with Brierly as translator and editor) was published in 1968, based on David's 1966 book Grands Systèmes de Droit Contemporains.

1016	Canute becomes king of England
1066 (January)	Edward the Confessor dies and Harold Godwinson assumes English crown
1066 (October)	William of Normandy defeats Harold at the Battle of Hastings
1066 (Christmas)	William crowned king of England
1085/6	Domesday Book prepared and issued
1150 (approx.)	Vacarius begins teaching Roman civil law at Oxford
1215	Magna Carta signed by King John at Runnymede
1250s	Bracton writes *On the Laws and Customs of England*
1258	Provisions of Oxford enacted
1285	Statute of Westminster II enacted
1290	Statute *Quia Emptores* enacted
1481	Littleton's *Treatise on Tenures* (English land law) published in Law French
1530s	King Henry VIII breaks relations with the Church in Rome
1606	King James I appoints Edward Coke Chief Justice of Court of Common Pleas
1615	*Earl of Oxford* case
1616	"Compromise of 1616" settles jurisdictional disputes between courts
1765–1769	Blackstone's *Commentaries on the Laws of England* published
1750s–1780s	commercial law absorbed by common law, through Lord Mansfield's efforts
1832	reform of English procedural law
1873–1875	Judicature Acts (merging courts of law and equity)
1972	UK enters EEC (later EU)

I. Pre-Norman English Law

A. *The Celts and the Romans in Britain*

Professor Francis Heller, a legal historian and long-time faculty member at the University of Kansas, offers this synopsis of the early growth of the law in England, starting with the Celts and continuing with the Romans.

> The land bridge that tied Britain to the present Low Countries did not disappear until ca. 6000 B.C. There is archaeological evidence that people had moved back and forth across this link but it is not known who these people were. The Celts arrived by sea beginning late in the eighth century B.C. and, apparently, had conquered and/or absorbed most of the original population by the end of the eighth century. Again, however, we have little beyond stone and metal relics; we know that the Celts wrote (in runes) but they have not left us anything that would allow us to know how they were governed and what laws they had (if any).

> In fact, the first written evidence of any significance is Julius Caesar's account in *De bello gallico* of his conquest of the southern portion of the island in 55 (or 54) B.C. It tells us a good deal about Caesar's military accomplishments but very

little about the people he forced to acknowledge Roman sovereignty. It was not until a hundred years later (43 A.D.) that Rome established full control over the southern part of Britain (allowing the troublesome Picts, on the other side of Hadrian's Wall, to remain free). But Roman control never extended beyond the garrison cities and their number soon began to relinquish (e.g., to "balance the budget" the emperor Domitian in the year 90 reduced the force in Britain to a mere three legions). In practice most of Britain remained essentially free and Roman institutions (including Roman law) had little effect on the Celtic population. By 410 A.D. the last vestiges of Roman overlordship had come to an end. Modern scholarship attributes seeming remnants of Roman legal influence not to the imperial occupation but to later influence of the Roman church.[2]

Another source offers a similar view regarding the absence of lingering legal influence of Roman occupation in Britain:

> Romans ruled parts of the island for nearly four centuries. England was marked indelibly with Roman culture—the rose, road system, Latin language and central heating—but the Romans did not bestow upon the inhabitants the Roman legal system. England had not been developed, it had been occupied.... What Rome contributed to the English legal system was indirect, occurring through the survival of remnants of institutional structures of a civilized society.[3]

We might contrast (i) the post-5th-century *absence* of any lingering legal influence of Roman occupation of Britain with (ii) the post-5th-century *presence* of a lingering legal influence of the Roman occupation in many other parts of the Roman Empire. Our historical survey in Chapter Two revealed that such influence was strong enough in many parts of Europe to allow some features of Roman law to survive the collapse of the western part of the Empire in 476, albeit in a vulgarized form as it blended with Germanic law. This did not occur in Britain. Despite Roman occupation of Britain for over four centuries, the Romans left almost no legal "imprint" on the country, which was regarded by the Romans as a primitive frontier.

B. The Anglo-Saxon Period

1. Germanic Tribes and the Importance of Customs

Instead, in the long millennium running from the arrival of the Romans up through the year 1066, the main "imprint" on the law of what came to be known as England was made not by the Romans but by the Germanic tribes that came across from the continent and pushed the Celts further west and south. Heller gives this brief account:

> [By the early 4th century, the] Celts had evolved into a number of tribal groups, each headed by a king and most of them continually at war with each other. In fact, the first arrivals from Germany, the Saxons, were not invaders but had been invited by one of the kings to aid him in his battles with other kings. Nor did the Saxons (or, for that matter, the Angles and the Jutes) arrive in one single movement. Although history books tend to focus on the year 442, the migration spread over the entire century. What is rather amazing is that by the year 600 the Britons

---

2. Francis H. Heller, *The Growth of the Law in England* (unpublished, on file with the author).
3. Mary Ann Glendon, Palo G. Carozza, and Colin B. Picker, COMPARATIVE LEGAL TRADITIONS IN A NUTSHELL 154–155 (2008) [hereinafter Nutshell-2008].

have been pushed out of the main island into the peninsulas of Cornwall and Wales; within another century the descendants of the three Germanics tribes have come to be known as "English" and the country they inhabit as "England."

We have some understanding of the societal and legal arrangements of these people, partly because some written evidence has survived and partly because it is clear that their institutions and their practices closely resembled those of the Germanic tribes on the continent (including those of the Franks, the ancestors of today's French). Even so, Pollock and Maitland, the authors of the classic account of The History of English Law before the Time of Edward I (1895), observe that "in truth, the manners, dress and dialects of our ancestors before the Norman conquest are far better knows to us than their laws" (pp. 24–25).

We have available to us today the laws of king Æthelbert of Kent (ca. 600), the code of the Alfred the Great (ca. 890) and the laws of Canute (or Cnut), or ca. 1020. None of these has survived in its entirety and, more importantly, we have no indication that any of them were in fact followed. Æthelbert's laws, most scholars believe, were either prepared by or at least heavily influenced by St. Augustine who had persuaded Æthelbert to convert to Christianity. His laws reflect essentiality Christian morality and one may doubt that they had much impact on his pagan subjects. Alfred, though they called him "the Great," spent most of his years as king of England (871–900) battling the Danes. His laws were essentially a compilation of custom and of edicts of his predecessors; he sought to minimize the blood feud as a means of settling disputes—but English kings were still doing this two hundred years later. The principal importance of the laws of Canute (1016–1035), essentially a smattering of edicts on a variety of subjects, is that they were promulgated with the consent of the Witan (sometimes also called witenagemot), an assembly of the leaders and elders of the nation.[4]

Excerpts from the first of three sets of royal laws Heller refers to—those of King Æthelbert, promulgated around 600 CE—appear in Appendix 4.1, at the end of this chapter. They give the initial impression of a predominantly criminal code, specifying punishments for a variety of acts; and several of them pay special attention to crimes committed against the king or his interests. Some of the provisions look very similar to the "if-then" statements appearing in Chinese dynastic codes, which we shall examine below in Chapter Six. See also Appendix 4.2 for a brief biographical sketch of King Æthelbert and a more comprehensive explanation of his code of laws (or "dooms"); in addition, see Appendix 4.3 for a brief biographical sketch of King Canute.

It should not be assumed, however, that any of these three sets of royal laws during the Anglo-Saxon period—those of Æthelbert, of Alfred, or of Canute—had very comprehensive geographic coverage and application in England. In fact, just the opposite held true: in this period England was characterized by fragmented political control and by a patchwork of customary laws. As Heller explains, "even though we speak of a "king of England," the dominant fact was that there were seven kingdoms within England and that there were significant differences in the laws (and customs) observed throughout the land."[5]

How important were these "significant differences in the laws (and customs)" applicable in different parts of England during the Anglo-Saxon period? Some impression of this emerges from the following description:

---

4. Heller, *supra* note 2, at 7–8.
5. *Id.* at 8.

[The] customary law as administered in Essex might differ considerably from that which was administered in Kent. For instance, primogeniture, the right of the eldest son to inherit the whole of the real property where there was no will, applied almost universally throughout England; but in Kent there existed a system of land-holding called gavelkind tenure whereby all the sons inherited equally; while in Nottingham and Bristol, under the custom of Borough-English, the property passed to the youngest son.[6]

2. Courts in Anglo-Saxon England

As we shall see throughout this chapter, a defining feature of the common law is the importance of *courts*—and especially two particular aspects of courts and their operation. Those aspects are (i) the competition between different court systems (a competition that ultimately was resolved in England only in the late 1800s) and (ii) the central role of judges sitting on those courts, whose decisions formed the core of the common law. Hence it makes sense for us to consider briefly the operation of courts in the Anglo-Saxon period. It was those courts, after all, that William of Normandy "inherited" in 1066.

Although details of courts in the Anglo-Saxon period are sketchy, it is possible to gain some impression of their operation in the years preceding 1066 by projecting backward from the years just following 1066, by which time the centralized administration of legal and political power had improved the system of record-keeping. The following excerpt does just that: it projects backward from the 1270s to the period just before 1066, thereby providing a description of a principal category of courts in Anglo-Saxon England—the "hundreds" courts.

> In the 1270s there were 628 hundreds or wapentakes (the Danelaw equivalent)[7] in England, and it is unlikely that the figure in the Anglo-Norman period was much lower. The number of hundreds in each shire varied; there were thirty-five in Devon, fourteen in Oxfordshire in the 1270s. So, too, did the size of individual hundreds; a hundred reeve might well have ten to twenty villages in his hundred, but some in Kent had only two. Some hundreds customarily met as groups, others did so on occasion by royal order. In 1066 lords held possibly about 100 wapentakes or hundreds from the king, and the number had increased markedly by the early thirteenth century, doubling or trebling in Wiltshire. Such hundreds

---

6. Kenneth Smith and Denis J. Keenan, English Law 1 (2d ed., 1966).

7. A "hundred" or "wapentake" is a territorial and administrative division. One source (adequate for our purposes) explains that "[i]n England a hundred was the division of a shire for administrative, military and judicial purposes.... Originally, when introduced by the Saxons..., a hundred had enough land to sustain approximately one hundred households headed by a *hundred-man* or *hundred eolder*. He was responsible for administration, justice, and supplying military troops, as well as leading its forces." See Wikipedia entry for "Hundred (county subdivision)", http://en.wikipedia.org/wiki/Hundred_%28county_subdivision%29 (citing *A Vision of Britain Through Time* (University of Portsmouth)); http://www.visionofbritain.org.uk/types/status_page.jsp?unit_status=Hundred. The term "wapentake", which is derived from the Old Norse word *vápnatak*, constitutes a rough equivalent of an Anglo-Saxon hundred. The word "wapentake" denotes an administrative meeting place, typically a crossroads or a ford in a river. While the origin of the word is not clear, it might be related to the practice by which voting at such a meeting place would be conducted by the show of weapons. See the Wikipedia site cited above and authorities provided there.

were not evenly spread throughout the realm, being far more common, for example, in the south-west than in the east. Hundreds were important sources of revenue, and indeed lords may have desired them primarily for financial rather than judicial benefits.

The Anglo-Saxon evidence ... [indicates] hundred courts being held once every month or four weeks, unless there was more pressing royal or public business.... Each session seems to have lasted a single day. Courts met in a variety of places, for example in churchyards or at thorn trees. Judgments rested with the suitors, generally presided over by a bailiff, appointed by the sheriff or by the lord.... The obligation to attend again rested on the larger land-holders of the hundred, ...

... If we accept an estimate of a population of 1.5 million in 1086, we can be reasonably sure that at least one percent of the population attended hundred courts, and the proportion of adult males doing so might easily be one in twenty. Moreover, there were each year two particularly large sessions, to be attended by all freemen....[8]

The "hundreds" courts were not the only courts in Anglo-Saxon England. Other types of courts included manorial courts, shire courts, county courts, "honorial" courts, seignorial courts, and others.[9] Those courts, like the "hundreds" courts, were predominantly local in their scope of operation; in other words, the imprint of central administrative authority was weak or nonexistent.

To summarize: at the time of the arrival of the Normans — discussed in some detail below — the laws of England were largely customary in character, varying significantly from one locale to another, despite the attempts by several kings to promulgate legislation in some geographic areas and on some substantive issues. During the Anglo-Saxon centuries a variety of courts developed at the local level based largely on the division of land-holding among lords and barons; and the operations of such courts were public affairs that involved a significant proportion of the population.

---

8. John Hudson, THE FORMATION OF THE ENGLISH COMMON LAW: LAW AND SOCIETY IN ENGLAND FROM THE NORMAN CONQUEST TO MAGNA CARTA 37–39 (1996).

9. For a description of county courts in Anglo-Saxon England, see *id.* at 35–37. See also Smith & Keenan, *supra* note 6, at 1:

[In the period preceding] the Norman Conquest [in 1066] the law was administered by the Lords of the Manor in the manorial courts, and by the County Sheriffs, often sitting with the Earl and the Bishop, in the courts of the Shires and Hundreds. They administered the law for the King in their respective areas and decided the cases which came before them on the basis of local custom.

Other sources refer to a rich variety of other Anglo-Saxon courts, such as the *burhgemot* (borough courts), *folcgemot* (folk courts), *sciregemot* (shire courts), and *witanagemote* ("council of wise men"). For a description of some of these, and some others, see Joseph Jackson, ENGLISH LEGAL HISTORY 18–19 (1955); Frederick G. Kempin, Jr., HISTORICAL INTRODUCTION TO ANGLO-AMERICAN LAW IN A NUTSHELL 22–28 (3d ed. 1990). That latter authority explains that in this Anglo-Saxon period, and indeed for some time after the Norman arrival, "judges were unknown. There were 'courts,' but they were composed of lay persons called suitors." *Id.* at 22–23. Supporting the proposition that the laws at the time took the form of customs, this same authority notes that those suitors "answered questions of 'law' on the basis of their knowledge of local customs. The heads of these bodies — the reeves, sheriffs, lords, and stewards — merely presided. Law was not yet a specialized body of knowledge that needed professional judges." *Id.*

II. The Rise of Common Law after the Norman Conquest

Let us turn, then, to the Norman "conquest" and to the development of the common law of England. What we shall see is a gradual but comprehensive change in England's law away from Anglo-Saxon customary law toward a law that had several key features: (i) it was common to all of England, (ii) it emerged out of a jurisdictional battle involving royal courts and local courts, (iii) it therefore paralleled the seemingly irrepressible trend toward centralization of political power in the country, and (iv) it proved ultimately fragile and unsustainable on its own because of its procedural complexity and its limited applicability.

A. The Norman Takeover and William's Reforms

1. An Overview of the Significance of 1066

The events of 1066, and those of the next century and a half, are so central to the development of the common law that they warrant special attention. The following pages present four perspectives on that important period, drawn from four sources. The first perspective takes the form of an excerpt from the writings of Francis Heller, who offers this look at William of Normandy's seizing of control of England in 1066 and the development of royal courts:

> The year 1066 may well be the most important date in the history of English law. Duke William of Normandy (where history remembers him not as "the Conqueror" but, because of his illegitimate background, as "the Bastard") had as tenuous a claim to the crown of England as his cousin Harold [Godwinson], the incumbent whom he defeated (and who died) in the battle of Hastings.[10] William's first priority was, therefore, to entrench his position in England, (As duke of Normandy he found it necessary to divide his time between the two countries he now ruled.) He did this mainly by two bold assertions of royal prerogative: He declared that all land in England belonged to the king and he proclaimed himself the fountainhead of justice in the realm.
>
> To buttress the first claim William ordered an inventory taken of all land in England and who occupied it (the Domesday Book [1086]). He then distributed the land in such a fashion as to assure Norman control of the countryside; at the

---

10. While it is not essential to our story here, it is worth noting just *why* William won the battle of Hastings, since the reason for his victory reflects the political disarray in England in the period immediately preceding the Norman invasion. Following Edward the Confessor's death in January 1066, Harold Godwinson secured the support of the Witenagemot (the Anglo-Saxon assembly of nobles) and had himself crowned king. He faced challengers, however, to his claim and to his control over England. In September 1066, about three weeks before the battle at Hastings, Harold Godwinson had taken his army north to repel Viking forces led by Harald Hardråda. He did so at the battle of Stamford Bridge. Then, on learning that William's forces had landed near Pevensy, Harold Godwinson hurried southward to meet this new challenge. Some advisors urged a delay while more men could be assembled, but Harold was determined to prove his ability to defend his new kingdom decisively against any invader. His proof failed; on 14 October 1066 the battle with William's forces ended in Harold's death, reportedly by an arrow through his eye.

same time he dispersed his Norman knights so as to minimize the danger of a possible revolt by them against the king, especially during his absences. Theoretically all land titles in England derive from the Domesday Book and, until about 150 years ago, the law maintained the fiction that the land belonged to the king and whoever held it was, in one form or another, no more than a lessee.

The assertion that all law emanated from the king was at least as important. Whenever he could do so, William traveled about the country and in every town he came to be summoned the elders and demanded to know what offenses had been committed, who had broken "the king's peace." In effect, this was the beginning of the grand jury. The king then had the accused brought before him, heard the parties, and rendered judgment. In doing so, however, he again consulted the elders and ascertained from them what the customary verdict and sentence was. When he heard cases involving the crown—which he did at Westminster, the seat of the government—he applied his understanding of the laws of various parts of the kingdom as he had come to learn them on his travels—a law common to the kingdom, the "common" law.

His successors (Rufus [William II], Henry I, and Stephen), not nearly as energetic as he had been and often preoccupied with foreign and domestic warfare, dispatched members of their retinue, the curia regis (the king's court), and instructed them to follow the law as King William had pronounced it—the beginning of the system of precedent. Henry II (1135–80) then systematized the judiciary, bringing order to the system of formulas (writs) that determined who would have access to the king's court and the king's justice. Every expansion of the jurisdiction of the king's court, of course, meant a reduction of the judicial power held by the barons (the "manorial" courts) whose resentment of this (and other) assertions of the royal prerogative led to the confrontation at Runnymede and the issuance of the Great Charter of 1215.[11]

Heller's reference to the year 1066 as perhaps "the most important date in the history of English law" calls to mind some of the key dates in the history of European civil law. As we saw in Chapter Two, these would certainly include such dates as 450 BCE (with the promulgation of the Twelve Tables), 532 CE (with the completion of Justinian's *Digest* and *Institutes*), a date in the late 11th century that we cannot pinpoint exactly (when the *Digest* was rediscovered in Italy), and 1804 (with the enactment of the French Civil Code). Surely 1066 is as important for the common law as those dates are for European civil law.

2. The Bayeux Tapestry

Fortunately, some of the events of 1066—and particularly the Battle of Hastings that marked William of Normandy's successful invasion of England—were recorded in a remarkable work of art completed only a couple of decades after the events it depicts. Box #4.2 presents an excerpt from an art history book describing that work of art and the events it memorializes.

---

11. Heller, *supra* note 2, at 8.

Box #4.2 The Bayeux Tapestry and the Battle of Hastings[12]

[A] single large-scale example of pictorial art [from the feudal Romanesque period] is the so-called "Bayeux Tapestry," one of the most eloquent documents of this or any other time. Here, in visual form, is the story of the conquest of England by William the Conqueror recounted from the Norman point of view, in the course of which a vivid picture of the life and attitudes of feudal man unfolds. The term *tapestry* is a misnomer, justified in this case because of its function as a wall hanging. Since the design is applied in woolen yarn to a coarse linen surface rather than woven into the cloth itself, it is more accurately described as an embroidery.... [The Bayeux Tapestry measures] 20 inches wide and 231 feet long ... [and] was probably the product of one of the renowned English embroidery workshops and apparently was completed about 20 years after the great battle it describes. The central figure is, of course, William the Conqueror, who indelibly stamped his powerful personality on the north European scene throughout the latter half of the 11th century. The span of time is from the closing months of the reign of Edward the Confessor to that fateful day in 1066 when the Conqueror made good his claim to the throne by putting the English forces to rout at the Battle of Hastings.

The Bayeux Tapestry, in complete presentations, is divided into 79 panels, or scenes. The first part ... is concerned with William's reception of Harold, an English duke, whose mission to Normandy ostensibly was to tell William that he [William] was to succeed Edward the Confessor as king of England. In one of these scenes, William and Harold are seen at Bayeux (Fig. 194), *where Harold took an oath to Duke William.* (The italics here and later are literal translations of the Latin inscriptions that run along the top of the Tapestry above the scenes they describe.) Placing his hands on the reliquaries that repose on the two altars, Harold apparently swears to uphold William's claim, although the exact nature of the oath is left vague. This is, however, the episode that later became the justification for [William's] English campaign — because Harold, false to his supposed sworn word, had had himself crowned king. In these early panels, in the upper and lower borders, a running commentary on the action continues a tradition begun in manuscript illuminations. Here the commentary is in the form of animal figures that were familiar to the people of the time from bestiaries and sculpture and the allusion is to certain fables of Aesop. The choice of the fox and crow, the wolf and stork, and the ewe, goat, and cow in the presence of the lion all have to do with treachery and violence and serve to point out the perfidious character of Harold.

William is seated serenely on his ducal throne, foreshadowing his future dignity as king. The scene, furthermore, actually is located in Bayeux Cathedral, the exterior of which is shown in the curious representation to the left of the seated William. Bayeux's bishop was none other than Odo, William's half brother, who in all probability commissioned the tapestry. If the visual evidence is taken literally, Odo's part in subsequent events was considerable....

The main course of action in the Bayeux Tapestry moves like the words on a printed page — that is, from left to right. At times, however, it was necessary to represent a pertinent episode apart from the principal action, whereupon the pictorial narrator simply reversed the usual order and moved his scene from right to left, thus, in effect, achieving a kind of visual parenthesis and avoiding any confusion with the flow of the main story. Such a reversal is employed in the scene depicting the death and burial of the Confessor (Fig. 195). On the right and side near the top is *King Edward in his bed* as he *addresses his faithful retainers.* On one side of him is a priest; Harold is on the other; while the queen and her lady-in-waiting are mourning at the foot of the bed. Below, under the words *here he has died*, the body is being prepared for the last rites. Moving toward the left, the funeral procession approaches *the church of St. Peter the Apostle*, the Romanesque predecessor of Westminster Abbey in London, which Edward had built and dedicated but ten years before, while the hand of God descends in blessing. The procession includes a group of tonsured monks reading prayers and two acolytes ringing the funeral bells.

---

12. The account in Box #4.2 is drawn from William Fleming, Arts & Ideas 160–166 (3d ed. 1974).

When William received word that Harold had been crowned, he immediately determined on invasion, and the second part of the Tapestry … is concerned with the preparations for his revenge up to the eve of the battle. After all was in readiness, he set sail *and crossed the sea* (Fig. 196). The ships seen in the Tapestry are similar to those in which William's restless Viking ancestors invaded the French coast two centuries before…, and it was just such ships that Leif Eriksen and his fellow mariners apparently reached the eastern coast of North America earlier in the same century.

After the landing, the grand finale begins with the assembling of forces for the great battle (panels 54–79). The Norman side has both archers on foot and knights on horseback, while the English fight in a solid phalanx with immense battleaxes, small spears, and clubs with stone heads. The Normans move in from left to right and the English from the opposite direction. The climax of the battle is reached in a wild scene at a ravine [Fig. 197], where men and horses are tumbling about while the *English and French fall together in battle*. Shortly after, Harold is killed, and the fighting concludes with the *English turned in flight*. The lower border in these scenes spares none of the horrors of warfare; dismembered limbs are strewn about, scavengers strip coats of mail from the bodies of the fallen, and naked corpses are left on the field.

Figure 194. Harold swearing oath to William.

Figure 195. Death and Burial of Edward the Confessor

Figure 196. Norman Ships Sailing toward the English Coast

Figure 197. Climax of the Battle of Hastings.

3. Feudalism, Centralization, and the Common Law

The third perspective (of four) on the events of 1066 and the century and a half that followed them is drawn from the famous work of René David, who offers an overview of the Norman "conquest", the restructuring of English political authority that it brought, and the early creation of a "common law" of England. David makes several key points about the legal and administrative effects of the Norman invasion, about the nature of feudalism, and about the common law that emerged from the gradual centralization of power.

First, René David emphasizes that "[t]he Norman Conquest did not in itself alter the state of things" in terms of the laws in place when William arrived on the scene, although the governance of the kingdom changed dramatically:

> [William] expressly proclaimed the maintenance in force of Anglo-Saxon law; and even now it is sometimes possible for English lawyers and judges to invoke, and even apply, a rule of law dating from the Anglo-Saxon period.

> The Norman Conquest, however, is an event of the utmost importance in English legal history because it brought to England, in addition to the foreign occupation, a strong and centralised administrative organization, rich in experience, that had shown its worth in the Duchy of Normandy. With the Norman Conquest, the period of tribal rule is finished and feudalism is installed.[13]

René David then explains what sort of feudalism was "installed" in England under William's centralized administration:

> The English form of feudalism was very different from that existing in France, Germany or Italy at the same period. The *seigneurs* of Normandy who accompanied William to England were in a conquered country, they did not speak the language of the inhabitants and they were scornful of local habits and manners. They felt the need to band around their sovereign in order to maintain the conquest and defend their lands. The Conqueror, for his part, knew how to ward off the danger of over-powerful vassals; in the distribution of land made to his supporters, no very large fief was constituted and thus no baron was able to challenge his power.[14]

---

13. David & Brierly, *supra* note 1, at 311.

14. Despite this policy imposed by William, and despite the recording of land that had been undertaken in the Domesday Book, circumstances gradually changed over the following years, so that by the 13th century the title to land had become seriously clouded in many cases and was often in dispute. Moreover, some landholders purported to transfer claims over their land to others (technically sub-tenants), such that the lords who held outright title to such land did not in fact have any power over the sub-tenant to collect taxes or enforce feudal duties. This practice of "alienation" made a great many parcels of land subject to "subinfeudation". In 1290, in an attempt to counteract this trend, and hence to press for more centralized royal power, the statute *Quia Emptores* was enacted to prohibit most

It was rather as though an army were encamped in England; that there was a sense of discipline and organisation was shown by the drafting, as early as 1086, of the *Domesday Book*, a document in which 15,000 manor estates and 200,000 homes were inventoried. This military and highly organised character of English feudalism, so unlike that of the European continent, prepared the way for the development of the Common law.[15]

René David then offers an explanation of the "Common law" that emerged against the backdrop of this highly centralized administrative structure of government following the Norman "conquest"—and he emphasizes how that common law differed from the pre-Norman Anglo-Saxon law:

> What was this Common law—at the time called *commune ley* in "law French" which, from the reign of Edward I (1272–1307) to the seventeenth century, was the spoken language of law[16] while the written language, as in the rest of Europe, was Latin?
>
> *Comune ley* or Common law, as distinct from local customs, is the law common to all England[,] but in 1066 it did not exist. The assemblies of free men, called County or Hundred Courts, applied only local custom [before 1066]; in other words they only decided, according to custom, which of the parties had to establish his claim by submitting to a system of proof that had no pretentions to rationality. Although they remained competent in principle even after the Conquest, the Hundred or County Courts were gradually replaced by new feudal courts (Courts Baron, Court Leet, Manorial Courts), but these also decided disputes by applying the local customary law. Ecclesiastical courts set up after the Conquest applied Canon law, common to all Christianity. The creation of the *comune ley*, an English law truly common to the whole of England, was to be the exclusive work of the royal courts of justice, commonly called the Courts of Westminster, and so named after the place where they sat from the thirteenth century.[17]

4. The Royal Courts

A final reference to the Norman invasion of England and the early development of the common law also emphasizes the operation of courts, and particularly the growth of the royal courts at Westminster:

> The administrative ability of the Normans began the process destined to lead to a unified system of law which was nevertheless evolutionary in its development.

---

forms of such subinfeudation; thenceforth, all the nobles were directly subordinate to the king, so that when land was alienated, the grantee was required to assume all tax and feudal obligations of the original tenant—a status known as "substitution". For further details on the statute *Quia Emptores*, see Kempin, *supra* note 9, at 147–148.

15. David & Brierly, *supra* note 1, at 311–312.

16. [*footnote in original*] French was the language of the royal court until the Tudors came to the throne at the end of the fifteenth century, and was therefore naturally used in the royal courts of justice. Use of English declined as the jurisdiction of the royal courts was extended. French, however, was *spoken* less and was also gradually abandoned from the sixteenth century by legal writers who preferred English. Unsuccessful attempts in [the 17th century] were made to establish English officially to the exclusion of French and Latin; this was only achieved in 1731. On the subject of "law French," *cf.* Maitland's Introduction to Volume 17 of the *Selden Society*, pp. xxiii–lxxxix. Baker (J.A.), *Manual of Law French* (1979).

17. David & Brierly, *supra* note 1, at 312–313.

The Normans were not concerned to change English customary law by imposing Norman law on England. Indeed, many charters of William I giving English boroughs the right to hold courts stated that the laws dispensed in these courts should be the laws of Edward the Confessor, which meant that English customary law was to be applied.

The Normans did, however, strive to make the law of England uniform and the chief means by which this was achieved was the introduction of the General Eyre whereby representatives of the King were sent from Westminster on a tour of the Shires for the purpose of checking on the local administration. During the period of their visit they would sit in the local court and hear cases, and gradually they came to have a judicial rather than an administrative function....

The General Eyre disappeared in the reign of Richard III (1377–1399) [*sic*; should read "Richard II"],[18] but a system of circuit judges from the King's Bench took its place [beginning shortly thereafter]. By selecting the best customary rulings and applying these outside their county of origin, the circuit judges gradually moulded the numerous local customary laws into one uniform law "common" to the whole kingdom. Thus, customs originally local ultimately applied throughout the whole of the realm. However, there was no absolute unification even as late as 1389, and in a case in the Common Pleas in that year, a custom of Selby in Yorkshire was admitted to show that a husband was not in that area liable for his wife's trading debts, though the common law elsewhere regarded him as liable.

When not on circuit the justices sat in the Royal Courts at Westminster, and it was probably at Westminster that they discussed the differences in the customary law on the various circuits, selecting the best rulings and applying them both at Westminster and on circuit.

The Royal Courts of Westminster developed out of the *Curia Regis* (or King's Council) which was originally a body of noblemen advising the King. The Court of Exchequer was the first court to emerge from the *Curia Regis* and dealt initially with disputes connected with royal revenues; later it dealt with many common law actions not necessarily connected with revenue. The Court of Common Pleas was set up in the time of Henry II to hear disputes between the King's subjects. The Court of King's Bench was the last to emerge from the *Curia Regis*....[19]

B. A Tug-of-War of Courts — National versus Local

1. Peculiarities of Courts — Further Details

The account offered above focuses on courts, and particularly on the interplay of two types of jurisdiction — locally-based jurisdiction and centrally-based jurisdiction. Our understanding of the significance of courts in the common law tradition requires that we dig somewhat deeper into these topics.

---

18. A simplified chart of the sovereigns of England (including their "houses" or "dynasties") from 1066 onward appears in Appendix 4.6.

19. Smith & Keenan, *supra* note 6, at 1–2. Another source emphasizes that English government structure at this early stage was unified: "No separation of government functions existed in early Norman England. The king, acting with close advisors in council ... exercised judicial as well as executive and legislative powers." Nutshell-2008, *supra* note 3, at 157.

A principal type of court with locally-based (rural) jurisdiction during the period just preceding and just following 1066 was the "hundreds court", as described earlier. Another type was the county court. These were soon joined, following 1066, by feudal courts — that is, those courts at the local level that were presided over by the feudal lords to whom the grants of land had been made by the king. Another type of locally-based focused courts also arose because of William's arrival in England: the ecclesiastical courts.

> Moves towards the existence of separate ecclesiastical courts, with their own procedure, areas of jurisdiction, and largely clerical personnel, started soon after the Norman Conquest as part of more general Church reform. In the early or mid-1070s William I ordered that [bishops could hear cases in separate courts — not the hundreds courts, that is — and apply the "canons and Episcopal laws"].
>
> ... Ecclesiastical courts heard disputes involving lay people, cases of marriage and bastardy, of the bequest of moveables after death, and — although the surviving evidence is sparse — of lay sin. They also heard accusations of clerical offenses, although many of these would have been settled out of court, for example in the monastery. In the Anglo-Norman period the punishment of clerical offenders seems often to have involved cooperation with lay powers, perhaps after the cleric had been deprived of his orders. Cases between great ecclesiastics, for example over the relationship of two churches, were often heard by the king, or by a combination of royal and ecclesiastical courts. Likewise, a wide range of cases involving ecclesiastical lands or other rights took place either in royal courts or those of ecclesiastics in their role as lords. Certainly, in the latter there might be a large ecclesiastical element, but they must still be distinguished from, for example, diocesan courts. Conflicts of jurisdiction did occasionally arise, and tended to be decided by the king and his court. However, overall before 1154 there is little evidence of conflict, much more of cooperation between ecclesiastical and lay courts.[20]

It was by the operation of this rich variety of locally-based courts that practically all law in England was applied in the years immediately following the Norman invasion. And yet this situation was not to persist; the local courts would come encounter a formidable challenger in the form of centralized jurisdiction. René David has explained the situation in this way:

> The king [at first] only exercised "high justice" ... in very exceptional cases, such as when the peace of the kingdom was threatened and circumstances made it impossible for justice to be rendered in the usual forum. The *Curia Regis*, from which the king dispensed justice assisted by his closest officials and the persons of highest rank in the kingdom, was a court for only the most important personalities and disputes; it was not an ordinary court open to all and sundry.
>
> But from the thirteenth century certain parts of the *Curia Regis* gradually became ... autonomous bodies ... [and] ceased to accompany the King in his pro-

---

20. Hudson, *supra* note 8, at 48–50. Another authority offers these further insights into the reason for the ecclesiastical courts:

> Before the Norman Conquest the then existing courts heard all suits, both lay and ecclesiastical, and the Bishop and the Earl sat as joint judges. These joint courts were disliked by the Papacy because of the quarrels which took place between the lay and ecclesiastical members of the various tribunals. Prior to his conquest of England, William I had promised to set up separate ecclesiastical courts in [England] in return for the Pope's blessing of his proposed campaign. After the Conquest, William carried out his promise....

Smith & Keenan, *supra* note 6, at 9–10.

gresses about the country and established their seat at Westminster. But these royal courts of justice by no means had general jurisdiction. [They] ... had to treat with some consideration the sensibilities of the feudal barons who wanted to be their own masters and were not, therefore, very willing to submit to the justice of these new courts.... The royal courts, furthermore, were not really equipped to render justice, even on appeal, in all the different kinds of contestation that arose in the kingdom. Their intervention was thus at first limited essentially to three main types of cases where it did appear more or less natural; royal finances, matters respecting the ownership and possession of land[21] and serious criminal matters affecting the peace of the kingdom. Three different courts — Court of Exchequer, Court of Common Pleas, Court of King's Bench — heard matters coming within each of these categories at the beginning, but very soon this division of jurisdiction disappeared and each of the three courts at Westminster could hear any dispute brought before the royal courts.

Apart from these three categories, all other disputes were settled by the Hundred or County Courts, feudal courts, ecclesiastical courts — and later, as well, when this became necessary, by different commercial or municipal courts. The privilege of rendering justice was granted for certain types of cases to the latter and they applied the international customary law of commerce, the *lex mercatoria* or *ley merchant*, or municipal regulations.[22]

This was a system that, viewed from the perspective of hindsight, was destined to crumble eventually: as the powers of the king grew, the jurisdiction of the royal courts tended to grow. There were also some other reasons for such a growth in jurisdiction. Those reasons centered on money and modernity.

The expanding jurisdiction of the royal courts centered on money in the sense that access to those courts involved the payment of fees by the parties. That is, the Chancellor and the royal judges earned fees from hearing cases and deciding them.[23] The expanding jurisdiction of the royal courts at Westminster centered on "modernity" in the sense that those courts departed from the old procedures — including the various methods of proof by "ordeal" of one sort or another[24] — that were still followed in the hundreds courts and other local courts. Moreover, "[i]t was only the royal courts that had the means

---

21. [*footnote in original*] An owner is master in his own house, but who is an owner? To decide this it was natural to resort to the royal courts. Questions of rights to possession of land concerned the public order and peace of the kingdom.

22. David & Brierly, *supra* note 1, at 313–315.

23. *Id.* at 314. See also Nutshell-2008, *supra* note 3, at 158 (noting that preference among litigants for the royal courts "eroded the role of local courts and reduced [the] court fees revenue which was intensely coveted by ... the barons").

24. According to one source, the principal forms of ordeal in English practice, at least up through part of the 13th century, included ordeal by fire, ordeal by water, and ordeal by battle. In the ordeal of fire, the accused person was required to carry a red-hot bar of iron for three feet; if within three days his hand was healed, he was deemed innocent; if not, he was deemed guilty. In the ordeal by water, the accused person was required to plunge his hand into boiling water and draw out a stone; if within three days his hand had healed, he was deemed innocent; if not, he was deemed guilty. See Jackson, *supra* note 9, at 19–20. Another source describes another form of ordeal by water: in this form, an accused person was secured by a rope and let down into a pool of cold water; "if the water received him and he sank, he was thereby proved innocent." Kempin, *supra* note 9, at 59. That source also describes trial by battle, which was not officially abolished in England until 1819, after centuries of disuse. *Id.* at 51–52.

to summon witnesses and to enforce judgments; and only the king, apart from the church, could require the swearing of an oath."[25]

For these and other reasons, the royal courts gradually enlarged their jurisdiction, at the expense of the local courts. "The feudal courts were eclipsed, as the Hundred Courts had been; municipal and commercial courts handled matters of only minor importance; and the ecclesiastical courts only heard cases in relation to marriage and the discipline of clergy."[26]

2. The Writ System

The reason this centralization of the court system was fraught with difficulty revolves around the limitations noted earlier on the royal courts' jurisdiction. Those limitations took the form of the writ system. Two brief explanations will illuminate the writ system adequately for our purposes. The first places special emphasis on its rigidity:

> Jurisdiction of the common law courts was limited severely by a writ system. A civil action lay before one of the courts only where a specific writ was available from a high official ("where there is no writ, there is no right"). Issued in the name of and constituting a command from the king, writs were addressed to an official authorizing commencement of specific suits, later known as "forms of action." The system was rigid; selection of the wrong writ resulted in dismissal.[27]

A second explanation, by René David, offers a similar account but emphasizes the discretionary nature of the writ system and how it gradually expanded:

> [T]o press a claim before the king's courts was not a right but a favour which the royal authority might or might not grant. The person who solicited this privilege had first of all to address his request to an important royal official, the Chancellor, asking him to deliver a writ (*breve*), the effect of which was to enable the royal courts to be seized of the matter upon the payment of fees to the Chancery....

> It was not automatic that a writ would issue from the royal Chancery or that the judges would be convinced that they should take up a matter upon which a complaint was lodged.... For some considerable time, each instance had to be individually examined to determine whether it was expedient that the writ should issue, and the list of established situations where writs were granted automatically ... was slow to grow. A first list of writs, drawn up in 1227, reveals that there were 56, and there were only 76 in 1832 when the system was considerably modified.[28]

The writ system may therefore be regarded as a method by which a balance was struck between (i) enlarging the jurisdiction of the royal courts at Westminster and (ii) retaining jurisdiction at the local level in the various forms of local courts. Another method for striking that balance was attempted in 1215, when the local barons forced King John to sign the Magna Carta. Although the Magna Carta did include some provisions relating to per-

---

25. David & Brierly, *supra* note 1, at 314.

26. *Id.* at 314–315.

27. Nutshell-2008, *supra* note 3, at 158.

28. David & Brierly, *supra* note 1, at 315. For a list and brief synopsis of the most important of the writs—going by such names as "attaint", "*capias ad respondendum*", "*certiorari*", "*fieri facias*", "*monstrans de droit*", "*warrantia cartae*", and various forms of "*habeas corpus*", see Jackson, *supra* note 9, at 90–107.

sonal rights (for which it is generally remembered today), it was more noteworthy at the time for its overall aim of circumscribing the powers of the king—so that he would no longer allow the jurisdiction of his courts to continue expanding at the expense of the local courts. Here is one account of the Magna Carta and its legal ais and consequences:

> The progressive loss of jurisdiction of the rural courts, among other things, induced revolt among the English barons. Joined by a similarly aggrieved clergy[,] the barons in 1215 extracted a charter from King John, later to become venerated as the Magna Carta. It was a self-serving document for the barons, who viewed the charter as a contract to halt their losses of feudal privileges.[29]

Some further details in this regard appear in the biographical sketch of King John offered in Appendix 4.7. (Note that a simplified chart of the sovereigns of England from 1066 onward appears in Appendix 4.6.)

Other efforts at striking a balance between the powers of the central courts and the powers of the local courts occurred in the decades just following the Magna Carta. For example, in 1258, the Provisions of Oxford were issued;[30] one effect they had—or at least attempted—was to prohibit any further expansion of the writ system—a prohibition that was later discarded but attempted again in 1285 with the Statute of Westminster II.[31]

3. Consequences of this Peculiar Course of Development

What possible significance might these hoary facts[32] have for a modern understanding of the common law? René David offers these observations:

> These circumstances in which the Common law developed are not of merely historical interest. From at least four points of view they have left their mark upon

---

29. Nutshell-2008, *supra* note 3, at 159–160.

30. The Provisions of Oxford have been regarded by some as a first constitution for England, inasmuch as they purported to force King Henry II to recognize the rights and powers of Parliament. Moreover, they were published in English—the first English government document to be published in the English language since the Norman "conquest" two hundred years earlier. For further details, see the entry for "Provisions of Oxford" in the *Classic Encyclopedia*, based on the 1911 version of the Encyclopedia Brittanica, at http://www.1911encyclopedia.org/Provisions_Of_Oxford. See also "English and Its Historical Development", in *English-Word Information*, at http://wordinfo.info/unit/4208?letter=E&spage=5.

31. One source offers this summary of the interplay of the Provisions of Oxford and the Statute of Westminster:

> [A] practice grew up under which the clerks in Chancery framed new writs even though the complaint was not quite covered by an existing writ ... This appeared to Parliament to be a usurpation of its powers as the supreme lawgiver. Further, it took much work away from the local courts, diminishing the income of the local barons who persuaded Parliament to pass a statute called the Provisions of Oxford in 1258, forbidding in effect the practice of creating new writs to fit new cases. This proved so inconvenient that an attempt to remedy the situation was made by the Statute of Westminster II in 1285, which empowered the clerks in Chancery to issue new writs *in consimili casu* (in similar cases), thus adapting existing writs to fit new circumstances. The common law began to expand again....

Smith & Keenan, *supra* note 6, at 3–4.

32. The adjective "hoary" has been defined as carrying these three main denotations: (1) gray or white with age (as in "an old dog with a hoary muzzle"; (2) ancient or venerable (as in "hoary myths"); (3) tedious from familiarity. See dictionary.com, particularly http://dictionary.reference.com/browse/hoary. The noun "hoar" is commonly associated with frost (as in "hoarfrost", which the Oxford English Dictionary dates to 1290), presumably expressing the resemblance of the white features of frost to an old man's beard. The German language still retains a form of the word "hoar" as a title of respect, in "Herr".

English law and even today their influence can be detected. English jurists have, in the first place, traditionally emphasised matters of procedure. Secondly, many of the categories and concepts of English law have been shaped by these historical circumstances; they have, in the third place, led to the rejection in English law of the distinction between public and private law. Finally the early development of the Common law was an obstacle to the reception of Roman law categories and concepts.[33]

Let us briefly examine each of these four points in order,[34] beginning with some observations on English common law's remarkable (one might say obsessive) emphasis on procedure:

a. Emphasis on procedure

In the long period in which the common law was developing, and indeed up to the 19th century, when dramatic legislative reforms were undertaken, the principal focus of English lawyers and commentators—including "jurists" of the sort described more fully below—was on procedure, not on substance or principle. In particular, they concentrated on the operation of the writ system outlined above, so as to determine how particular legal disputes might (or might not) be framed in such a way as to provide the necessary "key" (writ) to obtain entry into the royal courts at Westminster. A phrase often used to capture this reality is "remedies precede rights". This approach, so different from the approach taken in the development of European civil law (where emphasis on substance far outweighed emphasis on procedure), was driven in part by the use of the jury system in England. Growing out of ancient usage, and formed in fact well before the Norman arrival,[35] the jury system as a method of settling issues in both criminal and civil cases influenced the manner in which lawyers approached the law. A lawyer's attention was focused on issues of procedure because the overall aim was to formulate questions of fact in a way to ensure getting them before a jury. In that setting, the substance of the law, "to adopt the striking phrase of Sir Henry Maine (1822–1888), appears to have been 'secreted in the interstices of procedure'... [and indeed the common law] did not appear to be so much a system attempting to bring justice as a conglomeration of procedures designed, in more and more cases, to achieve solutions to disputes."[36]

b. Categories and concepts

This heavy emphasis on procedural matters, and on the development of law by the gradual accretion of rules emerging from the disposition of specific disputes brought before courts, has had a plainly visible effect on the structure and classification of common law. Recall from the discussion in Chapters Two and Three that European civil law developed

---

33. David & Brierly, *supra* note 1, at 317.

34. The following details are drawn from several sources, especially David & Brierly, *supra* note 1, at 317–323.

35. For a brief summary of the historical roots of the jury in England, see Kempin, *supra* note 9, at 54–68.

36. David & Brierly, *supra* note 1, at 317–318, citing Sir Henry Maine, EARLY LAW AND CUSTOM 389 (1861). David explains that the 12th-century author Glanvill and the 13th-century author Bracton described "the whole of English law" by focusing on procedure and the writ system, as did that "chronicles known as the *Year Books*, written in Law French, which inform us of the state of the law between 1290 and 1536 [and which] concentrate principally on relating matters of procedure and often omit altogether whatever solutions were given in the disputes themselves which they recorded.

a highly classified "taxonomy" of rules and principles. English law developed differently. Unlike European civil law, English law "never achieved a general principle linking [the liability for civil wrongs] to a comprehensive idea of fault, but [instead] developed a series of special or nominate civil wrongs: deceipt, nuisance, trespass, conversion, libel and slander, … and so on."[37] This is different from the approach taken in the French civil code, which (as described in Chapter Two) included a general maxim that the causing of injury by one person to another creates an obligation of compensation. Such a norm, drawn from Roman law antecedents, was absent from English law because of the emphasis on procedure over substance. It was, as David says, "only with some effort that a general principle of civil liability was developed" rather recently in English law.[38]

c. Public law and private law

Indeed, even the central distinction found in European civil law — the public law/private law distinction — is necessarily missing from English common law. In a sense, all law was "public" law because it emerged from the judgments of courts that technically had jurisdiction only over those matters that were of interest to the public at large, the kingdom as a whole. David describes this "wasting away" of private law in the English experience:

> The royal courts enlarged their jurisdiction by developing the basic idea that their intervention was justified in the interests of the crown and kingdom. Other courts in this way of thinking were, therefore, available only if private interests were in question. But these other courts gradually declined [for reasons noted above, including reasons centering on money and "modernity"], and with them the very idea of private law disappeared in England. All cases submitted to the English royal courts thus had the appearance, as it were, of being public law disputes.

> The "public law" aspect of English law emerges from an examination of the special technique of the *writ* by which the action before the royal courts began. The writ was not simply the plaintiff's authorisation to act; technically it was an order given by the king commanding his officers to order the defendant to act according to the law by satisfying the claim of the plaintiff. If the defendant refused to obey the order, the plaintiff could then proceed against him; his action before the royal court would be justified not so much because of the opposition made to his claim but because of the defendant's disobedience of an order of the administration. The English trial is a matter of public not private law. It was essentially a debate as to whether an administrative act, the writ, issuing from the royal chancery, was properly issued and whether the order it embodied to the defendant was to be maintained. The trial was not for the purpose of setting aside an administrative act prejudicial to the person who requested it; on the contrary, he who obtained and meant to take advantage of it instituted an action in order that the procedure, if contested, be confirmed.[39]

d. Barriers to the reception of Roman law

The last of the four points made by René David regarding the contemporary significance of the early (and peculiar) development of English common law focuses on how

---

37. David & Brierly, *supra* note 1, at 320.
38. *Id.* at 320–321.
39. *Id.* at 321.

that course of development made it impossible for England to "receive" Roman law. Re-call from the discussion in Chapter Two the manner in which "reception" of Roman law, and of the *jus commune* more generally, took place to a greater or lesser extent all across the face of Europe, especially in Germany. This would obviously have been impossible at the beginning of Norman political control over England, since the rediscovery and study of Justinian's *Digest* had not occurred as of 1066. However, no reception *ever* occurred in England, for reasons that again relate to the peculiarities of courts and jurisdiction in that country.

> [In terms of the substantive rules and principles that courts could rely on in pro-viding solutions to disputes brought before them,] English law has a different appearance from continental laws. The courts of Westminster were in a situa-tion very dissimilar to that of the various traditional European continental courts.... From the beginning [those continental] courts had general jurisdic-tion in all litigation; they were never restricted to only certain kinds of cases made possible through special procedures. And since they were free from such obstacles, the continental courts were able to modernise their procedures gen-erally by turning to the new, written procedures of Canon law. Having general jurisdiction, they were also able to concentrate upon the systematic development of principles of justice and to allow themselves to be guided in this respect by the model offered by Roman law.
>
> In England on the other hand the situation was totally different because the royal courts, the courts of Westminster, were special courts only having jurisdiction in special cases for each of which there was a particular procedure; they had come into existence because of a completely new factor — the development of a centralised royal power. The royal courts, emerging as independent branches of the *curia Regis*, were first of all political rather than judicial organs because it was intended that they resolve problems involving the interest of the king and the kingdom — in other words, the general interest — and not principally, in theory at least, the private interests of individuals. For the new kinds of problems that had arisen a new kind of law was therefore required.... And of course the over-riding necessity that all questions be handled within the traditional procedural framework was a major obstacle to the reception of the rules and concepts of Roman law.
>
> In these circumstances, the courts of Westminster had to construct a new law.... [This new law] took some elements from Roman law; it is established, for instance, that in Bracton's thirteenth century description of legal institutions much was bor-rowed from the post-glossator Azo (*d.* 1230).[40] All these elements, however, were re-shaped and melded in the procedural moulds used by the courts. Moreover, their origin was never divulged by the judges; the Common law, constructed de-cision by decision by the courts, was presented as essentially a work of reason.... Later, the so-called *general immemorial custom of the realm*, of which the judges were the oracles, was said to be the basis for this work of reason. But one must not be misled by such language: this general immemorial custom was a pure fic-tion; the only true customs existing in England in the twelfth and thirteenth cen-turies were *local* customs. It was in order to provide the Common law with a foundation in agreement with the traditional, canonic and Roman theories of the

---

40. [*footnote in original*] Maitland (F.W.), *Select Passages from the works of Bracton and Azo* (1895); Winfield (P.H.), *Chief Sources of English Legal History* (1925), p. 60.

sources of law that this concept of general immemorial custom was, *a posteriori*, invented. It was not based on any reality.

The rigor of the Common law procedures and the need to conform to a traditional framework were the main reasons preventing the wholesale reception of Roman legal concepts in England, at a time when the courts at Westminster, extending their original jurisdiction, gradually made it complete and most often were deciding purely private law disputes. These procedures, from many points of view archaic and typically English, forced a process of "anglicisation" to take place when substantive elements were borrowed from Roman or Canon law.[41]

To the points made in this excerpt from René David I would add only two further observations. First, it is worth noting that although the odd historical development of English common law served as an obstacle to the (visible) reception of Roman law categories and concepts, there was nevertheless a significant degree of indirect "importation" of Roman civil law into England during these early days of the common law's development. As described more fully in Appendix 4.8, the scholar Vacarius—having been trained at the University of Bologna in the early days of the Glossatorial School there—came to England in the early 12th century and taught courses in Roman law at Oxford for many years. This is but one illustration of how, according to modern research, continental law had much more of an impact on the early development of English law than was earlier thought.[42] As noted in the preceding excerpt from David, another early English scholar —Henry de Bracton—also borrowed from the Roman legal scholarship of the day.[43] For a biographical sketch of Bracton, who wrote his famous treatise *On the Laws and Customs of England* in the 1250s, see Appendix 4.9. As noted there, Bracton wrote in Law French, which was the spoken language of law from the late 13th century to the 17th century.[44]

Second, the emphasis on procedure and the lack of emphasis on Roman law in the development of English common law led to another important phenomenon—the training of English lawyers not through academic training but through a form of apprenticeship. Heller offers this explanation:

> The rigidity of the writ system and the emergence of formal procedures (the latter strongly influenced by canon law) made it necessary that litigants have the assistance of persons learned in these rules and the courts soon demanded that

---

41. David & Brierly, *supra* note 1, at 321–323.

42. See R.H. Helmholz, *The Origins of Magna Carta (1215) and the European Ius Commune* (draft article, about 1996, on file with author) (asserting "that the *ius commune*, the amalgam of Roman and canon laws that governed legal education and influenced legal practice in Europe from the twelfth century onwards, played a significant role in the drafting of the [Magna Carta's] provisions"). See also *Influences of Roman Law on the Common Law of England*, available on the Creighton University website at http://www.creighton.edu/law/library/rarebookroom/moreonthecommonlaw/index.php (asserting that "[t]he Norman conquest of 1066 reintroduced continental ideas including Roman ones" and specifically that "Christianity and the emergence of Canon law also helped preserve Roman legal concepts" and introduce them into England in the 12th century, when "[m]ost lawyers and judges ... were churchmen [who were] schooled in Canon and Civil law" and whose "training in method and principle enabled them to construct a rational, a general, a definite system of law out of the vague and conflicting mass of customs, half tribal, half feudal of which the English law [under the Anglo-Saxons] consisted").

43. Another early treatise on the law of England, this one by Glanvil, also reflects a strong influence of Roman rules and principles. The great English jurist Maitland is quoted as having said that "[t]here are very few sentences in [Glanvil's text] which can be traced to any Roman book, and yet in a sense the whole book is Roman." *Influence of Roman Law, supra* note 42.

44. See *supra* note 16 and accompanying text.

those who would appear before them in that capacity be certified as to their learning. Thus persons who would aspire to make advocacy there profession found it advantageous to seek out older practitioners and become their apprentices. Because the royal courts all sat at Westminster, these attorneys (as they soon came to be called) tended to reside at the same inns during the terms of court and the prospective lawyer would seek permission to lodge at one of these inns, take his meals with the seniors and listen to their discussions of rules and cases. In due course, formal readings during the meals took the place of informal talk and the "Inns of Court" became recognized as the exclusive route into the legal profession.[45]

Taking both of these two observations together presents a picture of early English law that resembles in some way dynastic Chinese law. As we shall see later in Chapters Six and Seven, several factors combined to make Chinese law rather impervious to *direct* influence from foreign legal rules and concepts — encouraging it, in other words, to develop largely "indigenously" or "insularly", without having either the benefit or the annoyance of having to adjust (at least on the surface) to outside legal forces. In some ways English law in its early formative years displayed a similar character, partly because of the two factors noted immediately above: that is, (i) that as a general rule the odd historical development of English common law served as an obstacle to the *obvious* or *direct* reception of Roman law categories and concepts, although below the surface there were in fact significant subtle and indirect forms of influence that we can discern in retrospect; and (ii) that the training of English lawyers in the early years of the common law's development (and indeed until fairly recently) occurred not through academic training but almost exclusively through a form of apprenticeship conducted in London, the seat of power for the state.

In sum, English law took on an insular character. Consistent with the view, still held by a great many English nationals, that the United Kingdom (and especially England) is not part of Europe,[46] English law developed in a fashion that provides a sharp contrast with continental European law. J.A.C. Thomas, most famous for his explanations of Roman law (and relied on in Appendix 2.18 for an overview of the "second life" of Roman law), has offered these observations about some of the factors that have helped create the insularity of English law:

> In the first place, there is the obvious geographical separation from the mainland of the continent which in earlier times made for a greater distinctness. Then William I, who established the Norman kingdom, claimed to be the legitimate successor to Edward the Confessor whose laws and customs he swore to uphold; he was also the first of a strong line of kings who early established the central authority of the crown and substituted royal courts administering the "common custom of the realm" for the local jurisdictions. This early unification of common law was further facilitated by the centralisation of the legal profession in the capital, away from the universities and near the courts. The Inns of Courts, in their earlier days, may be thought of as universities of law: but the teachers and the taught were actual and aspiring practitioners[,] and the law that they practiced and studied was the common law of England, a practical law the preparation for which was not education as such but experience and example. Thus

---

45. Heller, *supra* note 2, at 9–10.

46. For some enlightening and some amusing views on this, conduct a Google search for "English views on whether England is part of Europe".

there developed a tough insular legal system capable of resisting the blandishments of Romanism in the sixteenth century.[47]

III. The Need for and Rise of Equity

Let us pause for a moment to consider this question: What, if anything, was wrong with the system of common law around the 15th century, as it had emerged from the various influences described above? If we were to compare English common law of that time to the law that had developed on the continent of Europe — evolving, as we know through our earlier examination in Chapter Two, from a melding of Roman civil law, canon law, and commercial law — could we identify any specific defects in the English common law?

We might consider this question from five perspectives. First, from the perspective of the monarch, the common law of the 15th century probably seemed adequate; after all, in the two centuries that had passed since the Magna Carta, the jurisdiction of the royal courts at Westminster had gradually expanded, to the benefit of the king.[48] Second, from the perspective of the royal courts themselves (that is, their judges), the system probably seemed adequate; although complex, the writ system was workable, despite the fact that the substantive rules to be applied by the courts were not, as on the European continent, based in a centuries-old academically-rich tradition. Third, from the perspective of the practicing bar (that is, legal professionals practicing before the royal courts) in London, the system also probably seemed adequate, or at least lucrative and workable — and perhaps less intellectually demanding than legal practice on the continent because of the heavier emphasis on procedure and lighter emphasis on substance.

However, the view of the English legal system in the 15th century might be different, and much less favorable, from two other perspectives. From the perspective of those lords and barons and other members of the local aristocracy responsible for administration of government and justice throughout the rest of the country (that is, outside London), the common law system described above probably represented an unsatisfactory and deeply irritating power-grab by the central royal and judicial authorities in Westminster, whose constant expansion of jurisdiction came at the expense of those lords and barons, leading toward a wasting away of the courts they operated. Moreover, from the perspective of the litigants themselves — that is, persons all over England wishing to gain some relief and satisfaction out of legal disputes — the system as it had developed by the 15th century also probably appeared unsatisfactory.

These problems led to an imaginative solution — the development of a separate "corrective" system of courts. This development did not come easily; instead, it involved a strenuous political conflict. Let us examine that conflict and its resolution.

A. Law and Equity in Conflict

A combination of factors led to the creation of a rival system of courts that, over the course of several centuries, vied with the royal courts for jurisdiction and power. One

---

47. J.A.C. Thomas, Textbook of Roman Law 11 (1976).

48. Heller notes that "[a]lthough each king at his coronation reaffirmed the Magna Carta, both legislation and practice strengthened the royal courts". *Id.* at 9.

such factor was what we might call the brittleness of the writ system. As described above, that system threw up many obstacles to the administration of justice within the royal courts at Westminster. Many a party seeking such justice might be disappointed, either (i) because the dispute that he wanted those courts to handle (in his favor, of course) did not fall within the parameters of one of the writs through which access to the courts was possible or (ii) because even if a writ were available, other limitations in the remedies available from the royal courts left him dissatisfied. From that party's perspective, then, some alternative approach — some corrective action — was needed.

This need for corrective action was then joined by a second factor: the momentum toward centralization of power within the monarchy. That momentum toward central-ization, it will be recalled, began explosively when William I arrived on the scene fol-lowing the Battle of Hastings; and then William's successors had gradually expanded the monarchy's central powers. Therefore, when some corrective alternative to an inadequate system of justice became evident, an obvious solution came to the mind of the dissatis-fied litigant: he should take his case directly to the king.

> If the royal courts were unable to give satisfaction[,] could not the king remedy the malfunctioning of his courts? To the medieval mind, this final appeal to the king was very natural and the royal courts were not offended, at least at the beginning, to see the parties requesting the King to exercise his "prerogative." After all, the royal courts themselves owed their development to the operation of the same prin-ciple — that one could, in exceptional cases, appeal to the king to obtain justice.[49]

This is in fact what occurred. Beginning especially in the 14th century, a private per-son who was not able to have his case heard in the royal courts (because of the rigors of the writ system), or who could claim that the outcome of his case in those courts was shocking to the conscience, found it increasingly attractive and feasible to seek interven-tion from the king as a matter of the king's grace and special prerogative. This special re-course typically was handled by the office of the chancellor, who was thought to have a special responsibility for guiding the king's conscience and therefore could be relied on (or so it was hoped) to transmit to the king the request for special relief. One source of-fers the following summary of this new form of relief:

> To counter the severity of the writ system and provide relief other than money damages, the king and later his Chancellor, the "keeper of the king's conscience," accepted petitions for equitable relief. Heard in an inquisitorial fashion mod-eled on canon and Roman law, these equitable proceedings focused on avoid-ing the strictures of the common law. It was successful, and a formal Court of Chancery soon assumed jurisdiction of pleas in equity.[50]

Once planted, these seeds of change — we shall soon see that they were the seeds of a fierce jurisdictional battle — grew and flourished. Beginning around the middle part of the 15th century, and especially during the Wars of the Roses (1453–1485), the chancel-lor became increasingly autonomous in handling appeals brought to him by litigants dis-satisfied by their treatment at the hands of the royal courts. From an objective standpoint (if there is one), it might seem perfectly appropriate that the chancellor would assume this role. René David explains:

> [The chancellor's interventions were] more and more frequently requested be-cause procedural difficulties and judicial traditionalism stood in the way of the

---

49. David & Brierly, *supra* note 1, at 324.
50. Nutshell-2008, *supra* note 3, at 161.

necessary development of the Common law. His decisions, in the beginning made on the basis of "the equity of the case", became increasingly systematised and the application of "equitable" doctrines soon amounted to additions and correctives to the "legal" principles applied by the royal courts.[51]

The seeming attractiveness—maybe even innocuousness—of this trend was not entirely pure, however, from a political standpoint. The late 15th century and early 16th century saw the house of Tudor rise to power.[52] Its urge toward absolutism, evident for example in the reign of Henry VIII, made the expansion of the chancellor's powers quite attractive. Hence such an expansion seemed likely both from the perspective of its political appeal (to the king, that is) and from the perspective of its substantive fairness. David offers an explanation of how these two considerations intertwined to encourage the legal expansion of the chancellor's "corrective" powers to do equity:

> Tudor absolutism of the sixteenth century was based on an extensive use of the royal prerogative. In criminal law, the famous Court of "Star Chamber" (*camera stellata*), after having been usefully employed to re-establish order following the civil war, was a formidable threat to the liberty of subjects. In civil matters, the equitable jurisdiction of the chancellor, founded as well on royal prerogative, was also considerably broadened. After 1529, the chancellor ... was not an ecclesiastic but usually a lawyer. The chancellor examined the petitions addressed to him as a real judge, and [he did so] in observation of a written procedure inspired by Canon law, one entirely different from the principles of procedure observed at Common law [in the royal courts]. The substantive principles he applied were also largely taken from Roman law and Canon law to whose reception procedure was no obstacle in this case as it was at Common law. These principles[,] rather than the very often archaic and outmoded Common law rules, generally gave more satisfaction to the Renaissance ideas of social good and justice. And because of their concern for justice and good administration, the English sovereigns of this period favored the chancellor's jurisdiction.
>
> The play of political considerations was also in its favor. The private, written and inquisitorial procedure of chancery which never made use of the jury, rather than the oral and public Common law procedure, may also have been preferred by a monarch of authoritarian disposition. There was also probably some idea that if Roman law were to be adopted by the chancellor[,] the law would then ... be limited to private relations, thereby giving greater scope to royal absolutism and executive discretion. *Princeps legibus solutus est.*[53] *Quod principi placuit, legis habet vigorem.*[54] How were such attractive maxims found in the Digest to be resisted? It may also have seemed simpler, in fact, to evolve an entirely new legal system and judicial administration than to attempt to bring about the reforms in the Common law that were so necessary at this time. *English law thus narrowly escaped joining the European continental legal family in the sixteenth century* because of the success of the chancellor's equitable jurisdiction and the decay of the Common law. There was a risk that disputing parties would abandon the

---

51. David & Brierly, *supra* note 1, at 325.

52. A simplified chart of the sovereigns of England (including their "houses" or "dynasties") from 1066 onward appears in Appendix 4.15.

53. [*footnote in original*] Digest, 1.3.31. (The prince is above the law.)

54. [*footnote in original*] Digest, 1.4.1. (That which receives the assent of the prince has force of law.)

Common law courts and that these would fall into disuse, just as the Hundred Courts were deserted and abandoned three centuries before when the courts of Westminster, then in their full glory, offered a more modern justice administered according to a procedure superior to the traditional methods.[55]

A point in the foregoing excerpt by René David that warrants special attention appears near the end, where he refers to "the risk that disputing parties would abandon the Common law courts and that these would fall into disuse, just as the Hundred Courts were deserted and abandoned three centuries before when the courts of Westminster ... offered a more modern justice".[56] This passage might elicit the image of two "end runs". The first "end run" (like a football player running around the end of the opposing team's defensive line) was successful: a litigant who doubted the fairness or competence of the local courts (or who was disappointed at the result he received in such a court) could make an "end run" around those local courts and take his case to the royal courts at Westminster — *if* he could somehow navigate his way through the writ system by proving that his case was of sufficient significance to the kingdom as to justify jurisdiction by those courts rather than having the case ultimately resolved in the local courts. The second "end run", however, was only partially successful. That "end run" took the form of a litigant seeking redress in the courts of equity when it was clear that the courts of common law were going to be (or had already proven to be) inadequate to give the litigant the relief he thought he deserved. In this second attempt at an "end run", there was no *complete* escape from the common law and its courts; but some *partial* degree of relief or protection was in fact provided by the courts of equity. (It was as if the football player did indeed get tackled by the opposing team's defensive line, but the referee provided certain protections from undue roughness, as by awarding additional yardage to the player if the defensive linesmen tackled him too hard.)

These legal developments were taking place against the backdrop of other major political developments. Francis Heller offers this explanation of the political circumstances under which the Courts of Chancery arose:

> The turbulent years of the Hundred Years' War and the War of the Roses required the kings to give most of their attention to military matters. Two consequences grew out of this royal pre-occupation: First, to fight his wars the king needed money; trade, both foreign and domestic, had by this time produced accumulations of wealth in the cities; the addition of town representatives ("the Commons") to the council with whom the king discussed matters of state served to co-opt the merchant class and to make their wealth accessible to the king. This, thus, is one of the major causes for the development of Parliament (from the French *parler*, to talk); its legislative function had its origins in concessions the Commons extracted from the king in return for monetary contributions for the royal engagement in war.

> Secondly, as the kings concentrated their interest on foreign and domestic wars, they neglected the everyday conduct of government, allowing bureaucratic patterns to take hold. Thus legal institutions and practices came to be solidified and embedded in the social structure. Fortunately, the rigidity of the court system had by this time come to be counterweighted by the emergence of chancery, grown out of the king's discretionary power but evolved now into a system that com-

---

55. David & Brierly, *supra* note 1, at 325–326.
56. *Id.* at 326.

plemented the common law. Chancery (or "equity" because its beginnings had been appeals by aggrieved citizens to the king's sense of fairness and equity) developed direct remedies and applied them where "law" denied access to or relief from the courts.

The balance of the two systems had been fairly achieved by the time the Tudor dynasty gained the throne. History spends much time exploring Henry VIII's marital adventures and his break with Rome, "Bloody" Mary's efforts to restore Roman Catholicism and the first Elizabeth's achievements, both at home and abroad, but tends to gloss over the fact that the Tudor period is the closest to absolutism that England ever came. The courts, like Parliament, were dutifully subservient to the monarch.[57]

Ultimately, however, the momentum toward absolutism was arrested, and so the continued expansion of the powers of the courts of chancery was stopped. Heller explains that it was "when, with James I, a less effective ruler came to the throne", that Parliament and the common law courts pushed back.[58] David offers this explanation:

> ... Several reasons explain why [the abandonment of the common law courts and a surrender of their jurisdiction to the courts of equity] did not take place. The resistance of the common lawyers had to be taken into consideration by the monarchy. To defend their position and their work, and to support them against royal absolution, the Common law courts found an ally in Parliament. The poor organisation of Chancery, its congestion and venality were all weapons in the hands of its enemies. The revolution that might have brought England into the family of Romanist laws did not take place. In the end, a compromise was worked out which left the Common law courts and the court of the chancellor side by side, in a kind of equilibrium of power.
>
> This compromise was not the result of legislation or a formal decision by royal authority or the judges. Very much the contrary. At the end of an extremely violent conflict[59] between Chancery and the Common law courts represented by Chief Justice Coke (1552–1634), who was also leader of the liberal parliamentary opposition, James I pronounced in favour of the former in 1616. The danger, however, had been serious and the chancellors were wise enough not to abuse their victory, and thereby disarmed parliamentary hostility. Parliament

---

57. Heller, *supra* note 2, at 10–11.

58. *Id.* at 11. The reason why Parliament pushed back is to be found not only in the fact that James I was, as Heller says, a less effective ruler, but also in the fact that he was regarded as a foreigner whose claims of the monarchy's power were unpalatable. In another text, Heller offers this perspective:

James I came to London as a stranger. James VI as king of Scotland, he was, as far as the English were concerned, a foreigner. Worse yet, from the very beginning he insisted that as king he was all-powerful. He made this clear in his first Speech from the Trhone which he had then printed under the title *The Divine Right of Kngs*. The opposition to his rule increased with the years and soon included most of the nation's prominent citizens.

Francis H. Heller, AMERICAN LEGAL HISTORY 56 (1998) (unpublished, on file with author) [hereinafter AMERICAN LEGAL HISTORY). As noted in Appendix 4.6 at the end of this chapter, the reign of James I—the first monarch in the House of Stuart—began in 1603.

59. [*footnote in original*] The decisions or decrees of the Court of Chancery were not directly enforceable; their effectiveness, however, was assured by the possibility of imprisoning the contravening party or by the sequestration of his property. The common lawyers declared that they considered a person who opposed such measures, even to the point where he had killed an officer of the Chancery charged to enforce them, as having acted in legitimate self-defense.

was, in truth, more interested in ending another abuse of royal prerogative, the Court of Star Chamber (abolished in 1641), than it was in the disappearance of Equity as such. A tacit understanding was established on the basis of the *status quo*. It was understood that the jurisdiction of the chancellor was to remain but that it would attempt no new encroachments at the expense of the Common courts; it would also continue to adjudicate according to its precedents and thus escape from the criticism that it was arbitrary. It was further understood that the king would no longer use his prerogative to create new courts independent of the established Common law courts. Even the nature of Equity itself was to change: the chancellor, as a legal or political figure, was no longer seen as judging on the basis of morality alone and tended to act more and more as a true judge. Further, after 1621, the control by the House of Lords over the decisions of the court of Chancery was admitted. In these new conditions the Common law courts were inclined to admit those interventions of the chancellor which were authorised in virtue of precedents.[60]

The importance of the so-called "Compromise of 1616" warrants more attention than it receives in the foregoing excerpt from René David. Another source offers this somewhat clearer account of the conflict leading up to that compromise:

[The conflict between Law and Equity] arose out of the practice of the Court of Chancery which issued "common injunctions" forbidding a person on pain of imprisonment from bringing an action in the common law courts, or forbidding the enforcement of a common law judgment if such a judgment had been obtained.

Thus, if X by some unconscionable conduct, such as undue influence, had obtained an agreement with Y, whereby Y was to sell X certain land at much below its real value, then if Y refused to convey the land, X would have his remedy in damages at common law despite his unconscionable conduct. However, if Y appealed to the Chancellor, the latter might issue a common injunction which would prevent X from bringing his action at common law unless he wished to suffer punishment for defiance of the Chancellor's injunction. Similarly, if X had already obtained a judgment at common law, the Chancellor would prevent its enforcement by ordering X, on pain of imprisonment, not to execute judgment on Y's property.

However, the common law courts retaliated by waiting for the Chancellor to imprison the common law litigant for defiance of the injunction, and then the common law would release him by the process of *habeas corpus*.

This period of rivalry culminated in the *Earl of Oxford's* case in 1615, when it was decided that where common law and equity were in conflict Equity should prevail.[61]

The issue raised in the *Earl of Oxford* case (to express it in simplified form) was whether the result emerging from the common law courts or the result emerging from the courts of equity should prevail in a dispute in which Magdalene College (in Cambridge) had attempted to force the defendant to vacate certain land that the college had leased to the defendant for a long period of time. The college wanted to break the lease because the land had increased dramatically in commercial value (due to the efforts of the defendant), such that the college thought it would be able to gain a higher rent for it under these

---

60. David & Brierly, *supra* note 1, at 326–328 (emphasis added).
61. Smith & Keenan, *supra* note 6, at 5–6.

changed circumstances. The college asserted in part that the lease had been invalid from the beginning because the college had in fact never possessed the authority to grant a long-term lease in the first place. The college won the case in the common law courts, in an action presided over by Sir Edward Coke; however, the Lord Chancellor, Lord Ellesmere, applied the "clean hands" doctrine in issuing a common injunction out of the Court of Chancery to rule in favor of the defendant and prohibiting the college's enforcement of the common law order—on grounds that the college should not be permitted to benefit richly from its own *ultra vires* action. The two courts became locked in a stalemate, and the matter was eventually referred to the Attorney-General, Sir Francis Bacon. Sir Francis, by authority of King James I, upheld the use of the common injunction and concluded that in the event of any conflict between the common law and the equity, equity would prevail.[62] As noted above, it was the political decision following the Attorney-General's decision that constitutes the "Compromise of 1616".

B. The Post-Conflict Complementarity of Law and Equity

With the Compromise of 1616, the English legal system took on a distinctively odd dual character. "Alongside the Common law rules, the work of the royal courts of Westminster or, as they are also called, the 'Common law courts,' it also [applied] *rules of Equity* or 'equitable remedies' which complement and correct the Common law"[63]—and those rules and remedies in equity were applied exclusively by the Court of Chancery. (As we shall see below in subsection IVA, the courts of equity and common law were merged finally in the late 1800s.) In other words, in the centuries following 1616, the relationship between law and equity changed from one of conflict to one of complementarity.

For a diagrammatic representation of the long history of courts in the English system, see Box #4.3. It is intended to reflect, by using shaded circles, the growing or diminishing extent of the jurisdiction of various types of courts in England. It shows in column A the mixture of local courts—including mainly hundreds courts, county courts, and other Anglo-Saxon courts that existed before Norman times, as well as the feudal courts and ecclesiastical courts that emerged starting with the Norman "conquest" of 1066. The diagram shows in column B the royal courts at Westminster—that is, the common law courts. Lastly, it shows in column C the courts of Chancery (courts of equity) whose development has been described above.

The appearances (and disappearances) of shaded circles, as the centuries progress, reflect how the various local courts, the common law courts, and the courts of equity wax and wane over time. The two attempts at "end runs" that I discussed above—the first successful, the second only partially so—can be seen in the diagram. First, as the royal courts (common law courts) expanded their jurisdiction in the 12th through 14th centuries, they sucked jurisdiction away from the local courts, thereby permitting litigants to make an "end run" around those local courts and take their cases to the royal courts at Westminster—a solution that had serious deficiencies, however, because of the common law courts' heavy emphasis on procedure and the writ system. Second, as those deficien-

---

62. In the system of English case reports, see *Earl of Oxford's Case* (1615) I Ch Rep I, 21 ER 485, and *The Earl of Oxford's Case in Chancery* (1615) Mich 13 Jac 1; 21 ER 485. For further information on the case in Chancery, *see* the Oxford Authorship Site, at http://www.oxford-shakespeare.com/ (search for "Earl of Oxford" or "Earl of Oxford's Case in Chancery, 1615"). See also D.M. Kerly, Equitable Jurisdiction of the Court of Chancery 111–113 (1890).

63. David & Brierly, *supra* note 1, at 328 (emphasis in original).

cies of the common law courts became more and more evident, the court of Chancery expanded its jurisdiction in the 15th and 16th centuries, challenging the authority and effectiveness of those common law courts, thereby permitting some litigants to make an "end run" around those common law courts—a trend that was arrested, however, by the Compromise of 1616. That compromise, resulting in the system of "complementarity" in which the common law courts and the courts of equity operate in parallel, is reflected in the pair of equal-sized circles in the 17th and 18th centuries. Lastly, the merger of the courts of law and equity that occurred in the late 19th century is reflected in the long oblong shaded shapes appearing in the 19th and 20th centuries.

Box #4.3 *Diagrammatic Representation of the Development of Courts in England*

The peculiar nature of this parallel system—that is, the complementary functions of law and equity for over two centuries in English law—is important enough to warrant some closer attention. Let us give it that attention by examining several specific questions and illustrations regarding this complementarity.

A first question concerns the hierarchical relationship between law and equity—or, more precisely, between the operation of the common law courts and operation of the courts of equity. In a case involving both sets of courts, which one will prevail? The answer, though complicated, is captured in the phrase "equity follows the law", the meaning of which has been described in this way:

> The chancellor never intervened with a view to creating new legal rules which later judges would have to apply. He never purported to change the law, such as it had been established and applied by the Common law courts; quite the contrary—the chancellor professed his respect for the law: "Equity follows the law" was a maxim proclaimed by Chancery. But to "follow" the law did not necessarily mean that considerations of morality were to be put aside and it was in the name of morality that the chancellor intervened without, however, clashing the law. It could never be admitted in effect that the enforcement of a right might amount to an injustice; that a *summum ius* amounted to a *summa iniuria*. In other countries, the judges themselves could supply the required remedy by prohibiting the abuse of a right or fraud, or by applying the principle of public order and good morals; such remedies were possible on the European continent within the very framework of the legal principles. In England, however, the royal courts did not have the same freedom of action because that had never had the same general jurisdiction and were bound to observe rigid procedures. And so it was that, avoiding them and appealing to a special court created upon the authority of royal prerogative, solutions drawn from the dictates of conscience and morality were brought to bear as limitations upon or complements to a strict Common law....[64]

The image that emerges from the general description is that of a "dance" between law and equity (or between common law courts and courts of equity). Three examples might clarify the nature of this "dance". David offers two illustrations from contract law—one relating to the effectiveness of remedies and the other relating to the treatment of contracts entered into under duress—and a third illustration that focuses on the concept of the trust.

> [*Contract remedies.*] In the case of breach of contract, the prejudiced party could obtain only the [payment of] damages at Common law because the action of *assumpsit* for sanctioning contracts, delictual in origin (*trespass*), could only conclude for a condemnation to pay damages. It might happen, of course, that this sanction was inadequate and that the aggrieved party was more interested in obtaining the actual performance of the undertaking. There was, however, no action available before the Common law courts to obtain this result. By proceeding before the court of the Chancery a decree of "specific performance" enjoining performance could be obtained. Common law was not violated in any way; a remedy was simply granted that it [*i.e.*, the common law] was not able to provide.
>
> [*Forced "consent" in contracts.*] ... Further, the archaic Common law system had a doctrine of reality of consent ... in contract that was fairly primitive and underdeveloped. Its conception of *duress*, for example, covered only physical violence

---

64. David & Brierly, *supra* note 1, at 340–341.

and not moral coercion. The chancellor intervened therefore against those who unconscionably took advantage of their position as parent, guardian, master, confessor or physician to obtain a contract or some undue advantage from another; such person was prohibited from invoking the contract or demanding its performance. And in this way the doctrine of *undue influence*, as a moral imperative, was added to the legal rules of *duress*.

[*Concept of the trust.*] A person places property in the hands of another, because of the confidence he has in the latter, so that such property will be administered in the interest of a third person to whom it was inconvenient or even impossible to transfer ownership and to whom the revenues produced by such property must be remitted. At Common law the person who received the property, the trustee, became the outright owner; his undertaking to manage it in the interests of and to make over the revenues to a third person was not enforceable. The chancellor however gave effect to this agreement; he did not oppose the Common law rule by denying that the trustee was the owner of the property but complemented the rule by means of the effective sanction he gave to the obligation which, in conscience, the trustee has assumed.[65]

These illustrations suggest that great care was taken to avoid having the rules of equity violate the rules of common law, and to avoid having the courts of equity appear to be overriding the common law courts. Instead, the system of complementarity was conceived as permitting equity to supplement and improve upon the legal system as applied by the common law courts, in the interests of morality. Looking at the situation from an objective perspective, this seems like convenient fiction—or, to use the phrase Merryman often employs in describing certain aspects of the civil law tradition (such as the orthodox view that judges cannot make law), it seems like "folklore" plain and simple. From such a perspective, it would seem preferable to make modifications to the common law, and for the common law courts to develop and apply equity's "corrective" measures themselves. As we shall see below in subsection IVA of this chapter, the common law did finally undergo dramatic changes—in the 19th century. Until that time, the fragile compromise between the common law courts and the courts of equity did not permit such changes to be made.

Another question we might consider concerns terminology: what different terms were used in order to distinguish between the operations of the courts of equity and the common law courts, in order to reflect and respect their distinct functions? René David explains:

Because—in the beginning at least—the Chancery was not considered a court, it did not appear to be deciding "in law"; this would create a dangerous conflict with the law courts at Westminster which were financially and morally interested in retaining their monopoly over judicial administration. Even the terminology adopted by the Chancellor's court bears witness to this—procedure before the court is a "suit," not an "action," in certain "causes" or "matters"; one invokes "interests," not "rights"; the Chancellor grants a "decree," not a "judgment"; he may award "compensation," not "damages." The chancellor intervened "in equity" without purporting to modify the legal rules as administered by the courts. In every case it was by virtue of the demands of conscience that the intervention occurred.[66]

Yet another question relates to the power of the courts of equity to act "*in personam*". What does that phrase mean? It reflects the specific power of the Chancellor to physi-

---

65. *Id.* at 341–342.
66. *Id.* at 342–343.

cally coerce a person (on behalf of the king, of course, but largely because of the Chancellor's status as an ecclesiastic) to take certain action or refrain from taking it. For example, a person prevailing in a case in the common law courts might (by order of the courts of equity) be imprisoned to meditate upon the fallacious nature of a strict reliance upon his absolute "rights."

Another question relates to the mandatory or discretionary nature of legal and equitable remedies. The latter were almost always discretionary. Even as the intervention of the Chancellor, and later the operation of the courts of equity, became more systematic and predictable, equity remained discretionary, so that equity "only intervened if it was considered that the conduct of the defendant was contrary to conscience and if the plaintiff had no cause for reproaching himself: he, on his side, had to have 'clean hands' and must have acted without undue delay (*laches*) in asserting his right."[67]

Lastly, what about procedure? Where did the courts of equity draw rules of procedure for handling cases coming before them? Those courts were not bound by the procedural rules of the common law, of course, so they were at liberty to use a system entirely different from that of the common law. Proceedings in equity were largely written and inquisitorial in nature—drawing inspiration from the canon law; and in no cases did those proceedings in equity involve the participation of a jury.[68] In short, the procedure adopted by the courts of equity was in essence the "inquisitorial" system developed in continental European civil law countries, as discussed above in Chapter Three.

IV. Modestly Revolutionary Change and Legal Continuities

A. *The Rationalization of English Law*

Recall that the five "subtraditions" of the civil law tradition, as surveyed above in Chapter Two, were (1) Roman Civil Law, (2) canon law, (3) commercial law, (4) "the revolution", and (5) legal science. It is not too far a stretch to regard (1) the growth of the common law through the royal courts at Westminster and (2) the rise and stabilization of equity as being the counterparts in English legal history to the first two "subtraditions" in the civil law tradition. Moreover, like European civil law, English common law experienced the absorption of commercial law. The following paragraphs briefly explore that absorption and then discuss the role of jurists and the role of legislation in English legal history. All of these developments—occurring for the most part in the last 250 years— might be regarded as a period of "rationalization" of English law.

1. Commercial Law

The absorption of commercial law into the common law took place in the relative calmness (from a legal perspective) that followed the two major developments de-

---

67. *Id.* at 343. David explains, however, that "[f]rom the seventeenth century [onward,] precedents were established to 'guide' the chancellor in the exercise of discretionary power implied by such principles". *Id.* This reflects the changes imposed following the Compromise of 1616 described above.
68. *Id.* at 344.

scribed above—that is, the formation of the common law and the rise and stabilization of equity. Specifically, in the second half of the 18th century, largely through the efforts (including especially the judicial decisions) of Lord Mansfield, the law merchant that had developed over many centuries on the continent was integrated into English law.[69]

Another source gives the following more detailed account of the specific means by which Lord Mansfield made his contribution to the absorption of commercial law into English common law. (See also Appendix 4.13 for a biographical sketch of Lord Mansfield.)

> Mansfield was particularly qualified for the task of redefining commercial law because of his background and predispositions. As a Scotsman he was interested in, and learned in, Scottish law, which was based on the civil-law principles so basic to Continental mercantile law. As an individual, he was inclined to seek advice from merchants concerning mercantile practice and to adopt it as the law. In cases in which the law was in doubt, evidence of mercantile custom was admitted, and Mansfield used merchants on his juries.
>
> … [Mansfield's] primary contribution was in the refinement and definition of terms and the rights of parties. To the sparse comments of prior cases he added analysis, reason, and logic. Although it had been decided in 1699 that a good-faith holder for value of a bill of exchange had rights superior to one who lost it, Mansfield gave form and logic to the point in *Miller v. Race* (1768) whence the doctrine is often traced. Another such refinement was the famous case of *Price v. Neal* (1762) holding that a drawee cannot regain the money he has paid out on a forged bill of exchange. The liabilities and rights of the parties to negotiable instruments were thus settled by a series of decisions during Mansfield's tenure.[70]

2. Blackstone's *Commentaries*

Some references were made earlier to the work of legal scholars—in particular Bracton and Littleton. (See Appendices 4.9 and 4.10 for their biographical sketches.) The contribution of Lord Mansfield (born William Murray) was highlighted immediately above. One of the great masters of legal scholarship, however, for both English law and American law, was William Blackstone. A biographical sketch of Blackstone appears in Appendix 4.14.

Blackstone's classic work, *Commentaries on the Laws of England*, describes English law in the second half of the 18th century, when the common law was at its zenith. The *Commentaries*, published from 1765 to 1769, have been regarded as being comparable to the work of Pothier (1699–1772) in France. Blackstone's *Commentaries* had a tremendous influence because it defined the framework of English law and thus facilitated its expansion and reception.[71]

---

69. See *id.* at 328–329. David explains that until this absorption occurred, "commercial law in England was considered a distinct and international body of law, the application of which was to be reserved to merchants as such". *Id.* at 328.

70. Kempin, *supra* note 9, at 272–273. Another authority echoes this last point about the significance of bills of exchange: "Perhaps the most important mercantile custom recognised [and incorporated into the common law, largely through the efforts of Lord Mansfield] was that a bill of exchange was negotiable. In this way the custom of merchants relating to negotiable instruments and the sale of goods became part of the common law, and later, by codification, of statute law in the Bills of Exchange Act, 1882, and the Sale of Goods Act, 1893." Smith & Keenan, *supra* note 6, at 9.

71. See David & Brierly, *supra* note 1, 330.

Blackstone's work served also as a prelude to the English version of codification. Recall that the French Civil Code emerged from Napoleon's post-French-Revolution efforts in 1804. Just following that important development, and for some of the same reasons that had triggered it, codification efforts were undertaken in England as well. The fanatic revolutionary fervor that gripped France in the late 18th century did not cross the English Channel, but deep concerns over the allegedly anachronistic (some said venal) aspects of the English common law (and equity) prompted many reformers to attempt a wholesale revision of English law, principally through the enactment of legislation—and the issuance of the French Civil Code added fuel to the fire of their enthusiasm in this regard.

3. The 19th Century Reforms

René David offers this summary of the 19th century reforms in English law. In doing so, he gives special attention to (i) the contribution made by Jeremy Bentham, (ii) the procedural rationalization of the court systems in the 1830s and the 1870s, and (iii) the substantive reorganization of English law.

> After the thirteenth and sixteenth centuries, the nineteenth and twentieth centuries are periods of fundamental transformation in the history of English law. The striking feature of this period, with the triumph of democratic ideas and through the influence of Jeremy Bentham (1748–1832), is the unprecedented development of legislation. A great work of legal reform and modernisation was accomplished. Through the operation of radical reforms in procedure, especially in 1832–1833 and 1852, a veritable revolution took place.[72] Until that time English law had developed within the procedural framework of the different forms of action. Once freed from these fetters, English jurists, like their continental colleagues, paid greater attention to the substantive law and it was on this basis that Common law principles were henceforth systematically re-organised.

> Judicial organisation was also greatly changed by the *Judicature Acts* of 1873–1875 which removed the formal distinction between Common law courts and the court of the chancellor; all English courts became empowered to apply the rules of Common law as well as those of Equity, unlike the earlier position when a Common law court could only award a Common law remedy and one had to seek a remedy available in Equity from the Chancery Court.

> In substantive law, a considerable amount of re-organisation was accomplished through the abrogation of lapsed legislation and the process of statutory consolidation; English law was in this way purged of many archaisms and the systematic presentation of its rules in various areas was thus facilitated.[73]

Another source also emphasizes these two elements of change in the 19th century—that is, both procedure and substance—and again stresses the contribution of Jeremy Bentham:

> English law in the 19th century was altered by structural and social legislative reform. Jeremy Bentham and others who had little respect for tradition and the sanctity of precedent ... viewed the common law as inordinately slow in responding to social needs. They urged codification to provide certainty and com-

---

72. As part of this "veritable revolution", many aspects of the old writ system were dramatically simplified.

73. David & Brierly, *supra* note 1, at 330–331.

prehension to the law, and to avoid a social revolution. The conservative judiciary and bar neither desired reform nor believed that legislation should be its source. Parliament became the progenitor of social change, however, enacting laws extending education, creating a competitive civil service exam, broadening House of Commons representation, reforming child labor laws and the Poor Law system, centralizing such government activities as road construction and adopting a freer trade policy by reducing protective tariffs.[74]

Both of the preceding quoted passages refer to Jeremy Bentham and to codification. These references warrant some further elaboration. A biographical sketch of Jeremy Bentham appears in Appendix 4.15 at the end of this chapter; but it is important to note here just how dim a view he took of the common law and how radical a change he wished to bring to it. One author offers this summary:

> Bentham's critique of the common law—that it was 'dog law', whereby men were punished for their actions *ex post facto*, as you would beat a dog, that it existed nowhere but in the vague minds of the judges, and that it was in danger of being inflexible—led him, by the early 1780s, to seek to abandon it, or even a statutory digest of it, and put in its place a Pannomion, a complete and perfect code of laws. In doing so, Bentham had found his life's work: the creation and completion of such a code. This was to be the reverse of the common law method: in place of the dog-law, there would be a body of clearly defined rules for judges to apply; in place of the technical rigidity of common law procedure would come flexibility in adjudication, with an absence of strictly defined procedural rules.[75]

The first of these last two points—that there should be a body of "clearly defined rules for judges to apply"—closely resembles the view that energized continental European law reform movements in the same era. Likewise, Bentham's desire for a "complete and perfect code of laws" is the same that some Europeans, including Frederick of Prussia, acted upon in creating early codes. The same authority explains how contradictory Bentham's views were to the approach of the common law as it had developed over several centuries:

> The practical implications of Bentham's legislative view were profound. Bentham held that judges both should not and could not legislate: *ex post facto* decisions made a rule for the punished party, but made no future direct rule, since the judge's command was limited to the case. Hence, law required positive rules to be imposed by the legislator; but if the role of judges was to be limited to applying pre-determined rules, then the code of legislation needed to be complete....

> [Moreover, in terms of procedure] Bentham would ... do away with pleas entirely, and would allow the judge to hear everything that might be relevant, directly from the mouths of the parties.... [T]he parties would confront each other face to face, giving *viva voce* testimony in simple day-to-day language before a single judge who would hear the whole cause in a single sitting ... [characterized by a] looseness of procedure....

> This, then, would be the reverse of the common law method: a strong code of rules, a flexible code of procedure. It required a Herculean legislator, but this was not something that daunted Bentham.[76]

---

74. Nutshell-2008, *supra* note 3, at 1167–168.
75. Michael Lobban, THE COMMON LAW AND ENGLISH JURISPRUDENCE 116–117 (1991).
76. *Id.* at 123, 130.

The radical transformation Bentham sought did not occur. Several commissions were established to study various proposals for reform—of property law, of criminal law, of procedure, and of the legal profession itself. As shown in the following collection of snippets drawn from a treatise examining English law reform in the early 1800s, the actual result of all these efforts had two main features: (i) several significant changes were made to the content of the rules, both substantive and procedural, and even to the overall concept of law as a set of rules; but (ii) the more dramatic of Bentham's proposals—to replace the common law with a codified system and to abandon detailed forms of procedure in favor of much more flexible rules of procedure—were emphatically rejected.

[*Overview*] By the 1820s, even the most traditionally minded lawyer needed little convincing that the law was in dire need of reform. With the publication of detailed studies ... and ... revelations..., lawyers could see for themselves how anachronistic and senseless much of their law was.

... [However,] the sort of reform [the legal profession] was thinking about was ... a piecemeal one, [rather than Bentham's complete codification].... [One observer noted that there was a preference for] "the plan of inquiring into defects in our legal system productive of actual mischiefs, and remedying these by simple and practical corrections, to any bolder attempts at a general change of system"....

[*Law of real property*] The law of real property ... provides a good test of the climate for codification in the 1820s.... It is noteworthy how seriously the Real Property Commission [that was established to study reform of the law in that area] took not just the idea of reform, but the idea of codifying the law. It shows the pervasiveness and influence of a Benthamic concept of rules. However, when it came to a discussion of the code, it is clear that Bentham's influence had its limitations. The commissioners questioned [Bentham's disciple] James Humphreys on his proposals for a code ... [and Humphreys was forced to admit] that it was feasible only in *theory*: in practice, such a code was never likely to be adopted in Great Britain, and would take years to achieve. He preferred the idea of taking a single isolated area of law [of real property], to see if that could be made into a simple code.

[These admissions by Humphreys, along with other arguments,] influenced the Real Property Commission ... to reject Bentham's idea of a code.... [T]he commissioners noted that it was extremely difficult to alter the law, for even incorrect rules of law involved chains of judicial consequences which would have been acted and relied upon. "We dread the shock that would be occasioned by any precipitate attempt at emendation," the commissioners reported, "and we recollect that it is as impossible suddenly to change the laws as the language of any country." ...

The recommendations of the Real Property Commission thus ended by being uncontentious reforms of specific doctrines. Thus, it simplified conveyancing in order to simplify the many rules which had evolved in a haphazard manner to evade the statutory regulations such as the Statute of Uses.

[*Criminal law*] ... The most famous attempt at codification in England, and the one which came closest to success, was made by the Royal Commission on the Criminal Law, which produced eight reports between 1833 and 1845.... The task of these men was to digest all the criminal statutes into one, to digest the common law crimes, and to see if they could be united into one code.

... However, when [the commissioners] came to analysing the content of the law, they found it adequate, so that no Pannomion [of the sort Bentham had proposed] was needed.... [They concluded] that out of a mass of decisions and solutions could be teased definitions which were precise. [Indeed,] by the Seventh Report [the commissioners] claimed that statutes were less clear [than the common law was regarding criminal law]....

Ultimately, ... [w]hat they proposed was to create a simple digest of the law [that would itself] ... not be absolute; merely an authoritative reference....

[*Procedure*] Bentham's procedural ideas provided some of the greatest challenges to the common law, and his theories were debated strongly in the 1820s.... [Bentham's opponents on this topic favored making procedural rules more specific—just the opposite of Bentham's urging for a flexible "natural" system of procedure]. Therefore, while Bentham ... proposed the removal of pleading, the *Law Magazine* proposed making it stricter, so that the point defined [in a case before the court] would be clearer ... [by applying a] system of special pleading....

.... [Ultimately such a system of] special pleading, the antithesis of the ideal Benthamic procedure, was perceived to be the ideal vehicle to produce Benthamic rules....

[*Conclusion*] Thus, by the 1830s, the Benthamic idea of the Pannomion had failed to take root. In the sphere of substantive law, Bentham's positive proposals failed to make the impact he desired. Most common lawyers still saw their law as a growing body, flexible and responsive to the needs of society, ... However, they did take on board Bentham's ideas on the nature and form of the law, seeing law as a set of rules....[77]

The reforms undertaken in England in the early 1800s took the form of statutory enactments—legislative correctives to perceived inadequacies or dysfunctionalities in the common law. Likewise, the "merger of law and equity" that occurred as a result of the Judicature Acts of 1873–1875—more precisely, a merger of the *courts* in which legal and equitable cases could be brought—also took the form of legislation. Hence from the 19th century onward, English law has relied much more heavily on statutes than it previously did. This raises an obvious question: With those reforms in place now for nearly a century and a half, what difference (if any) is there between the contemporary common law tradition (or at least contemporary English law) and the contemporary civil law tradition? In order to begin addressing that question, which we shall return to later in Chapter Five, let us consider more closely how the role of legislation in England changed over the centuries. One authority offers this summary:

In early times [in England] there were few statutes and the bulk of law was case law, though legislation in one form or another dates from 600 A.D. The earliest Norman legislation was by means of Royal Charter, but the first great outburst of legislation came in the reign of Henry II (1154–1189). This legislation was called by various names: there were Assizes, Constitutions, and Provisions, as well as Charters. Legislation at this time was generally made by the King in council, but sometimes by a kind of Parliament which consisted in the main of a meeting of nobles and clergy summoned from the shires.

---

77. *Id.* at 189–222 *passim.*

In the fourteenth century parliamentary legislation became more general. Parliament at first requested or prayed the King to legislate, but later it presented a bill in its own wording. The Tudor period saw the development of modern procedure, in particular the practice of giving three readings to a bill; and this was also the age of the *Preamble*, which was a kind of preface to the enactment, describing often at great length the reasons for passing it and generally justifying the measure.

From the Tudor period onwards Parliament became more and more independent and the practice of law making by statute increased. Nevertheless statutes did not become an important source of law until the last two centuries, and *even now, although the bulk of legislation is large, statutes form a comparatively small part of the law as a whole. The basis of our law [i.e., English law] remains the common law, and if all the statutes were repealed we should still have a legal system, even if it were inadequate; whereas our statutes alone would not provide a system of law but merely a set of disjointed rules.*

Parliament's increasing incursions into economic and social affairs increased the need for statutes. Some aspects of law are so complicated or so novel that they can only be laid down in this form; they would not be likely to come into existence through the submission of cases in court. A statute is the ultimate source of law, and, even if a statute is in conflict with the common law, the statute must prevail. It is such an important source that it has been said—"A statute can do anything except change man to woman," although in a purely legal sense even this could be achieved. Statute law can be used to abolish common law rules which have outlived their usefulness, or to amend the common law to cope with the changing circumstances and values of society. Once enacted, statutes, even if obsolete, do not cease to have the force of law, but common sense usually prevents most obsolete laws from being invoked; nevertheless a statute stands as law until it is specifically repealed by Parliament. (*Prince of Hanover v. Attorney General*, 1956.)

As Act of Parliament is absolutely binding on everyone within the sphere of its jurisdiction, but all Acts of Parliament can be repealed by the same or subsequent Parliaments; and this is the only exception to the rule of the absolute sovereignty of Parliament—it cannot bind itself or its successors. (*Vauxhall Estates Ltd. v. Liverpool Corporation*, 1932.)[78]

It should be clear from this account that the role of legislation in England remains different from the role of legislation in a typical European civil law country. Having said that, it is equally clear that the 19th century brought dramatic changes to English law. They include the full absorption of commercial law into the common law, the rationalization of substantive law, the rise of legislation, the rationalization of procedural rules (including the complex system of writs), the merger of courts of equity with those of common law, and much more.

B. Modern Common Law in Mass Society

In subsection IIC of Chapter Two, I offered some observations about the "modern civil law in mass society". I highlighted there the political and demographic changes that

---

78. Smith & Keenan, *supra* note 6, at 6–7 (emphasis added).

characterize today's world, and I emphasized that because of these changes, the civil law tradition finds itself today in "an environment of fluidity at various levels".

The same can be said of the common law tradition. The forces at work in the civil law world are, after all, also at work in the common law world; it is largely a single world now. Which of the two traditions—civil law or common law—seems better suited to respond to these changes? This is a matter of speculation, of course. Here is how René David saw the situation, writing several decades ago:

> The work of modernisation that began in the nineteenth century continues today but with some new features. The liberalism dominant until 1914 has been replaced by a socialist trend attempting to create a new social order. With this change *the Common law is undergoing a serious crisis: the judicial and case by case methods characteristic of its original development are no longer suited to the idea of bringing about rapid and extensive social change.* Statutes and regulations now occupy a far more important place than they did in the past. The setting up of many new administrative regimes has brought about much litigation between citizen and government which numerous bodies, alongside the ordinary courts, have been established to handle. Because of the volume of this work and the need for special expertise in many fields which the regular judiciary did not have, it was thought inappropriate to place such matters within the jurisdiction of the regular courts. The same thinking that in France and elsewhere prompted the creation of administrative tribunals also occurred in England, and it matters little that England did not follow suit by setting up an independent hierarchy of courts. More important than the question of structure is the fact that a large number of cases—in fact not less than the volume handled in the ordinary courts—is heard before these bodies in which jurists may sit with non-jurists or are altogether absent. This new range of disputes is therefore often handled and resolved through the use of methods that are not those of the traditional Common law.
>
> For many of the new problems of the welfare state it seems that the Romanist system of the European continent, more familiar with a legislative and doctrinal construction of the law, is better prepared than English law. A *rapprochement* may thus come about between English and continental laws and some see signs of it already. Such a movement is encouraged by the needs of international commerce and by a clearer realisation that affinities do exist between all European countries linked as they are to the values of western civilisation; the entry of the United Kingdom into the European Economic Community in 1972 will undoubtedly give it further force.[79]

The emphasis that René David places on the rise of administrative regimes and tribunals could be added to the diagram in Box #4.3. That is, a new column D might be inserted at the far right-hand edge of that diagram to show administrative tribunals arising in the 20th century.

To a certain degree, of course, these England-specific developments are of only slight significance in the overall "story" of the common law tradition. The influence of the common law throughout the world results from the campaign of colonization and conquest that England engaged in beginning in the 16th century. Once the dismantling of the British Empire concluded in the 20th century, the particular legal developments in England waned in importance to the rest of the common law world. The common law that

---

79. David & Brierly, *supra* note 1, at 331–332 (emphasis added).

was "transplanted" to many parts of the rest of the world was the common law of *earlier* times, before the dawning of the 20th century. It is to that "transplantation" phenomenon that we now turn our attention.

V. Transplantation of the Common Law

In considering the *civil* law tradition, we postponed until Chapter Three our examination of how the civil law spread beyond Europe—instead of addressing that question in the Chapter Two summary of the history of the civil law. Why have I taken a different approach here in discussing the *common* law tradition, by including questions of its world-wide distribution with the historical survey of its development in England? Because I wish to incorporate into this historical development some details about how the English common law spread to North America, and particularly to the lands that became the USA. Accordingly, the discussion in this section gives (a) a brief description of the reasons for, and extent of, the common law's "transplantation" in various regions outside England, and then (b) a summary of the American experience with its English common law heritage.

A. *Reasons for, and Extent of, Distribution*

Looking at them from one perspective, we could dispose of the issues identified in the heading for this subsection (reasons for, and extent of, the distribution of the common law) very quickly—like a hot knife goes through butter. It might seem obvious that the *reason* why the common law tradition got distributed beyond the shores of England is the same as the reason why the civil law tradition got distributed in so many places outside continental Europe: the urge for empire. Indeed, I noted just at the close of the preceding section that "[t]he influence of the common law throughout the world results from the campaign of colonization and conquest that England engaged in beginning in the 16th century". Likewise, if we wish to explain the *extent* of the distribution of the common law tradition around the world, we could look to the extent of that campaign of colonization and conquest.

While true, these answer are overly simplistic. Recall that the Romans occupied Britain for roughly four centuries, and yet Roman law had virtually no lasting impact there. In order to consider more carefully the reason for, and extent of, the distribution of the common law around various parts of the world, we should focus also on its sustainability and appeal as a "deeply rooted ... set of attitudes about law" (recalling Merryman's definition of a legal tradition, first introduced above in Chapter One).

For this examination of the common law's sustainability and appeal, let us see what two observers emphasized about the common law in a series of radio broadcasts intended to summarize the "migration" of the common law. These broadcasts, emanating from the Overseas Service of the BBC (British Broadcasting Corporation), introduced audiences as of about 1960 to the distribution of the common law in such countries as Australia, India, Israel, Canada, and the USA.[80]

---

80. See generally *The Migration of the Common Law*, 76 Law Quarterly Review 39 (1960) [hereinafter *Migration*].

Two opening essays in the BBC radio series featured (i) the person serving at the time as Lord Chancellor (successor to the Chancellors under whom the courts of equity had evolved) and (ii) an Oxford law professor. They offered two rather different perspectives on the question of why the common law "migrated" and why it survived that process.

The Lord Chancellor begins his observations by explaining how the common law developed gradually through (1) the accumulation of decisions issued by judges in cases coming before them, accompanied with (2) the doctrine of *stare decisis*, under which later judges would abide by such earlier decisions when the same point came up in litigation.

> You may, then, well ask "was not the result of this that the law remained rigid and static?" Fortunately the answer is "No"; it is completely wrong to suppose that because the common law is based on precedent it is inflexible and incapable of expansion; when, hundreds of years ago, my predecessors on the Woolsack thought that the existing law was becoming too rigid they corrected this tendency by introducing new rules which became known as "the rules of equity" because they were designed to work substantial justice. For example, under the old law a man who mortgaged his house to raise a loan would find himself turned out of his home if he did not repay "on the nail"; equity stepped in to protect him and give him a further chance to pay. Moreover, judges have always extended old rules to new sets of circumstances and from this produced what were, in fact, new rules. They have, too, invoked the doctrine of public policy in order, for example, to declare contracts void as against public interest. This doctrine has been called "the prevailing opinion of wise men as to what is for the public good." A rule like this can obviously change with the changing conditions of society. Two great men as well as great lawyers, one an Englishman, Lord Wensleydale, and the other an American, Mr. Justice Holmes, have put it well: Wensleydale said that the common law was "a system which consisted in applying to new combinations of circumstances those rules which we derive from legal principles and judicial precedents"; Holmes thought that "the life of the law is not logic but experience."
>
> In the result, most of the fundamental principles of our constitutional law that maintain the freedom of the subject and limit the power of servants of the Crown are to be found in the common law alone. It is still largely true, as another classic writer, Professor Dicey, said, that "nine-tenths of the law of contract and nearly the whole of the law of torts (which are civil wrongs) are not to be discovered in any volume of the statutes." This is the law which has often been termed the "birthright" of an Englishman. I am glad to think the Englishman has not selfishly kept it to himself.[81]

Having offered these introductory comments, the Lord Chancellor then explains the process by which the common law spread and—most importantly for our inquiry—the reasons it has (in his view) "flourished":

> Every lawyer, if not every schoolboy, knows why the common law spread in the first place: it was the simple rule of law, enunciated as long ago as 1608 in *Calvin's Case*, that the English transported English law with them when they entered a territory where no civilised law was practiced. But the curious thing is that the common law has so flourished in those territories that, even where the original

---

81. *Id.* at 41–42.

political ties have been broken, the system of law has remained, and today nearly one-third of the population of the world is governed by that system.

I have had the advantage of meeting lawyers from all over the world, ... [and] I have learned that in every kind of civilisation the pursuit of justice is instinctive and that a legal system which gives this instinct freedom to express itself has an inherent strength which is not easily destroyed.

Now the first and most striking feature of the common law is that *it puts justice before truth*. The issue in a criminal prosecution is not, basically, "guilty or not guilty?" but "can the prosecution prove its case according to the rules?" These rules are designed to ensure "fair play," even at the expense of the truth. Perhaps the most obvious example of this principle is the rule that a prisoner cannot be made to expose himself to cross-examination if he does not want to. The attitude of the common law to a civil action is essentially the same: the question is "Has the plaintiff established his claim by lawful evidence?" not "has he really got a good claim?" Again, justice comes before truth. So, you see, there is more than meets the eye in the old story of the Irish prisoner who, when asked whether he pleaded "guilty" or "not guilty" replied "and how should I be knowing whether I am guilty until I have heard the evidence?"

Secondly, the common law developed in a country where the *"Rule of Law"*—which accords so well with that instinctive craving for justice—has long been observed. We have for centuries accepted as unquestionable the principle that anyone— whether a private citizen or high official—who interferes with the person or property of another can be made to answer for his actions before a court of law and will be liable in damages, if he has exceeded his legal powers. It is no defense to the policeman who arrests me illegally, or the customs officer who wrongly seizes my goods, that he had express orders to do so from his superiors. The Rule of Law is not, of course, a peculiarity of the common-law countries, but so steeped in it were, and are, the common lawyers that they have taken it with them wherever they have gone.

It is not only through its principles, but through its personalities that the English legal system has been so readily accepted by others. Our legal profession is peculiar, but its structure brings to the fore those practitioners who are honest, fearless and independent, and this in its turn has meant that the *common-law judges* have achieved a position in our society which is unrivalled by any foreign judiciary. Like other men they are fallible, but their integrity and independence have, and rights, earned the respect and confidence of the whole world. Again, the instinct for justice makes men of every nation ready to see their own disputes decided by impartial and independent tribunals, and a legal system which fosters a tradition of impartiality and independence in its judiciary is bound to derive therefrom a lasting strength which is independent of the substantive rules it applies.

Lastly, the common law has always relied largely on *the ordinary citizen*. There is the magistrate and the juror, who are not lawyers. And there is that familiar figure known to lawyers as "the reasonable man." He is the ordinary prudent person by whose standards civil liabilities are governed. Thus our lawyers and judges have a close relationship with people who are not experts practicing some esoteric science. This has made them particularly aware of change in ordinary standards of conduct and thought, and a legal system which keeps in touch with those for whose service it exists is one they will hesitate to throw lightly away. Those are, in my opinion, the basic reasons why the common law has proved such a successful migrant. How it has happened you will hear from others.[82]

Having identified these reasons for the survival of the common law outside England—specifically, (i) its placement of justice before truth, (ii) its faithfulness to the rule of law, (iii) its independent judges, and (iv) its focus on the ordinary citizen—the Lord Chancellor concludes his remarks by emphasizing the value he sees in applying certain strengths of the common law to an even wider stage—the international affairs of the modern world:

> I have already said that nearly one-third of the world's population are governed by laws which have the same basic principles. This can be a tremendous force for international understanding, the first essential for which is "speaking the same language." All common lawyers at least speak a similar language, whether the tongue they speak it in is English or Hindustani. To some extent they recognise the same rules of conduct as binding on them in their own affairs and they recognise the authority—both legal and moral—of their own tribunals. If that attitude to their own law and their own courts can be transferred to international affairs and disputes, we will have gone a long way to solving the political problems of the modern world. I believe that in the widely spread common law we have a powerful weapon in our hands which we can use to bring about this degree of international understanding. This, I am certain, is one of the greatest contributions the Commonwealth can make to our modern civilisation.[83]

The Lord Chancellor's view of the common law bubbles with praise and optimism. It would suggest that the common law has an appeal for all humans everywhere. Arthur Goodhart, a professor of Law at Oxford,[84] offers a very different perspective. In his remarks for the BBC broadcasts on the migration of the common law, Goodhart opens by pointing out why it is the civil law tradition—not the common law tradition—that has generally proven more attractive to cultures outside Europe and the British Isles:

> In his introduction to this series, the Lord Chancellor has emphasised with justifiable pride that nearly one-third of the world's population is governed by the rules of the common law. It may seem strange therefore, if I begin today by pointing out that no country which has not at some time or other been part of the British Empire has ever voluntarily adopted the common law. When Turkey, in 1926, decided to replace its antiquated legal system by a modern one it took its criminal law from the Italian code and its civil law from the Swiss and the German ones. In the same way, Japan based its new system on Continental law, in spite of its close commercial relationship with Great Britain and the United States. These are only two illustrations of the fact that whenever there has been choice between the common law and the Roman law, which is, of course, the basis of the modern Continental codes, the decision has always been in favor of the Roman law.

---

82. *Id.* at 42–44 (emphasis added).

83. *Id.* at 44.

84. Sir Arthur Goodhart, an American national, served as the Master of University College—the same college in Oxford that I attended as a young law student in the 1970s. He had retired by the time I arrived at University College, but he and his wife lived in the top floor of a building (named after him) that served as a dormitory for new students. I met him and his wife numerous times as she would guide his wheelchair to a nearby garden (named after her) on pleasant days.

There are, I believe, three reasons for this. The *first* is that this Roman law is in the form of a code, and is therefore far more convenient than is the common law which is a strange amalgam of case law and of statutes. The basic common law principles were originally established by the judges when they decided cases on the theory that they were declaring the customary law of the Kingdom. Today, statutes are far more important than case law, but this is a development in large part of the past two centuries....

The *second* reason is that the language of the common law is difficult to understand because it still contains many terms that are not only technical but are also medieval in character. Maitland has spoken of the "seamless web" of English history—this is true in particular of the English law which has all the strength of the English oak tree but also has some of its gnarled branches. The famous French author, Stendhal, so greatly admired the purity of the language in the French code that he made it his practice to read a few sections of it every morning before he began work on his novels. It is difficult to believe that an English novelist would read an English statute or a reported case in similar circumstances.

The *third* reason for the popularity of Roman law is that it is concerned primarily with private law as contrasted with public law. It deals with such subjects as private property, contracts, commercial law, and civil wrongs against individuals. These are clearly separated from the public law which directly concerns the State and controls the exercise of State authority. The Roman law, which of course, recognised the absolute authority of the Emperors, held that "What is pleasing to the Ruler has the force of law." It is, therefore, possible for any country to adopt the Roman civil law without creating a conflict between the law and its political system, however autocratic the system may be. Thus the most famous of all modern codes—the French code—was created by Napoleon and still bears his name.[85]

For Goodhart, then, the civil law tradition has many features that has made it attractive to nations having to choose what form of legal system to create upon independence. (Recall that in the 19th and 20th centuries there were a great many such nations.) He then turns his attention to the main theme of the radio series—*why* the common law has in fact survived in many of the countries where it was introduced. Here, some of his observations resemble those offered by the Lord Chancellor:

But when we turn to the different history of the common law we find that its most striking feature is its public law; it is primarily a method of administering justice. It was through the establishment of the Royal Courts of Justice that the common customs of the realm were transmuted to the common law. Almost from the beginning, and certainly from the thirteenth century onward, the principle was accepted that the King was under the law. This was finally established when in 1215 the barons met King John on the field of Runnymede, and forced him to affix his seal to the articles of the Magna Carta—the great Charter which we still recognise as the foundation stone of our liberties. From that day to this the basic principle has been that no man, however great and powerful, can disregard the ordinary law of the land. The law is our great protector because, in the splendid words of Chapter 39: "No free man shall be taken or imprisoned or disseised or outlawed or exiled or in any wise destroyed, save by the lawful judg-

---

85. *Migration, supra* note 80, at 45–46 (emphasis added).

ment of his peers and the law of the land." These words have been repeated in modern form in the constitutions of most of the common law countries—the United States, Ireland, India, Pakistan and Israel—and are implicit in all the others.

… Perhaps the most distinctive part of the common law was—and still is—the jury system under which no man can be convicted of felony unless he has been found guilty by a jury of twelve ordinary citizens. It is obvious that this system is the most effective guard against governmental tyranny ever devised if—and this is an essential *if*—the ordinary citizen is prepared to show courage and independence. The independence of the jury was finally established in 670 in *Bushel's* case. Bushel had been committed to prison when the jury, of which he was a member, had acquitted William Penn of unlawful assembly against the manifest evidence. Chief Justice Vaughan, however, held that a jury was not bound to follow the directions of the judge. Again, at the end of the eighteenth century the juries refused to convict the accused in a series of famous libel cases which established the freedom of the Press.

The second essential feature of the common law is found in the writ of habeas corpus. By that writ the body of any man who claims, or whose friends claim, that he is being unlawfully detained must be brought into court so that the legality of his detention may be established. It has been said that each word of this writ is of more value than is a library of books written in praise of liberty. Habeas corpus is the key that unlocks the door to freedom.

The third principle of the common law is found in the independence of the judiciary. The judges are not the servants of the government: they are the servants of justice, and it is their function to see that justice is done not only between individuals, but also between the individual and the State. This is due in part to a fortunate chance. Edward I, in the thirteenth century, chose his judges from the leaders of the Bar instead of from the civil service, and this method has been followed ever since in the common law countries. These leaders had not been subject to the orders of the Crown while they were at the Bar, so it was natural that when they became judges they showed the same independence.

This separation of the judges from the processes of government has led to the establishment of the adversary system of trial which is a unique feature of the common law. Under the Continental system the judge plays a leading and active part in attempting to establish the truth [in criminal proceedings]. It is for him to question the witnesses. As a result, the impression may be given that the judge is hostile to the prisoner who is being tried before him. The theory of the common law is that justice can best be achieved by giving each party the fullest opportunity to present his own case. The judge is the arbiter between two adversaries. This aloofness of the judge is a guarantee against the introduction of evidence which may be unfairly prejudicial to the accused, and against the use of arbitrary force by the police, because evidence so obtained will be rejected by the judge at the trial. It is for this reason that the judge has been rightly called the watch-dog of liberty.

The fourth principle is summed up in the phrase "An Englishman's home is his castle." This … expresses a most important truth. In simple language it means that under the common law no one, however great the position he may hold, may open my door unless he does so under the specific authority of the law. This is the hallmark of government under the law.

These are the principles which are recognised in all countries where the common law rules.... [In these principles] we find an expression of the ideals of government to which all of us subscribe—government under law, even-handed justice, and a due recognition of the rights of our fellow men.[86]

We shall see later, in Chapters Six and Seven, that at least one of the points Goodhart emphasizes in those closing observations—namely, the importance of government under law—would be largely rejected in dynastic Chinese culture. Naturally, the BBC radio series does not touch on that point. Instead, it proceeds to summarize the means by which the common law "migrated" to various other countries around the world, carried along by the English campaign of empire-building and then surviving for different reasons in different foreign environments. For a general impression of where those foreign environments were, see the map depicting colonial distributions appearing in Appendix 3.5 and Appendix 3.6 at the end of Chapter Three.

B. The American Experience

Our survey of the American experience with the common law—examining this topic mainly from a historical perspective for now—can draw from three sources. The first is the same BBC radio series referred to immediately above. The second is an introductory text on the US legal system. The third is a law journal article that focuses directly on a comparison of civil law, common law, and Chinese law from the perspective of legal codification.

In the BBC radio series referred to above, the essay on the "migration" of the common law to those portions of North America that became the territory of the USA (with the shameful extermination, displacement, and cultural emasculation, that is, of the native Americans) begins by explaining that the common law was only one part of the laws of England in the first years of colonial settlement of North America. Here is how the commentator, Professor Mark DeWolfe Howe, began his observations:

> The title of this series treats common law as immigrant. I make no protest against the image, but I suggest that our picture of history will be more true to life if we recognise that this particular immigrant came to American shores with distinguished companions.... For we must not forget ... that in the first years of colonial settlement the common law was merely a segment of the laws of England.
>
> ... [For example, when] the Puritans of Massachusetts Bay sought justification for their peculiar law of inheritance, they were able, with some colour of right, to claim that since it was consistent with the recognised customs of the County of Kent it could not be condemned for its repugnancy to the laws of England. When the King conferred a jurisdiction in equity upon a royal governor or established courts of Vice-Admiralty in the American colonies he could defend his action by reminding the resentful colonists that in his house of justice there were many

---

86. *Id.* at 48. The second paragraph in this excerpt stresses the importance of the independence of the jury. For a description of *Bushell's Case* (decided in 1670) and of the action taken three years earlier (1667) by the House of Commons to condemn the practice of punishing juries for failure to follow the prosecution, see AMERICAN LEGAL HISTORY, *supra* note 58, at 86–87.

mansions of law. When the colonists protested that parliamentary taxation without representation was tyranny, they reminded the King that his law—the law of the crown—and God's law—the law of nature—gave rights to Englishmen in the colonies as they did to those who stayed at home. [In short, both (i) certain ancient customary law and (ii) natural law were regarded as being part of English law at the time. (Howe also discusses the element of equity in English law at the time.)]

In the end, of course, the Americans [focused most of their attention on the common law; they] came to see that a lawyer's myth which had done political wonders in England could also do marvelous service overseas. Building upon legend which Coke had dignified with spurious annotation and English Puritans had sanctified with pious pedantry, the Americans discovered that the rights that really mattered to them had their roots in common law. Thomas Jefferson spoke as a disciple of Coke when he said that the "common law is that system of law which was introduced by the Saxons on their settlement of England" and which came to its end with Magna Carta. English legal history, in the eyes of Jefferson, was the grim narrative of the desecration of this law by Parliaments and Kings—a story which was less than tragic only because there had been times when learned and indignant Englishmen had redefined in Petitions and Bills of Rights the privileges and immunities of their Saxon ancestors. By these occasional restatements of the common law the rights of Englishmen—and therefore of Americans—had been kept alive.[87]

Howe then proceeds with a description of how the common law found its way into the actual laws and constitutions of the new republic following the American Revolution:

It was the prevalence of this wholesome myth, I suspect, that frequently led the draftsmen of state constitutions to include a provision that the common law of England should continue in force.... Of course, the continued vitality of common law also served the mundane purpose of providing the courts with rules of decision. Before many years had passed, ... [this practical function—of filling in gaps in the new American law by referring to the English common law—assumed primary importance. Soon the] Bar and the courts were [engaged in] showing that respect for the common law of England which the constitution required them to show at the same time that they molded the law to serve the exuberant purposes of a free people.

... [A practical statement of the] law was what the bench and bar wanted, and it was their good fortune that they could find it conveniently at hand in Blackstone's *Commentaries*.... [The] practitioners and judges were, most of them, so grateful for the order and clarity which the great commentator had imposed upon the common law that they forgave him his sins and blessed him for his achievement. Without his help American lawyers would have been forced to take their common law from the crabbed text of Coke's *Institutes* or to seek out the inaccessible reports and, if they were fortunate enough to find them, interpret their bewildering contents.

One aspect of the constitutional and statutory provisions by which the common law was continued in effect deserves particular emphasis. Because of the terms

---

87. *Migration, supra* note 80, at 49–50.

in which such provisions were written, the American courts exercised powers far more extensive than those possessed by judges in England administering the common law. For under the constitutions which gave them their authority the American judges were bound to enforce the common law of England *only if it was applicable to American circumstances.* As a consequence, they were quick to discard an English doctrine if, in the language of our own time, it seemed "un-American." ...

It is not surprising that many Americans saw dangers in the selective enforcement of the common law.... To democratic legislators it seemed a violation of the American principle of separation of powers that irresponsible judges should turn policies which they favored into law. To professional patriots it seemed intolerable that a revolution which had cast out English crown law and English statute law had not wholly destroyed the English common law. American disciples of Bentham saw American soil as most promising ground in which to plant the seeds of codification.[88]

We shall examine the American Codification Movement shortly. Howe summarizes why, in his view, a codification effort in the young USA, based on the French civil code that had recently been enacted, proved unsuccessful. For one thing, he says, the publication of Kent's *Commentaries on American Law*—supplementing and ultimately replacing Blackstone's *Commentaries* as practical guides for American lawyers—served to satisfy the thirst for clarity and internal consistency in the laws that had developed helter-skelter in the decades just following the Revolution.[89] For these and other reasons, the common law—first appearing on North American shores as an immigrant—before very long "became a naturalized citizen of the United States".[90]

Let us turn to a second source of information as we examine the "migration" or "transplantation" of common law into the territory that became the USA. This source is Allan Farnsworth, an American legal scholar famous world-wide for his work in contracts law. In his *Introduction to the Legal System of the United States*,[91] Farnsworth offers these observations about the early colonial period up to the time of the American Revolution:

> There were at least three impediments to the immediate acceptance of English law in the early colonial period. The first was the dissatisfaction with some aspects of English justice on the part of many of the colonists, who had migrated to the New World in order to escape from what they regarded as intolerable conditions in the mother country. This was particularly true for those who had come in search of religious, political, or economic freedom. A second and more significant impediment was the lack of trained lawyers, which continued to retard

---

88. *Id.* at 50–51.

89. For a fascinating account of how Kent formulated his view of English law, on the basis of which he prepared his *Commentarieis on American Law*, see Daniel J. Hulsebosch, *An Empire of Law: Chancellor Kent and the Revolution of Books in the Early Republic*, 2 UNIVERSITY OF ALABAMA MEADER LECTURE ON EMPIRE 1 (2007) (describing how Kent's law library reflects a "book revolution" in post-colonial America that expanded the influence of English legal writings there. See also Michael H. Hoeflich, *Comparative Law in Antebellum America*, 4 WASHINGTON UNIVERSITY GLOBAL STUDIES LAW REVIEW 535, 537 (2005) (reporting that "[e]arly American legal culture was awash in foreign law").

90. *Id.* at 52.

91. See E. Allen Farnsworth, INTRODUCTION TO THE LEGAL SYSTEM OF THE UNITED STATES (1983). A more recent edition, edited by Steve Sheppard, was released in 2010. Farnsworth died in 2005.

the development of American law throughout the seventeenth century. The rigorous life in the colonies had little attraction for English lawyers. English law books were not readily available, and few among the early settlers had any legal training. The third impediment was the disparity of the conditions in the two lands. Particularly in the beginning, life was more primitive in the colonies and familiar English institutions that were copied often produced rough copies at best. The early settlers did not carry English law in its entirety with them when they came, and the process by which it was absorbed in the face of these impediments was not a simple one.

The extent to which English case law, as distinguished from statute law, was in effect, either in theory or in practice, during the early history of the colonies is not free from dispute. It is clear that though the British Parliament had legislative power over the colonies, it was not fully exercised.... Power to legislate had been conferred upon the colonies themselves, and each had its own legislature with at least one elective branch and with considerable control over internal affairs. Codification [such as the *Laws and Liberties of Massachusetts*, discussed in Appendix 4.18 at the end of this chapter] was common in the early stages of some of the colonies partly because of the absence of law books and the lack of a trained bar, and partly because of colonial notions of law reform. Colonial legislation was reviewed by administrative authorities in the mother country and might be set aside if it was "contrary" or "repugnant" to the laws or commercial policy of England.... But no systematic control was exercised until the end of the seventeenth century.

During the seventeenth century the justice that was administered was often lacking in technicalities and was sometimes based on a general sense of right as derived from the Bible and the law of nature. Court procedure, at least outside of the superior courts, was tailored to suit American needs and was marked by an informality of proceedings and a simplicity of pleadings befitting a less technical system in which the judges were, for the most part, untutored in the law.... Substantive law, as well as procedure, began to respond to colonial needs. In England the feudal policy in favor of keeping estates in land intact had resulted in the rule of primogeniture, the exclusive right of the eldest son to inherit the land of the father. In America, however, this rule was rejected in favor of equal distribution among all children, subject to varying rights of a surviving spouse. This practice began in the northern colonies, was confirmed there by statute, and had spread southward by legislation to all of the states by the end of the eighteenth century.

The beginning of the eighteenth century saw considerable refinement of colonial law and a concurrent increase in the influence of English case law. Review of colonial legislation had become more thorough. With the growth of trade and the increase in population—to some three hundred thousand in 1700—the ranks of trained lawyers were swelled and the courts of review began to be manned by professionals.... English law books had become increasingly available and it had been said that by the time of the Revolution Williams Blackstone's widely read *Commentaries on the Laws of England*, which first appeared between 1765 and 1769, had sold nearly as many copies in America as in England. Interest in English law was stimulated by the necessity of dealing in commercial matters with English merchants trained in its ways and by the desirability of reliance upon its principles to support the colonists' grievances against the Crown. By the time of the

Revolution English law had come to be generally well regarded and each colony had a bar of trained, able, and respected professionals, capable of working with a refined and technical system. The colonial legal profession, especially in the cities, had achieved both social standing and economic success. It was also politically active: twenty-five of the fifty-six signers of the Declaration of Independence were lawyers.[92]

Farnsworth's account goes on to describe how English common law was "received" into the legal systems of the various US states following the end of the American Revolution. In doing so, he emphasizes the sense of disorder, bordering on chaos, that afflicted American law in those early post-colonial days. Those problems (as noted also in the observations by Howe, quoted above) led to a flirtation in the new USA with the prospect of codifying American law. Efforts in that direction gained close and sustained attention, especially in the 1820s and 1830s—the very time, we should recall, that codification efforts were underway in England, with special influence from Jeremy Bentham.

The early-19th-century American codification effort, however, was not the first one of its kind. Nearly two centuries earlier, laws in the Massachusetts Bay colony underwent a primitive form of codification, thereby providing a template for other colonial codification efforts. In fact, enthusiasm for legal codification has appeared at several times in American legal history. Because legal codification has played such a significant role in the development of European civil law—a matter explored earlier in Chapters Two and Three—we should pay some attention to codification in American law. Indeed, we shall see in Chapters Six and Seven the prominent role that codes and codification have played throughout Chinese legal history as well.

Against that backdrop, Appendix 4.18, at the end of this chapter, features excerpts from a law journal article undertaking a comparative study of codification in American law, European law, and Chinese law. American codification efforts receive the most attention in those excerpts, but enough reference to European and Chinese experience is included to draw a number of contrasts and similarities among the three legal traditions in this regard. I therefore close the main text of this chapter by referring the reader to Appendix 4.18.

---

92. *Id.* at 6–8. As an elaboration of Farnsworth's observation that in 17th-century America "the justice that was administered was often lacking in technicalities", consider this explanation from Francis Heller:

> It is important to bear in mind that the colonies were widely scattered along the eastern seaboard and that there was little interaction until, roughly, the middle of the 18th century (i.e. after the advent of steam power had revolutionized transportation). There was no center of either learning or culture, let along economic or political activity. Being a lawyer in this kind of society meant being a generalist, often little more than a "scrivener"—it is estimated that, at the time of the Revolution, two out of three of the male, white population of the colonies were illiterate. Printing, essential as it was to communication, was still entirely manual—a tedious, dirty task: There were few instances of printed reports of judicial decisions.

American Legal History, *supra* note 58, at 73.

Appendix 4.1
Excerpts from Laws of King Æthelbert, 600 CE

[*Note:* See also Appendix 4.2, giving background on King Æthelbert and observations about his laws, or "dooms", as excerpted below.]

THESE ARE THE DOOMS WHICH KING ÆTHELBERT ESTABLISHED IN THE DAYS OF AUGUSTINE

1. The property of God and of the church, twelve-fold; a bishop's property, eleven-fold; a priest's property, nine-fold; a deacon's property, six-fold; a clerk's property, three-fold; "church-frith," two-fold;....

2. If the king calls his "leod" to him, and any one there do them evil, [let him compensate with] a two-fold "bōt," and L. shillings to the king.

3. If the king drink at any one's home, and any one there do any "lyswe," let him make two-fold "bōt."

4. If a freeman steal from the king, let him pay nine-fold.

5. If a man slay another in the king's "tūn" let him make make "bōt" with L. shillings.

6. If any one slay a freeman, L. shillings to the king, as "drihtin-beah."

7. If the king's "ambiht-smith," or "laad-rinc," slay a man, let him pay a half "leod-geld."

8. The king's "mund-byrd," L. shillings.

9. If a freeman steal from a freeman, let him make three-fold "bōt"; and let the king have the "wite" and all the chattels.

10. If a man lie with the king's maiden, let him pay a "bōt" of L. shillings.

11. If she be a grinding slave, let him pay a "bōt" of XXV. shillings. The third [class] XII. shillings.

12. Let the king's "fed-esl" be paid with XX. shillings.

13. If a man slay another in an "eorl's" "tūn," let make "bōt" with XII. shillings.

14. If a man lie with an "eorl's" "birele," let him make "bōt" with XII. shillings.

15. A "ceorl's" "mund-byrd," VI. shillings.

16. If a man lie with a "ceorl's" "birele," let him make "bōt" with VI. shillings; with a slave of the second [class], L. "scaetts"; with one of the third, XXX. "scaetts."

17. If any one be the first to make an inroad into a man's "tūn," let him make "bōt" with VI. shillings; let him who follows, with III. shillings; after, each, a shilling.

18. If a man furnish weapons to another where there is strife, though no evil be done, let him make "bōt" with VI. shillings.

19. If "weg-reaf" be done, let him make "bōt" with VI. shillings.

20. If a man be slain, let him make "bōt" with XX. shillings.

21. If a man slay another, let him make "bōt" with a half "leod-geld" of C. shillings.

* * *

31. If a freeman lie with a freeman's wife, let him pay for it with his "wer-geld," and provide another wife with his own money, and bring her to the other.

32. If any one thrust through the "riht ham-scyld," let him adequately compensate.

33. If there be "feax-fang," let there be L. sceatts for "bōt".

34. If there be exposure of the bone, let "bōt" be made with III. shillings.

35. If there be an injury of the bone, let "bōt" be made with IV. shillings.

36. If the outer "hion" be broken, let "bōt" be made with X. shillings.

37. If it be both, let "bōt" be made with XX. shillings.

38. If a shoulder be lamed, let "bōt" be made with XXX. shillings.

39. If an ear be struck off, let "bōt" be made with XII. shillings.

40. If the other ear hear not, let "bōt" be made with XXV. shillings.

41. If an ear be pierced, let "bōt" be made with III. shillings.

42. If an ear be mutilated, let "bōt" be made with VI. shillings.

43. If an eye be [struck] out, let "bōt" be made with L. shillings.

44. If the mouth or an eye be injured, let "bōt" be made with XII. shillings.

45. If the nose be pierced, let "bōt" be made with IX. shillings.

46. If it be one "ala," let "bōt" be made with III. shillings.

47. If both be pierced, let "bōt" be made with VI. shillings.

48. If the nose be otherwise mutilated, for each let "bōt" be made with VI. shillings.

49. If it be pierced, let "bōt" be made with VI. shillings.

50. Let him who breaks the chin-bone pay for it with XX. shillings.

51. For each of the four front teeth, VI. shillings; for the tooth which stands next to them IV. shillings; for that which stands next to that, III. shillings; and then afterwards, for each a shilling.

52. If the speech be injured, XII. shillings. If the collar bone be broken, let "bōt" be made with VI. shillings.

53. Let him who stabs [another] through an arm make "bōt" with VI. shillings. If an arm be broken, let him make "bōt" with VI. shillings.

54. If a thumb be struck off, XX. shillings. If a thumb nail be off, let "bōt" be made with III. shillings. If the shooting (*i.e.* fore) finger be struck off, let "bōt".

* * *

Appendix 4.2
Biographical Sketch of King Æthelbert*

Æthelbert, born in approximately 560 CE, became king of Kent, in southeast England, sometime between 580 and 590, after the death of his father, King Irminric. During Æthelbert's lifetime, Kent was prosperous, due in large part to its strong trade ties with continental Europe. Kent was one of the seven English kingdoms composing the Heptarchy and Æthelbert was the *Bretwalda*, or dominant king among the group.

Æthelbert is known largely as having been the first English king to convert to Christianity. In 597 Pope Gregory I sent a missionary named Augustine to England. This mission is credited with Æthelbert's conversion to Christianity and also inspired his subsequent issuance of a code of law for Kent. This is also referred to as Æthelbert's Doom (with "Doom" meaning decrees). [See Appendix 4.1, above.] It is possible that hearing of Justinian's great legal compilation, and of the tradition of Roman codification more generally, may have inspired Æthelbert's efforts. Regardless of the motivation, he is thought to have become the first Anglo-Saxon king to reduce the customary laws to writing. Æthelbert's code is also the first known text containing the English language.

Although it would seem logical that the Catholic Church and Roman codification tradition might have influenced the content of the code that Æthelbert issued, this does not appear to be the case. Rather, the code for Kent is a unique conglomeration of customary laws and has sometimes been compared to the *Lex Salica*, a code of customary Frankish law. The Catholic Church is referenced in Æthelbert's code but does not appear to influence it. Likewise, there does not appear to be any direct influence from Justinian's Code or any other Roman codes, as the influence of Roman law never really took hold on the British Isles during the Roman Empire's existence.

The compilation of laws within Æthelbert's code takes the form of a restatement. Æthelbert's Doom identifies the transgressions and the proper penalties applied to each act. However, unlike Roman law, it does not announce any general principles of law. Consequently, Æthelbert's Doom lists specific monetary penalties for numerous specific in-

---

* This synopsis, prepared largely by Justin Waggoner, draws from various sources, both online and print, including Charles E. Tucker, Jr., *Anglo-Saxon Law: Its Development and Impact on the English Legal System*, 2 USAFA JOURNAL OF LEGAL STUDIES 127 (1991). The image is of a stained glass window in All Soul's College Chapel, Oxford. See http://en.wikipedia.org/wiki/File:Ethelbert,_King_of_Kent_from_All_Souls_College_Chapel.jpg.

juries suffered by the victim. The overarching goal of the code is the protection of the public peace. The intent of the actor was irrelevant, meaning that the fine was dependent solely upon whether or not the defendant caused harm to the victim. Therefore, the code operated under a strict liability tort law scheme, rather than a criminal act and punishment format. This made the cases simpler by preventing the rudimentary legal system from having to delve into several case-specific facts.

While no criminal law penalties such as death sentences or lifetime imprisonments were included in customary Anglo-Saxon law, there was a "blood feud" protection right. As a result, the members of a harmed family could lawfully avenge the death or injury caused to their kin by retaliating against the offender. However, the concern was that this could lead to an endless cycle of violence that would disrupt the peace. Such blood feuds were a common problem in late 6th century England. Therefore, Æthelbert's solution was to regulate the right to exact revenge by requiring payment to both the victim (or the victim's family) and to the central government for any vengeance acts. Over time, this change helped to transition the Anglo-Saxon society from one based on family loyalty (i.e., tribalism) to one based on governmental authority.

Interestingly, the code authorizes different penalties based upon the social class of the victim. This hierarchy identifies seven different classes, which in descending order of penalties received included: (1) clergy, (2) the king, (3) the noblemen, (4) the commoners, (5) the freedman, (6) indentured servants, and (7) slaves. Since the customary law already protected the interests of various classes of people, one of the key motivations for completing Æthelbert's Doom may have been to establish protection for the new arrivals from the Catholic Church.

Customary law in England after the issuance of Æthelbert's code tended to reflect the growing influence of the Roman Catholic Church. Despite the subsequent changes to Æthelbert's work, his code was an important development at the time and is an important piece through which legal historians can understand the largely intangible law that existed in England prior to the 11th century.

Æthelbert's lengthy reign ended with his death in 616. He was succeeded by his son, Eadbald. Æthelbert was later canonized by the Catholic Church.

Appendix 4.3
Biographical Sketch of King Canute*

Canute the Great was a Viking king who ruled England, Denmark, Norway, and some of Sweden in the early 11th century. Due to his success as a king and the breadth of his dominion, he was given the unofficial title of "Emperor of the North".

It is believed Canute was born in Denmark between the years of 985 and 995. He was the son of Danish king Sweyn Forkbeard and it is thought his mother had been a princess from Poland. Very little is known of Canute's life until 1013, when he joined his father in the invasion of England. He is described then as being very tall and exceptionally strong, while leading some of the Danish Viking warriors to battles. The Danes captured England rather quickly. However, King Sweyn Forkbeard died in 1014. The Danes in England then held out Canute as their king, but the English refused to recognize him as such.

Canute's older brother Harald then succeeded their father to the Danish throne. Harald then gave Canute another chance to lead a Viking invasion into England. Ultimately, this invasion would prove to have more staying power, as Canute was able to take over the entire kingdom and force a battle-wounded Edmund Ironside, then king of England, into a treaty. The vast majority of England would belong to Canute, while a small portion was left to Edmund. The treaty stated that the final survivor between Edmund and Canute would be king to all of England and pass the title on to their heirs. Likely as a result of his injuries, Edmund Ironside died just over a month after the treaty and Canute became king of all of England at the end of 1016. Harald died in 1018, after which Canute became king of Denmark. Canute gained control of Norway and part of Sweden during the 1020s.

Canute proved a very successful king with a relatively peaceful reign, most of which he spent in England. He strengthened the currency in use by the English and created freer trade by expanding the markets between England and Scandinavia. It is disputed whether Canute was a religious man, but regardless, he was very generous to the Church. He is also credited with dividing England into the four great Earldoms, which would be the basis for England's feudal baron system or many centuries. Canute, although already married, wed the widow of a former English king (and mother of Edward the Confessor) shortly after becoming king to shore up his and his heirs' claims to the English throne. Their son, Harthacanute, like his father, would briefly reign as king of both the Danes (1035 to 1042) and the English (1040 to 1042) after Canute's death in 1035.

Canute's reign did see the introduction of some interesting Danelaw measures. Canute issued some communal responsibilities in the law. For example, if a person witnessed a criminal commit a theft and did nothing to prevent the theft or apprehend the criminal, that witness could be liable to the victim for the damages suffered. Moreover, if one of the king's workers were killed in a particular community without any townspeople presenting evidence that might implicate the guilty party, the entire community would receive economic penalties. Canute also favored criminal punishments that were relatively

---

* This synopsis, prepared largely by Justin Waggoner, draws from various sources, both online and print, including Susan S. Kuo, *Bringing in the State: Toward a Constitutional Duty to Protect from Mob Violence*, 79 INDIANA LAW JOURNAL 177 (2004); Russell Glazer, *The Sherman Amendment: Congressional Rejection of Communal Liability for Civil Rights Violations*, 39 UCLA LAW REVIEW 1371 (1992); Desmond Manderson and Naomi Sharp, *Mandatory Sentences and the Constitution: Discretion, Responsibility, and Judicial Process*, 22 SYDNEY LAW REVIEW 585 (2000); Trisha Olson, *Of the Worshipful Warrior: Sanctuary and Punishment in the Middle Ages*, 16 ST. THOMAS LAW REVIEW 473 (2004).

gentle in comparison to other kings of his time. Eventually, the law Canute established would have little impact on the subsequent centuries of English law, as the Norman Conquest in 1066 would lead to the establishment of the common law tradition.

Appendix 4.4
Biographical Sketch of William of Normandy*

WILLIAM the CONQUEROR.

William of Normandy, also known as William the Conqueror or King William I of England, was born in Normandy (part of northwest France near southern England) in 1027. William was the illegitimate and only son of his father, the Duke of Normandy. Thus, when William's father died in 1035, William became Duke of Normandy. Young William and his supporters initially had a somewhat difficult time maintaining power, but they were eventually able get a solid footing in Normandy. In 1053 William wed his wife Matilda, with whom he would father ten children.

The story of William the Conqueror's rise to power in England involves competing claims, mismatched armies, and winds across the English Channel. Edward the Confessor died in January 1066 without any children, prompting three parties to stake competing claims to the throne: William, Harold Godwinson (Harold II), and the Viking King Harald III of Norway. As depicted in the Bayeux Tapestry [see Box #4.2 in subsection IIA of Chapter Four, above], William claimed that Edward the Confessor had promised him the English throne in 1051 or 1052. (By some accounts, this was either a false claim by William or a hollow promise from Edward; at that time, the kingship was not necessarily hereditary but was appointed by the witan, or council.) Moreover, William contended that Harold had sworn his allegiance to him in 1064, thus placing William next in line for the crown. Rather than naming either of the foreign claimants [William or Harald III] to the throne, the Anglo-Saxon government in England (acting through the witan) named Harold Godwinson as king. Additionally, the Anglo-Saxons asserted that this was in accordance with Edward's deathbed request.

In response to the crowning of Harold as king, William assembled an army to invade southern England. While William and his forces waited weeks for favorable winds, the Viking King Harald III of Norway began to invade England from the north, requiring the Anglo-Saxon army to advance north to stop them. This was a lucky break for William the Conqueror, as he was able to safely cross into England while Harold and his troops fought in the north. The Anglo-Saxons then headed south at full speed to confront the Normans. On October 13, 1066, Harold Godwinson's overworked army fell to William the Conqueror's forces in the Battle of Hastings. Harold was killed during the battle.

---

* This synopsis, prepared largely by Justin Waggoner, draws primarily from various print and on-line sources, including *William the Conqueror* entry in NEW ADVENT CATHOLIC ENCYCLOPEDIA, at http://www.newadvent.org/cathen/15642c.htm and Wikipedia entries for William the Conqueror, Domesday Book, and common law. The image is from Wikimedia.

William was formally crowned King of England at Westminster Abbey on Christmas Day of 1066.

Southern England quickly agreed to fall under King William's authority. However, much of northern England resisted the rule by the foreign Normans. William responded by ruthlessly burning and destroying much of the land in northern England. These actions succeeded in securing the obedience of northern England.

William the Conqueror centralized power to an degree unprecedented in England. As part of that effort he disenfranchised Anglo-Saxon landowners and instituted a brand of feudalism that strengthened the monarchy. William also ordered the compilation of the Domesday Book, an effort comparable to a modern census. Through the Domesday Book, completed in 1086, King William was able to identify all landholders, along with specific information regarding their wealth, such as the exact number of oxen each person owned. The Domesday Book thus proved useful for tax purposes. So successful was William's effort to centralize power and land ownership that (by one account) only two Anglo-Saxon barons that held lands before 1066 retained those lands twenty years later.

King William, an effective ruler and accomplished warrior, died after a battle in France from wounds suffered after falling off of his horse in 1087. William's eldest son Robert became the next Duke of Normandy. William's second oldest surviving son, William, would then become King William II of England, while his youngest son, Henry, would succeed William II as King Henry I.

Appendix 4.5
Biographical Sketch of Harold II*

King Harold II of England—Harold Godwinson—is historically known as having been the last Anglo-Saxon King of England. Harold was born in 1022. His father, Godwin, was a powerful lord under Canute the Great, and Harold's mother was Danish. Sometime before reaching the age of 23, Harold II had already been appointed to an earldom.

After his father's death in 1053, Harold II became the Earl of Wessex, covering the entire southern one-third of England. Consequently, he was the second most powerful man in the country behind King Edward (the Confessor). In fact, Harold may have been even more powerful than Edward the Confessor, as the King remained in exile for long stretches of time, and the latter part of Edward's reign has been described as, for all intents and purposes, having been Harold's. Harold also was responsible for defeating the Welsh in a significant 1062–1063 war.

Edward the Confessor died in January 1066. According to William of Normandy, both Edward the Confessor and Harold had claimed that William would inherit the crown after Edward's death. However, the Anglo-Saxons claimed that Edward the Confessor had pointed towards Harold on his deathbed, which was taken as a sign that he meant to name Harold as the successor. Harold was promptly crowned as Harold II in the first coronation at Westminster Abbey.

Shortly after being named king, Harold had to contend with invasions from both the south and the north. Viking King Harald III of Norway approached from the north, accompanied by Harold II's brother Tostig. Both the Viking King and Tostig died in combat, as Harold II won the battle. Meanwhile, however, William the Conqueror and his Norman forces had landed in southern England. Immediately after winning the battle against the Vikings, King Harold marched approximately 240 miles to south where he met William's troops in the Battle of Hastings. Harold II's beleaguered army lost to the Normans. Harold was killed in the battle and William then went on to become the next King of England. The story of the events leading up the Norman invasion of England and the invasion itself are famously displayed on the Bayeux Tapestry.

---

* This synopsis, prepared largely by Justin Waggoner, draws from various online sources, including the entry for *King Harold II* on the website of NNDB, at http://www.nndb.com/people/735/000093456/.

Appendix 4.6
List of English Sovereigns Beginning with William I
The Sovereigns since the Conquest and Their Regnal Years

House	Name	Accession	Years Reigned
NORMAN	William I	1066	21
	William II	1087	13
	Henry I	1100	35
	Stephen	1135	19
PLANTAGENET	Henry II	1154	35
	Richard I	1189	10
	John	1199	17
	Henry III	1216	56
	Edward I	1272	35
	Edward II	1307	20
	Edward III	1327	50
	Richard II	1377	22
LANCASTER	Henry IV	1399	14
	Henry V	1413	9
	Henry VI	1422	39
YORK	Edward IV	1461	22
	Edward V	1483	2 months
	Richard III	1483	2
TUDOR	Henry VII	1485	24
	Henry VIII	1509	38
	Edward VI	1547	6
	Mary	1553–4	5
	Philip and Mary	1554–8	
	Elizabeth I	1558	45
STUART	James I	1603	22
	Charles I	1625	24
	The Commonwealth	1649	–
	The Protectorate	1653	
	Charles II	1660	(a) 36
	James II	1685	4
	William and Mary	1689–94	13
	William III	1694–1702	
	Anne	1702	12
HANOVER	George I	1714	13
	George II	1727	33
	George III	1760	60
	George IV	1820	10
	William IV	1830	7
	Victoria	1837	64
SAXE-COBURG & GOTHA	Edward VII	1901	9
WINDSOR	George V	1910	26
	Edward VIII	Jan. 1936	11 months
	George VI	Dec. 1936	16
	Elizabeth II	1952	–

(a) In accordance with constitutional principle the reign of Charles II is deemed to have commenced at the death of Charles I in 1649, though in fact it began only in 1660.

Appendix 4.7
Biographical Sketch of King John*

King John ruled England from 1199 until his death in 1216. He is known largely for having signed the *Magna Carta* and also for various negative aspects of his reign.

In 1167, King John was born in Oxford. John was the youngest of eight children and five sons born to his father, King Henry II, and his mother, Eleanor of Aquitaine. Due to his junior position in birth order to his older brothers, John was not able to expect any inheritance and thus earned the nickname John "Lackland." John received an excellent education as a youth. However, his family life was very turbulent. His mother and older brothers were continually involved in plots against his father. When John was just six years old, his mother was imprisoned for what would be a sixteen year stint. John was his father's favorite son.

John was involved in numerous disputes with his brothers, especially with Richard, throughout his early adulthood. In 1185, John became the ruler of Ireland. However, the Irish despised him and he left after just eight months. Henry II died in 1189 and Richard, also known as Richard I and Richard the Lionhearted, acceded to the throne. While Richard was away during the Third Crusade between 1190 and 1194, John overthrew the person Richard had designated to rule in his absence. John promised Londoners the right to govern themselves if he would be recognized as Richard's heir presumptive. After Richard returned to England, he made peace with his youngest brother and named him as his heir.

Richard died in 1199. John was unable to gain full support in his bid for the crown as his young nephew Arthur also exerted a vocal claim. Ultimately, John captured Arthur and imprisoned him. Arthur died as a prisoner and some accounts (including those prevalent at the time) state that a drunken John had murdered him. The belief in these accounts led some of King John's French holdings to rebel against him. John also imprisoned Arthur's sister, Eleanor, his own niece, where she remained until her death in 1241. These acts surely help explain why John gained a reputation as a cruel and brutal king.

King John's unsuccessful efforts to retain the modern day French regions of Normandy and Aquitaine, both then held by England, was a major blow to his popularity in England. In fact, John earned the nickname "Soft-sword" for his clumsy battlefield exploits. Shortly after John's defeat in France, the majority of the local barons rallied against him and demanded concessions due to his failures in domestic governance (including high taxes), war, and his general abuses of power. Thus, the concessions the barons demanded were restraints on what the king could legally do. The signing of the Magna Carta marked the first time an English king had been forced by his own people to sign an agreement that limited his powers.

The Magna Carta was signed by King John in the meadow at Runnymede on June 15, 1215. The Magna Carta purportedly put a halt to the expansion of the king's expansion of the Royal Courts' jurisdiction. In effect, the barons were attempting to gain back some of the judicial power that had been seized by William the Conqueror and subsequent kings who centralized the English judicial system. This attempt proved ultimately unsuccessful.

---

* This synopsis, prepared largely by Justin Waggoner, draws from various sources, including Jane Rutherford, *The Myth of Due Process*, 72 BOSTON UNIVERSITY LAW REVIEW 1, 7 (1992).

The terms of the Magna Carta allowed the king to be overruled by a committee of barons called the Great Council. King John renounced the Magna Carta and its limiting terms once the barons had left London. King John also gained papal approval because his signature had allegedly been obtained under duress. This action led England into a civil war known as the First Barons' War. John died during the war a little more than a year after signing the Magna Carta. John's nine year-old son, Henry III, was then crowned and civil war ended.

The Magna Carta had an enormous impact on the development of the common law and also the composition of the United States Constitution. Some have even claimed that its terms amounted to the first step towards modern democracy. The Magna Carta was intermittently integral in the development of the English common law for several centuries after its issuance. During the 17th century English Civil War during the reigns of Charles I and II, the Magna Carta was viewed romantically as a golden-age of English citizens' liberties by those who opposed the monarchy. Although it no longer enjoys the force of law, some of the rights it provides to the common people are still in use today. For example, the right of habeas corpus was established in the Magna Carta. The Great Council, with its members who were charged with acting in the best interests of the country, was the predecessor of the modern Parliament in England.

King John's modern legacy is unfavorable, due to his reputation for cruelty, high taxes, failure to honor the *Magna Carta*, and forfeiture of French lands. In 2006 BBC History Magazine selected King John as the 13th century's worst Briton. King John also made an appearance in the stories of Robin Hood as an evil, cowardly king who acted arbitrarily and overtaxed his subjects.

Appendix 4.8
Biographical Sketch of Vacarius*

Born in approximately 1120, Vacarius was an Italian who became the first professor of law in England and the founder of the law school at Oxford University. It is believed that Vacarius was educated at Bologna and came to England in 1146 to serve as counsel to the Archbishop of Canterbury Theobald of Bec. Subsequently, Vacarius began teaching at Oxford University, then just a budding university.

Interestingly, Vacarius lectured to crowds both poor and rich alike. While teaching at Oxford, Vacarius published a nine-volume compendium of the *Codex Justinianus*, commonly referred to as the *Liber Pauperum*. The *Liber Pauperum* was actually intended for the poor students in Oxford and contained excerpts from the *Digest* and the *Institutes* for those who could not afford the full texts. The *Liber Pauperum* became a leading textbook at Oxford University. Claims were made that this book resolved all of the legal questions typically debated within law schools. However, King Stephen of England put a halt to all lectures on Roman law and ordered the destruction of the civil and canon law books that Vacarius had brought with him from Italy. Nevertheless, when King Stephen died in 1154, civil law regained its role as a course offering at Oxford. Civil law would continue to be the only law that was taught at Oxford until Sir William Blackstone made the common law part of the curriculum in 1758.

Following King Stephen's death, Vacarius gained an appointment as a legal adviser and ecclesiastical judge for the Archbishop of York. Vacarius served in this position for several decades up until he died around 1200. It is not clear whether Vacarius ever continued his lectures at Oxford after King Stephen's death. Regardless, Vacarius played a pivotal role in bringing the "rebirth" of Continental Europe's civil law across the English Channel, where it would ultimately have at least indirect influence England's legal system.

---

* This synopsis, prepared largely by Justin Waggoner, draws from various sources, including David E. Cole, *Judicial Discretion and the "Sunk Costs" Strategy of Government Agencies*, 30 British Columbia Environmental Affairs Law Review 689 (2003); and Richard A. Pacia and Raymond A. Pacia, *Roman Contributions to American Civil Jurisprudence*, 49 Rhode Island Bar Journal 5 n.52 (May 2001).

Appendix 4.9
Biographical Sketch of Henry de Bracton*

Henry de Bracton was a 13th century English jurist. His book *On the Laws and Customs of England* played a key role in the use of case law within the common law tradition. Bracton was also responsible for developing the requirement of *mens rea* or criminal intent for a defendant to be criminally culpable.

In approximately 1210 Bracton was born in Devonshire, a region in southwest England. Aside from his background in the Church, little else is known of Bracton's early life up until 1245 when he first became a justice. Bracton served as a criminal court judge from 1248 until his death in 1268. He also served as a justice in the predecessor to the King's Court. He resigned from this position prior to the Second Barons' War that began in 1258.

Bracton's writings drew heavily upon both the Roman law and sources of canon law. His major work was *On the Laws and Customs of England*, which he wrote between 1250 and 1256. Bracton had access to many rolls of recorded law cases from the then-equivalent of the King's Court called plea rolls. The plea rolls, which were generally not accessible even to someone in Bracton's position, contained information such as complete transcripts and pleadings in cases. At the time Bracton was alive, there was no effective *stare decisis* in the English legal system. Thus, in writing the treatise *On the Laws and Customs of England*, Bracton proved to be ahead of his time (at least in the common law tradition) by offering commentary with criticism and praise in regard to various decisions. Bracton often chose cases—most of which were approximately twenty years old at the time—in which he favored the judge's reasoning and could provide it as a model response to a particular factual situation. *On the Laws and Customs of England* was left unfinished because Bracton's access to the plea rolls was disrupted. Nevertheless, it was the most thorough English medieval law text.

Bracton's writings were heavily influential in medieval England as most of its 13th and 14th century lawyers read his material. In particular, his analysis of case law was passed on to future jurists. As with many jurists, the popularity of his writings over subsequent centuries fluctuated depending on the prevalent views. Bracton's writings were also read extensively by the founders of the US Constitution. Bracton also authored materials on the king's powers under the law, on the law of the Royal Courts, and on intestacy.

Bracton was integral in establishing the requirement that in order for a defendant's actions to be criminal he or she must have acted with criminal intent or the proper *mens rea* to commit the crime. Prior to Bracton's time, the distinction between a tort and a crime resulting in the same injury to a victim was not recognized. Although this distinction fell out of use for approximately two centuries after Bracton's life, it was reincorporated into English law around the beginning of the 16th century.

---

* This synopsis, prepared largely by Justin Waggoner, draws from various sources, including Martin R. Gardner, *The Mens Rea Enigma: Observations on the Role of Motive in the Criminal Law Past and Present*, 1993 Utah Law Review 635, 655 (1993); and David J. Seipp, *Symposium: The Distinction Between Crime and Tort in the Early Common Law*, 76 Brigham Young University Law Review 59, 81 (1996).

Appendix 4.10
Biographical Sketch of Thomas de Littleton*

Thomas de Littleton was a 15th century English judge and legal writer. He was born in approximately 1407 in Worcestershire (although some reports date his birth to as late as 1422), a region of west central England. Scant details are known of Littleton's early life, but it is believed he was a London barrister. His early career involved government appointments pertaining to property matters. In the 1450s he became a county court justice and in 1466 he was appointed as a judge of the Court of Common Pleas. Nine years later, in 1475, Littleton was knighted.

Thomas de Littleton's significance to the development of common law stems from his authorship of the *Treatise on Tenures*, which enjoyed more than three centuries as the standard real property law text for students of English law. Littleton wrote the treatise while he was a judge and it was first published in the same year he died (1481). The *Treatise on Tenures* was the first textbook written specifically on the topic of English property law, which in the 15th century focused primarily on real property. The timing of the *Treatise on Tenures* was impeccable, as English property law had been in a state of at least moderate uncertainty since the Norman conquest. The existing property law was an uneasy combination Anglo-Saxon customary law and Norman feudalism.

The *Treatise on Tenures* was written in law French, a unique blend of Norman French and English. Interestingly, unlike most previous authors of English law, Littleton did not draw any of his material from the sources of Roman law or the more contemporary commentators. He chose instead to write exclusively about English law.

In addressing one of the various real property issues in the *Treatise on Tenures*, Littleton first provides a definition of the class of rights with which he is dealing. Next, through either actual case decisions (which he cited) or, more frequently, hypothetical cases, Littleton then elucidates upon the key principles of English property law. Thus he used a system much like that of the Roman *jurisconsults*.

---

* This synopsis, prepared largely by Justin Waggoner, draws from various sources, including the Britannica Precise Encyclopedia, at http://www.answers.com/topic/thomas-de-littleton. The image is from an engraving by Thomas Trotter (ca. 1750–1803), after a 15th-century painting.

Appendix 4.11
Biographical Sketch of Henry VIII*

King Henry VIII of England, son of King Henry VII, was born in 1491. Henry was the third child of his father and had an older brother, Arthur. Since Arthur, as the Prince of Wales, was next in the line for succession, Henry was prepared for a career in the church. However, in 1502, Arthur died suddenly of an illness shortly after his marriage to Catherine of Aragon, the youngest daughter of the celebrated Spanish royal couple King Ferdinand II of Aragon and Queen Isabella I of Castille. Young Henry then became the Prince of Wales. After his father's death in 1509, Henry VIII, only seventeen years old, became king and married Catherine of Aragon, for whom a Papal dispensation had been acquired to invalidate Catherine's prior marriage to Arthur.

Henry VIII is famous in popular culture for having had six wives and the manner of his separations from these wives. However, Henry's personal life also had a surprisingly significant impact on England's religious move away from the Roman Catholic Church and, accordingly, England's legal developments.

---

* This synopsis, prepared largely by Justin Waggoner, draws from various sources, including Samuel Gregg, *Legal Revolution: St. Thomas More, Christopher St. German, and the Schism of King Henry VIII*, 5 Ave Maria Law Review 173 (2007); and C.M.A. McCauliff, *Book Review: Parliament and Supreme Headship: Church-State Relations According to Thomas More*, 48 Catholic University Law Review 653 (1999). The first image is from a portrait by Hans Holbein the Younger. The second image is from a woodcut by Hans Liefrinck.

Henry was an enthusiastic young king whose court was a key point for glamorous excess and Renaissance experiences including many concerts, dances, jousts, and hunting expeditions. Princess Mary, Henry and Catherine's first child to reach adulthood, was born in 1516. Catherine had a series of miscarriages and babies that died in their infancy. The inability of Catherine and Henry to produce a son to serve as Henry's heir caused considerable concern. Henry blamed Catherine. Meanwhile, Anne Boleyn, who served in Catherine's court, captured Henry's attention and ultimately his adoration. Nevertheless, Anne refused to merely be his mistress. Henry grew more infatuated with Anne and sought an annulment from Pope Clement for his marriage to Queen Catherine on the grounds that his brother and Catherine had consummated their marriage. The Pope did not act on the petition.

Henry VIII then used his considerable power to get leading theologians at Oxford and Cambridge to convince the Parliament that his marriage to Catherine had been unlawful. Consequently, when Henry could not get what was effectively a divorce from Rome, he was able to get his own government to grant him an annulment from Catherine. Interestingly, this break from papal authority would be repeated by other European countries during the rise of the nation-state.

Henry and Anne Boleyn were married in early 1533. She gave birth to Elizabeth I later that year. Also in 1533, the House of Commons forbade all appeals to Rome and prohibited the admission of papal bulls into England. After these measures were passed by England, Pope Clement finally denied the annulment between Henry and Catherine and also declared his marriage to Anne Boleyn as void. Both Rome and England passed measures that broke off communications between the parties. Subsequent measures were then passed making the King head of the Church of England. Moreover, Henry VIII removed the canon courts' ecclesiastical jurisdiction and made all clergymen directly answerable to the King.

Any dissenters to Henry VIII's religious policies were suppressed. Several people within the Church who did not agree with his policies were tortured or executed, including John Fisher, Bishop of Rochester, and Sir Thomas More, Henry's former Lord Chancellor, both of whom refused to take the oath to the King as "the only Supreme Head in Earth of the Church of England."

Henry and Anne's marriage deteriorated as the couple fought about the King's various infidelities. Moreover, after Elizabeth's birth, Anne miscarried twice, meaning that Henry still lacked the all-important male heir. After the second miscarriage in 1536, the King had Anne arrested for treason and she was executed that same year. Ten days later he married Jane Seymour, one of Anne Boleyn's ladies-in-waiting. In 1537, Jane gave birth to a son, Prince Edward—the future Edward VI—and she died shortly thereafter. The King's remaining three marriages, although significant in their own right, had less influence on the future of England.

Although Henry VIII never abandoned the Roman Catholic Church's principles, his break with Rome had enormous consequences on the course of English history. By breaking relations with Rome and creating a state-centered religion (Anglicanism), Henry seized economic and political power from the Church and made England into a more powerful nation. Among other things, this destroyed canon legal authority in England and allowed Chancery to fill the gap. Although Henry did not fully complete the break with the Roman Catholic Church, his daughter, Elizabeth I, did accomplish this.

Appendix 4.12
Biographical Sketch of Sir Edward Coke*

Sir Edward Coke, an extremely influential English jurist, provided many valuable contributions to English law and the common law tradition. Coke was born in eastern England in 1552 to a father who was a barrister. Coke gained his education at the Norwich School and Trinity College in Cambridge, prior to being called to the bar in 1578.

Coke served as a successful lawyer prior to becoming a Member of Parliament in 1589. He excelled in the Parliament and was named Speaker of the House of Commons in 1592. Between 1592 and 1594, Coke worked as Solicitor General. Then, in 1594, Sir Edward Coke was appointed by Queen Elizabeth I as Attorney General of England, a post in which he would serve as until 1606. While in this position, he was involved in the prosecution of Sir Walter Raleigh. In 1606, King James I appointed Coke as Chief Justice of the Court of Common Pleas. Seven years later, King James I again appointed Coke to a Chief Justice position, this time on the Court of the King's Bench. The King then removed Coke from the King's Bench in 1616 after his refusal to fall in line with the royalty's views. However, Coke would recover and be appointed to the Privy Council the following year. Coke also returned as a Member of Parliament between 1621 and 1628. He was imprisoned for six months during 1621 on false charges manufactured by those with opposing political views. He died in 1634.

During his lifetime, Sir Edward Coke was involved in a wide variety of contributions to the development of the common law. As a member of the King's Bench, Coke fervently defended the common law against overreaching by ecclesiastical bodies, courts controlled by local aristocrats, and also the King. One of Coke's more notable judicial opinions arose when he interpreted the Magna Carta to apply not only to the protection of nobles, but also to all other subjects under the Crown in an equal manner. Thus Coke established the law as a provider of rights among all citizens. (By some accounts, however, Coke's historical arguments, including those relating to the Magna Carta, were based on false interpretations.) Coke also played a prominent role in the drafting the Petition of Right (1628); his most important writings are the *Reports*, a series of detailed commentaries on cases in common law, and the *Institutes*, which includes his commentary on Littleton's *Tenures*.

Coke's judicial decisions provided the foundations for several key principles of English law. For example, he gave official weight to the proposition that a person's "home is his castle" in regard to self-defense. Coke also authored opinions that laid out the contractual parol evidence rule and formed what some analysts consider to be the basis of environmental law (in a pigsty nuisance case). Interestingly, Coke also took part in some early instances of judicial review during his tenure as a judge.

In addition to his work in politics and as a judge, Coke also authored numerous legal treatises and other materials. Coke's writings, some of which were aboard the Mayflower in 1620, were key in training all colonial and early US attorneys. Thus, it is fair to say he was the most renowned English jurist in early America. American revolutionists John Adams and Patrick Henry would argue from Sir Edward Coke's treatises to support their positions.

---

* This synopsis, prepared largely by Justin Waggoner, draws from various sources, including Harold J. Berman, *The Origins of Historical Jurisprudence: Coke, Selden, Hale*, 103 YALE LAW JOURNAL 1651, 1673–1681 (1994); Hila Keren, *Textual Harassment: A New Historicist Reappraisal of the Parol Evidence Rule with Gender in Mind*, 13 AMERICAN UNIVERSITY JOURNAL OF GENDER IN SOCIAL POLICY AND LAW 251, 301–303 (2005); and Paul Raffield, *Contract, Classicism, and the Common-Weal: Coke's Reports and the Foundations of the Modern English Constitution*, 17 CARDOZO STUDIES IN LAW AND LITERATURE 69 (2005).

Appendix 4.13
Biographical Sketch of Lord Mansfield*

Lord Mansfield was a famous 18th-century judge and politician. He was born William Murray in Scotland in 1705. His father was a poor Jacobite Scottish peer. Despite his family's humble status, Mansfield enjoyed an excellent education as a youth. Through the charity of his friends, Mansfield was then able to study law at Christ Church, in Oxford. While there, he gained significant training in Justinian's *Digest*.

After completing his legal studies, Lord Mansfield was called to the bar in 1730. Early in his career, he was a very popular barrister in Scotland, but he had difficulties attracting clients in England. However, after a stirring oral argument in a particularly noteworthy 1737 English trial, Mansfield became highly sought after as a barrister throughout England. Mansfield's political career began in 1742 upon his election to Parliament and his appointment as Solicitor General. He proved to be an outspoken politician during his fourteen years in Parliament. Mansfield was appointed Attorney General in 1754 and then 1756 to the position of Chief Justice of the King's Bench. He would serve in this capacity for 32 years, until 1788. He valued this position over any others and even declined an offer to become Lord Chancellor.

Lord Mansfield is recognized largely as the founder of English mercantile law, drawing on the commercial law used between merchants in Europe. Prior to Mansfield, the common law was ill equipped to deal with the numerous new cases and customs that transpired as commerce expanded rapidly. In most cases, the common law left commercial issues solely to juries; after cases were decided, no guiding principles were extracted to assist in the disposition of subsequent cases. Lord Mansfield responded to this chaotic situation by issuing decisions so comprehensive that they nearly equated to their own commercial code. Mansfield's contributions on commercial law created a more systematic and rational structure in which merchants could operate. Other courts were also able to apply a predictable set of rules to conflicts between the merchants.

Lord Mansfield's decision in the 1772 *Somersett* Case held that there was no legal backing for slavery in England. The ruling applied to England only, and not its colonies. Thus, slavery was allowed to continue within the United States, and would continue for nearly a century after the *Somersett* Case.

---

* This synopsis, prepared largely by Justin Waggoner, draws from various sources, including Daniel R. Coquiellete, *Legal Ideology and Incorporation IV: The Nature of Civilian Influence on Modern Anglo-American Commercial Law*, 67 Boston University Law Review 877, 948 (1987).

Appendix 4.14
Biographical Sketch of William Blackstone*

Sir William Blackstone was an English jurist and professor famous for his treatise *Commentaries on the Laws of England*. Blackstone was born in London in 1723. He gained a legal education at Pembroke College in Oxford. Blackstone served as a university fellow in Oxford, prior to being called to the bar in 1746. He then worked the next twelve years as a rather unsuccessful barrister in London. However, his break came in 1758 when he returned to Oxford as a law lecturer, in the newly-established Vinerian Professorship. His lectures were very successful and would eventually form the basis of the *Commentaries on the Laws of England*.

Between 1765 and 1769, the four volumes of Blackstone's *Commentaries on the Laws of England* were published. The *Commentaries* were treatises of English common law that were long regarded as the leading publications on the common law. The *Commentaries* were exceedingly popular because they were concise, readable, and (perhaps most importantly) portable summaries of the common law. Blackstone delved into the history behind the common law tradition and used broad strokes in describing the various areas of law. Blackstone's *Commentaries* played a special role in the development of the American legal system. They were required reading for most lawyers in the American Colonies. The United States Supreme Court still often cites to the *Commentaries on the Laws of England*, especially when attempting to discern the historical intent of the Framers of the Constitution. This is because the *Commentaries* are considered to be a definitive source of the common law in pre-Revolutionary America.

---

* This synopsis, prepared largely by Justin Waggoner, draws from various online sources. The first of the two images comes from a marble bas-relief—one of 23 reliefs of great historical lawgivers in the chamber of the U.S. House of Representatives in Washington, DC; this one was sculpted by Thomas Hudson Jones in 1950. The second image is from a portrait by Blackstone by Thomas Hamilton Crawford (1860–1948), after a Joshua Reynolds portrait.

The four volumes of the *Commentaries* were divided into different categories—reminiscent of treatises in the civil law tradition—including (i) the rights of persons, (ii) the rights over property, (iii) private wrongs, and (iv) public wrongs. Blackstone's definition in the *Commentaries* for property rights has provided the dominant Western concept of property. Blackstone also authored treatises on the Magna Carta and other topics. In addition, he served as a Member of Parliament starting in 1761. However, most of the last twenty years of his life were spent with his family in Castle Priory House, which he built at Wallingford. Blackstone had been chronically ill for much of his life and died in 1780.

Appendix 4.15
Biographical Sketch of Jeremy Bentham*

Born in 1748, Jeremy Bentham was an English legal and social theorist. He is perhaps best known for his advocacy of utilitarian philosophy—that is, determining the correct act or policy by that which would cause the greatest good for the greatest number of people. Bentham advocated tirelessly for legal reform based on utilitarianism. He was a prolific writer, predominantly focusing on law and legislation, and one of his goals in life was to create a "Pannomion"—a complete utilitarian code of law.

Bentham is also recognized for his concept of the Panopticon. Although it was never built, the Panopticon was a plan for a circular prison designed like a wheel with spokes. Bentham's model was designed so that "all its parts should be visible from a single point by means of a series of reflectors; that is to say, a prison in which an inspector would be able to see at a glance everything that was taking place, the inspector being himself concealed from the observation of the prisoners, so as to [create] 'the sentiment of an invisible omniscience.'" Bentham's Panopticon design influenced future social theorists, including Michel Foucalt.

Further details about the criticisms that Jeremy Bentham leveled at the common law system, and the impressive energies that he devoted to the project of legal codification in order to overcome the evils of that system, are offered in the main of this chapter, in subsection IVA.

---

* This synopsis, prepared largely by Erin Slinker Tomasic, draws from various online sources and from Charles Milner Atkinson, JEREMY BENTHAM: HIS LIFE AND WORK (1970, 1905); and A BENTHAM READER (Mary Peter Mack ed., 1969). The quoted phrases comes from the Atkinson book at 84–85. The image is from a painting by Henry William Pickersgill (died 1875).

Appendix 4.16
Biographical Sketch of James Kent*

James Kent was an American jurist and legal scholar born in New York in 1763. Kent was raised in Dutchess County New York (now Putnam County, located in the Hudson River Valley), where his father was a lawyer. At the age of eighteen, he graduated from Yale College in 1781. There were no professional American law schools at that time, but Kent developed an interest in law while reading Blackstone's *Commentaries* as independent study while courses were suspended at Yale during the Revolutionary War. Four years after graduating he began working as an attorney in Poughkeepsie, New York, near where he grew up. From 1791 to 1793, Kent served as a representative of Dutchess County in the New York State Assembly. Kent then relocated to New York City, where Governor John Jay appointed him a master in chancery for the city, probably due in part to Kent's pro-Federalist views.

Kent continued to work several diverse positions in academia, politics, and law. He became the first professor of law at Columbia University in 1793, a position he found to be especially frustrating and would hold until 1798. While teaching at Columbia, Kent also served another term in the New York State Assembly in 1796 and 1797. Kent became recorder of New York in 1797, in 1798 a justice of the New York Supreme Court (now the Court of Appeals, the highest court in New York), in 1804 Chief Justice, and in 1814 chancellor of New York, a position he held until his retirement in 1837. James Kent also was a member of the New York State Constitutional Convention in 1821. He lived until 1847. The Chicago-Kent College of Law was named in his honor.

James Kent is significant in the context of comparative legal studies largely because of his role as chancellor in New York. Chancery law (also known as "equity") was unpopular during the colonial period due to conflict with the British. Consequently, little development occurred in terms of case law in the courts of equity. However, Kent's sound judgments and written opinions (which he introduced to the court) became a building block for American equity jurisprudence. Prior to Kent's emergence as an authority, equity decisions were largely based upon the individual judge rather than on equity principles and precedent. Moreover, Kent was very much ahead of his time in his stance on judicial review, noting almost a decade prior to *Marbury v. Madison* that "[the judicial branch] ought not in sound theory be left naked without any constitutional means of defence". *See citation #1 below!*

Prior to his work as chancellor, Kent had also introduced the practice of drafting opinions to the New York Supreme Court, which had not been done by the Court prior to his tenure. Particularly noteworthy were his decisions on commercial law issues that provided important guidance and predictability, while also earning him the title as "the father of American commercial law."

One of Kent's most lasting achievements, however, is his *Commentaries on American Law*, originally published in four volumes (and six editions during Kent's lifetime) starting in 1826. This was a pioneering work on the part of Kent, as nobody had yet attempted to provide an examination of the American legal system. The *Commentaries on American Law* was very broad in its coverage, discussing state, federal, and international law, in addition to property rights matters. The *Commentaries* received significant praise in both the United States and England.

---

* This synopsis, prepared largely by Justin Waggoner, draws from various online sources and from Judith S. Kaye, *Symposium: Commentaries on Chancellor Kent*, 74 CHICAGO-KENT LAW REVIEW 11, 15 (1998), citing James Kent, *An Introductory Lecture to a Course of Law Lectures* (1794), reprinted in 3 COLUMBIA LAW REVIEW 330, 337 (1903). The quoted phrases come from the Kaye article, at pages 11, 15, and 19–20.

Appendix 4.17
Biographical Sketch of David Dudley Field*

David Dudley Field II was born in Connecticut in 1805. He was admitted to the bar in 1828 and moved to New York City, where he would remain during his career as an attorney and, more notably, as a law reformer. Field believed that common law in the United States, and especially in New York state, needed radical changes—specifically a unification and simplification of its procedure. During the 1830s, he visited several European states and investigated their courts, procedures, and codes.

Upon returning to the United States, Field set the goal of codifying common law procedure. He wanted to establish fixed and predictable rules, in terms of both procedural and substantive law. This was due in part to Field's abhorrence of judicial discretion. A key quotation expressing Field's views can be drawn from his address at the opening of the Law School of the University of Chicago in 1859, "If the decision of litigated questions were to depend on the will of the Judge or upon his notions of what was just, our property and our lives would be at the mercy of a fluctuating judgment, or of caprice. The ex-

---

* This synopsis, prepared largely by Justin Waggoner, draws from various online sources and from Stephen N. Subrin, *Uniformity in Procedural Rules and the Attributes of a Sound Procedural System: The Case for Presumptive Limits*, 49 ALABAMA LAW REVIEW 79 (1997); and Andrew P. Morriss, *Codification and Right Answers*, 74 CHICAGO-KENT LAW REVIEW 355 (1999). The second paragraph above is derived almost directly from the first source, at p. 86, and the quoted passage in the fourth paragraph is drawn from the second source, at p. 362. See also Helen K. Hoy, *David Dudley Field*, in GREAT AMERICAN LAWYERS, Vol. V: 125–74 (William D. Lewis ed., 1908). The image is from a black-and-white photograph that was taken between 1865 and 1880 and that is housed in the Library of Congress, according to which the image is in the public domain.

istence of a system of rules and conformity to them are the essential conditions of all free government, and of republican governments above all others. The law is our only sovereign. We have enthroned it."

When not working within his law practice, Field devoted his free time to this codification process. Initially, Field met strong resistance to his efforts. However, in 1847, he was appointed as the head of a committee to revise the practice and procedure of the New York courts. Three years later the Code of Civil Procedure, now known as the Field Code, was enacted by the New York legislature.

A key feature of the Field Code was its elimination of the distinction between forms of procedure between suits in law and equity requiring separate actions. Rather than maintaining the split between the two actions, Field unified both suits into the same procedure and simplified the process. Moreover, the Code of Civil Procedure boldly stated "there is no common law in any case where the law is declared by the [Code]," thus preempting any case law in existence prior to the enactment of the Code.

The Field Code was extremely influential on the development of law in both the United States and the rest of the common law world. Field's civil code was adopted in twenty-four states and his criminal code in eighteen more. Furthermore, England and several of its colonies instituted procedural reform based largely upon the Field Code. A subsequent work by Field involved a codification of almost all of New York's civil and political codes (although most of his work product was never adopted). Nevertheless, Field's work remained extremely influential because many states duplicated its format and structure. After completing his work on the Field Code, David Dudley Field continued to exert his influence on international codification efforts by preparing the *Draft Gistlines of an International Code* in 1872. This led to the formation of the Association for the Reform and Codification of the Laws of Nations, which Field served as president.

In addition to being the predominant codifier in the American legal system, Field was also involved in politics. Field was originally an anti-slavery Democrat, but he then switched his support to the Republican party in 1856 and to the Lincoln Administration throughout the Civil War. Field then returned to the Democratic party in 1876 and served the final three months of a New York Senator's unexpired term.

Appendix 4.18
Legal Codification in America
(excerpt of law journal article by Head)

[*Note:* The following text is excerpted from a pre-publication draft of the article appearing at 13 DUKE JOURNAL OF COMPARATIVE & INTERNATIONAL LAW 1 (2003). Almost all footnotes have been deleted; readers are advised to refer to the published article for citations to authority. The footnotes that remain carry different numbers from those that appeared in the final published version, and some have been shortened or modified. They appear in the typical style for US law journals. In one case (footnote 2), new material has been added to reflect more recent scholarship.]

Codes, Cultures, Chaos, and Champions:
Common Features of Legal Codification Experiences in
China, Europe, and North America
John W. Head

I.   Introduction
    A. Aims and Overview
    B. Definitions and Theories of Codification
       "Codification"
       Conditions and factors of codification

II. Chinese Experiences with Legal Codification
    A. Codification in the Qin period
       The historical setting
       Unification of China and promulgation of the Qin Code
       Conditions and factors of codification
    B. The Han Dynasty and Codification
       From Qin to Han
       The Han Code
       Conditions and factors of codification
    C. The Tang Dynasty and Codification
       Division, Confucianism, reunification
       The Tang Code
       Conditions and factors of codification
    D. The Ming Dynasty and Codification
       The historical setting
       The Ming Code
       Conditions and factors of codification
    E. Other Sources of Law in Dynastic China

III. European Experiences with Legal Codification
    A. Justinian's Codification
       The character of the work
       Conditions and factors of codification
    B. The French Experience with Codification under Napoleon
       Background to the Code Civil
       Revolution and codification
       Conditions and factors of codification

IV. American Experiences with Legal Codification
  A. The *Laws and Liberties of Massachusetts* of 1648
      American colonial legal systems
      The character of the Laws and Liberties
      Conditions and factors of codification
  B. The American Codification Movement of 1815–1840
      Post-Revolution legal developments
      The call for codification
      Conditions and factors of codification
  C. The Field Codes — Successes and Failures
      Field's legacy, aims, and inspiration
      Field's great success — codification of civil procedure
      Field's great failure — codification of substantive civil law
      Conditions and factors of codification
V. Concluding Observations

Synopsis

What are the key conditions and factors that contribute to a successful effort within a political unit to create a new legal code? This article builds on the existing "comparative codification" literature by examining that question in the context of three very different legal traditions: dynastic Chinese law, European civil law, and North American common law. Drawing on nine important codification experiences — four from China, two from Europe, and three from North America — the author posits that three conditions must exist in a legal system for codification to occur: (i) that written law is generally regarded favorably as a means of ordering society; (ii) that the top political authority in the society is powerful enough to impose a code; and (iii) that such top political authority is eager to champion the cause of codification. Assuming these three necessary conditions are present, several key contributing factors — for example, cultural change and legal chaos — further augur in favor of codification. The author identifies five such factors and illustrates their importance in each of the nine codification experiences. The article concludes with some observations about (i) the value of including traditional Chinese law in comparative codification studies and (ii) the interplay between the concentration of political power (lacking, for example, in the international legal system) and the likelihood of legal codification.

I. Introduction

A. Aims and Overview

Much has been written over the years about legal codification in Europe and, to a lesser extent, in North America. Indeed, an extensive "comparative codification" literature has developed. From this extensive legal scholarship have come various theories about the conditions and factors that contribute to a successful effort within a legal system to create a new legal code.

In contrast, relatively little attention has been given in the West to the dynastic Chinese experience with legal codification. This lack of attention derives in part from the paucity of reliable information available on the subject in Western languages. Recently, however, substantially more information has come to light in the West about Chinese legal codification, and about dynastic Chinese law generally. For example, in the last half-century numerous archeological finds have yielded remnants of legal codes dating from the Qin and Han eras. Moreover, just in the past decade, reliable English translations of two key dynastic codes from later eras — the Tang and the Qing — have appeared.

In this article, I attempt to broaden the scope of "comparative codification" to encompass Chinese experience with legal codes. Without attempting to be at all comprehensive, I offer illustrations of that experience and compare it with selected codification experiences in Europe and North America; and against that backdrop I explain my own perspective on the conditions and factors that can lead to codification.

For these purposes I have chosen nine codification experiences: four from China, two from Europe, and three from North America. For the first two Chinese examples, I look to the third century BCE, when the state of Qin unified China and then quickly fell to the Han dynasty. We have a thin but growing body of evidence regarding the codified issued law in this period. I then turn to the seventh century CE and the Tang dynasty, a high point in Chinese cultural development and also, because of its Tang Code, in Chinese legal development. Lastly I look to the fourteenth century CE, when the Ming dynasty succeeded the Mongol (Yuan) dynasty, thus returning China to ethnic Chinese rule, evidenced in part by the enactment of the Ming Code.

For the European examples, I briefly survey the codification efforts of Justinian and Napoleon, which resulted in perhaps the two most celebrated codes in the civil law tradition. My aim in doing so is to suggest some likenesses that these two efforts bear to the Qin, Han, Tang, and Ming codification experiences in China.

For my three North American examples, I consider first the seventeenth-century Massachusetts exercise that yielded the *Laws and Liberties of Massachusetts* and then turn to two codification efforts in nineteenth-century America: the national codification movement that reached a high point around the 1830s, and then a follow-on effort orchestrated mainly by David Dudley Field in New York. In examining these North American codification efforts, and comparing them with the Chinese and European examples, my aim is to illustrate some similarities and dissimilarities that I consider most important in discerning what conditions and factors — political, legal, and social in character — seem to be most important for codification efforts to succeed.

B. Definitions and Theories of Codification

Before describing specific codification experiences, I offer both a working definition of codification and the general thesis that I intend to develop in this article.

"Codification". In defining codification, I opt for simplicity, aware that many different definitions are possible and that choosing one can bear importantly on the analysis of conditions and factors of codification. For my purposes, "codification" is the process by which the top authority in a political unit puts into effect for the legal system of that political unit a single, newly-conceived, legally binding "code". I define a "code" in turn as a body of rules that, while not necessarily comprehensive or perfectly clear and consistent, is intended to cover all or most aspects of a major area of law within the legal system, such as civil law, criminal law, or procedural law. "Codification" excludes a reissuance or recension of an existing code of laws currently in force, or a revision of such a code unless the revision radically changes either the structure or content of that code. A "codification" is also to be distinguished from an unofficial "compilation" that constitutes a collection of legal rules (perhaps with added commentary or structure) but that does not itself have the force of law.

Conditions and factors of codification. Here is my central thesis: Codification, as I have defined it above, depends for its success on a convergence of various conditions and factors. Specifically, for codification to occur, three conditions must exist in the legal system:

- High regard for written law. The first condition is that written law is generally regarded favorably as a means of ordering society. That is, most persons having power and influence within the political unit find it appealing, or at least accept-able, that rules of behavior take the form of official law and that they be written. I refer to this hereinafter as the "regard-for-written-law" condition.

- High concentration of political power. The second condition is that the top po-litical authority is strong enough to impose a code. That is, the lawmaking power within the political unit is not so divided among competing players as to make it impossible to promulgate a comprehensive set of laws applicable to the entire po-litical unit. I refer to this hereinafter as the "power concentration" condition.

- A champion for codification. The third condition is that the top political author-ity has a strong enough desire to impose a code that he (or it) is prepared to cham-pion the cause. Expressed differently, there is a person or a set of persons with controlling authority who considers codification to be vitally important for some reason (typically a political reason, such as to strengthen nationalism or to earn a place in history) and is prepared to push for it. I refer to this hereinafter as the "champion-of-codification" condition.

Assuming the three necessary conditions for codification (as described above) are pre-sent, the following five factors augur in favor of codification. Not all of these five factors need to be present, but as more of them become present, codification becomes more likely.

- The existing law is chaotic or difficult to ascertain—for example, located in mul-tiple sources, partially or largely unwritten, internally inconsistent, or tangled in its structure. I refer to this hereinafter as the "legal chaos" factor.

- The existing law is inconsistent with radical political changes that have just oc-curred—for example, a change in the form of government, the overthrow of a monarchy, or the dissolution or merger of political units. I refer to this hereinafter as the "radical political change" factor.

- The existing law is behind the times generally—for example, substantially out of step with the social status of one or more segments of the population, or silent on matters now important because of technological or economic advances. I refer to this hereinafter as the "behind-the-times" factor. Whereas the "radical political change" factor turns on political structures and changes, this "behind-the-times" factor turns on other important changes of a cultural nature.

- A "model" code from an earlier time is available and is culturally relevant to the people of the political unit. I refer to this hereinafter as the "model code" factor.

- Legal scholars and jurists play a highly important or influential role in the legal sys-tem—such that it is natural for practicing attorneys, judges, and legislators to turn to the work of jurists and scholars for guidance in designing, drafting, and applying laws. I refer to this hereinafter referred as the "scholar/jurist influence" factor.

Why might any of this be interesting? Because, like other comparative studies of law, an examination of similarities and dissimilarities in the codification experiences of two or more legal systems can help us better understand each of those legal systems. More particularly, my aim in enumerating various conditions and factors of codification is to provide a framework in which to undertake such an examination. For me, this is not a predictive exercise—to anticipate, for example, where codification might strike next—but instead an explicative one. Ultimately, the value of the exercise rests in a deeper un-derstanding of the legal systems under consideration. One of them, the Chinese legal system, is not only intrinsically fascinating but also largely unfamiliar to most Western students of law. I begin with it.

[Note: Sections II, III, and IV are omitted here]

* * *

V. American Experiences with Legal Codification[1]

The story of legal codification in America is dramatically different from those of China and Europe, at least in the instances I have chosen for illustration. In the following paragraphs I describe three codification efforts in North America—a colonial effort in seventeenth-century Massachusetts, a more or less national effort in early nineteenth-century America, and an effort that concentrated on the state of New York later in the same century. The first effort may be regarded as a success, although it pales in significance when compared to the codification efforts I have told about above. The second effort ended in failure, except to the extent that it laid the groundwork for the third effort, which was a partial success although much narrower in scope than the Chinese and European efforts discussed above. I believe the fate of these three American efforts is at least partly explicable by reference to the various conditions and factors of codification that I have enumerated at the beginning of this article.

A. The *Laws and Liberties of Massachusetts* of 1648

American colonial legal systems. Two opposing assumptions—both of them false—might be made about the legal systems in the early days of the English colonies in America. One of these assumptions, probably the more common, is that those legal systems were essentially transplants of English law. As a practical matter, this would have been impossible, largely because the circumstances in the colonies were so radically different from those in England. As Roscoe Pound observed, the common law of England in colonial times was heavily burdened with formalism, and "[i]ts ideals were those of the relationally organized society of the Middle Ages and so quite out of line with the needs and ideas of men who were opening up the wilderness." Reflecting this reality, the colonial charters customarily provided that laws should be established in the colonies themselves in a way not contrary to the laws of England.

The fact that colonial conditions differed radically from those of England might lead to the opposite assumption about legal systems in the early days of the English colonies: that they were, as one author has put it, "home-spun, indigenous legal order[s]." This assumption is also false, although perhaps not so far wide of the mark as the first one is. The basic precepts of English law, including especially its emphasis on individual rights,

---

1. In writing this portion of the article, I have relied on the following authorities (listed in alphabetical order): Francis R. Aumann, The Changing American Legal System (1940); Charles M. Cook, The American Codification Movement (1981); David Dudley Field, Speeches, Arguments and Miscellaneous Papers of David Dudley Field (A. P. Sprague, ed., 1884); Lawrence M. Friedman, A History of American Law (2d ed. 1985); Kermit Hall et al., American Legal History—Cases and Materials (1991); George L. Haskins, *Codification of Law in Colonial Massachusetts: A Study in Comparative Law*, 30 Ind. L.J. 1 (1954); George L. Haskins, Law and Authority in Early Massachusetts: A Study in Tradition and Design (1960); Charles M. Hepburn, The Historical Development of Code Pleading in America and England (1897); The Life of the Law (John Honnold ed., 1964); John Henry Merryman, The Civil Law Tradition 26–33 (1985); Mathias Reimann, *The Historical School Against Codification: Savigny, Carter, and the Defeat of the New York Civil Code*, 37 Am. J. Comp. L. 95 (1989); Bernard Schwartz, Main Currents in American Legal Thought (1993); Thorp L. Wolford, *The Laws and Liberties of 1648*, 28 Boston U.L.R. 426 (1948).

definitely formed the foundation of law in the English colonies, and once the colonies had progressed beyond the earliest phase of their development—that is, beyond "the nasty, precarious life of pioneer settlement"—the rules and traditions of English law had an important abiding influence.

The most accurate picture of law in the colonies, therefore, has two main features: English legal heritage and indigenous legal rules. Both of these features were reflected, in varying proportions, in legal codes that several of the colonies established for themselves in the latter part of the seventeenth century. One of the earliest of these colonial codes, and apparently the most influential, was *The Laws and Liberties of Massachusetts* ("*Laws and Liberties*" or "*LLM*").[2]

The character of the Laws and Liberties. The *Laws and Liberties* was remarkable in several respects. For one thing, it was purported "to be a complete and comprehensive statement of the laws, privileges, duties, and rights in force" within the colony.

> The [*LLM*] was not only an authoritative compilation of constitutional provisions—regulations for the conduct of administration, courts and their jurisdiction, trade, military affairs, and the relation between church and state—but it included also the substantive law of crime, of property, and of domestic relations. Detailed provisions regulating prices and wages are also

---

2. FRIEDMAN, *supra* note 1 at 61, 91. Friedman refers to two earlier codes: Dale's laws in Virginia (1611), and the *Body of Liberties* adopted in Massachusetts in 1641. *Id.* at 68–70. *See also* AUMANN, *supra* note 1, at 12 (enumerating colonial "codification" efforts that predated the *LLM*). Introductory provisions of *The Laws and Liberties of Massachusetts* are reprinted in part in HALL, *supra* note 1, at 15–17. For an analysis of the content of the *LLM*, see Walford, *supra* note 1, at 431–62 (focusing on administrative and judicial provisions, religious and personal freedoms, public records, property, domestic relations, business regulation, and criminal law). Walford quotes from an introduction to a 1929 edition of the *LLM* for the proposition that it was "the first attempt at comprehensive reduction into one form of a body of legislation of an English-speaking country." *Id.* at 426. [*New material*: For a recent examination of the legal conditions in Massachusetts in its earliest colonial days, explored by contrasting those conditions with the conditions existing in Virginia's earliest colonial days, see WILLIAM E. NELSON, I THE COMMON LAW IN COLONIA AMERICA: THE CHESAPEAKE AND NEW ENGLAND, 1607–1660 (2008). This authority emphasizes the stark differences between those two colonies but their similarity in one respect—that in their earliest days neither of them relied much on the common law:

> [T]he leaders who initially governed Virginia and New England made little use of the common law as an instrument for social control. Virginia's rulers sought to accomplish their main chore, which was to coerce labour out of the local inhabitants, through intimidation and brutality, while New England's leaders strove to create a religious utopia by recourse to the law of God, not the law of England. The English legal heritage of the inhabitants of both Virginia and New England constituted a set of background norms to which they occasionally turned when convenient, but England's common law was not the initial foundation of their legal systems.

Id. at 8. The same authority posits that what pushed the law of both Virginia and Massachusetts toward some convergence around English common law was the concept of the rule of law—which in that context meant the "idea that society ought to be governed by ascertainable and unchanging rules capable of restraining arbitrary actions by those in power." The impetus for that push, however, differed: in Virginia, such stability in legal rules was necessary in order to attract investors whose loans would keep the colony afloat; in Massachusetts, stability in the legal rules was demanded in order to overcome the ambiguity inherent in having broad discretion rest with the elite magistrates. *Id.* at 8–9. For other observations about the diversity of law among the colonies, and the rather uncertain and uneven embrace of common law principles there, see FRANCIS H. HELLER, AMERICAN LEGAL HISTORY 92–119 (1998) (unpublished, on file with author) (exploring the "reception" of the common law in America as described in the 1996 Supreme Court's *Seminole Tribe* case and as illustrated in varying approaches to jury trials in the colonies).]

found, as well as a number of laws governing individual behavior and affecting the moral welfare of the community. For example, gaming for money is proscribed, and penalties are imposed for drunkenness, profanity, and the telling of lies.

A second noteworthy feature of the *Laws and Liberties* is its structure. Instead of being arranged in a logical, analytical fashion — as was, for example, Justinian's *Institutes* or the French *Code Civil* discussed above — the *LLM* was arranged alphabetically by subject. Following its introductory clauses, the *LLM* proceeded from a provision on "Abilitie" (regarding capacity of persons to make wills and dispose of property) to provisions on "Actions," "Age," and "Ana-Baptists," and concluded with a provision on "Wrecks of the Sea." In this respect, as I hinted above, the *LLM* pales in comparison to other codification efforts described in this article.

Conditions and factors of codification. A third noteworthy feature of the *Laws and Liberties* brings us back to the focal point of this article: conditions and factors of codification. The first of the three conditions that I have identified as necessary for successful codification is evident in the story of what led to the drafting and enactment of the *LLM*. That story centers around the efforts of the colonists to restrict the arbitrary powers of the governor and his assistants by forcing them to have the legal rules by which they governed written down and published. Here is how one authority on the *LLM* tells the story:

> It must be borne in mind that the organization of the Colony of Massachusetts Bay was autocratic from the start. At the time of settlement in 1630, the government of several thousand persons was in the hands of the governor and his seven or eight "assistants" or "magistrates."…. There was nothing in the political theory of this group which could be described as democratic…. [They] looked upon themselves as instruments in the divine hand for carrying out a great religious mission. Their voice was supreme in judicial as well as in legislative matters, and, during the three years following settlement of the Colony, they inflicted fines and imprisonment, levied taxes, and granted lands entirely within their own discretion. Although the basic aims of these leaders were generally accepted, the absolute authority wielded by this small oligarchic group provided an immediate source of dissatisfaction to the great bulk of the colonists, and a movement was soon under way aimed not only at broadening the basis of government but at obtaining security against the arbitrary power of the magistrates. Although in 1634 the government was placed upon a wider basis through extension of the suffrage, absence of knowledge as to what justice might be expected continued to be a principal basis for complaint. A considerable portion of the population felt that the magistrates … could not be trusted to decide fairly unless the rules which were to guide their decisions were public property.

These circumstances closely resemble those that led to the issuance of the Twelve Tables in Rome in 450 BCE — a large majority successfully pressuring a small minority of power-holders to write down the legal rules, with the aim of preventing the arbitrary exercise of that power. In the case of the Massachusetts experience, however, another element also contributed to this desire for the rules to be written down: the "traditional Puritan belief in the importance of the written word."

The colonists' insistence that a code of laws be drafted eventually resulted in the approval in 1641 of a document known as the "Body of Liberties." This document, however, "was less a code of laws than a kind of modern state constitution." It had such inadequate coverage — it did not, for example, incorporate particular laws that had already been enacted — that it failed to satisfy the colonists. Indeed, it "in fact increased their insistence upon having a comprehensive code of laws." Accordingly, committees "were therefore appointed once again with a view to preparing a comprehensive compilation of all applicable laws and regulations. Their work resulted in the detailed and comprehensive Code of 1648 ... which was printed for distribution in 1649," and this "brought to an end the long struggle over the power of the magistrates."

The desire to have the laws written down — what I have referred to as the "regard-for-written-law" condition to successful codification — is reflected in the provisions of the *LLM* itself. Its introductory clause posits the general thesis: "These Lawes which were made successively in divers former years, we have reduced under several heads in an alphabeticall method, that so they might the more readilye be found ... wherin (upon every occasion) you might readily see the rule which you ought to walke by." More specifically, other *LLM* provisions required "that both the judgment of any court and the reasons therefor should be recorded" — requirements that grew out of a campaign to force the governing authorities to reduce rules and judgments to writing in order to prevent arbitrary action.

What of the other two conditions of codification that I have identified — the "power concentration" condition and the "codification champion" condition? Are they evident in the circumstances that resulted in the issuance of the *Laws and Liberties*? They are, but their scope of coverage was fairly narrow. It could be said that these two other conditions occurred once the colonists broke the absolute power of the governor and magistrates and intensified their insistence on a set of written laws. However, that is all they got. The *LLM* was hardly the kind of sophisticated and structured code that emerged from the codification experiences discussed above — that is, in Qin, Han, Tang, or Ming China, in Justinian's empire, or in Napoleon's France — in which codification champions had a much greater concentration of power.

This leads me to a further, subsidiary thesis as to the conditions necessary for codification to occur: they have weight. Once all three of the conditions are present, codification can occur, assuming enough of the other factors also are present; but these conditions (perhaps unlike typical conditions precedent in some contracts) can also vary by weight. The degree to which they are present affects the kind of code they help create — its scope, its exclusivity, its break with the past. For example, the three conditions — "regard-for-written-law," "power concentration," and "codification champion" — were not only present in the case of the French *Code Civil*, but present to an unusually high degree. Napoleon's power and the importance he placed on codification were both very great. Perhaps as a consequence, the *Code Civil* had a broad scope of coverage and a high degree of exclusivity. It dominated the areas of its coverage, as shown by its displacement of all prior law and by Napoleon's hope (albeit short-lived) that it would not be made the subject of commentary and interpretation. In contrast, although all three conditions were present in the case of the *Laws and Liberties*, two of them — "power concentration" and "codification champion" — were much less pronounced. Perhaps as a consequence, the *LLM* lacks the kind of exclusivity and domination that characterized the *Code Civil*. There is no indication that the *LLM* was supposed to expand on or displace pre-existing law. Instead, its aim was to restate pre-existing law, as revealed in the introductory clause quoted above: the laws "which were made successively in divers former years, we have reduced ... so they might the more readilye be found."

This subsidiary thesis—that the conditions of codification can have more or less weight, and that their weight (the degree to which they are present, beyond a bare minimum) can affect the scope and exclusivity of the code that they help create—seems to be borne out in the Chinese experiences with codification as well. As explained above, codified law in the Qin, Han, Tang, and Ming periods had a limited scope of coverage, reflecting the competition between the Legalist preference for written law (*fa*) and the Confucianist preference for the mainly unwritten norms of *li*, which governed most activities of most Chinese most of the time. Because Chinese society did not regard written law (*fa*) favorably as a means of ordering society as a whole (as distinct from serving merely as a means of maintaining imperial rule sufficient to bring political order), one of the three conditions I have identified—the "regard-for-written-law" condition—did not have as much weight in China as in the two European codification experiences I have discussed above.

Hence, the presence of the conditions of codification is not a black-or-white proposition. There are shades of gray. The conditions of codification can be present in degrees, and the degree to which they are present bears on the character of the codification, and especially on the exclusivity and "reach" of a code.

The same shades of gray appear in the other five factors that I identified above as tending to favor codification. In the case of colonial Massachusetts, some of those factors existed, but in degrees that differed from their presence in some of the other codification experiences discussed above—especially that of France at the beginning of the nineteenth century. More specifically:

- The "legal chaos" factor was present to some degree in colonial Massachusetts. As explained above, one of the main ingredients to colonial American law was English legal heritage; but it would not be easy to identify clearly what were the laws of England in the seventeenth century, since they would have included a mish-mash of parliamentary statutes, case-law, local customs, ecclesiastical law, and other ingredients. It is unlikely, however, that the "legal chaos" in seventeenth century Massachusetts was as dramatic as that described by Portalis just before the promulgation of the *Code Civil*—"a mysterious labyrinth" and "an immense chaos."

- The "behind-the-times" factor was also present, and to a substantial degree. The *Laws and Liberties* reflects, according to one author, "a fresh and considered effort to establish new provisions which were suitable to new conditions in a frontier society," and specifically to Puritan emigrants whose announced purpose was "to create a kingdom of God in the wilderness." Again, however, this factor was probably more evident in some other codification exercises described above—for example, Justinian's codification, which drew from sources that dated from several centuries earlier, before Rome had embraced Christianity and before the empire had divided and the West had fallen.

- The "radical political change" factor was present to some extent in seventeenth century Massachusetts, as the frontier colonial circumstances had important political consequences, among them the concentration of discretion in a small oligarchy. However, there was no revolutionary political re-ordering on the scale of the French Revolution from which the *Code Civil* emerged.

- The Massachusetts codifiers had little in the way of a "model code" on which to draw. Although they might have found some guidance or inspiration in compilations of customary law that existed in some of the local English jurisdictions from which the colonists came, and the alphabetical arrangement they followed in preparing the *Laws and Liberties* might have been inspired by various earlier abridgments, these would almost surely have been of less use than Justinian's *Institutes* were to the drafters of the *Code Civil*, or than the Tang Code was to the commission responsible for creating the Ming Code.

- Lastly, the "scholar/jurist influence" factor would have been largely absent from the colonial Massachusetts codification experience, for a combination of reasons. First, although English law in the 1600s was the subject of some famous scholarly works, it was far less influenced by legal scholarship than European civil law, given the centuries of work by Glossators and Commentators poring over Justinian's *Digest* beginning in the twelfth century and sometimes giving opinions that were binding in courts, or than Chinese law, with its long march of Confucianist scholars whose work had become so influential in China by the time of the Ming dynasty. Besides, the availability of English legal treatises was slim in Massachusetts as of the mid-seventeenth century. Moreover, the American colonies at that time did not offer very hospitable circumstances for the kind of homegrown legal scholars that would become influential starting early in the nineteenth century.

In sum, the *Laws and Liberties* experience presents a mixed image of codification in early America. On the one hand, the *LLM* did constitute a code of sorts, and it is surely a noteworthy accomplishment given its circumstances and its consequences. In the years following its adoption in 1648, this compilation of laws was widely emulated. Despite differences among the colonies, many of them copied large portions of *The Laws and Liberties of Massachusetts*. Hence, the same basic structural framework — alphabetical arrangement of important laws — appeared in the statutory compilations, or "codes," adopted in many parts of the colonies, including Connecticut, New Hampshire, New York, Pennsylvania, Delaware, and East New Jersey.

On the other hand, the *LLM* pales in comparison to the other codes I have described, from Europe and China. I have suggested, as a reason for this, that two of the three necessary conditions for codification were only barely present, and several of the other factors favoring codification were less markedly present or influential than in those other codification experiences.

B. The American Codification Movement of 1815–1840

I turn now to the eighth of nine codification efforts discussed in this article — the great flirtation of the United States, shortly after it achieved national independence, with the idea of "substituting a general code for the whole of the common and statute law." That codification effort largely failed as a national movement, for reasons I summarize below.

Post-Revolution legal developments. The account of the American codification effort of the early nineteenth century begins with American independence in the late eighteenth. Unlike many political revolutions, the American Revolution did not involve demands for radical changes in laws or legal institutions. At least as far as private law was concerned, American patriots felt little need to bring revolutionary legal change. Indeed, most of the new states specifically provided by law (usually by constitutional provisions) that the laws in existence before independence would remain in force.

Several reasons have been identified for this preference for legal continuity over legal change. First, "an inequitable legal system had not been a source of revolutionary discontent" in America, as it had been in France. Second, the American Revolution had not involved radical ideological change, as was the case for example in the Russian revolution, and therefore "changes in the legal system were not ideologically mandated." Third, practical realities provided "pragmatic reasons for sustaining the inherited system." These practical realities included the difficulty of creating instantly a new system of law, as well as the instability that any attempts to do so would incite.

In short, the independence of the American states from England did not trigger any immediate drastic change in the laws and institutions that had developed in the colonies before the separation. It was as if an old house had been transferred to a new owner (by theft, perhaps, in the view of the English and the American loyalists), and the new owner had seen no immediate need to make major repairs or renovations to the house.

What happened over the next few years was predictable, at least for someone who has purchased and moved into an old house, and it can be seen as involving overlapping stages. First came a period of settling in and adjustment. Second, as circumstances changed, the need for repair and renovation became apparent. Third, a debate developed over how drastic the alterations should be, and indeed whether the entire structure should be destroyed and replaced by a different one. Lastly, the most expansive proposals for change were rejected, and a compromise solution for renovation was reached.

In the case of the "old house" of American law,[3] the period of settling in and adjustment lasted for roughly a generation following American independence, and it represented a balance between two urges: (i) to conserve and continue in force the pre-existing rules and institutions, in the interest of stability, and (ii) to overcome defects that independence created and that changing circumstances exacerbated.

One of the perceived defects in the inherited system was the inaccessibility and uncertainty of the law. Complaints along these lines, encouraged by the establishment of a republican form of government, were exemplified by the following comment made at the close of the eighteenth century:

> Every citizen ought to acquire a knowledge of those laws that govern his daily life and secure the invaluable blessings of life, liberty, and property.... [Y]et in no country is it more arduous and difficult to obtain a systematic understanding of the law.

Responding to this problem of uncertainty, most states undertook the "revision" of their statutory laws. This exercise did not, however, involve an actual reform of the substance of those laws; instead, it involved consolidating the statutes still in force in a state and putting them into some kind of order, usually chronological.

Even this seemingly modest exercise was daunting, as the laws enacted by colonial legislatures and later by the state legislatures had not to that point been widely distributed or well organized. By preparing their "revisions," the various states provided reliable and usable compilations of statutes currently in force. In New Jersey, for example, the revised laws as published in 1800 comprised one volume of 455 pages.

---

3. My research has revealed that I am not the first person to whom an "old house" analogy occurred in this context. *See* John Forrest Dillon, *Bentham's Influence in the Reforms of the Nineteenth Century,* in I SELECT ESSAYS IN ANGLO-AMERICAN LEGAL HISTORY 504 (1907) (remarking that Jeremy Bentham's remedy for English law, which he saw as "a system full of delays, frauds, snares, and uncertainties," was "not to stop leaks in the roof, put in new panes of glass, and otherwise repair the rotten and dilapidated structure, but to demolish it and rebuild anew").

In this way the immediate challenges were met of making the legal system (or systems) of the United States functional in the earliest years. However, this period of "settling in and adjustment," to use the old house analogy I introduced above, provided no permanent solutions. Although most American lawyers apparently regarded the state of American law by 1815 with satisfaction, the opposite opinion soon prevailed. By 1820, the dominant view was that legal reform was essential to meet the new circumstances in which the United States found itself.

Numerous specific ills were identified. Foremost among these, for our purposes, was that of complexity. One American legal historian says that "it appeared that American law was becoming an incomprehensible tower of Babel." Another asserts that by the early 1800s "a perfectly bewildering array of reported decisions" had been established, and provides these details:

> It has been estimated that by 1822 there were about "one hundred and forty volumes of American Reports, all published since the organization of the federal government." The rate of increase was so rapid that by 1824, complaints were being made concerning the "vast and increasing multiplication of reports...."

The call for codification. What was to be done? According to many—both lawyers and laypersons—codification offered the best answer. Thus began a great national flirtation of the United States with a comprehensive legal codification. It was a movement that generated a surprisingly high degree of attention and enthusiasm:

> For nearly three decades, law reform would remain a preoccupation of the legal profession. Few comparable periods exist in American legal history when reform was so prominent in professional life.[4]

> [Although legal reform had been espoused before, the factor that] differentiates the period after 1820 from the preceding years was the manifest vitality and comprehensiveness that law reform activity displayed. In the earlier years, overt programmatic improvement of the law was episodic and localized, as was discussion of major legal problems. After 1820, a general American law reform movement could be said to exist. While the states necessarily remained the focus of reform efforts, agitation and debate concerning the improvement of the legal system transcended local boundaries.

That "agitation and debate" centered on codification, and specifically, as one writer put it in the 1820s, on "the expedience and practicability of substituting a general code for the whole of the common and statute law."

Proponents of codification had a precedent for such an effort, of course, in the form of the French codification that had been completed only a few years earlier.[5] In particular, the *Code Civil* was an immediate and compelling source of inspiration. It was new, it was easily available in English, it had emerged in a country whose circumstances seemed similar to those of the United States, and it was widely regarded as a paradigm of grace

---

4. COOK, *supra* note 1, at 69. According to another text on American legal history, the proposals that emerged from the codification movement "distracted the attention of lawyers for most of the nineteenth century." HALL, *supra* note 1, at 316. *See also* GRANT GILMORE, THE AGES OF AMERICAN LAW 27 (1977) (noting "the influence which [the codification movement] exerted for the better part of half a century" and asserting that "[f]rom the 1820s until the Civil War, American lawyers lived with the idea that the common law not only could be but probably would be codified").

5. The five basic French codes—the *Code Civil*, the Code of Civil Procedure, the Penal Code, the Code of Criminal Procedure, and the Commercial Code—had been promulgated between 1804 and 1811.

and simplicity.[6] Morever, it was part of a continental European legal tradition that was gaining popularity in the United States, as reflected in the growing number of references in early nineteenth-century law reports to civil law authorities of various kinds, including Pothier and other scholars, Justinian's *Institutes* and *Digest*, and the *Code Civil* itself.

The French codification experience, of course, was a hard act to follow. A comprehensive national codification that would reform American law was obviously a radical idea, and like most radical ideas it would need strong, singular leadership and a clear, singular set of specific goals and of measures for achieving them. The codification movement of 1815 to 1840 lacked both. It "manifested a diffused expression of reformist energy rather than a picture of tightly knit organization activity."

For one thing, there was "no single person who can be considered the theorist of the movement" in this period. Although Jeremy Bentham and David Dudley Field are often cited as dominant figures in this regard, Bentham was in fact spurned by many Americans on both sides of the debate, and Field was instrumental only in the latter phases of the American codification movement, as discussed more fully below in part IVC. In the early, formative stages, the codification song was sung by several men, including William Sampson, Joseph Story, Charles Sumner, William Plumer, Thomas Cooper, Robert Rantoul, and others. Indeed, "[a]lmost every law writer after 1825 felt compelled to include his views" on the proposed reform of law through codification.

They did not sing the same tune. Except for the most general of grounds for espousing codification — the advisability in principle of bringing more control and clarity to the mounting volume of case law and statutes — there was no common thread in the movement, no single theory sufficiently compelling to translate proposals into effective action. Some proponents called for a radical reform of the law, designed to go back to first principles, perhaps based on natural law, and to create a distinct legal self-identity for the United States. Among those more radical proponents was William Sampson, who has been described by one source as "a flambouyant codifier who castigated the common law and urged the need for America to declare its independence from English jurisprudence," and whose 1823 address to the New York Historical Society encouraged codification by contrasting the defects of English common law with the glorious benefits that could come from a general code of American law. Other proponents also urged radical reform.

Others preferred a far more moderate or restrictive approach, under which codification would be undertaken for the purpose of rationalizing and systematizing the law by resolving inconsistences, pruning away obsolete rules, and remedying blemishes — but not to reform it substantively. Among these was Joseph Story, who first opposed codification but then in 1821 gave some encouragement to a general code, or at least to moving in the direction of such a code. He made this comment in 1829:

> The mass of the law is, to be sure, accumulating with an almost incredible rapidity.... It is impossible to look without some discouragement upon the ponderous volumes which the next half century will add to the groaning shelves of our jurists.... I know indeed of but one adequate remedy, and that is, by a gradual digest, under legislative authority, of those portions of our jurisprudence

---

6. Cook quotes one American lawyer as saying that the Code Civil had a structure that was marked by "lucid order, precision and method" and another as praising it for its "simple principles of right" written "in simple language." COOK, *supra* note 1, at 71. For some of its proponents, codification reflected not only grace but also mathematical certainties. AUMANN, *supra* note 1, at 150 (suggesting that "Napoleon's belief in legal logarithm tables undoubtedly led to the Civil Code" and that similar views existed in the United States).

which under the forming hand of the judiciary, shall from time to time acquire scientific accuracy. By thus reducing to a text the exact principles of the law, we shall, in a great measure, get rid of the necessity of appealing to volumes which contain jarring and discordant opinions; and thus we may pave the way to a general code, which will present in its positive and authoritative text, the most material rules to guide the lawyer, the statesman, and the private citizen.... [However], to attempt any more than this would be a hopeless labor, if not an absurd project. We ought not to permit ourselves to indulge in the theoretical extravagances of some well meaning philosophical jurists who believe that all human concerns for the future can be provided for in a code speaking a definite language. Sufficient for us will be the achievement to reduce the past to order and certainty.

In addition to being divided between radicals and moderates (with differing shades of each), the proponents of codification were also divided geographically. However much enthusiasm the codification movement was able to generate at the national level, legal codification in nineteenth-century America would have to be, in the end, largely a state-by-state process. Only a few states could have pro-codification leaders with the stature and endurance of Field, to whose efforts in New York we shall turn in part IVC of this article.

In short, the codification movement that began around 1815 lacked a clear focus, in that no one person or group gained ascendancy over the others and presented a singular theory and program for codifying American law. One reason for this is especially pertinent to our consideration of the conditions and factors of codification. A singular theory and program of codification would in any event have been difficult for most of the early proponents of codification to muster because of their own intellectual nature and professional bent: "Being, by and large, practical men of the common law, they were not comfortable with legal philosophy or theory.... Consequently, when it came to the formation of abstract principles on which a proposed system of codified law would operate, they were quite noticeably out of their element."

By 1840, the American codification movement had lost steam, at least as a national effort at comprehensive reform that attracted broad interest and support. One expert on the movement refers to its outcome as "tradition in triumph—almost."[7] Why did tradition triumph (almost)? Two factors seem to predominate: (i) the strength of the common law tradition itself in America and (ii) the emergence by the mid-1800s of a broad range of American legal literature—chiefly treatises and digests—that provided tools for lawyers and judges and largely obviated comprehensive codification of the type originally propounded.

The first factor—strength of the common law tradition itself—can be seen in the intense criticisms voiced by the opponents to codification right from the beginning of the movement. Whether through fear of change or through sincere devotion to the common law, those opponents of codification strenuously defended the status quo. A largely conservative majority of the American bar consistently resisted law reform, and thus codification.[8] More importantly, perhaps, the common law was able to meet the demands of the rapidly developing American society in the antebellum period. The English legal system was replaced by the 1840s with an indigenous and distinct system of American common law that was "com-

---

7. Cook, *supra* note 1, at 201. *See also* Gilmore, *supra* note 4, at 27 (noting that "the pre-Civil War codification movement ultimately failed").

8. *See* Cook, *supra* note 1, at 202 (explaining that "[a] conservative faction of the bar, often a majority, had consistently fought demands for legal reform whenever they had appeared"). *See also* Lawrence M. Friedman, *Law Reform in Historical Perspective*, 13 St. Louis U. L.J. 351, 369–70 (1969) (discussing the opposition of the American bar to substantive reforms of law).

patible with American circumstances and capable of solving the legal problems created by a rapidly changing society." The establishment of the uniquely American common law doctrines, the "Americanization" of the common law, diminished the appeal of codification.

The second factor that alleviated the need for codification was the "development of a body of American legal literature, chiefly treatises and digests."[9] Treatises and digests by American scholars appeared as early as the 1820s and included such influential works as Nathan Dane's *A General Abridgement and Digest of American Law* and James Kent's *Commentaries on American Law*. The 1830s and 1840s, however, brought what can only be described as a flood of American legal literature, with such works as the *Treatise on the Law of Private Corporations Aggregate* by Joseph K. Angell and Samuel Ames (1832), *Elements of International Law* by Henry Wheaton (1836), *Introduction to American Law* by Timothy Walker (1837), *Evidence* by Simon Greenleaf (1847), and *Treatise on the Measure of Damages* by Theodore Sedgwick (1847) leading the way.[10] Joseph Story, one of the most influential of the American jurists of the first half of the nineteenth century, published at least eight textbooks on a wide variety of legal topics between 1832 and 1845. The writings of Story and Kent in particular "discouraged the possibilities of a reception of French law, since they presented in a systematic, orderly, reasoned fashion what was in substance sound common law." In sum, the treatises by American jurists provided judges and lawyers with practical guidelines and gave the American common law a sufficient theoretical foundation to withstand the sway of civil law.

Conditions and factors of codification. If we examine the American codification movement of 1815–1840 in terms of the various conditions and factors of codification that I identified earlier, we see some of them present but most of them lacking. I assess them as follows:

- The "regard-for-written-law" condition was surely present in early nineteenth-century America, as in all Western law — in contrast, for example, to the Confucianist views discussed above, under which a rule of law (*fa*) was seen as inferior to a rule by men who knew and practiced the precepts of *li*[93] — but this regard for written law was also tempered by a high regard for the approach that English common law had taken for the development of new law. Growing largely through the accretion of judicial decisions announced in particular cases, English common law clearly did not have a primarily statutory character. "Legislation ... has traditionally occupied only a secondary position in English law and was limited to correcting or complementing the work accomplished by judicial decisions." The appeal of the common law's reliance on case-by-case development was perhaps reflected in Joseph Story's declaration in 1817 that it is "impossible to provide by any code ... for the infinite variety of distinctions" necessary for justice to be done in particular cases, and in his later warning against the "theoretical extravagances of some well meaning philosophical jurists who be-

---

9. COOK, *supra* note 1, at 204. The reports of the American state courts' decisions also played an important role in strengthening the common law tradition, because they "were building blocks for an indigenous system of law...." FRIEDMAN, *supra* note 1, at 325–26.

10. FRIEDMAN, *supra* note 1, at 328. *See also* COOK, *supra* note 1, at 204–07 (noting and discussing the significant increase in American legal literature after the 1830s). In addition to the original American digests and treatises, many of the works by the British legal scholars, such as Joseph Chitty's PRACTICAL TREATISE ON THE LAW OF CONTRACTS, were "adapted" to the American circumstances by adding American precedent and explanatory footnotes. FRIEDMAN, *supra* note 1, at 326. *See also* COOK, *supra* note 1, at 205 (discussing the "American editions" of English works).

93. [These notions of *li* and *fa* are explored in deetail in Chapters Six and Seven, below.]

lieve that all human concerns for the future can be provided for in a code speaking a definite language."

- The "power concentration" condition—under which the top political authority is strong enough to impose a code—was certainly absent if the aim of the movement was to create a national codification, as it was for some proponents.

- The "champion-of-codification" condition—under which there is a person or a set of persons at the top of the political unit's power structure to whom codification is vitally important for some reason—was also absent in the American codification movement of 1815–1840. As discussed above, no single person led the movement to give it a clear focus and strategy.

- The "legal chaos" factor was certainly present and indeed triggered much of the interest in codification, as discussed above, but the development of treatises took the edge off that interest by bringing an increasing degree of order out of the chaos.

- The "behind-the-times" factor—that is, whether the existing law is substantially out of step with social or economic developments—was probably present to some degree, as reflected in the criticism of the "continued close affinity of American law to English jurisprudence," but, as noted above, the American Revolution did not involve demands for radical changes in laws or legal institutions. Besides, ideological views changed over time (and at the urging of persuasive spokesmen) so that "the common law became synonymous with freedom and codification with restraint."

- The "radical political change" factor was obviously present to a certain degree—that is, the political circumstances of the newly independent United States obviously required new constitutional bases for law. However, for the reasons noted above, this political change did not in itself prompt broad support for radical change to the content of the laws.

- The "model code" factor was present but only to a limited degree. Under my formulation of this factor, the "model code" must be both available and culturally relevant. As explained above, the French *Code Civil* was available and, at first, emulated among some codification proponents. However, the enthusiasm for the *Code Civil* had substantially waned by about the 1830s, when it became clear that the *Code Civil* would be subject to continuous interpretation.[11] Moreover, any examination of the cultural context of the *Code Civil*, beyond merely its relationship with a revolution that had some similarities to the American revolution, would reveal that it rested on very different historical, social, and political foundations from those that were found in American law and that might support an American legal code.

- The "scholar/jurist influence" factor was largely absent. As noted above, the proponents were, for the most part, "not comfortable with legal philosophy or theory" and hence not cut of the same cloth as Justinian's team of compilers working under Tribonian, or Napoleon's drafting commission drawing on Pothier and other legal scholars, or the Chinese codifiers so heavily influenced by Legalist and later Confucianist scholarship. Moreover, to the extent that legal scholarship was pertinent to the American codification debate, it increasingly urged against radical codification based on "theoretical extravagance."

---

11. Codification opponents pointed to the numerous reports of the *Cour de Cassation* and various commentaries and digests of the codified French law as evidence that the code had not reduced uncertainty or the workload of legal practitioners. *See* Cook, *supra* note 1, at 115.

C. The Field Codes—Successes and Failures

Field's legacy, aims, and inspiration. David Dudley Field[12] was the key figure in the second phase of the nineteenth-century American codification movement. From the appearance of his first published work on law reform in 1839 to the time of his death in 1894, Field was a tireless promoter and theoretician of codification in the United States. The major portion of Field's codification efforts occupied about forty years, beginning in 1847, when he was appointed by the New York legislature with the aim of codifying the laws of New York. As I explain in the following paragraphs, this forty-year period was marked by some success but fell far short of the goal Field had set.

What was that goal? Although his efforts were focused on the codification of state law, his ultimate goal (as he expressed it) was to create a universal "CODE AMERICAN, not insular but continental." His reasons for setting this goal were familiar ones. Echoing the law reformers of the early 1800s, Field criticized the common law of the United States for being "filled with tumult and disorder." He asserted that the only solution to the problem of chaos and uncertainty in law was comprehensive codification.

More specifically, Field saw two main purposes for codification of the common law: (i) the "reduction of existing laws into a more accessible form, resolving doubts, removing vexed questions, and abolishing useless distinctions"; and (ii) the "introduction of such modifications as are plainly indicated by our own judgment or the experience of others." He claimed that codification would bring both practical and theoretical advantages: it would result in "dispens[ing] with a great number of the books" that encumber lawyers' libraries; it would save a "vast amount of labor" that lawyers spent on research; it would "settl[e], by legislative enactment, many disputed questions, which the Courts have never been able to settle;" it would allow the legislature to "effect reforms in different branches of the law;" and finally, it would make knowledge of the law accessible to common people.

As vehicles for delivering these benefits to New York, Field planned for implementation of five different codes in that state; together they would constitute a comprehensive code governing all aspects of the law. The codes were to include "a political code, embracing all the laws relating to government and official relations; a code of civil procedure, or remedies in civil cases; a code of criminal procedure, or remedies in criminal cases; a code of private rights and obligations; and a code of crimes and punishments." Field himself wrote and revised significant portions of the proposed codes and led efforts to adopt them in the New York legislature.

In doing so, Field took cues from Bentham, Story, the drafters of the French codes, and other codification proponents. In particular, he incorporated into his codes many principles of the civil law codes and their writers. Field's Civil Code, for example, included sources that were "judicial, statutory, doctrinal, and codal," and it contained "over fifty citations to the French and Louisiana Civil Codes, the French Code of Commerce, ... and references to Justinian's Digest and Code." The structure of Field's Civil Code was closely modeled on the Louisiana code and the French code, and it contained "four general divisions; the first relating to persons, the second to property, the third to obligations, and the fourth containing general provisions relating to these different subjects."

Field not only borrowed freely from the other codes in devising his Civil Code but also had a similar vision of the purpose of the Civil Code as had codifiers in the civil law countries. For him a civil code was "to be a statement of the general principles of pri-

---

12. [See Appendix 4.17 for a biographical sketch of David Dudley Field.]

vate law, from which most specific rules can be directly ascertained — either because they are directly expressed or because they can be directly deduced." Thus Field asserted that his Civil Code "can not provide for all possible cases which the future may disclose," and that the purpose of the code was to "give the general rules upon the subjects to which it relates."

Field's great success — codification of civil procedure. I have focused most attention on Field's Civil Code because it was the core of Field's effort, in that it "constituted Field's attempt to codify the common law." In this attempt, Field failed. Let us look first, though, at the area of his success.

The first of the Field codes, the Code of Civil Procedure, was enacted in New York in 1848 and soon became a "landmark in the movement for law reform." Field intended to prepare a procedural code that would "make legal proceedings more intelligible, more certain, more speedy, and less expensive." To a large degree Field achieved these goals. Field's Code of Civil Procedure consisted of only 391 sections, and "was couched in brief, gnomic, Napoleonic sections, tightly worded and skeletal." Among other things, it "eliminated the common-law forms of action and the distinction between actions at law and actions in equity," thus replacing the dual system of justice with "one unified system administered by one court of general jurisdiction." The code's provisions also substantially simplified the pleading procedure and spelled "the death sentence of common-law pleading."

Had New York been the only state to adopt Field's code of civil procedure, the success would have been significant, although not great. However, Field's Code of Civil Procedure took root all across the country: "The enactment of this New York code opened ... the floodgates of reformatory legislation, and determined the course of its progress." About half of the American states had adopted codes based on the Field's Code of Civil Procedure by 1900. At the forefront of the American states' adoption of Field's Code of Civil Procedure were the western states, with Missouri approving an analogous code in 1849 and California approving a similar code in 1850. While the codes adopted by different states differed in some details from Field's Code of Civil Procedure of 1848, all codes embraced the essential principles of the civil pleading, permitting only "one form of civil action" and streamlining the procedures of pleading amendment.

A central reason for the success of Field's Code of Civil Procedure was the support of the legal profession and the commercial elite for procedural reform. The procedural law in New York before Field's reforms was indeed antiquated and confusing, and while there was some opposition to the reform of procedural law, the benefits of codifying the legal procedure outweighed the reservations of the codification's opponents.

Field's great failure — codification of substantive civil law. Field's success in having his Code of Civil Procedure adopted in New York and elsewhere contrasted with his failure to codify substantive law. In 1857 the New York legislature appointed Field to head a commission charged with drafting codes of substantive law. The commission was instructed "to reduce the substantive law of the state to a systematic code consisting of three parts, a 'political,' a 'civil,' and a 'penal code.'" Field's Code Commission submitted nine reports to the New York Legislature, with the final report and draft of the Civil Code submitted on February 13, 1865. To Field's dismay, the Civil Code then "spent the next fourteen years under the legislative rug." In 1879 both houses of New York's legislature passed bills adopting the Civil Code, only to be vetoed by the Governor. In 1882, Field's Civil Code was again approved by New York's legislature and again vetoed by the Governor. The 1882 effort proved to be "the last time the [Civil] Code got as far as the Governor's desk," although the codification debate continued undiminished for a number of years.

The main reason for the failure of Field's Civil Code was the strong opposition within the legal profession, especially by the New York Bar, to the reform of substantive law through general codification. The New York lawyers, while not fully satisfied with the substantive law, were not ready to embrace full-scale codification. The opposition to general codification came from three main lawyer groups: those who considered codification an "economic threat" to their livelihood; those "learned and honest visionaries" that "opposed codification on theoretical grounds"; and those lawyers who "generally favored codification but opposed the Field Codes because they thought that the codes were poorly prepared."

The leader of the anti-codification forces was prominent New York lawyer James C. Carter. Carter argued that "codification was fundamentally at odds with the true nature of law, in particular with the common law and its tradition of flexibility and growth." Carter also opposed the idea of legislative interference in law-making, asserting that "a legislative body consisting principally of laymen, possesses no single qualification which enables it to prosecute the cultivation and improvement of this science, and its adaptation to human affairs." Field viewed the legislature somewhat differently, considering it a proper vehicle for improvement of laws, but was careful to address the accusations that there was "something dangerous or revolutionary in the [proposed Civil] Code." Field envisioned that the entire codification would be "the work of experts—jurists like Field himself," while the legislature "would simply take the codes and give them its stamp of validity."

In the end, New York lawyers and legislators sided with Carter, and by 1887 Field's substantive codes were defeated. They had been proposed as legislation various times between 1879 and 1887 in New York but could never muster enough political clout to survive the legislative obstacles or the Governor's opposition.

Field's Civil Code was given a somewhat warmer reception outside New York. Even before the final failure in New York, a few western states and territories—including the Dakotas, Idaho, Montana, and California—had enacted codes modeled on Field's Civil Code. The acceptance of Field's Civil Code in those states did not translate, however, into the replacement of the common law with the codified law, as seen in the fate of California's Civil Code. That Civil Code, which "consolidated all of the state's statutory and common-law rules governing private relations ... into one meticulously arranged volume," generally met little opposition at its inception in 1872. In 1884, though, John Norton Pomeroy, a dean of the law school at Berkeley, launched an attack on the California's Civil Code in a series of articles entitled *The True Method of Interpreting the Civil Code*. Pomeroy criticized the alleged defects of the code, including "its disregard for established terminology, its incompleteness, its strangeness of organization, and above all its inaccuracy." Pomeroy's criticism of the Civil Code was based on a belief that "only judge-made law was expansive and flexible enough to meet the needs of a rapidly evolving society." Thus he argued that California courts should consider the Civil Code as declarative of common law and, accordingly, interpret its provisions "using common-law precedents and customs." The California courts, starting with the state's 1888 Supreme Court decision in *Sharon v. Sharon*, adopted Pomeroy's approach to code interpretation. Thereafter, the Civil Code largely lost its significance in California's jurisprudence, and the codification effects were negated. The fate of the Civil Codes in other states, with the exception of Louisiana, was similar to that of California's: "The [civil] code did not become the dominant source of law in any state."[16]

---

16. Gunther A. Weiss, *The Enchantment of Codification in the Common-Law World*, 25 YALE J. INT'L L. 435, 516 (2000). It is worth noting in passing that Georgia had a codification movement distinct from the one led by Field and in 1861 adopted a comprehensive code that included a political

In the final analysis, then, despite Field's failure to become "the American Justinian" as a result of his unsuccessful attempt to codify the American common law, his fight for codification did have a lasting impact on the development of American law. All of his codes focused the attention of the legal profession and legislators on "some of the drawbacks of common law." His Code of Civil Procedure substantially changed the procedural formalities of common law. Even the defeat of most of his codes on the state level constituted, perhaps ironically, an important contribution to American legal development by giving impetus to a new enthusiasm for national codification, as sponsored and encouraged by the American Bar Association. This process was to result in the Restatement movement of the 1920s, which brought back with renewed force many of Field's arguments.[17]

Conditions and factors of codification. How does the Field codification exercise square with the conditions and factors of codification that I have identified in this article? The answer turns in some respects on which aspect of the Field codification exercise we examine —the fairly successful efforts in the area of civil procedure or the largely unsuccessful efforts in substantive areas, especially a substantive civil law codification. In some other respects, of course, the assessments I offered above in part IVB, discussing the national codification movement of 1815–1840, also apply to the later efforts by Field, focused in New York.

- As noted above, the "regard-for-written law" condition was obviously present in nineteenth-century America—although tempered by a high regard for the special character of common law as relying on the accretion of caselaw. Perhaps the distrust that many American lawyers and commercial elites had in legislatures helps explain the experience of codification in California, which continued to endorse case-by-case development of legal principles even though a civil code was enacted.

- The "power concentration" condition was largely absent. Even though the Field efforts took place mainly at the state level (unlike some efforts in the earlier phase of the codification movement), the political power to adopt a code was divided between the legislature and the Governor; complicating the matter further, by exercising its own political clout, was the New York Bar. Although enough support was garnered among these various power-holders to enact the Code of Civil Procedure, the same was not true of the substantive Civil Code: the legislature was won over twice, but the Governor vetoed the adoption of that code.

- The "champion-of-codification" condition was absent under my formulation of that condition. Field himself was a ceaseless champion of codification, of course, and he was not without some political influence. However, he was not even an officeholder, much less a political leader with the sort of power that we see in most earlier codification experiences described in this article. Expressed differently, his enthusiasm far outstripped his authority. Nor was the American legislature in the nineteenth century eager or adequately prepared institutionally for the reform of

---

code, a civil code, a code of practice, and a penal code. *See generally* Marion Smith, *The First Codification of the Substantive Common Law,* 4 Tul. L. Rev. 178 (1930). The civil code of Georgia consisted of 1,576 sections, each of which was characterized as a brief, concise statement of a basic principle. *Id.* at 185. That code was in operation until 1933, although its legal success has been disputed.

17. *See generally* Natham M. Crystal, *Codification and the Rise of the Restatement Movement,* 54 Wash. L. Rev. 239 (1979) (discussing connections and similarities between the Restatement movement and the codification movements of the late nineteenth century). *See also* Friedman *supra* note 1, at 406 (calling the Field codes "the spiritual parents of the Restatements of the Law"). The first Restatements were widely perceived at the time as a foundation for the codification of American law. *See* Samuel Williston, *Written and Unwritten Law,* 17 A.B.A. J. 39, 41 (1931) (asserting that the Restatements "will serve as a better foundation for a Code").

substantive law: "It had neither the interest nor the ability to undertake the rigorous and technical task of codifying the law."

- The "legal chaos" and "behind-the-times" factors were both present in respect of the effort to codify civil procedure. Field repeatedly emphasized the chaotic and anachronistic features of procedure, and the common perception of civil procedure as archaic, confusing, and inflexible clearly helped assure the passage of Field's Code of Civil Procedure. However, these two factors were probably absent at the time with respect to substantive aspects of the civil law, at least in the minds of a great many New York lawyers, whose conservatism and faith in the common law James Carter appealed to in order to stymie Field's efforts at substantive codification. In addition, as noted earlier, the continuing development of American legal literature had taken much of the punch out of the claim that substantive American law was chaotic or antiquated.

- The "radical political change" factor was not present during the Field's codification movement. While the Civil War represented a "profound constitutional crisis," it did not, of itself, prompt any reactive urge toward codification, such as that prompted by the French Revolution or the overthrow of a Chinese dynasty.

- The "model code" factor played an influential role in Field's own work—he continuously invoked and drew from the principles and provisions of earlier civil law codes—but the wider popularity and influence of the French and other codes were scant. As noted above, for example, enthusiasm for the *Code Civil* had waned by around the 1830s.

- The "scholar/jurist influence" factor was probably absent, as it was a few decades earlier during the first flirtation with codification of American law. Even if American legal scholars were growing in influence with a broad array of publications, the debate over Field's codes in New York was dominated by practitioners and men of commerce. Furthermore, a good number of those legal scholars who did enter the debate either argued against codification, and many advocates of codification generally regarded Field's Civil Code as fundamentally flawed.

VI. Concluding Observations

I have had two goals here. First, I have tried to show that the scope of "comparative codification" can and should be broadened to encompass Chinese experiences with legal codes. Second, against that broader backdrop, I have tried to identify some key conditions and factors that seem important to the success of a codification effort. Although I have not attempted to be comprehensive[18] or to provide factual information not already familiar to specialists in the legal histories of China, Europe, or North America, I do believe the broadening of scope and the identification of conditions and factors can serve several useful purposes.

For one thing, the juxtaposition of these various codification experiences, particularly those of China, can enrich our understanding of the distinct legal cultures from which

---

18. My selection of codification experiences in China, Europe, and North America is intended to be illustrative, not exhaustive. I have not, for example, examined how the conditions and factors of codification that I have identified here might play out in the case of the Theodosian Code of the late fifth century CE, the German Civil Code of the late nineteenth century, other European codes, modern Chinese and Japanese legal codes, or some other well-known codification experiences.

they arose. For example, inclusion of Chinese codification into the overall "comparative codification" exercise helps us recognize one key condition to codification that has not so far received much attention in the literature—what I call the "regard for written law" condition. My discussion of the great debate, and subsequent compromise, between the Legalist and Confucianist views of law in the Qin-Han period aims to focus attention on this "regard for written law" condition. Once we do so, we see some parallels in both European and North American experience. Ever since the time of the Twelve Tables, European culture has broadly accepted the proposition that law should be written and published and accessible as a protection against the unfettered discretion of a small governing elite. The same proposition appears in seventeenth century Massachusetts with the *Laws and Liberties* of 1648.

Including Chinese law also draws attention to another of the factors that commonly appear in successful codification efforts—the existence of a culturally appropriate "model code." It appears that codification was relatively easy in China in every dynasty after the Qin because of an increasing body of precedents—especially the Qin Code, the Han Code, and the Tang Code. In contrast, codification was difficult in eighteenth-century America in part for lack of such a precedent; English common law had not been codified, and the European civil law codes were too foreign to serve as a guide acceptable to most Americans interested in legal reform at the time.

Another observation that emerges from this three-cornered comparison relates to the second and third conditions to which I have drawn attention: codification efforts need strong, concentrated political power and will. The Chinese codification experiences highlight this. The tremendous power wielded by the Chinese emperors and by Justinian and Napoleon stand in contrast to the situation in nineteenth century America—and perhaps this difference helps explain the differences in outcomes. Indeed, we might even speculate that legal codification was seen as a means by which the extremely powerful Chinese and European codifiers I have mentioned acted both to exhibit that power and to secure it.

Some new insight might also come from the distinction I have proposed between conditions and factors. Those circumstances that I regard as conditions—a high regard for written law, power concentration, and a champion of codification—are necessary to a successful codification effort. The five other circumstances—the "legal chaos," "behind the times," "radical political change," "model code," and "scholar/jurist influence" factors—are not each individually necessary but can, in aggregate, augur in favor of a successful codification effort. Again applying this rubric, we might speculate that a legal system that exhibits all or nearly all of those five factors would still remain uncodified if the system lacks a central concentration of political authority (either in an individual or in a small nucleus of persons) and a strong will to codify. The international legal system comes to mind.

In order to sum up my views on the conditions and factors of codification as applied to the nine specific instances described above, I close with the following tabular presentation. It gives a rough indication (using "X" and "O" notations) of the presence or absence of each of the conditions and factors in each of those nine codification efforts. Some explanations appear in notes following the table. Even with these explanations, the table represents an exercise in oversimplification. For example, it glosses over the differing degrees to which the various conditions or factors were present in each of those nine codification experiences.[19] Despite these shortcomings, I believe the table reflects the main

19. In discussing the *Laws and Liberties* of 1648, I introduced "a subsidiary thesis—that the conditions of codification can have more or less weight, and that their weight (the degree to which they

thesis I introduced at the beginning of this article—that codification, broadly defined, depends for its success on a convergence of several specific conditions and factors. In my view, these conditions and factors of codification provide a useful framework in which to examine, and better understand, widely divergent legal systems.

* * *

Presence or Absence of Key Conditions and Factors of Codification in Selected Codification Efforts

	Qin Code[a]	Han Code[b]	Tang Code[c]	Ming Code[d]	Justinian's Codification[e]	Code Civil[f]	Laws and Liberties[g]	USA 1815–1840[h]	New York (Field)[i]
CONDITIONS									
Regard for written law	X	X	X	X	X	X	X	X	X
Power concentration	X	X	X	X	X	X	X ?	O	X ? / O ?
Champion of codification	X	X	X	X	X	X	X ?	O	X ? / O
FACTORS									
Legal chaos	X	O	O	X	X	X	X	X	X / O
Radical political change	X	X	X	X	X	X	X	X	O
Behind the times	O ?	O	O	X ?	O ?	X	X	X	X / O
Model code	X ?	X	X	X	X / O	X	O ?	O	O
Scholar/jurist influence	X	X	X	X	X	X	O	O	O

NOTES TO TABLE

a *See supra* part IIA. As explained there, the "behind-the-times" factor was probably absent, given the continuity that existed between the state of Qin and the Qin empire. It is difficult to assess the presence of the "model code" factor because of the paucity of written evidence; but at least Shang Yang's code would presumably have served as a model for the Qin code.

b *See supra* part IIB. As explained there, the radical political change represented by the replacement of the Qin dynasty with the Han probably was not accompanied by any legal chaos or by a view that the laws were behind the times as a social or cultural matter.

c *See supra* part IIC. As explained there, the Tang Code showed considerable continuity from the Sui Code, suggesting that the Tang draftsmen were not facing a tangled web of inconsistent laws from multiple. Moreover, they were not trying to take account of any dramatic social, cultural, or economic change. Instead, the dramatic change from the Sui to the Tang was primarily a political one.

d *See supra* part IID. As explained there, the law was seen as somewhat behind the times because some Chinese intellectuals had shunned government service under the Yuan dynasty of the Mongols; on the other hand, the latter years of the Yuan dynasty had seen a progressive sinicization of the Mongol influence.

e *See supra* part IIIA. As explained there, while Justinian's urge for codification reflected his concern over the chaotic character of sources of Roman law and his desire to regain a centralized political

---

are present, beyond the minimum) can affect the scope and exclusivity of the code that they help create." *See supra* part IVA.

and legal control over the empire, there was no remarkable mismatch between the content of law and contemporary social developments or demands. Hence, the "behind-the-times" factor was probably absent. My inclusion of a "X/O" notation for the "model code" factor reflects the fact that Justinian's *Institutes* was based on a model (Gaius' *Institutes*), but the Digest had no such model.

f   *See supra* part IIIB.

g   *See supra* part IVA. The "X ?" notations for the "power concentration" condition and the "codification champion" condition reflect my view, expressed there, that these two conditions were barely present in seventeenth-century Massachusetts. The "O ?" notation for the "model code" factor reflects the fact that the only common-law precedents on which the drafters of the *Laws and Liberties* might have relied are various earlier English abridgments that seem to have been available in Massachusetts at the time.

h   *See supra* part IVB. As explained there, two of the three conditions for codification were absent in the efforts to create a national code in early nineteenth-century America.

i   *See supra* part IVC. This column reflects both the relatively successful effort to codify civil procedure in New York and the failed effort to codify substantive civil law there. All three conditions were probably present for the first of these efforts (procedural codification), although the merger of concentrated political power with strong political will did not survive long. As for the substantive codification, the "champion of codification" condition was absent despite the leadership showed by Field, as his enthusiasm for codification far outstripped his actual political power to effect it, especially in view of the division of power between the legislature (which Field persuaded) and the Governor (whom he did not). As also explained above in part IVC, the "legal chaos" and "behind-the-times" factors were present in the case of civil procedure—it was very broadly regarded as chaotic and archaic—but not in the case of substantive civil law, which many opponents of codification thought should grow gradually through the common-law process of accretion of case law. For reasons also explained in part IVC, the other three factors were also largely absent.

Appendix 4.19
History of the Common Law Tradition in Song
Common Law, My Friend
(to the tune of *Blowin' in the Wind*)

How many years has the common law been
The envy of all the human race?
It started in 1066, so they say
When William threw Harold on his face.

In 1215 at the fields of Runnymede,
The barons put King John in his place.
but in 1285, Westminster II came alive
And the common law grew at a faster pace.

Common law was narrow, based on writs, that's the thing.
It was brittle by the 15th century,
So the Chancellor, acting on behalf of the king,
Developed the Courts of Equity.

They grew in strength and almost gave the Brits the civil law,
Which would been delicious irony,
But 1616 saw a compromise with common law
The two systems would have rough equality.

That's how things stayed until 1-8-7-5,
Except, of course, in North America.
In the primitive conditions of the colonies, it seems,
It was hard to know and use the common law.

We flirted with the notion of a civil law regime,
Especially in the 19th century
But in the end we saw that we should stick with common law,
And the rest, as they say, is history.

Chapter Five

The Common Law Tradition in Operational Perspective

Outline

Study Questions

SQ #5.1 What are the main sources of law in the English legal system today, and how (if at all) do they differ from the main sources of law in England before 1800?

SQ #5.2 Can we generalize as to what the main sources of law are today in common law systems *other* than England, such as the USA or Canada or Australia?

SQ #5.3 What is the relationship in English law today between caselaw and legislation ("statutes")? How (if at all) does this differ from the relationship in English law between caselaw and statutes in 1800? ... in 1900?

SQ #5.4 Is the "ideology of codification" different in the common law tradition from that in the civil law tradition?

SQ #5.5   How (if at all) does the concept of a legal rule differ in the common law tra-
            dition from that in the civil law tradition, and what practical implications
            might this have?

SQ #5.6   Of what significance is the law/equity distinction today in English law? How
            (if at all) does this differ from the significance of that distinction in English
            law in 1800? ... in American law today?

SQ #5.7   In what sense can custom be a source of law in the English legal system?

SQ #5.8   Of what significance is legal writing as a source of law in the common law
            tradition?

SQ #5.9   Does the common law tradition rely less on "reason" than the civil law tradi-
            tion does?

SQ #5.10   Are the procedures used in criminal cases in the USA mainly derived from
            (mainly required by) the common law tradition? ... or by American tradi-
            tions and values?

SQ #5.11   Is the American system of criminal procedure adequately protective of the in-
            dividual? ... of the society?

SQ #5.12   Should civil litigation and criminal prosecutions be carried out with funda-
            mentally similar procedures?

SQ #5.13   How important, efficient, and fair is it to use jury trials in civil litigation?

SQ #5.14   What are the advantages and disadvantages of having a single, unified, pyra-
            midal system of courts (as opposed to two or three separate systems of courts,
            as in most civil law countries)?

SQ #5.15   What role has religion played in the development of the common law tradi-
            tion? What role has ideology played?

SQ #5.16   What would you identify as the "soul" of the English legal system? ... the
            American legal system?

Introductory Comments

From the historical account of the common law tradition offered above in Chapter
Four, we turn now to an operational account—highlighting certain aspects of how common law systems in several nations around the world actually operate. Three preliminary
matters need to be highlighted before we begin that exercise.

As a first preliminary matter, we need to decide which common law systems to use. They
differ from each other, sometimes quite widely. Today's United Kingdom is, as a territorial matter, the birthplace of the common law; but its legal system has changed substantially since the time that the common law was "exported" (or "migrated") from England
to various other territories of the world. Therefore India, the USA, and some other countries (for various reasons) display their own important additions and modifications. The
USA in particular has a legal system marked by "exceptionalism" in several ways. Yet even
Canada, Australia, and New Zealand also differ importantly from England in their legal
systems, despite the fact that those countries gained independence more recently from

England than did the USA, and despite the fact that those lands (unlike India) had little in the way of existing indigenous law that could effectively impede the "transplantation" of a foreign legal tradition on their soil.[1]

In short, it is not as easy to find the high degree of commonality among common law systems—and therefore to identify a "typical" common law country or to draw generalizations—as is the case with European civil law. After all, several countries in the very region where the civil law tradition was born (that is, continental Europe) still retain the clear stamp of that tradition. The UK is not part of the same sort of "neighborhood" of countries sharing the common law tradition with it.

I have settled on a mix of English and US law. That is, for purposes of illuminating the common law in operational perspective, the following pages will bounce back and forth between those two systems—with more emphasis on US law, which I will sometimes refer to as "American law"—in the hope that doing so will provide a broad enough array of examples to serve as a basis for comparing the common law tradition in operational perspective with the civil law tradition in operational perspective. That, after all, is the overall goal here—not to provide detailed or comprehensive descriptions of one or another aspect of national law but rather to provide a representative basis for general comparison, adequate to serve the various purposes identified in Chapter One when we surveyed the reasons for engaging in a comparative study of law.[2]

As a second preliminary matter, it is worth noting that this chapter is a great deal shorter than most others in the book, with considerably fewer footnote citations. The reason for this is that many points about English and US law that are important to us in this context—sources of law, the role of judges, the contours of criminal procedure, etc.—have already been discussed more or less directly and comprehensively in the course of Chapter 3. That chapter, surveying the civil law tradition in operational perspective, offered numerous observations that compared the civil law with the common law.

Hence, our effort in this chapter will focus mainly on (i) offering some brief reminders of key points already identified earlier as being characteristic of the common law in actual operation, (ii) expanding as necessary on a few of those points, and (iii) filling some gaps on topics that have few or no counterparts in the civil law world, such as the current applicability and significance of the distinction between law and equity.

In order to carry out the first of these tasks—offering brief reminders—I have used a special technique in this chapter that does not appear in the other chapters in this book. Following each main subheading, I have provided a short, indented "Highlights" paragraph intended to capture the essence of the subject. Indeed, in some cases such a short "Highlights" paragraph stands alone because the subject has been adequately discussed earlier.

As a final preliminary matter, I would draw special attention to Study Question #5.16, asking about the "soul" of English and American law. As we shall see, Chapter Seven includes an inquiry into the "soul" of contemporary Chinese law. Considering that topic here in the context of common law can serve as both preview and practice for that later exercise.

---

1. As we saw above in section V of Chapter Four, these notions of "exportation", "migration", and "transplantation" all serve as metaphors for the adoption of English law outside the British Isles.

2. As noted in subsection IIB of Chapter One, the "possible aims" of such a study include such things as legal self-awareness, law reform, sociological understanding, and cross-border legal practice.

I. Sources of Law

A. *Sources of Law in General*

Highlights. Although caselaw served as the main source of English common law for many centuries, the rise of legislation as a "new" source of law (especially beginning in the 1800s) has resulted in a rough equality today between caselaw and legislation in England (and in other common law systems) as primary sources of law. Other main sources include regulations (increasingly important), custom, and constitutional law.

In Chapter Four we surveyed the history of English law. From that survey, it should be evident that caselaw — "judge-made law" — sits at the center of English common law, and that legislation (statutes) played a subsidiary role until relatively recently. Now these two sources (caselaw and legislation) have roughly equal weight in most common law systems. The following summary by René David explains the relationship between them and mentions three other "secondary sources" of English law.

English law, the Common law fashioned by the Courts of Westminster and Equity by the Court of Chancery, is not a judge-made law only by reason of its historic origins. Since the influence of the universities and of legal writing has been less in England than on the continent and since no complete re-shaping of the law has ever taken place through the technique of codification, English law has retained its original characteristics as much with respect to its sources ... as in its structure. It is, typically, a judge-made law, a *case law....*

Legislation — *statute law* to employ the English usage — has traditionally occupied only a secondary position in English law and was limited to correcting or complementing the work accomplished by judicial decisions. In truth, however, the position today is reversed to a large extent. In England, statutes and delegated or subordinate legislation can no longer be considered as secondary; their importance is in fact equal to that enjoyed by these same sources on the European continent. However, for historical reasons, the role of legislation in England is still somewhat different; and, because of English law's structure, the work of the English legislators is not fully the equivalent of continental codes and legislation.

Compared to the decisions of the courts and statutes, the other sources of English law — custom, legal writing and reason — do rank as secondary sources. Their importance however is far from negligible and it is, accordingly, important to take them into account as well.[3]

The preceding observations by David appear at the beginning of the chapter on "sources of English Law" in his book *Major Legal Systems in the World Today* — or, in its original French title, *Grands Systèmes de Droit Contemporains*. (David's co-author, J.E.C. Brierly, is largely responsible for the English translation.) Our survey of English legal history, in

---

3. René David & John E.C. Brierly, Major Legal Systems in the World Today 366 (2d ed., 1985).

Chapter Four, drew heavily from that treatise. In the course of his explanation of "sources of English law", David explores each of the five elements referred to in the three introductory paragraphs quoted above — namely, caselaw, legislation, custom, legal writing, and reason. At the conclusion of his chapter on "sources", David offers a "summing-up" on each of them. Let us examine what David says — as a civil law lawyer writing about the premier common law system — but starting not with either caselaw or legislation but rather with custom.

... Custom

In the first place the idea — extremely current — that English law is a customary law should be abandoned immediately. This misconception, entertained by many continental European jurists, is derived from the idea that one of two alternatives must be true: *either* the law is "written" and is therefore based on codes, *or* it is "unwritten" and is therefore customary. English law has never been a customary law: it is a judge-made law. The impact of the Common law was to bring about the disappearance of whatever local custom there was. The concept of an obligatory line of court decisions (*jurisprudence constante, ständige Rechtsprechung*), in itself related to that of custom, is unknown in the present operation of the rule of precedent; in England a single decision rendered by a court of a certain degree is enough to constitute a binding precedent.[4]

David's rejection of the notion that English law is customary law does not, of course, tell the entire story. In some limited respects, custom still serves as a source of law in England. This is one way in which England probably stands entirely alone in the common law world. Although many common law countries today might allow for some circumstances in which customary rules — distinct, that is, from caselaw and statutes — can serve as sources, the specific substantive rules "carried" in those customs are almost surely country-specific. We shall examine quickly the particular role that custom plays in English law later, in subsection ID of this chapter. For now, the principal point is the one David emphasizes — that English common law, built on caselaw, gradually but effectively displaced custom beginning with the Norman period.

David then turns his attention to legislation, explaining how the developments of the past two hundred years have dramatically increased the significance of legislation as a source of law in England:

... Legislation

... [T]he idea that legislation in English law is a source of only secondary importance should also be laid to rest. This point of view is no longer acceptable today.... [I]t is true that England has no codes of the Napoleonic type, but "written law" is, in practice, and in almost all respect, as important and as developed as it is in continental Europe. Today statutes contain much more than merely corrections to the Common law; there are vast areas of social activity for which the very principles of the legal order are to be looked for in legislation. However it is still true that a similar legislative tradition does not

---

4. *Id.* at 391–392. David's last point — that a single decision can constitute a binding precedent — has only been true relatively recently. See Geoffrey Sawer, *The Western Conception of Law*, appearing as section II in Chapter 1 (Different Conceptions of the Law) of II INTERNATIONAL ENCYCLOPEDIA OF COMPARATIVE LAW (Legal Systems of the World — Their Comparison and Unification, 1975), at 24 (noting that in England, "the very high degree of authority attributed to decided cases, in particular to a *single* precedent, was not reached until the nineteenth century").

prevail in England and on the continent; the formulation of legislative legal rules of general scope or application is generally badly done in England. And it is also true that English lawyers still have some difficulty in adapting to the techniques of legal rules expressed legislatively. English statutes have a casuistic character or case-by-case approach not found in continental legislation ... In English legislation an attempt is made to situate legal rules as much as possible at the level of the judge-made rule, still considered its only normal form of expression. The principles expressed in the statute are not, moreover, fully recognised by English jurists, and therefore truly integrated in the Common law, until they have been applied, reformulated and developed by decision of the courts.[5]

The observation made in the last paragraph of the passage quoted above—that statutory provisions are not "fully recognised by English jurists" until they have been applied by the courts—is worth considering carefully. It is important to bear in mind that David's book dates from the 1960s, although it was updated later. However, even if that observation was true a few decades ago, it might be subject to some skepticism today, at least by English lawyers in general (note that David refers to the views of "English jurists", by which he presumably means judges). In any event, David's observation might not apply to other common law systems. In the USA, a lawyer (whether a judge or a corporate counsel or a litigator in a large law firm) giving his attention to a statutory provision would probably regard the provision as being "integrated into" the laws of his or her jurisdiction immediately upon its enactment—although its precise *meaning* as applied in specific circumstances might be unclear until tested through actual litigation and judgment.

David's underlying point, however, almost surely does apply in most common law countries: legislation constitutes a centrally important source of law, and yet the way in which a typical common law lawyer regards legislation does differ from how a typical civil law lawyer views legislation—and the reason for this can be found largely in the importance of caselaw in the common law tradition. It is to that topic that David then turns. He emphasizes the flexibility of caselaw:

... *Rule of precedent*

... [T]he idea that the rule of precedent is applied with a kind of automatism, thereby paralysing the evolution of English law, must also be dismissed. History has show the falsity that such was ever the meaning of the rule....

The only purpose of the rule of precedent is to provide a framework [for] English law and this through the conservation of its traditional "judge-made" structure.... [It was applied with an apparently great strictness in the nineteenth century ... [because] conditions of the time required this rigour ... [On the other hand,] [p]resent social evolution requires a greater flexibility because of the accelerated rhythm with which these social changes are taking place.... [This flexibility has come through] the use of the technique of "distinguishing" the judicial decisions. And the evolution has been rapid enough in the traditional areas of Common law that the legislators have only rarely been required to intervene.[6]

Having identified "the technique of 'distinguishing'... judicial decisions" as a means by which law can adapt to societal changes, David then elaborates on that technique:

---

5. David & Brierly, *supra* note 3, at 392.
6. *Id.* at 392–393.

... *Technique of distinctions*

The technique of "distinguishing" judicial decisions is fundamental in English law. The legal education of an English jurist is largely devoted to mastering this technique and learning its possibilities and limitations.... A reversal in the case law (*revirement de jurisprudence*) is, in principle, excluded in England because the affirmation of a rule of precedent is necessary to judge-made legal system. Analogous results are however achieved in fact through the technique of distinctions, without damage to the legal edifice, and new developments in the law brought about....

... This technique of distinctions is therefore very closely linked to the analysis of the *legal rule* found in English law. Through suggested distinctions, the English jurist endeavors to limit increasingly the extent and the wording of a rule which inevitably seems to have originally been expressed in too general terms. It is thus not a matter of chance that the English concept of the *legal rule* is much narrower than the continental *régle de droit*. Not only is it natural, it is also necessary in a judge-made law. And the English theory of the sources of the law is a logical result of this point of view.[7]

Recall that René David's summary of "sources of English law" identified five items: caselaw, legislation, custom, legal writing, and reason. Having elaborated briefly on the first three of these, he then discusses the last two. Before seeing what he says about them, we should pause to consider the role that each of those first three have in both an "orthodox" legal system and a more modern legal system—as that distinction was introduced near the beginning of Chapter Three. Recall that caselaw would not have been acknowledged as having any role as a source of law in the "orthodox" view, but that it will often be recognized (that is, in most contemporary civil law systems) as today having a secondary role or status as an "indirect source". Legislation, the relative late-comer to the common law list of sources, has been the dominant source of law in the civil law world for many centuries, with even stronger credentials there since the time of what John Henry Merryman has called "the revolution"—that broad movement intended to make law more rational and secularist. That same movement, of course, pressed for a greatly reduced role for custom as a source of law. English legal developments also brought about a reduced role for custom, but for completely different reasons.

David then turns to legal writing and "reason" as sources of English law. In both respects he addresses (and criticizes) the notion that English law is less logical and more practical than continental European law:

... *Legal Writing*

... It is generally true that in England the law owes less to professors than it does on the continent and more to judges. Here again however care must be observed. England is a country where certain legal works—written mostly, it is true, by judges—were treated as *books of authority*: the works of Glanvill, Bracton, Littleton and Coke had such prestige that they were considered, in the courts, to be the most authoritative expositions of the law of their time and were endowed with a status that Europeans would only accord to legislation itself.

Since the nineteenth century, the role of legal writing has changed and developed. Today law students are more and more educated in universities. They study

---

7. *Id.* at 393–394.

law more in the courses, writings of their teachers, treatises and text-books, than in the colleges or digest of judicial decisions complied for legal practitioners: the teaching of law concentrates today on substantive law, and procedure and practice is now only exceptionally taught in English law faculties....

... Reason

English Law is very clearly a product of English history when one considers particularly its categories and concepts and the prominent role played by the courts. "The life of the law" wrote Holmes "has not been logic: the life of the law has been experience". We must however be careful not to exaggerate the difference which is sometimes said to exist between French and English law on this point. Romanist laws are in no sense less a product of history than English law. Their history however has been different: it gave a greater place to university teaching, *la doctrine* and legislation, and the result has been that Romanist law appears structurally more systematic and, perhaps, more apparently rational than English law. But is English law really less logical and more practical than the Romanist laws? This is at least doubtful. Between the practical sense dear to the English and the logic dear to the French, there is a middle path, a factor that reconciles them because it is at the heart of each law, and this is reason (*la raison*).

... While constructing the Common law system it was always necessary to seek the solution most in agreement with reason, and a deciding factor in the discovery of this solution was the desire to achieve a consistency in legal decision-making. This necessarily supposed a recourse to logic.

... There are of course in practice very real differences in the laws of different Common law countries.... It is useful however, ... to emphasise that, because it is founded on reason, the Common law has a non-national dimension. It is ... the element creating a unity among the laws of the western world because reason sets them above the arbitrariness of national politics and thus distinguishes them from [other, non-Western, concepts].[8]

The closing comments by David in the passage quoted above raises some intriguing questions regarding the "universality" or "unity" of the common law as compared with the civil law tradition. For example, how valid is the proposition that the common law has more of a "non-national dimension" than civil law does? Recall that in subsection VA of Chapter Four we read Arthur Goodhart's explanation of why it has always been the civil law, never the common law, that countries have chosen when they had a choice of a new legal system. One reason he identified for this is that civil law—or at least the private law within the civil law tradition—is more flexible and forgiving, amenable for use by any particular form of government, whereas common law does (according to Goodhart) require some restrictions on government. If that is true, to what extent might that fact augur in favor of a greater "non-national dimension" for the common law?

B. The Interplay of Statutes and Caselaw

Highlights. A more detailed examination confirms that whereas legislation was originally viewed (in English legal history) mainly as "corrective" in character,

---

8. Id. at 394–396.

to re-direct some misdirected caselaw, the strong reform movements of the 1800s (involving some efforts even at codification) greatly elevated the significance of legislation as a source of law, so that today legislation and case-law act as largely co-equal sources of law in common law systems.

The relationship in English law, and in common law systems more generally, between legislation and caselaw warrants further attention, partly because that relationship is so widely cited as a point of sharp distinction between civil law and common law countries. One source offers the following observations regarding both the historical foundations and the contemporary practice of these two sources of law in common law systems. The first few paragraphs quoted here appeared in more complete form in our Chapter Four examination of the historical development of English common law through case decisions.

> The system of [caselaw in England, as it developed over the centuries,] was held together by the doctrine of *stare decisis*, or standing by previous decisions.... In later times this practice crystallised into the form which is known as the binding force of judicial precedent, and the judges felt bound to follow previous decisions instead of merely looking to them for guidance. By these means the common law earned the status of a system....

> In early times there were few statutes and the bulk of law was case law, though legislation in one form or another dates from 600 A.D. [with the Laws of King Æthelbert, appearing above in Appendix 4.1].... The ... first great outburst of legislation came in the reign of Henry II (1154–1189).... Legislation at this time was generally made by the King in Council, but sometimes by a kind of Parliament which consisted in the main of a meeting of nobles and clergy summoned from the shires.

> In the fourteenth century parliamentary legislation became more general. Parliament at first requested or prayed the King to legislate, but later it presented a bill in its own wording. The Tudor period saw the development of modern procedure [in legislative activity]....

> From the Tudor period onwards Parliament became more and more independent and the practice of law making by statute increased. Nevertheless statutes did not become an important source of law until the last two centuries....

> Parliament's increasing incursions into economic and social affairs increased the need for statutes. Some aspects of law are so complicated or so novel that they can only be laid down in this form; they would not be likely to come into existence through the submission of cases in court....

> *Delegated Legislation*

> Many modern statutes require much detailed work to implement and operate them, and such details are not normally contained in the statute itself, but are filled in from some other source. For example, the National Insurance Act, 1946, only gives the general provisions of a complex scheme of national insurance, and an immense number of detailed regulations have to be made by civil servants in the name of, and under the authority of the Minister of Pensions and National Insurance. These regulations, when made in the approved manner, are just as much law as the parent statute itself. This form of law is known as delegated legislation.[9]

---

9. Kenneth Smith and Denis J. Keenan, ENGLISH LAW 2–3, 6–7 (2d ed., 1966).

Some aspects of that description are England-specific and do not apply in other common law countries. For example, the account offered above of the role of precedent in English common law does *not* accurately reflect the reality in US law. In US law, there is no formal rule of *stare decisis*—that is, that courts can never depart from their earlier decisions. However, as a practical matter, the importance of consistency plays an enormous role in the behavior of US courts, so that *stare decisis* is a powerful influence. Merryman makes this point:

> Judges [in the USA] may refer to a precedent because they are impressed by the authority of the prior court, because they are persuaded by its reasoning, because they are too lazy to think the problem through themselves, because they do not want to risk reversal on appeal, or for a variety of other reasons. These are the principal reasons for the use of authority in the common law tradition, and the absence of any formal rule of *stare decisis* is relatively unimportant.[10]

C. *Law and Equity*

Highlights. The distinction between law and equity, and some of the specific rules and procedures of the courts of Chancery as they emerged from the Compromise of 1616, still exist in England, and to varying extents in other common law countries—including the USA. An illustrative substantive equitable concept is that of the trust; and numerous procedural rules reflect the corrective and *in personam* aspects of equity.

As we saw in Chapter Four, the common law courts—that is to say, the royal courts at Westminster—were challenged in the 16th century by the competing courts of Chancery, or courts of equity. Although a compromise was reached between the two competing court systems, and a "merger" of the two court systems occurred in the late 1800s, the distinction between law and equity retains deep significance in the common law tradition. Accordingly, the account offered above relating generically to "caselaw" is incomplete; it must be supplemented by a reference to the development of equity—including in particular its remaining relevance today.

The story differs from one common law country to another—with England perhaps being the one in which the law-versus-equity distinction holds the most relevance today. With regard to England, two accounts can provide an overview of how the distinction operates in practice. Although both accounts date from about three decades ago, and therefore do not reflect certain recent reforms in court structures and other details, they are still generally valid. The first, from the authoritative *International Encyclopedia of Comparative Law*, offers this synopsis:

> "[T]he effect of [the] success [of the Court of Chancery in creating a jurisdiction independent from that of the common law courts] has been to split the English legal system into two halves." Law and equity have been administered in the same courts for [over] a century now, since the administration of the two systems was fused in 1873–1875; but the distinction is still entrenched in the midns of English lawyers and is still an actuality in English legal practice.

> ... For barristers, who have had to pass separate examination papers in equity and common law, it is the fundamental division, since it determines where they

---

10. John Henry Merryman and Rogelio Pérez-Perdomo, THE CIVIL LAW TRADITION 47 (3d ed. 2007) [hereinafter Merryman-2007].

have their offices; the Strand in London, where the Law Courts are, physically divides Lincoln's Inn, where most equity barristers have chambers, from the common law Inns to the South nearer the Thames....

In the law schools a separate course on equity is very generally taught and is usually compulsory, and teachers expounding the law in many other subjects constantly find themselves saying "At law ... but in equity ..." Many monographs and textbooks deal exclusively with equity.... It is always known whether a judge, who must apply both law and equity, was trained and practised on one or other side. Judges almost invariably state the rules of the two systems separately. Furthermore, they readily confess their unfamiliarity with the other system and sometimes castigate the unfamiliarity of their colleagues with their own. The division is frequently recognised in statutes....[11]

A second account is offered by René David, who focuses on the practical issue of how to determine which set of procedures—law or equity—should apply to particular proceedings:

A question relevant in the early days and still relevant after [the reforms made via the Judicature Acts, completed in] 1875 was this: of the two very different procedures available at Common law or in Equity, which should be selected in any given matter? Both in fact have been retained. Within the divisions of the High Court of Justice created by the legislation some judges sitting in the Queen's Bench Division decide according to the oral and contradictory procedures of traditional Common law and others, in the Chancery Division, according to the written, inquisitorial procedures derived from the old Equity proceedings. The same barristers do not plead in both divisions; the tradition of being either a "common lawyer" or an "Equity lawyer" persists, and the two callings do not suppose the same tastes, training or even the same kind of ability.

... [Hence the key issue revolves around] which of the two procedures, that of the Common law or that of Equity, is most appropriate in the circumstances.... Equity now includes that series of subjects in which it appears appropriate to proceed by way of written procedures, whereas the Common law comprises those in which the oral procedures of the past are retained.

Generally speaking, today, in order to know whether one is within the area of the Common law or that of Equity, it is more important to know which branch of law is involved rather than what sanction is available. Common law thus comprises, besides criminal law, the whole of the law of contract and torts; but the "common lawyers" of today apply, without any difficulty, such doctrines as misrepresentation, undue influence and estoppels, now perfectly integrated into Common law and which, it is perhaps only barely remembered, once had their origins in Equity. On the other hand, Equity includes the law of real property, trusts, partnerships, bankruptcy, the interpretation of wills and the winding up of estates. Historically, some of these subjects belong to Equity but with regard to others, on the contrary, it has simply been deemed more advantageous that they be handled by "equity lawyers" according to their own procedures and methods rather than those of the Common law....

---

11. Tony Weir, *The Common Law System*, appearing as section III in Chapter 2 (Structure and the Divisions of the Law) of II INTERNATIONAL ENCYCLOPEDIA OF COMPARATIVE LAW (The Legal Systems of the World—Their Comparison and Unification, 1975), at 80–81.

[Hence there has been] a rationalisation of English law, made possible by the nineteenth century reforms on procedure and judicial organisation. But this process has taken place within the traditional framework and in particular without abandoning the deeply rooted legal categories of Common law and Equity.[12]

In the US legal system, the role of equity—and, more generally, the points of distinction between law and equity—would be more difficult for a US lawyer to identify. The following account summarizes the importance of the law-versus-equity distinction in US law, both today and in earlier periods.

In the United States today, the federal courts and most state courts have merged law and equity in the courts of general jurisdiction, such as county courts. However, the substantive distinction between law and equity has retained its old vitality. This difference is not a mere technicality, because the successful handling of certain law cases is difficult or impossible unless a temporary restraining order (TRO) or preliminary injunction is issued at the outset, to restrain someone from fleeing the jurisdiction taking the only property available to satisfy a judgment, for instance.

Equity courts were widely distrusted in the northeastern U.S. following the American Revolution, and the northern states eliminated their equity courts by the late 1700s. However, the mid-Atlantic and southern states were slower to abandon their equity courts. The federal courts did not abandon the old law/equity separation until the promulgation of the Federal Rules of Civil Procedure in 1938.

Even today, a number of states still have separate courts for law and equity. Delaware is one notable example, as its Court of Chancery is where most cases involving Delaware corporations are decided. Some other states (such as Illinois and New Jersey) have separate divisions for legal and equitable matters in a single court. Although Virginia consolidated the two courts in 2006, it maintains much of the same actions and remedies. Besides corporate law, which developed out of the law of trusts, areas traditionally handled by chancery courts included wills and probate, adoptions and guardianships, and marriage and divorce.

After U.S. courts merged law and equity, American law courts adopted many of the procedures of equity courts. The procedures in a court of equity were much more flexible than the courts at common law. In American practice, certain devices such as joinder, counterclaim, cross-claim and interpleader originated in the courts of equity. Also, the modern class action evolved out of the equitable doctrine of virtual representation, which enabled a court of equity to fully dispose of an estate even though it might contain contingent interests held by persons which the court did not have direct jurisdiction over.[13]

---

12. David & Brierly, *supra* note 3, at 345–347.

13. See the Wikipedia entry for *Equity (law)* at http://en.wikipedia.org/wiki/Equity_%28law%29, citing writings by various authors, a US Supreme Court case, and Virginia rules of procedure. For additional information about the law-versus-equity distinction in the USA and in some other common law countries, see Weir, *supra* note 11, at 92–94.

D. Custom

Although the discussion in subsection IA above identified custom as a source of law in English law (and in some other common law systems, but in different forms), we did not examine there the specifics of how custom can be used in England. After all, despite the fact that the common law represents a displacement of local custom by general national rules, some rare circumstances still exist in which a rule of custom can be applicable in England. The following excerpt explains how this can occur. Note that it concludes by emphasizing the very narrow role custom now plays in England as a source of law.

[I]t is still possible, even today, to argue the existence of a custom before the courts [in England] and have it accepted as law, though its operation is usually restricted to a particular area, or to a particular trade or profession. Such customs may be local, general or convention.

1. Local Custom. Such a custom may be raised to the level of law in a particular area. To be recognised by the courts as having the force of law, a local custom must fulfil the following requirements—

[*1a.*] *Immemorial Existence.* It must have existed at the commencement of legal memory—"from the time when the memory of man runneth not to the contrary" (Blackstone). Actually the limit of legal memory is arbitrarily fixed at A.D. 1189, and existence from this date will be readily presumed. In fact, proof of existence within living memory will shift the burden of proof on to the person who asserts that the custom did not exist in 1189.... The 1189 rule appeared in the sixteenth century and seems to have been applied because customary rights were becoming too easy to establish. In particular, too much land was being transferred from Lords of the Manor to their tenants under supposed customary rights.

[*1b.*] *Continuity.* The claim to enforce the customary right must have been continuous, and the right to exercise it must not have been interrupted. This does not mean that the right must have been continuously exercised, so long as the claim to enforce it has not been abandoned or positively disputed....

[*1c.*] *Certainty.* The area of the application of the custom must be certain, and the subject matter and the persons benefited by the custom must be capable of precise identification.

[*1d.*] *User must be nec vi, nec claim, nec precario.* This means without force, stealth or permission. In particular it must be noted that, where the so-called custom has been exercised by permission or licence, it will be impossible to establish it as a custom....

[*1e.*] *User must be Reasonable.* The courts are not anxious to establish a custom which is manifestly unreasonable....

[*1f.*] *The Custom must have Obligatory Force.* People must feel bound to observe it. Thus, while it is a custom of sorts to wear black at a funeral, it is unlikely to become law, because people do not feel bound to observe it.

[*1g.*] *Consistency.* A custom can only be admitted as law if it is consistent with other customs, and is not contrary to statute or to a rule of common law.

[*1h.*] *Locality*. It would be difficult for people in Cumberland to set up customary rights in Kent. If they have such rights, they must be part of the common law and not based on local custom.

2. General Custom or Usage. Such customs are to be found mainly in mercantile transactions. The cases show a certain amount of conflict, and it is not certain whether it is still possible to incorporate new mercantile customs into the common law.... The test which the courts apply in establishing general custom is universality of observance rather than immemorial antiquity.

3. Conventional Custom. [Some] customary rulings are never raised to the level of the common law, but may affect the rights of parties to a contract who, because they are members of a certain trade or profession, find that certain customary usages have been incorporated into their contract. Here again the test is universality of observance rather than immemorial existence. Such usages are found in the customs of the Stock Exchange and the rules relating to the Sale of Goods and to Bills of Exchange, although most of the latter have been incorporated in the Sale of Goods Act, 1893, and the Bills of Exchange Act, 1882. Generally both parties must belong to the same trade or profession before the application of a custom will be implied.

As an instrument for the development of English law, custom has almost ceased to exist, since the stringent requirements set out above limit its efficacy as a law-creating force.[14]

E. The Role of Jurists and Legal Writing

Highlights. It is the *practicing* jurist, not the *academic* jurist, who has provided some overriding structure to the English common law. University education for lawyers has traditionally (until recently) been seen as unnecessary (perhaps even distracting) because of the common law's intense concentration on procedure and cases. Such practicing jurists as Bracton, Littleton, and Blackstone have in a sense saved common law from being "civilized".

Note from subsection IA above that René David identifies "legal writing" — particularly by men who served as judges — as a source of law in England. Our discussion of sources of law in the civil law world revealed that a somewhat different sort of "legal writing" — particularly by academic lawyers — served as a foundational element to law, sometimes referred to as a "formant" of law or an "indirect source". Characterizing law as a machine that is designed by the legal scholar, built by the legislator, and operated by the judge, Merryman concludes that "law in a civil law jurisdiction is what the scholars say it is".[15] Such a conclusion would be difficult to reach in the common law world. Legal academics (that is, law teachers) have risen in importance in England for some of the reasons David offers — most importantly, the shift of legal education to universities — but they still occupy a lower position than their civil law counterparts.

Having explored several aspects of sources of law in the common law world, let us expand on this last point regarding the relative importance of legal scholars in the com-

---

14. Smith & Keenan, *supra* note 9, at 7–9.
15. Merryman-2007, *supra* note 10, at 60.

mon law versus the civil law tradition, along with some comparative reference also between other types of legal professionals.

II. Categories of Law and Lawyers

A. *The Legal Profession*

> *Highlights.* Given the importance of caselaw, it is no surprise that judges and advocates are the "heroes" of the common law—especially judges, since they have a law-creating function under the traditional view of case-law as a major source of law. This high status of judges helps distinguish common law from civil law perspectives on the role of various legal professionals.

Chapter Three offered extensive observations about the role of various legal professionals in a typical civil law country, with special emphasis on Italy as an illustration. Our examination of those issues involved numerous points of comparison with common law countries—including, for example, details of differing approaches toward legal training and licensing. Further discussion of those points seems unnecessary here; instead, a review of subsections IC and ID3 of Chapter Three should suffice.

B. *Private Law and Public Law*

> *Highlights.* The public/private distinction that is so central to an understanding of civil law systems is largely absent, or of only minor significance, in most common law systems.

Our review of English legal history in Chapter Three highlighted the peculiar historical development of the English legal system (as birthplace of the common law tradition). One consequence of the odd "end-run" that the royal courts at Westminster made around the local, rural courts (at the expense of the barons and to the benefit of the centralized governmental and judicial authority) is that all common law was in a sense "public" law, for two related reasons. First, the jurisdiction of the royal courts at Westminster depended on some genuine showing that the claimants wishing to bring their dispute to those courts were raising an issue that was of interest to the kingdom "in common". Second, the issuance of a writ permitting such a case to be brought was a thoroughly public, governmental act. In that sense public law "squeezed out" private law. It is by no means silly or impossible to make some classification of law in a common law system into "private" and "public" categories similar to those that exist in European civil law tradition,[16] but those

---

16. Indeed, a popular summary of US law makes such a distinction, placing (in its table of contents) the subjects of contracts, torts, property, family law, commercial law, and the law of business enterprises under the chapter heading of "Private Law" and placing the subjects of constitutional law, administrative law, trade regulation, labor law, criminal law, and environmental law under the chapter heading of "Public Law". See E. Allan Farnsworth, AN INTRODUCTION TO THE LEGAL SYSTEM OF THE UNITED STATES ix (4th ed., 2010, as edited by Steve Sheppard). Significantly, the same table of contents precedes both of the chapters on those topics with a chapter on "Procedure", so important to common law tradition. *Id.* The author also makes this observation: "The division of substantive law into public and private law is ... of more questionable utility than the division of law into substance and procedure". *Id.* at 106. For a broader examination of how the distinction between public

categories, and the distinction between them, surely cannot be seen as having overriding significance in common law countries.

III. Content and Operation

A. *Criminal Procedure*

> *Highlights.* Notwithstanding (i) the fact that some civil law countries have undertaken reforms in their systems of criminal procedure (especially in Italy since the 1980s) and (ii) the fact that great diversity exists between common law countries' approach to criminal procedure, it remains true that common law country, in their criminal procedure, generally take more of an accusatorial or adversarial approach than is typical in the civil law world.

Our discussion of criminal procedure in civil law countries occupied a substantial portion of Chapter Three. The discussion included a close examination both of (1) specific rules (including such issues as hearsay, presumption of innocence, the use of lay triers of facts, and much more) and (2) underlying principles and ideologies at work in the design and operation of civil law systems of criminal procedure. One method of undertaking that examination was to consider how the O.J. Simpson trial of the 1990s in California might have looked in a continental European court; another method involved studying a recent murder trial in Italy, also with a comparative perspective.

Only a few points need be made now to supplement the discussion in Chapter Three. The first focuses on England; the next two relate to criminal procedure in the USA; the last applies to both countries.

One source offers the following nutshell account of criminal procedure in the "United Kingdom" (although the author probably draws only or mostly from England; details are likely to differ in other portions of the UK).

> In the United Kingdom, … the suspect is arrested and produced before a court (in the UK system, the Magistrates' Court). The decision to produce the suspect in the Magistrates' Court is taken by the Crown Prosecution Service, based on a realistic prospect of securing a conviction against that individual. In the Magistrates' Court, if the allegation against the accused relates to a summary offense (an offense that the Magistrates' Court has the jurisdiction to try directly), the accused is tried immediately. Cases involving offenses that require the accused to be tried on indictment (that is, more serious offenses) are sent to the Crown Court. Cases relating to a third category of offenses — those over which both the Magistrates' Court and the Crown Court have trial jurisdiction — are considered separately by the magistrate, who determines whether the magistrates will try the accused or whether the case will be sent to the Crown Court.

> Cases before the Crown Court are heard by a judge sitting with a jury. The trial process is generally similar in nature and procedure to that in the U.S. system [de-

---

law and private law can be applied in English law, see Weir, *supra* note 11, at 94–103. Weir also discusses the distinction between commercial law and civil law in common law jurisdictions. *Id*. at 103–113.

scribed below], with the burden of proof lying with the prosecution — that is, the prosecutor must prove the accused has committed the offense contained in the indictment.[17]

The same source offers a somewhat longer sketch of criminal procedure in the USA. The author notes at the outset that rules governing criminal prosecutions appear largely at the state rather than at the national level; but then he traces the main contours of the procedure followed in most states.

> Unlike most countries, the United States does not have a single criminal justice system. Instead, systems vary from state to state.

> The U.S. criminal justice system comes into play with the commission of an offense. In most instances, information relating to that act is received by the relevant law enforcement agency from indirect sources, including the victim of the offense, a witness to the crime, nongovernmental organizations such as neighborhood groups, or state agencies such as public health organizations. On other occasions, information is directly received by law enforcement agencies — for example, if the offense is committed in the presence of law enforcement officers. After the information relating to the commission of a criminal offense has been received and the relevant law enforcement agency has established that an offense was, in fact, committed, the law imposes a duty on the relevant agency to conduct a criminal investigation.

> A vital milestone in the process is the apprehension (arrest) of the suspect. If the investigation reveals the innocence of the arrested suspect, the investigator releases him or her from custody even if the suspect has not been produced before a court of law. The suspect is so produced only if there are reasonable grounds to believe he or she was involved in committing the crime. At this stage, information relating to the criminal act and any evidence currently available are reported to the prosecutor, who uses that information to decide whether to file formal charges in court. The law requires that suspects in custody of the police be produced before a court of law without unnecessary delay. Once the suspect appears in court, the judge must decide whether to continue to detain the individual or to release him or her before trial. If the charge being leveled against the accused is of a minor nature, he or she may opt to plead guilty to the charge (without opting to proceed to trial); the judge will then be required to convict the accused based on the plea of guilt and decide on the penal sanctions to be imposed.

> After the completion of the investigation and the initial appearance of the suspect in a court of law, there is a preliminary hearing, during which efforts are made to determine whether probable cause exists to believe the accused has committed the offense charged and whether that offense is within the jurisdiction of the relevant court. At this stage, a detailed inquiry is not envisaged, and courts are required only to consider the basic nature and reliability of the available material, enabling a decision on the justification of the charge. If the judge determines that no probable cause exists, the accused is dismissed from further proceedings. If not, the case is bound over to a grand jury. In the grand jury, the prosecutor presents the available evidence against the accused, which the

---

17. Herbert M. Kritzer, LEGAL SYSTEMS OF THE WORLD: A POLITICAL AND SOCIAL ENCYCLOPEDIA 382–383 (2008).

jury then weighs in deciding whether there is sufficient evidence to try the accused. If the grand jury decides in favor of the prosecutor, it is required to submit to the court an indictment (containing details of the offense allegedly committed by the accused), together with a written statement of the essential facts of the offense at issue. After the presentation of an indictment, or "information" (generally issued in cases involving misdemeanors), the accused is arraigned in court. At the arraignment, the charges are read to the accused, and he or she is informed of his or her rights; then, the accused's plea of guilt or nonguilt is recorded. On this occasion, the accused has the option of (1) pleading guilty to the charge, (2) negotiating an amendment to the indictment by pleading guilty to a lesser charge, (3) pleading "nolo contendere" (an acceptance of penal sanctions without admitting guilt to the charge), or (4) pleading not guilty. If he or she pleads not guilty, the case will be set for trial. In all other instances, the court proceeds to convict and sentence the accused. On rare occasions when the judge believes that the guilty plea has been tendered by an accused who does not comprehend the consequences of such a plea or who has been coerced, the plea may be rejected and the case will be set for trial.

The U.S. system guarantees a trial by jury to every individual accused of having committed a serious crime. However, in some instances, the accused is entitled to elect a bench trial, wherein it is the judge and not the jury that serves as the finder of fact. In either circumstance, however, it is the judge who decides questions of law. The trial proceeds on the premise that the prosecution has to prove the guilt of the accused and that until such an obligation is fulfilled, the accused is not required to prove his or her innocence. At the conclusion of the trial, the accused is either acquitted or convicted of the original charges or lesser charges. If the accused is convicted, he or she may seek review of the conviction or the sentence through an appeal process.[18]

Recall that in Chapter Three, our discussion of criminal procedure in civil law countries began by exploring the topic of arrest and detention of a person suspected of committing a crime. An excerpt from the Schlesinger treatise highlighted the fact in the civil law world would it would be "unthinkable to use physical arrest as a routine measure against a suspect who has not yet been tried and who, consequently, must be presumed innocent."[19] Now that our attention has turned to the common law (especially English and American) legal systems, it is worth seeing the remainder of the comparison the Schlesinger text offers:

Compare this rational design of pretrial detention with our traditional law of arrest and bail [in the USA]. Probable cause that the suspect has committed the crime, a ground merely supporting the initiation of prosecution, suffices for arrest. Once arrested, the suspect's release depends on his capacity to post bail. Under procedures still prevailing in many states, an indigent defendant can thus be kept in jail despite the absence of any rational justification for detaining him, while the wealthy suspect may be released even though he is likely to flee or to intimidate witnesses. [Although some important modifications to this approach have been made in such legislation as the Federal Bail Reform Act, the provi-

---

18. *Id.* at 382.

19. See text accompanying note 72 in Chapter 3, citing Ugo A. Mattei, Teemu Ruskola, and Antonio Gidi, SCHLESINGER'S COMPARATIVE LAW: CASES, TEXT, MATERIALS (7th ed. 2009) (quoting from a 1974 work by S. A. Cohn).

sions of that and similar legislation require a release of the detained suspect] only after the suspect has been subjected to the (frequently unnecessary) indignity of the initial arrest.... It follows, I submit, that even in our most liberal jurisdictions something might yet be gained by comparative study of the subject of arrest and pretrial detention.[20]

A last observation about the system of criminal procedure used generally in the common law world (including England and the USA) comes from Merryman, who explains the "mixed" aspect of the rules and approach used in handling criminal cases. The mixture he refers to combines some elements of an accusatory and some elements of an inquisitorial system.

> [In the early days of its development, criminal procedure] in the common law tradition ... was basically accusatorial in nature, and the early development of the jury as a necessary participant in the criminal proceeding in England tended to prevent any strong movement toward excesses like those of the Continental inquisitorial system. If a jury was to have the power to determine guilt of innocence of the accused, the proceedings would necessarily have to be oral and be conducted in the presence of the jury. Although it became the rule early in the development of the English criminal trial that the accuser need not employ and compensate the prosecuting attorney, the public prosecutor came very late to the common law. Even today, in England, a member of the practicing bar will be retained to represent the public interest in a criminal proceeding, and will be compensated from public funds. The creation of a professional police force and of a public prosecutor to investigate the commission of crimes, compile evidence, seek authority to prosecute, and actually conduct the criminal proceeding on behalf of the state are comparatively recent developments in the common law world. In effect, they represent a shift away from the accusatorial and toward the inquisitorial system. But the public nature of the trial, the orality of the proceedings in the trial, the existence of a jury, and the limitations on the power of the judge, all combine to perpetuate some of the more desirable features of the accusatory system. The result is a kind of mixed system of criminal procedure.[21]

In sum, our view of criminal procedure in both the civil law tradition and the common law tradition needs to take into account both (1) Merryman's explanation of how common law approaches to criminal procedure now have a "mixed" character and (2) the ways in which some civil law countries have recently introduced reforms to reduce some of the unappealing aspects of a pure inquisitorial system. Both sides of the divide between civil law and common law have moved toward each other in this regard. We should watch for signs of such movement when we turn to the operational aspect of Chinese law, in Chapter Seven. Our examination of Chinese criminal procedure in Chapter Seven will also afford an opportunity to consider some specific points — relating to the requirements or incentives for the accused person to testify at his or her trial — that distinguish the English, American, European, and Chinese systems.

B. Civil Procedure

Highlights. Perhaps curiously, the typical common law country handles civil litigation in a manner very similar to that of criminal prosecution (or maybe the

---

20. *Id.* at 836–837.
21. Merryman-2007, *supra* note 10, at 128–129.

curiosity runs the other direction). The paradigm of the common law's use (or expectation) of a public trial, with a jury, helps explain this.

This topic was explored in some detail also in Chapter Three, and no further elaboration seems necessary here. The principal discussion appeared in subsection IIB of Chapter Three, in subsections that addressed these topics: (1) where is the trial?; (2) matters relating to evidence and proof; and (3) matters relating to judgments, enforcement, and appeals.

C. Division of Court Structures and Jurisdiction

Highlights. The typical common law system has a unified court system, unlike the typical civil law system. There is, however, in English law a parallel construction, at least until 1875, to the civil law's division of jurisdiction (courts) along the lines of the division of categories (private law versus public law); but that separation of courts into law and equity was dismantled by the Judicature Acts in the late 19th century.

This topic also was explored in some detail in Chapter Three, and no further elaboration seems necessary here. The principal discussion appeared in subsection IIC of Chapter Three, in subsections that examined (1) ordinary courts; (2) administrative courts; and (3) constitutional courts (or, in the case of France, a constitutional council). The reasons for those divisions of jurisdiction did not exist in England's legal development. The very different division between courts of common law (the royal courts at Westminster) and courts of equity (Chancery) was ultimately eliminated by the Judicature Acts of 1873–1875, as discussed in subsection IVA of Chapter Four.

D. The Role of Religion and Ideology

Highlights. Like the civil law, the common law stands apart from religion — in the sense that the law is influenced by religious norms but is separate from them. If anything, English law developed with less direct religious elements than European civil law. However, common law exhibits a more prominent ideological "skeleton" than does the civil law.

Some observations appeared in subsection IIIB2 of Chapter Three regarding religion and ideology as influences on law. Those observations appeared in the context of considering the future of the civil law, and they focused on the relationship between "western law" generally (not just civil law or continental European law in particular) and Islamic law. To that earlier discussion perhaps one further observation might be made, regarding common law in particular.

Unlike the development of European civil law, the development of English common law had relatively little direct influence from a competition with (or absorption of) canon law. It is true, as we saw in Chapter Four, that ecclesiastical courts were established in England (with William's arrival in 1066) and that both substantive and procedural components of canon law entered through indirect means into the common law. However, the scholarly elaboration of canon law, its interplay with Roman civil law, the competition between the two with the rise of the nation-states in continental Europe — all these were much more prominent themes in the story of continental developments than in the story of English law and governance.

Having said that, we must acknowledge that the peculiarities of English legal history have left an ideological imprint on the common law. Several of the points made by those commenting on the "migration" of the common law reflected such an ideological imprint—or perhaps it might be seen as an ideological "skeleton" on which muscles and fat and flesh have developed. The Lord Chancellor's reference to the value placed on the independence of judges and the importance of the "common man", as well as Arthur Goodhart's reference to the common law's insistence on limitations on government, may be regarded as ideological in nature. They are elements of a distinction between the common law and the civil law—and an even more substantial distinction between the common law and Chinese law, as we shall see in Chapter Seven, when we examine the underlying ideological values, or the "soul", of the Chinese legal system.[22]

IV. Closing Observations

Two points may be added in closing this very short chapter. The first relates to empire and decolonization, the second to legal peculiarity.

We briefly explored at the end of Chapter Three the legal impact caused by a great explosion of colonization and conquest that a handful of European powers engaged in starting around the 16th century. As explained there, this remarkable surge of influence had a lasting effect, even after it was followed by a wave of decolonization.

No continental European country could outperform England, though, in this undertaking. According to one source, an 1821 newspaper wrote this of the British Empire: "On her dominions the sun never sets; before his evening rays leave the spires of Quebec, his morning beams have shone three hours on Port Jackson, and while sinking from the waters of Lake Superior, his eye opens upon the Mouth of the Ganges".[23] At one time or another between 1500 and 1970, England claimed power over great portions of North America, the entire Indian Subcontinent, Australia and New Zealand, and some portions of Africa and the Middle East. As we saw in the last portion of Chapter Four, it is this remarkable, if tarnished, record of colonization and conquest that explains in large part the "migration" of the common law—that is, its exportation out of the tiny island country of England to vast territories around the world.

Similar legal "exportation" came from the USA. Although it did not develop the same far-flung system of possessions through formal colonization, the USA exercised a heavy influence over the economic and legal systems of many countries around the world. Among the more notable instances of this are the Philippines and Japan. Both of those countries felt some US influence on their legal systems, although for totally different reasons, in the 20th century. In the case of Japan, it was largely the US post-war occupation

---

22. One observer of American law has identified four elements of the American "legal culture" that have endured from the founding of the USA and shaped the evolution of the American legal system: "liberty, distrust of government, tolerance, and optimism". David S. Clark, *The American Legal System and Legal Culture*, appearing as chapter 1 in Introduction to the Law of the United States (David S. Clark & Tuğrul Ansay eds., 1992), at 1. For other observations about the American legal culture or legal "soul", see subsection IVB3a of Chapter Seven, below.

23. *The British Empire, in* Caledonian Mercury, Oct., 15, 1821 at 4, as cited in the Wikipedia entry for *The Empire on Which the Sun Never Sets*, at http://en.wikipedia.org/wiki/The_empire_on_whichthe_sun_never_sets.

that served as the vehicle for such influence. In the case of the Philippines, it was the roughly half-century leading up to formal independence in the 1940s.

The story of American legal influence over the legal systems of countries all around the world has continued in recent years. Along with other western countries, the USA has engaged in efforts at legal reform — praised by some observers as laying the groundwork for economic and social development but condemned by others as another form of alleged neo-colonialism — and these efforts have carried American legal concepts with them. In the 1960s and 1970s, as one source explains, "[t]he 'law and development' movement ... was ... [an] effort to export a set of institutions and practices supposed to build the rule of law"; and then the 1990s also "witnessed a tremendous growth in 'rule doctors' armed with their own competing prescriptions for legal reforms and new legal institutions at the national and transnational levels."[24] Although these efforts assumed their most visible form in the context of the World Bank and other international institution, the real impetus behind them came from the USA and other western countries. As a result, both common law and civil law influences have been urged on countries all around the world.

A second closing observation serves as a transition to the study of Chinese law, to which we turn in the next two chapters. In many respects, English law — and the common law that emerged from it and was spread to countries all around the globe — has a peculiarity to it that the civil law does not share. The reasons for this peculiarity should by now be evident. The common law is much younger than the civil law. The common law, at least through most of its development, has been subjected to much less external pressure from other cultures. The common law had severe limitations on its jurisdictional reach, and therefore an odd focus on procedure over substance, that emerged from political developments that were unique to England. We could point to other reasons as well for considering English law, and the common law more generally that emerged from it, as peculiar in a way that does not come to mind (at least not as quickly) when we think about the civil law tradition.

Aside from having some vague curiosity value, this observation is intended to provide food for thought as we turn our attention to Chinese law. In that case, the age of the legal tradition is much greater than either civil law or common law. However, the isolation of China, the nature of its language, a cluster of specific political and military events and leaders from twenty-two centuries ago — all these factors and more resulted in the creation of a legal tradition, at least until almost exactly one hundred years ago, that we might regard as even odder than the common law tradition. On the other hand, had China embarked on the sort of global imperialist mission that European countries and England did starting five hundred years ago, perhaps the legal system on which China's greatness was built would not look odd at all but instead would appear rather commonplace around the world today.

---

24. Bryant G. Garth and Yves Dezalay, *Introduction*, in GLOBAL PRESCRIPTIONS: THE PRODUC-TION, EXPORTATION, AND IMPORTANT OF A NEW LEGAL ORTHODOXY 1 (Yves Dezalay and Bryant G. Garth eds., 2002), as excerpted in John Henry Merryman, David S. Clark, and John Owen Haley, COMPARATIVE LAW: HISTORICAL DEVELOPMENT OF THE CIVIL LAW TRADITION IN EUROPE, LATIN AMERICA, AND EAST ASIA 63 (2010). These authors paint an unimpressive picture of the record of such efforts to export the rule of law. *Id.* at 64. Another observer — Randall Peerenboom, whose views on the rule of law we shall examine in some detail in Chapter Seven — also refers to the "perceived failures" of the law and development movement and notes that some critics of that movement worry that such efforts might in fact "strengthen authoritarian regimes and undermine efforts to promote political reforms and democratization". Randall Peerenboom, *Varieties of Rule of Law*, in ASIAN DISCOURSES OF RULE OF LAW: THEORIES AND IMPLEMENTATION OF RULE OF LAW IN TWELVE ASIAN COUNTRIES, FRANCE AND THE U.S. 1, 37 (2004), as appearing in Merryman, Clark, and Haley, *supra*, at 67.

Chapter Six

The Chinese Legal Tradition in Historical Perspective

Outline

Study Questions

SQ #6.1   About when in Chinese history did each of these dynasties occur?

    (a) Zhou

    (b) Qin

    (c) Han

    (d) Tang

    (e) Song

    (f) Yüan

    (g) Ming

    (h) Qing

SQ #6.2   What is the "dynastic cycle", and what is its significance?

SQ #6.3   How old is the Chinese legal tradition?

SQ #6.4   What role did each of these persons play in the early development of the Chinese legal tradition?

    (a) the "Duke of Chou"

    (b) Confucius

    (c) Mengzi and Xunzi

     (d)   Shang Yang

     (e)   Qin Shi Huangdi

     (f)   Li Si

SQ #6.5   What is the meaning of each of these terms?

     (a)   Confucianism

     (b)   Legalism

     (c)   *xing* [or *hsing*]

     (d)   *lǐ*

     (e)   *fǎ*

     (f)   *lü*

     (g)   *lì*

SQ #6.6   What was the key aim of the Legalists, and how did it motivate them to insist on the use of law as a means of social control?

SQ #6.7   What (and when) was the earliest known Chinese officially-promulgated written law in China—something we might (with a stretch) call a "code"?

SQ #6.8   On what grounds did some leaders in early Chinese society object to the promulgation of written laws, such as the *xíng shū* ordered inscribed on bronze tripod vessels in the 6th century BCE?

SQ #6.9   What were the main values and aims of the Confucianists?

SQ #6.10   Why would members of traditional Chinese society be especially concerned about violations or disruptions of the social order?

SQ #6.11   What is the relation between law and religion in traditional China?

SQ #6.12   What is the origin of law, according to Chinese legend?

SQ #6.13   Which side of the debate—the Confucianists or the Legalists—won the day in 221 BCE?

SQ #6.14   Why might we accurately refer to the "Legalist triumph but Confucianization of the law" in the Qin-Han period?

SQ #6.15   What role did Dong Zhongshu play in the development of the Chinese legal tradition?

SQ #6.16   What was "Imperial Confucianism"?

SQ #6.17   What were the most important codes in the Chinese legal tradition?

SQ #6.18   How much continuity was there from the codes of one dynasty to another?

SQ #6.19   How did the approach taken by the second "alien dynasty" (the Qing) differ from the approach taken by the first "alien dynasty" (the Yüan), in terms of the law?

SQ #6.20   What were some key features and characteristics of the dynastic Chinese law codes, and how much "civil law" did they cover?

SQ #6.21   What punishments were administered for violations of rules set forth in the dynastic Chinese codes?

SQ #6.22   In what sense was traditional Chinese law "vertical" rather than "horizontal" in its operation?

SQ #6.23   How would you describe the office of the district (*hsien, xian*) magistrate and his role in the operation of the law in traditional China?

SQ #6.24   How would a person become a district magistrate, or a member of the imperial civil service more generally, in traditional China?

SQ #6.25   How welcoming was dynastic China to foreign influences, especially those relating somehow to law?

SQ #6.26   How did the list and hierarchy of sources of law in dynastic China tradition differ from those of the common law tradition and the civil law tradition?

SQ #6.27   How do the fundamental goals underlying the codes in traditional Chinese law differ from the goals present in the codification efforts in the civil law tradition and in American law?

SQ #6.28   What is the fundamental legal division in traditional Chinese law, roughly analogous to the private-public division in civil law and the law-equity division in common law?

SQ #6.29   When did dynastic rule end in China?

SQ #6.30   What was the legal significance of the May Fourth Movement?

SQ #6.31   What sort of law was there in China in the first half of the 20th century?

SQ #6.32   Of what legal significance was the long conflict between the Guomindang and the Communists, culminating in the late 1940s?

SQ #6.33   What legal changes occurred in China with the declaration of the founding of the People's Republic of China?

SQ #6.34   In what sense was China ruled "by movement" rather than by policy in the 1940s through the 1960s?

SQ #6.35   What would you consider the two or three most important legal developments in the second half of the 20th century?

SQ #6.36   From a legal and political perspective, what other periods in Chinese history does the 20th century resemble?

SQ #6.37   Why might we say that the legal reforms beginning around 1979 represent a great "paroxysm" of effort?

SQ #6.38   How many constitutions has the PRC had since its founding?

SQ #6.39   How might we view the Chinese legal system as having "matured" in the past 100 years?

Introductory Comments

The third of the three great legal traditions on which this book focuses is the Chinese legal tradition. Some of the observations made at the close of Chapter Five—relating to the ideological content, the distribution, and the peculiarity of common law—serve as a fitting segue to this chapter. Like the civil law and common law traditions, Chinese law has its share of ideological content and peculiarity. As we shall see, those features have contributed to one of the striking differences between Chinese legal history and the histories of the two main western legal traditions. Unlike them, Chinese law retained — for century upon century, dynasty upon dynasty — a distinctly inward focus, not only developing with little direct external influences but also remaining "at home" rather than getting transported around the world through colonization and conquest.

In this chapter we shall see the historical processes that shaped a remarkably stable legal tradition with views about the role of law in society that look dramatically different from those of the western legal traditions we have studied so far. The account of these historical processes fall into two parts, reflecting the breathtaking shift in fortunes and philosophies of China that occurred almost exactly a century ago. Before that shift, dynastic Chinese law reflected a curious and effective blend of two competing legal philosophies; after the shift, modern Chinese law has followed a tumultuous path, buffeted by a series of political, economic, and social storms. After surveying that story in this chapter, we shall turn in Chapter Seven to consider where Chinese law stands today.

———————

I. Dynastic China's Legal Development

Highlights. The development of the Chinese legal tradition spans many centuries. The following account tries to convey the broad sweep of that story, first by identifying important highlights and patterns (such as the dynastic cycle), then summarizing the great ideological conflict between the Confucianists and the Legalists that was resolved in about the 2nd century BCE. From then on the story is remarkable for its continuity: for many centuries the "alloy" between Confucianism and Legalism, as reflected in detailed legal codes fine-tuned and administered by an imperial bureaucracy with a common ethic and purpose, contributed to a political stability unmatched elsewhere in the world. This section summarizes that story and ponders a cluster of important themes emerging from it.

A. *Overview and Patterns*[1]

To a surprising degree, some of China's oldest history — including its legal history — is in a sense quite new. Recent archaeological discoveries, some of them unearthed in

———————

1. The account in this section, and throughout this chapter, draws liberally from two of my works: John W. Head & Yanping Wang, Law Codes in Dynastic China: A Synopsis of Chinese Legal History in the Thirty Centuries from Zhou to Qing (2005) [hereinafter LCDC]; and John W. Head, China's Legal Soul (2009). Those works, in turn, rely on a mix of English-language and Chinese-language works. Several of those are cited in the Selected Bibliography at the end of this book. Most prominent among them for this chapter are the following (in alphabetical order by author or editor, beginning with books): Derk Bodde and Clarence Morris, Law in Imperial China (1967); T'ung-Tsu Ch'ü, Law and Society in Traditional China (1961); John King Fairbank, China — A New History (1992); Wallace Johnson, The T'ang Code (vol. I, 1979) [hereinafer Johnson-1979]; Wallace Johnson, The T'ang Code (vol. II, 1997) [hereinafter Johnson-1997]; William C. Jones, The Great Qing Code (1994); Hyung I. Kim, Fundamental Legal Concepts of China and the West: A Comparative Study (1981); Geoffrey MacCormack, The Spirit of Traditional Chinese Law (1996) [hereinafter MacCormack-1996]; F.W. Mote, Imperial China 900–1800 (1999); Lucian W. Pye, China — An Introduction (4th ed., 1991); J.A.G. Roberts, A Concise History of China (1999); Bradley Smith and Wan-go Weng, China — A History in Art (1973); Michael Sullivan, The

only the past three decades as China has embarked on building projects at an unprecedented pace, have provided fresh information dating back many centuries.[2] Moreover, the opening of certain archives in China to Western scholars in the 1980s has led to a substantial re-evaluation of the role that civil law (as distinct from criminal law) played in the Qing Code[3] (referred to below).

The basic outline of Chinese legal history, however, has long been well established, and it closely follows the dynastic cycle that is so central to all aspects of Chinese history. In order to supply that basic outline, Box #6.2 provides a chronological summary of Chinese dynastic history generally (with a reference at the end to post-1911 developments)—a summary that is presented in even more simplified form in a "time line" format in the Box #6.1. Box #6.3 then provides a chronological summary of Chinese *legal* history. Explanatory text follows the boxes.

Box # 6.1 Simplified Time Line of Most Significant Chinese Dynasties[4] (with approximate starting dates, if known)

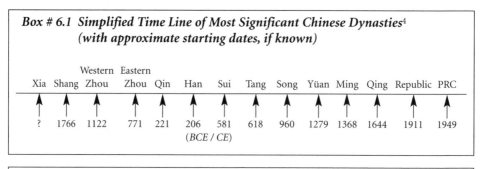

		Western	Eastern										
Xia	Shang	Zhou	Zhou	Qin	Han	Sui	Tang	Song	Yüan	Ming	Qing	Republic	PRC
?	1766	1122	771	221	206	581	618	960	1279	1368	1644	1911	1949

(*BCE / CE*)

Box #6.2 Main Chinese Dynasties and Periods

(*Note:* Dynasties or periods of principal interest for purposes of legal history appear in **bold**)

[*"Feudalism" or "Slavery" Era*—from about the 22nd century to the 5th century BCE]

- **Xia Dynasty** .... about 22nd century to 18th century BCE
- **Shang Dynasty** .... about early 18th century to 12th century BCE (traditional dates are 1766–1122 BCE, but sources vary)
- **Zhou Dynasty** .... 11th or 12th century to 221 (or 256) BCE

ARTS OF CHINA (3rd ed.1984); and various essays in BASIC CONCEPTS OF CHINESE LAW (Tahirih V. Lee, ed., 1997).

2. For example, a set of bamboo slips found in the 1970s provided much new information about the Qin code. *See* LCDC, *supra* note 1, at 68. As explained in an official Chinese website (china.cn.org), "from the Shang and Zhou right through to the Wei (220–265[CE]) and Jin (265–420[CE]), bamboo and wood were ... the main writing materials. This prolonged period of some 2,000 years has come to be known in Chinese history as the Age of the Bamboo Slip". An online description (http://www.crystalinks.com/chinascript.html) explains that to create bamboo slips for writing purposes, a piece of bamboo would be cut into sections, then into strips, then dried by fire to prevent rotting and attack by worms in the future. The finished bamboo slips would be 20 to 70 cm in length. A brush was used in writing, working from top to bottom, with each line comprising from 10 to at most 40 characters. To write a work of some length, one would need thousands of slips. The written slips would then be bound together with strips into a book. Some books were so heavy that they had to be carried in carts.

3. LCDC, *supra* note 1, at 223–224.

4. This time line is obviously not constructed to scale. For more definitive information on dates, see Box #6.2. As in Box #6.2, the two post-dynastic political regimes—the Republic of China and the People's Republic of China, have also been included in this diagram.

Western Zhou	....	11th or 12th century (1122?; 1027?) to 771 BCE	
Eastern Zhou	....	771 to 221 (or 256) BCE	
* Spring and Autumn period		(771 to 481 BCE)	

[*"Dynastic" or "Feudalism" Era* — from the 5th century BCE to the 20th century CE]

* Warring States period		(403 to 221 BCE)	
• **Qin Dynasty**	....	221 to 206 BCE	3 emperors
• **Han Dynasty**	....	206 BCE to 220 CE	
* Western or Former Han		(206 BCE to 8 CE)	14 emperors
[Han Dynasty was interrupted by Hsin Dynasty, 9 to 23 CE]			
* Eastern or Later Han		(25 CE to 220 CE)	12 emperors

[*All dates from here on are CE*]

• **Period of Three Kingdoms**	....	220 to 280	
* Wei			
* Shu			
* Wu			
• **Jin** (or Chin or Tsin) **Dynasty**	....	265 to 420	
* Western Jin			
* Eastern Jin			
• **Nan-Bei Dynasties**	....	420 to 589	
(Southern and Northern Dynasties)			
• **Sui Dynasty**	....	581 (or 589) to 618	2 emperors
• **Tang Dynasty**	....	618 to 907	24 emperors
• **Song** (or Sung) **Dynasty**	....	960 to 1279	
* Northern Song		(960 to 1126)	9 emperors
* Southern Song		(1127 to 1279)	9 emperors
• **Yüan** (Mongol) **Dynasty**	....	1279 to 1368	18 emperors
• **Ming Dynasty**	....	1368 to 1644	17 emperors
• **Qing Dynasty**	....	1644 to 1911	10 emperors

[*Modern Era* — from 1911 to the present]

• Republic of China	....	1911 to 1949	
• People's Republic of China	....	1949 to present	

Box #6.3 *Highlights of Chinese Legal History*

Western Zhou Dynasty: (ca. 1100–771 BCE)	• development by Duke of Zhou of *lǐ* concept as a central element of relations within the aristocratic class • development of *Lü Xing* (criminal laws) by Lü Hou
Eastern Zhou Dynasty: – Spring & Autumn Period (770–476 BCE)	• *Xíng shū* ("books of punishment") inscribed on bronze and iron tripod vessels and on bamboo tablets (536–501 BCE) • Confucius' writings, expanding on the concept of *lǐ* and advocating government by virtuous example (ca. 500 BCE) • early development of views from which the Legalist school arose
– Warring States Period (475–221 BCE)	• Mengzi's writings and Xunzi's writings, developing and modifying Confucius' views (about 325–250 BCE) • writings by main representatives of the Legalist school (ca. 430–230 BCE). • supposed publication of Li Kui's *Canon of Laws* or *Fa Jing* (400 BCE)
Qin Dynasty: (221–207 BCE)	• adoption of Legalist philosophy in government • promulgation of Qin Code

Han Dynasty: (206 BCE–220 CE)	• partial rejection of Legalism; return to Confucianist views; "Confucianization of the Law" • promulgation of Han Code (ca. 200 BCE)
Sui Dynasty: (581–617)	• promulgation of *K'ai-huang lü* (Sui Code) (581 CE)
Tang Dynasty (618–907)	• promulgation of Tang Code (653, 737)
Song Dynasty: (960–1279)	• promulgation of Song Code (963) — largely repeating Tang Code — and later compilations of guidelines to aid judges and clerks
Yüan Dynasty: (1279–1368)	• promulgation of several "codes", including most prominently the Treatises issued in 1291 and 1331
Ming Dynasty: (1368–1644)	• promulgation of *Da Ming lü* (Great Ming Code) (1389) • promulgation of *Wen xing t'iao-li* (Ad hoc Provisions) (1500)
Qing Dynasty: (1644–1911)	• promulgation of first *Da Qing lü* (Great Ching Code) (1646) and later *Da Qing lü-li* (Statutes and sub-statutes) (1740)
Republic of China (1911–1940s)	• promulgation of proposed constitutions and legal codes, in an effort to create a modern Western-like legal system
Qing Dynasty: (1949–present)	• further legal reform followed by suppression of law (1966–1976), then followed by dramatic legislative activity

Throughout the chronology reflected in Boxes #6.1, #6.2, and #6.3 are several important patterns that warrant our attention. One authority has offered this overview:

> What are the major patterns or movements of Chinese history? Space permits a summary description of only four. By far the most important is *the passage from feudalism to empire* during the first millennium B.C. During most of this millennium, the then "China" consisted of a coterie of small principalities mostly clustered in the north around the Yellow River valley and westward, plus one or two others in the Yantgtze valley farther south. These principalities were ruled by hereditary noble houses....
>
> [Then came empire, in the third century BCE.] The most important single date in Chinese history before the abolition of the monarchy in 1912 is 221 B.C. In that year the state of Ch'in [Qin] brought Chinese feudalism to an end by conquering the last opposing principality and creating for the first time a truly universal Chinese empire. (The name "China," from Ch'in, commemorates the Ch'in achievement, but has never been used by the Chinese themselves....) This event begins the age of imperial China and with it the bureaucratic state....
>
> [A second] historical pattern most emphasized by Chinese historians themselves has been that of *the dynastic cycle*: a sequence of major dynasties, each having a usual duration of somewhat under three hundred years, in the course of which it would come into being, flourish and expand, then decline, and finally disintegrate. Each such cycle would usually be closed by a much briefer period of political disorder and warlordism, out of which, eventually, a new dynasty would arise....
>
> A third pattern has been that of the recurring *tension between the agrarian Chinese and the pastoral peoples of the steppes and deserts north and northwest of China proper*. The Great Wall was first built under the Ch'in empire as an arbitrary and only partially effective attempt to demarcate the two ways of life. In the

long run, neither the Chinese nor the nomads could impose their life patterns on each other, but in the short run (which in China might mean a century or more), China proper repeatedly expanded to embrace greater China during the peaks of major dynasties, but contracted again under "barbarian" pressure during the intervening troughs. Twice in late imperial times, all of China fell under barbarian rule: first under the Mongols (the Yuan dynasty, 1279–1368) and again, more effectively, under the Manchus (the Ch'ing [Qing] dynasty, 1644–1912).

A fourth and very significant but little understood development is that of the growing *urbanization and commercialization of Chinese life beginning during the late T'ang dynasty* (ninth century) and perhaps reaching its peak under the Sung (960–1279). During these centuries, commercial and industrial activity, especially in Central and South China, enormously increased.... [W]hat was to begin in Renaissance Europe several centuries later seemed already to be beginning in China, with all the potential changes this implied. But then something happened or rather failed to happen: the forces that were to lead to capitalism and industrialism in Western Europe failed to achieve ongoing momentum in China. The West was to change into a modern society, China did not. Why this should have been—whether it resulted from the Mongol invasion or the resiliency of the Confucian bureaucratic state or other factors—is one of the major unanswerables in Chinese history.[5]

With that as background, let us turn to a brief survey of China's dynastic legal development, starting with the great ideological conflict that is so central to that story.

B. Confucianism and Legalism

1. Foundations of *Lǐ* and the Confucianist Tradition

a. Confucius and the *lǐ*

Although Chinese history can be traced back to about forty centuries ago, the story begins for our purposes with the Zhou Dynasty, dating from the 12th or 11th century BCE. Indeed, the Zhou Dynasty marks the start of China's true *legal* history, as the precedents upon which Confucius based his philosophy of proper behavior and proper governance were set during the Western Zhou period, which dates from about 1100 BCE to around 771 BCE.[6] Confucius saw the Western Zhou period as a golden age from which lessons could be drawn for his own age. He lived around 500 BCE, just before the chaotic Spring and Autumn period of the Eastern Zhou Dynasty gave way to the equally or more chaotic Warring States period (see Box #6.1, above). Both of these periods saw the rise in power of relatively small states "which professed only symbolic allegiance to the Zhou kings, who in the end only ruled a small area around Luoyang",[7] the capital city of the Eastern Zhou.

---

5. Smith and Weng, *supra* note 1, at 12–13 (introductory comments by Derk Bodde) (emphasis added).

6. As suggested in Box #6.2, different sources assign different dates to events and developments in ancient China. For various dates assigned to the founding of the Western Zhou, for example, compare J.A.G. Roberts, *supra* note 1, at 7, and Pye, *supra* note 1, at 6 (both give the date 1122 BCE) to J.M. Roberts, A CONCISE HISTORY OF THE WORLD 72 (1995) (he gives the date 1027 BCE).

7. J.A.G. Roberts, *supra* note 1, at 11.

In short, Confucius was witnessing the disintegration of the Zhou Dynasty and dedicated his efforts to restoring China to the unity and stability he saw in the earliest periods of that dynasty. In particular, he emphasized the need for virtuous leaders to govern the people by enlightened example, following a strict code of behavior that centered on observance of ritual and respect for certain fundamental relationships, such as that between father and son and that between emperor and subject.

For inspiration in developing this strict code of behavior, Confucius relied on an early Zhou Dynasty leader, the so-called "Duke of Zhou".[8] Around 1000 BCE, the Duke of Zhou took the view that the supreme goal of a political leader, in order to maintain the "mandate of heaven" (*tianming*) that legitimized his rule, was to bring harmony both to the universe and to society. Accomplishing such a goal, according to the Duke of Zhou, required close and constant attention to ceremonies and proprieties.

The concept of *lǐ* 礼 was conscripted into duty for this purpose. An explanation of *lǐ*, along with certain other key Chinese legal terms and concepts, can be found in Box #6.4, below. As indicated there, the notion of *lǐ* was originally confined in meaning to refer largely to rituals relating to burial and honoring of the dead to receive the blessing of ancestors. Over many centuries its scope gradually enlarged. The Duke of Zhou's contribution to this process, according to the generally-accepted view, was to expand *lǐ* to make it a code of behavior that regulated the internal relations among the members of China's aristocratic class, including the various levels of political leaders (*zhong*).[9]

The following excerpt from a text on Chinese legal philosophy offers some insight into the actual content of the *Zhou lǐ*:

> The basic principles of the *Zhou lǐ* can be summarized in the phrase "*qin qin, zhun zhun, zhang zhang, nan nü you bie*".
>
> The idea of *qin qin* is that one must love his relatives, especially the older relatives on his father's side; a son and younger brother must be loyal, faithful, and subordinate to the father and older brother; the small *zhong* [clan leader] must obey the big *zhong* [king]; and officials must be selected according to the degree of closeness.
>
> The idea of *zhun zhun* is that the inferior must respect and obey the superior — and in particular must respect and obey the *tian zi* (son of heaven) of the Zhou

---

8. This man's actual name was Ji Dan. Ji was his family name and Dan was his given name. In China, a person's surname (family name) is typically said or written first and his or her given name is said or written second. The given name can consist of either one part (as, for example, in Ji Dan) or two parts (as, for example, in Mao Zedong).

9. In addition to developing the *lǐ* to regulate relations in the ruling class, the Duke of Zhou is also credited with having devised and established the political structure — the so-called *zhong fa* pyramid — by which that ruling class exercised its control over the country. The term *zhong fa* refers to the system of social and political organization and clan inheritance. The Western Zhou's *zhong fa* pyramid consisted of three big *zhong* (leaders) and numerous small *zhong*. The Western Zhou King, considered the son of heaven, was the biggest *zhong*, the supreme ruler of the government. The kingdom itself could be inherited only by the eldest son. The other sons of the king were feudal lords. They had their own feudal states, which were relatively independent of central control. Compared to the Western Zhou King, these feudal lords were small *zhong*, but within each feudal state the feudal lord was the big *zhong*. The title and position of a feudal lord could be inherited only by his eldest son; the other sons of such feudal lord would have the status of Qing Da Fu; these were principal royal officials in each feudal state. Under this *zhong fa* pyramid system, the feudal lords maintained a dual relationship with the king — political and familial. In terms of the political relationship, the feudal lord was a vassal; in terms of blood ties he was the head of a local branch of the royal clan. Thus political allegiance had as its foundation family allegiance.

people and, in turn, also respect and obey the kings of the individual states within the Zhou dynasty (which are the smaller *zhong*, subordinate to the big *zhong*). The distinction between the upper class and the lower class cannot be ignored.

The idea of *zhang zhang* is that the younger must respect the older.... The idea of *nan nü you bie* is that man is superior to woman....

Of these principles, the core ones are *qin qin* and *zhun zhun*. *Qin qin* is the principle governing the *zhong fa* [clan and leadership system]; *zhun zhun* is the principle of distinguishing between classes. The core element within *qin qin* is a recognition that the father is the most authoritative [head] in the family; the core element within *zhun zhun* is a recognition that the king is the most authoritative [head] in the political structure.

Between *qin qin* and *zhun zhun*, *qin qin* takes priority. This is because the Zhou dynasty's political structure was built on the structure of *zhong fa*. The content of *qin qin* includes the content of *zhun zhun*. Therefore, in the Zhou dynasty, "lack of filial piety" is the most serious offense.[10]

Box #6.4 Chinese Legal Terms and Concepts[11]

lǐ 礼, 豐 rules of proper behavior; a code of propriety. Although originally confined in meaning to refer to rituals relating to burial and honoring of the dead, the concept of *lǐ* gradually expanded in scope. In Western Zhou times, it referred to proper courtly behavior of the aristocracy in their dealings among themselves. Confucius broadened the meaning of *lǐ* to refer to proper behavior generally, based on the place or status of a person within the family or the social and political system. Western analogues to *lǐ* might include such concepts as ritual, chivalry, courtesy, morality, and ethical behavior. [Two Chinese characters for *lǐ* are given above; the first is the modern version, and the second is the older version.]

fǎ 法 published law (in general, not a particular published law); positive law (posited by an official such as the emperor). The Legalist philosophy, emphasizing man's selfish nature, favored the use of *fǎ* instead of relying on the less objective rules of *lǐ*. Whereas reliance on *lǐ* is consistent with a "rule of men," reliance on *fǎ* is more consistent with a "rule of law." The ancient Chinese character for *fǎ* is 灋. The left part means water. The right part is a combination of two words, one of which refers to a one-horned goat or ram called the *xie zhi* (*hs'ieh-chai*), which existed in legend, and the other of which means "leave" or "go." It was said that during the rule of Shun—some sources say the rule of Yao (both were famous leaders in the legendary golden age referred to above as occurring in the second half of the third millennium BCE)— a famous judge named Gao Yao (Kao Yao) tried cases by using such a one-horned goat. When the goat found that a defendant had committed the crime with which he was charged, the goat

---

10. See LCDC, *supra* note 1, at 30, and sources cited there. (This excerpt comes from a major Chinese-language source of legal philosophy, as translated by Yanping Wang.) The word *qin* can mean both "love" and "relative"; so *qin qin* can be roughly translated as "love your relative". The word *zhun* can mean both "respect" and "the superior"; so *zhun zhun* can be roughly translated as "respect your superior." The word *zhang* has the meaning "the older"; so *zhang zhang* can be taken as "treat the older as the older." The phrase *nan nü you bie* can be translated as "there exists a distinction between men and women." *Nan* = male; *nü* = female; *you* = there exists; *bie* = distinction, difference.

11. Information included in Box #6.4 is drawn from various sources. For further details and citations, see LCDC, *supra* note 1, at 17–18. For a fascinating account of the meanings of *lǐ*, *fǎ*, and *lü* —based in the case of *fǎ*, for example, on a detailed analysis of the radicals (component parts) of the characters 法 (modern version of *fǎ*) and 灋 (ancient version of *fǎ*)—see generally Zeng Xianyi and Ma Xiaohong, *A Dialectic Study of the Structure and Basic Concepts of Traditional Chinese Law and an Analysis of the Relationship Between Li (Ceremony) and Fa (Law)*, 1 FRONTIERS OF LAW IN CHINA 34 (2006).

would gore him, thereby releasing an evil spirit from his body. As a result, justice was achieved, which was represented by water.

*xíng*xíng 刑 punishment. The *xíng shū* (literally, "punishment books") that first appeared on bronze tripod vessels around 536 BCE set forth prescribed punishments for various illegal acts.

lü 律 statute; a particular law (as opposed to *fǎ*, which usually means written law in general). The term *fǎlü* means "legal provision," as in a code. The original Qing Code, promulgated in 1646, was called the *Da Qing lü* ("Great Qing Code", or "Code of the Great Qing").

lì 例 a subsidiary rule or regulation, or a sub-statute, or "codified precedent." The 1740 version of the Qing Code was called the *Da Qing lü-lì* ("Statutes and Sub-statutes of the Great Qing Code"). The *lì* (not to be confused with *lǐ* 礼 described above) comprised detailed rules that were normally based on decisions or interpretations and were printed following the article of the Code to which they referred.

tianming 天命 mandate of heaven (*tian* = heaven; *ming* = mandate). Beginning as early as the Zhou Dynasty, the concept developed that emperors had legitimate authority to rule only so long as their conduct was consistent with the will of heaven. If heaven became displeased with the ruler, the mandate to rule could be revoked; in that case revolt would be legitimate.

About five centuries after the Duke of Zhou established the *Zhou lǐ*,[12] Confucius put it to broader use. "Confucius" is the Latinized form of the name Kung Fuzi, or Kungzi, which is the formal name often used in referring to the man whose personal name was Kung Qiu or Kung Chung-ni.[13] Confucius was born in Zou Yi (now in the southern part of the area of Qu Fu, in what is now Shandong Province), in the small state of Lu. It was a happy accident that he should be born there, because the feudal lord of the state of Lu, whose name was Bo Qin, had a reputation for following the prescriptions and ceremonies of the *Zhou lǐ* better than most.

It was in this setting that Confucius, whose parents probably belonged to the minor aristocracy,[14] gained a profound admiration for the Duke of Zhou's *Zhou lǐ* and, over time, developed it as a broader personal and political code of behavior. Specifically, Confucius' teachings rested on a cluster of key principles: people can be educated; they can be taught virtue; they can learn by example from a virtuous king; a king should there-

---

12. The Duke of Zhou is not the only individual, of course, who had a noteworthy influence on the earliest development of Chinese law. As noted above in Box #6.3, another Western Zhou figure —Lü Hou—is credited in traditional Chinese legal history with having concentrated his efforts on criminal law, and in particular on criminal punishments (*xíng* 刑). Specifically, Lü Hou, in his capacity as a judge, compiled a body of rules called the *Lü Xing*, which set forth certain key principles in trying cases and applying punishments. See LCDC, *supra* note 1, at 30–31, citing both Chinese-language sources and writings by Geoffrey MacCormack.

13. "Kung zi" might roughly translate to "man whose family name is Kung." Confucius' given name was Qiu (Chiu), which means "small mountain"—supposedly a reference to the shape or appearance of his head when he was born. "Zhongni" (Chung-ni) was another of Confucius' given names; it signifies that he was the second son of his father. See LCDC, *supra* note 1, at 32, and sources cited there.

14. See J.A.G. Roberts, *supra* note 1, at 14. Confucius himself "was appointed to a junior post in his own state until he was forced to go into exile." *Id.* According to another source, Confucius "spent some time as a minister of state and an overseer of granaries." J.M. Roberts, *supra* note 6, at 78. For other information about Confucius, see THE ANALECTS OF CONFUCIUS (Simon Leys tr., 1997), in which the translator, Simon Leys, emphasizes that Confucius himself chose "*enthusiasm* as the main defining aspect of his character", which suggests that the popular image of Confucius "as a solemn old preacher, always proper, a bit pompous, slightly boring" is mistaken.

fore rule by virtue, setting a moral example by his behavior; and such behavior should rest on precepts and relationships that trace their roots to the *Zhou lǐ*.

Confucius went beyond the *Zhou lǐ*, however, in some important respects. Three warrant special mention: (i) Confucius expanded the scope of the notion of *lǐ*, so that it would thenceforth apply not just to the aristocracy but to social relations generally; (ii) Confucius emphasized the dominant role that *lǐ* should play in the conduct of government— almost to the exclusion, that is, of written law— and (iii) Confucius established a direct link from education to ethics and from ethics to politics, under which the authority to govern was to be reserved to an intellectual elite.

What specifically were the rules of *lǐ* that Confucius believed in or emphasized, and where are they written down? These very questions would perhaps make Confucius sigh with frustration, because they reveal a misunderstanding of the character of *lǐ*. Before Confucius— that is, during most of the Zhou Dynasty— the rules of *lǐ* "were transmitted in unwritten form only."[15] After Confucius emphasized and broadened these rules, it is said that "Confucianists ... prepare[d] several written compilations of *lǐ*."[16] One such compilation is the so-called Book of Rites, or *Li ji* (*Li chi*). However, even that large compilation cannot be regarded as a full statement of the rules of *lǐ*, partly because different rules apply to different persons depending on their status in the family and society (indeed, this is a fundamental principle of *lǐ*) and on other factors such as time and place.[17]

What does *lǐ* have to do, in specific terms, with law as it was made and applied in dynastic China? A great deal. Confucius relegated law to a very minor role as a method of ruling society. He thought the cohesion and well-being of society are to be secured not through legal rules but through the observance of proper rituals of *lǐ*. While punishment (*xíng*) will be necessary in some cases, virtue is to be the principal means of ruling the country. The following passages from the *Analects*— the classic statement of Confucius' philosophy[18]— illustrate Confucius' thoughts in this regard:

> The Master said: "Lead them by political maneuvers, restrain them with punishments [and] the people will become cunning and shameless. [But] [l]ead them by virtue, restrain them with ritual [and] they will develop a sense of shame and a sense of participation.
>
> Lord Ji Kang asked Confucius about government. Confucius replied: "To govern is to be straight. If you steer straight, who would dare not to go straight?"
>
> Lord Ji Kang asked Confucius about government, saying: "Suppose I were to kill the bad to help the good: how about that?" Confucius replied: "You are here to govern; what need is there to kill? If you desire what is good, the people will be

---

15. Bodde and Morris, *supra* note 1, at 19.

16. *Id.*

17. See LCDC, *supra* note 1, at 36, and sources cited there.

18. See generally ANALECTS, *supra* note 14. Simon Leys, the translator, explains the significance of the *Analects*: "[N]o book in the entire history of the world has exerted, over a longer period of time, a greater influence on a larger number of people than this slim little volume." He cautions: "[I]f we ignore this book, we are missing the single most important key that can give us access to the Chinese world. And whoever remains ignorant of this civilization, in the end can only reach a limited understanding of the human experience." *Id.* at xvi–xvii. According to Leys, "[t]he *Analects* is to Confucius what the Gospels are to Jesus. The text, which consists of a discontinuous series of brief statements, short dialogues and anecdotes, was compiled by two successive generations of disciples ... over some seventy-five years after Confucius's death— which means that the compilation was probably completed a little before, or around, 400 BC." *Id.* at xix.

good. The moral power of the gentleman is wind, the moral power of the common man is grass. Under the wind, the grass must bend.[19]

In discussing Confucius' disdain for law, one author begins by explaining the meaning of "rites" and "ritual," in which Confucius placed so much faith:

> The central importance of *rites* in the Confucian order may at first appear disconcerting to some Western readers (conjuring up in their minds quaint images of smiling Oriental gentlemen, bowing endlessly to each other), but the oddity is merely semantic; one needs only to substitute for the word "rites" concepts such as "*moeurs,*" "civilized usages," "moral conventions," or even "common decency," and one immediately realizes that the Confucian values are remarkably close to the principles of political philosophy which the Western world inherited from the Enlightenment. Montesquieu in particular ... developed notions which unwittingly recouped Confucius's views that a government of rites is to be preferred to a government of laws; Montesquieu considered that an increase in law-making activity was not a sign of civilization — it indicated on the contrary a breakdown of social morality, and his famous statement "*Quand un people a de bonne moeurs, les lois deviennent simples*" could have been lifted straight from the *Analects*.[20]

To summarize about Confucius: Drawing inspiration from the Duke of Zhou, Confucius formulated an expanded version of *lĭ* that would govern politics and social relations much more broadly than did the old *Zhou lĭ*,[21] with government to be placed in the hands of true gentlemen who were dedicated to the ritual and ceremony that (Confucius thought) had been the hallmark of a glorious past, and with law and punishment relegated to a very meager role.

b. Mengzi and Xunzi

Mengzi (Meng-tzu, Latinized as Mencius) and Xunzi (Hsun-tzu) are seen as following in Confucius' footsteps, but in fact they departed in important ways from his philosophy — at least as that philosophy appears in the *Analects*. Two such departures relate to (i) the stratification of society by distinctions in status, and (ii) the role of punishment in government.

Mengzi (372–289 BCE),[22] like Confucius, thought that men are by nature good and moral, and that if a man is taught proper behavior, then presumably his natural tendency toward morality will compel him to put that knowledge into practice and behave properly. Xunzi (313–238 BCE) took a different view on the nature of men. He said "[t]he nature of man is evil; his goodness is acquired"; and "the original nature of man is evil, so he must submit himself to teachers and laws before he can be just;

---

19. These passages are drawn from ANALECTS, *supra* note 14, at Chapter 2 (passage 2.3) and Chapter 12 (passages 12.17 and 12.19).

20. *Id.* at xxv–xxvi. A rough translation of Montesquieu's words would be "When a people has good morals, its laws will be simple."

21. For an intriguing account of the possible similarity between the *lĭ* and modern constitutions, see Ma Xiaohong, *A Reflection on the History of Chinese Constitutionalism of Last Century*, 2 FRONTIERS OF LAW IN CHINA 44, 66 (2007) (asserting that "in ancient China, rule by *lĭ* actually had the status and role similar to that of Western constitutions").

22. The man's name was in fact Mengke, and the name of the book he wrote was "Mengzi". However, he has become known by the name of his book. By some accounts, Mengzi (or Mengke) lived from 390 to 305 BCE.

he must submit himself to the rules of decorum and righteousness before he can be orderly."[23]

Although they differed on the nature of man, it appears that Mengzi and Xunzi agreed with each other (and differed from the Confucius of the *Analects*) on the nature of society. For Mengzi and Xunzi, society was inherently non-uniform and unequal. Human beings "were characterized by differences in intelligence and in virtue, and these differences set the stage for the division of labor."[24] The *Mencius* elaborates:

> Great men have their proper business, and little men have their proper business.... Some labor with their minds, and some labor with their strength. Those who labor with their minds govern others; those who labor with their strength are governed by others. Those who are governed by others support them; those who govern others are supported by them. This is a principle universally recognized.[25]

As a consequence of these distinctions, society was characterized by relationships of subordination and superordination: "The young serve the old; the inferior serve the noble; the degenerate serve the worthy."[26] Moreover, for Mengzi and Xunzi, it was the role of *li* to maintain such distinctions.

Confucius would have rejected much of this, for he "simply did not talk in terms of an upper class and a lower class, or of the necessity that the latter be kept in their proper place, or in ignorance." Instead, he "told the men in power that they could secure the adherence of the people only by setting them an example of moral conduct—which, he usually implied, they signally failed to do." Indeed, he "worked to destroy arbitrary barriers between classes".[27]

The second point of departure that Mengzi and Xunzi made from Confucius' views relates to the role of punishment in government. It appears from the *Analects* that Confucius took a very dim view of the use of punishment, regarding punishment as vastly inferior to benevolence and good moral example as a means of persuading the people to behave well. These were utopian views, so it should come as no surprise that later Confucianists would temper them, especially in times of political and social unrest. Both Mengzi and Xunzi gave greater prominence than Confucius did to the proper role of punishment as a tool of governance.

In short, the teachings of Confucius underwent significant modification even in the two centuries after his death. (As we shall see below, further modifications would also come later.) No doubt those modifications reflected in part the fact that Confucius' views in their pure form seemed both radically utopian and politically threatening to the governing elite of his time. But other influences were also at work: at the same time that Confucius was spreading his gospel, sharply contrasting views were being espoused rather successfully by another group—the Legalists.

---

23. J.A.G. Roberts, *supra* note 1, at 18, citing (for the first quoted passage) an English-language text on sources of Chinese tradition. See also Geoffrey MacCormack, *Mythology and the Origin of Law in Early Chinese Thought*, 1 JOURNAL OF ASIAN LEGAL HISTORY 4–5 (2001) (describing Xunzi's views and giving birth and death dates of ca. 310 and ca. 211 BCE).

24. Ch'ü, *supra* note 1, at 226.

25. *Id.* at 226, citing MENG-TZU CHU-SU, 5B, 1b-2a.

26. *Id.* at 227, citing HSUN-TZU 3, 28a.

27. Herrlee Glessner Creel, *Legal Institutions and Procedures During the Chou Dynasty*, appearing in Alan Cohen, R. Randle Edwards, and Fu-mei Chang Chen, eds, ESSAYS ON CHINA'S LEGAL TRADITION (1980), at 38–39.

2. Legalism and the "Confucianization" of the Law

a. The Legalists, Fǎ, and the Qin Dynasty

During the latter part of the Eastern Zhou period (771–221 BCE), it became possible for control over land to be sold—that is, transferred to persons outside the family. As a result, new landlords appeared. Under the prevailing rules and relationships of the *lǐ*, the status of these new landlords was inferior to that of the nobles who were part of the (blood-related) ruling family.[28] Not surprisingly, the new landlords chafed under this old order and wanted a new one.

They found several proponents. We need not concern ourselves with individual theoreticians and politicians—Li Kui, Shang Yang, and Han Fei, for example[29]—but can refer to them in aggregate by the label history has given them: Legalists. In general, the views of the Legalists ran counter to Confucianist views in three key inter-related areas. First, they asserted that the government should rest not on social distinctions of *lǐ* but instead on law applied equally to all persons. Second, a realistic view of human nature, they said, dictated that people can be persuaded primarily by punishments, and not by moral example provided by the leaders. Third, as a corollary to the first and second points, a rule by law was superior to a rule of men.

One author offers some details on these points, emphasizing the third one in particular:

> The Legalists' position ... was diametrically opposed to that of the Confucianists. The [Legalists] denied that moral influence alone could determine the social order and that some one or two persons could wield enough power to transform the customs of the land and create either order or disorder within the state. They strongly rejected the rule-by-man principle.... Instead they sought a principle of governing that would assure a long, even a permanent peaceful order of society, and not one whose uncertainties could only lead to intermittent periods of order and disorder.

> Therefore the Legalists did not believe in the principle of "ruling-by-man." They claimed that "a sage ruler relied upon law, not upon wisdom;" ... The Legalists usually drew an analogy between the workings of law and the compass and the square. A sage could no more give up law in governing than an artisan could correct a circle without a compass, or a square without a square.[30]

Central to the Legalist philosophy was the notion of *fǎ* 法. As reflected above in Box #6.4, *fǎ* may be defined as published, posited law setting forth rules that were relatively egalitarian in their effect and that created known disincentives for transgressions. Indeed, *fǎ* entailed, at least for the Legalists, harsh punishments that would create adequate "shock and awe" (in today's terms) to assure compliance by all in society.

These seemingly incompatible ideologies—Confucianism and Legalism—occupied legal and political discourse and practice for roughly three hundred years between about 550 and 230 BCE. In the interest of brevity, we must pass over numerous developments and frictions that occurred in that period—including the issuance in 536 BCE of the *Xíng shū* ("books of punishment") on bronze tripod vessels, seen as a clear manifestation of Legalism.[31] For our purposes, the most important aspect of the great Confucian-

---

28. For an explanation of the *zhong fa* system, see *supra* note 9.

29. For descriptions of these men and their work, see LCDC, *supra* note 1, at 45–46, 63–73.

30. Ch'ü, *supra* note 1, at 242–250.

31. Another significant development was the issuance of the *Fa Jing* ("Canon of Laws") around 400 BCE. This too was a manifestation of Legalism. Yet the powerful influence of Confucianism con-

ist-Legalist debate was its surprising outcome. In short, there was a compromise reached between the two—or, to use a metaphor that appeals to me, a strong new alloy was created by melting the two competing ideologies together.

The cauldron in which that alloy was produced took the form of an intense hundred-year period between about 224 BCE and 124 BCE.[32] That period saw seven key developments of profound legal and political significance. They are listed here in rough chronological order:

- The bloody climax of the ages-old Warring States period, with the state of Qin progressively crushing the other states into which the old Zhou Dynasty had fractured.

- The unification of China in 221 BCE by Ying Zheng, the king of the state of Qin, who then assumed the title of Qin Shi Huangdi (First Emperor of Qin).[33]

- The imposition of a harsh Legalist ideology under the Qin Code, with punishments that reportedly created a population seething in bitterness against the Qin leaders; and, correspondingly, the official outlawing of Confucianism—taking the form of fires that were set at the orders of Qin Shi Huangdi and his prime minister, Li Si, to burn the classical Confucianist literature.[34]

- The collapse of the Qin Dynasty after a mere fifteen years (in 206 BCE) and the establishment of the Han Dynasty in its place.

- A reintroduction of Confucianist values as the basis for imperial government, but within the framework of a written code (the Han Code).

- An amalgamation and rationalization of competing strains of philosophical and religious teachings into a body of doctrine that we now refer to as Imperial Confucianism.

- The solidification of the role of Confucianist scholars in the imperial bureaucracy, responsible thenceforth for the empire's law and governance.

Each of these developments deserves separate treatment, but let us concentrate on only the last three, which all occurred as the Han Dynasty began its rise to a glory that earned it an image for generations to come as a "golden age".

---

tinued to be felt as well in this period, especially in literature and theory. For details, see LCDC, *supra* note 1, at 48–70.

32. I have selected these dates because, as noted below, the first one is shortly before the unification of China and the second one is the year in which the imperial academy was founded.

33. The king of the state of Qin is referred to variously as King Zheng or Ying Zheng. His given name was Zheng (Cheng, meaning "correct" or "upright"), and his family name was Zhao. See LCDC, *supra* note 1, at 70 n. 31, and sources cited there.

34. Around 213 BCE, prime minister Li Si "presented a memorial to the emperor suggesting that scholars, other than those attached to the court, should surrender all historical records other than those of Qin and that these should be burned." J.A.G. Roberts, *supra* note 1, at 24. Smith and Weng, *supra* note 1, at 60, quote from Li Si's memorial to the emperor:

> Your servant suggests that all books in the imperial archives, save the memoirs of Ch'in, be burned. All persons in the empire, except members of the Academy of Learned Scholars, in possession of the Book of Odes, the Book of History and discourses of the hundred philosophers should take them to the local governors and have them indiscriminately burned. Those who dare talk to each other about the Book of Odes and the Book of History should be executed and their bodies exposed in the market place. Anyone referring to the past to criticize the present should, together with all members of his family, be put to death.

b. The Han Dynasty and Dong Zhongshu

The founding emperor of the Han Dynasty was Liu Bang (247–195 BCE), who took the reign name of Gaozu[35] shortly after consolidating his power following his successful effort to defeat the Qin regime. One of the measures sometimes cited as contributing to his success in this effort was to permit the reintroduction "of Confucian values as the basis for imperial government",[36] notwithstanding his reputation for holding scholars in contempt.[37]

Gaozu's reign lasted until 195 BCE. His two sons and his grandson also ruled (as did his widow, the Empress Lü, for a few years), covering a period until 141 BCE. It was in the latter years of that period—under the Emperor Wenti and his son who reigned as Jingdi—that the empire achieved new levels of stability and prosperity. But the most glorious period came with the next emperor, Wudi, who reigned between 141 and 87 BCE. Under his rule, the frontiers of the empire were extended, in part because of successful military campaigns against the Xiongnu (Hsiung-nu) people to the north.[38] Following that victory, Wudi sent 700,000 people to the northwest to colonize the conquered territories and sent emissaries west as far as India—an expedition that "opened the overland route later known as the Silk Road, which became the main artery of material and cultural exchange between the East and the West, from the Han capital Ch'ang-an to the Mediterranean shore."[39] Further expansions occurred southward to Vietnam and northeast to Korea, resulting in the infiltration of Chinese culture into Japan.[40] By around 100 BC the Han empire had extended its reach much further than ever before. In addition, cultural achievements abounded: the first dictionary was compiled; lacquer work and painting reached high levels; astronomy was developed; and textbooks on arithmetic and medicine were produced.[41]

More important to us than the military, territorial, and cultural successes presided over by the Han leaders, however, were their legal initiatives—and in particular the reintroduction of Confucianism as a guiding ethic for the legal system. In the following passage, the historian Harry Gelber highlights this change:

> What the Han rulers, and especially Wudi, did *not* stick to was [Qin Shi] Huangdi's legalism. Instead, *the Han revived, endorsed, and embedded Confucian principles.*
> So Wudi repealed the Qin edict ordering book-burning[42] and revived the idea that imperial authority came from heaven, not merely from whatever laws had been decreed. He strengthened the bureaucracy further and saw to the selection of candidates for his civil service. The way in which students trained in this [manner] were appointed to government posts was the start of the famous Chi-

---

35. Emperors of China typically adopted "temple names" or "reign names", and often had still different names applied to them posthumously as well. See Pye, *supra* note 1, at 64.

36. J.A.G. Roberts, *supra* note 1, at 28.

37. Indeed, "Gaozu ... declar[ed] that he had won the empire on horseback and had no time for the Confucian classics. However, a Confucian scholar named Lu Jia, who had been an early supporter of the emperor, compiled for him the *New Analects*, a collection of essays which identified the shortcomings of the Qin dynasty and recommended that the new emperor's government should observe ethical standards." *Id.*

38. *Id.* at 29–30.

39. Smith and Weng, *supra* note 1, at 68–69.

40. *Id.* at 69.

41. Harry G. Gelber, THE DRAGON AND THE FOREIGN DEVILS: CHINA AND THE WORLD, 1100 BC TO THE PRESENT 24 (2007).

42. See *supra* note 34 and accompanying text.

nese system of civil-service appointments by examination that later became a model for the civil services of the modern Western world. The later Han emperors themselves were given a proper Confucian education and most high officials came to be educated in the same tradition. The emperor was personally responsible for carrying out seasonal rituals to ensure good harvests and the people's welfare.[43]

We have seen earlier in this chapter some of the key elements of Confucius' teachings and some aspects in which Mengzi, Xunzi, and others modified those teachings in the two centuries or so after Confucius. More modifications occurred during the Han Dynasty. Indeed, the modifications were so great in some cases that they might better be called departures or even emasculation, largely because they arose out of a series of accommodations that were necessary in order that Confucianism could withstand challenges from other influences. Some of the challenges came from other philosophical views or religions, some came from antipathy or hostility on the part of emperors. Confucianism withstood such challenges by evolving into what has been called "Imperial Confucianism".[44]

One authority paints a striking, if perhaps oversimplified, picture of a key phase in that process of evolution:

> Confucianism gained eminence during the Han period because of the meeting of minds of a monarch in search of a clear mandate from Heaven and a scholar with an ambition to dominate the current ideologies, which included earlier Legalist, Taoist and Confucian theories. Their formula was simple — they interpreted the past to suit the present. The scholar Tung Chung-shu [Dong Zhongshu], hand-picked in an examination by Emperor Wu [Wudi] soon after his ascension to the throne [in 141 BCE], claimed authority from the Confucian ideal of a perfect social order and from the cosmological theory of the Book of Changes and the Yin-yang Five Elements School to support his own concept of the "Oneness of Heaven and Man."[45]

The quoted passage goes on to give details of Dong Zhongshu's teachings, but we should pause here to get oriented. The emperor Wudi — unlike Gaozu, the first Han emperor — had been educated in the Confucianist tradition;[46] and it was consistent with that background for Wudi to recruit for his bureaucracy "men of talent who had been educated through the medium of the Confucian texts."[47] Between 141 and 124 BCE, several steps were taken to strengthen the link between Confucianist training and government service by establishing official posts for academics intending to specialize in the interpretation of Confucianist texts and then by establishing an imperial academy where students would study those texts for an examination that would make the successful students eligible for an official appointment.[48]

---

43. Gelber, *supra* note 41, at 23 (emphasis added).

44. Fairbank, *supra* note 1, at 62. As Fairbank explains, the term "Imperial Confucianism" is used "to distinguish it both from the original teaching of Confucius, Mencius, et al. and from the secular and personal Confucian philosophy that arose during Song times and has since then guided so many lives in the East Asian countries of the old Chinese culture area — China, Korea, Vietnam, and Japan." *Id.*

45. Smith and Weng, *supra* note 1, at 79.

46. J.A.G. Roberts, *supra* note 1, at 28, 30.

47. *Id.* at 31.

48. *Id.*

There were other influences at work, however, besides Confucianism. Daoism (Taoism) was one of them. One author offers this summary of Daoism in the early Chinese context:

> *Dao* means "the path," "the way." It expressed the common people's naturalistic cosmology and belief in the unseen spirits of nature, much of which was shared by the scholar-elite. Daoism was an enormous reservoir of popular lore.
>
> Traditionally Daoism stemmed from Laozi…, who was claimed by his followers to have been an elder contemporary of Confucius.[49] The school of thought ascribed to him [Laozi] became a repository for a variety of beliefs and practices that Confucianism had refused, including early popular animism, alchemy, ancient magic, the search for the elixir of immortality…, early Chinese medicine, and mysticism generally, both native and imported from India.
>
> … [T]he early Daoists argued that human moral ideas are the reflection of human depravity, that the idea of filial piety springs from the fact of impiety, that the Confucian statement of the rules of propriety is really a reflection of the world's moral disorder. Following this line of thought, the typical Daoist took refuge in a philosophy of passivity expressed in the term *wuwei*, meaning "action by inaction" or "effortlessness."[50]

Another outside influence—outside the traditional Confucianism, that is, as it had originated with Confucius himself and then undergone modifications by such disciples as Mengzi and Xunzi—was the concept of *yin* and *yang* forces. Under this concept, two primal forces are at work in nature: *yin*, the negative, and *yang*, the positive. *Yin* and *yang* complement each other; but of the two *yang* is inherently nobler. "*Yang* is the substance and always leads, but *yin* is the shadow and always follows."[51]

Yet another outside influence at play in early Han times was the concept of the five elements. These were wood, fire, soil, metal, and water.[52] The number 3 also carried significance; another organizing principle centered on the three major human relationships (ruler and subject, father and son, husband and wife),[53] as well as on the threefold obligations of the ruler: to serve Heaven by making sacrifices, to serve earth by performing symbolic acts such as ploughing a furrow, and to serve man by enlightening the people through education.[54]

It might seem impossible to reconcile these various concepts and influences into a unified theory, but Dong Zhongshu did it.

> From the earlier Confucian doctrine he took the view that stability in society depends on three major human relationships: ruler and subject, father and son, and husband and wife; and that the morality of the individual depends on five constant virtues: humanity, righteousness, propriety, wisdom and good faith.

---

49. Although rubbings exist showing Confucius paying respects to Laozi (Lao Tzu), the story of such a meeting "was a Taoist invention"—although such a popular one that "even Confucianists repeated it to prove their founder's receptiveness to noble teachings." Smith and Weng, *supra* note 1, at 81.

50. Fairbank, *supra* note 1, at 53–54. For other accounts of the rise and influence of Daoism in China, see J.M. Roberts, *supra* note 6, at 78; Pye, *supra* note 1, at 37, 53–54; Mote, *supra* note 1, at 497–498. In addition to Laozi, another principal name in the early development of Daoism is Zhuangzi, a philosopher from the fourth century BCE. Mote, *supra*, at 497.

51. Smith and Weng, *supra* note 1, at 79–80.

52. J.A.G. Roberts, *supra* note 1, at 31; Smith and Weng, *supra* note 1, at 79.

53. Smith and Weng, *supra* note 1, at 79.

54. J.A.G. Roberts, *supra* note 1, at 30.

From the Book of Changes and the Yin-yang School he adopted the concept that the universe comprises Heaven, Earth and Man — the basic trilogy. These are made up of five elements: wood, fire, soil, metal and water. They are controlled by two primal forces: *yin*, the negative, and *yang*, the positive.... The essence of Heaven and Earth, when combined, is oneness; when separated, becomes two, *yin* and *yang*.... Man is born with the nature of Heaven; therefore, he also inherits the qualities of *yin*, *yang* and the five elements and is responsive to Heaven. When human events are in harmony with Heaven, great peace prevails; when they are contrary to Heaven, great upheavals occur. Heaven produces the ruler for the people but not the people for the ruler. At the same time, Heaven favors *yang* and shuns *yin*; therefore, favors benevolence and shuns punishments. Thus Heaven always supports the benevolent ruler and removes the tyrant.

... By injecting political significance into natural disasters, such as earthquakes and floods, Tung Chung-shu was able to derive constructive results from his emperor's belief in cosmology. Citing political philosophy, implied by Confucius..., [Tung Chung-shu] pointed out that unity was the universal virtue and Confucianism the only way to unified authority. Yet many of his philosophical ideas had no relationship to earlier Confucianism. He reinterpreted history and arranged the past dynasties as Three Reigns and Five Sovereigns (to match the three relationships and five virtues) to prove that Han was now the dynasty favored by Heaven. Hearing Tung's arguments..., Emperor Wu established Confucianism as the official government doctrine.[55]

To a modern Westerner, this sounds like hocus-pocus; or, as one author has expressed it, "this is a game any number of philosophers can play."[56] Yet as the same author has explained, the manipulation and integration of these various ideas — Daoism, *yin* and *yang*, five elements, and so on — became a tool that the Confucianist advisers could use to great effect in influencing the emperors' behavior:

> [T]hey claimed to be, and became, indispensable advisers to the emperor [based on their command of the classic writings. It could be said that] ... the literate elite ... had entered into an alliance with monarchy. The monarch provided the symbols and the sinews of power.... The literati provided the knowledge of precedent and statecraft that could legitimize power and make the state work.[57]

One natural consequence of the adoption of an "Imperial Confucianism" along the lines described above has already been noted: the establishment of the civil service examination system and the educational academy that supported it. As one authority has explained, "Han Confucianism came into its own when the imperial academy was founded in 124 BC."[58]

---

55. Smith and Weng, *supra* note 1, at 79–80. Derk Bodde writes that "the Confucianism which triumphed in Han times was a highly eclectic thought system ... that borrowed extensively from its philosophical rivals," including those that focused on *yin* and *yang*, the five Chinese elements, and other "cosmologists" or "naturalists." Bodde and Morris, *supra* note 1, at 27, 43–44. As we shall see later, especially in section IVB1a of Chapter Seven, further "borrowings" from competing philosophies occurred several centuries later in developing so-called "Neo-Confucianism". These include Buddhism, although only indirectly. See also notes 129–133 and accompanying text, *infra* in this chapter.

56. Fairbank, *supra* note 1, at 64.

57. *Id.*, quoting Arthur F. Wright.

58. Fairbank, *supra* note 1, at 67. The academy's students — which numbered 30,000 at one point in the Han Dynasty — studied the five Confucian classics: the *Yijing* or *Classic of Changes* (for divini-

It is that year — 124 BCE — that I used as the ending date for the period in which the seven key developments noted above occurred in the span of merely a hundred years. Whereas the beginning of that period saw the rise of the Qin Dynasty and the crushing of Confucianism at the hands of proponents of Legalism, the end of that hundred-year period saw Confucianism resurrected and placed in a position of authority — in the form of an alliance between the Confucianist legal scholars and the imperial rulers.

Another natural consequence of this alliance between Confucianism and imperial governance is that Confucianist ideas (whether orthodox or hybrid) would find expression in the application, and eventually the substance, of legal codes. It is to that subject that we now turn.

C. Law Codes in Dynastic China

1. The Han Code

Recall that the Legalist ideology called for written law, and that the first emperor of a united China — Qin Shi Huangdi — used the Qin Code as the vehicle for imposing Legalism over his newly-founded Qin empire. Of central significance in the developments described above is this fact: the dramatic rejection of the Qin Dynasty around 206 BCE did *not* involve a rejection of codification. Instead, the Han leaders adopted a legal code almost immediately after overthrowing the Qin. Indeed, that Han Code, first prepared around 200 BCE, drew from precedents it received from the Qin Dynasty, including perhaps the *Fa Jing* ("Canon of Laws") referred to earlier.

Although we know very little about the specific provisions or even the overall structure of the Han Code because it has been almost completely lost through the ages,[59] we do know that it reflected both Confucianist and Legalist aspects and indeed constituted an "alloy" of the two. A leading expert on the Han Code, A.F.P. Hulsewé, explains:

> Han law is the outcome of two streams of thought, an archaic one, filled with the magico-mythical concepts of "primitive" society, and a very matter-of-fact one, purely practical and political, with the *raison d'état* as its primary motive. To put it differently: Han law partook on the one hand in the general Chinese heritage with its particular views on the order of the universe, on the interdependence of all the parts of this universe and consequently on the responsibility of the individual to act conformably to its rules as these had been established by society so as not to disturb cosmic harmony, or else to suffer the consequences. On the other hand, Han law took over the administrative and legal rules of the Ch'in [Qi] empire and their practical application in the government organisation. These rules ... had the very practical political purpose of maintaining the stability of the government and of increasing its power by means of detailed regulations affecting the behaviour of its subjects.[60]

---

ation), the *Shujing* or *Classic of Documents* (or *History*), the *Shijing* or *Classic of Songs* (*Odes*, ancient folk poems), the *Chinqiu* or *Spring and Autumn Annals* (chronicles of Confucius' own state of Lu in Shandong, with their commentaries), and the *Liji* or *Record of Ceremonies and Proper Conduct*. *Id.*

59. Only some scattered remnants of the Han Code have survived. For the landmark study of the Han Code by a Western authority, based on a careful and skeptical reading of the literature available to him at the time, see generally A.F.P. Hulsewé, REMNANTS OF HAN LAW (1955).

60. *Id.* at 5.

The first of the two "streams of thought" Hulsewé refers to is Imperial Confucianism, that amalgam of traditional Confucianism (already modified by followers of Confucius after his death) and other elements of "correlative cosmology" described above, as espoused by Dong Zhongshu. The second is Legalism. Hulsewé is describing a process that has been widely referred to as the "Confucianization of Law",[61] by which the Legalist doctrine that the Qin state and dynasty applied so strictly (and, for a time, successfully) was counterbalanced by the very Confucianist doctrine that the Qin leaders had tried to squelch.[62] This process had already begun in the early stages of the Han Dynasty, and it was to continue for the entire remaining twenty centuries of dynastic Chinese history— perhaps most gloriously in the Tang Code of the 7th century CE.

2. The Kaihuang Code and the Tang Code

a. Yang Jian

A recurrent theme in Chinese history is that of ambitious non-Chinese peoples from the north and west taking control of the central plains around the Yellow River (Huang He) and, from there, striving toward a unified empire. This was true of the Qin people in the fourth and third centuries BCE (the state of Qin was the westernmost of the so-called "Warring States"), and it was true several centuries later when the Sui people from north China established the Sui Dynasty in 581 CE, unifying China after a period of fragmentation following the collapse of the Han Dynasty in 220 CE.[63]

The central figure in that unification was the leader of the Sui people, a man named Yang Jian (often referred to in histories by his posthumous reign name of Wendi). One of the first initiatives taken by Yang Jian after assuming control over a significant portion of China was to strengthen the examination system:

> Examinations were conducted by the Board of Civil Office, they were held triennially and degrees were awarded at three levels. To obtain a lower degree a candidate had to demonstrate literary ability and knowledge of a classical work. The most prestigious degree ... assessed the candidate's broader learning. Successful candidates were appointed to official positions....[64]

---

61. This term is used in Ch'ü, *supra* note 1, esp. at 267 et seq. It is also used in Bodde and Morris, *supra* note 1, at 27.

62. For other references to the process by which Confucianist doctrine was re-introduced, see LCDC, *supra* note 1, at 98 n. 145, and sources cited there.

63. That period of fragmentation from 220 CE to 581 CE is reflected in the listing of principal Chinese dynasties and eras appearing in Box #6.2 *supra*. For a narrative describing that period of fragmentation, see J.A.G. Roberts, *supra* note 1, at 40. Roberts gives this summary:

> Between 220 and 589, apart from a brief interlude between 280 and 316, no one dynasty ruled the whole of China. Between 220 and 280 the empire was divided into three kingdoms. The Western Jin then briefly and ineffectually reunited the country, but from 316 there was a prolonged division between the north and the south. In the south, six dynasties established their capital at Jiankang, that is modern Nanjing. In the north, until 384 there was a period of extreme fragmentation known as the time of the Sixteen Kingdoms. Then the Toba, a branch of the Xianbei, established the Northern Wei dynasty with its capital at Luoyang. In 435 the dynasty split and a further period of political fragmentation ensued until Yang Jian not only conquered the north but also subdued the south and in 589, having established the Sui dynasty, reunified China. In 618 this dynasty was replaced by the Tang, and one of the most glorious periods in Chinese history commenced.

64. *Id.* at 48–49.

Another early initiative taken by Yang Jian was to promulgate the Kaihuang Code (*Kai Huang Lü*). He did this first in 581 (which was the same year he captured the capital city and assumed the throne in the north), and then he revised it in 583.[65] Although the Kaihuang Code also has been lost, it is considered "[a] major turning point" in the development of legal codes in China, in that its "format was adopted virtually unchanged by the earliest *surviving* code, that of T'ang of 653."[66]

b. The Tang Code

The recurrent theme mentioned above — that of tribes from the north and west taking control of China and proclaiming dynastic authority — is only the first part of a two-stage theme. The second stage involves a collapse of that dynasty within only a short time and the rise of a new, more durable dynasty in its place. Thus the Han replaced the Qin in about 206 BCE. Likewise, the Tang replaced the Sui in about 617 CE. It was in that year, 617, that the founding emperor of the Tang Dynasty promulgated the first version of the Tang Code, just after he had wrested control from the Sui emperor. The founding Tang emperor was Li Yuan; his reign name was Gaozu, the same (curiously and confusingly) as the reign name of the founding emperor of the Han Dynasty. Of most importance to us is that the Tang Code promulgated in 617 — as well as the most celebrated version of the Tang Code, which was promulgated in 653[67] — adopted Imperial Confucianism, that unified theory which took account of the *yin-yang* distinction and the seemingly all-pervasive significance of the "five elements", with a view to providing guidance for proper governance of the empire by carefully maintaining balance and what one authority has called the "Oneness of Heaven and Man."[68]

The Tang Code manifests this central concern for harmony in several ways. For example, the Code itself is to be regarded as representing the *yin* — the dark side of social control — in contrast with the *yang* influence of ritual, morality, and education. More concretely, the definition and imposition of punishment by death also reflects the *yin-yang* distinction. Death was under the *yin* or negative power, and so there were two death penalties — strangulation and decapitation — reflecting the fact that two is a *yin* number.[69]

Likewise, the Code is full of fives. For example, it establishes five principal types of punishments: beating with the light stick, beating with the heavy stick, penal servitude, life exile, and death. As shown in Box #6.5, the first Article in the Code lists five gradations of the first of those punishments. An accompanying commentary explains that this number is "in imitation" of the five elements. Several of the other types of punishments also have five gradations each. In addition, the number five appears in counting the degrees of family relationship and in indicating the significance of official privilege, both of which bear on the punishment prescribed in various provisions of the Code. A few representative specific provisions appear in Box #6.6.

---

65. See Johnson-1979, *supra* note 1, at 39. For details on the Kaihuang Code, see LCDC, *supra* note 1, at 114.

66. Bodde and Morris, *supra* note 1, at 58 (emphasis added).

67. J.A.G. Roberts, *supra* note 1, at 50.

68. The quoted phrase is from Smith and Weng, *supra* note 1, at 79.

69. As Professor Johnson notes, a discussion of this point appears also in Bodde and Morris, *supra* note 1, at 46–48. Johnson-1979, *supra* note 1, at 14.

Box #6.5 The Tang Code—Article 1[70]

Article 1
The Five Punishments with the Light Stick

Article: There are ten, twenty, thirty, forty, and fifty blows with the light stick (*ch'ih*).[a]

Commentary: Redemption by payment of copper (*shu*) is respectively one, two, three, four, and five *chin.*

Subcommentary: Ch'ih "light stick" means *chi* "to beat," and is also glossed as meaning *ch'ih* "to shame."[b] It means that if a person commits a small offense the law must discipline him. Therefore beating is used to shame him.

During the Han dynasty the light stick was made of bamboo. But at the present time it is made of *ch'u* wood. Thus the *Book of History* states: "The stick is employed in teaching [persons to be moral]." This is its meaning here.

.... The punishment of beating with the light stick is the lightest of punishments. During the changes of successive periods the severity of the punishments has varied. But all dynasties have looked toward a time when there would be no punishments. There would be only righteousness, and punishments would be discarded.

The *Hsiao ching yüan shen ch'i* [an apocryphal text on the *Book of Filial Piety*] states: "The sages made the five punishments in imitation of the five elements."

.... The light stick has five degrees, from ten to fifty blows. Therefore it is stated that the punishments with the light stick are five. The degrees of penal servitude and of beating with the heavy stick also conform to the same standard.

   a Ratchnevsky ... points out that this punishment of beating with the light stick was first used in the Han dynasty. It replaced mutilation following the edict of Emperor Wen in 167 B.C.... The light stick used during the T'ang dynasty was 3.5 *ch'ih* in length and 0.2 *ts'un* and 0.15 *ts'un* in diameter at the large and small ends, respectively....

   b [The second part of this definition] rests upon the homophones *ch'ih*, "light stick" and *ch'ih*, "to shame." This kind of definition occurs several times in the Code.

Box #6.6 The Tang Code—Selected Specific Provisions[71]

Article 122
Criticizing the Emperor

Article: 122.1a—All cases of criticizing the emperor where the circumstances are completely reprehensible are punished by decapitation.

     122.1b—If the circumstances are not completely reprehensible, the punishment is two years of penal servitude.

Article 367
Forging an Imperial Decree

Article: 367.1a—All cases of forging an imperial decree or of adding to or subtracting from the language in one are punished by strangulation.

     367.1b—If the imperial decree has not yet been put into force, the punishment is reduced one degree....

---

   70. The text of this Box #6.5 is quoted directly from Johnson-1979, *supra* note 1, at 55–57. Lettered footnotes in Box #6.5 appear as numbered footnotes in the original. Several other footnotes have been omitted, and Chinese characters have been omitted. The footnote reference to Rachnevsky is to Paul Ratchnevsky, Un Code des Yuan (1937).

   71. The text of this Box #6.6 is quoted directly from Johnson-1979, *supra* note 1, at the section numbers noted above.

Article 412
Illicit Sexual Intercourse with Great Aunts in the Male Line and
Female First Cousins Once Removed in the Male Line

Article: 412.1—All cases of illicit sexual intercourse with great aunts in the male line, female first cousins once removed in the male line, one's own female first cousins in
the male line, one's maternal aunts, the wives of one's brothers, and the wives of
one's brothers' sons, are punished by life exile at a distance of 2,000 *li.*

412.2—If force is used, the punishment is strangulation. . . .

Article 462
Drifting Aimlessly to Other Places

Article: 462.1a—All cases of those who do not run away but drift aimlessly to other places
are punished by ten blows with the light stick for the first ten days, increased by
one degree for each further ten days, and with a maximum punishment of one
hundred blows with the heavy stick. . . .

Article 499
Sentencing Decapitation for a Crime that Requires Strangulation

Article: 499.1a—All cases of sentencing a crime that should be punished by strangulation
to be punished by decapitation, or sentencing a crime that should be punished be
decapitation to be punished by strangulation, are punished by one year of penal
servitude.

499.1b—The punishment is the same with regard to suicide. . . .

As discussed above, the notion of harmony is also central to the concept of *lǐ*, especially in the form as developed by Confucius based on his view of the Western Zhou Dynasty. Indeed, as Derk Bodde has pointed out, the imperial codes can be viewed as
exemplifications of, or vehicles for, the principles of *lǐ*.[72] In particular, the concept of *lǐ*
places special emphasis on social status, on filial piety, and on loyalty to the emperor.[73]

The Tang Code also serves these values. It provides, for example, that social and political status will affect a person's liability for punishment. Political status is explicitly
taken into account in determining the amount of punishment to be imposed. One way
it does so appears in the so-called "Eight Deliberations", under which relatives of the emperor and persons in high position—defined as "active duty officials of the third rank
and above, titular officials of the second rank and above, and persons with noble titles of
the first rank"—are to be given special consideration in the imposition of punishment.

As for social status, similar differentiation of punishments appears quite clearly in the
Code. An offense by a commoner against a slave, for example, would generally trigger a
punishment that was two degrees less than if the offense were committed against another
commoner—such as 20 blows of the light bamboo instead of 40 blows of the light bamboo. An offense by a slave against a commoner would generally be punished two degrees
heavier than had the offender been a commoner. If a slave hit or beat a commoner so as
to break a limb, the punishment was strangulation. But if a master killed a slave who had
committed some offense, the penalty was one hundred blows with the heavy stick.

---

72. See Bodde and Morris, *supra* note 1, at 29–38. See also Ch'ü, *supra* note 1 at 278–279.

73. As noted above, the original views of Confucius, especially on social status, were later modified by his disciples, beginning with Mengzi and Xunzi.

Even more striking—and, again, entirely consistent with the principles of *lǐ*—is the Code's treatment of filial piety. One of the "Ten Abominations" (most heinous crimes) is "lack of filial piety," and it triggered special punishment. As Professor Johnson expresses it, "[f]ew greater crimes were possible in T'ang China than for a son to strike his father, while a father who beat his son was not committing any crime at all."[74]

The Tang Code established a pattern that would be followed with little interruption for the next thousand years of Chinese legal history. That long stretch of time saw four main dynasties: the Song, the Yüan, the Ming, and the Qing. Each of those dynasties added its own stitches to the pattern set by the Tang Code.[75]

3. The Song, Yüan, Ming, and Qing Codes
a. *Song, Yüan, and Ming continuity*

For example, the Song Dynasty (starting around 960 CE) almost immediately re-enacted the Tang Code intact, and then gradually supplemented its provisions with new edicts and regulations. The Yüan rulers (starting with Kublai Khan around 1279) at first took a different approach, temporarily displacing traditional codes with rules that drew from the customary laws of the Mongols, but then the Yüan rulers produced legal "codes" that increasingly lost their Mongolian character in favor of Chinese culture and institutions.[76] Thus the momentum of the Chinese tradition of legal codification carried through the Song and the Yüan dynasties despite the fact that the latter represented the first complete conquest of China by a foreign power.

The return of China to Chinese control in the Ming Dynasty (starting around 1368) brought a renewed enthusiasm for the codification process, resulting in the promulgation of several versions of a Ming Code, the most important of which appeared in 1389. That Ming Code introduced some important structural changes but nevertheless retained the central features of the Tang Code promulgated about seven centuries earlier. That is, it was fundamentally penal in character, prescribing specific, graduated punishments for precisely-defined crimes that were regarded as threatening to a centralized, authoritarian political order that itself reflected Imperial Confucianism.

In the interest of brevity, let us pass over these Song, Yüan, and Ming dynasties and codes without pausing[77] and direct our attention instead to the Qing legal system—and in that way view the dynastic legal codes at their highest point of sophistication. In particular, let us look at (1) some structural and substantive matters, (2) the role of the district magistrate in applying the law, (3) how the Qing Code (and those applying it) dealt with matters that Western lawyers would call "civil law", and (4) what portion of people's

---

74. Johnson-1979, *supra* note 1, at 31–32. He points out that close family relationships would reduce the degree of punishment for robbery, although it would generally increase it for crimes against the person. *Id.* at 32.

75. See Box #6.2, *supra*, for a nutshell account of Chinese dynastic history, and Box #6.3, *supra* for highlights of Chinese legal history—including some of the developments referred to in the following several paragraphs.

76. The Yüan legislation lacked the degree of structural integrity and rational organization that the Song and Tang codes had. Hence my use of quotation marks around the word "codes" and the reference in Box #6.3, *supra*, to the Treatises of 1291 and 1331.

77. For a discussion of these periods of Chinese dynastic legal history, with special emphasis on codes and other forms of law and government, see LCDC, *supra* note 1, at Chapter V and section I of Chapter VI.

behavior was governed by the Code and what portion was governed instead by extra-legal influences and institutions.

b. Qing Code—general structure and substance

In terms of structure, the Qing Code simply repeated its predecessor, the Ming Code, in which one large chapter or book dealt with "terms and general principles"—covering such things as the five punishments, the ten "great wrongs" (referred to earlier in the context of the Tang Code, as the "Ten Abominations"), and the like—and another six chapters or books had rules relating to each of the six government departments into which the imperial bureaucracy was divided. By the time of the first Qing Code, which was issued in 1646 (a mere two years after the Qing Dynasty had established itself upon defeating the Ming leadership), that over-all structure had been in place (via the Ming Code) for several hundred years.

The continuity in structure was matched by a continuity in substance—that is, in the number of and even the specific content of the provisions of the Qing Code. The first Qing Code was "largely a copy of the Ming Code."[78] Only after about 80 years had gone by were any substantial changes made to the Qing Code, and even then the number of articles in the Code was reduced by only five percent—from 460, as inherited from the Ming Code of 1389, to 436.[79] Moreover, the content of many articles also remained largely unchanged.

Indeed, the continuity of Chinese codification extends beyond merely this Ming-Qing similarity. As noted above, the Tang Code drew heavily on the Sui (Kaihuang) Code. Later, numerous provisions of Yüan law had been drawn directly from Tang law; now, corresponding provisions, often with rather similar formulations, were also to be found in the Qing Code. Indeed, a review of many Qing Code provisions shows a direct line of ancestry—a sort of "pedigree"—going right on back to provisions first appearing roughly a thousand years earlier in the Tang Code,[80] the earliest of the codes available to us. In fact, one source asserts "that 30 to 40 per cent of the statutes of the Ch'ing [Qing] Code go back unchanged to the T'ang Code of 635."[81]

c. The district magistrate

How were these provisions, and the Qing Code in general, actually applied in practice? To understand this requires a summary of the role of a particular class of government official—the district magistrate. The district (*xian, hsien*) was the lowest territorial level in the bureaucratic hierarchy.[82] Qing China had about 1,200 districts, each with a population of 200,000 or more.[83] The following description explains the role of the magistrate within each district.

---

78. Bodde and Morris, *supra* note 1, at 60.

79. *Id.*

80. For a review of several sets of such provisions, see LCDC, *supra* note 1, at 201–205.

81. Bodde and Morris, *supra* note 1, at 63, citing a Chinese legal historian. See also Johnson-1979, *supra* note 1, at 9.

82. *Id.* at 4. The *xian* (*hsien*) was ultimately responsible to the emperor, who ruled through the various boards and commissions. "Each of the eighteen provinces was headed by a governor (often two or three provinces came under a governor-general) who directed the activities of the mandarins [Confucian bureaucrats] at the subdivision levels of circuit, prefecture, department, and district." Richard C. DeAngelis, "People's Republic of China," appearing as Chapter 12 in A.N. Katz, ed., Legal Traditions and Systems (1986), at 247.

83. DeAngelis, *supra* note 82, at 247. For an account of the development of the *xian* (*hsien*) in ancient China, see Derk Bodde, China's First Unifier: A Study of the Ch'in Dynasty as Seen in

The magistrate's office (*yamen*) was located in one of the larger cities [in the *hsien*, or *xian*] with a population that numbered in the tens of thousands and bore the entire responsibility for local government of the hsien, including the rural villages that ranged in size from a few hundred people to market town communities of several thousands.

Although the local magistrate was the lowest ranking officer in the imperial hierarchy, his position is not analogous to the lowest echelon of Western civil service bureaucrats. The magistrate was not on the bottom rung of a career ladder ...; more often than not, the office represented the apex of a government career....

Candidates for the imperial civil service prepared themselves through a classical Chinese education that placed emphasis on Confucian philosophy and literary and artistic achievement. This education virtually assured that most, though not all, came from comfortable economic backgrounds....

The education and examination of scholars showed little regard for training in the mundane administrative, economic, or legal skills associated with the post of magistrate....

Well versed in poetry and literature, ... the magistrate often lacked training in his two most important responsibilities: judicial administration and tax collection. The duties of the magistrate were awesome. His trust was to maintain the peace of the hsien, to serve as the highest judicial officer, and to ensure the economic well-being of the community by overseeing public works, flood control, disaster relief, government granaries, and an equitable tax administration....

The routine work of the yamen [magistrate's office] was handled by the magistrate's staff. This included personnel of various grades such as runner and clerks.... The clerks were government-paid employees whose ... primary responsibility was record-keeping and processing of enormous numbers of documents.... [T]he clerks posed a constant threat to the new magistrate of limited experience. That the magistrate was at all able to carry out the responsibilities associated with his office was due to the use of private secretaries.

The private secretaries were experts in the administration of law and taxation.... Private secretaries were not government officials but were considered the equal of officials and superior to the clerks. They were paid by the magistrate and given room and board within the yamen, where they maintained close contact with the magistrate.

The most important of the private secretaries was the legal secretary, whose status and salary were greater than the others.... The legal secretary had the enormous responsibility of managing the magistrate's legal work, closely scrutinized by the magistrate's superiors, in a system involving a complex law code and detailed corpus of administrative regulations.... All cases of homicide and larceny came directly under the secretary of law; [he] would review complaints and write a formal rescript for the magistrate's approval.

THE LIFE OF LI Ssü 238–243 (1938 & 1967). For extensive accounts of the *xian* (*hsien*), the district magistrate, and the Qing administrative regime into which they fit, see generally T'ung-Tsu Ch'ü, LOCAL GOVERNMENT IN CHINA UNDER THE CH'ING (1962), and Thomas A. Metzger, THE INTERNAL ORGANIZATION OF CH'ING BUREAUCRACY: LEGAL, NORMATIVE, AND COMMUNICATION ASPECTS (1973).

The magistrate was the only official who served as trial judge in his district of several hundred thousand people. Court was held only six or seven months a year due to prescribed recesses and holidays. Criminal cases attracted his immediate attention and, upon the registration of a complaint, were investigated under the auspices of the legal secretary.[84]

From this excerpt we see the pivotal role played by the district magistrate. Viewed from his perspective, the Qing Code represented a set of instructions about how to handle a broad variety of circumstances that bore on the ability of the emperor to govern the empire. Given the lack of formal training in matters of law and public policy,[85] it is hardly surprising that this set of instructions (the Code) needed to be extremely detailed.

d. Civil law under the Qing Code

Most of the Qing Code provisions give the appearance of criminal law rather than civil law. In other words, from a Western perspective, the Qing Code (like all of its predecessors as referred to earlier in this book) seems to constitute a criminal code that focuses entirely on the imposition of specific punishments for specific behavior that is regarded as dangerous to the state in some way. This impression is supported by the formulation of the provisions themselves: each was constructed as an "if-then" statement. The "if" part of the statement described a certain type of act or behavior; the "then" part of the statement prescribes a specific punishment. A few representative provisions of the Qing Code, for example, appear in Box #6.7.

Box #6.7 Sample Provisions from the Qing Code[86]

Plotting Rebellion

In the case of plotting rebellion and high treason, where there is joint plotting, ... all will be put to death by slicing. [The perpetrator's] paternal grandfather, father, sons, sons' sons, brothers, and those living in the same household ... [and male relatives] sixteen years or older, ... will all be beheaded. His [male relatives] fifteen years or under, as well as [his] mother, daughter, wife, concubines, [unmarried sisters, and certain other named relatives] will all be given into the households of meritorious officials as slaves. The property [of the perpetrator] will be forfeit to the government.

Illicit Sexual Relations (Fornication)

In the case of fornication with consent, the punishment is 80 strokes of the heavy bamboo. If [the woman] has a husband, the punishment is 90 strokes of the heavy bamboo.

If there is fornication with force, the punishment is strangulation. If it is not consummated, the punishment is 100 strokes of the heavy bamboo and exile to 3000 *li*....

In the case of fornication with force, the woman is not punished.

Beating Another Person

Everyone who engages in an affray or inflicts blows and, using hands or feet, strikes another but does not cause injury, will receive 20 strokes of the light bamboo. If he causes injury,

---

84. DeAngelis, *supra* note 82, at 247–251.

85. "The practice of earlier dynasties that the education of officials show[s] some concern with matters of law and public policy was abandoned in the Ming and Qing era, when the emphasis shifted to Confucian orthodoxy and literary accomplishments." *Id.* at 247.

86. As translated by Professor Jones in William C. Jones, THE GREAT QING CODE (1994), at pages 237 (rebellion), 285 (beating), 347 (fornication), and 360 (escape). For purposes of illustration, I have omitted most of the interlineary commentary appearing in Jones' translation of the Qing Code.

or if, by using some other object, he inflicts a blow on another and does not cause injury, he will receive 10 strokes of the light bamboo. [If the skin which is struck] turns blue or red [and] there is a swelling, this is an "injury".... If someone pulls out a square *cun* of hair or more, then punish with 50 strokes of the light bamboo. [If someone strikes another] and blood flows from the ears or eyes and there is internal injury and [the victim] spits blood, then punish with 80 strokes of the heavy bamboo....

If someone breaks another's tooth, or tears off a finger from the hand, or a toe from the foot, or injures one eye or wounds another's ear or nose ... then the punishment is 100 strokes of the heavy bamboo.... If someone breaks two teeth, or two fingers, or toes, or above, ... then the penalty is 60 strokes of the heavy bamboo and penal servitude of one year.

Officers Who Allow Thieves to Escape

Everyone charged with arresting persons who receives [an] order to pursue an offender and presents pretexts [for not going] and does not go will ... receive the penalty for the offence [committed by] the offender reduced one degree.

The provisions shown in Box #6.7 do indeed give the Qing Code the appearance of a body of criminal law, at least when viewed from a Western perspective. Appearances can be deceiving, however, and perspectives can be narrow. One of the most strongly-held convictions expressed by careful observers of China—its history, its culture, its law—is that Western concepts translate poorly into that setting. Some writers, for example, warn Westerners about the danger of trying to examine China through a telescope and seeing only their own reflection in the lens.[87] Professor Jones, in introducing his translation of the Qing Code, emphasizes the inappropriateness and futility of trying to understand Chinese law on Western terms and "with expectations formed by exposure to Western ideas about law."[88]

In particular, Jones makes the following observations that bear on the question of whether the law of the Qing Code is "civil law" or "criminal law."

One of the aspects [of the Qing Code] that especially strikes the Western observer is that the Code is not much concerned with the disputes of private individuals, nor with the notion of 'rights'. We are accustomed to think that a legal system is primarily a social institution within which 'persons'—private individuals, or groups of individuals, or even the state—can make claims against other persons and have these resolved by a neutral trier of fact and law.... We also tend to think that the laws applied by the courts will deal to a very considerable extent with private law—torts, contracts, property, and the like.... These are all aspects of the legal systems we are familiar with ... [and] they reflect the [fact that much of Western law] was formed by Roman law, ... [which arose] in a very small and predominately agricultural community with a weak government. As a consequence, the legal problems that it dealt with in the formative period [focused on] disputes between private individuals that arose out of torts, simple contracts, and succession.... This approach has been maintained down to the present.... Civil law is at the heart of Western law, and ... Western jurists use a model of the universe composed of discrete entities—persons who create legal obligations by the exercise of their individuals wills....

---

87. "China is so distant, culturally as well as geographically, that the metaphor of gazing outward through a telescope seems natural. Unless we focus well, however, another metaphor may better describe what takes place: If our gaze searches for what our preconceptions suggest we should find, we may see only Others, who are reverse images of ourselves." Stanley B. Lubman, BIRD IN A CAGE: LEGAL REFORM IN CHINA AFTER MAO 12 (1999), citing Victor H. Li, LAW WITHOUT LAWYERS (1977).

88. Jones, *supra* note 1, at 4.

The situation in China was radically different. The polity of China consisted of a highly centralized government headed by an absolute ruler who ruled by means of a bureaucracy. The primary obligation of every Chinese was to fulfil the duties assigned to him by the Emperor. All human activities had to be carried on so as to fit into his scheme for directing society. Consequently one would expect the imperial law or Code to take note of human activity only as it was perceived to affect imperial policies. It was natural that the primary focus of attention would be the activities of bureaucrats in the performance of their duties, not the activities of ordinary human beings in their private lives.... In China the subject matter of Roman civil law was considered only when it affected the interests of the Emperor.

Thus marriage was rather thoroughly dealt with since marriage and the family system were basic to the polity. [Likewise, an] institution that was similar to the English mortgage, the *dian*, was given considerable space, presumably because it was important to know who owned land so that the government could collect the taxes on it.... But except for torts, which are treated together with crimes, very little attention is paid to private matters....

One consequence of the difference in points of view is that the categories of Western law are meaningless within the Chinese system of formal law, that is, the Code. One cannot speak of the Code as being a body of civil or criminal law nor of its being a combination of the two. It is obvious that civil law as the law which deals with the private concerns of citizens from the point of view of those citizens did not exist in the Code. There were no citizens for one thing, only subjects. More importantly the Code dealt with all matters from the point of view of the ruler.[89]

The Code itself, according to this view, is neither criminal nor civil in character, if we use those terms from a Western perspective. Perhaps Professor Jones would have us see it as a complex network of rules and procedures, worked out over many centuries, directing the bureaucrats serving the Emperor (especially the district magistrates primarily responsible for applying the law) as to how they should handle the vast array of circumstances and behavior that were important to the Emperor, whose responsibility it was to maintain political control and social harmony within the territory of China. Although the Code's concentration on imposing punishments for specified behaviors gives it the look of a criminal code, perhaps its many provisions on administrative and personnel matters give it the look of a code of government structure and procedure; and its many provisions on tax, land registration, and imperial treasuries might give it the look of a set of fiscal regulations; and maybe its many provisions on sacrifices, imperial ceremonies, and care for family members give it the look of a moral or religious

---

89. Jones, *supra* note 1, at 4–8. Father Laszlo Ladany, a Hungarian born Jesuit who went to China as a missionary and then became an expert on Chinese law and politics, offers a similar view of the difference between Western law and Chinese law:

> The Chinese and European legal systems are different in basic structure. The *praetor* in classical Roman law adjudicated the complaints of individuals. Law, one can say, came from below. In China it came from above. The Chinese legal system defined the duties and obligations of individuals and this in turn indirectly protected the rights of the individuals.... [So it] is far from the truth to say that in ancient Chinese law there was no 'civil law', but the starting points in China and in the West were different. The Western system takes as its starting-point the rights claimed by the individual. The Chinese system begins with the state as the guardian of rights and the punisher of transgressors.

Laszlo Ladany, LAW AND LEGALITY IN CHINA: THE TESTAMENT OF A CHINA WATCHER 33 (1992).

code. In all these respects, however, the Code must be seen as having a different audience from that which much of Western law (whether codified or not) typically has. The audience of the Qing Code, and that of its predecessors, was the official bureaucracy responsible for keeping the machinery of dynastic administrative control in good running order.

If the Code is viewed from that perspective, it actually becomes easier to regard it as speaking to many of the same issues as Western law does. Some important recent scholarship does view the code from that perspective. For example, a collection of articles emerging from a 1991 conference on "Civil Law in Chinese History" examines the treatment that the Qing Code gave to matters of private property, succession, marital relations, contract, and debt.[90] Far from concluding that these matters were outside the ambit of the Code and its application, the articles taken together suggest that despite the different audience to which the Code was primarily addressed (the bureaucracy rather than the individual), the Code did in fact serve, at least in its later versions, as the foundation for protecting a wide range of private interests — or *minshi*, which is typically translated as "people's matters."[91] More specifically, these key points emerge from this recent scholarship[92]:

- Although the Qing Code dealt mainly, at least on the surface, with *xingshi*, or "punishment matters," it also addressed at least obliquely some topics covered by what is now referred to as *minshi* (people's matters) — for instance, debt, markets, land and houses, marriages, succession, and family division.

- Past American scholarship focused on criminal law (that is, viewing the dynastic codes, including that of the Qing, as being predominantly criminal in nature), mainly because of the limitations of available materials. In particular, (i) "[i]mportant civil stipulations in the Qing code … are often buried in the middle of paragraphs under misleading headings, and wrapped up in administrative concerns such as taxation," and (ii) disputes over such civil matters "were to be handled on the authority of the local magistrates, without review by upper levels" and therefore those disputes did not show up in compilations of cases, especially the records of local courts.

- Not only was the substantive law regarding *minshi* hidden from the view of Westerners; the procedural law (that is, whether and how *minshi* litigation occurred) was also hidden. As a result, past scholarship on the Qing legal system "added up to an image of that system either as little concerned with civil matters or, when it did deal with civil cases, as operating at best as a mediator, relying on Confucian morality and human compassion for guidance."

---

90. Kathryn Bernhardt and Philip C.C. Huang, eds., CIVIL LAW IN QING AND REPUBLICAN CHINA (1994) [hereinafter cited as Bernhardt-Huang-1991]. For a follow-up work on related topics, see Philip C.C. Huang, CIVIL JUSTICE IN CHINA: REPRESENTATION AND PRACTICE IN THE QING (1996), and Philip C.C.Huang, CODE, CUSTOM, AND LEGAL PRACTICE IN CHINA: THE QING AND THE REPUBLIC COMPARED (2001).

91. See generally Kathryn Bernhardt and Philip C.C. Huang, *Civil Law in Qing and Republican China: The Issues* [hereinafter cited as Bernhardt-Huang-Issues], appearing as the introductory Chapter 1 in Bernhardt-Huang-1991, *supra* note 90. Another translation of *minshi* would be "civil matters", rather than "people's matters". The use of the term "civil matters" would better highlight the distinction between *minshi* and *xingshi* (punishment matters, or criminal law). However, Bernhardt and Huang opt for "people's matters" in translating *minshi*.

92. All of the details, including quoted passages, given below are drawn from Bernhardt-Huang-Issues, *supra* note 91.

- However, that view is distorted. "The opening of local archives in China to Western scholars in the 1980s" has led to research proving that by the late 1800s "civil
  cases formed a major part of the caseload of local courts." Moreover, court judgments arising from those cases "were almost always based on readily identifiable
  statutes and sub-statutes" in the Qing Code, so that "operationally the most important parts of the Qing code consisted in later adjustments and additions that
  were made in response to changing social realities."

The view that is emerging, then, from recent research is that of a "layered" Qing Code.[93]
The most prominent layers reflect the ancient debate between Legalists and Confucianists — a debate that I highlighted above in subsection IB2 of this chapter. The Code is Legalist in its emphasis on punishment, and it is Confucianist in the emphasis it gives to various
matters of ritual and the differentiation of proper roles in society. Underneath these
prominent layers, however, according to views emerging very recently, is a third layer of
provisions that address *minshi* (people's matters). These, it is said, took on great importance during the period of the Qing Dynasty as a "way in which codified law adapted to
social change."[94]

e. Rules of behavior outside the code

But did it adapt fast enough? That is, just how impressed should we be by recent findings and analyses showing that the Qing Code, at least in its closing decades, did respond
to changing realities and social demands by adding a third (and deeper) layer of provisions focusing on *minshi* (people's matters)?

In my view, these discoveries are intriguing but should not blind us to the fundamental characteristic of all the dynastic Chinese legal codes: their substantive coverage was inherently limited because their audience and their aims were limited. Derk Bodde has pointed
out that "Chinese traditional society ... was by no means a legally oriented society despite
the fact that it produced a large and intellectually impressive body of codified law."[95] Instead,
the ordinary man's behavior, in China perhaps more than in most other civilizations,

> was shaped far more by the pervasive influence of custom and the usages of pro-
> priety than by any formally enacted system of law. The clan into which he was
> born, the guild of which he might become a member, the group of gentry el-
> ders holding informal sway in his rural community — these and other extra-legal
> bodies helped to smooth the inevitable frictions in Chinese society by inculcat-
> ing moral precepts upon their members, mediating disputes, or, if need arose,
> imposing disciplinary sanctions and penalties.[96]

As another author has expressed it, "Chinese society had built in powerful forces for
self-regulation" which included "traditions of the family and clan and other associations

---

93. This image of "layering" in the Qing Code is drawn from the 1996 and 2001 works of Huang,
cited *supra* note 90.

94. Bernhardt-Huang-Issues, *supra* note 91, at 7, summarizing the findings in Jing Junjian, *Legislation Related to the Civil Economy in the Qing Dynasty*, appearing as Chapter 3 in Bernhardt-Huang-
1991, *supra* note 90, at 42–84.

95. Bodde and Morris, *supra* note 1, at 3–4.

96. *Id.* at 5–6.

and occupational grouping"; and so for the most part, "disputes were settled informally and by appealing to middlemen and village elders, with as little recourse as possible to courts of law."[97]

To place this in the context of Qing China: for the bulk of the populace, personal behavior was most directly and importantly influenced not by the Qing Code but instead by traditional rules of moral and ethical conduct among members of family and society. The *content* of those traditional rules, like the content of the Code, was heavily influenced by Confucianist values that had matured and infiltrated Chinese culture over the centuries that had elapsed since Confucius had lived and taught. But the *medium* by which those rules became part of society was not so much the Code itself as it was the network of other, "extra-legal" institutions.

As Chinese society changed—especially with increasingly intense intercourse of all kinds with Western society—pressure grew for legal rules whose *audience* was wider than merely the bureaucracy of the imperial government and whose *aims* were wider than merely to protect the society from chaos and the emperor from challenge. In short, the law codes that so distinguish Chinese dynastic legal tradition—even the Qing Code at its highest degree of sophistication—did not occupy a very large portion of the total area of rules governing human behavior in China.[98]

D. Key Themes in Dynastic Chinese Law

The preceding sections of this chapter have offered a brief overview of Chinese dynastic legal history, giving some special attention to two aspects that played especially leading roles in that history: (i) the Confucianist-Legalist debate that was settled for the most part in the third and second centuries BCE and (ii) the law codes that served, in part, as the vehicles by which the outcome of that debate was carried forward with remarkable continuity for many centuries—indeed, all the way up to the early 20th century. Let us now consider a cluster of important themes that emerge from that historical survey. Doing so will help us compare China's dynastic legal tradition with China's contemporary legal system.

Four key themes will receive our attention in the following paragraphs. They relate to (i) the remarkable continuity of China's traditional law, (ii) how Chinese dynastic law consistently deflected, filtered, or swallowed outside influences that might easily have displaced the traditional structure had it been weaker or less well-entrenched, (iii) what role, if any, there was for the "rule of law" in dynastic China, and (iv) the manner in which Imperial Confucianism served as a central "legal ethic" in dynastic China.

---

97. Pye, *supra* note 1, at 72.

98. For further discussion of this point, see Johnson-1997, *supra* note 1, at 5 (noting that the Tang Code "was regarded as the last means by which to protect society when all other attempts to promote desirable behavior in an individual or family had failed"); Kim, *supra* note 1, at 20 (asserting that traditional Chinese law is more of a customary law based on *lǐ* than a positive, written statutory law). This point also runs throughout Ch'ü, *supra* note 1.

1. Law and Continuity

To a Western observer, one of the most remarkable features of China is the continuity of its civilization, however one may wish to define "civilization." Using China's own definition of civilization as bound up importantly with writing—indeed, the Chinese word for "civilization" refers explicitly to writing[99]—one could conclude that China has been *legally* civilized for at least two and a half millennia, since the time that the first *xíng shū* (books of punishment) were etched on the bronze tripod vessels in 536 BCE,[100] and possibly for many centuries before that.[101] Moreover, China's history shows another kind of continuity: political continuity. At least since the centralization of control that occurred in the Qin Dynasty, China has seen a degree of political continuity (manifesting itself in the "dynastic cycle" referred to early in this chapter) that is unmatched by societies elsewhere— or at least by those in Western Europe, whose influence on the rest of the world (through colonization and conquest) has been so heavy. For example, while Western Europe went through a series of different forms of political organization—an integrated empire followed by highly disintegrated feudal fragmentation followed by a cluster of nation-states— China's form of dynastic political organization endured for century after century.

I have tried to capture in diagram in Box #6.8 the image that comes to mind for me as I consider the contrast between (1) China's form of dynastic political organization and (2) the varying forms of political organization in Western European countries over many centuries, through the end of the 19th century. The relatively continuous thick line in the top portion of the diagram in Box #6.8 represents, in stylized form, dynastic China's relative political unity, durability, and continuity—undulating somewhat and with some interruptions to reflect periods of instability that were part of the dynastic cycle from about the time of the Qin Dynasty. By contrast, the sequence of lines—some solid, some dashed, some dotted—in the middle portion of the diagram in Box #6.8 represents Western Europe's political development over roughly the same period, and particularly its shift from unity (under the Roman Republic and then Roman Empire) to disunity (following the collapse of the Roman Empire in the West) and the gradual coalescence of separate nation-states starting around about 1500. Out of deference to the many indigenous peoples of the world who have tried (largely without success) to withstand the attacks of Western powers—particularly since the time that those powers began their frenzy of colonization and conquest starting around 1500—I have included at the lower portion of the diagram in Box #6.8 a single thin line representing (collectively) the native (Indian) tribes and nations of the North American continent.

---

99. The following explanation by the great authority on Chinese law, Derk Bodde, as quoted in LCDC, *supra* note 1, at 83–84, attests to this connection: "Our word 'civilization' goes back to a Latin root having to do with 'citizen' and 'city.' The Chinese counterpart, actually a binom, *wen hua*, literally means 'the transforming [i.e., civilizing] influence of writing.' In other words, for us the essence of civilization is urbanization; for the Chinese it is the art of writing."

100. This event was referred to above. See text accompanying note 31, *supra*, as well as reference to the *xíng shū* in Box #6.3 and Box #6.4. For further details on the *xíng shū* and their significance, see LCDC, *supra* note 1, at 48–58.

101. See LCDC, *supra* note 1, at 54–56 for the view that written law, even codified law of a sort, existed as early as the very beginning of the Zhou dynasty, perhaps around 1100 BCE.

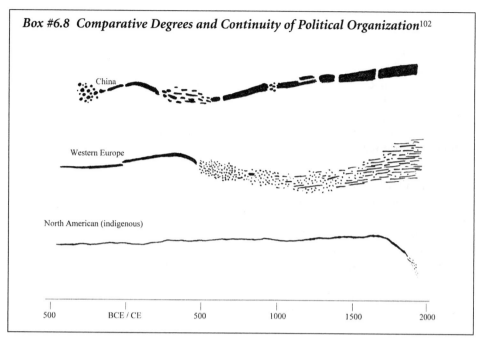

Box #6.8 Comparative Degrees and Continuity of Political Organization[102]

What kind of relationship, if any, might we see between (i) China's continuity of civilization and continuity of political organization (ii) China's legal codification efforts as I have summarized them earlier in this section? I offer below, in an abbreviated form, my own views on this question—cognizant, of course, of the likelihood that numerous factors are surely at play in these kinds of continuity that I have highlighted.[103]

---

102. The different hefts of the lines are intended to reflect (in very rough fashion) different sizes of population in the societies represented. The rising or falling of lines is intended to reflect changes in economic and political power.

103. One such possible factor, unrelated to law, is what Professor Mary Wong has observed in helping me think through these issues:

> [An interesting question is] why the Chinese system seems to be relatively stable throughout the millennia. One distinctive aspect of Chinese culture is the compliance or submissiveness of the general populace, unless faced with extreme poverty or calamities. Compare and contrast this with the Western way, which is much more out-spoken, ready to revolt or react. Consider the reason behind this stark difference. Buddhism and Taoism are both philosophies and religions. They are more powerful as philosophies and a few emperors (and empress) of China were Buddhists and Taoists. They are religions at the secular level with key concepts of Buddhist nirvana and other-worldliness and placidness and Daoist "wu-wei" (no aggressive pro-action). [Some of these points appear in the discussion of Neo-Confucianism in Chapter Seven, below.] The preachings of release from worldly affairs and transcendence had permeated the entire Chinese civilization for the past thousand of years. I think the impact of these two philosophies and religions on the general beatitude of the Chinese populace contributed to the non-resistance [to and long durability of] dynastic rule.

E-mail correspondence with Professor Mary Wong, June 29, 2008. John King Fairbank has made a similar observation in noting "the docility of the Chinese peasantry, who were remarkably inured to following the dictates of authority because it represented the peace and order on which their livelihood depended." Fairbank, *supra* note 1, at 369. Another way of characterizing Chinese culture, similar to focusing on its "compliance" or "submissiveness", is to emphasize that it is comfortable with paternalism.

a. Qin unification

The Qin Dynasty (221–206 BCE) was a time of meltdown for both Confucianism (already modified from the form that Confucius first espoused) and Legalism (which had already proven effective in the Qin state before the unification under Qin Shi Huangdi). Indeed, one might see the fires that were set at the orders of Li Si and Qin Shi Huangdi to burn the classical Confucianist literature[104] as serving only to melt Confucianism rather than to burn it away; and, in like fashion, one might see the intensity with which the Qin leaders imposed Legalist theories as causing those theories also to overheat and melt down.

In short, to use the metaphor that I introduced earlier, the Qin Dynasty may be characterized as a fiercely hot cauldron that melted and merged those two ingredients—Confucianism and Legalism—which had developed in the sixth, fifth, and fourth centuries BCE. When the molten mass cooled—that is, when the Han Dynasty had succeeded in extinguishing the fires of the Qin Dynasty—Legalism and Confucianism were inextricably bound together, in a new compound material, a legal alloy, that was strong enough to last for the next two thousand years as a central core for China's government and culture. A principal manifestation of this new alloy was the Han Code, which revealed a merger of practical Legalism and Imperial Confucianism.

b. Continuity and legal conservatism

Once the pattern for Chinese codification was set in the Han Code, that pattern stood the tests of time. We might see the first and most important of those tests coming with the reunification of China under the Sui, in the late 6th century. Perhaps Yang Jian, the founder of the Sui Dynasty, should receive credit not just for the reunification itself[105] but also for having revived and refined the pattern of codification, for it was he (born and raised a Buddhist, ironically) who promulgated the Kaihuang Code and gave shape to the examination system that was to endure throughout the remainder of dynastic Chinese history.[106] The Kaihuang Code, by formalizing the five punishments and the Ten Abominations, reasserted the importance of the Legalist-Confucianist alloy that had been forged in the Qin-Han period, and the Sui then passed along that alloy to the Tang.

The Tang emperors, especially the first two of them, used that Legalist-Confucianist alloy in creating various versions of the Tang Code, which then served as a model for all the Chinese dynastic legal codes that followed, in ways that are obvious to us in comparing provisions in those various codes, especially the Ming and Qing codes. As noted above, many provisions of the Qing Code can be traced directly to (and have

---

If Western (especially American) society can be likened to a population of dragonflies, with each dragonfly operating more or less independently, Chinese society might be likened to a colony of honeybees, with each bee operating entirely within a paternalistic (or more precisely maternalistic) structure. The former emphasizes individualism; the latter emphasizes collectivism. All such images, naturally, are broad generalizations.

104. See *supra* note 34 and accompanying text.

105. For a more complete description than was offered above regarding Yang Jian's rise to prominence, the establishment of the Sui dynasty, and the reunification and "sinicization" of the country, see LCDC, *supra* note 1, at 113–114.

106. For a more complete account of the examination system and the Kaihuang Code, see *id.* at 114–115.

formulations that are nearly identical to) those of the Tang Code. Thus the continuity of the codes may be seen as a form of legal conservatism—a conserving of the grand solution (the Legalist-Confucianist alloy) that had emerged from the Qin-Han period.

c. Codes as cultural constitutions

This might seem strange. That is, it probably strikes most modern Western observers as quite odd that many of the same provisions appearing in the Tang Code would appear also in the Qing Code. One might be tempted to ask, "would not the natural changes occurring in economic, political, and social circumstances require substantial changes in the legal provisions as well?"

My own view is that this question itself reveals two assumptions that probably do not have much validity in the context of dynastic China. The first assumption is that change is natural; the second assumption is that when change does occur, the law should bend to accommodate it. Perhaps a society whose underlying cultural philosophy centers on harmony, ritual, stability, and moral virtue—as dynastic Chinese society clearly did[107]—does not have much interest in change, does not regard it as natural, and in particular does not see the law as a servant of change, bending to the vagaries (and mistakes) of new and untried ideas.

In this regard, the Chinese dynastic codes may be viewed as constitutions rather than ordinary laws. By their nature, constitutions (as we see them in nation-states today) set forth the less changeable, more fundamental principles that a political society regards as central to its identity. Some countries, especially the United States with its relatively old constitution, are loath to tinker and fiddle with those fundamental principles, even if they sometimes seem unresponsive to contemporary problems. In other countries, especially civil law countries, the same function—expressing key legal principles—is served by a civil code. This is true for the French, whose civil code, dating from Napoleon, is nearly as old as the U.S. constitution, commands similar respect, and has retained most of the same structure (and some of the same content) with which it was first born two hundred years ago.

The same was true of the Chinese codes. The founding emperors of several new dynasties apparently regarded the enactment of a legal code as essential to their efforts to take control and prove their legitimacy. For example, as noted earlier in this chapter, Yang Jian issued a legal code in the first year of his newly-declared Sui Dynasty (581);[108] Gaozu (Li Yuan), the founder of the Tang Dynasty, issued a legal code as soon as he gained control of the capital city in 617, which was actually before his reign officially began, and then promulgated revised codes in 619 and 624, drawing heavily on the Sui Code;[109] the Song Code was issued in just the fourth year after the founding of the dynasty, and it preserved the Tang Code in its entirety.[110] It probably did so in part because the Tang Code was regarded as a "constitutional" document. Indeed, although the Song government essentially re-issued the Tang Code, it also attached

---

107. For accounts of how Confucianism includes these features, see *id.* at 35–36, 49. For a description of these influences at work in the Tang Code, see *id.* at 119–121.

108. For further details in this regard, see *id.* at 114.

109. See *id.* at 118.

110. See *id.* at 143–144.

new provisions to several sections of that code, and the new provisions took priority over the old ones.[111]

Likewise, later dynasties (especially the Qing) developed elaborate systems of sub-statutes and commentaries by which the codes sought to address new circumstances as they arose—for example, economic concerns and "civil" demands of the 19th century[112]—while preserving the structure and content of the time-tested and revered document and the cultural values of Confucianism that that document reflected and represented.

In short, dynastic China's experience with legal codification seems importantly bound up with the overall political continuity and durability that makes China's history so remarkable. Beginning with a fierce ideological debate that reached a climax and compromise in the second and third centuries BCE, the codification experience took on a character of conservatism and yielded a form of constitutionalism that lasted through to the end of the Qing era in the early 1900s, at which point the force of external political circumstances, and the weakness of the Qing leadership, finally brought the demise of dynastic law.

2. Law and Dynastic China's Rejection of Challengers

Perhaps another factor contributing to the remarkable political and cultural continuity in dynastic China appears in its traditional response to foreign influence. The Chinese history summarized earlier in this chapter reveals many episodes in which serious challenges from outside China were made to the political, ideological, economic, or social status quo inside the country. Several such challenges came, for example, in the form of military attack from outside China, especially from the north and west. Other challenges came in the form of new religious and cultural influences, as when Daoism and Buddhism were introduced. Still other challenges appeared in the form of European ideas and economic pressures.

Let us explore a few such episodes in an effort to generalize about how China reacted to these various types of influence and challenge. As we shall see, that reaction typically featured a cluster of elements, including arrogance, ignorance, disinterest, rejection, and "filtering" of foreign influences.

a. Military and political challenges

A persistent theme in Chinese history revolves around military challenges from the north and west. To me, the best visual image of this theme comes in the form of a metaphor offered by Nelson Ikon Wu. Although the image Wu offers focuses on cultural influences, the same applies to military attacks:

> The invisible continuity of the Chinese cultural metamorphosis always seems to me like a giant with his two feet firmly planted in the soil somewhere between Ch'ang-an and Loyang in the northern heartland where farther to the east continental Asia meets the Pacific Ocean. Seen from above and judged by the position of his broad shoulders, the giant appears to be facing south-southeast, with

---

111. *Id.* at 143–145. My view of the codes as "constitutional documents" resembles a view taken by at least one scholar of Chinese law that "the codes to some extent implement a moral orthodoxy that itself was maintained through the various dynasties in essentially the same form by the Confucian literati." Geoffrey MacCormack, TRADITIONAL CHINESE PENAL LAW 290 (1990) [hereinafter Mac-Cormack-1990].

112. See *supra* notes 90–94 and accompanying text.

his back toward the desert plateau whose western limits border Asia Minor and point to Europe. Rising high over the terrain as he grows, he ... does not enlarge his form in a radial-symmetrical way; [instead,] he moves forward and reaches to the left and to the right. The Himalayan Mountains block him from uniting with India, and *invaders sneak up to enter him from behind.*[113]

Harry Gelber, in his recent book *The Dragon and the Foreign Devils*, documents the many attacks that invaders have waged on China over the centuries but that the Chinese ultimately repelled or reversed. An abbreviated list of these would include the following:[114]

- the Xiongnu tribal attacks, beginning in the 2nd century BCE and launched from their nomadic ranges in the steppes to the north and northwest of China in an effort to gain access to food sources, especially in winter.

- the Tubo Turks' attacks in the early 4th century CE, resulting in the capture of the city of Loyang and the then of the emperor himself.

- the Tibetans' incursions in both the north and the south later in the 4th century CE; and

- the takeover of the northern part of China in the 12th century CE by the Jin people, forcing the Song dynastic leaders south (thereby starting the so-called "Southern Song" Dynasty).

Of course, the two most massive external military and political attacks came from the Mongols and the Manchus. As explained earlier in this chapter, these attacks—one occurring in the 13th century CE and the other occurring in the 17th century CE—resulted in "alien" control of China for well over half of the last six centuries of its dynastic history.[115] And yet the Chinese culture, and even the core of Chinese political integrity, may be said to have prevailed throughout those centuries. Why? Because in the first of these cases the foreign control was short-lived and left little imprint, and in the second of these cases the invaders were in a sense "converted" to Chinese.

As for the Mongols, their Yüan Dynasty faced strong resistance at every attempt to replace Chinese values and institutions with Mongol values and institutions,[116] including attempts to introduce legal enactments inconsistent with the codes that had emerged from the Song, Tang, and Sui dynasties that preceded the Yüan. For example, the Yüan legal enactment of 1291 (Treatise of Yüan New Regulations, or *Chih-yüan-hsin-ko*) represented a sharp departure from the pattern of those earlier codes[117]

---

113. Nelson Ikon Wu, *Introduction to the Art of China*, in Smith and Weng, *supra* note 1, at 13 (emphasis added).

114. See Gelber, *supra* note 41, at 26–28 (Xiongnu, whom the Han emperors fought off and on between about 140 and 51 BCE), 40 (Tubo Turks and Tibetans), and 57 (Jin).

115. For other accounts of the Mongol and Manchu invasions and empires, see LCDC, *supra* note 1, at 150–155, 193–196 and sources cited there. See also the pertinent chapters in Volume 6 of the CAMBRIDGE HISTORY OF CHINA (1994), which deals with alien regimes and border states. In a larger sense, attacks and challenges from the north and west also appeared in the form of the Qin state's aggressive conquest of the other warring states in 221 BCE and the Sui people's aggressive reunification of China in 581 CE. These aggressions were not quite as "alien" or "external" as were those of the Mongols or Manchus, but they were nearly so.

116. See LCDC, *supra* note 1, at 155, suggesting that Mongol and Chinese forms of government were like oil and water.

117. That 1291 Treatise had a different structure and did not take the form of a predominantly criminal code. See LCDC, *supra* note 1, at 161–165. The 1291 Treatise is listed in Box #6.3, *supra*, along with the 1331 Treatise referred to in text accompanying note 118, *infra*. Numerous other Yüan legal enactments that are not reflected in Box #6.3 are discussed in LCDC, *supra* note 1, at 158–161.

and had to be replaced just forty years later by a legal enactment (the 1331 Treatise of Punishment and Law, or *Hsing-fa chih*) that bore a remarkably close resemblance, both in structure and (especially) in content, to the Tang Code.[118] And of course it should be borne in mind that the Yüan Dynasty, partly for the very reason that it did not adapt well and quickly to many Chinese values and institutions, lasted for less than a century

As for the Manchus, the fact that they enjoyed a much longer and stronger dynasty (the Qing Dynasty) than did the Mongols (the Yüan Dynasty) surely resulted in large part from the Manchus' careful and thorough adoption of Chinese values and institutions. Indeed, the Manchus seem to have recognized immediately the importance of adopting Chinese culture as their own. Their conscious effort to do so appears in many of their actions just before and during their attempts to supplant Ming rule:

- In 1625, well before trying to take over China, the founder of Manchu power built a new imperial palace in Manchuria that was modeled on that in Beijing.[119]

- In taking control of Beijing in June 1644, the Manchu leader Dorgon "rode in the imperial palanquin into the palace grounds" and declared that because the Qing had driven away the rebels responsible for the Ming emperor's suicide, "[n]one in history have ever more properly succeeded to the Mandate [of Heaven]."[120] He also asserted that "the empire is a single whole. There are no distinctions between Manchus and Hans."[121]

- In October 1644, the Qing government moved its capital from Manchuria to Beijing.[122]

- The first Manchu emperor to occupy the capital in Beijing not only "worked hard to master Chinese" but also "continued [his uncle] Dorgon's practice of heeding the advice of senior Chinese advisors" and "pointedly adhered to the institutional structure of the Ming dynasty."[123] Indeed, he saw to it that the civil service examination system was quickly resumed in 1646.[124]

- The first long-serving Manchu emperor, Kangxi (reigned 1662–1722) "committ[ed] himself whole-heartedly to the business of being a Chinese emperor"[125] and in 1670 circulated a "Sacred Edict" expounding numerous principles of Neo-Confucianism, which included "the total subjection of women, the indisputable authority of fathers and the unquestioning loyalty of subjects to rulers."[126]

---

118. See LCDC, *supra* note 1, at 166–170 (documenting the similarities between the 1331 Treatise and the Tang Code).

119. Mote, *supra* note 1, at 790.

120. *Id.* at 819.

121. J.A.G. Roberts, *supra* note 1, at 143.

122. Mote, *supra* note 1, at 819.

123. *Id.* at 823.

124. *Id.* at 824. In doing so, the emperor was in fact following the lead of his father, who had adopted the Ming system of examinations (given in the Manchu, Mongol, and Chinese languages) for use in Manchuria even before the Qing gained control over China. Smith & Weng, *supra* note 1, at 242.

125. J.A.G. Roberts, *supra* note 1, at 148. His government largely "continued the practices of the Ming." *Id.* at 149. The emperor Kangxi is the subject of an elegant book that tells, from the emperor's own writings, the story of his reign, his ambitions, and his thoughts. See Jonathan D. Spence, Emperor of China: Self-Portrait of K'ang-hsi (1974).

126. J.A.G. Roberts, *supra* note 1, at 154.

In short, as one historian has remarked, "[i]t was the Chinese system, Chinese officials, and Chinese ideas that enabled the Manchus to conquer China."[127] And as explained earlier in this chapter, this program of adopting Chinese ways was reflected also in the Qing approach to codified law. The first Qing Code of 1646 was largely a copy of the Ming Code, and even the revisions adopted about eighty years later made remarkably few substantive changes.

b. Religious and intellectual challenges

The same notion of "conquest by absorption" or "conquest by translation" also applies to China's response to the religious and intellectual challenges that have faced China over the centuries. For example, as noted earlier, Dong Zhongshu—the scholar of the 2nd century BCE who had the ear of the Han emperor Wudi—crafted the rather odd package of "Imperial Confucianism" that reconciled a cacophony of concepts and influences into a unified theory,[128] thus taking the punch out of Daoism and other cosmologies.

Likewise, the teachings of Buddhism, which gained a strong foothold in China in the 4th century CE, were in effect subverted and overcome by traditional Chinese thought and culture.[129] Here is how one scholar has explained how the Chinese language served as a filter for Buddhist doctrine:

> In attempting to transfer or "translate" their new and alien ideas into terms meaningful for their Chinese audience, the early Buddhist missionaries ran into the problem that has faced all purveyors of foreign ideas in China ever since: how to select certain Chinese terms, written characters already invested with established meanings, and invest them with new significance without letting the foreign ideas be subtly modified, in fact sinified, in the process.[130]

It was perhaps because of this "sinification" or "sinicization"[131] that Buddhism took hold in China. That is, some Buddhist concepts—on the relatively high position that Buddhism gave to women, for example—were simply changed to fit with existing Chinese culture: "Husband supports wife", for instance, was translated into "The husband controls his wife".[132] Thus made culturally appropriate, Buddhism found receptive audiences in both south and north China—making the new religion, according to one author's speculations, perhaps "China's most important cultural import before the 19th century."[133]

c. European ideas and economic pressure

One of the most fascinating forms of Chinese contact with foreigners came through trade with people far to the west of China, especially the Europeans. Although ideas and

---

127. *Id.* at 140, quoting Franz Michael.

128. See text accompanying notes 45–55, *supra.*

129. For a brief account of the spread of Buddhism in China, see Smith and Weng, *supra* note 1, at 94–98. They state that the "first historical mention of a Chinese Buddhist community was recorded in A.D. 65. One hundred years later Buddha was being worshipped along with the Taoist deities. But the ideological fortress of Confucianism, armed with an ethical system governing man's social relations, was not easily penetrated. Not until the collapse of both the social order and the political system ... [in the period of division following the Han dynasty] did Buddhism gain momentum." *Id.*

130. Fairbank, *supra* note 1, at 75. See also J.M. Roberts, *supra* note 6, at 73 (explaining that by the eighth century, "Buddhist doctrine had become sinicized").

131. The terms "sinification" and "sinicization" may be, and often are, used interchangeably.

132. Fairbank, *supra* note 1, at 75.

133. See J.M. Roberts, *supra* note 6, at 215.

pressures of this sort became especially important beginning in the 18th century, they began as early as the time of the Roman Republic[134]—and by 166 CE "the Romans sent envoys to the Han capital at Loyang."[135] But the Chinese were hardly enthusiastic about interacting with the Europeans:

> From the beginning the Westerners—traders and others—were highly interested in China and its ways. The Chinese, by contrast, showed no interest in exploration or travel to the far West, as distinct from some trade. Pliny the Elder, for example, noted that 'like savages, the Seres [Chinese] shun the company of others and wait for traders to seek them out'. That contrast between the Europeans' desire for distant exploration and adventure, and the altogether more narrow and domestic focus of China, would continue.[136]

From the European perspective, of course, continued interest in exploration and adventure eventually came to have two related motivating forces: (1) the spread of what the Europeans saw as their own superior civilization (including Christianity), and (2) profit. Pressure on China to accept European delegations, typically for the purpose of facilitating commercial transactions, grew steadily from the 18th century onward. Gelber offers this series of observations about the receptiveness—or rather the non-receptiveness—of the Chinese to such entreaties:[137]

> [I]t hardly occurred to the Chinese ruling classes that—apart from such oddments [as some scientific and astronomical information]—the Europeans might have anything to say that would be of great interest, still less anything that might cause China to amend its political or diplomatic habits.

> China's rulers distrusted foreign traders, especially perhaps Western ones, as liable to disturb the empire's domestic peace.

> [Reflecting that distrust, starting in the middle of the eighteenth century, all] foreign trade was concentrated at Canton (Guangzhou), which became the filter shielding the [Chinese] population in general, and the official world in particular, from foreign disturbance. Contact was maintained through a selected group of Chinese merchants, known as the Cohong, who operated both as brokers and as superintendents of the foreign traders.... Communications had to go through the Cohong. They had to be worded as 'petitions'.... The smallest detail of the foreigners' lives and goods were subject to regulation.

> [In an effort to remove these restrictions and expand trade, a mission from Britain in 1791] sought permission for a permanent British ambassador to settle in Beijing. Though London may not have realised it, for the Chinese emperor and a culturally conservative autocracy, that was almost sure to be an entirely

---

134. See Gelber, *supra* note 41, at 35 (noting that "by the fourth century BC the Romans and Greeks began to speak of the 'Seres', the silk people").

135. *Id.*

136. *Id.* at 36. Gelber offers this explanation of China's "narrow and domestic focus", and its dismissive attitude more generally toward foreigners:

> [Chinese] people and officials continued to assume as self-evident that the Chinese state, headed by the Son of Heaven, could not be merely one state among many. Instead, it was the society of the civilised world, with 'China' and 'Civilisation' two sides of the same conceptual coin.... [People] beyond [China's] borders ... were, by definition, 'barbarians', in the obvious sense that they were not part of the central civilisation.

Id. at 33.

137. The following excerpts are draw from *id.* at 149, 155, 156, 160, and 163–164.

unacceptable and revolutionary demand. It meant that this strange kingdom on the other side of the world [Britain] would claim a kind of equality with the Celestial Empire. It would even, and quite intolerably, imply that the emperor was no longer a universal monarch.

[In response to the British trade mission, the Chinese made it clear that they] would insist on homage to the emperor taking the normal form of the demonstrative kowtow,[138] which was especially important for domestic consumption. China's highest officials, and even principles of the blood, performed it. The 1655 Dutch mission had kowtowed not just to the emperor, but to the empty throne and even to mere documents carrying the imperial seal. Several other foreign missions had since then had no difficulty complying with the established Chinese ceremonial forms.

[When the British trade envoy, Lord George Macartney, expressed his unwillingness to perform the kowtow, the Chinese authorities ushered him away with a dismissive imperial edict addressed to King George III, saying:]

> Our dynasty's majestic virtue has penetrated into every country under Heaven, and Kings of all nations have offered their costly tribute by land and sea ... I set no value on objects strange or ingenious, and have no use for your country's manufactures ... It behoves [sic] you, O King, to respect my sentiments and to display even greater devotion and loyalty in future ...

[Despite its failure to secure an embassy in Beijing, Macartney's mission] did serve important purposes. The mission brought back first-hand reports of the magnificence of China's culture ... [as well as] Beijing's lack of interest in, and ignorance of, the non-Chinese world, the role of Western industry, or the changing conditions of the balance of power or the conditions of trade. Even on lesser questions, the British encountered simple incredulity. For instance they found the Chinese simply refused to believe that in Europe firearms had long since superseded bows and arrows.

This reported combination of ignorance, dismissiveness, and arrogance—and particularly the last of these—is even seen by some as the true cause of the Opium War between Britain and China in the 1840s. No less prominent a personage than John Quincy Adams (sixth president of the USA) explained that opium was

> a mere incident to the dispute, but no more the cause of the war than the throwing overboard of tea in Boston harbor was the cause of the American revolution ... [T]he cause of the war is the kowtow—the arrogant and insupportable pretensions of China that she will hold commercial intercourse with the rest of mankind not upon terms of equal reciprocity, but upon the insulting and degrading forms of the relation between lord and vassal.[139]

However fair or unfair Adams' characterization might have been, it reflects the deep reluctance and resistance shown by the Chinese government toward European influence.

---

138. Gelber explains that in early days, the *kowtow*—consisting typically of three kneelings and nine bowings of the head to the floor—arose from the manner of sitting at a time when there were no formal benches or chairs in China. *Id.* at 33. Later, it evolved into the full pattern of three separate prostrations, with the forehead touching the ground three times with each prostration. *Id.* at 170.

139. *Id.* at 188.

Expressed differently, China proved in this way (as it had in terms of religion and military attacks) to be not only *disinclined* culturally and institutionally to respond to European influence, but strong enough to withstand most such influence—coming in this case in the form of trade.

d. Durability in China's response to external influence

Why would this be? Why would the Chinese culture and institutions prove so durable—at least until the very end of the dynastic period—as to withstand the full impact of these various challenges, whether military, political, religious, ideological, or economic? Many answers could be offered, but I would suggest a law-related answer.

I believe the legal codes, and in particular their manifestation of the "alloy" I referred to above (Legalism and Confucianism melted together), are closely related to China's rejection—or more precisely its "conquest-by-absorption"—of all its main challengers. It is difficult to say whether (i) China's experience with codification is a contributing cause of its ability to withstand challenges to the political or cultural status quo, or whether instead (ii) both of these features—China's ability to withstand challenges and its long, consistent record of codification—are themselves the result of some other yet more influential feature. In either event, we can see an increasingly close connection between those two features through China's dynastic history.

For example, by the time of the Tang Dynasty, the pattern of codification was well formed. Also by the time of the Tang Dynasty, the period of Chinese disunity was largely a thing of the past. Another look at Box #6.2, near the beginning of this chapter, reveals that the two principal periods of disunity in China were in the five centuries or so that preceded the Qin Dynasty (the Spring and Autumn period, followed by the Warring States period[140]) and just after the Han Dynasty, the dissolution of which led to about 350 years of fragmentation in which, "apart from a brief interlude between 280 and 316, no one dynasty ruled the whole of China."[141] After the pattern of Chinese codification was firmly set in the Sui-Tang period, China no longer suffered any significant periods of fragmentation—that is, division into a large number of sections. Instead, aside from a division of China into north and south for about a century and a half from 1127 to 1279, most of the period from the end of the Tang to the end of the Qing—a stretch of almost exactly one thousand years (907 to 1911 CE)—saw a unified China.

Whether the relationship I see in dynastic China between legal codification and the sort of cultural "durability" referred to above is as close as I portray it, the fact remains that the durability itself is real and extraordinary. I believe dynastic China exhibits these features in dealing with literal and figurative "attacks" (or "leakage" into China) from outside its borders: (i) an arrogant lack of interest in the ideas that the challengers presented, (ii) a rejection of the challengers themselves whenever possible, and (iii) a thorough "filtering" of the foreign influences when they could not be rejected or deflected. We shall return to these themes in subsection IIE of this chapter in considering how contemporary China has reacted to foreign influences—especially foreign legal influences—in its recent law reform movements.

---

140. Although the names of these two periods suggest that the earlier one was relatively more peaceful than the later one, in fact "wars were equally frequent in both periods." J.A.G. Roberts, *supra* note 1, at 13.

141. *Id.* at 40.

3. The Rule of Law versus Political Control

Having looked so far at two key themes emerging from the survey of dynastic Chinese law offered earlier in this chapter—namely, (1) law and continuity and (2) law and dynastic China's rejection of challengers—let us now turn to a third theme. This theme revolves around the rule of law, the role of law, and political control.

Few legal notions attract as much attention these days as does the notion of the "rule of law". Even a cursory review of contemporary legal literature in the areas of international and comparative law reveals countless books, articles, definitions, and declarations on the topic. I shall discuss some of the competing ideas on the "rule of law"—and offer in some detail my own assessment of what it entails—in Chapter Seven of this book, which examines the rule of law in *contemporary* China. For present purposes, however, let us use the rough-and-ready general definition of the "rule of law" set forth in Box #6.9.

Box #6.9 *General Definition of "Rule of Law"*[142]

A society may be said to adhere to the rule of law if the rules in its legal system are publicly promulgated, reasonably clear in their formulation, prospective in their effect, reasonably stable over time, reasonably consistent with each other, applicable to all segments of the society (including the government, so as to prevent the government elite from acting arbitrarily), reasonably comprehensive in their coverage of substantive issues facing the society and its people, and reasonably effective, in the sense that the rules are broadly adhered to by the people in the society—voluntarily by most, and through officially forced compliance where necessary.

Based on that general definition of "rule of law", what might we conclude about the presence or absence of the rule of law in dynastic China? I would suggest that the picture is mixed. On the one hand, there is perhaps no legal system on Earth that has created and sustained any more sophisticated written system of laws than the Chinese did over the many centuries of that country's dynastic history.[143] On the other hand, we must bear in mind that the Western powers dealing with China at a high point in its development —in the latter part of the Qing Dynasty—found its legal system so profoundly deficient as to demand extraterritorial privileges in the 19th century.[144] Were those Western concerns—which if expressed in modern terminology would amount to a claim that there was no "rule of law" in China—totally baseless?

No. For reasons that I shall only sketch out briefly here, it seems clear that the dynastic Chinese legal system as described in this chapter would not meet the requirements of the rough-and-ready definition I offered above for "rule of law"—a definition, by the way, that (as we shall explore in Chapter Seven) would be regarded as weak and inadequate by many Westerners.[145]

---

142. I have formulated this definition from a variety of sources, including in particular the works of Lon Fuller, as explained in Chapter Seven of this book.

143. As one observer has stated, "the Chinese gave us the concept of the scholar official, the Mandarin, of law of a sophistication and detail that today we can barely imagine." Anne-Marie Slaughter, *Closing Remarks*, appearing in DEMOCRACY AND THE RULE OF LAW 64 (Norman Dorsen and Prosser Gifford eds., 2001).

144. I shall refer to this development at the beginning of section II of this chapter.

145. As indicated above, a much more detailed discussion of how to define "rule of law" will be undertaken in Chapter Seven. At that point we shall see competing and additional factors to those included in the "rough-and-ready" definition offered in Box #6.9. Some of those possible factors include procedural rights and protections, proportionality (of punishment to "fit the crime"), individ-

China's dynastic legal system, even at its most sophisticated, would fail to meet at least two of the standards included in the "rule of law" definition offered above in Box #6.9. First, the legal system—centered on the legal codes as described earlier in this chapter—was not *applicable to all segments of the society* because it did not apply to the ruling elite in the government. In a system dominated by an all-powerful emperor who exercises totalitarian control and is above the law—indeed, is the sole ultimate author of the law, with recognized authority to change it at will—the rule of law cannot be said to exist.

Second, the rules set forth in the dynastic Chinese legal codes were by no means *comprehensive in their coverage of substantive issues facing the society and its people*. As explained above in subsection IC3 of this chapter, the fact that rules relating more directly to *minshi* (people's matters) started appearing in the Qing Code—in the form of a "third layer" of provisions—does not overcome this reality: for the bulk of the populace, personal behavior was most directly and importantly influenced not by the Qing Code but instead by traditional rules of moral and ethical conduct among members of family and society, so that even at their most sophisticated, the law codes that distinguish the Chinese dynastic legal tradition did not occupy a very large portion of the total area of rules governing human behavior in China.

As explained earlier in this chapter, both of these key features of Chinese dynastic law are noted in the following words of Professor Bill Jones (who translated the Qing Code into English in the 1990s):

> The polity of China consisted of a highly centralized government headed by an absolute ruler who ruled by means of a bureaucracy. The primary obligation of every Chinese was to fulfil the duties assigned to him by the Emperor. All human activities had to be carried on so as to fit into his scheme for directing society. Consequently one would expect the imperial law or Code to take note of human activity only as it was perceived to affect imperial policies. It was natural that the primary focus of attention would be the activities of bureaucrats in the performance of their duties, not the activities of ordinary human beings in their private lives....[146]

It is worth noting that the other factors included in the general "rule of law" definition appearing above in Box #6.9 *do* seem present in dynastic Chinese law, at least based on the brief survey offered in this chapter. The rules set forth in the law codes were for the most part *publicly promulgated*,[147] reasonably *clear* in their formulation (sometimes extremely detailed, in fact, so as to reduce the likelihood of misapplication of punishments for their transgression), typically *prospective* in their effect, reasonably *stable* over time (enduring in some cases for centuries with little change), reasonably *consistent* with each other (as a result of intense study and fine-tuning by the Confucianist scholars at the im-

---

ual civil liberties, democratic participation in rule-making, protections against discriminatory treatment based on race or gender, rights of private parties to sue the government for misfeasance, and independence of the organs of judicial power.

146. See *supra* note 89.

147. A significant exception to this appeared in the Song dynasty. One authority notes that "[t]he Sung [Song] authorities prohibited private individuals both from printing or copying any laws and from possessing any code provisions" on grounds that "the laws belonged exclusively to the emperor and were never to be made accessible to the people". Ichisada Miyazaki, *The Administration of Justice During the Sung Dynasty*, appearing as Chapter 3 in ESSAYS ON CHINA'S LEGAL TRADITION (Jerome Alan Cohen, R. Randle Edwards, and Fu-mei Chang Chen, eds., 1980). Of course, it must be borne in mind that (i) most private individuals at the time would have been unable to read the law codes anyway and (ii) the intended *audience* for the law codes was, as noted above, the officers in the imperial bureaucracy—and especially the district magistrates—instead of the public at large, and this fact undercuts somewhat the effectiveness of whatever promulgation of the rules did take place.

perial court[148]), and reasonably *effective*—with, indeed, immense coercive power available for and devoted to their enforcement.

Despite the fact that Chinese dynastic law does seem to meet the "rule of law" standards in these several aspects, its failure to meet the other two standards—those regarding applicability to the government and comprehensiveness of coverage—is fatal. I would conclude that dynastic China was not governed by the "rule of law" as defined above. In Chapter Seven below we shall consider whether *contemporary* China is governed by the rule of law, and how (if at all) the country's dynastic legal tradition bears on that question.

4. The Guiding Ethic in Law and Government

In the closing paragraphs of this section I shall address the last of the four key themes emerging from the survey of dynastic Chinese law offered earlier in this chapter. This theme revolves around the role that Imperial Confucianism played as the central *legal ethic* or "soul" of dynastic Chinese law. Like the discussion in the preceding paragraphs regarding the "rule of law" in dynastic China, the discussion here is preliminary in nature. Its aim is to set the stage for the detailed treatment in Chapter Seven of this more important question: What is the central legal ethic or "spirit" or "soul", if any, in *contemporary* Chinese law?

We must begin, naturally, with some general observations about what the terms "legal ethic" and "legal soul" mean in this context. Let us begin with the word "ethic" itself. For present purposes, the word "ethic" may be defined as "a set of principles of right conduct" or "a theory or a system of moral values", and the word draws some of its meaning from the notion of "character", to which the word "ethic" is related in its Greek roots. I distinguish "ethic" from "ethics": "ethics" typically would refer to either "the study of the general nature of morals" or to more specific "rules or standards governing the conduct of a person or the members of a profession". As a more familiar or colloquial term, I use "legal soul" to convey the same general meaning—and I could also use such terms as "ideology",[149] "spirit",[150] "value orientation", or "heart".

Based on this description of the meaning of "ethic", the term "legal ethic" would mean the set of fundamental legal principles or values that give a legal system its unique spirit and character—its "soul".[151] Another way to view the concept of "legal ethic" would be

---

148. A significant exception to this appeared in the Ming dynasty—indeed, during the reign of the founding emperor, Zhu Yuanzhang. He consistently violated the basic requirement of consistency. One authority describes the situation in this way:

> While the emperor was determined to produce a universal code that could be minutely followed, he undermined that intent by constantly issuing laws which met immediate needs and which often contradicted his Great Ming Code, thereby producing the anomaly of a Code that all officials were required to follow, and a body of his edicts (typically ordering much harsher, often cruel punishments that his code specifically abolished) which transcended the Code's authority; that would prove to be typical of his imperial style.

Mote, *supra* note 1, at 570. For further detail, see LCDC, *supra* note 1, at 187–189.

149. The term "ideology" would work about as well as "ethic" or "soul" for my purposes, given the usual definition of "ideology" as meaning a body of ideas reflecting the social needs and aspirations of a group or culture, or a set of doctrines or beliefs that form the basis of a system (such as a legal system). The term "ideology" lacks, however, the notions of morality and essential character that the terms "ethic" and "soul" connote.

150. One common connotation of "spirit" is that of the "vital principle or animating force within living beings", with such synonyms as core, essence, heart, marrow, pith, and substance.

151. For these purposes, I am using the term "legal system" to mean the network of rules—both "primary" rules and "secondary" rules as described by H.L.A. Hart (former holder of the chair in jurisprudence at Oxford, and a hero of mine there in the 1970s) and the set of institutions governing

as a sort of glue, because a key function of a legal ethic is to serve as a cohesive element, binding together a society by means of a common understanding and shared set of values that are predominantly legal (but also perhaps moral and social) in character.

My task in defining "legal ethic" or "legal soul" in this context is in fact much easier than it first appears. After all, as noted above, the ultimate goal that I am aiming at in this respect is straightforward: to try to identify what, if anything, in *contemporary* Chinese law plays the role that Imperial Confucianism played in *dynastic* Chinese law. For this purpose, I could in fact use nearly any label at all. The label "legal ethic" appeals to me as most adequate.

More important than the label to be used is an explanation of why it might be reasonable for us to regard Imperial Confucianism as playing the central role that I am ascribing to it. In other words, why do I consider Imperial Confucianism to be so crucial an ingredient in dynastic Chinese law as to prompt me to search for a modern correlative to it in contemporary Chinese law?

The answer to that question, I believe, should be clear from the survey of Chinese legal history that I have offered above. Let me briefly reiterate in a simplified way some aspects of Imperial Confucianism—what it was, how it developed, and what role it played in the creation of the longest-running legal tradition the world has ever seen. In short, I shall try to summarize why Imperial Confucianism qualifies as a "legal ethic" or "soul"[152] or "ideology" or "spirit" or "heart" or "glue" for dynastic Chinese law.

- As explained above,[153] what came to be known as Imperial Confucianism grew out of the teachings of Confucius, who concentrated on the power of *lǐ* 礼 in governing society. Those teachings, as revised (and made more acceptable to power-holders) by Mengzi and other later disciples, stood on one side of a great intellectual and political tug-of-war with the opposing teachings of Legalism—a debate that lasted from roughly the 6th century to the 3rd century BCE.

- Although that debate was won temporarily by Legalism with the establishment of the Qin Dynasty by Qin Shi Huangdi, the victory was short-lived. On displacing the Qin leaders, the new Han Dynasty—through its founding emperor Liu Bang—soon reintroduced Confucian values as the basis for imperial government. This created an "alloy" by which Legalist and Confucianist approaches to government were melted together and compromised.

- As also noted above, "Confucianism [shortly] gained [further] eminence during the Han period because of the meeting of minds of a monarch [Wudi] in search of a clear mandate from Heaven and a scholar [Dong Zhongshu] with an ambition to dominate the current ideologies."[154] Dong Zhongshu did that by imaginatively amalgamating Confucianist teachings with those revolving around Daoism, yin and yang, the five elements, cosmology, numerology, and more.

---

legal relations that comprise the law applicable in a specific nation-state or similar entity in international law. For further details on the terms "legal tradition" and "legal system", see discussion in subsection IA of Chapter One.

152. The characterization of Imperial Confucianism—and the *lǐ* that lay at the center of it—as the "soul" of Chinese law is not original with me. See Zeng and Ma, *supra* note 11, at 49 (asserting that in the Han dynasty, "'fa was the body and 'li' was the soul" of traditional Chinese law). In other passages, these authors also characterize *lǐ* as the "spirit of traditional Chinese law". *Id.* at 52.

153. See especially subsection IB of this chapter.

154. Smith and Weng, *supra* note 1, at 79.

- Through the creation (and repeated rehabilitation when necessary) of an examination system for the selection of the imperial bureaucracy, this conglomeration of doctrine anchored itself more and more deeply into the system of governance, including (most importantly for our purposes) the legal system through the long series of dynastic legal codes. Thus the teachings themselves and the process of governing were fused, so that even though the emperors and their immediate advisors undisputedly held ultimate authority and wielded it always to their own perceived advantage, the detailed tasks of drafting, interpreting, amending, and implementing the law codes all lay in the province of persons whose ideology and world view revolved around Imperial Confucianism.[155]

- Despite various modifications through time,[156] the same general "alloy" of Imperial Confucianism (with its emphasis of *lǐ* in a hierarchical society devoted to harmony) and Legalist thought (with its emphasis on *fǎ* and *xíng*) helped sustain a dynastic order[157] with a legal system dominated by codes that endured over many centuries,[158] until a combination of factors — weak governance, rampant corruption, interaction with the West, and more — spelled the demise of that dynastic order.

- While in place, those legal codes revealed Confucianist doctrine in many ways — such as the numbers and types of punishments, the adjustment of punishment depending on the social status of the perpetrator and victim, the glorification of filial duty and duty to state, and the overarching aim of harmony — and amounted to instructions issued by the emperor to officials in the imperial bureaucracy responsible for sustaining order in society and power in the emperor.

I have painted above with a broad brush, in order to emphasize the centrality of Imperial Confucianism in dynastic Chinese law. It played the role of a "legal ethic" or "soul". In Chapter Seven we shall consider what, if anything, we can find in *contemporary* Chinese law that plays that role.

---

155. For explanations of how, from the Han era onward, Confucianist ideas found expression in the application of the law codes, and how Confucianist scholars were commonly involved also in the drafting of the codes, see LCDC, *supra* note 1, at 96–97 (Han), 109–112 (between Han and Tang), and 119–121 (Tang), 191–192 (Ming), and 212–216 (Qing).

156. Some of these, such as the rise of Neo-Confucianism, along with other influences, will be explored in Chapter Seven. The fact that these modifications may make Imperial Confucianism appear to us as a rather sloppy mish-mash of factors does not diminish the importance of the role that Imperial Confucianism played during the dynastic period; even a confused or hazy ideology can provide a core of shared belief adequate to solidify a society's identity and claim the loyalty of its members.

157. As noted above, this result — sustaining the dynastic order — may be viewed as the intended product of an alliance that the Confucianist scholars entered into with the emperor as monarch: "The monarch provided the symbols and the sinews of power.... The literati provided the knowledge of precedent and statecraft that could legitimize power and make the state work." See *supra* note 57.

158. Another observer takes a similar perspective on the combination of Legalism and Confucianism:

> Traditional imperial China was governed by a dual authority, one element of which was the statutory basis of law enforcement through punishments to ensure the government's political will; the other was the Confucian code, a moral source of authority akin to natural law that regulated the behavior of the Confucian scholars themselves, the guardians of this moral system who handed it down to later generations. The long history of Chinese imperial culture serves as testimony to the fact that these dual sources of authority reinforced each other in support of a system that, despite crises, survived the rise and fall of successive dynasties for almost two millennia of Chinese history.

DeAngelis, *supra* note 82, at 246.

II. Modern China's Legal Development

Highlights. Having offered a synopsis of Chinese dynastic law, with particular reference to some of its key characteristics, we turn now to modern Chinese law—by which I mean the law of the PRC and its immediate political predecessors. Just as the story of dynastic China ends with the collapse of the Qing Dynasty at the dawn of the 20th century, the story we turn to now begins with that collapse and continues to the present day. In particular, this section focuses on the legal reform efforts that have been undertaken in fits and starts over the past hundred years or so. The story falls rather easily into three segments—(i) from the Qing downfall at the turn of the century until early 1949, (ii) from 1949 to 1978, and (iii) from 1979 to the present. The section closes by considering two questions that bear on modern China's legal identity: (1) does contemporary Chinese law show the same remarkable continuity that is evident in dynastic Chinese law and (2) has contemporary Chinese law consistently deflected and filtered outside influences, as dynastic Chinese law did?

A. *Overview and Patterns*[159]

The year 2009 marked a "triple anniversary" for Chinese law reform. Thirty years earlier, in 1979, the newly established People's Republic of China ("PRC") embarked on a dramatic new phase of legal reform.[160] Having just emerged from the chaotic era—one

---

159. The account in this section draws liberally from a range of sources, some of which are cited in the Selected Bibliography at the end of this book. Most prominent among them (in addition to those cited *supra* note 1) are the following (in alphabetical order by author or editor, beginning with books): Ronald C. Brown, Understanding Chinese Courts and Legal Process (1997); Bin Liang, The Changing Chinese Legal System, 1978–Present (2008); Albert H.Y. Chen, An Introduction to the Legal System of the People's Republic of China (3d ed. 2004); Daniel C.K. Chow, The Legal System of the People's Republic of China (2003); Kenneth A. Cutshaw et al, Corporate Counsel's Guide to Doing Business in China (2d ed., looseleaf); Pitman B. Potter, The Chinese Legal System: Globalization and Local Legal Culture (2001) [hereinafter Potter-2001]; China's Legal Reforms and Their Political Limits (Eduard B. Vermeer and Ingrid d'Hooghe, eds., 2002); Introduction to Chinese Law (Wang Chenguang and Zhang Xianchu, eds., 1997) [hereinafter Wang & Zhang]; Xin Ren, Tradition of the Law and Law of the Tradition: Law, State, and Social Control in China (1997); James M. Zimmerman, China Law Deskbook: A Legal Guide for Foreign-Invested Enterprises; Zou Keyuan, China's Legal Reform—Towards the Rule of Law (2006); Volker Behr, *Development of a New Legal System in the People's Republic of China*, 67 Louisiana Law Review 1161 (2007); Jianfu Chen, *The Transformation of Chinese Law—From Formal to Substantial*, 37 Hong Kong Law Journal 689 (2007); Ma Xiaohong, *A Reflection on the History of Chinese Constitutionalism of Last Century*, 2 Frontiers of Law in China 44 (2007); Randall Peerenboom, *The X-Files: Past and Present Portrayals of China's Alien "Legal System"*, 2 Washington University Global Studies Law Review 37 (2003); Pitman B. Potter, *Globalization and Economic Regulation in China: Selective Adaptation of Globalized Norms and Practices*, 2 Washington University Global Studies Law Review 119 (2003) [hereinafter Potter-2003].

160. As a precise technical matter, this latest legal reform movement could be dated either (i) from December 1978, when the Third Plenary Session of the Eleventh Central Committee adopted dramatic changes that were mainly economic in character but that also had important legal components and implications, or (ii) from early 1979, when legislative efforts began in earnest—as illustrated by the adoption in that year of the criminal code and the criminal procedure code. For details on the late-1978 Plenary Session, see Kenneth Lieberthal, Governing China: From Revolution Through Reform 133 (1995).

might say disastrous era — in which Mao Zedong had delivered such disasters as the Great Leap Forward and the Cultural Revolution (discussed briefly below), China and its leaders began charting a dramatically different economic course which in turn required fundamental changes in the nation's laws and legal concepts.

The year 2009 also marked the sixtieth anniversary of the founding of the PRC. That point in history, punctuated by the great celebration at Tiananmen Square on October 1, 1949, was also one of dramatic legal change in the country — in addition, of course, to being the official beginning of a momentous political transformation.

Moreover, the year 2009 marked the ninetieth anniversary of the May Fourth Movement (discussed briefly below), which also had legal reform at its core. In addition to voicing other complaints, the thousands of protesters who took to the streets of Beijing on May 4, 1919 were expressing outrage at the refusal of the negotiators at Versailles (following World War I) to honor their earlier promises to end the practice by powerful European powers (and the USA) of exercising legal jurisdiction within the territory of China on grounds that China's own legal system was inadequate or uncivilized.

Having now passed this "30-60-90" year anniversary, China once again may be viewed as having opened a new chapter of legal reform. Hence it seems particularly appropriate to use that theme — legal reform — as an organizing theme as we examine law in contemporary China.

Let us begin that examination at the very close of the 19th century, when China was struggling to make the transition to a new political and legal system as the dynastic system was collapsing. That tumultuous moment serves as a starting point for the selective list of legal and political developments that I provide in Box #6.10, which I shall refer to in the course of this section. Special attention is given throughout Box #6.10 to various statutes and constitutions emerging in China over the past hundred-plus years; and the first part of Box #6.10 highlights some key political developments by which the Communist Party of China ("CPC") came to control the PRC.

Box #6.10 Selected Chinese Legal and Political Developments from about 1900[161]

1898 · The Emperor Guangxu issues an edict in June favoring constitutional and political reform (as urged by Kang Youwei, a reformist leader); but 103 days later, conservative forces headed by the Empress Dowager Cixi confine the emperor, bringing that reform effort to a close.

1900 · The Boxer Uprising comes to its climax with the execution of several dozen foreigners in missionary families and a 55-day siege of the foreign legation in Beijing; the siege is broken by a relief expedition of foreign forces marching on that city in August.

1901 · The Empress Dowager Cixi (in exile in Xian while Western powers occupy the capital following the Boxer Uprising) issues an edict soliciting suggestions for the reform of Chinese law along the lines of Western models.

1902 · The Imperial Court appeals in March to all Chinese ambassadors residing abroad to examine the laws in various countries and report back to the Ministry of Foreign Af-

---

161. Entries in Box #6.10 are drawn largely from the following sources: Albert H.Y. Chen, *supra* note 159, especially pages 23–45; Wang & Zhang, *supra* note 159, especially pages 9–13; Zou Keyuan, *supra* note 159, especially pages 2, 4, 12, 13, 24, 161, 207, and 217; Jianfu Chen, *supra* note 159, *passim*; Chow, *supra* note 159, especially at pages 9–11, 118–119, and 230; Ma Xiaohong, *supra* note 159, especially pages 47–53; J.A.G. Roberts, *supra* note 1, especially pages 201–266. Pinpoint citations have been omitted for brevity.

fairs; and in May the Imperial Court appoints a group to examine all laws currently in force in China with an eye to reform.

1903 · The *Company Law* and the *Bankruptcy Law* are promulgated, along with the *General Principles for Merchants*

1904 · A Law Codification Commission is established, thereby making the reform of Chinese law (and the corresponding study of foreign law) a new cause for the Imperial Court.

1905 · The Empress Dowager announces (i) her conversion to constitutionalism and (ii) an immediate end to the imperial examinations.

1906 · The *Law for the Organization of the Supreme Court* is issued, and the Supreme Court is established; and the Imperial Court issues an edict declaring that China will introduce a constitutional polity within nine years.

1908 · The *Imperial Outline of Constitution* is promulgated. The Empress Dowager and the Emperor Guangxu die.

1909 · Some provincial assemblies, chosen by an electorate composed of men over the age of 25 who either meet an educational qualification or own property, begin to meet for the purpose of making recommendations to provincial authorities.

1910 · The *Law for the Organization of the Courts* is promulgated; the *Current Criminal Code* is also issued, distinguishing for the first time in history between civil and criminal cases; and other legislative activity begins (involving the drafting of codes for civil law, civil procedure, and commercial law) that reflects a process of rapid Westernization of Chinese law.

1911 · With an uprising in Wuhan leading to a defection of most of China's provinces, the Qing empire is overthrown and a provisional government begins to take shape.

1912 · Sun Zhongshan (Sun Yatsen) promulgates in March a provisional constitution of the Republic of China; a Presidential Decree of March 10 declares that all imperial laws remain effective unless they are modified by new laws or they are contrary to the principles of the Republic. Later in March, the military leader Yuan Shikai succeeds Sun Zhongshan as president of the Republic of China.

1914 · A *Temple of Heaven Draft of Constitution* is promulgated in May, reflecting the dictatorial inclinations of Yuan Shikai.

1916 · Yuan Shikai begins his reign as (purported) emperor on January 1; but in June he dies, plunging China even deeper into an era of warlordism in which the Beijing government ceases to exercise effective authority over the country. In December Chen Duxiu publishes *The Way of Confucius and Modern Life*, criticizing Confucianist teachings on filial piety and on the subservience of women.

1919 · On May 4, a crowd of 3,000 students assembles at Tiananmen Square in Beijing and marches on the foreign legations to protest China's treatment at the Versailles Peace Conference — thus creating the flashpoint of the May Fourth Movement, which also features attacks on Confucianism.

1921 · The Communist Party of China (CPC) is founded with the objective of overthrowing the bourgeoisie by a proletarian revolution; it holds is first party congress in Shanghai in July (with about 50 members).

1923 · Another constitution is promulgated, but without much success.

1924 · The Guomindang (Nationalist) Party Congress passes resolutions concerning the equality of the sexes, thereby attempting to establish formally (for the first time in Chinese history) equality of woman with men.

1927 · The "Northern Expedition", a military campaign launched in 1926 by Guomindang leader Jiang Jieshi (Chiang Kaishek), succeeds in consolidated the power of the Guomindang Party by defeating or absorbing warlord forces; and the Guomindang (Nationalist) Government is established in Nanjing, starting an extensive program of legislation.

1928 · The concept of law—as set forth in Sun Zhongshan's *San Min Zhu Yi* ("Three Principles of the People")—is explained by the first president of the Guomindang-dominated legislature at its opening session in November, with the assertion that *San Min Zhu Yi* legislation, unlike traditional Chinese law, is designed to protect collective national interests instead of family and clan interests and that this concept of law is superior to the Western concept of law making the interests of the individual of paramount importance. Also in this year, work starts on the creation of a series of fairly comprehensive codes of law known collectively as the Collection of the Six Laws (*Liufa Quanshu*).

1930 · The Nationalist Army makes its first determined attack on Communist bases in Jiangxi province but is forced to withdraw.

1931 · Japanese forces occupy Manchuria. The CPC, while in control of Jiangxi, issues the *Constitutional Outline of the Chinese Soviet Republic*, calling for a five-branch system of government comprising the executive, legislative, judiciary, examinations, and control bureaux.

1934 · In view of repeated Guomindang attacks on the CPC in Jiangxi province, the CPC abandons its base there and begins the "Long March"—an arduous trek of Communist stalwarts fleeing the Guomindang's campaign of extermination—and provides the setting for Mao Zedong to achieve primacy within the CPC. Jiang Jieshi launches the New Life Movement, aimed at encouraging certain Confucianist values (and holding up Jesus Christ as a model to emulate).

1935 · The Long March concludes in northern Shaanxi province, having extended over 5,000 miles.

1937 · Japan launches an invasion of China, setting off a war in which China's civilian population suffers under some of the worst and most sadistic atrocities in modern warfare; faced with this threat, the Guomindang Party is forced to form a united front with the Communists, despite the distrust between Jiang Jieshi and Mao Zedong.

1938 · The Guomindang, having transferred to Chongqing, loses more battles against the Japanese, who occupy Wuhan and Guangzhou; a Guomindang leader defects to establish a collaborationist regime with its capital at Nanjing.

1941 · The CPC issues the *Principles of Government of the Shaanxi-Gansu-Ningxia Border Regions.*

1944 · The CPC claims by now to control four "border regions", including the Shaanxi-Gansu-Ningxia Border Region, and about a dozen "liberated areas" in central China.

1945 · The August US bombing of Hiroshima and Nagasaki brings the Sino-Japanese War (and World War II generally) to an end and leaves the Guomindang and Communists jostling for power. The CPC holds its seventh party congress, with a membership that has grown to 1.2 million (from 50 members in 1921).

1946 · The Guomindang and the Communists are persuaded by US Ambassador George Marshall to agree to a ceasefire, but both sides use it as a pretense to disguise their preparations for war. The CPC issues the *Constitutional Principles of the Shaanxi-Gansu-Ningxia Border Regions.*

1947 · The war between the Guomintang and the Communists begins to shift in favor of the latter.

1949 · In February, the CPC's Central Committee issues the *Instructions on the Abolition of the Collection of the Six Laws of the Kuomintang and on Confirmation of the Judicial*

Principles of the Liberated Areas—under which all existing laws of the Guomindang regime are declared abolished. In September, the Chinese People's Political Consultative Conference adopts the *Common Program*, which promises to establish a new legal system and serves as a provisional constitution; in October, the People's Republic of China is officially established and announced by Mao Zedong in Beijing's Tiananmen Square. In December, Jiang Jieshi and two million of his supporters flee to Taiwan; and Mao Zedong travels to Moscow to negotiate with Stalin.

1950 · Tibet, which came under Chinese political control in the 18th century but had been autonomous since 1913, is "liberated" by the People's Liberation Army. China intervenes in the Korean conflict, pushing UN forces back to the 389th parallel, thus deepening the PRC's rift with the USA, which now becomes committed to supporting the Nationalists on Taiwan.

1951 · The *Organic Law of the People's Courts* is adopted.

1952 · The "Movement of Judicial Reform" is begun, prompting (i) the removal of about 80% of the judges that had been appointed by the Guomindang government and (ii) the enactment of new laws and regulations.

1954 · The first Constitution of the PRC, heavily influenced by the 1936 Constitution of the Soviet Union, is promulgated by the new National People's Congress (NPC). This 1954 Constitution, emerging from the "Movement of Judicial Reform", emphasizes "socialist legality". In addition, the *Organic Law for the People's Procuratorates*, also influenced by the Soviet model, is promulgated.

1955 · The Supreme People's Court issues its *Reply on the Non-Desirability of Referring to the Constitution in the Determination of Crimes and Sentences in Criminal Judgments*, which is regarded as prohibiting courts from relying on constitutional provisions directly in deciding a case—in other words, prescribing that courts can apply only the ordinary legislation (if any) through which the Constitution was implemented.

1956 · The CPC, at its Eighth National Congress, confirms the policy of building "the people's democratic legal system" and declares that one of the most pressing tasks of the country is to codify the laws systematically. In addition, the CPC announces a policy of "letting a hundred flowers bloom and a hundred schools contend"—that is, encouraging all people to express their opinions and criticisms freely.

1957 · The "Hundred Flowers" movement (begun in 1956) unleashes a barrage of criticism regarding the CPC's repressive policies, defects in the legal system, and other issues; in response, the CPC launches the "Anti-Rightist Campaign", under which hundreds of thousands of people are labeled "rightists" and sent to "rehabilitation" farms for "re-education through labour" without recourse to any formal court procedure. Consequently, the prestige of courts and other legal institutions falls sharply.

1958 · The newly-established courts and procuratorates begin to be merged into the public security organs, starting at the county level.

1959 · The Ministry of Justice and the organs of judicial administration under it are abolished, as part of a campaign in which the CPC denounces certain key principles as bourgeois and reactionary, including judicial independence, equality before the law, the system of defense lawyers in criminal trials, proportionality of punishment, the presumption of innocence, and the idea of human rights.

1962 · In a slight abatement of the assault on law and legal principles, Mao Zedong declares in March that there is in fact a need to enact both criminal and civil laws; drafting work on codes of criminal law and criminal procedure is therefore recommended.

1966 · In another reversal, Mao Zedong launches (in May) the "Great Proletarian Cultural Revolution" to purge all "counter-revolutionaries" including the "revisionists" and "capital roaders" in the CPC. Thus begins a tragic period in which Mao, through his personality cult, mobilizes millions of "Red Guards" (mainly students and youths) all over China to create civil anarchy and a reign of terror in which nearly 100 million people are subjected to persecution or victimization in one way or another; in the process, law schools are closed and the entire legal system is essentially destroyed.

1967 · The *People's Daily*, the CPC's leading newspaper, publishes an article entitled "In Praise of Lawlessness", denouncing law as a bourgeois form of restraint on the revolutionary masses and claiming that the legal system is a "strait-jacket' holding back the mass movement.

1968 · In October, Liu Shaoqi is removed from the state presidency by the CPC Central Committee, in disregard of the Constitutional provision that the President of the PRC can be removed only by the NPC.

1969 · The People's Procuratorate is formally abolished.

1975 · The 1975 Constitution is promulgated, reflecting the extreme leftist ideology of the Cultural Revolution era—for example, by deleting provisions from the 1954 Constitution on equality of citizens under the law, judicial independence, and legal protection of private property rights. CPC control over the political and legal system is expanded.

1976 · In September, Mao Zedong dies; and in the following month, the members of the so-called "Gang of Four" (alleged ringleaders of the chaos spawned by the Cultural Revolution) are arrested by the "pragmatists" (including Deng Xiaoping).

1978 · In February, the NPC is convened and enacts the 1978 Constitution, which marks a partial departure from the most radical ideology and policies of the Cultural Revolution but does not directly repudiate it (and indeed maintains the CPC's control over the political and legal system). In December, Deng Xiaoping insists that "the legal system must be strengthened" in such a way as to ensure that "laws would not change merely because of a change of leadership or a change in the leaders' views and attention." The procuratorates are re-established. The CPC by now has 35 million members.

1979 · The Ministry of Justice is re-established; organic laws on courts and on procuratorates are adopted; the *Equity Joint Venture Law* is enacted.

1980 · The *Provisional Regulations on Lawyers* are issued in August by the NPC Standing Committee.

1981 · The *Contract Law* is adopted, with a strong flavor of Soviet influence. In June, the CPC adopts the *Resolution on Questions of Party History Since the Establishment of the PRC*, which urged that law and the legal system must be emphasized to prevent the recurrence of errors committed during the Cultural Revolution.

1982 · The 1982 Constitution is adopted in December, representing a return to the "socialist legality" model of the 1954 Constitution. The *Trademarks Law* is also adopted, reflecting the influence of Western Law. The Chinese Law Society is established.

1983 · The Ministry of Education approves more than 30 universities to set up law departments, and a national conference on legal education (held in Beijing) calls for the enrollment of up to 10,000 law students by the end of 1987. Some decisions of the Supreme People's Court begin to be distributed within the court system.

1984 · The *Patent Law* is adopted, again reflecting the influence of Western law.

1985 · The *Gazette of the Supreme People's Court* begins publication, thus expanding the range of court decisions publicly available and providing a mechanism by which the Supreme People's Court provides guidance to lower courts.

1986 · By the end of this year, numerous courts have been established, including 29 high courts, 337 intermediate courts, 2,907 basic courts, and over 14,000 people's tribunals, with a total of nearly 99,000 judges. The *General Principles of Civil Law* is adopted, based directly on the German model; and a relatively comprehensive legal regime for foreign investment has been established.

1988 · The 1982 Constitution is amended to legitimize the private economy and to legalize the leasing of land and the transfer of land-use rights and the *Cooperative Joint Venture Law* is adopted.

1989 · By the end of this year, about 150 national statutes, more than 500 administrative regulations and rules, and more than 1,000 local rules have been issued, covering all major aspects of social and economic life; and legislative focus on administrative law results in the *Law on Administrative Litigation*, laying down detailed standards defining which administrative activities are legal or illegal. In May, the protests and crackdown at Tiananmen Square bring international criticism and reveal CPC concerns over risks associated with political reform.

1991 · The State Council issues its white paper on *Human Rights in China*, suggesting an about-turn in the official attitude toward the discourse of human rights (by claiming that "[i]t remains a long-term historical task for the Chinese people and government to continue to promote human rights")

1992 · In January, Deng Xiaoping takes his "Southern Tour" and is reported as saying that "reforms and greater openness are China's only way out" and that "if capitalism has something good, then socialism should bring it over and use it". In addition, the *Maritime Code* is adopted and is heralded as an example for harmonizing Chinese law with international practice.

1993 · The 1982 Constitution is amended again, this time replacing the reference to a "planned economy" with that of a "socialist market economy" and also replacing "state-run economy" with "state-owned economy" (implying that the public sector of the economy will no longer be operated by bureaucratic administration but will be regulated by market mechanisms); and the *Company Law* is enacted.

1994 · The *Foreign Trade Law*, the *Arbitration Law*, and the *Audit Law* are adopted, along with the *State Compensation Law* (supplementing the *Law on Administrative Litigation* adopted in 1989); and the legal aid system begins operations.

1995 · The *Securities Law*, the *Law on Accounting*, and the *Insurance Law* are adopted. There are by this time (according to one account), 89,000 lawyers and 7,200 law firms, and legal education has flourished, with the number of law schools having risen from two by the end of 1977 to more than 80.

1996 · Revisions to the *Criminal Law* and the *Criminal Procedural Law* are undertaken, with a stated aim of absorbing commonly accepted international standards on justice and the rule of law; and the NPC Standing Committee enacts the *Law on Lawyers*, which seeks to strengthen and modernize the legal profession and to recasting lawyers as professionals providing services to clients (instead of as state workers)

1997 · The *Law on Administrative Punishment* is adopted, complementing the earlier laws on administrative law and procedure; and an "Intensified Educational Rectification Movement" within the judiciary is undertaken, resulting in the reshuffling, disciplining, and removal of thousands of judges. Deng Xiaoping dies, and the CPC adopts "Deng Xiaoping Theory" as part of the CPC's official ideology (along with Marixism-Leninism and "Mao Zedong Thought"). In addition, China signs the International Covenant on Economic, Social and Cultural Rights.

1998 · Several changes are initiated in the judicial system, including (i) improving a "lay assessor" system in which laypersons assist judges in making court judgments; (ii) strengthening township courts in order to expand the judiciary's role in rural areas, (iii) appointing certain senior judges as superintendents responsible for offering advice in handing major or difficult cases, (iv) opening most trials and hearings to the public, (v) introducing the practice of advising victims, witnesses, and suspects in criminal cases of their legal rights, and (vi) changing the system of recruitment of judges. In addition, China signs the International Covenant on Civil and Political Rights.

1999 · The 1981 version of the *Contract Law* is replaced with a revised *Contract Law* that reflects a "pluralist approach" to legislation, drawing on experience from foreign and international sources; and the 1982 Constitution is amended again, this time (i) to reflect the NPC's strategy (urged by CPC Secretary-General Jiang Zemin) to "rule the country according to law" (以法治国, *yifa zhiguo*) and "build a socialist country governed by law" (建设社会主义 法制国家, *jianshe shehui zhuyi fazhi guojia*), and (ii) to give further prominence to the role of the private sector in China's economy.

2001 · The Supreme People's Court, in its "Reply to the Shandong High Court" regarding the case of *Qi Yuling v. Chen Xiaoqi and others*, suggested that courts may refer to and rely on provisions of the Constitution in deciding cases—thereby departing from the position established on this issue in 1955. China is admitted to the World Trade Organization.

2002 · Upon the retirement of Jiang Zemin from the position of CPC Secretary-General (succeeded by Hu Jintao), Jiang's "theory of the Three Represents" is formalized in the CPC constitution, setting the stage for the incorporation of that theory into the PRC Constitution in 2004. In addition, the CPC constitution is amended (i) to delete references to the ultimate abolition of capitalism, and (ii) to open CPC membership to a broad range of people, including private entrepreneurs; and by 2002 the CPC has 66 million members.

2003 · As of the end of the year, over 560,000 undergraduate and nearly 11,000 graduate students are enrolled in several hundred law departments and schools within Chinese universities.

2004 · In March, the 1982 Constitution is amended again—this time mainly (i) to provide expressly that the state respects and protects human rights, (ii) to provide expressly for the protection of citizens' private property rights, and (iii) to adopt Jiang Zemin's "theory of the three represents". The NPC and its Standing Committee have adopted (as of June of this year) a total of 323 laws, 138 resolutions, and 10 sets of legislative interpretations since 1979, and the State Council had issued 970 administrative regulations; local legislatures has also issued thousands of rules. There are over 3,500 courts and more than 190,000 judges, whose qualifications are regulated by national laws and examinations; and there are roughly 120,000 practicing lawyers, of whom nearly 5,000 work in the 3,023 legal aid organizations.

2005 · The Public Servants Law is adopted, setting a high standard for conduct by government officials.

2006 · The NPC adopts the *Supervision Law*, which authorizes the NPC to exercise supervisory control over the operations of courts—not (as earlier proposed) over individual cases handled by the courts but rather on a collective basis and relating to "specific issues".

2007 · The Property Law is enacted, covering all three types of property in the PRC—state, collective, and private—and giving legislative detail to the constitutional provisions added in 2004 guaranteeing private property rights.

2008 · The NPC Standing Committee announces that draft laws submitted to it for review will be published on the NPC's website and in some cases also published in major newspapers, to permit comments to be provided by the public.

B. The Republic of China (1911–1949)

As should be clear from the entries given in the "time line" of Box #6.10, the development of law in modern China has been both figuratively and literally "revolutionary". To borrow a phrase that an authority on Chinese law has used in a different context, there has been "a mighty paroxysm of effort"[162]—or, more precisely, numerous such "paroxysms"[163] of effort—on the part of China in reformulating its law.

1. The Qing Collapse, Legal Reform, and the May Fourth Movement

At the very beginning of the period covered in Box #6.10—that is, as the 19th century was giving way to the 20th—the incentive to undertake significant legal reform in China came from a cluster of factors, but one central factor was China's desire to put an end to the system of "extraterritorial privileges." That system, which dated back to the previous century, has been described in this way:

> [F]oreign subjects were exempt from local jurisdiction, and, instead, were subject to their own national authorities for conduct while physically present in China. Extraterritorial privileges include an exemption from jurisdiction of local courts; freedom from arrest by local officials; and the right to a criminal or civil trial by consular or national courts.... The United States, for example, secured its extraterritorial privilege in its treaty with China, concluded on July 3, 1844. The China Treaty of 1844 provides that "citizens of the United States who may commit any crime in China shall be subject to be tried and punished only by the consul, or other public functionary of the United States, thereto authorized, according to the laws of the United States" [and that] "all questions in regard to rights, whether of property or person, arising between citizens of the United States in China, shall be subject to the jurisdiction of and regulated by the authority of their own Government."[164]

In the waning days of the Qing Dynasty, and with the dawning of a new day that its collapse promised to China, Chinese authorities condemned the system of extraterritorial privileges and pressed for the practice to be terminated. Their complaints got results—or at least promises:

> After the practice [of extraterritorial privileges had] existed for over 60 years, and on the demand of the Chinese government, Great Britain and the United States promised to abolish the extraterritorial system on the condition that China establish a legal system consistent with international norms. Article 15 of the commercial treaty between the United States and China of 1903 [formalized that promise on the part of the United States].[165]

---

162. Daniel Chow uses this phrase in connection with the country's Great Leap Forward (described briefly later in this chapter):
> Just as the nation was consumed and united by a mighty paroxysm of effort during the disastrous Great Leap Forward, China is now also consumed by a drive to lift itself up to the level of advanced industrialized nations and to resume its place among the leading nations of the world. Law and legality need to be understood in the context of the nation's all-consuming goal.

Chow, *supra* note 159, at 37.

163. A "paroxysm" may be defined as a "sudden outburst of emotion or action", "a sudden attack or spasm or fit", or "a convulsion". The word derives in part from Greek roots that mean "to stimulate" or "to irritate" or "to goad".

164. Zimmerman, *supra* note 159, at 38 (citations omitted).

165. *Id.* at 43 (citations omitted).

On the strength of that commitment, the Chinese government "took steps to reform its legal system, including the establishment of an independent judiciary and codification of its law."[166] Some details in that regard appear in Box #6.10, which identifies a series of initiatives in the years immediately before the Qing Dynasty collapsed in 1911.

We might regard those efforts at legal reform as both effective and ineffective. Obviously, they were *ineffective* if effectiveness is to be measured in terms of sustaining the Qing leaders in power. The Chinese political system was so weakened by the turn of the 20th century that legal reforms, however bold, could not keep it from falling. And fall it did:

> On 10 October 1911, a date thereafter known as the 'Double Tenth', a mutiny headed by New Army officers broke out at Wuchang. They seized the city and obtained the support of the Hubei provincial assembly, which declared the province independent from the empire. By December all the provinces of central and southern China had followed suit. A republic was declared and Sun Zhongshan (Sun Yatsen) was invited to become provisional president. The Qing court appealed to Yuan Shikai, the most influential military commander in the north, to come to its support, but instead he decided to support the republic and to force the emperor to abdicate.[167]

In another sense, however, the late-Qing efforts at legal reform were *effective*: they laid the groundwork, both in terms of outlook and in terms of tangible documents, for the legal reform efforts that continued after the Qing Dynasty was replaced by the Republic in 1912. As shown in Box #6.10, numerous steps were taken then to adopt new criminal and commercial laws.[168] Indeed, by the time of the 1919 Paris Peace Conference following World War I, although the efforts at legal reform had met with serious obstacles because of China's post-Qing political instability,[169] some impressive changes had in fact been made:

> At the time of the Paris Peace Conference, China had adopted a National Constitution; developed civil, criminal, commercial, and procedural codes; established new court systems; improved legal training; and reformed the prison and police systems. [The legal codes were] based upon the codes of several Continental European countries including France, Germany, and Switzerland.[170]

---

166. *Id.* "In 1902, the Emperor Guangxu issued an order to reform China's legal system and established a law reform commission headed by jurist Shen Jiaben. The Qing Dynasty established China's new Supreme Court in 1906." *Id.* See also Wang and Zhang, *supra* note 159, at 8 (describing legal reform efforts in the late Qing period). See also Chow, *supra* note 159, at 53–54 (noting that "efforts during the final stage of the Qing dynasty were made to adopt various modern laws based upon the laws of western nations and the newly modernized Japanese legal system").

167. J.A.G. Roberts, *supra* note 1, at 206. As Roberts explains, the Qing collapse probably had less to do with the role of such revolutionaries as Sun Zhongshan (Sun Yatsen) than with the degree of decay already afflicting the Qing leadership, exacerbated by specific developments revolving around railroad nationalizations, military modernization, economic depression in Central China, and flooding along the Yangzi and Han rivers that claimed over two million lives. These facts make it questionable whether the events of 1911, which were in any event followed by the decline of the Republic into warlordism — "should be counted as a genuine revolution" at all. *Id.* at 213.

168. See also Zimmerman, *supra* note 159, at 43.

169. Some sources emphasize the shortcomings of the legal reform efforts during this period. See, e.g., Chow, *supra* note 159, at 54 (noting that the post-Qing legal reforms "were never fully implemented"); Wang and Zhang, *supra* note 159, at 8 (explaining that the laws drafted by the Nationalist Government "were never effectively implemented throughout the country, due to the failure of the Nationalist Government to unify the country").

170. Zimmerman, *supra* note 159, at 44 n.39 (citing S. Liu, EXTRATERRITORIALITY: ITS RISE AND ITS DECLINE 23 (1925)).

Despite these initiatives, which the Chinese government emphasized to the foreign powers gathered at the Paris Peace Conference, no action was taken there to dismantle the extraterritorial privileges. This inaction, which the Chinese government interpreted as unjustified intransigence, was only one part of a package of insults and injury (from the Chinese perspective) that emerged at the Conference and that led to the May Fourth Movement:

> The treatment of China at Versailles [site of negotiations for the Paris Peace Conference] led to mass protests in Tiananmen Square on May 4, 1919, thereby launching what is known as the May Fourth Movement, which is characterized as the first true nationalist movement in China. Thousands of students took to the streets in Beijing in the largest and most violent demonstration yet seen in the capital. The demonstrators were incensed by the hypocrisy of the Western powers, which raised China's hopes that the "unequal treaties would be abolished and Chinese sovereignty restored." The protests in Beijing led to nationwide demonstrations throughout China and reshaped intellectual thought in China over the next decades. The May Fourth Movement inspired Chinese activists of all types of ideologies.[171]

2. Nationalists and Communists

There was no shortage of activists and ideologies — and struggles for power — at this time in China. Indeed, for most of the three decades from 1919 to 1949, China could be regarded as a bipolar country, with political, military, and ideological loyalties falling largely into two camps: that of the Guomindang (Nationalist) Party and that of the Communist Party of China. As reflected in some of the entries shown in Box #6.10 for those three decades, the two rival parties vied strenuously for power in a competition that waxed and waned (even exhibiting some degree of détente in response to the Japanese invasion of the late 1930s) and that featured two mighty foes in Jiang Jieshi (Chiang Kaishek) and Mao Zedong.

A flavor for the tumult during this time can be found in this synopsis of the period from 1919 to 1949:

> During these years [beginning in 1919 with the May Fourth Movement] several important events took place: ... the founding of the Chinese Communist Party CCP [CPC[172]] in 1921; the reorganization of the Guomindang, or Nationalist Party; and the Northern Expedition of 1926–8 which led to the nominal reunification of the country.... [Then,] [b]etween 1928 and 1937 the Guomindang attempted to transform China into a modern state, while at the same time harassing the CCP, with which it had split in 1927. In 1931 Japan seized Manchuria but Jiang Jieshi [Chiang Kaishek], now leading the Guomindang, refused to respond. He preferred to pursue the Communists, who set out on the Long March in 1934. By 1936 Japanese encroachment on north China forced Jiang Jieshi to agree [on a] united front with the Communists, and in the following year the Sino-Japanese War broke out. After an initial period of heroic

---

171. *Id.* at 44–45 n.40, quoting from Jonathan Spence, THE SEARCH FOR MODERN CHINA 293–294, 310–319 (1990).

172. As noted earlier, the abbreviations CCP (standing for Chinese Communist Party) and CPC (Communist Party of China) are used interchangeably in the literature. In my own writing, I use the acronym CPC; but in quoted material I have, for the most part, left references to "CCP" undisturbed.

resistance, the Guomindang retreated to Chongqing while the Communists fought on from their base at Yan'an. After the defeat of Japan in 1945, the Guomindang and CCP fought a civil war which resulted in the Communist victory of 1949.[173]

Given that tumultuous political environment, it should come as no surprise that efforts toward legal reform in China in the 1920s, 1930s, and 1940s present a mixed picture. There were, as reflected in Box #6.10, laws, legal policy instruments, and competing constitutions emerging from the Guomindang and CPC camps. These efforts drew from a variety of sources and promised an array of new directions.

The Communists, for example, took inspiration from Soviet experience. Some of the Guomindang initiatives, in contrast, built upon Chinese experience in recent decades with Western-inspired legislation; but some Guomindang initiatives proposed improvements on the Western model.[174]

These efforts contributed to laying the groundwork for later legislative and legal initiatives. They could not, however, succeed in providing China with a stable legal system — either on a predominantly Western model, as the Guomindang generally favored, or on a Marxist-Leninist model, as the Communists preferred.

C. The PRC in Mao Zedong's Grip (1949–1978)

1. A Sharp Left Turn

The next milepost in the story of modern China's legal system appeared in 1949. With the establishment of the PRC in that year, the country's legal reform set upon a definite and radical ideological course. Emphatically rejecting the goal of creating a new legal system compatible with Western expectations and experience, the Communist leadership adopted a completely different approach:

> In February of 1949, the CCP [CPC] forcefully removed the Guomindang Government, including its judiciary and the entire body of laws. The CCP issued a directive abolishing the Guomindang's six codes, all modeled after European legal codes, including the Constitution, the Commercial law, Civil Law, Civil Code of Procedure, and Criminal Code.[[175]] In September of 1949, the CCP is-

---

173. J.A.G. Roberts, *supra* note 1, at 206–207.

174. See, e.g., the reference in Box #6.10 to the *San Min Zhu Yi* legislative initiative launched in 1928. That initiative is noteworthy for its claim to improve both on traditional Chinese law and on Western law by focusing on the protection of collective national interests instead of either (i) family and clan interests or (ii) the interests of the individual.

175. As explained by Albert Chen, the use of the term "Collection of the Six Laws" (sometimes referred to as the "Six Codes") is curious:

> [The term] does not mean six codes only but in fact refers to the total of all enacted laws and regulations of the Republic of China under the [Guomindang] government. It is not completely clear what exactly was the original meaning of 'Six Laws' — one view is that it referred to constitutional law, civil law, commercial law, criminal law, the law of civil procedure, and the law of criminal procedure [in which case it would correspond to the five codes typical for European civil law countries, plus the constitution]; another view is that it embraced constitutional law, civil law, commercial law, criminal law, procedural law and the organic law of the courts.

Albert H.Y. Chen, *supra* note 159, at 24 n.11.

sued the *Common Program of the Chinese People's Consultative Conference*, which became the temporary basic law of China.[176]

In October 1949, Mao Zedong officially announced the establishment of the PRC and of a new political system that was based on Marxist-Leninist ideas. This was to have obvious and dramatic implications for the legal system in the years to follow:

> Based on orthodox Marxism, the Chinese communist government strongly repudiated Western democracy and its justifications of an autonomous legal system (i.e., ideas of separation of power and [of] checks and balances). Rather, it declared that law is associated with the nature of the state and therefore by no means impartial. It is a tool for the maintenance of state domination. Consistent with this understanding, class struggle [was] viewed as an effective means to push forward development of society.... From the "Anti-Rightists" campaign and the "Great Leap Forward" movement in the 1950s to the Cultural Revolution in the 1960s and 1970s, law and the legal system were used as tools for class struggle, and their existence and functions were subject to politicians' discretions. In 1959, for instance, the Ministry of Justice (MOJ) and the Bureau of Legislative Affairs (under the State Council) were both closed, following by abolishment of justice bureaus in provinces, autonomous regions, and municipalities.[177]

2. Governing by Movement

Let us take a short detour — away from legal affairs and into political and economic affairs — in order to sharpen our understanding of what transpired in China during this period of "campaigns" and "movements". The passage quoted immediately above refers (as do some entries in Box #6.10 above) to the "Anti-Rightist" campaign and the "Great Leap Forward" movement. Each of these represents a significant event in 20th-century Chinese history, and each illustrates something of the chaos and irrationality that China suffered under while in the grip of Mao Zedong. Box #6.11 offers a thumbnail sketch of the "Anti-Rightist" campaign, and Box #6.12 gives a synopsis of the "Great Leap Forward" movement.

Box #6.11 The "Anti-Rightist" Campaign[178]

The Anti-Rightist Campaign was a rectification movement directed against some party members and intellectuals who expressed their criticism of the Communist Party regime during the Hundred Flowers Campaign of 1956–57 — so named for the phrase, "Let a hundred flowers bloom together, let the hundred schools of thought contend." In a speech entitled "On the Correct Handling of Contradictions among the People", Mao had encouraged intellectuals to voice their criticism of the Party, asserting that "non-antagonistic contradictions" could help speed progress toward socialism. After some hesitation, the critics surfaced with their complaints. Some were published, and some appeared in the form of posters hung on a "democracy wall" in Beijing by Peking University students critical of some officials. Apparently surprised by the severity of the attacks that the Hundred Flowers campaign elicited, Mao struck back with a counter-attack, in the form of the Anti-Rightist Campaign. Designed to purge its critics both inside and outside Party ranks, the campaign developed into a vehicle for violent, brutal political revenge. One of the most famous victims was the writer Ding Ling, who was accused

---

176. Zimmerman, *supra* note 159, at 46–47.
177. Bin, *supra* note 159, at 19 (citations omitted).
178. This account draws, in part *verbatim*, from the following sources: Albert H.Y. Chen, *supra* note 159, at 29; Chow, *supra* note 159, at 15; J.A.G. Roberts, *supra* note 1, at 266.

of having opposed the Party leadership in her literary work. She, like many others, was sent to redeem herself through labor on a farm near the Soviet border—all without recourse to any formal court procedure. Another victim was Lin Xiling, a 20-year-old law student a Beijing's Renmin (People's) University of China and a CPC member herself. During the Hundred Flowers Campaign, she made some public speeches containing criticisms of the authorities. She was reported to have been sentenced to 20 years of re-education through labor with deprivation of civil rights for life.

Box #6.12 The "Great Leap Forward" Movement[179]

One of Mao's earliest economic reforms, the Great Leap Forward (GLF), led directly to a famine that killed some 20 to 30 million people from 1958 [to] 1960. The GLF was a misguided and aborted attempt to leapfrog China into the modern age. In 1958, the nation began a mighty effort to build new roads, factories, dikes, dams, and lakes. One of the most quixotic feats of the GLF was the campaign begun in July 1958 to produce steel in backyard furnaces. By some accounts, by October 1958 some 1 million backyard furnaces were set up and 100 million people were busy melting their farming and household implements to make steel that proved largely unusable. The GLF demonstrated the capacity of the Chinese people to unite in a national effort of great magnitude and intensity as never before even if the results were ultimately devastating and catastrophic. The national mood of fervent self-sacrifice and devotion to the nation infused many cadres with the desire to continually break production records and led to the totally unrealistic and false reporting of agricultural production figures. The reports of miraculous increases in productivity led to increases in requisitions from Beijing. At the same time, diversion of water for public works and poor weather led to decreases in crop production. The combination of increased requisition [and decreased] productivity … led to a man-made disaster of mass starvation in China's villages. Several years of more rational economic policies in the 1960s were necessary to bring China back to pre-GLF production levels.

Some of the same elements of passionate irrationality and brutal perversity that appeared in the Anti-Rightist campaign and the Great Leap Forward movement showed up also in "many other smaller movements designed to raise the political consciousness of the general populace";[180] and in some of those movements "law and the legal system were used as tools for class struggle".[181] Specifically, in the place of the formal institutions of justice arose "mass trials held all over the country in which mobs of angry citizens meted out a rough revolutionary justice on class enemies of the old order".[182] The account of those trials is grim indeed:

These so-called trials were held in public before frenzied crowds where the victims were bound, made to kneel, and had to suffer verbal and physical attacks without

---

179. This account draws *verbatim* from Chow, *supra* note 159, at 15–16.

180. Chow, *supra* note 159, at 54–55.

181. Bin, *supra* note 159, at 19.

182. Chow, *supra* note 159, at 55. Simon Leys (translator of the *Analects* of Confucius quoted earlier in this chapter) has offered this account of one such "trial", held in 1971:

> The accused person's crime was the defacing of a portrait of Mao Zedong; the accused had been denounced by his own daughter, a twelve-year-old child. On the basis of the child's testimony, he was convicted and sentenced to death; as was usually the case in these mass-accusation meetings, there was no right of appeal, and the sentence was carried out immediately, by firing squad. The child was officially extolled as a hero; she disclaimed any relationship with the dead man and proclaimed publicly her resolution to become from then on "with her whole heart and her whole will, the good daughter of the Party."

Simon Leys, *The Burning Forest—Human Rights in China*, appearing on the Morning Sun Website [about the Cultural Revolution], at http://www.morningsun.org/stages/leys_humanrights.html.

any opportunity to defend themselves. By Mao Zedong's own account as many as 800,000 people met their deaths through these cruel and brutal methods.[183]

3. Revolutionary Meltdown

Then came the Cultural Revolution. As noted in Box #6.10, the Great Proletarian Cultural Revolution was launched by Mao in May 1966 with the stated purpose of purging all "counter-revolutionaries", including the "revisionists" and "capital roaders" in the CPC. From then until Mao's death in 1976, the shutdown of the legal system was nearly complete:

> [I]n this 10-year period, the Third Session of the National People's Congress (NPC), as the national legislative organization, could not hold its regular meetings, even though the national Constitution required its annual meetings. Only one law, the Platform for the Development of the National Agriculture ... was made during this period. The revised Constitution in 1975 contained merely 30 articles, a sharp reduction from a total of 106 articles in the 1954 Constitution. The People's Procuratorates were completely abolished and regrouped into public security organizations. The remaining organizations of the legal system also could not function normally in this period. It was not unusual that the *Gong, Jian, Fa* (police, procuracy, and court) were smashed by extremely feverous youths, the Red Guards, in social movements. This period of time was later described by scholars as lawless or a period of the "rule of man."[184]

As another author has expressed it, "the so-called Cultural Revolution ground the administration of justice to a halt,"[185] and efforts at productive law reform were abandoned:

> Contracts were considered to be symbols of a capitalistic system; hence, the contract system was abolished. For about twenty years no contract law was enacted, nor was contract law practiced in the courts. Since 1950 Socialist China had tried to develop a criminal code. In the course of time, thirty-three drafts of such a code had been completed, but it was only in 1980, after the end of the Cultural Revolution, that the completed code was finally enacted.[186]

D. The PRC in Reform Mode (1979–Present)

1. Legal and Economic Reclamation

Mao's death in 1976—arguably the greatest favor he did for the Chinese people—set the stage for a new start in China; and that new start included the current phase of the country's legal reform. This phase, no less wrenching than the earlier "paroxysms of effort" described above, began with an acknowledgment that the abandonment of law under Mao had been disastrous for the country and that efforts to reclaim legal order were now urgently needed:

> The Chinese government [after Mao's death] ... emphasized that the excesses of the Cultural Revolution occurred as a result of certain officials taking advantage of China's incomplete legal system to seize power. To guard China from returning to a similar situation, the NPC stressed the need to develop a legal system that

---

183. Chow, *supra* note 159, at 55.
184. Bin, *supra* note 159, at 19–20 (citations omitted).
185. Behr, *supra* note 159, at 1163.
186. *Id.* at 1164 (citations omitted).

ensures the stability and continuity of the laws; guarantees the equality of all the people before the laws and to deny anyone the privilege of being above the law; and that the law may be revised only through legal procedures and not at the personal whim of a particular leader.[187]

Let us pause for a moment to consider how this line of thinking—focusing on the need for laws that would be stable, applicable to all in society, and not subject to "the whim of a particular leader"—resembles the line of thinking described in section I of this chapter when we examined the views of Legalism as it was developed over twenty centuries ago. Here is the description we saw there:

> The Legalists ... strongly rejected the rule-by-man principle.... Instead they sought a principle of governing that would assure a long, even a permanent peaceful order of society, and not one whose uncertainties could only lead to in-termittent periods of order and disorder.[188]

One sort of "disorder" that was uppermost in the minds of China's leaders immediately after Mao's death freed the country from maniacal one-man rule was *economic* disorder. Almost immediately after Mao had left the scene, the new leadership, under the control of Deng Xiaoping, started adopting dramatic (though partially disguised) economic changes. Those economic changes, and the results they brought, were breathtaking:

> 1978 marked a watershed in Chinese history. After the 3rd plenary session of the 11th Central Committee, the CCP officially acknowledged that "the principle [*sic*] contradiction in China today is no longer class struggle but between the growing material and cultural needs of the people and the backwardness of so-cial production". This call was to end the class struggle that had persisted in China for more than 20 years and to shift the government's priority back to eco-nomic development. In the next three decades, China's economy quickly took off and began to catch up with advanced developed nations. For example, in 1978, both the gross national product (GNP) and the gross domestic product (GDP) were a little more than 364 billion yuan, and the per capita GDP was just 381 yuan. Then the GDP grew at an average of 9.6% (adjusted) per year from 1979 to 2005. By 2005, both GNP and GDP reached more than 18.3 trillion yuan (more than a 1,198% index increase with 1978 = 100), and the per capita GDP jumped to 14,040 yuan (more than a 878% index increase with 1978 = 100). The most re-cent data reported China's GDP as 20.94 trillion yuan in 2006, a 10.7% increase from 2005.[189]

The same adjective I used above to describe these economic developments—"breath-taking"—also describes the *legal* reforms that were undertaken to facilitate the PRC's economic reorientation. The following few paragraphs supplement the information ap-pearing in Box #6.10 to illustrate how remarkable these legal reforms have been both in terms of legislative activity and in terms of institutional recovery.

2. A Legislative and Regulatory Frenzy

Between 1978 and 1992, according to one source, the PRC's government "promulgated more than two thousand laws, statutes, amendments, and decrees, exceeding the total

---

187. Zimmerman, *supra* note 159, at 49 (citing Chiu, *Certain Problems in Recent Law Reform in the People's Republic of China*, 3 COMPARATIVE LAW YEAR BOOK 1, 12 (1979)).

188. Ch'ü, *supra* note 1, at 242–250.

189. Bin, *supra* note 159, at 21 (citations omitted).

number of laws enacted in its first three decades under Communist rule."[190] If anything, the pace has quickened in more recent years: according to another authority, the number of laws and regulations promulgated at the national level and by local peoples' "congresses" between 1992 and 2004 exceeds 7,100,[191] causing one observer to remark that legal reform in China "is an area of frenzied activity"[192] and another to note that "[t]he pace of reform makes it difficult even for those within China to keep abreast of the latest developments [because] ... [n]ew laws and regulations are being issued at breakneck speed, old laws and regulations are amended continually, and whole new regulatory regimes and institutions are being created."[193]

What is the legislative state of play today, a little more than thirty years after this high-speed legal reform process got underway in 1979? Naturally, it is beyond the scope of our discussion here to offer a substantive survey of the laws now in force in the PRC. Excellent sources of information are available for that purpose.[194] Suffice it to say that the PRC now has a comprehensive body of statutory and regulatory law that addresses the whole range of economic issues — contracts, property, tax, labor and employment, government procurement, banking, insurance, consumer protection, intellectual property, trade, securities, insolvency, and business associations — as well as civil law, civil procedure, criminal law, criminal procedure, family law, mediation and arbitration, environmental protection, and more.[195] An illustrative sample listing of such laws and regulations, with the dates of their adoption, appears in Box #6.13.

Box #6.13 Post-1979 Chinese Laws — Selected Listing[196]

Air Pollution Law (2000)

Arbitration Law (1994)

Agriculture Law (1993)

---

190. Xin Ren, *supra* note 159, at 2.

191. Bin, *supra* note 159, at 44 (table 3.1). Another source reports that "local people's congresses have adopted over 5,000 local laws since 1979, ranging from traffic rules and foreign investment incentives to domestic relations laws" and that the NPC's Standing Committee, which has important legislative authority, has enacted over 300 laws since 1979. Zimmerman, *supra* note 159, at 53. Similar figures emphasizing the impressive volume of legislative activity appear in the entries for 1989 and 2004 in Box #6.10, *supra*.

192. Edward B. Vermeer, *Introduction* in Vermeer and d'Hooghe, *supra* note 159, at ix.

193. Peerenboom, *supra* note 159, at 38.

194. See, e.g., Wang & Zhang, *supra* note 159; Guanghua Yu and Minkang Gu, Laws Affecting Business Transactions in the PRC (2001); Wang Guiguo and John Mo, Chinese Law (1999); Zimmerman, *supra* note 159.

195. This list of topics is drawn from the chapter headings in Zimmerman, *supra* note 159, and in Wang and Mo, *supra* note 194. In addition to these laws and regulations, of course, and serving as some form of guide for the legal system as a whole, is the PRC's current constitution, first adopted in 1982 and amended four times since then. For the text of the constitution, detailing amendments at the end, see http://english.peopledaily.com.cn/constitution/constitution.html. As reflected in Box #6.10, and discussed more fully later in this chapter and the next, the amendments were adopted in 1988, 1993, 1999, and 2004. Preceding the 1982 constitution, as also reflected in Box #6.10, were three earlier constitutions. For a synopsis of those constitutions, as well as the 1982 Constitution and its amendments, see Arjun Subrahmanyan, *Constitutionalism in China: Changing Dynamics in Legal and Political Debates*, China Law & Practice, May 1, 2004, available at http://www.chinalawand-practice.com.

196. This listing is drawn almost entirely from Albert H.Y Chen, *supra* note 159, at 318–332 and does not purport to reflect legislative and regulatory changes since the publication of Chen's book in early 2004. A few of the laws and regulations listed here might have been superseded or reformulated by later enactments.

Audit Law (1994)

Basic Norms of Professional Ethics of Judges (2001)

Budget Law (1994)

Company Law (1993)

Consumer Protection Law (1993)

Copyright Law (1990)

Criminal Code (1997)

Decision of the NPC Standing Committee on Drug Control (1990)

Environmental Protection Law (1989)

General Principles of Civil Law (1986)

Guarantee Law (1995)

Highway Law (1999)

Income Tax Laws (various)

Implementing Measures for the National Judicial Examination (2001)

Insurance Law (1995)

Labour Law (1994)

Law Against Improper Competition (1993)

Law of Administrative Licensing (2003)

Law of Administrative Litigation (1989)

Law of Administrative Punishment (1996)

Law of Administrative Review (1999)

Law of Administrative Supervision (1997)

Law of Chinese-foreign Co-operative Joint Ventures (1988)

Law of Chinese-foreign Equity Joint Ventures (1979)

Law of Civil Procedure (1991)

Law of Contract (1999)

Law of Criminal Procedure (1996)

Law of Government Purchases (2002)

Law of Individuals' Solely-Owned Enterprises (1999)

Law of Negotiable Instruments (1995)

Law of Partnership Enterprises (1997)

Law of Rural Land Contracts (2002)

Law of Township and Town Enterprises (1996)

Law of Trust (2001)

Law on Advertisements (1994)

Law on Commercial Banks (1995)

Law on Judges (1995)

Law on Lawyers (1996)

Law on Legislation (2001)

Law on Procurators (1995)

Law on Tenders (1999)

Law on the Management of Urban Real Estate (1994)

Law on the People's Bank of China (1995)

Law on the Protection of the Rights of the Elderly (1996)

Law on the Special Procedure of Maritime Litigation (1999)

Legal Aid Regulations (2003)

Management Measures on Aid to Vagrants and Beggars (2003)

Management Measures on Basic-level Legal Workers (2000)

Management Measures on Lawyers' Practising Certificates (1996)

Management Measures on Legal Professional Qualification Certificates (2002)

Maritime Law (1992)

Marriage Law (1980)

Measures on the Custody and Education of Prostitutes and their Customers (1993)

Measures on the Handling of Official Documents (2000)

Measures on the Handling of Road Traffic Accidents (1991)

Measures on the Management of Co-operative Law Firms (1996)

Measures on the Management of Partnership Law Firms (1996)

Military Service Law (1984)

Mineral Resources Law (1986)

National Security Law (1993)

Norms on Lawyers' Professional Ethics and Practice Rules (1996)

Opinions of the Supreme People's Court on the Professionalisation of the Judiciary (2002)

Organic Law of the NPC (1982)

Organic Law of the People's Courts (1979)

Organic Law of the People's Procuratorates (1979)

Organic Law of the State Council (1982)

Organic Law of Villagers' Committees (1998)

Patent Law (1984)

Pricing Law (1997)

Procedural Rules of the NPC (1989)

Procedural Rules of the NPC Standing Committee (1987)

Product Quality Law (1993)

Provisions on People's Mediation Work (2002)

Regulations on Administrative Review (1990)

Regulations on Arrest and Detention (1979)

Regulations on Collectively-owned Enterprises in Cities and Towns (1991)

Regulations on Collectively-owned Enterprises in Villages (1990)

Regulations on Detention Centers (1990)

Regulations on the Handling of Enterprise Labour Disputes (1993)

Regulations on the Management of Representative Organs of Foreign Law Firms (2001)

Regulations on the Management and Registration of Social Organisations (1998)

Road Traffic Safety Law (2003)

Rules of Conduct for NPC Standing Committee Members (1993)

Rules on Lawyers' Disciplinary Sanctions (1992)

Rules on Notarial Procedure (2002)

Securities Law (1998)

State Compensation Law (1994)

Succession Law (1985)

Supreme People's Court's Provisions on Evidence in Administrative Litigation (2002)

Supreme People's Court's Provisions on Evidence in Civil Litigation (2001)

Supreme People's Court's Provisions on Judicial Interpretation Work (1997)

Supreme People's Court's Provisions on the System of Public Trial (1999)

Trademark Law (1982)

Water Law (1988)

Water Pollution Law (1984)

3. Institutional Recovery

A legal system comprises much more, of course, than promulgated laws and regulations. It also includes institutions, personnel, and operations — most notably enforcement operations. Obviously, China's law-making (that is, legislative) institutions are in place and keeping busy, as evidenced by the large numbers of laws that have been promulgated. Indeed, these institutions constitute a remarkably complex network of congresses, standing committees, and councils at national level as well as lower levels (provinces, special municipalities, autonomous regions, etc.).[197] In addition, a court system, a procuracy system,[198] and an increasingly active community of practicing lawyers have devel-

---

197. For details regarding these various legislative bodies, see, e.g., Zimmerman, *supra* note 159, at 52–63; Chow, *supra* note 159, at 142–167. For information on the degree to which the members of these various legislative bodies are chosen by means of open elections with popular voting, see Box #7.5 in Chapter Seven, below.

198. The institution of a procuracy is unfamiliar to lawyers in many common law countries, including the USA. In general legal terms, a procurator — a term that derives from the Latin verb *procurare*, which means "to take care" — supposedly serves as a watchdog of legality, overseeing the observance of the laws in the system, especially by government officials. One authority offers this description of the procuracy as it exists in China:

> As in other civil law systems, China has a procuracy system that parallels the court system but is independent from both the courts and the Ministry of Justice, and is responsible for supervision of the judicial system.... [T]he Organic Law of the People's Procuratorates ... provides that the procurators are entrusted with supervision of the courts and administrative tribunals; investigation and prosecution of illegal conduct committed by government officials and judicial officers ... ; and investigation and prosecution of activities deemed to be a threat to public security.... The procuratorates act independently and are not subject to interference by government agencies or individuals.... The Supreme People's Procuratorate answers directly to the NPC and its Standing Committee, and is responsible for supervising the local and special procuratorates.

Zimmerman, *supra* note 159, at 66. For further discussion of the procuracy (or Procuratorate), see subsection IIIC4 in Chapter Seven, below.

oped in recent years in the PRC,[199] and an explosion in the volume of litigation has taken place in recent years. One authority, in describing the "amazing increase in cases,"[200] offers these statistics:

> In 1978, the total number of cases accepted by the courts was 447,755. The number skyrocketed to more than 5 million after 1996, reached a record high of 5,692,434 in 1999, and then slowly decreased to 5,161,170 by 2005. In 27 years, the total number of cases increased more than tenfold. When broken down, data showed remarkable increases in all types of cases. From 1978 to 2005, the numbers increased more than 13-fold for general civil cases and almost fourfold for criminal cases; economic dispute cases increased more than 295-fold from 1980 to 2001; and administrative cases increased more than 181-fold from 1983 to 2005.[201]

Legal training also has expanded dramatically in the PRC in the past thirty-five years or so from its moribund state at the close of the Cultural Revolution:

> Only after 1978 did legal education finally gain a rebirth. In the next 10 years from 1978 to 1987, the number of law colleges and departments increased from 6 to 86; the number of teachers increased from 178 to 5,216; and the number of law graduates increased from 99 to 12,639. These numbers continued to grow in the 1990s and in the new millennium. By 2006, more than 600 law programs were open nationwide with more than 200,000 students.[202]

There is obviously a linkage between these factors of (i) a rejuvenated court system, (ii) a quickening pace of litigation, and (iii) an increased supply of lawyers. Taken together, they could in time surely be expected to bring about the effective implementation and enforcement of laws, which is something that any legal system ultimately depends on. While numerous shortcomings persist in that respect (a point that will be explored in Chapter Seven, below), a shift in that direction does in fact seem to be occurring.

4. Summing Up as of 2010

The legislative, institutional, and operational aspects of the legal system of the PRC today—only a little more than thirty years since the new chapter of remarkable reform began at the end of 1978 and early 1979—are thoroughly impressive in scope and volume, and would be so even if the system had developed over three hundred years rather than over just thirty years. Our principal interest at this juncture, however, lies not in the system's scope and volume but in its character today, viewed from a historical perspective.

Recall that in subsection ID2 of this chapter, we examined four themes relating to the character of *dynastic* Chinese law; they focused on (i) the remarkable continuity of China's

---

199. For details, see Zimmerman, *supra* note 159, at 64–70 (courts, procuracy, lawyers); Wang and Mo, *supra* note 194, at 15–19 (courts); Chow, *supra* note 159, at 225–247 (lawyers); Brown, *supra* note 159, at 24–27 (lawyers) and 51–83 (courts). According to one source, the number of lawyers in China rose from about 2,000 in 1979 to nearly 154,000 in 2005. Bin, *supra* note 159, at 51. See the entry for 2004 in Box #6.10, *supra*, for a somewhat lower figure for 2004.

200. Bin, *supra* note 159, at 45.

201. *Id.*

202. *Id.* at 55. The same author explains that the numbers of graduate law programs and students also have increased. *Id.* at 55–57. For figures from another source regarding the numbers of law students in 2003, see Box #6.10, *supra*.

traditional law, (ii) how Chinese dynastic law consistently deflected or filtered outside influences; (iii) whether the "rule of law" prevailed in dynastic China, and (iv) the manner in which Imperial Confucianism served as a central "legal ethic" in dynastic China. The stage is set now for us to examine the character of *contemporary* Chinese law in terms of those same four themes. The first two of those themes are predominantly historical in nature, so we shall consider them in the final paragraphs of this chapter. The other two—rule of law and "legal ethic"—require more extensive treatment and will be dealt with in Chapter Seven.

E. Discontinuities and Disconnections in Contemporary Chinese Law

Of the two questions at issue here—(i) does contemporary Chinese law show the same remarkable continuity that we saw in section I as a hallmark of dynastic Chinese law? and (ii) has contemporary Chinese law consistently deflected and filtered outside influences, as dynastic Chinese law did?—the first one is easy to answer. The answer is an emphatic "no". Let us explore that point briefly and then turn to the second question.

1. A Termination of Dynastic Chinese Law's Continuity

As should be clear from the account offered in section I of this chapter, dynastic Chinese law could be regarded as a model—even a miracle—of stability and continuity compared to the other great legal traditions of the world. The central elements of China's dynastic legal system, founded on the Confucianist-Legalist compromise emerging around the 3rd century BCE, remained in place with relatively little disruption or fundamental alteration despite numerous political, social, demographic, and economic developments. This differentiates the Chinese dynastic legal system from the European civil law tradition, which has an origin of comparable age[203] but which has experienced a parade of tumultuous political and institutional transformations—splintering, reunification, colonization, and independence, as well as the influences of canon law, commercial law, and other subtraditions. (I tried to illustrate this distinction between Chinese dynastic law and European civil law in Diagram #6.8, above.) And of course the English common law tradition and Islamic legal tradition are of much more recent origin.[204]

The stability and continuity that made traditional Chinese law unique ended about a hundred years ago. Some of the highlights of its demise, which came with the collapse of the Qing Dynasty, have been recounted earlier in this chapter.

It might be tempting to regard what has occurred in China over the last ten or twelve decades *not* as a complete termination of dynastic Chinese law's remarkable continuity but

---

203. Recall from Chapter Two that the issuance of the Twelve Tables in Rome in 450 BCE is commonly accepted as a beginning-mark for the European civil law tradition.

204. Recall from Chapter Four that the (English) common law tradition is generally regarded as beginning in 1066 CE when William of Normandy, having defeated Harold at the Battle of Hastings, established a strong central government at Westminster and began building a system of royal courts that gradually expanded jurisdiction to create, through judicial decisions in specific legal disputes, a body of rules common to the kingdom as a whole, thus largely displacing localized customary rules. The Islamic law tradition is generally regarded as beginning with the prophet Muhamed, and particularly with his move to Medina in 622 CE.

merely as a temporary interruption of it.[205] As noted in the first portion of this chapter, several such temporary interruptions occurred throughout Chinese history. They include, for example, (i) the three-century period of disunity between the end of the Han Dynasty in 220 CE and the beginning of the Sui Dynasty in the late 6th century CE,[206] (ii) the years of unrest and uprising that occurred just before the successful replacement of the Tang Dynasty with the Song Dynasty in the late 9th and early 10th centuries CE,[207] and (iii) the similar disorder that accompanied the replacement of the Yüan Dynasty with the Ming Dynasty in the 14th century CE.[208]

In my view, we cannot reasonably equate those earlier periods of political disorder with the last ten or twelve decades—that is, with the period encompassing the final decline and collapse of the Qing Dynasty and the instability and political changes that followed— not, at least, from a legal perspective. Recall that one of the first steps taken by most founding emperors of new dynasties was to enact a legal code intended to restore the glory of an earlier dynasty,[209] often accompanied by initiatives to rejuvenate Confucianist tradition.[210] Contrast that with the course of events in China since the late 1800s as summarized earlier in this chapter, and especially in Box #6.10. From a legal perspective, there has been

---

205. The characterization of Mao Zedong as the founding emperor of a new dynasty—a possibility that I explore briefly at the beginning of section IV of Chapter Seven—is consistent with this view that the legal chaos following the collapse of the Qing Dynasty merely represented an interruption, not a termination, of the dynastic legal tradition.

206. For a summary of the political events during that period of disunity, see *supra* note 63.

207. This transition occupied a period of nearly a century (starting from the collapse of the Tang to the solidification of the Song), and it was indeed a chaotic time. One authority offers this summary of the first half of the transition, as the Tang Dynasty was falling apart:

In its final half century the Tang was an object-lesson in anarchy. Officials, both civil and military, became so cynically corrupt and village peasants so ruthlessly oppressed that the abominable became commonplace. Loyalty disappeared. Banditry took over. Gangs swelled into armed mobs, plundering all in their path as they roamed from province to province. Emperors, their eunuchs, and officials lost control and were despised. For six years (878–884) the major bandit Huang Chao led his horde up and down the face of China, from Shandong to Fuzhou and Guangzhou, then to Luoyang and Chang'an, which was destroyed. By 907, the official end of the Tang dynasty, Turkic and other non-Chinese peoples occupied much of North China and warlordism flourished elsewhere.

Fairbank, *supra* note 1, at 86–87. Following the collapse of the Tang Dynasty, it took roughly another half-century (to 960 CE) for the Song leaders to solidify power. See LCDC, *supra* note 1, at 140–141.

208. This transition lasted roughly a third of a century. During the 1330s, minor social disturbances began to break out in isolated instances of banditry. In the 1340s, some towns were attacked by bands of people whom worsening economic conditions had made desperate and whom ambitious leaders could easily incite to action; and by the 1350s, "Chinese society was rent by disorder on a scale that had not been seen for centuries." Mote, *supra* note 1, at 520–521. Mote, one of the great authorities on dynastic China, offers this cautionary note after his description of the chaos occurring between the Yüan and Ming dynasties:

In the face of general chaos, powerful regional movements developed; some merely defended their local interests, while others were ambitious to bring down the imperial government. We have here a rare case study of what could happen in China when a society long accustomed to being ruled by a coherent centralized governing authority found itself without one.

Id. at 521.

209. As explained above, the exception in this pattern appears with the establishment of the Yüan Dynasty—the first and by far the less successful of the two main "alien" dynasties in China. See text accompanying notes 116–118, *supra*.

210. See, e.g., LCDC, *supra* note 1, at 191–192 (explaining the steps take by Zhu Yuanzhang, the founding emperor of the Ming Dynasty, including "steps to further enhance Confucianism", as part of a "program to return to traditional Chinese values").

virtually no interest in the past century or so in *resuscitating* China's traditional past from a legal perspective;[211] quite to the contrary, the interest has been in *abandoning* dynastic Chinese law (particularly the codes) in favor of new approaches. Expressed differently, I see in the Chinese experience of the past century or so not a mere *interruption* of a continuing Chinese legal tradition but instead a complete and irreversible *discontinuity* of that tradition.

A principal reason for this discontinuity, in my view, is China's exposure to the Western world. Until relatively recently, it was both possible and likely that China—and indeed all of East Asia—would have little contact with the West. Distances were great and travel was slow and dangerous. When the intellectual and industrial revolutions came into full bloom in Europe (but not in China[212]) starting just a few hundred years ago, and prompted Western interests to press their way into China with growing insistence in the 19th century, the tables were turned: it became not only feasible but also inevitable that the people of China would interact with the West. A Korean government official has offered these observations on the result of that interaction and on the comparison that the interaction led some Asians to make:

> Once Asia was great. Asia has ... a history of brilliant civilization at least 5,000 years old, ... [and] has been the envy of other continents since the publication of *The Book of Marco Polo*. However, the Asians, who constitute more than half of the world population, lay dormant in Asiatic resignation. We slept under the beautiful silk blanket of 5,000 years of history of glorious civilization. Then the Western people came to Asia to wake us up. When we were awakened from the long dream, we found ourselves suffering from poverty and hunger, disease and ignorance.[213]

However suitable China's dynastic legal tradition might have been for the centuries before the modern world—with all its faults—arose, it had clearly ceased being suitable ten or twelve decades ago, not only according to the Western powers demanding "extraterritorial privileges" as described at the opening of this chapter but also according to Chinese observers and leaders (including many within the Qing regime itself). Dramatic change, including an abandonment of the traditional system, was inevitable. The only question was what shape that dramatic change would take. And part of that question was whether, and to what extent, the new version of Chinese law would be influenced by Western models, concepts, and values. This brings us to the second question posed above: has contemporary Chinese law consistently deflected and filtered outside influences, just as dynastic Chinese law did? Expressed differently, has China's resistance to outside legal influences endured?

---

211. As I shall explain below, there clearly *is* a contemporary interest—indeed, a passionate fervor—in restoring to China the political strength and autonomy it once enjoyed. See subsection IVC2 of Chapter Seven, below.

212. Recall the fourth of the four major patterns in Chinese history described by Derk Bodde, as quoted above in section I of this chapter:
> [Although a flowering of] commercial and industrial activity [occurred in Song China, so that] what was to begin in Renaissance Europe several centuries later seemed already to be beginning in China ... then something happened or rather failed to happen: the forces that were to lead to capitalism and industrialism in Western Europe failed to achieve ongoing momentum in China. The West was to change into a modern society, [but] China did not. Why this should have been ... is one of the major unanswerables in Chinese history.

See *supra* note 5.

213. Dick Wilson, A BANK FOR HALF THE WORLD 2 (1966), quoting from a November 1966 address by Kim Hak-Yul, the first Korean Governor of the Asian Development Bank.

2. The Balance between Indigenous and Exogenous Influences
a. Striking the balance in dynastic Chinese law

Recall the observations I offered above in subsection ID2 of this chapter about China's resistance to external influences in the development of its legal system during the centuries-long dynastic period. As suggested there, the strength of the "alloy" that was forged in the Qin-Han period and then incorporated effectively into the legal codes governing the empire seems to have contributed to the fashioning of an armor that deflected outside influences of various sorts.

Of course, the picture is not so simple as that "armor" image suggests. For one thing, there were other factors (besides the Confucianist-Legalist alloy) that made China resistant to outside influence, such as geographic isolation, especially from Europe. (We must bear in mind that until less than two centuries ago, the speed with which people, goods, and information could move was largely limited by how fast a horse could run and a boat could sail.) In addition, not all foreign influences faced by China were deflected like arrows careening off of metal armor but were instead filtered and "sinified" by a language that was not amenable to foreign concepts.[214] Still, much of Chinese history, including its legal history, is remarkable for its rejection of (or heavy filtering of) foreign influences.

b. Striking the balance in contemporary Chinese law

Has this attitude continued in the past thirty years as the PRC has created, in an extremely fast-track fashion, a new matrix of legal rules, institutions, and processes? Numerous experts have addressed this question, although typically without trying to make the comparison I am offering to dynastic Chinese law. I summarize in the following paragraphs some of their observations.[215]

In a book published in 1999, with thirteen contributors from the City University of Hong Kong, Professor Wang Guiguo paints a mixed picture of how external legal systems and approaches have influenced Chinese law during the PRC's recent legal reform movement:

> Looking back at the path of China's legal reforms of the last 20 years, China has demonstrated its willingness to learn from the experience of the developed economies in establishing a suitable legal system for strengthening the socialist market economy. China was even prepared to adopt the whole sector of a foreign legal system. In this regard, the tax system (heavily influenced by the US tax system) and the industrial property laws (i.e. patents, designs and trademarks—a copy of the German system) are examples. In most cases, however, *China appeared to be more willing to accept the provisions and concepts of foreign laws than their values and underlying principles.* As a result, China has resisted the notion of 'copying' or 'transplantation'.... [Nonetheless, the] interdependence be-

---

214. For a discussion of the difficulties the Chinese language poses for the adoption of foreign concepts, see text accompanying notes 130–133, *supra.*

215. I have not addressed here the period from the collapse of Qing rule at the turn of the twentieth century to the most recent surge of legal reform beginning in 1979. For a detailed survey of the influence (especially in legal theory) felt in China from the growing contacts with the West from the mid-1800s to the mid-1900s, see generally He Qinhua, *The Birth and Growth of Modern Jurisprudence in China,* 1 FRONTIERS OF LAW IN CHINA 486 (2006).

tween China and the rest of the world makes it impossible for China to resist cultural, political and legal influence—including values and beliefs—of foreign countries ... [and therefore in recent years] foreign concepts, values, etc. slowly entered into China and influenced Chinese laws.[216]

Wang and his colleagues emphasize the particular influence that other legal systems have had on Chinese law in the area of business and finance, partly in the context of the PRC's accession to the WTO. In these areas, the influence has been very substantial. In areas of law *other* than those relating to business and finance, however, the PRC has been much less receptive to Western influence. Two of Wang's colleagues, for example, explain that marriage in China "is different from that in the capitalist states in terms of its meaning, its social foundation and its social consequences. For instance, a marriage is, unlike in common law jurisdictions, not regarded as a contract but rather a crystal of love within the purview of the socialist public family."[217]

Another expert, Professor Xin Ren, writes in her 1997 book *Tradition of the Law and Law of the Tradition* that "the current modernization of law in China emerged as a hybrid of the Chinese imperial legal tradition, Western law, and Soviet socialist law,"[218] and then she proceeds to explain that although the last of these, Soviet socialist law, seems most significant,[219] China has in fact taken its own unique approach to law:

> [T]he administration of law in China differs so substantially from the system in the former Soviet Union. For example, the Chinese legal system is typically characterized as having the vast participation of the political party in the actual dispensation of justice, an informality of law and the legal process, and strong moral characteristics in legal education and training as well as in the administration of adjudication, while the former Soviet Union maintained a much more formalized rule of law and judicial procedure.[220]

Xin Ren also observes that although the PRC's legal reform in recent years seems to have adopted numerous attributes of a Western legal system—extensive legislation, for example, and the development of a class of legal professionals to serve as judges and as advocates in litigation "pursued by ordinary citizens"[221]—the underlying ideology and expectations in the PRC's legal system clearly do *not* follow a Western model:

> Excited with China's economic reform, many Western observers are watching whether China is going to succumb to the influence of the Western model of law—which often means the separation of law from other political institutions, a professional class of jurists, an independent judiciary, a system of due process,

---

216. Wang Guiguo, *The Legal System of China*, appearing as Chapter 1 in Wang and Mo, *supra* note 194, at 3–4 (emphasis added).

217. Anthony M.W. Law and Alisa W.C. Kwan, *Law of Family, Marriage and Succession*, appearing as Chapter 11 in Wang and Mo, *supra* note 194, at 418.

218. Xin, *supra* note 159, at 3.

219. *Id.* (noting that "the legality of the Communist Party's ruling power over the legislative and judicial processes, the domination of Marxist ideology in legal education and the training of jurists, and the protection of the interests, status, and priviledge [*sic*] of the Communist Party in the administration of justice are profoundly accentuated as the common features of socialist law"). Xin also notes other evidence of "the assimilation of former Soviet socialist law into Chinese law, not so much in terms of the procedural rules but primarily in terms of the ideological foundation of law." *Id.* at 4.

220. *Id.*

221. *Id.* at 2.

a principle of presumed innocence, and the right to competent legal representation—and eventually to abandon its anti-individualism and nondemocratic legal tradition.…

Apparently, China's economic openness and privatization have not changed its authoritarian tradition and lack of democratic voice in state-commanded social control efforts. What is even more puzzling to Western observers is that though China might have created what can be called laws, they are often side-stepped by the government officials. There have been institutions that are called public security, people's procurate, and people's courts, but they seem to have no independent role in resolving the disputes brought before them. There have been defense counsels appointed or hired by the accused, but they have very limited access to the power and privilege that their Western counterparts can enjoy in defending their clients' innocence beyond a reasonable doubt. There has been a constitution that guarantees the rights of free speech, press, and assembly, but its insistence on individuals' obligation to the state and the Communist Party often leaves little room for individuals to exercise their rights.[222]

Another author, Professor Pitman Potter of the University of British Columbia, also explores the interplay between external and indigenous influences on Chinese law during the PRC's recent legal reform movement. In the opening passages of his book *The Chinese Legal System—Globalization and Local Legal Culture*, Potter offers this summary:

Legal reform [in China since 1978] has … been complicated by … ambivalence about the introduction of ideals of governance associated with the West.… Foreign perspectives on China's legal system often presume that the legal reforms of the Deng Xiaoping era are more or less natural complements to economic and social reform—and possibly a harbinger to political reform. *Foreign observers are invited to conclude that Chinese legal reforms express an evolving willingness to approach governance in ways that are roughly comparable to or at least compatible with those of the industrialized democracies. These presumptions appear to be supported by the use in China of institutional forms described in the familiar nomenclature of the liberal legal tradition.* Foreign observers are given to understand that Chinese courts, lawyers, and judges are categorically comparable with those of liberal legal systems, and that various categories of substantive and procedural law in China parallel their liberal legal counterparts.

However, the legal system of the PRC offers students of law a signal lesson in the dangers in uncritical acceptance of such easy comparisons. The record of foreign involvement in China's post-Mao legal and economic reforms suggests the very real costs that ensue from the failure to understand the ways in which legal institutions and processes borrowed from abroad are driven by local conditions to operate in unexpected ways.…

… Much of the story of the PRC's legal reform effort concerns the struggle to adapt international norms to local conditions. Local legal culture refers to the system of Chinese values and practices that informs legally significant behavior. *Despite the influences exerted by foreign legal norms, Chinese law remains dominated by local*

---

222. *Id.* at 2–3.

legal culture. The development of the Chinese legal system over the past twenty years has reflected a process of selective adaptation, by which borrowed foreign norms about law and legal institutions have been mediated by local legal culture.[223]

Potter describes various sorts of interaction that have occurred between PRC government officials, including those working at the National People's Congress, and counterparts in Canada, Europe, the USA, and elsewhere in the world, particularly on topics relating to such "institutional" matters as legislative procedure and administrative law.[224] He asserts, however, that in the area of legislative procedure "foreign influences have been limited to internal procedures and the organization of legislative organs and have not extended to the broader questions of [Communist] Party dominance,"[225] and although the PRC's Administrative Litigation Law "was heavily influenced by the US Federal Administrative Procedure Act,"[226] in fact "foreign influences have had little effect on the basic normative premise underlying China's administrative law system, namely that administrative law remains an instrument in the service of Party-led governance."[227]

The picture that emerges from the analysis offered by Wang, Xin, Potter, and other authorities is that the PRC's legal reform effort of the past thirty years has exhibited three related characteristics in terms of the significance of external influence. I suggest this synopsis:

- There has been very extensive *interest in, and study of, foreign legal systems* — their norms, operations, and institutions — as China has struggled to create a legal system on a hurry-up basis to accommodate and facilitate the dramatic economic changes that the country's leadership set in motion thirty years ago following the death of Mao and his failed policies.

- From this consideration of foreign legal systems there has emerged a *mixed set of reforms*, so that (1) in some respects (especially matters of economic law) laws and institutions in today's China bear a resemblance, at least on the surface, to Western laws and institutions,[228] while (2) in other respects (family law, for example), PRC law bears little or no such resemblance to Western counterparts.

- Even in those aspects of the PRC's legal system that do reveal significant external influences, there has been *a thorough filtering* (or "screening" or "translation") of

---

223. Potter-2001, *supra* note 159, at 1–2 (emphasis added).

224. *Id.* at 35.

225. *Id.*

226. *Id.*

227. *Id.* at 36. Potter also describes how some specific substantive areas of Chinese law, as adopted or revised in recent years, reflect or resist foreign influence and models. For example, he offers this explanation of property law reform:

> [I]n the main Chinese legal specialists working on property rights were compelled to look abroad [including to Japan, Europe, and the Anglo-North-American tradition] for guidance. The adoption of foreign law norms, however, is moderated by local tradition and norms of political and legal culture. In particular, the individualist orientation of liberal property rights regimes conflicts with the collectivist norms in China, while private rights discourses of liberalism conflict with the public law norms of Chinese tradition and PRC policy. The development of property rights in the PRC is largely a process of mediating these conflicts.

Id. at 56. See also Potter-2003, *supra* note 159, at 126–127 (further describing the interaction of Western influence and local legal culture in the PRC's reform of property law).

228. It is worth noting that there are substantial differences between various sorts of "Western laws and institutions", particularly those of the civil law tradition and those of the common law tradition. As a broad generalization, it can be said that China has been more receptive to the former (especially German law) than to the latter. I am indebted to Lin Miao for emphasizing this point.

those external influences in an attempt to make the foreign elements compatible with underlying elements of Chinese legal and political culture—and that filtering is sometimes nearly invisible to outsiders unfamiliar with those underlying elements of Chinese legal and political culture.

Here is how Potter expresses some of the ideas I have offered in the above synopsis—especially the idea of "filtering":

> To a large extent, the development of Chinese legal institutions and practices has reflected the dynamics of local legal culture, and particularly the imperatives of political control for the Chinese Communist Party. While the structures of legislative, administrative and dispute resolution institutions appear quite recognizable to foreign-trained lawyers, the norms and practices of these institutions often depart quite significantly from the expectations of those familiar with liberal legal systems. This reflects the influence of *local legal culture*, which *acts* as *a normative filter through which flow the influences of foreign and international legal models.*[229]

c. Reasons for a thorough filtering

Potter's reference to "local legal culture" and my own reference (also above) to "underlying elements of China's legal and political culture" invite us to consider just what those elements are. That is what we shall turn to in Chapter Seven as we continue to explore contemporary China's legal identity. Before doing so, however, I wish to close this chapter with some further observations regarding the issue at play here—the effect of external influences on contemporary Chinese law—and especially the "filtering" of such external influences.

How is China different in this respect from any other country undertaking legal reform? Would it not be true of any such country (as I have asserted above in respect of the PRC) that some external models and pressures for change would be rejected, some would be accepted, and all those that are accepted would be filtered ("translated") so as to make them compatible with underlying elements of local legal and political culture? Indeed, is this not precisely the process that European countries went through when the "reception" of the Roman-canon *jus commune* was occurred, as described above in Chapter Two? Is this not the process that the American colonies—and, after independence, the US states—went through in determining how closely American law would hew to English law?

Probably so; but I regard China's experience in this regard as importantly different—indeed, unique—in two respects, both of which relate to the dynastic legal tradition that I summarized in the first section of this chapter. First, the fact that that the Chinese legal tradition is (as already emphasized above) in a league of its own when judged in terms of age, stability, and effectiveness would suggest that the "local legal and political culture" is likewise more stable, more homogenous, more clearly developed, and more deeply rooted than those in the West. These features, in turn, should allow us to explain and perhaps even predict how it is that we can expect local law in China to resist and filter foreign legal influences—much more so than in any other legal system undergoing substantial reform.

Second, I believe that this same stable continuity that puts Chinese law, as part of Chinese civilization more generally, in a league of its own has given China as a society a deep

---

229. Potter-2001, *supra* note 159, at 37 (emphasis added).

pride in its past that has made China's withering humiliation at the hands of Western powers in the 19th century all the more ignominious and embarrassing. The past seems to be "closer" to many Chinese than it is to most Westerners—especially to Americans, with such a short national history of their own and so little interest in history more generally. As a result, I believe the flaccid ineptness of the late Qing leaders in dealing with the challenge of aggressive, overreaching Western powers has planted in many Chinese a bitterness and suspicion against all things Western, including Western (especially American) legal structures that seem to demand and celebrate individual self-sufficiency at the expense of family and community interdependence and responsibility.

It is partly a reflection of my views on this topic that I have highlighted earlier in this section the ninetieth anniversary of the May Fourth Movement.[230] That episode from 1919, like the Boxer Rebellion that preceded it by two decades,[231] revealed profound anti-Western sentiments—and for good reason, given the abusive treatment that the Chinese had suffered at the hands of Western powers in the periods leading up to those eruptions of violence.

---

230. My wife and I recall the seventy-fifth anniversary of the May Fourth Movement, which was celebrated at Renmin University (where we were living at the time) with fireworks.

231. One source offers this synopsis of the Boxer Rebellion and the circumstances that both triggered it and followed it:

> By the end of the nineteenth century, Britain, France, Germany, Russia, and Japan all held control over a major naval port and over railways leading to mines in China's interior. The growing foreign influence led to a local backlash in the form of the Boxer Uprising of 1898–1901, which incited punitive measures by foreign nations that only compounded China's misery. One of the best known events of the nineteenth century because a large number of diplomats, journalists, and their families were besieged in the legation quarters in Beijing, the Boxer Rebellion was a peasant-based uprising based upon principles of spirituality and martial arts and fueled by a fanatical hatred of foreigners. The Boxers killed at least 250 foreigners before the Rebellion was crushed by an alliance of eight national armies. To punish China, the alliance of foreign nations imposed the draconian Boxer Protocol of 1901 on the Qing government. The Protocol required the destruction of some twenty-five Qing forts and the imposition of a crippling $333 million indemnity. The Boxer Protocol further weakened China just as foreign nations seemed prepared to launch an all-out race for imperial conquest of China. Like a ripe melon, China was about to be carved up by foreign nations eager to stake their claims. By the beginning of the twentieth century, the future of China as a nation was in peril. Whether China would survive or perish was unclear.

Chow, *supra* note 159, at 5–6.

Appendix 6.1
History of the Chinese Legal Tradition in Song
Red China Ballad

(to the tune of *Red River Valley*)

The *Chou Li* emerged around 1000 BC.
The *xing shu* came out in 536.
221 saw the Q'in push Legalism,
But after 15 years the Chinese folks said "nix!"

So in 206 the Han ruled all the country,
And they stayed in power 'til two-two-oh AD
After four hundred years of big divisions
The T'ang Code came out in 653.

Well, that T'ang Code was the model for the Ming Code
Which in 1368 was first composed.
And the Ming Code was the model for the Qing Code
Whose Dynasty in 1616 rose.

The Qing leaders had a bad 1800s.
Even though they thought they were the sons of heaven.
The Republican insurgents fully captured
The Forbidden City in 1911.

1949 begins Modern China;
Mao Tse Tung gave Chinese folks a crazy fate.
1960s brought the Cultural Revolution,
But the '90s brought a capitalistic state.

Now we've reached the end of Chinese legal history.
It's a story that is rich and very long.
Please remember: dates don't have to be a mystery;
All you really have to do is sing this song.

Chapter Seven

The Chinese Legal Tradition in Operational Perspective

Outline

Study Questions

SQ #7.1   What is meant, in general, by the terms "rule of man", "rule of law", and "rule by law"?

SQ #7.2   What does the Chinese constitution say about the rule of law?

SQ #7.3   What is the character, and in particular the binding character, of the Chinese constitution?

SQ #7.4   Did traditional (dynastic) China exhibit "rule of man" or "rule of law" or "rule by law"?

SQ #7.5   What difference is there between a "thick" and a "thin" version of the rule of law?

SQ #7.6   Would Lon Fuller have said that a "legal system" existed in dynastic China? … in the PRC in 1968? … in the USA today?

SQ #7.7   Do any contemporary Chinese academic lawyers support proposals for China's adoption of a liberal democratic version of the rule of law?

SQ #7.8   What distinction might be drawn between an "individualist mentality" and a "collectivist mentality", and how might such a distinction apply (if at all) to law?

SQ #7.09   What are the most appealing aspects of today's Chinese legal system?

SQ #7.10   How would you compare contemporary Chinese law with (i) modern civil law systems and (ii) today's US legal system(s) in terms of

    (a)   the sources of law?

    (b)   the role of legislation, constitutions, and caselaw?

    (c)   the role of scholars?

    (d)   the role of judges, and particularly the independence and competence of judges?

    (e)   legal categories (*e.g.*, is the private-public distinction significant)?

SQ #7.11   Merryman asserts that in the orthodox civil law tradition, law is regarded as a machine that is designed by the scholar, built by the legislator and operated by the judge. We might say that in the orthodox common law tradition, law is regarded as a machine that is both built and operated by the judge, without any overall design—which necessitates minor occasional repairs and modifications by the legislator. How should we characterize Chinese law in such terms? Would our answer differ based on whether we are focusing on *dynastic* Chinese law versus *contemporary* Chinese law?

SQ #7.12   In looking specifically to contemporary Chinese criminal procedure,

(a) how might we characterize it overall, compared to criminal procedure in the USA or in a typical European civil law country?

(b) what aspects of it would be especially troubling to a US lawyer — especially a US criminal defense attorney?

(c) does a person accused of a crime have the right to legal counsel during interrogation? ... the right to remain silent during trial?

(d) how (if at all) do differences between it and US criminal procedure reflect different balances of values to be served?

(e) how would you evaluate the involvement of the public in criminal trials — for example, by the use of lay assessors?

SQ #7.13 What differences are there between Imperial Confucianism, Neo-Confucianism, and New Confucianism, in terms of their legal implications or applicability?

SQ #7.14 What is the significance in contemporary China of Marxist-Leninist-Maoist-Dengist thought?

SQ #7.15 What correlative, if any, is there in contemporary China to Imperial Confucianism in dynastic China?

SQ #7.16 Are we likely to see a convergence between the Chinese legal system and Western legal systems, including those in the USA and Europe?

SQ #7.17 Recall that Merryman offered several criticisms of the civil law (discussed above in Chapter Three). What criticisms would you level at Chinese law? ... at the common law in general or US law in particular?

SQ #7.18 How would we go about identifying the "legal soul" of China? ... of the USA? ... of Italy?

Introductory Comments

In this final chapter we conclude our survey of three great legal traditions. Having considered in Chapter Six the historical development of Chinese law, it is time now to consider Chinese law from an operational perspective. This chapter begins (in section I) by examining whether, and to what extent, the actual operation of *modern* Chinese law reflects a feature that was central to *dynastic* Chinese law — an emphasis on a "bureaucratic verticality" under which law was wielded by the emperor, addressed to the bureaucracy, and designed to serve as a key instrument of social control. With modern China's legal system having undergone so many changes in recent years, has this aspect of China's legal tradition survived in some form, or has it been totally discarded? Expressed more bluntly, is there a "rule of law" in China?

Sections II and III of this chapter shift our focus to more detailed aspects of the operation of law in today's China, by examining several of the same elements that were prominent in Chapter Three (civil law from an operational perspective) and Chapter Five (common law from an operational perspective). Specifically, section II summarizes the sources and categories of law and lawyers in contemporary China, and section III discusses China's procedure of criminal justice, both "on paper" as set forth in the 1996 Criminal Procedure Law and "in practice" according to various Chinese and foreign observers.

Lastly, section IV concentrates on this question: Given the breathtaking speed with which China has reformed its legal system over the past three decades, where can we now find its core of central enduring values, as a modern corollary to the Imperial Confucianism that gave ideological durability to the law and moral legitimacy to the government for century after century in dynastic China? In other words, what is the essence of China's "legal ethic" today? Where is its "legal soul"? Speculating about this topic invites us to bring our entire study to an end by asking the same question about countries in the civil law family and the common law family. After all, every legal system in today's world is being pressured to change, because society in all countries is changing. What does our comparative survey of three great legal traditions tell us about discovering or identifying the "legal soul" of any country?

I. Rule of Law in China

A. *Preliminary Definitions and Distinctions: Fazhi, Renzhi, and Instrumentalism*

Many observers have offered views on the question of whether there is or is not a "rule of law" in China. These views have appeared in many of the publications that have emerged recently on contemporary Chinese law—both English-language publications[1] and Chinese-language publications.[2] In order to make some sense of this question, let us first consider some definitions and distinctions.

---

1. See the Selected Bibliography at the end of this book for citations to some of the works I have relied on in formulating the views expressed in this chapter. Among the most important of those works, several of which are cited below in footnotes, are the following (listed in alphabetical order by author or editor, starting with books): Albert H.Y. Chen, An Introduction to the Legal System of the People's Republic of China (3d ed. 2004); Daniel C.K. Chow, The Legal System of the People's Republic of China (2003); Kenneth A. Cutshaw et al, Corporate Counsel's Guide to Doing Business in China (2d ed., looseleaf); John W. Head, China's Legal Soul (2009); Kenneth Lieberthal, Governing China: From Revolution Through Reform (1995); Stanley B. Lubman, Bird in a Cage: Legal Reform in China After Mao (1999) [hereinafter Lubman-1999]; Pitman B. Potter, The Chinese Legal System: Globalization and Local Legal Culture (2001); The Limits of the Rule of Law in China (Karen G. Turner, James V. Feinerman, and R. Kent Guy, eds., 2000); China's Legal Reforms and Their Practical Limits (Eduard B. Vermeer and Ingrid d'Hooghe, eds., 2002); Introduction to Chinese Law (Wang Chenguang and Zhang Xianchu, eds., 1997); Xin Ren, Tradition of the Law and Law of the Tradition: Law, State, and Social Control in China (1997); Guanghua Yu and Minkang Gu, Laws Affecting Business Transactions in the PRC (2001); James M. Zimmerman, China Law Deskbook: A Legal Guide for Foreign-Invested Enterprises (2d ed. 2004); Zou Keyuan, China's Legal Reform: Towards the Rule of Law (2006); Volker Behr, *Development of a New Legal System in the People's Republic of China*, 67 Louisiana Law Review 1161 (2007); Jianfu Chen, *The Transformation of Chinese Law—From Formal to Substantial*, 37 Hong Kong Law Journal 689 (2007); Randall Peerenboom, *The X-Files: Past and Present Portrayals of China's Alien "Legal System"*, 2 Washington University Global Studies Law Review 37 (2003) [hereinafter Peerenboom-2003].

2. In addition to the English-language works cited above in note 1, I have benefited from studying various works appearing in the very valuable journal titled Frontiers of Law in China, which since 2006 has provided English translations of important articles written (originally in Chinese) by

An elementary distinction may be drawn between three competing terms, and the concepts that they convey: "rule of law," "rule by law," and "rule of man." The third of these can be distinguished from the first and second by reference to the great debate referred to earlier in this book between the Confucianists and the Legalists. The former may be said to have favored the rule of man, and the latter to have favored the rule of law or perhaps rule *by* law. However, before we examine these three concepts in the Chinese context, let us consider a wider, more universal context. After all, the rule of law has recently become for many people and institutions around the world a goal, a requirement, a standard, a fetish, perhaps even a religion. But what does it mean?

1. Rule of Law—A Survey of Meanings

Even a quick perusal of literature relating to the rule of law[3] reveals a smorgasbord of formulations. Appendix 7.1, at the end of this chapter, provides a sampling of such rule-of-law definitions and descriptions, emerging from a survey of recent literature from various sources. I have distilled from those formulations a list of several elements that appear with some regularity in rule-of-law definitions. See Box #7.1 for my distillation of those elements. As would be expected, they are not by any means all consistent with each other, and they receive very different degrees of attention and nuances of meaning by various observers. (The listing of various elements and assertions in Box #7.1 is not intended to reflect their order of importance.)

> ### Box #7.1 *Rule-of-Law Definitions—An Array of Typical Elements*
>
> • The law must be consensual in its origin—that is, emerging from a general agreement or acceptance throughout the society, as opposed to being autocratic in origin.
>
> • The rules in the legal system are created democratically—that is, with some input (whether direct or indirect) by the subjects or citizens of the state.
>
> • The rules do not emerge from the arbitrary will or judgment of a person or group of persons wielding coercive governmental power.
>
> • The government officials are required to act in accordance with the (pre-existing) law.
>
> • The law therefore rules over the government and the governed alike.
>
> • The law is viewed as being (in part) a mechanism to prevent government agents from oppressing the rest of society.
>
> • The government is therefore restricted from infringing upon an inviolable realm of personal autonomy.

Chinese law professors. That journal is edited by two law professors from Renmin University of China, including my long-time friend Professor He Jiahong. Of particular importance for this chapter are the following articles appearing in various issues of that journal (which I have abbreviated in the following citations as "FLC"): Chen Weidong, *The Basic Concepts of Re-Modifying the Criminal Procedure Law,* 1 FLC 153 (2006); He Jiahong, *Ten Tendencies of Criminal Justice,* 2 FLC 1 (2007); Jiang Ming'an, *Public Participation and Administrative Rule of Law,* 2 FLC 353 (2007); Ma Huaide, *The Values of Administrative Procedure Law and the Meaning of its Codification in China,* 1 FLC 300 (2006); Ma Xiaohong, *A Reflection on the History of Chinese Constitutionalism of Last Century,* 2 FLC 44 (2007); Wang Chenguang, *Law-Making Functions of the Chinese Courts: Judicial Activism in a Country of Rapid Social Change,* 1 FLC 524 (2006); Wang Zhoujun, *Democracy, Rule of Law and Human Rights Protection Under Gradually Developed Constitutionalism,* 2 FLC 335 (2007); Zhang Wenxian, *China's Rule of Law in the Globalization Era,* 1 FLC 471 (2006).

3. Included in that literature are the works cited in Appendix 7.1 to this chapter, on which the following paragraphs draw liberally.

- The powers of the government are divided into separate compartments—typically legislative, executive, and judicial—with checks and balances preventing any one compartment from dominating the others (and therefore the entire legal system).

- The judicial power of the state is largely separate from and independent of the holders of the executive and legislative power.

- The people in the society have a right to determine who will govern them and how they will be governed.

- The people in the society also have certain other fundamental rights whose exercise helps prevent unfettered governmental power—these include rights to the freedom of speech, of assembly, of press, and of religion, as well as rights against arbitrary arrest and unjustified detention.

- The rules in the legal system, more particularly, reflect a theme of limited power of government, so that the rights and authority of the state are restricted, and all rights and authorities not expressly granted to the state are reserved to the people.

- The rules in the legal system are reasonably consistent over time.

- The rules in the legal system are applicable to all persons in the society.

- Nobody, therefore, is "above the law".

- The rules in the legal system are general, not particular, in the scope of their application.

- The legal system guarantees procedural fairness ("due process")—that is, certain basic rights of process must be followed in order for the government to act against the interests of an individual, including his or her economic interests.

- The legal system treats all people in the society with equality and with respect.

- The legality of a person's treatment by the organs of state power depends on its being shown to serve the common good—including the good that comes to all members of society by prohibiting harsh treatment of *any* member of society, including a member of an unpopular minority.

- Distinctions made between people or classes of people must be justifiable on rational grounds and not purely on the basis of race or religious belief or ethnicity or gender or on other grounds that reflect an attempt at dominance by one group over another.

- The law establishes limits on the state's power not only of a procedural character but also of a substantive character, so that certain fundamental substantive rights—usually set forth in a constitution—are guaranteed.

- The law should be employed to safeguard and advance the civil and political rights of the individual and to create conditions under which the individual's legitimate aspirations and dignity may be realized.

- The law also requires that the state take measures to prevent encroachment by powerful members of the society on the rights of other members of society.

- All members of the society are assumed to have moral rights and duties with respect to one another.

- Among the duties of citizens is the duty to submit to and obey the positive laws of the state, in order to preserve civil society and avoid anarchy or social chaos.

- The law provides people with the right to bring any non-frivolous allegation of government abuse before a competent court.

- The law acts as a constant impediment to arbitrary or overly discretionary authority on the part of the government.

- Any executive or administrative action infringing on individual rights must be authorized by law—that is, it must have a legal foundation conferring authority to act.

> - Any punishment that the law prescribes for a transgression of the rules should be proportionate in its severity to the seriousness of the transgression.
> - The law in the society must be clear and accessible to (and therefore understandable by) members of the society.
> - The law protects a broad range of economic rights, by which members of the society may keep what they earn and may enter into contracts and alliances (such as business entities) as they wish.
> - The law also provides at least a "safety net" of economic protections, so that members of society are not preyed upon by powerful and unscrupulous economic actors.

It is from this general array of various definitions of "rule of law" that I drew the rough-and-ready definition that I used for purposes of subsection ID3 in Chapter Six (see Box #6.9). That rough-and-ready definition reads as follows:

> *A society may be said to adhere to the rule of law if the rules in its legal system are publicly promulgated, reasonably clear in their formulation, prospective in their effect, reasonably stable over time, reasonably consistent with each other, applicable to all segments of the society (including the government, so as to prevent the government elite from acting arbitrarily), reasonably comprehensive in their coverage of substantive issues facing the society and its people, and reasonably effective, in the sense that the rules are broadly adhered to by the people in the society — voluntarily by most, and through officially forced compliance where necessary.*

Considered against the backdrop of the rich tapestry of possible "rule of law" elements offered in Box #7.1 (and in the more expansive account of "rule of law" definitions in Appendix 7.1), the above rough-and-ready definition now might seem overly narrow and simplistic. For example, it encompasses none of the substantive rights that some "rule of law" definitions insist on guaranteeing. Nor does it refer at all to democratic involvement (or consent or even acquiescence) in establishing the legal rules. Nor does it require a separation of governmental powers into offsetting compartments. We might find, therefore, that this rough-and-ready definition requires modification as we shift our perspective from a general context to a Chinese context — or we might not.

2. Rule of Law in a Chinese Context

a. In general

Let us start to make that shift in perspective now. One authority, Wejen Chang, offers this explanation of the rule of law versus the rule of man in a Chinese context — some of which reminds us of the Confucianist-Legalist debate that we examined in Chapter Six of this book:

> Since the late nineteenth century, when China began its modernization, *fazhi*, a translation of the Western term "the rule of law," has gained popularity among the Chinese — first the intellectuals, then the common people. Now most Chinese want to see *fazhi* established in China.... The concepts of *fazhi* and its opposite, *renzhi*, or the rule of man, are not entirely new to the Chinese. Ancient records indicate that similar ideas were the subject of serious discussions among earlier philosophers and led to heated debates between the Confucians and the Legalists. The first debate was probably provoked in 536 B.C., by an order of Zi Chan, the prime minister of the state of Zheng, to have the criminal law of his state inscribed on a bronze vessel put on public display. It was meant by him

and understood by his contemporaries as a dramatic gesture to demonstrate the permanence of the law and to assure the people that the law would be applied strictly according to its letter, free of government manipulation.[4]

This last element that Wejen Chang refers to in terms of the rule of law—that the application of the law would be "free of government manipulation"—is absent from the "rule of man" (*renzhi*) model that the Confucianists (and others opposing the Legalist view) found preferable. For the Confucianists, law (*fǎ*) was only one form of rules, and indeed not the most fundamental or effective form of rules. Chang explains this view as it existed in early China:

> In traditional China, *fa* (law), as a social norm, meant positive law only. In addition, there were many other norms, including *dao* (the Way), *de* (moral precepts), *li* (rites), and *xisu* (custom). In the past, only the Daoists (Taoists) and the Legalists advocated making the Way and the law, respectively, the sole norm; other ancient Chinese thinkers maintained that all of these norms were necessary for social order. Later, most Chinese accepted the basically Confucian view that the various norms form a hierarchy, with the Way at the top, the law at the bottom, and the others in between. When a lower norm was unclear or inadequate, it was to be interpreted or supplemented in accordance with the higher norms, and when a conflict existed between a higher and a lower norm, the higher one prevailed.[5]

As noted earlier in this book, a defining character of dynastic Chinese law under the great compromise between Confucianism and Legalism was that it sought to incorporate the higher norms—and in particular the *lǐ* as developed over centuries of studying the Confucian classics—into the comprehensive legal codes by which the bureaucracy governed the people and institutions of China. The *lǐ* was, in a sense, placed "inside" the *fǎ*. And yet there was an ultimate escape valve that allowed for an overriding of the law by one authority—that of the emperor, and particularly the founding emperor of a dynasty. As emphasized above, one of the first orders of business for any founding emperor was to establish a new legal code. The authority of the emperor to do so reflected the fundamentally hierarchical nature of Chinese society, in which (i) the most important relationship at the family level was that of the son to the father, whose authority over the son was virtually absolute and (ii) the most important relationship at the societal level was that of the subject to the emperor, whose authority over the subject was virtually absolute.[6]

It was that latter feature—the authority of the emperor over the subject—that gave Chinese dynastic law its character of *renzhi* (rule of man), if we assume the emperor was human and do not regard the emperor (as we are told many did at the time) as some sort of god. Therefore the dynastic Chinese legal system may be regarded as constituting a blend of the rule of law with the rule of man.

Indeed, we might expand on that point by observing which of these elements—rule of man versus rule of law—was more important, and from whose standpoint. From the standpoint of the district magistrate and others in the bureaucratic structure of govern-

---

4. Wejen Chang, *Foreword*, in Turner et al, *supra* note 1, at vii.

5. *Id.* at viii. Chang offers further explanation of this point by noting that "Chinese reluctance to sanction law as an ultimate authority [can be traced] to an early philosophical stance that assigned formal law a subordinate place in a hierarchy of norms." *Id.* at 7.

6. Indeed, these two types of relationship were essentially combined in the *zhong fa* system that the Duke of Zhou was said to have put in place early in the Western Zhou Dynasty (ca 11th century BCE). See note 9 in Chapter Six, above.

ment—with the exception, of course, of the emperor and those in his immediate circle—the legal codes constituted the rule of law. Their provisions were relatively clear, rigid, and binding with very little apparent scope for discretion. From the standpoint of the emperor, of course, the legal codes constituted a rule of man (and perhaps a rule *by* law, a matter explored below). Recall that it is in part for this reason—that the law codes were not at all binding on the emperor, as the head of the government—that I concluded in Chapter Six that there was not in fact a "rule of law" in dynastic China.[7]

b. Rule of man, rule of law, and rule by law

Let us turn our attention now to modern China (that is, following the collapse of the dynastic system with the end of the Qing Dynasty in 1911). In this era it seems easier to distinguish between rule of man versus rule of law, for Chinese law since 1911 has never achieved the sort of systemic sophistication that it had developed over centuries of cultivation under the generations of Confucian scholars in the Han, Tang, Sung, Ming, and Qing eras. Instead, Chinese law has in the past hundred years or so vacillated between two modes—that of a fairly obvious *renzhi* (rule of man, as for example during most of Mao Zedong's rule) and that of a hybrid system that gives some deference to *fazhi* (rule of law) but with elements also of *renzhi*.

It is at this point that we should examine the third of the three terms referred to above: "rule by law". Eduard Vermeer has referred to the distinction between "rule of law" and "rule by law" in his observation that "Chinese politicians claim they want to build a socialist country ruled by law. But Chinese reformists have gone further, and professed that instead of rule *by* law, one should strive after the rule *of* law."[8] The two notions can perhaps be best distinguished by focusing on two related elements: (i) the role of discretion and (ii) the application of the law to government officials. Under the former notion (rule *by* law), while government officials typically would rely on written rules (rather than pure discretion) in governing the state, those officials would ultimately have discretion to depart from the rules in circumstances that they deemed exceptional. Moreover, as such discretion would imply, the government officials would themselves not be bound by the rules. Under the latter notion (rule *of* law), the government officials *would* be bound by the rules and therefore would not have discretion to depart from them. Instead of exercising discretion in exceptional circumstances, the government officials would need to await the adoption of an official amendment of the rules to accommodate such exceptional circumstances.

A term often used to capture the same concept as "rule by law" (distinguishing that concept from a "rule of law") is "instrumentalism". Pitman Potter offers this explanation of that term in the context of contemporary Chinese law:

> The Chinese government's approach to law is fundamentally instrumentalist. This means that laws and regulations are intended to be instruments of policy enforcement. Legislative and regulatory enactments are not intended as expressions of immutable general norms that apply consistently in a variety of human endeavors, and neither are they constrained by such norms. Rather, laws and regulations are enacted explicitly to achieve the immediate policy objectives of the regime. Law is not a limit on state power; rather, it is a mechanism by which state power is exercised, as the legal forms and institutions that comprise the

---

7. See subsection ID3 of Chapter Six, above.
8. Eduard B. Vermeer, *Introduction* in Vermeer and d'Hooghe, *supra* note 1, at ix.

Chinese legal system are established and operate to protect the Party/state's political power.[9]

Stanley Lubman uses the same term — instrumentalism — in describing the course of legal reform in China since the new PRC regime was declared in 1949:

> The last two decades of the twentieth century saw the Chinese leadership begin to use law as an instrument of governance in a manner relatively more sophisticated than the crude and formalistic copying of Soviet law in the early 1950s or the blunt instrumentalism — and worse — that had followed.[10]

I interpret Lubman's observation to mean that following the establishment of the PRC in 1949, the Chinese leadership first mimicked Soviet law and then moved toward "blunt instrumentalism" of the sort I referred to above — in which law is seen purely as an instrument of state power — and then deteriorated into something worse during the Cultural Revolution when all law was essentially abolished, before entering into a new phase in the last two decades of the 20th century.

These three terms — rule of law, rule by law, and rule by man — may be seen, therefore, as describing three different points along a spectrum, with rule of law (*fazhi*) representing a system in which the actions of government authorities are subject entirely to the control of the written law, with rule of man (*renzhi*) representing a system in which government authorities sit outside the control of the law, and in fact govern not predominantly through law at all but instead through discretion (recall that for Confucius, the *lǐ* typically should not take written form and could in any event never be fully encompassed in written form[11]), and with rule *by* law representing a hybrid of the two, under which government officials apply formal, written, perhaps detailed rules but are not themselves bound by those rules.

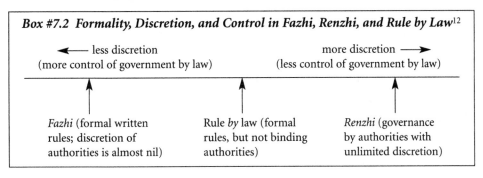

Box #7.2 Formality, Discretion, and Control in Fazhi, Renzhi, and Rule by Law[12]

◄———— less discretion
(more control of government by law)

more discretion ————►
(less control of government by law)

Fazhi (formal written rules; discretion of authorities is almost nil)

Rule *by* law (formal rules, but not binding authorities)

Renzhi (governance by authorities with unlimited discretion)

---

9. Potter, *supra* note 1, at 10.

10. Stanley Lubman, *The Study of Chinese Law in the United States: Reflections on the Past and Concerns About the Future*, 2 WASHINGTON UNIVERSITY GLOBAL STUDIES LAW REVIEW 1, 3 (2003).

11. See text accompanying notes 15–17 in Chapter Six, above.

12. Certain other elements of the rule of law are disregarded for purposes of this diagram. The diagram is simplified in other ways as well. For example, another intermediary position between *Fazhi* and *Renzhi* could be occupied by *Dongzhi* ("rule of Party") — as might be applicable in the case of China, whose system of law and governance is dominated by the CPC. The notion of *Dongzhi* can be attributed to the revolutionary Chinese writer Lu Xun. Active in the days of the post-Qing chaos, the May Fourth Movement, and rise of the CPC, Lu Xun criticized the Guomindang for its control over China as *Dongzhi*. For a biographical sketch of Lu Xun, see generally *Writing for the Revolution — The Story of Lu Xun (1881–1936)*, appearing in REVOLUTIONARY WORKER #970 (Aug. 23, 1998), available at http://revcom.us/a/v20/970-79/970/luxun.htm. I am indebted to Professor Mary Wong of Hong Kong University and to Wang Yanping for drawing these observations about *Dongzhi* and Lu Xun to my attention.

c. Constitutional considerations

In debating the question of what role law plays in today's China—that is, whether that country is best characterized now as having rule of law, rule by law, or rule by man—observers sometimes focus on the actual language of the Constitution of the PRC, and particularly the language appearing in the amendments made in 1999. The pertinent text of those amendments appears in Box #7.3, along with information about varying translations into English.

Box #7.3 Excerpts from 1999 Constitutional Amendments on "Rule of Law"[13]

Amendment Three (approved on March 15, 1999, by the 9th NPC at its 2nd Session)

- The English version of the text of the amendment, as reported on the People's Daily website—http://english.peopledaily.com.cn/constitution/constitution.html—reads as follows:

  One section is added to Article Five of the Constitution as the first section: "The People's Republic of China practices ruling the country in accordance with the law and building a socialist country of law."

- The key phrases are examined below—first in *pinyin*, then in Chinese characters, then in English translation using the People's Daily translation as above, then with some alternative translations from various sources.

  - *yifa zhiguo*
    - 依法治国
    - "ruling the country in accordance with the law" (People's Daily translation, found at http://english.peopledaily.com.cn/constitution/constitution.html)

    or "governs the country according to law"—according to the PRC Government's "official web portal", at http://www.google.com/gwt/n?u=http://english.gov.cn/2005-08/05/content_20813.htm

    or "governing the nation in accordance with law" (Wikipedia, found at http://en.wikipedia.org/wiki/Chinese_law)

    or "govern the country according to law" (Peerenboom—see text below)

  - *jianshe shehui zhuyi fazhi guojia*
    - 建设社会主义法治国家
    - "building a socialist country of law"

    or "makes it a socialist country ruled by law"—according to the PRC Government's "official web portal", at the address given above

    or "building a socialist rule of law state" (Wikipedia, as shown above)

    or "establish a socialist rule of law country" (Peerenboom—see text below)

---

13. The exact text in Chinese characters of the provision added to Article 5 by the 1999 amendment is beyond any question, of course. The key provisions of that text are shown in Box #7.3. Likewise, the exact text in *pinyin* of the provision added by the amendment is beyond any question. The key provisions of that *pinyin* text also appear in Box #7.3. What is subject to varying opinions is how the Chinese terms (whether in Chinese characters or in *pinyin*) are to be expressed in English. Some alternative translations are offered in Box #7.3.

As noted in Box #7.3, the key language (in *pinyin*) proclaims the policy "*yifa zhiguo, jianshe shehuizhuyi fazhiguo*", which has been translated literally by one (Western) expert—Randall Peerenboom—as "govern the country according to law, establish a socialist rule of law country".[14] Peerenboom offers this explanation of that language and suggests that it has been misinterpreted by some commentators who urge that China is not serious about the rule of law:

> [The assumption that a socialist system such as China's] could not be serious about legal reforms and the rule of law ... is evident in the way many Western reporters and some academics translate the phrase *fazhi*. This phrase by itself could be translated as either rule of law or rule by law, as there are no prepositions in the Chinese language. However, the phrase is part of a longer *tifa* or official policy statement of *yifa zhiguo, jianshe shehuizhuyi fazhiguo* [as noted above]. The commitment to governing the country according to law reflects the central tenet of rule of law: law is supreme and binds government officials and citizens alike. Indeed, the principle of supremacy of law and the notion that no party or person is above the law is explicitly stated in both the state and Party constitutions. Significantly, an alternative phrase *yifa zhiguo* using a different first character, which means "use law to govern the country," was explicitly rejected because it could be interpreted to support an instrumental rule of by law rather than rule of law in which all are bound by law. Because the difference between the two phrases had been the subject of much academic debate, the significance of the choice was well-known to all. There has also been considerable discussion of the difference between an instrumental rule by law and the rule of law among academics. PRC legal scholars who have given lectures on rule of law to Jiang Zemin and other senior leaders confirm that they understand the distinction between rule by law, in which government actors are not bound by law, and rule of law in which law is supreme.... Nevertheless, many reporters and some scholars insist on translating *fazhi* as rule by law and sometimes even go so far as to translate *yifa zhiguo* as "relying on law to rule the country" or "using law to govern" and other such more instrumental renderings. Such translations are not translations in the sense of direct rendering of the ordinary meaning of the words in Chinese. Rather, they are interpretations that reflect the translators' biases or assumptions about the nature of legal reform in China.[15]

By Peerenboom's account, China has pledged itself to the rule of law—understood as meaning that the government is bound by the rules of law—as part of its formal constitutional framework. While the Constitution of the PRC is not directly applicable in the same way that the US Constitution is,[16] the fact remains that China has officially adopted

---

14. Peerenboom-2003, *supra* note 1, at 37, 67.

15. *Id.* at 67 (citations omitted).

16. See Chow, *supra* note 1, at 71, 78 (explaining that "it is doubtful ... whether the current PRC Constitution has direct legal effect in the absence of implementing legislation" and that "[m]any scholars in the PRC view the Constitution as [merely] declaratory ... [since] courts in the PRC do not have the power to determine whether a constitutional violation has occurred or to interpret the Constitution. On the other hand, as noted in Chapter Six (see Box #6.10), an expansion of the jurisdiction of courts to apply the Constitution was confirmed in a 2001 statement by the Supreme People's Court. The citation that Professor Castellucci provides for that case is as follows: *Qi Yuling v. Chen Xiaoqi, Case of Infringement of Citizen's Fundamental Rights of Receiving Education Under the Protection of the Constitution by Means of Infringing Rights of Name*, 5 ZUIGAO RENMIN RAYUAN GANGBAO [Gazette of the Supreme People's Court of the People's Republic of China] 158 (2001).

the rule of law as formal legal policy[17]—and indeed congratulated itself recently for implementing that policy so admirably.[18]

Perhaps some further light may be shed on the issue of how *renzhi* should be translated by examining two points—one linguistic and the other historical. The first point revolves around the fact that the *pinyin* romanization *zhì* actually applies to two different Chinese characters (having some relationship to law, that is). The historical point revolves around Deng Xiaoping's role in developing the policies that the CPC would follow in respect of law and government. Both of these points appear in Box #7.4.

Box #7.4 *Focusing on Fazhi and the Role of Law in China*[19]

Using the *pinyin* romanization *fazhi* in discussions of the "rule of law" in China is subject to uncertainty at several levels. In addition to the fact that there are no prepositions in the Chinese language (as noted above) is the fact that *fazhi*—or, to be more precise by including the tonal marks, *fǎzhì*—can be used for two different Chinese characters. The first is 法治 and the second is 法制. The character 法, which appears in both binoms, is of course *fǎ*—law. [See Box #6.4 in Chapter Six for a detailed description of that term.] The character 治 (*zhì*) would typically be translated as "to rule" or "to govern" or "to manage" or "to control" or "to harness" as in the case of a river). The character 制 (*zhì*) would typically be translated slightly differently, as "system"—or "to control" or "to regulate".

Before 1997, the question of which of the two related but different conceptualizations of the role of law in China should be used—that is, whether 法治 or 法制 should be used—was debated among scholars and among top level government officials. In simplified form, the debate asked whether China should build a "rule of law" country or should instead build only a country with "laws and systems". The debate was settled in September 1997, when the CPC proclaimed (at its annual meeting) that China should be a rule of law country—and it was this concept that was adopted into the Constitution by the NPC in 1999.

Before 1997, however, the other conceptualization—法制—commanded much attention. It became well established that China was aiming to build a country with "laws and system" (法制). Indeed, Deng Xiaoping is the author (in this context) of the concept of 法制. On December 13, 1978, Deng Xiaoping proclaimed at an important government meeting that in order to build up the socialist legal system, China must follow four key principles. The first

---

17. For one authority's detailed account of what was intended at the time of the 1999 amendment of the PRC Constitution, see Zou Keyuan, *supra* note 1, at 34–35. Zou quotes from Jiang Zemin's 1997 report to the CPC for this explanation of what Jiang meant by "rule of law" as called for in what became the 1999 amendment:

> The development of democracy must combine the improvement of the legal system so as to govern the country by law. To govern the country with law means to manage the state affairs, economic and social affairs by the people under the leadership of the Party in accordance with the Constitution and law stipulations through various ways and forms. It should be guaranteed that all the work in the state is carried out under the law. Institutionalisation and legalisation of the socialist democracy should be progressively achieved so that the institution and the law will not be changed because of the change of the leadership and because of the change of views and attention of the leadership.

Zou also explains the earlier views of both Jiang and his predecessor Deng Xiaoping regarding the meaning of they ascribed to "rule of law". See *id.* at 35–37.

18. For a reference to the February 2008 White Paper issued by the PRC's State Council, see *infra* note 80 and accompanying text. While the White Paper catalogued innumerable ways in which the CPC has, by its own account, delivered to the country an increasingly strong system of law and governance, based on what it calls the rule of law, the White Paper does not actually define the term "rule of law".

19. I am indebted to Wang Yanping for assisting me with the content of Box #7.4. Some definitions offered in Box #7.4 are drawn primarily from the Chinese Character Dictionary appearing at http://www.mandarintools.com/chardict.html.

was 有法可依, which may be understood as follows: 有 (*you*, there should exist); 法 (*fa*, law); 可 (*ke*, may); 依 (*yi*, refer to) — or, in brief, there should be law [for the law officers] to refer to. The second was 有法必依, which may be understood as follows: 有 (*you*, there should exist); 法 (*fa*, law); 必 (*bi*, must); 依 (*yi*, refer to) — or, in brief, if there is law, one must refer to the law or comply with such law. The third was 执法必严, which may be understood as follows: 执 (*zhi*, enforce); 法 (*fa*, law); 必 (*bi*, must); 严 (*yan*, strict) — or, in brief, law enforcement officers should not be lenient; instead, enforcement of law must be strict. The fourth was 违法必究, which may be understood as follows: 违 (*wei*, violating); 法 (*fa*, law); 必 (*bi*, must); 究 (*jiu*, investigate, or prosecute) — or, in brief, if there is a violation of law, it must be prosecuted.

For Deng Xiaoping, then, it was the 法制 form of *fǎzhì* that China should focus on, not the 法治 form of *fǎzhì*. (Deng's explanation of the four key principles noted above appeared in DENG XIAOPING'S SELECTED ARTICLES (vol. 2, at 147, 322.) Not until 1997 was the 法治 form of *fǎzhì* accepted officially by China.

The preceding discussions focus intently on *words*, and especially on the translation of words from one language to another. Those discussions also focus on *classification*, with an eye to determining whether to classify certain words (and the concepts they name) into one class or another class (such as "rule of law" or "rule by law"). This is altogether natural, of course (at least in western intellectual discourse), because law, like language and culture more generally, relies on words, and because organizing the chaos of reality into recognizable and digestible categories helps us in understanding that reality. However, we should not lose sight of the fact that many words (and the concepts they name) are to some extent not amenable to either translation or classification, especially if the persons using the words are themselves inclined toward vagueness. Speaking directly about some of the key words at issue here — that is, relating specifically to "rule of law" considerations, Ignazio Castellucci offers these observations:

> [In many reports and commentaries, including especially those issued from official Chinese government agencies,] terms referring to both concepts of rule of law and rule by law can be found. Maybe [the effort to consider whether there is rule of law or rule by law in China] is all about a westerner's attitude in classification; the Chinese vagueness of terms reflects the inherent flexibility of the Chinese concept, able to cover several of our western ones; western scholars should avoid trying to make subtle, clear and rigid of what is a fundamentally fuzzy and flexible distinction, to say the least; and which might well be non-existent in the Chinese tradition and mentality. *Fa zhi*, after all, does not mean "rule by law," nor "rule of law"; in a leal sense, it only means ... *fa zhi*. A precise and accurate translation of *fa zhi* into English language [is not really] ... possible.... [In the end, the] actual legal meaning of *fa zhi* cannot come from any more or less accurate translation, but from observations of the Chinese history and present reality.[20]

Having issued that challenge to use "observations of the Chinese history and present reality" in order to understand the true meaning of *fa zhi*, Castellucci proceeds to do just

---

20. Ignazio Castellucci, *Rule of Law with Chinese Characteristics*, GOLDEN GATE UNIVERSITY ANNUAL SURVEY OF INTERNATIONAL & COMPARATIVE LAW 35, 39–40 (2007) [hereinafter Castellucci-2007]. Prof. Castellucci, a close friend of mine from the University of Trento, has taught and practiced law in Italy, China, and elsewhere and relies in the article cited here on a wide-ranging set of sources, including Soviet-era legal sources and analysis, to assess the Chinese legal system. For his survey of the Chinese legal tradition within the wider ambit of Asian law, see Ignazio Castellucci, LE GRANDI TRADIZIONI GIURIDICHE DELL'ASIA (2009).

that. In a fascinating survey of Chinese legal culture, Soviet legal culture from which Chinese law drew heavily in the mid-20th century, and European legal culture, Castellucci explains several points that help explain the meaning of *fa zhi*. Here are some highlights:

> The "rule of law" is a western concept, associated with societies regulated solely by the law. In such societies, the law is [or at least aspires to be] a set of general rules that apply to all its citizens, particularly the State and ruling elite, and which covers nearly all areas of life. Such rules are always enforceable by a court of law, according to legal procedures, free from any interference from other sources of behavioral rules—such as tradition, politics, religion, or administrative praxis.[21]

> [However,] the *role* of law in China is different than the Western one; consequently, even the Chinese notion of the rule of law differs from its western counterpart.[22]

> [For one thing,] [c]onstitutional provisions related to hierarchy of norms, providing for the usual Constitution-laws-regulations order of prevalence, remains to some extent ineffective [in China, which shares the typical socialist view in which] Constitutions are perceived as political documents rather than strictly legal ones.[23]

> [In addition, formal law in China does not have a monopoly over the direction and validity of state action. Instead,] *Party policy and documents play a key role in the construction and interpretation of Chinese law by making policy a part of the law, and the law itself a special type of political directive.* From a political point of view, it [*i.e.*, law] is another tool to disseminate and implement the directives of the central policy-making organs in the government apparatus and amongst the citizens.[24]

> [Specifically, in addition to courts issuing judgments in cases coming before them, several other organs of the state also direct state policy. One such] government institution playing administrative, supervisory and normative functions ... is the Supreme People's Procuratorate, [providing supervision to] the underlying system of the People's Procuratorates.[25]

> [Indeed, official] "political-legal committees (*zhengfa weiyuanhui*) [operate] at all levels of the courts and Procuratorates pyramids] ..., with the purpose of coordinating activities and establishing guidelines and policies in accordance with Party policy pertaining to the administration of justice and law enforcement.[26]

---

21. *Id.* at 35.

22. *Id.* at 36.

23. *Id.* at 41. Castellucci explains the long-term prohibition in China of making direct references to articles of the Constitution when making judgments—a matter discussed further below in subsection IVB3b of this chapter.

24. Castellucci-2007, *supra* note 20, at 51 (emphasis in original).

25. *Id.* at 52. Castellucci explains that the functions of the people's procuratorates "are not confined to prosecutorial work, as it happens in the Western legal systems for public prosecutors" but instead involves offering interpretations of the law, making "regulations and implementation rules on the work of the prosecution", handling political work for the state, and generally to "represent public interests in every court, [with] authority to intervene in civil and administrative cases and to supervise the courts' judicial work and law enforcement"—including "*supervising ... all other government organs at their corresponding level*". *Id.* at 53–54. For further information about the procuratorate, see *infra* note 157 and accompanying text.

26. Castellucci-2007, *supra* note 20, at 55. Castellucci goes on to explain the role of the "judicial committees" that also exist in every court, "formed by the most senior judges ... [and] the corresponding Procuratorate ... with the purpose of determining local guidelines for decisions and sometimes actually deciding sensitive cases". For further details on this practice, see the discussion in subsection IVD, below.

In fact, one specific feature of "political" legal systems [such as that of contemporary China] ... is *the severability of law from enforcement, where the law and its enforcement are actually two different issues.* Enforcement is neither a neutral, technical issue, nor an automatic consequence of law. In a "political" context (of which Chinese courts and law-enforcing agencies unquestionably are a part), law can be under-enforced or over-enforced according to policy needs.[27]

It follows from [the above points, and others,] that the western conception of the legal system ... does not apply to the Chinese reality, as it has developed in the last decades. The legal system is an isolated feature of the society, working for itself according to its rules, irrespective of other influences. Rather, it works as a part of an integrated political-legal system of governance.[28]

[Even though some recent developments suggest that the Chinese leadership is moving somewhat toward a more western view of the role of law in society,] the shift toward a stronger legal system and a rule of law does not necessarily imply that the Chinese political-legal system should share the same values of the Western legal traditions. A "socialist" rule of law still implies the guiding role of a single, or preeminent, party over the political and legal systems, as well as the prevalence of common interest over individual ones....[29]

This synopsis of Castellucci's explanation of key differences between the Chinese legal system and western legal systems highlights the differences in forms of political organization that can disguise to the careless observer the difficulties inherent in trying to engage in a simplistic translation exercise—converting, for example, *fa zhi* into an English phrase such as "rule of law" or "rule by law". As a practical matter, of course, we do need to engage in some sort of classification or "labeling" or "translating" exercise; so in the discussion that follows, the terms "rule of law" and "rule by law" (or "instrumentalism") will still be used—but with this entreaty that we remain aware of the inherent shortcomings in doing so.

B. Three Questions

Let us give some attention now to three questions as we continue to consider how, if at all, contemporary Chinese law reflects traditional views developed over centuries under the Chinese dynastic legal system—looking particularly, that is, at the question of whether today's China is indeed, as a practical matter, a "rule of law" country or a "rule by law" country or a "rule of man" country. The three questions are these: (1) who writes the rules? (2) to whom are the legal rules addressed? (3) how does the legal system balance the competing claims of control versus discretion—that is, the balance between (i) exercising control over government officials versus (ii) authorizing the use of discretion by those government officials. I shall address these three questions in reverse order.

---

27. Castellucci-2007, *supra* note 20, at 59. Castellucci points out that this severability of law from enforcement often results in China "in the total lack of enforcement, as happens for instance in the payment of indemnifications for requisitions of land for reasons of public interest". *Id.* As a result of this and other factors (including what Castellucci calls "local protectionism"), a very high proportion of judgments are not enforced. *Id.* at 60. See also Chow, *supra* note 1, at 226 (explaining how "[p]roblems in the enforcement of judgments and orders continue to plague the courts").

28. Castellucci-2007, *supra* note 20, at 63.

29. *Id.* at 64.

1. Control versus Discretion

Recall that in the dynastic Chinese legal system, the law codes provided for very little discretion on the part of the district magistrates, who were the members of the government bureaucracy most directly responsible for the application of those rules. Instead, the law codes prescribed an extraordinarily detailed matrix of punishments to accompany any form of conduct that bore on the imperial resources (for example, royal stables and palaces, military assets, and grain reserves) and on the maintenance of stability in society (for example, marital relations, religious observances, and violent physical behavior).[30] Underlying that detailed matrix of punishments was the Confucian notion that cosmic harmony could be preserved only by maintaining harmony in society, and maintaining harmony in society required a fastidious attention to balancing punishment not only with the severity of the transgression involved but also with the relative positions that the perpetrator and the victim held in the sophisticated network of relationships within the society and the polity. Accordingly, as noted above, from the perspective of the district magistrate and nearly all other officials within the government bureaucracy, the dynastic system represented a rule of law in the sense that it was binding on those officials—although obviously not binding on the very highest officials, including the emperor, from whose perspective the dynastic system represented a rule *by* law or a rule of man.

Is this still the case in the legal system of today's China? I believe the most accurate answer is "yes and no". On the one hand, the impression I draw from the work of numerous observers is that from the point of view of a government official, the rules set forth in the flood of new legislation of recent years strike a balance that is much closer to the "more control" end of the spectrum than to the "more discretion" end of the spectrum presented in the diagram appearing in Box #7.2 above. Granted, the underlying assumptions to the legal rules have changed significantly—for example, the social or political standing of the perpetrator and the victim no longer bears on the legal result—and indeed the laws no longer take a form that strikes a Western observer as overwhelmingly criminal in character, as was the case with the dynastic legal codes.[31] However, I believe that in general the fundamental character of the system remains the same from the perspective of the typical government bureaucrat: it is a system in which the rule of law prevails in the sense that the law is binding on such bureaucrats, at least up to the very highest levels in the government hierarchy.

On the other hand, a common complaint from legal practitioners, at least foreign practitioners, in China is that the laws—while binding—are vague, and that this vagueness has the practical effect of granting wide discretion to the government officials responsible for implementing those laws. Stanley Lubman makes this point:

> Loose drafting has long marked Chinese legislation and contributed to its lack of precision. National legislation is intentionally drafted in broad terms that per-

---

30. In one respect, the district magistrate *was* in fact given some degree of discretion in applying the provisions of the legal code: If the behavior at issue was simply not covered by the code's provisions but nonetheless clearly required some attention (and imposition of punishment) by the imperial bureaucracy because it bore on a matter of direct interest to the emperor or his rule, then the district magistrate was authorized (by code provisions) to reach a decision in the case through a process of reasoning by analogy—that is, finding the code provision(s) that addressed behavior most closely similar to the behavior in question and applying a punishment accordingly. It was partly in an effort to restrict the scope of such discretion that the code provisions were expressed in such detail.

31. For a discussion of the criminal-law appearance of the dynastic law codes, see subsection IC3d in Chapter Six, above.

mit bureaucrats to exercise considerable ingenuity in promoting local interests, which ... allows interpretations that stray widely from the legislative intent.[32]

Pitman Potter makes a similar point regarding the intentional ambiguity of laws that in effect give officials broad discretion:

> One consequence of legal instrumentalism as practiced in China is that laws and regulations are intentionally ambiguous so as to give policy makers and implementing officials alike significant flexibility in interpretation and implementation. Many Chinese laws and regulations are replete with vague passages that do not lend predictability or transparency to the regulatory process.[33]

A counter-example, however, appears in the fact that when the Criminal Code was most recently amended, provisions on "analogous crimes" (also called "pocket crimes") were deleted, thus narrowing the scope for discretion on the part of judges applying the provisions of that code.[34] In short, we might generalize by saying that discretion comes mainly in the indirect form of vagueness, as distinct from the direct form of authorization—and that the laws remain formally binding on the government officials responsible for applying them.

2. A Focus on *Minshi*

This leads to the second of the three questions: to whom are the legal rules addressed? In this respect, surely contemporary Chinese law departs dramatically from dynastic Chinese law. Whereas the latter amounted largely to a system of directives issued by the emperor (and those immediately surrounding the emperor) to the remainder of the bureaucracy —leaving all the rest of society in the class of "subjects" of the law who should steer clear of it if possible—China's legal system today is thoroughly different. The sorts of *minshi* (people's matters) that appeared only in the very latest phases of the dynastic eras[35] now predominate, especially in the area of economic laws governing contracts, business asso-

---

32. Stanley Lubman, *Looking for Law in China*, 20 Columbia Journal of Asian Law 1, 36 (2006) [hereinafter Lubman-2006]. Lubman also acknowledges some of the historical reasons for the low esteem in which law was held until recently in China, and suggests that to reduce the degree of discretion in implementation it "will be necessary to develop administrative procedures and administrative law". *Id.* at 47. As noted in Chapter Six above (especially Box #6.10), and in some of the writings cited later in this chapter by Chinese academics, much attention has been given in recent years to the adoption and implementation of administrative rules and procedures.

33. Potter, *supra* note 1, at 11.

34. See Wei Lo, The 1997 Criminal Code of the People's Republic of China 7–8 (1998). Wei Lo explains that Article 79 of the 1979 Criminal Code read as follows:

> A crime not specifically prescribed under the specific provisions of the present law may be confirmed a crime and sentence rendered in light of the most analogous article under the special provisions of the present law; provided, however, that the case shall be submitted to the Supreme People's Court for its approval.

Article 3 of the 1997 Criminal Code, in contrast, reads as follows:

> Anyone who commits an act deemed a crime by explicit stipulations of law shall be convicted and given punishment by law and any act not deemed a crime by explicit stipulation of law shall not be convicted or given punishment.

Id. at 8. Wei Lo states that "[t]he new approach may be conducive to preventing the practice of determining crimes at judges' discretion". *Id.* For further discussion of the degree to which contemporary Chinese laws provide discretion and flexibility ("wiggle room"), see Peerenboom-2003, *supra* note 1, at 77, 81 (criticizing exaggerations of how much such "wiggle room" actually exists).

35. For a discussion of *minshi*, see *supra* subsection IC3d of Chapter Six, above.

ciations, investment, finance, and the like.[36] Law in today's China, in short, reflects a form of "populism" that was largely absent from (and nearly invisible in) dynastic law.

A close reader might think this assessment conflates two similar but distinct matters. To say, as I have in the preceding paragraph, that law in contemporary China gives dramatically more attention than dynastic law did to *minshi*—that is, the matters that are of interest to regular people in their lives (for example, in facilitating economic transactions) —is not necessarily the same thing as to say that the law is *addressed* to those regular people. Especially in a political system that features such centralized governmental control as China does (today and always), the legal rules might plausibly be regarded as being addressed not to individuals per se but rather to bureaucrats responsible for administering those rules, even if the rules themselves relate to the lives and transactions of private individuals. Given this, it might be seen as inappropriate to regard the rules as "populist".

In my view, this reasoning rests on a distinction without a difference. The "populism" of any legal system—that is, the extent to which it gives attention mainly to the affairs of private individuals rather than mainly to the affairs of the state—is not much diluted merely by the fact that its norms are as a *procedural* matter expressed as instructions to official persons, such as judges or (in the case of dynastic China) district magistrates. What counts most is what types of behavior—that of private individuals or that of government officials—is ultimately being regulated. As explained above, the Qing Code became slightly more "populist" because provisions on "people's matters" were inserted into it—supplementing (not replacing, of course) the other provisions in the code, which dealt for the most part with the protection of imperial power, prerogatives, procedures, and personnel—even though the level of government control (and the fact that the Code still was administered by the district magistrates) remained unchanged.

Accordingly, in considering the question of "to whom are the rules addressed?"—or perhaps more precisely "to whose *interests* are the rules addressed?"—it seems clear that the answer for contemporary Chinese law, unlike dynastic Chinese law, is "the private side of society".

3. Who Writes the Rules?

Is this "populism" in terms of the *addressees* of today's Chinese law accompanied by a "populism" in terms of the *creators* of today's Chinese law? This is simply a different way of asking the remaining question identified above: who writes the rules? For some observers, this question goes to the heart of the overall question of whether the contemporary Chinese legal system is a system adhering to the rule of law or to the rule *by* law. One authority asserts that as a practical matter today's China still follows "legal instrumentalism"—that is, rule *by* law—in the sense that in the modern legal reform efforts "the [Communist] Party retains its authority to determine the content of law".[37]

Understanding the role of the Communist Party in Chinese law is of absolutely central importance to understanding law in modern China. In his "nutshell" account of Chinese law, Daniel Chow devotes an entire chapter to this topic. He offers this explanation:

> Given the pervasive role of the Communist Party of China in all facets of the
> Chinese state and society, any treatment of China's legal system would be wholly

---

36. For broad surveys of such economic laws, see generally Cutshaw et al, *supra* note 1, Yu & Gu, *supra* note 1, Wang & Zhang, *supra* note 1, and Zimmerman, *supra* note 1.

37. Potter, *supra* note 1, at 11.

inadequate without an examination of the CPC.... The PRC Constitution vests power and authority in the political and administrative structures that form the lawful government of China; the exercise of power through these structures is the legitimate exercise of power.... [T]he CPC ... is a political party and not a governmental entity. A political party is a body of voters formed for the purpose of influencing or controlling the policies and conduct of government through the nomination and election of its candidates for office. By installing its top leaders in leading government positions and its members throughout the PRC government apparatus, the CPC is able to influence and control the PRC government. At certain points, the organs of the PRC government and the CPC appear[] to be fused or merged together[,] with the CPC exercising effective power through its control of the government organs. When the CPC exercises power through the government apparatus of the PRC as set forth in the Constitution, it exercises legitimate power. If the CPC were to exercise powers directly and not through the filter of government organs, as appeared to be provided for under the 1975 and 1978 Constitutions, there might arise concerns about the legitimacy of its rule as it is not a government entity. *Under the present political system in the PRC, the government structure serves the important purpose of legitimizing the power exercised by the CPC.*[38]

We shall look further at the CPC, and its role in Chinese law and society, later in this chapter. For now, however, the key point to draw from Chow's explanation is his insistence on the legal legitimacy of the CPC's exercise of power. Such exercise of power is legitimate, he asserts, because of the CPC—which is not in fact the *only* political party in China but undisputedly the *key* political party[39]—has placed its leaders in government positions in ways that are entirely consistent with the PRC Constitution. Chow provides a further explanation of the constitutional provisions, and then of the specific mechanism by which the CPC exercise control over China through those provisions:

While the CPC has absolute authority in China, *the Party is careful to give the appearance of operating within a legal framework* and careful not to give the appearance, as was the case during the Cultural Revolution, of acting above the law. Provisions in the 1982 Constitution explicitly subject all political parties to the rule of law and make clear that no organization or individual is above the law [citing Article 5 of the PRC Constitution].... Operating within the legal constraints of a government system that appears to be representative and in which power is transferred from the people through popular elections to a parliamentary system in which lower level delegates elect higher level delegates allows the CPC to claim that its leadership is supported and affirmed by the will of the people.... *[H]owever, the political system actually operates quite in reverse of appearances. Decisions are actually made by a small group of Party leaders and then are*

---

38. Chow, *supra* note 1, at 115–116 (emphasis added). The literature is full of other similar accounts of the CPC and its relationship with the PRC's political and legal system. See, e.g., chapter 2 in Zou Keyuan, *supra* note 1; chapter 4 in Chow, *supra* note 1; Albert H.Y. Chen, *supra* note 1, at 58–73, 74–94.

39. Chow, *supra* note 1, at 120 (explaining that "China officially endorses a multi-party system of political parties under the leadership of the CPC", which "exercises firm financial and supervisory control over [the other eight] parties", many members of which are also members of the CPC); Xin Ren, *supra* note 1, at 56 (quoting a Chinese official as saying that "China is a one-party-ruling country in which the Chinese Communist Party is the core of the leadership with cooperation from other political parties who 'participate' in governing China but will never rule China").

ratified and rubber-stamped by Party and government organs under the control of a core of Party elites. The outcome of elections for all important government positions is controlled by the CPC through the nomenklatura system in which the CPC is able to place its approved candidates into those positions. The government of the PRC, under the control of the CPC, does not really exercise the independent powers of government. Rather, the CPC uses its control of the government apparatus to justify or legitimate the CPC's own actions, decisions, and policies. This may seem to be unnecessary given that the CPC has absolute authority, but the legitimating function of the current system is quite crucial to the CPC.[40]

Without a doubt, this system guarantees CPC control over China's legal system — control that Chow refers to (in the passage quoted above) as "absolute authority". Not surprisingly, many observers have emphasized this feature of China's system of law and governance, and have drawn special attention to the historical tradition that such centralized control reflects. For example, Xin Ren notes that the CPC's "paramount power in controlling the state and military forces remains largely unshakable",[41] and then she offers these observations about the "penetration of the state's power into the social fabric" of China, both as of the time she was writing (1997) and in times past:

> Over the centuries, China's rulers, regardless of their philosophical belief and political appeal, have displayed a consistent commitment to a model with the state's strong will in controlling and ordering Chinese society. Under this model, the state not only plays an active role in enforcing law and upholding order against undesirable human conducts but also aggressively penetrates into every thread of the social fabric, such as the family, kin, guild, trade union, school, and other social institutions. To the Chinese rulers, the ultimate goal of social control in Chinese society is far beyond the conventionally understood threshold — controlling human conduct. To the state officials the task of social control unmistakably means both behavioral conformity and thought uniformity. Regardless of its political shortfalls, such a model has been carried on for generations by Chinese rulers and thus forms a unique inherent feature of the legal tradition that predisposes China's propensity in the contemporary legalizing process.[42]

Let us return to the question at issue: Who writes the rules? The picture presented by these accounts is clearly *not* one in which the great masses of individuals within the society write the rules, either directly or through an elected representative parliament. Indeed, as was recently explained by John Thornton — a professor at Tsinghua University and chair of the Brookings Institution — it is only at the village level that Chinese citizens can elect their officials. See Box #7.5 for details.

---

40. Chow, *supra* note 1, at 131–132 (emphasis added). In another passage, Chow explains that the nomenklatura system "refers to a list of Party or government positions kept by Party leaders that can be filled only by certain persons whose names appear on a list of candidates or nominees for those positions.... Through the nomenklatura system, Party organs can determine the list of names of the candidate list, which often corresponds exactly with the number of positions available." *Id.* at 129.

41. Xin Ren, *supra* note 1, at 48. In another passage, Xin Ren acknowledges "the legality of the Communist Party's ruling power over the legislative and judicial processes". *Id.* at 3.

42. *Id.* at 1. As further evidence of the extensive control that the CPC exercise over Chinese law and society, Xin Ren explains that China lacks a fully independent judiciary — although she notes "that judicial independence is always relative rather than absolute in both totalitarian and democratic societies." *Id.* at 49.

Box #7.5 *"Democratic" Elections in China*[43]

There are several systems for selecting the officials responsible for enacting laws at the various levels of government in China. Some important features of those systems are summarized here:

- For about a decade, peasants in China's roughly 700,000 villages (that is, about 700 million farmers) have held competitive popular elections to choose government leaders for those villages.

- Those village-level elections began in some areas in the early 1980s. When it emerged in the 1990s that less than half of the officials so elected were CPC members, the Beijing authorities took corrective steps, so that today more village chiefs are CPC members.

- At the township level, which is the lowest rung in the Chinese government structure, some direct elections were held after the mid-1990s, but most townships use a different method — the "open recommendation and selection" system, under which any adult resident can become a candidate but a council of community leaders narrows the candidate pool to two persons and the local parliamentary body (the local People's Congress) makes the final selection. However, more experimentation is taking place at the township level, with some competitive elections being tried in some parts of the country.

- At the county level — one administrative rung up from a township — some "open recommendation and selection" polls (as described above) have been conducted, again on an experimental basis, for the position of county deputy chief in a very few areas (representing less than one-half of a percent of China's counties).

- In urban areas, some experimentation is also occurring. For example, in 2003, twelve private citizens ran as independent (non-CPC) candidates for district legislative positions in Shenzhen, and two of them won seats. And independent candidates have run for parliamentary positions also in other parts of the country, although almost none of them has ever gotten elected.

- China's leaders have in recent years also taken steps toward competitive elections with the CPC. Some observers regard this "intraparty democracy" as more important than the experiments referred to above in competitive elections at the local level.

- For example, in the 2006–2007 election cycle, the local CPC leaders in nearly 300 townships were chosen through direct voting by party members. And the forming of "interest groups" within the CPC is reportedly no longer prohibited.

- Still, these incidents represent the exception to the rule. For the most part, the selection of legislative authorities in China remains within the control of the CPC.

Hence, instead of seeing rules of law emanating directly from "the will of the people carried out through an elected body such as a parliament," as Xin Ren says is the expectation in Western culture,[44] we see law in today's China — like law in dynastic China — that is written by a very small cadre of officials who have gained power by birth, through force, or on the basis of their proven apparent fidelity to a favored ideology. Throughout nearly all of dynastic Chinese history, those officials would have been emperors and the cluster of close advisors, especially Confucian scholars, who surrounded them. In contemporary China, those officials are the most elite of CPC officials.

---

43. The information in Box #7.5 is drawn (and in a few passages reprinted *verbatim*) from John L. Thornton, *Long Time Coming: The Prospects for Democracy in China*, 87 FOREIGN AFFAIRS 2, 5 *et seq.* (2008).

44. *Id.* at 54.

C. Thick and Thin Versions of a Rule of Law

1. Peerenboom and Fuller

How, if at all, should these facts bear on our assessment of whether China's legal system does or does not reflect a "rule of law"? In other words, should the nearly absolute authority of the CPC over China's system of law and governance, coupled with the absence of a genuinely representative legislature reflecting direct influence by society at large, lead us to conclude that China is *not* in fact a "rule of law country" as its Constitution proclaims?

Randall Peerenboom has offered some views that would lead us away from any such conclusion. For Peerenboom (whom I quoted above for his explanation of the "rule of law" language added to the PRC Constitution in 1999[45]), the entire debate over whether today's China aspires to and adheres to a rule of law is plagued by sloppy and biased definitions, some of which he attributes in particular to Ugo Mattei, a comparative law expert at the University of Torino and the University of California at Hastings:

> China seems to be moving toward some form of rule of law, but not the liberal democratic form of rule of law that Mattei implicitly uses as his benchmark.... [S]ome of the traits found in China are hard to reconcile with such a system [that features a liberal democratic form of rule of law]: [those traits include] a hierarchical society, an emphasis on family, different gender roles, different conceptions of rights or at least a different balance between the interests of the individual and group, and different justifications and rationales for those outcomes.... But these features are not at odds with the rule of law per se, just with one particular version....
>
> Mattei ... equates rule of law with Western liberal democracy ... Mattei is not alone [in this respect;] ... For many, "the rule of law" means a liberal democratic version of rule of law.
>
> The tendency to equate rule of law with liberal democratic rule of law has led some Asian commentators to portray the attempts of Western governments and international organizations such as the World Bank and IMF to promote rule of law in Asian countries as a form of cultural, political, economic, and legal hegemony. Critics claim that liberal democratic rule of law is excessively individualist in its orientation and privileges individual autonomy and rights over duties and obligations to others, the interests of society, and social solidarity and harmony.
>
> *It may help in sorting out matters to distinguish between thick and thin versions of rule of law. Briefly put, a thin theory stresses the formal or instrumental aspects of rule of law*—those features that any legal system allegedly must possess to function effectively as a system of laws, regardless of whether the legal system is part of a democratic or non-democratic society, capitalist or socialists, liberal or theocratic. Although proponents of thin interpretation of rule of law define it in slightly different ways, there is considerable common ground, with many building on or modifying Lon Fuller's influential account that laws be general, public, prospective, clear, consistent, capable of being followed, stable, and enforced.

---

45. See *supra* text accompanying notes 14–15.

In contrast to thin versions, thick or substantive conceptions begin with the basic elements of a thin conception, but then incorporate elements of political morality such as particular economic arrangements (free-market capitalism, central planning, etc.), forms of government (democratic, single party socialism, etc.), or conceptions of human rights (liberal, communitarian, collectivist, "Asian values," etc.).

In China and other Asian countries for that matter, there is little debate about the requirements of a thin theory and the basic principle that rule of law refers to a system in which law is able to impose meaningful restraints on the state and individual members of the ruling elite, as captured in the rhetorically powerful if overly simplistic notions of a government of laws, the supremacy of the law, and equality of all before the law. However, there is considerable debate about competing thick conceptions of rule of law.[46]

I have quoted from Peerenboom at length because I find that his conceptual framework offers a powerful way of organizing our thoughts on the rule of law in China. Before embarking on that, however, it is worth giving special attention to one aspect of Peerenboom's conceptual framework: his reliance on the work of Lon Fuller. Recall that we saw in the first chapter of this book a synopsis of Fuller's views on the "morality" of law. See Box #1.1, in Chapter One, for a summary of those views. For convenience, an abbreviated form appears here in Box #7.6.

Box #7.6 Lon Fuller and the "Morality" of Law (abbreviated)[47]

In his great work, *The Morality of Law* (1964), Lon Fuller argues that law is subject to an internal morality consisting of eight principles relating to the rules that purportedly comprise the legal system. These principles may be summarized in this way:

- (P1) the rules must be expressed in general terms;

- (P2) the rules must be publicly promulgated;

- (P3) the rules must be (for the most part) prospective in effect;

- (P4) the rules must be expressed in understandable terms;

- (P5) the rules must be consistent with one another;

- (P6) the rules must not require conduct beyond the powers of the affected parties;

- (P7) the rules must not be changed so frequently that the subject cannot rely on them; and

- (P8) the rules must be administered in a manner consistent with their wording.

---

2. Proposing and Testing a Hypothesis

a. A hypothesis on aspirations

We might pull together (i) Peerenboom's views on a "thin" rule of law and (ii) Fuller's enumeration of attributes of legality to consider the following hypothesis about contemporary Chinese law: Even though China *does* aspire, according to its Constitution, to

---

46. Peerenboom-2003, *supra* note 1, at 55–58 (emphasis added). Peerenboom's work, and especially his distinction between "thin" and "thick" versions of the rule of law, has been widely cited. See, e.g., Albert H.Y. Chen, *supra* note 1, at 38; Jianfu Chen, *supra* note 1, at 730.

47. I have drawn this description in part from an account offered in the Internet Encyclopedia of Philosophy: A Peer Reviewed Academic Resource, at http://www.iep.utm.edu/l/legalpos.htm#SH4a. As noted in Chapter One, Lon Fuller was a professor of law at Harvard University for many years.

achieving a "thin" rule of law—under which the legal system would boast the attributes that Peerenboom draws from Lon Fuller's work—China *does not* aspire to the liberal democratic version of a "thick" rule of law; and if it can be said that China aspires to *any* thick version of the rule of law, it is one (or more) of the alternative versions of a "thick" rule of law that Peerenboom identifies. These include "statist socialist", "neo-authoritarian", and "communitarian" versions of a "thick" rule of law. Peerenboom briefly defines these various types of "thick" versions of a rule of law (including the "Liberal Democratic" version) as follows:

> [T]he Liberal Democratic version of rule of law incorporates free market capitalism (subject to qualifications that would allow various degrees of "legitimate" government regulation of the market), multiparty democracy in which citizens may choose their representatives at all levels of government, and a liberal interpretation of human rights that gives priority to civil and political rights over economic, social, cultural, and collective or group rights.

> Statist Socialists endorse a state-centered socialist rule of law defined by, *inter alia*, a socialist form of economy (which in today's China means an increasingly market-based economy but one in which public ownership still plays a somewhat larger role than in other market economies); a non-democratic system in which the [Communist] Party plays a leading role; and an interpretation of rights that emphasizes stability, collective rights over individual rights, and subsistence as the basic right rather than civil and political rights.

> There is also support for various forms of rule of law that fall between the Statist Socialism and the Liberal Democratic version. For example, there is some support for a democratic but non-liberal (New Confucian) Communitarian variant built on market capitalism, perhaps with a somewhat greater degree of government intervention than in the liberal version; some genuine form of multiparty democracy in which citizens choose their representatives at all levels of government; plus a communitarian or collectivist interpretation of rights that attaches relatively greater weight to the interests of the majority and collective rights as opposed to the civil and political rights of individuals.

> Another variant is a Neo-authoritarian or Soft Authoritarian form of rule of law that, like the Communitarian version, rejects a liberal interpretation of rights, but unlike its Communitarian cousin, also rejects democracy. Whereas Communitarians adopt a genuine multiparty democracy in which citizens choose their representatives at all levels of government, Neo-authoritarians permit democracy only at lower levels of government or not at all.[48]

---

48. Peerenboom-2003, *supra* note 1, at 58–59 n.87. As noted above, Appendix 7.3 to this chapter provides a sampling of rule-of-law definitions and descriptions emerging from a survey of recent literature from various sources. The overwhelming majority of those definitions and descriptions reflect what Peerenboom calls a Liberal Democratic "thick" version of the rule of law—and this is hardly surprising given the fact that most of those definitions and descriptions come from western sources. Peerenboom himself seems to prefer one of the latter two "thick" versions of the rule of law listed above —those emphasizing communitarian values. In his 2007 book on China, Peerenboom writes this:

> On the whole, I find the arguments in favor of the kind of communitarian or collectivist approach to rights issues found in some Asian countries … more persuasive, and the results on the whole more attractive, than the liberal approach as practiced particularly in the United States.… To put it simply, … liberalism tends to benefit the more talented, smarter, or already well-off individuals in a society at the expense of the vast majority. In contrast, communitarianism benefits the vast majority, albeit at times to the detriment of exceptional individuals.

Having now introduced Peerenboom's distinction between a "thin" version of the rule of law and several "thick" versions of the rule of law, it is appropriate for us to consider yet again the rough-and-ready definition of "rule of law" that I offered earlier. That definition (as posited in Box #6.9 in Chapter Six) reads as follows:

> *A society may be said to adhere to the rule of law if the rules in its legal system are publicly promulgated, reasonably clear in their formulation, prospective in their effect, reasonably stable over time, reasonably consistent with each other, applicable to all segments of the society (including the government, so as to prevent the government elite from acting arbitrarily), reasonably comprehensive in their coverage of substantive issues facing the society and its people, and reasonably effective, in the sense that the rules are broadly adhered to by the people in the society—voluntarily by most, and through officially forced compliance where necessary.*

Does that definition of the rule of law adequately take into account the important distinction that Peerenboom has offered between "thin" and "thick" versions of the rule of law? I believe it does—and indeed I intended for it to do so. The above definition *includes* most of Fuller's "morality of law" attributes, it *adds* a requirement that the rules be relatively comprehensive in coverage, and it *omits* elements that would appear in what Peerenboom refers to as a Liberal Democratic version of a "thick" rule of law definition. For example, my definition omits such elements as these:

- The law should be employed to safeguard and advance the civil and political rights of the individual—including most prominently the freedom of expression—and to create conditions under which the individual's legitimate aspirations and dignity may be realized.

- The legal system guarantees procedural fairness ("due process")—that is, certain basic rights of process must be followed in order for the government to act against the interests of an individual.

- The law emerges from democratic processes in which all citizens play a direct part in creating rules or in electing representatives who create the rules.

- The powers of the government are divided into separate compartments—typically legislative, executive, and judicial—with checks and balances preventing any one compartment from dominating the others (and therefore the entire legal system).[49]

Randall Peerenboom, CHINA MODERNIZES: THREAT TO THE WEST OR MODEL FOR THE REST? ix (2007) [hereinafter Peerenboom-2007]. For a psychological view of the "collective or interdependent nature of Asian society" as contrasted with the "individualistic or independent nature of Western society", see Richard E. Nisbett, THE GEOGRAPHY OF THOUGHT: HOW ASIANS AND WESTERNERS THINK DIFFERENTLY ... AND WHY (2003), reviewed at SCIENTIFIC AMERICAN, April 2003, at 98 (asserting that the first of these is "consistent with Asians' broad, contextual view of the world and their belief that events are highly complex and determined by many factors" and that the second "seems consistent with the Western focus on particular objects in isolation from their context and with Westerners' belief that they can know the rules governing objects and therefore can control the objects' behavior").

49. This list of elements, which I would include as central ingredients to a Liberal Democratic "thick" version of the rule of law—but which may be absent from the "thin" version of the rule of law—is inspired in part by my correspondence with James Dunlap of the Lovells firm in Hong Kong. According to Dunlap, democracy involves three main elements: free elections, freedom of expression, and limited government—which itself includes an independent judiciary to protect a core of non-derogable minority rights, as well as certain economic freedom and property rights. Correspondence with James Dunlap, Mar. 26, 2008.

I introduced (a few paragraphs previous to this one) the following hypothesis: Even though China *does* aspire, according to its Constitution, to achieving a "thin" rule of law—under which the legal system would boast the attributes that Peerenboom draws from Lon Fuller's work—China (or at least those of its CPC leadership) *does not* aspire to the liberal democratic version of a "thick" rule of law. Is that hypothesis correct? One way of testing it is to consider a range of views expressed in recent writings by certain Chinese legal scholars from some of the top universities in China. I shall do that in the following paragraphs, in which I summarize observations made by experts Wang Zhoujun, Jiang Ming'an, He Jiahong, Ma Huaide, Chen Weidong, and Ma Xiaohong.

b. "Feeling the stones when crossing the river"

Wang Zhoujun offers these observations about the meaning of the rule of law:[50]

> Rule of law requires that organizations of public power should possess and exercise public power to manage the society according to law. In other words, rule of law emphasizes government's compliance with the law. The three powers of legislation, law enforcement and administration all belong to the category of public power and must abide by the law.[51]

Two key themes in Wang Zhoujun's writing on democracy and the rule of law are these: (1) of the various forms of governmental power, it is *administrative* power that increasingly matters in the daily lives of individuals in today's China; and (2) China's contemporary legal system is, and should be, taking a *gradualist* approach to bringing administrative power under the control of the rule of law. As for the first of these themes, Wang Zhoujun gives this explanation:

> Modern administrative power keeps expanding and covers and manages everything from cradle to grave. In order to further improve the efficacy of social control, administrative organs have been granted certain legislative power and limited quasi power of law enforcement. Essentially a modern structure of public power has been formed with administrative power at the core, and ... the domination of administrative power is determined by the complexity of the modern society. We have no choice and there is no way out. Consequently, in the context of modern society, the core of the construction of rule of law is how to perform official duties according to law.[52]

Wang Zhoujun then proceeds to his second thesis: enhancing the rule of law in the administrative functions of government must be undertaken gradually—as in the case of "feeling the stones when crossing the river" in order to avoid falling headlong and drowning in a torrent of uncertainty and risk when making one's way to the other shore.[53] Noting that the basic strategy of exercising the "rule of law" was only officially

---

50. See generally Wang Zhoujun, *supra* note 2.

51. *Id.* at 339.

52. *Id.*

53. See *id.* at 346–348. For Wang Zhoujun, "feeling the stones when crossing the river" means that "in the whole reform process, every step taken has to be very cautious." In his view, the other shore of the river is "a prosperous and powerful, democratic and civilized socialist country". *Id.* at 348. Although Wang Zhoujun does not do so, the phrase "feeling the stones when crossing the river" is derived from Deng Xiaoping's phrase *mozhe shitou guo he* or "crossing the river by feeling for stones". Deng used the phrase in the context of experimenting with economic policies. For details, see Satya J. Gabriel, *Economic Liberalization in Post-Mao China: Crossing the River by Feeling for Stones* (Oct. 1998), appearing in Prof. Gabriel's CHINA ESSAY SERIES, available at http://www.mtholyoke.edu/courses/sgabriel/economics/china-essays/7.html.

formulated and adopted in 1999, Wang Zhoujun points to progress that has been made in implementing that strategy, particularly in the area of administrative law. In particular, he emphasizes the three stages of "startup", "accumulation", and "integration" that have occurred in China's development of the rule of law,[54] which Wang Zhoujun says "firstly requires government to abide by the law, and secondly requires that the law should comply with the essence of law, which contains justice, fairness, openness, credibility and efficacy."[55]

What Wang Zhoujun does *not* include in the notion of the rule of law—at least as it is pursued in China—is the principle of democracy by majority rule. He claims that China's cultural foundations are ill-suited to that form of democracy:

China's Confucian traditional culture is a value system of clannishness with the royal authority at its core.... Although traditional culture has been weakened to some extent since the beginning of modern China, it is still very influential and has produced many restrictions on the development of China's constitutionalism.

First, worship of power [that has its origin in] royal authority is poles apart from the ideas of modern democracy. Democracy is built upon the principle of "the minority is subordinate to the majority", while worship of power is in essence a rule of "the powerless are subordinate to the powerful".... In this view, "majority" is not necessarily an adequate reason for soliciting obedience. Mr. Bo Yang ... [has explained this:] I once saw in an English movie some children arguing over whether to go climbing trees or swimming. After a while they decided to vote and the decision was to climb trees. And everyone went climbing trees. I was very much impressed by this behavior, as democracy is not just a form, it is a part of life (Bo, 1986)." What Mr. Bo Yang said causes us to appreciate clearly the profound meaning of "all knowledge is local": the principle of majority rule is the foundation of the western democracy, while in Chinese culture, the principle of majority rule is not always true—if without authority and power as backup, more often than not the minority would not yield to the ruling of the majority; they would rather set up another faction and split from the majority....

Second, clannishness can cause alienation of the fragile democracy in our country, which is already gaining ground in China. Our country is promoting democracy at the village-level organizations.... However, due to the penetration of the traditional culture of clannishness, some negative impact has occurred.... The clan's control over local affairs [is tightening, and in some areas has displaced official government authority.] ...

Besides, worship of power is one of the reasons for the faint awareness of rule of law and human rights [in China, which had] ... a society of rule of man characterized by the emperor's autocratic rule that lasted for over 2000 years.... [Therefore,] it can be said that China's traditional culture is one of the reasons why China's constitutional reform flounders.... [Hence,] we should adopt a gradual process of cultural transformation ... [because China's development of

---

54. In this regard, Wang Zhoujun cites various administrative law statutes enacted in 1989, 1996, 2004, along with the draft administrative procedure code still under preparation. Wang Zhoujun, *supra* note 2, at 340–341.

55. *Id.* at 340.

the rule of law by] simply "copying" the constitutional system of the West will not work. We need stable and cautious development strategies.[56]

c. Democracy and rule of law

Another Chinese legal scholar, Jiang Ming'an of Peking University, also emphasizes the importance of (i) enhancing the rule of law in the exercise of *administrative* power, while (ii) taking a cautious and *gradual* approach to embracing certain aspects of democracy—what Jiang refers to as "participatory democracy".[57] For Jiang, "participatory democracy" can in fact be the enemy of the rule of law, as it was during the Cultural Revolution, "a period during which China's democracy ran out of control and was distorted, and legal system of destructed [*sic*]."[58] According to Jiang, "[i]t is obvious that 'mass participation democracy' (or 'direct democracy') without a legal system (and rule of law) is horrifying and will drive human beings back to the 'natural status' without any safety guarantee."[59]

In view of this danger, Jiang explains, the development of administrative rule of law in China (and the development there of the rule of law and constitutionalism more generally) has followed the path of "delegate democracy," which he claims has these advantages:

> [F]irst, the quality of the people's representatives is normally higher than that of the average citizens, hence the quality of the decisions made by the representative bodies is normally higher than that of the decisions made by the average citizens collectively; second, the people's congress has less people than the meeting of all citizens, so it is easier for it to reach consensus ... ; third, the representative congress usually follows relatively strict procedures in discussing issues, and as a result is likely to be cautious in making decisions ... [rather than being] affected by emotions and to be manipulated, which may result in some extreme decisions and may even lead to "majority tyranny" ... ; fourth, delegate democracy is more economical than direct participation democracy."[60]

Jiang's views would surely strike most readers as self-evident, although they do raise the question (at least in my mind) of why Jiang does not address this key issue: does the "representative congress" to which he refers actually exist in the PRC, where control over the election of persons to such a congress is so tightly held by the CPC? Perhaps as a silent acknowledgment of that issue, Jiang turns his attention to ways in which "delegate democracy" in China can in fact be supplemented by "participatory democracy". Such supplementation is needed, he says, because "delegate democracy" has drawbacks: (1) representatives have their own interests that sometimes differ from those of the public whose interests they are supposed to serve; (2) "members of the modern parliament are normally recommended by political parties, which have their own interests that are not always aligned with those of the public"; and (iii) "when making decisions the representative bodies usually adopt the principle that the minority shall be subordinate to the majority, thus sometimes the legitimate rights and interests of the minority cannot be protected effectively".[61]

In addition, Jiang observes, in modern society the issues that face a government become so complicated as to require greater and greater delegation to administrative agen-

---

56. *Id.* at 349–352.
57. See generally Jiang Ming'an, *supra* note 2.
58. *Id.* at 356.
59. *Id.*
60. *Id.* at 363–364.
61. *Id.* at 364–365.

cies, and this shift of authority can place even further distance between the authorities and the people in the society. This is the reason, he says, that administrative rule of law is so important. One means of ensuring such rule of law is to "protect freedom of speech, reinforce the report of public opinions by news media and perfect citizens' open discussion mechanism. Newspaper, radio, television and Internet and open discussions are important channels and forms of public participation".[62]

For Jiang, however, the (administrative) rule of law should *not* entail too much of these substantive freedoms of speech, press, and assembly:

> Of course, various media, especially open discussions over the internet, carry certain risks: some people may fabricate rumors and stir up troubles, make libelous, offensive and irresponsible remarks against the government and other people, mislead the public intentionally and create incidents.... Therefore, on the one hand, the law should protect freedom of speech, and on the other hand, it should regulate the operation of various news media.[63]

d. Importance of administrative procedure rules

A third Chinese legal scholar, Ma Huaide (vice president at the China University of Political Science and Law), also focuses on how administrative law, and especially administrative *procedure* law, bears on the rule of law in China.[64] Ma offers these observations:

> As a significant step toward constructing democracy and rule of law in China, codifying administrative procedural law has great implications in developing democratic politics, protecting citizen rights, controlling corruption, overcoming bureaucracy, accelerating administrative efficiency, improving the socialism market economy, and constructing socialism rule of law in the country, [especially] in constructing rule of law government.[65]

Ma Huaide seems to go further than many other Chinese scholars in embracing what would typically be regarded as liberal democratic political ideology. He asserts, for example, that "[a]s the basis of democratic politics, citizen's [*sic*] participation in the management of state affairs and democratic process should be greatly encouraged",[66] and Ma explains how codifying administrative procedural law can contribute importantly to democratic politics. Such codification can also, Ma points out, "be conducive to civil rights protection, and human rights promotion, which are the common duties of all countries around the world, and which are also the main aims of bettering rule of law."[67]

e. Restrictions on officials' power

He Jiahong, a friend of mine at Renmin University from the time of my Fulbright fellowship to Beijing in 1994, also defines and discusses issues relating to the rule of law.[68] For He, the movement toward the rule of law is one of ten key "tendencies" that he believes will dictate the development of criminal justice (He Jiahong's work focuses on crim-

---

62. *Id.* at 370.
63. *Id.*
64. See generally Ma Huaide, *supra* note 2.
65. *Id.* at 308.
66. *Id.*
67. *Id.*
68. See generally He Jiahong, *supra* note 2.

inal law.) He offers this succinct account of what the rule of law is, what it emerged from, and why it matters:

> Rule of man is a kind of government for primitive society. In primitive time, since there was no law, rule by man was the only choice, and rulers originally were people with strong body or high prestige.... In modern times, the emerging bourgeois in the western countries turned the "rule of law" into a banner and instrument for their fight for power, and one of their slogans was "the King shall not violate the law". Later, with social development and the accumulation of the experience of social administration, mankind became more and more aware of the superiority and essence of the rule of law. Thus, it is a necessary trend of human society to proceed from rule by man to rule of law.

> Currently, the rule of law is in global fashion. Similarly, China should also move along the track of "rule of law". The basic aim of the rule of law is to form a law-based stable and benign social order. The basic meaning of the rule of law consists of two focuses and one basic point.... The first "focus" of the rule of law is to formulate good laws. However, without strict observance, execution and justice, good legislation in itself will not be able to make for a genuine rule of law. The "non-observance" is equal to the lawlessness.... So, the second focus is to execute laws.... In modern law-ruled nations, social members, especially powerful government officials, must strictly observe laws. Though it is necessary for ordinary people to conform to laws, yet it is more so for officials. Hence the "basic point" of the rule of law is to restrict officials' power and to adhere to the principle that "officials shall not violate the law."[69]

f. Rule of law and international standards

Chen Weidong, another Chinese legal scholar at Renmin University, also examines the rule of law in the context of Chinese criminal law and procedure.[70] Chen discusses the "challenge" posed by a mismatch between certain international standards and certain Chinese rules governing criminal procedure. In particular, Chen notes that Chinese rules are inconsistent with provisions found in the International Covenant on Civil and Political Rights requiring a presumption of innocence, safeguards against self-incrimination, and protections against double jeopardy. "Hence," Chen says, "at present, applying the criminal justice guidelines stated in international covenants to our criminal procedure is a problem that needs to be resolved immediately".[71]

Chen Weidong's proposal for resolving that problem seems internally inconsistent. On the one hand, Chen posits that "all rules of criminal justice, which are ordained in international pacts that our nation has subscribed or has been affiliated to, should be carried out through this modification of [China's] Criminal Procedure Law". On the other hand, Chen claims that the PRC "should be able to set up some exceptional rules according to the situation of our nation."[72] There seems to be an unexplained inconsistency between these two approaches, which is odd given Chen's acknowledgement that "if there is discord between international treaties and the Criminal Procedure Law, the whole law system will arrive

---

69. *Id.* at 9–10.
70. See generally Chen Weidong, *supra* note 2.
71. *Id.* at 160.
72. *Id.* at 161.

at a state of confusion, which will then lead to contradictions and conflicts between law criterions [*sic*] and will go against the modernization of [China's] legal system."[73]

g. Rule of law or rule of lǐ?

The exceptionalism that Chen Weidong suggests also appears, but in a much bolder form, in the views of Ma Xiaohong of Renmin University.[74] This legal scholar takes the position that the current enthusiasm, in China and elsewhere, for the rule of law rests on the assumption that the rule of law is superior to the rule by *lǐ*, which Ma Xiaohong defines as "rites" — that is, "norms and concepts formed at the beginning of human society, including primitive religions (e.g. sacrificial rites), morals (kindness to tribe members and enmity towards adversaries), and habits (daily conducts and speeches)."[75] That assumption of superiority, Ma says, is incorrect; it merely reflects biased and racist views by Westerners (he cites the prominent 19th-century comparative jurist and legal historian Sir Henry Maine in particular) whose colonization of the world made them equate might with right.[76] As a result of that colonization, Ma asserts, "Western law had become a yardstick for judging whether a country/region's law was 'progressive' and 'civilized' or 'backward' and 'barbarous'".[77]

That biased and racist view, Ma Xiaohong implies, should be discarded. Neither one of the two different approaches to law is inferior to the other, Ma says:

> If we can say that after the lengthy period of the Customary Law, the West, on the basis of their specific economic and social conditions, chose to leave the clanship [that all societies have gone through] for the rule of law, then, China, on the other hand, choose [*sic*] to "reform the clanship" and enter into the stage of rule by *lǐ*. The two choices in themselves were not inferior to each other, [but rather] the formation and development of a civilization and a cultural mode [represented by these two different choices] were endowed by the environment and the history and [therefore] no one could be said to be advanced or underdeveloped".[78]

h. Pluralism in perspectives

It appears, then, that Ma Xiaohong is issuing a call for China to renounce the "rule of law" in favor of the "rule of *lǐ*". The former, he indicates, is a foreign element that will never be successfully imposed on Chinese society. The latter, he says, reflects China's deep Confucian traditional values.[79]

It should be obvious from the survey of views summarized in the preceding paragraphs that Chinese legal scholars bring a wide range of perspectives to the question of whether China aspires to, or should aspire to, a rule of law — and if so, what that means. Some scholars do seem to endorse not only the rule of law in its "thin" version but also certain aspects of a Western-oriented liberal democratic "thick" version of the rule of law — including, for example, participatory rights and other procedural safeguards in administrative

---

73. *Id.* at 163.
74. See generally Ma Xiaohong, *supra* note 2.
75. *Id.* at 57.
76. *Id.*
77. *Id.* This assertion by Ma is echoed, of course, by advocates of many indigenous and other peoples who have found themselves in unfortunate relationships with colonizers from the West.
78. *Id.* at 58.
79. *Id.* at 65–69.

law, and even certain substantive rights for individuals.[80] Other Chinese scholars take a more gradualist approach, urging caution in China's development of legal changes that could be incompatible with China's current circumstances or long-held values. And some Chinese scholars would apparently have the country return to some of those long-held values, thereby abandoning the efforts made in recent years to adopt any sort of rule of law ideology—including, presumably, even the "thin" version of the rule of law. That last view, however, would seem to be a minority position, and one that is inconsistent with the 1999 constitutional amendment.

We should hardly find this diversity of views among Chinese scholars surprising. Surely a diversity of views on such an issue would appear in any country, and particularly in one that has experienced such a "paroxysm" of legal reform as China has in recent years. Randall Peerenboom offers these observations about that country's varied views on the rule of law and how to achieve it:

> Although one can appreciate the desire for an overall, coherent plan for reforms, no country has ever successfully implemented rule of law in accordance with some preordained theoretical blueprint. Legal reforms are necessarily evolutionary, context-specific and path-dependent. Moreover, China is increasingly pluralistic. As noted, there are important differences in the conceptions of rule of law and the different emphases in the purposes of law among central leaders, local officials, academics, and Chinese citizens, and within these broad categories as well.... Thus, no single view of law or single theory can capture the diversity of perspectives.[81]

i. Consensus in observation?

Before concluding this examination of the rule of law in China, let us move from theory to practice—from "ought" to "is". In the preceding paragraphs I introduced and then tested this hypothesis: Even though China *does* aspire (in accordance with its Constitution) to achieving a "thin" rule of law, China *does not* aspire to the liberal democratic version of a "thick" rule of law. In my view, that hypothesis holds up well under scrutiny: there appears to be little consensus in terms of *aspirations* about rule of law in China, beyond the aim to achieve the rule of law in its "thin" form.

Is there, however, a consensus of *observation?* That is, can we say that China's current legal system does in fact have the attributes of a "thin" rule of law? Perhaps we can, although only barely. For these purposes, let us draw not directly on the "thin" version of the rule of law that Lon Fuller proposes (enumerating eight key attributes[82]) but instead

---

80. For Stanley Lubman's assessment on this point—concluding that several leading Chinese legal scholars have "call[ed] for establishment of the rule of law based on principles familiar in the West" (including a requirement that members of the NPC be elected in public campaigns and that they not provide a "rubber stamp" for CPC policies)—see Lubman-1999, *supra* note 1, at 124–125.

81. Peerenboom-2003, *supra* note 1, at 94. In another, more general context, Peerenboom asserts that it might even be better to "avoid reference to 'the rule of law,' which suggests that there is a single type of rule of law" and instead to "refer to the *concept* of 'the rule of law,' for which there are different possible *conceptions*." Randall Peerenboom, CHINA'S LONG MARCH TOWARD RULE OF LAW 5 (2002).

82. See Box #7.6, *supra*, summarizing Fuller's views. In simplified form, the attributes are that the rules in the legal system be general, public, prospective, understandable, reasonably consistent with each other, within the power of society to follow, fairly stable over time, and administered in a manner consistent with their wording.

on the slightly more demanding (but still "thin") one that I have proposed, as explained above.[83] Using that as our standard, it seems that law in today's China probably *does* possess the minimal attributes required to say that it does adhere to the rule of law — subject, however, to one point of uncertainty. That point of uncertainty relates to the requirement that the rules be "applicable to all segments of the society (including the government, so as to prevent the government elite from acting arbitrarily)". Given the peculiar and entrenched status of the CPC in the political system — and the opportunity for manipulation that this presents — it is not clear that the rules are in fact, when push comes to shove, fully applicable to the government.

Except for that point of uncertainty — which is by no means insignificant — it seems that China's system does have the rule of law under the "thin" standards explained above. The impressive legal reform efforts in China over the past ninety years, and especially in the last thirty, have created a system that is, for the most part, competent and effective.

We should, of course, not lose sight of the fact that several aspects of the system have attracted harsh criticism both from inside and from outside China. For example, as we shall examine more fully in subsection IIC below, the continuing lack of independence (and in some cases inadequate legal training) among members of the judiciary constitutes a major blemish on the system.[84] Similarly, improvements that several Chinese legal scholars cited above have proudly described regarding administrative law and procedure have in fact enjoyed only partial success, with some local officials in China's rural regions merely feigning compliance with the laws — or in some cases simply ignoring and breaking the law;[85]

---

83. That rule of law definition appears near the beginning of subsection IC2a above, as well as in Box #6.9 in Chapter Six, above. It requires that the rules in the legal system be publicly promulgated, reasonably clear in their formulation, prospective in their effect, reasonably stable over time, reasonably consistent with each other, applicable to all segments of the society (including the government, so as to prevent the government elite from acting arbitrarily), reasonably comprehensive in their coverage of substantive issues facing the society and its people, and reasonably effective, in the sense that the rules are broadly adhered to by the people in the society — voluntarily by most, and through officially forced compliance where necessary.

84. These and related issues are addressed in Albert H.Y. Chen, *supra* note 1, at 151–155. See also Jim Yardley, *A Judge Tests China's Courts, Making History*, NEW YORK TIMES, Nov. 28, 2005, available on www.nytimes.com (reporting that although "China's leaders have embraced the rule of law as the most efficient means of regulating society", a "central requirement in fulfilling that promise lies unresolved — whether the governing Communist Party intends to allow an independent judiciary"; and also asserting that "China's court system is far from an independent entity that can curb government power" and that instead the judges "remain a pliable tool to reinforce that power because they are often "poorly educated in the law and corrupt") Other articles in a series on the rule of law in China can also be found at http://www.nytimes.com. See, e.g., Joseph Kahn, *Deep Flaws, and Little Justice, in China's Court System*, NEW YORK TIMES, Sep. 21, 2005; see also Joseph Kahn, *When Chinese Sue the State, Cases are Often Smothered*, NEW YORK TIMES, Dec. 28, 2005.

85. See Kevin J. O'Brien and Lianjiang Li, *Suing the Local State: Administrative Litigation in Rural China*, appearing as chapter 2 in Neil J. Diamant, Stanley B. Lubman, and Kevin J. O'Brien, ENGAGING THE LAW IN CHINA: STATE, SOCIETY, AND POSSIBILITIES FOR JUSTICE (2005), at 31:

> The promulgation of the Administrative Litigation Law (ALL) in 1989 was hailed in China as a "milestone of democratic and legal construction." ... [However,] the law's implementation has been hounded by interference and feigned compliance. To this day, the law is widely regarded to be a "frail weapon" that has not greatly reduced administrative arbitrariness.... [Indeed,] in the countryside, ... many local officials continue to mistreat villagers in egregiously illegal ways.... [G]etting a case accepted is difficult, and long delays are common. Even when rural complainants manage to win a lawsuit, they often face uncertain enforcement or retaliation.

For a similar criticism regarding local indifference to national laws, see Elizabeth Economy, *The Great Leap Backward?*, 86 FOREIGN AFFAIRS 38, 43 (2007) ("One of the problems is that although China

and other shortcomings in the adherence to the law deeply trouble some observers.[86] Likewise, the Chinese government's treatment of minorities—Tibetans among them—also fuels concerns among many groups and nations around the world.[87] And throughout the system, the pernicious use of *guanxi* (special personal relationship) continues to serve as an "extra legal mechanism" for handling affairs in China.[88] As one observer has noted, "the extensive use of personal connections (*guanxi*) to circumvent the law or to gain leniency seriously undermines the public's confidence in the judicial system".[89]

These are important matters; some of them are deeply troubling deficiencies—and other such deficiencies in China's legal system can also be cited. Indeed, the PRC's State Council recently acknowledged serious shortcomings in the country's legal system.[90]

However, while such features as these are patently inconsistent with a liberal democratic "thick" version of the rule of law as championed by (though rarely achieved) in the West, perhaps they do not require us to conclude that the PRC's legal system falls fatally short of meeting the standards of the rule of law in some reasonable "thin" version. In other words, it would be difficult to conclude that China's legal system is generally dysfunctional or inherently corrupt or so technically deficient as to place the PRC in the same category as those many other countries around the world whose laws and institutions are plainly unable to fulfill what Fuller calls law's essential purpose of achieving social order through the use of rules that guide behavior.[91]

---

has plenty of laws and regulations designed to ensure clean water, factory owners and local officials do not enforce them").

86. See, e.g., Jianfu Chen, *supra* note 1, at 738 (emphasizing that "[l]aw-in-the-books is not necessarily the same as law-in-action" and citing "[t]he tremendous difficulties experienced by Chinese courts in enforcing court judgements [*sic*] or decisions"). Stanley Lubman offers this broad critique:

> [L]egal reform remain[s] [a] work in progress without clear goals. The Chinese Communist part ... values its control over Chinese society more than it does legal reform; the Party-state's institutions for making and implementing law remain in considerable disorder; strong controls over the Chinese bureaucracy's exercise of discretion are lacking; localism weakens the application of laws and policies adopted by Beijing; and Chinese society is beset by severe strains that weekend the force of law.

Lubman-2006, *supra* note 32, at 4.

87. See, e.g., Erich Follath, *Western Democracy Loses Ground To Autocrats* (Jun. 13, 2008), appearing in Speigel Online, available at http://freeinternetpress.com/story.php?sid=17131 (noting that although the Chinese Constitution guarantees "a right to freedom of speech, ... when a minority like the Tibetans voice the slightest protest this is seen as an attempt to destabilize the country and their voices are silenced with brute force").

88. Potter, *supra* note 1, at 12.

89. Zimmerman, *supra* note 1, at 71. Zimmerman also points out that a "by-product of *guanxi* is the institution of nepotism in China, which has allowed senior cadres and their children ... to monopolize key business and to hold substantial real property interests". *Id.* For similar comments on the pernicious uses and effects of *guanxi* in China, see Thornton, *supra* note 43, at 11, and Lubman-2006, *supra* note 32, at 70–74.

90. A government "White Paper" issued in February 2008 stated that "in some regions and departments, laws are not observed, or strictly enforced [and] violators are not brought to justice; [instances of] local protectionism [by which legal rules are bent in favor of local persons and interests] occur from time to time; some government functionaries take bribes [and] abuse their power when executing the law". PRC State Council Information Office, China's Efforts and Achievements in Promoting the Rule of Law, issued Feb. 28, 2008, available at http://www.chinadaily.com.cn/china/2008-02/28/content_6494029_11.htm. See also *White Paper Published on China's Rule of Law*, available on the China.org website at http://www.china.org.cn/government/news/2008-02/28/content_11025486.htm.

91. See Box #7.6, *supra*, for an elaboration on this purpose. Randall Peerenboom reminds us that the quality of a country's legal system is closely tied to the overall wealth (level of economic development) in that country. A country's economic development typically brings greater demand for, and therefore the emergence of, an efficient and fair legal system. Hence, the richer countries can be expected

The observations I have made in the preceding paragraph might be regarded as faint praise for the Chinese legal system. Alternatively, they might be regarded as a realistic assessment of that system, as judged against a different standard from the one often used in evaluating (and criticizing) Chinese law and governance.

D. A Summing-Up on the Rule of Law

With all this as background, I would offer six closing observations about the "rule of law" in today's China.

- First, as suggested above, China *does* seem to aspire — as an official policy and constitutional matter, with widespread support — to achieving a "thin" rule of law, under which the country's legal system would have the sorts of attributes Lon Fuller identifies. That is, the rules in the legal system would, for the most part, be general, public, prospective, clear, consistent, capable of being followed, stable, and enforced.[92]

- Second, the flurry of legal reform undertaken in China in the past three decades has moved the country at breathtaking speed toward meeting that goal of a "thin" rule of law. Considering the state of Chinese law when those efforts began,[93] progress has been remarkable, although shortcomings doubtless remain — as of course they do in all countries. Moreover, disagreements exist both within China and outside China as to whether the progress, speedy as it has been, should not be accelerated even more.

- Third, disagreements also exist as to just what version of a "thick" rule of law, if any, China aspires to today. While pronouncements from the CPC leadership typically seem to reject a liberal democratic version,[94] China may be, as Randall

---

to have much better legal systems, and adherence to the rule of law, than poorer countries. Indeed, Peerenboom cautions that "given the importance of wealth [in achieving the rule of law], comparing poor countries to rich countries is like comparing a piano to a duck." Peerenboom-2007, *supra* note 48, at 199.

92. Those attributes were enumerated in Box #7.6, *supra*.

93. As one source expresses it, "[a]s of 1977, ... China was governed by decrees, by bureaucratic regulations, and by the personal orders of various officials; it had no codes of law at all. In addition, many of the decrees, regulations, and so on were kept secret." Lieberthal, *supra* note 1, at 151.

94. See, e.g., Elisabeth Rosenthal, *China Trying to Crack Down on Liberal Intellectuals*, N.Y. Times (May 8, 2000), available at http://query.nytimes.com/gst/fullpage.html?res=9405E3DE1338 F93BA35756C0A9669C8B63 (noting that "China's leaders are trying to rein in a growing and increasingly assertive liberal intellectual movement" because "China's leaders clearly view this trend as a threat to their political power", and that the leadership has taken "a series of punitive action against writers perceived as straying too far in a liberal or reformist direction"); see also Xin Ren, *supra* note 1, at 56 (quoting a chief justice of the People's Supreme Court as having instructed fellow judges that "the courts must exercise the independent power of the judiciary under the leadership of the Party"); see also Joseph Fewsmith, *China Under Hu Jintao*, appearing in Joseph Fewsmith, China Leadership Monitor, No.14 (Hoover Institution, spring 2005), available at http://media.hoover.org/documents/clm14_jf.pdf (noting that the Hu administration "has actively backed a campaign to criticize "neoliberalism" and has cracked down on the expression of liberal opinion"); see also Yu Zheng, *Communist Reform Broadens Democracy*, appearing in Scientific Outlook on Development (report on 17th Annual CPC Congress (October 17, 2007), available at http://news.xinhuanet.com/english/2007-10/17/content_6898247.htm (reporting that Chinese leader Hu Jintao asserted in visiting the USA in April 2006 that "China would not embrace Western-style democracy"). These relatively recent rejections of democratic liberalism have deep roots, of course. Deng Xiaoping, for example, condemned as proponents of "bourgeois liberalisation" those who wanted Western-style political freedoms in China. See Manoranjan Mohanty, *Development and Democracy: The Indian and Chinese*

Peerenboom asserts, "increasingly pluralistic" and exhibiting "important differences in the conceptions of rule of law and the different emphases in the purposes of law among central leaders, local officials, academics, and Chinese citizens".[95]

- Fourth, China does not today meet the standards of a liberal democratic version of a "thick" rule of law.[96] Illuminating the distinction between "thin" and "thick" rule of law concepts allows us to consider more intelligently why this is the case — that is, to consider whether the absence of a liberal democratic "thick" rule of law in China reflects either (i) an outright disregard for the PRC Constitution's requirement for a "rule of law country", or (ii) instead (which seems more likely), a reluctance on the part of China's leadership to aim for a liberal democratic version of a "thick" rule of law and its acceptance instead of a different version.

- Fifth, contrasting law in today's China with dynastic Chinese law can provide some context for the recent legal reform efforts. For example, (i) unlike dynastic Chinese law, contemporary Chinese law is addressed to the people in ways that bear on their daily lives, instead of being addressed narrowly to the government bureaucrats responsible for maintaining control over the people; (ii) still, the balance between control over the bureaucrats and discretion on the part of the bureaucrats seems similar now to the balance struck in the dynastic codes, although certain underlying assumptions about social hierarchy have disappeared; and (iii) the urge of the CPC in modern China to exercise firm control over the country's people, and over the state apparatus in its entirety, reflects an ages-old approach that dominates Chinese dynastic legal history.

- Taking all these factors into consideration, here is my own conclusion, with which other observers might of course disagree: subject to one point of uncertainty, I take the view that a "thin" rule of law—consistent with the standards I have discussed above—*does* exist in today's China, although only barely. The point of uncertainty revolves around the standard requiring that the rules be applicable to all segments of the society, including the government. The peculiar entrenchment of the CPC in the political system presents a substantial risk of manipulation.

II. Sources and Categories of Law and Lawyers

Now we change our focus. The preceding section of this chapter introduced contemporary Chinese law from an operational perspective by examining a fundamental issue cutting across that country's entire legal system—namely, its acceptance of some sort of rule of law (and by considering in particular *what* sort of rule of law applies in that legal system). As should have been clear from the discussions of these issues in sec-

---

Experience, appearing as Chapter 26 in Across the Himalayan Gap: An Indian Quest for Understanding China (Tan Chung ed., 1998), available at http://ignca.nic.in/ks_41030.htm.

95. Peerenboom-2003, *supra* note 1, at 94.

96. For an engaging and detailed assessment of China's performance in reaching three goals identified by Premier Wen Jiabao in late 2006 as central to "democracy"—"elections, judicial independence and supervision based on checks and balances"—see generally John Thornton, *Slowly Does It: China's Embrace of Democracy*, Australian Financial Review, Feb. 8, 2008. See also text accompanying notes 84–90, *supra*.

tion I, such a broad-based inquiry seems appropriate given the deep differences between Chinese law and western law, including China's historical peculiarities as outlined above in Chapter Six.

From these deep issues we turn to a survey of certain features of Chinese law "on the surface". Recall that in Chapters Three and Five above, our surveys of the civil law tradition and the common law tradition (respectively) from an operational perspective focused on such topics as the sources of law, the categories of law, the roles of lawyers, and the operation of rules relating to criminal procedure and civil procedure. The same types of topics are addressed in this section and the next section, beginning here with the sources and categories of law and lawyers.[97]

A. Formal and Informal Sources of Law

Broad consensus exists among Chinese legal scholars about the classification of laws and regulations. One of the most famous contemporary Chinese legal scholars, Wenxian Zhang, identifies the formal sources as these:

- the constitution
- laws as enacted by the National People's Congress and its Standing Committee
- administrative regulations and departmental rules
- local laws and local government rules
- military regulations and rules
- regulations relating to the autonomous regions, administrative regions, and special economic zones (that is, both the national-level rules applicable to those sorts of governmental units and their internal rules, such as basic laws, regular laws, and regulations of the autonomous regions)
- international treaties and practice.[98]

Wenxian Zhang goes on to offer these summaries relating to the most important of these various types of laws in the Chinese system:

> *Constitution.* As the fundamental statute of the nation, the constitution is the most important source of contemporary Chinese law. The highest organ of state power—the National People's Congress (NPC)—enjoys the power to enact, adopt and amend the Constitution, which regulates the most fundamental and important issues in contemporary China. The Constitution is the "mother-law" of other laws and regulations, and, on the reverse, other laws and regulations give specific terms expanding on the Constitution.[99]

---

97. The account in the following paragraphs was drafted largely by Ms. Lijuan Xing, my SJD student and research assistant at the University of Kansas. I have made some alterations in style and format, and I have added some material.

98. Wenxian Zhang, JURISPRUDENCE 133 (2007) (as translated by Ms. Lijuan Xing with stylistic editing for cross-language clarity and consistency).

99. For further discussion of the role of the constitution in China, and how it differs from the role played by the constitution in the USA, see *infra* subsection IVB3 of this chapter. See also the details given in Chapter Six (especially in Box #6.10) regarding the contradictory positions taken in 1955 (prohibiting courts from relying on constitutional provisions directly in deciding cases) and 2001 (reversing that position in certain respects). One author makes this observation in that respect:

Laws. Laws, as the second-most important source of the contemporary Chinese legal system, laws are enacted by the NPC and its Standing Committee.[100] According to the Constitution, laws are composed of basic ones and non-basic ones. The NPC enacts and amends basic laws governing the fundamental issues of the nation and its social life, such as criminal offences, civil affairs, procedures, the State organs and other matters; the NPC's Standing Committee enacts and amends the non-basic laws that involve the issues other than the ones that should be enacted by the NPC—for example, the Law of the People's Republic of China on State Compensation, the Law of the People's Republic of China on the Protection of Minors, and the Copyright Law of People's Republic of China.

Moreover, decisions of the NPC and its Standing Committee containing regulatory contents have the same effect of the laws, such as the Decision to Set Up Maritime Courts in Coastal Cities, and the Decision on National Security Organs' Authorization in Investigation, Detention, Preliminary Inquiry and Execution of Arrests Enjoyed by Public Security Organs.

Administrative regulations and departmental rules. The term "administrative regulations" refers to the regulatory documentation made by the highest administrative organ—the State Council—in accordance with the Constitution and the laws. The status and effect of administrative regulations are lower than the Constitution and the laws.

The ministries and commissions of the State Council, the People's Bank of China, the State Audit Administration, and other organs endowed with administrative functions directly under the State Council may—in accordance with the laws as well as the administrative regulations, decisions and orders of the State Council, and within the limits of their power—formulate rules that are referred to as "the rules of the departments," in accordance with the Constitution and the Legislation Law of the PRC.

Military regulations and rules. Although the Constitution of 1982 does not clarify the authorization to develop the military regulations and rules, it stipulates that the Central Military Commission of the People's Republic of China directs the armed forces of the country and that the Chairman of the Central Military Commission is responsible to the National People's Congress and its Standing Committee. Article 93(1) of the Legislation Law provides that "the Central Military Commission shall, in accordance with the Constitution and laws, formulated military regulations." Article 93 (2) regulates that "the General Departments,

---

Due to the Chinese culture and the socialist ideology that would not permit challenges to the constitutionality of the Chinese Communist Party ... as the ruling party and the government, the *Constitution* has been limited to general principles almost all the time, until some recent controversial attempts to make it a law alive in practice by relying on certain provisions of the *Constitution* in court proceedings.

Xianchu Zhang, *Business Law in Mainland China*, appearing as Chapter Three in A GUIDE TO BUSINESS LAW IN ASIA 49, 53 (Pitman B. Potter & Ljiljana Biuković, eds., 2008) (emphasis in original).

100. The method used for enacting laws was regularized by the Legislation Law adopted by the National People's Congress in 2000. That law "intends to improve the legislation process and quality by introducing 'three readings', hearings, public consultations, and publication procedures. [Hence, according to one observer], the entire legal system has made significant progress in democratizing the law-making process, improving transparency and encouraging public participation." Xianchu Zhang, *supra* note 99, at 56.

the various services and arms and the military commands of the Central Military Commission may, in accordance with laws and the military regulations, decisions and orders of the Commission, formulate military rules within the limits of their power." Moreover, "military regulations and military rules shall be implemented within the armed forces." "Measures for formulating, revising and nullifying military regulations and military rules shall be formulated by the Central Military Commission in accordance with the principles laid down in this Law."

Based on the wording of the Constitution, the status and effect of military regulations are inferior to the Constitution and laws, and the status and effect of military rules are lower than the Constitution, laws, administrative regulations and military regulations.

Local laws and local government rules. Among the sources of contemporary Chinese law, local laws constitute the largest amount. According to the Constitution and the Legislation Law, the local laws can be divided into several types.

[First, the] people's congresses or their standing committees of the provinces, autonomous regions and municipalities directly under the Central Government may, in light of the specific conditions and actual needs of their respective administrative areas, formulate local regulations, provided that such regulations do not contradict the Constitution, the laws and the administrative regulations.

[Second, the] people's congresses or their standing committees of the comparatively larger cities may, in light of the specific local conditions and actual needs, formulate local regulations, provided that they do not contradict the Constitution, the laws, the administrative regulations and the local regulations of their respective provinces or autonomous regions, and they shall submit the regulations to the standing committees of the people's congresses of the provinces or autonomous regions for approval before implementation.

Local people's congresses at various levels and their standing committees, within the limits of their authority as prescribed by law, can adopt and issue resolutions and examine and decide on plans for local economic and cultural development and for the development of public services, according to the Constitution and the organic laws. If these decisions are regulatory, they should be regarded as a source of law within their jurisdiction and enjoy the same effect as local laws, even though they are not called "local laws."

In contemporary Chinese law, local government rules are another type of source. As the Constitution and the Legislation Law provide, the people's governments of the provinces, autonomous regions, municipalities directly under the Central Government and the comparatively larger cities may, in accordance with laws and administrative regulations and the local regulations of their respective province, autonomous regions or municipalities, formulate rules that are named as "local government rules." The local government rules are differentiated from the departmental rules in that the effect of local government rules are inferior to the Constitution, laws, administrative regulations and local laws.[101]

---

101. Wenxian Zhang, *supra* note 98, at 133–136.

Wenxian Zhang then discusses the regime of rules that govern certain special types of governmental units within the PRC, such as autonomous regions and special economic zones—they are of little special interest to us in this context—before proceeding to discuss the role of international law as a source of law in contemporary China.

> International treaties refer to bilateral or multilateral treaties and agreements and other instruments of the nature of a treaty or agreement concluded between the People's Republic of China and foreign States. On the one hand, the international treaties are the major source of international law; on the other hand, since they are binding to signatory states, all the international treaties signed by the PRC are another source of contemporary Chinese law.

> According to the Law of the People's Republic of China on the Procedure of the Conclusion of Treaties enacted by the NPC's Standing Committee in 1990, the power to conclude international treaties are separated. The State Council of the People's Republic of China concludes treaties and agreements with foreign States. The NPC's Standing Committee decides on the ratification and abrogation of treaties and important agreements concluded with foreign States. The President of the People's Republic of China, in accordance with decisions of the NPC's Standing Committee, ratifies and abrogates treaties and important agreements concluded with foreign States.

> International customs, despite their limited application, are another source of contemporary Chinese law. In general, the prerequisites to apply international customs are not clarified in Chinese laws or treaties. The General Principles of the Civil Law of the People's Republic of China, however, contains a provision relation to their application. Article 142 provides that "If any international treaty concluded or acceded to by the People's Republic of China contains provisions differing from those in the civil laws of the People's Republic of China, the provisions of the international treaty shall apply, unless the provisions are ones on which the People's Republic of China has announced reservations. International practice may be applied on matters for which neither the law of the People's Republic of China nor any international treaty concluded or acceded to by the People's Republic of China has any provisions." Additionally, Article 150 stipulates that "the application of foreign laws or international practice in accordance with the provisions of this chapter shall not violate the public interest of the People's Republic of China."[102]

Having given our attention earlier to the sources of law in civil law and common law systems, it should be apparent now what items are missing from the list that Wenxian Zhang has offered of the sources of law in contemporary Chinese law. For example, compare that listing with the listing in Box #3.2 in Chapter Three, showing the "modern view" of the sources and authorities of law in the civil law tradition. Box #3.2 showed these six formal or "primary" sources in most civil law systems:

- constitution
- statutes
- regulations
- custom

---

102. *Id.* at 137.

- initiative & referendum
- international law

In addition to those six "primary" sources, Box #3.2 also showed these two "secondary" sources or "informal sources" — or, in the case of the second of the two, we could call them "authorities" or "*formants*":

- caselaw
- legal scholarship

Wenxian Zhang's enumeration of sources of law in the Chinese legal system does not include counterparts to two of the "direct sources" shown in Box #3.2 — namely, custom and initiative & referendum. Moreover, Zhang's enumeration of sources makes no mention of caselaw and legal scholarship.

What role, if any, does each of those four items — custom, initiative & referendum, caselaw, and legal scholarship — play in the contemporary Chinese legal system? One of them — initiative & referendum — is easy to dispose of: given what we have seen of the very large role played by the CPC, and the correspondingly small role played by any form of direct democracy, we can conclude that initiative & referendum are absent from the Chinese legal system.

As for custom, we have seen what a profound influence traditional Confucianist values have played for many centuries in Chinese culture and law. From this we might easily view custom as present in the contemporary Chinese legal system — but "below the line", as a "secondary source" instead of a primary source of law. The other two items — caselaw and legal scholarship — also may be said to exist in today's Chinese legal system, but also "below the line".[103]

The status of one of these — caselaw — warrants further attention. One expert offers this summary:

> China follows a continental legal system model in which court decisions [do] not have binding precedential value as in a common law system such as that of the United States. In many cases, a [Chinese] court will decide a case by issuing an order that is no more than one or two sentences in length with no legal reasoning or analysis. There is no comprehensive national reporting system in China in which all court opinions are officially recorded. Since 1985, the Supreme People's Court has published the *Gazette of the Supreme People's Court of the People's Republic of China* for the purpose of providing instruction and guidance to lower courts and lower level procuratorates. The *Gazette* is published four times each year and contains notable cases decided by the SPC in addition to important national legislation, official documents, and judicial interpretations.... In recent years, some provincial level courts have also compiled collections of cases for the purpose of instructing lower courts.[104]

The picture that emerges from this survey of sources in Chinese law is quite similar, then, to the picture of sources in the civil law tradition, but with certain significant adjustments (regarding custom and initiative & referendum) that reflect key political and

---

103. Some further explanation of this last point appears below in the discussions of the roles of judges and legal scholars in today's China. In particular, see the reference to "judicial explanation" in subsection IIC4.

104. Chow, *supra* note 1, at 214–215.

cultural realities of today's China. The same is true of some other structural aspects of Chinese law, including legal categories, to which we turn now.

B. *Legal Categories*

Our survey of the civil law tradition revealed a crucial distinction between public law and private law; and our survey of the common law tradition revealed a crucial distinction between law and equity. Both of these distinctions have deep historical roots. If we look for a correspondingly crucial distinction in Chinese law, especially one that has deep historical roots, we would surely seize upon the distinction between Confucianism and Legalism, or the closely related distinction between *lǐ* and *fǎ*.

However, that distinction between *lǐ* and *fǎ* is now submerged below the surface; it has become less important or less visible than other methods of categorizing law. This is similar to the fate that has befallen the distinction between law and equity, especially in the USA (more so than in England); and indeed, although the distinction between public law and private law is still of great significance in the civil law world, it has been partially overtaken by other legal developments that have thrown question on its usefulness. Those legal developments have included, as we saw in Chapter Three, the expanding importance of certain other categories of law.

In China, the various categories of law have been organized into what are referred to as seven legal "departments". They are:

- constitutional laws (*i.e.*, the constitution and some related laws)
- civil and commercial laws
- administrative laws
- economic laws
- social laws
- criminal laws
- procedural and nonprocedural laws[105]

This taxonomy of laws has been adopted not only by most Chinese legal scholars but also by the National People's Congress. Wenxian Zhang offers this description of these categories of laws, along with a few illustrations:

> *Constitution and related laws.* These regulate the fundamental issues of the nation, reflect the essence and basic principle of Chinese socialist laws, and establish the basic principles of the laws of various levels. The most fundamental provisions are contained in the Constitution of the People's Republic of China. The Constitution of 1982 and 31 articles of its four amendments of 1988, 1993, 1999 and 2004 constitute this dominant legal department. Its related laws include those on organization and operation of state organs,[106] regional national

---

105. Wenxian Zhang, *supra* note 98, at 154.

106. [*footnote in original*] For example: the Organic Law of the National People's Congress, the Organic Law of the State Council, the Organic Law of the Local People's Congresses and Local People's Governments, the Organic Law of the People's Courts, the Organic Law of the People's Procuratorates, the Rules of Procedure for the National People's Congress, and the Law on Deputies to the National People's Congress and to the Local People's Congresses at Various Levels.

autonomy,[107] basic issues of special administrative regions,[108] protecting and regulating the political rights of citizens,[109] national territory, national sovereignty,
national symbols, and nationality.[110]

Civil and commercial laws. Civil and commercial laws refer to the basic laws regulating civil and commercial social activities. Chinese legal system adopts the
mode of incorporation of civil law and commercial ... No civil code prevails in
China. The General Principles of the Civil Law of the People's Republic of China,
as the essence of the legal framework, together with some separate civil laws such
as the Contract Law, the Guaranty Law, the Auction Law, the Trademark Law,
the Patent Law, the Copyright Law, the Marriage Law, the Law of Succession,
the Adoption Law, the Law on Land Contract in Rural Areas, constitute the civil
legal system. Voluntariness, fairness, making compensation for equal value, honesty and credibility are the fundamental principles bearing on civil and commercial legal relations.

As a special part of civil law, commercial law was developed in order to meet the
requirements of efficiency in modern commercial activities. Commercial law is
the collection of laws regulating commercial relations and activities among persons and legal persons. The subject matters of commercial law and those of civil
law are similar to each other. For example, both commercial law and civil law regulate economic relations among parties with equal status. The difference between commercial law and civil law lies in that the civil law regulates mainly the
civil property and personal relations among parties with equal status while the
commercial law regulates mainly the commercial activities and relations among
parties with equal status. Not until the adoption of market economy within
China was the importance of commercial law recognized and stressed. Currently,
the Companies Law, the Law on Partnership Enterprises, the Law on Securities,
the Law on Negotiable Instruments, the Maritime Law, the Trust Law, the Law
on Individual Proprietorship Enterprises, and the Enterprise Bankruptcy Law
have taken effect as the key constituents of Chinese commercial law.

Administrative law. Administrative law refers to the collection of laws and regulations regulating the administrative management of the nation. It embraces the
laws and regulations on administrative subjects, administrative acts, administrative procedures, administrative supervision, and institution of public servants
of the state.[111] The administrative law covers a wide range of national defense,

---

107. [*footnote in original*] For example: the Law on Regional National Autonomy.

108. [*footnote in original*] For example: the Basic Law of the Hong Kong Special Administrative
Region, and the Basic Law of the Macao Special Administrative Region.

109. [*footnote in original*] For example: the Electoral Law of the National People's Congress and
Local People's Congresses, the Measures for Election of Deputies from the Chinese People's Libera-
tion Army to the National People's Congress and Local People's Congresses at or Above the County
Level, the Measure for Election of Deputies of the Hong Kong Special Administrative Region of the
People's Republic of China to the Eleventh National People's Congress, the Organic Law of the Urban
Residents Committees, and the Organic Law of the Villagers Committees.

110. [*footnote in original*] For example: the Law on the National Flag, the Law on the National
Emblem, the Nationality Law, the Law on Assemblies, Processions and Demonstrations, the Martial
Law, the Law on State Compensation, and the Law on Garrisoning the Macao Special Administrative
Region.

111. [*footnote in original*] On regulating the administrative authorization and strengthening internal supervision: for example, the Law on Administrative Punishments, the Law on Administrative
Supervision, the Law on Administrative Reconsideration, and the Administrative Permission Law.

diplomacy,[112] personnel, civil affairs, public security, national security,[113] nationalities, religions, affairs of overseas Chinese, education, science and technology, cultural, public health, sports,[114] urban construction and environment protection.[115]

Economic law. This refers to the collection of laws and regulations on social economic relations originating from the intervention, management or control of economic activities out of social interests. Two main parts constitute economic law: one aims at creating fair circumstance for competition and maintaining the market order, such as the laws on antitrust, anti-unfair competition, antidumping and countervailing; and the other part focuses on the state macro-control and economic management, including laws on finance, taxation, audit, statistics, price, technology supervision, business management, foreign trade and economic cooperation.[116]

Social law. Social law refers to the collection of laws and regulations on labor relationships, social insurance and social welfare. The main purpose of the social law is to guarantee the legal rights and interests of workers, jobless, persons with limited or no working capability and other persons in need of assistance, from the perspective of social welfare as a whole. Laws and regulations on labor, employment, wages, welfare, vocational safety and health, social insurance, social relief, and special insurance constitute the main content of the social law.[117]

---

112. [*footnote in original*] On national defense and diplomacy: for example, the Military Service Law, the Reserve Officers Law, the Law on the Protection of Military Installations, the Civil Air Defense Law, the Regulations Concerning Diplomatic Privileges and Immunities, the Regulations Concerning Consular Privileges and Immunities, and the Law on the Procedure of the Conclusion of Treaties.

113. [*footnote in original*] On public security and national security: for example, the People's Police Law, the Law on the Control of the Exit and Entry of Citizens, the Law on Control of the Entry and Exit of Aliens, the Regulations on Administrative Penalties for Public Security, the Law on Control of Guns, the Fire Protection Law, the State Security Law, the Law on Guarding State Secrets, and the Law on National Defense Education. On judicial administrative: for example, the Law on Lawyers, and the Prison Law.

114. [*footnote in original*] On education, science and technology, culture, public health, sports: for example, the Education Law, the Compulsory Education Law, the Vocational Education Law, the Higher Education Law, the Teachers Law, the Law on Popularization of Science and Technology, the Law on Progress of Science and Technology, and the Law on the Standard Spoken and Written Chinese Language.

115. [*footnote in original*] On environmental protection: for example, the Environmental Protection Law, the Marine Environment Protection Law, the Law on the Prevention and Control of Atmospheric Pollution, the Law on Prevention and Control of Water Pollution, the Law on Prevention and Control of Environmental Noise Pollution, the Law on Prevention and Control of Desertification, the Law on Promotion of Cleaner Production, the Law on Evaluation of Environmental Effects, and the Law on the Administration of the Use of Sea Areas.

116. [*footnote in original*] On macro-control: for example, the Budget Law, the Audit Law, the Accounting Law, the Law on the People's Bank of China, the Law on the Administration of Tax Collection, the Individual Income Tax Law, and the Securities Law. On market order and rules of competition: for example, the Law Against Unfair Competition, the Law on the Protection of Consumer Rights and Interests, the Law on Product Quality, and the Advertisement Law. On opening-up and foreign trade: for example, the Law on Chinese-Foreign Equity Joint Ventures, the Law on Chinese-Foreign Contractual Joint Ventures, the Law on Foreign-Capital Enterprises, and the Foreign Trade Law. On essential industries: for example, the Agriculture Law, the Seed Law, the Railway Law, the Civil Aviation Law, the Highway Law, the Electric Power Law, and the Law on the Coal Industry. On reservation and utilization of natural resources: for example, the Forestry Law, the Grassland Law, the Water Law, the Mineral Resources Law, and the Land Administration Law.

117. [*footnote in original*] Examples of prevailing social law: the Labor Law, the Law on Safety in Mines, the Law on Work Safety, the Law on the Protection of Disabled Persons, the Law on the Pro-

Criminal law. This refers to the collection of laws and regulations on crimes, criminal responsibilities and penalties. This category of law regulates the social relationships arising from crimes. The Criminal Law amended on March 14, 1997, its four amendments, and the Decision of the Standing Committee of the National People's Congress on Punishing Crimes of Fraudulently Purchasing, Evading, and Illegally Trading in Foreign Exchange represent the laws and regulations of the criminal law.

Procedural and nonprocedural laws. These are the various laws and regulations on social relationships arising from litigation and non-litigation activities, and they include laws and regulations on civil litigation, criminal litigation, administrative litigation, and arbitration. The Criminal Procedure Law, the Civil Procedure Law, the Administrative Procedure Law, the Special Maritime Procedure Law, and the Arbitration Law mainly constitute this legal category.[118]

C. The Roles of Judges and Legal Scholars

Some details regarding the training of practicing lawyers in China have already appeared in Chapter Three (particularly in Appendix 3.1, surveying the training of lawyers in four legal systems) and in Chapter Six (particularly Box #6.10, Box #6.13, and subsection IID3 of that chapter, relating to the expansion of legal training in recent years).[119] Let us concentrate our attention here, therefore, on the two types of legal professionals that have most occupied our interest in exploring differences between the civil law and common law traditions: judges and legal scholars.

Our surveys of the other two great legal traditions offered a contrast that may be summarized, in very simplified form, in this fashion: in the common law world, judges occupy a place of high prestige, reflecting in part the fact that for many centuries during the development of the common law they were the principal authors of the law, by virtue of the fact that caselaw — not legislation — constituted the main source of law; in the civil law world, by contrast, judges occupy a place of relatively low prestige (despite the obviously more specific professional training they receive compared with most common law judges), reflecting in large part the successful efforts at key junctures in European history to keep judges *out* of the business of law-making.

For reasons explored in the following paragraphs, we may conclude that judges in contemporary China occupy a role similar to that of judges in a typical civil law country, with two significant differences: (1) Chinese judges are widely regarded as having a responsibility to reflect in their operations (including their judgments) the policies of the

---

tection of Minors, the Law on Prevention of Juvenile Delinquency, the Law on the Protection of Women's Rights and Interests, and the Trade Union Law.

118. Wenxian Zhang, *supra* note 98, at 154–158.

119. For further information about the role of lawyers in today's China — with particular attention to the Lawyers Law (2007), the training and qualification of lawyers for practice, the regulation of lawyers, and the structure and operation of law firms — see Chow, *supra* note 1, at 228–243. The same source also provides a summary of the role of notaries. See *id.* at 248–250 (explaining that notaries "are state legal workers who provide the service of certifying that certain legal acts and legal documents have been properly executed and that certain facts have occurred" — similar to the description of notaries in typical European civil law systems). For a description of recent reforms in Chinese legal education, see generally *Legal Education Reform in China Through U.S.-Inspired Transplants*, 59 JOURNAL OF LEGAL EDUCATION 60 (2009).

state as designed by the CPC; and (2) until relatively recently, a great many members of the judiciary in China had little or no useful legal training. These and other points are explored below.

1. Judicial Jurisdiction Outside Trials

According to Article 5 of the Judges Law,[120] the role of Chinese judges mainly lies in application of laws to disputes. This is similar, of course, to the principal function of judges under both the civil law tradition and the common law tradition. However, Chinese judges also perform other functions beyond trials. Some of these functions overlap with those of procuratorates or public security organs, such as investigating criminal cases, deciding on the making of arrests, and collecting evidence in such cases. (Further details in this regard appear below in section III regarding Chinese criminal procedure.) The same applies in civil and administrative proceedings. Article 65 of the Civil Procedural Law[121] and Article 34(2) of the Administrative Procedure Law[122] also contain the similar authorization of courts to collect evidence.

With these responsibilities to carry out functions beyond purely judicial functions have come various forms and institutions of supervision—that is, other organs of government imposing external authority on the operations of the judges. These forms of supervision have been blamed for undermining the neutrality of the judges, a subject to which we now turn.

2. Questionable Independence of Judges

The concern over the independence of judges in China originates mainly from their relationship with organs of state power. One authority offers these observations:

> Chinese courts are subject to the leadership and supervision of a number of institutions. Politically, each court is under the leadership of the Chinese Communist Party at the local level. The local CCP committee appoints, reviews, promotes, and removes judges, especially those in management positions. The Party, through its Political and Legal Committee (PLC), determines the priority of judicial work, coordinates the court's relationships with other legal institutions, and even makes decisions in important and contentious cases.
>
> Constitutionally, the courts fall under the supervision of the local People's Congress. Since the late 1990s, in response to increased judicial corruption, some congresses at the provincial level have instituted a mechanism to supervise the courts more directly. The methods they use can place a court's operations under the systematic scrutiny of legislative "deputies."
>
> The process leaves individual judges vulnerable—before, during, and after trials—to demands that they decide a case as a deputy sees fit. In a very real sense, the deputies become judges over the judges.

---

120. Article 5 of the Judge Law states that "[t]he functions and duties of a judge are as follows: (1) to take part in a trial as a member of a collegial panel or to try a case alone according to law; and (2) to perform other functions and duties as provided by law."

121. Article 65 of the Civil Procedure Law states that "[t]he people's court shall have the right to make investigation and collect evidence from the relevant units or individuals; such units or individuals may not refuse to provide information and evidence."

122. Article 34(2) of the Administrative Procedure Law states that "[a] people's court shall have the authority to obtain evidence from the relevant administrative organs, other organizations or citizens."

Judicial work is also under the legal supervision of the Supreme People's Procuracy. The procuracy is defined in the Constitution (1982) as the legal supervisory organ of the state.... Once a procuracy protests a decision, the court is bound to reconsider the case (Fu 2000).

Financially, the courts are dependent on local government. A court's income through the budgetary fund, however, covers only part of its expenditures; it has to rely on an extrabudgetary fund (EBF) to cover the balance. The amount in a court's EBF comes from myriad fees and fines; donations and sponsorships solicited by the court; and loans taken by the court from organizations and individuals, even from judges themselves. In most of the jurisdictions in China, local governments provide about half of what the courts need to operate; the EBF provides the rest.[123]

Having identified various sources of influence to which Chinese courts and judges are exposed, the same observer then offers these details on the *forms* that such influence often take:

Much of the external interference in the courts arrives described as "leadership" or "supervision." There also is institutionalized political intervention: the CCP and the government—at the national or local level—direct the verdicts in cases of national or local importance. Major corruption cases involving senior CCP or government officials, for example, are decided beyond the courts. Political intervention also is common in economic cases where the outcome could affect the social stability of a region—a major labor dispute, for example, or an insolvency case that could lead to large-scale redundancies, any case that could stir the people to take to the streets in protest. In these cases, it is imperative for the courts to report to the local CCP committee and proceed under the committee's coordination. The task of the judiciary here is to comply with the political order and passively implement decisions made outside the court. A trial in these circumstances is a formality: the judges involved are well versed in the politics of compliance and political ceremony.

Although political intervention in the adjudication of a particular case is rare, it is important to note that it is difficult to distinguish that interference from the interference of officials in their personal capacity. The most popular form of interference is a written note to the court, instructing the court to adjudicate a case in a particular way. The notes are kept in an internal case file and are considered seriously by the court in making a decision. When they want their interference off the record, CCP and government leaders use the telephone or an in-person meeting to relay instructions or ask for a progress report on the court's handling of a particular case.

External pressure and interference notwithstanding, the courts still decide most of the criminal, civil, and economic cases on their own. It is in the institutional interest of the courts to assert judicial authority, to carve out their space and to protect it. A judge's job is to judge; and, like other professionals, judges are not willing to cede their authority to others. In most cases, judges are free to decide; only a small number of cases are directed by political forces.

Judges address external intervention in their work in a number of strategic ways. For example, they may delay a trial, effectively compromising the effect of in-

---

123. Hualing Fu, *Putting China's Judiciary into Perspective: Is It Independent, Competent, and Fair?*, appearing in Beyond Common Knowledge: Empirical Approaches to the Rule of Law 193, 203 (Erik G. Jensen & Thomas C. Heller eds., 2003). See also *supra* note 84 and accompanying text.

terference by stalling its implementation. Or, if they know political instructions are likely in a case, they may try the case quickly, rendering a judgment before the instructions arrive. Or judges may simply ignore political instructions.

In general, though, the courts follow instructions from the CCP. As noted earlier, when deciding difficult cases, the courts actually may invite the intervention of the CCP or the local government....[124]

Some of the same points explained above are summed up in this shorter excerpt, focusing on both the political control and the financial influence to which judges are subject:

To a large extent, the historical legal culture [in China] that "there was no formal separation of judicial powers from others and no developed doctrine of judicial independence" has continued in modern times. For example the judiciary in China has been subjected to political control by the CCP through its Political and Legal Affairs Committee ... in personnel affairs and judicial policy, and at the same time, subject to the local government in its financial affairs and budget allocation.[125]

Moreover, as noted above, the undercutting of a judge's independence comes not only from external forces but also from within the court structure in which the judge operates:

[Under the Chinese Constitution,] so-called judicial independence refers to only the independence of the relevant People's Court, not the individual judges. [Hence,] inside the People's Court, a judge may be subordinate to his division head, the president and vice president of the court, and the Trial Supervision Committee as the supervising organ to review all the complicated or high impact cases.... As a result [of these and other factors], the system makes it difficult for the courts and judges to be truly independent from the influence of other organs and individuals.[126]

Perhaps a useful method for understanding the significance of these various methods by which judicial independence is compromised in China is to consider this demand made in the "Charter 08" signed by a large number of prominent Chinese citizens in December 2008:

An Independent Judiciary. The rule of law must be above the interests of any particular political party and judges must be independent. We need to establish a constitutional supreme court and institute procedures for constitutional review. As soon as possible, we should abolish all of the Committees on Political and Legal Affairs that now allow Communist party officials at every level to decide politically sensitive cases in advance and out of court....[127]

3. Lingering Problems with Judicial Incompetence

In addition to being subject to influence of the sorts noted above—influence that would almost surely be regarded as inappropriate interference in the context of civil law

---

124. *Id.* at 206. Fu also notes that "government intervention is limited in ordinary civil and economic cases", since government authorities typically have no interest in divorces or some other such matters. *Id.* at 206. For similar observations about the various forms of influence to which courts and judges are subject, see Castellucci-2007, *supra* note 20, at 51–56. See also Chow, *supra* note 1, at 220–224.

125. Xianchu Zhang, *supra* note 99, at 55 (citing Albert Chen for the quoted passage).

126. *Id.* at 101.

127. *China's Charter 08* (translated by Perry Link), appearing in THE NEW YORK REVIEW OF BOOKS, vol. 56, no. 1, Jan. 15, 2008, available at http://www.nybooks.com/articles/22210?email.

or common law judges—many Chinese judges operate under some other clouds and constraints. These relate to their competence. For reasons founded purely in the historical chaos that China's legal system suffered through in the last ten to fifteen years of Mao's rule (that is, in the 1960s and 1970s), some judges have little legal training. Consider the observations offered by one expert around the year 2000 regarding the backgrounds of Chinese judges:

> Chinese judges come from three distinct backgrounds: government bureaucracies, the military, and the universities and law schools. Each of these groups has experienced different training and holds different ideologies....
>
> The first group of judges comes from government bureaucracies. In the past, whenever there was a shortage of court personnel, the government would transfer "suitable" people from other government departments to the courts. Suitable here generally meant "well connected."... Although those transfers tend to be described in terms of strengthening the judiciary, their effect has been a group of Chinese judges comprised of redundant government officials with no experience or schooling in the law. Most of the people in this group became judges in the 1980s; and their proportion in the judiciary has been dropping largely because of the availability of law school graduates and the increasingly high educational requirements for judges.... Still, local CCP and government officials can always find judicial posts for their relatives and friends.
>
> The second group of Chinese judges is made up of demobilized soldiers. The People's Republic of China has a long tradition of ex-soldiers serving as judges. In the CCP's ideology, both soldiers and judges are broadly defined as "instruments of the state." When they leave the military for the judiciary, demobilized soldiers are simply safeguarding the state in a different way....
>
> ... The judiciary has no choice but to accept demobilized soldiers and to place ex-soldiers of senior rank in senior management positions—notwithstanding their lack of relevant education and training. The government press portrays demobilized soldier-judges favorably, noting that their lack of education is compensated for by their "military characteristics"—discipline, determination, toughness, and a willingness to obey orders....
>
> ... The third group of Chinese judges is made up of graduates in law from universities and colleges. Most are junior judges because they are just out of school or lack experience. It remains the case in the Chinese courts that the most qualified judges—those with legal education—work at a junior level in the courts; those with fewer qualifications occupy more-senior positions; and those with no legal qualifications become court presidents or their deputies.
>
> The official thinking on judges with a law school background is that their knowledge is "theoretical"; they often are criticized for their lack of practical knowledge and experience and their inability to get things done.... There is a sense, too, that their liberal political views and relaxed lifestyle contribute to their failings.... In turn, judges with a law school background are highly critical of and look down on those who are not formally educated in law, especially those from a military background.
>
> Today, educated judges are gaining power in the judiciary: more law school graduates have entered the judiciary since the late 1990s, and they are becoming the largest group of judges in the Chinese courts. Many educated judges have begun to reach middle or high positions in the court system. In addition, they are the

legal experts in the courts; they have the ability to decide cases that raise difficult legal issues. And as the government increases its emphasis on professional-
ism and procedural justice, the judges with formal legal education will find
themselves in an advantageous position.[128]

The observations made above date from about the year 2000. However, similar observations about the continuing problems of incompetence among China's judges have been
made more recently as well. In a book published in 2008, one expert offers this assessment:

> Judicial quality and mishandling of cases have been major concerns for a long time.
> Most judges do not have experience as lawyers and were not subject to the uni-
> form national judicial examination until 2002. As a result, wrongly decided cases
> caused by lack of training, corruption, local protectionism, or political influ-
> ence have made headlines.[129]

As is clear from the account given in section II of Chapter Six, China's legal system —
including its system of legal education — has built up an enormous momentum of reform in the past three decades. Hence every passing year brings the replacement of older
judges with younger judges in China, thereby changing the overall mix of the "three distinct backgrounds of judges" described above.

In short, the lingering problems with judicial competence are probably evaporating —
at least if "competence" is regarded mainly from a technical standpoint. Our studies of
judges in the common law tradition (in Chapters Four and Five, above) would suggest that
there is a great deal more than mere *technical* competence required of a judge. As the most
prominent type of legal professional (the "hero") in the typical common law system, the
judge is also responsible for safeguarding the integrity of the legal system — a responsibility that is discharged in the USA, for example, in part by judicial review of legislative and
administrative action to ensure that such action is consistent with the fundamental rules
of a (binding) constitution. As we shall see later in examining "constitutionalism in China"
(see subsection IVB3, below), Chinese judges are not given a similar responsibility or power.

4. Judicial "Explanation" — Limited Legislative Power?

In one respect, however, a small set of Chinese judges — those on the Supreme People's
Court of the PRC — do have an unusually broad power. This power, which might be regarded
as a limited form of legislative power, comes in the form of the "judicial explanation". The
term "judicial explanation" refers to certain judicial documents issued by the Supreme People's Court for the purpose of clarifying the vagueness of legislative provisions.

Such judicial explanations are different from the "replies" that are also issued by the
Supreme People's Court. The latter ("replies") are made to respond to questions posed by
lower people's courts. These replies are not generally binding in other cases; however,
such replies will occasionally be referred to in cases presenting closely similar situations.

By contrast, the "judicial explanations" issued by the Supreme People's Court are regarded as binding supplements of the promulgated laws, and hence as a source of law in
and of themselves.[130] In this one respect, then, Chinese judges do enjoy limited legislation
power in the Chinese legal system — but *only* those judges on the Supreme People's Court.

---

128. Fu, *supra* note 123, at 206–208. See also *supra* note 84 and accompanying text.
129. Xianchu Zhang, *supra* note 99, at 102.
130. For further details on this process, see Xianchu Zhang, *supra* note 99, at 57:
    In practice, ... the Supreme People's Court has issued a large number of judicial interpre-
    tations and instructions not only on concrete issues arising from trials, but also on how to

5. The Role of Scholars

The role of legal scholars in contemporary Chinese law can usefully be viewed from two perspectives: (i) the general part they play in teaching about the law and in cultivating, developing, and evaluating it; and (ii) the different social functions performed by what one observer has identified as the "three generations" of legal scholars who have been active in the past few decades as China's legal system has undergone such a remarkable transformation.

One observer has offered this description regarding the first of these perspectives on the role of legal scholars:

> Legal scholars refer to those taking part in legal education and research, including mainly the professors, experts, and researchers of law.... Legal scholars are an essential force in state legal construction. The functions of legal scholars, as well as spreading legal knowledge and spirit and cultivating new emerging legal forces, are to carry out research on theories and practices of rule of law in China and to provide the government authorities with inexhaustible impetus. Legal construction in any country could not succeed without inheriting, integrating, and innovating legal thoughts. Legal scholars are an indispensible think tank in the Chinese legal construction and the guards of "rule of law." ... [Hence the] role of legal scholars is of the same importance as judges, prosecutors and lawyers.
>
> Compared to judges, prosecutors and lawyers, [however,] legal scholars make an additional contribution to the "rule of law." In a sense, judges, prosecutors, and lawyers are the "technicians" in the legal field, similar to the "operators" in the factories; while scholars are transmitters of legal knowledge, originators of legal spirits, builders of legal theories, advocates of legal reforms, and suppliers of legal thoughts.[131]

According to that description, legal scholars occupy a place in the Chinese legal system that closely resembles their place in civil law countries. In the metaphor that John Henry Merryman offers, law in the civil law world may be regarded as a machine that is designed by the scholars, built by the legislators, and operated by the judges.

However, there is more to the story. Because of the peculiar ideological and political tumult that China's legal system suffered through under Mao, followed by the headlong rush to reform that has occurred in the past three decades, legal scholars in China may also be viewed from a different perspective. The same observer offers this explanation regarding the functions of legal scholars in helping China navigate this tortuous path:

> Since the reform and opening up, three generations of legal scholars have grown in Chinese society. The first generation, represented by Youyu Zhang, mounted

---

understand and apply laws in general terms even before any trial. Such general interpretations ... may even rewrite the law adopted by the national legislature. In practice, these interpretations have played a very important role to remedy defective or outdated legislation. In recent years, the Supreme People's Court has taken a more proactive approach by exercising its interpreting power to develop new rules to deal with urgent issues newly arising where the formal legislation is not yet available.
See also Castellucci-2007, *supra* note 20, at 51 (noting that because of this function, "the Supreme Court exercises a *de facto* general normative power by means of issuing opinions on general matters of 'interpretation' of given laws").

131. Wenlong Shi, LEGAL ETHICS 149 (2006) (as translated by Ms. Lijuan Xing with stylistic editing for cross-language clarity and consistency).

the legal stage during a period of stagnancy, and these scholars' major achievements were to advocate vigorously the laws and to publicize the "rule of law" [following the virtual eradication of law during the Cultural Revolution]. The second generation, represented by Zongling Shen, was characterized by introducing foreign and international laws into China as well as succeeding to the tasks of the first generation. The third generation emerged by the end of 20th century and still is active. Their tasks are to explore the essence of "rule of law" and the laws with Chinese characteristics.[132]

It is time to take stock. The picture that emerges from all of these structural aspects of contemporary Chinese law—including the sources of law, the categories of law, the role and characteristics of judges, and the functions of legal scholars—seems to feature two main themes. First, contemporary Chinese law reflects the influence of the civil law tradition. Recall these facts: (1) the civil law is much more easily "transplanted" than the common law system (for reasons explored in the discussion of the "migration of the common law" in Chapter Four); (2) consistent with that, much of the legal reform efforts in China in the early 20th century—that is, after the fall of the Qing Dynasty in 1911 and until the creation of a communist state in 1949—drew from European models; and (3) economic and commercial law, which is one of the areas on which the more recent legal reform efforts in China have concentrated, is also largely European in its origin. Given these facts, it should come as no surprise that modern China's legal system reflects civil law influences. This is what we have seen in examining some structural aspects of that legal system—especially the sources of law and the roles of judges and scholars.

Second, contemporary Chinese law also reflects in its structural features a very different influence: the centuries-old traditions and ideologies of dynastic Chinese law. The view of law as an instrument of state power, to be wielded for the purpose of maintaining order, stability, and efficiency—a view that our earlier survey (in Chapter Six) showed to be central to dynastic Chinese law—finds its contemporary manifestation in several aspects of the account given above. These aspects include such things as (i) the absence of initiative and referendum from the list of sources of law, (ii) the overwhelming influence that political authorities exercise over the operations of judges and courts, (iii) the appointment of untrained and incompetent persons as judges, a practice whose effects have only recently dissipated, and (iv) the characterization of legal scholars as being servants of the state ("to provide the government authorities with inexhaustible impetus", as expressed in the observer's account quoted above).

III. Chinese Criminal Procedure[133]

Criminal procedure constituted one of the principal focal points of our earlier examination of the content and operation of both civil law and common law systems. Crimi-

---

132. *Id.* at 150.
133. Most of the content of section III has been drawn from pages 93–106 of a monograph prepared by my SJD student and research assistant at the University of Kansas. See Lijuan Xing, *Introduction of Chinese Criminal Procedure* (unpublished, 2010, on file with author, available on request). I have made only minor editing changes as necessary to conform to the structure of this chapter; in addition, I have made a few additions to her work. Ms. Xing's monograph relies on a combination of English-language and Chinese-language sources. Among the principal such sources are the following (in alphabetical order, with English translations of Chinese-language texts): Ronald C. Brown,

nal procedure will also be our focal point in this survey of contemporary Chinese law.[134] The following account touches on (i) the historical foundations of modern Chinese criminal procedure, (ii) the main features of the content of the 1996 Criminal Procedure Law, as implemented, (iii) the roles and rights of various parties involved in a criminal prosecution, and (iv) a cluster of issues recognized as needing attention regarding the operation of China's criminal justice system.

A. Historical Foundations in Modern China

1. Efforts before 1979

The government of China promulgated no criminal procedure code in the first thirty years following the establishment of the PRC in 1949. As explained above in Chapter Six, many of those years witnessed political and economic chaos, culminating in the devastating Cultural Revolution. "[E]fforts to devise a comprehensive criminal procedure code in China after 1949 were continuously disrupted by political campaigns and upheavals."[135] Despite the lack of a uniform code of criminal procedure, however, some laws and regulations were enacted that provided a foundation for the later emergence of criminal procedure law. These included the *Interim Organic Regulations of People's Courts of the People's Republic of China*, the *Interim Organic Regulations of the Supreme People's Procuratorate of the Central People's Government*, and the *General Organic Rules of People's Procuratorates of All Levels*, promulgated by the Committee of the Central People's Government in 1951. These enactments "laid the legal foundation for establishing uniform judicial authorities and litigation procedures within mainland China."[136]

Furthermore, in 1954, the National People's Congress passed the Organic Law of Courts of the PRC, the Organic Law of Procuratorates of the PRC, as well as the Regulations of the People's Republic of China on Arrest and Detention. These enactments clarified the

---

UNDERSTANDING CHINESE COURTS AND LEGAL PROCESS: LAW WITH CHINESE CHARACTERISTICS (1997); Jianfu Chen, *A Criminal Justice System for A New Millennium?*, in Vermeer & d'Hooghe, *supra* note 1; Mike P. H. Chu, *Criminal Procedure Reform in the People's Republic of China: The Dilemma of Crime Control and Regime Legitimacy*, 18 UCLA PACIFIC BASIN LAW JOURNAL 157 (2001); Jungui Shen, RESEARCH ON IDEOLOGY OF CRIMINAL LITIGATION AND PROCEDURAL IMPROVEMENT (2006); Shijie Song, STUDY ON INSTITUTIONS OF CRIMINAL TRIAL (2005); Li Yao, SCIENCE OF CRIMINAL PROCEDURE LAW (2006).

134. For a summary account of key aspects of *civil* litigation (as distinct from criminal prosecution), see Xianchu Zhang, *supra* note 99, at 100–105, along with pertinent segments of other sources on contemporary Chinese law cited in note 1, *supra*. Xianchu Zhang emphasizes the enormous importance of civil litigation in contemporary China by reporting that "[i]n 2006 the people's court at all levels heard 4.91 million civil cases (including trials of first instance and appellant cases), including 23,314 foreign-related cases." *Id.* at 100. Xianchu points out that one of the trends we saw in some European civil law countries regarding civil litigation has also emerged in China: "A clear direction of civil procedure reform since the 1990s is to 'privatize' civil litigation by discharging the court duties from the old inquisitorial model and assigning more duties and responsibilities to the parties concerned and making the judiciary more neutral.... [In short,] an adversarial system is taking shape in China." *Id.* at 101. For other details on civil procedure, with particular emphasis on various forms of mediation, see Philip C. C. Huang, CHINESE CIVIL JUSTICE, PAST AND PRESENT (2010). For a more practice-oriented summary of civil litigation in China, particularly from a commercial perspective, see Cutshaw et al, *supra* note 1, at 689–699 (providing also a synopsis of changes made by the 2007 amendments to the Civil Procedure Law).

135. Chu, *supra note* 133, at 165–166.

136. Li, *supra note* 133, at 21.

principles of separate functions, coordination, and mutual checking among public security organs, courts, and procuratorates. These 1954 laws also and "established some fundamental rules of trials."[137]

2. The Criminal Procedure Law of 1979

China's Criminal Procedure Law of 1979 (the "1979 CPL") was the first criminal procedure code enacted in China following the PRC's establishment in 1949. The 1979 CPL "was in many ways inspired by earlier drafts prepared during the 1950s and 1963 that had their roots in the civil law inquisitorial system of continental Europe."[138] The highly-charged political and ideological atmosphere of the time was evident in the fact that those earlier drafts had "also incorporated elements of Marxism and Leninism into the text, and the law was seen as a tool of the proletarian dictatorship designed to protect the people from enemies of the Communist Party."[139]

The twofold purpose of the 1979 CPL, according to Jianfu Chen, was "to elaborate the constitutional provisions regarding the division of powers and responsibilities among the people's court, the people's procuratorates and the public security organs, and to provide working procedures for criminal adjudication."[140] The ability of the 1979 CPL to achieve these goals, however, was hampered by certain systemic problems. "Major flaws" of the 1979 CPL included the "deficiencies and ambiguities present under the procedural law, and the lack of qualified legal professionals working within the system to comply with the rules."[141] Moreover, it has been pointed out that the 1979 CPL ignored some important principles of criminal procedure, such as presumption of innocence, due process, and the right to counsel.[142]

Moreover, the implementation of the 1979 CPL raised even more problems and criticism than the provisions themselves did. "The deficient law was made even worse by many decisions of the NPC's Standing Committee, issued during various anti-crime campaigns, and by the inability or unwillingness of the law enforcement organs to act with the law."[143]

---

137. *Id.*

138. Chu, *supra note* 133, at 166.

139. *Id.*

140. Jianfu Chen, *supra note* 133, at 78–79.

141. Chu, *supra note* 133, at 166–7.

142. *Id.* at 167–168. Chu offers this explanation:

> There was no presumption of innocence for the accused; rather the system incorporated the presumption of guilt as the standard for trying cases. Since suspects were objects of punishment, they were not guaranteed many rights, including early access to an attorney. Moreover, verdicts were usually decided before trial, frequently not by the judges who had investigated the cases themselves, making trial procedures a mere act of formality. These conditions led to numerous criticisms concerning the 1979 CPL's failure to adhere to international legal standards of presumption of innocence, due process, and the right to counsel.

Id. For a summary of certain other deficiencies of the 1979 Criminal Procedure Law, see Chow, *supra* note 1, at 267–268 (focusing particularly on "the notorious 'shelter for examination' procedure (*shourong shencha*) widely used by public security organs ... [that] allowed persons to be held in detention where there was concern about a person's identity or where the suspect might be roaming around to commit crimes"—a procedure that was so popular that an estimated "80% of all suspects arrested before the 1996 revision were first detained under this procedure"). For observations about the shortcomings of the 1979 Criminal Procedure Law in combatting "environmental crimes", see generally Yang Chun-xi, John W. Head, and Liu Sheng-rong, *China's Treatment of Crimes Against the Environment: Using Criminal Sanctions to Fight Environmental Degradation in the PRC*, 8 COLUMBIA JOURNAL OF CHINESE LAW 145 (1994).

143. Jianfu Chen, *supra note* 133, at 79.

The harmful roles that judicial authorities played in implementing the 1979 CPL were also criticized in terms of their incompetence:

> During the early stages of the procedural law's implementation, judges, prosecutors and police were unfamiliar with working under formal legal procedures and were thus unable to complete their tasks according to specified time constraints. The NPC Standing Committee, the State Council, the Supreme People's Court, the Supreme People's Procuratorate, and other state bodies subsequently amended several of the 1979 CPL provisions to extend the time frame for conducting investigation, prosecution, trial, and appeal, but those amendments did little to protect the rights of the accused.[144]

3. The Criminal Procedure Law of 1996

These various difficulties and inadequacies of the 1979 CPL prompted efforts at reform. In addition, a "dilemma of legitimacy" may partially account for the decision of the Communist Party of China ("CPC") to revise the 1979 CPL.

> The [CPC] top leadership's perpetual campaigns against crime and corruption have been key strategies employed by the leaders to prevent further erosion of Party legitimacy. Yet the attention focused on catching and penalizing criminals indiscriminately for the purpose of social stability likewise has had a negative impact on the Party's image. In their relentless efforts to combat corruption and crime, Party leaders neglected many of the rights granted to the citizens under the 1982 Constitution.[145]

Legal scholars played an active role in preparing a new criminal procedure code, which ultimately took the form of the 1996 Criminal Procedure Law ("1996 CPL"). As one observer has expressed it, the legal academy's "spirit and the calls for revision were aimed at finding a balance between punishing criminals and protecting individual right through the due process of law."[146]

The 1996 CPL was drafted mainly by legal scholars in criminal procedure. The process to have the draft commented on, modified, and enacted—a process that extended from 1993 through late 1995—was by no means easy and smooth because many governmental organs resisted the new legislation or insisted on certain regulations that they viewed as important for their own benefit. The ultimate enactment of the 1996 CPL in March 1996 (with effectiveness from January 1, 1997)[147] was "mainly a result of major compromises with opposing views and arguments among scholars, officials and different forces in the Chinese legal system."[148] Some observers regard the enactment of the 1996 CPL as "hasty" and flawed in certain respects; one expert, however, has applauded the new rules "in terms of eliminating the presumption of guilt, limiting police and prosecutorial discretion, providing a defendant with greater access to an attorney, and improving the impartiality and independence of the collegiate panel."[149] We shall see how those and other aspects of the 1996 CPL play out in practice.

---

144. Chu, *supra note* 133, at 167.
145. *Id*, at 168–169.
146. *Id*. at 169.
147. The CPL is available online at http://www.cecc.gov/pages/newLaws/criminalProcedureENG.php.
148. Jianfu Chen, *supra note* 133, at 78.
149. Chu, *supra note* 133, at 186.

4. Related Legislation

In addition to the 1996 CPL, certain other laws and regulations are worth mentioning for the contribution they make to the overall structure of Chinese criminal procedure. They include the following:

- The Organic Law of the People's Courts of the PRC (2006)
- The Organic Law of the People's Procuratorates of the PRC (1983)
- The Judges Law of the PRC (2001)
- The Public Procurators Law of the PRC (2001)
- The Law of the PRC on Lawyers (2007)
- The Decision to Improve the System of People's Assessors (2004)

B. General Procedure in Criminal Cases

The general criminal procedure in China contains four main stages: pretrial, first instance, second instance, and execution (*i.e.*, implementation of the judgment). It also includes a special procedure for the review of death sentences. Most of these will be summarized below—in some cases in abbreviated form by the use of bullet points.[150]

1. Pre-Trial Stage

- *Filing a case.* The public security organs or the People's Procuratorates have the right to file cases for investigation within the scope of their jurisdiction. As to a case of private prosecution, the victim has the right to bring a suit directly to a People's Court.
- *Investigation.* The public security organs mainly take the responsibility for investigation. In addition, the procuratorates and courts have the right to investigate certain criminal cases as stipulated by law.
- *Interrogation of the criminal suspect.* Interrogation of a criminal suspect can be conducted by the investigators of a People's Procuratorate, by a public security organ, or by a People's Court. When interrogating a criminal suspect, the investigators shall, according to Article 93 of the 1996 CPL, ask the criminal suspect whether or not he has committed any criminal act, and let him state the circumstances of his guilt or explain his innocence. Then they may ask him questions, which the suspect must answer truthfully; but he has the right to refuse to answer any questions that are irrelevant to the case. After the suspect is interrogated, he may appoint a lawyer to assist him with legal advice and to file any appropriate petitions and complaints. When the lawyer meets with the suspect in custody, the investigating organ may, depending on the seriousness of the charges, send its representative to be present at that meeting.
- *Initiation of a public prosecution.* All cases requiring initiation of a public prosecution shall be examined for decision by the People's Procuratorates. In examining

---

150. Most elements of the description offered here are governed by specific provisions of the 1996 CPL, a few of which are cited in the following paragraphs. For further details on Chinese criminal procedure, see Chow, *supra* note 1, at 263–284.

the case, the People's Procuratorate will (according to Article 137 of the 1996 CPL) ascertain whether the facts and circumstances of the crime are clear, with reliable and sufficient evidence, whether the investigation is being lawfully conducted, whether the case has an incidental civil action, and other aspects of the case.

2. First Instance

- *Jurisdiction.* A criminal case comes under the jurisdiction of the People's Court in the place where the crime was committed. Generally speaking, the Primary People's Courts have jurisdiction as courts of first instance over ordinary criminal cases. However, some first-instance cases may fall into the jurisdiction of people's courts at higher levels.

- *Layout of courtrooms.* The layout of courtrooms for criminal cases was regulated in a document of 1985 issued jointly by the Supreme People's Court and the Supreme People's Procuratorate, and was affirmed in a document of 1993 issued by the Supreme People's Court, the *Notice on Issues of Courtroom Names, Layout of Trial Areas, and Hanging of the National Emblem.* The positions of the judges, public prosecutors, defendants, and others were showed in a figure attached to the 1993 document. See Figure #7.1 for that diagram, and see Box #7.7 for a photograph taken recently in a primary People's Court in China.

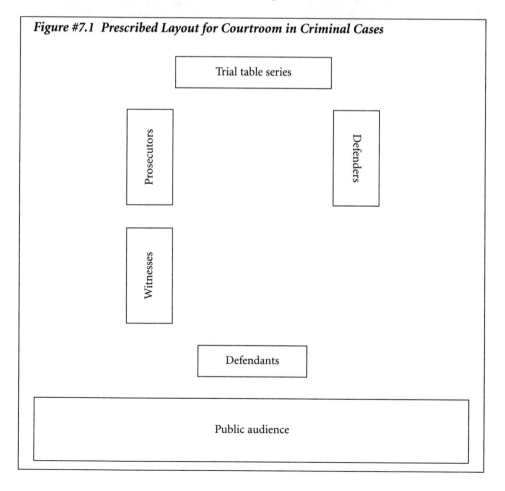

Figure #7.1 Prescribed Layout for Courtroom in Criminal Cases

Trial table series

Prosecutors

Defenders

Witnesses

Defendants

Public audience

Box #7.7 Photograph of Criminal Court in China[151]

- *Implications of this layout of courtrooms.* This layout has some intended implications, including the following: (i) the people's assessors are, by being seated with the professional judges, to be regarded as having equal importance with them; (ii) there is also an equality between prosecutor and defense attorney; and (iii) because the defendant is located separately from the defense attorney, the defendant is seen as *not* having equal status with the prosecutor.

- *Collegial panel.* Trials of cases of first instance in the Primary and Intermediate People's Courts are conducted by a collegial panel composed of three judges or of judges and people's assessors totaling three. However, cases in which summary procedure is applied in the Primary People's Courts may be tried by a single judge alone. Trials of cases of first instance in the Higher People's Courts or the Supreme People's Court are conducted by a collegial panel composed of three to seven judges or of judges and people's assessors totaling three to seven. The members of a collegial panel are odd in number. People's assessors cannot serve as presiding officer of the court. When a case is to be tried by a collegial panel composed of people's assessors and judges, the number of people's assessors in the collegial panel shall be not less than one-third of the total number of the persons in the panel.

- *Public trial or not?* Cases of first instance in a People's Court shall be heard in public. However, cases involving State secrets or private affairs of individuals shall not be heard in public.

- *Court session.* The court session typically involves these steps:

---

151. This photograph appears at http://jyqfy.chinacourt.org/public/detail.php?id=3.

Step 1: Ascertaining by presiding judge[152]

Step 2: Reading out the bill of prosecution by public prosecutor

Step 3: Presenting statements by defendant and victim

Step 4: Interrogating or questioning the defendant

Step 5: Giving testimony by witnesses

Step 6: Questioning of witnesses

Step 7: Showing of evidence by prosecutor and defenders[153]

Step 8: Stating and debating

Step 9: Final statement of defendants

Step 10: Adjournment

Step 11: Signing courtroom record

- *Sentencing.* Generally, a People's Court shall pronounce judgment on a case of public prosecution within one month (or one and a half months at the latest) after accepting the case.

- *Private prosecution; summary proceedings.* Cases of private prosecution and summary procedure are subject to some separate rules and procedures.

3. Second Instance

Upon the completion of a trial at first instance, an appeal and protest would lead to the so-called "second instance" procedure. The defendants' right to appeal is guaranteed by the law. In addition, the procuratorates enjoy the right to protest, and the victims and their legal representatives have the right to request protest from the procuratorates. A "protest" in this context means an assertion that some definite error in a judgment or order of first instance has been made by the court.

Both the facts and the application of law are subject to the review in second instance without limitation of the scope of appeal or protest. A public hearing is not a compulsory requirement, except for cases of protest.

Rejection, revision, and remand are three types of possible judgments of second instance. That is, the People's Court on appeal can issue a rejection of the appeal if it determines that the original judgment was correct; it can issue a revision if the original findings of fact were correct but the application of law (or the prescription of a punishment) were incorrect; and the People's Court on appeal can issue a remand if a new trial is required because of errors made in the ascertainment of facts (or in some other instances) in the original proceedings.

---

152. This involves an ascertainment if all the parties have appeared, an announcement of the case and its subject matter, a naming of the members of the collegial panel, the court clerk, the public prosecutor, the defense attorney, and others, and an informing of the defendant of his right to a defense. 1996 CPL, Art. 154.

153. This involves a presentation by the prosecutor and defense attorney to the court of material evidence for the parties to identify, along with the records of testimony of witnesses who are not present in the courtroom and the conclusions of expert witnesses who are not present in the courtroom. During a court hearing, if the collegial panel has doubts about the evidence, it may announce an adjournment in order to carry out an investigation to verify the evidence. 1996 CPL, Arts. 157, 158.

The People's Court of second instance may not increase the criminal punishment on the defendant if the second instance proceedings result from an appeal filed by the defendant. All judgments and orders of second instance and all judgments and orders of the Supreme People's Court are final.

4. Execution of Judgment

The People's Procuratorates have the right to supervise the carrying out ("execution") of criminal punishments by executing organs to see if the execution conforms to law.

China still officially sanctions the imposition of the death sentence.[154] Any such death sentence emerging from a court judgment is subject to approval by the Supreme People's Court.[155] In a case in which an Intermediate People's Court has imposed a death sentence with a two-year suspension of execution, that sentence shall be subject to approval by a Higher People's Court.

C. Roles and Rights of the Main Parties in Criminal Cases

1. The Criminal Suspect and Defendant

A criminal suspect or defendant enjoys the rights to request withdrawal (that is, the withdrawal from the case of any judicial or investigatory personnel who would have a conflict of interest), to have the advice of legal counsel, to demand cancellation of compulsory measures, to mount a defense, to apply for a guarantor pending trial, to apply supplementary or new expert verification, to make statements in trial, and to question witnesses. In addition, he or she has a right of appeal, a right of petition, and other related rights as stipulated in the CPL. Most of these rights are subject to certain limitations. (See subsection IIID3, below, for a discussion of the limitations on the right to have the advice of counsel.) In Chinese criminal procedure, a criminal suspect has no right to remain silent; and the same seems to apply to the accused person once he becomes a defendant at trial.[156]

---

154. "China remains the world's top executioner—the Dui Hua Foundation, a human rights group, estimates that China carried out 5,000 to 6,000 executions in 2007. The same year, the United States executed 42 people. On a per-capita basis, China is estimated to have carried out 30 times the number of executions the United States did." Maureen Fan and Ariana Eunjung Cha, *China's Capital Cases Still Secret, Arbitrary*, WASHINGTON POST, Dec. 24, 2008, available at http://www.washington-post.com/wp-dyn/content/article/2008/12/23/AR2008122302795.html.

155. "Starting in 2007, China began for the first time in more than two decades to require a final review of every capital case by the Supreme People's Court. The hope was to reduce the number of executions and bring some consistency to a process that had been handled unevenly by lower courts." *Id.*

156. 1996 CPL, Art. 93. This provision requires that the criminal suspect shall answer the investigator's questions truthfully; this implies that the suspect has no right to remain silent. The provision reads as follows in its entirety:

When interrogating a crime suspect, the investigating personnel shall first ask the crime suspect whether or not he has any criminal act, and allow him to state the circumstances of his guilt or give the explanation on his innocence, and then they may ask him questions. The crime suspect shall truthfully answer the questions raised by the investigating personnel. However, he shall have the right to refuse to answer any question irrelevant to the case.

Id., available at http://www.lehmanlaw.com/resource-centre/laws-and-regulations/general/criminal-procedure-law-of-the-peoples-republic-of-china-1996.html. The same absence of a right to remain silent seems to apply in the case of the defendant during trial. The pertinent provision reads as follows:

2. Victims

Victims enjoy the rights to report a crime, to be a party in public prosecution, to consent to being questioned, to bring private prosecution, to request withdrawal, to file an incidental civil action, to entrust agents, to complain about the refusal to file a case, to be informed the decision on whether initiating a prosecution (and to complain about that decision), to request supplementary or new expert verification, to make a statement in trial, to question witnesses in trial, to question a defendant in incidental civil actions, and to request the procuratorate to protest the outcome of a trial. According to the CPL, the victims are obliged to provide evidence and testimony truthfully.

3. Judges

The general functions and duties of judges are (1) to take part in a trial as a member of a collegial panel or to try a case alone according to law and (2) to perform other functions and duties as provided by law. The second of these includes a responsibility to guarantee the defendant's right to a defense, to protect the procedural rights of the parties, to investigate and handle private prosecution cases, to appoint legal aid, to insure the safety of witnesses and their near relatives, to accept reports and complaints, and to insure the safety of reporters, complainants, and informants and their near relatives.

The rights granted to judges by Chinese criminal procedure law mainly are the rights to collect or obtain evidence, to impose coercive measures, to grant a guarantor pending trial or residential surveillance, to make decisions regarding arrests, to interrogate, to cancel or modify coercive measures, and to seal up or freeze the property of a defendant.

4. Public Prosecutors

The major functions and duties of public procurators are: (1) to supervise the enforcement of laws according to law; (2) to mount a public prosecution on behalf of the State; (3) to investigate criminal cases directly accepted by the People's Procuratorates as provided by law; and (4) other functions and duties as provided by law.[157] In exercising the supervision on the enforcement of laws, the procuratorates are given the

---

> After the public prosecutor reads out the bill of prosecution in the court, the defendant and victim may make their respective statements on the crimes charged against in the bill of prosecution, and the public prosecutor may interrogate and question the defendant. The victim, and plaintiff and defender in an incidental civil action, as well as agents ad litem may, with permission of the presiding judge, put questions to the defendant. Judicial personnel also may interrogate and question the defendant.

Id., Art. 155.

157. Beyond the context of criminal law (which is the main focus here), the procuratorates have a wide range of responsibilities. See Castellucci-2007, *supra* note 20, at 52–55. Castellucci explains there the historical evolution of the procuratorate in China, which was built on the model of the Soviet version of the *Prokuraturar*, an institution that itself was created in 1722 in czarist Russia by Peter the Great to serve as "the eyes of the Czar". *Id.* at 53, citing a work by Picardi and Lantieri about civil justice in Russia from Peter the Great to Kruschev. For further information about the procuratorate, see Chow, *supra* note 1, at 218–220. Chow offers this brief explanation:

> While the procuratorate is equivalent in some respects to government organs that prosecute criminal cases in other legal systems, the procuratorate in the PRC is also an organ of legal supervision. Among its responsibilities, the procuratorate is to supervise the work of the courts and the public security organs to ensure that no errors are made in the administration of

right to supervise criminal proceedings, to supervise the investigatory activities of public security organs, to supervise the courts' compliance with litigation procedure, to exercise judicial supervision, and to supervise the execution of criminal punishments.

When performing the function of undertaking a public prosecution, the procuratorates have the authority to decide about arrests, to decide and initiate a public prosecution, and to file incidental civil actions on behalf of the state.

As to the power of investigating criminal cases, the procuratorates can file a case, undertake a direct investigation of certain cases, collect or obtain evidence, participate in a discussion of cases in public security organs, and interrogate criminal suspects. In addition, the procuratorates also bear the responsibilities to safeguard the procedural rights of the involved parties, to grant, cancel or modify compulsory measures, to accept reports, complaints, and information about the proceedings, and to insure the safety of reporters, complainants, informants, witnesses, and their near relatives.

5. People's Assessors

The Decision of the National People's Congress on People's Assessors sets out the qualifications for the people's assessors. They are granted the equal rights with judges as collegial members, except that they cannot serve as presiding officers in trials. They can vote independently, request further discussion of the cases, and participate in first-instance cases.[158]

6. Defense Lawyers

The general functions of lawyers in criminal cases are as follows: (i) to accept authorization by a criminal suspect involved in a criminal case to provide him with legal advice; (ii) to represent him in filing a petition or charge; (iii) to apply for bail for an arrested criminal suspect; and (iv) to accept authorization by a criminal suspect or defendant or appointment by a people's court to act as a defense attorney in trial. For those lawyers involved with the victim's representation, the main function is to act as an advisor and agent *ad litem* and to participate in the criminal proceedings.

If engaged as a defense attorney, a lawyer has the functions of providing legal advice, filing petitions and complaints, and applying to obtain a guarantor pending trial on behalf of arrested suspects. The defense attorney has a right to ascertain the nature of crimes, to meet with criminal suspects, to consult, extract and duplicate the judicial documents, and to collect information or request collection by procuratorates or courts. During trial, the lawyers have the rights to question defendants and witnesses, to show evidence, to request new witnesses or evidence, and to mount a defense on behalf of the defendants. When performing any of these functions, the lawyers are obligated to keep confidential the secrets and to avoid conflicts of interests with clients.

---

justice. This supervisory role over the courts distinguishes the procuratorate from government prosecuting organs in many other legal systems.
Id. at 218–219.

158. As has been pointed out, lay assessors are drawn largely from "those included on lists provided by the Party at the relevant level" of government; and therefore the inclusion of such lay assessors in the system provides an easy conduit for the imposition of CPC policy influence into the operations and judgments of the courts. See Castellucci-2007, *supra* note 20, at 56–57.

7. Public Security Organs

The general functions of public security organs in criminal cases are (1) to prevent, stop, and investigate illegal and criminal activities, and (2) to execute some kinds of criminal punishments.

In the context of criminal investigation, the public security organs have the authority to file cases, to collect evidence, to interrogate criminal suspects, to request for approval of arrests, to execute decision of arrest, to assist public prosecution, and to protest procuratorates' decisions not to arrest or not to prosecute.

The public security organs also perform the duties to execute criminal punishment with respect to criminals sentenced to public surveillance, criminal detention, or deprivation of political rights, as well as with respect to criminals serving sentences outside prison or who are granted parole.

D. Issues Concerning Criminal Justice in China

1. Judicial Independence

Some observations were made above, in subsection IIC2 of this chapter, regarding the independence of judges as a general matter in China. Several of the various factors identified there by which judicial independence is threatened or compromised play especially strong roles in the operations of the criminal justice system. After all, most governments regard law enforcement — maintaining peace and order — as one of their most central functions; and China's traditional political culture certainly reflects that view. Accordingly, judicial independence in the context of criminal procedure would seem especially vulnerable to attack by the government.

According to numerous observers, this is precisely what has happened. One Chinese legal scholar, writing just in the past decade, has asserted that "trial independence has never been realized in practice", since interference with the operations of courts and judges comes from CPC judicial committees, from courts of higher level, and from presidents and chief justices of courts, so that "[a]s a result, collegial panels enjoy only the power to try cases but now the power to make judgments, which seriously hinders the realization of trial independence."[159]

Perhaps this concern over judicial independence in criminal proceedings (or, more precisely, the lack thereof) is inherent to the Chinese system because of persistent uncertainty over what is meant by "independence", and over what is meant by its opposite — "interference". Even though Article 5 of the 1996 CPL states rather unequivocally that "the People's Courts shall exercise judicial power independently in accordance with law, and the People's Procuratorates shall exercise procuratorial power independently in accordance with law, and they shall be free from interference by any administrative organ, public organization or individual" — language that is largely similar to provisions of Article 126 of the Constitution of 1982, Article 4 of the Organic Law of the People's Courts, and Article 9 of the Organic Law of the People's Procuratorates — the fact remains that considerable disagreement remains over the requirement of "independence" and the pro-

---

159. Shen, *supra* note 133, at 76–77.

hibition on "interference". Some Chinese scholars assert that the meaning of judicial independence in the Chinese context is different from its meaning in western countries. Here is what one such scholar has written:

> [T]he term "interference" refers to conduct amounting to illegal interference, such as replacing laws with personal orders, suppressing the authority of laws by personal powers, and demanding the submission of courts or procuratorates to personal orders. [By contrast,] [s]uggestion or guidance within the scope of an official's responsibilities is not referred to as "interference" in this context.... It is worth mentioning here that the principle of "jurisprudence [judicial] independence" in the Chinese legal system is different from what it is in the western countries. "Jurisprudence [judicial] independence" in western countries is an important pillar of Power Separation, and a key element of political organization. In China, however, it is a working rule rather than a political principle. It emphasizes that the performance of the courts and procuratorates be free from illegal interference.[160]

2. Relationship between Courts, Procuratorates, and Public Security Organs

The descriptions offered above of the functions of various entities involved in criminal procedure showed considerable areas of overlap. For example, such overlap — particularly between courts, procuratorates, and the police (public security organs) — occurs in such areas as (i) investigating criminal cases (by all three), (ii) interrogating criminal suspects (by all three), (iii) deciding on arrests (by the courts and the procuratorates), (iv) collecting evidence (by all three), (v) insuring the safety of witnesses (by all three).[161]

Why would there be so many instances of overlapping functions between these different types of organs? Probably because of the heavy emphasis that Chinese criminal procedure law places on fighting crime and maintaining order in the society. It seems likely that some of the overlaps would severely impair the rights of criminal suspects to a fair trial. For example, questions naturally arise over the appropriateness of a judge trying a case for an alleged crime that was in fact investigated by that judge, and for which the evidence was obtained by himself or herself.

Moreover, the overlapping functions can contribute to a situation in which judges see themselves as being in a competitive relationship, or even an inferior position, with respect to the other entities involved in the process (procuratorates and police). For example, some rights of judicial "supervision" granted by the 1996 CPL to the procuratorate leads to an anomalous situation: in the context of the courtroom trial, the procuratorate is subject to the decisions of the judge; and yet after the trial the procuratorate has authority to challenge the court's judgment.

3. The Lawyer's Restricted Role in Defense

Criminal defense is one of the most controversial issues of Chinese criminal procedure. A principal concern in this regard centers on limitations that have been placed on the involvement of lawyers in defending persons accused of criminal activity.

---

160. Li Yao, *supra note* 133, at 42.
161. For further information about the procuratorate, see *supra* note 157 and accompanying text.

The point at which a defense lawyer can be involved in the process has been advanced to an earlier stage of the criminal process. That is, under the 1996 CPL, the defense counsel can be involved at the stage of investigation—as opposed to the earlier system in which a defense lawyer had no role until much later. However, even under the 1996 provisions, involvement by a defense lawyer is permitted only "[a]fter the criminal suspect is interrogated by an investigation organ for the first time or from the day on which compulsory measures are adopted against him."[162] Moreover, during the investigation stage of the procedure, the function of a defense lawyer is fairly narrow—that of an "agent" rather a "defender". As one authority explains, "[d]uring this stage, the lawyers have no right to provide defense for the suspects, [and] no sufficient rights to investigate and present."[163] In addition, the right of defense lawyers to collect or obtain evidence is also greatly limited by the CPL, because they have to get permission from the courts, procuratorates, victims, or witnesses. The lawyers also face difficulties in calling witnesses and cross-examining evidence in trial.

It is worth pointing out that the Law on Lawyers of 2007 aims at strengthening the rights of lawyers, including defense lawyers.[164] Although as a theoretical matter it would seem that the 2007 legislation would prevail over any inconsistent provisions within the 1996 CPL, the new provisions have not so far brought much difference to the actual practice of criminal defense.

Some other recent regulatory enactments also bear on the ability of defense lawyers to carry out their functions. In June, 2010, the Supreme People's Court and several other entities (including the Ministry of Public Security and the Ministry of Justice) jointly issued (i) the Regulation on Certain Issues of Reviewing and Judging Evidence in Dealing with Cases Involving the Death Penalty and (ii) the Regulation on Certain Issues of Excluding Illegal Evidence in Dealing with Criminal Cases. At first glance, these two regulations seem to address the main issues that have invited wide concerns in the criminal evidence system, including legitimacy of collecting procedure, cross-examination on evidence, and presence in court session of witnesses and expert witnesses. However, some observers have expressed concerns that the new regulations still permit the use of evidence that has serious deficiencies and that the new regulations still permit courts to undermine the right to cross-examination.

4. Testimony by the Suspect or Defendant

As noted above at the beginning of subsection IIIC1, under the approach followed in the 1996 CPL, a criminal suspect has no right to remain silent. It is worth examining how this practice—especially when viewed in tandem with the practice of disallowing a suspect the benefit of legal counsel when the suspect is first being interrogated—compares to the approach taken in European civil law countries and in the English and American legal systems. Consider the following general observations regarding the accused as a source of information in the course of criminal proceedings:

> The role of the accused as a source of information in the truthfinding process is an important and thorny topic in any system of criminal procedure. It is also the topic concerning which—upon superficial inspection—the gap between common law and civil law appears most unbridgeable.

---

162. 1996 CPL, Art. 96.

163. Song, *supra note* 133, at 57.

164. See, for example, Articles 33 and 34 of the Law on Lawyers of 2007, granting certain permissions to defense lawyers in respect to consulting with criminal suspects and obtaining from police authorities the evidence against them.

Closer analysis, however, shows that the rock-bottom principle that is the foundation of all specific rules in this area of the law today is shared by virtually all civilized legal systems: no physical compulsion may be used to make the suspect talk.[165] In this sense, almost all civilized legal systems give the suspect, even before he becomes the defendant, the right to remain silent. The more enlightened legal systems, whether of the common-law or the civil-law variety, also are in agreement today on the principle that from the very beginning of the investigation the accused is entitled to the assistance of counsel. It follows that when the suspect, at any stage of the proceedings, is called upon to exercise his all-important option—to talk or not to talk—at least the more enlightened legal systems will make it possible for him to be guided by counsel's advice.[166]

The author goes on to explain that crucial differences show up between legal systems when the next logical question is asked—that is, whether the lawyer advising the accused person will recommend that he talk or not. The author explains as follows: (i) that in the USA, the lawyer will almost always advise the client to make no statement to police under any circumstances, and also to remain silent at his trial because this will insulate him from cross-examination, including any inquiry into the suspect's prior convictions; (ii) that in England, the lawyer is likely to advise her client to speak, at least at the time of his trial, because the defendant's testimony will not, in and of itself, expose him to questions about prior convictions (and adverse inferences can be drawn from his silence); and (iii) in most European countries the defendant would almost always be advised not to remain silent at trial, not only because of the adverse inference that his silence could trigger but also because by his silence he would be squandering the opportunity to make statements that would tend to mitigate the punishment that a court would decide upon in the case of conviction. (It will be recalled from Chapter Three that in European civil law systems, the issues of culpability and sanction are typically considered together, not separately).

It would seem that Chinese criminal procedure does not follow any of those approaches, since it (1) does not afford an accused person the right to advice of counsel at the time of his initial interrogation and (2) does not afford an accused person the right to remain silent, either during that interrogation or at the time of his trial.

5. Other Issues

In addition to those noted above, concerns have been voiced about several other aspects of the criminal procedure rules and practice in China. Such concerns relate to an alleged undercutting of the presumption of innocence,[167] to the alleged abuse of special

---

165. The principle announced in this comment might be contrasted with the principle adopted by some US authorities in recent years regarding the permissibility of using torture (or "enhanced interrogation" techniques) to extract information from persons who are suspected of being involved in terrorist activity.

166. Ugo A. Mattei, Teemu Ruskola, and Antonio Gidi, Schlesinger's Comparative Law: Cases, Text, Materials 841–842 (7th ed. 2009) (quoting from a 1974 work by S. A. Cohn).

167. See, for example, Amanda Whitfort, *The Chinese Criminal Defense System: A Comparative Study of a System in Reform*, 35 Hong Kong Law Journal 695, 712–713 (2005); Robert Bejesky, *Political Pluralism and Its Institutional Impact on Criminal Procedure Protections in China: A Philosophical Evolution from "Li" to "Fa" and from "Collectivism" to "Individualism"*, 25 Loyola of Los Angeles International & Comparative Law Review 1, 24 (2002); Jianfu Chen, *supra* note 133, at 86–89, 94–95.

procedures applicable to cases involving state secrets,[168] and to claims of ineffectiveness of the system of lay assessors as participants in criminal trials.[169]

IV. Modern China's Legal Ethic

A. Preliminary Observations

We have already examined, both in this chapter and in Chapter Six, some issues regarding the "afterglow" of traditional Chinese law in contemporary China, and particularly in the Chinese legal system that has emerged from the "paroxysm" of reform efforts that began about thirty years ago. Thus far I have suggested that that "afterglow" is fairly strong in some respects—for example, in China's consistent rejection and "filtering" of external legal influences.

This is by no means a novel observation. Nearly two decades ago, one expert noted the same sort of "afterglow" in writing of Chinese political developments of the 20th century and how they reflected a long tradition:

> Politics under the rule of the Chinese Communist Party (CCP) cannot be divorced from the Chinese autocratic tradition. This tradition had been formed during more than two thousand years of imperial history and is deeply rooted in Chinese political culture. [For example, despite innovations brought by Communist rule,] one can detect traditional behavioral patterns among the majority of the peasantry, and these patterns are even more pronounced among the political elites. *Mao Zedong*, who is still regarded as a radical revolutionary by most Westerners, *is now perceived by most Chinese as a founding emperor and restorer of the imperial order*.[170]

The last five words in that quoted passage—"restorer of the imperial order"—can serve as a starting point for a discussion of modern China's "legal ethic". To what extent can we appropriately regard Mao Zedong's reassertion of strong centralized control (a centralized control that has been sustained since Mao's death by Deng Xiaoping and a succession of others) as a restoration of "the imperial order"?

Recall that a central feature of the imperial order in dynastic China was Imperial Confucianism. As explained above in Chapter Six, Imperial Confucianism constituted a colorful—one might easily say imaginative or even fanciful—conglomeration of elements drawn from numerology, cosmology, metaphysics, religion,[171] and of course the very se-

---

168. See, e.g., Bejesky, *supra* note 167, at 26.

169. See, e.g., Bin Liang, Changing Chinese Legal System, 1978–present: Centralization of Power and Rationalization of the Legal System 146 (2008). See also *supra* note 158. For more detailed discussion of these and other concerns, see generally Xing, *supra* note 133.

170. Zhengyuan Fu, *Continuities of Chinese Political Tradition*, in Studies in Comparative Communism, vol. XXIV, no. 3, September 1991, 257, at 260–261 (emphasis added). When I asked a graduate law student at Peking University in early 2008 how he views Mao Zedong, he expressed a view similar to that indicated above—that Mao was like the founding emperor of a dynasty, similar to those of numerous earlier dynasties.

171. See the discussion in subsection IB2b of Chapter Six, above, of how Dong Zhongshu accommodated into Confucianist thought the importance of the numbers 2, 3, and 5, yin and yang, the five elements, Daoism, and a miscellany of other influences.

rious and sophisticated teachings of Confucius himself as sustained and manipulated by such men as Mengze and Xunzi.[172] That conglomeration of elements became infused into the legal system beginning in the early Han period and was articulated and strengthened through many centuries of nurturing by a bureaucracy whose ranks were filled with persons well enough versed in Imperial Confucianism to pass the civil service examinations.

Our inquiry now centers on what, if anything, has replaced or succeeded Imperial Confucianism as a central ethic of Chinese law, with "ethic" carrying the same meaning ascribed to it above in Chapter Six.[173] This inquiry involves several questions. For example, what remnants of Imperial Confucianism *itself* can we see in contemporary Chinese law? Are the voices of the Confucianist scholars still echoing today, despite the several efforts that were made during the 20th century—in the May Fourth Movement, for example, and during the Cultural Revolution[174]—to silence them? If so, how do those Confucianist voices bear on the contemporary Chinese legal system? If not, where can we find some *other* key legal ethic underlying that system? Is there one at all?

In order to address these and related questions, let us examine the views of various observers writing from quite varied perspectives[175]—some of the most illuminating of which appear in the works of Chinese law professors associated with prestigious Chinese uni-

---

172. See the discussion in subsection IB1b of Chapter Six, above, of how Mengzi and Xunzi modified Confucius' original teachings in ways that made them more palatable and useful to a strong central government intent on retaining power.

173. As noted there, the essence of a "legal ethic" at issue here is that of "a set of fundamental legal principles or values that give a legal system its unique spirit and character". I have used the more common word "soul" interchangeably with the more precise word "ethic". See text accompany notes 149–151 in Chapter Six.

174. One element of the May Fourth Movement, discussed in section II of Chapter Six above, involved attempts "to abolish the out-of-date evils of the old China and establish new values for a new China", and this included a denunciation of Confucianism. John King Fairbank, CHINA—A NEW HISTORY 268 (1992). Similar attitudes prevailed in the Cultural Revolution, when the Red Guards energized by Mao Zedong attacked the "four olds"—old ideas, old culture, old customs, and old habits. *id*. at 393. Mao himself has been described as "a rebel against the Confucianism denounced in the May Fourth Movement." *Id*. at 374.

175. See the Selected Bibliography at the end of this book for citations to some of the works I have relied on in this chapter. Among the most important of those works that were originally written in English—several of which are cited below in footnotes—are the following (listed alphabetically by author or editor, beginning with books), some of which have also been cited *supra* note 1 but are cited again here for convenient reference: Daniel C.K. Chow, THE LEGAL SYSTEM OF THE PEOPLE'S REPUBLIC OF CHINA (2003); Kenneth A. Cutshaw et al, CORPORATE COUNSEL'S GUIDE TO DOING BUSINESS IN CHINA (2d ed., looseleaf); ENGAGING THE LAW IN CHINA (Neil J. Diamant, Stanley B. Lubman, and Kevin J. O'Brien eds, 2005); Kenneth Lieberthal, GOVERNING CHINA: FROM REVOLUTION THROUGH REFORM (1995); Stanley B. Lubman, BIRD IN A CAGE: LEGAL REFORM IN CHINA AFTER MAO (1999); Pitman B. Potter, THE CHINESE LEGAL SYSTEM: GLOBALIZATION AND LOCAL LEGAL CULTURE (2001); THE LIMITS OF THE RULE OF LAW IN CHINA (Karen G. Turner, James V. Feinerman, and R. Kent Guy, eds., 2000); CHINA'S LEGAL REFORMS AND THEIR PRACTICAL LIMITS (Eduard B. Vermeer and Ingrid d'Hooghe, eds., 2002); INTRODUCTION TO CHINESE LAW (Wang Chenguang and Zhang Xianchu, eds., 1997); Xin Ren, TRADITION OF THE LAW AND LAW OF THE TRADITION: LAW, STATE, AND SOCIAL CONTROL IN CHINA (1997); James M. Zimmerman, CHINA LAW DESKBOOK: A LEGAL GUIDE FOR FOREIGN-INVESTED ENTERPRISES (2d ed. 2004); Zou Keyuan, CHINA'S LEGAL REFORM: TOWARDS THE RULE OF LAW (2006); Volker Behr, *Development of a New Legal System in the People's Republic of China*, 67 LOUISIANA LAW REVIEW 1161 (2007); Albert H.Y. Chen, *Confucian Legal Culture and Its Modern Fate*, appearing as Chapter 16 in THE NEW LEGAL ORDER IN HONG KONG (Raymond Wacks, ed, 1999), online digital edition available at http://library.hku.hk/record=3136080 [hereinafter Chen-1999]; Albert H.Y. Chen, *Is Confucianism Compatible with Liberal Constitutional Democracy?*, 34 JOURNAL OF CHINESE PHILOSOPHY 195 (2007) [hereinafter Chen-2007]; Jianfu Chen, *The Transformation of Chinese Law—From Formal to Substantial*, 37 HONG KONG LAW JOURNAL 689

versities.[176] I have structured the discussion of their views by posing various possibilities or "candidates" for serving in the role of the central "ethic" lying at the heart of contemporary Chinese law and bringing moral legitimacy to government in China. I begin with the possibility of a new form of Confucianism itself, and then I consider, in turn, these other possibilities:

- Marxist-Leninist-Maoist-Dengist thought
- the rule of law
- constitutionalism
- religion
- nothing

In examining these possible "candidates" for the central legal ethic at work in contemporary Chinese law, let us keep in mind the fact that in today's China, as Randall Peerenboom has expressed it, "one of the government's most pressing problems is the unavailability of traditional bases of legitimacy and a moral vacuum resulting from the demise of traditional ethical systems."[177]

B. Where To Find the Central Legal Ethic — A Survey of Possibilities

1. A New Confucianism?

If there is any form of Confucianism at work in today's China, surely it must be a modern version of Confucianism rather than the old Imperial Confucianism described in Chapter Six. That is, it seems obvious and beyond any dispute that the conglomeration of numerology, cosmology, metaphysics, and so forth is so non-scientific and supernatural that no modern society would embrace it as a key ethic to its legal system. Besides, the institutional structure on which Imperial Confucianism rested — the examination system, the bureaucracy of Confucianist scholars, etc. — was dismantled long ago.

Hence the only form of Confucianism even eligible to serve as a key legal ethic in today's China must be a "New Confucianism" or a "Neo-Confucianism" that draws some elements from the old Imperial Confucianism and makes them workable in a contemporary setting. In order to examine this possibility, we first need to distinguish between two schools of thought referred to generally as "Neo-Confucianist" and "New Confucianist". The first of these actually dates back many centuries and reflects the perceived need to modify earlier versions of Confucianism in order to reflect the growing influence of Buddhist and Daoist thought in China. The second — "New Confucianism" — dates from the 20th century.

a. Neo-Confucianism

For our purposes, the following explanation will suffice to provide an overview of what key elements "Neo-Confucianism" encompasses:

(2007); Randall Peerenboom, *The X-Files: Past and Present Portrayals of China's Alien "Legal System"*, 2 Washington University Global Studies Law Review 37 (2003).

176. For those views, I have drawn from articles in the very valuable journal titled Frontiers of Law in China ("FLC"), referred to in footnote 2, *supra*. Of particular importance are the articles cited there by He Jiahong, Ma Xiaohong, Wang Zhoujun, and Zhang Wenxian.

177. Peerenboom-2003, *supra* note 1, at 53.

[*In general*] Neo-Confucianism is a form of Confucianism that was primarily developed during the Song Dynasty, but which can be traced back to [earlier scholars] in the Tang Dynasty. It formed the basis of Confucian orthodoxy in the Qing Dynasty of China. The term should not be mistaken for New Confucianism which is an effort to apply Confucianism to the modern times of China. It was a philosophy that attempted to merge certain basic elements of Confucian, Daoist, and Buddhist thought. Most important of the early Neo-Confucianists was the Chinese thinker Zhu Xi (1130–1200 [CE]).

[*Origins*] Confucians of the Song Dynasty (960–1279) studied the classical works of their faith, but were also familiar with Buddhist and Daoist teachings. Buddhist thought offered to them many things that they considered worthy of admiration, including ideas such as the nature of the soul and the relation of the individual to the cosmos, ideas not yet fully explored by Confucianism. Song Confucians drew greatly from Buddhist thought as well as their own traditions, thus giving rise to the English-language name of "Neo-Confucianism".

There were many competing views within the Neo-Confucian community, but overall, a system emerged that resembled both Buddhist and Taoist (Daoist) thought of the time and some of the ideas expressed in the Book of Changes (I Ching) as well as other yin [and] yang theories.... A well known Neo-Confucian motif is paintings of Confucius, Buddha, and Lao Tzu all drinking out of the same vinegar jar, paintings associated with the slogan "The three teachings are one!"

One of the most important exponents of Neo-Confucianism was Zhu Xi (1130–1200). He was a rather prolific writer, maintaining and defending his Confucian beliefs of social harmony and proper personal conduct. One of his most remembered was the book *Family Rituals*, where he provided detailed advice on how to conduct weddings, funerals, family ceremonies, and the veneration of ancestors. Buddhist thought soon attracted him, and he began to argue in Confucian style for the Buddhist observance of high moral standards. He also believed that it was important to practical affairs that one should engage in both academic and philosophical pursuits, although his writings are concentrated more on issues of theoretical (as opposed to practical) significance. It is reputed that he wrote many essays attempting to explain how his ideas were not Buddhist or Taoist, and included some heated denunciations of Buddhism and Taoism.

While Neo-Confucianism incorporated Buddhist and Taoist ideas, many Neo-Confucianists claimed to strongly oppose Buddhism and Taoism. Indeed, they rejected Buddhism as a faith.... Nonetheless, Neo-Confucian writings adapted Buddhist thoughts and beliefs to the Confucian interest. In China Neo-Confucianism was an officially-recognized creed from its development during the Song dynasty until the early twentieth century, and lands within the scope of Song China (Korea, Vietnam, and Japan) were all deeply influenced by Neo-Confucianism for more than half a millennium.

[*World View*] Zhu Xi's formulation of the Neo-Confucian world view is as follows. He believed that the Tao 道 (dào; literally "way") of Tian 天 (tiān; literally "heaven") is expressed in principle or *li* 理 (lǐ)[178], but that it is sheathed in

---

178. Note that this is a different form of *li* than the *li* that carries the meaning of "rules of proper behavior" (as described more fully in Box #6.4 in Chapter Six, above). The *pinyin* rendition, including the tonal marking, is the same for both words, but the Chinese characters are different. The Chi-

matter or *qi* 氣 (qì). In this, his system is based on Buddhist systems of the time that divided things into principle (again, li), and *shi* 事 (shì). In the Neo-Confucian formulation, *li* in itself is pure and perfect, but with the addition of *qi*, base emotions and conflicts arise. Human nature is originally good, the Neo-Confucians argued (following Mencius), but not pure unless action is taken to purify it. The imperative is then to purify one's *li*. However, in contrast to Buddhists and Taoists, neo-Confucians did not believe in an external world unconnected with the world of matter. In addition, Neo-Confucians in general rejected the idea of reincarnation and the associated idea of karma.

Different Neo-Confucians had differing ideas for how to do so. Zhu Xi believed in *gewu* 格物 (géwù), the Investigation of Things, essentially an academic form of observational science, based on the idea that *li* lies within the world. [On the other hand,] Wang Yangming (Wang Shouren), probably the second most influential Neo-Confucian, came to another conclusion: namely, that if *li* is in all things, and *li* is in one's heart, there is no better place to seek than within oneself.... Wang Yangming developed the idea of *innate knowing*, arguing that every person knows from birth the difference between good and evil. Such knowledge is intuitive and not rational. These revolutionizing ideas of Wang Yangming would later inspire prominent Japanese thinkers like Motoori Norinaga, who argued that because of the Shinto deities, Japanese people alone had the intuitive ability to distinguish good and evil without complex rationalization.... The importance of *lǐ* in Neo-Confucianism gave the movement its Chinese name.... [That name— *Lǐxué* 理學—could perhaps best be translated as] "The study of Li."

... [*Bureaucratic examinations* According to some sources,] Neo-Confucianism became the interpretation of Confucianism whose mastery was necessary to pass the bureaucratic examinations by the Ming, and continued in this way through the Qing dynasty until the end of the Imperial examination system in 1905. However, many scholars such as Benjamin Elman have questioned the degree to which their role as the orthodox interpretation in state examinations reflects the degree to which both the bureaucrats and Chinese gentry actually believed those interpretations, and point out that there were very active schools ... [of] learning which offered competing interpretations of Confucianism.... [One such] competing school of Confucianism was called the Evidential School or Han Learning ... [which] argued that Neo-Confucianism had caused the teachings of Confucianism to be hopelessly contaminated with Buddhist thinking. This school also criticized Neo-Confucianism for being overly concerned with empty philosophical speculation that was unconnected with reality.[179]

---

nese character for the former (rules of proper behavior) is 礼; the Chinese character for the latter (principle, or rationale) is 理.

179. This explanation is drawn from Wikipedia, probably an adequate source for a general description of this sort. See http://en.wikipedia.org/wiki/Neo-Confucianism (some parenthetical explanations of hyperlinked topics omitted). For another synopsis of Neo-Confucianism and its founding thinkers (especially Zhu Xi), see Fairbank, *supra* note 174, at 97–98. Fairbank notes that "Neo-Confucianism, as the Jesuits later named it, took shape in the Southern Song" with these key ideas (i) only through disciplined self-cultivation could a person get some understanding of the Dao, or Way, that "vast energizing force that pervades the universe and all things in it"; (ii) "the true Way for the moral improvement of the individual and the world had been set forth by Confucius and Mencius but had not been transmitted thereafter"; and therefore (iii) great emphasis should be placed, particularly by society's leaders, on "repossessing the Way" by studying certain classics from pre-Tang times. Due to the influence of Buddhism on Daoism, and vice versa, Fairbank observes that ""[i]n effect Zhu Xi

b. New Confucianism

Distinct from "Neo-Confucianism" is "New Confucianism", which is much more recent in origin. Even more than Neo-Confucianism, New Confucianism is subject to uncertainty as to content and application. A sense of that uncertainty emerges from this description:

> New Confucianism ... is a new movement of Confucianism that began in the twentieth century. It is deeply influenced by, but not identical with[,] the Neo-Confucianism of the Song and Ming dynasties.
>
> The term itself was first used as early as 1963 (in two articles in the Hong Kong journal *Rensheng*). However, it did not come into common use until the late 1970s. New Confucianism is often associated with the essay, "A Manifesto on Chinese Culture to the World," which was published in 1958.... This work is often referred to as the "New Confucian Manifesto," although that phrase never occurs in it. The Manifesto presents a vision of Chinese culture as having a fundamental unity throughout history, of which Confucianism is the highest expression. The particular interpretation of Confucianism given by the Manifesto is deeply influenced by Neo-Confucianism, and in particular the version of Neo-Confucianism most associated with Lu Xiangshan and Wang Yangming [who believed that if *lǐ* is in all things, including one's heart, then there is no better placed to seek the perfection of *lǐ* than within oneself, preferably through *jingquo*, a practice that strongly resembles Zen meditation] (as opposed to that [form of Neo-Confucianism that is] associated with Zhu Xi [who believed in *gewu*, the "investigation of things", essentially an academic form of observational science]). In addition, the Manifesto argues that while China must learn from the West [in terms of] modern science and democracy, the West must learn from China (and the Confucian tradition in particular) "a more all-encompassing wisdom."[180]

One form of New Confucianism calls especially for a return to old Chinese values, claiming that the alternative is continued social and spiritual degradation. Geor Hintzen explains these views:

> From the late [nineteen-]eighties onwards, there was a noticeable revival of Confucian 'culturalism'. Supported by some mainstream and conservative Marxist views of the 1980s, which claimed that China was following its own unique path to modernization through socialism with Chinese characteristics, re-born Confucianists started to point to the traditional basis of social relations which underlie Chinese culture.... For example, Li Zhengang proposed a traditional answer to a long list of problems of China's perceived 'spiritual disorientation' (*jingshen mishi*). There was a loss of reference for moral appraisal, value trends were confused, all kinds of immoral practices proliferated, the control mechanisms of social morality were weakened, and moral education had turned out all wrong and become deformed.... These problems, he believed, 'were seriously obstructing the development of the material and spiritual civilizations of so-

---

found a means of smuggling a needed element of Buddhist transcendentalism into Confucianism." *Id.* at 98.

180. See http://en.wikipedia.org/wiki/New_Confucianism.

cialism'. Pluralism was leading people to self-contradictory beliefs so that they 'no longer knew what constituted an ideal person'.... Quoting an array of Confucian maxims, Li proposed to 'use old morals in service of modern life'... and, amongst other things, to rectify ... the cultural market. This new-found morality, moreover, would not have to limit itself to the outward relations and ideals, but would try to reach people's innermost psychological make-up.[181]

Let me offer a summary of the picture that emerges from these descriptions of Neo-Confucianism and New Confucianism. It is a picture of both unity and diversity. That is, there is unity, or at least consensus, as to the central tenets of Confucianism. Focusing on lǐ 礼[182] which was developed early on through the efforts of the Duke of Zhou and Confucius,[183] Confucianism gradually expanded to encompass numerous related and rival philosophies—especially through the efforts of Dong Zhongshu in early Han times—to create Imperial Confucianism; and it was at that point that the *legal* character of Confucianism was further strengthened because of its involvement in law and governance.[184] In the centuries from the Han to the Qing dynasties, that Imperial Confucianism—based on the classic works that scholars had to master in order to pass the civil service examinations and thereby to gain positions in the imperial bureaucracy—gradually evolved and diversified as the influences of various persons and philosophies came to be felt. Among the more important of those influences, especially in the later dynasties (Ming and Qing), was *Lǐxué* 理學[185]—an assortment of varying theories[186] that western observers have generally labeled "Neo-Confucianism". In yet more recent times (after the demise of dynastic China), efforts to resuscitate Imperial Confucianism have taken the form of a "New Confucianism" that draws on (i) the central core ideas that course their way throughout the evolution of Confucianism, as well as (ii) the ideas of certain adherents of *Lǐxué* (Neo-Confucianism), and (iii) certain modern influences and realities. That "New Confucianism", however, lacks the degree of *legal* character that (as noted above) distinguished Imperial Confucianism and gave it its central place in law and governance in dynastic China.

---

181. Geor Hintzen, *To Have One's Cake and Eat It? Human Rights in Chinese Culture*, appearing as chapter 3 in Vermeer and d'Hooghe, *supra* note 1, at 59–60.

182. As indicated in note 178, *supra*, the word (and concept) lǐ 礼 (rules of proper behavior) that lies at the bottom of the *Zhou Li* is different from the word (and concept) lǐ that lies at the bottom of *Lǐxué* 理學 (Neo-Confucianism)—despite the otherwise close connection between Confucianism and Neo-Confucianism.

183. See the descriptions in Chapter Six, above, of the contributions each of these men made to defining and applying lǐ.

184. As noted earlier, the Confucianist scholars "claimed to be, and became, indispensable advisers to the emperor [based on their command of the classic writings. It could be said that] ... the literate elite ... had entered into an alliance with monarchy. The monarch provided the symbols and the sinews of power.... The literati provided the knowledge of precedent and statecraft that could legitimize power and make the state work." See note 57 in Chapter Six, above.

185. As noted above, the first character 理 (lǐ) in this context means "principle"; the second character 學 (xué) in this context means school or learning or knowledge.

186. As noted above, substantial divergence appears in competing versions of *Lǐxué*—particularly those of Zhu Xi versus those of Wang Yangming. See text accompanying note 179, *supra*. Moreover, Neo-Confucianism was derided by some other scholars as constituting merely "empty philosophical speculation that was unconnected with reality". See *id.* Indeed, some historians have speculated that the introspective philosophical tendencies of Neo-Confucianism in Song and Ming times might have helped generate the neglect on science and technological advancement that Derk Bodde calls one of "the major unanswerables in Chinese history". See text accompanying note 5 in Chapter Six, above. I am indebted to Professor Mary Wang for drawing my attention to this point.

c. Confucianist influence in today's China

Reflecting the emergence of interest in New Confucianism, Peerenboom points to the efforts by the Communist Party of China to weave such concepts into China's legal and political system:

> The Chinese Communist Party (CCP) has been searching rather desperately for some way to revamp its ideological basis by latching on to [several] ... vague and uninspiring ideas.... [In this effort, the] ruling regime has ... tried to revive Confucianism. However, after years of attack, the level of support for Confucianism is weak and its relevance debatable. At any rate, the Party's appeal to Confucianism is not based on some supernatural connection to *tian* [heaven] but rather on much more mundane pragmatic considerations. Confucian values—the importance of family, an emphasis on education and hard work, meritocratic advancement, a commitment to public service—are seen as conducive to economic growth and stability. From the Party's perspective, the politically conservative aspects of Confucianism—deference to authority, the lack of democracy, and the importance attached to order and political stability—are also attractive. From the perspective of reform-minded intellectuals, on the other hand, "New Confucianism" offers the possibility of a credible, alternative social-political philosophy to Western liberalism, one that is compatible with the main hallmarks of modernity—capitalism, democracy, rule of law, and human rights—but at the same time more faithful to China's indigenous traditions and current contingent circumstances (*guoqing*).[187]

One point Peerenboom makes warrants special emphasis: whatever promise some form of New Confucianism might hold for the *future* as an organizing and energizing force in China's legal and political system, New Confucianism *at present* fails to deliver much. Peerenboom's views on this point are woven together with his views on the rule of law in contemporary China. We explored this matter above in section I of this chapter, where we saw Peerenboom asserting that (i) whereas China seems well on its way to achieving a "thin" rule of law, it has not embraced (and likely will not embrace in the foreseeable future) the same sort of "thick" rule of law as Western critics urge on it—that is, a liberal democratic "thick" rule of law—and moreover (ii) that no alternative versions of a "thick" rule of law have yet been adequately developed.

Peerenboom expands on these thoughts, with particular attention to New Confucianism, as follows:

> [There has not yet] been enough work done on developing in a systematic way a comprehensive alternative political philosophy to liberal democracy to serve as the foundation for alternative thick conceptions of rule of law.... Whether [such alternative philosophies as] communitarianism, New Confucianism, or Neo-authoritarianism will be able to provide the basis for a normatively attractive alternative political philosophy to liberalism remains to be seen....

---

187. Peerenboom-2003, *supra* note 1, at 54. For other views on how "Confucianism ... is being re-discovered by Chinese political leaders, and is now being disseminated in the population ... as a valuable part of the Chinese heritage and maybe as a source of inspiration in order to solve some of the problems brought about by rampant capitalism and by the new China materialist society", see Castellucci-2007, *supra* note 20, at 48–49. Castellucci also explains a flirtation by the CPC with a related notion, that of "virtue"—and in fact a purported "rule of virtue" (*de zhi*), as mentioned in the recently-amended constitution of the CPC. See *id.* at 47–50.

To date, New Confucianism has attracted the most attention from scholars, not only in China but in other Asian countries and even in the West. New Confucians suggest that Confucianism can be adapted to modern times and that to claim otherwise is to essentialize Confucianism in an inappropriate way. This project seems worth pursuing, though there are a number of serious questions to be answered and obstacles to overcome.

First, there is no accepted definition of Confucianism.... Thus, identifying the key or core values or elements of Confucianism is problematic to say the least. Yet, in the absence of any attempt to state the key elements or parameters of Confucianism, advocates of New Confucianism are left to their own devices. One typical approach is to scan the tradition for values or practices that seem at least on their surface similar to values and practices associated with modernity, while ignoring the context in which these ideas were embedded and all of the related values and practices that are inimical to modernity. When undesirable features are noted, they are quickly dismissed. Confucianism is a living tradition, and traditions change. But that does not mean that one is free to attribute anything one wants to Confucianism. It may be possible to simply reject some ideas—such as the subjugation of women—in favor of other ideas. But can one reject the notion of a paternalistic government or the inegalitarianism inherent in the *li*/rites (assuming one would want to)? And can one simply substitute democracy and elections as the basis for legitimacy rather than the traditional moral cultivation of the leaders and the mandate of heaven? Advocates must address these thorny methodological issues that arise in rending Confucianism compatible with modernity.

[Moreover, the] empirical basis for the claim that Confucianism is still important in contemporary societies also seems rather weak. One might point to countries such as South Korea, Taiwan, and even Singapore as examples of modern states influenced by Confucianism Yet are these countries really Confucian in any meaningful sense? It is often difficult to empirically verify the link between Confucianism and contemporary institutions or practices. Frequently, Confucianism is simply assumed to be what is doing the explanatory work, when other alternatives seem just as likely. What remains of Confucianism seems less like a coherent system and more like isolated values, often hardly unique to Confucianism, that serve as a communitarian corrective on liberal extremism.[188]

I find Peerenboom's analysis persuasive. In this respect, perhaps my perspective is somewhat different from that of my friend Albert Chen at the University of Hong Kong. In two characteristically strong and elegantly-written pieces—one from 1999[189] and the other from 2007[190]—Professor Chen has explored the issue of what role, if any, China's Confucianist legal heritage plays in contemporary China and will (or can) play there in the future.[191] By my reading, Chen finds considerably more evidence than Peerenboom does of the continuing identity, relevance, and acceptance of Confucianist tradition in

---

188. Peerenboom-2003, *supra* note 1. at 90–92.
189. See generally Chen-1999, *supra* note 175.
190. See generally Chen-2007, *supra* note 175.
191. In addition to these works, Professor Chen has also written about modern relevance of Confucianist thought in another context. Albert H.Y. Chen, *Mediation, Litigation, and Justice: Confucian Reflections in a Modern Liberal Society,* appearing as chapter 11 in CONFUCIANISM FOR THE MODERN WORLD (Daniel A. Bell and Hahm Chaibong eds., 2003). This is but one of many books regarding modern iterations and applications of Confucianism.

today's China. For example, Chen draws attention to the numerous scholarly writers who
see that tradition as alive and well:

> [M]any writers point out that although the basic doctrines, modes of law-mak-
> ing, legal institutions, and procedures of traditional Chinese law have been dis-
> carded in the course of China's revolutionary transformations in the twentieth
> century, many of the traditional attitudes, perceptions, ideas, and values, and
> much of the traditional mentality, psychology, and behaviour relating to law still
> survive even today, and they constitute part of the 'deep structure' of the con-
> sciousness, psychology, and character of the Chinese people. Some scholars ex-
> press this point in the language of historical materialism, stating that unlike the
> west which underwent centuries of capitalist development after the decline of
> feudalism, China's present socialist society ... still exhibits features of the culture
> 'feudalism'... which only ended relatively recently.[192]

According to Albert Chen, some scholars writing about China's legal heritage — especially those scholars criticizing that heritage because of its incompatibility with "the Enlightenment values of liberty, equality, the rights of individuals and citizens, the rule of
law, and the sovereignty of the people" — have underestimated how strong a grip Confucianist legal tradition still has on present-day China and Chinese attitudes:

> I think these scholars have not gone far enough in exposing the fact that in
> some [fundamental] ways..., contemporary China has not yet grown out of
> its past. For instance, the one-party rule by one single ideology, with no tol-
> eration of pluralism in political and social thought, is still a reproduction or
> duplicate of the China that for over two millennia upheld Confucianism as
> the orthodoxy in matters of thought, so that the free and vibrant intellectual
> climate of the 'hundred schools of thought' in the Spring and Autumn and
> Warring States periods[[193]] never returned until the twentieth century, and
> then only briefly. Even today, the officials and cadres who control the fate of
> the most populous nation of the world are not subject to the kind of public ac-
> countability that is embodied in the political institutions of western liberal
> democracies. The moralistic tone of the state-controlled media and educa-
> tional system is reminiscent of the traditional style of Confucian moral in-
> struction, even though the content of the message is quite different from the
> content of Confucianism. China is still ruled by paternalistic rulers answer-
> able primarily only to their own consciences (as the emperors were answer-
> able only to heaven); thus the transformation which many generations of
> modern Chinese intellectuals have hoped for of the people from 'children-sub-
> jects' to 'citizens' has yet to be seen.[194]

Partly in view of this grip that China's past is said to have on its present, Albert Chen
implies that Confucianist legal tradition retains the strength — the "enduring significance"
as a source of the "spirit" of the Chinese people — to serve as the foundation for "a rejuvenated Chinese culture".[195] In this respect, Chen seems to challenge Peerenboom's assertion that the "empirical basis for the claim that Confucianism is still important in
contemporary societies ... seems rather weak".[196]

---

192. Chen-1999, *supra* note 175, at 15 (as numbered from the beginning of the chapter).
193. For a reference to these periods, see Box #6.2 in Chapter Six, above.
194. Chen-1999, *supra* note 175, at 17 (as numbered from the beginning of the chapter).
195. *Id.* at 18 (as numbered from the beginning of the chapter).
196. Peerenboom-2003, *supra* note 1, at 92.

Still, even Albert Chen does not assert that China's Confucianist legal tradition is *already playing* the same sort of role in contemporary Chinese law that Imperial Confucianism played in dynastic Chinese law. Instead, he posits that Confucianism has the *potential* for playing such a role. He closes his most recent article on this subject with an entreaty for that potential to be realized and actuated as part of China's move toward liberal constitutional democracy (which he abbreviates as "LCD") — a move that Chen strongly favors:

> [T]he Confucian concepts and practices of personal cultivation and human development, ... and of the moral responsibility of holders of political power can ... provide answers to the eternal questions about the meaning and significance of human existence and about the source of value, answers which LCD, either as a political system or a political philosophy, cannot provide. If liberal democracy is to serve humanity and to flourish..., it must be anchored in a culture, tradition, religion, or philosophy that upholds the higher humanistic, moral, and spiritual ideas of humankind. This ... could be the inspiration for a Confucian political philosophy for China's future.[197]

In sum, it would seem that Confucianism — whether in a "Neo" form or in a "New" form — lacks both the theoretical heft and the popular acceptance *today* that would be necessary to regard it as playing the role in contemporary Chinese law that Imperial Confucianism played in dynastic Chinese law. Therefore, let us move on to consider another possible candidate for that role.

2. Marxist-Leninist-Maoist-Dengist Thought?

As noted earlier, the most recent full version of the PRC's Constitution was adopted in December 1982 and has been amended four times since then. We saw in section I of this chapter the amendment that made explicit reference to "rule of law" (or "rule by law", depending on translation issues), and later in this chapter we shall consider other aspects of the Constitution. For now, let us concentrate on a certain constitutional provision that might be regarded as announcing a key ethic that provides ideological durability to the law and moral legitimacy to the government. I refer to the provision praising "Marxism-Leninism, Mao Zedong Thought, Deng Xiaoping Theory and the important thought of 'Three Represents'" as providing guidance to the Chinese people in (among other things) improving China's "socialist legal system".

a. Constitutional foundations

The third and fourth amendments to the PRC Constitution, approved in 1999 and 2004, respectively, trace the development of that provision. As shown in Box #7.8, which reprints excerpts from those amendments, the provision has evolved with the addition of new ideological and political heroes in China:

Box #7.8 Excerpts from 1999 and 2004 Constitutional Amendments on Ideology[198]

AMENDMENT THREE (approved on March 15, 1999, by the 9th NPC at its 2nd Session)

The *original text* of paragraph seven in the Preamble of the Constitution is: "Both the victory of China's new-democratic revolution and the successes of its socialist cause have

---

197. Chen-2007, *supra* note 175, at 211.

198. The excerpts in Box #7.7 are drawn from the website of the official English-language newspaper *People's Daily*. See http://english.people.com.cn/constitution/constitution.html (emphasis added).

been achieved by the Chinese people of all nationalities under the leadership of the Communist Party of China and the guidance of Marxism-Leninism and Mao Zedong Thought, and by upholding truth, correcting errors and overcoming numerous difficulties and hardships. China is currently in the primary stage of socialism. The basic task of the nation is to concentrate its effort on socialist modernization in accordance with the theory of building socialism with Chinese characteristics. *Under the leadership of the Communist Party of China and the guidance of Marxism-Leninism and Mao Zedong Thought*, the Chinese people of all nationalities will continue to adhere to the people's democratic dictatorship, follow the socialist road, persist in reform and opening-up, steadily improve socialist institutions, develop socialist democracy, improve the socialist legal system and work hard and self-reliantly to modernize industry, agriculture, national defense and science and technology step by step to turn China into a powerful and prosperous socialist country with a high level of culture and democracy."

It is *revised* into: "Both the victory of China's new-democratic revolution and the successes of its socialist cause have been achieved by the Chinese people of all nationalities under the leadership of the Communist Party of China and the guidance of Marxism-Leninism and Mao Zedong Thought, and by upholding truth, correcting errors and overcoming numerous difficulties and hardships. China will stay in the primary stage of socialism for a long period of time. The basic task of the nation is to concentrate its efforts on socialist modernization by following the road of building socialism with Chinese characteristics. *Under the leadership of the Communist Party of China and the guidance of Marxism-Leninism, Mao Zedong Thought and Deng Xiaoping Theory*, the Chinese people of all nationalities will continue to adhere to the people's democratic dictatorship, follow the socialist road, persist in reform and opening-up, steadily improve socialist institutions, develop a socialist market economy, advance socialist democracy, improve the socialist legal system and work hard and self-reliantly to modernize industry, agriculture, national defense and science and technology step by step to turn China into a powerful and prosperous socialist country with a high level of culture and democracy."

AMENDMENT FOUR (approved on March 14, 2004, by the 10th NPC at its 2nd Session)

1. "... along the road of building socialism with Chinese characteristics ..." and "... under the guidance of Marxism-Leninism, Mao Zedong Thought and Deng Xiaoping Theory ..."

Revised to: "... along the road of Chinese-style socialism ..." and "... under the guidance of Marxism-Leninism, Mao Zedong Thought, Deng Xiaoping Theory and the important thought of 'Three Represents' ..."

The reference in the 2004 amendment to the "Three Represents" gives constitutional status to policies that Jiang Zemin announced in November 2002 in this statement to the National Congress of the Communist Party of China ("CPC") in his capacity as leader of the CPC:

Reviewing the course of struggle and the basic experience over the past 80 years and looking ahead to the arduous tasks and bright future in the new century, our Party should continue to stand in the forefront of the times and lead the people in marching toward victory. In a word, the Party must always represent [1] the requirements of the development of China's advanced productive forces, [2] the orientation of the development of China's advanced culture, and [3] the fundamental interests of the overwhelming majority of the people in China.[199]

---

199. Statement by Jiang Zemin, November 8, 2002. For an explanatory account offered at the time by an official newspaper, see *Jiang Calls on CPC to Implement 'Three Represents' in All-round Way*, PEOPLE'S DAILY, available at http://english.people.com.cn/200211/08/eng20021108_106482.shtml.

The announcement of these policies has been said to signal an attempt to strengthen the position of the Chinese Communist Party by showing (i) its continued attention to economic production, (ii) its dedication to the glory and progress of China's unique culture, and perhaps most importantly (iii) a move away from its old image as a revolutionary party focusing its energies on serving the proletariat and toward a role in which it represents the majority of the people in the country, including members of the business class — that is, capitalists.

Taken together, the various elements included in the awkward phrase "under the guidance of Marxism-Leninism, Mao Zedong Thought, Deng Xiaoping Theory and the important thought of 'Three Represents'" serve as what the official website of the Communist Party of China calls its "Ideological and Theoretical Basis". The CPC explanatory statement on that point reads in pertinent part as follows:

> The Communist Party of China (CPC) takes *Marxism-Leninism, Mao Zedong Thought, Deng Xiaoping Theory and the important thought of Three Represents* as its guide to action and theoretical bases.
>
> *Marxism-Leninism* reveals the universal laws governing the development of history of human society. It analyzes the contradictions inherent in the capitalist system that it is incapable of resolving internally and shows that socialist society will inevitably replace capitalist society and ultimately develop into communist society....
>
> The Chinese Communists have untiringly striven to integrate Marxism with the concrete practice in China and adapted it to Chinese conditions. Combining Marxism-Leninism with the concrete practice of the Chinese revolution, the first generation of the CPC's central collective leadership, with Comrade Mao Zedong as its core, settled such basic questions as the nature, motive force and object of the new-democratic revolution and the road to socialism in China. And *Mao Zedong Thought* was thus established, which is Marxism-Leninism applied and developed in China. Mao Zedong ... established the theory for building a proletarian party in a semi-colonial, semi-feudal society constituted mainly of peasants and petty bourgeoisie.... Mao Zedong's theory of party building is the first historic leap of the Marxist theory of party building in China.
>
> After the Third Plenary Session of the Eleventh CPC Central Committee in 1978, the Chinese Communists, with Comrade Deng Xiaoping as their chief representative, reviewed their experience, both positive and negative, since the founding of the People's Republic. They emancipated their minds, sought truth from facts, shifted the focus of the work of the whole Party onto economic development and carried out reform and opening to the outside world; this ushered in a new era of development in the socialist cause. They gradually formulated ... *Deng Xiaoping Theory*. This theory is the outcome of integrating the basic tenets of Marxism-Leninism with the practical conditions in present-day China and the characteristics of the times; it is a continuation and development of Mao Zedong Thought under new historical conditions.... History has shown that Deng Xiaoping's theory of party building is the second historic leap of the Marxist theory of party building in China.
>
> Since the Fourth Plenary Session of the Thirteenth CPC Central Committee in 1989, the third generation of the central collective leadership, with Comrade Jiang Zemin as its core, has held high the great banner of Deng Xiaoping Theory, stayed on the road of socialism with Chinese characteristics and unswerv-

ingly concentrated on economic development.... Comrade Jiang Zemin set forth the new theory of party building that calls for the CPC to always represent the development trend of China's advanced productive forces, the orientation of China's advanced culture and the fundamental interests of the overwhelming majority of the Chinese people.... At its Sixteenth National Congress in November 2002, the Party established the important thought of *Three Represents*, together with Marxism-Leninism, Mao Zedong Thought and Deng Xiaoping Theory, as the long-term guiding ideology that it must uphold.... The Three Represents adheres to dialectical materialism and historical materialism, embodies Marxism's theoretical characteristic of advancing with the times and is imbued with the same spirit as the Marxist stand, viewpoint and methodology.... The important thought of Three Represents takes the theory of building the party in office as its main subject, promoting economic, political, and cultural advancement under socialism with Chinese characteristics and all-round social progress as its basic content, and the great rejuvenation of the Chinese nation as its goal.... The important thought of Three Represents has ushered in a new stage in the adaptation of Marxism to Chinese conditions.[200]

b. Party Line as a new legal ethic?

For the sake of simplicity, we might call this package of policies and ideologies the "CPC Party Line". Aside from the fact that the language in which the CPC Party Line is announced would strike most Western readers as stilted, self-congratulatory, and fluffy, might it in fact provide the "legal ethic" at issue here? That seems unlikely for three related reasons, which I shall label "inhospitability", "insufficienty", and "inconsistency".

First, the preponderance of the CPC Party Line is so *inhospitable* to law that it could not reasonably be regarded as the key ethic of the legal system. The inhospitability I refer to derives from how the law was viewed in both Marxist-Leninist ideology and Mao's revolutionary agenda. For both, law must be subsidiary to violent force. Xin Ren explains this point:

> To understand the nature and limitation of law and the legal system in China, an examination of two fundamental elements of the Marxist-Leninist ideological stands that significantly influenced Mao's political thinking will, perhaps, provide meaningful clues to Mao's revolutionary agenda. First, using brutal violence or armed force to establish a socialist state has been the heart of Marxist-Leninist ideology and has generally been practiced by Communists elsewhere as it has been by the Chinese. Marx suggested that "one of the final results of the proletarian revolution will be the gradual dissolution and ultimate disappearance of that political organization called the state ... [but that in working to achieve that result] ... abandoning the state machinery "would be to destroy the only organism by means of which the victorious working class can exert its newly conquered power, keep down its capitalist enemies and carry out that economic revolution of society without which the whole victory must end in a defeat and a massacre of the working class. [Hence, law and the state can not disappear immediately but first must be used, with violence if necessary, to create a dictatorship of the proletariat.]

> The same support for violence was also embraced by Mao Zedong in one of his earliest works, *Report on an Investigation of the Hunan Peasant Movement*, first published in 1927:

---

200. See http://english.cpc.people.com.cn/66739/4521326.html (emphasis added).

[A] revolution is not the same as inviting people to dinner, or writing an essay, or painting a picture, or doing fancy needlework; it cannot be anything so refined, so calm and gentle, or so mild, kind, courteous, restrained, and magnanimous. A revolution is an uprising, an act of violence whereby one class overthrows another.

Mao openly expressed his favorable attitude about armed force and violence as a necessary path way to overcoming the power of the old ruling class. As he stated so aptly, "political power comes from the barrel of a rifle." The socialist state could not survive without the consolidation of the military forces and the use of violence to overthrow the power of the antagonistic class.

... Because law has the political functions of advancing the socialist revolution toward communism and of protecting the interest of the newly established ruling class in China, "law is arbitrary in so far as it is treated not as a set of inviolable canons but as a site in constant need of rearticulation to aid the development of socialism." As it was suggested by Michael Dutton (1992), the CCP needed to be free from any procedural or substantive restraints of law and to limit public scrutiny on the administration of law in order to effectively utilize law and the judiciary, as a weapon of class struggle, for the furtherance of the socialist revolution.[201]

These observations suggest that in Marxist-Leninist-Maoist thought, law is arbitrary and is made subordinate to force and violence. Since Marxist-Leninist-Maoist thought comprises a substantial part of the CPC Party Line as described above, it would seem entirely incongruous to suggest that that Party Line could possibly serve as the "heart" or "soul" or "central ethic" of the legal system in contemporary China. Simply adding into the Party Line some references to Deng Xiaoping Theory and Jiang Zemin's "Three Represents" would seem inadequate to overcome the fundamental inhospitability that the older element of the Party Line exhibited toward law.

Second, if we were to ignore the violent aspects of the Communist foundations to the CPC Party Line, and focus solely on its socialist aspects, the Party Line still would seem to fall short of providing the sort of legal ethic at issue here. As Randall Peerenboom has put it succinctly, "[s]ocialism is surely *insufficient* as an ideology" by which to legitimize the legal and political system.[202]

Why is socialism—which is said to be at the heart of the CPC Party Line—inadequate for this purpose? For one thing, socialism is a predominantly economic ideology or system, and this would appear to prevent it from being robust enough to serve in the capacity of a legal ethic. Besides, the sort of socialism at play in the PRC—"Chinese-style socialism", in the words of the 2004 constitutional amendments—is by now heavily flavored (perhaps contaminated) by what most observers would regard as rather straightforward capitalism.

This brings us to the next related point as to why the CPC Party Line could not easily be regarded as supplying the legal ethic in contemporary China: the Party Line itself is

---

201. Xin Ren, *supra* note 1, at 50–52, quoting from writings by Marx, Engels, and Mao, and from Michael Dutton, POLICING AND PUNISHMENT IN CHINA (1992). Xin Ren goes on to say that, for Mao, "[t]he role of law and the legal system is, after all, to be a suppressive instrument against class enemies." In the same vein, she asserts that "[f]or Communists, the law is a political weapon for overcoming the power and resistance of their class enemies." *Id.* at 63. Likewise, she emphasizes "the legality of the Communist Party's ruling power over the legislative and judicial processes" as a feature of socialist ideology. *Id.* at 3.

202. Peerenboom-2003, *supra* note 1, at 53 (emphasis added).

so internally *inconsistent* on its own terms as to rob it of any persuasive meaning. Consider the basic differences between Marxist-Leninist thought, for example, and the enormous emphasis placed now by the PRC government on individual wealth generation and protection of private property—the latter of which is in fact enshrined in the PRC's Constitution as a result of the 1999 and 2004 amendments.[203] Indeed, each of the "layers" added through the years to the fundamental Marxist-Leninist ideology compounded the internal inconsistency in the CPC Party Line. "Mao Zedong Thought" differed, for example, from Marxist-Leninist theory in terms of the extent to which it sees a need for the Communist Party to seize control over all facets of the society. Xin Ren explains this point as follows:

> [W]hat is unique about Mao Zedong's approach is his obsession with the political roles of law and the judicial system, which held for him the same fascination he had expressed about literature, the arts, intellectuals, and education—the so-called components of the superstructure that Marx elaborated from the Hegelian dialectics of history. But Marx was an economic determinist. For him, change in the superstructure was determined by change in the economic basis, that is, the productive forces ... [and the] proletarian revolution occurs when the superstructure no longer matches up to the advanced productive forces in a capitalist society. The advancement of productive forces over the development of the superstructure was the central premise of Marxist political-economic theory. But for Mao Zedong, the impact of the superstructure on the economic basis was more than just important. It was crucial and vital for consolidating the political power of the Communist Party. In order to consolidate the victory of the revolution, Mao insisted that the CCP [Chinese Communist Party] must hold the commanding power over *all* facets of societal life—including the economy, politics, culture, and the judiciary—backed by the "iron-fist dictatorship" and the violent suppression of class enemies.[204]

That inconsistency between Maoist thought and Marxist-Leninist theory might be considered largely one of emphasis and extent. However, the next "layer" in the CPC Party Line—that of "Deng Xiaoping theory", added (as a constitutional matter) in 1999—introduced more dramatic incompatibility. Mao would have found surprising, perhaps abhorrent, the economic and legal changes set forth in the 1982 Constitution. Also known as the "Deng Xiaoping Constitution",[205] that instrument had as a "fundamental purpose ... to incorporate the new policies of economic reform"[206] that Deng Xiaoping had introduced in 1978, including "the protection of foreign investment and recognition of indi-

---

203. The 1999 Amendments inserted the "recognition of the private sector as an important component of the national economy", and the 2004 Amendments inserted stipulations governing "protection of private properties". For details, see Zou, *supra* note 1, at 3.

204. Xin Ren, *supra* note 1, at 53 (emphasis added). Xin Ren draws this contrast between Maoist thought and Marxist-Leninist theory after having explained that although Marxism "is purely a product of Western culture" and therefore would seem on the surface to have "little in common with Chinese tradition", it is in fact ideologically "'less alien than either Buddhism or Christianity' to the Chinese because of the longstanding cultivation of Confucian secular morality." *Id.* at 48, quoting from L. Shaffer, *Marxism Enters a Confucian Realm: The People's Republic in the Perspective of Chinese History*, 14 FLETCHER FORUM OF WORLD AFFAIRS 1 (1990).

205. See Zou, *supra* note 1, at 30. As noted above, the 1982 constitution was preceded by two constitutions of the 1970s: the so-called "Gang of Four Constitution" of 1975, growing out of the Cultural Revolution; and the so-called "Hua Guofeng Constitution" of 1978 that also served as an affirmation of the Cultural Revolution. *Id.* at 29–30.

206. *Id.* at 3.

vidual economy as complementary to the national economy".[207] And from a legal perspective, the departure from Maoist thought was even more dramatic. For example, "[t]he provision in the 1954 Constitution that 'all citizens are equal before the law' [was] restored" in the 1982 Constitution,[208] a change that directly repudiates the Maoist view that the key purpose of law was to be a weapon of class struggle and hence intrinsically unequal in its application. Indeed, as one authority has explained, that "legal equality" constitutional provision from 1954 had been rebuked by Mao and others as the CPC's powers grew:

> After 1957, the principle that "all citizens are equal before the law" was [criticized by CPC leaders for its tendency of] "getting rid of the elements of class in the law:' the emphasis on getting everything done according to law was said to be "a fallacy to put law above everything and to deny the Party's policy"; and the defence and lawyers' systems were labelled systems to "help the class enemy escape its due punishment". As a result, the 1954 Constitution was progressively more and more disregarded from its adoption and totally abandoned at the early stage of the Cultural Revolution, when the so-called class struggle reached its climax.[209]

Therefore, for the 1982 Constitution to have restored the "legal equality" provision represented a reversal of the Maoist view of the role of law in Chinese society and governance. Moreover, it was recognized as such at the time. Deng himself referred in 1978 to the mistakes that Mao had made and the need for China to learn from them and to make changes:

> Although various mistakes in the past were closely related to some leaders' ideas and working styles, problems involved in the organic system and working system should also be considered major culprits.... Even a man as great as Mao Zedong was seriously influenced by corrupt systems and consequently his actions made the Party, the country and him suffer. To guarantee people's democracy, a sound legal system must be strengthened, democracy must be institutionalised and legalised so that the system and laws won't change just because of a change in leadership or just because of changes in the leaders' ideas.[210]

In sum, whereas Mao saw law as "a suppressive instrument [to be used] against class enemies",[211] Deng saw that "the main purpose of law was to maintain social order".[212] There is, then, a crescendo of inconsistency in the ideological "layers" found in the CPC Party Line from Marxist-Leninist theory to Maoist thought to Deng Xiaoping theory. Each departed in important ways from its predecessor.

This pattern of departures continued in the 1990s as the CPC shifted its emphasis even more to economic productivity and to the rule of law — changes that were, as noted earlier, reflected in the 1993, 1999, and 2004 amendments to the 1982 Constitution and that seem to have been covered in the third of Jiang Zemin's "Three Represents". As explained

---

207. *Id.*, citing articles 11 and 18 of the 1982 constitution.

208. *Id.* at 30, citing article 33 of the 1982 constitution.

209. *Id.* at 29, quoting from Zhang Jinfan, *Tortuous Course of Development of Legal System of China in the Past 50 Years*, CHINA LAW, Oct. 25, 1999, at 47.

210. *Id.* at 31, drawing the Deng quotation from Zhang Jinfan, *supra* note 209, at 49. Deng made this statement at the famous Third Plenary Session of the 11th Central Committee, held in December 1978. It was at that meeting that the central committee of the CPC adopted dramatic changes that were mainly economic in character but that also had important legal components and implications, setting in motion the reforms that the PRC has undertaken over the past three decades.

211. Xin Ren, *supra* note 1, at 53.

212. Zou, *supra* note 1, at 32.

above, the third of Jiang's "Three Represents" calls for the CPC to represent "the fundamental interests of the overwhelming majority of the people in China". Although this language is vague, it appears to constitute yet a further movement away from the CPC's old
image of a revolutionary party focusing its energies on serving the proletariat and toward
a role in which it represents the majority of the people in the country, including members of the business class—that is, capitalists.[213]

My conclusion from the characterizations of the CPC Party Line that I have discussed
above is that it is inhospitable, insufficient, and inconsistent to serve as the sort of key legal
ethic—the "spirit" or "soul"—of contemporary Chinese law.[214] And so, again, let us
move on to consider yet another possible candidate for that role.

3. Constitutionalism?

Let us continue our search for a modern correlative to Imperial Confucianism by considering another possible candidate: constitutionalism, or perhaps more precisely the
specific substantive principles that the broad population in Chinese society finds in that
country's constitution.

a. A comparative detour

In order to assess this possibility, let us first take a detour and consider what core
legal ethic, if any, lies at the heart of the *American* legal system.[215] Giving some attention to that topic here might provide some useful context and contrast to our consideration of Chinese law; and it can also set the stage for a brief examination, in the
closing paragraphs of this chapter, of how we might discern the legal "soul" of other
countries.

We might speculate that the core legal ethic in the American system consists of a package of values that we could label the "American Constitutional Ethic". The main elements
in that package would include the following, probably along with several others:

- The substantive and procedural legal protections found in the US bill of rights
  (the first ten amendments to the US Constitution of 1787), and particularly such
  specific rules as these:

---

213. For a fascinating set of observations regarding how the CPC has tried to strike a viable balance between (i) reinventing itself in order to stay relevant in a rapidly changing economic and social environment and (ii) emphasizing the long-term historical constancy of the CPC's leadership role
in Chinese political society over time—in order to perpetuate its own power—see generally Arjun
Subrahmanyan, *Constitutionalism in China: Changing Dynamics in Legal and Political Debates*, CHINA
LAW & PRACTICE, May 1, 2004, available at http://www.chinalawandpractice.com (see specifically
http://www.chinalawandpractice.com/Article/1692820/Channel/9934/Constitutionalism-in-China-
Changing-Dynamics-in-Legal-and-Political-Debates.html).

214. In expressing a similar view, Stanley Lubman has offered this observation:
    Perhaps the most significant social change brought on by economic reform has been the
    loss among many Chinese of whatever faith they may have had in the ideology of Marx-
    ism-Leninism-Mao Zedong Thought. Together the Cultural Revolution and the great hard-
    ships caused by Mao's policies had already begun to weaken belief in the ideology, and the
    economic reforms have further accelerated its decline. The party's legitimacy will increas-
    ingly be questioned, especially if a stall in Chinese economic growth brings hard times.
Lubman-1999, *supra* note 1, at 121.

215. I use the term "American legal system" to refer generally to the US (federal) legal system and
the state legal systems.

- freedom of speech
- freedom of the press
- freedom of assembly and right to petition
- freedom of religion, both freedom from having to associate with a state-sponsored religion and freedom to practice the religion of one's choice (if any)
- freedom from arbitrary arrest and detention
- freedom from having private property for public purposes taken without compensation
- freedom of movement
- the right to have certain "due process" procedural requirements followed
- the right to trial by a jury of one's peers
- the freedom from arbitrary search and seizure

- Other substantive rights that people assume are guaranteed by the US Constitution, such as these:
  - the right to own handguns suitable for killing other humans
  - the right to privacy
  - the right to vote in elections for representatives in Congress

- Other substantive rights that are found primarily in the Declaration of Independence of 1776 (even though people might think they appear in the Constitution), such as these:
  - the right to equal treatment (on the basis that all people are created equal)
  - the right to "life, liberty, and the pursuit of happiness"

- Freedom from government interference of most types—and, to safeguard that freedom, a guarantee that the government will have only expressly limited powers.

Underlying several of the elements in the "package" described above are certain popular assumptions—that is, assumptions as to which there is broad consensus across the American population as a whole. These assumptions include (i) the assumption that the natural state of persons is a state of freedom,[216] and (ii) the related assumption that all powers of the government emanate from the people, in accordance with some form of "social contract" by which (as John Locke asserted) individuals agree (begrudgingly, perhaps) to surrender a limited set of specific rights to a central authority in return for assurances from that central authority that it will provide collective defense, both against external aggression and against internal lawlessness. Indeed, the US Constitution itself conveys the sense of a contract in several respects. The opening language enumerates specific purposes for which the people (acting in part through their state governments) have consented to enter into the federal arrangements that the constitution establishes. These specific purposes include such things as "to form a more perfect union", to "provide for the common defense", to "establish justice", to "promote the general welfare", and so forth.

---

216. As is well known, the US Constitution originally gave only limited scope to this assumption, especially in its accommodation of slavery.

The Tenth Amendment to the US Constitution, in turn, expressly limits the powers of the federal government by providing that "[t]he powers not delegated to the United States by the Constitution, nor prohibited by it to the states, are reserved to the states respectively, or to the people".

Much of the US Constitution, of course, addresses structural issues—how the federal government is to be organized and is to function, for example, and what relations (including "checks and balances") are to be maintained among the three branches of the government. These provisions can likewise be viewed—and, what is more important, *are* viewed by most Americans—as further manifestations of a fundamental organizing theme: the government is the servant of the people.

Whether or not this is a *good* theme is entirely beside the point here. I have expressed the various components of what I label the American Constitutional Ethic in terms that I believe reflect how most Americans view them. Ask a "man on the street" what lies at the very center of the American legal system, and I think you will get answers that closely resemble the points enumerated above. Objective observers, both inside and outside the USA, will readily point out the many ways in which the reality falls short of the ideal, but the important point for our present purposes is to recognize that there *is* an ideal, that it has developed over many scores of years, and that it constitutes a common popular understanding of how the American legal system should work.

What about the rule of law? Is "the rule of law" a part of the American Constitutional Ethic? No, but the opposite is true: the American Constitutional Ethic is part of the rule of law—or, more precisely, it is what provides the "thickening agent" that creates the American version of what Randall Peerenboom calls the "liberal democratic version" of the "thick" rule of law—a topic explored above. It should be obvious that several of the components I have enumerated above are clearly consistent with such a liberal democratic "thick" version of the rule of law that Peerenboom describes. Indeed, it might be that some Americans would, when asked to list features that lie at the core of the American legal system, include "the rule of law" on the list. However, I believe that if pressed for more detail, the respondents would identify various particular rights and freedoms I have enumerated above (especially those of a procedural nature). And in any event, the list would not end with "the rule of law" or the individual rights it encompasses; that is, the respondents would also name several other substantive elements such as freedom from government, freedom of religion, freedom of the press, and so forth.

Another feature also appears, I believe, in the American Constitutional Ethic, or perhaps underneath it: religion. I shall postpone for now a discussion of that point.

b. Constitutionalism in China

Now let us turn back to China. Does "constitutionalism"—that is, a strong popular embrace of a package of provisions of the Chinese constitution (or other fundamental legal or policy documents)—serve as the key legal ethic in today's China, in a way that is similar to how I have described the situation in the American legal system? I think the answer must be "no", for several reasons.

First, the current PRC Constitution is still relatively new, dating only from 1982. It has already undergone four significant amendments. As noted above, these occurred in 1988 (to define the status of the private sector and the country's policy on private businesses), in 1993 (when the position of democracy was upgraded), in 1999 (when the basic strategy of exercising the rule of law was formulated), and in 2004 (when, among other things, a provision asserting that "the state respects and protects human rights" was added).[217] Moreover, the current PRC Constitution was preceded by three other constitutions since 1949, and those constitutions show a great deal of discontinuity.[218]

Hence, there simply has not been adequate time for the substantive norms set forth in the PRC Constitution to have become internalized by the Chinese people. The norms themselves have changed too frequently and too dramatically for that.

Perhaps more importantly, the *idea* of constitutionalism—as distinct from the specific norms found in a particular constitution—has almost surely not been internalized by the Chinese people. In a fascinating article on Chinese constitutionalism, Ma Xiaohong of Renmin University of China has discussed this issue and offered some comparisons to western constitutions and constitutionalism:

> Like other colonial or semi-colonial countries, constitutionalism in modern China did not come from traditions but was passively imported from Western countries. Such passivity means, a colonization movement, following the heel of the Industrial Revolution, swept across the globe and the entire world was dragged rather than entered into by itself the "modern path", and China was no exception....
>
> Our mistakes began with our misunderstanding of "what is constitutionalism". Such misunderstanding is somewhat similar to that of "rule of law".... [However,] [o]ur misconception of constitutionalism is much greater.
>
> As to the origin of Western constitutionalism, no one will deny that it was based on specific traditions. In the works composed by ancient Greek thinkers, we can find the evidence for the checks and balances required by modern constitutionalism and democratic thinking. If we read and compare Plato's *Laws* and Aristotle's *Politics* with Montesquieu's *The Spirit of Laws*, we can readily discern a kind of succession between them.... Constitutionalism, with the support of traditions and history, acquired a kind of rationality and divinity. To talk about constitutionalism, we first have to mention something about the "Constitution", which is the text and guiding principle of constitutionalism. Westerners based their knowledge or understanding of the Constitution on traditions. Theoretically speaking, the Constitution is built upon social contracts and it defines citizens' basic rights and obligations in the form of basic law and prescribes the authority of the state's important institutions and their mutual relationship. From the aspect of social contract, the power of the state comes from citizens' authorization and the Constitution is a contract between the state and its citizens. The state, when exercising its authority, should not harm citizens' rights, and instead, it should try to protect their interests; the purpose of the checks and balances is to prevent power abuse. Such contractual nature will make every citizen feel his personal interest being tied to the Constitution and recognize its indispensability. What is more important and yet ignored by us is that the Constitution in Western countries is regarded as the representation and the essence of their national spirits, civilization and values.

---

217. This summary is drawn from Wang Zhoujun, *supra* note 2, at 336. Each of the amendments involved other changes not mentioned here.

218. See *supra* note 205 for references to the "Gang of Four Constitution" and the "Hua Guofeng Constitution", from 1975 and 1978, respectively.

... In the past one hundred years, Chinese ... scholars have diligently introduced the types and modes of Western Constitution and constitutionalism. But the connection between constitutionalism and [Chinese] historical traditions and the relationship between Constitution and [Chinese] national values have been overlooked or evaded.... What is unfortunate for modern Chinese constitutionalism is that, the constitutionalism arrived in China at a time of national crisis, and even people who truly admired the constitutionalism had no time to leisurely appreciate the historical and cultural elements behind the constitutionalism.

... The departure from traditions, disregard of national feelings and spirits, and the unrealistic expectation for foreign culture (constitutionalism) were underlying causes [for disappointing results in efforts to absorb constitutionalism into Chinese culture and society]. As to this, American jurisprudent Pond, as an onlooker, saw most clearly. Pond warned: "the constitutionalism cannot be created in the short term and out of aspiration. A constitutional government must gradually evolve from the native culture and traditional aspiration and is not something that, upon its maturity, can be willfully transplanted to other countries."[219]

According to Ma Xiaohong, then, constitutionalism has not succeeded in China, in the sense of providing a central legal ethic for the country. Ma points out that in dynastic times, there *was* such a legal ethic, and it was *lǐ*:

[I]n ancient China, rule by *lǐ* actually had the status and role similar to that of Western constitutions, and moreover, it was closely linked with national feelings.... Its values and spirits had imprinted an indelible mark upon every native.... Compared with modern people's indifference to violations of the [PRC] Constitution, in ancient China, *lǐ* or rule by *lǐ*, once endangered or damaged, people would rush to protect it.... In ancient China, rule by *lǐ* was not merely an instrument of governance it was also the standard with which people appraised their monarch and officials. It was a belief and a channel connected to various strata and precisely for this reason, *lǐ* and rule by *lǐ* had become the "basic law"

---

219. Ma Xiaohong, *supra* note 2, at 48–51 (emphasis added). I see a similarity between (i) Ma's emphasis of China's lack of a tradition of constitutionalism and (ii) William Jones' emphasis of the different aims and audience of law in Western culture (especially that most heavily influence by Roman tradition) as compared with the aims and audience of law in Chinese culture. Recall Jones' explanation of that difference, as evident in the Qing Code (which Jones' translated into English):

[T]he [Qing] Code is not much concerned with the disputes of private individuals.... We are accustomed to think that a legal system is primarily a social institution within which 'persons'—private individuals, or groups of individuals, or even the state—can make claims against other persons and have these resolved by a neutral trier of fact and law.... These are all aspects of the legal systems we are familiar with ... [and] they reflect the [fact that much of Western law] was formed by Roman law, ... [which arose] in a very small and predominately agricultural community with a weak government. As a consequence, the legal problems that it dealt with in the formative period [focused on] disputes between private individuals that arose out of torts, simple contracts, and succession.... The situation in China was radically different. The polity of China consisted of a highly centralized government headed by an absolute ruler who ruled by means of a bureaucracy. The primary obligation of every Chinese was to fulfil the duties assigned to him by the Emperor. All human activities had to be carried on so as to fit into his scheme for directing society. Consequently one would expect the imperial law or Code to take note of human activity only as it was perceived to affect imperial policies.

See note 89 in Chapter Six, above, and accompanying text.

of ancient China. Since the late Qing [Dynasty], the keynote was to relinquish *lǐ* and adopt laws (in its Western sense), and despite some opposition, the westernization had turned to be irresistible. Yet, in China, the hastily introduced Constitution appeared to be empty talk and, quite embarrassingly, was degraded to an instrument of power struggle.[220]

Another Chinese professor—Wang Zhoujun of Suzhou University—takes a somewhat more cheerful view toward the slow movement in developing a strong constitutionalism in China. Noting the common sense involved in "feeling the stones when crossing the river",[221] Wang applauds "progressive" or "gradual" constitutionalism:

> Social development and reform are just like "crossing the river" and are full of uncertainties, thus constant exploration and continuous choices are necessary.... Reforms have to be based on specific experience and move along cautiously, that is, have to "feel the stones".... There has to be planning, otherwise "gradual" progress will become "blind progress" without any sense of direction. We have to focus all the time on our goal—"the other side of the river"—a prosperous and powerful, democratic and civilized socialist country.[222]

Then Wang Zhoujun explains that constitutional reform in China "is different from the constitutional development that is initiated from within the West". Specifically, he quotes Deng Ziaoping's statement to then-former US President Jimmy Carter in June 1987: "China's main objective is to develop, shake off backwardness, strengthen the nation and gradually raise the standard of living. In order to accomplish this, it is essential to have a stable political environment."[223] For this reason, Wang asserts, China is conducting "constitutionalism with stability."[224]

Moreover, Wang Zhoujun emphasizes that this gradualist approach to building a sense of constitutionalism among the Chinese people is to a large extent a *cultural* mandate. That is, China should (Wang says) "adopt a gradual process of cultural transformation corresponding to that of constitutional evolution".[225] Otherwise China will remain backward and runs the risk of devolution into chaos and continuing to engage in a "worship of power" and "clannishness" and the rise of certain "grass-roots organs of power [that] are not democratic at all but enormously popular".[226]

To sum up: constitutionalism is by no means unimportant in China. At this stage, however, the PRC's Constitution itself is too new, and the Chinese people have not yet developed a tradition in which constitutionalism can truly take hold—and particularly constitutionalism along a western model, in which a country's constitution can acquire "a kind of rationality and divinity" and can be "regarded as the representation and the essence of their national spirits, civilizations, and values".[227]

---

220. Ma Xiaohong, *supra* note 2, at 66–67. Ma Xiaohong goes on to explain some aspects of that power struggle as exhibited in the development of Chinese constitutions and the degradation of Confucianism. See *id.* at 67–69.

221. See Wang Zhoujun, *supra* note 2, at 347.

222. *Id.* at 347–348.

223. *Id.* at 348.

224. *Id.*

225. *Id.* at 351.

226. *Id.*

227. Ma Xiaohong, *supra* note 2, at 49.

4. Religion?

I noted earlier in passing that I believe many Americans see a religious component, or perhaps underlayment, to what I have called the American Constitutional Ethic. Let consider that point further, in part to help us address this question: Does religion play a role in China's legal system today, so that we could find in such religion a contemporary correlative to Imperial Confucianism?

A lively debate has developed in recent years (made more accessible and extreme, probably, by the internet) as to whether the founders of the American legal and political system were predominantly Christian—and, if so, whether their religious beliefs were closely similar in content to the religious views held by many contemporary Americans (in particular radical Christian fundamentalist Americans).[228] Whether intelligently or not (I think not) a great many Americans seem quite comfortable attributing early-21st-century fundamentalist Christian religious beliefs to the founders of the American legal and political system; and therefore those modern-day Americans view the US Constitution and the American Declaration of Independence as importantly infused with religious content. Such Americans are thereby projecting and enhancing a myth in which the country's legal and political system carries a religious significance—specifically a Judeo-Christian religious significance.

It is a myth,[229] of course, that has the momentum of history behind it. Throughout the ages and around the world, law has often been viewed as having religious authorship or

---

228. See, e.g., Robert Ulrich, *Were the Founding Fathers Christian?*, available at http://www.shalom-jerusalem.com/heritage/heritage19.html (asserting that the Founding Fathers were Christians carrying out God's plan to create the USA for specific purposes, and that "[w]e must not permit revisionists to steal from us our Christian heritage by rewriting history"); http://www.christianparents.com/ffathers.htm (untitled, enumerating many pieces of evidence, including quotations, allegedly proving that the founding fathers, and the legal system they created, were deeply Christian); *Our Founding Fathers Were Not Christian*, available at http://freethought.mbdojo.com/foundingfathers.html (documenting the many ways in which Founding Fathers made clear that they were not founding the USA as a Christian nation—including a US treaty provision from the late 1700s asserting that "the United States was "in no sense founded on the Christian religion"). These and numerous other sites can be found from a simple Google search for "founding fathers were Christian". For more measured and nuanced assessments of the issue, see, e.g., Eyal Press, *In God's Country*, THE NATION, Nov. 2, 2006, available at http://www.thenation.com (acknowledging that "some right-wing demagogues now insist ... that the Founding Fathers were devout evangelicals who viewed America as a Christian nation and who would have sided with conservatives in today's culture wars"); and David Liss, *The Founding Fathers*, THE WASHINGTON POST, June 11, 2006, available at http://www.washingtonpost.com (reviewing several books taking opposing positions on the alleged Christian views of the founding fathers). Both of these articles explain that most of the founding fathers showed strong tendencies toward Deism and Unitarianism. According to the online version of the Encyclopedia Brittanica, "deism" generally "refers to what can be called natural religion, the acceptance of a certain body of religious knowledge that is inborn in every person or that can be acquired by the use of reason, as opposed to knowledge acquired through either revelation or the teaching of any church".

229. The word "myth" can carry many different shades of meaning. I use it here in the sense conveyed by these related definitions, which I have gleaned from several sources: (1) a traditional story accepted as history or drawn out of historical events, used to explain the world view of a people; (2) a narrative account or story which contains the collective wisdom of a society and articulates beliefs concerning key aspects of individual identity or collective life; (3) a sacred story that purports to explain or describe the origins and worldview of a culture; (4) a narrative—not necessarily an "untrue story"—that tells of origins.

inspiration. Here is how Derk Bodde has described this point, focusing particularly on early societies:

> A striking feature of the early written law of several major civilizations of antiquity has been its close association with religion. Not all of these civilizations, to be sure, actually produced systems of written law. When they did so, however, they commonly signalized this achievement by attributing, at least initially, a divine origin to the law they used—an origin signifying that such law had been given or revealed to mankind by a god or gods.
>
> This belief so obviously underlies Judaic and Islamic law that for them it requires no further elaboration. It is equally apparent, however, in the world's earliest written law as know to us from Mesopotamia. On the stele bearing the famed laws of Hammurabi (ca. 1728–1686 B.C.), for example, a sculptured relief shows Hammurabi receiving from Shamash, god of justice, a divine commission for his writing of the laws....
>
> Turning ... to Europe, we find Plato, in the famous opening passage of the *Laws*, making one of his protagonists unhesitatingly attribute the origin of law "to a god." In Rome, similarly, despite its early secularization of law, we find Cicero purporting to quote "the opinion of the wisest men of his day" to the effect that "Law is not the product of human thought, nor is it any enactment of peoples, but something which rules the whole universe.... Law is the primal and ultimate mind of God." Even in eighteenth-century England, indeed, after centuries of experience with a secularly based common law, we find a similar conception persisting in legal theory. Thus we are told concerning Sir William Blackstone, author of the famous *Commentaries* (1765), that he "regarded divine law as the corner-stone of the whole [legal] edifice," "declared that divine law had been specifically revealed to men through inspired writings," and "sought to make secular law approximate to the dictates of God and of nature."[230]

It should come as no surprise, therefore, that in a country (such as the USA) whose population at least claims to be relatively religious,[231] some connection might be seen between law and religion in general—and a view that religion is somehow centrally important to the country's legal system might be widespread. If we see a strong tendency of this sort in the USA, then we might see an even stronger tendency in certain Islamic countries. Take Iran as an example. There, the influence of religion (Islam) on the legal system is extremely far-reaching, and as one observer has explained, Islamic law is "so

---

230. Derk Bodde and Clarence Morris, Law in Imperial China 8–10 (1967).

231. A recent survey of 35,000 Americans by the Pew Research Center revealed the strength of religious affiliation among the US population: more than half of Americans rank the importance of religion very highly in their lives, attend religious services regularly and pray daily; more than nine in ten Americans (92%) believe in the existence of God or a universal spirit; six in ten believe that God is a person with whom people can have a relationship; roughly seven in ten say they are absolutely certain of God's existence; nearly two-thirds (63%) take the view that their faith's sacred texts are the word of God. Pew Forum on Religion & Public Life, *U.S. Religious Landscape Survey*, available at http://religions.pewforum.org/reports. All these data reveal an important difference between Americans and Europeans, who "generally place much less importance on religion in their lives, and general indicators show that major churches in Europe are declining in terms of membership, recruitment of clergy, financial contributions and overall public influence". Pew Forum on Religion & Public Life, *Secular Europe and Religious America: Implications for Transatlantic Relations* (April 2005), available at http://pewforum.org/events/index.php?EventID=76.

intimately connected with religion that [it (that is, the law)] cannot readily be disseverred from it [*i.e.*, separated from religion].[232] We examined this same phenomenon from a somewhat different angle in section IIB2 of Chapter Three (and in particular Box #3.15).

Another authority elaborates on this point about the intimate connection between Islamic law and religion:

> The fundamental principle of Islam is that of an essentially theocratic society, in which the state is only of value as the servant of revealed religion. Instead of simply proclaiming moral principles or articles of dogma to which Muslim communities would have to make their laws conform, Muslim jurists and theologians have built up a complete and detailed law on the basis of divine revelation.[233]

Iran is hardly alone, of course, in incorporating Islamic principles into its legal system. To varying extents, many countries with heavy Muslim populations do the same, and in those countries religion would seem strongly connected to the legal system. At this very moment, Turkey is the scene of a great contest between those parts of the society who would, and those who would not, end eighty-plus years of secular law and government in favor of a much more robust Islamic system.

This is not the place to evaluate the pros and cons of having a strong connection between law and religion in American, Iranian, Turkish, or any other society. The point here is merely that many—perhaps most—societies throughout history and even today would regard their legal systems as having some connection with religion. One society might consider the connection modest, perhaps taking the form of a non-denominational ceremonial deism; another society might consider the connection extremely strong. But many would see religion as a component of the "ethic" that lies at the heart of the legal system.

Having glanced at the role that religion plays in the American legal system and in certain Islamic-majority countries, let us return now to China. Could we accurately say that any sort of religion lies at the core, the heart, of contemporary Chinese law? Probably not. Throughout dynastic Chinese history, there was no appreciable religious component or origin to law. This point is emphasized by Derk Bodde, whose observations were quoted above regarding the close association that written law had with religion in several *other* major civilizations of antiquity:

> The contrast [between] the Chinese attitude [and the belief in those other major civilizations regarding] a divine origin of the law is indeed striking, for in China *no one at any time has ever hinted that any kind of written law*—even the best written law—*could have had a divine origin.*
>
> ... [Instead,] the ancient Chinese viewed the origins of law [quite differently]....
> A notable feature of Chinese historical and philosophical thinking, apparent already in early times, is its strongly secular tone. In general, it prefers to explain human events in terms of the rational (or what seems to it to be the rational) than

---

232. Asaf A.A. Fyzee, OUTLINES OF MUHAMMADAN LAW 15 (4th ed. 1974). A more recent treatment of the relation between law, religion, and the state confirms this explanation: "The most difficult part of Islamic Law for most westerners to grasp is that there is no separation of church and state. The religion of Islam and the government are one. Islamic Law is controlled, ruled and regulated by the Islamic religion. The theocracy controls all public and private matters. Government, law and religion are one." Denis J. Wiechman, Jerry D. Kendall, and Mohammad K. Azarian http://www.uic.edu/depts/cjus/, *Islamic Law: Myths and Realities*, appearing at http://muslim-canada.org/Islam_myths.htm.

233. Bodde & Morris, *supra* note 230, at 456.

in terms of the supernatural.... When we turn to the legal sphere, therefore, it should not surprise us that here too the atmosphere is secular. What is really arresting, however, especially when we remember the honored status of law in other civilizations, is the overt hostility with which its appearance is initially greeted in China—seemingly not only as a violation of human morality, but perhaps even of the total cosmic order....

An excellent example of this attitude is a story ... providing probably the earliest explanation for the origin of *fa*, written law.... [The story] attributes the invention of *fa* neither to a Chinese sage-king or even to a Chinese at all, but rather to a "barbarian" people, the Miao, [who were] alleged to have flourished during the ... twenty-third century B.C.... [and whose use of law to impose cruel punishments on innocent people prompted] Shang Ti or the "Lord on High" (the supreme god of the ancient Chinese), seeing the resulting disorder among the people ... [to feel] pity for the innocent and hence [he] exterminated the Miao, so that they had no descendents.

In later centuries, when law became more prevalent and the need for its existence became increasingly recognized, ... the origin of law [was still viewed] in strictly secular terms ... [as reflected in this explanation] from the Han empire ...: "Law is not something sent down by Heaven, nor is it something engendered by Earth. It springs from the midst of men themselves."[234]

It is true, as explained above, that Imperial Confucianism did incorporate Daoist influences—these were felt as early as the time of Dong Zhongshu[235] (in the latter part of the 2nd century BCE)—as well as some Buddhist influences, although later and less directly.[236] However, even if Buddhism or Daoism—or, for that matter, Imperial Confucianism itself—were to be regarded as a "religion" at all (as opposed to a philosophy of life), none of them resembles the type of monotheistic religious system from which other societies in the world have often considered law to have emanated. In short, as a historical matter, the Chinese—unlike many other societies—do not have a tradition of seeing religion as being central to law.

Does modern-day China seem different in that respect? Again, probably not. Chinese society today would seem to be so broadly secular[237]—a situation that sixty years of Com-

---

234. *Id.* at 10–15. This account by Bodde—suggesting that law in ancient China, instead of being regarded as having a divine origin, was actually considered so bad as to require divine intervention —is supported also by Randall Peerenboom's account of the connection between law and religion in dynastic China: "The dominant view among specialists in Chinese legal history is that religion exerted only a minimal influence on law in China." Peerenboom-2003, *supra* note 1, at 51.

235. See text accompanying notes 50 and 55 in Chapter Six, above.

236. Buddhism arrived in China largely with the Toba Turks in the late 4th century CE, and "the great age of Buddhism in China [was] from the fifth to the ninth centuries". Fairbank, *supra* note 174, at 73. In exerting influence in China, Buddhism underwent a substantial "sinification". See text accompanying notes 129–130 in Chapter Six, above. Moreover, during its early period of influence, during the Tang Dynasty, Buddhism (like Daoism) was "bureaucratized" in a way that made it (and Daoism) "quite unable to achieve independence from the state". *Id.* at 80–81. Hence "the field of practical action [was left] to the Confucians", although "Buddhism would have its indirect influence later in the amalgam known as Neo-Confucianism". *Id.* at 81. This influence was discussed above; see *supra* note 179 and accompanying text.

237. A recent study by the Pew Research Group found that only "31% of the Chinese public considers religion to be very or somewhat important in their lives", and that only "one-in-five Chinese adults ... say they are religiously affiliated. This would make China one of the least religiously affiliated countries in the world. In the United States, by contrast [as was pointed out in note 231, *supra*], more than eight-in-ten adults (83%) say they are religiously affiliated". Pew Forum on Religion & Public Life,

munist influence greatly facilitated, of course—as to leave no possibility for any religious influence on the legal system, much less any possibility that religion would lie at the core or "heart" of contemporary Chinese law.

5. Other Possibilities

So far we have considered four possible "candidates" for serving in the same sort of role in China's contemporary legal system that Imperial Confucianism served in dynastic China: (1) a new form of Confucianism; (2) the CPC's "Party Line" (Marxist-Leninist-Maoist-Dengist thought); (3) constitutionalism; and (4) religion. None of them, it seems, can properly be regarded as serving that purpose today, even though several of them—especially constitutionalism and a new Confucianism—are championed by some observers as *potential* sources for such a new legal ethic.

Does this mean that there is today *no such key "legal ethic" in China?* Some observers have expressed (or reported) views that can be interpreted as suggesting just that. Stanley Lubman, for example, offers these thoughts about law and political legitimacy in contemporary China:

> Many have exclaimed that China has no law at all, or, as one daughter of a high official said to me, Chinese law is "like a baby that has not grown up yet."...
>
> The leadership has tried unsuccessfully to find further philosophical justification for the continuation of one-party rule beyond simple affirmation of the need for unity and stability.[238]

Even an exceptionally optimistic and cheerful account of contemporary Chinese law, offered in 2007 by Jianfu Chen, a professor at LaTrobe University in Melbourne, concludes with a rather dark and cautionary assessment of what lies at the heart of law in today's China, and of how substantial are the challenges that lie ahead for that country's legal and political system. Chen's article begins with this sanguine, almost sassy, assertion:

> China ... is a transformed, and still rapidly changing society. Never in modern history has China enjoyed such economic prosperity and social stability. Never have the Chinese people felt so confident or has their future looked so promising. And never has China been so outward looking nor has the world paid so much attention to it. People have watched China, largely as bystanders, with amazement, bewilderment, and sometimes dismay.
>
> These continuing changes in China have not just been about economic development. There has been another quiet, peaceful, and largely successful "revolu-

---

Religion in China on the Eve of the 2008 Beijing Olympics (May 2, 2008), available at http://pewforum.org/docs/?DocID=301 (see specifically http://pewforum.org/Importance-of-Religion/Religion-in-China-on-the-Eve-of-the-2008-Beijing-Olympics.aspx).

238. Lubman-1999, *supra* note 1, at 126, 127. In another passage, appearing under the heading "Ideological Vacuum and Lack of Moral Compass", Lubman explains that "[n]o alternative system of belief has appeared to challenge an increasingly hollow Communism, and at this moment China seems to be drifting ideologically." *Id.* at 121. For similar views regarding "moral drift", see Philip P. Pan, OUT OF MAO'S SHADOW: THE STRUGGLE FOR THE SOUL OF A NEW CHINA (2008), quoted in Michiko Kakutani, *Dipatches from Capitalist China*, NEW YORK TIMES, July 15, 2008, at B1 (quoting Pan's reference to profound problems he sees in today's China: "the stifling limits on political and religious freedoms, the abuse of power by privileged officials, the sweatshop conditions in the factories, the persistent poverty in the countryside, the degradation of the environment, the moral drift of a cynical society").

tion" in the area of law, whose deficiencies have been more often mercilessly examined and documented than its historical achievements and significance.[239]

Jianfu Chen then proceeds to do just that—to document the historical achievements of Chinese law over the past few decades. Much of his account records efforts—some quickly successful, some slower in their results—to throw off outmoded or inappropriate legal ideologies and constraints. These include the efforts to escape the collapsing dynastic legal system at the turn of the 20th century,[240] the mid-century efforts to abandon the backwardness of Western law in favor of "a Marxist concept of law as being a tool to remould the society and to suppress class enemies",[241] the later efforts to move away from the Maoist extremism to a more moderate approach in which law's role is to provide "a social order conducive to economic development",[242] and the most recent efforts to "throw[] off the ideological shackles of the Soviet [instrumentalist and policy-based] conception of law in China".[243]

Chen's article closes, however, with an acknowledgment that "the present law and legal system are not without some serious problems", among which is that "Chinese law has become less Chinese than ever before, both in its form and [in its] substance".[244] He bemoans the fact that in its rush to make Chinese law more "Western", lawmakers in China have adopted foreign laws without trying to understand the context in which those foreign laws were created and implemented, and how they must be modified to fit into the very different context of China. "Too often", Chen writes, "local [Chinese] customary law and practice are dismissed as being "backwards" or "old and bad habits", ... but too few have bothered to explains the reasons for their existence"[245]—and therefore what disadvantage or danger might come from simply discarding and replacing them.

This fundamental problem that Jianfu Chen has identified—the precipitous pitching-out of old legal rules and concepts in favor of new ones from foreign legal cultures, and thereby creating a new legal landscape that is unfamiliar and therefore unsuited for China—seems closely related to a second fundamental problem that Chen identifies. That problem is the mismatch between rules and reality:

> Law-in-the-books is not necessarily the same as law-in-action. Herein lies the most glaring failure in modern legal development in China. The problems in this area are not minor, but massive and deeply rooted in the fundamental politico-economic system of China. Legal scholars have no difficulty in identifying a large number of fundamental problems existing in institutions and in performance by power bearers. These problems have been summarised in terms of some fundamental contradictions in the Chinese politico-legal system and its practice.... The tremendous difficulties experienced by Chinese courts in enforcing court judgements [*sic*] or decisions are but one example of the limitations on fundamental political reform that cannot be initiated by the judiciary or carried out without authorisation from the Party. The root of these problems is power, or more precisely, the lack of checks

---

239. Jianfu Chen, *supra* note 1, at 689–690.
240. *Id.* at 713–715.
241. *Id.* at 716.
242. *Id.* at 718.
243. *Id.* at 723. Here Jianfu Chen describes the transition from a piecemeal approach of policy initiatives taken by the government to a legitimate legal reform effort focusing on rights, so that "people [would] be liberated from constraints imposed by traditional duties, status and dictatorship". *Id.*
244. *Id.* at 736.
245. *Id.* at 737.

and balances of powers—a problem described by a Chinese economist as the "privatisation of public powers." If law cannot be independently enforced, as one Chinese scholar has noted, it is doubtful whether it is important to have law at all.[246]

Not until such fundamental problems as these are solved, Chen asserts, can the ongoing "transformation of law [in China] ... finally make Chinese law Chinese".[247]

This might strike some observers as a deeply troubling picture. What Jianfu Chen has written provides some confirmation of what we have found thus far in our search for a modern correlative to Imperial Confucianism, and therefore for the key ethic, the soul, of contemporary Chinese law. It is not clear that there is a popular consensus within China regarding any one of what would seem to be the most obvious "competitors" or "candidates" for serving as such a key legal ethic. In other words, if we ask "what is the new legal ethic in China?", none of those candidates—neither a new Confucianism, nor the CPC Party Line, nor constitutionalism, nor religion—appears to supply a persuasive answer.

If that is true, it suggests one of two conclusions. Either (1) there is no effective, broadly-accepted legal ethic *at all* at work today in China or, alternatively, (2) the content of such a new Chinese legal ethic is to be found elsewhere, in some ideology or set of values *other* than the ones we have examined above. Perhaps it is impossible at this point to know for sure which of these two conclusions is correct.

However, if the first of those possible conclusions is true—that is, if there is in fact no operative ethic at the heart of the contemporary Chinese legal system—this might be grounds for serious concern. Of course, we should bear in mind that even if contemporary China has undergone such wrenching changes in recent times that it now has *no* effective central legal ethic, that certainly does not make China unique in the world. The international community has numerous states whose legal systems are partially incomplete or immature or ineffective in any number of ways and for any number of reasons. Many, like China, have suffered degradation and ignominy at the hands of foreign powers, mainly Western powers, and some still suffer today under a range of heavy burdens—war, scarce resources, disease, and more. Other states, including some that emerged from the former Soviet empire, have struggled to overcome political and economic instability of daunting proportion. Such circumstances as these have made it impossible to create and sustain a workable legal system, founded on popular consensus about what lies at the heart of such a legal system, in scores of countries around the world.[248]

China, however, is different from other countries. It has been, currently is, and surely will continue to be one of the most important countries in the world. Hence, if it is true that China does not have a central legal ethic, this is cause for especially

---

246. *Id.* at 738.

247. *Id.*

248. Indeed, we might speculate that some countries that arguably *do* have workable legal systems today—based on a national legal ethic—might soon find this situation changing as time dilutes the sense of identity that new generations have with that national legal ethic. If so, the number of countries lacking a central legal ethic will increase over time. According to some observers, much of the world *already* lacks any legal ethic. For example, Vaclav Havel, the great Czech playwright and former Czech president, recently expressed his deep concern over the "rampant consumerism" and "anti-spirituality" that he sees in humanity today: "I get the sense that we are the first civilisation in the history of mankind ... [for which] [h]uman existence ... isn't metaphysically anchored in any way in a code of *moral* conduct, from which we could then derive a *legal* code." Stefan Wagstyl, *The Playwright Who Became President*, FINANCIAL TIMES, July 5–6, 2008, at 3 (emphasis added).

serious concern. Without broad consensus in a society about the core values that give energy and legitimacy to its legal system, that legal system can be hijacked by a persuasive dictatorship. Surely China, of all countries, hardly needs to be reminded of that danger.

Even beyond the dangers that could face *China* if it lacks a broad consensus about the core legal values are the dangers that could face the *rest* of the world if China lacks such a consensus. Some observers have asserted that China's surging economy and power create a "contested modernity"—that is, a competition (we might even say a fundamental disagreement) over what constitutes modernity in today's world. Martin Jacques suggests that although the dominant position achieved by western countries over the last several hundred years might make us assume that the West essentially defines modernity, this assumption might be completely false, since the specific reasons for the growth of western influence are probably (in his view) "relatively short-term factors rather than preordained" and universal factors.[249] Jacques explains his views in a series of paragraphs that I have drawn from several passages early in his book *When China Rules the World*:

> Europe was the birthplace of modernity. As its tentacles stretched around the globe during the course of the two centuries after 1750, so its ideas, institutions, values, religion, languages, ideologies, customs and armies left a huge and indelible imprint on the rest of the world. Modernity and Europe became inseparable, seemingly fused ... But though modernity was conceived in Europe, there is nothing intrinsically European about it: apart from an accident of birth it [*i.e.,* modernity] had, and has, no special connection to that continent and its civilization. Over the last half-century, as modernity has taken root in East Asia, it has drawn on the experience of European—or more precisely, Western—modernity. However, rather than simply being clones of it, East Asian modernities are highly distinctive, spawning institutions, customs, values and ideologies shaped by their own histories and cultures.

> [Accordingly, we need to regard modernity differently.] Far from Europe being the template of modernity which every subsequent transformation should conform to and be measured by, the European experience must be regarded — notwithstanding the fact that it was the first—as highly specific and particular.

> ... [That is,] Europe's journey to and through modernity took highly specific and unique forms—[most importantly] the relative absence of an external threat, colonialism, the preponderance of industry, relatively slow growth, a pattern of intra-European conflict..., and individualism.... Since Europe has enjoyed such a huge influence on the rest of the world, ... distinguishing between the specific [reasons for growing power] and the universal [reasons] is often difficult and elusive. Europeans, unsurprisingly, have long believed that what they have achieved must be of universal application, by force if necessary. It is only with the rise of a new range of modernities [—and particularly that of China—] that it is becoming possible to distinguish between what is universal and what is specific about the European experience.

> The West has shaped the world we live in. Even now, with signs of a growing challenge from China, the West remains the dominant geopolitical and cultural force. Such has been the extent of Western influence that it is impossible to think of the world without it, or imagine what the world would have been like if it

---

249. Martin Jacques, WHEN CHINA RULES THE WORLD 30 (2009).

had never happened. We have come to take Western hegemony for granted. It is so deeply rooted, so ubiquitous, that we think of it as somehow natural. The historian J.M. Roberts wrote, in a somewhat triumphalist vein: 'What seems to be clear is that the story of western civilisation is now the story of mankind, its influence so diffused that old oppositions and antitheses are now meaningless.' Not quite. Western hegemony is neither a product of nature nor is it eternal. On the contrary, at some point it will come to an end.[250]

One might justifiably say that Western hegemony has already come to an end. In any event, though, China's influence in the world—and the potential for its growing influence—is surely beyond question. What is also beyond question is that China's culture rests on foundations that differ radically from those underlying Western culture. We could fairly easily identify the core legal values—the "legal soul"—of most Western countries in whose hands most of the hegemonic power of recent decades and centuries has rested. By the same token, it is easy to *imagine* a China that also has a clearly recognizable core to its legal system—a "legal soul". However, reality does not match that imagination. That is, the survey we have undertaken in the preceding paragraphs has *not* revealed the content of such a "legal soul" for China. If, as Jacques and others have surmised, the arrival of China on the stage of world power amounts to the arrival of a new modernity, it would seem discomforting—one might even say dangerous—if China is conflicted about just what comprises its "legal soul".

C. Modern China's Legal Identity

Whether there is or is not a central "legal ethic" or "legal soul" in contemporary China, we certainly can identify certain key *features* that help define modern China from a legal perspective. In completing our survey of Chinese law, let us consider what fits within that package of features, taking into account the various observations made so far in this chapter and in Chapter Six.

In doing so, we might focus on six features that seem especially important to modern China's legal identity.[251] I list those six features[252] in Box #7.9, and in the text that follows I offer some brief observations about each of them, in reverse order.

> ### Box #7.9 Important Features of the Contemporary Chinese Legal Identity
>
> *Materialist Orientation.* An overriding orientation toward individual generation of personal wealth and toward substantial and sustained national economic expansion.
>
> *Legitimacy.* An insistence that the legal and political system have formal internal integrity so that political power is exercised in accordance with constitutional provisions.

---

250. *Id.* at 21–22, 32, 35–36, 45.

251. It undoubtedly has other features also. If we define "legal identity" broadly, to encompass all of a society's law and legal tradition—including its age, its degree of sophistication, its scope of coverage in terms of both population and geographic reach, its legal ethic (if there is one), its aspirations and attitudes, and whether or not it adheres to the "rule of law" in some form—then the six features highlighted here would be supplemented with several others discussed earlier.

252. In another context, I have noted that these six features can be formed into an acronym—MOLECARP. For a further explanation, along with an image of an odd (and imaginary) creature combining the attributes of a mole and a carp (a sort of fish), see the closing pages of John W. Head, CHINA'S LEGAL SOUL (2009).

> *Extrovertism.* An outward-looking disposition (as a reversal of many centuries of looking inward) in order to gain from the rest of the world and to play an influential role in international affairs.
>
> *China-Appropriateness.* An insistence on guarding against allowing external values or interests to operate within China unless they are in fact compatible with Chinese values and interests.
>
> *Restoration.* A determination to restore China to a place of greatness in the world, after a roughly 150-year period of distressing and embarrassing subjugation.
>
> *Progressivism.* A dedication to rapid forward movement to transform China into a society that is modern and that meets all important international standards.

1. Progressivism

China today is a country in transformation. The upbeat remarks quoted above from Jianfu Chen about China's recent developments[253] ring true: Chinese society is rushing forward enthusiastically into a new day. There is a vibrant, fresh, future-oriented outlook that shows up in technology,[254] education,[255] English language studies,[256] and many other ways. As stated in the Chinese Constitution, "the Chinese people ... [will] work hard and self-reliantly to modernize industry, agriculture, national defense and science and technology step by step to turn China into a socialist country with a high level of culture and democracy".[257] These aims—they are aims of progressivism—might well be seen as forming part of the overall legal identity that characterizes contemporary Chinese law.

From a legal perspective, this progressivism manifests itself in the impressive body of legislation adopted in China in recent years. Details appeared above in Chapter Six (especially in Box #6.13), along with the explanation of how a major emphasis in the legislative productivity has been economic in nature.

Progressivism is far different, however, from *revolution*. The sentiment expressed by Wang Zhoujun of Suzhou University—urging patience in developing a strong constitutionalism in China, like "feeling the stones when crossing the river"[258]—is probably shared by many Chinese. So disastrous have been the consequences of revolutionary changes in the past century, especially the Cultural Revolution from the mid-1960s to the mid-1970s, that the sense of urgency for a brighter future is tempered by a patience borne of experience.

---

253. See text accompanying note 239, *supra*.

254. See, e.g., David Lague, *Chinese Submarine Fleet Growing, Analysts Say*, THE NEW YORK TIMES, Feb. 25, 2008, at A10 (surveying China's technological progress in a variety of fields).

255. See, e.g., *Learn from Others*, CHINA DAILY, Dec. 12, 2006 (noting the significant number of Chinese students studying abroad and the knowledge gained from studying in advanced countries). See also *Carrot Tactics to Lure the Talented*, CHINA DAILY, Mar. 31, 2007 (examining the trend in which greater numbers of foreign-educated Chinese returning to China and the governmental incentives provided to encourage talented graduates to return to China).

256. See, e.g., Evan Osnos, *Crazy English: The National Scramble to Learn a New Language Before the Olympics*, 84 THE NEW YORKER, at 44 (April 28, 2008) (describing, as one of many efforts made by the Chinese government and by Chinese individuals to improve English-language skills, a system of instruction that involves instructors shouting English phrases to students to help them learn the language).

257. PRC 1982 Constitution, paragraph 7 of Preamble.

258. See subsections IC2b and IVB3, *supra*, in this chapter.

2. Restoration

We can also see in today's China an intense determination to restore China to the position of greatness that it once enjoyed. Viewed from the perspective of only the last century or two, perhaps China does not evoke for many westerners an image of greatness. My mother, for example, growing up in the 1930s, had an impression of a China that was pitiable for its poverty and disorganization. And yet the glories of China's past — its art, its inventiveness, its governmental effectiveness, its treasures — rivaled those of any of the greatest societies the world has known. These glories could be enjoyed, of course, only by those few Chinese who were fortunate enough to live in privilege — that is, the glories meant little to the vast bulk of the common people — but in that respect China was no different from most other societies throughout history.

In today's world, China stands alone among the great *former* great empires of the past in its opportunity to restore itself to its former glory. Which of the modern-day vestiges of other great empires can say the same — Egypt? Greece? Rome? Russia? Of course not. China is unique in this respect, and this opportunity for restoration to greatness seems uppermost in the minds of many Chinese. The taste of restoration will be especially sweet, of course, given the century or so of especially distressing subjugation that China suffered before reclaiming its independence in 1949.

As we saw earlier, this urge for restoration generally does *not* appear in the realm of law — although perhaps an exception may be found in some writings by Chinese legal experts who offer reminders of the elegance, morality, and effectiveness of the dynastic legal order. Ma Xiaohong and Albert Chen, for example, both express an almost sentimental nostalgia for *lǐ* as an organizing force for harmony in the traditional Chinese legal system.[259]

3. China-Appropriateness

The specific contours of China's approximately 150-year period of especially embarrassing subjugation might be seen to have caused the Chinese people to place an extremely high value on ensuring that the *restorative progressivism* described above is culturally appropriate to China. As noted above in Chapter Six, China lived under "alien dynasties" for over half of the last six hundred years of its dynastic period. Even so, neither the Yüan nor the Qing rulers succeeded in introducing into China many foreign influences. Instead, the Yüan and the Qing rulers themselves underwent rather thorough "sinification" (indeed, the Qing rulers generally did so quite willingly). The story was different, however, during the period in which China essentially shared its sovereignty with several foreign powers. Under the guise of the "extraterritorial privileges" described above in Chapter Six, China was in a sense carved up and subjected to several tides of foreign influence. Moreover, in the political and legal chaos that followed the collapse of the Qing Dynasty in 1911, exposure to — indeed, embrace of — foreign ideas and ideologies intensified.

That ended, for the most part, in 1949. Aside from the partial embrace for some years of Soviet models and ideologies, the course that China has set for itself in the past several decades has been consciously China-specific in content. As suggested is Chapter Six, when considering western and other foreign influences of a legal nature, China has typically shown a wariness that results in either a rejection or an extensive "filtering" of foreign ideas. Perhaps for this reason Randall Peerenboom's classification of different "thick"

---

259. See generally Ma Xiaohong, *supra* note 2, and text accompanying notes 194 and 220, *supra*.

versions of the rule of law—with the liberal democratic version being only one of several—will prove appealing to Chinese intellectuals because it tends to vindicate the Chinese claim of "Asian values" or "Chinese values".[260] In a similar sense, the seemingly vapid phrase "the road of Chinese-style socialism" (as introduced in the Fourth Amendment to the PRC Constitution) gains some substance.

Taken together, perhaps the two characteristics just discussed—"restoration" and "China-appropriateness"—can help explain the intense nationalistic fervor that now seems to be at work in Chinese society. What are the most high-profile and incendiary issues of recent years as China adjusts its place in the world? Hong Kong, Taiwan, Tibet, the Olympics, the US bombing of Chinese diplomatic facilities in Belgrade,[261] the alleged intrusion into Chinese territory of a US surveillance aircraft,[262] and so forth. Many of the issues revolve around sovereignty and national pride.

4. Extroversion

In embracing *Chinese-appropriate restorative progressivism* as a cluster of shared core attitudes—both as a legal matter and more broadly—the Chinese government and people seem to have shed their centuries-old introversion. The degree of haughty, egotistic arrogance exhibited by numerous Chinese emperors—as masterfully described by Harry Gelber in his recent book on China's relations to the outside world[263]—makes for amusing stories now, but it came at a numbingly high price. While China was resting on its laurels, the nation-states of the West were pushing their way through the great adventures

---

260. Stanley Lubman gives special emphasis to one sort of "Chinese value"—that of interpersonal relations, or *guanxi*. He offers these critical observations:

> A striking characteristic of Chinese legal culture has been the primacy of interpersonal relations over legal relationships. This is not only a theme that has been echoed in research [and practical experience].... It would be wrong to draw too strong a contrast between Westerners who conceive of their business relationships in terms of legal rights and duties and Chinese who are concerned only with personal qualities and relationships.... Nonetheless, the Chinese emphasis on relationships (*guanxi*) seems to have had a strength and durability for thousands of years that make it more powerful and pervasive than comparable Western emphases [and therefore] ... no assessment of Chinese law should fail to weigh heavily the interaction between law and traditional forms of *guanxi* and its modern manifestations.... [Among other things, the traditional value placed on *guanxi* is deeply significant because it] presents a considerable obstacle to the deepening of legal consciousness and the strengthening of legal institutions.

Lubman-1999, *supra* note 1, at 304. It would seem, then, that this sort of "Chinese value" might be serving to impede, not facilitate, a legal progressivism, at least in the eyes foreigners. For other comments on the role of *guanxi* in Chinese law and business, see *supra* notes 88–89.

261. On May 7, 1999, a NATO plane bombed the Chinese embassy in Belgrade. Three people died and at least twenty were injured in the attack. NATO released a statement claiming that the bombing of the embassy was a regrettable mistake. China responded with a strong condemnation of the attack and called for an end to the bombing in Yugoslavia. Several thousand Chinese protestors gathered outside the US embassy in Beijing, during which they became violent, throwing gas bombs and rocks. *See* http://www.cnn.com/WORLD/europe/9905/10/kosovo.01/#1 and http://www.cnn.com/WORLD/europe/9905/08/kosovo.01/.

262. In mid-2001, a US surveillance plane made an emergency landing in China after it went through a mid-air collision with a Chinese fighter plane. The 24-member U.S. crew was held in Chinese custody for eleven days, but the plane was not returned until more than three months after the incident. See United Press International, *Spy Plane Returns to U.S. for Assessment*, July 5, 2001.

263. See generally Harry G. Gelber, THE DRAGON AND THE FOREIGN DEVILS: CHINA AND THE WORLD, 1100 BC TO THE PRESENT (2007). See also text accompanying notes 137–138 in Chapter Six, above.

and struggles of political and ideological chaos, ocean exploration, religious battles, the scientific and industrial revolutions, and other episodes that allowed those countries to overwhelm China in military, economic, and even cultural terms. A more contemporary reminder of that, as if any such reminder were necessary, came in the form of Mao's foolish Great Leap Forward program, in which much of the Chinese population was evidently hoodwinked into believing that sheer willpower, without relying on technical and scientific knowledge available from the outside world, could propel China into modernity.[264]

It would seem that today's Chinese society, intent on avoiding any repeat of this history, now places great value on extroversion—and not just to learn from external sources but also to play a role on the world stage that is commensurate with its newly-reclaimed greatness. Unlike the situation thirty years ago, for example, the PRC now has a seat at the United Nations, the World Bank, the International Monetary Fund, the Asian Development Bank, and other international organizations. It has become party to scores of international treaties, and it has officially recognized the superiority of those treaties over domestic law.[265] More broadly, it recognizes that, as expressed in the PRC Constitution, "[t]he future of China is closely linked with that of the whole world ... [and] China ... works to strengthen unity with the people of other countries ... and strives to safeguard world peace and promote the cause of human progress".[266] These aims seem to constitute part of the overall legal identity of contemporary China.

5. Legitimacy

Whatever difficulties there might be (as explored above in the first section of this chapter) in distinguishing between "rule of law" and "rule by law"—and in determining which of these best characterizes the reality or even the goals in today's China—there is no such difficulty in distinguishing either of those from "rule of man". Following the disastrous Cultural Revolution—and indeed the terrible times that emerged time and again throughout Mao's dictatorial leadership—a consensus emerged in China that certain safeguards simply must be put in place to prevent a single person or an oligarchy from using the country's law as an instrument of personal power and aggrandizement. In short, legitimacy must be ensured in the exercise of state power.

An illustration of how this shift in attitude was signaled appeared earlier in this chapter, where Deng Xiaoping was quoted as telling the top CPC leadership in 1978 that "various mistakes in the past were closely related to some leaders'... working styles," and that "[e]ven a man as great as Mao Zedong was seriously influenced by corrupt systems", and that in order to avoid this in future, "a sound legal system must be strengthened, democracy must be institutionalised and legalised so that the system and laws won't change just because of a change in leadership or just because of changes in the leaders' ideas."[267]

---

264. For a synopsis of the Great Leap Forward, which killed some twenty to thirty million people from 1958 to 1960, see Box #6.12 in Chapter Six, above.

265. See Zhang Wenxian, *supra* note 2, at 484 (quoting the Administrative Procedural Law for the proposition that "[i]f an international treaty concluded or acceded [to] by the People's Republic of China contains provisions different from those found in this Law, the provisions of the international treaty shall apply, unless the provisions are ones on which the People's Republic of China has announced reservations"). Zhang Wenxian goes on to assert that "modernization and globalization are just two sides of the same coin". *Id.* at 485.

266. PRC 1982 Constitution, paragraph 12 of Preamble.

267. See *supra* note 210 and accompanying text.

As a legal matter, therefore, policy, party, and personality all were made subordinate to law—at least on paper—in the intricate provisions of the PRC 1982 Constitution that separated the CPC from direct law-making authority, while still guaranteeing to the CPC a central place of influence over the selection of persons who *would* have the direct authority in framing and enacting that legislation.[268] This requirement that there be some institutional legitimacy and integrity, and that the CPC would work within that institutional system, might also constitute a part of the "package" of content for the modern Chinese legal identity.

6. Materialist Orientation

When I began teaching business law in Beijing under a Fulbright fellowship in 1994, I asked students in my class to write a couple of sentences saying why they wanted to study this subject. To my surprise, several of them said that it was because Deng Xiaoping had said it was acceptable—and indeed consistent with *China's* national interest—that individuals look after *their own* interest by working to gain personal wealth.[269] Many US law students, of course, also have an eye on gaining personal wealth for themselves, but they would seldom express that interest as bluntly as did my Chinese students. Now, nearly 20 years later, might it be that some people in China despair because so many of their fellow Chinese seem to have the accumulation of material wealth as a central, all-consuming goal in life—and, more importantly, that so Chinese think that the main purpose of the government and of the legal system to facilitate the generation of wealth?[270]

If so, we might regard the first and last features under discussion—that is, "materialist orientation" and "progressivism"—as particularly important in describing the modern Chinese legal identity. That is, we might see at work in China today a materialist-oriented progressivism under which the key claim that the CPC-dominated government can make to the loyalty of Chinese society is the CPC's effectiveness in delivering financial success, both at the national level and at the personal level.[271]

In his masterful book *Bird in a Cage*, Stanley Lubman makes two specific points that bear on these issues, and more generally on a search for the modern Chinese legal identity. The first of Lubman's points coincides with the observations I have just made about the materialistic orientation of contemporary Chinese society. Under the heading of "The Frayed Chinese Social Fabric", Lubman writes this:

---

268. For a description of these arrangements, see the early passages in subsection IB3 of this chapter.

269. As one observer has explained, in the early 1980s "[t]he slogan 'To get rich is glorious' was coined". J.A.G. Roberts, A Concise History of China 289–290 (1999).

270. For illustrations of the interest being shown in China in recent years on the accumulation of personal wealth, see *Far East Prosperity a Boost to Rolls-Royce*, The Portsmouth Evening News, April 22, 2008 (noting the increase in sales of Rolls-Royce cars China, due to increased personal wealth and the car's position as a status symbol); *More Millionaires as Nation Gets Wealthier*, Business Daily Update, November 29, 2007 (describing a huge increase in the number of millionaires and billionaires within China); and *School Kids in Need of More Sleep*, Business Daily Update, March 19, 2007 (noting the long hours that many Chinese students spend studying and quoting a Chinese parent as saying that "if you give your child a happy childhood in China, you give him a failed adulthood" in terms of his ability to gain personal wealth and professional success).

271. Sounding a similar theme, one authority asserts that "the development of law in modern China has been directed to achieving the two goals of (1) safeguarding the nation against chaos through maintaining social control and (2) developing commerce, trade, and foreign investment. Chow, *supra* note 1, at 63. For a similar view, see Peerenboom-2003, *supra* note 1, at 54 (asserting that in seeking a base of legitimacy, "[n]owadays, the ruling regime relies primarily on appeals to economic growth and self-interest (in particular the material interests of citizens in a higher standard of living)").

One of the most dramatic changes in Chinese life is the new importance of wealth as a key to social status, which is an extraordinary reversal of Maoist egalitarianism. Many Chinese perceive that others are more blessed with material goods and economic opportunity than they, and the growth of "red-eye disease" (jealousy) has been much discussed in the Chinese media and noticed by foreign observers. The sudden importance of wealth has upset the long-held and widely-shared perceptions of many Chinese about how society should be organized. Traditional Chinese society was hierarchical, and social stability was deemed to depend on all knowing their place. China under Mao was also hierarchical, although categories of rank and status were politicized. Economic reform has totally upset former hierarchical orderings of society, causing alienation and anxiety. Older persons, for example, who sacrificed much, willingly or otherwise, to build and maintain socialism in China now see individualistic young people making fortunes without expecting to bear responsibilities toward the state.[272]

A second point in Lubman's book has a wider orbit. Lubman asserts that "China is presently undergoing a crisis of belief in an ideology that has become irrelevant and in a Party whose legitimacy is in doubt".[273] We explored that topic in section IVB of this chapter, and I suggested the conclusions not only (i) that the old ideology—that is, the CPC Party Line—has become irrelevant to most Chinese, but also (ii) that no other ideology of the sort that would seem most likely to be capable of replacing it (for example, some modified form of Confucianism, or the rule of law, or constitutionalism, or religion) has evidently done so. Materialism, after all, is not an ideology; nor is it an "ethic" of the sort we have been searching for in this chapter—in the way that Imperial Confucianism provided a legal ethic standing at the core of Chinese dynastic law. Nor, for that matter, would any of the elements that described above—legitimacy, extroversion, China-appropriateness, or even progressivism—qualify as an ideology or as an ethic. Each of these is more in the nature of a tendency or an orientation or an attitude than "a set of doctrines or beliefs that form the basis of a political, economic, or other system" (a working definition of "ideology") or "a set of principles of right conduct" or "a theory or a system of moral values" (two working definitions of an "ethic" in general).

V. Closing Observations

We have not exhausted the subjects of this book—the three great legal traditions—but we have exhausted the time and effort we can reasonably devote now to this broad sur-

---

272. Lubman-1999, *supra* note 1, at 120. We might see Lubman's views on this matter, expressed a decade ago (his book was published in 1999), being confirmed by reports of the sort cited in the preceding footnote and by my own personal interviews with thoughtful and forthcoming Chinese individuals. For example, in extended conversations with a law professor at the University of Hong Kong, I heard personal opinions that accorded with Lubman's views. When I asked what the central motivating force or value is in Chinese society today, the professor said it is personal material gain, facilitated by capitalist-oriented policies and fueled by greed. Similar views were expressed by others, including a university law professor in Beijing and a faculty member of a business school in Hong Kong, who claimed to be reflecting widespread opinion among intellectuals in China.

273. Lubman-1999, *supra* note1, at 3. This comment is in keeping with others Lubman makes about ideological drift and uncertain political legitimacy. See *supra* notes 233 and 267 and accompanying text.

vey of those subjects. In these final paragraphs, let us consider some issues that invite us to view those three great legal traditions from a "comparative distance". About half of this chapter, focusing on the Chinese legal tradition in operational perspective, has examined aspects of contemporary Chinese law "on the surface", such as the categories of law, the role of judges, the influence of the CPC, the status of the constitution, and the intricacies of criminal procedure. The other half of this chapter has looked "below the surface" in an effort to discern underlying features that make Chinese law distinctive.

How might we look "below the surface" in other legal systems to discern underlying features that make them distinctive? I offered some speculations earlier in this section (especially in section IVB3a) about the central "legal ethic" or "legal soul" of the USA. My speculation there revolved around a package of features I called the "American Constitutional Ethic". What similar package of features might comprise the core "legal ethic" or "legal soul" of Italy, or of Germany, or of England, or of Japan?

We cannot formulate full answers such large questions in these final pages of the book, of course, but our exposure to the three great legal *traditions*—and our understanding now of the meaning and significance of a legal tradition in the abstract—can enable us at least to visualize what types of inquiries we would undertake to search for the "legal soul" of a particular legal *system*. The inquiries would surely include these:

(1) How well-rooted a *history* does the current legal system have, and what are the main contours of that history?

(2) To what extent does the content of the current legal system reflect the *values* of the people in the society to which it relates—and what are those values?

(3) What degree of *homogeneity* exists within the society in terms of history, ethnicity, ideology, and religion—and what is the relationship, in particular, between the dominant religion (if any) and law?

(4) How clear and compelling a *narrative* (whether accurate or not) does the society have about its legal system?

(5) What degree of *technical sophistication* does the legal system have in terms of its specific rules, institutions, and procedures? (Codification would figure into this assessment.)

(6) What is the dominant view within the society of its own *future trajectory*, and the role (if any) that law will make in continuing that trajectory?

(7) More generally, *how important is law* in the minds of the members of the society, in terms of handling disputes, living life, and defining one's identity?

Our introduction in Chapters Two and Three to some aspects of a few legal systems in Europe—for example, those of Germany, Italy, and France—would allow us to formulate some answers to these seven questions when applied to those countries. We might, for instance, assert that in each of those countries, the current legal system is very deeply rooted in history, with a narrative that is quite clear and compelling—more so than would be the case for many non-European countries—and that the legal system has a very high degree of technical sophistication, contributed to by rich experiences in legal codification. Our answers, however, to items (2) and (3) might be less clear, since each of those three countries is now undergoing a change in ethnic composition—with in recent influx, for example, Turks in Germany and Africans of various nationalities and ethnicities in France and Italy. Maybe one reason our survey of possible answers to the question of "what is the legal soul of China" was inconclusive (and perhaps troubling) is that the answers to items (1), (4), (6), and (7) are unclear as applied to modern Chinese society. And we might speculate that the presence of a "legal soul" in the USA derives largely from the clear answers we could give—today, at least—to the questions in items (1), (2), (4), and (7) as applied to that country.

All of this is speculative and not worth spending too much time contemplating. What probably *is* worth contemplating, however, is a pair of concluding propositions.

The first concluding proposition, rather dark in nature, concerns the pace of change within all societies around the world. All countries—whether they are predominantly influenced by the civil law tradition, the common law tradition, or the Chinese legal tradition—are now experiencing change that is occurring extremely quickly. Even in those countries that have long histories and that currently enjoy stable legal and political systems, that fast pace of change might make it increasingly difficult to say with respect to *any* legal system just what lies at its core. In other words, the worrisome uncertainty that I have expressed above about China's "legal soul" might, before long, apply even to such countries as England France, Italy, and Germany—the main birthplaces of the common law and civil law—and indeed to the USA as well.

The second concluding proposition is brighter in nature, and it focuses on tradition—the very topic with which we embarked on our comparative study of law at the beginning of Chapter One. As suggested there, the concept of tradition involves notions of memory and self-identity, and it provides a foundation—a place to stand—in charting a future path in response to change and then continuing the journey that the tradition describes. Viewing the concept of a tradition in this manner provides grounds for optimsim. As the surveys of civil law, common law, and Chinese law have shown, each has a rich, fascinating, and enduring tradition that can help various legal systems and societies around the world, and perhaps the global society itself, meet the challenges of change. This can be the case, of course, only if we *know those traditions*. Perhaps the survey provided in this book helps us do that.

Appendix 7.1
A Sampling of Rule-of-Law Definitions

*The following array of definitions and descriptions of the "rule of law" emerges from a survey of recent literature—mainly as appearing in books and on websites (excerpts from books appear first, then excerpts from articles or postings on websites). Although the sources for these accounts are cited, what is more important than **who** has expressed the specific views summarized below is the broad variety in **what** views have been expressed on this topic. Some key elements appearing below have been distilled into the substance of Box #7.1 in the main text of Chapter Seven—and from that substance in Box #7.1 I have fashioned my own short rough-and-ready definition of "rule of law" as applied in this book.*

* * *

Robin L. West, Re-Imagining Justice: Progressive Interpretations of Formal Equality, Rights, and the Rule of Law (2003), at 4–5.

"Rule of law is to shield, or protect, both the individual and the community from the brunt of overly personally, tyrannical, whimsical, or brutal or 'naked' politics. The Rule of Law on this vision distinguishes legality from tyranny, distinguishes the orderly and benign control of the social behavior of free men by rules from the whimsical (or worse) command over individuals by unchecked and unduly personal authority. Law is power's antidote. Law is the antithesis of politics; law constrains, counters, and cabins politics. We organize authority in lawful forms so as to emasculate particular power holders or seekers; we establish law to frustrate the will to power. Law, and the Rule of Law, is that which protects individual freedom from political overreach, unites and perhaps partly explains a good deal of contemporary constitutional law."

* * *

T.R.S. Allan, Constitutional Justice: The Liberal Theory of the Rule of Law (2001), at 2–3.

"It is chiefly the combination of the principles of due process and equality that enables the rule of law to be properly characterized as a 'rule of reason': they amount to a basic requirement of justification, or condition of legitimacy, whereby the legality of a person's treatment, at the hands of the state, depends on its being shown to serve a defensible view of the common good (broadly understood to mean for the good of a community whose members are accorded equal respect and dignity, according to some rational account of their collective well-being). It is not sufficient for laws or government policies to be accurately applied to particular persons, in accordance with their true meaning or proper interpretation; the associated distinctions made between persons, or groups of persons, must also be capable of justification ... The principle of separation of powers enables the law to serve as a bulwark between governors and governed, excluding the exercise of arbitrary power. When the executive government must act within the constraints of general rules, formulated by the legislature without regard to the details of specific cases or the character of particular persons, a basic equality of treatment is ensured."

* * *

Luigi Ferrajoli, The Past and the Future of the Rule of Law, appearing as Chapter 8 in The Rule of Law: History, Theory, and Criticism (2007), at 323, 355.

Rule of law, in the "broadest sense ... means any legal system in which public powers are conferred by law and wielded in the forms and by means of the procedures the law prescribes ... In the second, strong and substantive sense, "rule of law" instead stands only for those systems in which public powers are also subject (and hence limited or constrained by) law not only in their form, but also in the content of their decision. In this meaning, prevalent in continental Europe, the phrase denotes legal and political systems in which all powers, including legislative power, are constrained by substantive principles normally provided for by the constitution, such as the separation of powers and fundamental rights" [p. 323]

"If we also turn our attention to the twentieth-century concept of constitutional democracy, we find three ideas underpinning the theory of the 'Rechtsstaat' (or the Rule of Law) incorporated within in: 1) the law gives shape to and in doing so limits state powers—the *pouvoirs constitutes*; 2) legal sovereignty is exercised according to the model of the government by law, hence the principle of "statutory reservation" becomes the central tenet of the classical doctrine of the Rechtsstaat (or rule of law); 3) judicial protection functions through the constitutional acknowledgment of the right to bring any abuse by private or public powers before a court." [p. 355]

* * *

John Philip Reid, Rule of Law: the Jurisprudence of Liberty in the Seventeenth and Eighteenth Century (2004), at 4, 8.

The rule of law doctrine is made up by "the general principle that 'individuals should be governed by law rather than the arbitrary will of others,' that is, of course, not by the arbitrary will and caprice of government officials but by law ruling over governor and governed alike. There are at least two principles explaining this rule … [The first principle is that] the purpose of the doctrine of the rule of law is to restrain the arbitrary exercise of power … The second principle is that rule of law by its very existence and by its enforcement employs institutional restraints, such as the writ of habeas corpus and the privilege of trial by a jury—constraints that prevent governmental agents from oppressing the rest of society." [p. 4]

"For [A.V.] Dicey [in his treatise, *Introduction to the Study of the Law of the Constitution*] rule of law means, in the first place, the absolute supremacy or predominance of regular law as opposed to the influence of arbitrary power, and it excludes the existence of arbitrariness or even of wide discretionary authority on the part of the government … It means, again, equality before the law, or the equal subjection of all classes to the ordinary law of the land administered by the ordinary law courts … The "rule of law" lastly, may be used as a formula for expressing the fact that with us the law of the constitution, the rules which in foreign countries naturally form part of a constitutional code, are not the source but the consequence of the rights of individuals as defined and enforced by the courts … thus the constitution is the result of the ordinary law of the land." [p. 8]

* * *

Paul W. Khan, The Cultural Study of Law: Reconstructing Legal Scholarship (1999), at 36.

"The rule of law is a social practice: it is a way of being in the world. To live under the rule of law is to maintain a set of beliefs about the self and community, time and space, authority and representation. It is to understand the actions of others and the possible actions of the self as expressions of these beliefs. Without these beliefs, the rule of law appears as just another form of coercive governmental authority. This is the way law appears to the alien who happens to find himself temporarily within the jurisdiction. He must negotiate around as set of rules, under a threat of coercion, without understanding the significance of the rules to those who see them as 'ours.' Law is something done to him, rather than something we do. Within the beliefs of the citizen, however, law appears as the legitimate and even 'natural' arrangement of our collective life."

* * *

Brian Z. Tamanaha, ON THE RULE OF LAW: HISTORY, POLITICS, THEORY (2004), at 9, 33, 92–93.

Aristotle's words on the rule of law: "The rule of law is preferable to that of any individual. On the same principle, even if it be better for certain individuals to govern, they should be made only guardians and ministers of the law ... Therefore, he who bids the law rule adds and element of the beast; for desire is a wild beast, and passion perverts the minds of rulers, even when they are the best of men. The law is reason unaffected by desire." [p. 9]

"The liberal orientation of the rule of law differs from pre-liberal sources" [such as Greek, Roman, and Medieval systems]. "In liberalism, rule of law emphasizes the preservation of individual liberty ... In societies oriented toward the community, or in fixed hierarchic societies, restraining the tyranny of the government does not enhance the liberty of individuals to be or do what they wish. Surrounding social and cultural constraints render such liberty irrelevant if not inconceivable." [p. 33]

Liberty here is divided into four compartments: [1] "the individual is free to the extent that the laws are created democratically. Citizens have thereby consented to, indeed authored, the rules they are obligated to follow. The individual is at once ruler and ruled ... [2] the individual is free to the extent that government officials are required to act in accordance with preexisting law. Citizens are subject only to the law, not to the arbitrary will or judgment of another who wields coercive government power. This entails that the laws be applied equally, and be interpreted and applied with certainty and reliability ... [3] "the individual is free in so far as the government is restricted from infringing upon an inviolable realm of personal autonomy ... [4] finally, freedom is enhanced when the powers of the government are divided into separate compartments—typically, legislative, executive, and judicial, and sometimes municipal, regional, and national—with the application of law entrusted to an independent judiciary ... This is the structural arrangement of enhancing liberty rather than a type of liberty itself." [p. 33]

[specific reference to China] "No western legal theorist identifies the rule of law entirely in terms of rule by law. Rule by law carries scant connotation of legal limitations on government, which is the sine qua non of the rule of law tradition. Nonetheless, a few contemporary regimes apparently adopt this understanding. Chinese legal scholars have claimed that this is the Chinese government's preferred understanding of the rule of law, although this take on the rule of law is not held by the Chinese alone—'Some Asian politicians focus on the regular, efficient application of law but do not stress the necessity of government subordination to it. In their view, law exists not to limit the state but to serve its power.'" [pp. 92–93]

* * *

Luc B. Tremblay, THE RULE OF LAW, JUSTICE, AND INTERPRETATION (1997), at 29.

Concept and conceptions of the rule of law include the follow ideas:

1. "Principle of legality: any executive and administrative action infringing upon individual rights must be authorized by law, that is, it must have a legal foundation conferring authority to act, understood in accordance with the formal validity thesis.

2. The separation of powers: according to WS Holdsworth, the core of the rule of law is that 'the judicial power of the state is, to a large extent, separate from the Executive and the Legislature.'

3. Procedural due process: the rule of law is a matter of abiding by the law and by various procedural guarantees in the administration of justice. This comes close to equating the rule of law with 'procedural due process' and with the 'principles of natural justice.

4. Certainty: According to Joseph Raz, the concept of the rule of law has two aspects: 1—that people should be ruled by the law and obey it; 2—the law should be such that people will be able to be guided by it.…

5. Promotion of material justice and individual rights: according to Ronald Dworkin, the ideal of the rule of law assumes that citizens have moral rights and duties with respect to one another, and political rights against the state as a whole. It insists that these moral and political rights be recognized in positive law, so that they may be enforced upon the demand of individual citizens through courts or other judicial institutions of the familial type, so fare as this is practicable …

6. Natural law: the rule of law supposes the existence of a transcendental just order, the validity of which derives from God, nature, or human reason and with which any positive law must be consonant.

7. Law and order: The rule of law expresses the idea that submission and obedience to positive laws (good or bad) constitute the foundation and the conditions for the preservation of civil society as opposed to anarchy, social chaos, state of war, and the like."

* * *

Spencer Zifcak, *Globalizing the Rule of Law: Rethinking Values and Reforming Institutions*, appearing as Chapter 2 in GLOBALISATION AND THE RULE OF LAW (Spencer Zifcak ed., 2005), at 35.

"Hayek … believed that the 'rule of law' implied that the law must be known and certain, prospective and never retrospective. No individual should be coerced except in the enforcement of rules having these attributes. Individuals should be equal before the law. It must therefore be general rather than particular in its application. A system based on the rule of law must embody the separation of powers. This requires that the law's interpretation and enforcement be vested in judges independent of executive government. Their application of the law must be faithful, open, and principled.… His [Hayek's] rule of law presumes both constitutionalism and democracy."

"The UN Commission on Global Governance affirmed the importance of applying the rule of law in the international arena in the strongest terms: the rule of law has been a critical civilizing influence in every free society. It distinguishes a democratic society from a tyrannical society; it secures liberty and justice against repression; it elevates equality above domination; it empowers the weak against the unjust claims of the strong. Its restrains, no less than the moral precepts it asserts, are essential to the well-being of society, both collectively and to individuals within it. Respect for the rule of law is thus a basic neighborhood value. And one that is certainly needed in the emerging global neighborhood."

* * *

Ross P. Buckley, *The Role of the Rule of Law in the Regulation of Global Capital Flows*, appearing as Chapter 7 in GLOBALISATION AND THE RULE OF LAW (Spencer Zifcak ed., 2005), at 141.

"For the rule of law to thrive, the legal system needs the following characteristics: 1) the laws need to be relatively clear, accessible and prospective in their operation; 2) the laws need to be seen to be legitimate and enjoy a broad measure of community support; this legitimacy and support usually derives from the laws being considered to be generally just; 3) the laws need to be interpreted and applied openly by an independent judiciary which itself enjoys a broad measure of community acceptance."

* * *

BLACK'S LAW DICTIONARY (5th ed. 1979).

The rule of law provides that decisions should be made by the application of known principles or laws without the intervention of discretion in their application.

* * *

Franz Michael, *Law: A Tool of Power*, appearing in HUMAN RIGHTS IN THE PEOPLE'S REPUBLIC OF CHINA (Yuan-li Wu et al. eds., 1988), at 33.

"Rule of law is the very foundation of human rights. In the Western legal tradition, law is applied equally to all; it is binding on the lawgiver and is meant to prevent arbitrary action by the ruler. Law guarantees a realm of freedom for the members of a political community that is essential to the protection of life and human dignity against tyrannical oppression and to the regulation of human relations within the community."

* * *

Jeremy Matam Farrall, UNITED NATIONS SANCTIONS AND THE RULE OF LAW (2007), at 31, 33–35, 40.

The basic premise of the rule of law is that it "aims to curb the arbitrary exercise of political power." [p. 31]

In the context of UN actions, "[f]ive basic clusters of meaning for the rule of law can be identified.... The first cluster of meaning is that of 'law and order'.... The second cluster of meaning equates the rule of law with efforts to hold criminals accountable for their crimes.... The third cluster of meaning equates the rule of law with principled governance ... [and encompasses] the importance of improving governance and eradicating corruption.... The fourth cluster of meaning associates the rule of law with the protection and promotion of human rights.... The fifth cluster of meaning entails resolving conflict in accordance with law." [pp. 33–34]

UN Secretary-General Kofi Annan has described the rule of law as "a principle of governance in which all persons, institutions and entities, public and private, including the State itself, are accountable to laws that are publicly promulgated, equally enforced and independently adjudicated, and which are consistent with international human rights norms and standards." Annan has also stated that the rule of law requires "measures to ensure adherence to the principles of supremacy of law, equality before the law, accountability to the law, fairness in the application of the law, separation of powers, participation in decision-making, legal certainty, avoidance of arbitrariness and procedural and legal transparency." [p. 35]

The rule of law can be regarded as "consist[ing] of five basic rule of law principles ...: transparency, consistency, equality, due process and proportionality." [p. 40]

* * *

Order in the Jungle, THE ECONOMIST, Mar 13th 2008. http://www.economist.com/dis-
playstory.cfm?story_id=10849115.

"Thick definitions treat the rule of law as the core of a just society. In this version, the
concept is inextricably linked to liberty and democracy. Its adherents say a country can
be spoken of as being ruled by law only if the state's power is constrained and if basic
freedoms, such as those of speech and association, are guaranteed. The "declaration of Delhi"
drawn up by the International Commission of Jurists in that city in 1959 followed this line
in saying that the rule of law "should be employed to safeguard and advance the civil and
political rights of the individual" and create "conditions under which his legitimate aspirations and dignity may be realised." Among other proponents of a thick definition are
Friedrich Hayek, an Austrian economist, and Cass Sunstein of the University of Chicago.
In their view, the rule of law includes elements of political morality.

Thin definitions are more formal. The important things, on this account, are not
democracy and morality but property rights and the efficient administration of justice.
Laws must provide stability. They do not necessarily have to be moral or promote human
rights. America's southern states in the Jim Crow era were governed by the rule of law
on thin definitions, but not on thick.

There have been huge improvements in monitoring and measuring the rule of law,
even though people cannot agree exactly what it is. "Fifteen years ago, we didn't talk about
this stuff," says Steve Radelet of the Centre for Global Development, a Washington think-
tank. "Ten years ago, there was no data." Now, the Worldwide Governance Indicators project — "one of the best kept secrets at the World Bank", believes Gordon Johnson, a grand
old man of aid-giving — is the state of the art. It gathers data on more than 60 indicators
(the extent of crime, the quality of police, judicial independence and so on) to create
rule-of-law and governance measures for virtually every country in the world. Aggregat-
ing like this (and being honest about the margin of error), says Mr Kaufmann, is far from
perfect, but is a decent approximation.

These measures confirm what is clear anyway: some countries have been able to improve their legal framework even in a short time. In 2000 Mikhail Saakashvili, then Georgia's minister of justice, sacked two-thirds of his country's judges for failing to pass an
exam. Four years later as president, he fired all the country's traffic police. Georgia's World
Bank rule-of-law score rose from nine out of 100 in 2002 (in the bottom 10%) to 33 at
the end of 2006 — low, but better. Central European and Baltic countries are doing better still: the radical legal changes required by membership of the EU improved their
economies as well as their judicial systems."

* * *

PRC State Council Information Office, *China's Efforts and Achievements in Promoting
the Rule of Law*, issued Feb. 28, 2008, available at http://www.chinadaily.com.cn/china/2008
npc/2008-02/28/content_6495385.htm, at parts I–IX.

"The rule of law has been established as a fundamental principle. It is a fundamental
state principle as well as the common understanding of all sectors of society to govern the
country according to law and build a socialist country under the rule of law. Moreover,
the socialist idea of the rule of law has been gradually established, with the rule of law at
the core, law enforcement for the people as an essential requirement, fairness and justice
as a value to be pursued, serving the overall interests as an important mission, and with
the leadership of the CPC as a fundamental guarantee." [part I]

"The precondition for building a socialist country under the rule of law is that there must be laws to go by. Unremitting efforts over many years have seen the establishment of a socialist legal framework with Chinese characteristics and with the Constitution at the core." [part II]

The rule of law in a country is determined by and conforms to its national conditions and social system. To govern the country according to law and build a socialist country under the rule of law is the Chinese people's demand, pursuit and practice. [foreword]

* * *

U.S. Department of State (formerly at http://usinfo.state.gov/dhr/democracy/ rule_of_law. html, now see http://www.america.gov/st/washfile-english/2006/January/20060118165638 maduobbA8.491153e-02.html).

"The rule of law is a fundamental component of democratic society and is defined broadly as the principle that all members of society—both citizens and rulers—are bound by a set of clearly defined and universally accepted laws. In a democracy, the rule of law is manifested in an independent judiciary, a free press and a system of checks and balances on leaders through free elections and separation of powers among the branches of government.

Although a written constitution is not a necessary component of democracy—for example, Great Britain does not have one—in the United States, the rule of law is based primarily on the U.S. Constitution and on the assurance that U.S. laws—in conjunction with the Constitution—are fair and are applied equally to all members of society."

* * *

U.S. Department of State (formerly at http://usinfo.state.gov/products/pubs/principles/law.htm), now see http://www.america.gov/st/democracyhr-english/2008/May/20080609204640eaifas0.7177698.html) [more detailed description, more particular to USA].

- "Rule of law means that no individual, president or private citizen, stands above law. Democratic governments exercise authority by way of law and are themselves subject to law's constraints.

- Laws should express the will of the people, not the whims of kings, dictators, military officials, religious leaders, or self-appointed political parties.

- Citizens in democracies are willing to obey the laws of their society, then, because they are submitting to their own rules and regulations. Justice is best achieved when the laws are established by the very people who must obey them.

- Under the rule of law, a system of strong, independent courts should have the power and authority, resources, and the prestige to hold government officials, even top leaders, accountable to the nation's laws and regulations.

- For this reason, judges should be well trained, professional, independent, and impartial. To serve their necessary role in the legal and political system, judges must be committed to the principles of democracy.

- The laws of a democracy may have many sources: written constitutions; statutes and regulations; religious and ethical teachings; and cultural traditions and practices. Regardless of origin the law should enshrine certain provisions to protect the rights and freedoms of citizens:

  - Under the requirement of equal protection under the law, the law may not be uniquely applicable to any single individual or group.

- Citizens must be secure from arbitrary arrest and unreasonable search of their homes or the seizure of their personal property.

- Citizens charged with crimes are entitled to a speedy and public trial, along with the opportunity to confront and question their accusers. If convicted, they may not be subjected to cruel or unusual punishment.

- Citizens cannot be forced to testify against themselves. This principle protects citizens from coercion, abuse, or torture and greatly reduces the temptation of police to employ such measures."

* * *

University of Iowa, Center for International Finance and Development http://www.uiowa.edu/ifdebook/faq/Rule_of_Law.shtml.

Rule of law "can be understood as a legal-political regime under which the law restrains the government by promoting certain liberties and creating order and predictability regarding how a country functions. In the most basic sense, the rule of law is a system that attempts to protect the rights of citizens from arbitrary and abusive use of government power."

National Constitution Center formerly at http://www.constitutioncenter.org/explore/BasicGoverningPrinciples/RuleofLaw.shtml, now at http://72.32.50.200/explore/BasicGoverningPrinciples/RuleofLaw.shtml

"The rule of law calls for both individuals and the government to submit to the law's supremacy. [Viewed in the context of the US system, by] precluding both the individual and the state from transcending the supreme law of the land, the Framers constructed another protective layer over individual rights and liberties".

* * *

US Agency for International Development http://www.usaid.gov/our_work/democracy_and_governance/technical_areas/rule_of_law/.

"The term 'rule of law' embodies the basic principles of equal treatment of all people before the law, fairness, and both constitutional and actual guarantees of basic human rights. A predictable legal system with fair, transparent, and effective judicial institutions is essential to the protection of citizens against the arbitrary use of state authority and lawless acts of both organizations and individuals. In many states with weak or newly-emerging democratic traditions, existing laws are not fair or are not fairly applied, judicial independence is compromised, individual and minority rights are not truly guaranteed, and institutions have not yet developed the capacity to administer existing laws. Weak legal institutions endanger democratic reform and sustainable development in developing countries.

Without the rule of law, the executive and legislative branches of government operate without checks and balances, free and fair elections are not possible, and civil society cannot flourish. Beyond the democracy and governance sector, the accomplishment of other USAID goals also relies on effective rule of law. For example, civil and commercial codes that respect private property and contracts are key ingredients for the development of market-based economies. USAID's efforts to strengthen legal systems fall under three inter-connected priority areas: supporting legal reform, improving the administration of justice, and increasing citizens' access to justice."

* * *

Thomas Carothers, *Promoting the Rule of Law Abroad: The Problem of Knowledge*, Democracy and Rule of Law Project, No. 34. January 2003.

Carnegie Endowment for International Peace.

http://www.carnegieendowment.org/files/wp34.pdf.

"Rule-of-law promoters tend to translate the rule of law into an institutional checklist, with primary emphasis on the judiciary.

- emphasis on judiciaries is widespread in the rule-of-law field, with the terms judicial reform and rule-of-law reform often used interchangeably.

- emphasis derives from the fact that most rule-of-law promotion specialists are lawyers and when lawyers think about what seems to be the nerve center of the rule of law they think about the core institutions of law enforcement. Yet it is by no means clear that courts are the essence of a rule-of-law system in a country. Only a small percentage of citizens in most Western rule-of-law systems ever have direct contact with courts. In a certain sense courts play a role late in the legal process—it might well be argued that the making of laws is the most generative part of a rule-of-law system. Yet rule-of-law programs have not much focused on legislatures or the role of executive branch agencies in law-making processes. The question of which institutions are most germane to the establishment of the rule of law in a country is actually quite complex and difficult. Yet for the last ten to fifteen years, rule-of-law programs have given dominant attention to judiciaries, without much examination of whether such a focus is really the right one. The uncertainty goes beyond the question of "which institutions?" Indeed, doubt exists about whether it is useful to conceive of and attempt to act upon rule-of-law development in primarily institutional terms. Clearly law is not just the sum of courts, legislatures, police, prosecutors, and other formal institutions with some direct connection to law. Law is also a normative system that resides in the minds of the citizens of a society. As rule-of-law providers seek to affect the rule of law in a country, it is not clear if they should focus on institution-building or instead try to intervene in ways that would affect how citizens understand, use, and value law. To take a simple example, many rule-of-law programs focus on improving a country's courts and police on the assumption that this is the most direct route to improve compliance with law in the country. Yet some research shows that compliance with law depends most heavily on the perceived fairness and legitimacy of the laws, characteristics that are not established primarily by the courts but by other means, such as the political process. An effort to improve compliance thus might more fruitfully take a completely different approach. In sum, the question of where the essence of the rule of law actually resides and therefore what should be the focal point of efforts to improve the rule of law remains notably unsettled. Rule-of-law practitioners have been following an institutional approach, concentrating on judiciaries, more out of instinct than well-researched knowledge".

* * *

Bo Li, *What is Rule of Law*, appearing in Perspectives [published by Overseas Young Chinese Forum] vol. 1, no. 5 (Apr. 30, 2000), available at

http://www.oycf.org/Perspectives/5_043000/what_is_rule_of_law.htm.

"I want to point out that when we say 'rule of law' these days, we mean something different from the instrumentalist conception of 'rule by law' of the legalist philosophers in ancient Chinese history. When we say 'rule of law' today we intend to describe a key component of the social and political orders found in the United States and other liberal democratic states of our time. In other words, by 'rule of law' we mean a western tradition that can be traced back to the Roman republics and was fully developed by the liberal constitutionalism. It is characterized, in the words of Max Weber, by 'legal domination.'

The difference between 'rule by law' and 'rule of law' is important. Under the rule 'by' law, law is an instrument of the government, and the government is above the law. In contrast, under the rule 'of' law, no one is above the law, not even the government. The core of 'rule of law' is an autonomous legal order. Under rule of law, the authority of law does not depend so much on law's instrumental capabilities, but on its degree of autonomy, that is, the degree to which law is distinct and separate from other normative structures such as politics and religion. As an autonomous legal order, rule of law has at least three meanings. First, rule of law is a regulator of government power. Second, rule of law means equality before law. Third, rule of law means procedural and formal justice.

Selected Bibliography

As noted in the *Preface and Acknowledgments*, my studies in comparative law, including the efforts resulting in this book, have relied heavily on the work of many experts. Some especially helpful contributions to the literature are listed here. Most of these, along with a great many other sources that I have drawn from in producing this book, are also cited in footnotes in the main text. For several sources specifically relating to the definition(s) of the rule of law, see the Appendix to Chapter Seven.

I. Comparative Legal Studies and Other General Sources

Harold **Berman**, Law and Revolution: The Formation of the Western Legal Tradition (1983)

Peter de **Cruz**, A Modern Approach to Comparative Law (1993)

Peter de **Cruz**, Comparative Law in a Changing World (1999)

René **David** and John E. C. **Brierley**, Major Legal Systems in the World Today: An Introduction to the Comparative Study of Law (3rd ed. 1985)

Lon **Fuller**, The Morality of Law (1964)

Mary Ann **Glendon**, Michael W. **Gordon**, and Christopher **Osakwe**, Comparative Legal Traditions in a Nutshell (1982)

Mary Ann **Glendon**, Michael W. **Gordon**, and Christopher **Osakwe**, Comparative Legal Traditions (1985)

Mary Ann **Glendon**, Michael W. **Gordon**, Paolo G. **Carozza**, Comparative Legal Traditions in a Nutshell (2nd ed. 1999)

Mary Ann **Glendon**, Paolo G. **Carozza**, and Colin B. **Picker**, Comparative Legal Traditions in a Nutshell (2008)

H. Patrick **Glenn**, Legal Traditions of the World (2007)

Erik G. **Jensen** and Thomas C. **Heller** eds., Beyond Common Knowledge: Empirical Approaches to the Rule of Law (2003)

Herbert M. **Kritzer**, ed., Legal Systems of the World: A Political and Social Encyclopedia (2008)

Ugo A. **Mattei**, Teemu **Ruskola**, and Antonio **Gidi**, Schlesinger's Comparative Law: Cases, Text, Materials (7th ed. 2009)

Mathias **Reimann** and Reinhard **Zimmerman**, The Oxford Handbook of Comparative Law (2006)

J.M. **Roberts**, A Concise History of the World (1993)

Rudolf B. **Schlesinger**, Hans W. **Baade**, Mirjan R. **Damaska**, and Peter E. **Herzog**, eds., Comparative Law: Cases, Text, Materials (5th ed. 1988)

Rudolf B. **Schlesinger**, Hans W. **Baade**, Peter E. **Herzog**, and Edward M **Wise**, eds., Comparative Law: Cases, Text, Materials (6th ed. 1998)

Konrad **Zweigert** and Hein Kötz, An Introduction to Comparative Law — the Framework (1977)

II. Civil Law Tradition and Continental European Law

Allan Chester **Johnson** et al., Ancient Roman Statutes (1961)

Hermann **Kantorosicz**, Studies in the Glossators of the Roman Law: Newly Discovered Writings of the Twelfth Century (1938)

F. H. **Lawson**, A Common Lawyer Looks at the Civil Law (1953)

John Henry **Merryman**, The Civil Law Tradition (2nd ed. 1985)

John Henry **Merryman** and Rogelio Pérez-Perdomo, The Civil Law Tradition (3rd ed. 2007)

John Henry **Merryman**, David S. **Clark**, and John Owen **Haley**, Comparative Law: Historical Development of the Civil Law Tradition in Europe, Latin America, and East Asia (2010)

O.F. **Robinson**, T.D. **Fergus**, and W.M. **Gordon**, European Legal History (2d ed. 1994)

Peter **Stein**, Roman Law in European History (1999)

J.A.C. **Thomas**, Textbook of Roman Law (1976)

Arthur Taylor **von Mehren** and James Russell **Gordley**, The Civil Law System (1977)

Thomas Glyn **Watkin**, An Historical Introduction to Modern Civil Law (1999)

III. Common Law Tradition and English and American Law

Charles M. **Cook**, The American Codification Movement (1981)

René **David** & John E.C. **Brierly**, Major Legal Systems in the World Today (3d ed. 1985)

E. Allen **Farnsworth**, Introduction to the Legal System of the United States (1983)

E. Allan **Farnsworth**, An Introduction to the Legal System of the United States (Steve Sheppard, ed., 2010)

Antonia **Fraser**, The Lives of the Kings and Queens of England (1975)

Lawrence M. **Friedman**, A HISTORY OF AMERICAN LAW (2d ed. 1985)

Francis H. **Heller**, *American Legal History* (unpublished, on file with the author)

Francis H. **Heller**, *The Growth of the Law in England* (unpublished, on file with the author)

John **Hudson**, THE FORMATION OF THE ENGLISH COMMON LAW: LAW AND SOCIETY IN ENGLAND FROM THE NORMAN CONQUEST TO MAGNA CARTA (1996)

Joseph **Jackson**, ENGLISH LEGAL HISTORY (1955)

Frederick G. **Kempin**, Jr., HISTORICAL INTRODUCTION TO ANGLO-AMERICAN LAW IN A NUTSHELL (3d ed. 1990)

Kenneth **Smith** and Denis J. **Keenan**, ENGLISH LAW 1 (2d ed., 1966)

IV. Contemporary Chinese Law

Books

Ronald C. **Brown**, UNDERSTANDING CHINESE COURTS AND LEGAL PROCESS (1997)

Bin Liang, THE CHANGING CHINESE LEGAL SYSTEM, 1978–PRESENT (2008)

Albert H.Y. **Chen**, AN INTRODUCTION TO THE LEGAL SYSTEM OF THE PEOPLE'S REPUBLIC OF CHINA (3d ed. 2004)

Daniel C.K. **Chow**, THE LEGAL SYSTEM OF THE PEOPLE'S REPUBLIC OF CHINA (2003 & 2009)

Kenneth A. **Cutshaw**, Michael E. **Burke**, and Christoper A. **Wagner**, CORPORATE COUNSEL'S GUIDE TO DOING BUSINESS IN CHINA (2009–2010 edition)

Philip C.C. **Huang**, CHINESE CIVIL JUSTICE, PAST AND PRESENT (2010)

Philip C.C. **Huang**, CODE, CUSTOM, AND LEGAL PRACTICE IN CHINA (2001)

Martin **Jacques**, WHEN CHINA RULES THE WORLD: THE END OF THE WESTERN WORLD AND THE BIRTH OF A NEW GLOBAL ORDER (2009)

Ronald C. **Keith**, CHINA'S STRUGGLE FOR THE RULE OF LAW (1994)

Hyung I. **Kim**, FUNDAMENTAL LEGAL CONCEPTS OF CHINA AND THE WEST (1981)

Stanley B. **Lubman**, BIRD IN A CAGE—LEGAL REFORM IN CHINA AFTER MAO (1999)

Jan Michiel **Otto**, Maurice V. **Polak**, Jianfu **Chen**, and Yuwen **Li**, eds., LAW-MAKING IN THE PEOPLE'S REPUBLIC OF CHINA (2000)

Pitman B. **Potter**, THE CHINESE LEGAL SYSTEM: GLOBALIZATION AND LOCAL LEGAL CULTURE (2001)

Karen G. **Turner**, James V. **Feinerman**, and R. Kent **Guy**, eds., THE LIMITS OF THE RULE OF LAW IN CHINA (2000)

Eduard B. **Vermeer** and Ingrid **d'Hooghe**, eds., CHINA'S LEGAL REFORMS AND THEIR POLITICAL LIMITS (2002)

Wang Chenguang and **Zhang** Xianchu, eds., INTRODUCTION TO CHINESE LAW (1997)

Wang Guiguo and John **Mo**, eds., CHINESE LAW (1999)

Xin Ren, TRADITION OF THE LAW AND LAW OF THE TRADITION: LAW, STATE, AND SOCIAL CONTROL IN CHINA (1997)

Guanghua Yu and Minkang Gu, LAWS AFFECTING BUSINESS TRANSACTIONS IN THE PRC (2001)

James M. Zimmerman, CHINA LAW DESKBOOK: A LEGAL GUIDE FOR FOREIGN-INVESTED ENTERPRISES (2004)

Law Journal Articles

Volker Behr, *Development of a New Legal System in the People's Republic of China*, 67 LOUISIANA LAW REVIEW 1161 (2007)

Chen Weidong, *The Basic Concepts of Re-Modifying the Criminal Procedure Law*, as appearing in English translation in 1 FRONTIERS OF LAW IN CHINA 153 (2006)

He Jiahong, *Ten Tendencies of Criminal Justice*, as appearing in English translation in 2 FRONTIERS OF LAW IN CHINA 1 (2007)

Jiang Ming'an, *Public Participation and Administrative Rule of Law*, 2004 JOURNAL OF CHINESE LAW [FAXUI YANJIU] 26 (2004), as appearing in English translation in 2 FRONTIERS OF LAW IN CHINA 353 (2007)

Stanley Lubman, *Looking for Law in China*, 20 COLUMBIA JOURNAL OF ASIAN LAW 1 (2006)

Ma Huaide, *The Values of Administrative Procedure Law and the Meaning of its Codification in China*, as appearing in English translation in 1 FRONTIERS OF LAW IN CHINA 300 (2006)

Ma Xiaohong, *A Reflection on the History of Chinese Constitutionalism of Last Century*, as appearing in English translation in 2 FRONTIERS OF LAW IN CHINA 44 (2007)

Randall Peerenboom, *The X-Files: Past and Present Portrayals of China's Alien "Legal System"*, 2 WASHINGTON UNIVERSITY GLOBAL STUDIES LAW REVIEW 37 (2003)

Pitman B. Potter, *Globalization and Economic Regulation in China: Selective Adaptation of Globalized Norms and Practices*, 2 WASHINGTON UNIVERSITY GLOBAL STUDIES LAW REVIEW 119 (2003)

Wang Chenguang, *Law-Making Functions of the Chinese Courts: Judicial Activism in a Country of Rapid Social Change*, as appearing in English translation in 1 FRONTIERS OF LAW IN CHINA 524 (2006)

Wang Zhoujun, *Democracy, Rule of Law and Human Rights Protection under Gradually Developed Constitutionalism*, 2004 JOURNAL OF CHINESE LAW [FAXUI YANJIU] 3 (2004), appearing in English translation in 2 FRONTIERS OF LAW IN CHINA 335 (2007)

Zhang Wenxian, *China's Rule of Law in the Globalization Era*, as appearing in English translation in 2 FRONTIERS OF LAW IN CHINA 335 (2007)

V. Dynastic Chinese Law

A more comprehensive listing of sources appears in the bibliography to my book LAW CODES IN DYNASTIC CHINA (co-authored with Wang Yanping). The following are worthy of specific mention here.

Kathryn Bernhardt and Philip C.C. Huang, editors, CIVIL LAW IN QING AND REPUBLICAN CHINA (1994)

Derk **Bodde** and Clarence **Morris**, Law in Imperial China, Exemplified by 190 Ch'ing Dynasty Cases (1967)

The **Cambridge History of China**, in multiple volumes, including in particular:

volume 1 — The Ch'in and Han Empires, 221 B.C.–A.D. 220, edited by Denis Twitchett and Michael Loewe (1986)

volume 2 — Sui and T'ang China, 589–906, part I, edited by Denis Twitchett (1979)

volume 6 — Alien Regimes and Border States, 907–1368, edited by Herbert Franke and Denis Twitchett (1994)

T'ung-Tsu **Ch'u**, Law and Society in Traditional China (1961)

John King **Fairbank**, China — A New History (1992)

John W. **Head**, China's Legal Soul: The Modern Chinese Legal Identity in Historical Context (2009)

John W. **Head** and Yanping Wang, Law Codes in Dynastic China: A Synopsis of Chinese Legal History in the Thirty Centuries from Zhou to Qing (2005)

A.F.P. **Hulsewé**, Remanants of Ch'in Law (1985)

A.F.P. **Hulsewé**, Remnants of Han Law (1955)

Jiang Yonglin, The Great Ming Code: *Da Ming lu* (2005)

Wallace **Johnson**, The T'ang Code, vol. I (1979)

Wallace **Johnson**, The T'ang Code, vol. II (1997)

William C. **Jones**, The Great Qing Code (1994)

Simon **Leys**, The Analects of Confucius (1997)

Geoffrey **MacCormack**, The Spirit of Traditional Chinese Law (1996)

F.W. **Mote**, Imperial China 900–1800 (1999)

Lucian W. **Pye**, China — An Introduction (1991)

J.A.G. **Roberts**, A Concise History of China (1999)

About the Author

John W. Head is a professor of international and comparative law at the University of Kansas, where he has been designated the Robert W. Wagstaff Distinguished Professor. He holds an English law degree from Oxford University (1977) and a U.S. law degree from the University of Virginia (1979). Before starting an academic career, he worked in the Washington, D.C., office of Cleary, Gottlieb, Steen & Hamilton (1980–1983), at the Asian Development Bank in Manila (1983–1988), and at the International Monetary Fund in Washington (1988–1990). Both his teaching and his published works concentrate on the areas of international business and finance, public international law, and comparative law. His principal books include CHINA'S LEGAL SOUL (Carolina Academic Press, 2009); LOSING THE GLOBAL DEVELOPMENT WAR—A CONTEMPORARY CRITIQUE OF THE IMF, THE WORLD BANK, AND THE WTO (Martinus Nijhoff, 2008); GENERAL PRINCIPLES OF BUSINESS AND ECONOMIC LAW (Carolina Academic Press, 2008); GLOBAL BUSINESS LAW—PRINCIPLES AND PRACTICE OF INTERNATIONAL COMMERCE AND INVESTMENT (Carolina Academic Press 2007), GLOBAL ECONOMIC ORGANIZATIONS—AN EVALUATION OF CRITICISMS LEVELED AT THE IMF, THE MULTILATERAL DEVELOPMENT BANKS, AND THE WTO (Transnational Publishers, 2005), and LAW CODES IN DYNASTIC CHINA—A SYNOPSIS OF CHINESE LEGAL HISTORY IN THE THIRTY CENTURIES FROM ZHOU TO QING (Carolina Academic Press, 2005, with Yanping Wang). He has been awarded Fulbright teaching fellowships to China and Italy and has also taught in Austria, Hong Kong, Jordan, Mexico, Mongolia, Turkey, and the United Kingdom and has undertaken special assignments in numerous locations around the world for international financial institutions and development agencies. Mr. Head is married to Lucia Orth, who is a lawyer, teacher, and novelist. He and his wife live in the quiet wooded countryside southwest of Lawrence, Kansas.

Index